FileMaker Pro 9

Geoff Coffey and Susan Prosser

Beijing · Cambridge · Farnham · Köln · Paris · Sebastopol · Taipei · Tokyo

FileMaker Pro 9: The Missing Manual
by Geoff Coffey and Susan Prosser

Printed in the United States of America.

Published by O'Reilly Media, Inc., 1005 Gravenstein Highway North, Sebastopol, CA 95472.

O'Reilly books may be purchased for educational, business, or sales promotional use. Online editions are also available for most titles (*safari.oreilly.com*). For more information, contact our corporate/institutional sales department: (800) 998-9938 or *corporate@oreilly.com*.

Printing History:

August 2007: First Edition.

This book uses RepKover™, a durable and flexible lay-flat binding.

ISBN-10: 0-596-51413-1

ISBN-13: 978-0-596-51413-6

[M]

Colophon

Philip Dangler and Adam Witwer provided quality control for *FileMaker Pro 9: The Missing Manual*. Ron Strauss wrote the index.

The cover of this book is based on a series design originally created by David Freedman and modified by Mike Kohnke, Karen Montgomery, and Fitch (*www.fitch.com*). Back cover design, dog illustration, and color selection by Fitch.

David Futato designed the interior layout, based on a series design by Phil Simpson. This book was converted by Abby Fox to FrameMaker 5.5.6. The text font is Adobe Minion; the heading font is Adobe Formata Condensed; and the code font is LucasFont's TheSans Mono Condensed. The illustrations that appear in the book were produced by Robert Romano and Jessamyn Read using Macromedia FreeHand MX and Adobe Photoshop CS.

FileMaker Pro 9

THE MISSING MANUAL

The book that should have been in the box®

Table of Contents

Part Two: Layout Basics

Part Three: Multiple Tables and Relationships

Part Six: Security and Integration

Part Seven: Appendixes

The Missing Credits

About the Authors

Geoff Coffey has been helping people solve problems with FileMaker Pro for over 10 years. He is a partner at Six Fried Rice (*http://sixfriedrice.com/*), a FileMaker Pro consulting and training firm based in Phoenix, Arizona. Six Fried Rice brings the power and simplicity of FileMaker Pro to individuals, workgroups, enterprise, and the Web through world-class training, expert advice, and custom development. In the past, Geoff has taught classes for FMPtraining.com and presented at the FileMaker Developer's Conference. He lives in downtown Phoenix with his wife of 14 years and his two daughters, Isabel (9) and Sophia (5). If you're a FileMaker fan, you can reach Geoff any time at *geoff@sixfriedrice.com*.

Susan Prosser is a certified FileMaker consultant, tinkerer, bicyclist, wife, and skill junkie. She makes her living creating databases and writing about creating them (*www.dbhq.net*). She can't, or won't, commit to being left-brain or right-brain dominant. Her mother thinks this is a delicate and artful balance, but husband Paul's cocked eyebrow suggests it *might* be too much caffeine. Whatever the cause, this mental fence straddling probably explains her love for FileMaker, since it's a great blend of style and substance, of form and function. Send questions about FileMaker, suggestions for alternative craft projects, or tear-stained essays about how doping is killing the beautiful sport of bicycling to *susanprosser@gmail.com*.

About the Creative Team

Nan Barber (editor) is associate editor for the Missing Manual series. She lives in Massachusetts with her husband and G4 Macintosh. Email: *nanbarber@gmail.com*.

Dawn Frausto (editor) is assistant editor for the Missing Manual series. When not working, she likes rock climbing, playing soccer, and causing trouble. Email: *dawn@oreilly.com*.

Jill Steinberg (copy editor) is a freelance writer and editor based in Seattle. O'Reilly, Intel, Microsoft, and the University of Washington have all published her work. Jill was educated at Brandeis University, Williams College, and Stanford University. Email: *saysjill@mac.com*.

Nellie McKesson (production editor) is a graduate of St. John's College in Santa Fe, New Mexico. She currently lives in Cambridge, Massachusetts, where her favorite places to eat are Punjabi Dhaba and Tacos Lupita. Email: *nellie@oreilly.com*.

Jesse Antunes (technical editor) is a specialist in complex FileMaker integrations, such as UPS, ICVerify, and PHP. He is a partner at Six Fried Rice (*http://sixfriedrice.com/*), which focuses on bringing easy-to-use professional solutions and expert training to its customers. If you have any questions about FileMaker basics or would like help accessing FileMaker's more complex and powerful abilities, you can reach Jesse any time at *jesse@sixfriedrice.com*.

Jerry Robin (technical editor) has been a FileMaker developer since 1988. He is owner and Chief Trainer of FMPtraining.com (www.fmptraining.com) and has produced a highly-acclaimed series of FileMaker training CDs. Jerry has presented at the FileMaker Developer Conference seven times; at the 2001 DevCon he won the Million-point prize in a special FileMaker version of *Who Wants to Be a Millionaire*. On weekends, Jerry performs improv and standup comedy in Phoenix (*www.jerryrobincomedy.com*).

The Missing Manual Series

Missing Manuals are witty, superbly written guides to computer products that don't come with printed manuals (which is just about all of them). Each book features a handcrafted index; cross-references to specific pages (not just chapters); and RepKover, a detached-spine binding that lets the book lie perfectly flat without the assistance of weights or cinder blocks.

Recent and upcoming titles include:

Access 2007: The Missing Manual by Matthew MacDonald

AppleScript: The Missing Manual by Adam Goldstein

AppleWorks 6: The Missing Manual by Jim Elferdink and David Reynolds

CSS: The Missing Manual by David Sawyer McFarland

Creating Web Sites: The Missing Manual by Matthew MacDonald

Digital Photography: The Missing Manual by Chris Grover and Barbara Brundage

Dreamweaver 8: The Missing Manual by David Sawyer McFarland

Dreamweaver CS3: The Missing Manual by David Sawyer McFarland

eBay: The Missing Manual by Nancy Conner

Excel 2003: The Missing Manual by Matthew MacDonald

Excel 2007: The Missing Manual by Matthew MacDonald

FileMaker Pro 8: The Missing Manual by Geoff Coffey and Susan Prosser

Flash 8: The Missing Manual by E.A. Vander Veer

Flash CS3: The Missing Manual by E.A. Vander Veer and Chris Grover

FrontPage 2003: The Missing Manual by Jessica Mantaro

GarageBand 2: The Missing Manual by David Pogue

Google: The Missing Manual, Second Edition by Sarah Milstein, J.D. Biersdorfer, and Matthew MacDonald

iMovie 6 & iDVD: The Missing Manual by David Pogue

iPhone: The Missing Manual by David Pogue

iPhoto 6: The Missing Manual by David Pogue

iPod: The Missing Manual, Fifth Edition by J.D. Biersdorfer

Mac OS X: The Missing Manual, Tiger Edition by David Pogue

Microsoft Project 2007: The Missing Manual by Bonnie Biafore

Office 2004 for Macintosh: The Missing Manual by Mark H. Walker and Franklin Tessler

Office 2007: The Missing Manual by Chris Grover, Matthew MacDonald, and E.A. Vander Veer

PCs: The Missing Manual by Andy Rathbone

Photoshop Elements 5: The Missing Manual by Barbara Brundage

PowerPoint 2007: The Missing Manual by E.A. Vander Veer

QuickBase: The Missing Manual by Nancy Conner

QuickBooks 2006: The Missing Manual by Bonnie Biafore

Switching to the Mac: The Missing Manual, Tiger Edition by David Pogue and Adam Goldstein

The Internet: The Missing Manual by David Pogue and J.D. Biersdorfer

Windows 2000 Pro: The Missing Manual by Sharon Crawford

Windows XP Home Edition: The Missing Manual, Second Edition by David Pogue

Windows Vista: The Missing Manual by David Pogue

Windows XP Pro: The Missing Manual, Second Edition by David Pogue, Craig Zacker, and Linda Zacker

Word 2007: The Missing Manual by Chris Grover

The "For Starters" books contain only the most essential information from their larger counterparts—in larger type, with a more spacious layout, and none of the more advanced sidebars. Recent titles include:

Access 2003 for Starters: The Missing Manual by Kate Chase and Scott Palmer

Access 2007 for Starters: The Missing Manual by Matthew MacDonald

Excel 2003 for Starters: The Missing Manual by Matthew MacDonald

Excel 2007 for Starters: The Missing Manual by Matthew MacDonald

Mac OS X Leopard for Starters: The Missing Manual by David Pogue

PowerPoint 2007 for Starters: The Missing Manual by E.A. Vander Veer

Quicken for Starters: The Missing Manual by Bonnie Biafore

Windows Vista for Starters: The Missing Manual by David Pogue

Windows XP for Starters: The Missing Manual by David Pogue

Word 2007 for Starters: The Missing Manual by Chris Grover

Introduction

For many people, the word "database" conjures up an image of a computer and a vast collection of information you can access only on a computer screen. But actually, databases are all around you—a phone book, a cookbook, and an encyclopedia are all databases. So is the stock page in your newspaper. In fact, if you look up the word "database" in a dictionary (which is a database, too), you'll probably read that a database is just a collection of information, or data.

Ideally, a database's information is organized so that you can easily find what you're looking for. For example, a Rolodex has information about people organized alphabetically. You can find any person's card pretty quickly because you know approximately where it is, even though there may be *hundreds* of cards to look through. But physical databases like this example all have major limitations compared to those that are stored on a computer. What if you want to get a list of all your associates in California? A Rolodex isn't organized that way, so you have to look through every card one by one. That kind of tedium is one of the reasons so many Rolodexes are now at the bottom of landfills, and it's one of the biggest problems a computer *database program* like FileMaker Pro can help you avoid.

The term *database program* means a computer program designed to help you build a database. Lots of computer programs use a database in one way or another; for example, your email program tracks hundreds of email messages you've sent and received, but it isn't a database program. A database program lets you build your own database and customize it to meet your specific needs.

A database stored on a computer isn't much different in theory than one painstakingly collected on Rolodex cards or other forms of paper. It contains lots of information, like addresses, Zip codes, and phone numbers, and organizes that info in useful ways (see Figure I-1 for an example). But because it's stored on a computer, you can organize the *same* information in numerous ways with ease—say, by name *or* by state. Computers also make searching databases a whole lot faster. In fact, a computer can often look through almost any amount of data in less than a second, which is a lot quicker than flipping through all your Rolodex cards to find everyone who lives in Kansas.

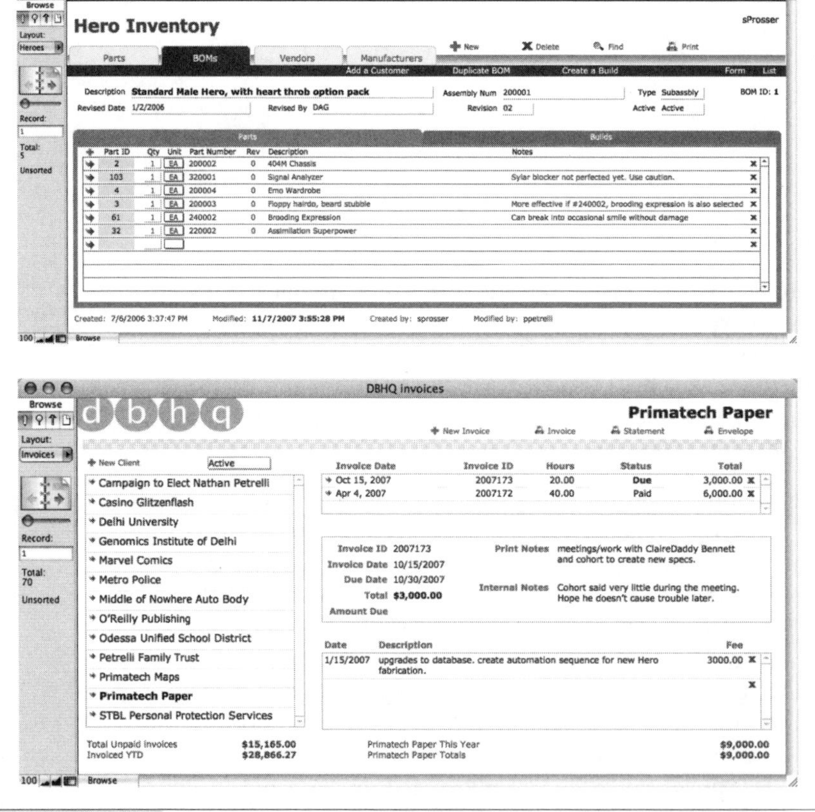

***Figure I-1:** FileMaker Pro lets you do just about anything with the information you give it. You can use it like a Rolodex to simply store and retrieve information, or run your entire business with this one program. FileMaker's built-in number-crunching and word-processing tools let you track people, processes, and things, creating all your reports, correspondence, and collateral documents along the way. Here are two examples of real-world FileMaker databases created for very different kinds of businesses.*

This book will teach you how FileMaker stores your information and how you can rearrange that information and get the answers to meaningful questions like which employees are due for performance reviews, who's coming to the company picnic, and which amusement park has the best deal on Laser Tag so you can throw a party for your top 50 performers. You won't have to learn to think like a programmer (or know the arcane terms they use), but you will learn how to bend FileMaker Pro's hidden power to your will and make it tell you everything it knows about your company, your stock portfolio, or how much you've spent on the replacement parts for the '58 Bonneville Sport Coupe you're rebuilding.

Why FileMaker Pro?

If you're reading this book, you've already decided to use a computer database instead of the mulched-up tree variety. *Choosing* a database program from the many options on the market is overwhelming. Some are enormously powerful but take years to learn how to use. Others are easy to get started with but don't offer much help when you're ready to incorporate some more advanced features. Here are a few reasons why FileMaker Pro is a great choice for most folks:

- **FileMaker Pro is the ease-of-use champion.** While other programs use funny words like *query*, *join*, and *alias*, FileMaker Pro uses simple concepts like *find*, *sort*, and *connect*. FileMaker is designed from the ground up for non-technical people who have a *real* job to do. It's designed to let you get in, get your database built, and get back to work.
- **FileMaker Pro can do almost anything.** Some other database programs are simple to use, but they're just plain simple, too—they can't do the kinds of things most businesses need to do. FileMaker Pro, despite its focus on ease of use, is very powerful. It can handle large amounts of data. It lets lots of people on different computers share data (even at different locations around the world). It even meets the needs of bigger companies, like integrating with high-end systems. And it's adaptable enough to solve most problems. If your home-based crafting business is taking off, and you need to figure out how much it costs you to create your top-selling items, FileMaker can do that. But if you're a large school district tracking dozens of test scores for more than 50,000 students in grades K-12, and you have to make sure those scores are tied to federal standards, FileMaker can handle that, too.
- **FileMaker Pro works on Macs or PCs.** If you or your company use both types of computers, FileMaker Pro makes the connection seamless. The exact same databases can be used on any computer, and even shared over the network simultaneously without a hitch (see page 676).
- **FileMaker Pro is fun!** It may sound corny, but it's exciting (and a little addictive) to have such a powerful tool at your fingertips. If you get the bug, you'll find yourself solving all kinds of problems you never knew you had. You might not think that getting married is an occasion for breaking out a new database, but you'll be amazed at how helpful it is. You can make a mailing list for your invitations, track RSVPs, note which favorite aunt sent you a whole set of bone china (and which cousin cheaped out by signing his name on his brother's gift card), and you can record what date you mailed the thank-you notes.
- **Everybody uses it.** Perhaps best of all, FileMaker Pro is very popular—more people buy FileMaker Pro than any other database program. And the program's fans love it so much they're actually willing to help *you* if you get stuck. You can find user groups, Web sites, discussion boards, chat rooms, mailing lists, and professional consultants all devoted to FileMaker Pro. This is one case where there's good reason to follow the crowd.

What's New in FileMaker Pro 9

FileMaker Pro is a single software package that serves two fundamentally different types of people: users and designers. Users are the folks who need a database to help them organize and manage the data they work with in order to do their jobs. Developers create the databases that users use. No matter which category you're in (and lots of people fall into both categories, sometimes popping back and forth dozens of times a day), you'll find that FileMaker doesn't play favorites. The features you need for both roles are equally accessible.

Day-to-day users appreciate features like the following, because they address many common tasks:

- When you create a new file, you get more options in the new **Quick Start** screen. You can create a new database from one of FileMaker's many templates, create a new file from scratch, or open an existing file, whether it's on your computer's hard drive or it's shared using FileMaker Server. The Learn More link serves as a clearing house for FileMaker help. Choose from links to the FileMaker Learning Center, a What's New guide, the User Guide, or FileMaker's Knowledge Base.
- The **enhanced Web viewer** you use to track FedEx and UPS packages (new since FileMaker 8.5) now gives you a progress bar as the page loads, so you don't have to wonder if your Internet connection is working. And when you pay for purchases, say on Amazon.com or eBay, the Web viewer shows a Lock icon to indicate that your connection is secure.
- If you need a quick refresher on, say, instant Web publishing, you don't have to scramble around your hard drive looking for FileMaker's documentation. The new **Product Documentation command** knows where to find help files and opens them without a fuss.
- **Multiple-level Undo** and **Redo of Typing** commands let you step backwards through your typing tasks. These features can come in handy when you're correcting data-entry mistakes, for example, which often requires many edits of data in the same field.
- With **field-level control for Visual Spell Checking**, you can turn off the display of squiggly lines under words FileMaker's spelling dictionary doesn't recognize. So if your database records patients' medical histories, FileMaker won't clutter up the name of every medication.
- Now you can send data to your boss who doesn't use FileMaker without even a trip to the File menu. The **toolbar** has new tools for "Save as Excel" and "Save as PDF."
- When you're installing FileMaker 9 for all the employees in your company, you don't want to spend time painstakingly entering staff names and other info so you can register each copy. But staff can use the **Register Now** command after you've finished.

- You can make ID tags for each piece of computer equipment in your office, complete with acquisition date, upgrades, and repair status by creating a new layout for Avery Label 6578. **Updated Avery Labels** include the latest copier styles and sizes, so you don't have to fuss with picky dimensions when you're in a hurry.
- No longer must you haunt user forums or make regular visits to FileMaker's Web site to make sure you've got the latest and greatest software. **Software Update Notification** checks weekly to make sure your copy of FileMaker Pro is up to date.

Database developers will appreciate these new features that help create databases (or improve those you already have):

- If you need to add a new calculation that totals up your monthly sales but aren't sure how, click the **Learn More** link in the Specify Calculation dialog box. This action launches FileMaker's Help file entry that explains the dialog box and all its secrets.
- When a new employee needs access to your shared databases, the **Send Link** command, found in the File menu, will generate an email with a clickable link to your files. No more writing lengthy instructions or standing over the new guy while he fumbles around a new network trying to find the files he needs to be productive on day one.
- **Conditional Formatting** lets you do neat tricks like display invoice totals in red if they're overdue, in blue if they're pending payment, or in gray if they've been paid.
- If you generate custom PDF catalogs for your customers and would like to add a few more items to an existing PDF, use **Append to PDF Script Step.** With this new command, you don't have to create a second document, or worse, start the whole catalog over from scratch.
- If your users have a wide range of monitor sizes, you'll love the new **Auto Resize Layout Objects.** You can anchor fields, tab controls, and other layout elements, and then they'll shrink or grow, depending on the screen size and resolution of each user.
- If you used to type extra spaces in the name of your tabs to force them to be the same width, you'll appreciate the improved **Tab Controls.** You can set a consistent tab width, and even make one tab the default, so that users always see it active when they navigate to the layout.
- **ScriptMaker** now lets more than one developer work on scripts at the same time. Script folders and separators let you organize scripts, and a search field filters long lists of scripts, making it easy to spot the one you need.
- If you've created a whizz-bang set of files for managing your home-based business, it's now a lot easier to sell well-behaved files to other users, because you can use one of FileMaker's new **Calculation Functions** to check which version of FileMaker Server your customer is running. That way, you can skip parts of your scripts that won't work on certain server versions.

- If you're keeping your college's course schedule in a FileMaker database, but registration data is stored in a SQL database, use the **External SQL Sources** (ESS) connection to share data between the two systems. See Chapter 17 for details.

If you use FileMaker Pro Advanced for its developers' tools (and if you aren't using it, you should), your professional life just got a whole lot easier. Here's a partial list of its new features:

- Finding out what went wrong with a script you're troubleshooting is easy with the **enhanced Script Debugger.** The script's last error code is displayed, so you don't have to capture it in a variable. Plus, the code is a handy link to the error code list. Just click to see, for example, that error 110 means the related tables referred to by your script are missing.
- The **Data Viewer** now displays a pop-up window with more room to read lengthy values that don't fit in the main window's columnar format. Even better, it automatically displays the value of all variables as your script runs them. No more time spent creating all the values you want to watch, or time wasted because you forgot to create an important one.
- To use FileMaker's new features effectively, you'll need to see them in the **Database Design Report** (DDR) when you analyze your system. Sure enough, FileMaker lists your external SQL tables and supplemental fields, grouped scripts, tab control properties, conditional formatting, and auto-resized layout objects in your DDRs.

If you share databases over the network, you'll be glad to know about FileMaker Server's new features. Here are the highlights:

- Server maintenance now takes place in a browser, so Mac and Windows fans alike see the same **Admin Console** with all the same features. If you use a Mac at work but a Windows machine at home, or if you have to administer the server from whatever machine you happen to be in front of when something crops up at work, you have only one screen to get used to.
- You'll know more about who's using your files, when they logged in, and even what account they've used to open those files with the improved **Client Administration** panel.
- **You can now run scripts from the server,** so you can set up a nightly maintenance routine that sweeps through your database, looking for all the records that were marked for deletion during the day. You can test each record with your script, and then delete or repair records while you and the rest of the staff are home resting.
- A new **PHP Site Assistant** lets you harness the power of PHP (a powerful, open-source coding language), without writing a single line of PHP code. The assistant helps you create a Web site using the tables and fields you've already created in your FileMaker database.

UP TO SPEED

What About the Big Guys?

The word *database* is a little abused in the computer world. Both FileMaker Pro and MySQL–an open-source database that you can use for free, if you have the skills, manpower, hardware, and know-how–are considered database programs, but they're about as similar as chocolate cake and dry flour. In reality, two kinds of database programs are available. One kind is very powerful (as in run-the-federal-government powerful) and *very* complicated. This type of database program just holds data, and computer programmers use sophisticated, and expensive, tools when they build big systems for big companies.

The other kind of database program–sometimes called a *desktop database*–is less powerful and a lot easier, but it actually has more features. In addition to holding lots of data, these programs provide an *interface* to access, organize, and search the data. This interface includes the menus, graphics, and text that let you work with the data, much like any other computer program. In other words, you don't need a computer science degree to create a powerful database with a desktop program like FileMaker Pro.

And with FileMaker Pro 9's powerful ESS connection feature, you can now have the best of both worlds. You (or even better, an IT person who's a database nerd) can create and administer a SQL database, and then you get to use FileMaker to create a snazzy interface for the SQL data. Your nerd colleague would say you're using FileMaker as a "front end" to the SQL database. You can just call it common sense.

The Very Basics

You'll find very little jargon or nerd terminology in this book. You will, however, encounter a few terms and concepts that you'll see frequently in your computer life. They include:

- **Clicking.** This book offers three kinds of instructions that require you to use the mouse or trackpad attached to your computer. To *click* means to point the arrow cursor at something onscreen and then—without moving the cursor at all—press and release the clicker button on the mouse (or laptop trackpad). Right-clicking works the same as clicking, but you use the right mouse button instead. (If you use a Mac and don't have a right mouse button, press the Control key as you click.) To *double-click*, of course, means to click twice in rapid succession, again without moving the cursor at all. And to *drag* means to move the cursor while keeping the button continuously pressed.

  When you're told to *Ctrl-click* something, you click while pressing the Ctrl key (the *Control* key on the Mac) on the bottom row of your keyboard. Such related procedures as *Shift-clicking* and *Alt-clicking* work the same way—just click while pressing the corresponding key.

Note: On the Mac, the key that does most of the Alt key functions is called the Option key. Macs also have an extra key called the Command key, which has a cloverleaf (⌘) on it. When the Mac keystroke is different from the one in Windows, this book gives it in parentheses.

- **Menus** are the lists of commands that you pull down from the words at the top of the FileMaker window. (On the Mac, they're always in the bar across the top of the screen.) There are two equally valid ways to choose from these pull-down menus with your mouse: Click once to open the menu, and then click again to choose a command; or click and *hold* the button as you drag down the menu, and release when you get to the desired command. Use whichever method you find easier.

- **Keyboard shortcuts.** Every time you take your hand off the keyboard to move the mouse, you lose time and potentially disrupt your creative flow. That's why many experienced computer jockeys use keystroke combinations instead of menu commands wherever possible. Ctrl-P (⌘-P) opens the Print dialog box, for example.

  When you see a shortcut like Ctrl-Q (⌘-Q), which closes the current program, it's telling you to hold down the Ctrl (⌘) key, and, while it's down, type the letter Q, and then release both keys.

If you've mastered this much information, you have all the technical background you need to enjoy *FileMaker Pro 9: The Missing Manual.*

About This Book

FileMaker Pro comes with a printed manual and an impressive online help system. These are actually pretty helpful resources—if you're a programmer, that is, or if you've been working with FileMaker for a while. Between the manual and the help system, you can figure out how FileMaker works. But you'll have to jump back and forth between page and screen to get the complete picture. And neither source does a great job of letting you know which features apply to the problem you're trying to solve.

This book is designed to serve as the FileMaker Pro manual, the book that should have been in the box. It explores each feature in depth, offers shortcuts and workarounds, and explains the ramifications of options that the manual doesn't even mention. Plus, it lets you know which features are really useful and which ones you should worry about only in very limited circumstances. Try putting sticky tabs in your help file or marking the good parts with a highlighter!

FileMaker comes in several flavors, and this book addresses them all. FileMaker Pro, the base program, takes up most of the book's focus. FileMaker Pro Advanced is an enhanced version of the program. Like the name promises, it contains advanced tools and utilities aimed at making development and maintenance of your databases easier. Its features are covered in Chapter 12 and 19. FileMaker Server lets you share your databases more safely and quickly than FileMaker Pro's peer-to-peer sharing. Learn about Server in Chapter 18.

About the Outline

FileMaker Pro 9: The Missing Manual is divided into seven parts.

- **Part One: Introduction to FileMaker Pro.** Here, you'll learn about FileMaker Pro's interface and how you perform basic tasks, like entering data and then sorting through it again. You'll also find out how FileMaker Pro stores your data inside fields and then organizes those fields into units called *records*. You'll see how to *define* fields and make them do some of the data entry work for you.
- **Part Two: Layout Basics.** Just as your actual data is organized into fields and records, the appearance of your database is organized into layouts. FileMaker Pro provides a whole raft of tools that make creating layouts fast and powerful. You'll find out how to use layouts to make data entry easier and how to create layouts that list and summarize your data.
- **Part Three: Multiple Tables and Relationships.** When you're storing lots of different types of data in a database, it's helpful to organize types of data using FileMaker's tables. And when you have more than one table, you need to figure out how the information in one table relates to the information in another. You'll learn how to create, connect, and manage multiple tables and how to set up complex relationships that show you just the data you need to see.
- **Part Four: Introduction to Calculations.** Most databases store lots of numbers, but the most important information in your database comes from performing some kind of math on those numbers. You'll learn how to use FileMaker Pro's more than 200 functions to do the math for you. Surprisingly, you can also use functions on fields that don't contain numbers. For example, there are functions for working with text, dates, and times. And some of the most powerful functions are the logical functions, which can perform tests on your data, and then give you results based on what the function finds out.
- **Part Five: Scripting.** Because there are so many things you have to do with a database that are repetitive, tedious, or just plain boring, FileMaker Pro provides a way for you to automate those tasks using scripts. You'll start with simple steps that teach you how scripting works, and learn how to make scripts for people to use. You'll see how to use scripts to work with fields and records, or with windows, or even with entire database files. And you'll explore more complex techniques, like making scripts pass information to one another and nesting scripts within other scripts.
- **Part Six: Security and Integration.** FileMaker knows your data's important enough to keep it safe from prying eyes. In this section, you'll learn how to protect your database with passwords and how to use privileges to determine what folks can do once they get into your database. This part also teaches you how to move data into and out of your database and how to share that data with other people and even with other databases. In the final chapter, you'll see the design and development tools provided in FileMaker Advanced to speed creation time and give you more control over how your database works.

- **Part Seven: Appendixes.** No book can include all the information you'll need for the rest of your FileMaker career. Well, it could, but you wouldn't be able to lift it. Eventually, you'll need to seek extra troubleshooting help or consult the program's online documentation. So, at the end of the book, Appendix A explains how to find your way around FileMaker's built-in help files and Web site. It also covers the vast online community of fans and experts: People are the best resource of all for fresh ideas and creative solutions. Appendix B lists FileMaker error codes.

Living Examples

Each chapter contains *living examples*—step-by-step tutorials that help you learn how to build a database by actually doing it. If you take the time to work through these examples at the computer, you'll discover that these tutorials give you invaluable insight into the way professional developers create databases. To help you along, online database files provide sample data for you to work with and completed examples against which to check your work.

You can get these files any time from the "Missing CD" page (see "About MissingManuals.com" on page 11). To download, simply click this book's title, and then click the link for the relevant chapter.

Macintosh and Windows

FileMaker Pro works almost precisely the same in its Macintosh and Windows versions. Every button in every dialog box is exactly the same; the software response to every command is identical. In this book, the illustrations get even-handed treatment, alternating between Windows Vista and Mac OS X.

One of the biggest differences between the Mac and Windows versions is the keystrokes, because the Ctrl key in Windows is the equivalent of the Macintosh ⌘ key.

Whenever this book refers to a key combination, you'll see the Windows keystroke listed first (with + symbols, as is customary in Windows documentation); the Macintosh keystroke follows in parentheses (with - symbols, in time-honored Mac fashion). In other words, you may read, "The keyboard shortcut for saving a file is Ctrl+S (⌘-S)."

About → These → Arrows

Throughout this book, and throughout the Missing Manual series, you'll find sentences like this one: "Open your Home → Library → Preferences folder." That's shorthand for a much longer instruction that directs you to open three nested folders in sequence, like this: "In the Finder, choose Go → Home. In your Home folder, you'll find a folder called Library. Open that. Inside the Library window is a folder called Preferences. Double-click to open it, too."

Similarly, this kind of arrow shorthand helps to simplify the business of choosing commands in menus, as shown in Figure I-2.

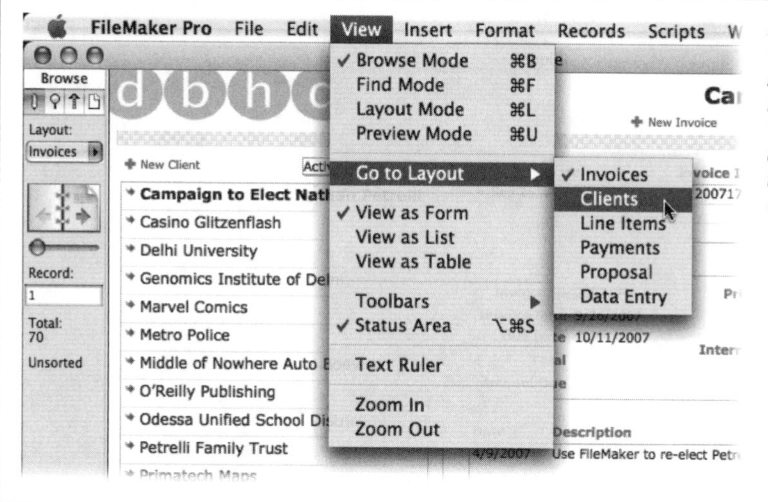

Figure I-2: *When you read in a Missing Manual, "Choose View → 'Go to Layout' → Clients," that means: "Click the View menu to open it, and then click 'Go to Layout' in that menu, and then choose Clients in the resulting submenu."*

About MissingManuals.com

At *www.missingmanuals.com*, you'll find news, articles, and updates to the books in this series. Click the "Missing CD-ROM" link to reveal a chapter-by-chapter list of the databases referred to in the book.

If you click the name of this book and then the Errata link, you'll find a unique resource: a list of corrections and updates that have been made in successive printings of this book. You can mark important corrections right in your own copy of the book, if you like.

In fact, the same page offers an invitation for you to submit such corrections and updates yourself. In an effort to keep the book as up-to-date and accurate as possible, each time we print more copies of this book, we'll make any confirmed corrections you've suggested. Thanks in advance for reporting any glitches you find!

In the meantime, we'd love to hear your suggestions for new books in the Missing Manual line. There's a place for that on the Web site, too, as well as a place to sign up for free email notification of new titles in the series.

Safari® Enabled

When you see a Safari® Enabled icon on the cover of your favorite technology book, that means it's available online through the O'Reilly Network Safari Bookshelf.

Safari offers a solution that's better than e-books: it's a virtual library that lets you easily search thousands of top tech books, cut and paste code samples, download chapters, and find quick answers when you need the most accurate, current information. Try it for free at *http://safari.oreilly.com*.

1

Part One: Introduction to FileMaker Pro

CHAPTER

1

Your First Database

FileMaker Pro databases can be as simple as a phone list for the soccer team or as complex as a company-wide system for purchasing, sales, inventory, invoicing, shipping, and customer tracking. But they all have a few important aspects in common and essentially *work* the same way. This chapter gives you a tour of FileMaker's major features and gets you up and running on your very first database.

FileMaker's vast assortment of tools and options can make its window as intimidating as a jumbo-jet cockpit. But the program's menu commands, dialog boxes, keyboard shortcuts, and other options stay largely consistent across all databases, from the most basic to the most high-powered. Almost everything you learn in the next few pages applies to every database you'll ever use.

Note: Because a database usually solves a *problem* of some kind, some FileMaker experts call a database a *solution*, as in, "I can create an inventory solution for your bakery, but it's going to cost you some dough." Usually, *database* and *solution* mean the same thing, although the term *solution* sometimes implies a system of several connected databases (more on that in Part 3).

A Very Quick Database Tour

Every FileMaker Pro database has two things in common: One, it stores heaps of information, and two, it gives you the tools to manage that information. Whether you start from one of FileMaker's templates (see page 20) or a completely blank slate (see page 94), your new database starts out data-free. It's an empty vessel waiting to be filled. (It would be nice if the program could figure out what data you want and enter it for you, but that probably won't happen until FileMaker Pro

9009.) You have to take care of the data entry yourself. At first, all you see in the window are the tools—buttons, controls, and pop-up menus—that you use to fill the database with data.

Every database window has the same basic structure. FileMaker provides a handful of special items around the window, as you can see in Figure 1-1.

Tip: You can download a sample database form the "Missing CD" page at *www.missingmanuals.com/cds*.

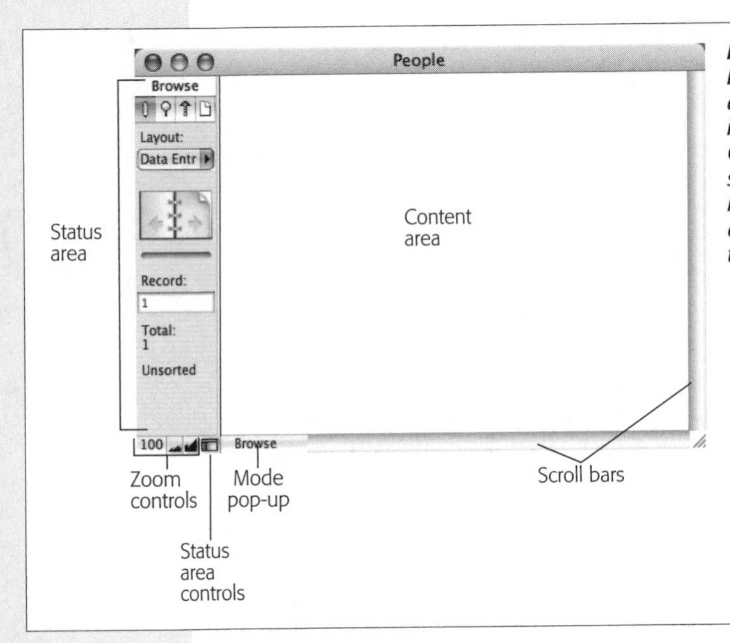

***Figure 1-1:** Every database window has the same apparatus around the edges–what's inside the window is up to you. Compare this window with the one shown in Figure 1-2, left. Both windows have a status area, zoom controls, and a Mode pop-up menu. The content is the only difference.*

Content Area

While some features like the status area, zoom controls, and Mode pop-up menu stay the same no matter which database you're using, what's inside the *content area* is the actual information (data) that makes each database unique.

When you create a new FileMaker database, you start with something that looks a little like Figure 1-1: plain and simple. That's because you haven't added any content yet. In Figure 1-2, you can see what your database will look like once you've started to fill it in. Depending on how you want to look at your information, you can use the controls described below to alter how your content appears onscreen.

Mode Pop-up Menu

This unassuming menu may not be the most prominent control in the window, but it's one of the most important. Each of FileMaker's four *modes* is a work environment unto itself, specially designed to help you view, edit, organize, or present your information in a specific way. Use this menu to switch modes depending on what you need to do.

- In contrast to rational expectations, you use **Browse mode** for more than browsing. In this mode, you can add, change, and view data in your database. Browse is the view shown in Figure 1-2, and it's where you'll spend most of this chapter.
- When you have a lot of data, looking through it all for a particular bit of information can be tedious. Use **Find mode** to let FileMaker do the looking for you. You tell FileMaker what you're looking for in Find mode; when it's done looking, FileMaker returns you to Browse mode and shows what it found. You'll see Find mode in action on page 35.

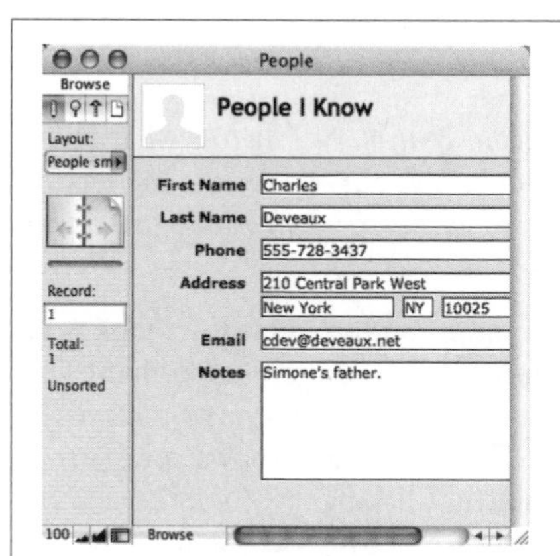

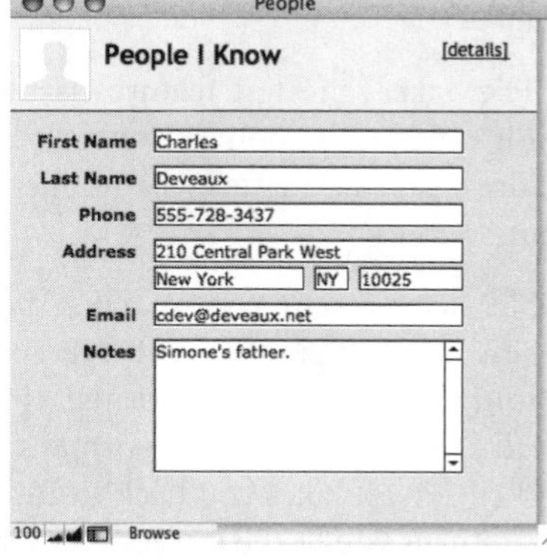

Figure 1-2: *Unlike the stark emptiness shown in Figure 1-1, this database is well underway, as you can see by the abundance of the content area.*

Left: The status area is part of all FileMaker databases, regardless of what they contain.

Right: Maximize your view of the content area by hiding the status area with a simple click on its control.

- In addition to using databases (viewing, finding, sorting, adding, and changing data), you can use FileMaker to *build* databases. **Layout mode** is where you design the screens (or *layouts*) that present your database information to best advantage. Part 2 is all about Layout mode.
- Although computers make maintaining and manipulating mountains of information a breeze, there's still no avoiding paper. Eventually you'll want to print something out, like a set of mailing labels or a paper backup of all your records. If you're ever curious about how something will look when printed, switch to **Preview mode**. It shows a one-page-at-a-time view of your data exactly as it will appear when printed.

To use the Mode pop-up menu, just click it and choose one of the four modes. Your FileMaker window instantly switches to the new mode. You can also glance at the pop-up menu to see which mode you're currently in. (The Mode pop-up menu is the most popular way to mode-hop, but there are plenty more; see the box on page 19.)

Status area and the status area controls

No matter what mode you're in, the *status area* (see Figure 1-1, left) is your central command center. This slim panel lets you see how much information you've got in your database and your current position within it. It also has the controls you'll use most often for both adding information to your database and accessing it later. If you're like most people, at some point you'll come to resent the fact that the status area takes up so much space on your screen. Despite the fact that it usually contains just a few numbers and icons, it eats up a good inch of space along the entire left edge of *every* window. Luckily, you can easily conceal the status area when you don't need it, as shown in Figure 1-2.

Zoom control

One of FileMaker's neatest features is the *zoom control.* No matter what you're doing, you can always zoom in for a closer look or zoom out for the big picture. This feature works no matter what mode you're in—even when you're previewing a printout.

To use FileMaker's zoom control, click the Zoom In button for a closer look (each click zooms in a little more). You can zoom in up to 400 percent, so that everything is four times bigger than normal. If you click Zoom Out, everything shrinks, to as small as one quarter of its normal size. The Zoom Level shows your current level, and clicking it takes you back to 100 percent. Clicking the Zoom Level a second time returns you to the *last* zoom level you were viewing (see Figure 1-3).

Note: Since you probably don't need to examine the words and numbers in your database on a microscopic level, you'll probably use the zoom control mostly in Preview mode to fit the whole page on the screen, or to adjust the contents of your FileMaker window to the most easily readable size (depending on the resolution of your monitor). It is not recommended that you use zoom control in place of reading glasses, though.

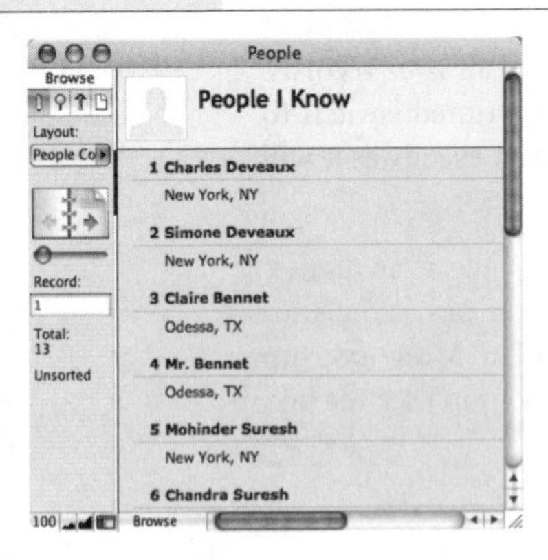

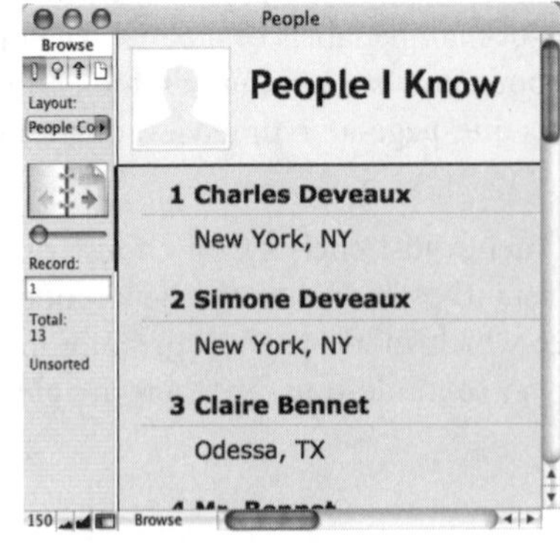

Figure 1-3: *Left: The zoom level in this window is set to 100%.*

Right: Clicking the Zoom Level button once switches you the zoom level you last looked at (200 percent, in this case). Click it again to return to 100%. You can zoom in or out until you find a happy place, and then click Zoom Level again and again. This process can be a form of meditation?or procrastination, depending on your point of view.

Scroll bars

Every window has horizontal and vertical scroll bars that appear whenever you have more content than the window can display. (For an example, see Figure 1-3.) If everything in the content area fits in the window, you won't see scroll bars—after all, you don't need them. FileMaker's scroll bars work just like the ones in any other program, and you can use your keyboard to scroll up and down as well. Press Page Up to scroll up one screenful. Page Down scrolls the other direction. To scroll right and left, use the Home and End keys respectively.

If your mouse has a scroll wheel, you'll notice that it works a little differently in FileMaker. What you scroll through varies based on where you put your mouse cursor—a feature called *contextual* scrolling. The wheel scrolls through the *window* when the cursor is inside the content area of the window. It scrolls through the *records* in your database if you run the cursor over the Book icon in the status area (see page 18). And if you put your cursor over a field that has a scroll bar (see page 162), the scroll wheel scrolls through the text in the field.

UP TO SPEED

Changing Modes

Switching between FileMaker's four modes is such a common task that the program actually gives you *four* ways to do it. The Mode pop-up menu (see page 16) is just one way. You can also use the Mode tabs in the status area (Figure 1-4, this page), or pick a mode from FileMaker's View menu.

The keyboard shortcuts are speediest of all:

- Press Ctrl+B (⌘-B) to switch to Browse mode.
- Press Ctrl+F (⌘-F) to switch to Find mode.
- Press Ctrl+L (⌘-L) to switch to Layout mode.
- Press Ctrl+U (⌘-U) to switch to Preview mode.

If you ever forget these shortcuts, check the View menu to refresh your memory.

FileMaker also gives you several ways to find out which mode you're *in*. The Mode pop-up menu always displays the current mode, and since it's always visible, it's the easiest place to check your mode. But the Mode tabs also reveal the current mode, and the View menu indicates the current mode with a checkmark. So when you return to FileMaker after checking email, you've got plenty of ways to reorient yourself. See Figure 1-4 for pictures of some of these mode-changing tools.

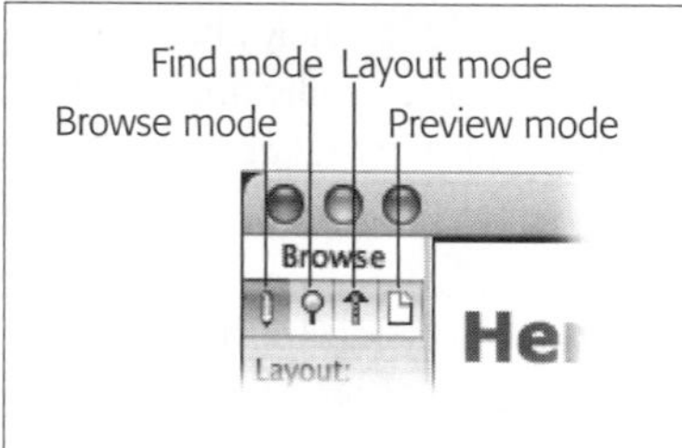

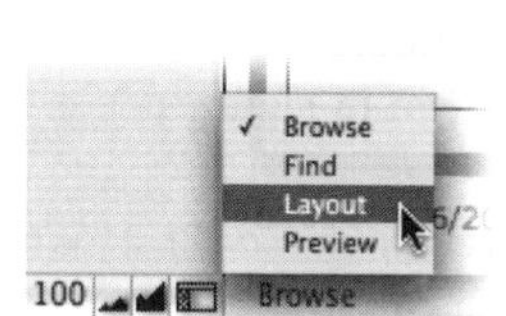

Figure 1-4: *There are lots of ways to change modes. You've got a View menu (like the ones you've seen in countless other programs), FileMaker's own Mode tabs, and a Mode pop-up menu. And if you resent the wasted energy of swinging your mouse to make things happen, you can use keyboard shortcuts, as noted on the View menu (see the box above). FileMaker believes in giving you choices, because that's how it rolls.*

Note: Don't be alarmed when the menus across the top of your screen change a bit when you switch modes. That's just FileMaker being smart. Some commands aren't useful in some modes, so the program doesn't clutter up your screen–or your brain space–with menus when you don't need them. For example, the Insert and Format menus change from black to gray (meaning *unavailable*) when you enter Find mode. The Request menu, though, appears *only* in Find mode.

Creating a New Database

The best way to understand the concepts introduced in this chapter is to get some mouse-on experience. Fortunately, FileMaker Pro gives you a quick way to jump-start a new database.

Although a database can do just about anything, most people want to do a few of the same things (like keep track of their contacts). Accordingly, FileMaker Pro comes with dozens of prebuilt *Starter Solutions*: sample databases that you can fill in with your own data and even customize as you see fit. A Starter Solution, or template, is essentially a sample database, without any information filled in yet. Templates let you start up a database quickly, and as you go along, change or expand it to suit your needs. Almost any conceivable database can be built on one of these foundational layouts; see the box on page 22 for the full catalog.

Tip: If you're the do-it-yourself type, see Chapter 3 for instructions on designing your own database layout from scratch.

Since just about everybody in the world needs to keep track of people, a good place to start your FileMaker experience is with a Contact Management database, which does just what its name suggests: It keeps track of people and their various numbers and addresses. This is the template you can use if, for example, you volunteer for a local repertory company and need a place to store the names and addresses of all season ticket holders. Once you've entered all the information, you can use the database to, say, print letters asking your subscribers for donations to provide new cup holders for the orchestra pit.

Choosing a Starter Solution

To create a new database from a template, you start launching FileMaker Pro (by using the Start → Programs menu in Windows, for example, or clicking its Dock icon on the Mac). Then choose File → New Database. The FileMaker Quick Start dialog box appears, as shown in Figure 1-5.

Warning: Keyboard shortcut aficionados beware. If you're used to typing Ctrl+N (⌘-N) for a new document, you're in for a surprise. In FileMaker, that command makes a new *record*, not a new file. So when you really do want a new file, you'll have to resort to using the mouse and the menu.

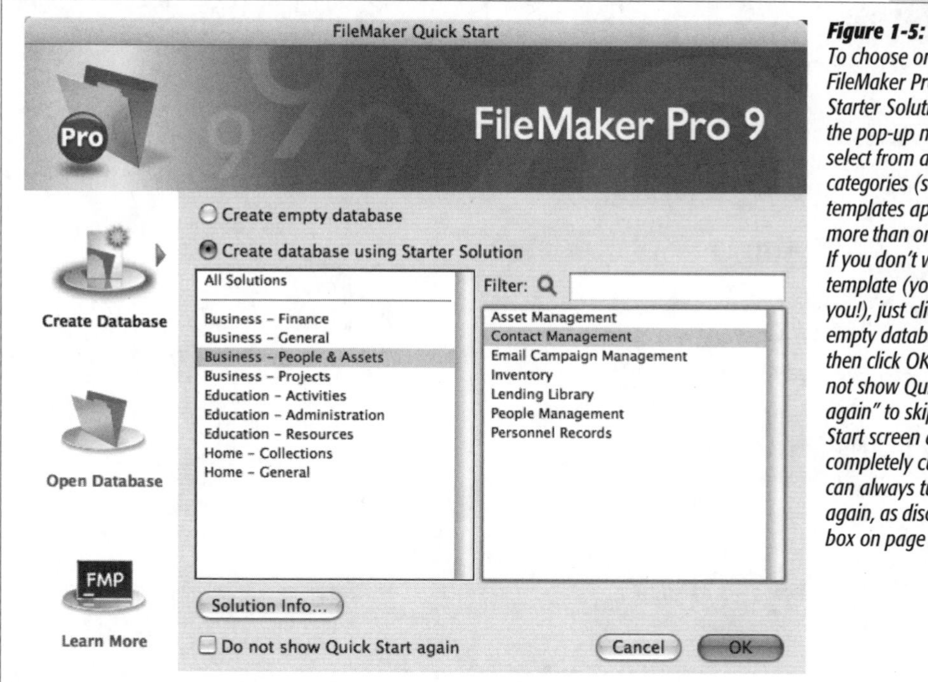

Figure 1-5:
To choose one of FileMaker Pro's built-in Starter Solutions, click the pop-up menu and select from a list of categories (some templates appear in more than one category). If you don't want to use a template (you rebel, you!), just click "Create empty database," and then click OK. Select "Do not show Quick Start again" to skip the Quick Start screen and go completely custom. You can always turn it on again, as discussed in the box on page 24.

To open the Contact Management template:

1. **In the New Database dialog box, select the "Business – People & Assets" category from the pop-up menu.**

   The list shows each template in this category. You can, of course, choose any template that looks like the database of your dreams, but in this example you're looking for Contact Management.

2. **In the "Business – People & Assets" list, select Contact Management.fp7, and then click OK.**

   FileMaker displays a standard Save dialog box.

3. **Name the new database and save it somewhere on your hard drive.**

   The new database appears onscreen, as shown in Figure 1-6.

Opening and Closing Database Files

Each database you create with FileMaker Pro is stored in a *file* on your hard drive—just like your Microsoft Word documents, Excel spreadsheets, and all the PowerPoint presentations you've ever created. This file contains all the information about how the database is structured, plus all the information stored inside it, which means you can open, close, copy, or back up a database as you would any other file. But if you need a bit more explanation, this section explains how to do those tasks, including some quirks that are particular to FileMaker files.

UP TO SPEED

A Tour of the Templates

FileMaker Pro's standard templates make it easy to perform routine tasks found in typical businesses, schools, and homes. Just choose a template and get right to work. Chances are one of the 40 templates built into FileMaker is set up to manage the kind of information you're working with, so you waste no time on setup. Here's an overview of the nine basic template categories:

- The **Business - Finance** set has the bean counters in mind. Track employee expenses and work hours (billable or otherwise), and generate purchase orders.
- The **Business - General** category is an assortment of useful templates from document management to to-do lists. With this category, you can keep track of computer files, create a searchable and printable product catalog, and more.
- If you need to keep track of real things–physical assets, customers, inventory, or just about anything else–use the **Business - People & Assets** category.
- Managers and planners can start in the **Business - Projects** category, where they'll find databases to help plan events, track problems, schedule people and other resources, and manage tasks and projects.
- See **Education - Activities** if you're organizing field trips or other events that require you to keep track of who's coming or who made a nice donation to the school boosters' fund.
- The **Education - Administration** set helps you administer your school's tasks. You can send emails to groups of people (to get a big turnout at your fundraising event), store notes about the research you're doing into how long sleepy students stay awake after lunch, or just keep track of student's names, addresses, and how to get in touch with their parents if they play hooky.
- **Education - Resources** is for collectors and those who keep track of collections. Librarians can manage a lending library, IT departments can make lists of their computer equipment, and anybody who needs to manage electronic assets, like graphics files or PDF documents, can do so right in FileMaker.
- The **Home - Collections** category includes databases to tell you who borrowed your OK Go CD and which computer has your vacation photos from your bike tour of Italy last summer.
- FileMaker is the people's database, so it's no surprise it comes prepared to tackle real problems. **Home - General** gives you a place to store Grandma's vegan apple pie recipe, helps you send email invitations to the big family reunion picnic, and lets you keep track of who's allergic to bee stings.

Opening a Database

To open a database that already exists, open FileMaker Pro and choose File → Open Database. Now select the file you want to work with (see Figure 1-7). If you prefer, you can find the file using Windows Explorer (Windows) or the Finder (Mac OS X), and double-click its icon.

When you open a database, you'll see one or more windows on your screen. If you've opened the Contact Management template you created on page 20, you have one database open, and that database has one window displayed.

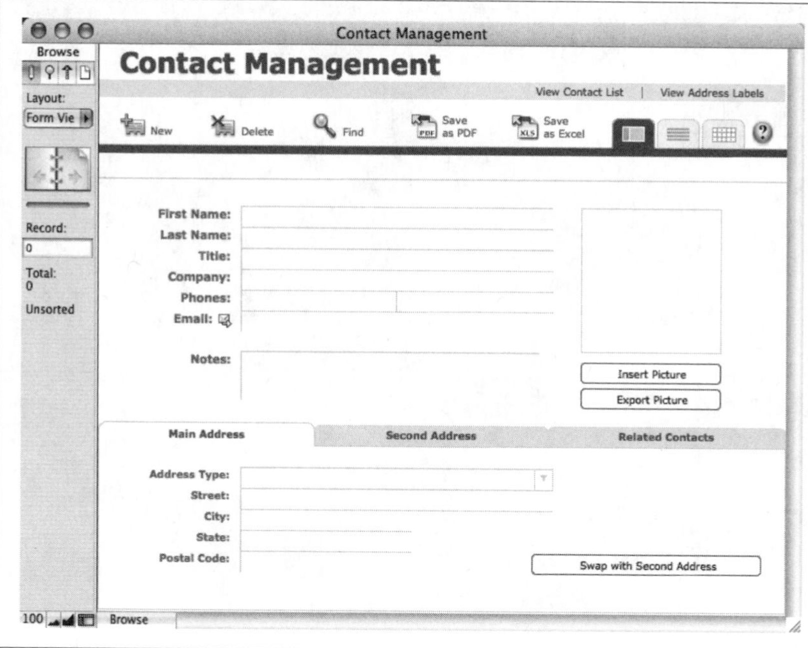

Figure 1-6: *The Contact Management template is an ideal way to create a simple database that contains information about people, like their names, email addresses, and phone numbers. It can hold up to two addresses for each person, and you can even store a picture with each contact—a handy feature if you have trouble putting a face to a name.*

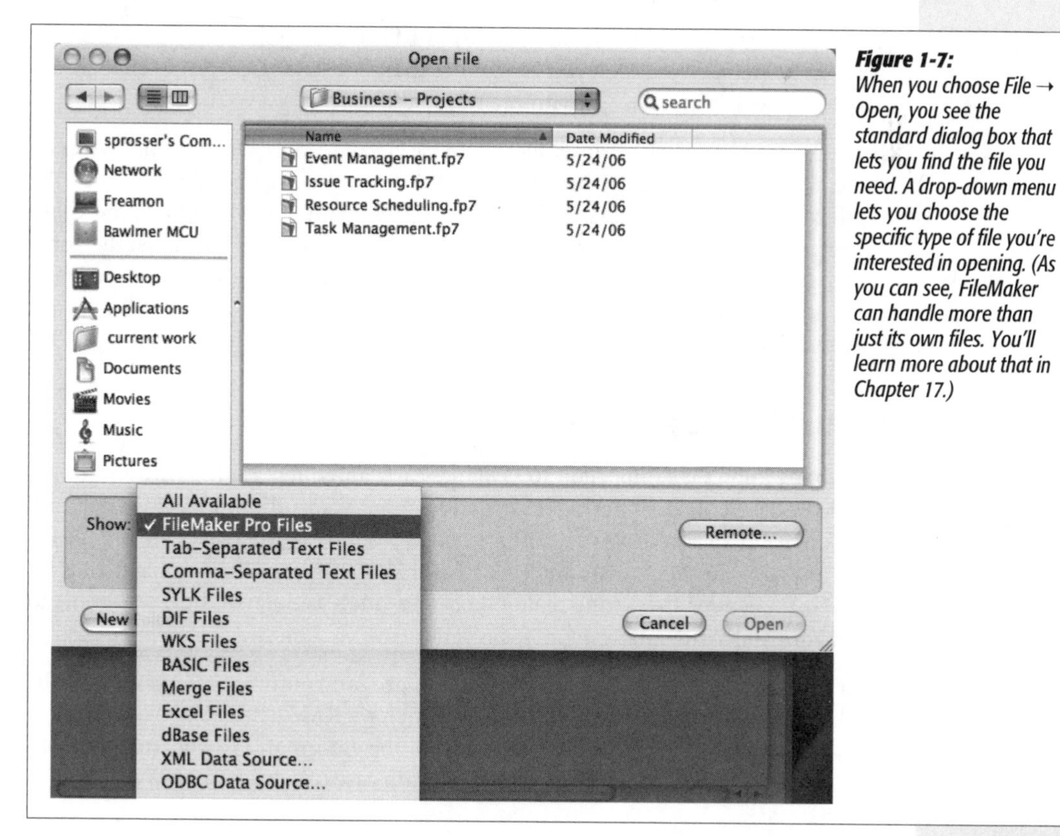

Figure 1-7: *When you choose File → Open, you see the standard dialog box that lets you find the file you need. A drop-down menu lets you choose the specific type of file you're interested in opening. (As you can see, FileMaker can handle more than just its own files. You'll learn more about that in Chapter 17.)*

WORKAROUND WORKSHOP

The Other New Database Dialog Box

If you don't see the box pictured in Figure 1-5 when you choose File → New Database, you may have told FileMaker to stop showing it to you (probably by turning on the "Do not show Quick Start again" checkbox also shown in that figure). To get the template-filled box back, follow these steps:

1. Click Cancel in the dialog box that did appear, if you haven't already. The imposter window goes away.
2. If you're on Mac OS X, choose FileMaker Pro → Preferences. If you're on Windows, choose Edit → Preferences. The Application Preferences dialog box appears automatically, with the General tab in front. At this point, you can change a handful of settings that apply to the FileMaker Pro program itself.

   Make sure "Show FileMaker Quick Start Screen" is turned on.
3. Click OK. Bye-bye preferences.
4. Choose File → New Database again. Now the window shows, with the full complement of templates.

If templates aren't your bag, you may find the New Database dialog box a bit of a drag, since you have to turn on "Create empty database," and then click OK *every* time you make a new database. Instead, just follow the steps above, but turn "Show FileMaker Quick Start Screen" *off*. Now, when you choose File → New Database, you'll see the stock-standard "Create a new file named" dialog box right away.

Closing a Database

To close a database, close all its windows in FileMaker: Choose File → Close or press Ctrl+W (⌘-W). When you have more than one database open, it isn't always easy to tell which windows go with each database.

If you're not sure what to close, there's an easy way to close all the windows in all the databases you currently have open. Hold down the Alt key (Windows) or the Option key (Mac), and then click the trusty File menu. On Mac OS X, the Close command is gone, replaced by a more powerful Close All. On Windows, the command is still called Close, but despite the name, it too closes all open windows. Choose it and FileMaker closes all its open windows, which also closes all your open databases.

Saving Your Databases

Everybody knows it's important to save files early and often, right? So you're working along in FileMaker entering information about your office birthday roster, and as good habit dictates, you type the keyboard shortcut that saves in practically every program in the known universe (that'd be Ctrl+S on Windows and ⌘-S on the Mac). Up pops the wrong dialog box. This one's asking you how you want to sort your data! What gives?

Don't worry, FileMaker has you covered. The program automatically saves all your work in a *cache*, which is part of your computer's RAM (Random Access Memory). Then, periodically, FileMaker transfers the information from the cache to your hard drive, where it's less likely to be lost in case of a crash.

You can control how much work is held in cache before it's saved to your hard drive, as described in Figure 1-8. In Windows, choose Edit → Preferences, and then click the Memory tab. On the Mac, choose FileMaker Pro → Preferences, and then click the Memory tab.

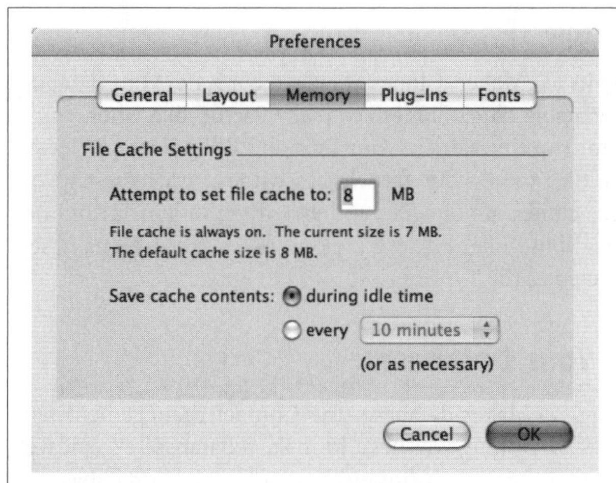

Figure 1-8:
Specify the size of FileMaker's cache and how often your work is moved from the cache to your hard drive. (Nerds call that flushing the cache.*) A larger cache yields better performance but leaves more data in RAM. If you're working on a laptop, you can conserve battery power by saving cache contents less frequently. Just remember, in case of a power outage or other catastrophe, the work that's in cache is more likely to be lost than what FileMaker has saved to your hard drive.*

Saving a Copy of Your Database

Chances are the data in your database is important. (Would you really go to all this trouble if it weren't?) Although FileMaker automatically saves your work as you go, what if the database file itself gets lost or suffers some digital harm? It's in your best interest to *back up* your database periodically. You can perform a backup by simply copying the database file. For example, you can copy it to a CD, email it to a friend, or duplicate it and tuck the copy away in another folder. The easiest way to make a backup is to choose File → "Save a Copy As." You'll see the typical Save dialog box. Just make sure that "copy of current file" is selected as the Type option. When you click OK, FileMaker makes your copy in the background, and you can continue working in the original file.

But if you want to start working in the copy you've just made, select the "Automatically open file" option before you click OK. FileMaker makes the copy of your file, and then helpfully opens it for you. FileMaker doesn't close the original file for you, so if you're finished with the original, choose it from the Window menu, and then close it to avoid confusion. Now only your new copy of the file is open.

If you want to make a copy of your database to send to an associate in another office, chose the "Create email with file as attachment" option. FileMaker copies your file, and then launches your email program, creates a new email, and attaches your newly minted file copy to it. All you have to do is provide an email address, type your message, and click Send. See page 638 to see how you can use similar options if you only want to send data to your associate in another format, like Excel or a PDF file.

Warning: You should always make sure a database is *closed* before you copy its file using any of the desktop methods (like Edit → Copy in Windows Explorer or the Mac's Finder, for example). If you copy the database file onto another disk while it's open in FileMaker, the copy you made may be damaged or missing information.

Saving a clone of your database

There's no ban on cloning in FileMaker. Clones are clean copies of your database, but without any of your valuable data. Clones are really useful, like when you've designed a killer database for running sales in your Dart and Billiards Supply Shop, and you want to send the files to all your franchisees without giving away your store's sales data. Just make clones of your files and give them to your proud new owners. To make a clone, choose File → "Save a Copy As," and then make sure "clone (no records)" is selected as the Type option.

Adding Records to Your Database

When you first open a new FileMaker database (the Contact Management template in this example), it has everything you need to make a database except, well, data. Now that you understand the basic components of a FileMaker database, it's time to start adding your own content. Whether your database contains information about individual persons, objects, pictures, dung beetles, or whatever, FileMaker always thinks of that information in individual chunks called *records*. Each record contains everything the database knows about that person, thing, insect, or whatever.

UP TO SPEED

Refining Your Finds

When FileMaker looks for records, it expects them to match your find request *exactly*. For example, if you put "Mohinder" in the First Name field, and "Suresh" in the Last Name field, FileMaker only finds Mohinder Suresh. Mohinder Ashtapur won't cut it, and neither will Arup Suresh. FileMaker ignores any fields that are empty in your request, so it doesn't matter what Mohinder's title is because you didn't include a Title field in your find request.

Although FileMaker insists that every field in each found record match each field in your request, the data *inside* each field doesn't have to be a perfect match. The next chapter explains how FileMaker decides when a match is good enough, and how you can change its decision-making process.

Finding the right records can be a real balancing act. Be too specific and you may not find anything at all; be too vague and you'll find more than you can handle.

Bear these in mind when you enter your find requests:

- Since FileMaker matches field values flexibly, you can often save typing and improve accuracy by being brief. For example, if you're looking for someone named "Rufus Xavier Sarsaparilla," just type *ruf* in the First Name field and *sar* in the Last Name field. Chances are you'll find the right guy, and you don't have to worry about spelling out the whole name.
- Enter data only in fields you're sure you need. For example, even if you know Rufus lives in Montana, you don't have to put Montana in the State field in your find request.
- If you find more records than you wanted, just go back to Find mode and enter data in more fields to narrow the search. Better yet, read Chapter 2, where you'll learn about the many powers of Find mode.

Now, because you need to store many smaller pieces of information in each record (like a person's phone number, address, birthday, and so on), FileMaker can bestow each record with an almost infinite number of *fields*—the specific bits of data that define each record and make it unique.

For example, each person in a database of magazine subscribers gets her own record. Her first name, last name, phone number, street address, city, state, Zip code, and the expiration date of her subscription are all examples of fields each record can include.

The techniques in this section work the same whether you're creating a new database for the first time (from the Contact Management template you created on page 20, for example), or adding to an existing one.

Note: All records in a database must contain the same fields, but that doesn't mean you fill them all in. For instance, in a gift list database, if your boyfriend refuses to disclose his hat size, you can just leave that field blank in his record.

Creating a Record

When you opened the template for your Contact Management database (see page 21), it was blank and lacking even a single record, so the first thing you need to do is create one. It's simple: Choose Records → New Record or press Ctrl+N (⌘-N). (Since you'll be creating lots of records in your FileMaker career, this is one keyboard shortcut you'll want to memorize.)

Note: When you're adding new records, you must be in Browse mode (see page 17).

Editing a Record

Now that you've created a record, you can enter information about the first person you want to keep track of. This is where those fields come in handy. To enter information in any field in a record, just point, click, and type. What to type? As Figure 1-9 illustrates, each field in this database has a label to its left, which indicates the type of information the field contains. Each field is also outlined in a light gray color.

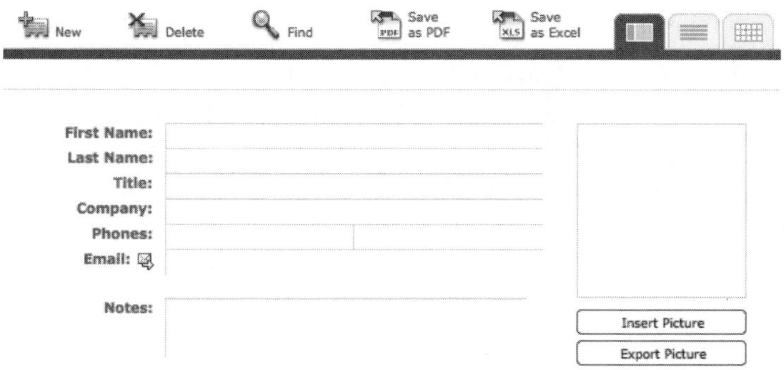

Figure 1-9: *Fields can look like just about anything, but in the Contact Management database, they're pretty simple. When you click in the content area, the fields you can edit are indicated by dotted borders. The field you're currently editing gets a solid border.*

UP TO SPEED

The Many Faces of a Field

Fields are inside the content area (see page 16), so don't be surprised if they don't always look the same. See Figure 1-10 for some variations on the same field. Unlike the status area, FileMaker Pro's content area is one place you can let your creative urges go wild. You can design your database to make fields look almost any way you want. A field can have a label to the right of–or below or above–where you enter text, or no label at all.

A field can be white, blue, green, or any other color. The same goes for the border around a field. In fact, if mystery is your thing, you can make your field invisible–no label, no border, and no color. (But here's a tip: When designing your own databases, make sure folks can tell where the fields are and what goes in them.)

Usually, if you click in a blank space in the content area, all the fields appear with the dotted outline shown in Figure 1-9, but you can't count on this (you can turn this feature off, as described on page 146). So don't expect every field to look like those shown here.

See Chapter 3 for more detail on customizing and beautifying the fields in your database.

Field Label	The Field	Description
Tagline	Save the Cheerleader, Save the World	No border
Tagline	Save the Cheerleader, Save the World	Black border, grey fill
Tagline	Save the Cheerleader, Save the World	Embossed, grey fill
Tagline:	Save the Cheerleader, Save the World	Engraved, grey fill
Tagline	Save the Cheerleader, Save the World	Black border, Drop Shadow
Tagline	Save the Cheerleader, Save the World	No border
	Tagline Save the Cheerleader, Save the World	Field Label on top
	Save the Cheerleader, Save the World Tagline	Field Label on bottom

Figure 1-10: *As you can see, the same field can appear many different ways, even on the same layout. Not all the graphic ideas in this illustration help make a field's contents more readable, as you can see. In general, the smallest amount of extra detail, like a pale border, or even no border at all, is better.*

Moving between fields

To get from the field you're in to another where you can add or edit text, the most obvious way is to reach for the mouse, slide over to the new field, and click. Unless you're eager to burn that extra half a calorie, you may want to try a quicker, less exercise-intensive way, like the following:

- Press the Tab key to move to the next field. If you're not in any field, the Tab key puts you in the first field.
- Hold down the Shift key and press Tab to move to the previous field. This time, if you're not in any field, FileMaker puts you in the *last* field.

Note: If you're wondering who decides which field is *next* or *previous*, dig this: *you* do. When you design a database, you get to set the *Tab order*, or the order FileMaker follows when you press Tab or Shift-Tab to move among fields. See page 269 for details.

UP TO SPEED

Lost in the Wilderness

The database template you're using in this chapter has an assortment of *buttons* in its content area (some are labeled in Figure 1-11). They can look like tabs, text links, or just about anything else (a few even look like buttons). A click on one of these may show you things you're not familiar with–maybe even make you feel like you've lost your place.

To avoid an accidental left turn when you try to commit the record, try not to click a button. Instead click somewhere in the empty white area around the fields.

If you've already clicked a button, and now you're lost in the wilderness, finding your way back won't require a trail of breadcrumbs.

Just follow these steps, in order:

- If you see a button in the status area called Continue, click it. (If you don't see that button, don't worry–just skip to the next step.)
- If the Mode pop-up menu doesn't say Browse, click it, and then choose Browse from the menu that appears.
- In the status area, under Layout, you should see a pop-up menu. Make sure this menu reads "Form View."

You should now be back in your comfort zone. Phew!

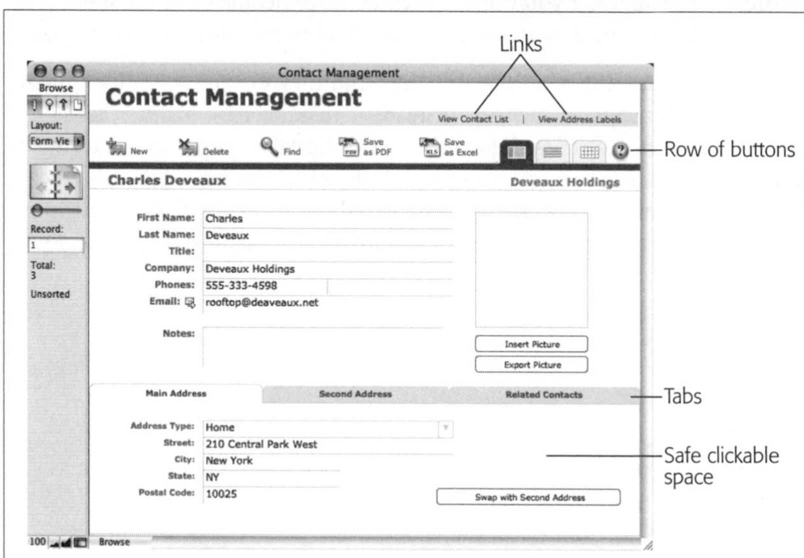

***Figure 1-11:** Just like their designers, all FileMaker databases are a little different, with different fields, buttons, and clickable things. But they all share some basic behaviors, so getting accustomed to basic behavior will stand you in good stead when you start poking around in other people's databases.*

Adding More Records

When you've filled in all the fields and you're ready to move on to your next subscriber, you must create an additional record to hold that contact, as each record can contain only one person's information. You've probably already figured out that you can just select Records → New Record again, and get another empty record to fill. You've also figured out you'll be creating records *a lot* as you enter all your subscribers. To speed things along, you can use the New Record keyboard shortcut: Ctrl+N (⌘-N).

UP TO SPEED

On the Record

To get *out* of all fields–so you're not in any field at all–press Enter (use the one on your numeric keypad, not the one that makes line breaks), or click a blank spot in the content area. This process is called *committing* the record. No, you're not sending the record away for a little quiet time; rather, you're telling FileMaker you're ready to commit to the changes you've made. (If you don't want to commit to the changes you've made, you can choose Records → Revert Record to get out of all fields and discard those changes. This command is explained more fully on page 32.)

When you first click in a field, you've *opened* the record. If you imagine an old-fashioned file cabinet, you'd have to open someone's file before you could change something in it.

As long as you have a record open, you're *in* the record. You can be in only one record at any given moment, and that record is said to be *active*. Rounding out this nonsense, when you've committed the record, you're *on* the record but you're not *in* the record. Believe it or not, getting this terminology straight makes things easier later on.

Duplicating a record

While no two people are alike, it may not always seem that way from their contact information. For instance, if you want to include three people from the same company in your database, the data in the Company field is the same for each person.

The Email and Phone fields won't be the same, but they may be close. It's time for a little organized laziness to kick in: Instead of making new blank records and retyping all that stuff, just choose Records → Duplicate Record (see Figure 1-12). FileMaker displays a new record containing all the same information as the record you chose to duplicate. (FileMaker copied everything from the first record into a new one for you.) Now you can just edit the information that needs to be changed.

Tip: Be sure you don't accidentally leave in the first person's email address or phone number, lest a message or phone call get misdirected later.

Deleting records

Last but not least, getting rid of a record you no longer need is a breeze. FileMaker Pro gives you three commands that let you delete one record, a group of records, or even *all* the records in your database.

Warning: Deleting records can't be reversed. There's no Undo option, since FileMaker saves changes automatically (see page 24). So when you delete a record (or all the records in a database), make sure you're ready to part with the data.

- **One record.** Just choose Records → Delete Record to delete the record you're currently on. FileMaker asks if you're sure you want to delete the record, lest you accidentally send, say, your aunt's address to the trash bin. If you've indeed written her—or anyone else—out of your life, simply click Delete in the message box to complete the purge.

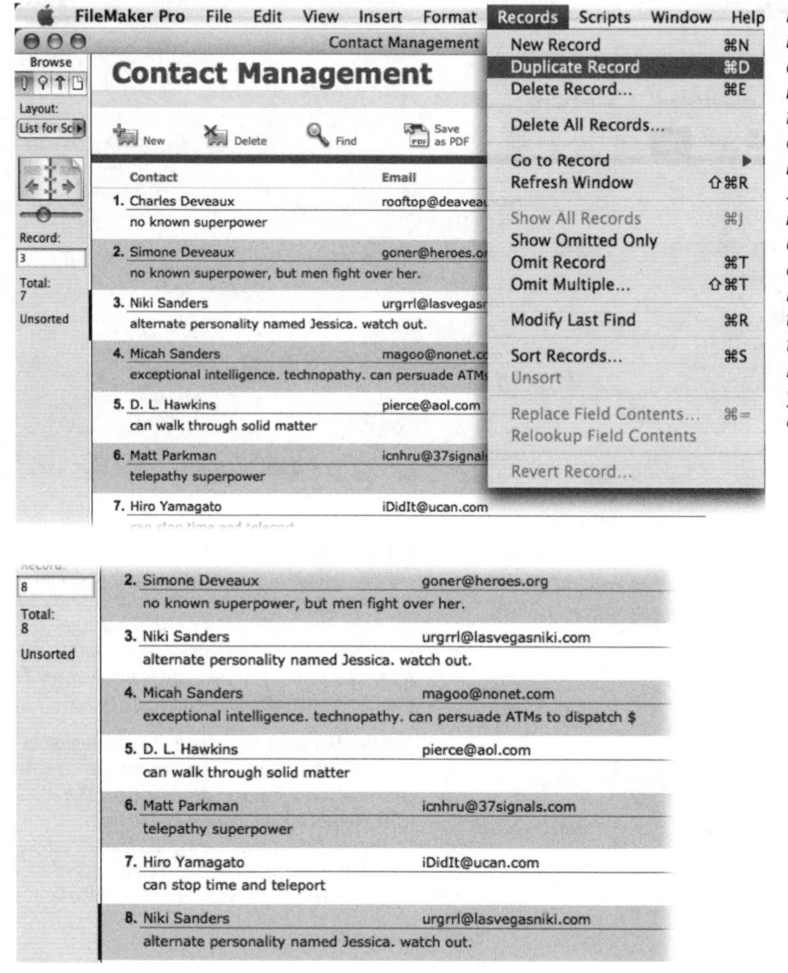

Figure 1-12: *If you go looking for your duplicated record later, you may be surprised where you find it. No matter where the original record is, the new record is created at the end. So if you have seven records in your database and you duplicate record #3, the duplicated record is #8. Notice the thin black line just to the left of record #3 in the top picture. That's FileMaker's way of telling you which record is active in a list.*

- **Multiple records.** FileMaker has a neat command (Records → Delete Found Records) that trashes any group of records of your choosing. Before you can use this command, you have to tell FileMaker what those records are, which you do by using the Find command (see page 35). In your FileMaker career, you'll often use the Find command to locate the records you want to act upon *before* you tell FileMaker what to do with them.

- **All records.** In some cases, you may want to delete all the records in a database. Maybe your friend wants an empty copy of your database for his own use. Or perhaps your database holds data you just don't need anymore, like test results you're about to reproduce. Complete record elimination is easily accomplished by way of two menu commands: Just choose Records → Show All Records, and then choose Records → Delete All Records.

WORKAROUND WORKSHOP

An Error a Day

When you create a database, FileMaker is nice enough to create the first record for you, so you can start typing right away. But when you start a database using a template, you're not so lucky. If you try clicking in a field, you're met with the error message shown at the top of Figure 1-13. Luckily, that error message tells you exactly what you need to do: Choose File → New Record first.

This minor annoyance is forgivable, since it's so easy to work around (and frankly, most databases don't stay empty for long). Unfortunately, another common error message is twice as annoying. If you try typing something *before you've* clicked in a field, FileMaker decides it better warn you with the box shown at the botton of Figure 1-13. Apparently, the folks at FileMaker are afraid you'll type madly away before you figure out nothing's showing up onscreen.

So instead, you'll have to dismiss an error message every time you bump a key on your keyboard. This gets annoying quickly, but there's no way to get rid of the error message for good. Just remember that you have to be *in* a field before you can start typing.

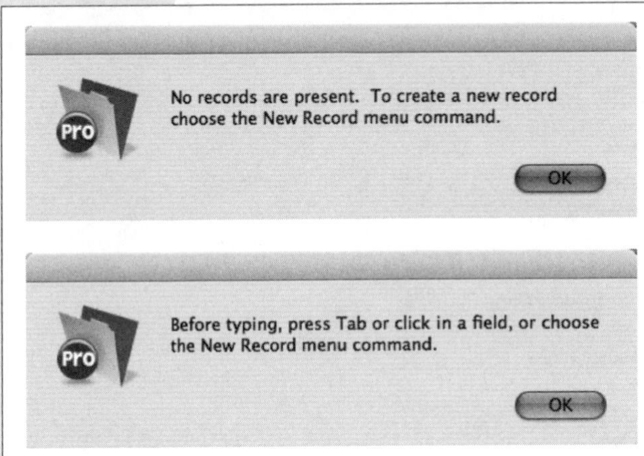
No records are present. To create a new record choose the New Record menu command.
OK
Before typing, press Tab or click in a field, or choose the New Record menu command.
OK

Figure 1-13:
Top: It's annoying to start typing only to get an error message before the first character is dry on the page. But FileMaker is trying to tell you something akin to "put some paper in this typewriter before you start typing madly away." (You do remember typewriters, don't you?)

Bottom: This error message is the companion to the one in the previous figure. In this communique, FileMaker needs you to tell it where to put all that data your 110 wpm processing power is delivering. Without direction, your data is going into the vast emptiness of space, instead of into your Contact database.

Tip: If you're feeling confident about a delete choice and want FileMaker to skip its "Are you sure?" confirmation message, hold down the Shift (Option) key while choosing Records → Delete Record.

Revert the record

Now that you know how to edit a record, and what it means to be in a record (see the box on page 30), you can learn about one of FileMaker's most overlooked features: the Revert Record command. Its purpose is simple: Choose Records → Revert Record and FileMaker throws away any changes you made since you first entered the record. This trick comes in handy when you accidentally modify a field by bumping into the keyboard, or realize you accidentally entered Steve Jobs' address in Bill Gates' record. Just revert the record and you can be confident that whatever you did has been forgotten.

But keep in mind that the Revert Record command is available only when you're in a record *and* you've made changes. If you don't have the record open, or you haven't made any changes since you last committed the record, the Revert Record command is grayed out.

Note: Committing a record isn't exactly difficult: You just press Enter or click somewhere in the window, and FileMaker dutifully saves the record without a peep. Once this happens, you can no longer choose the Revert Record command. (How's that for commitment?) If you want a little more control, you can tell FileMaker to ask you for confirmation before a record is committed. You'll learn how to do this on page 146.

Using the tools described so far for adding, deleting, and editing records in your database, you can quickly amass a large number of records. The next section explains how to find your way around this vast body of information.

Navigating Your Database

As exciting as it is to enter data into a database—well, the first time anyway—chances are you'll want to look at those records again at some point. In fact, some may say that's the whole point of building a database. But first, you need to learn how to *navigate* the records in the database, which this section explains. Fortunately, moving around a database isn't nearly as tough as following maps and highway signs in a foreign country. FileMaker makes it easy to skip from one record to the next, all the while keeping you abreast of where you are.

Tip: As you go through this section on navigating, it helps to have a database open in front of you so you can follow along and try some of these techniques. Since you probably don't have many records in the Contact Management database you just created, there's a sample one for you to download on the "Missing CD" page at *www.missingmanuals.com/cds*.

Navigating Record by Record

In the Contact Management database, you can add as many records as you want. But you can view only one at a time in the window FileMaker displays. To tell FileMaker which record you want to look at, you have three options:

- The **book icon** lets you flip from record to record one at a time. Pretend your database is a book, with each record on its own page. To get to the next record, click the right-hand page. To go back, click the left-hand page. If you can't go any further in one direction, the appearance of the icon's "page" changes, as shown in Figure 1-14.
- The **slider** is kind of a turbo-charged version of the Book icon. Instead of clicking once for each record, you can advance through a bunch of records by dragging. If you know approximately where you want to go (like "around halfway" or "about one-third from the end"), then the slider is the quickest way to get there. The slider is most handy when you want to get to the beginning or the end of the database. In that case, just drag the slider as far as it will go in either direction.

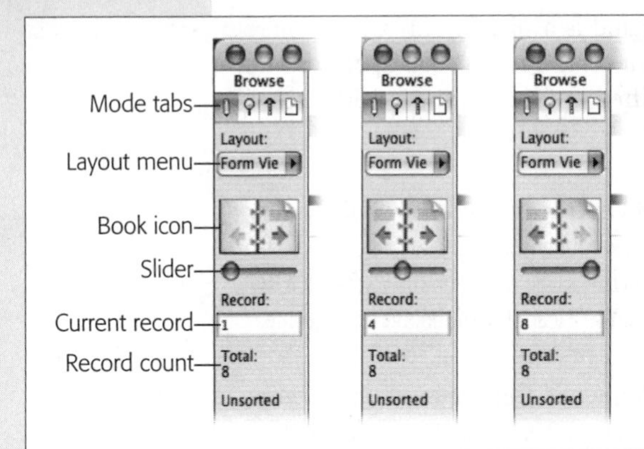

Figure 1-14:
The status area is the key to record navigation. In addition to displaying the controls for switching records, the status area indicates where you are in the database. This series of pictures, for example, shows the status area when you're on the first record in the database (left), a record in the middle of the database (middle), and the last record (right). Notice how the appearance of the Book icon and slider changes in each picture.

- The **Current Record** indicator serves two purposes. First, it shows you which record you're on. Second, if you know which record you *want* to be on, you can simply type in the record number to jump to it. Below the Current Record, the status area also shows you how many records are in your database.

Note: All navigation methods let you move within what FileMaker calls a *found set*, which lets you look at a specific set of records at one time. Learn more about finds and found sets on page 35.

Keyboard Shortcuts

FileMaker also has a few keyboard shortcuts to make record navigation painless. If you haven't used a database program before, you'll notice that some keys act in ways you may not expect—like the Enter key, as described below. Still, spending a little time getting used to using these keystrokes will save you hours of time down the road.

- To go to the next record, press **Ctrl (Control)-Down Arrow.**
- To move to the previous record, press **Ctrl (Control)-Up Arrow.**
- To activate the Current Record indicator without using the mouse, press **Esc.** Now type a record number and press Enter to go to that record. (This shortcut works only when you're not in the record; see page 30.)
- Pressing the **Enter** key *commits* the record, rather than inserting a new line in a field, as you may expect based on what the Enter key does in other programs. To insert a new line in FileMaker, press the **Return** key.

Note: On some keyboards, there isn't a Return key—instead, two keys are labeled Enter. In this case, the Enter key that's near the number keypad commits the record, while the other (normal) Enter key enters a blank line in the field.

- Pressing the **Tab** key moves you from one field to another. (To indent a line you have to *type* a tab character into a field, by pressing Ctrl+Tab [Option-Tab].)

Finally, bear in mind that you can change these things on a field-by-field basis when you're designing a database, as you'll learn in Chapter 3. For instance, File-Maker lets you decide that Return—not Tab—should move you from field to field. If you make that choice, Tab types a *tab* into a field, and Return doesn't insert a blank line. Unfortunately, there's no way for you to tell which key does what by looking at a field; you just have to try some of these keys to find out.

UP TO SPEED

Numbers Sometimes Lie

When you first create a database, FileMaker numbers each new record as you add it–with a record number that appears in the book icon (see Figure 1-14). You may think that this number is a great way to locate a particular record later: "I need to give Jim over at Dunder-Mifflin a call to reorder supplies. I put his contact information in record #79. I'll just go to that number." Since record numbers may change as you add and delete records from a database, though, the record number isn't necessarily a reliable way to identify one particular record.

For instance, if you delete the first record in a database, every record below it moves up one slot. Now, what used to be record #2 becomes record #1, what used to be #3 is now #2, and so on. Jim could've transferred out of the Scranton branch before you find his record that way. If you want to assign every record its own number, and have that number stay with the record forever, then you want *serial numbers*. They're discussed in Chapter 3.

Finding Records

When your database really gains some size, you'll realize that even keyboard shortcuts aren't the fastest way to get to the record you want. You need to *tell* FileMaker to pull up the record for you. For example, you have a season ticket holder whose last name is Spinnet and who just renewed her subscription for a year. You need to find her record and make the update, and you don't have all day.

Once you have hundreds of records in your Contact Management database, it could take ages to find the one you want by clicking the Book icon. Instead, switch to Find mode and tell FileMaker what you're looking for, and the program finds it for you. This section explains how to use Find mode to search for a record or group of records, and how to edit your search if you don't get the results you anticipated. (If you downloaded the example file discussed on page 16, you can open it and try out Find mode now.)

You can get to Find mode in four ways:

- Select Find from the Mode pop-up menu.
- Choose View → Find Mode.
- Click the Find mode tab in the status area.
- Press Ctrl+F (⌘-F).

The Mode pop-up menu, Mode tabs, and View menu all indicate what mode you're currently in. Once you're in Find mode, your window should look like Figure 1-15.

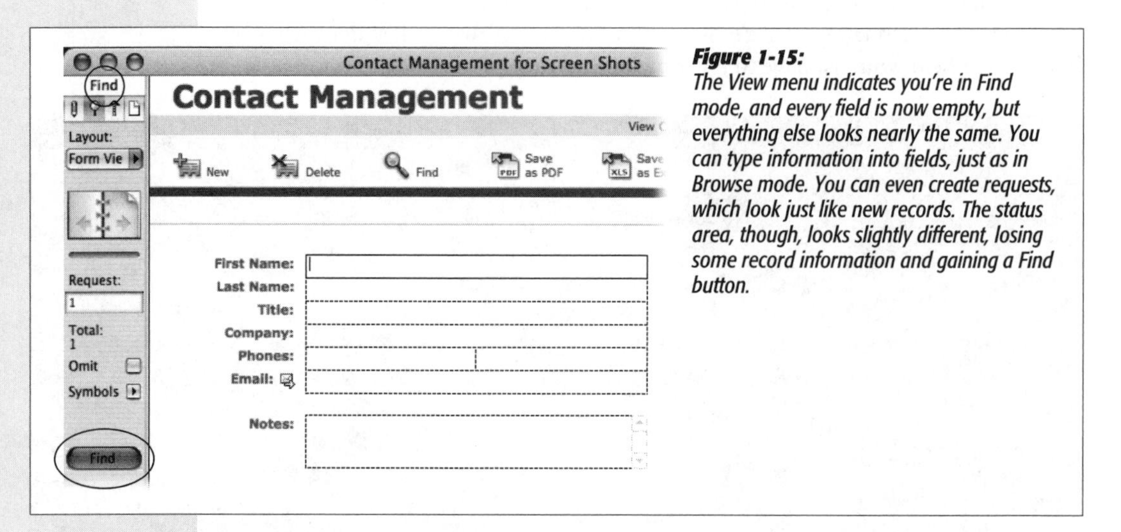

Figure 1-15: *The View menu indicates you're in Find mode, and every field is now empty, but everything else looks nearly the same. You can type information into fields, just as in Browse mode. You can even create requests, which look just like new records. The status area, though, looks slightly different, losing some record information and gaining a Find button.*

Find mode looks just like Browse mode (where you've spent all your time up until now). The best way to tell that you're in Find mode is to look for clues in the status area or Mode pop-up menu. Find mode also seems to work the same way—you can edit data in your fields and add, delete, or navigate through records. But don't be deceived: Find mode is very different from Browse mode.

Note: Another subtle clue indicates you're in Find mode: The borders around fields have a dashed-line appearance when the record is active. In Browse mode, active fields are bordered by a *dotted* line.

Even though it may seem like you're editing records in Find mode, you're actually not—you're editing *requests* instead. Requests describe what certain records look like, so FileMaker can find them for you.

You just need to enter enough information to tell FileMaker what you want. It then looks for records that have the same information you entered, much like searches you conduct using other programs.

Performing a find

Say you want to find every person in your Contact Management database whose last name is Sanders. Here's what you do:

1. **Choose View → Find Mode (or use any of the other methods described above to get to Find mode).**

   The window is now in Find mode, as you can tell by a quick glance at the Mode pop-up menu.

2. **Type *Sanders* into the Last Name field.**

   This works just like Browse mode: Simply click to place your cursor in the field, and then type. (Remember, you aren't editing a record—you're editing a *request*.)

3. **Click the Find button in the status area.**

   (You can also choose Requests → Perform Find or simply press Enter.)

FileMaker then looks for any records that have "Sanders" in the Last Name field. If the program doesn't find any, you see the message pictured in Figure 1-16. On the other hand, if FileMaker *did* find some records, you wind up back in Browse mode, presented with the records FileMaker found. (Technically, these records are called a *found set*. You'll learn much more about found sets in the next chapter.)

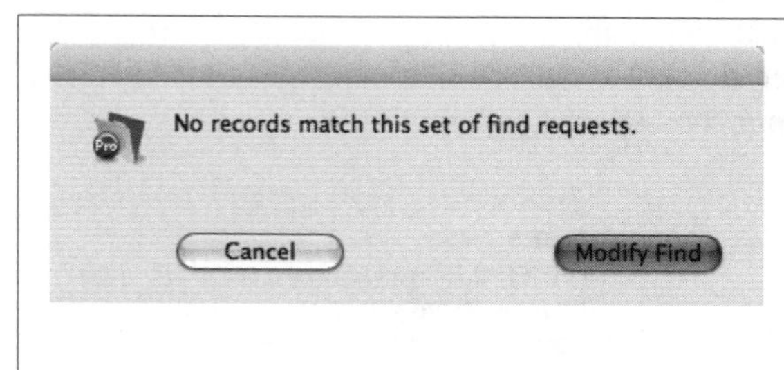

Figure 1-16:
If FileMaker can't find any records that match what you're looking for, you see the message pictured in this dialog box. If that's all you needed to know, just click Cancel and you'll wind up back in Browse mode as though you'd never performed a find. But if you realize you misspelled your search term or were a little too specific in describing what you wanted, click Modify Find. FileMaker sends you back to Find mode, where you can edit your request and click Find again.

After you perform a find, FileMaker displays the set of records that matched your find request (in this case, all the records with the last name Sanders). You can see how many records you found by looking at the count in the status area, as shown in Figure 1-17.

Figure 1-17:
After you perform a find, the status area shows how many records match your request. In this case, FileMaker found three records with the last name of Sanders. You can flip through these three records to your heart's content, but you can't see any records not in your found set. If you want to look at all your other records (you're done with those Sanders people), then choose Records → Show Omitted Only. FileMaker swaps your found set and shows you the other five records in your database. Then, when you're ready to look at all your records again, choose Records → Show All Records and it's one big, happy family again.

Although you're in Browse mode, you can't look through every record in the database—just the ones FileMaker found.

Tip: If your find didn't come out exactly the way you wanted, don't just return to Find mode. If you do, you'll have an empty request, and have to start all over again. Instead, choose Records → Modify Last Find, which takes you to Find mode and displays the request you used last. Now you can simply make any necessary modifications and perform the find again.

FastMatch

In the previous find examples, you had FileMaker search for records by telling it what to look for. But sometimes you're already looking at a record that has the right information in it—you just want to find more that match.

Say you need a list of everybody in the Contact Management file who has a superpower. Flip to any record with the word "superpower" in the Notes field. Drag to select the word "superpower." Right-click the highlighted text (Control-click on a Mac).

From the shortcut menu that pops up, select Find Matching Records (see Figure 1-18). Shazaam! Faster than you can say "ordinary people," FileMaker shows you a found set of all your contacts with superpowers.

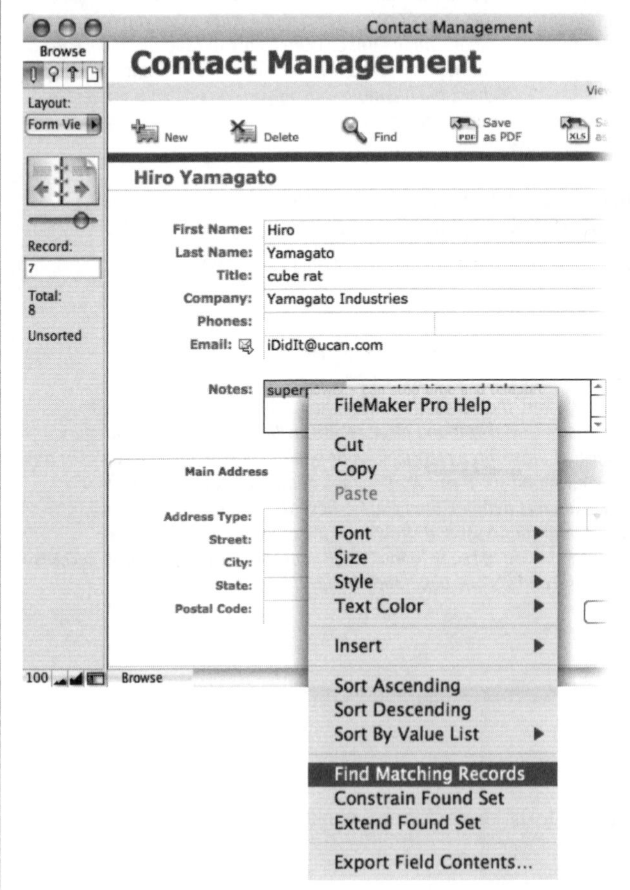

Figure 1-18: *FastMatch lets you select a piece of information from the record you're viewing (in this case, it's "superpower" from the Notes field) and find all other records that match it without the rigmarole of switching to Find mode. Right-click the selection and choose Find Matching Records from the shortcut menu.*

GEM IN THE ROUGH

Don't Forget You're in Find Mode

Find mode looks so much like Browse mode that it's easy to forget which mode you're in. This may not seem like a big deal, but it can be a real drag if you *think* you're in Browse mode and you start entering data. Since find requests look a lot like records, you can make quite a bit of progress entering records and never realize your mistake. When you finally do figure it out, it's a rude awakening: None of the requests you've just entered can be turned into real records; you must reenter them all in Browse mode.

Luckily, FileMaker is nice enough to give you a warning if it thinks you may be confused. See Figure 1-19 to see what you're in for. If you create more than ten find requests while in Find mode, FileMaker shows this message. If you were entering data in Find mode by mistake (at least you're finding out now, not after you've typed for three hours), just click No, switch to Browse mode, and start over with your data entry. If you know you're in Find mode, and you really want to add all these requests, just click Yes. FileMaker won't bother you again.

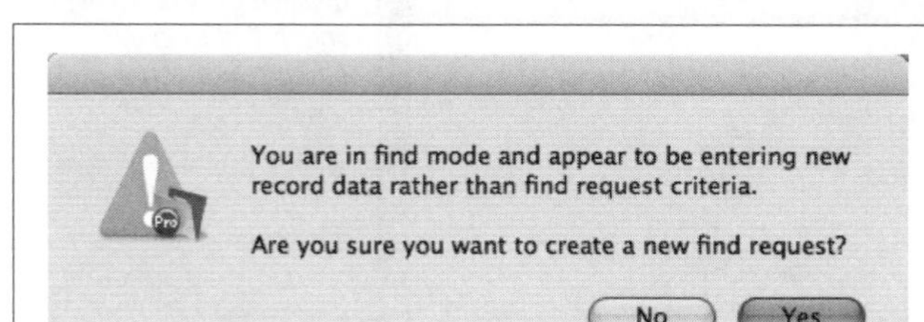

Figure 1-19:
If you create more than ten requests in Find Mode, FileMaker wonders if you're actually trying to enter data. If you're setting up a magnificently complex find, you may be annoyed. Just click Yes and keep up the good work. But if you just forgot to switch back to Browse mode, this warning can save you lots of lost keystrokes.

Same Database, Multiple Windows

So far, you've spent all your time in the same Contact Management window. If you're feeling a little claustrophobic, fear not. At any time, you can get yourself another window by choosing Window → New Window. You'll get an exact copy of the window you were just looking at. What's the big deal, you ask? The big deal is that you can switch to another record or do almost anything else in the new window, without affecting what's displayed in the first one.

When you have multiple windows open, you can change most of the settings you've seen so far for each window. For example, if you want to compare two contacts side by side, you can show one contact in each window.

You can even zoom one window in and another one out, or show the status area in one window but not the other (if that's your idea of fun). Another time multiple windows are useful is when you're working with one set of found records (see page 38) but need to do another search. You can perform a find in a new window without disrupting your work in the original window. Say you've been fiddling with the Find command to come up with all your contacts with superpowers, and then suddenly get the paperwork you need to edit the detail on another record. Although you could enter data on the list layout, all the fields you need may not be available. Just create a new window and look up the record you want to edit (see Figure 1-20). Your superpower group is safe and sound in the first window. See the box about Record Locking on page 42 to see what problems could occur with this kind of data entry.

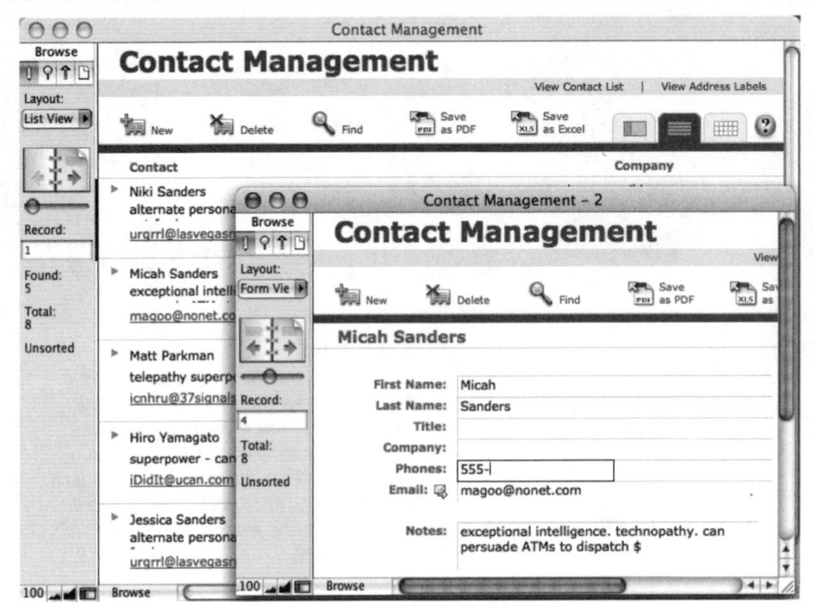

Figure 1-20: *In this example, the window in the back shows several records in the database on the List View layout. But the window in the front shows one record in detail. You can flip through records in the front window in their detailed glory and leave your list intact in the background.*

Note: If you have two windows open, both of them *are* connected in one way. If you edit the data in one window, the changes show up in the other window (or every window you have open, if you're working with multiple windows). Since FileMaker's windows display only the records in your database, a second window doesn't mean you have a second database–instead, both windows share the same data

---

Automatically Arranging Windows

If you have a lot of windows on your screen and don't feel like rearranging them yourself, you can use one of several commands that arrange the windows for you—or at least try to. Using FileMaker's Window menu, you can choose one of three commands: Tile Vertically, Tile Horizontally, or Cascade. Each command rearranges the windows in a different manner, as shown in Figure 1-21.

The Window menu commands are a great place to start when you have so many windows open, you don't even know which one you're looking for! However, 99 times out of 100, these automatic rearrangements somehow seem to make every window the wrong size, and put each window in the wrong place. So use these commands with the understanding that you may *still* have to do some rearranging yourself.

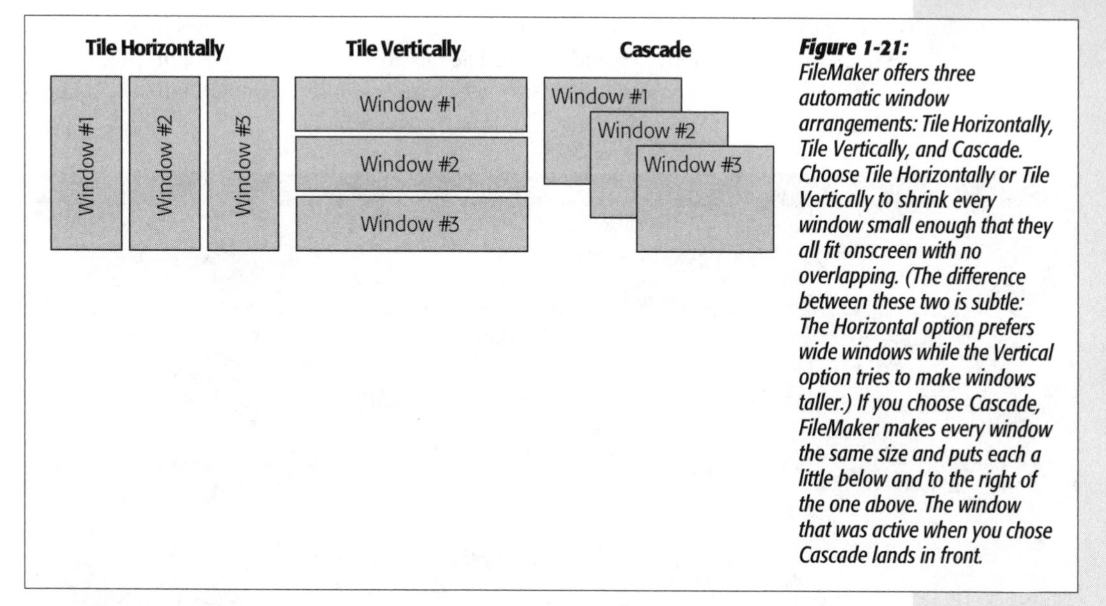

Figure 1-21: *FileMaker offers three automatic window arrangements: Tile Horizontally, Tile Vertically, and Cascade. Choose Tile Horizontally or Tile Vertically to shrink every window small enough that they all fit onscreen with no overlapping. (The difference between these two is subtle: The Horizontal option prefers wide windows while the Vertical option tries to make windows taller.) If you choose Cascade, FileMaker makes every window the same size and puts each a little below and to the right of the one above. The window that was active when you chose Cascade lands in front.*

Hiding Windows

If you have a window just the way you want it (for example, showing a list of customers Assistant Manager Dwight Schrute left behind when he went to work for Staples), but it's in your way onscreen, you can *hide* it instead of closing it. (When you close a window after using the Find command, your results disappear.) Hiding a window makes it disappear from your screen, but keeps the information stashed in a handy place in your computer so you can get it back if you want it. It's a neat timesaver when your screen is crowded—or when you want to keep prying eyes away from your information.

To hide the window displayed on the front of your screen, choose Window → Hide Window. To bring it back again, choose Window → Show Window, and pick the window you want back from the list. In order for this to work, you have to remember the *name* of the window you hid (its name appears in the title bar, across the top of the window).

Warning: You may be in the habit of using your operating system's built-in features for dealing with windows, like minimizing them to the Mac OS X Dock. These techniques work just fine in FileMaker, but they can play havoc when a FileMaker *script* needs to control the same window. If you're using any of these little software robots to automate tasks, as you'll learn in Chapter 13, it's best to stick to FileMaker's own window commands.

Closing hidden windows

On page 24, you learned that the way to close a database is to simply close its windows. As with most rules, there's an exception: Even if you close all visible windows, the database itself may still be open—in a hidden window.

The easiest way to close all FileMaker's open windows, hidden ones included, is to press the Alt (Option) key and choose File → Close (File → Close All on Mac OS X). The ordinary Close command closes every window, hidden or not, when this key is held down.

POWER USERS' CLINIC

Record Locking

If you try editing a record in one window while it's showing in another window, you'll notice that your changes don't appear in the second window as you type. In order for the changes to appear, you must first commit the record (see the box on page 30). Once you do, the changes appear everywhere else.

Here's a hypothetical example. Suppose you start making changes to Jim Halpert's contact information in one window, but you're interrupted by a phone call before you finish. To help the caller, you need to look something up in the database. Since you're a savvy FileMaker guru, you make a new window and look it up there so you don't have to lose track of the changes you're making to Jim. (He's getting all Dwight's former customers.)

Unfortunately, by the time you finish the phone call, you've forgotten that you already started editing Jim's record. Now you go to Jim's record *in the new window* to make the changes. Bear in mind the record is already half-changed but uncommitted in the first window.

What happens if you start making changes now? Which set of changes wins?

To avoid the problem of which changes "win," FileMaker automatically performs *record locking* for you. If you try to edit a record that's already being edited in another window, you see an error message that reads, "This record cannot be modified in this window because it is already being modified in a different window." Yes, it's frustrating to get this message, but just remember that automatic record locking really is your protection against major problems. (This is especially true when you have multiple users accessing your database at the same time–see Chapter 18.) This message is your friend.

CHAPTER

2

Organizing and Editing Records

With all its advanced database options—like Find mode in this chapter and the relational database features covered in the later parts of this book—FileMaker is a pretty good deal for $299. But you're getting way more for your money than a powerhouse database program. FileMaker has many of the capabilities of a basic word processor built right in, so you can unleash your creative text-formatting urges using tools that look and feel quite familiar. What you can do with FileMaker is limited only by your imagination and willingness to plunge into a few dialog boxes.

Once you have even a few records entered into your database, clicking through them all whenever you want to make changes gets cumbersome. This chapter shows you how to pull up the records you want to work with. Then once you've got 'em, the real fun begins. You'll find out all the ways you can format text in FileMaker to get just the right look for your project, and how to print it out on paper.

Views

In the Contact Management database example, you learned how to add to and edit your new database with only one record onscreen at a time (see page 26). This view is a common way to look at your information, but it's far from the only way. In fact, there are three possible ways to look at a database: form view, list view, and table view.

The one-at-a-time approach to viewing records you saw in Chapter 1 is called *form view*. In *list view*, you see lots of records in, well, a list. If they don't all fit in the window, you can use the vertical scroll bar to scroll through them. If you've used a spreadsheet program like Microsoft Excel, *table view* will look familiar—it looks a lot like a spreadsheet, with one row for each record and one column for each field.

To switch among views in any FileMaker database, use the View menu. Choose View → As Form, View → As List, or View → As Table. You'll see what each view looks like as you learn about them on the following pages.

Note: When you design a database, you can add clickable buttons, tabs, or other handy means to switch among views. For example, the Contact Management database you used in Chapter 1 has view tabs built into the template (see Figure 1-5). You can even turn *off* certain views if you want. If your database holds mostly digital photographs and makes no sense in table view, then you can make sure no one ever sees it that way. (You'll learn how in Chapter 5.)

Form View

In form view, you see only one record at a time. If you want to see the next record, you must click the pages of the Book icon, press Control-down arrow, or use some other method of switching records (see page 33). Most of the database work you've done so far has been in form view, and you can see an example in Figure 2-1. You can use form view when you have a lot of information to see about one record, or when you want to focus on just one record without being distracted by all the others.

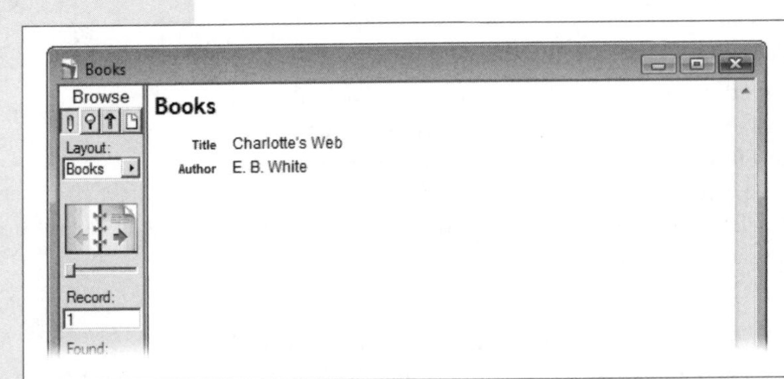

Figure 2-1: *This layout is set to form view right now. Looks familiar, huh? You've already spent some time in form view. Notice that you see only one record, although there are 25 in this database. You can page through records one by one by clicking the Book icon.*

List View

List view works *almost* exactly like form view. It shows your layout complete with its pretty design, but instead of limiting you to one record at a time, it shows you multiple records in a scrolling list. It also adds another element of feedback to the status area, as shown in Figure 2-2.

When you're working with a *group* of records—updating one field in several records or browsing through all your records in search of something—list view comes in handy.

Table View

If List view looks a lot like form view, then table view, well, doesn't. This view appeals to spreadsheet fans since it offers a consistent rows-and-columns design, the ability to sort with the click of a button, and the freedom to rearrange columns by dragging them around. Of course you can add, edit, delete, and find records in table view, just like the others.

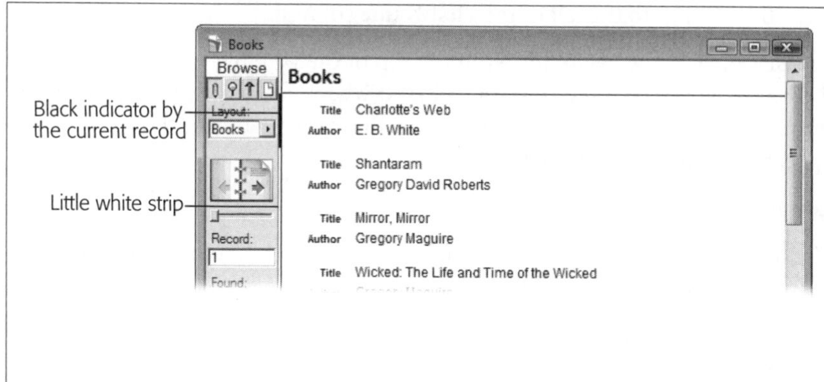

***Figure 2-2:** This database is the same one shown in Figure 2-1 but this time the layout is in list view. The little white strip along the right edge of the status bar tells you you're in list view. Its job is to show you which record is currently selected. The strip is filled with black along the edge of the current record. In this example, the first record is selected.*

When you put your layout into table view, any graphical embellishments disappear. Instead, FileMaker displays the fields of your layout in a no-nonsense, spreadsheet arrangement (Figure 2-3).

Each column represents one of your fields, and the order of the columns matches the order you go through the fields when tabbing. For example, the first column is the field you wind up in if you press Tab for the first time. Another Tab takes you to the second column.

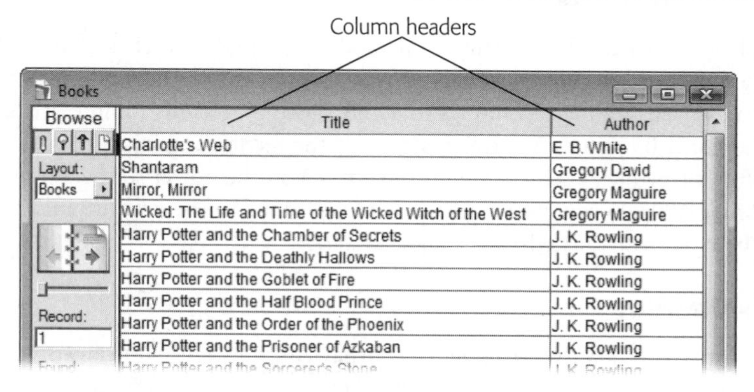

***Figure 2-3:** In table view, FileMaker ignores your layout's extra pictures, text, and other embellishments and shows you just the fields. Like a real spreadsheet, you can drag columns around to rearrange them. You can also click a column header at the top of any column to instantly sort the records by that field. Table view shows the same vertical white strip that you see in list view.*

In table view, you can move columns around by dragging them. To switch the First Name and Last Name columns, for example, do the following:

1. **Point to the words Last Name and hold down the mouse button.**

   FileMaker darkens the column header to show you it's selected.

2. **Drag the column to the left of the First Name column.**

   You see a black line extending from the top of the window to the bottom. This line shows you where the column will land when you let go. All the other columns will shift around to make room. In this case, you want the black line to appear to the left of the First Name column.

3. **Let go of the mouse button.**

   FileMaker moves the Last Name column to its new home, shifting other columns to the right to make room.

The column headings also make it easy to *sort* your data, as shown in Figure 2-4.

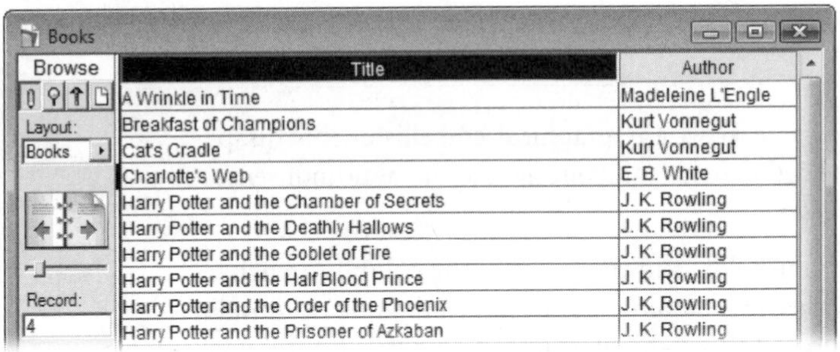

Figure 2-4: *When you click a column header, FileMaker darkens that header and sorts the list. This list, for example, is sorted by Title. If you sort the records using the Records → Sort Records command instead, FileMaker doesn't try to figure out which column was used. Instead, it simply lightens all the column headers.*

Advanced Find Mode

In Chapter 1 you learned about using Find mode for simple searches—but you only scratched the surface. The more records you have in your database, the more you'll need advanced finding techniques to avoid wasting precious minutes clicking the Book icon 1,057 times in a row just to find the record or records you want to display, edit, or print. FileMaker's Find tools give you the power to track down the one record in 100,000 you need *right this minute*, or the five records with missing phone numbers that you created a week ago Tuesday.

Finding by Omitting

If you know what you *don't* want better than what you do want, you can use the Omit checkbox. This feature comes in handy when the records you're looking for can best be described by what they aren't. For example, "every person who isn't from California" is a lot easier to say than "everyone from Alabama, Alaska, Arizona, Arkansas, Colorado…" In this case, you can get what you want by creating one find request, with California in the State field. Then, before you perform the find, simply turn on the Omit checkbox, which appears in the status area only when you're in Find mode (Figure 2-5). That's all there is to it. FileMaker starts with every record in the table, then throws out all the records with "California" in the State field, so you're left with everything else.

Omit also works with multiple find requests (see the box on page 50). If *all* your requests have the Omit option turned on, then all the records that match *any* of your requests are thrown out. Whatever's left over goes in your found set. If you have a mix of requests with and without Omit turned on, FileMaker goes through them in order. If the first request isn't an omit request, FileMaker finds all the matching records. If your first request is an omit, FileMaker finds every record that doesn't match and then moves on to the next request. That request may add new records to the found set, or remove records that are already there. In fact, a record could be found by one request, omitted by the next, and then found again by the third, so the record would be included in the found set since the last request added it. In the end, you're left with a found set in which every record matches at least one of your requests. Other records that would have matched may have instead been thrown out by omits.

Constraining and Extending the Found Set

When you perform a find normally, it effectively throws away any found set you had before, searches through all the records in the database, and produces a *new* found set. But you can also tell FileMaker to *constrain* the found set (that is, search within your last find results) or *extend* it (add matching records to the current found set).

Constraining the found set

Suppose you've just created a great product, and want to send out some free samples to see how people like it. You can't afford the postage to send everyone in your database a sample, so you decide to start with a smaller sampling—just people named Smith.

Problem is, a simple find reveals that your database has hundreds of Smiths. Some quick math in your head reveals that it's still too expensive. How about sending samples to just the Smiths in California? You *could* go back to Find mode and construct a request to find based on both criteria instead (by putting *Smith* in the Last Name field and *California* in the State field), but there's an easier way. After all, you've already got all the Smiths in your found set. What you really want to do is search *inside this found set* for all the records with California in the State field.

Here's how the procedure goes:

1. **Switch to Find mode, type *Smith* in the Last Name field, and then press Enter.**

   FileMaker searches the database and, in Browse mode, shows you the records with Smith for the last name. You glance at the status area—678 records! You now need to search through these records for those whose state is California. That's *exactly* what the Constrain Found Set command does.

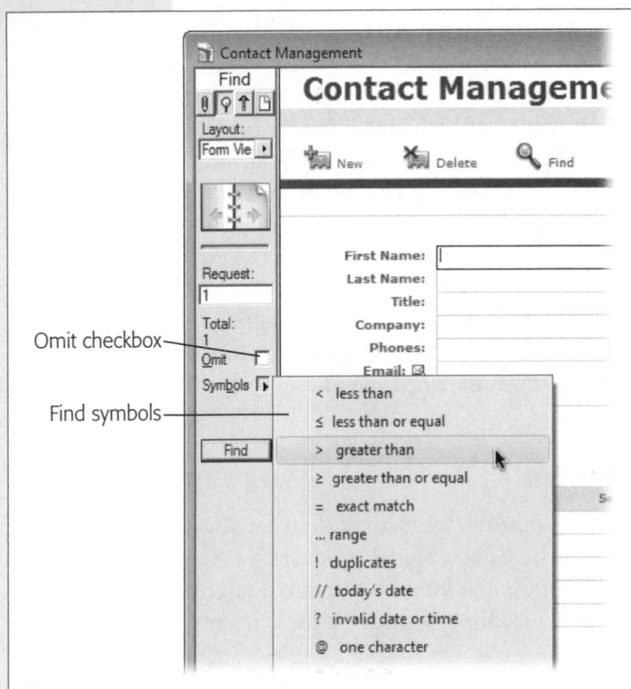

Figure 2-5: *Find mode offers up some new status area options. The Omit checkbox basically tells FileMaker to do an un-find: It finds all the records that* don't *look like your request. The Find symbols give you more control over how FileMaker decides whether it's found a match. They're described in detail starting on page 49.*

2. **Immediately switch to Find mode again using any of the methods described on page 19.**

   In other words, don't choose Records → Show All Records, and don't do anything to tamper with the current found set (678 records, in this example). You're now in Find mode again, ready to enter a request.

Note: In Find mode, there's no way to see what your current found set is. You just have to remember that you last searched for Smith. If you need to see the found set, just switch back to Browse mode and flip through the records.

3. **Type *California* in the State field.**

   Since the found set already has only Smiths in it, there's no need to repeat that information.

4. **Choose Requests → Constrain Found Set.**

   FileMaker searches out the people from California, but this time it looks only in the current found set. In the end, you get what you want with less typing.

Warning: Once you're in Find mode, FileMaker is itching for you to perform a find. If you just press Enter, it assumes you want to throw away your last found set and make a new one. Once it's gone, there's no way to return to the old found set and constrain or extend it. Likewise, if you accidentally choose the wrong command from the Requests menu, there's no going back. If you want to constrain or extend, be sure you choose wisely or you'll have to start all over again.

Extending the found set

Extending the found set works similarly. This time, though, you're asking FileMaker to perform a new find (through all records in the database) and then *add* the records it finds into your found set. What you end up with is all the records you already had, plus any new ones that were found. Suppose you've already found the Smiths, and you want all the Johnsons as well.

1. **In Find mode, type *Johnson* in the Last Name field.**

   So far, you're doing exactly what you would do in every other find. You just have all the Smiths in your found set, even though you can't see that in Find mode.

2. **Choose Requests → Extend Found Set.**

   This time, FileMaker looks through every record in the database for any Johnsons. Each time it finds one, it adds it to your existing found set. When it's done, you have all the Smiths *and* Johnsons in one found set.

Refining Searches with Find Symbols

Normally, FileMaker uses a pretty simple rule to decide whether a field value matches the field in your request (the *criteria*): If every word in the criteria appears at the *beginning* of any word in the field, FileMaker considers it a match.

For example, if you put *for* in the Note field in a find request, any of these notes would match:

- All for one and one for all.
- We will forever remember.
- Back and forth it went.

On the other hand, neither of these would match:

- Wherefore art thou, Romeo?
- Before there was art, there was an artist.

Note: This match-the-beginning mode of operation may seem odd, but it's surprisingly useful. Imagine you're looking for someone named Ahrmshulla Maharajapuram in your database. Of course, you could find the record by typing the full name, but chances are you'll get the same results if you search for *Ah Maha* instead. Since Ahrmshulla starts with Ah and Maharajapuram starts with Maha, FileMaker will find her with this abbreviated request, saving you from all that typing–and remembering how to spell the full name.

How do you tell FileMaker that you're looking for "for" *wherever* it appears in a word, not just at the beginning? You can use a special *symbol*—a character that has special meaning in a Find request—to stand for part of a word.

POWER USERS' CLINIC

Multiple Requests

It's rarely strictly necessary to use Constrain or Extend to get exactly what you want. To get the effect of a Constrain, just fill out multiple fields in your find request. Since a record has to match every field in the request, a computer geek would say you're doing an *AND search*. This odd term simply means you're asking for records where both the First Name is "John," for example, *AND* the last name is "Smith." Extend Found Set, by contrast, is analogous to an *OR search*, meaning it locates all the records that have *either* search term. An OR search is like saying, "Show me all the records where a student is either a 'Head Boy' or a 'Prefect.'" Another way to get an OR search is with *multiple* find requests. Remember that a request is the Find mode equivalent of a record. When you're in Find mode, you're free to create as many as you want (choose Requests → New Request) and you can flip through them using all the same tools you use to flip through records. Here's how to make your own OR search using multiple requests:

1. Enter Find mode using any of the methods described on page 19. FileMaker opens a blank request.
2. Type *Smith* in the Last Name field. You're describing one kind of record–the kind with "Smith" in the Last Name field. If you add any more criteria to this request, you'll just be excluding some Smiths from your found set. So instead...
3. Choose Requests → New Request. FileMaker gives you a second empty request. The first request is still there, although you can't see it. Since requests work just like records, you can use the Book icon, the Slider, or the keyboard shortcuts to switch between them. Or you can switch the layout to list view.
4. Type *Johnson* in the Last Name field. You're describing the other kind of record you want. Since you have two requests, FileMaker treats them separately, finding all the Smiths, then finding all the Johnsons, and finally putting both lists into the found set.

Essentially, each request represents another extension of the found set. Many FileMaker power users, once they've mastered multiple requests, find they can perform some complex searches using multiple requests with fewer clicks and keystrokes than the Constrain and Extend Found Set commands. For others, the Constrain and Extend commands offer a more straightforward, intuitive approach to complex requests. And there are some kinds of searches that are unwieldy using multiple requests, which are a breeze with Constrain and Extend. In the end, it usually comes down to preference.

Finally, there's no reason you can't mix these techniques, using Constrain and Extend *and* multiple requests at the same time. For instance, you could use multiple requests to find all your customers who live in Florida, Hawaii, and California, then use the Constrain Found Set command to find just the people named Fred who live in those three states.

The Symbol pop-up menu, which appears in the status area when you're in Find mode, lets you add these special characters to your searches, thus gaining more control over FileMaker's decision-making process when it's looking for records. There are plenty more special symbols, and each is described below.

The wildcard (*)

In the "Wherefore art thou Romeo" example, you would use the * wildcard symbol, which stands for "anything." It tells FileMaker that you don't mind if there's something *right before or right after* the "for." If you type **for** as your find criteria, FileMaker will display records that contain "therefore," "before," "George Foreman," and so on. (Of course, if you only want things that end with "for," you can type **for* in the find request.)

Less Than (<), Less Than or Equal To (≤), Greater Than (>), and Greater Than or Equal To (≥)

These symbols tell FileMaker to use your criteria as a maximum or minimum rather than a direct match. For example, the criteria *<David* will find every person whose name comes before David alphabetically. *≤David* is just about the same, but it will include any Davids as well.

Note: In Mac OS X, the Less Than or Equal To symbol shows up as ≤, but on Windows, it shows up as <= instead. You can type the ≤ symbol on Mac OS X (hold down the Option key and press the comma key) but it works just as well to type <= as you would on Windows. The same thing goes for the Greater Than or Equal To symbol, which you can type as >=.

These symbols are smart enough to understand different kinds of information. For example, *<10* in a field that expects numbers will find real numbers less than 10 (like 9). FileMaker performs the correct function with dates and times as well, in which case Less Than means *before* and Greater Than means *after*.

Exact Match (=), Literal Text (""), and Field Content Match (==)

The rule FileMaker uses automatically for determining a match is pretty loose. But sometimes you want exactly what you say: "Smith," not "Smithers" or "Smithey" or "Smithsonian." In this case, use the Exact Match symbol (=). In this example, type *=Smith* in the Last Name field, and perform your find.

If you want to exactly match *more* than one word, put the words in quotes instead. This Literal Text match is also good for criteria that contain punctuation, like "Mr. Smith."

Note: Like French fries, quotes come in two varieties: curly and straight. If you're someone who notices this kind of thing, you may wonder if it matters which kind you use. It doesn't. Usually FileMaker turns your quotes curly for you, but you can turn off smart quotes for a database in the File → File Options dialog box.

For the ultimate in specificity, use the Field Content Match symbol (==) instead. Exact Match requires that each *word* in your criteria match one or more words in the field. Literal Text seeks to match only what is in the quotes *anywhere* in the field. Field Content Match insists that the entire field matches the criteria text exactly. For example, *=Smith* matches "Smith," "Mr. Smith," and "Smith-Johnson." However, *==Smith* matches only "Smith" in the field and nothing else.

Note: Literal Text doesn't actually match text *anywhere* in the field. The criteria text must match starting at the beginning of a word. For instance, a search for "Mr. Smith" would match "Mr. Smith" and "Mr. Smithers," but if you searched for "*r. Smith*" (no M) instead, you'd find no matches.

Range (...)

The Range symbol is like the Greater Than or Equal To and Less Than or Equal To symbols combined. The criteria "David...Michael" matches everyone from David to Michael, alphabetically speaking. Just like the other symbols, the Range symbol is smart enough to understand numbers, dates, and times, as long as the field expects them. (You'll learn more about field types in the next chapter.)

Duplicates (!)

The Duplicates symbol (!) can be hard to get the hang of. When you put *!* in a field in Find mode, FileMaker finds records with *duplicate data* in that field. In other words, it looks for records with the *same* value in that particular field. The same as *what,* you ask? The same as *any other record*. Think of it this way: If you have only *one* person in your database from Idaho, and you perform a find with *!* in the State field, the person from Idaho won't appear. That's because—when considering the State field alone—the person from Idaho has no duplicates. On the other hand, if you have 11 people from Oklahoma, they'll *all* be found because they all have duplicates (each one has 10 others just like it, statewise).

Unlike most other symbols, the ! symbol is always used alone in a field in Find mode. You would never put *! Smith* in the last name field. Instead, you'd just put *!* all by itself.

POWER USERS' CLINIC

Finding Duplicate Records

Every database user eventually makes the mistake of entering the same data twice. Maybe you assume a person isn't in your database and add him, only to discover months later that he was there all along. The ! symbol can help you hunt this sort of thing down.

If you want to find *whole records* that are exact duplicates, you'll have to put *!* in every field when you're in Find mode. But it isn't at all uncommon for "duplicate" records to be slightly different. Maybe you updated the phone number in one but not the other, for instance.

Or perhaps you misspelled the street name the first time you entered this person, and spelled it right the second time. Finding exact duplicate records wouldn't catch these kinds of so-called duplicates.

If you're looking for duplicate records, you're usually best off putting the ! symbol in as few fields as possible. Try to pick fields that tend to be entered the same every time and stand a good chance of identifying an individual person. You can use just First Name and Last Name, for instance.

Today's Date (//) and Invalid Date or Time (?)

Like the ! symbol, these symbols can go in a field in Find mode all by themselves. The double slash is convenient shorthand for the current date. If you're looking for all the payments due today, you can type // in the Due field more quickly than "September 15, 2007."

The Invalid Date or Time symbol (?) is another helper when it comes time to clean house. It's possible to end up with the wrong kind of data in fields that are supposed to hold dates or times (like "N/A," "Never," or "Next Week"). Put *?* in the Due field, and FileMaker finds every payment whose due date is not valid, giving you an opportunity to fix them. (You'll learn more about fields that hold special kinds of data in Chapter 3.)

Note: You can mix and match these symbols in any combinations that make sense. For example, to find everything after today's date, just search for *>//* instead of *>12/21/2007*.

One Character (@), One Digit (#), and Zero or More Characters (*)

These symbols are like the wildcard characters you sometimes see in other programs. You already saw the Zero or More Characters symbol (*) at the beginning of this section. It simply tells FileMaker you're willing to accept some text—*any* text—in place of the * symbol. If you're not ready to go that far, you can instead permit just one character (letter, number, or punctuation) with the One Character (@) symbol. When matching numbers, you can be even more specific, permitting just one numerical digit with the One Digit (#) symbol. Here are a few examples:

- **smith** matches "Smith," "blacksmith," "Smithsonian," and "blacksmiths"
- **smith* matches "Smith" and "blacksmith," but not "blacksmiths" or "Smithsonian"
- *smith@* matches "smithy" but not "smithers"
- *@*smith* matches "blacksmith" but not "Smith" or "blacksmiths"
- *smith#* matches "smith1" and "smith2" but not "smithy"

Note: As discussed on page 49, when you do a Find, FileMaker matches the *beginning* of a word in the field. But as soon as you add these wildcard symbols to your search, it becomes a little less lenient: FileMaker insists on a complete word match. You can see this in the second example above. You might expect **smith* to match "blacksmiths" but it doesn't because FileMaker now wants the whole word to match.

Relaxed Search (~)

The last symbol, called Relaxed Search (~) applies only to searching Japanese language text. It instructs FileMaker to consider characters to match if they make the same sound, even if they aren't exactly the same character. Alas, in English, spelling always counts (you can't expect "~korn" to match "corn").

Refining a Found Set with Omit Commands

FileMaker provides a few menu commands to help you fine-tune your found set. Sometimes, after you've done the best find request you can, you still end up with a couple of records in the found set that you don't really want to see. FileMaker offers three commands that make tossing out misfit records as easy as pie.

POWER USERS' CLINIC

Finding Hot Dates

That heading got your attention, didn't it? Well, as long as you're here, you might as well read about some cool ways to get date fields to yield their secrets.

- If you need to find all invoices generated in September this year, type *9/2007*.
- To find out who received large bonuses while the boss was on sabbatical last year, type *12/2005...5/2006*.
- Keep tabs on payday sales by typing **/15/**.
- See if there's slow performance in the sales department on Monday morning by typing *Monday* in a date field. You can even just type *Mon* if you'd rather not bother with those extra keystrokes.
- To find out if the lull lasts through Tuesday, type *Mon...Tue*. (Full day names or three letter abbreviations work.)
- Find invoices generated just before the monthly incentive period closes by typing **/{29...31}/2004*.

Timestamp fields (see page 104) hold date and time information. You'd use a bunch of them to design a Time Clock Punching system. They also have some nifty search capabilities.

- Find out who clocked out between 4 p.m. and 4:59 p.m. today by typing *//4 pm*.
- See who your star performers and workaholics are (everybody in on any day between 6 and 7 a.m.), by typing *6 am*.
- Find out who left work early to pick up their preorder copy of *Harry Potter and the Deathly Hallows* by typing *7/21/2007 3 pm*.
- Check on anybody leaving after lunch any day in July by typing *7/2005 2 pm*.

Omit Record

Go to the record you don't want (using the Book icon, for example) and choose Records → Omit Record. This one-off command tosses the record out of the found set, reducing your found count by one. Don't confuse it with the Omit checkbox that shows up in the status bar when you're in Find mode (see page 46), which tells FileMaker to omit all the records that match your find request. The Records → Omit Record command omits just the single record you're sitting on.

FREQUENTLY ASKED QUESTION

Finding Special Characters

How do I find mrbill@microsoft.com when "@" means something special?

If what you're actually looking for includes one of these special symbols, you need to take extra precaution. When searching for mrbill@microsoft.com, the wildcard "@" symbol will match any letter, number, or punctuation mark. But the @ in the email address is none of these, so the search won't work.

To prevent FileMaker from interpreting the @ as a special character, use the Literal Text symbols you learned about above. In other words, putting the search text in quotes ("mrbill@microsoft.com") will do the trick. You could also search for *mrbill Microsoft*, since FileMaker sees these as two separate words.

Omit Multiple

If you have a whole stretch of records you don't want, use Records → Omit Multiple. It omits a contiguous group of records from the found set, starting with the current record. For instance, if you want to omit ten records in a row, navigate to the *first* record of the ten. Choose Records → Omit Multiple, and then type *10* in the dialog box that appears. Click Omit and the job is done.

Note: When you're done with your found set, and you want to see all the records again, choose Records → Show All Records.

Show Omitted Only

You can use this option when you're printing two separate lists—one of the California customers, and one of everyone else, for example. Once you've printed the California records, your found set happens to be exactly what you *don't* need. Choose Records → Show Omitted Only. This command effectively puts every record that's *not* in the found set into the new found set, and takes every currently found record out.

Here's how it works: Perform a find for the customers who have "CA" in the State field. FileMaker produces a found set of all California records for you, ready to print. After printing, choose Records → Show Omitted Only.

Now you have everyone *not* in California in your found set, and you're ready to print again.

POWER USERS' CLINIC

Over-Omitted

If you try to omit more records than possible (for example, you're on the third-to-last record and you ask FileMaker to omit 12 records), FileMaker will complain. But don't take offense: It's also nice enough to fix the problem for you. When you click OK, FileMaker returns you to the Omit dialog box and changes the number you entered to the maximum number possible. You only need to click Omit again to get what you probably wanted in the first place.

If you're looking at a record, and you know you want to omit it and every record after it, you might be tempted to look at the Record Number and the Found Count to figure out how many need to be omitted. But that's more trouble than it's worth. Just choose Records → Omit Multiple and enter something really big, like 999, or 9999999. When you click Omit, FileMaker will complain, do the math for you, and enter the right value.

This routine may sound contrived, but it's actually not all that uncommon among FileMaker pros. Imagine you're doing a direct-mail campaign and you can only afford to send 1,200 postcards. Your find request, however, produces 1,931 potential recipients. Rather than do the math, just go to record 1201 and use this Omit Multiple trick.

Note: You can also use Show Omitted Only if you forgot to turn on the Omit box in your find request. Instead of going back to Find mode to fix your request, just choose Records → Show Omitted Only and you'll get the same effect.

Changing Multiple Records

Sometimes the whole reason you performed a find is to change something in several records. If one of the companies you work with changes its name, you may have several records that need to be updated. The first step to fixing them is to *find* them. Once your found set includes the people at that company, you could change the Company Name field one record at a time (especially if you're billing by the hour). But a better use of your time is to use the Replace Field Contents command. Here's how it works:

1. **Click in the Company Name field (it doesn't matter which record), and correct the company name.**

   You've just fixed one of the records. All the others in the found set need the same fix. (Make sure you're still in the Company Name field or the next step won't work.)

2. **Choose Records → Replace Field Contents.**

   The Replace Field Contents dialog box appears (Figure 2-6). It has a handful of options that may not make sense to you yet. That's OK; just choose the first one: "Replace with." The new data you just typed is listed beside this option.

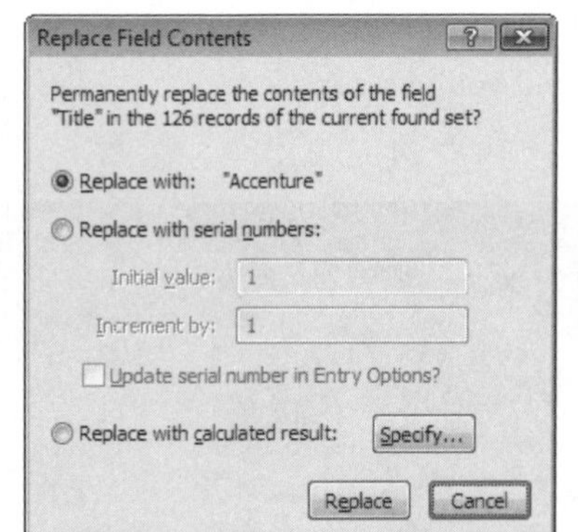

Figure 2-6:
The Replace Field Contents dialog box has three options: "Replace with," "Replace with serial numbers," and "Replace with calculated result." The first option is the only one you're concerned with right now. It replaces the contents of the current field in every record in the found set with whatever is in the current record when you click Replace. So, in the current record, type what you want to be in every record before you call up this dialog box. (You'll learn about serial numbers in Chapter 3 and calculations in Chapter 9.)

3. **Click Replace.**

   FileMaker now updates the Company Name field in *every record in the found set* to match what you typed in the current record. When it's done, you're still sitting on the same record, but if you use the Book icon to click through the records, you'll see that they've all been changed.

Warning: The Replace Field Contents command can be dangerous. It really does change every record in the found set, even if that wasn't your intent. Make sure you're absolutely certain you have the right found set before clicking Replace. Once it's done, there's no Undo command.

Sorting Records

Your Rolodex may be limited to an alphabetical (by last name) arrangement, but a FileMaker database has no such limitation. You can sort the records in any order you want, as often as you want. You can even do a sort-within-a-sort, as you'll see later in this section.

Don't confuse sorting with finding. When you sort, FileMaker doesn't change which records are in the found set. Instead, it simply rearranges the records you're already working on into a new order. For example, if you need a short-term loan, you can sort your contacts by annual income. FileMaker still shows all your contacts, but with Uncle Moneybags at the very top of the list.

The process always begins the same way: Choose Records → Sort Records. You'll see the Sort Records dialog box shown in Figure 2-7, with all available fields listed on the left. You tell FileMaker how to sort by moving a field to the list on the right.

Note: By "available," FileMaker means only the fields showing on the current Layout. If you want to see all the fields because the field you want to sort by isn't in the list, for example, choose the second item from the pop-up menu above the list–the one that starts with Current Table.

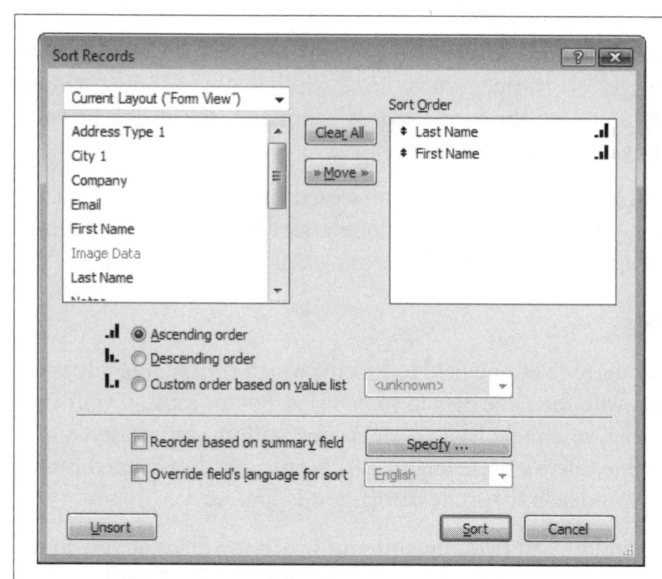

Figure 2-7: *The Sort Records dialog box offers a lot of options, but the two lists on top and the first two radio buttons are critical to every sort you'll ever do in FileMaker. In a nutshell, you pick the fields you want to sort by and the order in which they should be sorted, and then click Sort. That's the essence of any sort, from the simple to the most complex.*

Follow the steps below to sort by, say, Last Name:

1. **Choose Records → Sort or press Ctrl+S (⌘-S).**

   The Sort Records dialog box (Figure 2-7) appears.

2. **Select the Last Name field from the list on the left, and then click Move.**

   The field name appears in the Sort Order list on the right. You can save a little mouse mileage by double-clicking a field on the left instead of selecting it, and then clicking Move.

3. **Click Sort.**

   FileMaker sorts the records in the traditional alphabetical-by-last-name order. You can tell by flipping through the records or switching to table view.

Each sort field has an *order* associated with it as well. Right now, you only need to worry about two of these orders: "Ascending order" and "Descending order." You can click one of these radio buttons *before* you click Move, and the field will have the setting by the time it makes it to the Sort Order list. More often than not, though, you'll move the field over before you think about the order. In this case, just click to select the field from the Sort Order list and then pick the order. Each field in the Sort Order list shows a little bar-chart icon representing the order assigned to it, which matches the icons next to each radio button.

Tip: If you change your mind about one of the fields in the Sort Order list, click it. The Move button changes to say Clear, and a click removes the selected field from the list. If you want to remove every field from the Sort Order list, click Clear All.

When you're all done, click Sort. If you change your mind, click Cancel instead and FileMaker will forget everything you've done while in this window. Otherwise, the next time you choose the Sort Records command, the dialog box will show the same settings you used most recently.

The status area lets you know if your records are sorted (no surprise there). Below the Record Count, it says "Sorted" if you've done a sort, and "Unsorted" otherwise. (See the box on page 60 to learn what it means when it says "Semi-sorted.")

Multiple Sort Fields

FileMaker lets you pick more than one field to sort by, which comes in handy when you have lots of records with the same data in some fields. For example, if your People database gets really big, you might have several people with the same last name. If you just sort by last name, there's no telling in which order the like-named people will fall. In this case, it would help to sort by last name *and* first name.

When you use more than one sort field, the order in which the fields appear in the Sort Order list is important, because it determines which field FileMaker uses first. For example, if you sort a list of family members by First Name, then Last Name, you might wind up with records ordered like those shown at bottom in Figure 2-8.

Since the order of the sort fields is so important, FileMaker provides a convenient way to shuffle them around in the Sort Records dialog box after you've added them to the Sort Order list. Figure 2-9 sheds some light on how it works.

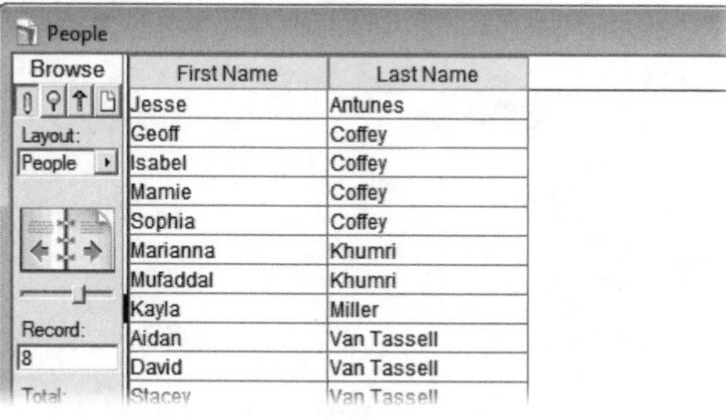

Figure 2-8:
Top: The records in this window are sorted by Last Name only. If you slide your eyes down the Last Name column, you can see that they're in alphabetical order, but several people have the same last name. FileMaker has done nothing to organize the four Coffeys in a reasonable order.

Bottom: Now the records are sorted by Last Name and *First Name. The last names are still in alphabetical order, but this time, when several people have the same last name, they appear together alphabetized by First Name.*

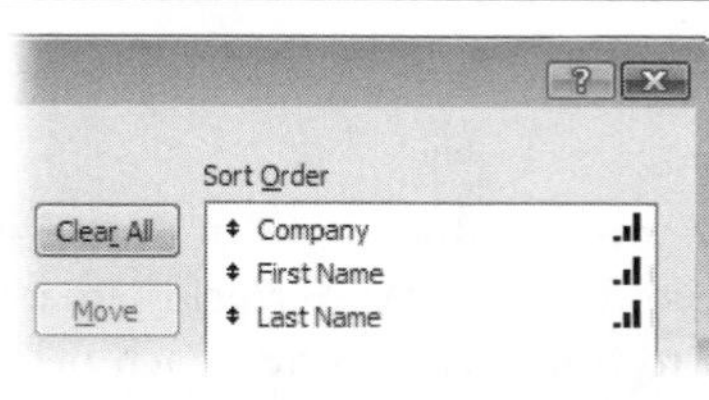

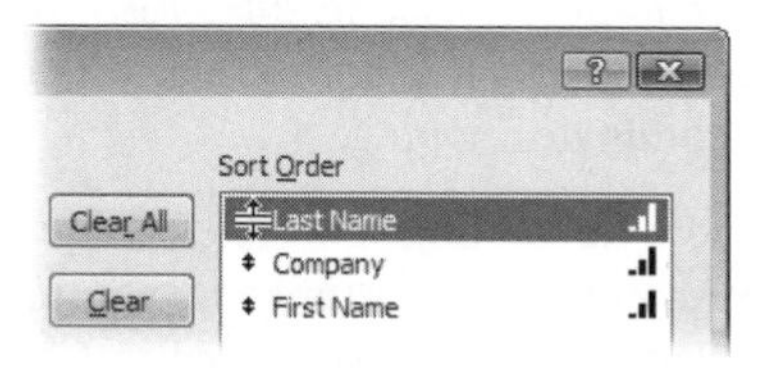

Figure 2-9:
Top: Each field in the Sort Order list has a little double-headed arrow before its name.

Middle: To change the order in which the fields are listed, first point to one of the arrows. Notice that your cursor changes shape. Instead of a normal arrow, you now have a double-headed arrow. FileMaker is letting you know that you can drag the item up or down in the list.

Bottom: Drag the item to its new position. If you prefer the keyboard, use the arrow keys to highlight the field you want to move. Then press the Ctrl (⌘) key along with the arrow keys to move the selected field. When you're done, and you click Sort, FileMaker will sort your records using each field in order, starting with the top field in the list.

If you do a multi-field sort and then discover you didn't get quite what you expected (because you had the fields in the wrong order), just choose Records → Sort Records again, move the fields in the Sort Order list to the right places, and then click Sort.

FREQUENTLY ASKED QUESTION

Sort of Sorted

When I haven't sorted my records, the status area says "Unsorted." What order is that, exactly? Is it completely random? Also, sometimes it says "Semi-Sorted." What in the world does that mean?

Remain calm. When the records are unsorted, they're in creation order. The first record you ever created (and haven't deleted yet) shows first, followed by the next one you created, and so on. Creation order is FileMaker's natural order for the records. Once you sort the records one way, they stay that way until you sort again or explicitly unsort them. (There's a button to do just that in the Sort dialog box, although why you'd want to use it is up to you.)

Now then: If the records are sorted and you add a new record, FileMaker doesn't put that record in its properly sorted place. Instead, it always goes right after the current record. Likewise, if you modify the data in a field your records are sorted by, FileMaker doesn't move the record to a new spot to keep things sorted. So if you add Adam Aaronson to your sorted address list, he winds up after Zorba Zuckerman, and if you change Zorba's name to Andrew, he stays at the end of the list anyway. When either happens, the status area changes to say "Semi-Sorted." For the most part, the data is sorted, but one or more records are out of place. Even if you then change the records back, it'll still say Semi-Sorted. FileMaker isn't smart enough to realize the data is back in sorted order until you tell it to sort again.

Editing What's in Your Fields

Once you've found the records you want to work on, it's time to learn timesaving and creative ways to revise and format your record text. FileMaker fields are a lot more capable than the little fields you're used to from dialog boxes. Each field is like a mini–word processor, with features that you're familiar with if you've ever written a letter on a computer. Of course, you can do basic things like select text, and cut, copy, and paste. There's even a Find and Replace feature and flexible text formatting powers. Read on to find out what you can do.

Find and Replace

Like your word processor, FileMaker has a Find and Replace feature. Also as in your word processor, you can (and should) use Find and Replace tools as often as possible to automate your editing process and eliminate retyping.

Suppose one of your clients is called Anderson Consulting. For one reason or another, they decide to change their name to Accenture. Unfortunately, you have 27 folks in your database with the old name, and the name is sprinkled in Company Name fields, Notes fields, and so on. You could look through your records one by one and fix them yourself, but you're never going to become a database guru that way. Instead, do a Find/Replace operation.

FileMaker fields can hold a lot of information, and it's not at all uncommon to put things like letters, emails, product descriptions, and other potentially long documents into a field. In cases like this, the Find/Replace command is just as useful as it is in your word processing program.

Since FileMaker has fields and records to worry about, though, its Find/Replace dialog box is a little more complicated than what you may be familiar with. Luckily, the concepts are simple, as shown in Figure 2-10. The Find/Replace dialog box lets you search a field, a record, or all records for a little snippet of text. It can also replace every occurrence of that text with something new—either one at a time, or all at once.

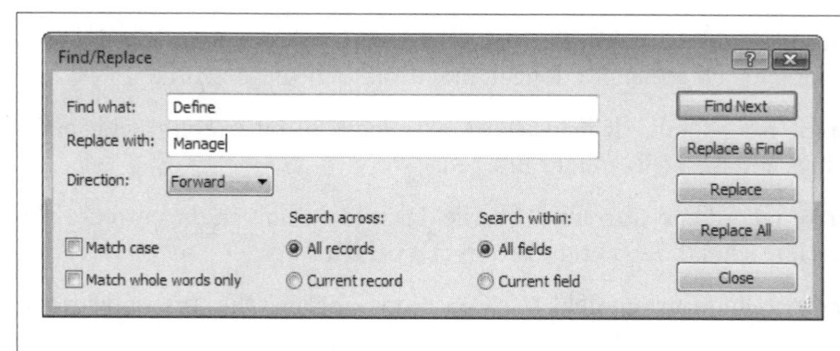

Figure 2-10: *In FileMaker, you use the same dialog box both to find text and to find and replace text. If you aren't replacing anything, don't click any of the Replace buttons. The text you're looking for goes in the "Find what" text box. If you're replacing it with something new, type that text in the "Replace with" text box. (If you want to replace some text with nothing, making it go away, leave the "Replace with" box empty.)*

Note: Don't confuse Find/Replace with Find mode. Find/Replace is for finding *text* in one or more fields and one or more records. Find mode is for finding *records*. You'll probably use Find mode much more often than Find/Replace. For the full story, see the box on page 64.

Here's FileMaker's version of Find and Replace:

1. **Choose Edit → Find/Replace → Find/Replace.**

   The Find/Replace dialog box opens, as shown in Figure 2-10.

2. **In the lower-left corner of the dialog box, turn on "Match case" and/or "Match whole words only" to tell FileMaker how you want it to match the text you're looking for.**

   Turning on "Match case" ensures that FileMaker looks for an exact uppercase and lowercase match. For example, when "Match case" is turned on, "Kite" and "kite" don't come up as a match.

   If you turn on "Match whole words only," FileMaker eliminates partial word matches. For example, "Drag" matches "Drag" and not "Dragon."

3. **Under "Search across," select either "All records" or "Current record."**

   You've just told FileMaker whether you want it to look through all the records in the found set, or only the record you're currently on. In a case like the Anderson/Accenture example, choose "All records."

4. **Under "Search within," select either "All fields" or "Current field."**

   "Current field" refers to the field you were editing when you opened the Find/Replace dialog box. If you weren't editing one, FileMaker will let you pick Current field, but when you try to find, it will complain with an error message. You're allowed to select any combination of Search across and Search within. Here's how that shakes out:

   - **All records and All fields.** FileMaker looks through every field in the window for a match. When it's done, it moves on to the next record.
   - **Current record and All fields.** FileMaker looks through every field in the window, and then tells you it's finished.
   - **Current record and Current field.** FileMaker looks only in the current field. When it reaches the end of the text in that field, it stops.
   - **All records and Current field.** FileMaker looks through the current field, and then moves to the next record. It keeps looking through records for more matches, but it pays attention only to the current field.

5. **From the Direction pop-up menu, choose Forward, Backward, or All.**

   The Direction pop-up menu controls which way FileMaker goes when it starts its search. To figure out what that means, imagine there's a long string running through your database. One end is tied to the first letter of the first field of the first record. The other end is tied to the last letter of the last field of the last record. This concept is pictured in Figure 2-11.

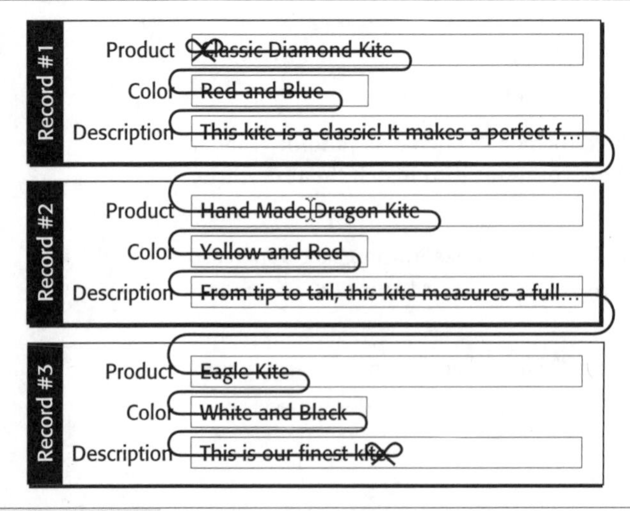

***Figure 2-11:** The Find/Replace command expects you to give it a direction. To decipher what that means, you have to do a little visualization. Here's a picture of the imaginary string, starting at the beginning of the first record, and stopping at the end of the last. When you click into a field, and the insertion point sits there blinking in front of a letter, it's marking a spot on the imaginary string. If you're not clicked into a field, FileMaker decides to mark the string right before the first letter of the first field of the current record. In this example, your cursor is sitting right there between "Made" and "Dragon."*

- **Forward.** FileMaker starts looking at your current spot on the string, and moves *forward* (towards the end of the string). When it gets to the end, it beeps.
- **Backward.** FileMaker starts looking at your current spot on the string, and moves *backward* (towards the beginning of the string). When it gets to the beginning, it beeps.
- **All.** FileMaker starts off just like a Forward search. When it reaches the end of the string, instead of beeping, it skips to the start of the string and keeps looking. It finally beeps and stops when it gets back where it started.

Now that you're through setting all your Find/Replace options, it's time to decide which button to click:

1. **Click either Find Next, Replace & Find, or Replace All.**
   - **Find Next** starts FileMaker looking. When it finds a match, it highlights it right in the field. The Find/Replace window doesn't go away yet, though. This way, you can click Find Next as many times as necessary to find what you're looking for, and then click Replace to change it to your replacement text. Click Find Next again to go to the next match.
   - If you feel the need to work more quickly—say you've done Find Next and Replace a couple times and everything looks in order—click **Replace & Find** instead. It replaces the current match, and then finds the next one all in one step. Repeat as many times as necessary.
   - Finally, if you're sure you want *every* match replaced, click **Replace All**, and FileMaker will do the entire find-replace-find-replace dance for you. FileMaker always asks you if you're sure about Replace All first, just in case. For instance, if you have some clients whose last name is Anderson and others whose company name is Anderson, you may *not* want to use the Replace All option. You'll need to check each occurrence individually to make sure you don't accidentally change someone's last name to Accenture.
2. **When you're done with the Find/Replace window, just click Close.**

Warning: Find/Replace has no undo, and since you can replace across all records and fields, it can be dangerous. Be careful with this command. Also, it can take a long time because it looks through the individual words in each field. If you're searching across all records, and you have lots of records, be prepared to wait a while as FileMaker does its magic.

Fields for Lots of Text

Click in the Notes field in the Contact Management database. Notice that when you do, a scroll bar appears on the right side of the field. If you type lots of notes, you'll be able to scroll through them. FileMaker fields can hold *a lot* of text. Technically, each field is limited to two gigabytes of data *per record*, which is a fancy way of saying "way more than you'll ever need." (When you design a database, you get to decide which fields have scroll bars, as discussed on page 163.)

UP TO SPEED

Find with Replace vs Find/Replace

You may be wondering how Find mode combined with Replace Field Contents is different from Find/Replace (discussed earlier in this chapter). In fact, they're very different, but deciding which to use can be confusing. Here are some guidelines:

- Find mode is significantly faster at finding things than Find/Replace. In Find mode, FileMaker uses something called an *index*, which lets it find ten matching records out of 293,000 in an instant. Find/Replace, on the other hand, looks through the fields the same way you would: one by one. It's faster than you, but it still takes time.
- Replace Field Contents always operates on one field across the entire found set. Find/Replace, on the other hand, also lets you replace across all fields in just the current record, as well as all fields and all records in the found set.
- Replace Field Contents always replaces the *entire* contents of the field. You can't replace every occurrence of "teh" with "the" for example. You can only give a new value that replaces whatever is in the field.
- Most important, Replace Field Contents assumes you've already found the records you want, and always modifies every record in the found set. Find/Replace adds a second layer of searching, as it scours the record or the found set looking for matches.

So why would you ever use Replace Field Contents? Sometimes you really do want to replace everything in the field every time, just like in the Company Name example on page 60. Also, Replace Field Contents is *significantly* faster at changing lots of records than Find/Replace. It takes just a few seconds to accomplish what Find/Replace would spend several minutes doing.

In general, if you want to find records, use Find mode, but if you want to find certain bits of text, use Find/Replace. Likewise, if you want to replace everything in a field in *every* record, use Replace Field Contents, but if you want to replace little bits of text, use Find/Replace. (If you want to replace little bits of text across thousands of records, study Chapter 7 first, or be prepared to take a vacation while your computer thinks about it.)

Finally, there's no reason you can't mix Find/Replace with Find mode. Since Find/Replace only searches records in the found set, you can establish a good found set *first* to make your Find/Replace go faster. (For example, if you're replacing "teh" with "the" in the Notes field, you may as well find all the records that have "teh" in their Notes field first, since Find mode is so much faster than Find/Replace.)

You can enter text into a field in all the usual ways, like typing on your keyboard or pasting text you copied from another field or another program.

Note: Even if a field doesn't have scroll bars, you can still add lots of text. In this case, FileMaker just makes the field grow to hold whatever you type. When you leave the field, it shrinks back to its normal size, hiding anything that goes outside the edges. Don't worry, though, the text reappears when you click back into the field.

Drag-and-drop Editing

In addition to copying and pasting, you can drag text from one place to another. But first, you have to turn it on in FileMaker's preferences, like so:

WORKAROUND WORKSHOP

Get Out of My Way

Unlike the Find/Replace window in most other programs, FileMaker's won't politely step aside. If you try to click in your database window to switch back to it, FileMaker just beeps at you. In fact, you can't do *anything else* but find and replace unless you close the Find/Replace window first. You can always move the Find/Replace window around the screen by dragging it, but if your database window is big, or your screen is small, the Find/Replace window can really get in the way, keeping the very results it's finding hidden behind it. Here are a few pointers to help you cope:

Make sure the Find/Replace window is as small as possible by dragging the resize handle in the lower-right corner. Like most windows, it's resizable, but its smallest size is almost always big enough.

If you close the Find/Replace window (click Close or just press Escape), FileMaker keeps the last-found item highlighted. Since FileMaker remembers all your settings, you can always open the Find/Replace window again and continue searching where you left off.

Wouldn't it be great if you could click the buttons in the Find/Replace window without having it open onscreen? Fact is, you can. In the Edit → Find/Replace menu, you'll see two handy commands: Find Again and Replace & Find Again.

Choosing these menu commands is just like clicking the Find Next and Replace & Find buttons in the Find/Replace dialog box.

FileMaker also offers one more convenient shortcut. If you have some text already in a field, and you want to find *the next* occurrence of the same text, you can choose Edit → Find/Replace → Find Selected. This one command does the same thing as copying the text, opening the Find/Replace window, pasting into the "Find what" box, clicking Find Next, and then clicking Close. All the other options in the Find/Replace window stay just as when you last used them.

Best of all, these handy commands all have keyboard shortcuts:

- To find the next occurrence (Find Again), just press Ctrl+G (⌘-G).
- To replace the currently selected text and find the next occurrence (Replace & Find Again), press Ctrl+Shift+G (Option-⌘-G).
- To find other occurrences of the selected text, press Ctrl+Shift+H (Option-⌘-H).

1. **On Windows, choose Edit → Preferences. On Mac OS X, choose FileMaker Pro → Preferences.**

   The Preferences dialog box emerges.

2. **Confirm that "Allow drag and drop text selection" is checked.**

   If you decide you don't like using drag and drop, just come back here and turn it off.

3. **Click OK.**

   The dialog box disappears.

Now that dragging is turned on, here's how it works:

1. **Make a new record (Records → New Record).**

   Now you've got a nice clean work surface.

2. **In the Notes field, type *Editing text a is drag.***

   Yes, it says "text a is." Type the mistake and all. Next you'll drag to fix it.

3. **Double-click the word "is."**

   The word is highlighted to let you know it's selected.

4. **Drag the selected word between "text" and "a."**

   Figuring out where dragged text is going to land can be tricky. If you look closely, you'll see that in addition to the text you're dragging, a little vertical line moves along under your arrow. You can see this in action in Figure 2-12. (Unless you have excruciatingly precise mouse movements, you'll probably have to fix the spaces between words. Unlike most word processors, FileMaker isn't smart enough to figure out where they go for you.)

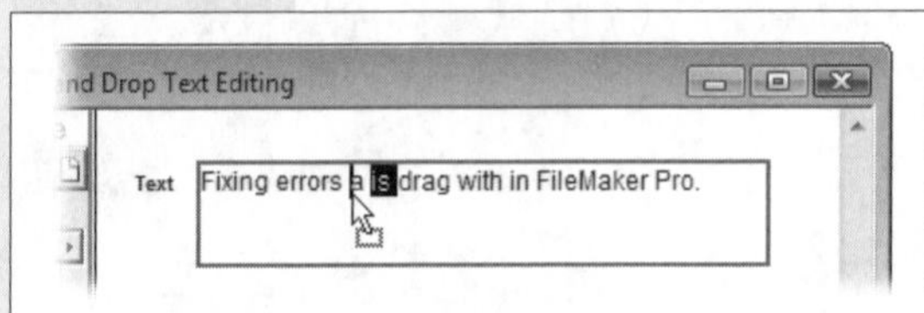

Figure 2-12: *When you turn on "Allow drag and drop text selection" in Preferences, FileMaker lets you drag selected text around with the mouse. Here, the word "is" is being moved after "errors" by dragging. The little vertical line under the arrow shows you exactly where the text will go when you drop it.*

Note: You can also drag text from one *field* to another. Instead of *moving* the text, FileMaker *copies* it. In other words, once you let go of the mouse button, the text will be both where it started *and* where you dropped it. If you want this behavior when dragging *within* a field, hold down the Ctrl (Option) key while you drag.

Text Formatting

Just like a word processor, FileMaker has commands to set the font, size, and style of the text in a field. (Figure 2-13 shows a field with formatted text.) This feature comes in handy for many reasons. For instance, imagine you have some really important information about a customer ("NEVER PAYS HIS BILL") that you want to keep in the Notes field. To make sure it gets noticed, you can make the note big, bold, and red. You can even use one of those fancy frilly fonts just to keep things interesting.

The formatting commands for font, font size, and type style are in the Format menu. But before you change anything, you'll notice that all FileMaker fields come with a preset (and pretty boring) standard formatting. (Part 2 of this book explains how you can change this automatic formatting.) Each of the formatting commands covered in this section lets you override the standard formatting for a field on a record-by-record basis.

Warning: Consider (and remember) the full implications of the paragraph above: *All* of the techniques described in the rest of this chapter pertain only to editing and formatting *individual* records. If you would like to change a field's formatting across the board, you need to make that change to your database's *layout*. For example, you might want all last names in your database to appear in boldface letters, or to put a box around everyone's phone number. You'll learn how in Part 2 of this book.

Figure 2-13: *You can format the text in any field just like text in a word processor. FileMaker lets you assign fonts, sizes, styles, colors, and more. You can even adjust paragraph attributes like line spacing, indenting, and alignment. In this record (from the Contact Management database) every field but Email Address has had its contents stylized.*

Font

FileMaker lets you pick from all the fonts you have on your computer (see the box on page 68 if you don't believe it). Using a font is a breeze if you're one of those FileMaker users who's heard of a computer. Just select the text you want to change, and then choose the font you want from the Format → Font menu. (If you're the type who plans ahead, you can also choose a font *before* you start typing.)

Note: As with all FileMaker editing commands, if you make a mistake, just choose Edit → Undo. Or use your trusty Undo keystroke: Ctrl+Z (Windows) or ⌘-Z (Mac). Unlike most everything else in FileMaker, when it comes to editing fields, you can undo as many times as you want as long as you haven't left the field yet.

Size

Changing the size of text is equally easy. Like changing fonts, you simply select the text and pick a size, in points, from the Format → Size menu. (Again, you can pick the size *before* you type if that's your thing.) The Format → Size menu lists only a few standard sizes. If you need a size that's not listed, just choose Format → Size → Custom and FileMaker will let you enter any point size from one to 500.

Immediately after Custom, one last size is listed. This one isn't separated from the rest just to be cute—it shows the last *custom* size you used. If you prefer 11-point, you only need to visit the Custom command once.

Once you've made the change, 11 will be listed at the bottom of the menu, that is, until you decide that 13-point type is your new favorite.

UP TO SPEED

More Fonts on Windows

On Windows, the Font menu may not show the fonts you want–it normally shows only a few (on Mac OS X, the Font menu *always* displays all your fonts). To get to the rest, choose Format → Font → Configure/More Fonts to show the Configure Font Menu dialog box. Once here, you can do three things: Pick fonts that don't show in the menu, control which fonts *do* show in the menu, and change how they display.

- The Available Fonts list shows every font installed on your computer. If you want to choose a font that isn't in the Font menu, select it from the Available Fonts list and click Apply. Unlike every other Apply button you've ever seen, this one applies the new font selection *and* dismisses the window.
- To add a font to the Font menu, select it from the Available Fonts list and click Move to add it to the "Appear in Menu" list. If you want the menu to show *every* possible font, click Move All instead. When you select a font from the "Appear in Menu" list, the Move button changes to Clear, and a click removes the font from the list. As usual, you can double-click font names to mimic the Move or Clear buttons.
- FileMaker can show fonts in the menu *in their own typeface*. For instance, the words "Times New Roman" will actually be *in* Times New Roman in the menu. If you don't want this behavior, turn off Show Fonts in Typeface. This setting also affects the display of fonts in the "Appear in Menu" list right in this dialog box.

When you've finished configuring, click OK. Your selected text won't be changed, but the font menu will now list the fonts you put in the "Appear in Menu" list. If you want to change the font of the selected text at the same time, select the font and click Apply instead.

Style

Using styles is a snap. Pick the style from the Format → Style menu and start typing, or select some text and apply a style. In addition to the industry-standard Bold, Italic, and Underline styles, FileMaker adds a few less common options to the mix. Except where noted here, you can mix and match styles to your heart's content (see the Notes field in Figure 2-13).

- **Word Underline** underlines each word, but not the space(s) between words. *Double Underline* puts two lines under your text. Each of the Underline styles is mutually exclusive, meaning you can't have text that's double underlined *and* word underlined.
- **Condense** squishes the text together so it takes up less space. *Extend* does just the opposite, putting a little extra space between each letter. Since these choices are opposites, you can't use both at the same time.

- **Strike Thru** draws a line right thru…uh, *through* the middle of each line of text. Use it when you want something to look like it's been crossed out—perhaps you have some data in the Notes field that no longer applies, but you want it there anyway in case it's important later.
- **Small Caps** replaces all the lowercase letters in your text with uppercase letters in a slightly smaller size, for an effect like you often see on fancy lawyer's stationery or wedding invitations.
- **Uppercase**, **Lowercase**, and **Title Case** are handy for those times when you've already typed text and later realize that you capitalized it incorrectly. Maybe your Caps Lock key got stuck halfway through someone's name, or you realize that you forgot to capitalize every word of a street address. You can use these commands to repair the damage. Uppercase and Lowercase turn all selected letters to capital or small, respectively. Title Case makes the first letter of each word uppercase, and every other letter lowercase.

Note: Using one of these styles doesn't change the actual text in the field at all. If you type *Mr. President* into a field, and then change its style to Uppercase, it will show as MR. PRESIDENT. But at any time, you can go back and remove the Uppercase style, and you'll get the original capitalization back unchanged.

- **Superscript** (Ctrl+Shift+plus sign or ⌘-Shift-plus sign) makes the text a little smaller and raises it up on the line, as in x^2. Subscript (Ctrl+Shift+minus sign or ⌘-Shift-minus sign) comes in handy when you're entering chemical formulas. (You *do* enter chemical formulas a lot, don't you?) You can't use superscript and subscript simultaneously on the same letter or number.

Note: The keyboard shortcuts for text styles in FileMaker are non-standard. While in most programs Ctrl+B (⌘-B) means Bold, in FileMaker it's Ctrl+*Shift*+B (⌘-Shift-B). The same goes for Italic and Underline. This change takes a little getting used to. Basically, take the keyboard shortcut you use in all your other programs, and add the Shift key.

Text Color

The mini word processor wouldn't be complete without colors. The Format → Text Color menu gives you a handful of colors to choose from. If you don't like those options, you can select Other Color (located below all the little color squares in the menu) to pick any color you want, as described in Figure 2-14.

If you don't like the assortment of colors FileMaker provides, you can change them by choosing Edit → Preferences (Windows) or FileMaker Pro → Preferences (Mac). In either case, switch to the Layout tab. Here, you get three choices: System subset, Standard system palette, and Web palette. The normal palette (System subset) gives you 88 colors, which most FileMaker mavens find more than sufficient. It's also nice because it's small enough for you to remember what color you've been using ("the third red from the top").

If you find the System subset palette too limiting though, feel free to try one of the others. The Standard system option displays the color palette built into your computer's operating system—Windows or Mac. Since you've probably seen this color arrangement elsewhere on your computer, you may find it easiest to use.

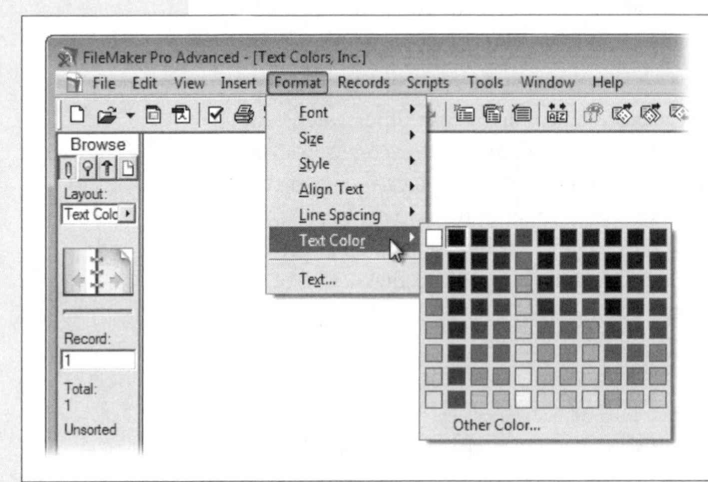

Figure 2-14: *The Format → Text Color menu offers a handful of canned color choices. If you're not happy with the colors you see, you can pick from two other palettes in FileMaker's Preferences dialog box. Whichever palette you choose determines the selection of colors you get when you choose from the Text Color submenu. Choosing "Standard system palette" gives you the most colors to work with.*

The Web palette lets you choose from the set of 216 colors commonly considered Web *safe*—that is, they're guaranteed to look pretty much the same in any browser on any computer. At one time, you needed to stick to only these colors if planning to publish your database on a Web site (Chapter 18), but the truth is you don't really need to worry about Web safe colors anymore. Every computer sold since, oh, about 1997, can display more colors than you ever dreamed of.

Note: The Format → Text Color menu is just one of several places where a color palette shows up in FileMaker. You'll see the others in Part 2. Just remember that if you change the color palette selection in preferences, the change affects the color palettes throughout FileMaker.

The Text Format dialog box

FileMaker provides one-stop shopping for all your text-formatting needs. Suppose you want to change a word to red 13-point bold-italic-underline-uppercase-condensed. That looks to be about seven trips to the Format menu. Instead, choose Format → Text to summon the Text Format dialog box (Figure 2-15). This one little window combines the Font, Size, Style, and Color menus described in the previous pages into one convenient place, turning seven menu commands into one. (Now if only it had a keyboard shortcut.)

Note: The Paragraph button reveals the Paragraph dialog box. It's covered on page 73.

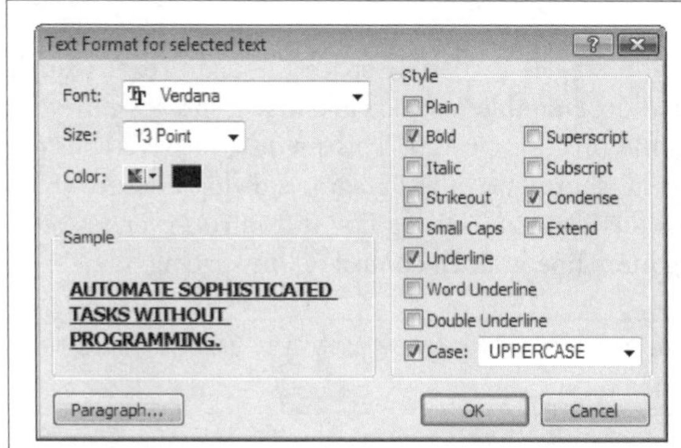

Figure 2-15:
The Text Format dialog box (Format → Text) helps cut down your mouse mileage. It combines Font, Size, and Color (exact copies of their counterparts in the Format menu) with individual checkboxes for each style. As you make selections, the text in the Sample box reflects your changes.

Paragraph Formatting

Sometimes you put *lots* of information in a field. For example, suppose you decide to keep track of all your correspondence with your customers. You can make a database to store letters and emails so you can search them or print them out, as needed. In a database like this, you usually end up typing (or pasting) long blocks of text into a field, where you need to control more than just the font, size, style, and color.

Align Text

Text alignment is perhaps the most important aspect of your document's appearance. You can have text rigidly justified on both right and left, or with a loose right margin for a more casual look. If you use FileMaker to send party invitations to your contacts, you can use centered alignment for an attractive, social look. People may not think about text alignment much, but it really sets the whole tone of a document. FileMaker puts these settings right on the Format menu.

The Format → Align Text menu offers four useful choices:

- Choose **Left** to make every line of text start at the left edge of the field. As the text wraps from line to line, the right edge appears jagged.
- Choose **Center** to make every line of text center itself in the field. In this case, both edges are jagged.
- Choose **Right** if you want every line to end exactly at the right edge of the field. As you can probably guess, this option means the *left* edge is jagged.
- The **Full** text alignment (sometimes called Justified in other programs) tells FileMaker to take special care to make every line start on the left edge of the field and end on the right edge. It adds a little space between words and letters as necessary so that everything lines up.

Note: The Format → Align Text menu also has three perpetually disabled items: Top, Center, and Bottom. These items control *vertical* alignment of the text within the field. The reason they're gray is that you can choose them only when you're designing your layouts (Chapter 4), not when you're entering data.

Line Spacing

Format → Line Spacing lets you single- or double-space the text. Text is single spaced normally, and if you choose double instead, FileMaker spreads out your lines of text, giving them a little breathing room. This menu also has a Custom option, which is primarily just a shortcut to the Paragraph dialog box. As you'll learn on page 73, you can use the Paragraph dialog box to control several aspects of text formatting—including more fine-grained control of line spacing.

Note: Unlike the other format options, alignment and line spacing apply to an entire paragraph, even if you have just a word or two selected.

The Text Ruler

A FileMaker field is much more than a mere container for plain text. Like a mini-word processor, you can set left and right indents and FileMaker makes sure your text stays between them. You can even set a first-line indent so the first line of each paragraph is automatically indented a little more (or less) than the rest of the text. Finally, you have complete control over tab stops: where they are and which direction the text goes when you tab to them.

The Text Ruler (View → Text Ruler) lets you set indents and tab stops for instant visual gratification. The ruler has an arrow icon for the Left, Right, and First Line indent settings (Figure 2-16), which you just drag to the spot on the ruler where you want the indent set. (For greater precision, you can also set indents in the Paragraph dialog box, as discussed in the next section.) You'll learn how to set tab stops on page 74.

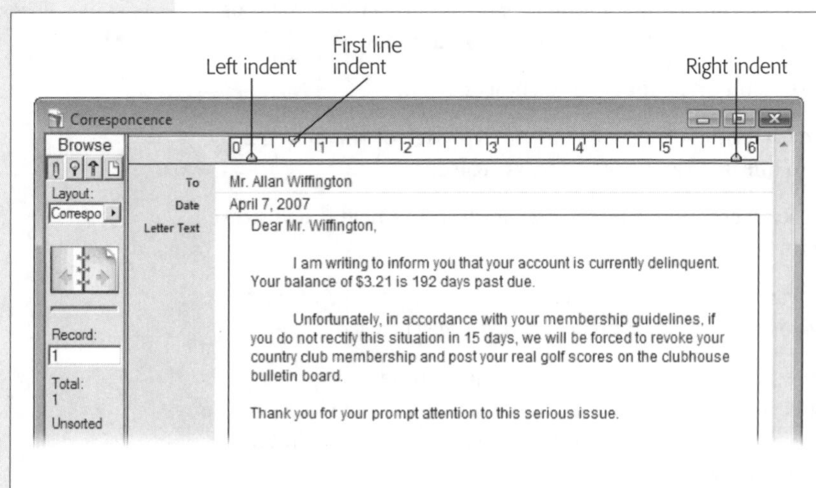

***Figure 2-16:** Like most word processors, FileMaker has a text ruler that lets you position margin markers right where you want them. When you drag the Left indent arrow, it moves the First Line arrow with it, so first drag the Left indent arrow where you want it, and then move the First Line arrow. If you want to move the Left Indent arrow without moving the First Line arrow, hold down the Alt (Option) key while you drag.*

When you turn on the Text Ruler, FileMaker adds a space along the top of the window to hold the ruler. When you're in a field, the ruler itself appears in the portion of this space that is directly above the field, with the zero point on the ruler lined up with the left edge of the field. (When you're not in a field, the ruler just measures the width of the content area.)

Detailed Formatting in the Paragraph Box

This multitalented window offers three groups of settings: Alignment, Line Spacing, and Indents. You can get to the Paragraph dialog box in one of two ways. Either choose Format → Line Spacing → Custom, or choose Format → Text and then click Paragraph. The dialog box opens, as shown in Figure 2-17.

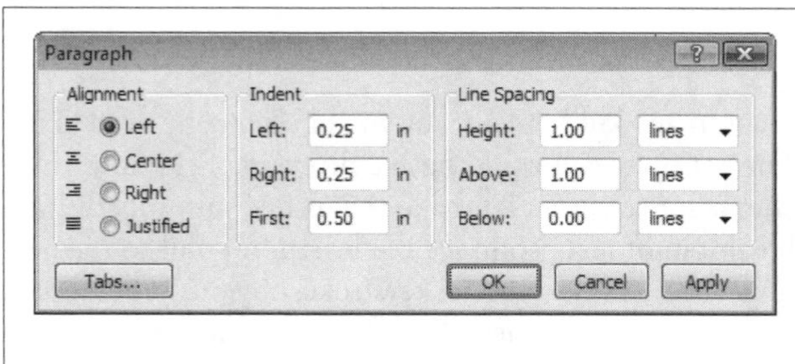

Figure 2-17: *The Paragraph dialog box lets you define a paragraph's alignment, indentation, and a whole lot more. If the Single and Double options in the Format → Line Spacing menu seem lacking, you can use this dialog box to control line spacing precisely. Just enter any number you want in the Height box, and choose your units (lines, inches, centimeters, or pixels). You can also opt to add extra space above or below each paragraph by modifying the Before and After settings.*

Warning: When you click Paragraph in the Text Format dialog box, FileMaker immediately applies any formatting settings you've made. To avoid unintentional reformatting, make sure you don't have any text selected when you choose Format → Text. (Better yet, bypass the Text Format dialog box altogether by choosing Format → Line Spacing → Custom instead.)

- The **Alignment** options are almost exactly the same as those found in the Format → Align Text menu. There is one small exception, though: Full alignment is called Justified, though it means the exact same thing. (Don't ask.)
- Next in line are the **Indent** settings. Here, you can specify how far the text indents from the left and right edges of the field. The Left setting applies to every line in the field, giving you the specified space between the left edge of the field and the beginning of each line. The Right setting works the same way, only it applies to the right edge of the field. The First setting, meanwhile, applies only to the *first* line of each paragraph. It tells FileMaker to insert more space before the first line, in addition to what's specified for the Left indent.

Note: If you want a *hanging indent*, where the first line sticks out to the left of the rest of the paragraph, specify a negative value for the First indent option, and a positive value for the Left indent.

- The Paragraph window also gives you more fine-grained control over **Line Spacing**. For instance, you can give your text 1.5 line spacing instead of single- or double-spacing by entering 1.5 in the Height box and choosing "lines" from the pop-up menu beside it. The Above and Below options refer to spacing before and after each paragraph. Unlike the indent settings, the spacing options let you pick the units right in the dialog box. You can choose Pixels (little dots on the screen), Inches, or Centimeters from the pop-up menu.

When your text is positioned and aligned just the way you want it, you have two options: Click OK to make the changes and close the Paragraph dialog box, or click Apply to inspect your changes so far. The Apply button leaves the Paragraph box open, so you can peek at your database window and see how it looks, then continue tweaking. Click OK when you're satisfied.

Tabs

Since a field can hold just about any kind of text, you might eventually need to use tab stops *within* a field. For example, you could have a nice large field into which you paste rows of text from a spreadsheet. To make things line up properly, you can set tab stops for each column of text. To move the insertion point to the next tab, press Ctrl+Tab (Option-Tab). This is a special keystroke, obviously, because in FileMaker pressing Tab jumps you to the next *field*. See page 236 to learn how Field Controls make plain old tabs work the way you're used to.

Like most word processing programs, FileMaker provides two ways to create tab stops: the Text Ruler described on page 72 and the Tabs dialog box.

Setting tabs in the Text Ruler

To insert a new tab stop, simply click anywhere in the ruler. A small right-pointing arrow appears where you clicked, representing a *left* tab stop. (The arrow shows you what direction text will go when you start typing.) FileMaker also supports other kinds of tab stops, but to get them, you have to visit the Tabs dialog box, described next.

Setting tabs in the Tabs dialog box

The Tabs dialog box is a laborious way of setting tabs, but it gives you more options because you can control all aspects of each tab stop manually. Here's the drill:

1. **Choose Format → Text.**

   The Text Format dialog box appears.

2. **Click Paragraph.**

   The Paragraph dialog box makes its entrance.

3. **Click Tabs.**

   Ta-da! You found the Tabs dialog box (Figure 2-18).

TROUBLESHOOTING MOMENT

Units

In the figures in this chapter, the Indent options are specified in Inches (you see "in" next to each text box). FileMaker actually has a setting for the unit used here and other places. FileMaker comes factory-set to inches, but it's nothing if not flexible. You can use inches, centimeters, or pixels—the choice is yours. If you're used to the metric system, by all means tell FileMaker to use centimeters. Or choose pixels for *really* precise control over text positioning. Here's how to change how FileMaker displays measurements:

If the Paragraph dialog box is open, click Cancel. The remainder of these steps will work only if your database's main window is in front.

- Choose View → Layout Mode. In this mode, the content area of the window changes somewhat. Don't be alarmed…and don't click anything in the window. (If you accidentally change something, that's OK. FileMaker will soon ask if you want to save.)
- Choose Layouts → Set Rulers to open the Set Rulers dialog box.
- In the Units pop-up menu, choose Pixels. (If you'd rather use different units, you can select anything you like. You can always repeat these steps later to get things back.)
- Click OK, and then choose View → Browse Mode.

You should be back where you started now. If you get a message asking if you want to save your changes, click Don't Save; this question refers to any accidental changes you made to the layout itself, not to the change of ruler units.

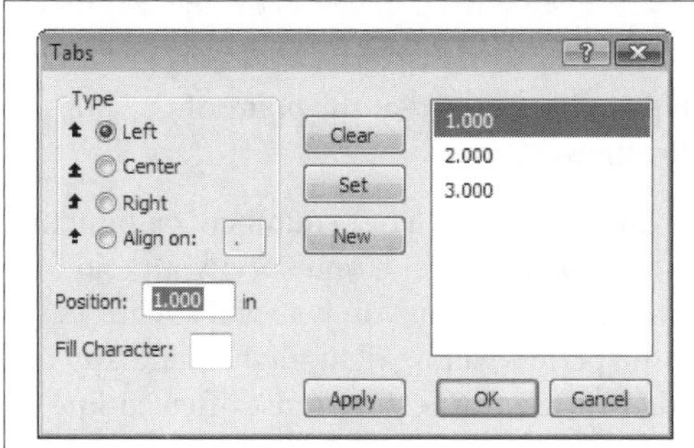

Figure 2-18: *The Tabs dialog box lists all the tab stops set for a field in the list on the right. You can also adjust a tab stop, delete it, or add a new one. Each stop has a Type, Position, and Fill Character. To change the settings for any stop, first select the stop, then edit the settings, and click Set.*

Note: If the Text Ruler is showing (Figure 2-19), you can get to the Tabs dialog box quickly. Just double-click any tab stop in the ruler. The Tabs dialog box opens with the clicked tab preselected.

To make a new tab stop, simply select the appropriate options as described below, and then click New. A new entry will appear in the list named after the Position you specified. You can create up to 20 tab stops, after which the New button becomes disabled. If you try to add a tab stop at a ruler position where one already exists, the new stop simply replaces the old one.

Editing tab stops in the Tabs dialog box

Once you've created tab stops, you can change them any time using the same Tabs dialog box. Select a Tab stop in the list to see its settings. The Type radio buttons, as well as the Position and Fill Character fields, change to reveal the settings for the selected stop. To change them, modify the values in any way, and then click Set. To delete the selected tab stop, click Clear.

Finally, you've probably noticed that the Tabs dialog box has an Apply button just like the Paragraph dialog box, and it works the same way. Click Apply, and the tab stops showing in the list will be reflected in the current field. Sometimes it can be tough to position your tab stops in just the right place. Use the Apply button to see how things line up. When you're satisfied with the tabs, click OK.

Tip: Adjusting tab stops by typing in numbers can be a real drag. Bear in mind that once you've established the settings for the tab stop (direction and fill character), you can set its position simply by dragging in the ruler. In the Tabs dialog box, just estimate the best spot, and then click OK, and use the Text Ruler to put it where you *really* want it.

Type. A tab stop's *type* effects how text entry behaves when you tab to that particular stop. Figure 2-19 shows how these different tab stops look in action.

- A **Left** tab causes the next text you type to be anchored to the tab stop on its left side. As you type, the text moves to the right just like normal left-aligned text.
- A **Right** tab works in the other direction. When you tab to one, everything you type is anchored on the right, like right-aligned text. As you type, the text moves to the left, towards the beginning of the line.
- A **Center** tab causes the text you type to be centered at the point of the stop. As you type, the text moves in both directions.
- The **Align on** tab lets you specify any character (letter, number, or punctuation) to act as the point of alignment. For instance, if you specify a period for the alignment character, the period or decimal point you type will anchor to the tab stop. Any text you type before the period will be right-aligned and any text after the period will be left-aligned. You use this feature most often to line up lists of numbers by their decimal points.

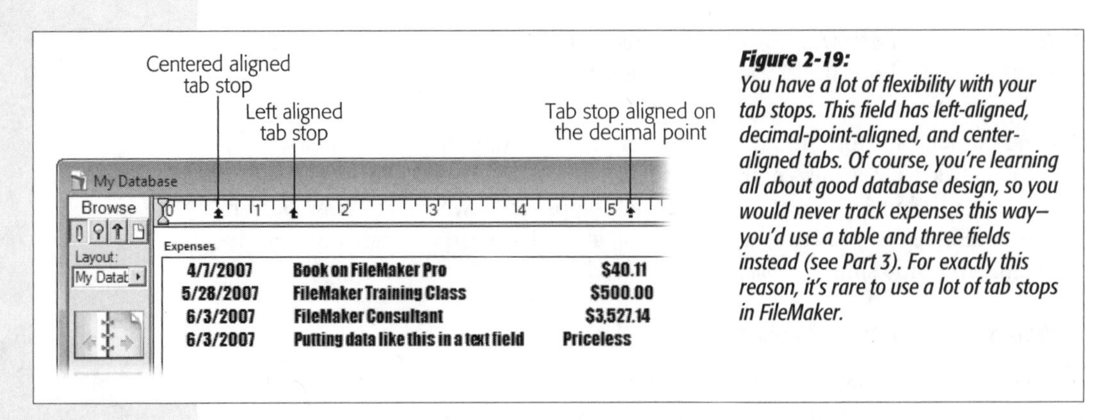

Figure 2-19: *You have a lot of flexibility with your tab stops. This field has left-aligned, decimal-point-aligned, and center-aligned tabs. Of course, you're learning all about good database design, so you would never track expenses this way—you'd use a table and three fields instead (see Part 3). For exactly this reason, it's rare to use a lot of tab stops in FileMaker.*

Position. In addition to a type, every stop has a *position*, which is measured from the left edge of the field, in the same units used for Indent settings (such as inches and centimeters). For example, if you're storing a little two-column list in a text field, you might set tab stops at .5 inches and 2 inches.

Fill Character. FileMaker also accepts a *fill character* for each tab. This character is repeated as many times as necessary to fill the blank space leading up to a tab. Most often you use a period for the fill character (as shown in Figure 2-20), but any character is allowed.

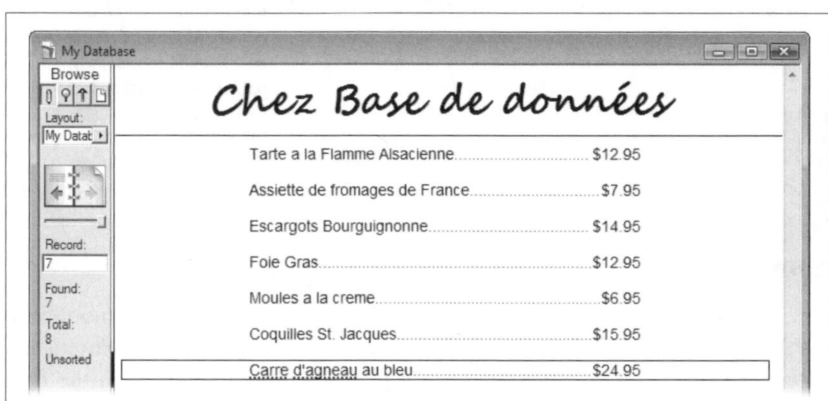

***Figure 2-20:** When a tab stop has a fill character, FileMaker uses it to fill the space leading up to the text at the tab stop. A period is by far the most common fill character. This database, which holds a restaurant's dinner menu, uses fill characters to produce a familiar look.*

Beyond Text: Container Fields

Words and numbers form the bulk of most databases. All these letters and figures convey important information, but they can be pretty boring. Increasingly, people are using FileMaker databases to store images, movies, and other bits of multimedia. For example, you can store a photograph of each employee right along with their personnel records. Or add product shots to your inventory database.

The Contact Management database has one field you may have been ignoring until now: Image. Unlike all the other fields in this database, the Image field doesn't expect (and won't accept) typed text. It's a special kind of field called a *container* field. Container fields can hold just about anything you want, including pictures, sounds, animation, music, and movies. You can even put any file from your hard drive into a container field, like a PDF file or a Word document. You can see container fields holding assorted things in Figure 2-21.

Whether you're using FileMaker as a full-blown asset management system, or you just want to keep a photo next to each employee record, FileMaker sees your container data as one of four distinct types: picture, QuickTime, sound, and file.

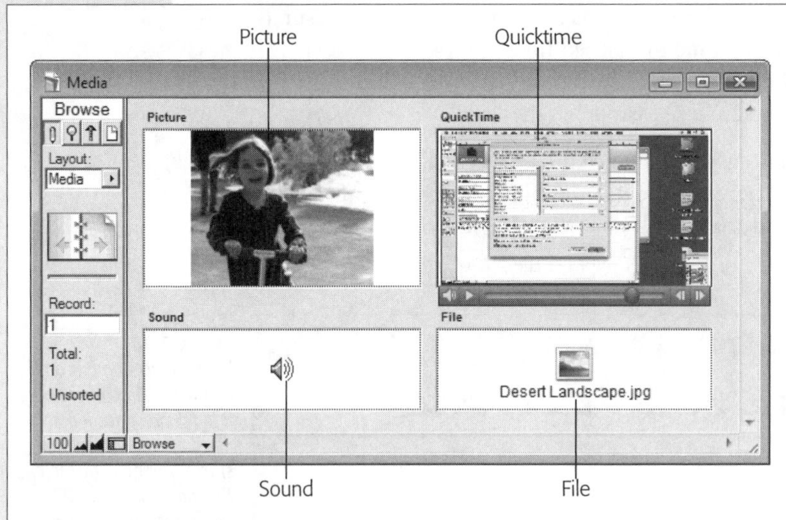

Figure 2-21: *A container field can hold any file, but it can be smarter about some file types than others–so long as you tell it what you're giving it. If you put a picture into a container field, FileMaker shows you the picture. If you insert a sound file, FileMaker gives you a special speaker icon that plays the sound when clicked. Music and movie files give you the typical play, pause, fast-forward, and rewind controls, just like movies on the Web. For other kinds of files, FileMaker just shows you the file's icon.*

Pictures

A *picture* can be in any of more than a dozen formats, including the common kinds like JPEG, GIF, PNG, TIFF, PICT, and BMP. FileMaker will also accept Photoshop and PostScript (.eps) files. When you put a picture in a container field, the field displays the picture itself.

The following methods for copying, pasting, and inserting pictures into container fields are the same whether you're inserting a movie, a PDF, text, or another type of file. You see the same type of Insert dialog box for navigating your hard drive each time.

Copy and paste

The most obvious way to put a picture into a container field is to paste it in. You can copy a picture from just about anywhere, click once in the field, and then choose Edit → Paste (Ctrl+V or ⌘-V).

You can also copy data from the container field. Again, simply click once on the field, and choose Edit → Copy (Ctrl+C or ⌘-C) or Edit → Cut (Ctrl+X or ⌘-X). Whatever was in the field is now ready to paste into another field, record, or program.

Insert → Picture

If the picture you want in a container field is stored in a file, copy and paste doesn't do you much good. You'd have to open the file in some program first, and then copy it from there—and that's no fun. Instead, you can insert the file directly into the field without ever leaving the comfort of FileMaker. Here's how:

1. **Click in the Image field.**

   You've now entered the record, and the Image field in particular.

2. **Choose Insert → Picture.**

   The Insert Picture dialog box appears. This window looks almost exactly like a typical Open File dialog box in Windows or Mac OS X. You can use it to find the picture you want to insert.

3. **Click Open.**

   FileMaker grabs the picture and puts it in the Image field.

Note: If you need to insert *lots* of pictures into a database, you can save yourself a lot of trouble by using the File → Import Records → Folder command. See page 666 for the full explanation.

QuickTime

QuickTime data includes anything supported by QuickTime Player, the multimedia software from Apple. FileMaker uses QuickTime to help it deal with multimedia files. The file types include QuickTime files (.mov); Flash animations; video files like AVI, DV, MPEG, and MPEG4; virtual reality files (VR); and music files like WAV, AIFF, MP3, and AAC. Because FileMaker uses QuickTime, and QuickTime is frequently upgraded, the exact list of formats FileMaker supports also changes. For the most part, QuickTime can handle most standard music, video, and animation formats.

When a container field holds a QuickTime file, you normally see the movie's *poster frame*, which is usually just the first frame of the movie. When you click the movie, a standard movie controller appears (like the one at the upper-right of Figure 2-21), so you can play, pause, fast-forward, and rewind it. The controller also has a button to adjust the volume and a little knob that shows you where you are in the movie.

Just as with a picture (see page 78), you use the Insert → QuickTime menu command to select a QuickTime file from the hard drive.

Note: Unlike pictures and files, FileMaker *never* stores QuickTime movies in the database. Instead, the program remembers where the original file is on your hard drive, and loads the data from it as needed. If you move or delete the original file, you'll see a message in your container field telling you FileMaker can no longer find the file.

Sound

A *sound* is a recorded bit of audio. FileMaker actually lets you record sounds right into the field. You can keep audio notes with a project record, or record your practice speeches and save them for when you're famous. When a container field holds a sound, it displays a little speaker icon; double-click it to hear the recorded sound.

POWER USERS' CLINIC

Store a Reference

When inserting a picture or file (see page 78), the dialog box includes an option to "Store only a reference to the file." When this option is turned off, FileMaker copies the actual file into your database. You can move or delete the original file and the data will still appear in the field, because the database now contains all the file's information within itself. If you turn on "Store only a reference to the file," FileMaker doesn't copy the file into the field at all. Instead, it just remembers the file you wanted. Each time you look at this record, FileMaker returns to the disk and finds the original file so it can display the data. In this respect, it works exactly like a shortcut or alias. If the file is gone (moved, deleted, or renamed), FileMaker leaves the field empty except for a short message that tells you the file could not be found.

There's no simple rule for when you should store the actual file, and when you should store a reference instead. Most people decide to store the file itself, because it saves the trouble of keeping the files and the database together.

This is especially true when multiple people are using the database from different computers. However, here are a couple of reasons you might want to store a reference instead:

- Storing many *larger* files can make your database get big—really big—which can cause a number of problems. It's harder to back up and move a huge database file from one place to another. If you're trying to email the database to your home office, your ISP may not appreciate (or allow) a 3 GB attachment, for example. If the inserted files aren't critical to the record data, it may make sense to leave them out of the database so it's easier to work with.
- Sometimes you want to catalog files inside FileMaker even though they might change over time. For example, if you wanted to put promotional images into a database so they're easy to locate, you probably *don't* want to make editing those images difficult. If you store a reference to these images, you can still edit the originals any time. As long as you haven't changed their name or location, when you look in FileMaker, you'll see the latest edits.

Otherwise, when you're using your database day to day, it usually doesn't matter whether you've inserted a reference or the actual file. For the most part, both kinds work exactly the same way. This book explains the differences as they come up.

Recording sound

The Insert → Sound command doesn't bring up the same dialog box as the other Insert commands. Instead, it shows the Record dialog box (that's the verb version of record, not the noun, as in "Record a greeting"—see Figure 2-22). If your computer has a microphone attached, you can record any sound directly into the field.

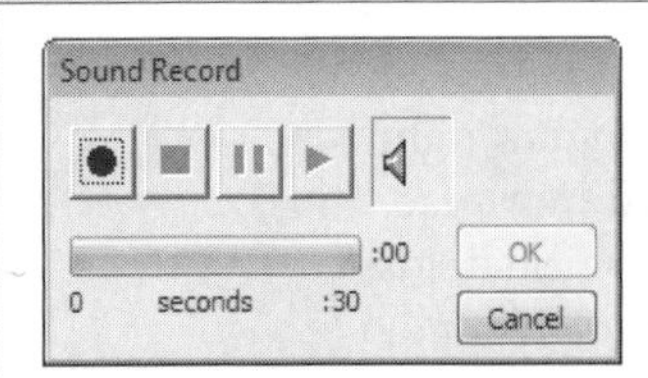

Figure 2-22: *FileMaker records sound from the sound input device you set up in your control panel (Windows) or System Preferences (Mac OS X). Most computers let you use more than just a microphone as the sound input device. For example, you can usually record sound from audio CDs in your CD-ROM drive.*

The Record dialog box is simple, but capable. The speaker icon provides feedback about what the microphone is picking up, by showing little sound waves indicating the sounds it's hearing. The more sound waves you see, the louder the recording. In fact, the speaker icon lets you check for sound waves even when you're *not* recording, so use it to do a quick sound check ("Testing, testing, 1, 2, 3"). If you don't see waves when you talk, make sure the microphone is plugged in.

When you're ready to record, proceed as follows:

1. **Click the Record button.**

   FileMaker immediately begins recording everything the microphone hears. As it does, the Recording Time progress bar fills slowly. When the progress bar reaches the end, you've recorded as much as you have room for.

2. **When you've finished recording, click Stop.**

   At this point, you have some sound recorded. The length of the recording shows to the right of the Recording Time progress bar.

3. **To hear what you got, click Play.**

   Once the recording is playing, you can use the Stop or Pause button to stop it. Clicking Stop will stop it completely. (The next time you press Play, it starts over from the beginning.) Pause, on the other hand, lets you stop the playback momentarily. (Clicking Pause or Play again starts the playback right where it left off.)

4. **If you're satisfied with what was recorded, click Save to store the sound in the container field.**

   If you click Cancel, FileMaker completely erases the sound you recorded with no warning, so be sure you click the correct button.

Note: The Insert → Sound command is specifically for recording sound directly into the field. If you have a sound file of some kind already on your hard drive (an MP3 for example), choose Insert → QuickTime instead. In general, if the data you're putting in the field has a *time component* (meaning it happens over time, like video or sound), treat it like a QuickTime file.

File

A container field can also hold a *file*. Since FileMaker doesn't know what the file is supposed to be, it simply shows you the file's name and icon. Unfortunately, you can't do anything with a file like this while it's in FileMaker. You can't edit it. You can't even open it and view its contents. Rather, the container field simply holds the file for you. (Soon you'll learn how to get it back out.)

If you can't use the file in FileMaker, why put it there at all? Sometimes people need to keep track of lots of files. They might need to organize them in ways that make sense only to their business. Keeping all these files in a folder on your hard drive can be a real drag since they can be slow to search and hard to reorganize. With FileMaker, you can

GEM IN THE ROUGH

PDFs in Mac OS X

The ability to store pictures, movies, sounds, and files in your database can be useful for lots of reasons. For example, if you're a recruiter, you could store resumes in Microsoft Word or PDF format right in the database alongside the info about a particular candidate. In fact, the Adobe PDF format is so common that people often need to keep track of PDF files--the brochure, flyer, or documentation for each of your products, the prospectus for each of your investments, or a floor plan for each of your properties.

You already know you can use the Insert → File command to store the PDF document right in a container field (and get it back out again later to look at it). But if you're on Mac OS X, you can do one better. Choose Insert → Image and then select a PDF file. FileMaker shows you the PDF (the first page of it, anyway) right in the container field. If your document has more than one page, you need to export the PDF out of the container field (see below) to read the whole thing.

Or, try this unexpected twist: You can read multipage PDFs right in FileMaker if you use Insert → QuickTime instead.

This time, when you click the container field itself, the standard QuickTime movie controls appear. Using these controls, you can flip through the pages in the PDF: Fast Forward goes to the next page, Rewind goes to the previous page. If you press Play, FileMaker flips through the pages one after the other until it reaches the end of the document.

If you need to search within a PDF file, try this. Open the PDF file, select all the text, copy it, and then paste it in a regular text field. FileMaker can search the text field, but you can view the PDF in all its glory in the container field.

keep the files right alongside other important data. For example, you can store project specifications (in Microsoft Word format) and diagrams (in Visio format) in your database along with tasks, team members, and timelines.

The most common way to place a file into a container field is to use the Insert → File command. On Windows, you can also copy a file on the desktop and paste it into a container field. When you insert a file, FileMaker makes no effort to figure out what's *in* the file. If you choose a picture, you'll still get just the name and icon. If you want to *see* the picture itself in FileMaker, you must choose Insert → Picture, as described on page 78.

Exporting data from container fields

Inserting files into container fields is all well and good, but it's just as important to get them back out again. When you use the Insert → File command, all you get to see is an icon and file name. Copying the file from the field with Edit → Copy, doesn't even do you much good, since FileMaker can't *paste* files to the desktop where you might actually be able to open and read them. A better way is to use the Export Field Contents command. Just click in the container field in question, and choose Edit → Export Field Contents. FileMaker asks you where you want to put the file, and what to name it. Click Save, and FileMaker creates a new file that's an exact copy of the one you put in the container field.

Note: If you turned on the "Store only a reference to the file" option (see the box on page 80) when you added the file, you don't need to get it back out again (after all, the file is on your hard drive somewhere). Instead, double-click the container field to open the original file in the appropriate program.

POWER USERS' CLINIC

Getting the Most Out of Your Fields

The Edit → Export Field Contents command isn't limited to container fields. With very few exceptions, you can export the contents of *any* field to a file. By contrast, you can't export a sound you recorded in FileMaker and you can't export the contents of a field you can't click into. (To help understand why you can't click in some fields, read about field behavior in Chapter 6, and about security in Chapter 16.)

Here are some examples of how to export to your advantage:

- Use Edit → Export Field Contents to create a file without having to retype what you've stored in FileMaker. But if you just whiz by the Export Field Contents dialog box without looking, you'll miss a couple of options that will save you buckets of time. If you want to watch a QuickTime video at a size larger than the skimpy container field, just click the "Automatically open file" option as you export the contents of your field. FileMaker creates a duplicate video file for you, and then opens a QuickTime player for your viewing pleasure.
- In fact, FileMaker is smart enough to open the right program for whatever you've exported. You'll get a text editor for text, a PDF viewer for a PDF, or a graphics viewer for graphics. You don't have to scramble around looking for a program that can handle your file, because FileMaker figures it out for you.
- If you want to spread the wealth around–let your colleagues know about a customer who always makes a big order at the beginning of the new quarter, say–then turn on the "Create email with file as attachment" option when you export your field contents. FileMaker makes a file, and then launches your email program, starts a new email, and attaches your new file to the email. All you have to do is type in a name, subject, and some text, and then send the email on its merry way.

Let FileMaker really impress you by clicking both options at once. You'll get a copy of the file open for reference and a fresh, shiny email nearly ready for sending. If you've got the screen real estate, you can look at both these little jewels while you're checking out the FileMaker record that spawned them.

Checking Spelling

Considering all the tools FileMaker provides for editing your records, it'll come as no surprise that it also has a full spell checker built right in.

Spell Checking in One Pass

Before printing out your database or otherwise sharing it with the greater public, you'll want to make sure your spelling is correct. If you've been typing new records at lightning speed, there are bound to be some typos. And nothing screams "amateur" louder than a City field that reads "Chciago." All the spell-checking commands are found under the Edit → Spelling menu. Here you have three choices:

- Choose Edit → Spelling → Check Selection to spell-check selected text only. This method comes in handy when you've just typed a word and it doesn't quite look right.
- To check the entire record, choose Edit → Spelling → Check Record.

- Finally, you might want to check spelling on many records at once. In this case, choose Edit → Spelling → Check All. When you choose this option, you're telling the spell checker to look at every field of every record in the current found set (choose Records → Show All first if you want to check *every* record in the database).

No matter how many records you're checking, FileMaker opens the same Spelling dialog box shown in Figure 2-23.

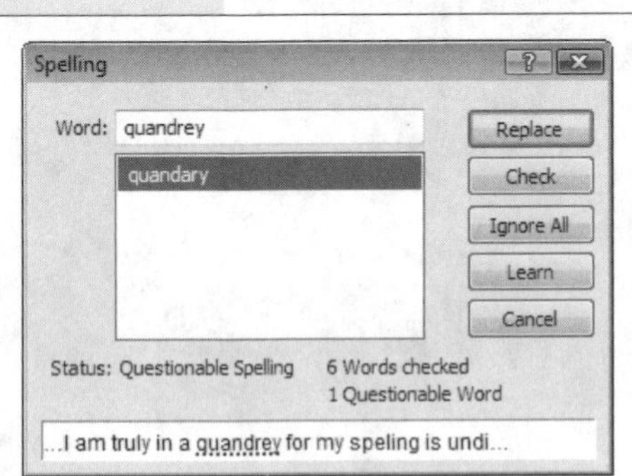

Figure 2-23: *The spell checker found a typo—"quandrey." You can see the misspelled word in the Word box and underlined in red in the box at the bottom of the window. If FileMaker figures out the correct spelling, it selects it in the list under the Word box. And if you're the type who calculates your gas mileage every time you fuel up, you'll be delighted to discover that FileMaker keeps track of how many words you've spelled wrong so far, and tells you at the bottom of the window.*

Note: Even if, by the magic of planetary alignment, you have no misspellings, FileMaker still opens the Spelling dialog box. In this case, though, it says "Status: Finished Spelling" in small print in the middle of the busy window. You're supposed to spot this right away and know the program's done. Of course, if you're like most people, you'll stare blankly at the screen for 30 seconds trying to figure out what went wrong first. Save yourself the confusion: Check the Status line when the window first appears. If FileMaker is finished, click Done.

At the bottom, the Spelling window says Status: Questionable Spelling. The Word text box displays the word in question. There are a few different ways things can proceed from here:

- More often than not, the correctly spelled word appears in the list below. In this case, just click the correct spelling, and then click Replace. (Alternately, you can simply double-click the correctly spelled word and save the trip to the Replace button.)
- If you don't see the right spelling, you can correct it yourself. Type the correct spelling into the Word box, right over the misspelled word. To confirm that your new spelling is correct, click Check; the status line changes to say Correct Spelling if you got it right. Otherwise, you'll be back where you started, with a misspelled word and a few suggestions below it.
- If you spelled it right originally, but FileMaker doesn't agree, you can click Ignore All to tell FileMaker to ignore this so-called misspelling. Better yet, click Learn to teach FileMaker the word so it won't bother you about it in the future. (Clicking Learn adds the word to your current user dictionary, which is explained below. Ignore All only ignores the word temporarily; if you quit FileMaker and come back later, it will think the word is misspelled again.)

- If you change your mind and want to stop the spell checker, just click Cancel. When the spell checker has finished its work, the status line changes again, this time to say Finished Spelling.

Note: Clicking Cancel doesn't undo all the changes you've made in the spell checker. It simply stops any further checking. If you've already corrected some words, the corrections will stick around after you cancel.

Spell Checking as You Type

FileMaker's spell checker also works automatically as you type. This *visual* spell check is a per-database setting, so you control it from the File Options dialog box. Choose File → File Options, and then click the Spelling tab. You'll find two options that you can mix and match to help you spell better, run faster, and jump higher. Well, you'll spell better, anyway.

The first option is "Indicate questionable spellings with special underline." If you miss your word processor, this one will make you feel right at home. You'll see that familiar red line underneath any word FileMaker doesn't like the looks of. Plus, if you right-click (Control-click on the Mac) the underlined word, and then choose Suggested Spellings from the shortcut menu, FileMaker offers suggestions for spelling the word properly. From the same menu, you can also tell FileMaker to learn the word or ignore it.

If red lines aren't annoying enough, you could turn on "Beep on questionable spellings," and FileMaker will make your computer beep when you type a space after a misspelled word. Unfortunately, it's just the same old alert beep that your computer makes in all kinds of other situations—so it can be easy to miss. But in combination with the red line, this pair could be a formidable reminder to spell better.

Note: Having FileMaker check your spelling as you type is exceedingly handy. But sometimes (especially in a database) your data entry will include things that don't need to be spell checked (like inventory codes, abbreviations, email addresses, and the like). Luckily, when you design your own databases, you can turn off the as-you-type version of spell checking for any particular field. See page 237 for details.

Managing Spelling Dictionaries

FileMaker comes with spelling dictionaries for various languages and choosing among them is easy. Just choose Edit → Spelling → Select Dictionaries. The Select Dictionaries window lets you choose the language to use for all spell-checking operations. You can see it in Figure 2-24.

User dictionaries

Remember from page 84 when you clicked the Learn button to teach FileMaker a new word? When you did so, behind the scenes, FileMaker actually added that word to the *user dictionary*, which is separate from the normal dictionary that comes with FileMaker.

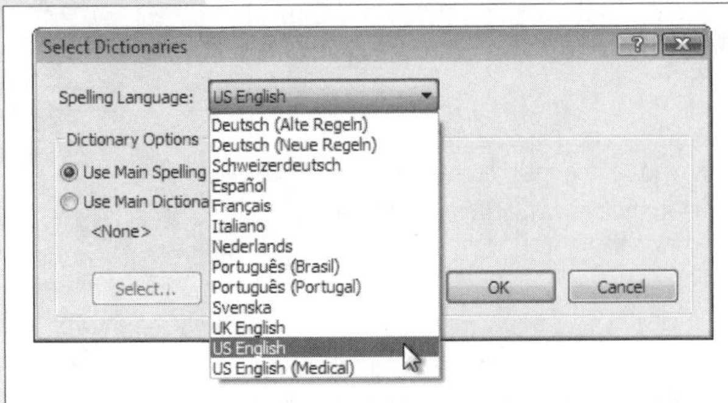

Figure 2-24:
The Select Dictionaries window lets you pick the spell checker language. You can also opt to use a User Spelling Dictionary (which happens automatically unless you come here and say otherwise). You can actually create as many user dictionaries as you want, and then select the one you want to use for a particular database.

In the Select Dictionaries window shown in Figure 2-24, you can choose whether or not to use the user dictionary. You can select an existing user dictionary (presumably, one you created previously), or create a new one. You can even have multiple user dictionaries for different purposes. For example, if you have two databases, one that tracks your apparel products and one that stores information about tools, it might make sense to keep two user dictionaries. The tools version might include words like "mm" and "pcs" while the apparel version would have "XXL" and "CottonPoly."

POWER USERS' CLINIC

Rewriting the Dictionary

You've already learned how to add to your dictionary using the Learn button in the spell checker. Well, if you've ever wanted to just *tell* it what words you want it to skip, you can. Just choose Edit → Spelling → Edit User Dictionary to open the User Dictionary dialog box. Here you can add new entries to the dictionary (type the word and click Add), or remove existing entries (select the word and click Remove).

You can also export all the entries to a text file where you can edit them to your heart's content. When you click Export, FileMaker asks where it should save the export file. The file you get is simply a plain text file with one word on each line. You can then edit in a text-editing program.

If you already have a file that has words you want, you can import those words into your user dictionary en masse. For instance, if you use a lot of technical terms, you might be able to download a list of terms from your industry and load them into a dictionary in one shot. The file has to have each word on its own line, so if it's in some other format, you'll need to clean it up first. (For example, use your word processor's Find/Replace function to turn a comma-separated list into one with a carriage return between each word.)

Also, make sure the file is plain text. A Microsoft Word file (.doc) or other special format won't work. (Making a plain-text file on Windows is a breeze: Just use Notepad, the simple text-editor program in the Accessories folder in your Start menu. On Mac OS X, however, you need a little more care. You can use Text Edit—it's in your Applications folder—but you must tell it you want plain text. Just choose Format → Make Plain Text before you save the file.)

Using the Import and Export features together can be particularly useful. You can export your user dictionary, edit it manually in the text-editing program (where making lots of edits might be easier), and then import it back in.

Note: In reality, it's nine times easier to just use one user dictionary, so you don't have to worry about which one is selected. (It generally doesn't hurt to have *too many* words in your user dictionary, while not having enough makes spell checking much more time consuming. Nothing's worse than having to wade through a dozen correctly spelled words every time.) Nevertheless, if you feel the need for more than one, the option is there.

Printing and Preview Mode

All this talk about the wonders of an *electronic* database may leave you thinking FileMaker has nothing to do with paper, but that's not true. It's a cruel fact of life that eventually you'll need to put your data on paper. You might want mailing labels for all your customers in Canada, or a special printed form prefilled with patient information for insurance filing. Sometimes you just need your data with you when you're away from your computer. As you'll learn in Part 2, you can arrange the data any way you want in FileMaker, and make certain *layouts* that are particularly suitable for printing. But for now, remember that FileMaker lets you print *anything* you see onscreen (just choose File → Print). Its Print dialog box has a few special options. Figure 2-25 show the Windows version. You can see the Mac OS X version (which requires a little more digging) in Figure 2-26.

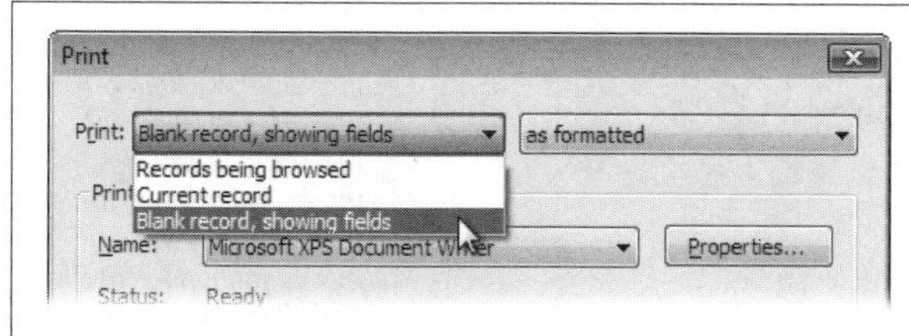

Figure 2-25: *FileMaker's Print dialog box gives you all the standard options, plus a little more. The Print pop-up menu (at the top in the dialog box in Windows) lets you tell FileMaker which records to print.*

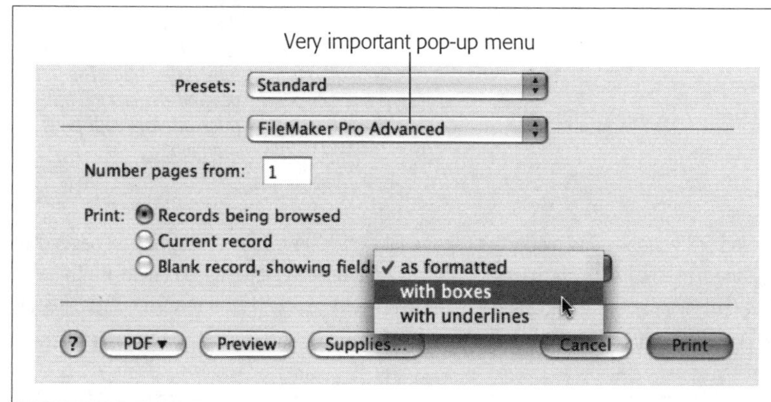

Figure 2-26: *On Mac OS X, FileMaker's special print options are tucked away in a secret place. You have to choose FileMaker Pro or FileMaker Pro Advanced from this unnamed but very important pop-up menu. In this example, you can see the field styles you can pick from if you elect to print a "Blank record, showing fields."*

- **Records being browsed** tells FileMaker to print every record in the found set. If you want to print all your Canadian customers, choose this option.

- **Current record** will print just the current record, which comes in handy when you just want to print *one* thing: your doctor's contact information to keep in the car, perhaps, or maybe Aunt Edna's candied yams recipe.
- **Blank record, showing fields** causes FileMaker to print what's onscreen with no data at all. You can change the look of each field to a box or an underline if you want (just pick your choice from the pop-up menu shown in Figure 2-25 and Figure 2-26). You would choose this option if you wanted to hand out pages for people to fill out with a pen (it's a kind of antique writing device), and later type their responses into the real database.

To see how the printout is going to look without committing trees to it, you can use *Preview mode* (Figure 2-27). You access Preview mode via the View menu, the Mode pop-up menu, or the Mode tabs (see page 19).

Preview mode shows you what your database looks like as though it were printed on paper. For instance, you can see whether FileMaker's going to chop off any information to fit on the page (anything beyond the width of the page simply isn't printed). Preview mode also indicates the margins and lets you flip through the file page by page using the Book icon.

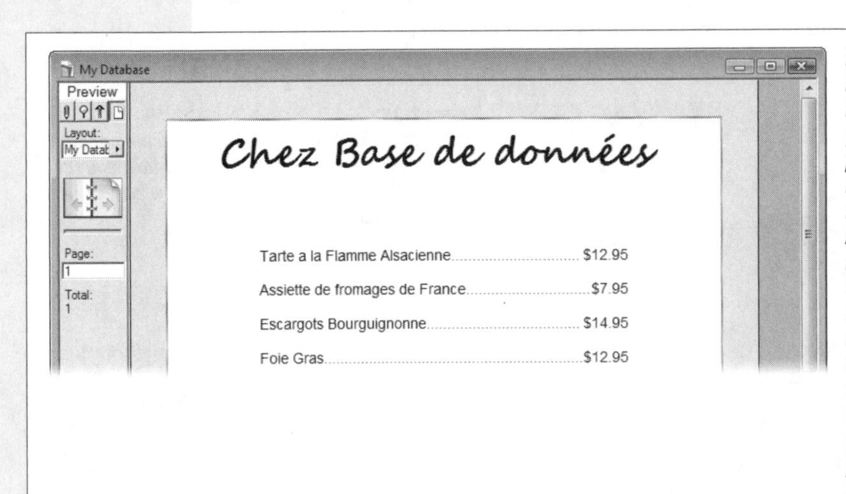

Figure 2-27: *In Preview mode, FileMaker reveals how your data will look when printed. You can't edit records in Preview mode–only view them. Also, the Book icon moves you a page at a time, instead of one record at a time, and the status area shows you the current page (not record) number and the total page count. The gray border around the page displays your page margin.*

Note: When you first go to Preview mode, the page count says "?" instead of the number of pages. FileMaker actually doesn't know how many pages it's going to print until you force it to count them. To do so, just drag the Record Slider all the way to the right, which tells FileMaker you want to see the last page. On its way there, FileMaker counts the pages, too. The process may take some time but FileMaker will catch up eventually.

All the standard page-setup options affect what you see in Preview mode. For example, if you change the paper orientation, Preview mode reflects the change right away.

On some computers and printers, you can reduce the printout by a percentage. When you do, Preview mode shows the page proportionately larger or smaller so you can see how the content area will fit on the page. (Which of these options are available to you depends upon the computer, operating system, and printer you're using.) The Zoom controls (see page 18) work in Preview mode, too. If the full page is too big to fit on your screen, just zoom out a bit to see the whole thing.

CHAPTER

3

Building a New Database

In Chapter 1, you jump-started your first database using one of FileMaker Pro's built-in templates. All FileMaker templates started out as blank databases. Some diligent FileMaker employees set up the fields and the formatting to get you started quickly, but there's no magic involved. With just a little knowledge and experience, you can create a database with all the power and fancy features of any FileMaker template. This chapter shows you how to build a contact management database from the ground up.

You really get FileMaker to work for you when you build your own databases. Lots of programs out there can help you keep track of one thing or another, but when you build your own database, it "thinks" the way you think and works the way your business works. You can design it to capture, organize, and display the information you need to know, when you need to know it—rather than bending your business (or life) to fit the software. It's time to learn how to custom-craft a database just for *you*.

Tables and Fields

So you're getting tired of your job, and you decide it would be exciting to get into the private investigator business. You found an office, ordered business cards, secured a phone line, and purchased some snazzy furniture. But have you thought about how you're going to *run* your business? Chances are, you could use some help from a database. And the first thing you need to think about when building a database is *what kind of information* it's going to track. For example, a private investigator may want to keep track of people—names, phone numbers, aliases, passport numbers, and so on. Someone in retail, however, may want to track inventory—product names, descriptions, item numbers, prices, quantities, and similar details.

Tables: The Foundation of Your Database

You already know that whatever information you put in your database goes into fields—and that's where your database building begins. These fields in turn comprise a *table*. Tables are at the heart of the database, holding all the information and keeping it organized. Everything else in a database works in service of the tables in some way, letting you edit, extract, or view the information.

Conceptually, a table has rows and columns. The fields you create become the columns in the table. As you add records, you add new rows to the table. It's called a table because it stores information in a tabular form, just like the table of values in the back of a college math book. When you first start out with FileMaker, you may not even be aware that tables exist, but you have one anyway. FileMaker always creates one table for you when you make a new database, and that's where it puts all your information. It doesn't matter how your database *looks*—even if you never see any rows and columns, you still have a table inside where the data lives.

Note: In this chapter, you're going to build a database based on a single table. As you've probably guessed, a database can have more than one table. A database can also have no tables at all–instead, it can work with tables from other databases. You can even hook several tables together so they can share data and keep track of *relationships* between records. That's why FileMaker Pro is called a *relational* database program. In Part 4, you'll learn all about multiple table databases and hooking multiple databases together.

Figuring Out What Fields You Need

You decide the first thing your new business needs is a database to keep track of the people you deal with. Figuring out what fields your table should have is one of the most important decisions you'll make. To make the right choices, think carefully about *what* you need to track.

There's a lot of detail to consider when you plan a database. As you work, you may find it helpful to take some notes or even draw a picture. You'll learn more tips for this kind of planning in Chapter 7. For starters, use these guidelines:

- **Records** are *things*, like people, buildings, invoices, payments, products, or orders. If a single record holds information about more than one thing, you're probably making a mistake. For example, in the database you're building now, the records represent *people*. If you later want to keep track of the invoices you send to your customers, you don't want to add fields like Invoice Number, Amount, and Due Date to this table.

  Why not? Because if you did that, each person's record would have room for only one invoice. If the same customer makes another purchase, you'd have to create a new record for each invoice *and* enter the person's information all over again. Even worse, when the customer gets a new address or phone number, you'd have to change it individually in *every* record.

Note: If you have more than one thing to keep track of, there's a solution: Have more than one table–one for people and one for invoices, for example. If your business starts branching out, you may even need more than one database. You'll get into that in Part 4.

- **Fields** are *attributes* of the item in each record. First Name, for example, is an attribute of a person. Most things have lots of attributes, and that's why most records have lots of fields. Unfortunately, there's some gray area here. For instance, is Company Name an attribute of a *person* (the company he works for), or is it a separate *thing*? The answer depends on what you want to do with the Company Name information. Again, Part 4 will help you work through these tough issues. For now, a simple rule to follow is, if you're only tracking one attribute of a thing, it's usually safe to make it a field. For instance, if you just want to keep track of the company a person works for, and don't plan to use the company's main address, phone number, or Web address, then you probably need only a simple Company Name field on each record.

UP TO SPEED

Think Table

Understanding the concept of a *table* is crucial when you're creating a database. In any particular table, every record has room to store the *same kind* of information. If you see a field called Email Address on one record, there's a place to put an email address on every record. If you want to record someone's birth date, you need to add a field for it. When you do, every record gets a Birth Date field, even if you type it only on one record.

When you're deciding what fields to put in your database, it helps to imagine a real table, or a spreadsheet.

Spreadsheets have rows, which are the records, and they have columns, which are the fields. If you have a column in one row, obviously, it's there for every row. If you add a new column, even after you've added 100 rows, that column is available to all the rows at once. See Figure 3-1.

	Name	Phone Number	Email Address
1	Harry Potter	+44 (020) 5555 7022	h.potter@hogwarts.ed.uk
2	Hermione Granger	+44 (020) 5555 2193	h.granger@hogwarts.ed.uk
3	Ronald Weasley	N/A	r.weasley@hogwarts.ed.uk
4	Vernon Dursley	+44 (011) 5555 9930	vdursley@grunnings.co.uk
5	Mr. Olivander	N/A	wandman27@hotmail.com
6	Stan Shunpike	N/A	stan@knightbusindustries.co.uk

Figure 3-1:
Even if you never see your data arranged this way in FileMaker, it's helpful to think of your data in terms of a table or a spreadsheet. If you visualize your data arranged in columns and rows, it's easier to figure out which fields you need to create in a new database.

So far, you know that your database will track people, and its fields will include any important attributes about a person. You may be tempted to have Name, Address, Phone Number, and Email Address as your fields—but you'd be making a mistake. What happens when you want to find all the people in Washington State? A search for Washington in the Address field will find them, as well as everyone on any Washington street and everyone in a town called Washington. Same goes for first and last name. You need a little experience and some careful thought to pick just the right fields. It's usually a bad move to have different kinds of information in the same field. Instead, think about what elements—no matter how small—are important to how you'll search, sort, analyze, or otherwise access your records later. In database lingo, those bits of information are *individually significant*, and each one should get its own field.

For example, the first line of a person's address often contains several pieces of information: a street number, street name, direction (north, south, east, west), and an apartment, building, or suite number. Should these all be separate fields, or is one field enough to hold the whole street address? Are all these bits of data *individually significant*?

Most people will use just one field for the entire street address, since you never have reason to divide it into smaller elements and work with them separately. But suppose your work requires you to send different marketing materials to different people depending on which part of town they live in. You'd need to isolate people by street name (all the people on Hawthorne Street) or by ranges of street numbers (1000 to 1400 Elm). In this example, street name and house number are individually significant, and you'd want to create a separate field for each.

For your People database, you'll start off with fields to hold all the basics: Name, Phone Number, Street Address, City, State, Zip Code, and Email Address.

Defining Fields

As you know by now, every FileMaker database starts with a table. And since fields and tables are so fundamental to a database, FileMaker asks you to create them as soon as you start. FileMaker assumes your needs are pretty simple, and starts right off asking what fields you want in this single table.

1. **Choose File → New Database.**

   Up comes the FileMaker Quick Start dialog box, just like the one back in Figure 1-5. This time you're *not* going to start with a template. Instead, you're starting with a clean slate, so you can build a database that's all your own. (Can't you just feel the excitement?)

2. **Select the "Create empty database" option, and then click OK.**

   FileMaker asks you what to name your new database and where to put it.

3. **Call this database People since that's what you're going to track.**

   In the Save As box (Mac OS X) or the "File name" box (Windows), type *People*, and then click Save.

   FileMaker creates the new file and automatically adds the .fp7 file name extension to your database name.

Note: That's not a typo. The extension .fp7 from FileMaker Pro 7 is the same for version 9. Good thing, too: It means people who still have versions 7 or 8 can use your version 9 files, although some of the new features won't work for them.

Just as promised, FileMaker asks you what fields you want—you see the Manage Database dialog box shown in Figure 3-2. This little beauty is where you build and manage tables. There's a tab for the tables themselves, a tab for the fields in those tables, and a tab called Relationships, where you tell FileMaker how different tables work together. For now, you can simply ignore Tables and Relationships. Your one free table has already been created (it's called People, just like the database), and you're ready to give it some fields.

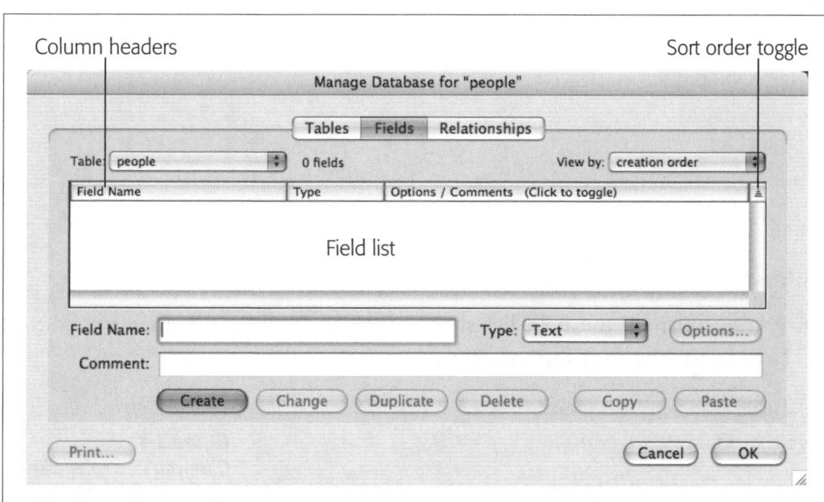

Figure 3-2: *In the Manage Database dialog box (File → Manage → Database), the Fields tab is where you go to tell FileMaker about the fields in your database. The field list shows all the fields in the selected table.*

Since you've already decided what fields you want, all that's left is to tell FileMaker what you've planned. First, create a field to hold a person's first name:

1. **In the Field Name box, type *First Name*.**

   Every field has a name—you can choose almost anything you want. (For some guidelines, see the box on page 97.)

2. **In the Type pop-up menu, make sure Text is selected.**

   Every field has a *type*, which you'll learn about shortly. You're creating Text type fields right now.

3. **In the Comment box, type *this is the person's first name* to help you remember what kind of data goes into the field.**

   Every field can have a comment to help you, the developer, remember what it's for. In this case, it's pretty obvious, so you could certainly leave the comment blank instead.

Note: Field comments don't show up when someone's *using* the database. They show only in this window. If you need extra information on the screen for the user to see, you'll want to *customize the layout*, as explained in Chapter 4.

4. **Click Create.**

   FileMaker creates the First Name field and adds it to the field list.

Now that you've created the first field, the rest are a snap. Following the same steps as above, create Text fields with the following names:

- Last Name
- Phone Number
- Street Address
- City
- State
- Zip
- Email Address
- Notes

When you're finished, the field list should look like Figure 3-3. (See the box on page 113 to learn why your Zip field must be a text field.)

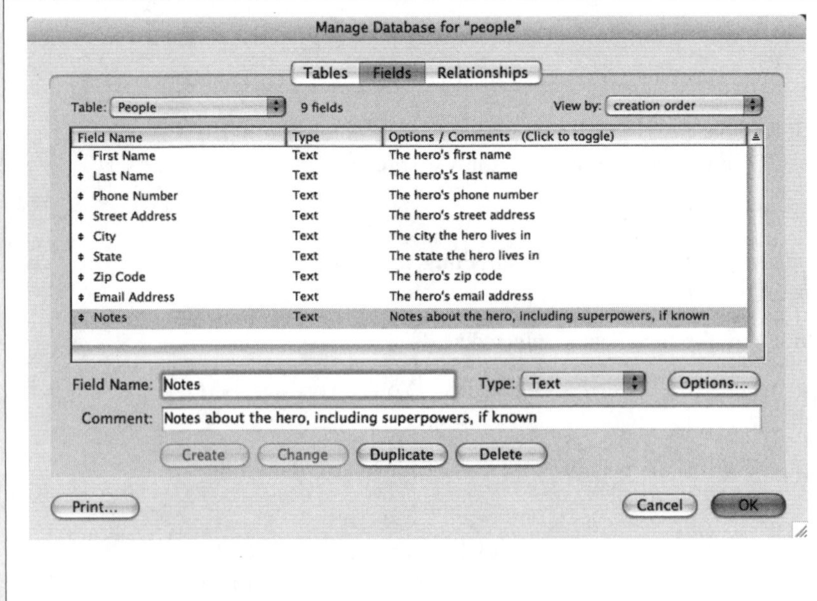

Figure 3-3: *Once you've created the necessary fields, the field list should look like this example. You may not see the field comments in the third column–this column can show comments or options. To switch between these two possibilities, click the column header. In this example, the fields' comments seem redundant. When your fields have descriptive names, comments may not be necessary. But as you start to create fields that perform math (Chapter 9) or do behind-the-scenes work (Chapter 7), you'll find comments more helpful.*

Changing a Field's Name

While you're here, you may as well try some more field-defining tricks. Say you want to change the name of the Zip field to Zip Code. It's very easy:

1. **Highlight the Zip field in the field list.**

   FileMaker fills in the Field Name, Type, and Comment boxes with the information about the Zip field.

2. **Change the field name to Zip Code, and then click Change.**

   When you have a field selected in the field list, the Change button becomes available. Instead of creating a *new* field called Zip Code, FileMaker just changes the name of the Zip field.

Note: If you select a field and make modifications to any of the settings at the bottom of the Manage Database window, FileMaker guesses you may want to click Change. If you try to select *another* field without clicking Change, FileMaker asks if you want to Save first. Clicking Save is the same as clicking Change: It updates the selected field with the new settings.

FREQUENTLY ASKED QUESTION

Field Naming Conventions

I've seen databases with all kinds of funny field names. I've seen all caps, no spaces, lots of odd prefixes, and plenty of funny punctuation. How should I name fields?

People can get downright philosophical discussing the best way to name fields, and it seems everyone has an opinion. So how should you name your fields? Well, here are some of the common suggestions, as well as some discussion about why you would or wouldn't want to follow them.

- Field names should have a prefix or suffix indicating their type.

FileMaker Pro developers often indicate the type of field in the field name. The reasoning is simple: You often have to pick a field from a list when you're building a database. All you see is its name, and you often want to know the type as well. In that spirit, people may name the First Name field something like "tFirst Name" where that "t" at the start means "text."

For most ordinary databases (in other words, not the really complicated stuff), you can usually figure out the type of a field by its name. For example, a field called Birth Date is probably a date field, while First Name is almost certainly text. You also don't often care about a field's type. For these reasons, you can usually ignore this advice and keep your field names prettier and more readable.

- Field names should have a prefix or suffix indicating their purpose.

When a table starts to get a lot of fields, it can really be hard to keep track of which one does what. For example, a big database that keeps track of products can have dozens of fields.

Some would be about inventory levels (like Quantity on Hand, Quantity on Order, Quantity Desired, and Quantity Back Ordered). Others would be about pricing (like Base Price, Price for 10 or More, Price for 20 or More, Price for 30 or More, and so on). Some people like to come up with special codes to represent different types of information, to keep the field names more compact: QTY In Stock, QTY Order, QTY Desired, QTY Backorder, QTY Average. Again, for most databases this problem doesn't occur very often. Consistent field names usually tend to develop their own English-language prefixes anyway (like all the Quantity fields). It's true, though, that field names can start to get long, and long names are more difficult to work with. In this case, abbreviations make good sense.

- Some database programs aren't so flexible with names. To be safe, FileMaker field names should follow the same rules as everybody else.

This rule usually *doesn't* apply. Why settle for names like "FNAME" and "LNAME" when FileMaker happily accepts "First Name" and "Last Name" instead? If you actually need to create the same database in another program some day, you'll have a lot more to worry about than renaming the fields. You can just ignore this rule unless you simply prefer geeky-sounding names.

Duplicating a Field

The Duplicate button creates a new field that's an exact copy of what's selected in the field list. The new field's name says *Copy* at the end, which is the only difference.

Fields can have many special options in addition to the name, type, and comment. You'll learn about them later in this chapter. Duplicate comes in handy when you want a second field with many options in common with the first. Just click Duplicate, and then change the new field's name.

Deleting a Field

As you create your fields, you may get partway through your list, and then decide to name *all* your fields differently, say, or combine two fields into one. You may find it easier to delete some fields and start fresh than to painstakingly modify each one. To delete a field, highlight it, and then click Delete.

FREQUENTLY ASKED QUESTION

Field Naming Problems

When I try to name my field "Customer Order/Preferred Delivery," FileMaker gives me some guff about not being able to "easily" use the name in a formula. Should I worry?

Well, maybe. Later on, when you read about calculation fields (see Chapter 9), you'll see that you can add the contents of two fields together, for example, or multiply the contents of one field by the contents of another. In fact, you can make field contents do just about any arithmetic dance you want them to do. When you perform math on fields, you're probably using number fields, but you can also do a surprising amount of work with calculations on text fields.

The specific problem with the field name above is that pesky "/" sign, which, in the language of math, means *divided by*. So if you try to use the contents of that field to do math, FileMaker gets confused about where the field name ends and the calculation begins.

Some people religiously avoid the use of certain characters. But you don't have to limit yourself if there's no reason to. The rule of thumb is that if there's a chance you'll need to do some math on a field, don't use any character that looks like a mathematical operation in the field's name. Characters to avoid are: + - * / ^ = ≠ < > _ _ ( ), ; " [ ] : $ { }. You also want to avoid using the names of functions in your field names. See page 413 for more about number functions. FileMaker's Help file also has a complete list of all functions, listed by name.

There are some other reasons, though, to avoid spaces and special punctuation in your field names. If you plan on building a Web site that interacts with your database using FileMaker's Web Publishing Engine, or that shares data with other database systems using ODBC or JDBC, you'll save yourself a lot of headaches if your field names don't start with numbers, don't contain any spaces, and contain only alphanumeric characters.

Reordering the Field List

Now that you have several fields, you may decide you don't like the *order* they're listed in. Perhaps you want all the address fields first, or maybe you're a big fan of reverse-alphabetical lists. You can rearrange the fields in the field list any time you want.

To *manually* arrange the fields, just drag the little up and down arrows beside a field name. Figure 3-4 shows you how.

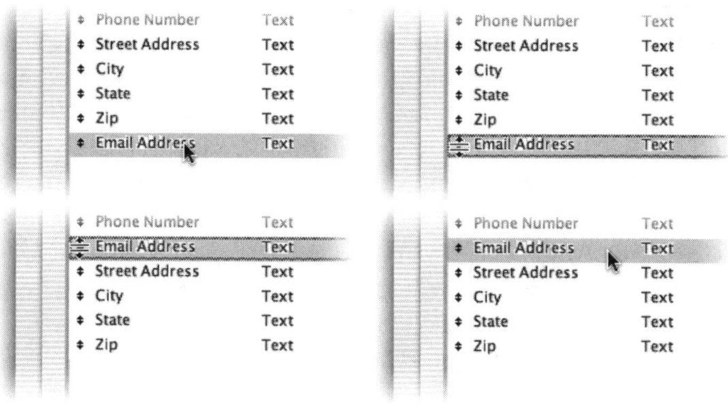

Figure 3-4:
This series of pictures shows how you can manually rearrange fields in the field list. When you mouse over the up and down arrows to the left of the word Email, the pointer changes to a new symbol that lets you know you can drag the item up or down (top right). As you drag, other fields in the list move out of the way to make room (bottom left). Use this maneuver to move all kinds of things in FileMaker.

If you'd rather let FileMaker order them for you, make a selection from the "View by" pop-up menu. This menu gives you four choices:

- **Creation order** is the order in which the fields were originally created. Sometimes you have a lot of fields, and you just can't remember what one of them is called. If you *do* remember that you created it relatively recently, you can view by creation order and look for it near the end of the list.
- **Field name** orders the fields alphabetically by name. This view is an easy way to find the field you want when you *do* know its name.
- **Field type** groups fields of the same type together. It puts the different types in the same order as they appear in the Type pop-up menu: text fields first, then number fields, then date fields, and so on. If you know you're looking for a calculation field (and that's all you know), view by type can help.
- **Custom order** is the order you put things in when you drag fields around in the list. Since you sometimes spend a lot of time getting the fields arranged in just the right way, you may be afraid to sometimes sort them by name instead, ruining your perfect custom order. But don't worry: After viewing them by name, you can easily switch *back* to custom order and see your perfect arrangement again.

Warning: If you're one of those funny people who like to keep everything organized *just right*, beware this classic bugaboo: If you sort the field list another way (like by name), and *then* move a field manually, the *new* order becomes your custom order. You'll lose all your hours of hard work. Therefore, once you've set up a custom order just the way you want it, make sure you switch *back* to it before you move any fields.

You can also click the Field Name or Type column headers to sort the list by that column. If you want to *reverse* the sort order, click the Sort toggle button. This button is at the right edge of the column headers, just above the scroll bar. Clicking the Options/Comments column header doesn't sort; instead, it switches what you see in that column. Normally, FileMaker shows you the options for each field. Clicking the header shows you comments instead.

Printing Field Definitions

Finally, if you click Print, FileMaker prints all the details about the fields you've selected. The printout resembles the field list, except that it's expanded to make room for *everything* about a field. You can print such a list if you want to keep your field names and types handy while you're working with your database, or if you need to send a list of fields to an associate so she can send you the right information.

Tip: You have to select at least one field for the Print button to become clickable. Then, when you click Print, you'll get details for any field that's highlighted. To print just a few, Ctrl+click (⌘-click on the Mac) each field you want to print. If you want a printout of *all* the fields in the table, first select one field, and then choose Edit → Select All. Now every field is selected, and the Print button prints them all.

Click OK when you're done creating and changing fields. FileMaker adds your fields to the database window. Congratulations! You've just built a database. It isn't pretty—as Figure 3-5 proves—but it works. The status area shows that your database has one record. Add data for a few records, using any of the techniques you learned in Chapter 1. You can even find, sort, print, and Find/Replace in this simple database.

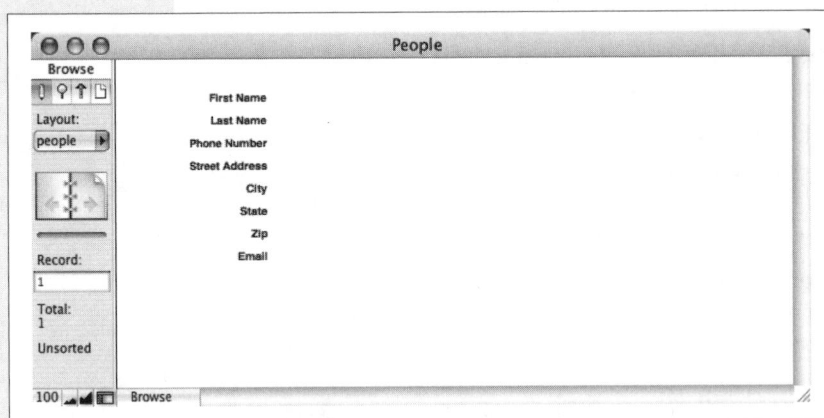

Figure 3-5: *Your first database! It has the same features as every other database you've seen, and you should have no trouble adding and editing records. It may not be pretty, but it works. You'll learn how to improve its looks in the next chapter.*

Field Types

Every field you create has a *type*, which determines what kind of information it holds. All the fields you just created are *text* fields—they're designed to hold various kinds of text. Back on page 77, you saw how container fields can hold pictures, movies, sounds, and files. But FileMaker actually has eight different field types, each designed for a slightly different task. For just a moment, you'll step away from the database you're building to get a brief introduction to each field type. You'll actually use these field types in various databases throughout the rest of this book.

You specify a field's type when you create it by selecting an option in the Type pop-up menu. The pop-up menu also shows handy keyboard shortcuts for each field type, so you can quickly create a series of fields without clicking the mouse.

UP TO SPEED

Use the Keyboard

You can get to almost everything in the Manage Database window's Fields tab from the keyboard alone. If you are a speed freak, you can avoid the mouse almost entirely. Here's how:

- On Windows, use the Tab key to move among buttons, text boxes, and pop-up menus. Unfortunately, FileMaker doesn't honor Mac OS X's Full Keyboard Access settings.
- On Mac OS X, press the Tab key to move between the Field Name, Comment, and field list.
- While the field list is active, use the up and down arrow keys to select the next and previous fields.
- Hold down Ctrl (⌘) while pressing the arrow keys, to move the selected field up or down in the list.
- Use the keyboard shortcuts for each field type. (Look in the Type pop-up menu to see them.)
- Press Alt + N (⌘-O) to see the field options dialog box for the selected field.
- Press the Delete key to delete the selected field,. Then, when you're asked if you're sure you want to delete the field, press D.
- Press the first letter of a button name in any of FileMaker's alert message boxes instead of clicking the button.
- Press the Escape key, then the Discard button to close the Manage Database window, and throw away all your changes.

Text

Text fields are the most common type—they hold any kind of text information like a name, phone number, or email message. A text field can store up to two gigabytes of information, so there's plenty of room for any realistic purpose. Whatever you type into a text field shows up just as you typed it, and you can use any of the formatting options described in Chapter 2.

Number

As if it isn't obvious, *number* fields hold numbers. Like a text field, you can type in just about anything you want, but as soon as you leave the field, FileMaker does its best to turn your data into a number, and that's what it shows you. What's not so obvious is that not all numerical values are numbers. Use a number field if you're going to be performing *math* with the numbers in your database. But for things like Zip codes and telephone numbers, use text fields instead. See the box on page 113 for the full explanation.

Numbers can be very large or very small, and they're *very* precise. The actual limits are thus:

- Numbers must be between 10^{800} and -10^{800} (it's actually 9.99999999...e799, because -10^{800} itself isn't included). If you're counting something reasonable—say, the number of protons in the universe—you'll be just fine.
- You get 800 significant digits in all. If you don't know what that means, ask a high-school algebra student.

- Only the first 400 digits are indexed in all, significant or otherwise. So if you're searching for numbers, you have a little less precision to work with.

FileMaker's number-handling capability is absolutely top-notch. If your work requires very precise mathematics, you'll be thrilled. For example, FileMaker is *much* more precise with numbers than Microsoft Excel.

You can enter numbers in FileMaker as you would in most any program. Type the number and any symbols that define it, like a negative sign or a decimal point. You can also use *scientific notation*. For example, if you have a burning desire to count the air molecules in your living room, you can put 6.02E23 into a number field. That means 6.02 times 10^{23} and it's a lot easier to type than 60,200,000,000,000,000,000,000,000. Of course, the exponent part (after the E) can be negative if really small numbers make your socks go up and down.

Date

At the risk of being obvious, a *date* field holds a date. FileMaker thinks of dates in numerical form by month, day, and year. You can put various punctuation marks *between* these numbers, but most people use a slash, a dash, or a period. For instance, 2/25/1975, 2-25-1975, and 2.25.1975 are all valid dates. If you type a date the wrong way, you see the error message in Figure 3-6.

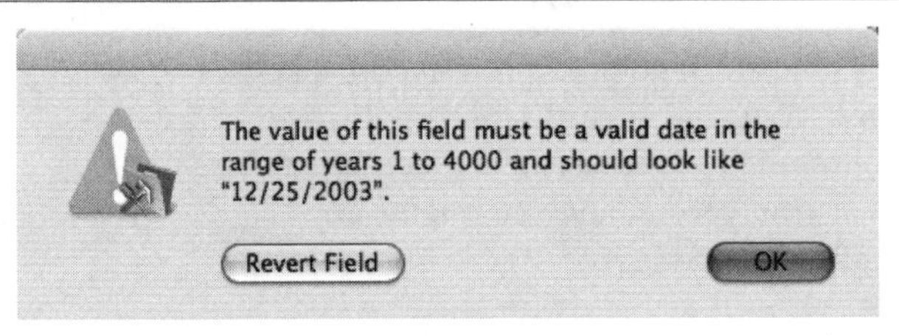
The value of this field must be a valid date in the range of years 1 to 4000 and should look like "12/25/2003".
Revert Field
OK

Figure 3-6:
If FileMaker doesn't like the date the way you entered it, it tells you so. The message ends with an example of a correctly formatted date.

Tip: If your date's in the current calendar year, you can save time by typing just the day and month. FileMaker fills in the current year for you. Don't add that second punctuation mark, though, or FileMaker will bark at you. Save even more time with the Insert → Date command. Just hold down Ctrl (windows) or ⌘ (Mac) and press the hyphen key (-).

FileMaker accepts dates from the year 1 (AD) to the year 4000, but since most databases don't have *that* long a lifespan, the program lets you enter a two-digit year and takes its best guess as to which century you're talking about. Here's how it works: If you type a two-digit year, FileMaker tries putting *20* in front of it. If that year is *more* than 30 years from now, FileMaker assumes you really meant 19-something and adds the *19* for you. Otherwise, it adds *20* for the first two digits. For example, if it's 2007 and you put *37* in for the year, you get 2037, but if you enter *38*, you get 1938. Confusing? Avoid all this runaround by entering four-digit years.

UP TO SPEED

System Formats

Your computer's settings determine how FileMaker wants numbers, dates, and times entered into fields. For example, in the United States, 7/12/2007 means July 12, but in Europe, it means December 7. In Windows, you change the settings in the Date and Time control panel. In Mac OS X's System Preferences, you use the International pane. When you create a database, FileMaker notes your Operating System settings and uses them. If you open the same database on a computer with different settings, you'll get a message asking if you want to use the *system* format, or the format stored with the database (see Figure 3-7).

If you don't want this message to appear, go to the File Options dialog box and make your preference known.

1. Choose File → File Options. This window lets you control a handful of settings for the current database.
2. Select the Text tab.

In this tab, the Data Entry section lets you control how the database handles varying format settings. The first two radio buttons prevent the message box from showing up. The third is for when you *want* FileMaker to ask every time.

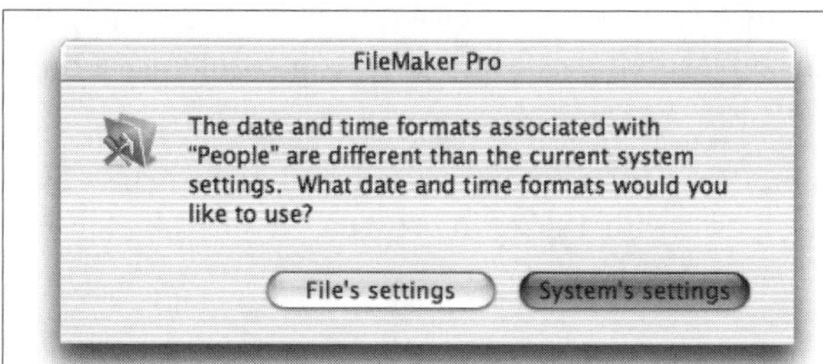

Figure 3-7:
FileMaker shows you this message when you first open a file that was created on a computer that uses different formats from yours. FileMaker just wants to make sure that you see the formats you want.

Time

You can probably guess what goes into a *time* field. Time fields actually serve two purposes, though. First, you can enter a time of day, like 4:30 PM or 1:27:03 AM. But you can also enter a *duration* instead, like 123:38:22 (meaning 123 hours, 38 minutes, 22 seconds). Even though this sequence isn't a valid time of day, it's an acceptable time value.

Times are easy to enter. They always go in like so: hours:minutes:seconds, and the seconds can also have a decimal part for fractions of a second. If you don't need seconds, you can just type in hours:minutes. Likewise, if you don't need minutes either, you can just enter a number of hours.

If you're entering a time of day, you can put an AM or PM after the time if you want, or you can use 24-hour notation. Either way, FileMaker can fix weird time entries, like 1:82:17, for you. In this case, you *can't* have 82 minutes because that's the same as 1 hour, 22 minutes, so FileMaker would change it to its more normal equivalent: 2:22:17. To have FileMaker check and repair time values, apply a time *format* to your time fields (see page 253).

Note: When entering time values, you *always* start with hours. If you're trying to enter just 12 minutes, 37 seconds, then you have to enter *00:12:37* or *0:12:37* so FileMaker doesn't think you mean 12 *hours*.

Time values are also quite precise. If you're recording track event times for your school, you can enter *00:00:27.180* for 27 seconds, 180 milliseconds. You can put up to six digits to the right of the decimal point.

Timestamp

A *timestamp* field is kind of like a date field and a time field combined. It holds *both* a date *and* a time. You use this kind of field to record when an event occurred, or when it will occur. If you want, you can create two fields, one for the date and one for the time. But FileMaker has all kinds of special abilities when it works with timestamp values that you'd have to otherwise try to figure out yourself. For example, it can figure out how much time has passed between two timestamp values with a simple calculation: End Timestamp – Start Timestamp (that's a minus sign). If you use separate date and time fields, the necessary calculation is anything but simple. If something happens on a specific date and time, you should use a timestamp field for it.

Timestamps support the same less-than-a-second accuracy as time fields. They show up as a date followed by a time with a space in between. All the rules for date and time entry apply: 2/25/1975 2:45 AM.

Container

You've already learned what a *container* field can do (see page 77). It holds pictures, sounds, QuickTime multimedia files, and ordinary files. Containers can hold up to two gigabytes of data, just like text fields.

Calculation and summary

Unlike the other field types discussed so far, *calculation* and *summary* fields don't hold your stuff at all. Instead, they make up their own values based on the settings you give them. For calculation fields, you can specify a special *formula* that it uses to determine its value. For instance, if you had a field called Birth Date, you could create a calculation field that shows the person's age. The Age field automatically updates to stay correct as time goes by, so you don't have to change it. You'll learn all about calculations in Part 3.

Summary fields are the strangest of all. They aren't even associated with a record. Instead, their value depends on the values of other fields across some set of records. For instance, a summary field could show you the number of people in the database who are from California, or the total dollar value of all outstanding invoices for a customer. You'll learn about summary fields in Chapter 6.

Advanced Field Options

At this point your database is simple, but entirely usable. In fact, you could stop reading right now, and you'd be able to build super-simple databases to solve all kinds of problems. But the Fields tab in FileMaker's Manage Database dialog box has lots more settings to make your database even smarter, easier to use, and more consistent.

Auto-Enter Options

All your fields are completely empty when you create a new record. Often, but not always, that's what you want—a completely blank slate. With FileMaker, you have a handful of other possibilities. Suppose most of your clients are from Phoenix, for example. It would be nice if FileMaker could put Phoenix in the City field for you—you can always change it later. In fact, this situation is so common that every field has a group of *Auto-Enter* settings where you can tell FileMaker exactly what to put in the field for you (see Figure 3-8).

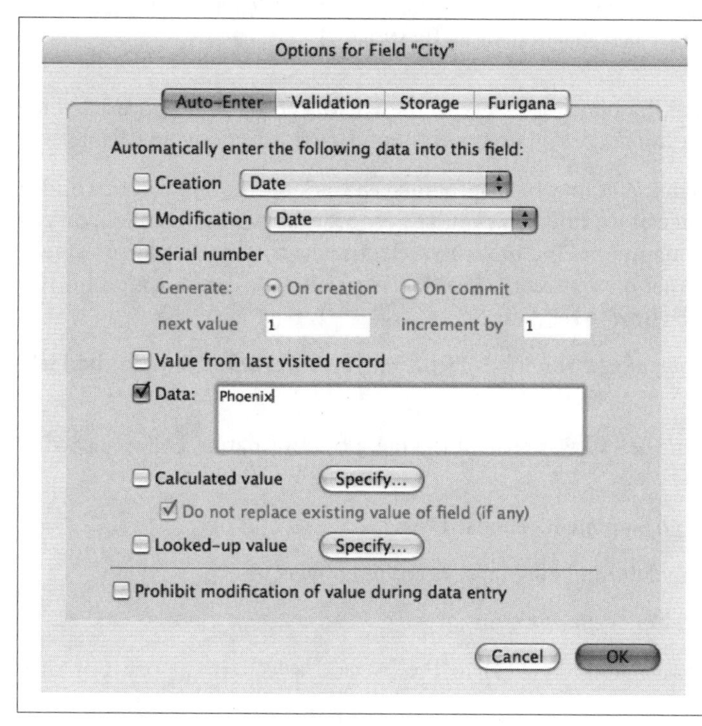

Figure 3-8: *FileMaker has several options for automatically entering information into a field. Most happen just once–when the record is created. The Modification, "Calculated value," and "Looked-up value" options, however, can automatically enter information in fields at other times as well.*

When you first create a field, all the Auto-Enter options are turned off, so the field stays empty. To turn one on, follow these steps:

1. **Choose File → Manage → Database.**

   Or press Ctrl+Shift+D (⌘-Shift-D). The Manage Database window appears.

2. **Click the Fields tab. In the field list, select any field, and then click Options.**

   Even quicker, just double-click the field. The Field Options dialog box emerges.

3. **In this window, click the Auto-Enter tab.**

   Now you see all FileMaker's Auto-Enter options (Figure 3-8), in all their glory.

Creation values

When a record is *first created*, FileMaker can enter some information about the circumstances under which it was created. You can record the date, time, or timestamp at the moment of creation.

The Name option refers to the name of the person who created the record. FileMaker gets this information from your operating system. On most systems, you must log into the computer before you can run programs. FileMaker uses the name of the system account you logged in with.

Note: You can tell FileMaker to use a custom name instead. Choose FileMaker → Preferences (Edit → Preferences), and then type your custom name in the User Name field.

The Account Name, by contrast, refers to the FileMaker account you used when you logged into the *database*. You can read about database accounts in Chapter 16.

In your People database, it may be helpful to keep track of the date you first added each record, so you can tell how long you've been working with someone. You can even use this information in Find mode to seek out new customers, old customers, or customers you met on a Tuesday. FileMaker has an Auto-Enter option for this very purpose. Here's how to set it up:

1. **In the Manage Database window's Fields tab, type *Creation Date* in the Field Name box.**

   Since the date the record was created is a piece of information being tracked, it needs to go in a field.

2. **From the Type pop-up menu, choose Date.**

   This field holds a date, and FileMaker needs to know it.

3. **Click Create, and then click Options.**

   The Create button adds the field to the list and selects it, so you can click Options right away.

4. **In the Field Options dialog box's Auto-Enter tab, turn on the Creation checkbox.**

   This setting lets you store information about the creation of a record. Since you're working on a date field, only the Date option is available in the associated pop-up menu.

5. **From the Creation pop-up menu, choose Date.**

   In this case, you want the date the record is created. Figure 3-9 shows the finished product.

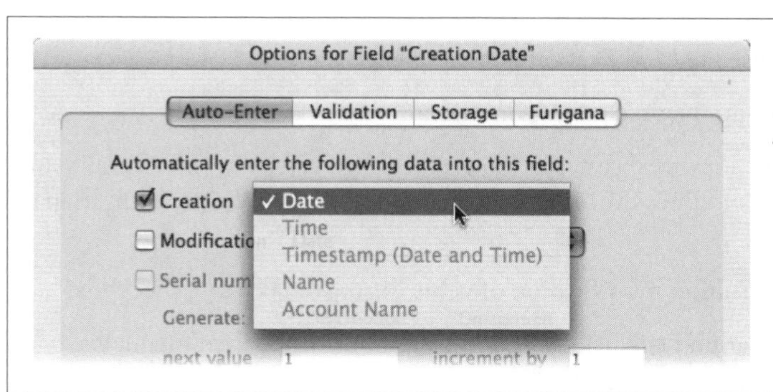

Figure 3-9: *When you set the field options, the dialog box shows you've turned on the Creation Auto-Enter option and selected Date. In English, that means you've told FileMaker to automatically record the date you add a new person to your database.*

6. **Turn on the "Prohibit modification of value during data entry" checkbox.**

   Because this field *always* automatically gets the right value, you don't need to change it in Browse mode. Editing this data would probably be a mistake, so you can tell FileMaker not to allow it.

7. **Click OK, and then, in the Manage Database window, click OK again.**

   You're now ready to test your new field. The existing record won't have the current date in it, because it was created before you made the Creation Date field. Create a record and see how FileMaker automatically enters the current date.

Tip: If you already have a lot of records in your table before you create the Creation Date field, you can enter dates manually by turning off the "Prohibit modification of value during data entry" option temporarily. Just be sure to turn it back on when you're done.

Modification values

Sometimes you want to keep track of when you last changed the data in your records. FileMaker can track the same information when you *modify* a record as when you create one. So if you adjust an interest rate in your database, for example, you can tell how long ago the change occurred. Furthermore, because records can change often, more than once a day even, you may need to know what *time* a record changed, not just the date. The Timestamp field is just the ticket. Here are the steps:

1. **In the Manage Database window's Fields tab, type *Modification Timestamp* in the Field Name box. From the Type pop-up menu, choose Timestamp.**

   Every field needs a name and a type, so you have to get those details out of the way first.

2. **Click Create, and then click Options.**

   The Field Options dialog box returns.

3. **In the Field Options dialog box's Auto-Enter tab, turn on the Modification checkbox.**

   Now you can use the Modification pop-up menu.

4. **From that pop-up menu, choose Timestamp.**

   As with record creation, you can have FileMaker enter any of several values when someone modifies the record. In this case, you want the program to make a Timestamp.

5. **Turn on the "Prohibit modification of value during data entry" checkbox.**

   As with the Creation Date field, you don't want this field edited manually.

6. **Click OK, and then, in the Manage Database window, OK again.**

   You're now ready to test your new field. Create a record, wait a minute, then edit it and see how FileMaker automatically enters the current date and time.

Unlike the Data and Creation Auto-Enter options, the Modification setting affects the value of the field *after* you create a record. This option updates the value every time the record changes. In fact, if you don't select the "Prohibit modification of value during data entry" option, the Modification setting will overwrite whatever you type in your Modification Timestamp field, since the timestamp occurs when you commit the record (see the box on page 109).

Note: If it sounds strange that you can use the "Prohibit modification of value during data entry" checkbox on a Modification field, never fear. FileMaker's Auto-Enter mechanism isn't considered *data entry*. Other times when records can change outside of data entry are when you're importing records (see Chapter 17) or setting fields via a script (see Chapter 13).

Serial number

Back in Chapter 1, you learned that record numbers can change as you delete or sort the records. If you want to assign a unique number to your record, you can use the "Serial number" Auto-Enter option. In the Field Options dialog box, you can specify the "next value," which is the value FileMaker uses for the next record that you create. The "increment by" value tells FileMaker how to change the number each time someone creates a record. For example, suppose "next value" is 1, and "increment by" is 2. If you create three records, FileMaker numbers them 1, 3, and 5.

You can specify non-numerical values for "next value" if you want. For example, if your field is a text field, you can put INV00001 in the "next value" box. Your first record would then get INV00001, followed by INV00002 and INV00003.

The Generate radio buttons under "Serial number" control *when* the serial number is assigned. If you select "On creation," then as soon as you create a record, FileMaker puts the serial number in the field. If you then decide you don't want the record, and you delete it right away, that serial number value has been *used up*, and the next record you make will have a new value. If you instead select "On commit," the serial number doesn't show up in the field until you exit the record. In other words, you can delete without committing and you won't use up any serial numbers.

You'll use serial numbers most often when connecting multiple tables (see Part 4). Serial numbers also come in handy when the items in your database don't have a convenient name. In a database of invoices, it can be tough to talk about one particular invoice ("You know, that one we sent last Thursday. No, not that one, the *other* one"). People generally use serial numbers to clarify things.

POWER USERS' CLINIC

Embracing Commitment

The word *commit* refers to a semi-technical database concept. When you create a new record, you haven't actually added a record to the table yet. Instead, you get a blank record on the screen, and the information you enter is stored in a temporary working area in your computer's memory. When you exit the record, the information in that working area is *committed*–or written–to the database.

When you edit a record, the same principle holds: As soon as you enter the record, it's copied to the working area. While you edit it, you're actually editing this copy. When you exit the record, FileMaker puts your edited copy back in the table. In general, think of *committing* a record as the same thing as *exiting* a record. When you exit the record, you commit it.

Value from last visited record

Some databases need a lot of repetitive data entry. If you take a trip to Los Angeles, you may meet 12 people who should go into your People database. When you get home, you have to type them all in. Rather than type *Los Angeles* and *California* over and over again, you can tell FileMaker to automatically fill the City and State fields for you. If you turn on "Value from last visited record," you'll need to type only *Los Angeles* and *California* once. When you choose Records → New Record, FileMaker copies the city and state from the current record into the new record for you.

1. **Choose File → Manage → Database.**

   The Manage Database window reappears. If the Fields tab isn't selected, click it.

2. **Select the City field, and then click Options.**

   The Field Options dialog box puts in an appearance. With this window, you can tweak several options for each individual field.

3. **Click the Auto-Enter tab, if necessary.**

   You see the same window shown in Figure 3-8.

4. **Turn on "Value from last visited record."**

   There are no additional settings for this option: Just turn it on. In this case, you *don't* want to turn on the "Prohibit modification of value during data entry" option, because you want to be able to change what's in the City field.

5. **Click OK. In the Manage Database dialog box, select the State field, and then click Options.**

   This time you want to auto-enter *CA*. Make the necessary settings, and then click OK.

6. **Click OK again to dismiss the Manage Database dialog box.**

   You're back in your database. Notice that the City and State fields in your current record didn't get the new information, though. The Auto-Enter options tell FileMaker what to put in fields only when you *create* a record.

   Now when you choose Records → New Record, the new record shows the correct city and state.

Tip: "Value from last visited record" is really cool when you're entering a bunch of records one right after another, but it can cause confusion if you poke around in your database before you start creating records. FileMaker thinks of your "last record" as the last record you *clicked in* or *opened*, not the last one you looked at. (See page 30 for the deal on opening records.) So make sure you open the record you want the value to come from just before you create a new record.

Data

This is the simplest Auto-Enter option. It puts data you specify into the field every time you create a record. You can specify text, date, time, and timestamp values by entering the information just as you would type it in a field.

If 99 percent of your associates are from your hometown, it makes sense to have your database automatically enter your city and state for you.

Calculated value

Sometimes you want to take advantage of the power of calculations, but you also want to be able to change the field if you need to. Since calculation fields always create their own (unchangeable) value, they don't work. Instead, you can create a normal field and have FileMaker automatically enter a calculated value into it. You can then change the value later if you want. You'll learn how to create calculations in Part 3.

Looked-up value

As you've already heard, FileMaker lets you connect multiple tables together in various ways. When you've done that, you can tell FileMaker to automatically fetch a value from some record in another table and plop it in the field. This feature is called a *lookup*, and you'll learn about it in Part 4.

Prohibit modification of value during data entry

Usually, when you use an Auto-Enter option, it's just to save you some typing. You may end up needing to change the value to something else, though. But sometimes the value is automatically entered, and it should stay that way forever. The Creation and Modification options most often fall into this category. If you're trying to keep track of when the record was created, there's no reason to ever change the date field. If you turn on the "Prohibit modification of value during data entry" checkbox, FileMaker doesn't let you change the field's value at all.

Validation Options

Auto-enter options tell FileMaker to enter some things for you. *Validation* options sort of do the opposite: They tell FileMaker what *not* to let you put in a field. You decide what kind of information *should* go there, and FileMaker warns you when you enter something that doesn't look right. In your People database, you may want to make sure the Zip Code field always looks like a real Zip code.

1. **Open the Field Options dialog box for the Zip Code field.**

   You should be an expert at this by now. In the list, just double-click the field.

2. **Select the Validation tab.**

   As you can see in Figure 3-10, you have a lot of choices when it comes to field validation.

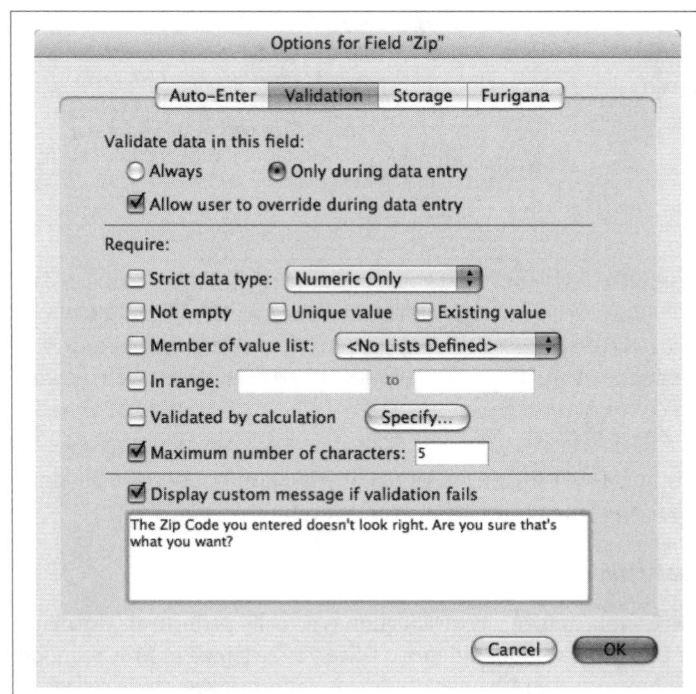

***Figure 3-10:** The Validation tab in the Field Options dialog box lets you check for errors before placing information into fields. You can, for example, make sure only numbers are entered, or that the first name is no more than 30 characters. You can apply as many validation rules as you want, and FileMaker checks each one whenever someone modifies the field.*

3. **Turn on the "Strict data type" checkbox, and from its pop-up menu, select Numeric Only.**

   These settings tell FileMaker to expect only numerals in this field.

4. **Click the "Maximum number of characters" checkbox and enter** *5*.

   You can do better than just require numbers. This option tells FileMaker to accept no more than five digits in the Zip Code field.

5. **Turn on the "Display custom message if validation fails" checkbox.**

   FileMaker automatically shows a message when a value in a field doesn't match the validation settings, but it's often more considerate to give the message in your own words. That's what this setting does.

6. **In the text box below this checkbox, type** ***The Zip code you entered doesn't look right. Are you sure that's what you want?***

   FileMaker displays this message if the validation fails. (For a little guidance on what these messages should say, see the box on page 114.)

7. **Click OK and OK again.**

   You're back in Browse mode and ready to test. Try entering too many characters into the Zip Code field, and you'll see your message when you exit the field, as shown in Figure 3-11.

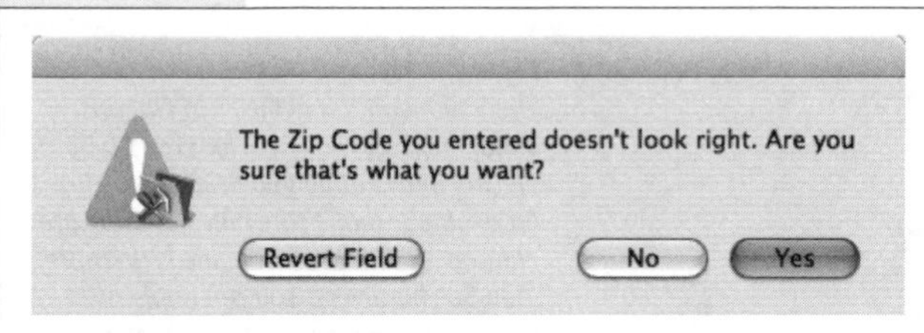

Figure 3-11:
If you enter a bogus Zip code in your database, you'll see your custom message. Click Yes to keep the invalid Zip code. If you want to fix it, click No and you'll be back in the field. If you click Revert Field, the field value changes back to what it was before you started editing.

Note: It's true that the validation settings you selected in the previous tutorial aren't perfect. They don't allow Zip+4 codes (46077-1039), but they would let you enter something like *123*, which isn't a valid Zip code at all. To handle such nuances of the simple Zip code, you need to use the "Validate by calculation" option, which lets you set much more specific validation standards. You'll learn about FileMaker's calculation features in Part 3.

Now that you know how to set them, you can tailor validation options to all kinds of situations. Here are your many choices in greater detail:

When to perform validation

The first two choices let you control when validation is actually performed. Normally, you want to validate only what you put into fields when you're typing in Browse mode. If you *import* data (more on that in Chapter 17) or enter information from a *script* (see Part 5), FileMaker completely bypasses the validation step. If you want to be strict

FREQUENTLY ASKED QUESTION

Numbers and Text

You have to set an awful lot of validation options to make sure people enter only Zip codes into a text field. Can't I just make the Zip Code field a number field instead?

No, you can't. Zip codes are numerical values, but they're not *numbers*, and that makes a big difference as far as FileMaker is concerned. For example, number fields don't recognize leading zeros–like the ones at the beginning of 00501 and scores of other perfectly valid Zip codes. If you enter *00501* in a number field, FileMaker thinks you meant to type the number *501* and "helpfully" removes those extra zeros when you exit the record. That's just not going to get your mail to Holtsville, New York anytime soon.

The Numeric Only validation option lets the field stay a Text field (which preserves all entered characters) but still accept only numerical digits on entry, which is exactly what you want for a Zip code.

Some people also assume that a phone number should be stored in a number field. Wrong again. Phone numbers contain not only numerals but also dashes, parentheses, and sometimes other special characters–all mere text to FileMaker. As a general rule, only make a field a Number field if you may have to perform some math with it. You'll learn all about using fields in calculations in Chapter 9.

about it, select the Always radio button under "Validate data in this field." FileMaker does as promised: It *always* performs the validation, even during automated processes.

Overriding validation

In the Zip code example, you were given the option of accepting a bogus Zip code if you wanted to. FileMaker simply *warned* you that things didn't look right. It was up to you to decide if it should be fixed. If you uncheck "Allow user to override during data entry," FileMaker takes away the choice. Instead, it simply refuses to accept invalid data.

Validation Requirements

When you added validation to the Zip Code field (see page 111), you asked FileMaker to accept only numbers and allow only five digits.

But data type and character count are just two of the eight kinds of validations FileMaker has up its sleeve. In the Validation tab of the Field Options dialog box, there are six more checkboxes. Most of them work much the same way: They check what you type against some specific condition. But one option, "Validate by calculation," offers a completely flexible way to describe exactly what you're looking for. Unfortunately, to use it, you need to learn how to perform *calculations* (mathematical or logical formulas) with your FileMaker data. They're covered in Part 3. Until then, here's what the other options do:

Strict data type

This option lets you pick four specific validations. You've already seen Numeric Only, which insists every character in your text field be a number. 4-Digit Year Date tells FileMaker to expect a date value, and that the year must be four digits long (2007 instead of 07). This choice works with text, date, and timestamp fields.

UP TO SPEED

Validation Messages

Custom validation messages (like the one in Figure 3-11) give you a chance to communicate directly with whoever uses your database. If you don't provide a custom message when you set up field validation, FileMaker uses a generic message of its own. This message explains the validation option that's being violated in language only a software engineer would love. This message may be confusing to whoever's using your database. Once you understand how FileMaker's validation messages work, try to improve upon them. You'll make your database a pleasure to use and give it a professional quality.

For example, if you've turned on the "Allow user to override during data entry" option, FileMaker asks if you want to allow the value anyway (Figure 3-12, top). Otherwise, it tells you to fix the field (Figure 3-12, bottom). In either case, the message box includes a Revert Field button. This button takes away any changes made to the field so that it returns to its previous *valid* value, but how's the user supposed to know that?

Instead, phrase the custom message as a question where Yes means "I want to keep what I've entered," and No means "I'll change it." When it shows your message, FileMaker automatically provides the Yes and No buttons, along with the Revert button.

If you turn off the ability to override the validation, and you're showing a custom message, FileMaker replaces Yes and No buttons with an OK button. In this case, the message should *not* be in question form. Instead, it should simply tell them what's wrong.

Finally, if the field value violates *several* validation options, the user must click Yes to a message about each one before FileMaker allows the value. Since all these error messages are annoying, you're better off using a custom message that explains all requirements.

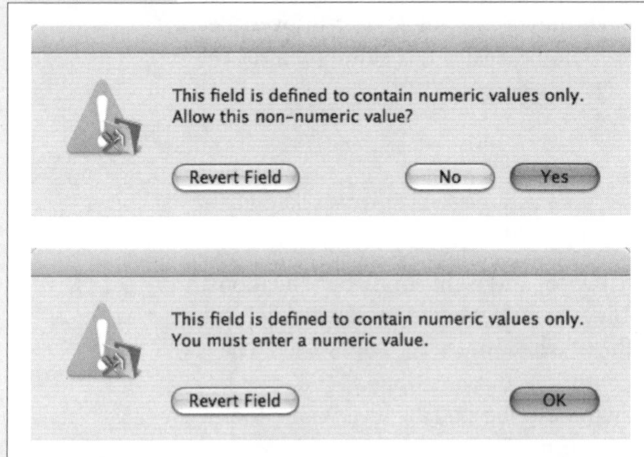

Figure 3-12:
Top: You'll see this dialog box if you select the "Allow user to override during data entry" option on your validated field. Hitting Return automatically chooses Yes, which can cause trouble if your users are quick on the Return key, since that tells FileMaker to accept the invalid data.

Bottom: This message, by contrast, doesn't give users the choice of accepting the invalid data they've entered. When you set up validation on your fields, you have to strike a balance between annoying your users and making sure they enter data properly.

"Time of Day" tells FileMaker that only time values that represent real clock times are acceptable. Since time fields can hold any number of hours, minutes, and seconds, you can enter something like *237:34:11* to mean "237 hours, 34 minutes, 11 seconds." But if the field is *supposed* to be the time of your lunch meeting, that value doesn't make sense. This option prevents its entry. It applies to text and time fields (Timestamp fields *always* require a time of day).

Not empty

If you insist on having *something* in a field, select the "Not empty" validation option. That makes FileMaker complain if you try to exit the record without entering a value. This option is the only simple validation option for container fields.

Unique

The "Unique value" option prevents you from putting the same thing in a field for two different records. For example, if you set this option for the First Name field in your database, you can't enter two people with the name "Bill," so you won't use this option for most data. You would use it for ID numbers, user names, or other information that should identify a single person uniquely.

Existing value

"Existing value" is just the opposite of "Unique value"; it doesn't allow any value that isn't already in that field on some record in the database. This option usually doesn't make much sense unless you turn it on *after* you've entered a representative amount of information into the database. Otherwise, the first record you enter would dictate the field value for every record created thereafter.

Member of value list

You often have a field that can contain any one of a predetermined set of things. In your database, for example, you may want to ensure that the State field contains a valid abbreviation for one of the 50 American states. This is where the "Member of value list" option comes in.

FileMaker lets you create *value lists*, which (not surprisingly) are lists of values: Red, Green, Blue; or Small, Medium, Large, for instance. You can make as many value lists as you want.

Note: You can see a value list in action in your Contact Management database. Just click the Address Type field. The items in this list let you mark the kind of address you're storing in each record.

---

1. **Open the Field Options dialog box for the State field.**

   Your trusty mouse can probably scramble the maze on its own by now.

2. **On the Validation tab, turn on the "Member of value list" checkbox. Then, from the associated pop-up menu, choose Manage Value Lists.**

   FileMaker shows you the Create Value Lists dialog box.

3. **Click New.**

   FileMaker creates a new empty value list and shows it to you in the Edit Value List window (shown in Figure 3-13).

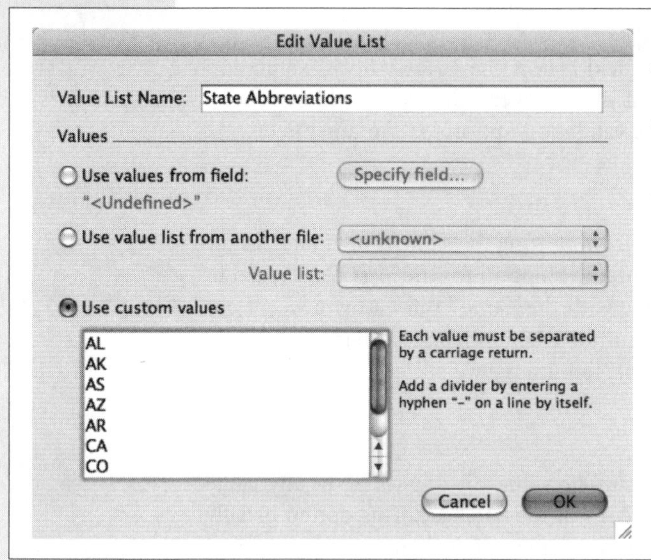

Figure 3-13: *A value list lets you specify exactly what entries a field can accept. This value list contains the postal abbreviations for the 50 states in the U.S. The finished database for this chapter has a value list with all the abbreviations. Download it at www.missingmanuals.com/cds.*

4. **In the Value List Name field, enter *State Abbreviations*.**

   Each value list needs a unique name.

5. **Make sure the "Use custom values" radio button is selected, and type state names in the list box under it.**

   As usual, you'll need to ignore several available options for now, and focus on "Use custom values." Each item in a value list must be on its own line. You can paste into this box as well, so if you find a list of states on the Internet, you can save yourself a lot of typing.

6. **Click OK to close the Edit Value List window.**

   The Manage Value Lists window now shows your new value list.

7. **Click OK again to close the Manage Value Lists dialog box.**

   Back in the Field Options window, the value list you just created should now be selected in the "Member of value list" pop-up menu. If it isn't, select it now.

8. **Click OK two more times, until you're back to your database.**

   Try entering a value in the State field that *isn't* in the value list. FileMaker will let you know you've messed up.

Note: Value lists are actually used for more than just validation. You'll learn how to create and edit them outside this dialog box in Chapter 6. You'll learn other uses for value lists throughout the book.

In range

"In range" lets you specify a minimum and maximum allowable value. FileMaker then protests if you enter a value outside this range. This method works for all the standard data types, since they all have a concept of order. For example, if you specify a range of *Adam* to *Johnson* for a text field, validation fails for *Schultz*. Range validation is most common, however, with number, date, and time values. You can require the Age field to be between 0 and 100, for example, or the Birth Date to be between 1/1/1900 and 12/31/2007.

Maximum number of characters

As previously mentioned, this option enforces a limit on the number of characters you can enter into a field. FileMaker fields can normally hold a huge amount of text. This option lets you keep things under control. You can use it to require specific kinds of information, like the five-digit Zip code above, or to prevent abuse of the database (for example, by limiting the First Name field to 30 characters so someone doesn't get carried away and paste the complete works of Shakespeare into it).

WORKAROUND WORKSHOP

Minimum Number of Characters

For some strange reason, FileMaker doesn't provide a simple validation option to enforce a minimum number of characters in a field. You often need to limit characters, but you have to dip into validation calculations to meet it. Luckily, the calculation to do it is really simple. Here's a validation calculation for requiring *at least* five characters in the field:

```
Length(My Field) >= 5
```

To use this calculation, turn on the "Validate by calculation" option. In the window that appears, type this calculation. You'll have to change "My Field" to the name of your field. If you want a number other than five, simply change it in the calculation. When you're done, click OK.

If you want *more than* five characters, change >= to >. If you want *exactly* five characters (no more, no less) then change >= to =. You don't need a lot of expertise for this calculation. (See Chapter 9 for much more on using calculations.)

Storage Options

It's time to get a little technical. Sorry. In the Field Options dialog box the Storage tab (see Figure 3-14) lets you control aspects of a field related to the nebulous concept of *storage*. Like a highly organized attic, FileMaker both holds onto your information *and* makes it easy to take out again. There are lots of details involved in how FileMaker compartmentalizes and maintains that information.

You can actually tell FileMaker to store only one value in a field, no matter how many records you have, or to allow one field to hold *more than one value* in each record. Strange, but true. Also, you get control over *indexing*, as described in the next section.

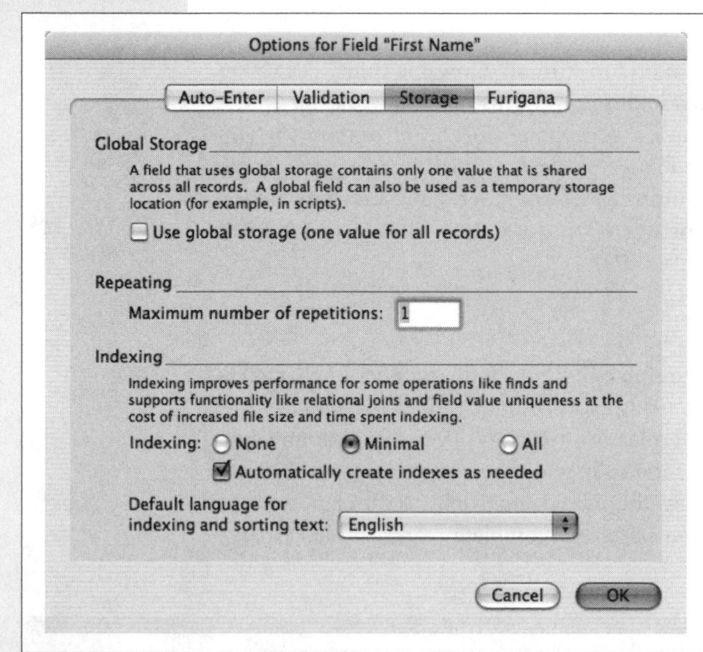
Options for Field "First Name"
Auto-Enter
Validation
Storage
Furigana
Global Storage
A field that uses global storage contains only one value that is shared across all records. A global field can also be used as a temporary storage location (for example, in scripts).
Use global storage (one value for all records)
Repeating
Maximum number of repetitions: 1
Indexing
Indexing improves performance for some operations like finds and supports functionality like relational joins and field value uniqueness at the cost of increased file size and time spent indexing.
Indexing: None
Minimal
All
Automatically create indexes as needed
Default language for indexing and sorting text: English
Cancel
OK

Figure 3-14: *The Storage tab is where various behind-the-scenes field settings lurk. Here, you can make a field global so it has only one value for the whole table, or make it repeating so it has several values in each record. You'll set options like these mostly when you're defining a database, not during day-to-day use.*

Global storage

"A field that uses global storage contains only one value that is shared across all records." So says the explanatory text in the dialog box, but what's that in English? When you use the "Use global storage" option, everything you learned about tables goes out the window. A *global field* isn't a column in the table at all. Rather, it's a single bit of storage that can hold one value, no matter how many records you have. In other words, if you change the contents of a global field on one record, FileMaker instantly changes it in every other record as well. Now every record has the same value for that field.

Suppose your company is planning a move or name change in the future, but you aren't ready to change your database just yet. In that case, you can make your company's name, address and phone number fields use global storage. You can even make a global container field and pop your company logo into it. Then, you'd just make your database's layouts display those *fields* instead of typing company information on a layout. (See Chapter 4 for details on designing layouts.) When the company makes its move, you just place the new name, address, logo, and so on into your global fields, and *voila!*—FileMaker changes the data instantly. You don't even have to remember every place you put the company information. When you update a global field, FileMaker finds every place that field shows up and makes the change consistently.

Note: There's an exception to everything, and indeed there's one situation where global fields don't instantly change everywhere for everybody. For details on how globals operate in shared files, see the box on page 688.

Repeating fields

A field can hold only a single value, right? Erm…well, not really. If you want to, you can turn any field into a *repeating field*. These fields can hold more than one value, each kept in a separate spot (and each shown in its own little field in the database window). In the Field Options dialog box, you specify the maximum number of values the field can hold. When would you want to use repeating fields? Almost never. See the box below for more info.

Note: The last tab in the Field Options dialog box applies only to Japanese text entry and isn't covered in this book. Fortunately, should you ever need to add furigana to your kanji, you can read how right in the dialog box.

WORKAROUND WORKSHOP

Repeating Fields Aren't Your Friends

With very few exceptions, repeating fields cause more trouble than they're worth. The truth is, they only exist because years ago when FileMaker was a youngster, it wasn't a *relational* database. That means it didn't have any way to tie multiple tables together so that they can share information and make connections between things in each table. When you were learning about how to pick fields, you were introduced to the concept that you need a table for each kind of thing you're keeping track of. In a database that's not relational (called a *flat file database*), there's no good way to track lots of different kinds of things in one database, so FileMaker had repeating fields to let you store more than one thing in a single record. For example, you could have an Invoice table with one record for each invoice. The individual items on the invoice need a place to live too, so you would create repeating fields. That way, each individual invoice could hold, say, 20 items.

But this is the 21st century, and FileMaker's come a long way. Nobody in her right mind would build an invoice database that way anymore (they'd hook together two tables instead—see Part 4). Since FileMaker had repeating fields ten years ago, and since it's really friendly about supporting all your ancient databases, it still supports repeating fields today.

That said, repeating fields are *occasionally* useful when writing calculations (see Part 3) and scripts (see Part 5). Other than that, you should avoid them like the plague for a few reasons:

- Repeating fields are uniquely FileMaker. If you want to take data out of your database and put it in some other program (like a spreadsheet or another database program), repeating fields can produce one serious pain in the neck. Likewise for getting data from other programs *into* repeating fields.
- If your database is accessed by Web pages or other outside programs, repeating fields make everything more complicated.

Repeating fields are inherently limited: If you create a field with 20 repetitions, you get 20 spots for data. If you need less, you're looking at empty fields all the time. If you need more, you have to modify your fields and make room on your screen. A relational database, on the other hand, can grow and shrink as needed without modifying the database structure at all.

Indexing

Since you're reading this book, you're probably hoping FileMaker can help you search through volumes of information faster than you could do it yourself, especially as your database grows from a simple electronic Rolodex to a humungous mailing list. When you're looking for the three people out of 5,000 whose birthday is February 29, FileMaker can find them in an instant because it doesn't really look at the birthday field on each record one by one. Instead, it uses the field's *index* to skip straight to the appropriate records. It's similar to the way you'd use a book's index to go directly to the pages that mention the topic you're interested in, rather than skimming every single page in the book.

Note: FileMaker uses a field's index in other ways, too. You need an index if you want to use the "Unique value" option in the field Validation screen. You also need indexed fields to create *relationships* in your data, as explained in Part 3.

FileMaker's indexing feature takes its own computerized notes on your fields *in advance*, so that when you enter Find mode (see page 35), the hard work's already been done, and your finds go that much faster. To take a peek at what a field index may look like, see Figure 3-15.

Figure 3-15: *You can see what's in a field's index right from Browse mode. Just click in the field and choose Insert → From Index. This command lets you put a value in a field that you know is already in the same field on a different record. A field's index shows you one instance of each value that's used in any record. In the sample database, there are two Deveaux and two Sanderses, but only a single instance of each name shows in the index. The "Show individual words" option shows a list of individual words in the index–every word in this field across all records. This option isn't very exciting in a last name field, where most entries are already individual words. It's most helpful in a lengthy field, like a Note field.*

Just like a book, you can have a field without an index. When FileMaker needs to find records based on what's in that field, it has to check every single record—a process that can take noticeably longer in big databases. On the down side, an index takes up space. If this book didn't have an index, it would be a fair bit shorter, and the same goes for a field's index. A database with indexed fields takes up significantly more space on your hard drive than one with no indexed fields. See the box below for more detail on this dilemma.

FREQUENTLY ASKED QUESTION

The Dark Side of Indexing

If indexing makes searching faster, why not just index every field?

Indexes have disadvantages as well. An index is useful only if it's up to date. When you change a field value, FileMaker has to store that new value in the table. If the field is indexed, FileMaker has to change the data you've typed, and it *also* has to update the index so that it knows about the changes to the field. Updating the index takes time (not much time, mind you, but it does take time).

When you're editing records in Browse mode, you'll *never* notice because updating the index for a handful of fields takes FileMaker less time than it takes you to realize you've pressed Enter. But if you're entering *lots* of information (like when you're *importing* records, as discussed in Chapter 16), the index updating can slow things down noticeably.

Also, indexes take up space. A relatively small database that has indexing turned on for every field could be much larger than the same file without indexes. For most users, this isn't an issue, but if you have a very large file, and saving space is a priority, turn off indexing where it isn't needed to save space.

Automatic indexing

The good news is you almost never need to think about indexing. FileMaker has a really smart way of dealing automatically with indexing: Every field starts out with no index at all, to save space and keep things as lean as possible. Later, while you're working with your database, if you do something that would be made faster with an index, like use the field in a find request, FileMaker automatically turns indexing on for you. That first find is slow since FileMaker looks through records one by one and builds the index (showing a progress bar in really big files), but once the field is indexed, subsequent finds happen quickly. You almost always want this automatic behavior.

Controlling indexing manually

In very large databases, there may come a time when you want to adjust indexing manually. For instance, if you know you won't ever search for someone by middle initial, you can turn off that field's indexing to reclaim the space it's using. Click the None radio button to turn indexing off completely. If you want to be able to search efficiently in a field, turn on All instead. The third choice—Minimal—creates a smaller index for the field. This index has everything FileMaker needs for relationships and field uniqueness, but not enough for fast searching. If you *don't* need to search in a field, but you *do* need it indexed for other reasons, choose Minimal.

When None is selected, you can keep FileMaker's automatically-turn-it-on-when-I-need-it behavior by turning on "Automatically create indexes as needed."

Note: FileMaker uses the field index when you do a find from Find mode, but *not* when you use the Find/Replace command. The index points FileMaker to *records*, and since Find/Replace doesn't find records (as discussed on page 60), the index does it no good. Therefore, when you do a Find/Replace, you don't make FileMaker automatically index a field. Several actions trigger indexing: including using the field in a find request or value list, turning on Unique or Existing validation, and, and using the field in a *relationship*. You'll learn about relationships in Part 4.

POWER USERS' CLINIC

Put Automatic Indexing to Use

FileMaker's ability to automatically index a field when it becomes necessary doesn't just save you the trouble of thinking about all this stuff. You can also use it to your advantage in some situations. Sometimes people need to distribute databases full of information.

For example, suppose you have a large parts catalog that's stored in a database, and you want your distributors to be able to use the database themselves to find parts. You can make a real FileMaker database available on your Web site for them to download, complete with your 10,000 parts records.

If there's a lot of information about parts, that database is pretty big. To make the download more palatable, tell FileMaker not to index *any* of the fields. But leave "Automatically turn indexing on if needed" turned on, to make the database as small as possible when people download it. Once people get it, they can start performing finds. As they do, FileMaker automatically indexes fields, making searches faster, and ballooning the size of the database.

Indexing language

To keep its indexes as small and tidy as possible, FileMaker doesn't actually store all a field's text in the index. Instead, it performs a little cleanup on the field values first. Most notably, it gets rid of the notion of uppercase and lowercase letters: "Peter" and "peter" become the same entry in the index. The entry you see in the index is the one that comes first in the file. So if you put "Peter Petrelli" in the first record of your database, and "peter jackson" in the second one, the index will show "Peter" as its entry. (See the box on page 123 for an exception to this rule.)

The index also splits the field value up into individual words and removes any characters that aren't generally part of a normal word. In order to do that, it needs to know what language the text in the field is in. If your computer's regional settings are for English, then FileMaker's field indexes will use English, too. Usually, that's exactly what you want. But in some cases, FileMaker's following the same language rules as your computer can cause a problem. For example, if you enter another language in a field without changing the index, your searches can give you unexpected results. If you search in an English-indexed field for *lang* (German for "long"), you'd get both "lang" and "länger" ("longer"), but if you set the index to German, you only get "lang." (In German, "ä" is a different character from "a.")

You can select a different language from the dialog box's Indexing section's pop-up menu. A field's language setting also comes into play when you sort records. To use the example given above, when you're sorting in ascending order (from A-Z), "länger" comes before "lang" in a field indexed as German (since "ä" comes before "a" in the German alphabet), but after it if the field's index is set to English (which doesn't consider accents in alphabetization).

Note: If the Language pop-up menu is unavailable, the field is probably not a text field. You can specify the language only for text fields.

POWER USERS' CLINIC

Unicode Indexing

One language option, called "Unicode," isn't a language at all. This setting tells FileMaker to forget everything it knows about languages and use the internal code numbers for each character as is. When indexing with this language option, FileMaker doesn't remove any special characters from the index, and it doesn't ignore uppercase and lowercase letters.

A find in such a field is *case sensitive*. When sorting, FileMaker also uses the character code numbers. Whichever code is lower comes first in the sort order, so capital "Z" comes before lowercase "a."

It's rare that you'll want your searches and sorts to be case sensitive, but if you do, you have the option. You're more likely to use Unicode indexing when you want to easily search for punctuation. For example, a field that holds text from a business-to-business Electronic Data Interchange (EDI) document can be well served by Unicode indexing so you can easily find the records that contain "~BIG."

Bringing It All Together

You've just learned a lot about the various options and settings in FileMaker's Manage Database window. At this point, it would be a good idea to take them for a test drive by adding some more functionality to your database. While you're at it, you'll get a chance to add a new field to an existing database (something you haven't done yet) and see how FileMaker responds—see the box on page 124.

A private investigator has to deal with all kinds of characters. You've decided you may need a little help separating the good guys from the bad guys. Of course, Mom always said there's some good in everybody, so what you *really* need is a field that holds a Goodness Rating: George Costanza gets a zero, Mrs. Cleaver gets a five, and everybody else gets something in between. You want to make sure the rating is between zero and five, and you'd like it to be three unless you manually change it.

1. **In the Manage Database dialog box, type *Goodness Rating* in the Field Name box and, from the Type pop-up menu, pick Number. Click Create.**

   You now have a field to hold the goodness rating, and the Options button is now available.

2. **Click the Options button, and then select the Auto-Enter tab.**

   The Auto-Enter options appear.

3. **Click the Data checkbox, and then, in the text box next to it, type *3*.**

   This option tells FileMaker to place some fixed piece of information in the field when you *first* create the record. Since you're assuming people are usually a three, it makes sense to let FileMaker fill in that value for you automatically, saving you time for more important tasks.

4. **Click the Validation tab, turn on "In range," and type *0 to 5* for the range options.**

   This action tells FileMaker to expect goodness ratings between zero and five.

5. **Uncheck "Allow user to override during data entry."**

   You don't want to allow values outside the range *at all*.

6. **Turn on "Display custom message if validation fails."**

   A custom message makes this whole thing feel more personal.

7. **In the custom message box, type *Please specify a Goodness Rating between 0 and 5*.**

   You may as well give a message that is as meaningful as possible. Since the user can't override this validation, the message is a statement, not a question.

8. **Click OK, and then OK again to close the Manage Database window.**

   You're back in your database again, and ready to test the Goodness Rating field. If it doesn't appear on your screen, see the box below.

That about does it. You now have a database that handily tracks people, including how good they are, and you can search it, sort it, print it, zoom it, and generally have a good time with it. In the next chapter, you'll learn how to gussy it up.

WORKAROUND WORKSHOP

Missing Fields

Normally, when you add new fields to a database, they show up automatically in the database window so you can work with them. However, you can tell FileMaker not to show them. If you do, it's your job to put the fields in the window yourself (which you'll learn to do in the next chapter). If FileMaker isn't showing you the fields, you need to fix the preferences:

1. Open the Application Preferences and select the Layout tab. You can find the Application Preferences by choosing Edit → Preferences (Windows) or FileMaker Pro → Preferences (Mac OS X).
2. Make sure the "Add newly defined fields to current layout" checkbox is turned on.

When this option is turned on, fields automatically show up in Browse mode as soon as you create them. You won't see any fields you created before you turn this option back on, though. See page 149 to learn how to use the field tool to drag new fields onto your layouts. Eventually, you'll probably want to turn this option off and manage your layouts manually.

2

Part Two: Layout Basics

CHAPTER

4

Layout Basics

In the last chapter you created your first database, and it really works. Unfortunately, it doesn't *look* all that great. For example, the Street Address field is the same width as the State field, even though street addresses are usually much longer than state names. The Goodness Rating field is *much* longer than it needs to be. And unless you're a real minimalist, the whole thing just looks boring (see Figure 4-1).

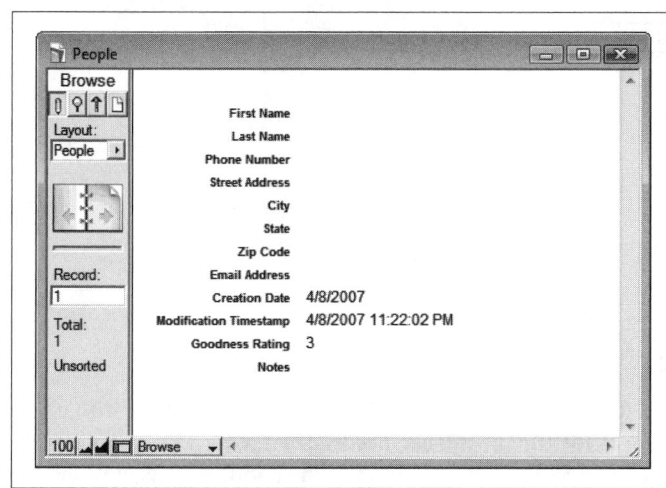

Figure 4-1:
This database works, but it could work—and look—better. What if you want to see lots of people at once? What if you want to print address labels for all these people? What if you want to arrange these fields in logical groups so they're easier to figure out? This database can't do any of those things, but if you give it a few new layouts, you can do all of them—and lots more.

There are other things to worry about as well. There's no good way to see lots of people at one time—in a nice list, for example. A list would also be handy for printing. As it stands, you have to print a whole page for each person in the database if you want a hard copy.

The FileMaker concept of *layouts* solves all these problems and more. While the Manage Database window lets you define the structure of your database (its fields and tables), layouts let you design the look and feel.

What Is a Layout?

If the tables form the heart of a database, layouts give it a face. When you design a layout, you feel like you're working in a graphics program: You can change the fonts, paste in your logo, make the background light fuchsia, and drag the fields around as though they're little onscreen Lego blocks. A single database may look like a White Pages, a "Hello! My Name Is" name tag, a glossy brochure, or a library card catalog index card. FileMaker displays the same information—but *how* it displays that information is up to you.

Better yet, a single database can contain as many layouts as you want; each shows the data in a certain way for a specific purpose. Figure 4-2 shows the People database with one possible layout.

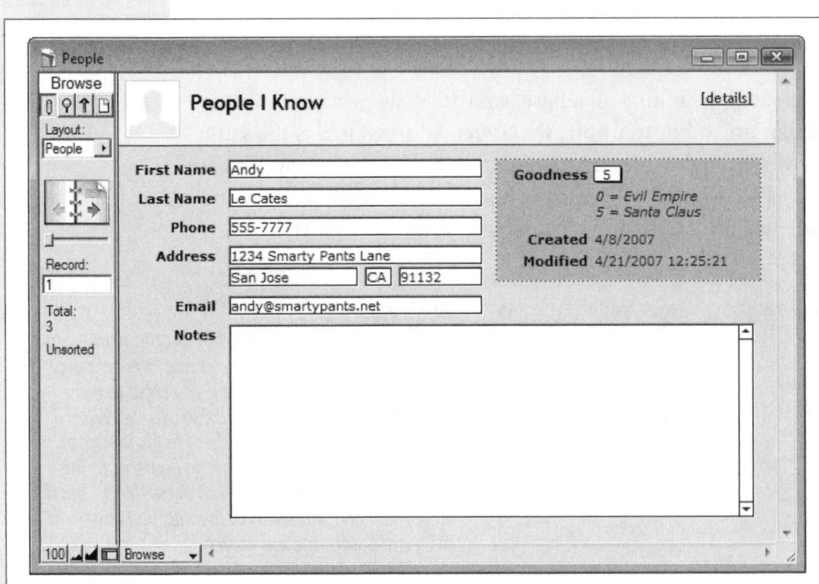

Figure 4-2: *This is the People database, too. It has the same fields and the same records as Figure 4-1–it's even the same file. Only the layout has changed. It's been redesigned and has a pop-up menu to make for easier data entry.*

Types of Layouts

You can make layouts for just about anything. Most databases start off with a few common kinds of layouts for the most basic needs. Then, over time, you usually add more layouts to meet specific needs. When thinking about layouts, you should be thinking about how you'll want to see the data—what kinds of information should be onscreen at the same time, for example—and how you want to *print* your data (printable lists, name tags, special forms, envelopes, statements, reports, and so on). Here are some common kinds of layouts:

- **Detail** layouts show all (or nearly all) fields on the screen for one record at a time—a full employee profile, for example. You use detail layouts for most, if not all, of your data entry. If you have a lot of fields, you can even create more than one detail layout: Contact Info, Emergency Info, and Payroll Info, for example.

Note: You've already encountered a detail layout. *Every* FileMaker database is born with one starter detail layout. It always looks like the one in your People database in the previous chapter–downright boring.

- **List** layouts show multiple records at one time, in a scrolling list. They usually show *less* information from each record than a detail layout so that more records can fit on the screen.
- **Table** layouts are designed to work best in table view (see page 44). Like a list layout, they show lots of records at once, but unlike a list layout, it doesn't matter how the fields are arranged on the layout itself, since table view always looks like a spreadsheet.
- **Report** layouts are designed for printing (see page 87). They usually show multiple records in a list form, often with a title at the top and summary information at the bottom. Reports can even have groups of data and intermediate summaries or running totals.
- **Envelope and Label** layouts format the data so that you can print it directly onto an envelope or a sheet of peel-and-stick labels. This layout makes addressing envelopes to people in your database a breeze. FileMaker can automatically create layouts for many envelope sizes and common label formats.

UP TO SPEED

Views and Layouts

FileMaker learners often confuse views and layouts. Both affect the way FileMaker displays your data. You can switch from layout to layout or view to view with ease. And you hear a lot about lists, tables, forms, and so forth when talking about either. So what's the scoop?

First of all, in every FileMaker window, you have a layout *and* a view selected at all times. Each layout is usually designed to work best with a certain view. Detail layouts are usually shown in form view, while list and report layouts usually use list view. For instance, if you have a Client List layout, you typically use list view.

Most of the time, the layout tells FileMaker how each record should look on the screen: where different fields appear, what fonts, sizes, colors, and pictures show up, and how much space it all takes up. When you pick a layout, FileMaker uses it to decide how things look.

The view, on the other hand, tells FileMaker what to *do* with the layout. In form view, it shows one record, using the layout to decide how that single record should look. In list view, it shows all the found records, each below the one before it. The layout dictates how each of those records should look, and you use the scroll bar to zip through them. In table view, FileMaker ignores the layout almost entirely. It pays no attention to how fields are arranged, or what colors or pictures you've used to decorate things. Instead, it shows a clean, simple list just like a spreadsheet. The only say the layout has in how things look is in which fields you see, and how FileMaker formats each individual field.

Very often, you create both a detail layout and a list layout for each table in your database. The list provides an easy way to scroll through records and find what you're looking for without getting data overload. When you're ready to see *all* the data, you switch to the one-at-a-time detail layout.

Switching Between Layouts

The ever-helpful status area tells you what layout you're on *and* lets you switch to another one. The Layout pop-up menu (Figure 4-3) is one of the most prominent elements of the status area. You can also see the same list of layouts in the View → "Go to Layout" menu.

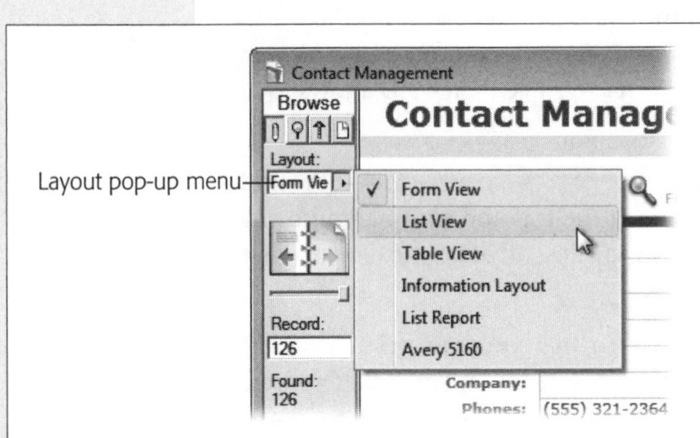

Figure 4-3:
In the status area, click the Layout pop-up menu to see a list of layouts in the database. To switch to a layout, choose it from the list. The Layout pop-up menu also shows you which layout you're using when you haven't clicked it.

Note: The Layout pop-up menu doesn't necessarily show *every* layout. You can actually tell FileMaker to hide certain layout names in this menu. You'll learn how on page 145.

Your People database has only one layout, making for a poor demonstration. To get a feel for how layouts work, you can use the Contact Management database instead (you created this database from a template in Chapter 1).

1. **Open the Contact Management database.**

   If you need a sample database to play with, you can find it on the "Missing CD" page (*www.missingmanuals.com/cds*), complete with sample data.

2. **If the status area isn't showing, click the status area control to show it.**

   You now see the status area. (The status area control is explained back in Figure 1-2.)

3. **From the Layout pop-up menu, choose List View.**

   Now that you finally understand the difference between layouts and views, the silly database has the nerve to name a layout "List View." Remain calm: The name just happens to be the best way to describe the layout (at least the developer thought so), because this layout is a list and it's displayed in list view.

   The List View layout shows in the window. FileMaker remembers which view you last used with each layout.

Since the layout affects only how the data shows, your found set and current record stay consistent as you change layouts. The following two steps show how this layout works.

4. **From the List View layout, use the status area's book icon to switch to another record.**

   Since you are viewing this layout as a list, as you change records, the little black line along the left edge of the window moves, as explained on page 45.

5. **From the Layout pop-up menu, choose Form – Main Address.**

   You're now viewing details of the record you selected when in list view. In other words, FileMaker stayed on the same record while you switched layouts.

Likewise, if you do a find on the Form – Main Address layout, and then switch to the List View layout, you'll see just the found records in the list. Since FileMaker is all about making all your data easy to see, search, print, and otherwise use, switching among various layouts is a big part of the game.

Note: As you spend more time with your own databases, you'll probably discover that you switch layouts *a lot*. You may decide all those trips to the tiny Layout pop-up menu are slowing you down. That's why most databases (the Contact Management template included) use *buttons* to make layout switching faster.

In Chapter 1, you learned how to click the tab graphics to switch between viewing record details, a list, or a table (see page 29). Now you know these tabs simply switch between three distinct layouts. You too can create buttons to switch between layouts, and you'll learn how in Chapter 6.

What Makes a Layout

A layout is made up of layout parts—sections that each behave a little differently when displaying or printing multiple records. Even the simplest layout has at least one part, and each part has objects on it. One kind of object is a field, which you've seen plenty of so far in this book. Each field in your database has a little label beside it that tells you which field it is. These labels are another kind of object: They're text objects. It just so happens those objects all belong to a part called the *body*, and if you need to talk about your layout, you'd say they are *on the body*.

Parts tell FileMaker how to treat the objects inside them when it displays or prints the layout. One part might show just once at the top of the window, while another shows over and over again for each record. This section tells you exactly what each part type does and when to use it. Finally, you'll learn how they work together and how they behave in each mode.

Layout Parts

FileMaker has eight different kinds of parts in all. Every layout uses at least one of these parts, and often several—although not all databases need all eight kinds of parts. Most types can occur only once on each layout (like a header), while others can appear several times.

- **Title Header.** The title header part holds things you want to appear only at the top of the very first printed page. Use it for a descriptive title, larger column labels, a company logo, or you can even make it the height of your paper, and it acts as a cover page.
- **Header.** The header part prints at the top of every page—unless you also use a title header, in which case the title header is on page one and the regular header is at the top of all other pages. In Browse mode, the header shows up at the top of the window. This part is where you might put a date and time, small title, smaller column labels, and anything else that you want on every page of the printout.
- **Leading Grand Summary.** This part prints below the header but above the records themselves. It's meant to contain totals and similar fields that add up, average, or in some way round up the results of your records, which FileMaker calls *summarizing*.

Note: Leading grand summary and all the other "summary" parts are how FileMaker creates *reports*. Reports, which help you compile and analyze your data, are nothing more than layouts designed for the job, as you'll learn in Chapter 6.

- **Body.** The body shows the actual record information. In list view, or when printed, it repeats once for every record.
- **Sub-Summary.** These parts help you add things like subtotals to complex reports. You'll learn all about this in Chapter 6.
- **Trailing Grand Summary.** If you prefer totals and overall summary information at the *bottom* of a report, they would go in this part.
- **Footer.** The footer prints at the *bottom* of every page—unless you also use a title footer, in which case, the title footer appears on page one and the regular footer appears on all other pages. The footer also appears at the bottom of the window in Browse mode. The footer's a perfect place for page numbers, copyright notices, and anything that ought to appear at the bottom of every page of your printout.
- **Title Footer.** The Title Footer part shows at the bottom of just the first page. Use it for special footer info that only needs to show once.

Figure 4-4 shows a layout with seven parts—one of each type except Sub-Summary.

Parts in form view

When in Browse mode, and viewing the layout as a form, you see every part except Sub-Summary parts. As Figure 4-4 shows, the parts go in the same order as in the list above. In practice, you'll probably never use *all* these parts on a layout you plan on viewing this way. In fact, if you only ever want to view a layout as a form in Browse mode, you really need only a Body part.

If the window isn't big enough to show every part, you get scroll bars as usual. In form view, the entire layout scrolls up and down, as shown in Figure 4-5.

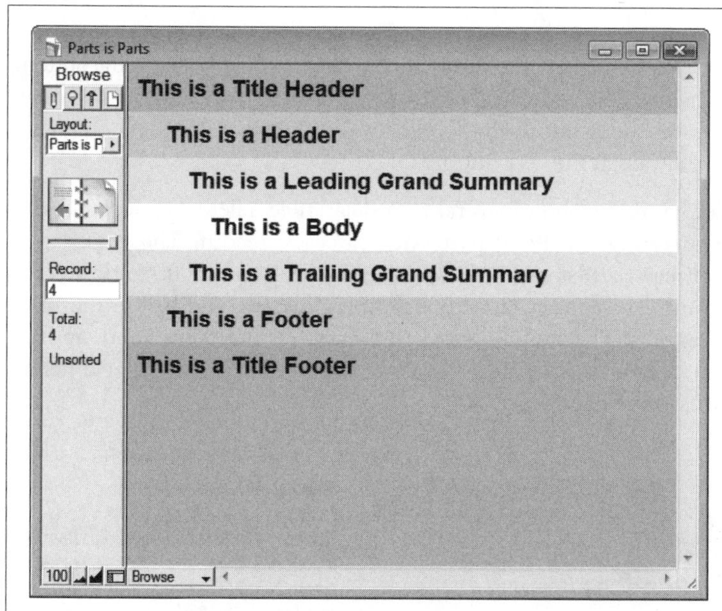

Figure 4-4:
This layout has a lot of parts: one of every type except Sub-Summary. In form view, as shown here, you can see every one of those parts. You'll see this same layout in various views (Form, List, or Table) and modes (Browse or Preview) over the next several pages.

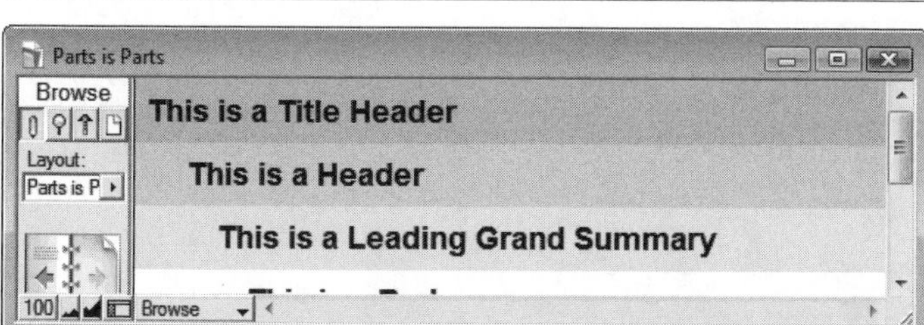

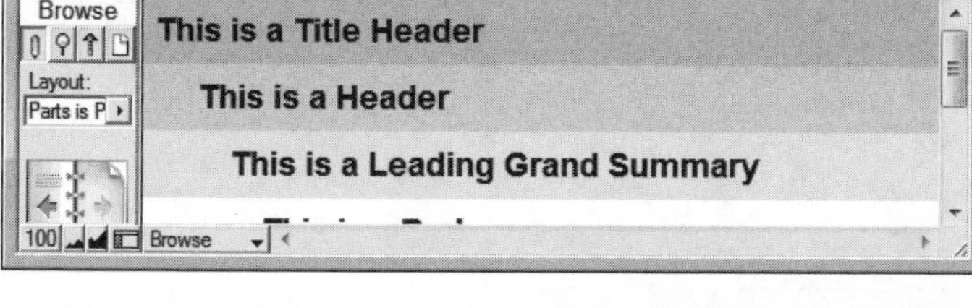

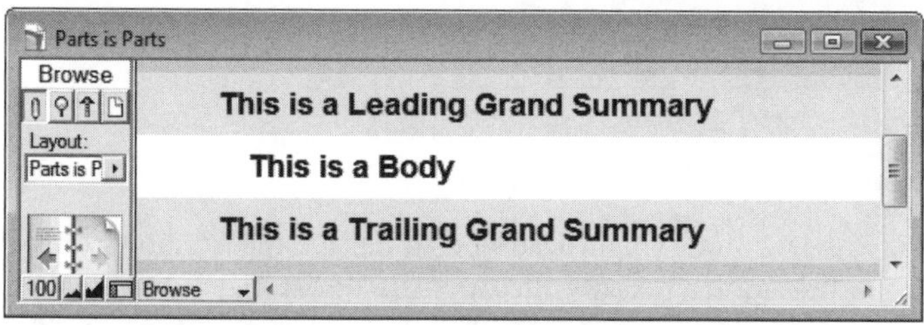

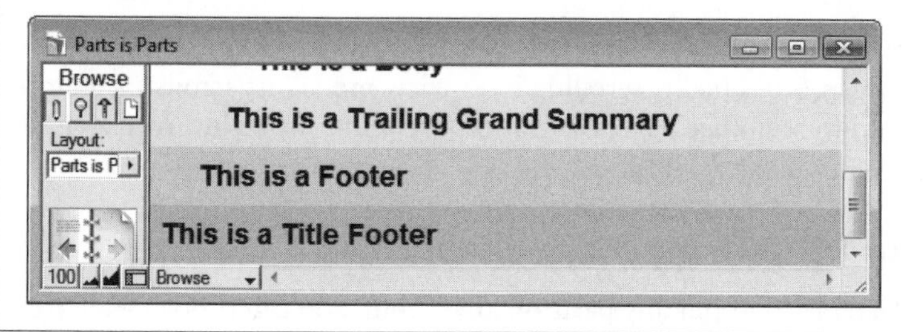

Figure 4-5:
This series of images shows the same layout in form view as you scroll. In the top image, the window is scrolled all the way to the top.

Middle: It's scrolled halfway down the layout.

Bottom: Finally, you can see the layout scrolled all the way to the bottom. In form view, the entire layout, including all parts, scrolls as one unit.

Parts in list view

In list view, the header is anchored to the top of the page and the footer to the bottom. When you use the scroll bars, the header and footer stay in place and the Body part scrolls. If you resize the window, the footer moves with it so that it's always the same height, and always at the very bottom.

List view is a *list* because it shows several records at once. FileMaker accomplishes this magic by repeating the Body part once for each record. The database in Figure 4-6 has three records, so in effect, the Body part repeats three times. The leading grand summary appears directly below the header, and before the Body part's first appearance. The trailing grand summary, on the other hand, appears right after the last record's Body part. Scrolling in list view is altogether different from form view, as shown in Figure 4-7.

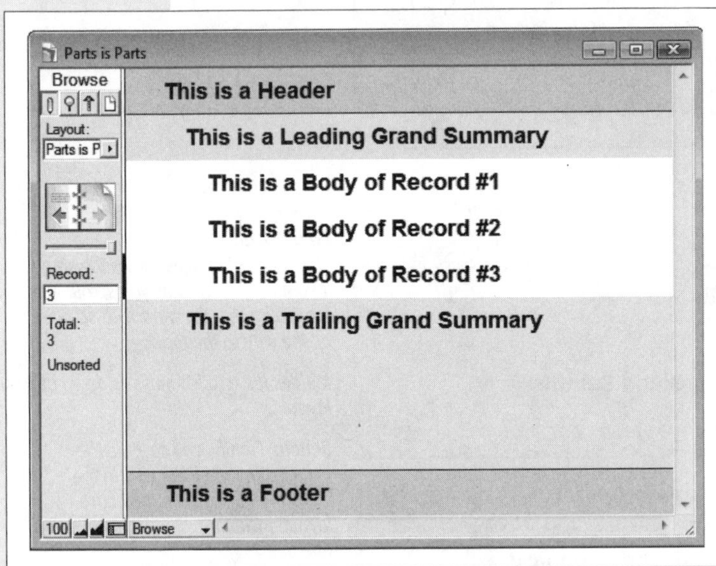

Figure 4-6: *Here's the same layout from Figure 4-4 in list view. Although this layout has all the same parts, list view doesn't show the title header and the title footer. The Body part repeats three times–once for each record in the table–and the trailing grand summary is bigger. FileMaker has increased its size so it fills up all the remaining space between the last record's body and the footer.*

Parts in Preview mode

A quick glance at Preview mode might lead you to believe that it shows only the title header and the title footer (exactly the opposite of list view), but that's not entirely true. Turn your eyes to Figure 4-8 for the whole story.

Just like list view, the grand summary parts place themselves before the first record and after the last record. Finally, scrolling in Preview mode just scrolls the current page. If you need to see other pages of your report while you're in Preview mode, use the Book icon to move around.

When to use 'em

While it's perfectly legal to put any parts on any layout, you can probably tell from the discussion above that some arrangements are more common than others:

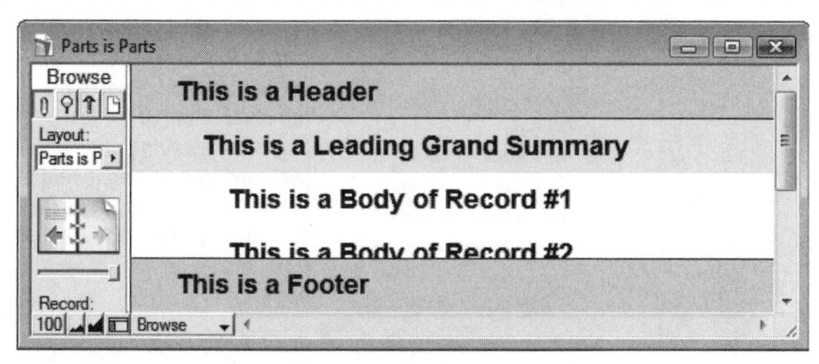

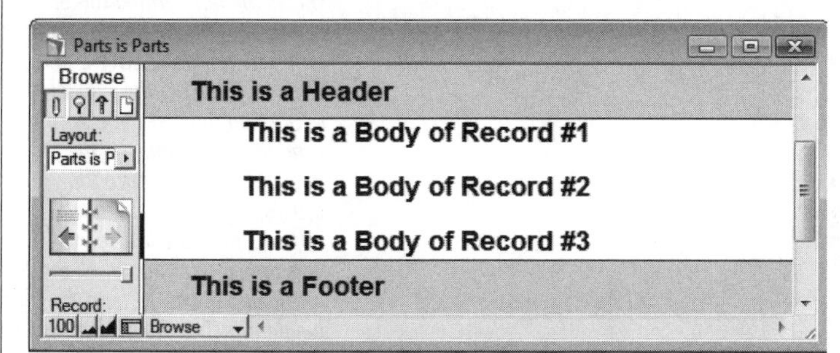

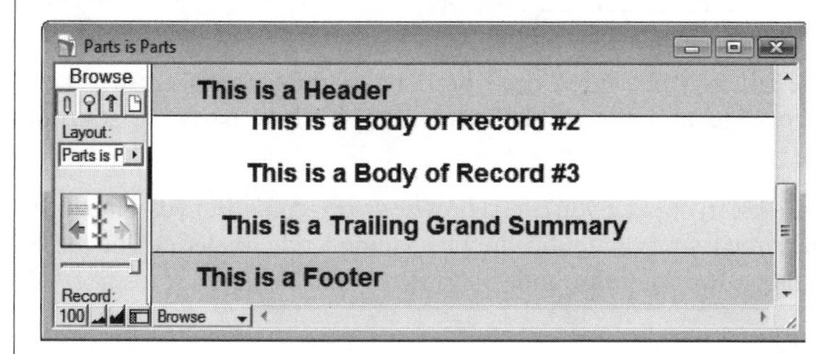

Figure 4-7:
Top: This sequence shows the same layout as Figure 4-5 scrolled to various places. In this case, since you're viewing the layout as a list, the header and footer stay put even when scrolling: They're always at the top and bottom of the window.

Middle: With the window scrolled halfway, the header and footer have not moved, but the leading grand summary has scrolled out of view. Each Body part is moving as well.

Bottom: When you reach the bottom of the list of records, the trailing grand summary comes into view.

- Detail layouts usually have just a Body part, or some combination of header, body, and footer. These layouts may show only a single record, so there isn't much point to Summary parts since there's no list of data to summarize.
- List layouts usually have a header and a body, and sometimes a footer. Occasionally, you want a trailing grand summary on your list layout as well, since it can show summary information after all the records without taking up precious space like a footer.
- Printed reports come in many forms. People often use all the parts shown above on a report: a large title header for the first page, and a smaller header for each additional page; a leading grand summary that shows below the title header and before the first record; a Body part for each record; a trailing grand summary to show totals from all records, and a footer to show page numbers and the like.

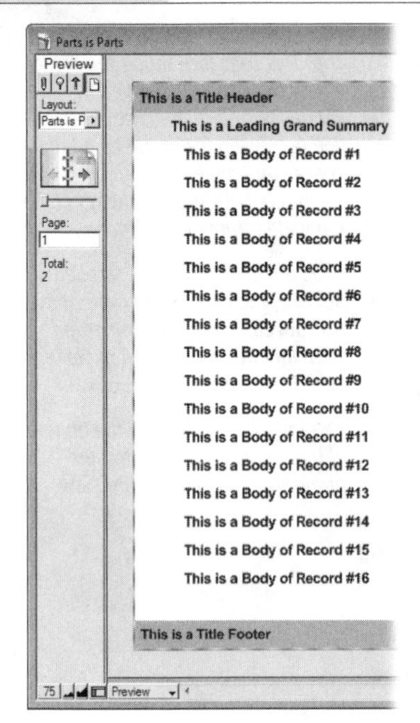

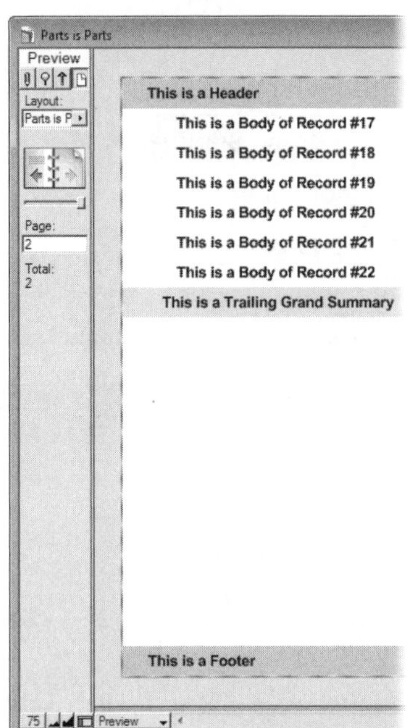

Figure 4-8:
Left: In Preview mode, the title header and footer are at the top and bottom of the first page. The leading grand summary appears right before the first record, and FileMaker adds a copy of the body for every record until it fills up the page.

Right: Every page thereafter shows the header and footer instead of the title header and footer. If you don't have a title header, you'll get the regular header on the first page, too (and the same goes for the title footer). Also notice that the trailing grand summary appears after the last record. This time it does not fill all the remaining space. Instead, its height matches the height you gave it on the layout.

- Envelope and label layouts often need headers and/or footers just to get the record data to align properly on the printed page. These parts are generally empty.
- You may have a list layout that you use to browse your records, but you often print it as well. Make the layout do double duty by adding a title header or title footer. They'll show only when you print, and you can save valuable screen real estate.

Layout Objects

Parts aren't so useful by themselves. They control how the items in your layout arrange themselves on the screen or on the page, but they need to have *things* in them to be really useful. You call those things *layout objects*. Layout objects come in seven flavors: Text objects, lines and shapes, images, fields, portals, tab controls, and Web viewers.

Note: Portals are all about relationships, and you won't learn about relationships–or portals–until Part 4. You'll take up tab controls and Web viewers a little sooner. Look for them in Chapter 6.

Text objects

Almost every layout ever created has included text objects: little blocks of text that are the same on every record displayed using that layout. Think about what happens when you move from record to record. The text labels for each field stay the same, even though the data inside each field changes with every record. Text objects give you one form of stability in the ever-changing world of database records.

When you design a layout, you can control every aspect of a text object, from the words in it to the font, size, style, color, line spacing, tab stops, and so on. (In fact, everything you learned in Chapter 2 related to formatting text in fields applies to text objects on layouts as well.)

Note: FileMaker's spell checker works in Layout mode too. Just choose Spelling → Check Layout. It looks and works just as it does in Browse mode—except that it checks text objects on the current layout. Also, the *visual* spell-checking feature (see page 85) works in Layout mode as well, so watch for dotted red underlines if you're a chronic misspeller.

Lines and shapes

If you need simple graphic embellishments in your layouts, FileMaker has built-in tools. For example, you might want to put a box around a person's address information, and another around the Notes field, so they are visually separated. You can draw lines, rectangles, ovals, and round-cornered rectangles right on your layout. You can also control the line color, thickness, and pattern for lines and shapes; and the fill color and pattern for shapes.

Images

If simple shapes can't properly convey your artistic vision for your layout, you have recourse: You can paste any picture right onto the layout. You can also insert a picture from a file on your hard drive. Database developers often add icons, logos, and other decorations this way. For example, you might add your company logo to the top-right corner of your layout, or put a cute little envelope icon by the Email Address field. Just remember a little of this "eye candy" goes a long way. If you get carried away, you can actually create so much visual clutter that people using the program are confused, instead of enlightened. Also, large images can make your layouts slow to load, especially when you share the database over a network (which you'll learn how to do in Chapter 18).

Fields

A layout without fields is just a picture. Perhaps it's a very complex picture that changes as you switch from list view to form view, and has an entirely different effect when printed (thank you, parts!), but it's a picture nonetheless.

To get *data* into your layout, you add field objects. For instance, if you make a new layout in the People database, and you want to show the person's address, you can add the Street Address, City, State, and Zip Code fields to the Body part of the layout. If the field is in the Body part (the most common place), then it shows data from the current record (or each record when you view the layout as a list). In list view, fields in Header, Footer, or Grand Summary parts show the values from the first or last record in the found set. In Preview mode (or when printing), headers and footers show data from the first or last record on each page.

Note: You won't usually put ordinary fields in Header, Footer, and Grand Summary parts. These parts usually contain global fields, summary fields (see page 286), page numbering, dates, or just text and pictures.

With a firm understanding of layouts, views, parts, and objects, you're ready to get down to business. The next section shows you how to put all these ideas to work in your own databases.

Layout Mode

OK. It's time to dive into Layout mode and see what it's all about. You'll probably spend most of your time in Browse, Find, and Preview modes, but despite this fact, Layout mode has more options, more buttons, more menu commands, and more hidden features than any other mode. As you explore Layout mode in this section, you'll work with the People database you created in the last chapter, so to start things off, open that database and switch to Layout mode:

1. **Open the People database you created in Chapter 3.**

   The database appears on the screen, in Browse mode. If you don't have the People database, you can download a copy from the "Missing CD" page from *www.missingmanuals.com*.

2. **Choose View → Layout Mode.**

Whoa! Welcome to Layout mode…and you thought you had this FileMaker stuff figured out. (Figure 4-9 shows what you should see on your screen.)

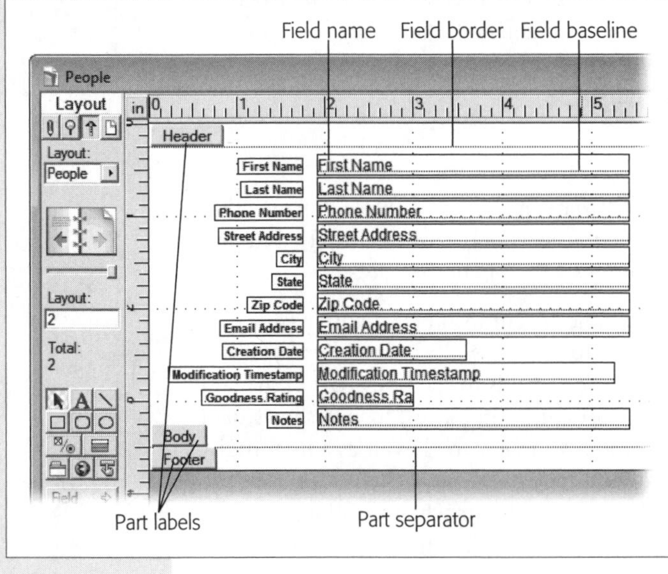

***Figure 4-9:** In Layout mode, your database looks a lot different. Each field on the layout shows its name where the data used to be, has a black border, and has a dotted line baseline. You can also see labels and separators for the three parts on this layout: header, body, and footer.*

The Status Area

You don't have to look too closely to see that the status area has changed significantly (Figure 4-10):

- Instead of the current record number and record count, the status area now shows the current layout number and the layout count. (You can't tell yet since you have only one layout, but the Book icon now moves you through layouts rather than records.)
- A handful of tools—little square buttons with icons on them—appear. (Read on to find out what they do.)
- In the bottom-left corner of the window, a new control called the *part label toggle* has joined the usual zoom controls and status area control.
- The Mode pop-up menu and mode tabs now show that you're in Layout mode.

It isn't just the status area that changes, though. Take a look at the menus. The Insert and Format menus, which are almost always gray in Browse mode, are fully functional now. And you have two new menus to help you design: Layout and Arrange. Finally, the Records menu has completely disappeared.

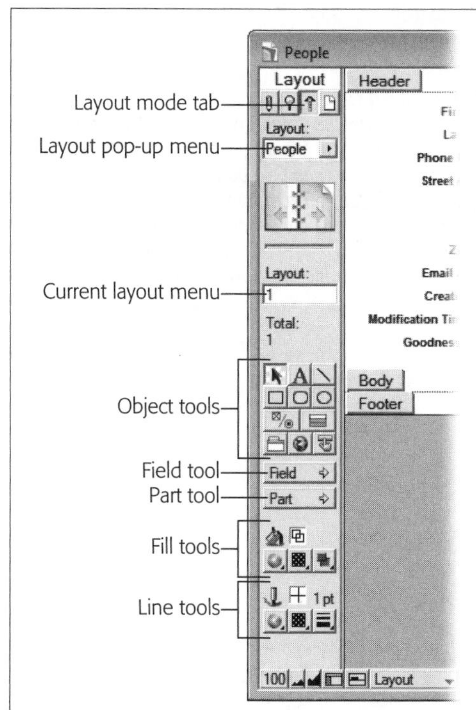

Figure 4-10: *In Layout mode the status area has a lot more going on. Some things haven't changed, though. The Layout pop-up menu still shows you layouts and lets you instantly switch from one to another. As usual, you can hide the status area with the status area control. And the zoom controls are perhaps more handy in Layout mode than they are in any other mode, since this is the place where you're likely to be fine-tuning little details.*

Tip: You may need to make your window taller to see everything the status area has to offer in Layout mode. In Windows, drag the top edge of the window up, or the bottom edge of the window down. In Mac OS X, drag the resize box at the bottom-right corner of the window.

View Options

Although Figure 4-9 shows how your database normally looks in Layout mode, FileMaker offers a host of options to change it. Each of these options has absolutely no effect on the finished look of your layout in Browse mode; rather, they help you while you're designing the layout. The View menu keeps those old standby commands (Browse mode, Find mode, Layout mode, Preview mode, and "Go to Layout") right there where they belong. But you get choices that are more suitable for layout tasks.

Go to Layout

This hierarchical menu gives you an alternative to using the status area's Layout pop-up menu to move to all your layouts. In Browse mode, the "Go to Layout" submenu shows only those layouts that you've specified for inclusion in Layout menus. But in Layout mode, *all* layouts are listed, so you can switch quickly as you work.

Page Margins

If you want a better feel for how your layout will look when printed, choose View → Page Margins (Figure 4-11). FileMaker shows a light gray border around your layout, representing your current page margins.

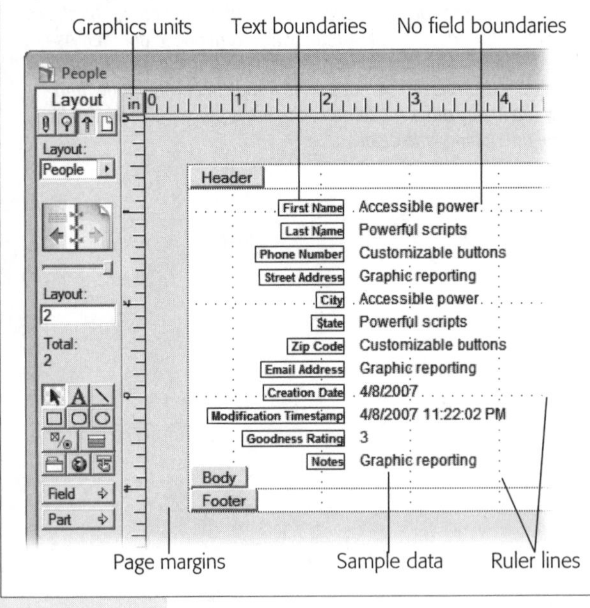

Figure 4-11: *In this picture, the graphic rulers, ruler lines, text boundaries, page margins, and sample data have been turned on; and field boundaries have been turned off. You can compare this illustration with Figure 4-9 to see how things have changed. You decide which settings you use, according to your personal preference. And you can turn any of them off or on with ease, so feel free to experiment.*

Note: Remember that the parts *all* show in Layout mode, but in Browse mode or when printing, parts come and go. So even when you display page margins in Layout mode, the height of the *layout* doesn't directly translate to the height of the printed page.

Graphic Rulers

Choose View → Graphic Rulers to get a handle on the actual size of the layout and the objects on it. When they're turned on, you see a ruler running up the left edge of the layout, and another across the top (see Figure 4-11). You can use this ruler to measure how big layout objects are and align things perfectly to a spot on the printed page, since an inch, centimeter, or pixels on the ruler matches the same unit when printed. Change the rulers' unit of measurement by clicking the square where they intersect. Units cycle through a series of presets: inches, centimeters, and pixels.

Text Ruler

You might not care how tall your page is, but you do want to know how wide objects are. If so, choose View → Text Ruler. When you have no text objects selected on a layout, the text ruler looks just like the graphic rulers above, except there's no ruler along the left margin. You see the text ruler in action when you have a text object selected. Then the ruler shrinks to the width of your object, and displays margins, indents, and tabs—an ideal tool for judging space when you're trying to cram a lot of information onto a small screen.

POWER USERS' CLINIC

Configuring Rulers and Lines

You don't have to be content with the lines and rulers FileMaker gives you. If your rulers are in inches, for example, and you prefer to work in pixels, you can easily make the change. When in Layout mode, simply choose Layouts → Set Rulers. In this window, you can choose the units your ruler uses. If you choose inches, FileMaker draws ruler lines one inch apart. If you choose centimeters, your lines are one centimeter apart instead. When you set your ruler units to pixels, the lines are 100 pixels apart (a line every pixel would probably be counter-productive).

If you have graphics rulers showing, you can avoid the trip to the Set Rulers dialog box. Your current choice of units is in the top-left corner of the layout, where the horizontal and vertical rulers meet. If you click this unit label, it changes. Each time you click, the units change again, rotating between all three options.

This dialog box also has a setting for grid spacing. See the box on page 170 for an explanation.

Ruler Lines

Rulers running along the edge of the window may not provide enough visual alignment aid to suit your tastes. In that case, choose View → Ruler Lines. FileMaker draws dotted lines along your layout in a grid pattern. With this grid, you can more easily see how things line up on the layout, and get objects just where you want them on the printed page.

T-Squares

Choose View → T-Squares to show the T-squares (Figure 4-12). When FileMaker shows you the T-squares, they always land aligned smack-dab in the middle of your layout. To move them where *you* want them, just drag them into place.

Unfortunately, you have to move them one at the time. Practice your multiplication tables while you do this tedious task.

You can even use the T-squares to line up objects on more than one layout. Align something to the T-squares, and then switch to a different layout and align another object to them. Now, as you switch between these layouts, the two objects stay in the same place. So what, you say? Most often, the two objects are really two copies of the same thing, say a button you want in the same place on two different layouts. If these two objects aren't precisely aligned on each layout, you'll see a very distracting flash when you switch between those two layouts. Sure, it takes a little time, but this kind of precision will give your database polish and a professional look.

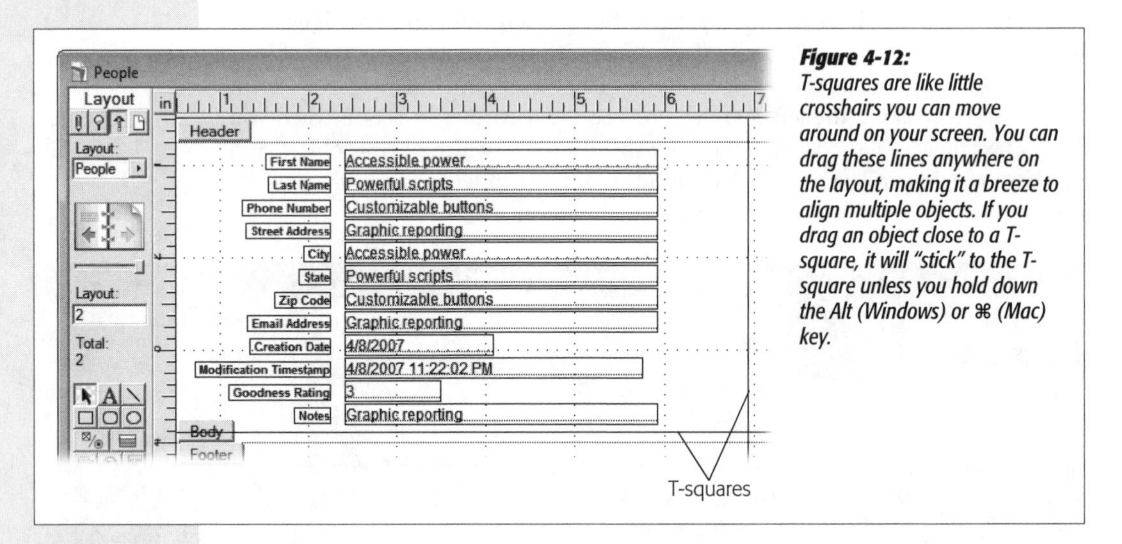

Figure 4-12: *T-squares are like little crosshairs you can move around on your screen. You can drag these lines anywhere on the layout, making it a breeze to align multiple objects. If you drag an object close to a T-square, it will "stick" to the T-square unless you hold down the Alt (Windows) or ⌘ (Mac) key.*

Object Info

This tiny window is a powerhouse of formatting options. You can position and size objects with numerical precision, give your objects their own names (which comes in handy when scripting, as you'll see in Chapter 13), and control how each object moves and resizes as you resize the window in Browse mode.

Buttons

Contrary to what you might think, View → Show → Buttons doesn't show or hide your buttons. Instead, this command puts a thick gray line around all objects you've defined as buttons. You haven't learned about buttons yet, so see page 258 for directions on how to make objects bend to your will and turn into buttons.

Sample Data

As mentioned above, FileMaker normally shows the name of each field inside the field itself. To get a real-world impression of your database, you can choose View → Show → Sample Data. FileMaker shows data from your records instead, just as you'd see in Browse mode. This feature can give you a visual clue about what kind of data a field holds (text, numbers, dates, and so forth), and how FileMaker is formatting these values. (If you don't *have* any records, you see semi-random sample data instead. Figure 4-11 shows fields with sample data.)

Text Boundaries

Normally, text objects on a layout (like the field labels you see now) have no border around them. Sometimes, though, you can have a tough time visually lining up text since different letters have different shapes and sizes. If you choose View → Show → Text Boundaries, you see a tidy box surrounding each text object. When you line up these boxes, you ensure that the text inside them is lined up, too.

Note: In case it isn't obvious, you can turn any of the above options *off* by choosing the appropriate command a second time.

Field Boundaries

All the view options available in Layout mode are turned *off* unless you turn them on yourself—except for this one. FileMaker normally shows a border around every field in Layout mode no matter how you have that field formatted for Browse mode. If you don't want to see this border, choose View → Show → Field Boundaries. Figure 4-11 shows how the layout looks with field boundaries turned off.

Note: Don't confuse field boundaries with text boundaries. Field boundaries show around field objects (of any type) while text boundaries show around text objects.

Sliding Objects

This command (View → Show → Sliding Objects) places small, black arrows near the top of any item that's been set to slide during printing. See page 210 to learn how to make objects slide.

Non-Printing Objects

This command puts a dotted gray border around any object that's set as non-printing. See page 244 to learn how to make objects non-printing.

Tooltips

As you'll learn in Chapter 19, FileMaker Pro Advanced allows you to attach helpful tooltips to your layout objects. When you turn on View → Show → Tooltips, you'll see a little sticky note icon attached to any object that has its own tooltip. As with all these view options, this icon appears only in Layout mode.

Note: If a FileMaker icon or button doesn't immediately convey meaning to you, let your mouse pointer hover over it to see the tooltip. FileMaker's buttons have tooltips of their own.

Toolbars

You can find all FileMaker's toolbar commands in either the menus or on the status bar. But if the fascination of menus has lost its steely grip on you, you can show or hide any of FileMaker's toolbars at will. They come in four flavors:

- **Standard.** This toolbar contains the stuff you find in most applications' toolbars. There are buttons for creating new files, for opening existing files, for saving, for undo, and for cut, copy and paste, among many others.
- **Text Formatting.** Here you'll find the stuff you need to make your text look great. You can change fonts, sizes, styles, alignment, and spacing.
- **Arrange.** These oddly marked buttons let you align objects, move them backwards and forward in layers, and rotate them.
- **Tools.** This powerful little bar gives you the strength to draw simple objects and to create those objects that make a database do what it does best. You can make fields, buttons, portals, tab controls, and Web viewers, as well as insert parts into your layout. Any of those items mentioned here that don't make sense yet will make sense in due time, Grasshopper. Keep reading this chapter and the next one. Soon, you'll be ready to leave the temple and embark on your own journey of discovery and saving the world through better databases.

The first time you see these toolbars, they're anchored near the top of the screen, just under the menu bar. But they all have dotted gray lines at their left edges. Just use these lines to drag the toolbars wherever you want them. They are powerless to resist you and will stay where they're put. Use the close box to make them go away.

Status area

This is a menu-based choice for showing and hiding the status area. If you have to work on a laptop, or any other computer with a small screen, you'll be grateful for the extra pixels you can squeeze out by hiding the status area while you're designing your layouts.

Zoom in and out

The View menu also has options to zoom the layout in or out (View → Zoom In and View → Zoom Out). If the thrill of clicking the zoom controls in the status area isn't enough for you, you can alternate between zoom buttons below and zoom menus above. You do have some control over what area of the screen is magnified. If there's an object you need to see, select it before zooming in. FileMaker tries to keep that object centered as it zooms.

Layout Setup

Most of your layout work simply involves creating and adjusting layout parts, and filling them with things. But some important aspects of a layout aren't visible on the layout itself. These settings are tucked away in the Layout Setup dialog box

(Figure 4-13) instead. You can call this window into action by choosing Layouts → Layout Setup. With the People database open, switch to Layout mode. Now's a good time to set some options.

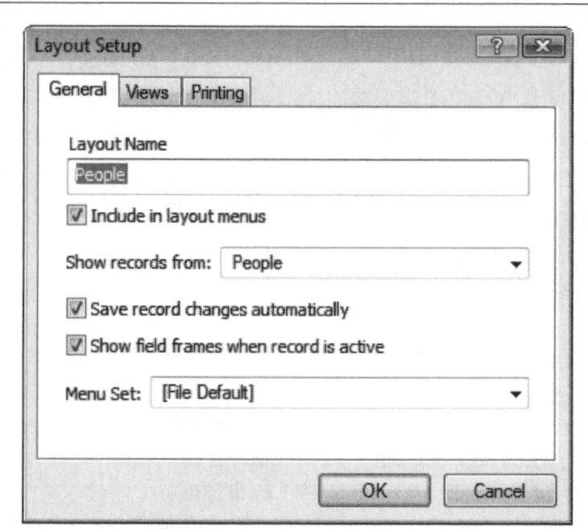

Figure 4-13: *The Layout Setup dialog box (Layouts → Layout Setup) gives you control over the layout's basic attributes. Under the General tab you can change the layout's name, for example. The "Show records from" pop-up menu controls which table the layout is connected to. Since your database only has one table, you don't have to worry about this option just yet. It's covered in full in Part 4.*

Layout name

First up, suppose your People database holds all your clients. You might want to change the name of this layout to "Personal Details." This change clears the way for a "People List" layout down the road.

1. **Choose Layouts → Layout Setup.**

   The Layout Setup dialog box appears.

2. **In the Layout Name box, type *Personal Details*.**

   You can give a layout just about any name you want, so long as it's no more than 100 characters long. You can even have more than one layout with the same name, if you're a fan of confusion. FileMaker keeps track of layouts using an internal ID number, so it always knows which layout is which. But you have to depend on the names you give your layouts, so name them wisely.

3. **Make sure the "Include in layout menus" checkbox is turned on.**

   Normally, each layout is listed in the Layouts pop-up menu, so that when you're using the database you can switch to that layout at any moment. In this case, you want to be able to check out client details at an instant's notice.

   Sometimes, you'll turn this checkbox off when a layout serves a special purpose: Perhaps it's a report that makes sense only after performing a special find and sort; or a search screen that works only in Find mode. In cases like these, you can turn off the "Include in layout menus" checkbox and use a script (see Part 5) to go to the layout instead. When you do, the layout no longer shows up in the Layouts pop-up menu or the View → "Go to Layout" menu in Browse, Preview, or Find modes. *Every* layout shows in these menus in Layout mode, no matter how you set this checkbox.

4. **Turn off the "Save record changes automatically" checkbox.**

   This way, FileMaker displays the message shown in Figure 4-14 whenever you try to exit a record after making edits to it using this layout. It's confirming that you want to save those changes when you commit the record.

   If you leave this checkbox turned on, this saving happens quietly in the background. FileMaker's factory setting is to commit changes the moment you leave the record, as you learned on page 24. But say you run a growing business and plan to hire a helper to update client information. Until that person gets up to speed in FileMaker, you want to give him a chance to double-check his work before saving it, so you don't want records saved automatically.

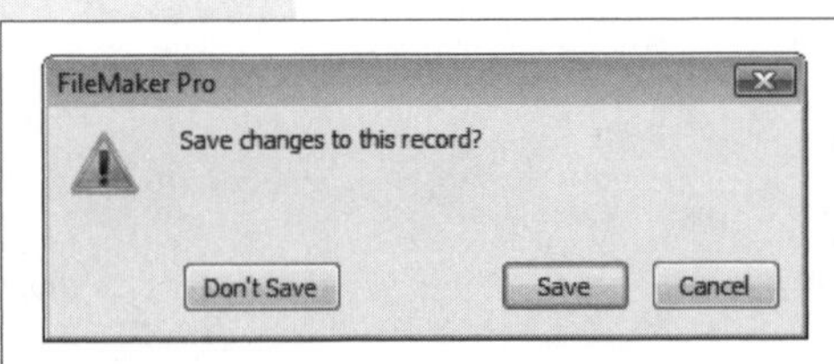

Figure 4-14:
When the "Save record changes automatically" option is turned off, you see this message when you exit a record to which you've made any changes. If you'd rather not keep the changes you made, click Don't Save. Click Cancel if you want to stay in the record, changes intact and unsaved. Click Save to exit the record and save the changes.

Note: Pay close attention to the fact that this is a *layout* setting. If you want to make sure record changes are always confirmed before being saved, you have to turn this setting on for every layout. There's a point to turning it on, though: Suppose you don't want to confirm changes to most of your fields, but you do want this behavior for the Notes field. You can simply leave the Notes field off the main layout, and create a separate notes layout. When you create this layout, you get the ask-before-saving feature for the Notes field without the hassle for every other field.

5. **Turn off "Show field frames when record is active."**

   The "Show field frames when record is active" option affects how FileMaker shows fields in Browse and Find modes. You've probably noticed that whenever you're in a field, every field on the layout has a dotted-line border around it. These borders help people figure out where the enterable fields are. Figure 4-15 illustrates the difference.

   Using the tools in this chapter, you, O savvy database developer, can make your layout clear and user-friendly without the unsightly dotted lines, so turn them off.

   You can always return to this dialog box (Layout → Layout Setup) if you ever get confused and want to use the dotted fields as a guide.

Tip: The Menu Set pop-up menu gives you heretofore unheard-of power. Using FileMaker Advanced, you can control which menus and commands are available when your users view a layout. But you won't learn how to do that until Chapter 19, so don't touch that dial just yet.

Now, if you switch to Browse mode, you see the new name in the Layout pop-up menu, and no frames when you click a field. Of course, without the field frames, your invisible fields look a little odd. You'll fix this problem shortly. But first, you need to learn about the tools you have in Layout mode.

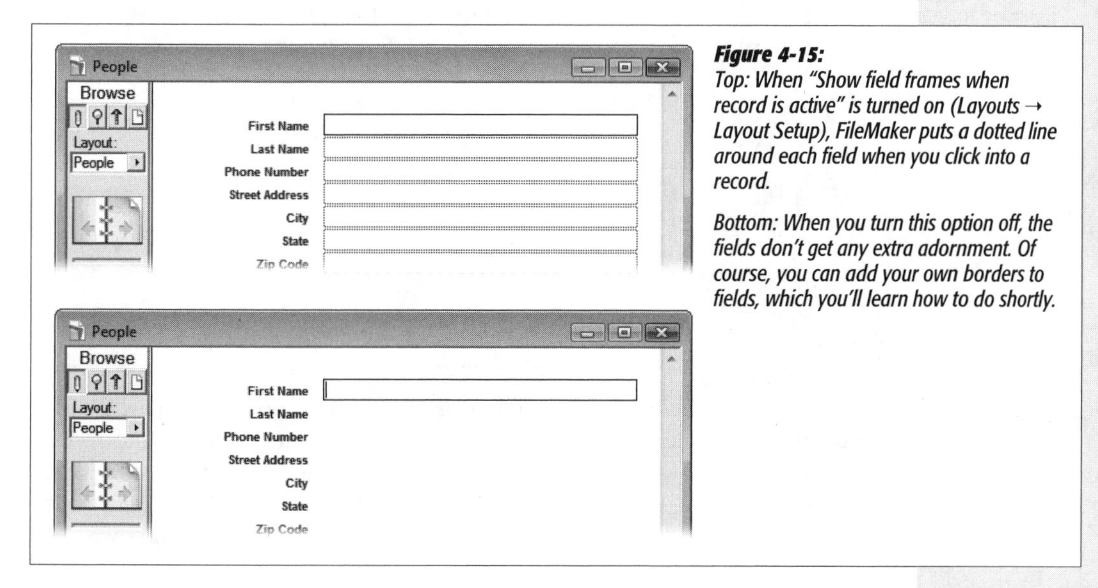

Figure 4-15:
Top: When "Show field frames when record is active" is turned on (Layouts → Layout Setup), FileMaker puts a dotted line around each field when you click into a record.

Bottom: When you turn this option off, the fields don't get any extra adornment. Of course, you can add your own borders to fields, which you'll learn how to do shortly.

Layout Tools

The vast majority of new goodies in the status area are *tools*. Like their real-world counterparts, you use tools to build things—in this case, your layout. You can see all the tools in the status area in Figure 4-10.

The drawing tools

The first set of tools in the status area is the *drawing tools*. These tools, for the most part, just let you draw decorations on the layout. They're the top two rows of the main tools panel, and you see them up close in Figure 4-16.

- The **selection** tool is active when you first enter Layout mode, and whenever you've finished using another tool, it immediately becomes active again. If you're not using some special tool, FileMaker assumes you want to use this one. Its only purpose in life is selecting objects on the layout. Once an object is selected, you can do things to it (like move it, resize it, or adjust the way it looks).
- The **text** tool lets you put text on your layout. For the most part, this text is unchanging—it's the same no matter what record you're looking at. The most common example of text on layouts is field labels, which you've seen in every database you've used so far. See page 153 for the skinny on working with text on a layout.

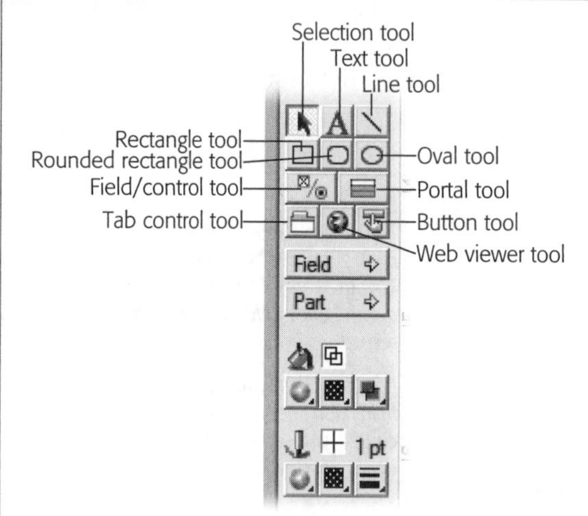

Figure 4-16:
These are the drawing tools. In this picture, the selection tool is active (it appears pressed down). To choose a different tool, click it. Once active, you can click or drag on the layout to draw a shape or add some text. When you release the mouse button, FileMaker automatically activates the selection tool again.

- FileMaker has a built-in understanding of a few basic shapes. You can use the **line**, **rectangle**, **rounded rectangle**, and **oval** tools to draw lines, squares and rectangles, circles and ovals, and rounded rectangles (rectangles or squares with round corners). Figure 4-17 shows a few ways people often use these shapes on layouts. On page 170, you'll get a chance to create some shapes and lines of your own.

Note: If you find FileMaker's drawing tools limited, fear not. You can create icons, buttons, or any other elements in any drawing program, and then place these images on your layout. Find out how on page 137.

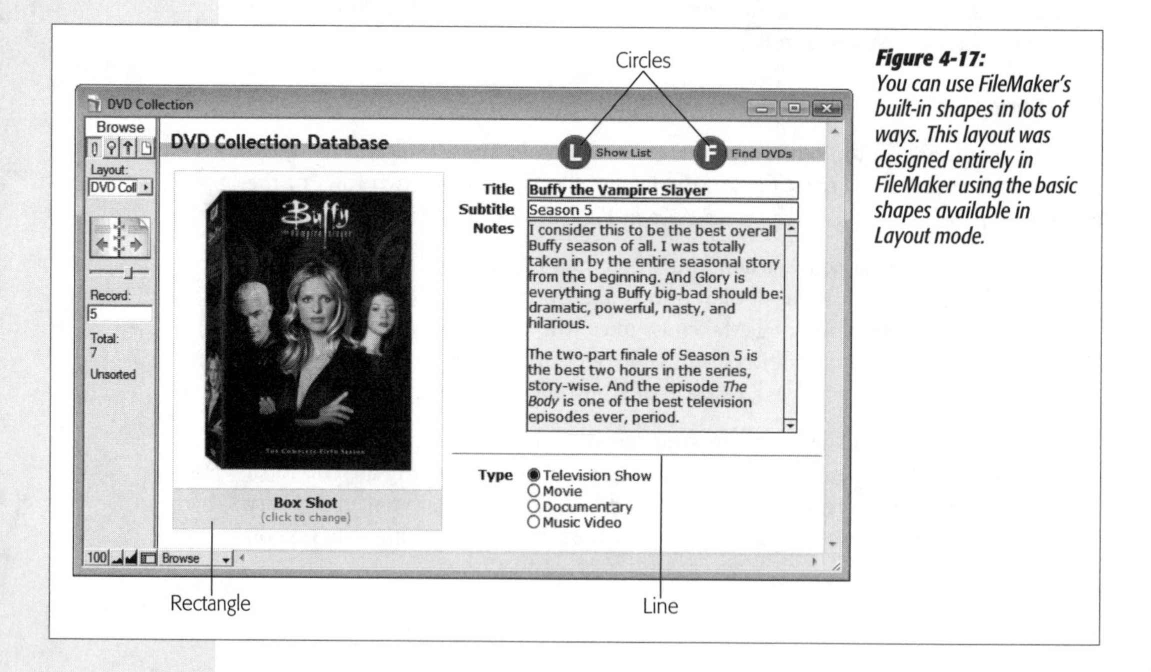

Figure 4-17:
You can use FileMaker's built-in shapes in lots of ways. This layout was designed entirely in FileMaker using the basic shapes available in Layout mode.

The control tools

The drawing tools let you gussy up your layout. But the control tools let the layout get down to business. With this party of five, you tell the layout where to put data and where it should go looking for that data. You can also create buttons to automate tedious or lengthy processes, and you can create tab controls, which make designing complex databases a breeze.

- The **button** tool helps you create a button which, when you click it, tells FileMaker to do something interesting—create a new record, switch to a different layout, or even run a script. You'll learn how to create buttons in Chapter 6 and how to write scripts in Chapter 13.
- The **field control** tool lets you determine everything that's important about a field except what's inside it. You can control a field's placement on your layout, its shape and size, and even what it looks like. The first part of Chapter 5 is all about field controls.
- The **tab control** tool gives you a major leg up on placing lots of information on a single layout without clutter. Look to Chapter 6 for the full scoop on how tab control makes your life easier.
- The **portal** tool creates portals—mysterious passageways to a different dimension. Wait...that can't be right. Portals actually show data from a *different* table right on your layout. You'll learn more in Part 4.
- The **Web viewer** tool lets you display Web pages directly on your FileMaker layout—maps, tracking information, *and so on)*. You'll learn about these in Chapter 6.

The field and part tools

The next tools in line are the **field** and **part** tools, which simply let you add fields and parts to your layout. To create a new field, drag the field tool onto your layout. When you let go of the mouse, FileMaker draws the field and pops up the "Specify Field" dialog box. Click the "Create label" option if you need a field label. Click OK and your field is created.

Note: The field tool and the field control tool let you add fields to your layout. Why the duplication? The answer is flexibility. With the field tool, you can quickly add a simple field to the layout with just *one* click. But if you want to manipulate it further, you need to take additional steps. With the field control tool, adding a field requires more clicks, but you get all the options up front.

In practice, you'll usually use the field control tool to save a little time when you know you want something more complex than the most basic field. Either tool produces a field that's equally customizable, so you can't make a *wrong* choice here.

The line and fill tools

Next up are the fill and line attribute tools, shown more closely in Figure 4-18. When you click these buttons, you get menus from which to pick colors, patterns, line thicknesses, and other special effects, each of which you can apply to assorted objects on the layout. For example, when you have a shape selected, you can choose from the menu under the fill color tool and change the shape's color. You'll use these tools all throughout this chapter.

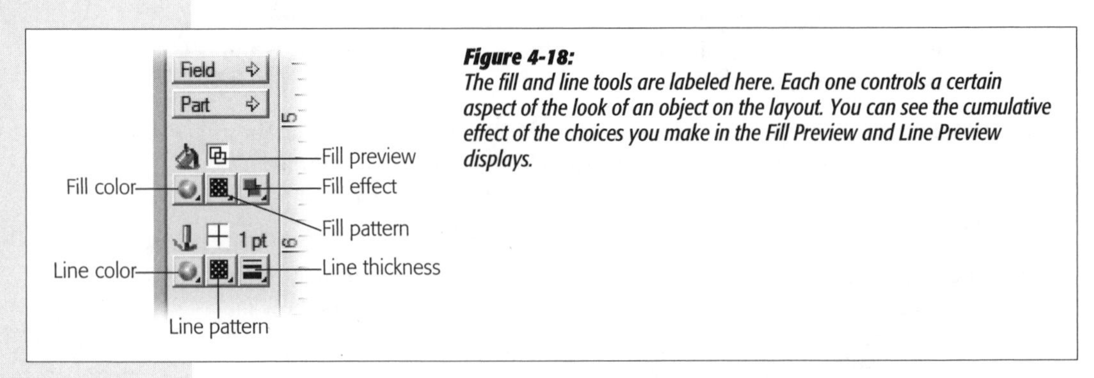

Figure 4-18: *The fill and line tools are labeled here. Each one controls a certain aspect of the look of an object on the layout. You can see the cumulative effect of the choices you make in the Fill Preview and Line Preview displays.*

- **Fill color, pattern, and effect.** When you select an object on the layout, the fill color changes the color of the object itself. You can also apply a repeating pattern to the object for that oh-so-80s look. If the early 90s is more your style, the fill effects tool lets you apply a simple drop shadow, an embossed effect, or an engraved effect. Figure 4-19 shows some rectangles with various fills.
- **Line color, pattern, and weight.** The next three tools affect the outline of an object, rather than its fill. You can again control color and pattern. The line weight tool also lets you adjust the thickness of the outline itself. You can see some line settings in action in Figure 4-20.

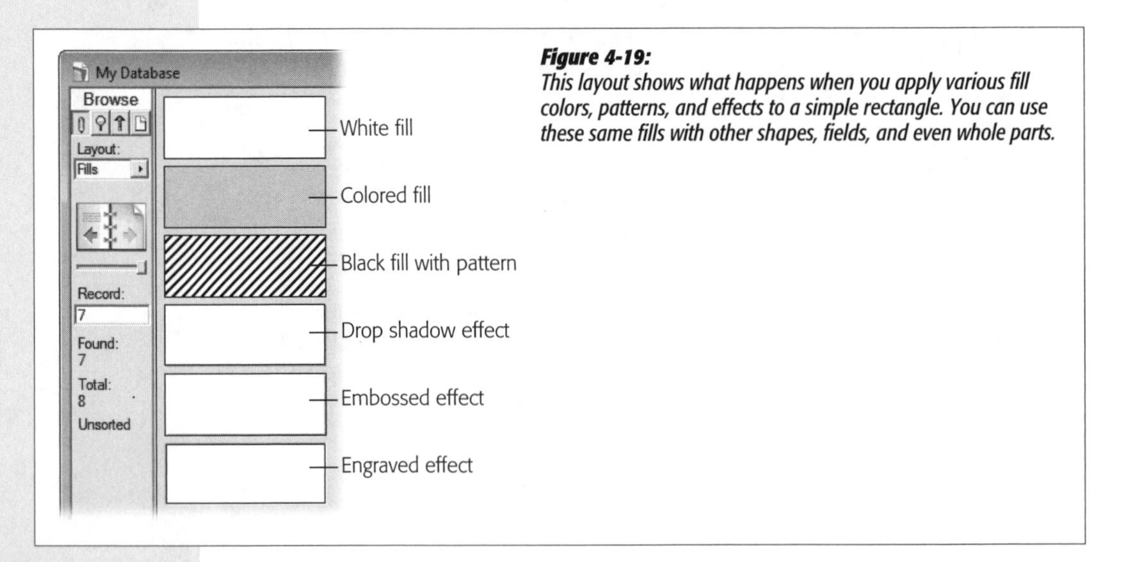

Figure 4-19: *This layout shows what happens when you apply various fill colors, patterns, and effects to a simple rectangle. You can use these same fills with other shapes, fields, and even whole parts.*

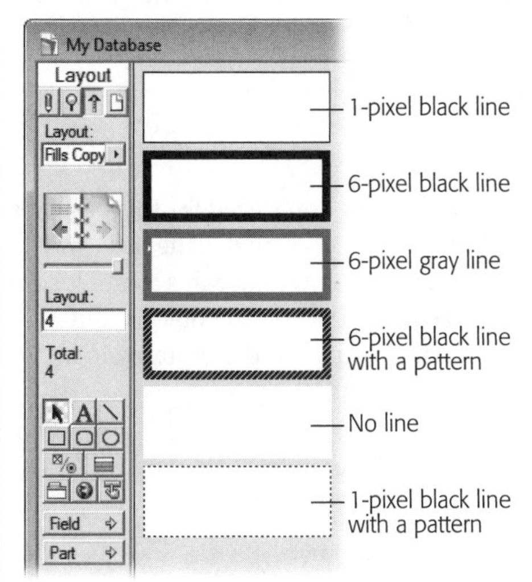

Figure 4-20:
Here you can see the same rectangles with various line styles. When you adjust the line color, pattern, and thickness, you can get many effects, from no line at all to a dashed line, to a thick black line. You can apply line effects to shapes, lines, and fields with borders.

Working with Parts

The first step to any layout design is to put the parts where they belong (or at least *approximately* where they belong; you can always tweak them later). In the beginning of this chapter you learned about the kinds of parts a layout can have, and it's your job to decide which ones you want for the layout you're building.

In your People database, your first job is simple—to pretty up the layout FileMaker created for you. It makes sense that such a layout would have a Header part (where you can announce the layout's title) and a body (where you can put the actual fields). Figure 4-21 shows one person's idea of a nicer looking detail layout.

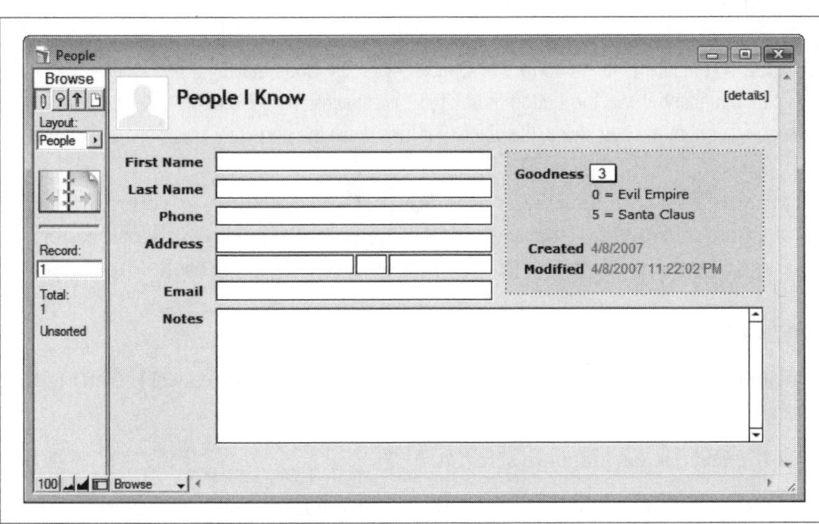

Figure 4-21:
Unless you're a real minimalist, you probably agree this layout looks nicer here than it did when FileMaker first created it. Here you can see the Header part and the Body part. Your first mission is to get these parts–and just these parts–on your layout.

Tip: You can get some hints on prettying up this layout and actually watch it being done. Check out the screencast at *www.missingmanuals.com*.

Deleting a part

The quickest way to delete the Footer part (which you don't need for this particular layout) is to click its part label and press Delete. (The part label is the little gray tag that says Footer.) Go ahead and delete the Footer part now. Since this footer is completely empty, it simply goes away immediately. If a part has any objects in it at all, FileMaker asks you if you're sure before removing the part and everything in it.

Warning: Look closely at those last three words. When you delete a part, *everything in it gets deleted too*. Be careful.

Resizing parts

Your next job is to make the header a little larger. Just drag the part label straight down a bit. As you drag, a dotted line tells you where the part will land when you let go. For now, make it about double its original size.

Every part below the one you resize moves down to make room, which is *almost* always what you want. But suppose your overall layout size is just where you want it (perhaps it's designed to print on a special form, and the exact size is critical). In a case like this, if you want to resize the header, you probably *don't* want it to push other parts down. Instead, as the header grows, you want the body to shrink a little, so that the header eats into the body. To get this effect, hold down the Alt (Windows) or Option (Mac) key while you drag the part label. When you do, the border between parts changes, but the overall layout size remains the same, and the objects on the layout don't move at all.

Note: Unless you hold the Alt (Windows) or Option (Mac) key when making a part smaller, you can't drag the part boundary above the bottommost object it contains. To get around this glitch, you must move the objects out of the way, delete the objects, or hold down the necessary keys while you drag.

FileMaker won't let you put objects *outside* a part, so sometimes as you're arranging things you get cramped for space. To make the rest of your layout work easier, go ahead and make the Body part taller as well—you can shrink it back down later.

Coloring a part

The finished detail layout should have a shaded header (Figure 4-21). Getting this effect is a breeze:

1. **Click the Header part label to select it.**

   The label itself darkens to let you know it's selected.

2. **Click the fill color tool in the status area (it's shown in Figure 4-18).**

   A menu of available colors pops up.

3. **From the menu, select the color you want for the header.**

   The Header part changes to match the selected color.

Note: You can apply a pattern to a part as well, but parts can't have fill effects.

Repeat the steps above, this time selecting the Body part and a different color (like light gray). When you color a part, this color becomes the background color both in the database window and when you print. With this phenomenon in mind, you should probably avoid excessively dark or otherwise awful colors and patterns. Of course, you can also elect to leave the body white, if you wish.

Adding and Editing Text

Figure 4-21 shows how your layout's going to look when you're done. Your next assignment is to put the text in the header. FileMaker's text tool makes it a cinch to click anywhere in a layout part and type away.

Adding new text

The first piece of text in the header should say "People I Know." This is a title for your entire database (in other words, your list layout will say the same thing on top). Here's how to do it:

1. **In the status area, click the text tool (it has an "A" on it).**

   The text tool button darkens to let you know it's active.

2. **Choose Format → Font → Trebuchet MS.**

   The text you're about to create will appear in this font.

3. **Choose Format → Size → 18 Point.**

   Now you're telling the text tool you want it to create larger text.

4. **Choose Format → Style → Bold.**

   And finally, you want this title to be bold.

Note: You can dress up your text in any font, size, and style you like. But don't forget that the computer your database is *used* on must have the font installed. If you have fine-and-fancy $300 fonts on your computer, but your employees will be using the database on stripped-down PCs, you want to pick a font that comes standard with your operating system so everybody sees the same lovely letterforms.

5. **Click somewhere in the header.**

   A new text box appears (Figure 4-22). This text box is FileMaker's way of saying "Go ahead and type."

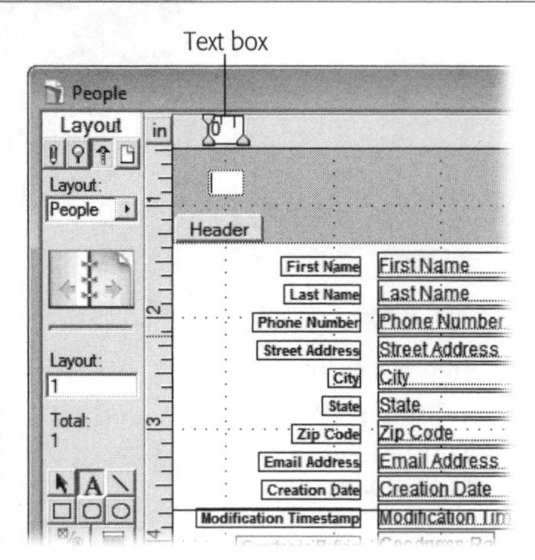

Figure 4-22: *When you click with the text tool, FileMaker shows a text box–you can type right in it. You can tell this text box is ready for typing because it has a dotted outline and a flashing insertion point. When you've finished entering text, just press Enter in the number keypad area of your keyboard, or click anywhere outside the text box.*

6. **In the text box, type *People I Know*.**

   As you type, the words appear in the box.

Note: Almost everything you know about entering text in Browse mode applies right here as well: you can change fonts, sizes, and styles, adjust tab stops, check spelling, and more. You can even choose Edit → Undo if you make a mistake (or choose it seven times if you make seven mistakes in a row).

7. **Press the Enter key by the number keypad on your keyboard, or click somewhere on the layout outside the text object itself.**

   The dotted outline and flashing insertion point disappear and you're left with a full-fledged text object. This object is automatically selected for you.

8. **If necessary, move the new text object to its proper place, using Figure 4-21 as a guide.**

   You move a text object like any other object: Just drag it.

As well as the main title, a header often also includes something to remind you (and the people who use your database) what layout you're looking at—the "[Detail]" text in this case. You already know how to do it:

1. **Using the text tool, click somewhere in the Header part, being careful not to click the existing text object.**

   A new text box appears, ready for typing.

2. **Type *[Detail]*.**

   The text box reflects your typing, but the text isn't the right size or style.

3. **Press Enter.**

   Again, the signs of an editable text box disappear and FileMaker selects the new text object.

POWER USERS' CLINIC

Locking the Layout Tools

After you create a text object with the text tool, the selection tool is automatically activated. FileMaker assumes you want just one text object, and saves you the trouble of switching back to the selection tool. If you anticipate creating several objects of the same type, give the tool icon a *double*-click instead of a single-click. The icon on the button turns white to let you know the tool is now locked. With a locked text tool, you can create as many text objects as you want: Click to create the text box, type the text, click again for another text box, and so forth. When you're finished, click the selection tool again to make it active, or just press the Esc key.

If, for some reason, you don't like FileMaker always switching back to the selection tool on your behalf, you can instruct it to lock the drawing tools automatically–so even a single-click keeps a tool active until you say otherwise. In Windows, choose Edit → Preferences. In Mac OS X, choose FileMaker Pro → Preferences. In the preferences window, select the Layout tab and turn on the "Always lock layout tools" checkbox. If you're like most people, you want to switch this checkbox off after trying it for about ten seconds; just revisit the Layout tab of the preferences window and make the change.

4. **Choose Format → Size → Custom.**

   The Custom dialog box pops up.

5. **Enter *11* in the "Custom font size" box, and then click OK.**

   The text you just created immediately changes size.

Note: Since 11 point isn't normally in the Format → Size menu, you have to use the Custom size option instead. This option works the same in Layout mode as it does in Browse mode (see page 67).

6. **Choose Format → Style → Plain Text.**

   The text object loses its bold formatting.

7. **Move the text object to its proper place.**

   You can see it coming: Just drag.

Changing text font, size, and style

FileMaker created a handful of text objects for you when it made this layout—the field labels. You can change the font and style of each label to make them attractive and easy to read, and you can also adjust the size to make sure everything fits. Figure 4-21 shows 11-point Verdana—a simple style that looks tidy and readable on most monitors.

Note: If you're designing a database on the Mac for use on PCs, you'll need to make all your text objects just a little larger than you (and FileMaker) think they need to be, because PCs display fonts larger than their Mac brethren do. It helps to check your layouts on a PC, because any text object that isn't wide enough will flow over onto another line, which probably isn't what you intended.

UP TO SPEED

Find and Replace Revisited

Layout mode retains some features you've already learned from Browse mode–albeit slightly modified to make sense to a database designer rather than a database user. For example, you might want to find and replace text on a layout, on occasion. Imagine you have decided to call the Zip Code field *Postal Code* instead, since you're planning a big drive into Canada. You can use Find/Replace to fix every field label on a layout in just one shot. When you're in Layout mode, the Find/Replace command searches through text on the layout itself rather than the data in fields and records.

The slightly pared-down dialog box you see when you choose Edit → Find/Replace → Find/Replace in Layout mode looks and works just like its Browse mode counterpart, aside from the lack of "Search across" and "Search within" options.

The other commands on the Edit → Find/Replace submenu–Find Again, Replace and Find Again, and Find Selected–also work exactly as they do in Browse mode. (See page 60 for details on the ins and outs of Find/Replace.)

You've probably already figured out that to change something about an object, you first need to select it. You can select the first object, change its font, change its size, change its style, and then select the second object and repeat…over and over until you're done or until you've torn out your last remaining hair. Or you can select *all* the field labels and change them in one shot. The box on page 157 describes several ways of selecting multiple layout objects, but the quickest way is often to *rubber band* them—that is, you drag to encompass the objects with your mouse. Here's how:

1. **With your mouse, position the selection tool just below and to the right of the Notes field label, and then click.**

   This spot is where you'll start your rubber band. Notice that as you drag around, a dotted rectangle follows you—that's the rubber band.

2. **Drag from this point up and to the left until the dotted rectangle completely surrounds the field labels.**

   Every object you want to select must be *inside* the rubber band—it can't hang out the edge—so be sure you go far enough to the left. Figure 4-23 shows how it looks when you're done dragging, *before* you release the mouse button.

3. **Release the mouse button.**

   You should see all the field labels selected. This process is easier to do than to explain, so the best way to learn how is to try it.

Note: To be sure you got what you want, make sure every field label has its own selection handles (the little black squares on each corner). If you missed one, just hold down the Shift key and click it–this action adds it to your current selection. Now that you have all the labels selected, you can start formatting them en masse.

4. **Choose Format → Font → Verdana.**

   Poof! All the labels change fonts.

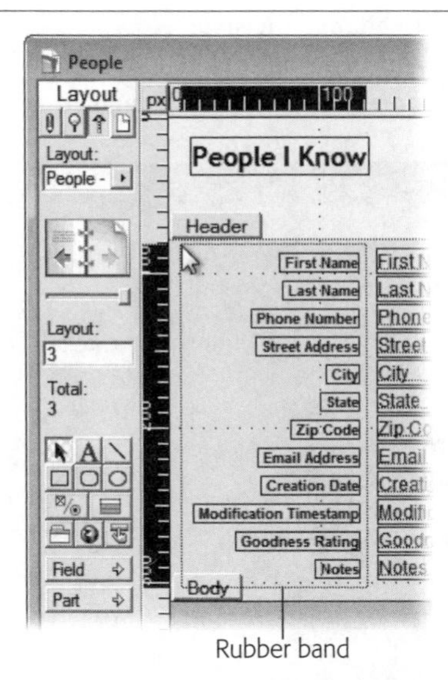

Figure 4-23: *You can use the rubber band technique to select several items at once. Just start on an empty spot on the layout and drag a rectangle around the objects you want to select. For more multiple selection tips, see the box below.*

5. **Choose Format → Size → 11 Point.**

   Double poof! All the labels change size.

Note: Since the *last* custom size you used was 11 point (when adding the "[Detail]" text on page 176), FileMaker now lists it at the bottom of the Format → Size menu. (If it isn't there, shame on you for not following directions! Only kidding. Simply choose Format → Size → Custom instead.)

POWER USERS' CLINIC

Selecting Lots of Objects

Selecting objects on a layout is such a common task that FileMaker gives you several ways to do it. You can always click an object to select it, but you can use any of the following methods as well:

If you want to select more than one object (so you can operate on them all at once), select the first object, and then press the Shift key and click each additional object. As you click, each object joins the selection. If you accidentally select an object, Shift-click it again to deselect it.

To select *everything* on the layout, choose Edit → Select All or press Control-A (Windows) or ⌘-A (Mac).

You can even select every object of a certain type (every field, for example). First select one object of the type you want. On Windows, hold down the Shift key and choose Edit → Select All. On Mac OS X, hold down the Option key and choose Edit → Select Same. FileMaker selects every object that is similar to the one you selected yourself.

If you have more than one object selected when you choose this command, FileMaker selects every object like any of the selected objects. For example, to select every field *and* every text object, select one field and one text object, and then choose this command.

Finally, you can easily select objects that are close together on the layout using the rubber band technique described on page 156.

See the box on page 160 for a few more commands that help when you work with lots of objects.

The labels were already bold, so you don't need to change the style. Now you have labels that look right, but their positions are all out of whack. That's OK, though, 'cause you're about to move them all anyway—after one more text-editing maneuver.

UP TO SPEED

Text Format Dialog Box Revisited

If you've read Chapter 2, you know that you can choose Format → Text to summon the Format Text dialog box, a one-stop shop for all your text-formatting needs. This handy window is fully accessible in Layout mode as well (the Text command is just a little lower down in the Format menu). From here, you can adjust the font, size, and style in one shot if you prefer. You can also change text color and paragraph settings, both of which work just as well for text objects in Layout mode as they do for field data in Browse mode.

For example, if you want to make the field labels bold, italic, red, 16-point Times New Roman, you can click the Format menu five separate times, choosing a different submenu each time. Or you can do the steps below. You get to decide which method to use. Ahhhh...choice.

1. Select the text object. As usual, you have to tell FileMaker *which* object to work with.
2. Choose Format → Text to open the Text Format dialog box.
3. From the Font pop-up menu, choose Times New Roman.
4. From the Size pop-up menu, choose 16 Point.
5. From the Color pop-up menu, pick a lovely shade of red.
6. Turn on the Bold and Italic checkboxes.

Editing existing text

If you compare the field labels you have now to those in Figure 4-21, you'll see you have a little more editing to do. The final layout has these field label changes:

- City, State, and Zip go away.
- Phone Number becomes Phone.
- Street Address becomes Address.
- Email Address becomes Email.
- Goodness Rating becomes Goodness.
- Creation Date becomes Created, and Modification Date becomes Modified.

Now you need to make these changes to *your* field labels.

First, get rid of the City, State, and Zip labels. Zapping them is a breeze: Select them all (using any of the methods described on the previous pages) and choose Edit → Clear or press the Delete or Backspace key. (If you're good with the mouse, you can use the rubber band trick (see page 156) to select them all, but it's probably just as easy to Shift-click each one.)

Now edit the remaining labels. Start with the Phone Number field:

1. **In the status area, double-click the text tool.**

   Your mouse pointer now has the typical text-editing I-beam shape. As an added bonus, the text tool is locked so you won't have to pick it again to fix the next field label.

2. **In the Phone Number label, double-click the word Number.**

   The text object turns back into an editable text box, with dotted outline and all.

3. **Press the Delete key twice.**

   The first delete removes the word Number. The second wipes away the blank space after Phone.

Note: When you're editing a text object like this, you're free to use the mouse or arrow keys to move about the object. It works just like entering text in a field in Browse mode. You can even apply fonts, sizes, and styles to individual letters or words inside a text object. For example, you could make the "e" in Phone bold (if you really wanted to).

---

4. **Press Enter.**

   The label is now selected, and it says Phone, just like it's supposed to.

Three more labels need fixing: Street Address, Email Address, and Goodness Rating. Repeat steps two through four above to make the necessary edits. (Don't forget that you're just changing the field *label* here, not the actual field name (as you did back on page 96). You can confirm this by looking inside the field in Layout mode, or by making a quick trip to the Manage Database window. You can even give the same field different labels on different layouts.)

Note: By almost every measure, a field label is just like any other text object. But the labels FileMaker creates for you have one hidden property that makes them special: When you change a field's name in the Manage Database window, its label automatically changes to match. As soon as you *edit* the text in a field label, though, this magical bond is broken. This break may be a good thing or a bad thing depending on your point of view. Some people edit their field labels manually so they can pick just the right name given the available space and the nature of the layout. Other people find that keeping their field labels and field names in sync helps them keep things straight in their heads. Thou mayest choose for thyself.

Figure 4-24 gives a quick sanity check. Your layout should look something like this.

Formatting Fields

Before you get to arranging the fields on the layout, you need to make one more adjustment. In the previous section, you formatted the labels—the text that identifies your fields onscreen at all times. FileMaker also lets you control how text appears when someone *types* into those fields later.

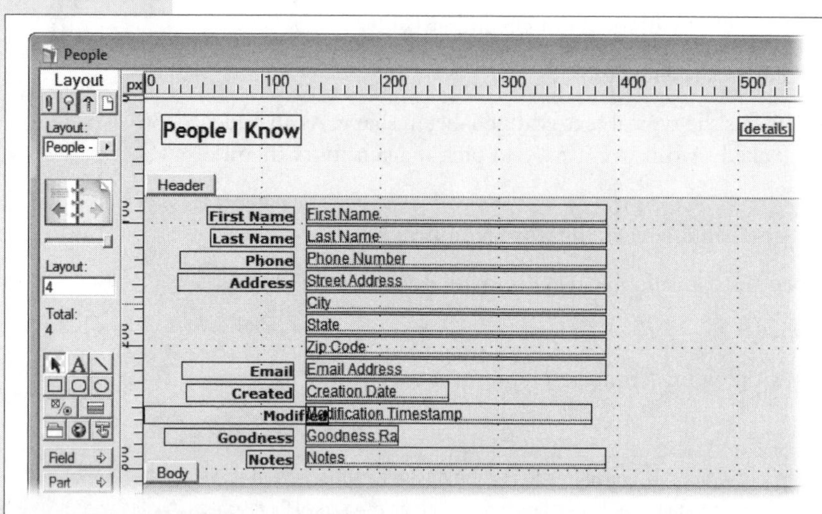

***Figure 4-24:** Here's how your layout should look (in Layout mode) after you've added header text, edited the text of the field labels, and formatted them with a new font, size, and style. The labels don't line up very well, but you'll fix that later.*

POWER USERS' CLINIC

Locking and Grouping

Sometimes an object just keeps getting in the way when you try to work with another one. For example, you might paste a large picture as the background of your layout. Every time you try to rubber band some objects, you end up moving this picture instead, since it fills all the otherwise empty space. To put this problem to rest once and for all, just lock the offending object. First, select the object or objects you want to lock. Then choose Arrange → Lock. Now you can't move, resize, or otherwise edit the object. If you need to do any of these things to it, just click it once, and then choose Arrange → Unlock to bring it back to normal.

On the other hand, if you find you're working with a particular set of objects very often, you can group them (Arrange → Group) to make them act as one. Once grouped, anything you do to one of them happens to them all. If you move one, they all follow. If you delete one, they all go away. And if you change any attributes—like font size—all of them change. The only thing you can do to an individual item that is part of a group is edit its text—the text tool can cut right through the group and let you edit an individual object. When you're ready to treat them as separate objects again, just select the group and choose Arrange → Ungroup.

Text formats

Formatting the text in fields works just like formatting field labels. The trick is to select the actual fields first. You want all your fields to be in 11-point Verdana. You could select each field one by one, or use the rubber band to select them all with one drag. But since you want to select *every* field on the layout, you can use the Select Same feature instead.

Just select one field (it doesn't matter which one). Then hold down the Shift key (Windows) or the Option key (Mac) and choose Edit → Select All (Windows) or Edit → Select Same (Mac). Although the menu command differs by platform, the effect is the same: All the fields are now selected.

Now that you have the fields selected, your first job is to adjust the text formatting—the way text will look when someone types in Browse mode. You've done this with text objects already (see page 155), and there's no difference here. Use the Format → Text command to bring up the Text Format dialog box, where you can choose 11-point Verdana.

Other field type formats

If you've worked with numbers in other programs, like other databases or a spreadsheet program, you know that number formatting can save lots of keystrokes and help you organize numbers so they're more legible. Likewise, entering in Date, Time, and Timestamp fields can have their challenges when you're trying to get the data to look a certain way. See page 246 for details on formatting these alternate field types.

Field Controls

A field is a field is a field. At least, that's what most people think. But FileMaker makes a distinction between the field in the table (where the actual data is stored) and the field on the layout, which is more correctly called a Field Control. Like the controls on the dashboard of your car, FileMaker controls are a method for inputting information into a field. In addition to plain old text fields for typing into, controls can be checkboxes, radio buttons, calendars or menus for fast and accurate data entry. Field controls have styles, borders, and behaviors that you can edit. This section gives you a taste of FileMaker's power, but complete coverage comes up in Chapter 6.

Note: When FileMaker experts get together around the water cooler, they use the terms *field* and *field control* interchangeably–even when referring to field controls on layouts. This book uses them interchangeably, too

Field/Control setup

Up to now, you've been learning about formatting the text, or the stuff that's in a field. But now, you'll see that the field control itself can be formatted with styles that have nothing to do with text. When FileMaker threw those first fields you defined out on the layout for you, it just made plain old fields, called Edit Boxes. But with Field/Control, you're in charge of how the field accepts information.

To choose a field type, first select one or more fields, and then choose Format → Field/Control → Setup. You can see the result in Figure 4-25. To see how it all works, you're going to turn your Goodness Rating field into a pop-up menu field and assign it a value list.

In the People database you've been working on so far, the Goodness Rating field works just like any other: It lets anyone using your database type any number into it, including things you don't want, like 21.785 or 4E27. You've already decided it should only take whole numbers between zero and five.

The perfect solution is to make the Goodness Rating field a pop-up menu showing the choices 0–5. That way, anyone using the database can immediately see what the expected options are and choose one with a swift flick of the mouse. By providing only acceptable choices, a pop-up menu ensures that the right kind of information ends up in the field—and makes data entry easier to boot.

1. **Click the Goodness Rating field to select it.**

   It grows selection handles.

2. **Choose Format → Field/Control → Setup.**

   You see the Field/Control Setup dialog box. (You can see it in Figure 4-25, too.)

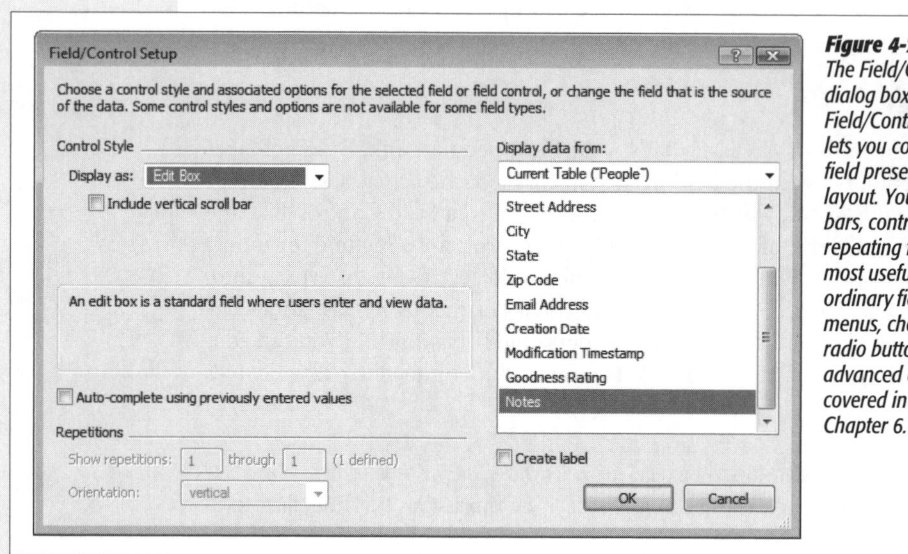

Figure 4-25: *The Field/Control Setup dialog box (Format → Field/Control → Setup) lets you control how a field presents itself on the layout. You can add scroll bars, control the display of repeating fields, and–most useful of all–turn ordinary fields into pop-up menus, checkboxes, or radio buttons. All of these advanced options are covered in detail in Chapter 6.*

3. **From the "Display as" pop-up menu, choose Pop-up Menu.**

   The "Include vertical scroll bar" checkbox disappears and a new pop-up menu takes its place.

4. **From the "Display values from" pop-up menu, choose Manage Value Lists.**

   The Manage Value Lists dialog box swings into view. The details of creating value lists are explained in Chapter 3; flip back to page 115 if you need a refresher.

5. **Create a new value list with the values 0, 1, 2, 3, 4, and 5. Click OK when you're done to close the Field Format box.**

   The Goodness Rating field now looks like a pop-up menu (a retro-80s pop-up menu, but a pop-up menu nonetheless). In Figure 4-26, you can see how it displays the value list you just created.

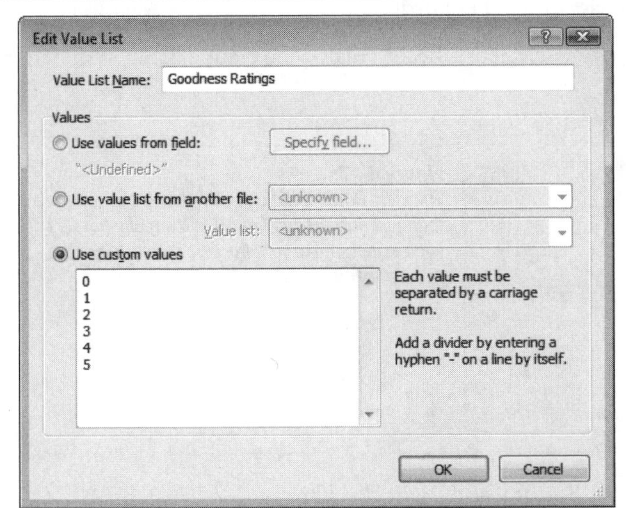

Figure 4-26: *A pop-up menu needs a value list to determine what choices it shows. Here, you're defining a value list called Goodness Ratings with values for zero through five. When you're done, click OK, and then OK again to return to the Field Format dialog box.*

While you're at it, the Notes field could use a scroll bar. (It could be a lot bigger too, and you'll learn how to do that shortly. For now, though, you'll just give it a scroll bar since you know it will hold lots of text.) To add a scroll bar, follow these steps:

1. **Select the Notes field.**

   Any time you make changes to a field control, you must select it first.

2. **Choose Format → Field/Control → Setup again.**

   The Field/Control Setup dialog box makes its triumphant return.

3. **Turn on "Include vertical scroll bar" and then click OK.**

   This option tells FileMaker to expect lots of text in this field. It will add a scroll bar to make *seeing that text easier.*

Field borders

Next up are the field *borders*. In Layout mode, your fields probably have black borders and dotted baselines, but in Browse mode, they're just floating bits of text. To give them a little more substance, you can put a true border around them, and then give them a nice engraved effect:

1. **Select all fields on the layout.**

   You can rubber band them, click them one by one, or use the Select Same feature.

2. **Press Shift and then click the Goodness Rating field, the Creation Date field, and the Modification Timestamp field.**

   These fields don't need the same formatting as all the others. By Shift-clicking, you tell FileMaker to deselect them.

3. **Choose Format → Field/Control → Borders.**

   The "Field Borders for selected objects" dialog box appears. It's shown in Figure 4-27.

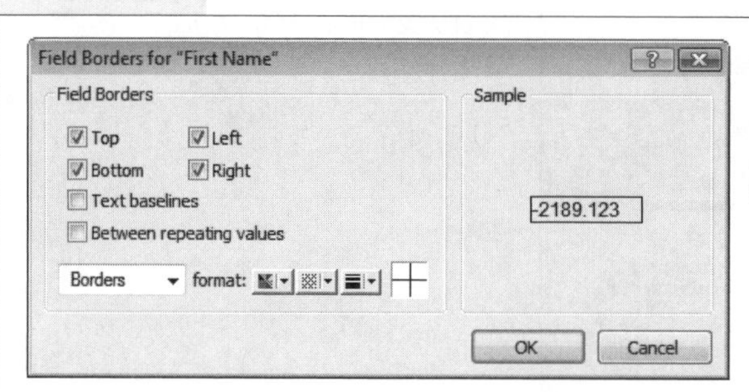

Figure 4-27: *The Field Borders dialog box lets you control more than just borders (go figure). If it's really borders you're after, make sure Borders is selected in the pop-up menu.*

4. **Turn on the Top, Left, Bottom, and Right checkboxes.**

   The Sample area shows how your field will look with borders applied to all four sides.

5. **Click OK.**

   The Field Borders dialog box goes away. You probably won't notice any change since FileMaker normally shows a thin border around fields in Layout mode, but your fields really do have borders now, even in Browse mode.

6. **In the status area, click the Fill Effects button** (it has two blue squares on it), **and choose Engraved.**

   FileMaker draws a beveled edge around each field. It also fills each field with white (you must have a fill color for the effects to work, so FileMaker adds one for you).

The fields now look a little more like…well…fields. But you've unwittingly created a new problem: The fields are now too short. When you added the engraved effect, FileMaker put an extra border around each field. This extra border uses up one pixel on each side, reducing the vertical space *inside* the field by two pixels. These few pixels make a difference—look at the City field, for example, whose "y" has lost its tail.

To remedy this problem, you need to make each field a little taller. But how much taller? Luckily, FileMaker knows just how tall a field needs to be, and it's ready to help you out. When you resize a field with the mouse, FileMaker won't let it get smaller than it needs to be to properly show one line of text in the selected font and size. You just need to manually resize the fields, letting FileMaker do its thing.

If you're feeling queasy at the prospect of resizing each of those fields manually, take heart. FileMaker has tools to make this sort of mass-resize job a snap. Here's how:

1. **Resize one of the fields so that it's just the right height.**

   The easiest way to do this is in two steps: First drag its lower-right handle straight down until it's obviously too large. Then drag the handle back up again. FileMaker stops it from getting smaller than the perfect height.

2. **Select every field by holding the Alt (Windows) or Option (Mac) key and then choosing Edit → Select All (Select Same on the Mac).**

   Now every field is selected, including the Goodness Rating field, which doesn't *need* to be resized.

3. **Shift-click the Goodness Rating field to deselect it.**

   You've got all the fields you want to resize; the tallest among them is the one with the correct height.

4. **Choose Arrange → Resize To → Largest Height.**

   FileMaker changes the height of every selected field control to the proper height.

   The options in Arrange → Resize To make it a snap to keep things clean and consistent on your layout.

You'll learn lots more about resizing, moving, and aligning objects in the next section.

Laying Out the Layout

You're finally ready to organize the fields on the layout. The goal of a layout is to present information in a clear and attractive manner—in this case, the details for the people in your database. Turn back to Figure 4-21 to remind yourself how this layout is supposed to look.

Right now, though, your window probably shows something of a mess. More like Figure 4-28, perhaps. To organize and beautify your layout, you need to move and resize your fields, and line things up, as described in this section.

Resizing objects

Turn on text boundaries (View → Show → Text Boundaries) and take a look at the labels you edited a few pages back. You see that some text objects are quite a bit longer than the text they contain. When you delete part of a label, the object itself doesn't get shorter. FileMaker doesn't let objects extend off the edge of a layout, so those long text boxes don't allow room to put the labels as far to the left as you want. You'll need to shorten them.

The First Name, Last Name, Phone Number, and Email Address fields are bigger than they need to be, too. You can easily fix them all at once. Select each object (Shift-click or use the rubber band), and then resize one of them using its handles (it doesn't matter which one you resize). When you finish, every selected field changes size to match the one you dragged. If the fields aren't the same size to begin with, choose Arrange → Resize To → Smallest Width after selecting them, and then use the resize handles.

UP TO SPEED

Formatting Different Field Types

Most people think of formatting as something you do to text—change the font, make it boldface, or whatever. That's also true in FileMaker when it comes to formatting *text*. But when you're talking about formatting *fields*, you begin by choosing the overall *style* of field you want in the first place. In FileMaker, that's called the *control style*, which is why the Field/Control Setup dialog box includes options like Pop-up Menu and Checkbox Set. There you can apply various options and settings depending on the basic field format.

Chapter 6 goes into great detail about how these different field formats work and how to choose options for them. Here's a brief rundown:

- **Edit Box** is the fancy term for a plain old entry field, like the ones that hold first and last names. You can type freely into this type of field.
- **Drop-down List** fields look just like Edit Box fields, but when you click or tab into one, it shows a list of choices below the field. You can either pick from the list, or click again and type something else. (The list of choices is defined by a value list, like those you created on page 162.)
- **Pop-up Menu** fields look and work like normal pop-up menus, forcing you to pick an item from a list. The Goodness Rating field in this chapter (see page 162) is an example.
- A **Checkbox Set** is a block of choices, each with a checkbox beside it. You can turn items off and on at will, just like normal checkboxes. When you turn more than one item on, the field value is set to both items, each on a line by itself.
- A **Radio Button Set** looks a lot like a Checkbox Set, except you can pick only one item at a time.
- A **Drop-down Calendar** makes entering proper dates drop-dead easy. FileMaker is really particular about the data it's willing to accept in a date field (it has to be a proper date after all). But if you attach a calendar to your date fields, you can just click on a date, and FileMaker pops it right into the field for you. It even circles today's date in the calendar for you, making finding it a breeze. (Bear in mind, though, that no matter which format you choose, anyone can still paste any data they want into a field, unless you use data validation, as described on page 111.)

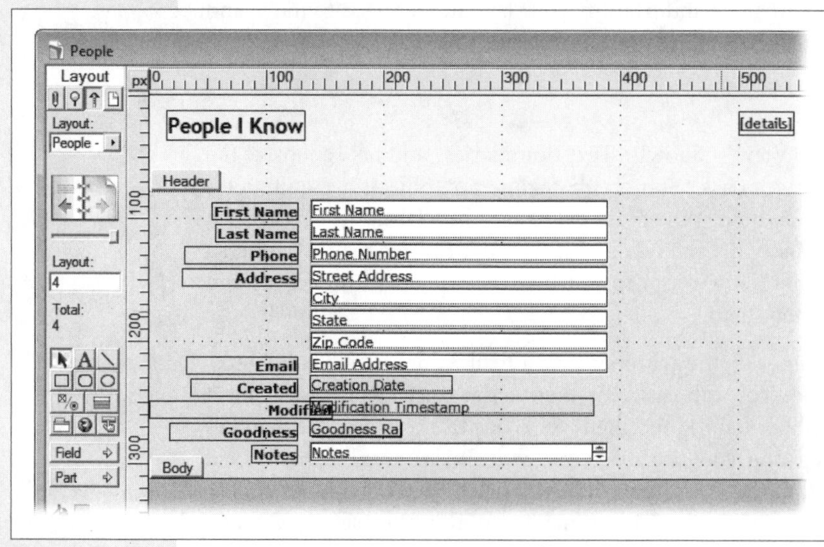

Figure 4-28: *Here's how your database looks now. The field and label formatting is in place, but the layout itself is a mess. Some fields are too big for the data they need to hold, others aren't big enough. And this layout needs some pizzazz. It's time to tackle field arrangement.*

Tip: Here's an old FileMaker trick to simplify this sort of text-object shortening task. For reasons known only to FileMaker Inc., FileMaker perfectly sizes a text object when you select the text and choose Format → Style → Underline or press Ctrl-Shift-U (⌘-Shift-U). When you turn the underline style back off, the object remains properly sized. Since this trick works even when you have several items selected (and since the command has a keyboard shortcut), it's by far the fastest and easiest way to clean up your labels. Just select them all, then turn underlining on and back off again.

While you're at it, make the Goodness Rating field narrower too. It can be very small since it shows only one digit. Finally, make the Notes field nice and tall so it can hold lots of notes. (You may need to make the Body part larger to make room. Just drag its part label down.)

POWER USERS' CLINIC

Super-Sizing

Dragging and the Arrange menu aren't the only ways to resize objects. If you're a numbers person, you can use the Object Info palette instead. Use the View → Object Info menu command to bring up this tiny window. It shows information about the selected object–namely, its position (how far the left, right, top, and bottom edges of the object are from the top-left corner of the layout) and its height and width.

But the power of the palette doesn't stop there. You can also type numbers into the palette, and the selected object will move or resize appropriately. If you have two similar objects on two different layouts, and you want to make sure they're the same width on both layouts, the Object Info palette is the easiest way:

1. Select the first object. Note its width in the Object Info palette.
2. Switch to the other layout.
3. Select the second object.
4. Type the same width in the Object Info palette.

When you're done, you can be absolutely certain both fields are the same width. Of course, you can also use this technique to set an object's height. You can even change an object's position and both dimensions in the same trip. If your memory is good, remember all four numbers. If you're middle-aged, write them down, because you'll have forgotten at least one of the numbers by the time you switch to the second layout.

The Object Info palette uses the same units you have your graphics rulers configured to use. But don't waste a trip to the Layout → Set Rulers menu just to change it. Instead, you can click the units displayed on the palette. As you click, FileMaker cycles between the supported unit types–inches, centimeters, and pixels; keep clicking until you find the one you want.

Aligning objects

Most of the field labels on the finished layout are right-aligned against an imaginary line running down the layout, as shown in Figure 4-29. But the Goodness Rating, Creation Date, and Modification Timestamp fields and their labels don't follow this rule. To get them out of the way, just move them all to the right of the rest of the fields for now.

The other field labels on your layout are probably lined up nicely along their right edges. If not, though, you can line them up easily. Select all the field labels that should be aligned, and then choose Arrange → Align → Right Edges. They leap to attention, all with their right edges in line with the text object that had been farthest to the right.

You can use this same command on the Goodness, Created, and Modified labels to get them aligned as well. Finally, move these three labels to the left so they sit properly next to their fields.

Note: If you have fields that are lined up vertically, but the spacing between them isn't even, use the Arrange → Distribute → Vertically command to make the spacing regular. There's also an Arrange → Distribute → Horizontally command to make your life a little bit easier.

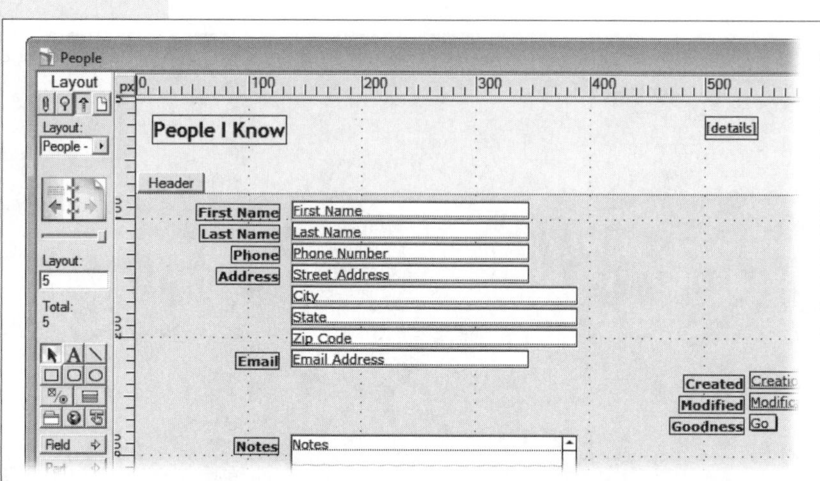

Figure 4-29: *There are two kinds of FileMaker layout designers: those who see imaginary lines and those who don't. Some people think a messy pile of fields and labels is just fine, but in most databases (and in this book), you'll see things lined up nicely.*

Moving objects

Now that the field labels are lined up, you can move them to their final resting place. Just select them all and then drag them a little to the left. Hold down the Shift key to make sure they don't drift up or down while you drag. When you Shift-drag objects, FileMaker makes sure they move only in *one* direction: up and down or left to right.

Note: You have to press the Shift key *after* you press the mouse button to start dragging. If you don't, FileMaker just sees a Shift-click, and deselects the object. Luckily, you can press the Shift key any time during a drag, and FileMaker will instantly snap the object to a perfect trajectory. You can even release Shift mid-drag if you decide you don't want constrained movement after all.

Using all the arrangement powers you now possess, it's time to line things up so the fields sit next to their labels. If you're using the Object Grids command (see the box on page 170) or you have very sharp eyes, you can probably just drag the fields next to their labels and get perfect alignment.

Tip: If you're having trouble getting perfect alignment, try this technique: Click a text object and keep the mouse button pressed, and FileMaker extends its baseline all the way across the layout in both directions. Since the field controls on the layout also have visible baselines (the dotted lines below their names), you can achieve perfect alignment as you drag by making sure the extended baseline from the text object you're dragging runs right through the field's baseline.

You can even check baseline alignment without moving the field. For instance, use the arrow keys to nudge all the text labels up or down a pixel, then click and hold one of the text labels to see if it lines up. If not, keep nudging until all the fields and labels are aligned.

The City, State, and Zip fields don't have labels of their own. Instead, they line up side by side under the Street Address field. Make the City field about half the width of the Street Address field. Then place the State field next to it, and make it wide enough to hold two letters. Finally, drop the Zip field in place next to the State field. Chances are you can't align the Zip field perfectly with the right edge of the Street Address field. If necessary, use the T-squares, the Object Size palette, and the arrow keys to bring things into alignment. Next, adjust the fields on the left side so that they're arranged in a pleasing way. Lastly, put the Goodness Rating, Created, and Modified fields and labels in the right spot, as shown in Figure 4-30.

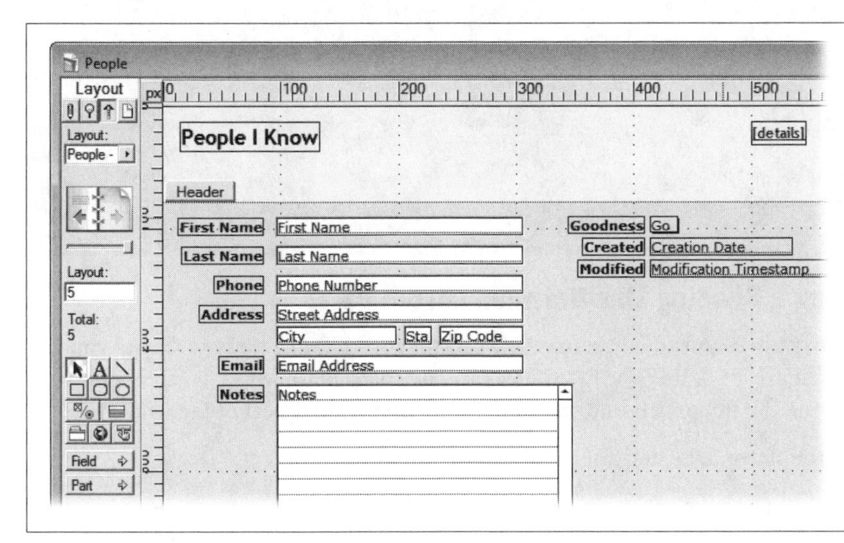

Figure 4-30: *Your database is starting to come together. The fields and labels are aligned, everything's in the right place, and you have the start of a decorative header.*

Adding images

The finished layout has a cute person icon next to the People I Know text. To add a picture to the layout, you can copy it from any other program, and then paste it directly on the layout. If the picture you want is in a file on your hard drive, use the Insert → Picture command instead. When you do, FileMaker will ask you to pick a picture file, and then insert it on the layout.

Once the picture is added to the layout, drag it into position in the header. If necessary, resize the header to accommodate it, and move the People I Know text object out of the way.

POWER USERS' CLINIC

Exercise Some Constraint

FileMaker developers often resize and move layout objects. Bearing this in mind, FileMaker has a few tricks up its sleeve to make things easier. You already know how to hold down the Shift key to constrain mouse movement (see page 168). Here are a few more goodies:

- Hold down the Control (Windows) or Option (Mac) key while creating or resizing a rectangle, rounded rectangle, or oval to make a perfect square or circle. When working with a line, this key makes it perfectly horizontal, perfectly vertical, or exactly 45° from one of these directions.
- With an object selected, press any of the arrow keys to move the object one pixel in the appropriate direction.
- Make a copy of an object by holding down the Ctrl (Windows) or Option (Mac) key while you drag it. Add the Shift key to the mix to make sure the object stays aligned with the original.
- Use the Duplicate command to create a new object that's 6 pixels to the right and 6 pixels below the original.
- Choose Align → Object Grids to turn another alignment feature on or off. Instead of moving with pixel-by-pixel freedom—which can make things nearly impossible to line up—things on the layout automatically align themselves to an invisible grid as you drag them. You can set the spacing of this grid by choosing Layout → Set Rulers and adjusting the "Grid spacing" value.

As if that weren't enough, you can use the Object Info palette introduced above to move objects as well. If the palette says the left edge of an object is two inches from the ruler origin, you can type *4* instead to move it farther into the layout.

Adding a Dividing Line Between Layout Parts

You may also want to add a line between the Header and Body parts. As you can see in Figure 4-30, this line helps break up the space in the window, and helps your eye locate the important information in the lower (Body) part of the window.

1. **In the status area, activate the line tool.**

   The mouse arrow changes to a crosshair.

2. **With the Shift key held down, drag a horizontal line about the desired width of the layout.**

   As you drag, a dotted line shows you what your line will look like. (Since you have the Shift key down, it sticks to a straight trajectory.) When you release the mouse button, the line appears.

3. **Drag the new line as far to the right as it will go, and place it as close to the Header part boundary as you can.**

   The Object Grids might prevent you from getting it right on the part boundary.

4. **Using the up or down arrow keys, nudge the line so that it covers the dotted part boundary perfectly.**

   The dotted part boundary line marks the *end* of the part above it, so this line is at the bottom of the header, not the top of the body.

5. **If necessary, resize the line so that it ends just a bit to the right of the [Detail] text object.**

   As you drag, hold the Shift key while you resize the line to make sure it stays perfectly horizontal. The line now marks the desired width for the layout.

Finishing Touches

You have only a few last touches to complete your layout. First, add a text object to hold the Goodness Rating key and type into it:

0 = Evil Empire

5 = Santa Claus

Tip: If you're like most people, your Font menu is half a mile long. It can be a real drag finding and selecting just the font you want. To save the trouble, duplicate one of your field labels and use that for the Goodness Rating key instead (Edit → Duplicate). Just edit it to show the correct text, and then change it to 9-point, align it to the left, and remove the bold style. You have an easier time duplicating an existing object than you do making a new one, since the duplicate picks up all the attributes you painstakingly set.

Next you need to add the box that holds the Goodness Rating, Creation Date, and Modification Time Stamp fields. Use the rectangle tool (see page 148) to create a rectangle about the right size. Set its line thickness to 1 pixel, choose a diagonal stripe line pattern, and then fill it with a light color of your choice. Because you added the rectangle *after* everything else, FileMaker shows it above the fields. When you move it into place, it hides the objects underneath. To move the rectangle behind the objects that you want to see, select it and choose Arrange → "Send to Back."

Using your personal design sensibilities, arrange the three fields inside the rectangle (resizing as necessary). You'll need to make the Modification Timestamp field narrower, for example, which is bigger than it needs to be anyway.

The Goodness Rating field should be filled with white, and it looks nicer with center-aligned text. Make these two changes now. (The Modification Timestamp and Creation Date fields can keep their transparent background since you won't be typing into them. You'll reserve the white fill for fields that expect data entry, as a little cue to the user.)

Finally, stretch the Notes field so its right edge lines up with the right edge of the rectangle. Compare your layout with the one in Figure 4-31 and make any additional adjustments that are needed.

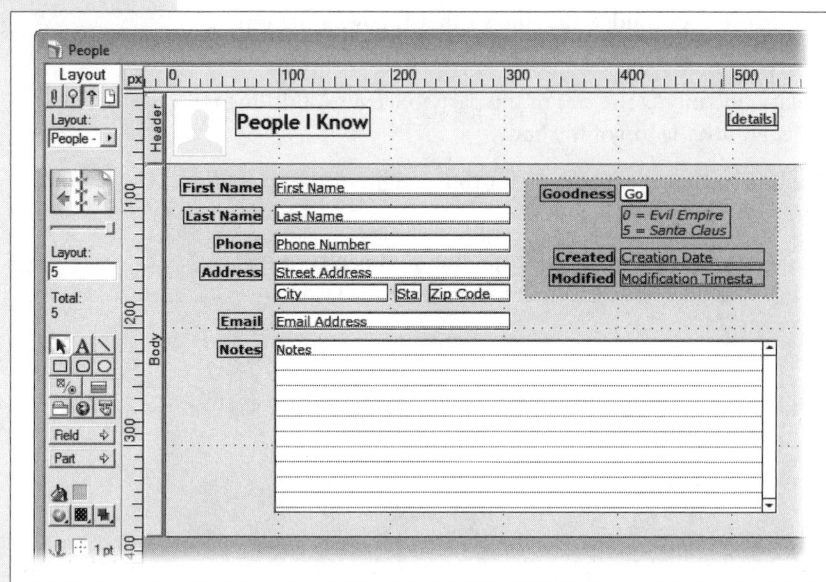

Figure 4-31: *Here's your finished layout. If yours doesn't look like this, make the necessary adjustments (or wear your distinctiveness as a badge of honor).*

You're ready to switch to Browse mode. When you do, FileMaker asks if you'd like to save your changes. Click Save. Now you see your new layout in action.

Autoresize

If you have a larger screen, chances are you want to take advantage of it. In Browse mode, try making the database window bigger. You'll quickly discover that FileMaker doesn't have the same idea you do about good use of screen real estate. Figure 4-32 shows what you get.

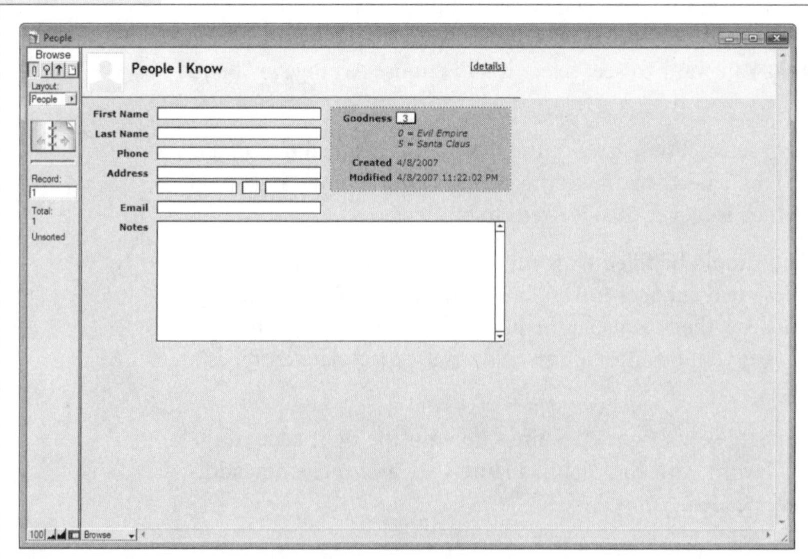

Figure 4-32: *Out of the box, FileMaker keeps the contents of that window the same size no matter how big you make the database window. Unhelpfully, the window's resize handles don't give you more room to view the contents. But fear not—you can tell FileMaker how to stretch and move things when you resize a window.*

Truth be told, FileMaker knows a great deal about how to fill up a window. But it needs a few hints from you before it can put all that power to work. You have to tell it which objects should move, which should stay put, and which ones should grow. With a few clicks in the now-familiar Object Info palette, you can make this layout perfectly at home on a big screen or a tiny one.

Anchors

Out of the box, every object on a FileMaker layout stays in exactly the same place no matter the size of the window. To change these settings, you use the Object Info palette. Chances are you've noticed the new anchor checkboxes in this window, but you can refresh your memory by peeking at Figure 4-33.

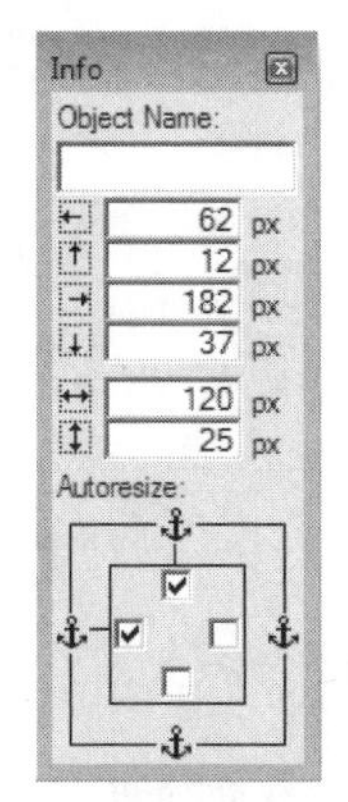

Figure 4-33:
The bottom half of the Object Info palette is devoted to the Autoresize settings. The four checkboxes tell FileMaker to anchor the object to the corresponding side of the window (notice the little anchor icons). Right now, all the objects on your layout are anchored at the top and left. In other words, their distance from the top and left edges of the window never changes, even as the window gets bigger.

To change how an object moves when the window is resized, you simply turn on and off the various checkboxes. As Figure 4-34 shows, FileMaker objects start out life with the top and left anchors in the Object Info palette turned on. Turning on one of these checkboxes causes the corresponding edge of the object to hold onto that edge of the window. If you want, you can make an object cling to the right edge of a window instead. Or the bottom edge. Or both (Figure 4-35).

You might think that you could throw FileMaker for a serious loop by anchoring an object to the left *and* the right (or the top and bottom). In fact, FileMaker is one step ahead of you: If you do this, it stretches the object, making it as big as necessary to keep both sides anchored. Figure 4-36 shows just such a setup.

As the various figures here show, which checkbox you turn on has a major impact on the position of the objects. By mixing and matching, you can make objects that stay in the top-right corner, move down but not right, grow in height *and* width, or a dozen other possibilities. But there's one more possibility that may not jump out at you—turning off *all* anchor checkboxes. In fact, this option is useful in its own right, as Figure 4-37 shows.

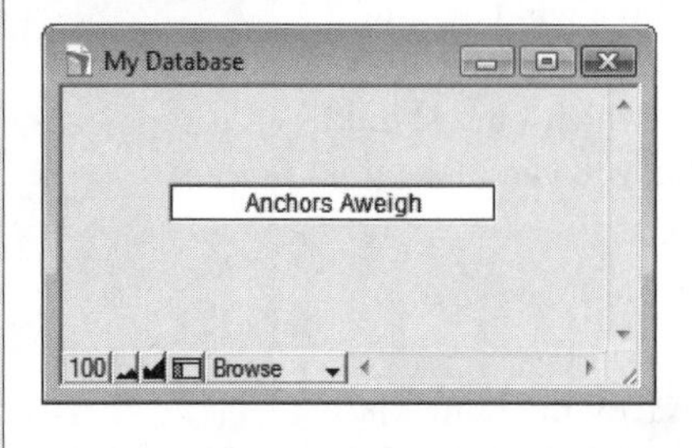

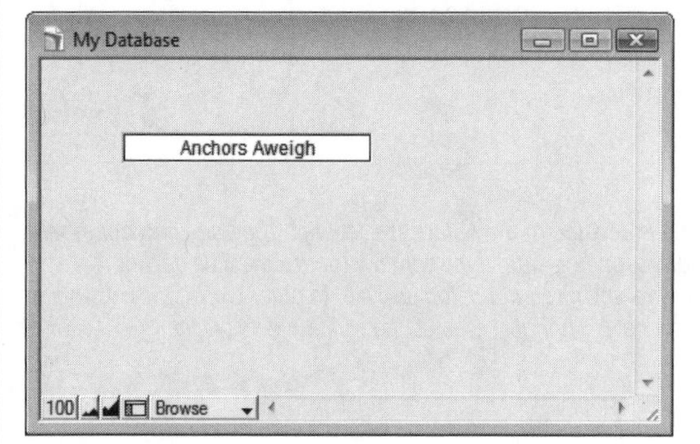

Figure 4-34:
Top: The one field on this layout is anchored to the top and left of the window (according to its factory settings in the Object Info palette).

Bottom: When you make the window larger, FileMaker keeps the top edge of the object the same distance from the top of the window. The left edge holds its place compared to the left side of the window as well.

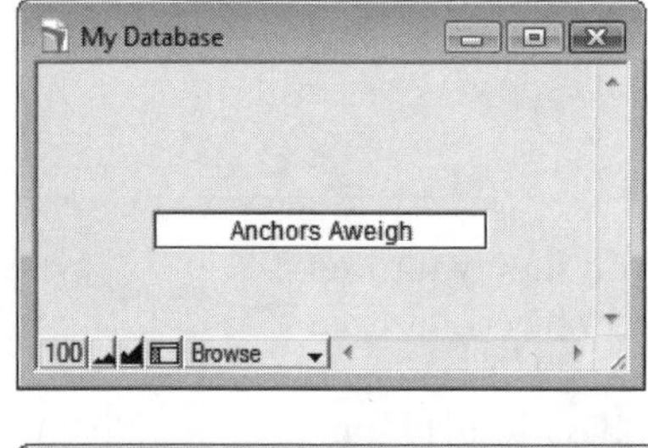

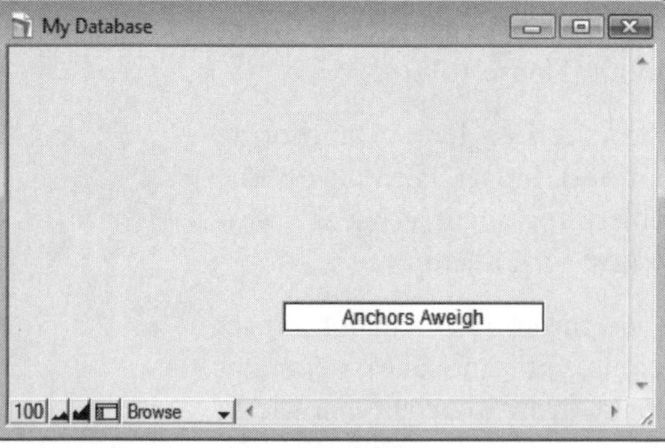

Figure 4-35:
Top: This time the same object as in Figure 4-34 is anchored on the bottom and right instead.

Bottom: Enlarging the window shows a very different result. FileMaker moves the object down and to the right to ensure that it keeps a constant distance from its anchored edges.

An unanchored object splits the difference: If the window gets 100 pixels wider, the object moves 50 pixels. The net effect is that the object stays in the same place relative to the overall size. If it was a third of the way down, and half way over, it will

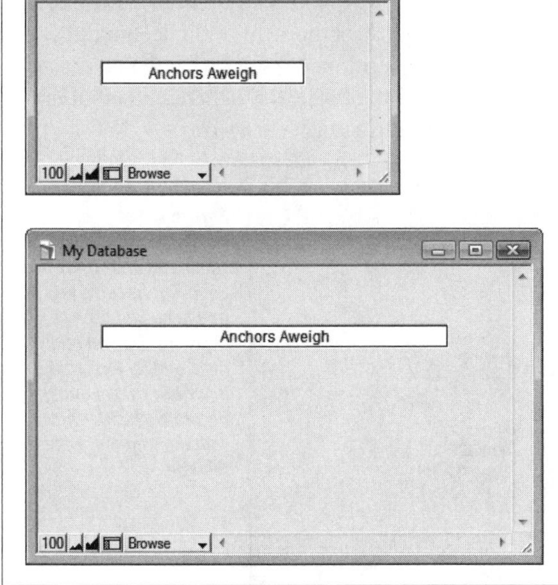

Figure 4-36:
Top: What if you anchor an object on two opposing sides? The field is now anchored on the top, left, and right.

Bottom: Rather than throw its hands up in despair, FileMaker bends to your will. It keeps the edges anchored by making the field bigger.

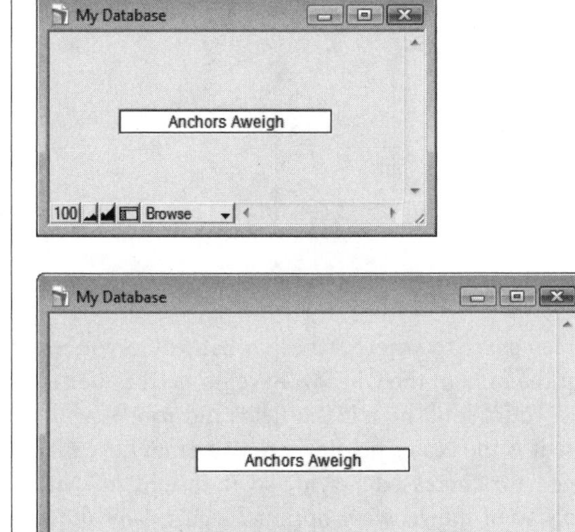

Figure 4-37:
Top: There's so much you can do with the Object Info palette's anchor checkboxes, you might forget you can turn them off altogether. In this window, the field has no anchors at all. Notice that it's positioned right in the middle of the layout.

Bottom: When the window gets bigger, FileMaker keeps the relative position of the object the same. Since it was in the middle before, it stays in the middle of the bigger window.

stay that way. Of course, you can anchor an object, for example, on the top or bottom, but not on the left or right. Such an object will float side to side, keeping its relative position, but will stay anchored if the window gets taller.

Making Autoresize work for your layout

To make your layout look great at any window size, you need to set the anchors carefully for each object. Before you start clicking, take a moment to think about how you want the layout to resize. When making this decision, consider what would make the layout better if you had more screen real estate to devote to it—there's no point in bigger for bigger's sake. Figure 4-38 shows an example of what *not* to do.

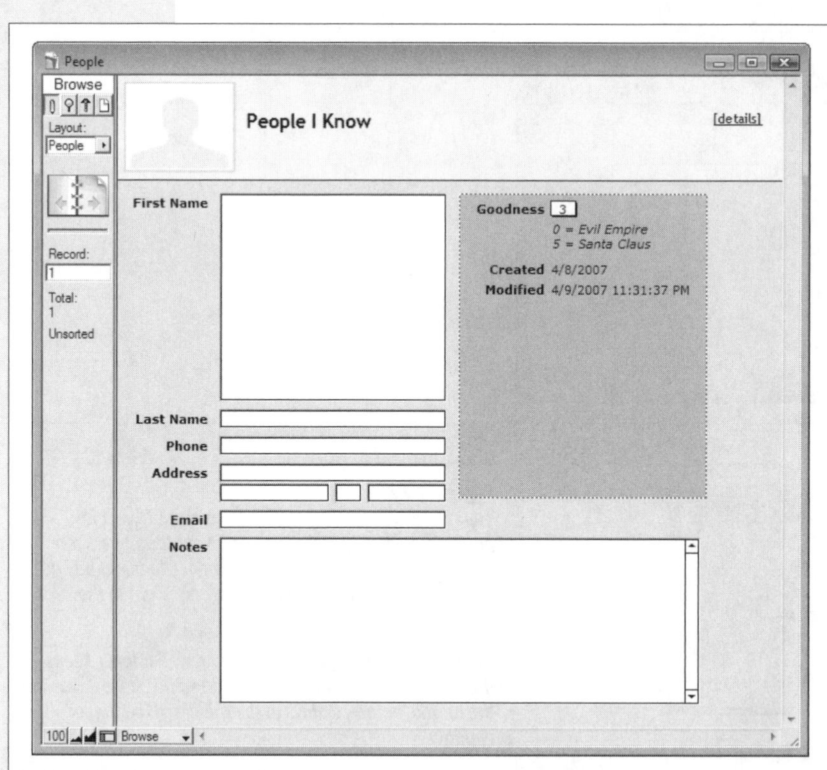

***Figure 4-38:** FileMaker puts you in complete control of resize behavior. As such, you're free to make bad decisions. Do you really need a taller First Name field? Is it critical that the decorative header grows with the window? Didn't think so.*

If you decide to devote more screen space to your database, what would you use it for? First, the fields that make up the bulk of the window have no need to be taller, but if the window gets wider, it would look nice if the fields did too. If you get more height, the best place to use it is the Notes field, where you often have lots of text. Everything else has no need for increased height, so it should just move appropriately to keep out of the way of the growing options. Figure 4-39 shows a better resize configuration.

Here's how to make your layout resize attractively, like the one in Figure 4-39:

1. **Open the People database and switch to Layout mode. Select the "[details]" text on the right side of the header.**

   You want this object to stick to the right edge of the window.

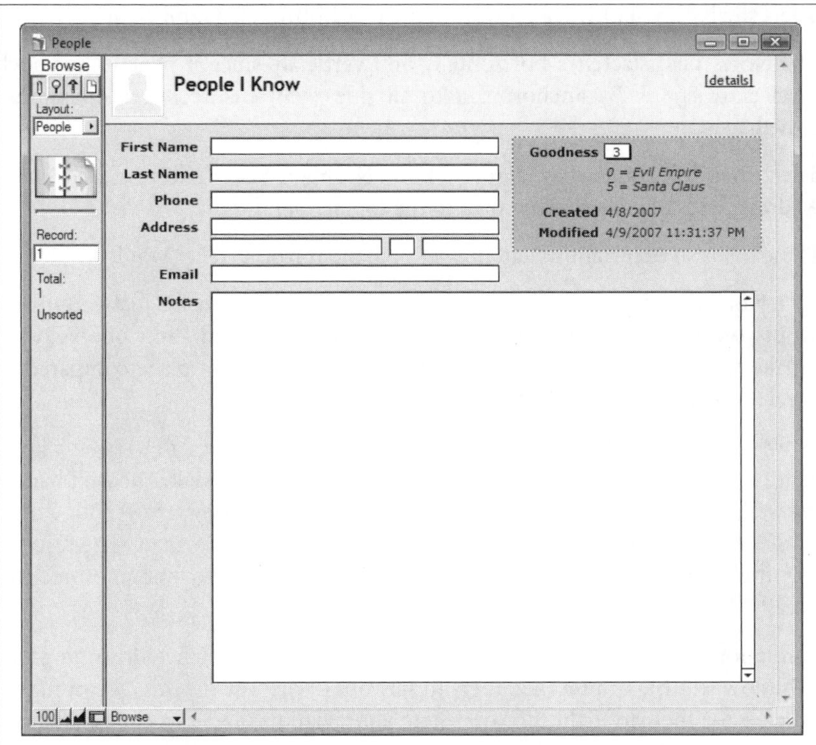

Figure 4-39: *In this version of the layout, a bigger window actually yields some improvement. The Notes field is bigger. Most of the other fields are wider. And the less size-critical elements move as appropriate to stay out of the way and preserve the overall look of the layout.*

2. **In the Object Info palette (View → Object Info), turn on the right anchor checkbox and turn off the left anchor checkbox. Keep the top anchor checkbox turned on and the bottom anchor checkbox turned off.**

   These settings tell FileMaker to keep the object in the top-right corner no matter the window size.

3. **Using the rubber band technique (see page 156), select the Goodness Rating field, the Created Date field, the Modification Timestamp field, all the associated text labels, and the box around them all.**

   All these elements live in a box in the top-right corner of the body. You want them all to move together, so you'll set their anchors in one shot.

4. **Use the checkboxes in the Object Info palette to anchor these selected elements to the top and right.**

   Now these elements stick to the top-right corner.

5. **Select the line between the body and header and anchor it to the top, left, and right.**

   This way, the line holds its position vertically but stretches horizontally to fill the window, no matter its size.

6. **Select the Notes field and anchor it to the top, bottom, left, and right.**

   The Notes field stretches horizontally and vertically since it benefits so much from extra space. By anchoring it to all sides, you ensure it gets maximum growth.

7. **Select the First Name, Last Name, Phone Number, Street Address, and Email Address fields and anchor them all to the top, left, and right.**

   These fields stretch right to left, but get no benefit from a taller window.

If you try out your layout in Browse mode now, you'll see that it's just about perfect. But you haven't done anything with the City, State, and Zip Code fields. If you make the window wider, these fields begin to look out of place compared to the Street Address field, which stretches with the window.

But how do you make these fields stretch as well? If you set them all to stretch horizontally (by anchoring to the left and right), you'll see that FileMaker doesn't handle it very well. Each field grows one pixel for each pixel the window grows. But a one-pixel increase in window width only leaves room for *one* field to grow. The result is that as the window gets wider, the fields begin to bump into one another, and eventually they drastically overlap.

In a situation like this, you have to choose *one* object to stretch (consuming any new window width), and set the others to stay out of the way. In this case, it makes most sense for the City field to grow. State abbreviations and Zip codes, after all, have a consistent width.

1. **Anchor the City field on the top, left, and right.**

   This field does the growing.

2. **Anchor the State and Zip Code fields to the top and right.**

   Since these fields are to the right of the City field, they stick to the right to stay out of the way.

Give your layout a shot in Browse mode now. If you followed the steps above, it should have much better resize behavior.

Keeping it small

Now your layout looks great when the window gets bigger. What about if you make the window *smaller*? Try it and you'll see that you can only go so far. Once the objects get as small as they are on the layout itself in Layout mode, FileMaker stops shrinking and moving things. Instead, the window gains some scroll bars and the layout gets cut off.

This points out an important Autoresize consideration: The size you make things in Layout mode sets the *minimum size* for the layout itself. If you're trying to ensure maximum flexibility, you should design your layouts as small as possible.

Your People database could probably be perfectly usable at a smaller size. If that's your goal, using the powers you've learned in this chapter, make the layout look like Figure 4-40.

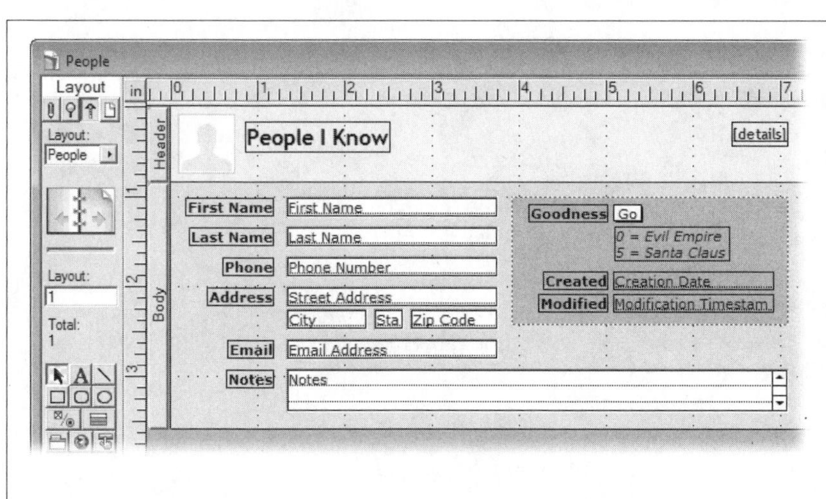

Figure 4-40: *Honey, I shrunk the layout! If you view this version of the layout in Browse mode, it will look exactly the same as before. That's because FileMaker scales it to fit your window size. But since you've made everything smaller in Layout mode, FileMaker lets the layout get smaller along with the Browse mode window before it begins to scroll. Therefore, when designing a layout for maximum flexibility, design it as small as possible.*

Wrapping up

Phew! That felt like a lot of work. Designing a FileMaker layout is a very visual process. That's really good news since it makes the process pretty *obvious* once you learn the tools. This chapter may make it seem laborious, but making a layout like this will quickly become second nature—you'll be able to crank one out in just a few minutes.

UP TO SPEED

Set the Width

FileMaker objects have four anchors, but the right anchor poses a particular challenge. How does FileMaker know where the right edge of your layout is? The top and left edges of the layout are well defined by the edges of the window itself. And you tell FileMaker exactly where the bottom is by positioning the bottommost part. But nothing on the screen tells FileMaker where you want the right edge of the window.

Suppose you have a field that's anchored on the right. When you're in Layout mode, you have 111 inches of space to its right. If you switch to Browse mode, FileMaker can't leave all that blank space there. So it assumes you want your layout to end at the right edge of the rightmost element. If the right-anchored field is this rightmost object, then it bumps right against the edge of the window. More often than not, though, you don't want your fields actually touching the window's border because it looks cramped. To fix the problem, you have to use some layout object to set the width.

In the People database, the line separating the body and header serves this purpose. No object is as far to the right as this line, so it sets the width. No matter how you size the window, in Browse mode this line touches the edge of the screen.

Any layout you create for onscreen use will probably need some object to set the width. Here are some options:

- Like the People database, use a line the full width of the layout. It doesn't have to be black, or only one pixel tall. A thicker colored line would look better on some layouts, and would do the job just as well.
- Instead of a background fill for the body or the header, place a colored rectangle on the layout and use it to set the width. Anchor it to the right and left, and it always fills the window, just like a colored part.
- Use a graphic like a company logo with a little built-in space on the right edge, and anchor it to the right.
- If all else fails, make a vertical line, place it on the layout where you want the right edge to be, and make it invisible (that is, give it a line thickness of None). A method that uses an invisible object is a last resort, because you may forget the object is there (and not understand why your layout is acting the way it does). But if your layout design is too Spartan for obvious lines and rectangles, an invisible line may be the only visually acceptable way.

CHAPTER

5

Creating Layouts

The last chapter introduced a lot of layout concepts, but you worked on only one layout. Most databases use many layouts, each designed for a different task. Your People database has a great detail layout, but what else could it use? For starters, a neatly arranged list of people would be nice. And how about a way to print mailing labels? You probably have some ideas about what *you'd* like your database to do, and FileMaker itself has some ideas of its own to help you along.

In this chapter, you'll learn the two main ways of designing and implementing your own layouts in FileMaker. You can create a unique new layout from scratch, in case you want to print all your worldly information on index cards (you know who you are). Or, if your needs are more down-to-earth, you can let a layout assistant save you some time. Just answer a few questions, and the assistant plugs your answers into standard forms like mailing labels. You'll also learn about special FileMaker layouts called *reports*, which sort, filter, or summarize your data before presenting it.

The Lowdown on Layouts

Although you can create an infinite variety of layouts in FileMaker, they all boil down to a few basic types. You get a chance to try each of them as you proceed through this chapter. Here's a brief overview of each.

Standard Form

The "Standard form" choice creates a layout just like the one FileMaker creates automatically when you start your database—a simple detail layout (see page 100). This time, though, you get to decide which fields to include. You also have some control over the fonts and colors. FileMaker calls these design controls "themes."

Columnar List/Report

If you want to show lots of records on the screen or page at one time, choose "Columnar list/report" instead. You still get to pick which fields to include and what theme to use, but FileMaker sets up the new layout as a list of records with one column per field, as shown in Figure 5-1.

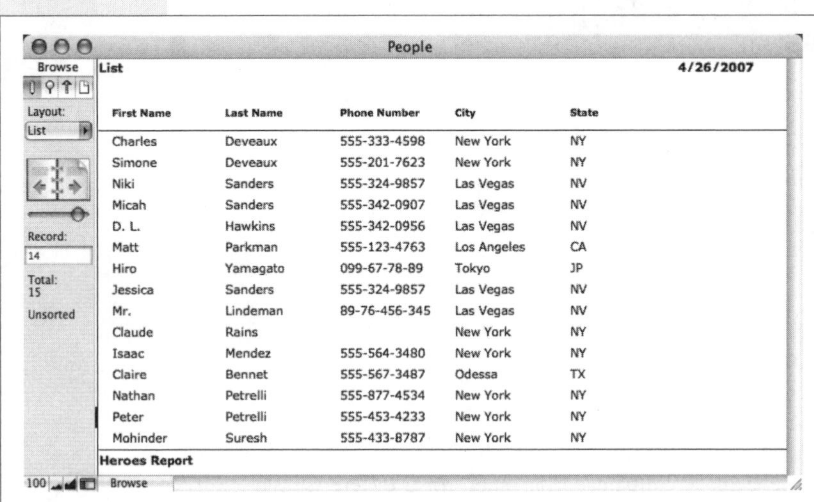

Figure 5-1: *This "Columnar list/ report" layout shows several people at a time in a space-efficient form. FileMaker plugs in header and footer data, plus column headings automatically when you create the layout. (You'll find out how to adjust all these settings on page 204.)*

Table View

When you select "Table view," FileMaker creates a layout much like "Standard form," but the layout is set to table view automatically. Actually, the pros (yourself included) know that you can choose View → "View as Table" in Browse mode to see *any* layout in table view (see page 44), so you rarely need to create a separate layout of this type. But if you're new to this whole database thing and want a layout that looks and acts like the spreadsheets you're accustomed to, the table view layout is your fastest way there.

Labels or Vertical Labels

If you ever need to print a sheet of peel-and-stick labels from your database—to make nametags for every attendee to your conference, or address labels for all those follow-up letters—the Labels layout type is your best friend (it's shown in Figure 5-2). FileMaker is smart enough to know how to set up a layout for any of the standard Avery label types. You just pick your type, and FileMaker does all the work. If you're not using Avery labels, you can plug in your own measurements.

Note: The "Vertical labels" type applies only to people with Asian language text in their database. This type rotates this kind of text to create *vertical* text labels.

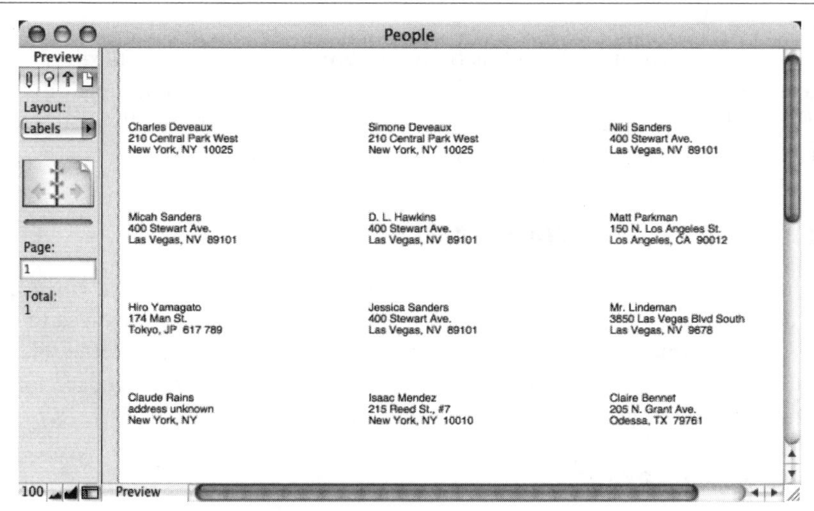

***Figure 5-2:** When you create a Labels layout, you can easily decide how all the field data mixes together to display as you want it. In this example, the First Name and Last Name fields are on the first line, with a single space between them. On the third line, City, State, and Zip Code fields have been combined appropriately.*

Envelope

If you'd rather print right on the envelope than stick a label on it, use the Envelope layout type. FileMaker creates a layout specially designed to print on a Number 10 size envelope (see Figure 5-3). You can even customize it with your company's logo and return address.

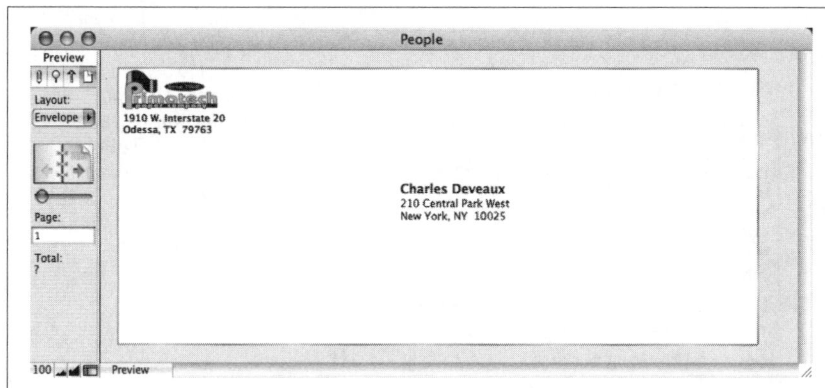

***Figure 5-3:** You can address envelopes in a heartbeat to everyone with a layout like this one. Just find the people you want, load a stack of envelopes in your printer, and print them out.*

Since every printer handles envelopes a little differently, the layout needs a little adjusting to print perfectly. Luckily, it's almost always a cinch to put things right. You can usually just delete the Header part from the layout. On more persnickety printers, you may have to leave the header in place, and adjust its height. Getting things lined up always involves a few test prints, but once you've got it working, you never have to fuss with it again. Well, until you get a new printer.

Blank Layout

The last type, called Blank layout, is both the simplest and the most flexible. You get a layout with a small header and footer, and a big body. It has nothing on it at all. If you like setting things up by hand, or your layout doesn't rightly match *any* of the types above, drawing a blank may be your best choice.

Creating a Layout from Scratch

FileMaker's built-in layout types are nice for quick-and-dirty work, but if you want your database to look great *and* work exactly the way you say, you may need to do some heavy customization. In fact, you'll often find it easier to start with a blank layout and add exactly what you need than to try to slice'n'dice a standard form into the avant-garde arrangement you have in mind.

Adding a New Layout

However they may end up, all new layouts start the same way. Open a database, switch to Layout mode, and choose Layout → New Layout/Report. You see the window shown in Figure 5-4—the New Layout/Report dialog box.

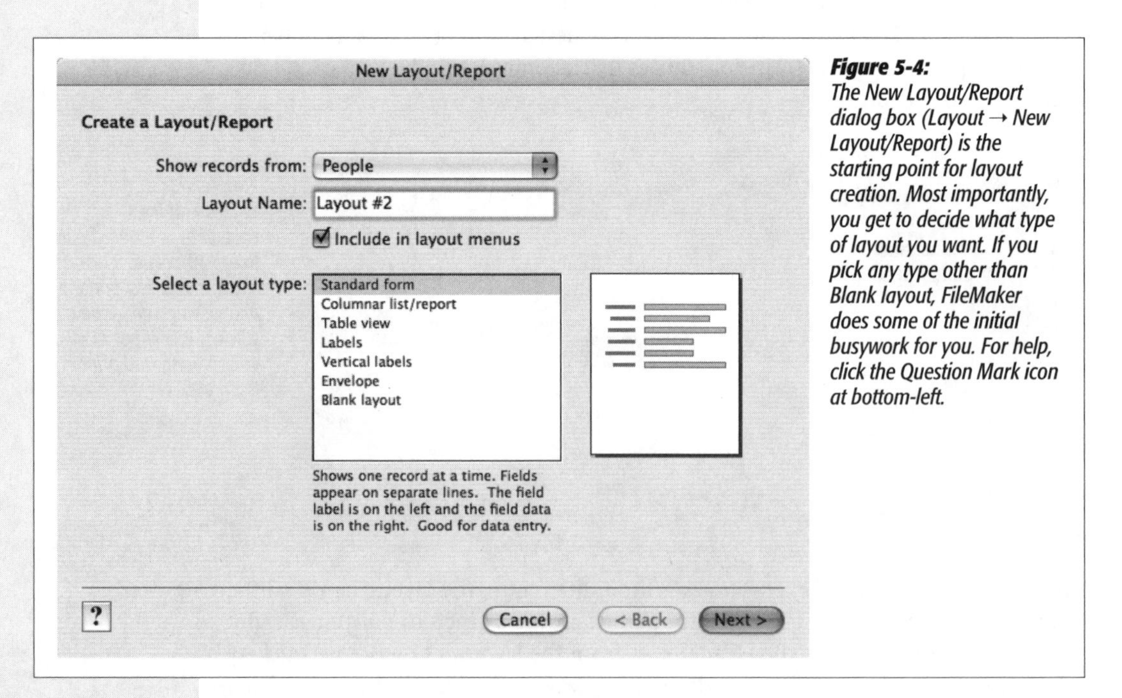

Figure 5-4: *The New Layout/Report dialog box (Layout → New Layout/Report) is the starting point for layout creation. Most importantly, you get to decide what type of layout you want. If you pick any type other than Blank layout, FileMaker does some of the initial busywork for you. For help, click the Question Mark icon at bottom-left.*

Note: As its name suggests, you'll see this dialog box again when you learn how to create reports, on page 202.

In this box, you tell FileMaker a few basic facts about the new layout you have in mind. (You can always tweak these settings later.) From top to bottom, here's how it works:

- **Show records from.** For now, you can just ignore this pop-up menu. (It lets you choose a table, but you have only one table so far.)
- **Layout Name.** Enter a name for your layout here. You can use any name you want, but you have to keep it to 100 characters or less.
- **Include in Layout menu.** Use this checkbox to tell FileMaker whether or not your new layout shows up in the status area's Layout pop-up menu. Most new developers turn on this option for every layout, to make sure they can always find their work. As your databases get more advanced, you may have special layouts that you want people to access only under certain circumstances. When you get that fancy, you can turn this checkbox off so folks can't switch to the layout any time they want.

Note: Every layout shows in the Layout pop-up menu when you're in Layout mode. This checkbox controls what shows up when you're in other modes.

Right now, the most important decision you make in this window is the choice of items in the "Select a layout type" list. FileMaker asks you questions specific to the type of layout you ask for, and then creates the layout based on your answer. When you select a layout type, FileMaker shows a little graphic mock-up of what this kind of layout looks like, just to the right of the list.

To get a feel for how it works, you'll create a layout in the People database like the one shown in Figure 5-5. Because this layout doesn't match any of the canned layout types in the New Layout/Report window, you'll start with a blank layout and build everything by hand. The goal is to see several people at once, so you'll tailor it with list view in mind.

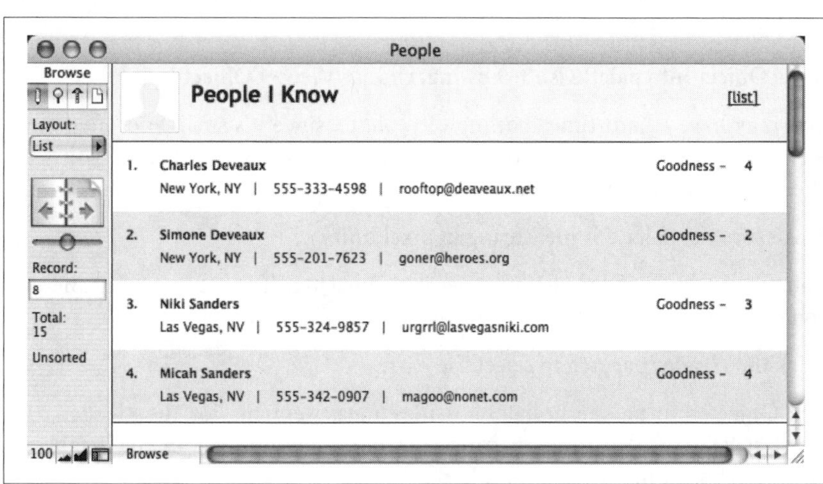

Figure 5-5: *The new list layout shows some information about a lot of people. As in all good list layouts, you can scroll through the records in the found set. Unlike your everyday, ordinary list, though, this layout doesn't have a strict columnar design.*

First, create the layout:

1. **Open the People database (see page 11 for download instructions). In Layout mode, choose Layout → New Layout/Report.**

   The New Layout/Report window pops up.

2. **In the Layout Name box, type a fitting name, like *List*. Then, from the "Select a layout type" list, choose "Blank layout."**

   The Next button changes to Finish, since you don't have any more choices for a blank layout.

3. **Click Finish.**

   FileMaker returns you to your database, and shows you the new blank layout.

Set Up the Header

This layout needs a header almost exactly like the one on the People layout. Unfortunately, you can't copy and paste the Header part (see page 132) itself, but you *can* copy everything on the header, and paste it on this new layout.

Before you do, you need to make this header the same size as the other so everything fits properly. As with many things in FileMaker, you have at least two good ways to perform this task. Which one you use depends entirely on your personal taste.

Matching part sizes with the Object Info palette

If you're a numbers person, this method is for you. Using the Object Info palette (see Figure 4-33), you can resize or reposition any layout object with pixel-perfect precision. To learn how to tackle it, you first check the exact size of the Header part on the People layout, and then adjust the new header so its size matches.

1. **Switch to the People layout.**

   You can switch using the Layout pop-up menu, or simply by clicking the left-hand page on the Book icon.

2. **If the Object Info palette isn't showing, choose View → Object Info.**

   You may have a hard time spotting the palette, since it's small and often lands way at the bottom-right of your screen. You know it's out there if you see a checkmark next to Object Info in the View menu.

3. **Make sure the palette is measuring in pixel units.**

   You should see "px" by each number in the palette. If you don't, click the unit you do see repeatedly until "px" shows.

4. **Click the Header part tag to select the part.**

   The Object Info palette updates to show measurements for the Header part. The last field—with a double arrow pointing up and down—is the height. Jot down the height number you see there.

5. **Switch to the new list layout, and then select the header by clicking its tag.**

   The Object Info palette now measures this part.

6. **Type the number you got in step 5 into the Height field on the Object Info palette, and then press Enter.**

   The part doesn't move while you type; you have to press Enter to see your change take effect. When you do, the Header part resizes and now perfectly matches the header on the People layout.

If you prefer less typing and more mousing, you can use the T-squares instead.

Matching part sizes with the T-squares

In the last chapter, you learned about the T-squares (see page 141). These handy liner-uppers don't just help you keep objects on the layout straight. They can also help you make sure parts and objects are in the same place on *different* layouts. Start on the People layout, and then follow these steps:

1. **If the T-squares aren't showing, choose View → T-Squares.**

   The T-square lines appear.

Note: On a busy layout, the T-squares can be hard to spot. If you know they're showing, but you can't *find* them, just turn them off and then back on. When you do, they reappear smack-dab in the center of the layout.

---

2. **Position the horizontal T-square between the header and the body.**

   The T-square floats above everything else on a layout, so it covers the dotted part boundary line perfectly. If you add a black line between your header and body, you may not see the boundary. Just put the T-square over your line instead.

Note: If you're having trouble getting the lines to match perfectly, the Object Grids may be holding you back. Choose Align → Object Grids to tell FileMaker to let you move the T-squares exactly where you want them.

---

3. **Switch to the new list layout, and then drag the Header part tag into the right place, using the T-square as a guide.**

   Since T-squares stay in the same spot as you switch layouts, you can rest assured your new header is just the right size.

Now that the header is the right size, you can fill it with the necessary objects. You could drag objects into the header manually, just as you did in the last chapter when you built the People layout. But you've already done that work once. Why not take advantage of it here as well? You can easily reuse these items: Copy and paste them from the People layout. You use copy and paste *a lot* when you design layouts.

1. **Switch back to the People layout. Select the graphic, "People I Know" text, and "[details]" text.**

   You can Shift-click or use the rubber band to select both objects. If you have a horizontal line on your layout, select it, too.

2. **Choose Edit → Copy.**

   Nothing changes on the screen, but FileMaker copies the objects to your operating system's clipboard.

3. **Switch back to the list layout, and then choose Edit → Paste.**

   The objects appear on the new layout, probably in the wrong place.

4. **Drag the objects (as a group) into their proper place in the header.**

   Since they're all selected, if you drag one object, the others follow.

Note: To give your database that professional touch (or if you're just a stickler for details), you can use the T-squares or the Object Info palette to be sure everything's in the same place on both layouts. If you do, just check *one* of the objects. Since they were copied, pasted, and moved as a group, if one is in place, the others are too.

Adding the finishing touches

Your Header part is nearly complete. To finish it, give it a colored fill (see page 150). Finally, since you're not making a detail layout, it probably shouldn't say "[details]" in the header. Change that text object to say "[list]" instead, so it matches the name of the layout. Figure 5-6 shows how your layout should look now.

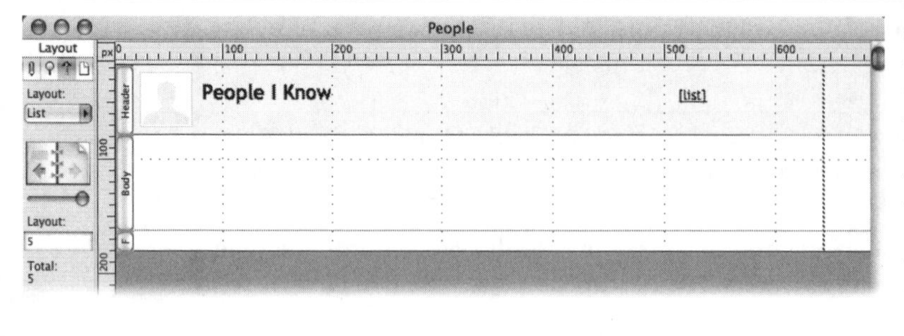

Figure 5-6: *Now that you've gussied up your header, it looks something like this example. The header's looking good, but the body could still use some work–it's empty right now. Since the body of the list layout repeats over and over for each record, the body should avoid wasted space. In Browse mode, the list scrolls so you can see all the records in your found set.*

Set Up the Body

Now that the header is in place, it's time to work on the body—and learn a few new tricks. You'll add the First Name and Last Name fields to the layout, and make them flow nicely together. You'll also tell FileMaker to show the record number next to each person's name.

Making data flow with merge fields

Knowing what you know now, if you set out to build this layout yourself, you'd probably jump right for the field tool and start dragging the new field on the layout. But look closely at Figure 5-7 first.

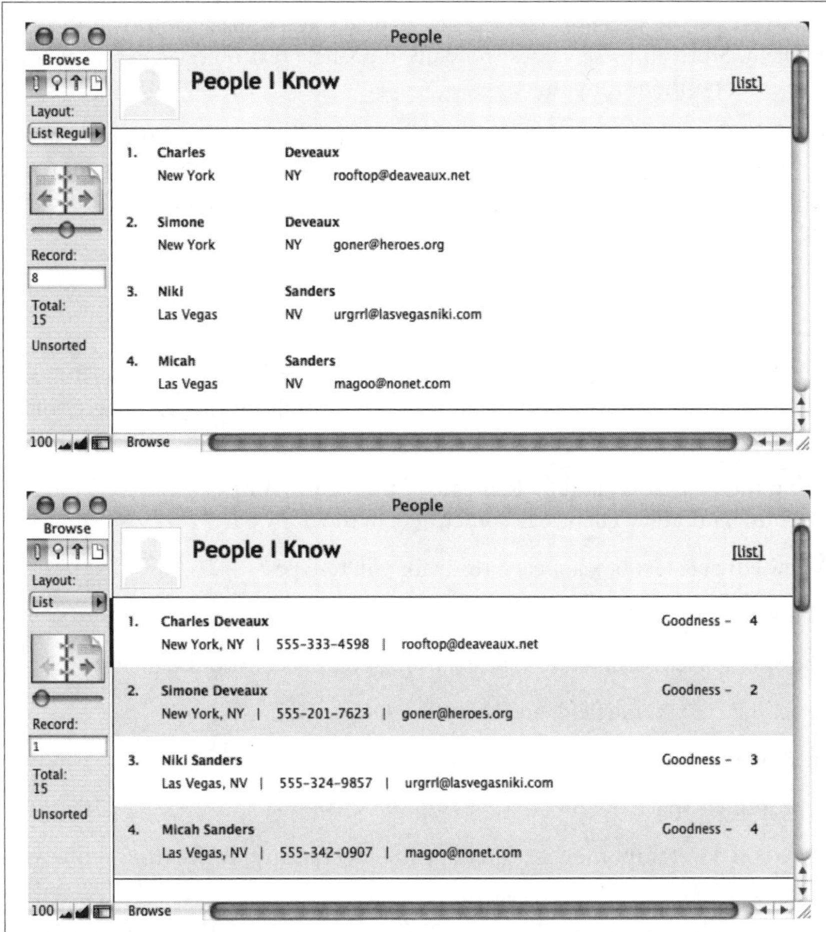

Figure 5-7: *Top: This layout uses normal fields, which are always in the same place on the layout, no matter what record you're on. Notice how the spacing between the contents of each field, particularly the First Name and Last Name fields, looks odd because it's inflexible.*

Bottom: By using merge fields, you can create a more professional-looking result. Plus, it can be a lot more efficient. Since there isn't much dead space between your merge fields, you can often get more information in about the same amount of space. This layout also has an alternating background (see page 195), which makes it easy to see where one record leaves off and the next one begins.

When you put a field on a layout, you're putting it *exactly* where you want it. No matter what record you're on when you look at the layout, that field value is in the same spot. Usually, that's where you want it to be, but sometimes—like in the new list layout—you want something a little more flexible. You want the Last Name field to start where the first name ends. Since some first names are longer than others, this spot changes from record to record.

In FileMaker, you solve this problem using *merge fields*. These work a lot like a mail merge in a word-processing program. You create an ordinary text object on your layout (not a field object), and then tell FileMaker to merge different field values into the text. For example, to put the first and last names together on your new layout, you create a text object like this:

```
<<First Name>> <<Last Name>>
```

Merge fields always show up in Layout mode with angle brackets around their names, just like <<this>>. When you look at this text object in Browse mode, though, you see the value of the First Name field, then a space, and then the Last Name field. Since all these values show up in a single text object, FileMaker sorts out the exact positions for you.

Merge fields have a downside, though: They're for display only. You need a real field if you want your users to be able to get into a field and change its contents. Your database already has a layout with real fields just for editing data (the detail layout), so in this case, merge fields are just what the doctor ordered.

Putting merge fields into a text object is easy:

1. **In the status area, click the text tool.**

   FileMaker activates the text tool; it changes your mouse arrow to an I-beam, and darkens the text tool button. Now set up the font for the text object you're about to create.

2. **Using the Font, Size, and Style menus (in the Format menu) choose Verdana, 11 Point, and Bold. Then click somewhere in the Body part.**

   A new editable text box appears, ready for you to type.

3. **Choose Insert → Merge Field.**

   The Specify Field dialog box appears, listing every field in your database.

4. **Select the First Name field, and then click OK.**

   FileMaker inserts <<*First Name*>> into the text object for you.

5. **Type a single space.**

   Since you don't want the first and last name *right* next to each other, you've just added a space.

6. **Choose Insert → Merge Field again. When the Specify Field dialog box returns, select the Last Name field, and then click OK.**

   FileMaker adds the Last Name merge field to the text object.

You now have a text object that shows the first and last names with a single space between them (you can switch to Browse mode and try it out if you want). You just need to put it into place.

The address, phone, and email information should also be in a merge field (study Figure 5-7 to see why—they all flow together in a nicely formatted line). In this case you want Verdana, 9-Point, Plain. You can also select a gray color (or any color you like) from the Format → Text Color menu. Repeat the steps above to build a text object like this:

```
<<City>>, <<State>> | <<Phone>>  | <<Email Address>>
```

Tip: You can mix and match merge fields and normal text to your heart's content. When you were setting up the first and last name, you added a space between the merge fields. This time you add even more. After you add the City merge field, type a comma and a space. After the State and Phone Number merge fields, type space-pipe-space.

Using symbols to show important info

Merge fields aren't the only things FileMaker can squeeze into a text object on the fly. You can also insert a handful of special *symbols*—stand-in characters that you can replace with useful information when you view your database in Browse or Preview mode. For instance, notice in Figure 5-7 how each record in the list is numbered. You can accomplish this effect with the record number symbol.

Tip: FileMaker offers a host of other symbols besides the record number symbol. See the box on page 192 for full detail.

Since you're creating a *list* layout, it would be nice to show record numbers. That way you can easily see where you are in the list at any time, even if you've scrolled down from the top. You use the record number symbol to make it happen.

1. **Select the first and last name text object you just created.**

   If you just make a new text object with the text tool, you have to set the font, size, style, and possibly color. Instead, you can take a text object that already has *all* the attributes you want and use it as a starting point.

2. **Choose Edit → Duplicate.**

   A copy of the first and last name object appears.

3. **In the status area, click the text tool. Click anywhere in the new text object you're about to edit.**

   FileMaker outlines the text object and adds a flashing insertion point. Now select all the text in the object.

4. **Choose Edit → Select All, and then press Delete or Backspace.**

   The selected text disappears, leaving an empty text box.

5. **Choose Insert → Record Number Symbol.**

   "@@" appears in the text box.

6. **Type a period, and then press Enter.**

   If you want a period after the record number symbol, you have to type it yourself. Pressing Enter tells FileMaker you're done editing the text object.

You now have a text object that contains "@@." But if you peek at it in Browse mode, you see that FileMaker actually puts the current record number in its place.

The record number symbol is useful for helping you keep track of where you are in a list, but it doesn't actually identify a record in a fixed way. It just numbers the records based on the current found set and sort order. You can see how this works by sorting the records differently. When you're done, they'll be in a different order, and each one could have a different number. See page 318 for a way to assign a permanent ID number, or a key, to a record.

UP TO SPEED

Other Symbols

FileMaker includes symbols for several special values you may want to show on a layout, as shown in Figure 5-8. You insert these symbols on the layout because you don't know in advance what they're going to be, such as the current date or record number. Then, when you switch to Browse mode (or Preview mode), FileMaker replaces the symbol with the up-to-the-moment correct value. You can read about the record number symbol on page 191. Here are the others:

- The **date symbol** (//) is replaced by the current date. People often include this symbol on printed reports so you can easily see when they were generated.
- The **time symbol** (::) is replaced by the current time.
- The **user name symbol** (||) is replaced by the current user's name. FileMaker takes the user name of whoever's logged into your computer. (That's two *pipe* symbols—Shift-backslash on most keyboards—typed side by side.)
- The **page number symbol** (##) is replaced by the page number in Preview mode or when you print. Otherwise, it just shows as a question mark.

The Insert menu has three related options as well, but unlike symbols, these don't get replaced by anything in Browse or Preview mode. When you use the Insert → Current Date command, for instance, FileMaker simply adds today's date to the text object in Layout mode. It will show this same date forever in either mode.

You can use the Insert menu to place symbols where you need them, but it's faster and easier to type them in manually. So once you've seen that "##" makes a page number, forget about mousing around and just type the two number signs.

Tip: You can apply the same formatting to date and time symbols as you do to regular versions of those fields. Just select the text block that contains your date symbol ("//"), and then select Format → Date and choose the formatting you want. You can add Time formatting to the time symbol ("::"), too.

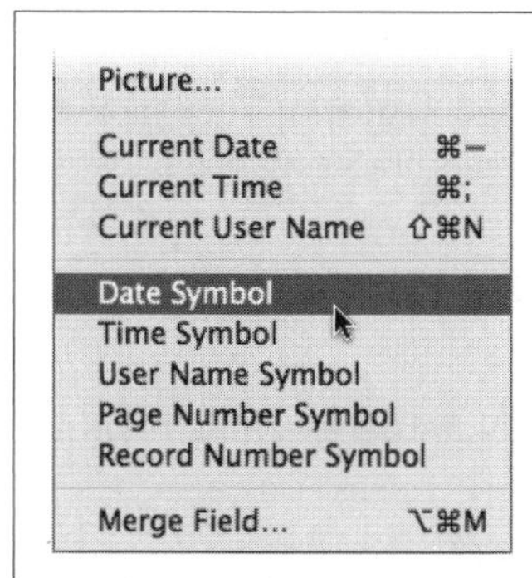

Figure 5-8:
You can use the Insert menu to insert the symbols FileMaker uses on layouts (see the box on page 192). But once you're familiar with those symbols, you can type them yourself. (That way, you can keep down your mouse's mileage and retain its maximum resale value.)

Arranging the objects

Now that you've added three new text objects to the Body part, you can arrange them on the layout. Using Figure 5-9 as a guide, apply the techniques you learned on page 165 to move the text objects into a clear, attractive arrangement. Once they're in place, you just need to add the Goodness Rating field and make a few adjustments to the Body part. You're almost done!

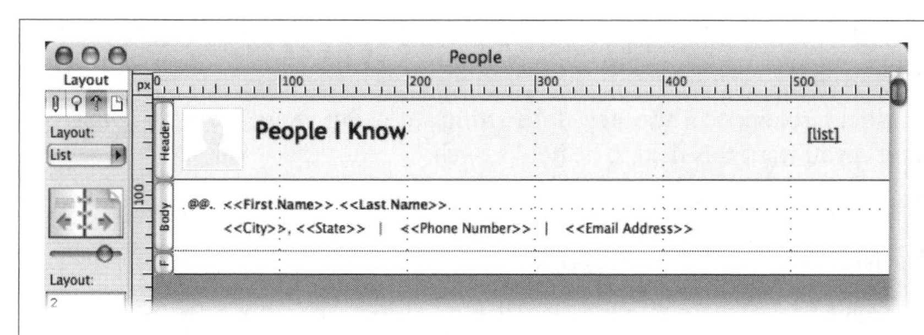

Figure 5-9:
Use the View Ruler Lines command to help you line up objects. Also as you drag a text object, you'll see a dotted line, called the baseline, *that helps you line text up neatly.*

Adding a field

The Goodness Rating is always a single-digit number, so unlike the First Name and Last Name fields, you don't need a merge field (see page 189) to get its spacing right. You use an ordinary field instead.

1. **From the status area, drag the field tool onto the layout.**

   The Specify Field dialog box appears.

2. **Make sure the "Create field label" checkbox is turned on.**

   When this option is on, FileMaker automatically adds a text object to serve as a label for your field.

3. **Select the Goodness Rating field, and then click OK.**

   FileMaker adds the Goodness Rating field to the layout, along with a new text object that says "Goodness Rating."

Copying formatting with the Format Painter

Unfortunately, the new field and label aren't formatted properly. They have the wrong font, size, style, and color. Instead of fixing each object manually as you learned in Chapter 2, you can use the *Format Painter*.

This intuitive tool copies all the formatting from one object and applies it to another. Here's how to use it:

1. **Click the text object that shows City, State, Phone Number, and Email Address to select it.**

   That object has the very formatting you want to copy.

2. **Choose Format → Format Painter.**

   Your mouse arrow changes to include a tiny paintbrush. The next thing you click with this special cursor takes on the copied format like a fresh coat of paint.

3. **Click the Goodness Rating label.**

   The label instantly changes to reflect the correct formatting. Also, it's already selected, so copying its formatting to the Goodness Rating field is a snap.

4. **Choose Format → Format Painter again, and then click the Goodness Rating field.**

   The field changes to the new formatting, too. But it isn't exactly what you want—you want this field to be bold as well.

5. **Choose Format → Style → Bold.**

   The label now has just the right formatting.

The Format Painter is certainly easier than choosing each formatting option individually, but it seems to work for only one object at a time. There are actually a couple of ways to extend the Format Painter's abilities. If the objects you want to format together are close enough, you can rubber band them with the Format Painter and they all change together. Just like the regular rubber band, you have to fully enclose each object for the change to take place. But pressing the Ctrl (⌘) key lets you merely *touch* an object with the rubber band to get the same effect.

But maybe even that method doesn't work for you, because your objects are all over the place. Wouldn't it be nice if the Format Painter were a button like the other tools? Then you could double-click it to lock it. Well, you're in luck, because that's just how it works.

1. **Choose View → Toolbars → Standard.**

   The Standard toolbar appears at the top of your screen.

2. **Select the object that has the formatting you want to copy.**

   You've just copied a text block's formatting, but you can also use a field, a drawn object, or anything that has formatting.

3. **Double-click the Format Painter tool—the one that looks like a paintbrush—and then click each object you need to format.**

   Double-clicking locks the tool, so you can use it over and over. You can even grab some rubber band selections if you want to.

4. **Click the Selection tool to let FileMaker know you're finished formatting (or use the Esc key).**

   All good things must come to an end.

You now just need to make the Goodness Rating field smaller (just wide enough to hold one number) and put it in its place on the right side of the layout. Delete the word "Rating" from the Goodness Rating label, and then add a "-" to the end and position it just to the left of the field. Figure 5-10 shows where you're at.

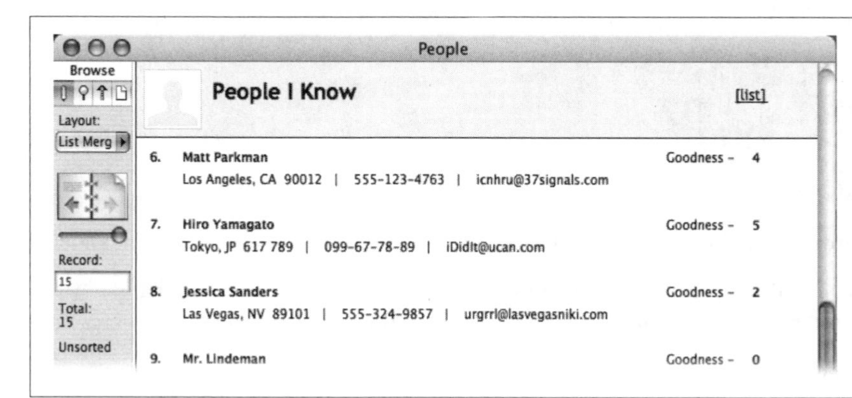

Figure 5-10: *With the Goodness Rating field in place, your layout is almost complete. Switch to Browse mode to admire the results of your labor. Notice that the list scrolls, so you can scan lots of records quickly.*

Alternating the body color

As Figure 5-5 plainly shows, the rows on this list layout are supposed to alternate between gray and white. FileMaker gives you this effect for free; you just have to turn it on. To do that, you pay a visit to the Part Definition dialog box via the Part Setup dialog box.

1. **Choose Layout → Part Setup.**

   The Part Setup dialog box appears, as described in the box on page 197.

2. **In the Part Setup dialog box's list, select Body, and then click Change.**

   This window lists every part in your layout. To select a part, just click its name. When you click Change, the Part Definition window opens (see Figure 5-11).

Tip: There's a shortcut to the Part Definition dialog box: Double-click the part tag you want to edit.

3. **Turn on the "Alternate background fill" checkbox.**

   The Fill Color menu and Fill Pattern menu buttons, which had been grayed out, become available and ready for you to make a choice.

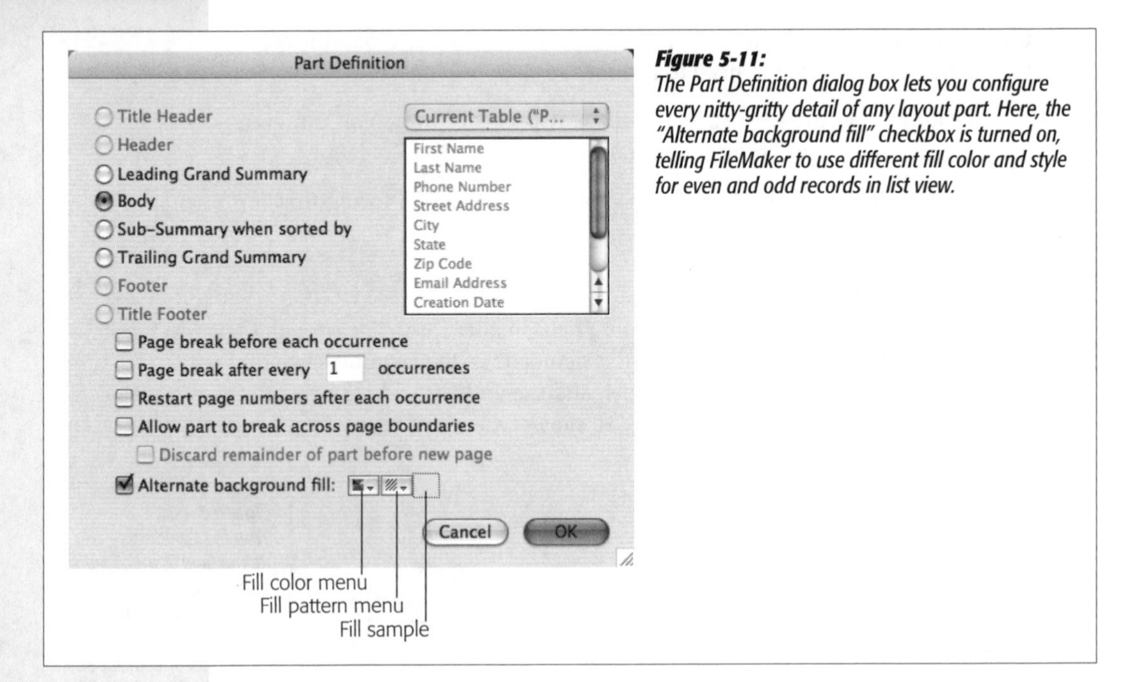

Figure 5-11:
The Part Definition dialog box lets you configure every nitty-gritty detail of any layout part. Here, the "Alternate background fill" checkbox is turned on, telling FileMaker to use different fill color and style for even and odd records in list view.

4. **From the Fill Color menu, choose a color to use for your alternate row color.**

   The Fill Sample changes to show your selection. Choose a color that's not too dark, or you'll have trouble seeing the text on the beautiful layout you've created.

5. **Click OK, and then click Done.**

   Nothing changes in Layout mode, but if you switch to Browse mode, you see the new effect.

When you use the "Alternate background fill" option, the settings you make in the Part Definition window apply to the even numbered records. You can still control the fill for odd numbered records by adjusting the Body part fill right on the layout, just like you did with the Header part. In this example, you tell FileMaker to color the even rows gray and leave the odd rows white. You can use this feature any time you want to make it easier to see where one record ends and another begins, in a list.

Now all you need to do is resize the Body part so it just fits its contents, using any of the methods described earlier in this chapter. When you've done that, your layout design is nearly finished.

Setting Layout View

Switch to Browse mode to admire your handiwork. If you're seeing only one record at a time, switch to list view (choose View → "View as List"). When you choose the blank layout template, you get complete freedom to make the layout look just the way you want. But one tradeoff is that you have to remember to tell the layout which view it's supposed to be in.

UP TO SPEED

Part Setup Dialog Box

When you choose Layout → Part Setup, FileMaker shows you the Part Setup dialog box (see Figure 5-12). This often-ignored box isn't just a slower way to get to the Part Definition window, though. From this one screen, you can create new parts and edit, delete, and rearrange existing parts. But, as you'll read on page 293, you can do most of this work more easily *without* this window, so you won't use it very often.

To add a new part, click Create. You're presented with the Part Definition dialog box, where you can decide what kind of part to create, and set various options. You can do the same thing by dragging the part tool from the status area or choosing Insert → Part.

To see the part definition for an existing part, select it and click Change. This maneuver too has a shortcut: Just double-click any part tag in Layout mode.

To delete a part, select it and click Delete. If the part contains any objects on the layout, FileMaker asks you if you're sure, because when you delete a part, you delete everything on it as well. You've already deleted parts without using this window, though, by selecting the part and choosing Edit → Clear. But if you hate menus, you can also just press Delete.

You can also rearrange parts using the same technique you use to order fields in the Manage Database window. Just drag the arrow icon next to a part name. But some parts (most parts, in fact) have a padlock symbol instead of an arrow icon. This symbol tells you the part is *locked* in place and you can't move it. The reason is simple: It doesn't make sense to move most parts. For example, the header is always below the title header and above everything else. You really only need to rearrange parts when creating *sub-summary reports*, which the next chapter covers.

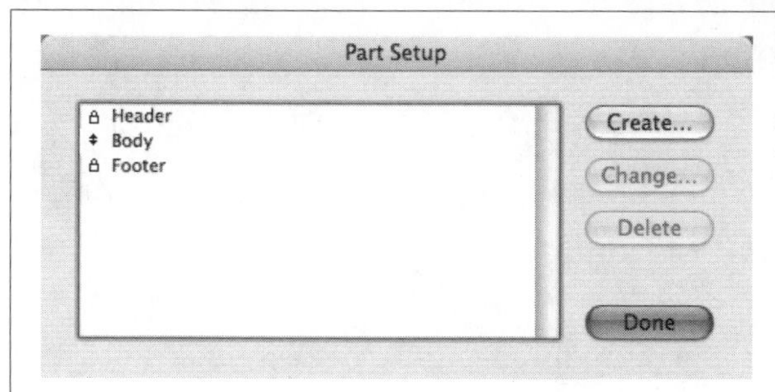

Figure 5-12:
The Part Setup dialog box is a catchall for the options pertinent to layout parts. You'll find it especially useful for rearranging parts of your layout.

Since FileMaker always starts out showing form view, that's what you see until you tell the layout something different.

1. **Switch to Layout mode, then choose Layouts → Layout Setup.**

   Remember, Layout mode is the only place you can make changes to a layout. The Layout Setup box is where you work this particular piece of magic.

2. **On the Views tab, turn off Form View and Table View.**

   You've just told FileMaker to make these two menu choices off-limits in Browse and Find modes. After all, they don't make much sense in a layout that's designed specifically to work as a list.

3. **Click OK to dismiss the dialog box.**

   Honestly, you have to tell some programs *everything*.

Now, when you switch to Browse mode and look at the View menu, "View as Form" and "View as Table" are grayed out. FileMaker won't let you accidentally switch your list to a useless view of the data.

POWER USERS' CLINIC

Getting Table View to Mind Its Manners

Table view is a real boon if you want a quick and easy way to make your data look like a spreadsheet. With one command, your layout displays data in rows and columns, which you can rearrange and sort. But if you dig a little deeper, you find that you have a lot of control over how table view works. These controls lurk under the Layout Setup command. When you click the Views tab, you see that the Table View option has a button that leads you one dialog box deeper–into Table View Properties.

- With the **Grid** controls, you can show or hide table view's horizontal and vertical gridlines. Try switching off the vertical gridlines to make rows more prominent. This way, it's easier to read across the data pertaining to a single record.
- With the **Grid Style** option comes two familiar pop-up menus. You can choose a new color for the grids with the color pop-up menu or apply a pattern to them from the pattern pop-up menu. A sample swatch shows you the choices you've made.
- Under **Header and Parts**, you control the header, footer, and column headers. Headers and footers anchor to the top or bottom of the screen while the records scroll through long lists. Column headers are the field names at the top of each column.
- Headers and footers are normally suppressed when a layout's in table view. Choose **Include header part** or **Include footer part** to display those parts of the layout. (For obvious reasons, these options have no effect on a layout in which you don't have those particular parts.)
- Since the column headers tell you what information you're looking at, you don't often find a reason to turn off their display. But you can do it if you want to, by unchecking **Include column headers**.
- More commonly, you may want to turn off some of the column headers' other features. Stop users from resizing columns by unchecking **Resizable columns**. Turn off **Reorderable columns** to keep folks from rearranging their order on the table. That way, nobody can move the First Name field so far away from the Last Name field that the data loses its meaning. Nobody can sort records if you uncheck **Sort data when selecting column**.
- Choose **Use custom height** to set rows to a specific height, and then select one of the measurement systems and type the height you want.

Setting Anchors in List Layouts

The layout you've created works great for certain tasks, like if you need an onscreen list of all the folks you have to call in certain areas of the country. You can see each person's name, city, state, and phone number. But wouldn't it be helpful to see the notes about each person, so you can have background information available when you make your calls?

Since this layout makes heavy use of merge fields, your first impulse may be to throw a merge field version of the Notes field on the layout. But if you do that, you can't take advantage of FileMaker's autoresizing (see page 172) of layout objects. And since the Notes field can hold varying amounts of data for each record, it would be helpful if its size could automatically adjust itself on your list layout, just as it does on the detail layout.

Anchors don't work quite the same way on a list layout as on a detail layout. Because the Body part has to repeat over and over for each record in your found set, anchored fields on list layouts expand horizontally, but not vertically. Still, you can use autoresizing to expand fields to reveal just a little bit more text if the screen size permits. To see how autoresizing works on a list, switch to Layout mode and create a regular Notes field on your layout. See Figure 5-13 for size and placement.

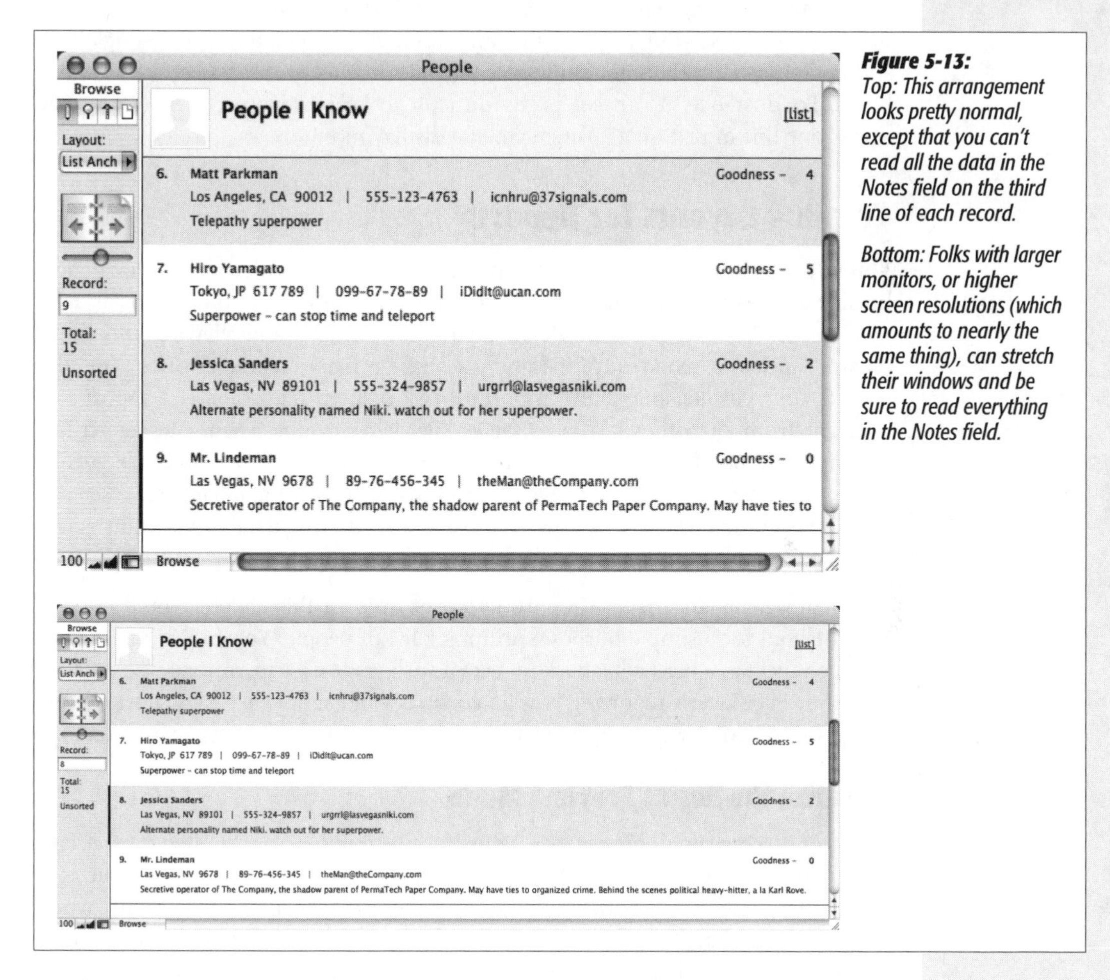

Figure 5-13: *Top: This arrangement looks pretty normal, except that you can't read all the data in the Notes field on the third line of each record.*

Bottom: Folks with larger monitors, or higher screen resolutions (which amounts to nearly the same thing), can stretch their windows and be sure to read everything in the Notes field.

1. **Choose View → Object Info.**

   You can skip this step if you're in the habit of working with the Object Info palette in view.

2. **Click the List label in the header, and then Shift-click the Goodness Rating field and its label. Finally, Shift-click the Notes field.**

   With multiple items selected, you can apply autoresizing to them all with a single click.

3. **Select the right anchor option.**

   FileMaker anchors all three items to the right edge of the window. If you test your layout in Browse mode, as you resize your window, the Notes field expands to reveal extra text, and the List text block and Goodness Rating field (and its label) scoot to the right.

If you have a big enough monitor, you can see a whole lot of text in the Notes field when you increase your window's width, although it's spread out on a single line. Although it's better than not being able to read some text at all, this effect has some limits. For instance, it can get pretty difficult to keep your place when you read across one line of text on a 30-inch cinema display monitor.

Creating Layouts for Reports

You've now knocked out two good layouts—a detail layout (see Chapter 4) and a list layout (described in this chapter). Layouts like these meet many typical database needs: You've got your detail layout for finding and viewing individual records, and your list layout for rapidly scanning many records at once. You also want to do *reporting*, an equally important task in a typical database. A report's no different from any other layout as far as FileMaker is concerned. But report layouts are designed from the ground up to be *printed*. Almost no database gets by without some kind of a report layout, and most important databases have several, from straightforward lists to powerful snapshots of your data's important statistics, like sales by region or inventory by product category.

The People database needs a reporting layout, too. In this chapter you'll create a report layout for a simple purpose: printing a list of people. You can print a report, and then file it as a hard copy backup, take it with you on a trip, or mail it to an associate. But FileMaker's reporting powers go far beyond simple lists. The next chapter introduces FileMaker's powerful data summarization and reporting capabilities.

Visualize the Result Preview Mode

First, you need a rough idea of how your layout should look. This step is especially important when you create a report, since the physical constraints of a piece of paper often dictate the working space you have. When you create a detail layout, you're free to make it large or small, tall or short, narrow or wide—whatever meets the needs of your data, and your computer's monitor. You'll have to live with some common restraints if you want to print your layout.

In the spirit of visualization, how about a picture? From the Preview illustration in Figure 5-14, you can get a pretty good idea of how this layout is going to come together. It has a header, a body, and a footer. The header includes a title, the date, and some column labels, and the footer has just a page number (these parts print on the top and bottom of each page). The body is the most important part: It has all the fields that show your information.

You can see the report in Layout mode in Figure 5-15.

Note: To see your layout in Preview Mode, choose View → Preview Mode.

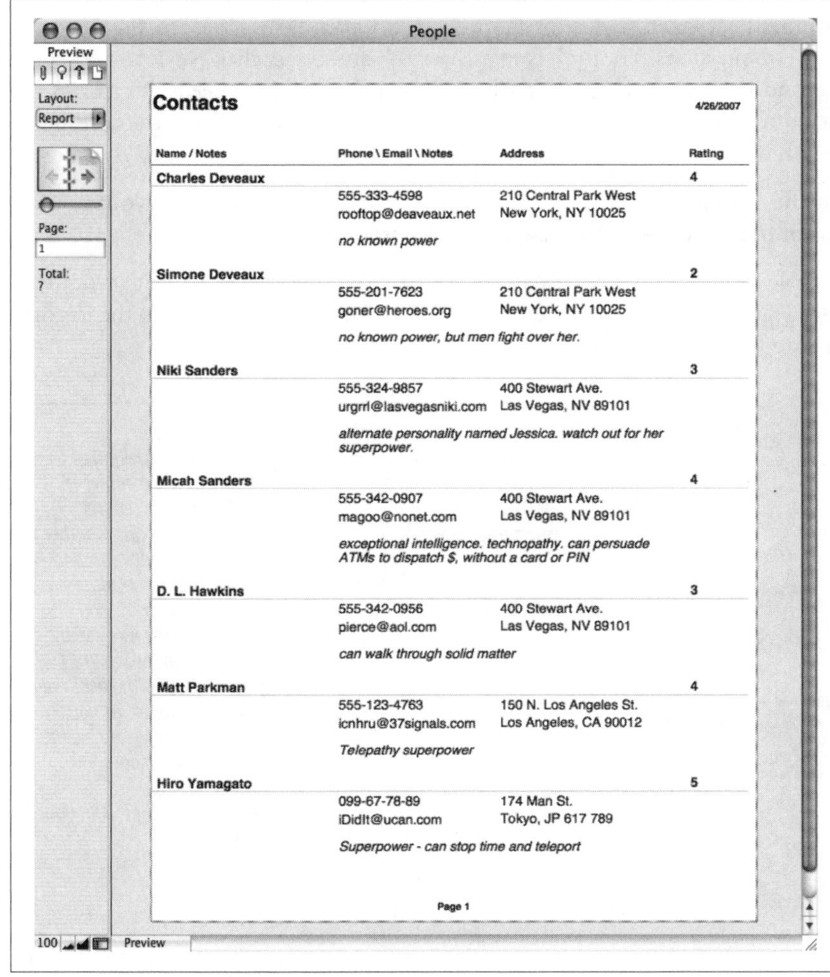

Figure 5-14: *In the steps on page 202, you'll add this report to the People database. Notice it's formatted to fit nicely on letter-sized paper when printed (it's in Preview mode here). You can also see the date the report was printed in the top-right corner, and a page number at the bottom of each page.*

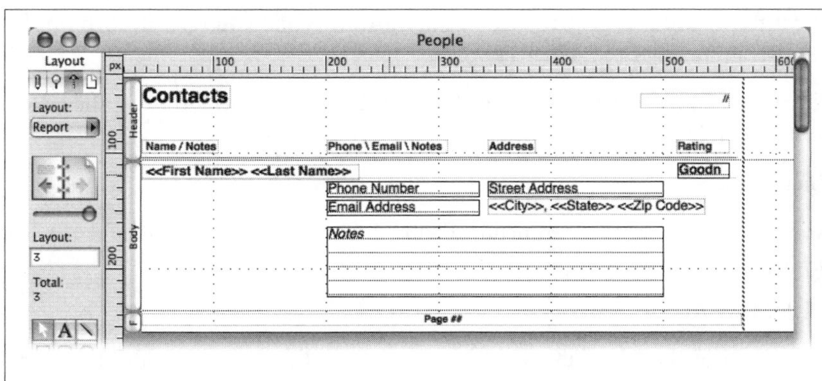

Figure 5-15: *In Layout mode, you can see how this layout comes together. Everything here should look familiar to you: parts, text objects, lines, fields, and merge fields. But don't fear—there's plenty left to learn, from FileMaker's automatic layout assistant to the ins and outs of printing a layout.*

Creating a Report Layout with an Assistant

In the example in the previous section, you started with FileMaker's blank layout. Since blank layouts are always just blank, there were no more choices to make. This time, FileMaker does a lot more work for you. Before it does, it asks you a handful of questions. Your job is to answer the questions, click Next, answer some more, and so on. When FileMaker has all the information it needs, it changes the Next button to a Finish button. FileMaker then creates the layout according to your specifications. Here's how to proceed:

1. **In the People database, switch to Layout mode and choose Layout → New Layout/Report. Name the new layout *Report.***

   You've been through these steps before (see page 184). Next, select a layout type (see Figure 5-16), so FileMaker knows which choices to offer you in the upcoming steps. Different layout types, different options.

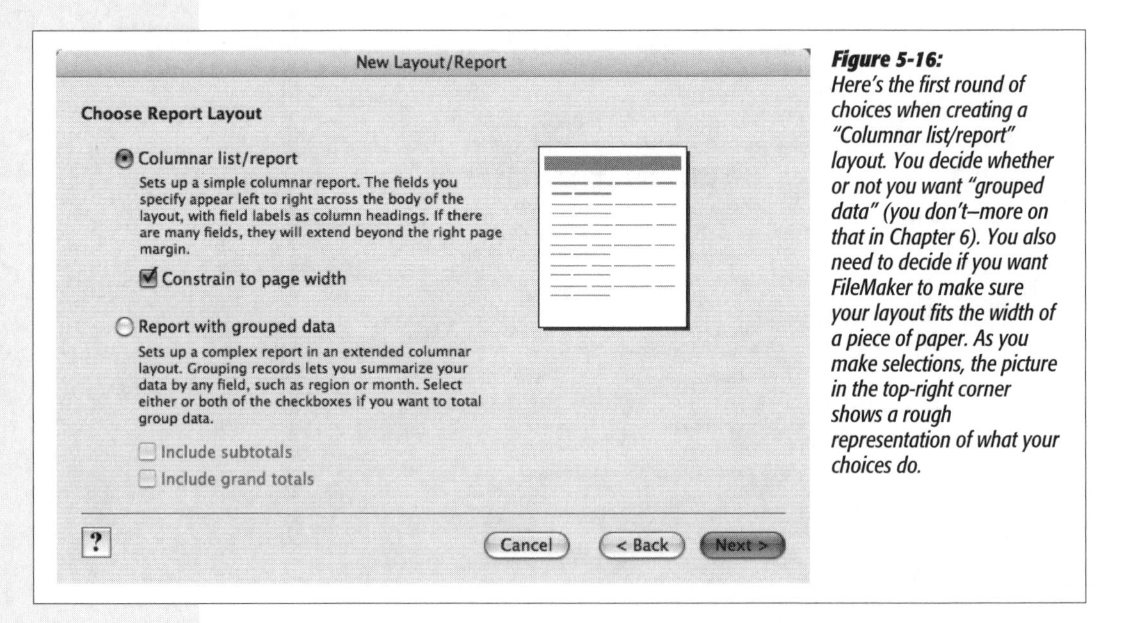

Figure 5-16: *Here's the first round of choices when creating a "Columnar list/report" layout. You decide whether or not you want "grouped data" (you don't–more on that in Chapter 6). You also need to decide if you want FileMaker to make sure your layout fits the width of a piece of paper. As you make selections, the picture in the top-right corner shows a rough representation of what your choices do.*

2. **Select the "Columnar list/report" radio button. While you're at it, turn on the "Constrain to page width" checkbox.**

   The picture in the top-right corner of the window changes to show that the layout won't extend past the width of a page.

3. **Click Next.**

   Now you see the window shown in Figure 5-17, where you tell FileMaker what fields to add to the layout.

4. **Click Move All.**

   Every field in the "Available fields" list moves to the "Layout fields" list. Click Next.

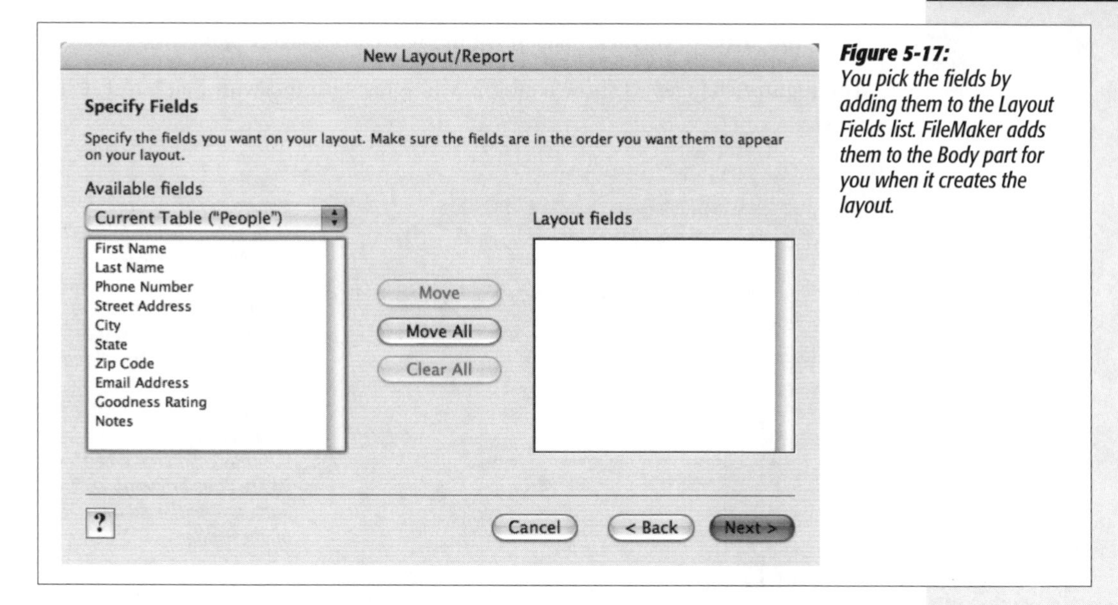

***Figure 5-17:** You pick the fields by adding them to the Layout Fields list. FileMaker adds them to the Body part for you when it creates the layout.*

5. **As shown in Figure 5-18, add the Last Name field to the "Sort order" list.**

   In the "Report fields" list, click Last Name, and then click Move.

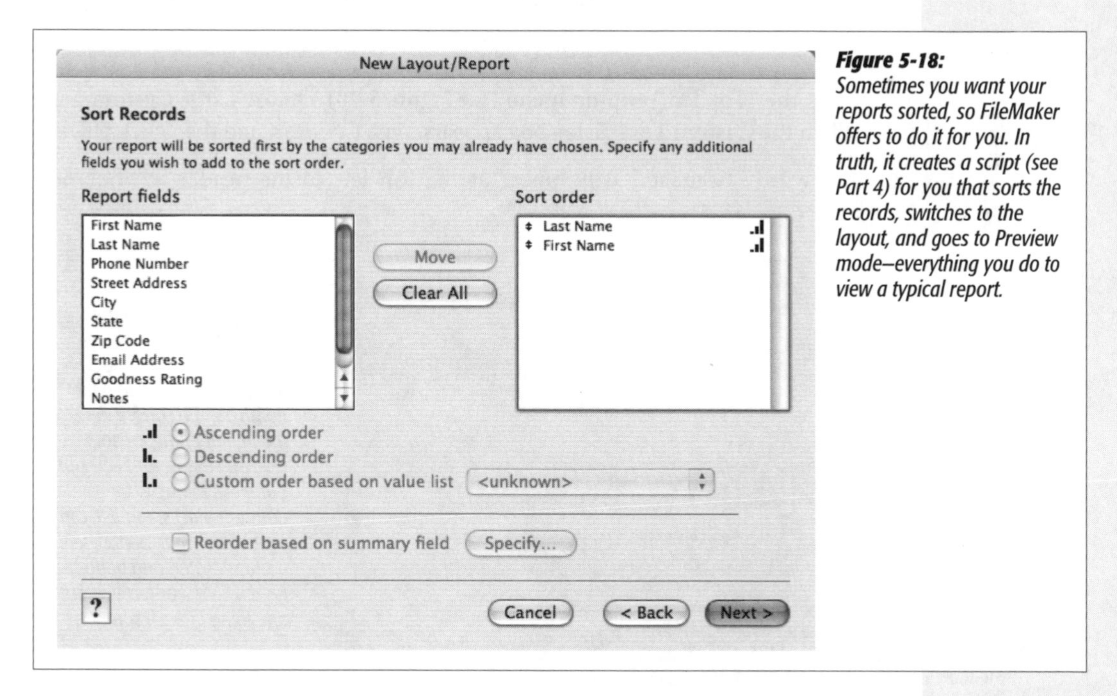

***Figure 5-18:** Sometimes you want your reports sorted, so FileMaker offers to do it for you. In truth, it creates a script (see Part 4) for you that sorts the records, switches to the layout, and goes to Preview mode–everything you do to view a typical report.*

6. **In the same way, add the First Name field to the "Sort order" list.**

   The "Sort order" list now shows the Last Name field, then the First Name field. This arrangement tells FileMaker to sort first by Last Name, then by First Name. Click Next.

7. **From the "Layout themes" list shown in Figure 5-19, select Standard.**

   The picture changes to show a simple white background with black text. Click Next.

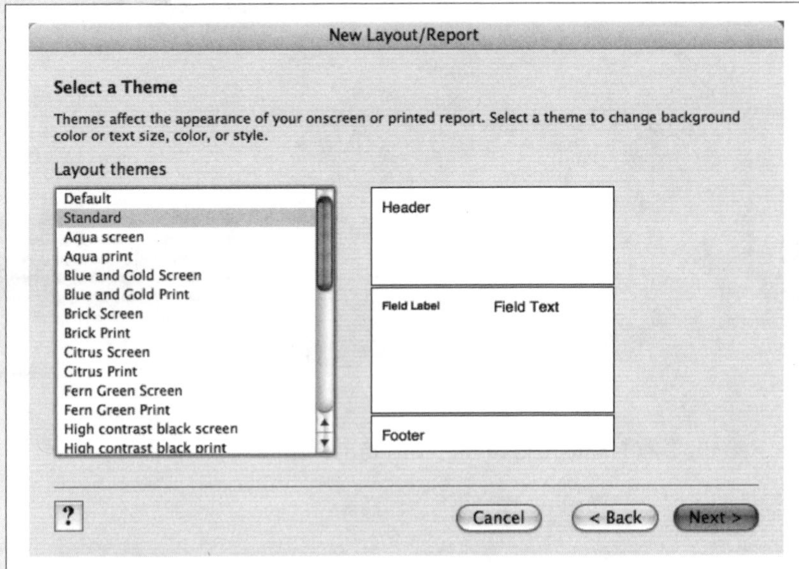

***Figure 5-19:** Here's your chance to select a theme. As you make selections from the "Layout themes" list, the picture changes to show how the theme will look. Click all you want–it's pretty much guaranteed that none of them will match your business collateral. When you're done browsing, pick Standard for the example on these pages.*

8. **From the "Top left" pop-up menu (see Figure 5-20), choose Large Custom Text. When the Custom Text dialog box appears, type *Contacts*, and then click OK.**

   The word "Contacts" will appear at the top left of the header in your new report.

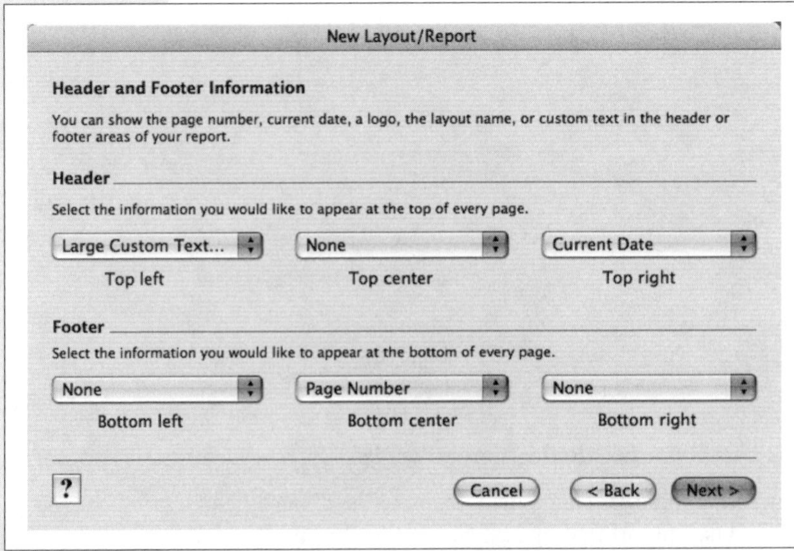

***Figure 5-20:** Once you have a theme, you get to choose what to put in the headers and footers. You can add page numbers, the current date, the layout name, custom text, and logos. And you can put these things in six different places: top left, top center, top right, bottom left, bottom center, and bottom right. FileMaker lets you put one thing in each spot.*

9. **From the "Top right" pop-up menu, choose Current Date. Then, from the "Bottom center" pop-up menu, choose Page Number. Then click Next.**

   Expect to see the Current Date appear at the top-right side of your header. A page number will appear in the center of each report page's footer.

10. **Select the "Create a script" radio button. Then, in the "Script name" box, type *Report*. Click Next.**

    As explained in Figure 5-21, you've just told FileMaker to add a command named "Report" to the Script menu. You can choose this menu command to run the report.

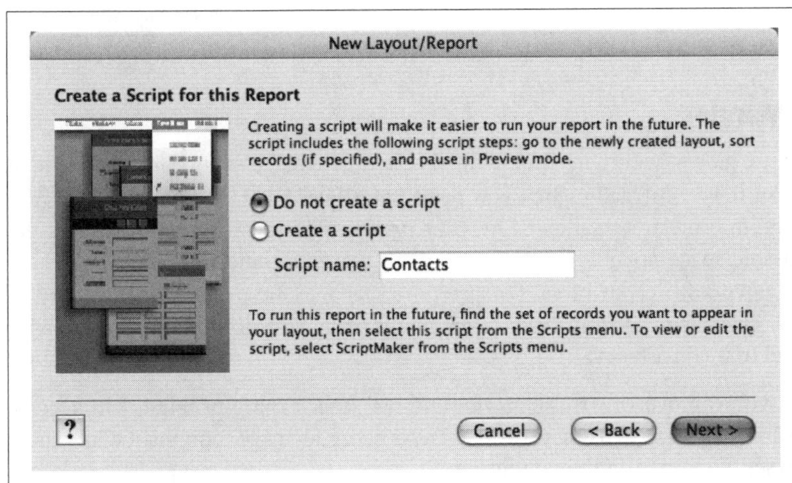

Figure 5-21: *Almost done! Remember a couple steps back when you defined a sort order for this report? As you learned then, FileMaker can create a script for you to perform the sort and show the report in Preview mode. Now you get to decide if you want it to or not. If you turn on "Do not create a script," then the sort order you specified before does you no good–without a script you have to sort the records yourself.*

11. **In the assistant's final screen (see Figure 5-22), turn on "View the report in Layout mode."**

    This tells FileMaker to deposit you in Layout mode after it finishes creating the report. Click Finish.

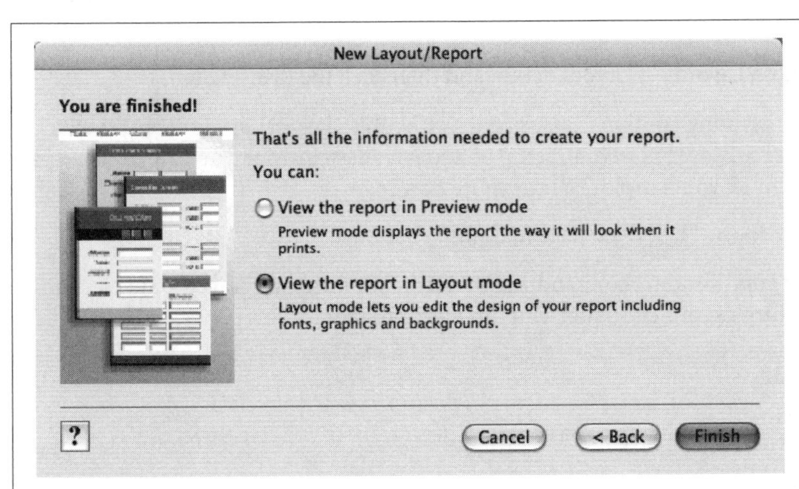

Figure 5-22: *Time to make your last choice. You can opt to view the report directly in Preview mode, or you can view the new layout in Layout mode. Since you're going to need to make some adjustments to the layout, choose "View the report in Layout mode."*

Phew! You're finished at last. Your new report layout should look something like Figure 5-23.

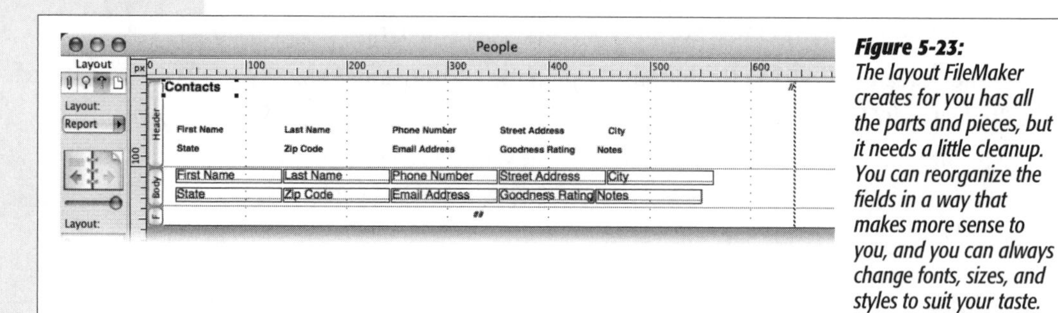

***Figure 5-23:** The layout FileMaker creates for you has all the parts and pieces, but it needs a little cleanup. You can reorganize the fields in a way that makes more sense to you, and you can always change fonts, sizes, and styles to suit your taste.*

Print Margins

Before you begin arranging things on the layout, you need to know how much space you have. Normally when you print from FileMaker, the page margins are set to the minimum size allowed by your printer. This arrangement provides the most usable space possible, but at a cost: The margins—and the printable area—change as you switch printers. For a report that may be printed on a variety of printers, all of which could have different margins, you don't want to deal with that kind of inconsistency.

Luckily, you can override this behavior and set explicit margins. First, you need to make sure FileMaker is using units that make sense for page margins. Follow these steps to set the units and the margins:

1. **Choose Layouts → Set Rulers.**

   The Set Rulers window appears (see the box on page 141).

2. **From the Units pop-up menu, choose Inches, and then click OK.**

   You're back on your new layout, where you've just told FileMaker to use inches for just about everything.

3. **Choose Layouts → Layout Setup, and then click the Printing tab.**

   The printing options associated with this layout appear, as shown in Figure 5-24. (This Layout Setup window is the same one you saw on page 145. This time, you'll explore a little more deeply.)

4. **Turn on the "Use fixed page margins" checkbox.**

   The Top, Bottom, Left, and Right text boxes start out grayed out. As soon as you turn on this checkbox, you can type into them.

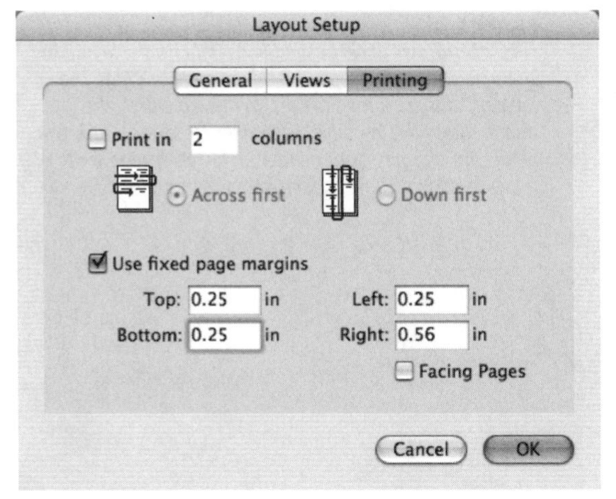

Figure 5-24:
These settings affect the way the current layout prints. For example, you can create a layout that prints in multiple columns (imagine printing sticky labels). You'll learn more about that in the next chapter. For now, draw your attention to the "Use fixed page margins" checkbox, which you need to turn on if you want this layout to have hard-coded (and consistent) page margins.

Note: The numbers you see in these boxes (before you type anything into them, that is) are the margins associated with the printer you're hooked up to. That's why they probably look different from what you see in Figure 5-24.

5. **In each of the Top, Bottom, Left, and Right text boxes, type .5.**

   Don't forget to type the decimal point. Your goal is to set the margin on all sides to half an inch.

6. **Click OK.**

   If your printer's driver software hogs up even more margin space, you'll see a warning message, but it won't tell you which margin setting is too narrow. Tweak the margins until the warning no longer appears. The Layout Setup dialog box disappears and you're looking at your layout again. If you have sharp eyes, you notice the page width has shrunk a bit, as shown in Figure 5-25.

Tip: If you like working in pixels and don't want the bother of switching units, take heart. You can probably do the math in your head even faster. Remember, there are 72 pixels per inch: A one-inch margin would be 72 pixels, and a half-inch margin would be 36. (If you like centimeters, figure there are 28 pixels per centimeter.)

Improving the Report Layout

Now that you've specified your page size, you can begin to lay out the report. FileMaker already created Header, Body, and Footer parts. It already set the layout to list view. And it already added a title, date stamp, page number, column labels, and fields in the proper parts. As usual, it just isn't very pretty. (Remember, Figure 5-34 shows the finished product.)

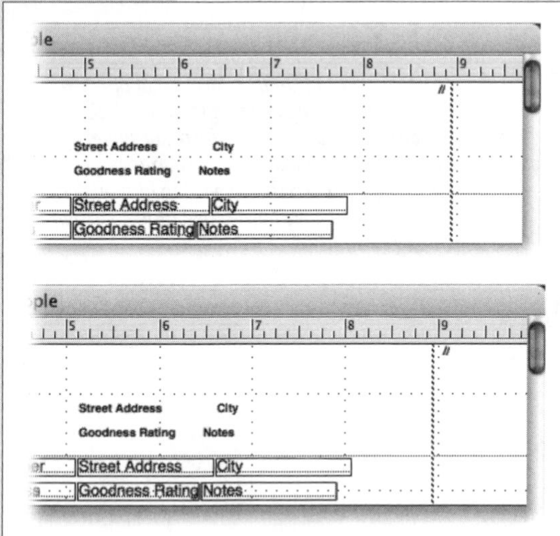

Figure 5-25:
FileMaker draws thick, hashed lines right on the layout to show page breaks. When you adjust page margins, the location of these lines changes. In these pictures, the top image shows the layout as FileMaker created it. Once you adjust the margins, your header no longer fits the width of a page, as shown in the bottom image.

Tidy up the header

Your first job is to clean up the Header part. As shown in Figure 5-26 for guidance, your tasks involve mostly text formatting and dragging things around.

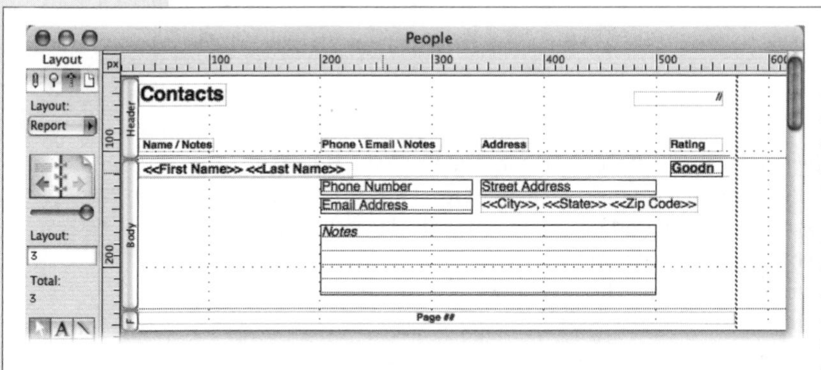

Figure 5-26:
To fix up the header, you need to do a little rearranging and change some fonts. For the look shown here, resize the "Contacts" title to 18-point. Simplify the column headings and change them to 12-point bold. Slide the date stamp (the "//" text object in the top-right corner) left so it doesn't extend off the page. Finally, add a 1-point black line the full width of the page along the bottom of the header. (see the box on page 209.)

Rearrange the body

In Figure 5-26, you can also see what your report layout will look like when you're done rearranging it. Again, you know everything you need to know. You want to replace the First Name and Last Name fields with larger merge fields (see page 189), rearrange the rest of the fields, and give them new font, size, and style formatting. This time, though, there are a few extra steps.

UP TO SPEED

Adding Straight Lines

You often see horizontal lines that cross the width of a page in printed reports. Many reports include a line between the header and the body of the page. (Technically, such a line is *in* the Header part.) Creating these lines is a snap:

1. In the status area, click the line tool. The mouse arrow changes to a cross-hair icon.
2. With the Shift key held down, drag a straight horizontal line anywhere on the layout. Don't worry about getting the line in the right place. You can more easily move it later.
3. Drag the new line all the way to the left, so that its left end touches the left side of the layout. As you drag left, FileMaker won't let you drag the line past the edge of the layout.
4. With the Shift key held down, drag the selection handle on the right end of the line until it touches the vertical page break line. Again, since you have the Shift key down, the line stays straight.
5. Using the mouse or the arrow keys, move the line up or down until it's positioned properly.

Using these steps, you can be sure your line is straight and exactly the width of a page.

First, you can delete the First Name, Last Name, City, State, and Zip Code fields. In their place, add two new text objects. One—formatted as 12-point bold text—should hold merge fields for the First Name and Last Name fields, with a space between them. In the second, add City, and comma and space, State, another space, and Zip Code. Finally, italicize the Notes field.

Once you've made these changes, you can rearrange the fields and objects using Figure 5-26 as a guide. (Don't worry about matching the example exactly. Periodically inspect your work in Browse mode and adjust the arrangement until it pleases your eye. Use your individual sense of style!)

With the fields in place, you have just one finishing touch to add to the body. It's hard to see in Figure 5-26, but there's a hairline-width line underneath the Name and Goodness Rating fields. You can save some effort by duplicating the horizontal line you added to the header. Select the line and choose Edit → Duplicate. A new line appears just below the first. Move it into position, and use the line thickness tool to make it a hairline.

Tip: You can copy an object *and* position it in one quick move: Ctrl-drag (Option-drag) it. The Ctrl or Option key tells FileMaker to copy the object instead of move it. To constrain the movement, press *Shift* as you drag. Your new object stays right in line with the original.

Tweak the footer

Next up is the Footer part. It's already almost perfect. But it would be nice if the report showed the word "Page" on the bottom of the third page, instead of just the mysterious "3." Use the text tool to edit the page number text object ("##"), typing *Page* and a space before the page number symbol.

Tip: If the text block for your page number doesn't center properly, stretch the block so that it extends from the left to right margin. It'll center perfectly now.

Sliding Layout Objects

Your layout is essentially finished; time to take a look. Choose Scripts → Report to run the script you told FileMaker to create for your report on "Creating a Report Layout with an Assistant." As Figure 5-27 confirms, this report has one minor problem: It's not very paper-efficient. All that blank space beneath most items is the Notes field, which may have lots of information, but usually doesn't. Wouldn't it be cool if you could tell FileMaker to slide the next record up if the Notes field didn't need all that space? The engineers at FileMaker thought so too, and added a feature called *sliding*.

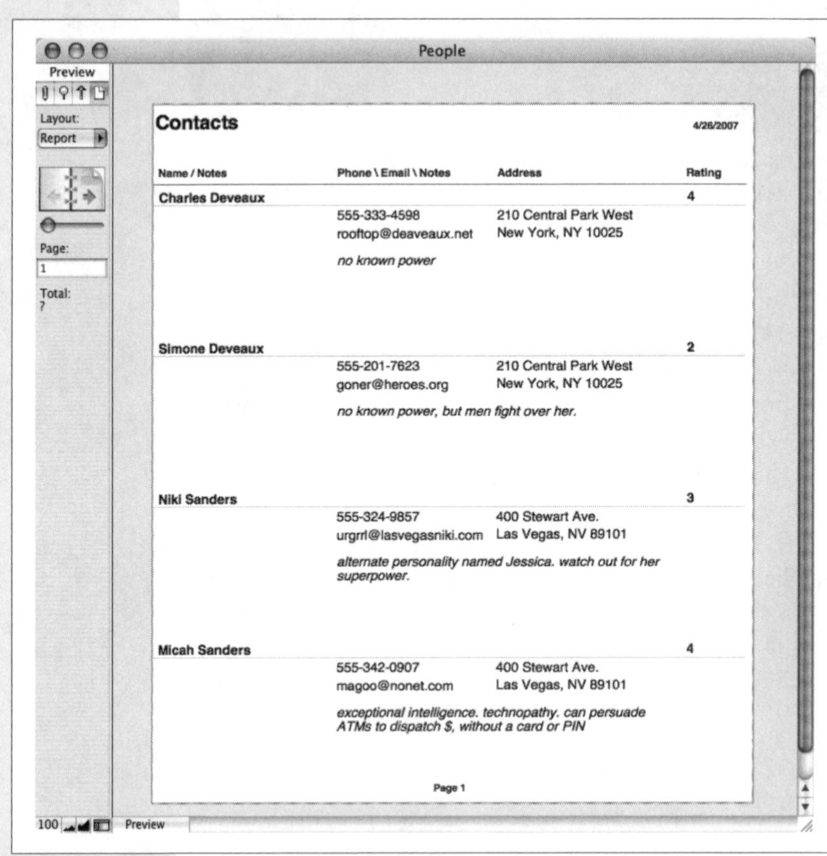

Figure 5-27: *The report is looking better, but it sure wastes a lot of space. The longest note on the page has only two lines. But when you were arranging fields on the body, you told FileMaker to make the Notes field about five lines tall, and that's how much space it reserves.*

When to use sliding

Since the data in a field changes from record to record, the amount of space it takes up often changes, too. Usually this behavior doesn't cause a problem. After all, you may *want* that empty space because you're printing onto a preprinted form, and everything needs to go in just the right spot on the page, or maybe your report design counts on consistent field sizes so things line up properly. But sometimes you can't get the effect you want without adjusting the layout based on the amount of data—usually when you're trying to tighten things up on the printed page to avoid wasted paper or excessive spacing around data.

Sliding does three things to help in this situation. First, it lets fields *shrink* to just the right size for their data. After a field has shrunk, any object on the layout can slide up or to the left to fill the space left behind.

Fortunately, whole layout parts can shrink vertically to compensate for their shrinking contents. It's an idea that's much easier to see than to explain, so turn your attention to Figure 5-28.

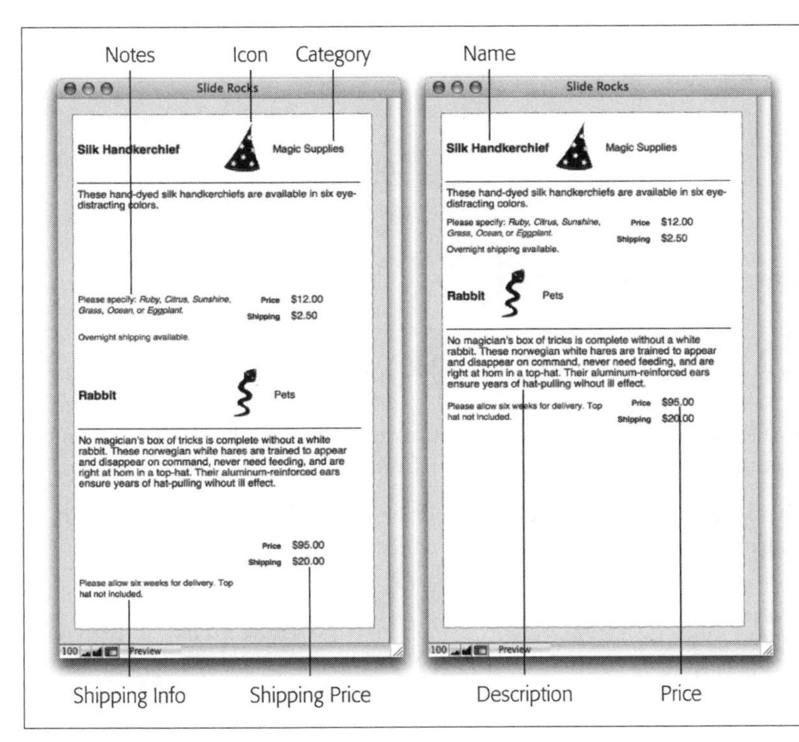

Figure 5-28: *These windows show the same thing: a page with two product records. The version on the left uses sliding to get rid of unsightly extra space. The width of the Name field shrinks to fit its contents. The height of the Description field shrinks to fit as well. The icon and category both slide left. The Notes field, Shipping Info field, Price field, and Shipping Price field all slide up. Finally, the entire Body part shrinks to fit its contents (notice how the second product record starts higher on the page in the right window).*

Choosing the objects to slide

Object sliding in FileMaker is notoriously hard to figure out. It's a bit like that board game "Go." The rules take a minute to learn but a lifetime to master. Here goes:

Sliding exists for only one reason: to compensate for changing field data. Therefore, unless you set at least one field to shrink, *nothing* on the layout moves. Unfortunately, you can't explicitly set a field to shrink. Instead, you set it to *slide*—and FileMaker makes sure it shrinks too. This seemingly simple principle is guaranteed to confuse you at least 36 times in the near future. You've been warned. Figure 5-29 shows how this field-shrinking business works.

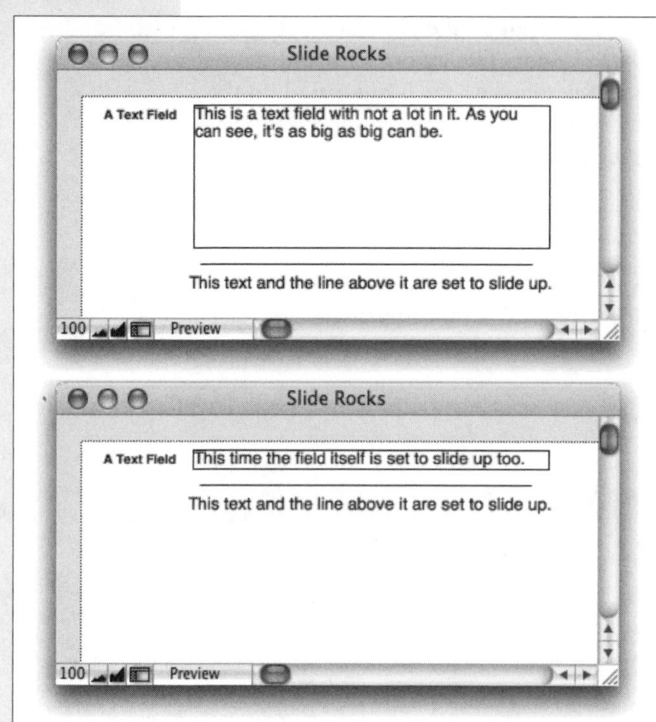

Figure 5-29: *In the top window, the line and text object are set to slide up…but as you can see, there's no sliding going on. That's because the field above them isn't set to slide. In the bottom window, the field has been set to slide up too, and now things are clearly sliding and shrinking.*

Once you've figured out which fields should shrink to fit their contents, you need to decide which objects should slide. What does that mean exactly? Normally, when you add an object to a layout, you specify exactly where it goes. But when the object is set to slide, its position is no longer fixed at an exact spot on the layout.

Instead, it moves up (or to the left) if other objects above it (or to the left of it) move or shrink. Figure 5-30 illustrates this concept.

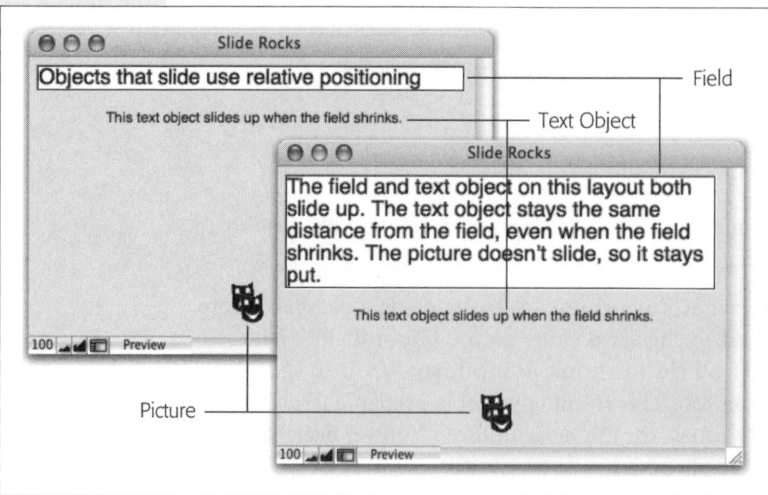

Figure 5-30: *Sliding objects (like the field and text object on this layout) position themselves relative to other objects on the layout. For example, since this field shrinks, and the text object slides up, the text object is always the same distance from the field. Its position on the page, though, changes from one record to another. The picture isn't set to slide, so it doesn't move at all.*

Setting sliding options

Once you have a general idea of which elements need to slide (and which fields must shrink accordingly), you can start telling FileMaker.

FREQUENTLY ASKED QUESTION

Merge Fields vs. Sliding

Why should I bother with sliding? Isn't that what merge fields are for?

It's true that merge fields and sliding objects have some things in common. Both adjust the data shown on a layout, squeezing things together in the process. But they have some major differences:

- Merge fields work everywhere, even in Browse mode. Sliding objects, on the other hand, have no effect on Browse mode (or Find mode). Instead, they do their thing only in Preview mode and when printing.
- Any object on a layout, including pictures, can slide. There's no way to incorporate pictures into merge fields.
- Fields that slide act just like normal fields in Browse mode, in that you can edit the data in them. Merge fields are just text objects, and are only for display.

Bearing all these differences in mind, you can easily figure out which method to use. If you have a few fields that you want to display as a single block of text, use merge fields. If your needs are more complex (incorporating graphics, for instance), or you need to be able to edit data on the layout, use sliding objects instead.

Also, there's absolutely nothing wrong with using both on one layout. In fact, the layout you just created uses merge fields for the name and address, but you're about to add sliding to the Notes field. You could even tell a text object containing merge fields to slide if you want. (Phew!)

The general process works like this:

1. **Select one or more objects on the layout.**

   FileMaker puts handles on the corners of each selected object.

2. **Choose Format → Set Sliding/Printing.**

   The Sliding/Printing window appears. (It's shown in Figure 5-31.)

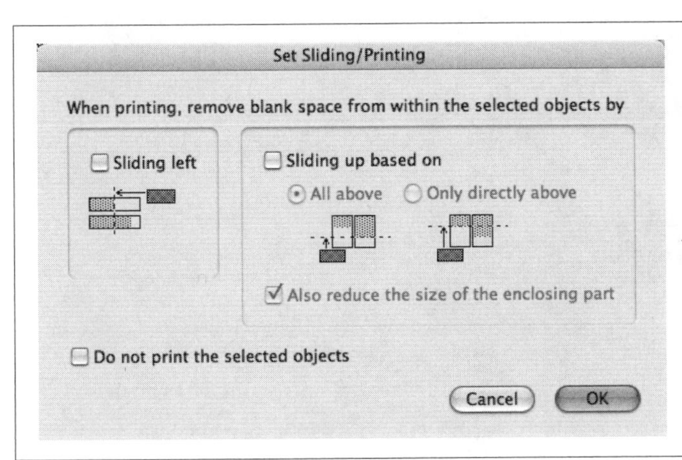

Figure 5-31: *The Sliding/Printing dialog box is where you go to tell FileMaker how an object should slide, if at all. You can also turn on "Do not print the selected objects," which does exactly what it says—hence the "/Printing" in this dialog box's name. You'll learn about all those other buttons soon.*

3. **Make your selections.**

   Right now you're just getting comfortable, so feel free to choose whatever you want. For example, choose Sliding Left to make your selected objects slide to the left to get rid of excess space. Each option will be explained in the next section.

4. **Click OK.**

   FileMaker returns you to your layout.

Since sliding affects the way your layout looks only in Preview mode and when printing, your layout won't look any different after you've made these changes. You can choose View → Show → Sliding Objects to identify the objects that will slide. With this option turned on, FileMaker draws tiny arrows on each sliding object, showing the direction it will slide.

Tip: Since setting sliding options requires a trip to a special window—and all those clicks—it can be tedious. If you have more than one object that will get the exact same settings, save yourself trouble by selecting them all first. If you plan ahead, you can usually set up even a complex sliding arrangement in just a few batches.

Now that you've *seen* the Sliding/Printing window, it's time to learn how to make sense of all those options.

FREQUENTLY ASKED QUESTION

This Field Slides and That Field Shrinks

What if I have a field that should shrink but not slide? How do I do that?

Would you believe, "You can't?" Sadly, it's almost entirely true. The series of images in Figure 5-32 shows the problem, and one workaround. Imagine you use FileMaker to keep track of the kinds of boards you sell. You record the material and the length, width, and height of the board. Sometimes you print this layout, and the first picture shows the result. It's not bad, but you decide you want the "ft" and "in" unit labels to slide left so they're closer to the numbers.

You remind yourself that the fields need to shrink for the sliding to work, and that shrink means slide. So you set the Length, Width, and Height fields, the "ft" text object, and the two "in" text objects all to slide left. The second image shows the result—not exactly what you had in mind.

What happened? Since the fields are set to slide, they did—right into one another. What you really want is for the fields to shrink but not slide. Alas, FileMaker has no such setting.

If you really want this to work, you have to get creative. The fields don't slide left if there's something in the way. Instead, they maintain their position relative to whatever is to their left. As shown in the third picture, you can put simple vertical lines next to the Width and Height fields. Since they're not set to slide, these lines act as little roadblocks for the slippery fields. To complete the effect, set the line thickness of the little lines to None. They disappear from the layout completely, but since they still exist, they still stop the sliding.

This workaround isn't perfect. It leaves invisible objects on your layout, which is always a recipe for trouble down the road ("Where is that line?!" or "What is this thing?"). But if you must have shrinking without sliding, a trick like this is all you've got.

The Sliding/Printing dialog box

The Sliding/Printing dialog box has several options to control just how the selected objects slide (and shrink if appropriate). In general, an object can slide left, up, or both.

If you want something to just slide left, you're in luck. Simply turn on the "Sliding left" checkbox and you're done. When you print or preview the layout, the objects slide to the left when field data isn't long enough to fill the full width of the field.

Objects that slide up, on the other hand, need a little more thought. To start, turn on the "Sliding up based on" checkbox.

When you turn this checkbox on, you make three more options available.

The "All above" and "Only directly above" radio buttons are hard to explain in words. Luckily, FileMaker gives you a picture to help you understand what they mean.

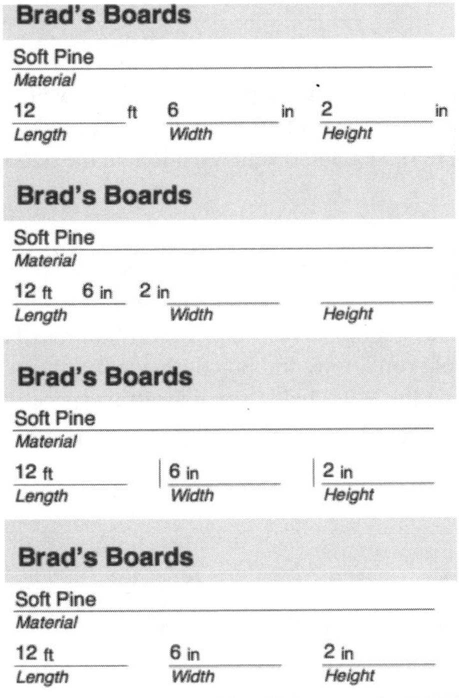

Figure 5-32:
In the top sample, the "ft" and "in" abbreviations are too far from the numbers they label. But if you set them to slide, they end up looking like the second sample–not an improvement. In the third sample, a short line acts as a barrier so the field and label can't slide their way past. If you want this effect, but without the unsightly lines, set their weight to "None," and they'll do their gatekeepers' work invisibly.

Remember an object that slides up stays the same distance from the object above it. But which object? See Figure 5-33.

Finally, if you turn on "Also reduce the size of the enclosing part," the part the object is on shrinks to fit its contents. This setting is a little misleading, though. For example, imagine you have two sliding objects on the Body part. One of these is set to reduce the Body part, while the other isn't. How can the body both reduce and not reduce at the same time?

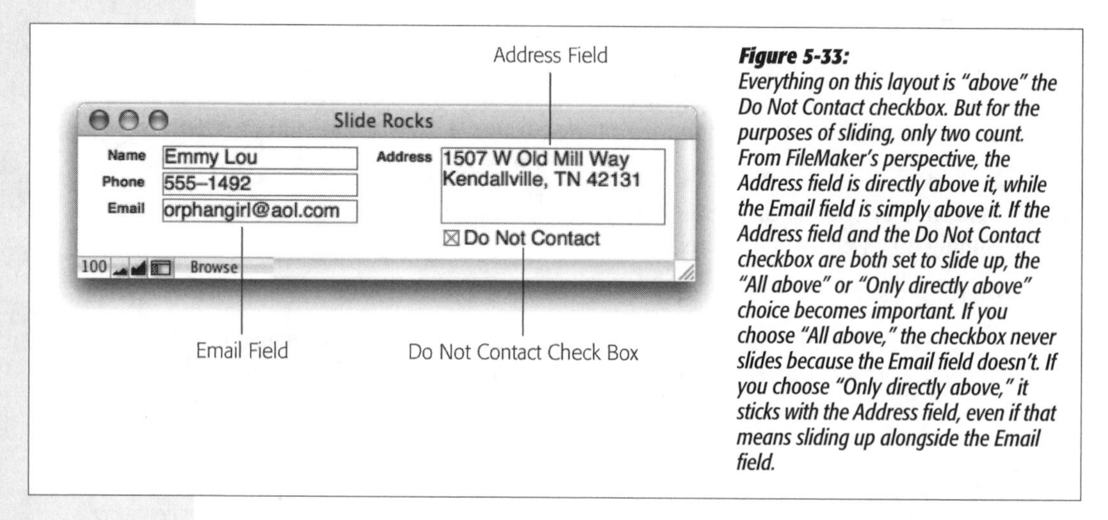

Figure 5-33: *Everything on this layout is "above" the Do Not Contact checkbox. But for the purposes of sliding, only two count. From FileMaker's perspective, the Address field is directly above it, while the Email field is simply above it. If the Address field and the Do Not Contact checkbox are both set to slide up, the "All above" or "Only directly above" choice becomes important. If you choose "All above," the checkbox never slides because the Email field doesn't. If you choose "Only directly above," it sticks with the Address field, even if that means sliding up alongside the Email field.*

In truth, the "Also reduce the size of the enclosing part" setting only matters for the *lowest* object on the part. If that object wants the part to reduce, it will. If it doesn't, the part won't. Anything you set on any other object doesn't matter. The lesson: If you're trying to get your part to reduce, focus your attention on the bottom-most object on your layout.

Using sliding on the report layout

The report layout you've been working on provides a dramatic example of how sliding can both save space and produce a more attractive printout. You may have lengthy notes about some of the people you know, and no comment about others. Here are the specific steps for shrinking the Notes field to avoid wasting space.

1. **Select the Notes field and the hairline below it.**

   Both objects have selection handles, and the Format → Sliding/Printing command is no longer grayed out.

2. **Choose Format → Sliding/Printing.**

   The now-familiar Sliding/Printing window appears.

3. **Turn on "Sliding up based on," and select "All above."**

   You want the Notes field to shrink vertically, and the line to slide up next to it, so up makes sense.

4. **In this case, you're interested in sliding things up, so turn on the "Sliding up based on" checkbox. With this option selected, the Notes field shrinks vertically to hold just its contents. The hairline also slides up, maintaining its distance from the Notes field as it shrinks.**

If you stop here, you won't quite have your problem solved. Even though the hairline slides up as much as possible, the Body part itself doesn't shrink, and your report still wastes paper. To solve this problem, turn on "Also reduce the size of the enclosing part." When you're done, click OK.

If you view your report now (Scripts → Report), things should look much better. Figure 5-34 agrees.

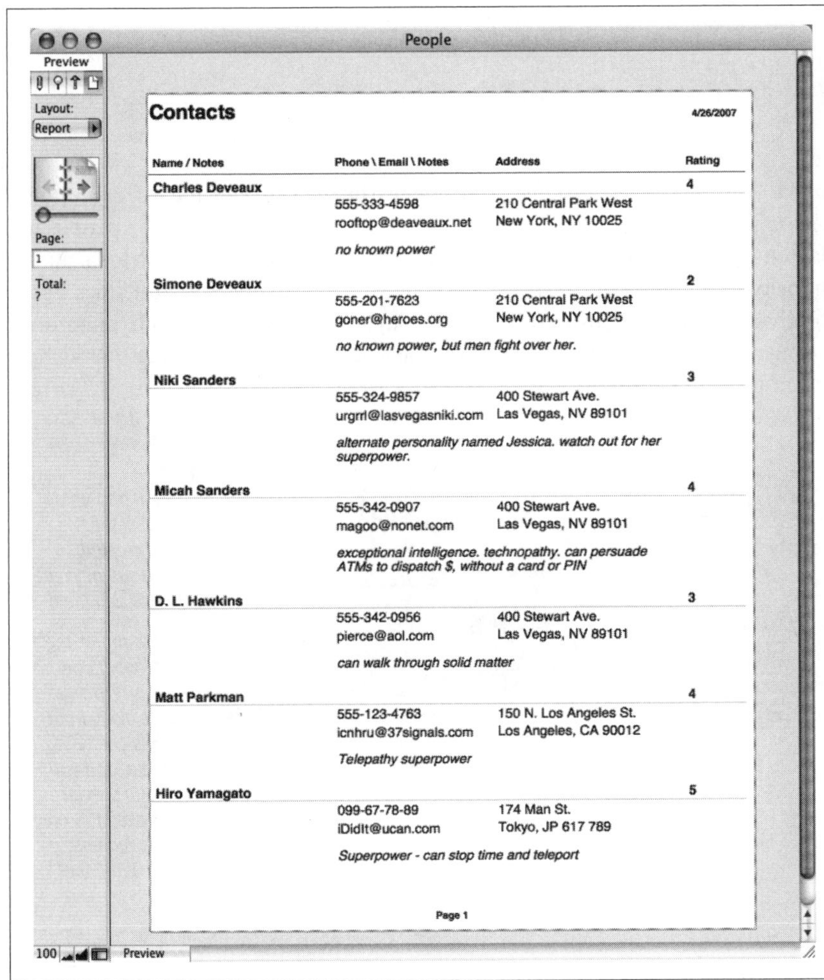

Figure 5-34: Feel free to make your layouts look the way you want–it's your database. The key thing to remember is that Preview mode, shown here, is remarkably like the printed page you'll get when you choose File → Print.

Setting Layout Order

Now that you know how to create new layouts, you'll find dozens of uses for them. Pretty soon, your pop-up menu of layouts will get lengthy. And, unless you're some kind of organizational genius, you probably won't create your layouts in exactly the order you want them to appear in the list. There's an easy way to manage the list, though. In Layout Mode, choose Layouts → Set Layout Order. You'll see the dialog box in Figure 5-35.

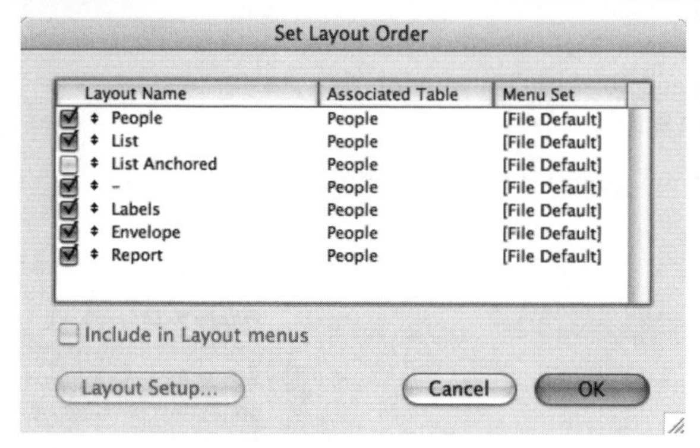

Figure 5-35: *Drag the double-arrow to reorder the list. The checkbox in the left column lets you determine whether a layout will appear in the Layout pop-up menu. When you select a layout from the list, the Layout Setup button becomes available, and you can go directly to the dialog box to rename a layout, change its views, and so on.*

To make your life easier, arrange your layouts in the order of most frequent use. Since you'll be working with your data mainly while you're viewing the people and list layouts, put them up top. Then you can move the layouts meant for printing down below, so they're grouped by function. You can make separator lines in the list to divide the groups. Just create a blank layout named - (that's a hyphen, with no extra spaces). Make as many "-" layouts as you need, and then drag them where you want them in the list.

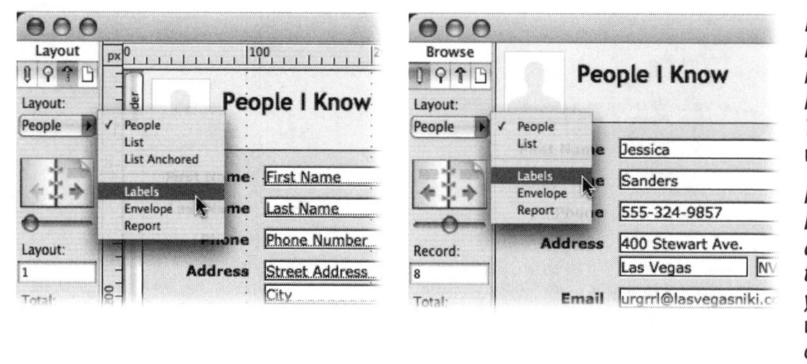

Figure 5-36: *Left: The Layout pop-up menu displays all the layouts you've created. That's how you can navigate when it's time to edit them.*

Right: In Browse mode, the List Anchored layout doesn't appear. Use this technique to keep layouts away from your users while you're working on them, or if you create them for a special purpose that's available only while a script is running. You'll learn all about that in Part 5.

Tip: To save time bouncing back and forth between creating new layouts and the Set Layout Order dialog box, create a bunch of spare separator layouts at the bottom of your list right away. Then you can move them up into place as you need them. (Don't display the separators in the Layout menu until they're in place, though.)

CHAPTER

6

Advanced Layouts and Reports

Believe it or not, Layout mode has *even more* tricks up its sleeve. In the last couple of chapters, you've learned how to use the basic layout tools to position fields, create text labels, add graphics, and more. You've experienced stress-free layout creation with the layout assistant and seen reports in action. You even know how to design full-fledged layouts from the ground up.

Now, you're ready to learn the more advanced layout concepts: controlling how fields look and act, and adding buttons to perform customized tasks. You'll also learn how text and field object formats can change based on the data in your fields. Next, you'll see how you can add real live Web page content directly to your FileMaker layout. Finally, you'll find out how to develop massively powerful reports by using summary and sub-summary parts to add groups, subtotals, and grand totals.

Value Lists

You flirted a bit with the Field/Control Setup dialog box in Chapter 4, when turning the Goodness Rating field into a pop-up menu (see page 162). Field controls can be more than pop-up menus, though. The six main field styles are Edit Box, Drop-down List, Pop-up Menu, Checkbox Set, Radio Button Set, and Drop-down Calendar.

Each style (except Edit Box and Drop-down Calendar) lets you associate a *value list* with the field. Value lists give you more efficient access to a few frequently used terms, numbers, dates, or times. Using a field control, you can then easily enter a value from the value list into the field. You tell FileMaker how you want these choices presented, by selecting one of the field control styles.

Using a value list-based field control helps in two ways. First, you can more easily enter data into your database. If folks need to put a part number into a field, for example, they can just pick it from a list and avoid typing it exactly. Just as important, fields formatted with a value list help ensure *consistency*. As your database grows, one of the toughest challenges you face is inconsistent data. For example, suppose you have two people entering addresses in your database. Cheryl is a fussbudget, and she *always* spells things out. Frank, on the other hand, is, ahem, keystroke efficient. He likes to abbreviate wherever possible. If all your customers are in central Arizona, you may wind up with some people in *Phoenix* and others in *PHX*, some in *Tucson* and others in *Tcsn*. Even worse, Frank, like most of his kind, can't even keep his own abbreviations consistent. He's got customers in *Chnd, Chndlr, Chand*, and (on a particularly bad day) *Ch*.

Even *horrendous* abbreviations may not cause a big problem to the human eye. After all, you can probably figure out where the person lives just by reading the City field. But what happens when you need to use FileMaker's find tools to find all the Chandler, AZ customers in your database? Searching for "Chandler" won't turn them all up. Instead, you have to try to think of all the different ways it could be abbreviated and search for each one. If you use a field formatted with a value list, however, you can make sure that everybody enters data the same way every time.

A value list has two parts. First, you decide which items appear in your value list. In this part, you're limiting the scope of the data your users can enter in a field. Creating value lists isn't technically a task that belongs to the Field/Control Setup dialog box—you can manage them at any time, using the File → Manage → Value List dialog box. In fact, as you learned on page 115, value lists aren't used just for field entry. You can also use a value list to validate field entry or to manipulate sort order.

Creating Value Lists

Creating a value list is a breeze. In fact, if you've read this book up to this point, you've already created two (see page 115 and page 162). The most direct way to create a value list is to choose File → Manage → Value Lists. FileMaker also includes a Manage Value Lists option in pop-up menus on dialog boxes throughout the program. Any time you're asked to *choose* a value list, FileMaker gives you a shortcut to the Manage Value Lists dialog box, too.

No matter how you get there, though, the Manage Value Lists dialog box looks just like the one in Figure 6-1.

Imagine you want to simplify data entry in your People database. One good candidate is the City field. Although a person could be from just about any city, you know that in your case, *most* of the people you deal with live near you. You can use a value list to speed entries in the City field by providing a list of the most common cities. First up, you need to create the value list:

1. **Open your People database.**

   If you haven't been following along, you can download a file with the fields listed in these steps from the Missing Manual Web site (*www.missingmanuals.com*).

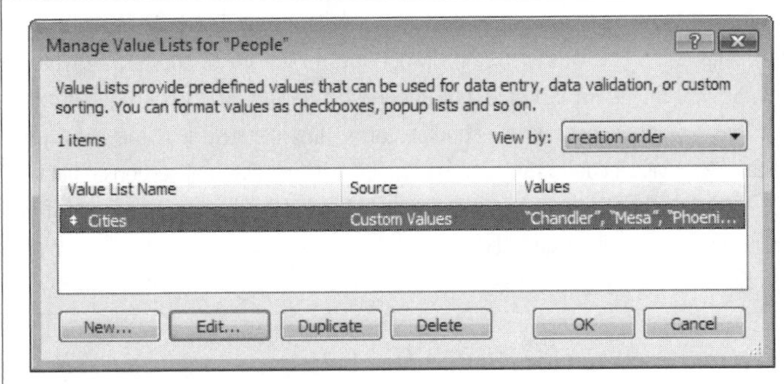

Figure 6-1:
The Manage Value Lists dialog box (File → Manage → Value Lists) is a one-stop shop for value list manipulation. You can add new value lists, modify the ones you already have, and delete the leftovers you're no longer using. As a budding FileMaker expert, you already know how to use this window: It works a lot like the Fields tab of the Manage Database dialog box.

2. **Choose File → Manage → Value Lists**

   The Manage Value Lists dialog box appears. Notice that FileMaker's considerate enough to tell you the name of the file you're working in.

3. **In the Manage Value Lists dialog box, click New, and then, when the Edit Value List dialog box opens (see Figure 6-2), give your new value list a name.**

   A name like *Cities* makes sense. But if you prefer, you can call it *Towns*, *Villages*, *Municipalities*, or whatever.

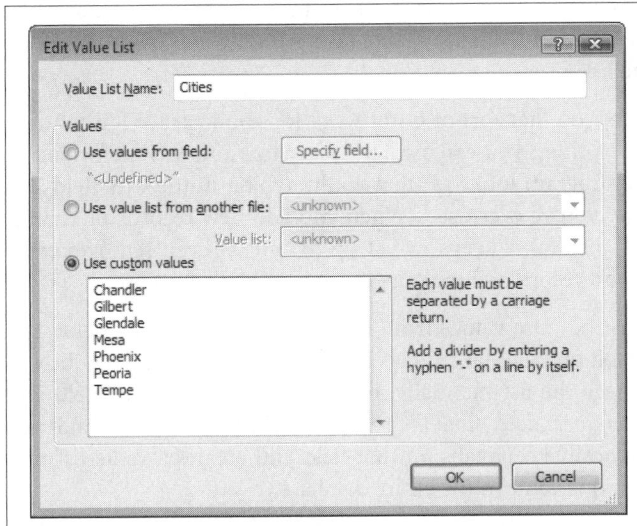

Figure 6-2:
The Edit Value List window is also where you create new lists. Start by giving it a good, descriptive name. Then choose one of the three basic value list flavors. If you have some specific ideas for what should go in the field, create a custom value list, as shown here. You can also use values from an existing field or a separate FileMaker file.

4. **Make sure "Use custom values" is turned on, and then, in the associated box, type the values you want to appear in your list.**

   Be sure to separate each item in your list with a line break (press Return at the end of each line). For example, you might enter Chandler, Gilbert, Glendale, Mesa, Phoenix, Peoria, and Tempe if you live in Phoenix, Arizona. Just remember to put each city name on its own line.

Note: You can put the values in any order you want, and FileMaker will preserve this order when it offers up a list of choices during data entry. You can even add divider lines to the list of choices, by typing a hyphen on a line by itself. So you might, for example, put Phoenix first in the list, then a separator line, and then the remaining cities in alphabetical order. Phoenix comes first because it is the most likely choice. The divider line serves as a visual cue to the user that the list has two different sections. That way, Phoenix doesn't look out of place when everything else is alphabetized. Also, bear in mind that if you leave blank lines in your list, FileMaker will include blanks in the list of choices, which is usually not what you want. So be careful to clean up any stray line breaks.

5. **Click OK, and then OK again to close both dialog boxes.**

   You're back in your database.

To attach this value list to the City field, select the field, and then choose Format → Field/Control → Setup. From the "Display as" pop-up menu, choose Drop-down List. Then choose your value list from the "Display values from" pop-up menu. (You're using a drop-down list because it lets you type anything you want in the field if the city you're after isn't in the list.)

Values from a field

Suppose you take a trip to Spokane and fit in with the folks there like a native. Suddenly you find your list of acquaintances from that city growing vigorously. You can very easily return to the Manage Value Lists window, edit your value list, and add Spokane to the list.

But why not let FileMaker do that sort of grunt work for you instead? Rather than sit there and type a list of cities, you can ask FileMaker to build the list for you as you add new data. The program looks at what you're typing in the City field and builds a list of every city you've ever used. When you add new records or change the city on old records, FileMaker keeps its list up to date. It even removes cities from the list if you delete a record and that city is not in any other record.

The key to this power is the "Use values from field" option in the Edit Value List window. When you turn it on, FileMaker grays out the "Use custom values" box so you can no longer manage the list manually. Instead, you click Specify Field and pick a field (*any text, number, date, time, or timestamp field*) from your database. FileMaker then automatically keeps tabs on that field and creates a value list that always includes every unique value in the entire database.

To do this in your People database, return to the Manage Value Lists window, select the value list you just created, and click Edit. Now turn on "Use values from field." You see the "Specify Fields for Value List" dialog box (see Figure 6-3).

In the "Specify Fields for Value List" dialog box, you see a pop-up menu labeled "Use values from first field." This pop-up menu lets you pick a table. Since you have only one table in your database right now, your choice is obvious: choose People. File-Maker immediately lists the fields in your database; select City. When you've made the selection, click OK in the three dialog boxes you've managed to pile up to get

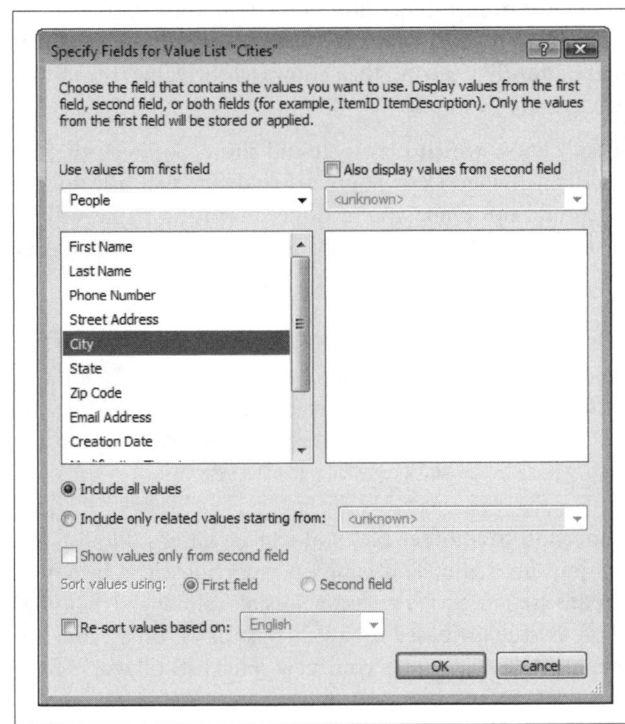

Figure 6-3: *The "Specify Fields for Value List" dialog box lets you tell FileMaker how to build the value list for you based on data already in the database. There's a lot more power here than you're ready to learn about just yet. You'll find out about adding a second field and the "Include only related values" option on page 350 (Chapter 11). For now, pay attention to the "Use values from first field" pop-up menu and the list below it.*

back to your database window. If you later want to change the field your value list is based on, return to the Edit Value List window and click Specify Field.

Note: The "Re-sort values based on" pop-up menu at the bottom of this window lets you tell FileMaker to use sorting rules from a different language for this value list. Whatever you pick, FileMaker *always* sorts these field-based value lists alphabetically. So you no longer have a chance to put more common items first in the list, or add separators.

Value list from another file

If you have another database that already contains just the right value list, you don't have to recreate it here. For example, your People database can use a Zip code value list containing all the Zip codes in your state from a different database on your hard drive. Instead of copying all that info into your People database, you can create a value list that simply goes and looks up the information in the other database—*refers* to it, in other words. If you later change the original value list (when the post office adds a new Zip code, say), People reflects that change as well. You don't have to make the change twice.

Note: When you build a large and complex database, it is sometimes advantageous to use more than one FileMaker file to keep things more manageable. You use this sort of value list most often when your *system* consists of several files. You'll learn more about complex databases in Part 3.

When you turn on "Use value list from another file" in the Edit Value List window, FileMaker shows you two pop-up menus. From the first, you choose the file that contains the value list you're after. The second then shows all the value lists in that file, so you can simply pick the one you want.

Trouble is, FileMaker doesn't know which files it should show. So, from the top pop-up menu, choose Add FileMaker Data Source. FileMaker will ask you to choose a file, which you should do. Once you're done, that file's name will be added to the "Use value list from another file" pop-up menu for eternity. You only have to go find it once.

Note: You may see two other choices on the pop-up menu: Add ODBC Data Source and Manage Data Sources. FileMaker uses the term *data source* to refer to just about anything in the world it might get some data from: an Excel spreadsheet, for instance, or some super-complicated corporate database, or another FileMaker file. You'll learn boatloads about other data sources in future chapters–they pop their heads up when you're scripting, using relationships, and integrating with other systems.

Now that you have a connection to another file, you can pick the value list you want from the "Value list" pop-up menu. The value list you choose can be any of the three types explained in this section. So it's perfectly possible (although confusing) to have a value list based on a value list based on a value list based on a value list. Also, if you *change* a referenced value list's type, your new value list still works fine.

Editing Value Lists

If your short list of approved part numbers changes, you need a way to edit your custom value list to reflect the new company policy. Choose Manage → Value Lists, select the value list you need to change, and then click Edit.

When you're through editing a value list, just click OK. If you decide you don't want to change it after all, click Cancel instead. Either way, you wind up back in the Manage Value Lists window. Just like in the Manage Database window, if you instead click Cancel, *everything* you've changed is tossed out. The value lists go back to the way they were before you opened Manage Value Lists. FileMaker asks you if you're sure first, since the Cancel button is precariously close to the OK button.

In addition to the New and Edit buttons, this Manage Value Lists dialog box has a Duplicate button. It does just what you'd expect: creates a new value list that's an exact copy of one you already have. You can live a long, healthy life without ever using this button, because once you create a value list in FileMaker, you can use the same list over and over in a multitude of fields and databases. (But isn't it nice to know you have the option?)

The Delete button deletes the selected value list, after an appropriate warning. As usual, you can hold down the Shift (Option) key as you press Delete to skip the warning.

Advanced Field Controls

As you've seen throughout the last few chapters, FileMaker field controls can take on many forms. In this section you'll learn exactly how each of these works, and

GEM IN THE ROUGH

Custom Sort Orders with Value Lists

Value lists play a part in so many database activities, it's a wonder they didn't call it ValueListMaker Pro. The Sort dialog box is another place value lists show up. Suppose you have a database of clothing products, each with a size: Small, Medium, Large, X-Large. (If you want to follow along, you can find just such a database on the Missing Manuals Web site at *www.missingmanuals.com*.) If you sort these records by size, they show up in alphabetical order:

- Large
- Medium
- Small
- X-Large

Chances are, that's *not* what you want–you want them in order from smallest to largest, or largest to smallest. To arrange that, simply create a value list with custom values: each size in the proper order.

You can then tell FileMaker to sort the record by size, but to use the order of this value list instead of alphabetical order:

1. Choose Records → Sort Records. You see the Sort Records dialog box.
2. Clear any existing fields from the Sort Order list and add the Size field. Remember you can quickly add items to the list by double-clicking them.
3. From the Sort Order list, select Size. The radio buttons below the list are now clickable.
4. Turn on "Custom order based on value list". This option informs FileMaker to order the sizes according to a value list.
5. Select the Sizes value list from the pop-up menu. Here's where you pick which value list to use.
6. Click Move. The Size field moves to the Sort Order list. The little bar chart icon beside this field matches the "Custom order based on value list" icon.
7. Click Sort. FileMaker sorts the records according to size. This time, the records are in a good logical order.

how you can configure them to get just the behavior you want. As a refresher, Figure 6-4 shows the Field/Control Setup dialog box.

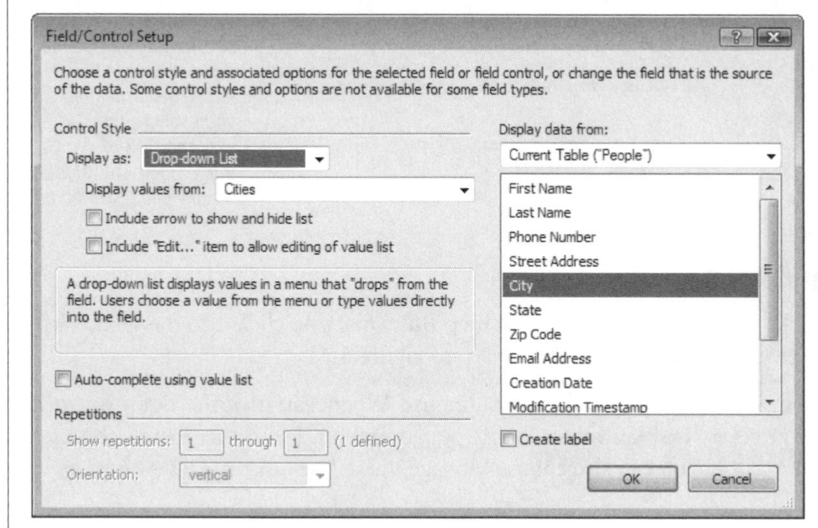

***Figure 6-4:** The Field/Control Setup dialog box (Format → Field/Control → Setup) lets you pick one of six different field control styles. Control styles are like electronic schoolmarms who watch over data entry. Drop-down lists and pop-up menus stand guard over your fields, to make sure the rules you set up are followed.*

Edit Box

Most of the fields you've used so far have been *Edit Boxes*. These are the click-and-type variety that normal people call a *text box*. Distinctive as always, FileMaker has its own moniker. No matter what you call it—Edit Box or text box—this sort of control isn't limited to just text. You can use an Edit Box with number fields, date fields, and so on.

When you select the Edit Box format, you have the choice of turning on the "Include vertical scroll bar" checkbox. You saw this option when you added a scroll bar to the Notes field on page 162. If you anticipate that a field will hold lots of information, a scroll bar can be a good idea, as Figure 6-5 shows.

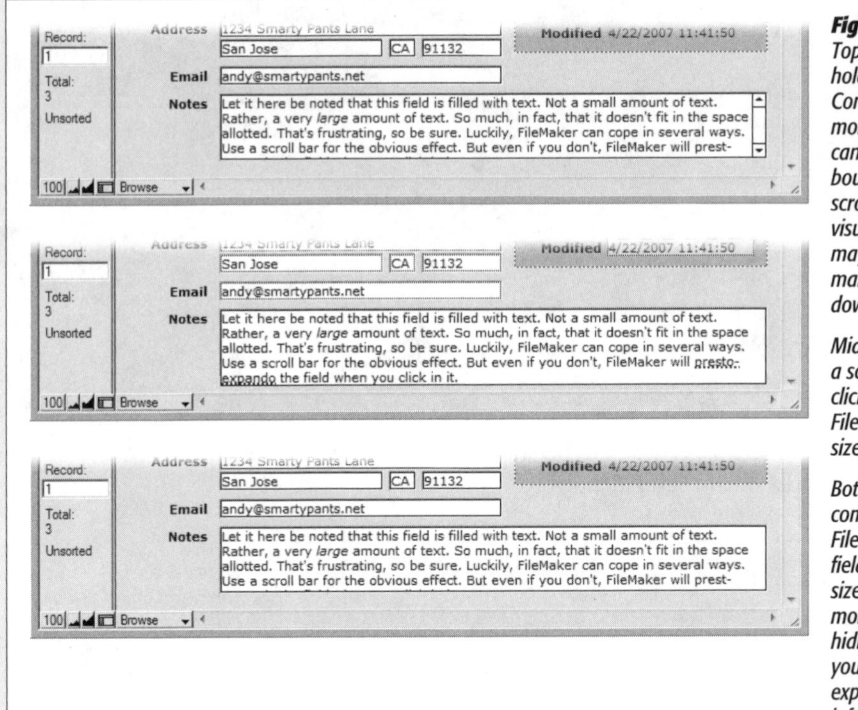

Figure 6-5: *Top: FileMaker fields can hold a lot of text. The Comments field here has more information than can fit in the field boundaries. Adding a scroll bar gives you a visual clue that there may be more, and makes it easy to scroll down to see it.*

Middle: If you don't have a scroll bar, when you click in the field, FileMaker increases its size to show all the text.

Bottom: When you commit the record, FileMaker shrinks the field back to its original size, leaving no clue that more text might be hiding below the fold. If you know you're expecting lots of information, you should usually add a scroll bar.

Drop-down List

This field type *looks* just like an edit box. But when you click into the field, a list of available choices appears just below it (see Figure 6-6).

The items in the list come from a value list. When you pick the Drop-down List type, you get a "Display values from" pop-up menu. From this menu, choose the value list to use. You can also choose Manage Value Lists to create a new one.

UP TO SPEED

Drop Down, Pop Up, Turn On

You may wonder how a drop-down list differs from a pop-up menu. They're similar in purpose, but have three differences:

- A pop-up menu requires you to make a choice when entering data–there's no way to type into the field unless you specifically tell FileMaker to allow it. With a drop-down list, on the other hand, you can always dismiss the list and type directly into the field instead. When the list pops up, just click the field again to make the list go away, and then start typing. From the keyboard, press Enter (Return) to make the list go away, or press Esc to toggle the list on and off.
- Drop-down lists work just fine with *thousands* of items in them. Since the list scrolls, it doesn't much matter how long it is. Pop-up menus, by contrast, get very cumbersome with more than a dozen or so items.
- Finally, folks can make selections from a drop-down list using just the keyboard, while a pop-up menu requires a trip to the mouse. The drop-down list's keyboard ability makes it preferable in cases where speed of entry is the priority.

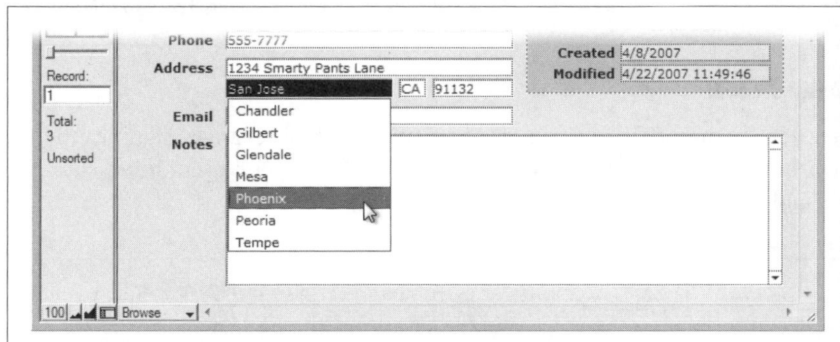

Figure 6-6: *A drop-down list like the one showing cities here gives you a scrolling list of choices to save you the trouble of typing the one you want. Just click an item in the list, and FileMaker enters it into the field. You can also use the up and down arrow keys to select an item in the list. Finally, you can type the first few letters of an item's name to select it. Once you have an item selected, press Enter (Return) to accept it.*

Note: If you don't apply borders to a drop-down list, the show/hide arrow appears only when the field is active. Add field borders (at least a right border–page 163) to make the arrow show.

Drop-down lists look just like edit boxes until you click them or tab into the field. Then the list drops down for your data-entry pleasure. But it could get annoying to have lists flashing at you just because you happen to be tabbing through the data in a record, so FileMaker lets you stop the list waving by choosing "Include arrow to show and hide list." Now the list is a little more polite. When the field is active, the list doesn't drop down until you click the arrow. If you make a choice from the list, it disappears. Or, if you don't want to enter anything into the field after all, just click the arrow and the list goes back home.

Finally, turn on "Include 'Edit…' item to allow editing of value list" if you want your users to be able to easily modify the list of choices. When folks choose "Edit…" (always the last item in the list), the window in Figure 6-7 shows up so they can modify the value list.

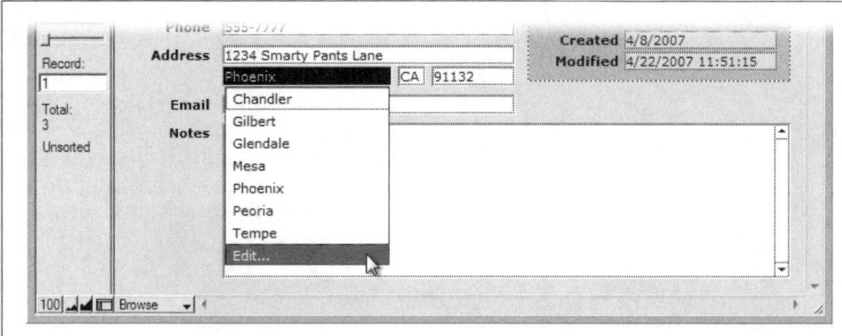

Figure 6-7: *You can include an Edit item in your drop-down list. When folks choose it, this little Edit Value List box appears. From here, they can add new items, delete items, or Edit items in the list–all by typing directly in the text box. All of this assumes your value list has "Use custom values" turned on. You can't edit the items in a value list based on field values.*

Pop-up Menu

When you format a field as a pop-up menu, the look changes significantly, as shown in Figure 6-8. Rather than type into the field, your users must click the menu and make a choice.

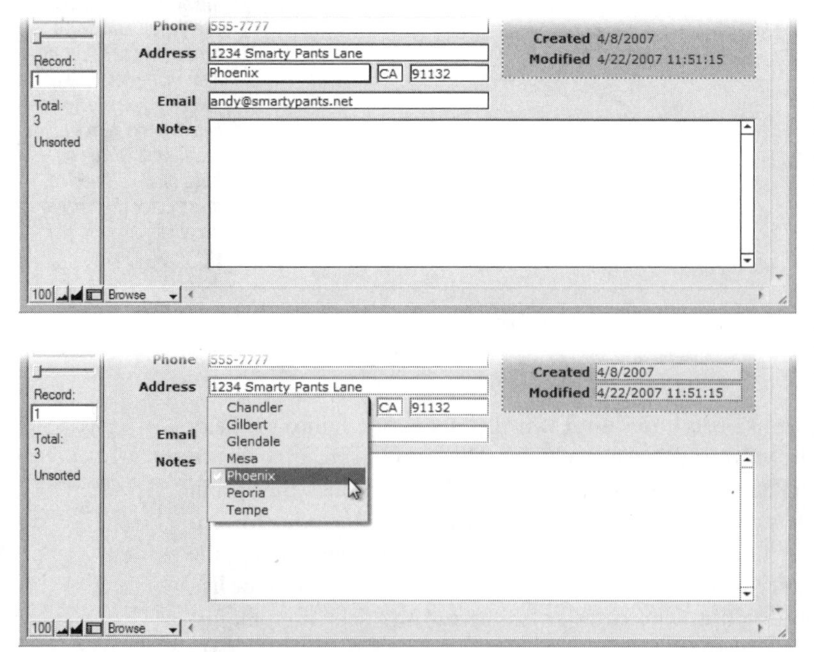

Figure 6-8: *Top: When the City field is formatted as a pop-up menu, it no longer looks like an ordinary field. Instead, it has a somewhat three-dimensional look.*

Bottom: When you click the pop-up menu, the value list appears, and you have to make a choice. Unlike a drop-down list, you can't click again and start typing.

Like drop-down lists, pop-up menus let mere mortals edit value lists, plus they up the ante by including an Other item. When people pick "Other…" from the menu, they see the window in Figure 6-9. Entering a value in this window puts it in the field but *doesn't* add it to the value list. Turn on "Include 'Other…' item to allow entry of other values" to grant this power to the masses. (See the box on page 230 for advice on the ramifications of letting your users edit or bypass your carefully crafted value lists.)

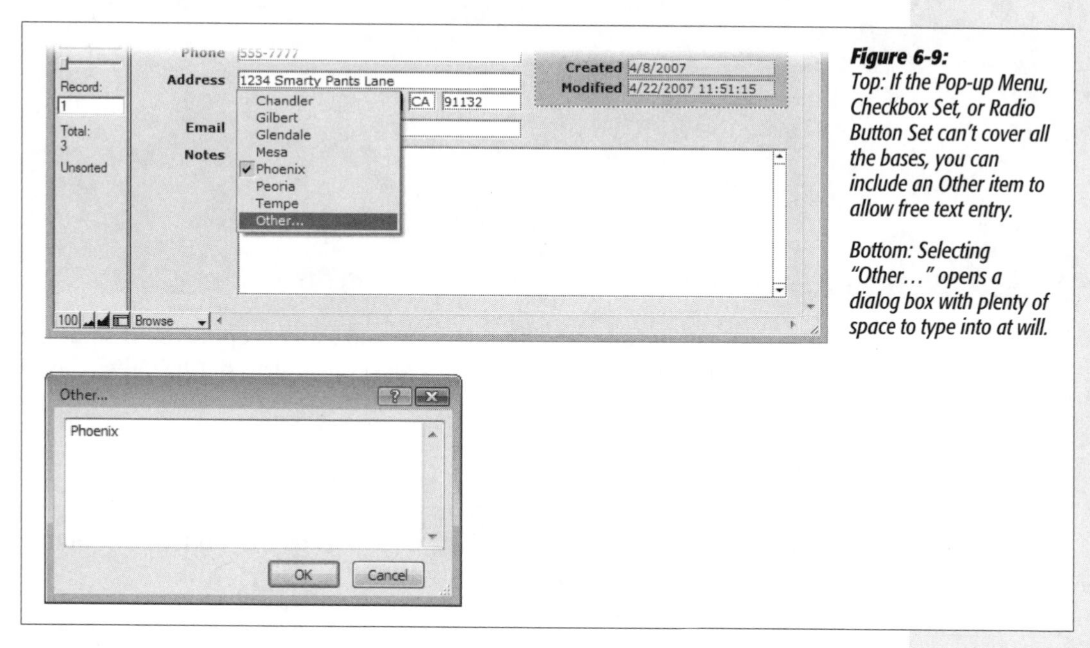

***Figure 6-9:** Top: If the Pop-up Menu, Checkbox Set, or Radio Button Set can't cover all the bases, you can include an Other item to allow free text entry.*

Bottom: Selecting "Other…" opens a dialog box with plenty of space to type into at will.

Checkbox Set

Figure 6-10 shows a field formatted as a Checkbox Set. With this format, database users can simply click each item to turn it on or off. As they do, the data in the field changes to reflect the checked items.

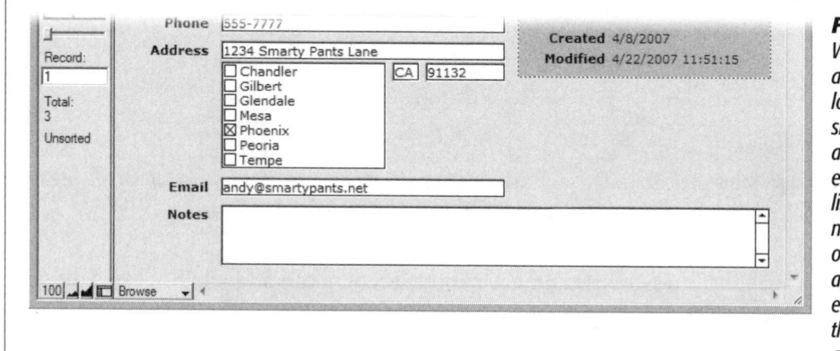

***Figure 6-10:** When you format a field as a Checkbox Set, it looks like the City field shown here. FileMaker adds one checkbox for each item in the value list, and arranges them to neatly fill the boundaries of the field. You can apply borders, fills, and effects to a field like this—they affect the entire area the Checkbox Set covers.*

UP TO SPEED

A Cautionary Tale

Not even the most highly paid database developer can think of everything folks might want to enter in a database, and a drop-down list with a handy edit option seems an obvious solution. But use it with caution. When some villainous or misguided soul chooses Edit, they're doing just that: editing your *value list* and potentially defeating the purpose for which you created it. Furthermore, if other fields in your database are formatted to use the same value list, *their* list of choices changes, too, because the underlying value list itself has changed.

So remember that value-list-based fields serve *two* purposes: simplicity and consistency. If you make it easy for folks to add their own items to a value list, you're also making it easy for the value list to get inconsistent and disorganized.

Adding an Other item can undermine consistency even more, because it encourages quick-handed mousers to simply bypass the value list entirely.

If the primary purpose of your value list is to gain consistency, you should consider leaving the Edit and Other options turned off. You can always add new choices to the value list yourself at any time as the need arises.

Checkbox Sets can include the Other item, just like a pop-up menu. If someone enters a value that isn't in the value list, FileMaker just turns on the Other checkbox to indicate the field has something more in it.

Radio Button Set

A Radio Button Set (see Figure 6-11) works much like a Checkbox Set. The only distinction is that folks can turn on only *one* item. If they try to turn on another item, FileMaker turns off items as necessary.

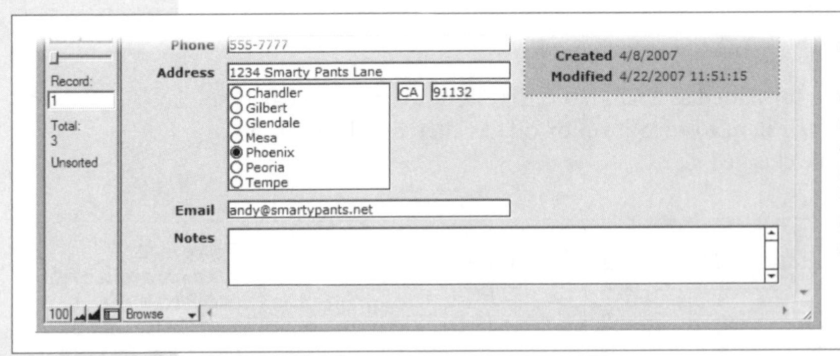

Figure 6-11: *This time the City field is formatted as a Radio Button Set. Now you can simply click the right city to set the field, making this one of the fastest field formats for mouse-based entry.*

Warning: Some users know they can Shift-click to select multiple items in a radio button set. See page 234 to learn how calculations can control these users' urge to get around the system.

Just as with drop-down lists and Checkbox Sets, you can add an Other or Edit item to the Radio Button Set. (See the box above for more detail.)

GEM IN THE ROUGH

Checkboxes Behind the Scenes

The beauty of Checkbox Set fields is that they let folks click *more than one* checkbox. In other words, you can capture several values in one easy-to-use field. This method comes in handy when the things you're tracking in your database have fields like Available Sizes, Available Colors, Warehouses, or any other attribute of the *one or more* variety. But wait, you say—how can a single field hold *more* than one value?

Simple, if you're FileMaker. Just give each checkbox its own line. In other words, if you have a Checkbox Set showing colors, and you turn on Red, Green, and Blue, FileMaker actually thinks of the field like this:

Red

Green

Blue

You can show the same field on another layout—or even the same layout if you want—without the checkbox formatting. If you do, you see the selected items: one on each line. This is called a "return-separated list." If you change what's in the field without using the checkboxes, you could end up with lines that don't match any of the value list items. In that case, the Checkbox Set turns on its Other item if it has one. (If not, the extra items simply don't show at all.)

A final note: Because Checkbox Sets need to be able to put several lines in the field, they're really suitable only for *text* fields. Other field types don't support multiline values.

Drop-down Calendar

In FileMaker, you can easily read date fields, and easily set them up. But actually typing dates into them is notoriously tricky. If you don't get just the right combination of numbers and tiny little separators, FileMaker gets all huffy and tells you the value you've just typed isn't valid. And if somebody swipes your desk calendar, how are you supposed to know what numbers to type in the first place? FileMaker Pro 9 can handle both these problems. It lets you give your date fields a nifty drop-down calendar where anyone can simply point and click to enter a date.

When you first format a field with a drop-down calendar, FileMaker doesn't give you any visual feedback letting you know a calendar's lurking there, waiting to drop down when you tab into the field. If you want to provide a visual clue, select "Include icon to show and hide calendar." Then you see a teeny, tiny calendar at the right side of your field (see Figure 6-12). Tiny as it is, the calendar icon still takes up some room, so you may have to make the field a little wider to display the entire date plus the new icon.

Note: Like the show/hide arrow on drop-down lists, the calendar icon shows up in an inactive field only if the field has a border. If you're a minimalist on the field border issue, you can format your field with only a right border to force the icon to appear.

The calendar itself is a little dynamo. To enter a date, click the Month Year display at the top and you see a pop-up menu that lets you jump to a specific month in the current calendar year.

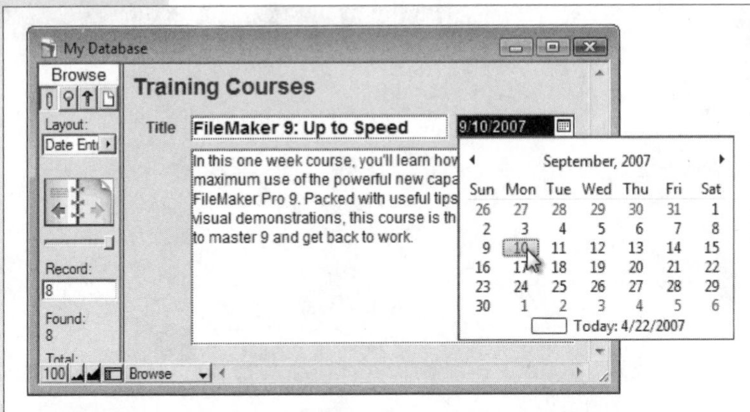

Figure 6-12: *The drop-down calendar makes entering dates a snap. It has some sweet controls, too. When the field's empty, the current date is highlighted when the field drops down. Or, if there's data in the field already, FileMaker highlights that date when the calendar appears.*

Right-click anywhere on the calendar (or Control-click on the Mac if you don't have a two-button mouse), and the pop-up menu changes to read "Go to today." The calendar closes and plunks the current date into the field.

You can also change the month with the right and left arrows at either side. The left arrow icon moves you backward in time (careful, don't touch anything or you could change the course of human history…), and the right one moves you forward. The up and down arrow icons change the display of years. Finally, you can move the highlighted date with your keyboard's arrow keys. Tap the down arrow key a few times to see how fast time flies.

But if you get carried away playing the controls ("Is my birthday on a Friday in 2015?"), the calendar's footer always displays the current date. Just click that display to enter the current date, and then click to open up the calendar again. It reorients to today's date.

Auto-Complete

Auto-Complete is a strong ally both for database designers who care about data consistency and for data entry folk who hate to type. Unlike the other Field/Control field styles, you can apply this little beauty to a regular Edit Box. Once you've turned on the option to "auto-complete using previously entered values," the field gets ESP and tries to figure out what you want to enter. Where do these superhuman powers come from? From that old friend, the field's index (see page 119).

Auto-Complete isn't a control style in and of itself; rather, you use it in conjunction with either an Edit Box or a drop-down list (the option isn't available for other styles). But Auto-Complete behaves a little differently on Edit Boxes than it does on drop-down lists. The differences are discussed in the following sections.

Auto-Complete in Edit Boxes

To turn on Auto-Complete for an Edit Box field control, visit the Format → Field/Control → Setup dialog box and turn on "Auto-complete using previously entered values." (This checkbox only shows up when you have "Display as" set to Edit Box.)

UP TO SPEED

When Is Auto-Complete Not Useful?

With such a cool feature, one that seems to know what people want to type before *they* do, you may be tempted to add auto-complete powers to most of your fields. But there are cases when it just isn't very helpful.

Auto-Complete depends on the index to know what to show in its list. There has to be data in at least one field for FileMaker to have any entries in the index. And indexes add a lot of size to your files, so if you index a lot of fields so that Auto-Complete works, you may find that the file size balloons. Remember, this feature comes with all of indexing's dark sides as a tradeoff for its power.

Another weakness: When someone types a letter that's not used much–like X, J, or Z–Auto-Complete may not produce a drop-down list.

This lack of a list doesn't mean Auto-Complete is broken. It just means the index doesn't have any entries beginning with that letter. The index saves no time in such cases.

Auto-Complete works best in larger databases where there are lots of records. And it's usually most effective if the records have a fairly wide range of data in them. For example, if a field is going to have only a few possible values (G, PG, PG-13, R, NC-17), then a drop-down menu or a pop-up list is a better choice than an Auto-Complete Edit Box.

None of these cautions means that you shouldn't use Auto-Complete. Just be aware of its limitations and the overhead it places on your file.

When you start typing into a field configured this way, FileMaker scans the field's index and drops down a list of matching entries. There *is no value list* in this case—it always draws from field values on other records. If you type *T*, for example, you see a list of entries that begin with the letter T. If you type *R* next, the list shortens to only words beginning with "TR." Once the list is short enough for you to find what you want, just click the list item to select it.

Tip: The Auto-Complete list behaves just like a regular drop-down list, so if you prefer, you can highlight items with arrow keys, and then press Enter.

Auto-Complete in drop-down lists

If your field is formatted as a drop-down list, you can make it even smarter by adding auto-complete behavior. Visit the Field/Control Setup dialog box, make sure "Display as" is set to Drop-down List, and turn on "Auto-complete using value list." When used in conjunction with a drop-down list, Auto-Complete instead uses the values from the associated value list. In fact, in many ways, it works just like an ordinary drop-down list. Now, though, you get the automatic type-ahead behavior you've come to know and love: As you begin to type, FileMaker automatically narrows the list to include items that start with what you've entered so far. This can make your drop-down lists even faster and easier to use.

Note: When you click into an Auto-Complete drop-down list that's formatted with a show/hide arrow, the list doesn't appear until you click the arrow or pres the Esc key. If you want the list to display as soon as the field is entered, then don't select the "Include arrow to show and hide list" option.

WORKAROUND WORKSHOP

One or Many?

Strange as it sounds, pop-up menus and radio buttons both allow *multiple selections*, just like Checkbox Sets. Just hold down the Shift key while you select an item, and FileMaker dutifully turns it on without turning off the item that's already selected. Handy though it may be, however, chances are you don't want anyone to use this trick and choose more than one value—otherwise you use checkboxes to make it obvious that multiple choices are desirable.

Unfortunately, there's no direct way to turn off this feature. If you want to prevent your users from picking too many items, you have to get creative. Here's one way of doing so:

Chapter 3 introduced you to Auto-Enter calculations (see page 110). They let you automatically change the value in a field, based on a *calculation*. You'll learn all about calculations in Part 4, so for now you just have to have some blind faith.

Here's how to limit your fields to a *single* value:

1. In the Manage Database window, select the field you want to fix and click Options. The Field Options dialog box appears. If it isn't already selected, click the Auto-Enter tab.
2. Turn on the "Calculated value" checkbox. The Specify Calculation dialog box appears.
3. In the big free-entry box on the bottom half of the window, type *LeftValues (Self ; 1)*. This calculation tells FileMaker you want to keep only the left-most—or *first*—value in the field.
4. Click OK. You're now back in the Field Options dialog box.
5. Turn off "Do not replace existing value (if any)" and click OK.

You're back in your database.

Now if you try to Shift-click a second item, FileMaker immediately throws it out. In practice, it *looks* like it simply doesn't let you Shift-click.

Repetitions

On page 119, you learned about repeating fields, which let you put several values in one field, with a separate Edit Box for each one. Remember, when you put a repeating field on a layout, you get to decide how many times it shows up. Even if a field has 200 repetitions, you don't *have* to show them all on the layout. You can elect to show just the first ten. Or just the last ten. Or numbers 37 through 118.

To control how repeating fields display, you use the same Field Control/Setup dialog box shown in Figure 6-4. This time, focus your attention at the bottom of this dialog box under Repetitions. Just enter the first repetition you want in the "Show repetitions" box, and the last one in the "through" box. You can't show noncontiguous repetitions here—you have to enter one beginning and one end, and FileMaker will show those and every repetition in between. But try this technique instead: Put multiple copies of the field on the layout, but specify that each copy displays a different range of repeats. You'll get much the same effect, as described in the box on page 235.

Note: If the "Show repetitions" and "through" options are grayed out, it probably means you didn't have a repeating field selected when you chose the Format → Field Format command.

Once you've figured out which repetitions to show, you get to pick an orientation. Your choices are Horizontal and Vertical, and Figure 6-13 makes sense of them.

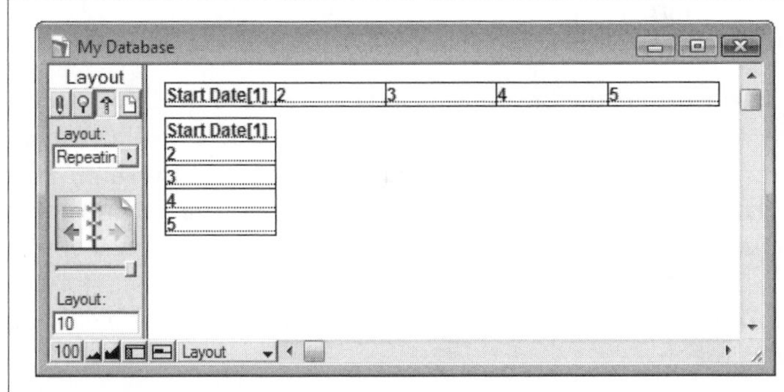

Figure 6-13: *This layout shows two repeating fields, one with horizontal orientation, and one with vertical. (See the box below for further advice.) In Layout mode, FileMaker numbers each repetition in a repeating field to let you know which one it is. The first repetition shows the full field name and–if there's room–the repetition number in brackets.*

POWER USERS' CLINIC

Flexible Repetitions

Suppose you *want* to show noncontiguous ranges of repeating fields. Or you need something more flexible than a straight up-and-down or side-to-side orientation. For example, your layout may be easier on the eyes if it shows the first ten repetitions in one stack, and the next ten in another stack right beside the first set. Or you may want to show just the even-numbered repetitions. Or perhaps you're determined to see repetition number 1, then 11 through 13, then 7 and 8, and finally number 281. No matter how capricious your desires, FileMaker's up to the job.

Here's the trick: Put the field on the layout *more than once*. Or, more correctly, put several field controls on the layout, all associated with the same field. For example, suppose you have a repeating field called Dimensions. It holds all the various measurements for a particular sprocket in your catalog. Now imagine you want to show the first 10 repetitions in a vertical stack, with the next 10 beside it.

First, add the field to the layout using the Field tool. From the Format → Field/Control → Setup dialog box, configure it to show repetitions 1 through 10 in a vertical orientation, and then click OK. Now duplicate the whole shebang. Select the copy, move it to its own plot of layout land, and visit the Field/Control Setup dialog box once more. Configure this version of the field control to show repetitions 11 through 20. If you head back to Browse mode, you'll see that you have all 20 repetitions on the layout, arranged the way you wanted.

By using various combinations of repeating field controls in various configurations, you can arrange field repetitions any way you want–even if you have to add a separate control for each repetitions.

Display Data From

So far, you haven't explored the right side of the Field/Control Setup dialog box, where there lives an incredibly powerful feature—the "Display data from" option. With this powerful tool, you can make one field display the contents of…another field. But why? While you ponder that Zen-like paradox, read the following example.

Say your database has a series of similar fields—Email, Mail, and Phone—each of which indicates whether or not you have permission to contact a customer using that method. You add the Email field to the layout and format it with a nice pop-up control and a value list with the custom values of Yes and No. You shorten it to just the right width and apply beautiful font formatting. Now, you have to add the Mail and Phone fields in turn and give them the same controls and text formatting. But that would take forever—twice!

Instead, do the following: Copy the Email field, and paste it onto the layout twice. Move one copy where the Mail field should be and the other where the Phone field wants to live. Next, use the Field/Control Setup dialog box to tell the duplicated Email field to display data from Mail instead. Do the same for the second copy, changing it to display data from the Phone field. With a few quick clicks, you're done. You've just borrowed the formatting from one field to display the information from another. The moral of the story: Use "Display data from" to avoid doing work you've already done.

Field Behavior

The Field/Control Setup dialog box controls how a field looks and works. FileMaker has another dialog box, called the Field Behavior dialog box, that also influences how a field works, but in a different way. This time, you get to decide when (if ever) a person should be allowed to click into the field, how it handles certain special keystrokes, and whether or not it should be spell-checked. The Format → Field Behavior command shows this dialog box, and so does Figure 6-14.

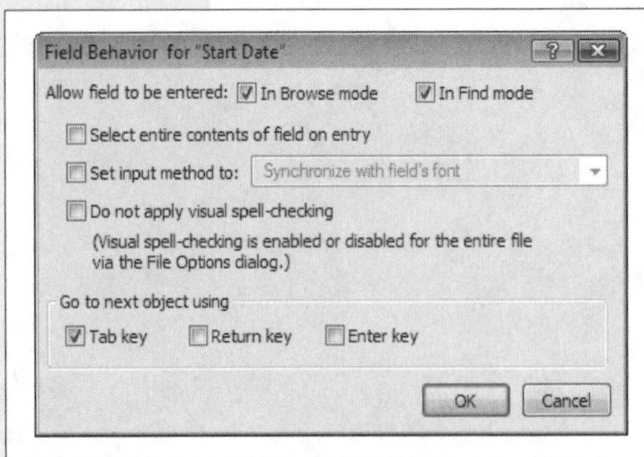

Figure 6-14:
By "behavior," FileMaker means five things: Can you click into the field? What happens when you do? How do you type into the field? When you do type, should FileMaker bother checking your spelling? And what do the special keys (Tab, Return, and Enter) do when in the field?

Field Entry

Sometimes you want to *show* a field value on a particular layout, but you don't want any one *changing* it. If that's your fancy, select the field in Layout mode and choose Format → Field Behavior. Then simply turn off the "In Browse mode" checkbox (next to "Allow field to be entered").

Just because you don't want this field being *modified* on this layout doesn't mean you don't want to use it in a find request. If you leave "In Find mode" turned on, your users can still type into the field in Find mode. If you don't want that either, turn off "In Find mode." If you want to let people modify a field but not search in it, then turn on "In

Browse mode" and turn off "In Find mode." For example, turn off Find if the field isn't indexed (see page 119) and you don't want people stuck with slow finds.

Select Entire Contents of Field on Entry

If a field is formatted as an Edit Box or a pop-up list, folks can click it to type a value. Normally, when they first click the field, a flashing insertion point marks the spot they clicked. When they type, FileMaker inserts the text at that point. If you prefer, you can instead have the field start out with all its content selected. For example, if the First Name field contains "Stacey," a single click on the "c" selects the entire name. To get this behavior, turn on "Select entire contents of field on entry." This option is ideal when editing the field usually means replacing the existing value with whatever you're typing. It's also great for date fields and other fields that contain a lot of punctuation that gets in the way of double-clicks. If, on the other hand, you often make minor tweaks to the field (think about the Notes field), then you would want to turn this option off.

Note: If you do select the entire contents of a field with "Select entire contents of field on entry" turned on, you can use your mouse or arrow keys to set the insertion point, just the way you edit text in any other program. Likewise, if you don't have this option turned on, you can still select the entire field contents by choosing Edit → Select All once you're in the field.

Input Method

Unless you work for the UN, you probably never use the "Set input method" setting, but for the sake of completeness, here's what it does: In some languages, entering text isn't as simple as in English. For example, Japanese has many more characters than fit comfortably on a keyboard. To get the job done, a Japanese typist must use an *input method*—the set of rules and software interfaces used to get text into the computer. Unfortunately, there isn't just one method, and FileMaker lets you pick which one you want. Normally, the "Synchronize with field's font" option is selected. This option just means FileMaker automatically picks the input method based on the font you've selected. If you want to override this behavior and specify a hard-coded input method, turn on this checkbox and, from the pop-up menu, choose the input method.

Field-level Visual Spell Checking

As described in Chapter 2, when FileMaker's visual spell checker is turned on, FileMaker underlines suspicious spellings when you are editing a field (see page 85). This feature is delightful until you realize that it dutifully tries to spell check the Part Number field in your Products database, the Password field in your Suppliers database, and the First Name field in your Russian Relatives database. In each of these cases (and many more), the field is pretty much guaranteed to contain a word or two that doesn't appear in FileMaker's spelling dictionary. Simply turn on "Do not apply visual spell-checking," and FileMaker won't bother marking misspelled words in that particular field.

UP TO SPEED

Borders and Repeating Fields

While you've got repeating fields on the brain, there's one more formatting choice worth talking about. You can put a border around a repeating field just like any other field. But this border goes around the entire set of fields, not each individual repetition. You wind up with what looks like one big field, and it can be a surprise when you click it and discover those repetitions. Wouldn't it be nicer if you could format those repeating fields to look like a sensible set of fields?

Nicer, yes. And possible, too. Just select the repeating field in Layout mode and visit the Format → Field Borders window. If you look at this dialog box with a repeating field selected, you have one additional option: "Between repeating values." When this checkbox is turned on, you get your borderline *between* each repetition, as well as around the whole thing.

Note: Turning this option *off* doesn't ensure that visual spell checking will kick in. You still need to turn the feature on in the Spelling tab of the File → File Options dialog box.

Go To Next Field Using

Way back in Chapter 1 you learned to use the Tab key to move from field to field. It turns out you can actually change this behavior, too: You can designate the Tab key, Return key, or Enter key to jump to the next field. Or pick any combination of the three (you don't have to press them *all at once* if you turn on more than one; rather, you can use *any* of the keys you turn on here).

Note: When one of these keys isn't assigned to go to the next field, its more normal behavior takes over: The Tab key inserts a tab into the field; the Return key inserts a new line into the field; and the Enter key exits the record.

You may want to change these settings for two reasons. First, if you have a field that *often* needs tabs typed into it (like a field that holds an ingredient list—quantity [Tab] unit [Tab] ingredient [Return]...), it can be annoying to have to press Ctrl+Tab (Option-Tab) all the time. You can turn off "Tab key" in the Field Behavior dialog box and make typing tabs easier. Since field behaviors are set for *each field*, you can give the Ingredients field this behavior, and keep the normal tabbing behavior for all the other fields on the layout.

The second reason comes down to the fact that humans are funny creatures. People are smart enough to put a man on the moon, but for some reason they *hate* to learn new ways to work. If you're creating a database for people whose old computer system used, for example, the Enter key to move between fields, you may decide to make FileMaker mimic that behavior to make their lives easier.

Conditional Formatting

In Chapter 4, you learned how to apply fonts, text styles, colors, and so on to many of FileMaker's layout objects. You can make fields, text objects, and shapes look almost any way you want with a little mouse gymnastics, but you're limited to just *one look* for any particular object. Particularly with fields and their labels, though, you may want to make the look *change* depending on exactly what is going on in the database. Suppose some of the people in your database have a very low Goodness Rating (less than three, say). It would be fantastic if this fact could be reflected by a more eye-catching visual clue than just a below-average single-digit number. What if the whole Goodness Rating field and its label turned red when the rating was below a certain threshold? Then the low rating would stand out immediately as you flip through records. You *can* apply just this sort of automatic reformatting in FileMaker Pro 9, using a new feature called *conditional formatting*.

Conditional formatting works by letting you specify a series of conditions and the specific formatting changes that go along with them. FileMaker means *condition* in the "I'll give you a hand on one condition..." sense. As long as certain restrictions are met, the formatting applies.

Conditional Formatting of Fields

You can apply conditional formatting to any text object, button, field control, or web viewer. Follow these steps to make your database really announce a low Goodness Rating:

1. **Open the People database, and go to the detail layout.**

   Make sure you're in Layout mode.

2. **Select the Goodness Rating field (not the text label beside it), and then choose Format → Conditional.**

   You see the Conditional Formatting dialog box pictured in Figure 6-15.

3. **Click Add.**

   A new condition appears in the list at the top of the window. Also, the Condition and Format sections of the dialog box become active (they were grayed out until now).

4. **From the first pop-up menu under Condition, make sure "Value is" is chosen.**

   You can configure your condition in two different ways. Either you place simple rules on the value of a field, or, if your needs are more complex, you use a *formula*. You'll learn about the Formula options on page 459 when you're learning about calculations.

5. **From the second pop-up menu under Condition, choose "less than."**

   In this case, you want the conditional formatting to apply when the Goodness Rating is less than three, so you tell FileMaker that's the kind of comparison it should do.

6. **In the box to the right of the pop-up menu, type *3*.**

   Here's where you enter the comparison value. (If you'd had chosen a comparison type other than "less than," the dialog box may have shown you different options.)

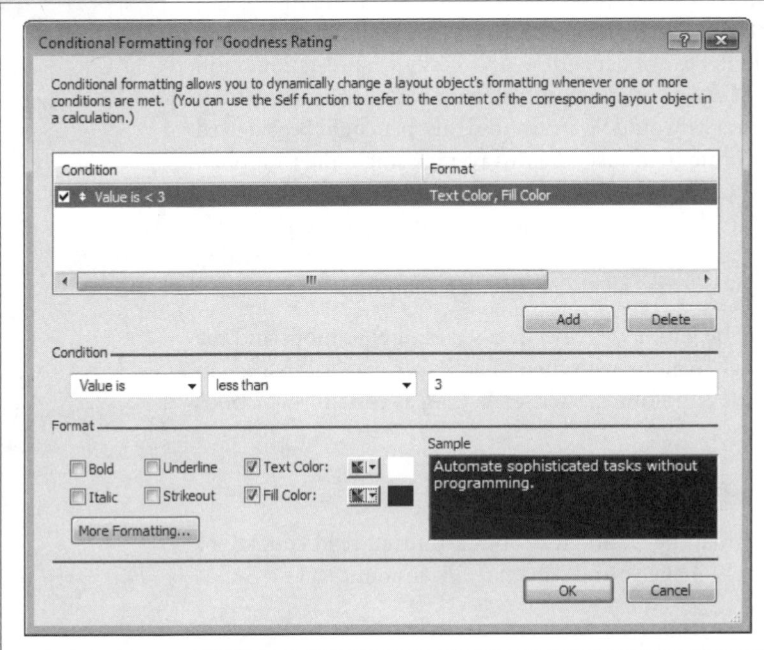

Figure 6-15: *The Conditional Formatting dialog box lets you assign formatting to a field, button, or text object that kicks in only when certain conditions are met. Simply click Add to add a new condition. Use the pop-up menus and boxes below the Condition line to tell FileMaker under what conditions the formatting should apply, and tell it what formatting you want by tweaking the options under Format.*

FileMaker adjusts the display of the dialog box so that the condition line reads like a meaningful sentence: "Value is → less than → 3."

7. **From the Fill Color pop-up menu, choose a dark red color. Then from the Text Color pop-up menu, choose white.**

   As soon as you make a selection from either pop-up menu, FileMaker turns on the checkbox to the left of its label. This checkbox tells FileMaker you want it to go ahead and apply this style when the condition is met. If you decide you don't want to change the fill color after all, you can simply uncheck the box.

Note: You don't have to provide any formatting rules for Goodness Ratings of three or more. When none of the conditions in the Conditional Formatting dialog box apply (you can add as many as you want), FileMaker leaves the object formatted as it shows in Layout mode, so you don't need to add a condition for the *normal* case.

8. **Click OK.**

   The Conditional Formatting dialog box disappears, and your layout looks utterly unchanged. Unfortunately, there's no way to tell an object has conditional formatting rules in Layout mode just by looking. You have to select the item, choose Format → Conditional again, and see if any conditions appear in the list.

Although the layout looks unchanged, if you switch to Browse mode and fiddle with the Goodness Rating field, you'll see it works as advertised. When you pick a rating of 1 or 2, the field turns red. Switch it to 3 and the field returns to its *normal* formatting. You can see the new Goodness Rating field in action in Figure 6-16.

Conditional Formatting of Text Objects

For even more punch, you can make the text label on the Goodness Rating field stand out as well. Applying conditional formatting to a text object works just like it did for a field, with one tiny twist: You have to type a formula instead of just typing a value. The following steps make everything clear.

1. **Select the Goodness text label, and then choose Format → Conditional. When the Conditional Formatting dialog box opens, click Add.**

   Once again, FileMaker adds a condition to the list. And once again, the pop-up menus, checkboxes, and entry fields below have come to life. Notice, though, that this time the first pop-up menu under Condition says, "Formula is." If you click it, you see that the "Value is" option is no longer available.

2. **In the entry box next to "Formula is," type *People::Goodness Rating* < *3*. (Make sure you don't type the period at the end.)**

   This simple formula tells FileMaker to look at the Goodness Rating field in the People table and see if its value is less than three.

Tip: Don't worry if what you just typed doesn't make complete sense just yet. Once you've read Part 4, that formula will feel comfy in your brain.

3. **From the Text Color pop-up menu, choose a red color. Click OK when you're done.**

   Once again, you're back on your visually unchanged layout. If you switch to Browse mode now (or glance at Figure 6-16), you'll see the formatting in action.

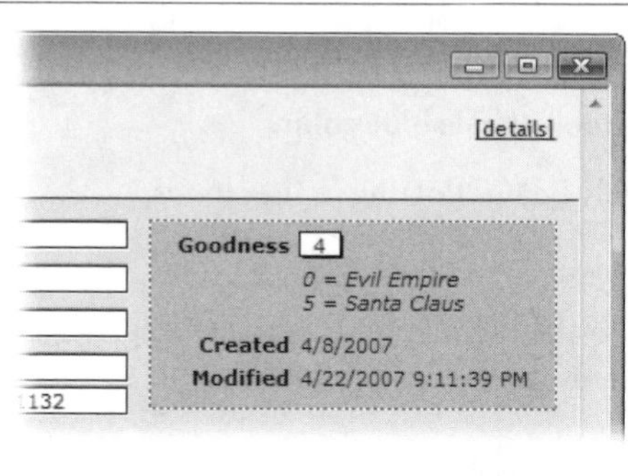

Figure 6-16:
Top: When the Goodness Rating is 4, the formatting looks just like it always has.

Bottom: When you change the Goodness Rating to 2, the conditional formatting kicks in, so the field is red with white text.

Multiple Conditions

In both the previous examples, you added only one condition to the list in the Conditional Formatting dialog box. But it wouldn't be a list if you couldn't add more than one. When you do, FileMaker looks at every condition on the list and makes the formatting changes for each one that applies. As a result, you can easily create several different formats for several different conditions. For example, you can make numbers in your budget database turn red when you're getting behind, stay black when you're right on target, and turn green when you're beating expectations. In the People database, you can do something similar, like make the Goodness Rating field take on progressively darker shades of red as the rating gets worse. Here's how:

1. **Select the Goodness Rating field, and then choose Format → Conditional. When the Conditional Formatting dialog box opens, select the condition in the list at the top of the window and click Delete.**

   FileMaker removes the condition from the list, effectively turning off the conditional formatting you added earlier.

2. **Click Add.**

   Now you get a new condition in the list, ready to configure.

3. **Make sure the first pop-up menu under Condition says "Value is" and, from the second, choose "Equal to."**

   This time you're going to add a condition for *each* Goodness Rating value. So for this first condition, you want to check only one particular value.

4. **In the box, type *5*.**

   This condition formats the field when the Goodness Rating is set to 5.

5. **From the Fill Color pop-up menu, choose a pale blue color.**

   People like this remind you of heavenly beings floating in the clouds.

6. **Click Add again.**

   FileMaker adds a second condition to the list. The program also explains each condition in the list, including what the rule is and what kinds of formatting apply.

7. **Choose "Value is" from the first pop-up menu, and "Equal to" from the second. This time, type *4* in the box.**

   You're specifying the formatting for a Goodness Rating of 4.

8. **From the Fill Color pop-up menu, choose a very pale red.**

   This person has just a tinge of imperfection.

   So far you've defined formats for two of the five possible Goodness Rating values.

9. **Repeat steps 6 through 8 three more times to give distinct fill colors to ratings of 3, 2, and 1.**

   Use a darker shade of red each time. When you're finished, you can test your labors. In Browse mode, the field's color changes every time you pick a new value. But depending on the colors you chose, you may have a minor problem. The text in the Goodness Rating field is black, and your lowest couple of ratings may be a very dark red. Black text on dark red is probably not easy enough to read, so you may wish to change the text color to white when the rating is 1 or 2. You *could* go back to each condition and turn on the Text Color formatting option, but there's a more elegant way that involves adding only one more condition:

10. **Revisit the Conditional Formatting dialog box and add another new condition: "Value is → between → 1 → and → 2."**

    When you choose the "between" option, you get *two* text boxes so you can enter the start and end values for a range.

11. **From the Text Color pop-up menu, choose the white color. When you're finished, click OK.**

    Now, when the Goodness Rating is 1, FileMaker notices that *two* conditions apply. One colors the background of the field dark red, and the other makes the text white. FileMaker applies as many conditional formatting rules as it finds, as long as the conditions are met.

Note: It's possible for two matching conditions to have competing formatting rules. For instance, you can set the text color to something different in each rule, even though they both apply to some values. In that case, FileMaker chooses the format from the condition that comes *last* in the list. You can move these conditions around using their little arrows to influence its decision. Just put the condition that should take precedence lower in the list.

More Formatting Options

If you don't see the formatting choice you want in the Conditional Formatting dialog box, just click More Formatting, and chances are you'll find what you want. This button opens a dialog box that, like FileMaker's usual Text Format window, lets you adjust additional formatting including font, size, and a few extra styles.

The only difference between this window and the other Text Format dialog box is that this one has a checkbox beside the Font, Size, and Color pop-up menus. So if you don't want FileMaker to change the font, for example, don't turn on its checkbox. When FileMaker applies a conditional format, it starts with the formatting you've applied to the object in the normal way (using the Format menu in Layout mode). It then folds in the formatting choices you've turned on here. For example, if you change the font of the Goodness Rating field on the layout, that new font will still apply when the conditional formatting rules are applied, so you aren't forced to make the font change in two places—as long as you don't set and turn on Font formatting here. As a general rule, turn on as few options in the Format section of the Conditional Formatting dialog box as necessary.

Removing Conditional Formatting

If an object has conditional formatting behavior that you don't want anymore (which often happens if you duplicate one field and change it to another), you can easily turn it off. Just select the object, choose Format → Conditional, and delete the conditions from the list. You can Shift-click to delete them all at once, or just click the first, and then click Delete repeatedly until they're all gone.

If you spent long hours adding complex conditions and you're not quite ready to commit to losing them forever, you can *turn them off* instead. Each condition in the list has a checkbox beside it. If you turn off a condition's checkbox, FileMaker no longer uses that condition. You can always get the condition back later by turning it back on. You can turn multiple checkboxes on or off at once as well: Just Shift-click the conditions you want to switch so they're all selected. Then turn off the checkbox beside *one* of them, and FileMaker turns all the others off as well.

Print-related Layout Options

Your layout needs are often different when viewing data onscreen versus on a printed page. For instance, you may want text blocks, fields, or other objects to show onscreen, but to disappear completely when printed. Also, when printing, you're often concerned about wasted paper, but few people worry about using too much scrolling window. FileMaker gives you a handful of layout options to control how things print.

Non-printing Objects

Sometimes you have something on a layout that you don't want to print. Imagine, for example, a layout that's designed to print over the top of preprinted invoice forms. When you view this layout in Browse mode, you want the appropriate boxes and labels to show so you can tell where to type and what to type there. But when you print, you want only the field data.

You can easily tell FileMaker exactly which layout objects you don't want it to print. The objects still show up in Layout mode, Browse mode, and Find mode, but if you switch to Preview mode or print the layout, they simply disappear. First select the object (or objects). Then choose Format → Sliding/Printing to open the Set Sliding/Printing dialog box, which you learned about in the last chapter. What you *didn't* learn about is the "Do not print selected objects" checkbox at the bottom of this window. Turn this checkbox *on* to turn printing *off*.

Columns

Occasionally your printed page needs to spread records across several *columns*. For example, when you print on address label sheets, the sheets you buy usually have two or three columns of labels on one page. Even when printing a list or detail layout, if your data's narrow, you can save paper by printing two records side by side. FileMaker has a built-in solution to just this problem: Choose Layout → Layout

Setup, switch to the Printing tab, and turn on the "Print in" checkbox. When you do, you can tell FileMaker *how* many columns you want by typing a number in the little entry box by the checkbox. When you turn on column printing for a layout, FileMaker shows you what's going on in Layout mode, as Figure 6-17 shows.

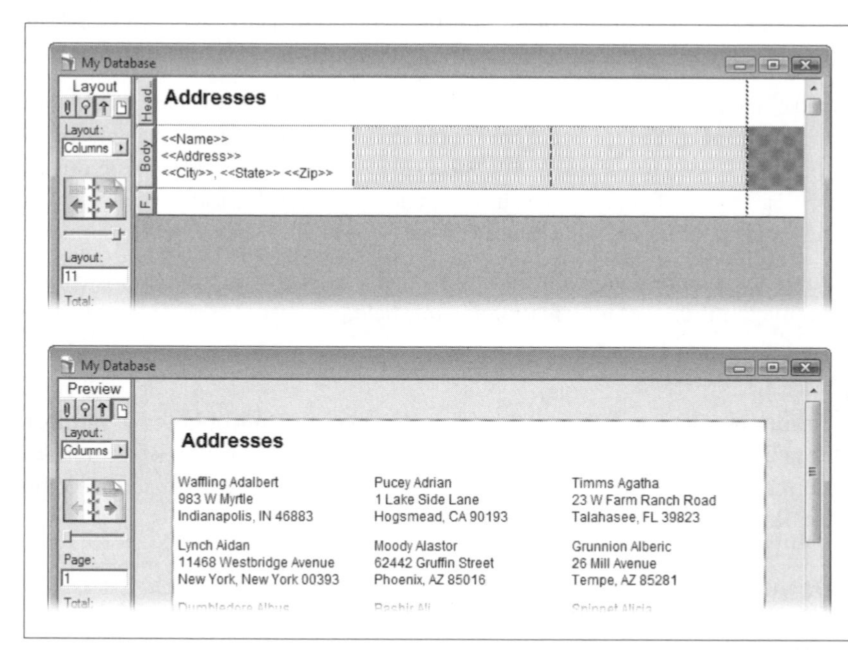

Figure 6-17: *Top: FileMaker draws a dashed line through your layout to show you where the columns land. It also covers every column but the first with a dotted pattern. This pattern is its way of saying, "Don't expect anything you put here to print." Since every column is identical, you just have to lay out the first. FileMaker repeats it for the rest.*

Bottom: With the layout set to print in three columns, everything comes together in Preview mode or when you print.

The column setting has no effect on your layout in Browse or Find modes. But if you print or switch to Preview mode, you can see the effect. Instead of repeating the Body part just vertically, FileMaker *tiles* the Body part both horizontally and vertically so that it fills the page.

Every column has to be the same width (this makes sense because every column contains the same kind of information). FileMaker automatically sets the column width so that the columns perfectly divide the page. But it bases its assumptions about the size of the page on the settings in the Print Setup (Windows) or the Page Setup (Mac OS X) dialog box at the time you turn on columns. If you later switch to a different paper size or orientation, you probably want to resize the columns. To do so, just drag the first (left-most) dashed line on the layout. When you finish, FileMaker makes every column the same width as the first one.

Lastly, FileMaker gives you two choices for the way it arranges records in the columns. Choose "Across first" in the Layout Setup dialog box if you want the *second* record to be at the top of the *second* column. Choose "Down first" if it should be the second item in the *first* column. The flow arrows on the icons in the Layout Setup dialog box show how the data flows onto the printout.

Format the Number/Date/Time/Graphic

All this talk about how fields look and work is well and good, but what if you want to change how the *data* inside them looks? A price and a weight both go in a Number field, but they are different types of values and should *look* different. FileMaker provides a series of formatting options for the data inside fields, giving you loads of control over how numbers, dates, times, and pictures look.

FileMaker has a special formatting dialog box for each kind of data a field can hold: Text, Number, Date, Time, and Container. (Timestamps are just a date and a time together, so you can format both parts separately.) You've already seen one of these dialog boxes—Text Format—in Chapter 4 (see page 155). It's the thing you see when, in Layout mode, you choose Format → Text.

Below this menu command, you find four others, each of which accesses a dialog box specific to the type of information in your field.

Number Formatting

Select a number field and choose Format → Number to control how the number inside the field is displayed. The Number Format dialog box has a lot of options, as you can see in Figure 6-18. You can use most of these in any combination, so the possibilities are vast.

Note: As with most layout settings, if you choose this command *without* selecting a field, FileMaker lets you edit the *default* formats. In other words, the settings you pick apply to every number field you add to the layout thereafter.

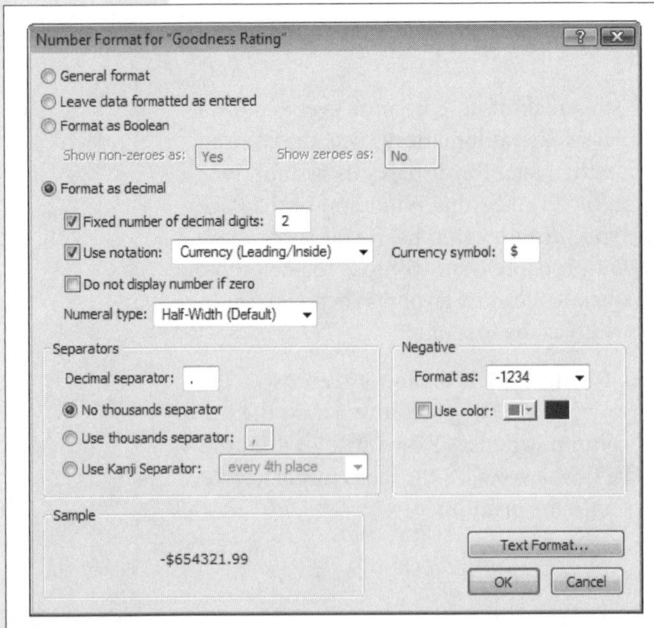

Figure 6-18: *FileMaker has four top-level number format settings: "General format," "Leave data formatted as entered," "Format as Boolean," and "Format as decimal." If you choose either of the last two, you get still more choices. If you're looking for the kind of number formatting options you're accustomed to in a spreadsheet program, turn on "Format as decimal" and go to town. The sample at the bottom of the dialog box shows how a number looks with your settings applied.*

General format

If you don't tell it otherwise, FileMaker assigns the General format to any new number fields you create. Usually, this format means, "show numbers the same way someone types them." But if your number has too many digits (either a very large number, or a number with lots of decimal places), FileMaker rounds the number or uses scientific notation to shorten it.

Leave data formatted as entered

If you don't want the automatic rounding and scientific notation you get with General Format, choose "Leave data formatted as entered" instead. FileMaker leaves your numbers alone, so they appear exactly as typed.

Format as Boolean

Sometimes you use a number field simply as a Boolean value. For instance, pretend you have a field that flags customers who get holiday cards. You could use a number field for this one, with a *1* in it if you want to send a card, and a *0* if you don't. But someone looking at the layout later could mistake all those 1s and 0s for so much computer gibberish (even if that someone is yourself).

For this reason alone, the Number Format dialog box has a choice called "Format as Boolean." With this setting, a number field shows one of two text values. The first ("Show non-zero as") shows if the number field has any non-zero value. The second ("Show zero as") shows only when the field has a zero in it. In the holiday card example, you may be tempted to turn this option on and use Send Card and Don't Send Card as the display values. Unfortunately, FileMaker only lets you enter a maximum of *seven* characters for each display value. So you have to stick with short-and-sweet values, like Yes and No.

Format as decimal

The most flexible setting is called "Format as decimal." When you choose this option, you activate a host of new settings:

Fixed number of digits. Turn on "Fixed number of decimal digits" if you want to force every number to have the same number of decimal places. Of course, FileMaker also lets you say *how many* decimal places you want. If the number in the field doesn't have a decimal part, FileMaker just fills in zeros after the decimal point.

Notation and symbols. The "Use notation" checkbox lets you add currency symbols, units, or other labels to your numbers:

- Choose **Percent** to turn the number into a percent value. FileMaker automatically multiplies the number by 100 and puts a percent sign after it. That way, your users can enter *.1* for 10 percent. (Entering the number this way makes math with percentages easier since you can simply multiply. After all, 10% of 20 is 2, not 200. You'll learn how to do math in FileMaker in Part 4.)

- Choose one of the **Currency** options to format the number as a monetary value. When you do, you can supply an appropriate currency symbol as well. The four currency options in the pop-up menu have to do with *where* the symbol is placed, as explained in Figure 6-19.

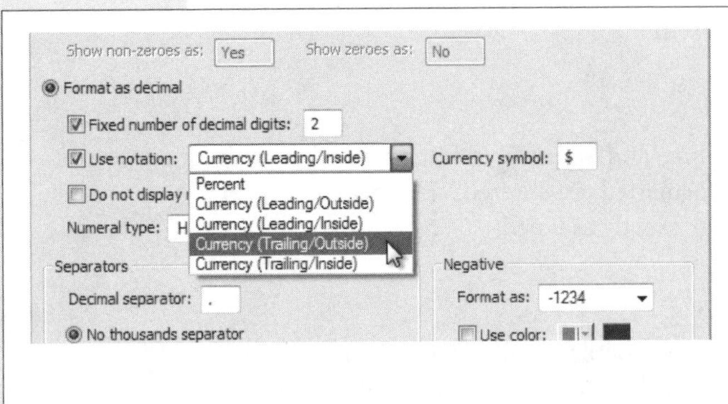

Figure 6-19: *FileMaker has four different currency options: Leading/Outside, Leading/Inside, Trailing/Outside, and Trailing/Inside. Leading and Trailing determine on which side of the number the currency symbol should live. Inside and Outside matter only for negative numbers. As this picture shows, the currency symbol goes between the negative sign and the number with the Leading/Inside option, and before the negative sign with the Leading/Outside option. FileMaker also lets you put parentheses around negative numbers if you want. In this case, you get an Inside/Outside choice for trailing currency symbols, too.*

Do not display number if zero. Suppose you have a report with lots of numbers, where many of those numbers are zero. For example, a financial report that shows who owes you money (like the Aging Receivables Report in Figure 6-20) often has more zeros than anything else. All those zeros can make the report cluttered and hard to read. Turn on the "Do not display number if zero" option to make the zeros go away.

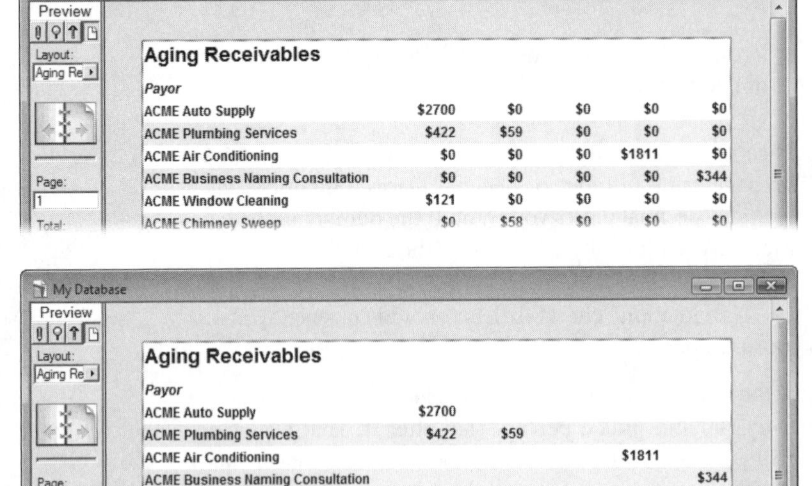

Figure 6-20: *These two windows show the same report, an Aging Receivables report just like you might get from your accountant.*

Top: Unfortunately, with all those zeros, it's hard to see the useful information.

Bottom: Here's how the report looks when each field has its "Do not display number if zero" option turned on (in the Number Format dialog box). The zeros go away, revealing the real picture.

WORKAROUND WORKSHOP

Currency-ish

The currency symbol is, in a sense, just an expression of *units*. It isn't at all uncommon to want to put *other* unit labels on your numbers too. But FileMaker doesn't have an option for any other variation. It seems hopelessly in love with currency.

Don't let the word "currency" in the "Use notation" pop-up menu get you down. Since you can type anything you want for the currency symbol (including multiple letters, numbers, spaces, or punctuation symbols), you're welcome to use one of the currency options for any other kind of unit too:

- Choose Currency (Trailing/Outside) from the pop-up menu, and put " cm" in the Currency Symbol box. The number 3.7 will now show as "3.7 cm" automatcally. Use this same technique with any unit abbreviation you want. (Note that you need a space before the abbreviation so they label doesn't run in to the number itself.)
- If you have part numbers, serial numbers, or other meaningful codes that should display with an informative prefix, you can accomplish that too. For example, choose the Current (Leading/Outside) option and put "PN/" in the Currency Symbol box. Now a part number field with "17789" in it will show "PN/17789." This might be handy on a report, for example.

The Currency Symbol box accepts only up to five characters (and that includes the leading space if you need one) so it isn't perfect. But in many cases it gets the job done.

Separators. Numbers use special symbols to separate their parts. For example, you usually see a decimal point between the whole and fractional parts of a number, and a comma after the thousands place. FileMaker uses whatever symbols your operating system dictates for these special purposes, but you're free to override them if you want. For instance, you can use a space instead of a comma between each third digit.

In the "Decimal separator" box, type the character you want in place of a decimal point. The box accepts only a single character. FileMaker calls the comma between every third digit a "thousands separator" and you can opt to leave them out by turning on "No thousands separator." Turn on "Use thousands separator" if you want them, and feel free to enter something other than a comma in the associated box.

Formatting negative values. The last thing you get to control with the "Format as decimal" option is the way FileMaker represents negative numbers. In the "Format as" pop-up menu, you can choose any one of six negative number formats:

- **-1234** puts a negative sign before the number in the usual fashion.
- **1234-** puts the sign on the *end* instead, if that's the kind of thing that makes your socks go up and down.
- For that oh-so-financial look, choose **(1234)** instead. It puts negative numbers in parentheses.
- **<1234>** is similar, but it uses angle brackets instead of parentheses.

- If you're an accountant, hold onto your hat. The **1234 CR** option will make you feel right at home when crediting those accounts.
- The last choice, ▲1234 puts that funny triangle before negative numbers. No idea what that's all about. If you know, more power to you.

To draw more attention to a negative number, you can have FileMaker automatically color it. Turn on "Use color," and then pick a color by clicking the little icon button to its right.

Note: The "Use color" option for negative numbers may seem a little redundant considering you can get exactly the same effect using Conditional Formatting, as you learned above (see page 238). Before FileMaker Pro 9, the "Use color" option was the only way to apply a different color to negative numbers. These days, you can use whichever method you prefer.

Formatting a number's text. At the end of the day, a number is text, too, really. It's made up of numbers and symbols using some font, size, style, and color. As such, you can choose the Format → Text command with a number field selected. If you're already in the Format Number dialog box, and you want to format the text as well, the Text Format button serves as a shortcut to the Text Format dialog box.

Note: This window has two more choices–"Numeral type" and "Use kanji separator." These options are specific to Japanese numbers and aren't covered in this book.

Date Formatting

The Date Format dialog box works a lot like its number-oriented sister. This time, though, you tell FileMaker how you want *dates* to look. This date could be the value in a date field, or the date part of a timestamp field. For example, the date at the top of a letter may look best spelled out, while the due date on a list of 25 invoices may best be served by an abbreviated numbers-only format. Figure 6-21 shows the Date Format dialog box (no surprises here: just choose Format → Date).

Leave data formatted as entered

When you choose "Leave data formatted as entered," FileMaker shows the date *almost* the same way you type it. If you type a two-digit year, the program changes it to four digits. Otherwise, it leaves the data alone.

Format as

If you choose "Format as" instead, you can pick from six common date formats in its pop-up menu, as shown in Figure 6-22.

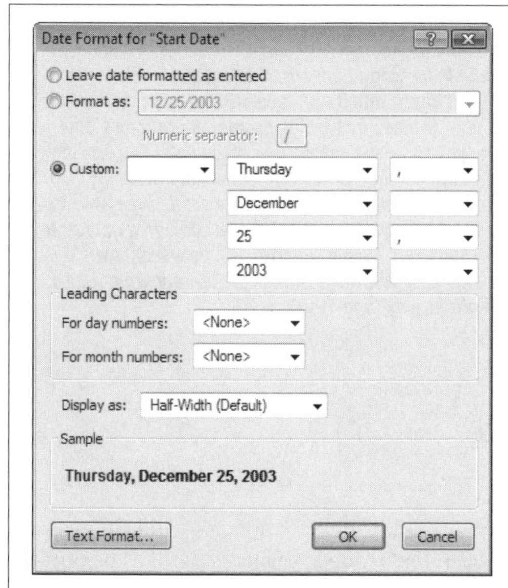

Figure 6-21:
The Date Format dialog box gives you lots of control over how dates look. You get three primary choices ("Leave data formatted as entered," "Format as," and Custom), the last two with assorted settings. And you get a sample demonstrating your choices as well.

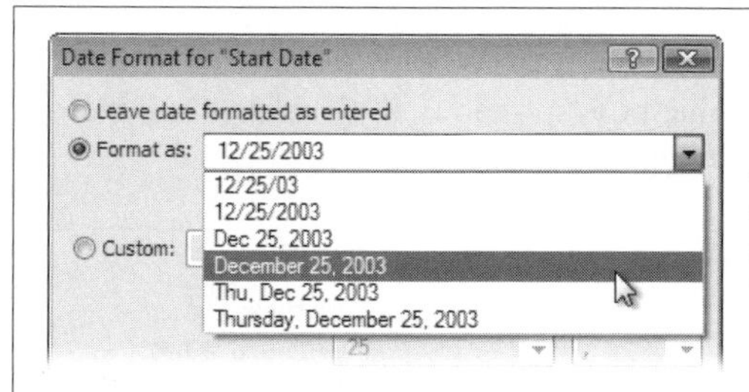

Figure 6-22:
The "Format as" pop-up menu gives you six canned date formats to pick from. If you choose either of the first two, you can pick something other than "/" to go between each number by typing it in the "Numeric separator" box (it's covered by the menu in this picture). You can also add a leading zero or a space to single-digit day and month numbers by picking from the Leading Characters area's pop-up menus.

Custom

For the ultimate in control, choose Custom. When you do, the mysterious unlabelled boxes, buttons, and pop-up menus to the right become usable. By selecting different parts of a date from the pop-up menus and adding your own text as appropriate to the boxes, you tell FileMaker exactly how you want the date formatted. You would use this option when none of the "Format as" formats (Figure 6-23) are exactly right. For example, if you're in the U.S., FileMaker suggests date formats that follow typical U.S. standards (month, then day, then year). But if people in England use your database, you may want to construct a custom format in line with their expectations (day, then month, then year).

When you tell FileMaker to format a date with the Custom option, it assembles the final date value piece by piece according to your specifications. Whatever you type in the Start Text box comes first, followed by the first date value. FileMaker then adds the text from the top Between Text box. Next comes another date value and more between text. This process continues until the last text box is added to the result. By mixing and matching text and date values, you can make a date look any way you want.

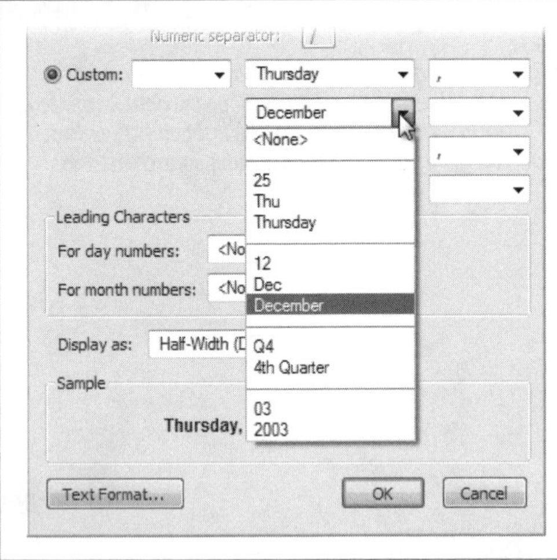

Figure 6-23: *The Custom date format options consist of a series of text boxes and four Date Value pop-up menus. You can put anything you want in the text boxes, and it will appear between portions of the date. Each pop-up menu includes the same set of choices. The first three let you show the day portion of the date. You can show the day-of-month number, or the day-of-week name as an abbreviation or full name. Next, you get the same three ways to display the month. If you're so inclined, you can add a quarter to your date in two ways. Finally, you can pick between a two-digit and a four-digit year. FileMaker strings the text and date values together to produce the final result.*

If you don't want to use one of the date values, choose "<none>" from the relevant pop-up menu. Likewise, to skip a between text value, clear its text box. The pop-up menu buttons to the right of each text box give you a choice of common date-related symbols for easy picking. They have a "<none>" option as well, if you want to quickly clear the associated box.

In addition to "<none>," the date value pop-up menus all have identical choices, divided into four sections, as shown in Figure 6-24.

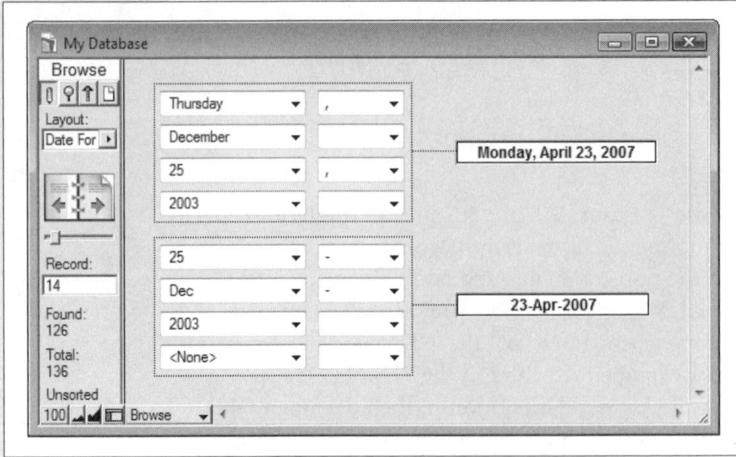

Figure 6-24: *This database shows the same exact date formatted in two different ways. As an added bonus, you can see the configuration of the Custom section of the Date Format dialog box for each one. As you can see, a date can be displayed just about any way you want.*

With either the "Format as" or the Custom option, you can use the pop-up menus in the Leading Characters area of this window to tell FileMaker how to handle single-digit month and day numbers. If you want them left alone, choose "<none>." To insert a leading space, choose Space, and for a leading zero, choose Zero.

Note: The "Display as" pop-up menu applies only to Japanese dates. And if you don't recognize these choices, you probably don't need to use this pop-up menu.

POWER USERS' CLINIC

International Super-date

If people all over the world use your database, you quickly discover that date formats can lead to unending confusion. A date like 1/11/07 could mean January 11 or November 1, depending on your persuasion. To avoid all this confusion, consider a date format that strikes a nice balance between efficient display and unambiguous interpretation: 11-Jan-2007.

To get this format, select a date field, choose Format → Date, and turn on the Custom option. Then configure it thusly:

- In the first pop-up menu, choose the number version of the day. (It's the number in the first group of options, right below "<none>".)
- In the top text box, enter a hyphen (-).
- In the second pop-up menu, choose the abbreviated month name.
- In the next text box, enter another hyphen (-).
- In the third pop-up menu, choose the year (you can use either the two- or four-digit version).
- Clear the contents of the two remaining text boxes, and in the last pop-up menu, choose "<none>".

Now click OK and switch to Browse mode. Your date field should show this svelte-yet-satisfying format. You can see this format, and its configuration, in Figure 6-24.

Time Formatting

Compared to dates and numbers, formatting time values is a breeze—FileMaker gives you just a few simple choices. Figure 6-25 shows the Time Format dialog box (Format → Time).

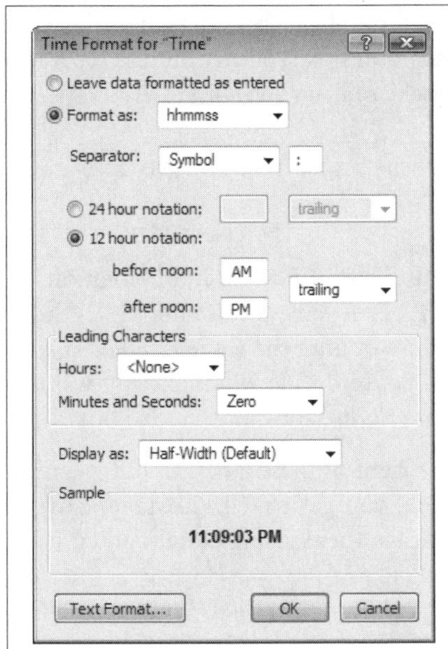

Figure 6-25:
To have FileMaker show your time values exactly the way you type them, choose "Leave data formatted as entered." If you want to standardize the display of time values, choose "Format as" instead, and then pick your options. Unsurprisingly, the sample area shows you a sample time formatted according to your specifications.

Leave data formatted as entered

This time, "Leave data formatted as entered" really means it. The time value shows exactly as you typed it.

Format as

The only other formatting option you get with time values is "Format as" and its related options. From the "Format as" pop-up menu, choose what time information you want to include:

- **hhmmss** tells FileMaker to show hours, minutes, and seconds.
- **hhmm** says you want hours and minutes, but no seconds. If your time value has seconds, FileMaker just ignores them.
- **mmss** limits the display to just minutes and seconds. If the time value has hours, the minutes are increased accordingly. For instance, if your field has *1:13:27* and you format it without hours, you see *73:27*—each hour adds 60 minutes.
- **hh** gives you a field that shows just the hours. Any minutes and seconds are left off.
- **mm** tells FileMaker to show the number of minutes. Again, any hours in the time value are counted as 60 minutes, and any seconds are ignored.
- **ss** shows a time as just a number of seconds. Every minute counts as 60 seconds, and every hour as 60 minutes. They're added up along with the seconds themselves to produce the final number.

Normally time values show a colon between each number. You can change this look if you want by typing something else in the Separator box. To leave out the separator entirely, clear the box. (This method lets you make military style times: *0730*.)

Note: As with date formatting, the pop-up menu between this box and its label lets you opt for a Japanese time separator instead.

When displaying clock time, FileMaker can use 24-hour or 12-hour notation. In other words, do you want to see *14:23* or *2:23 PM*? When you choose "24 hour notation," you can add some arbitrary text before or after the value (23:00UTC, for instance). When using 12-hour notation, you get to decide what text you want to represent a.m. and p.m. by typing in the "before noon" and "after noon" boxes.

You can choose from the pop-up menu to the right of these labels to put them on either side of the time value. Like a date value, you get to tell FileMaker how to handle single-digit numbers. Again, you can leave them a single digit, add a leading space, or add a leading zero.

Timestamp Formatting

Although FileMaker has a timestamp *field* (see page 104), there's no Timestamp option in the Format menu. Remember that timestamp fields really contain two

FREQUENTLY ASKED QUESTION

Formatting Fractional Seconds

I have times in my fields that have a decimal part in the seconds. Is there any way for me to control how these fractions of a second show up in FileMaker?

For most people who actually care about fractions of seconds (you nerds know who you are), the visual appeal of your database is the least of your worries. But for the guy out there with a double major in nuclear physics and interior design, FileMaker has just what you need.

The Time Format dialog box doesn't give you options for fractional seconds, leading many people to believe you have no control over how these are formatted. In fact, you do have control.

Just select your time field, and then choose Format → Number. Many of the number formatting options have no effect on a time field, but the "Fixed number of decimal places" and "Decimal separator" options work as expected. In other words, they let you control how many decimal places show and what character to use for your decimal "point."

There's an important caveat to this tip, though. If you have your time field set to "Leave data formatted as entered" in the Time Format dialog box, nothing you do in the Number Format window works. You must explicitly format the time value if you want to use number formatting on the seconds.

values: a date and a time. So, you use the Format → Date command to control how the date part of a timestamp looks, and the Format → Time command for the time portion. Like time values, you can also use Format → Number to control decimal places and points in the seconds part.

In order for a timestamp field to show your settings, though, you have to format *both* the date *and* the time parts. If either is set to "Leave data formatted as entered," the timestamp field just puts its hands over its ears and hums so it can't hear you trying to format it. Once you enter both the date and the time formats, the timestamp field straightens up and follows your formatting instructions.

You *do not* have to set the number format if you don't want to. If you don't choose a number format, FileMaker leaves the decimal part of your time values formatted as people enter them.

Note: Timestamp formats are a little tough to read because the date and time just sort of run together with a scrawny single space separating them. Make a custom format with " at" (that's *space*-a-t) in the last placeholder, and you get "Fri, May 6, 2005 at 12:30 pm." Much better.

Graphic Formatting

In Chapter 2 you learned how to put pictures, sounds, QuickTime data, and files into container fields. Remember that with pictures and QuickTime data, FileMaker actually shows the content right on the layout. When you design that layout, you have some control over how that content is displayed (see Figure 6-26).

Note: If someone records a sound (Insert → Sound) or puts a file (Insert → File) in your container field, you have no control over how FileMaker displays it. FileMaker automatically shows the appropriate icon and leaves it at that.

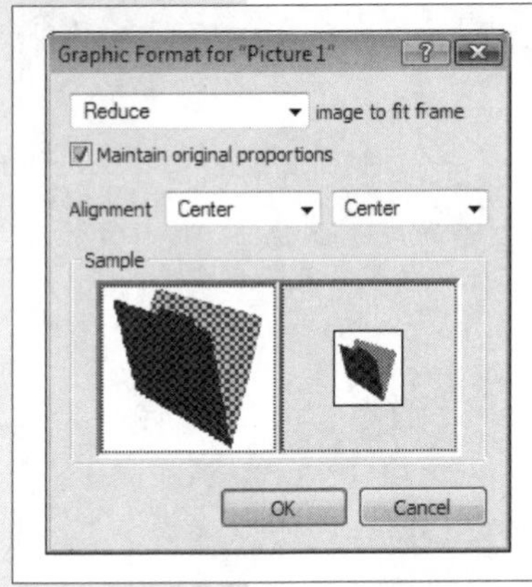

Figure 6-26:
With the Graphic Format dialog box you can tell FileMaker to shrink and/or enlarge a picture to fit the field boundaries, or to crop it–showing only what fits. You also get to decide where the picture lives inside the field, or what part gets cropped. If you don't mind wildly skewed images, you can also tell FileMaker to stop keeping your pictures properly proportioned.

Because the pictures and movies you put in the field may not always be exactly the same size and dimensions as the field control itself, FileMaker has to decide how to make things fit. Should it shrink a big picture down so it all shows, or let it get cut off on the edges? For a tiny picture, should FileMaker blow it up to use the available space, even though it may look a little blocky? For that matter, should it stretch and skew the image willy-nilly to force a fit, or leave some of the field empty? FileMaker lets you decide. When you choose Format → Graphic, you can control scale, position, and proportions.

Scale

The Scale pop-up menu lets you decide how FileMaker should handle pictures that aren't exactly the right size:

- Choose **Crop** if you want FileMaker to crop large pictures, showing only what fits. Figure 6-27 shows how this method works.
- Choose **Reduce** if you want FileMaker to shrink large pictures to fit, but leave small pictures alone. This setting is what you automatically get if you don't change it yourself.
- Choose **Enlarge** to make small pictures grow so they fit the field but are as big as possible. (The more FileMaker has to enlarge the image, the blockier it looks.) Large pictures get cropped.
- Choose **Reduce or Enlarge** if you want FileMaker to shrink big pictures and grow small ones. This setting ensures that every picture in the field (on each record) is the about the same size.

Alignment

If the picture is small and hasn't been enlarged, the alignment pop-up menus control *where* in the field the picture appears. For example, choose Right from the Horizontal Alignment pop-up menu and Top from the Vertical Alignment pop-up menu to nestle the picture in the top-right corner of the field.

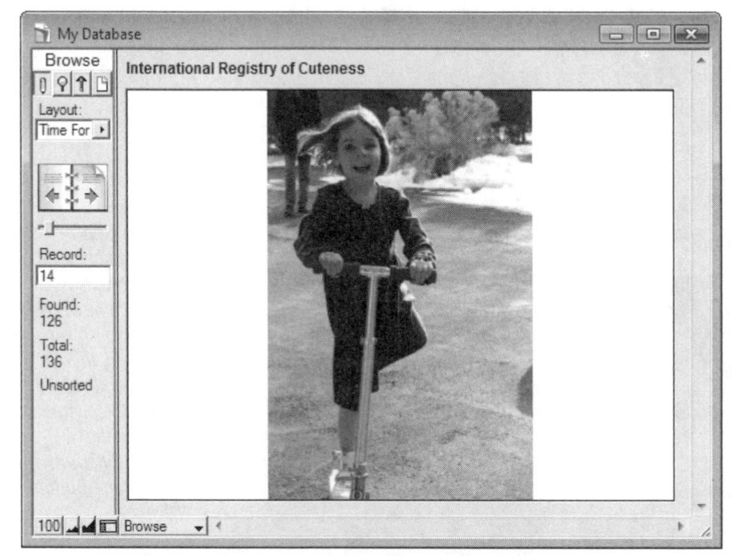

Figure 6-27:
Top: The image in this container field is too big to fit. But since the container field is formatted to reduce the image if necessary, it shrinks it down so the whole thing fits. FileMaker formats container fields this way when you first add them to the layout.

Bottom: This version, shows the Crop graphic field format, with the second Alignment pop-up menu set to Top. FileMaker shows the image at full size, and cuts off the portion of the bottom that doesn't fit.

If a picture has been reduced or enlarged so that it fills the field, it might still be smaller than the field in one dimension. In this case, the alignment pop-up menus tell FileMaker where to put the picture along this dimension. Figure 6-28 shows this process in action.

Finally, for large images that have been cropped, alignment controls which portion of the larger image you see. If you align to the top and left, for instance, you see as much of the top-left corner of the image as possible. You can see the same cropped picture with each possible alignment in Figure 6-29.

Note: When FileMaker reduces or enlarges a picture, it keeps the picture's aspect ratio the same. In other words, a picture that's four inches by six inches may not be that *size* in the container field, but its height *is* two-thirds of its width. If you'd rather FileMaker make the picture *exactly* the size of the container field, even if it means distorting it, turn on "Maintain original proportions."

Figure 6-28: *If a picture is smaller than the container field, or when FileMaker reduces a picture whose aspect ratio doesn't match the field, there's space left over. In these three fields, the picture is the same, but the alignment is different: Top, Center, and Bottom respectively.*

Figure 6-29: *This window has three container fields, all containing an image that's too big to fit. Each field is set to crop, but with different alignments. On the left, the image is set to align left. The center image is set to align center. Finally, the right image is set to align right. As you can see, FileMaker cuts off each image, but the alignment setting determines which portion of the image is visible.*

Adding Buttons

The first FileMaker database you looked at (the Contact Management template on page 20) has a pretty slick system for switching between list and detail layouts. Instead of fiddling with the tiny Layout pop-up menu, you can just click tab graphics right on the screen. Each click magically transports you to a different layout. (Of course, at the time you didn't know it was changing layouts. You didn't even know what a layout was. But the buttons still made sense to you.)

You can easily duplicate this magic in your own databases. Just use FileMaker's Button tool, shown in Figure 6-30. But don't let the tool's name and appearance mislead you. You're not limited to the rectangular beveled buttons this tool creates. In fact, you can turn *any* object on a layout—an imported graphic or even a field—into a button. When folks click the mouse button while pointing to such an object, FileMaker highlights it so they know they're about to perform some kind of action. When they let go, something happens. You get to decide what that *something* is.

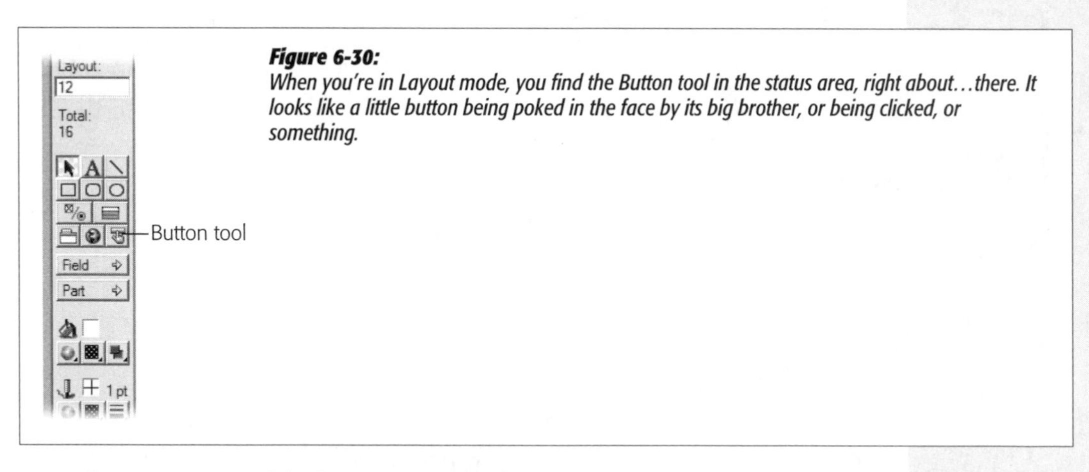

Figure 6-30:
When you're in Layout mode, you find the Button tool in the status area, right about...there. It looks like a little button being poked in the face by its big brother, or being clicked, or something.

Creating Buttons with the Button Tool

You want to add a "Go to List" button to the detail layout in your People database, so open the database now and switch to the detail layout.

To add a button, first click the Button tool, and then *draw* the button on the layout as though you were drawing a rectangle. Figure 6-31 shows you where you may want to put it.

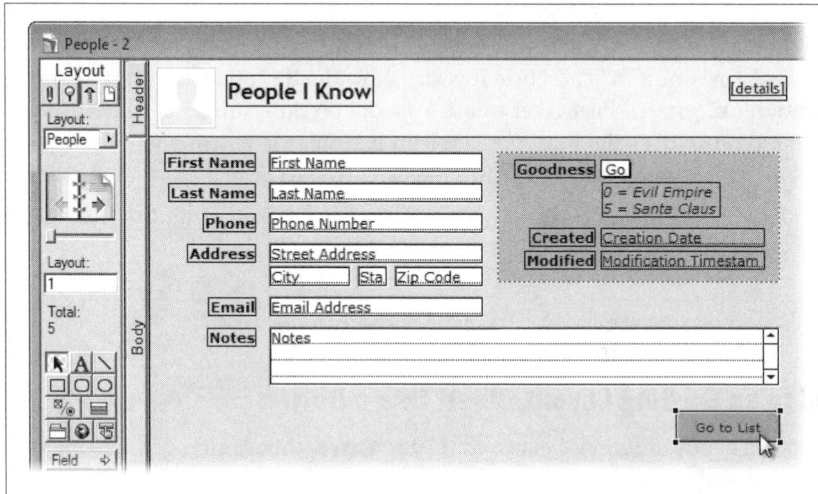

Figure 6-31:
You can put your button anywhere you want, and make it any size you want to. But if it's going to look like a button with the "Go to List" label, it should be close to the size of the button shown in the bottom-right corner of this window. Also, don't forget to set the button's autoresize anchors appropriately (see page 172). If you put it here, be sure to anchor it on the bottom and right.

When you release the mouse button, FileMaker immediately pops up the Button Setup dialog box (see Figure 6-32).

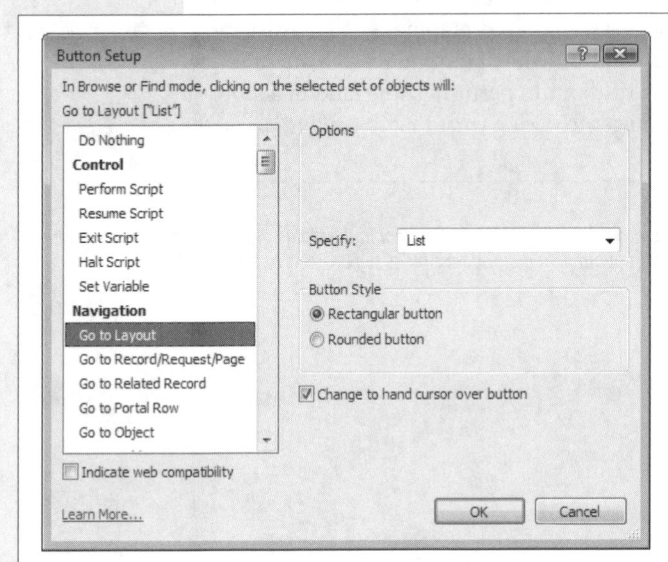

Figure 6-32: *The Button Setup dialog box shows up whenever you create a new button. You get to pick one action from the Button Action list. Most actions require a little configuration. When you pick one, its options appear in the Options area. You can come back to this box and make changes to an existing button: Just double-click the button in Layout mode (or choose Format → Button) to open it.*

You want this button to switch to a different layout whenever someone clicks it, so find "Go to Layout" in the action list and select it (it's right under the boldface Navigation item). When you do, the Options area shows you a pop-up menu labeled Specify. You can pick any layout in your database from this menu. For this button, choose List.

If you're picky about such things, you can even control whether your button has square corners or slightly rounded corners. Choose, for example, the "Rounded button" option for an elegant, classy look. (If you don't make a choice, square is what you get.)

Something else changes when you select a button command: The "Change to a hand cursor over button" checkbox appears below the Button Style area. By turning this option on, you tell FileMaker to use a special pointing-finger cursor whenever someone mouses over the button. (The icon is similar to the one you usually see when you point to a link in a Web browser—the universal cue that an area is clickable.)

When you're done making choices, click OK. You can now switch to Browse mode and give your button a try.

Note: Buttons work in Browse mode and Find mode, but not in Preview mode.

Turning an Existing Layout Object into a Button

Buttons are handy, but they can be redundant. Often, there's already something on your layout—like a picture or even a field—that would make a perfectly good button. For example, if you've got your company's logo in the top-right corner of the layout, you can make it link to the main page of your Web site. A separate button reading "Go to Home Page" would be unnecessary clutter. (Incidentally, in this case you would use the Open URL button action; see page 560.)

Here's another common example: Now that you have a button that goes from the detail layout to the list layout, you may want to give folks an easy way to get *back* where they came from. Rather than add a button to the already full Body part on the list layout, why not turn the person's name into a link of sorts? When you click the name, FileMaker shows you details on that person.

Turning one of a record's existing fields into a button capitalizes on the fact that FileMaker *always* selects a record when you click it in list view. And when you switch layouts, it always stays on the same record no matter which layout you use. This time you've added a button to the works, but the original behavior is unchanged: Clicking the list switches records, and the button switches layouts.

Here's how:

1. **If necessary, switch to Layout mode and to the list layout. Then, select the text object that holds the First Name and Last Name merge fields.**

   This is the object you want to turn into a button. You have to select it before you can work on it.

2. **Choose Format → Button Setup.**

   The Button Setup dialog box (see Figure 6-32) makes its return. This time, though, you're not making a *new* button. Instead, you're turning the selected object *into* a button.

3. **Choose the "Go to Layout" button action. When the Options area shows the Specify pop-up menu, choose Detail.**

   This action tells the button *which* layout it should go to.

4. **Click OK.**

   The window disappears and you're back on your layout. You don't see a change because you can't normally *see* if an object has been turned into a button. If you try the button now, it works fine, but it doesn't do your users much good if they don't know it's there. To make it obvious that the name links to the detail layout, why not make it *look* like a link?

Note: When you're in Layout mode, you can choose View → Show → Buttons. When this option is turned on, FileMaker outlines every button with a thick dotted line (it shows up only in Layout mode). Choose the same command again to turn it off.

5. **Using any of FileMaker's text formatting tools (see page 160), turns the text blue and gives it an underline.**

   Now your list layout looks like the one in Figure 6-33, and it works beautifully.

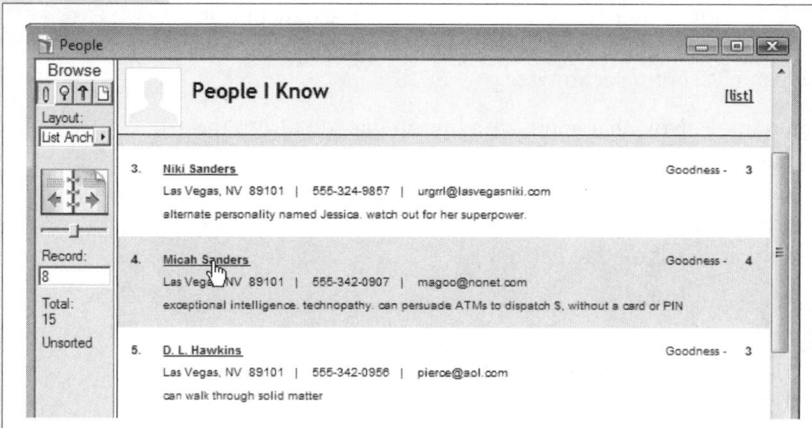

Figure 6-33: *Your list layout (in Browse mode) should look something like this window. When you point to a name, your mouse arrow changes to the little hand icon, and when you click, the name highlights. After the button is released, you see the detail layout for the correct person.*

If you select more than one layout object before you choose the Format → Button command, FileMaker automatically groups the objects and turns the entire group into a single button. These objects now act like any other grouped objects: Anything you do to one in Layout mode happens to all of them. If you later *ungroup* a grouped button, FileMaker warns you and removes the button behavior as well.

Note: If you want four *different* buttons that do the same thing (so you can work with them individually), you have to button-ize them one at a time.

Making a Button Not a Button

If you have a layout object that's already a button, and you don't want it to be a button anymore, you need a way to *turn off* its button-ness. It's easy to do but not very intuitive: Select the button and choose Format → Button Setup (or double-click the button). In the Button Action list (Figure 6-32), choose Do Nothing, and then click OK. Now the object isn't a button anymore.

Note: Here's a faster way, even though it's cheating. Just click a button and choose the Arrange → Ungroup command (or better yet, press Ctrl+Shift+R or Shift-⌘-R). Even if the button *isn't* part of a group, FileMaker pops open a message box asking if you want to remove the buttons. Just click OK, and your object is no longer a button.

You can even remove the button action from the "real" buttons you create with the button tool. That's because, in reality, the button tool just creates a specially formatted text object and automatically turns it into a button. If you switch it to Do Nothing, you're just left with a fancy text object. (You may want to deactivate a button when you're troubleshooting your database—or for a little April Fool's Day fun.)

POWER USERS' CLINIC

Making a Button Appear Grayed Out

Lots of programs on your computer include buttons that aren't always clickable. FileMaker itself, for instance, won't let you click Delete in the Fields tab of the Manage Database window if you don't have a field selected. The universally accepted look for a button that isn't quite ready to be clicked is a grayed-out label.

Accomplishing this feat is a breeze in FileMaker. Suppose you have a button that sends an email to the address in the Email Address field, logically labeled Send Email. But the label should be grayed out if there's no address in the field. How can you adjust the format of the button depending on what's in the field? FileMaker Pro 9's conditional formatting (see page 238) comes to the rescue again.

Since a button doesn't have a value of its own, you have to use the "Formula is" condition type, which you'll learn about more in Chapter 11. Here's a sneak peek to whet your appetite: Select the button and choose Format → Conditional Formatting. Click Add to add a new condition. In the box next to the "Formula is" pop-up menu, type the following exactly as shown:

```
People::Email Address = ""
```

In this formula, People is the table and Email Address is the field. In English, this formula says: *The Email Address field is equal to ""*. In other words, it's empty.

When this condition is true, use the settings in the Conditional Formatting dialog box to tell FileMaker to turn the button text gray. You can also lighten the background color of the button itself if you want. However you decide to make it look, you now have a button that automatically gives your user a visual clue when it doesn't apply.

Button Actions

The Button Setup window has dozens of available actions, as you can see at the left side in Figure 6-32. In the previous section, you created buttons for the "Go to Layout" action, but there are many more. As you scan through these commands, you probably notice that many of them repeat the same functions you find in FileMaker's menus. That's not just meaningless redundancy. By giving your databases buttons for lots of everyday commands, you can make FileMaker even easier to use than it already is. Design some icons (perhaps in your corporate colors), attach buttons to them, and you may find you hardly have to train your colleagues at all, because the buttons and their labels help explain what they need to do to use the database.

Here's a brief rundown on what some of these actions do.

Note: This section explains the button actions you're ready to use right now. Many available actions simply won't make sense to you until you've learned more about FileMaker. These buttons mimic the *steps* you can use when you write *scripts* to automate FileMaker procedures. (In fact, you can use *any* button action in a script.) You'll learn about scripts in detail in Part 5.

Go to Layout

"Go to Layout" is the action you used for the two buttons you created earlier in this chapter. It transports those who click it to another layout instantly. You get to pick which layout to visit.

Go to Record/Request/Page

The "Go to Record/Request/Page" action lets you switch to the next, previous, first, or last record in the found set. If you're in Find mode, it navigates find requests instead. Despite the word "Page" in its name, it doesn't navigate pages in Preview mode because buttons don't work in Preview mode. (The reason it has this name is because you can navigate pages with a script in Preview mode. See Chapter 13 for more.)

Go to Field

Use "Go to Field" if you want a button that delivers its clickers into a specific field. You get to pick the field by clicking the Options area's Specify button. For example, you could create a button that says "Back to Square One," which places the cursor in the first field in the tab order. (If you don't pick a field, this step goes to *no* field. In other words, it gets the user out of whatever field she's in.)

The Options area also has a "Select/perform" checkbox. For text, number, date, time, and timestamp fields, turn on this option if you also want FileMaker to select the contents of the field, so folks can just start typing to replace it. For container fields, this option tells FileMaker to *perform* the field contents. In other words, play the movie or sound, open the file, and so forth. This way, you could have a button that opens up a file (see page 81), stored in a container field. For the "Go to Field" action to work, the target field must be on the layout.

Go to Next Field and Go to Previous Field

The "Go to Next Field" and "Go to Previous Field" actions have no options at all. They simulate the Tab and Shift-Tab keystrokes, bouncing to the next or previous field in the tab order.

Note: It would be more correct to say these commands simulate whatever keystrokes you have configured to go to the next object in the Format → Field/Control → Behavior dialog box (see page 236). In fact, even if you have nothing selected here, these steps still do what they say. There's no need to fixate on the Tab key here.

Enter Browse Mode, Enter Find Mode, and Enter Preview Mode

The last three actions in the Navigation section—Enter Browse Mode, Enter Find Mode, and Enter Preview Mode—do just what you'd expect. Want a Find button on your layout? Assign it the Enter Find Mode action and you're done.

Note: The Enter Find Mode button has a "Specify find requests" option. You can use this power-user feature to preload the find requests and save your database's searchers a little time. You'll learn how to use the complex dialog box that this button conjures in Chapter 13.

Editing actions

FileMaker has seven editing actions, whose names are largely self-explanatory:

- Undo
- Cut
- Copy
- Paste
- Clear
- Select All
- Perform Find/Replace

The Undo action takes no options at all; it simply runs the normal Edit → Undo menu command. Select All also has no options. It works exactly like the Edit → Select All command.

Cut, Copy, Paste, and Clear all let you specify the field to act on. If you don't specify a field, they act on the field your user is in when he clicks the button. You can also turn on "Select entire contents" for these actions if you want FileMaker to do a Select All before it cuts, copies, pastes, or clears. Again, if you don't, it works on whatever the user has already selected.

Perform Find/Replace lets you pop up the Find/Replace dialog box. You can click Specify to preload the dialog box with your own choices. And you can turn on "Perform without dialog" if you want it to perform your user's Find/Replace choices without showing the dialog box at all.

Note: The Editing section also has an action called Set Selection. You're not ready for this one yet, but it's covered in Chapter 14.

Field actions

In the Fields section you find several useful and familiar commands.

Insert Text lets you stick predetermined text into a field. You can tell FileMaker *which* field to put it in, or leave "Go to target field" unchecked to have it land in the field the user's currently in. You also get a "Select entire contents" checkbox if you want the inserted text to *replace* whatever's in the field. Click the *bottom* Specify button to tell FileMaker what text to insert.

Several actions mimic the choices in the Insert menu (in Browse mode):

- Insert from Index
- Insert from Last Visited (Insert → From Last Visited Record)
- Insert Current Date

- Insert Current Time
- Insert Current User Name
- Insert Picture
- Insert QuickTime
- Insert File

For each of these, you can optionally choose the field to use, and whether or not to select everything in the field before inserting.

Finally, the Replace Field Contents action runs the Records → Replace Field Contents command. This time, you get to pick the field to replace into if you want. You can also predetermine what goes in the Replace Field Contents dialog box. If you turn on "Perform without dialog," your users never even see the dialog box. Instead, the replace *just happens*. You could use this action, for example, to add a Flag button to your layout. It would automatically flag every record in the found set by putting a Y in the same field on each of those records.

Record actions

Use the New Record/Request action to make a button create a new record. To duplicate the current record instead, choose Duplicate Record/Request. To delete a record, use Delete Record/Request. This action has one option: "Perform without dialog." Turn this action on if you want your button to delete the record with no warning message.

Warning: Turn off the warning message only if the people using your database are very experienced (or very trustworthy). The Undo command can't undo a deletion, so there's no going back–yet another reason for a good backup routine.

The Open Record/Request action locks the record without actually entering any fields. Chances are you *never* need to do this action from a button. Use Revert Record/Request to mimic the Records → Revert Record menu command. This one has a "Perform without dialog" option as well.

To give folks an obvious Save button, assign it to the Commit Record/Request action. This action is just like clicking out of the record. It's useful, though. If you have your layout set to show a "Do you want to save…" message whenever someone edits the record, you can add a Save button to the layout, using this command with the "Perform without dialog" option turned on. Whenever anyone clicks the button, FileMaker saves the record straightaway without the annoying dialog box.

Found Set actions

If you have certain finds that you perform a lot, you can create buttons to run them directly. Use the Perform Find, Constrain Found Set, and Extend Found Set actions to get the job done. Each action lets you specify what find requests you want them to use. See page 548 for an explanation of how to specify these requests manually.

For now, though, you can easily use them like this: First, perform the find you want the button to do (just go to Find mode, enter your criteria, and click Find). Then add the button to the layout and pick one of the find actions. Turn on "Specify find requests" and FileMaker shows you its complicated Specify Find Requests dialog box. But the box *already* has the requests you used last, so you can just click OK. Now your button performs the right find.

The last few actions work just like their counterparts in the Records menu:

- Modify Last Find
- Show All Records
- Show Omitted Only
- Omit Record
- Omit Multiple Records (this action has two options: how many records to omit, and the now-familiar "Perform without dialog")
- Sort Records (this one also lets you predetermine the desired sort order, and avoid the dialog box if you want)
- Unsort Records

Window actions

Windows are, after all, where FileMaker displays your information, so it pays to be familiar with the button commands that control them. With these actions, you can adjust an open window so your data fits more comfortably, or even create a new window to navigate in while the first stays intact in the background.

- Use **New Window** to make a button that creates a new window. You can determine its name, size, and position, but it always shows the layout you're already on, so its usefulness is pretty limited. It's more typically used in a script (see Part 5).
- The **Select Window** action lets you switch to a different window if you know its name. Click Specify, choose Window Name, and type in the name of the window. (The Current Window option makes sense only when scripting.)
- **Close Window** simply closes the active window. You can also supply the name of *another* window, and FileMaker closes that window instead.
- The **Scroll Window** action gives the button rudimentary control over the window's scroll bars. Choose Home to scroll to the very top. If you choose End, a button click scrolls to the very end. Page Up and Page Down work like scroll bar clicks, moving it one screenful up or down.

  You can scroll a window while you're in a field. If you do, the field you're in may no longer be visible on the screen. The Scroll Window action's To Selection option tells FileMaker to scroll the window so that the field you're in is visible.

- Use **Show/Hide Status Area** and **Show/Hide Text Ruler** to show or hide each embellishment. Your button can explicitly show or hide the item, or you can choose Toggle to have the button *switch* the setting with each click. The Show/Hide Status Area action also has a Lock checkbox. Turn this checkbox on if you want the status area control to become inactive when your button is clicked. With an inactive status area control, nobody can show or hide the status area without using your buttons.
- The **Set Zoom Level** action lets you make your own zoom buttons as well. This action also has a Lock option if you want to lock out the normal zoom control.
- **Adjust Window** lets you minimize, maximize, resize to fit, restore (to its last size), or hide the frontmost window.
- **Arrange All Windows** gives you the Tile Horizontally, Tile Vertically, Cascade, and "Bring All to Front" options from the Window menu.
- **View As** has an option for "View as Form," "View as List," and "View as Table." You can also choose Cycle to have one button that cycles through all three views.

Note: The options to lock the status area and zoom controls may seem a little odd for button actions. Why would a person ever click a button to lock herself out of something useful? Actually, you'll usually use these options as part of a *script* (Chapter 13). You see them here since button actions and script steps always have the same options.

Print actions

The Files section has two important actions: Print Setup and Print. These give you control over the File → Print and File → Print Setup or File → Page Setup commands. Optionally, you can preselect the options in each dialog box, and use the "Perform without dialog" checkbox to perform the action with no user intervention. You could, for instance, have buttons that switch to landscape and portrait page layouts, and a third button to directly print the current record.

Open actions

The Open Menu Item section gives you button access to several common dialog boxes. You can add them to a layout to save people a trip to the menu bar, which is especially useful if they don't know where the menu bar *is*.

- Open Preferences
- Open File Options
- Open Manage Database
- Open Manage Value Lists
- Open Find/Replace
- Open Help

Exiting FileMaker

If you want a button that exits or quits FileMaker itself, use the very last action in the list: Exit Application.

Tab Order

When you press Tab while editing a field, FileMaker automatically jumps you to the next field. But what does *next* mean? Normally, FileMaker moves through fields in a left-to-right, then top-to-bottom direction, but that's only one possible *tab order*, as Figure 6-34 illustrates.

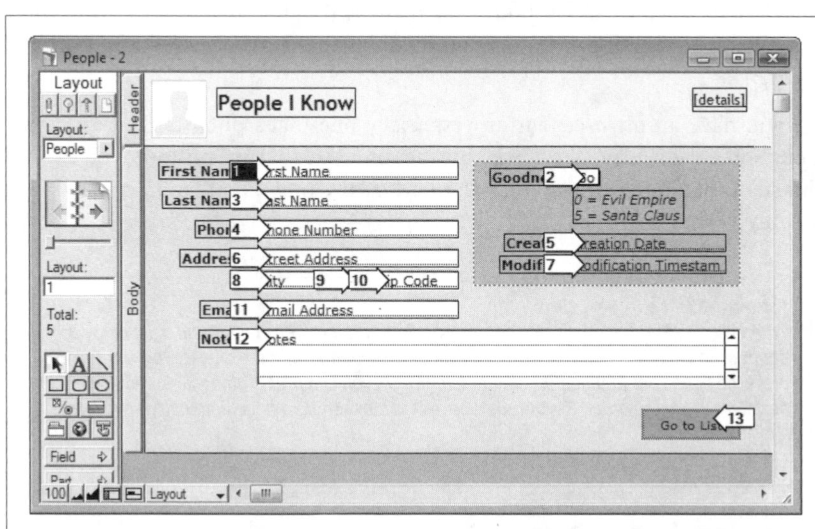

Figure 6-34: *Top: The numbers in the arrows show what order you'll follow when you tab through the record. FileMaker's automatic order has the Goodness Rating field just after the First Name field (because it goes left-to-right first) and before the Last Name field. But that's not an ideal setup.*

Bottom: This tab order makes more sense. The fields you don't type into are not in the tab order at all, the data entry fields go in a logical order.

As often as not, this automatic ordering is not ideal. For instance, in your People database, the automatic tab order puts Goodness Rating immediately after First Name. It makes more sense to put Last Name next instead for two reasons: First, you *expect* to enter the last name after typing a first name. Second, the Goodness Rating field is a pop-up menu, which you can't type into, so it probably shouldn't be tabbed into at all.

Buttons in the Tab Order

Even if you don't have a field ordering problem, you may still want to customize the tab order for another major reason: you can *tab to buttons* if you want. Because keyboard controlled buttons require a little planning (you don't want to make people feel like a pinball by bouncing them through dozens of buttons while they're furiously entering data), FileMaker skips them completely in its standard tab order.

But if you have an oft-used button (especially one that's often clicked after performing some data entry, like a Next button, or a New Record button), you can tell FileMaker to let you get to it with the keyboard alone. Figure 6-35 explains this more fully.

Figure 6-35:
When you tab to a button, FileMaker draws a dramatic black border around it, leaving no doubt as to what has its focus. Instead of clicking the button with the mouse, you can simply press the Space bar to trigger its action. Alternately, you can press Tab again to move on to the next item in the tab order. Keyboard-powered buttons can be a huge data entry timesaver.

Customizing the Tab Order

Whatever your reasons for doing so, FileMaker lets you completely customize the tab order for any layout. To fix the tab order on the detail layout of your People database, first choose Layouts → Set Tab Order. A few things happen onscreen: You see the arrows indicating tab order, and the Set Tab Order dialog box appears (Figure 6-36). You tell FileMaker what order to use by putting appropriate numbers into the tab order arrows. Put a *1* in the arrow that points to the button or field that should get your attention when you first press Tab. Put a *2* in the next object in line, and so forth.

Chances are, all the arrows that point to fields already have numbers in them reflecting FileMaker's automatic tab order. Clearing and typing into each arrow can thus be a form of digital torture. To ease the pain, FileMaker offers up the Set Tab Order window, which appears at the bottom-right corner of the screen. This window lets you make a few targeted bulk changes to the tab order.

First of all, you can clear the numbers from every arrow by clicking Clear All. This trick is great because once all the arrows are empty, you no longer have to type.

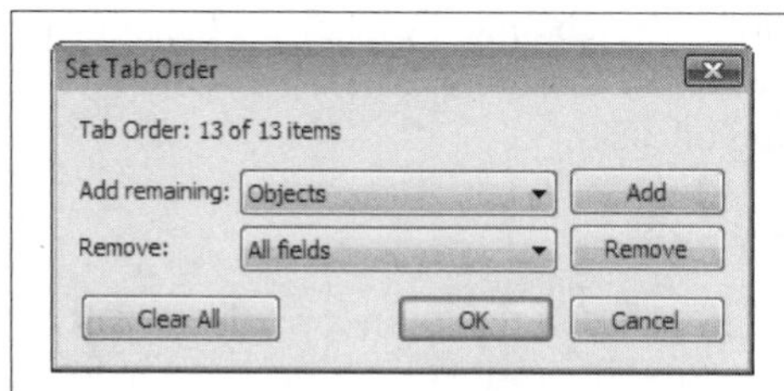

Figure 6-36:
When you choose Layouts → Set Tab Order, the Set Tab Order window appears. Meanwhile, FileMaker also adds the arrows shown in Figure 6-34 to the layout while this dialog box is open. From here, you can make bulk adjustments to the tab order, clear it, and start over, or manipulate the numbers one by one to get exactly the order you want.

Just click each arrow (or the field or button it points to) in succession, and FileMaker enters the numbers for you. If you want to remove only the fields or only the buttons from the tab order instead, choose the appropriate option from the Remove pop-up menu and click Remove.

If you click Add and choose from the "Add remaining" pop-up menu, you can add unnumbered fields, buttons, or both to the order. FileMaker numbers them for you using the same right-to-left, top-to-bottom philosophy that the automatic tab order uses. This option comes in handy if, for example, you want to set up a specific tab order for a few buttons first, and then use the automatic ordering for all fields thereafter.

When you're done making changes, either in the window or by editing the arrows directly, click OK. If you decide you've caused more harm than good in this tab order editing session, click Cancel instead, and the tab order reverts back to the way it was before you opened the Set Tab Order box.

Fixing the Tab Order in the People Database

As for the People database, you want to fix the tab order on the detail layout so that Last Name comes after First Name. You can approach this task in several ways, but the following steps show you a trick that makes it easier. You may be tempted to Clear All and then renumber all the arrows yourself. But since you're *removing* only a field from the tab order (the Goodness Rating field) you can save yourself the trouble:

1. **Choose Layouts → Set Tab Order.**

   The Set Tab Order window and its flock of arrows appear.

2. **Click the arrow pointing to the Goodness Rating field and delete the number.**

   The arrow pointing to Goodness Rating is now empty. Your order also now goes straight from 1 to 3, skipping right over 2. Pay no attention to this problem (that's the trick).

3. **Click OK in the Set Tab Order window.**

   If you switch to Browse mode and try out your tab order, you see that you can now tab right from First Name to Last Name.

This trick works because FileMaker establishes the tab order by following the numbers in the arrows in order. It doesn't give a hoot if those numbers aren't contiguous. You've fixed your layout with a minimum of clicks.

Preserving the Automatic Order

As long as you never choose the Set Tab Order command on a particular layout, FileMaker automatically manages the tab order for you. For example, if you add a Middle Name field to the layout, and place it between the First Name and Last Name fields, it automatically goes into the right spot in the tab order—between First Name and Last Name. If you switch the positions of the First Name and Last Name fields, Last Name becomes the first field in the tab order, and First Name comes next.

Once you click the Set Tab Order window's OK button, though, FileMaker hands full responsibility thereafter over to you. If you add a new field to the layout, it just gets stuck to the *end* of the tab order, no matter where you put that field on the layout. If you move fields around so that the tab order makes absolutely no sense, FileMaker doesn't care. It keeps the tab order exactly as you specified in Set Tab Order.

Web Viewer Controls

Imagine you want to view a map of someone's address in your People database. Getting a map isn't a problem; they're readily available on the Web. Google Maps (*http://maps.google.com*) and MapQuest (*www.mapquest.com*) both provide them for free. Still, it's a lot of work to copy address information, change programs, find the right page, and paste the address into your database for each record. Or maybe you want to show the map right on the layout, instantly available at a glance. You could draw your own maps and store them in a container field, or even take screen shots right off of Google and paste them in. But that's an awful lot of work, too.

Instead, simply ask FileMaker to go get the maps from the Internet for you. Using a FileMaker Web viewer, you can get FileMaker to automatically and instantly fetch almost anything available on the Web and display it directly on the layout. FileMaker even takes care of keeping things up to date: Every time you visit a record on the layout, it checks to see if newer information is available and automatically fetches the most up-to-date version, just like your Web browser.

You create Web viewers with the Web viewer tool. This globe-decorated tool button lives right between the Tab control tool and the Button tool on the status area when you're in Layout mode. (You can see these tools in Figure 4-16 if you need a refresher.) It works like most FileMaker tools: First click the tool button in the status area, and then drag a rectangle on the Layout to tell FileMaker where to put the Web viewer and how big to make it.

GEM IN THE ROUGH

Tab Order and Repeating Fields

Each repetition of a repeating field is treated as a separate entity as far as tab order is concerned. It's perfectly legal to have the *last* repetition come right after the *first*–if you're into aggravating the people using your database. But it can be a real drag to have to click each and every one of those repetitions when you set the tab order. FileMaker has a nice feature to save you the trouble.

When you click the first repetition of a repeating field (while setting tab orders), FileMaker gives it a number–and the arrow begins to flash. If you click this flashing arrow *again*, FileMaker numbers that field's additional repetitions for you, in the logical order.

But the magic doesn't stop there: Suppose you have a series of repeating fields, as shown here. The standard tab order would go *down* each column before moving to the next one, but you'd prefer to tab *across* the rows first. For example, if you're sitting in the first Quantity field, you want to tab into the Product field, then the Price field. Then once you've completed a row, you want the next tab to take you to the next one.

FileMaker can automatically do this kind of numbering for you, too. When setting the tab order, click the first Quantity field. It gets a number and begins to flash. Now click the first Product field, and then the first Price field, as pictured here. You notice that the arrow by the Quantity field continues to flash. Once you've done these three clicks, click the flashing arrow again. FileMaker now numbers all your repetitions properly.

In general, you click each repeating field in the order you want them tabbed to. When you're done, click the *first* one again to let FileMaker know. FileMaker fills out each row of repetitions matching this order.

(It should be gently suggested here that you should never, ever build a database like the one shown here. Ever. Period. If you want to track line items on an order, read Part 3 of this book first. Nonetheless, this repeating field trick still comes in handy on rare occasions.)

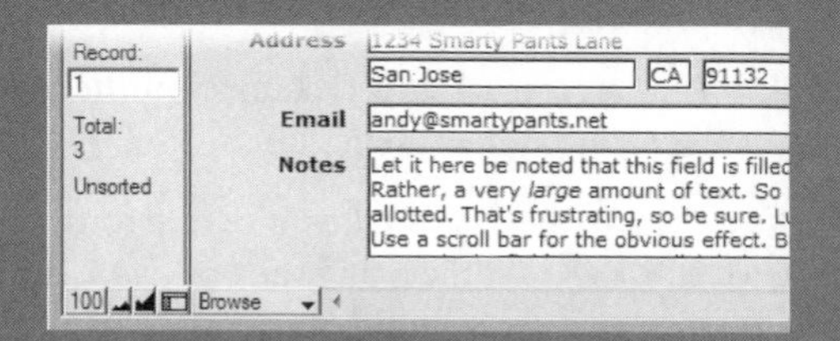

Putting a Web Viewer on a Layout

Here's how to get FileMaker to do all your map-surfing work for you:

1. **Switch to Layout mode in your People database, and get ready to edit the detail layout.**

   Since a map can be large, it makes sense to put it on the detail layout, where you have some room to work with.

2. **Make the Body part much taller by dragging its label downward.**

   The idea is to make room for the Web viewer on this otherwise-crowded layout.

3. **Select the Web viewer tool in the status area.**

   This tool has a picture of the earth on it. It is in the bottom row of tools, right in the middle.

FREQUENTLY ASKED QUESTION

FileMaker's Web Browser

Is the Web viewer a modern browser? Is it standards-compliant? Can it run JavaScript, or use browser plug-ins? Should I be worried about compatibility with various pages?

FileMaker doesn't actually have a Web browser of its own lurking underneath your layout. Instead, it calls upon the services of the Web browser engine most readily available—the one that came with your computer. On Windows, FileMaker uses Internet Explorer as its underlying browser technology. On Mac OS X, it uses Safari instead. This arrangement has a few important implications:

- FileMaker is using a tried-and-true browser technology, so you know it'll work well with most Web pages It has support for all the major Web technologies, just like its real Web browser counterparts.
- If you install any plug-ins for your Web browser, FileMaker uses them as well.
- If you upgrade your operating system or Web browser, FileMaker's Web viewer gets the benefits of the upgrade as well. For example, if you install Internet Explorer 7 (or use Windows Vista), then the Web viewer gets all its page-handling capabilities. If you have Internet Explorer 6 installed instead, your Web viewers have its limitations.

4. **Draw a rectangle on the page roughly the same width as the Notes field and a few inches tall.**

   As usual, you're free to tweak the exact size and position of the Web viewer any time you want, so you don't have to be perfect here. Figure 6-37 shows an example of what you're aiming for. As soon as you let go of the mouse button, FileMaker shows you the Web Viewer Setup dialog box (Figure 6-38).

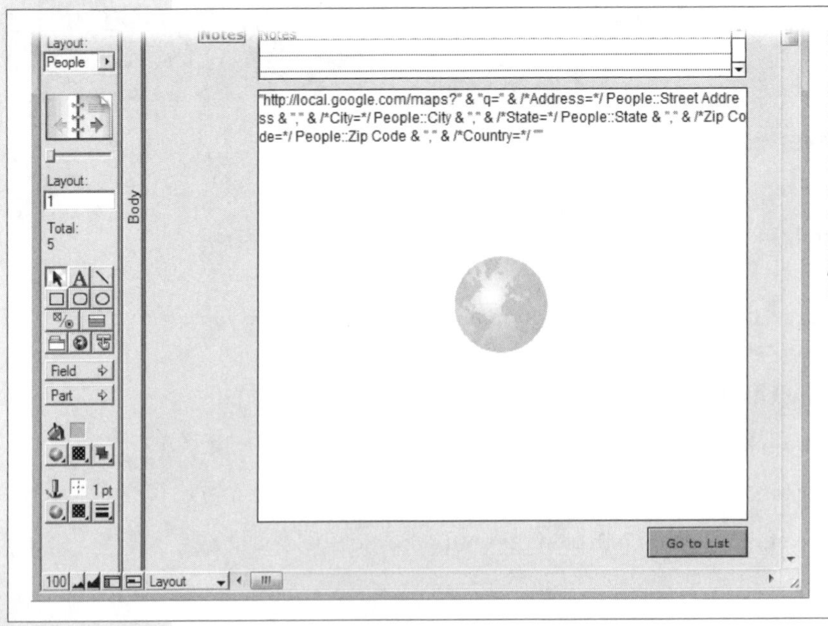

***Figure 6-37:** This version of the layout has a Web viewer below the Notes field (you can tell it's a Web viewer because it has a picture of the earth in the middle of it). You should put yours in about the same place and make it at least this tall.*

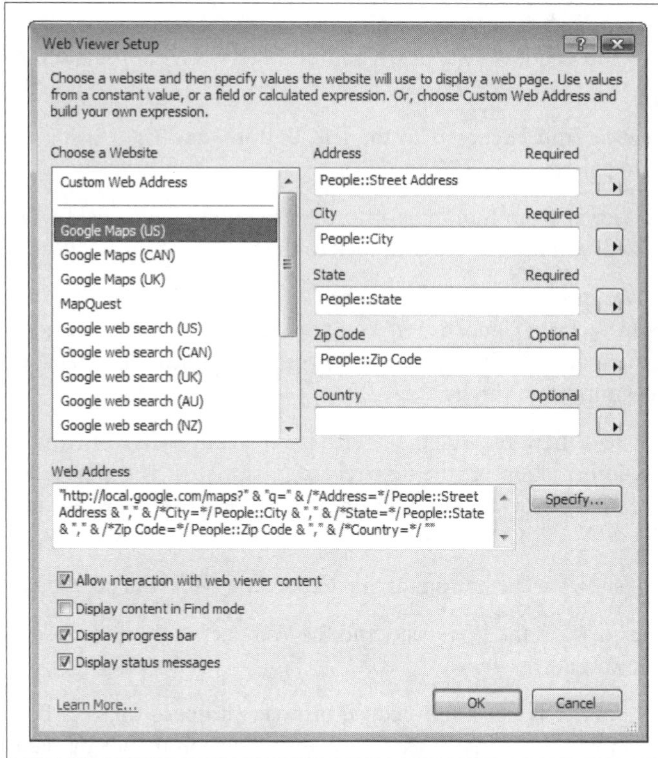

Figure 6-38: *The Web Viewer Setup dialog box has a lot of options. First, pick the Web site you want to show from the list on the left. Then fill in the appropriate boxes on the right. If you choose Custom Web Address, you can use the Web Address box at the bottom of the window to type in any URL you want.*

5. **In the "Choose a Website" list, select Google Maps (US).**

   You're telling FileMaker you want this Web viewer to show information from the Google Maps Web site. As soon as you make this selection, several entry boxes appear on the right side of the dialog box.

6. **Click the square button to the right of the Address entry box and, from the resulting pop-up menu, choose Specify Field.**

   FileMaker pops up the standard Specify Field dialog box. Here you'll tell FileMaker which field to pull the street address from when it goes to find a map.

7. **In the Specify Field window, select Street Address, and then click OK.**

   FileMaker now knows the first piece of information it needs to find the appropriate map. Notice that the Address box now shows People::Street Address.

8. **Repeat step 7 for the City, State, and Zip Code boxes. In each case, pick the appropriate field.**

   As you make selections, FileMaker fills in the various boxes. The Web Address box at the bottom of the window also changes, but you don't need to concern yourself with that just yet.

9. **Click OK.**

   The Web Viewer Setup window disappears, and the Web viewer appears on the layout.

10. **Select the Web viewer and anchor it to the left, bottom, and right using the View → Object Info palette.**

    To keep the Web viewer from bumping in to the expanding Notes field when the window is resized, you need to tell it to stick to the bottom of the window.

If you switch to Browse mode, you should see the Google Maps page with a map for the current person record (Figure 6-39). You may need to make the window bigger in order for the map to display properly. If you fiddle with the database a bit, you'll notice a few important things:

- When you switch to a new record, the Web viewer changes its contents to reflect the address information on the new record. Likewise, if you *change* the data in any of the address fields, the map instantly updates to show the new address.
- Status information shows at the bottom of the Web viewer while the page loads.
- You are free to click links in the Web page, and the Web viewer dutifully follows your clicks and shows a new page.
- Although the Web viewer is not a full-fledged browser (it doesn't have a Back button, for instance) you can access most typical browsing commands by right-clicking (Windows) or Control-clicking (Mac) anywhere on the Web page. In fact, the menu that appears when you do is just like the one you would see if you did the same in your real Web browser. For instance, choose Back from this menu to go to the previous page.

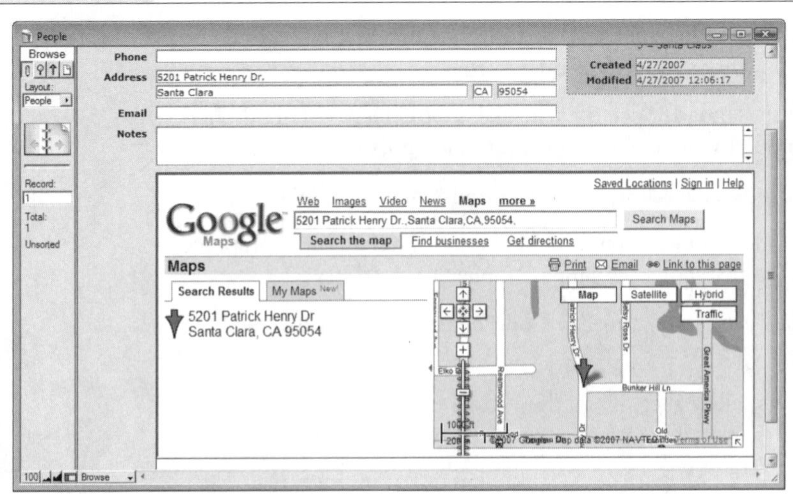

Figure 6-39: *The People database now has a Google Maps Web page showing right on the detail layout. FileMaker's Web viewer lets you embed any Web page on the layout, so you can save countless trips to your favorite Web resources. Unfortunately, Web pages tend to be big. You'll learn how to give this map more breathing room without investing in a 30-inch screen on page 279.*

POWER USERS' CLINIC

Beyond the Built-in Sites

When you added a Google Maps page to your layout, you didn't have to figure out how Google expects to receive address information. Instead, you simply picked Google Maps from a list and filled in the blanks. This easy-to-integrate approach is possible because FileMaker already knows how to connect to Google Maps. FileMaker has built-in support for nine popular Web sites (you see each one listed in the Web Viewer Setup dialog box). When you pick from this list, FileMaker shows a series of entry boxes appropriate for that site. For example, with Google Maps selected, the dialog box asks for Address, City, State, Zip Code, and Country. If you pick FedEx instead, FileMaker asks for a Tracking Number instead. In every case, you can pick a field FileMaker should use to get the data it wants, or you can type a value instead, like *USA* for Country if all your addresses are in the United States. (You can also opt to supply the data using a calculation. You'll learn all about calculations in Chapter 9.)

But don't let FileMaker's list of companion sites trick you into thinking they're the only ones that will work. You can connect a Web viewer to *any site*. Just choose Custom Web Address at the top of the "Choose a Website" list. Then type any URL you want in the Web Address box at the bottom of the window (or copy one from a Web page and paste it in).

Unfortunately, if you want the exact page information to be tied to data in the record (just like the Google Maps example) you'll have to supply a calculation for the Web Address. On the bright side, you'll learn how to write calculations in Part 4, which is right around the corner.

Web Viewer Options

FileMaker offers up a few configuration options for Web viewers in addition to the page they should load. The bottom of the Web Viewer Setup dialog box (Figure 6-38) includes four checkboxes to adjust the behavior of this particular Web viewer.

Allow interaction with Web viewer content

When the "Allow interaction with web viewer content" option is turned on (as it is for your map), FileMaker lets you actually *use* the Web page it loads. Specifically, you can click a link on the page to navigate to a new page. You can also use shopping carts, send email messages, watch video, or use any other features on the page.

When you turn this option off, all page behavior is deactivated. A click on the page produces no more response than a click on a blank spot on the layout. You can't even scroll the page. If a page is too big to fit in the space you've given it on the layout, FileMaker simply cuts it off.

Turn this option on when the page you are showing is just a starting point (like the login screen for your Orders Web page, or the first step in the application process). You should also leave this option on when the page is larger or its size is variable. On the other hand, you can turn "Allow interaction with Web viewer content" off when you're showing a small page that contains all the information needed.

Display content in Find mode

Normally, when you switch to Find mode, the Web viewer just goes blank. Which makes sense, since a Web viewer is usually showing a page associated with data in the current record. After all, if you go to Find mode, where you're no longer necessarily looking at a particular record, then FileMaker may not be able to tell which Web address goes in the Web viewer.

You can change this behavior, though, by turning on "Display content in Find mode." When you do, FileMaker makes its best effort to display the Web page even when you are in Find mode. For example, if you've typed a URL directly into the Web Viewer Setup dialog box, then FileMaker can continue to display the page properly no matter which mode you use (except Layout mode). If you're using a Web site that needs information from the database, FileMaker feeds it the data from the find request instead. This behavior could come in handy if the Web page information would be helpful to a person trying to construct a find request, but usually you'll want to leave this option off. It can be jarring to watch a Web viewer constantly refresh itself as you enter your find criteria.

Display progress bar

Unlike everything else on your layout, Web page content isn't always immediately accessible by FileMaker. The program has to go to the Internet and pull up the page, which can take some time (just as it takes time for a page to load in your browser). If you turn on "Display progress bar" (it's on until you turn it off, in fact), then FileMaker shows a subtle progress bar at the bottom of the Web viewer (Figure 6-40).

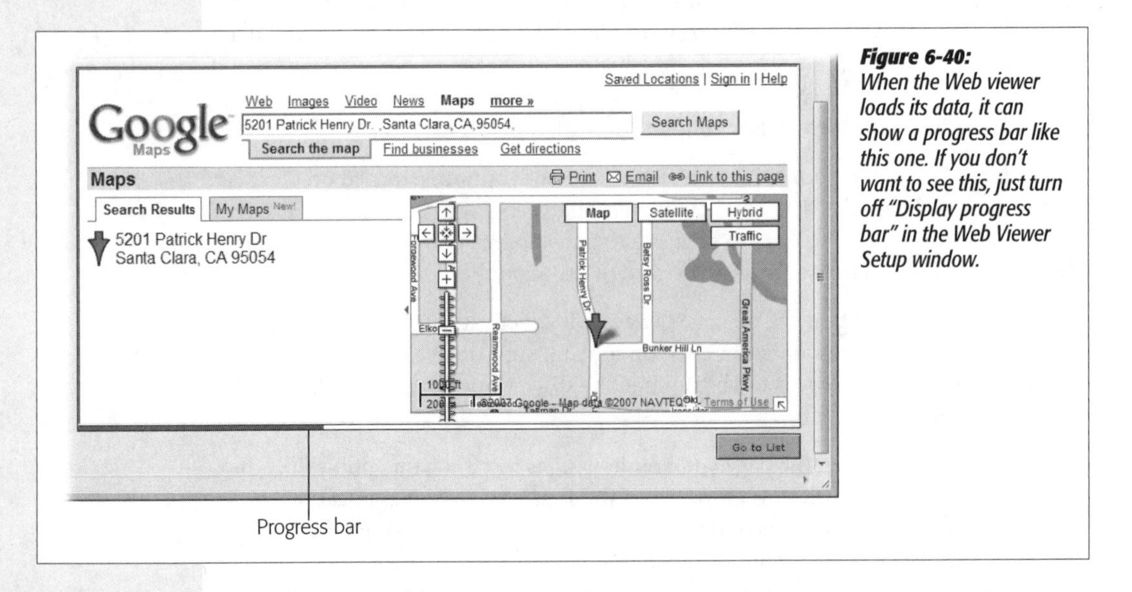

Figure 6-40: *When the Web viewer loads its data, it can show a progress bar like this one. If you don't want to see this, just turn off "Display progress bar" in the Web Viewer Setup window.*

Display status message

Another option that FileMaker automatically turns on is the "Display status message" checkbox. This option tells the Web viewer to reserve a little space along its bottom edge to show status information (Figure 6-41). Status information typically means the "Loading..." messages you see at the bottom of a Web browser window. Turn this option off if you'd rather not sacrifice precious layout space for not much more information than what the progress bar already gives you. That way, the Web viewer can use all its space on the layout for Web page content.

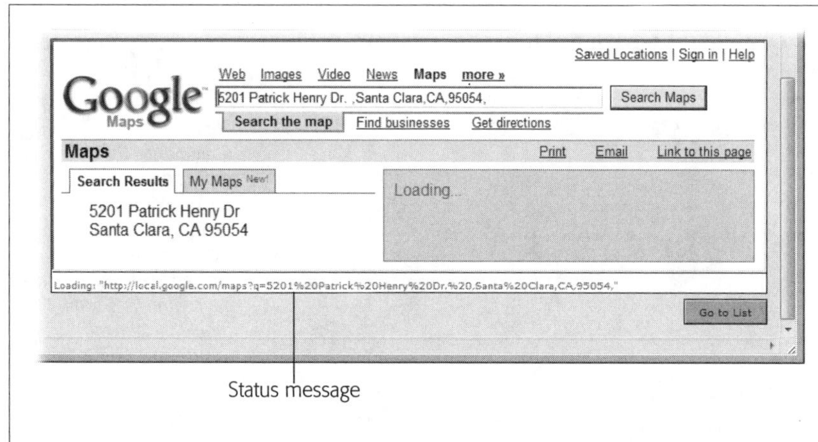

***Figure 6-41:** The Web viewer's status information mirrors the messages that appear along the bottom edge of your browser window (assuming you have this option turned on). If you'd rather not reserve this much screen space for a message that shows for less than half a second, then turn off "Display status message" in the Web Viewer Setup dialog box.*

Tab Controls

When a window needs to show you more information than fits comfortably on one screen, software designers resort to dividing it up onto an array of tabs. Just about every dialog box these days has a few tabs scattered across the top. For example, the Layout Setup dialog box in Figure 5-24 has tabs for General, Views, and Printing. Most Web browsers offer tabbed browsing so you can switch among different Web pages open in the same window.

FileMaker windows can get overcrowded, too. The Google Maps Web viewer you just added, for example, makes your overall layout quite large, and honestly, the map page would be happier with even *more* space. There are times when you just can't stretch a layout any farther. Maybe some of your employees have smaller monitors and you don't want them to have to scroll to see everything on the layout. Or you may feel you've already created a beautiful layout, with perfect proportions, and stretching it to fit a big map viewer would ruin the design you worked so hard to create. Whatever the reason, if you don't want to make a layout bigger, you can organize lots more fields by adding a tab panel (Figure 6-42). Then you can simply click the tab to see the map (which is still much less work than visiting a separate Web browser).

Creating a Tab Control

If you want to add another set of fields to hold the work addresses of the contacts in your People database, you have to make the layout bigger in order to hold your new fields. The hardest part of adding a tab control is getting everything out of the way to make room for it. Here are the steps:

1. **In the People database, go to detail layout and switch to Layout mode.**

   You're now ready to shuffle in a tab control.

2. **Scroll to the right so you have a large amount of empty layout space to work on.**

   You'll build the tab control here, and then move it into place when you're done.

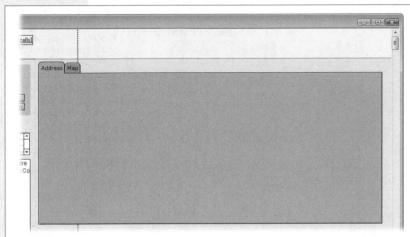

Figure 6-42: *As you draw the tab control on the layout, FileMaker outlines the space it will occupy, including the tab at the top and the space for the tab control itself. You should make a tab control about this size.*

3. **Click the Tab Control tool in the status area (it looks like a file folder at the bottom-left corner of the collection of tools). Then, draw a tab panel like the one in Figure 6-43.**

   You draw a tab panel the same way you draw a rectangle—click and drag. Make it about the same size as the space taken up by the fields you moved out of the way (you can always resize it later). When you release the mouse button, the Tab Control Setup dialog box appears. Here's where you tell the panel how many tabs it needs and what to name them.

4. **In the Tab Name field, type Address, and then click the Create button.**

   FileMaker adds the word Address to the Tabs list. Repeat this step for one more tab: Map.

5. **When you're done, click OK to close the Tab Control Setup dialog box.**

   Your new tab panel, complete with two tabs, sits highlighted in place on your layout. Notice that there are four selection handles at each corner, and a dark box around each of the three tabs. Any changes you make to the tab panel now affects both tabs.

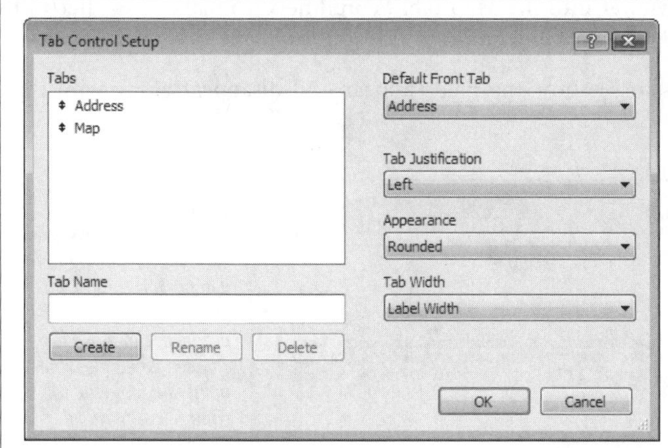

Figure 6-43:
The standard settings for tabs are left aligned, with rounded corners. But you can have square corners instead if you like them better. Left, center, and right justified tabs are just wide enough to enclose the names you give them. But fully justified tabs stretch out and divide the space to fill the width of the entire panel.

You've just added a tab control to your layout with two tabs, which you can see labeled along the top of the control—Address and Map. If you stop right now and switch to Browse mode, you'll see that your tab control is already working. You can click tabs, and they toggle. But a tab control is pretty useless until you put something on its tabs. Switch back to Layout mode, and then continue with these steps:

1. **Click the Address tab to make it active.**

   You can tell the Address tab is active when it's united with the gray rectangle of the tab control (the other tabs are separated from the rectangle by a dark line).

2. **Select all the fields, labels, and the Goodness Rating box, and drag them onto the Address panel.**

   When you put an object (or several objects) right on top of a tab control, they go into the tab. Now, if you move the tab control, all these objects move, too. If that isn't the case for you, your tab control may not be quite big enough. Every element has to be completely inside the tab control.

Note: The objects you've moved into the Address tab now operate completely within the tab. If you move the tab control, they move, too, without needing to be selected. And if you use the Arrange → "Send to Back" command, the selected object goes behind other objects *on the same tab*, but not behind the tab control itself.

3. **Resize the tab control if necessary so it's just the right size to hold the objects in it.**

   Since this tab is more complicated than the Map tab (which has to hold only the map), you can use it to determine how big the tab control itself should be. (You'll resize the map to fit accordingly.)

4. **Switch to the Map tab by clicking its label.**

   The tabs work like normal tabs even in Layout mode. When you switch tabs, all the fields you put on the first tab disappear, leaving a new box of empty space ready to fill.

5. **Move the Web viewer into the Map tab. (You'll need to make it smaller to fit properly—use Figure 6-44 as a guide.)**

   Click the panels to see how the fields appear and disappear along with their panels.

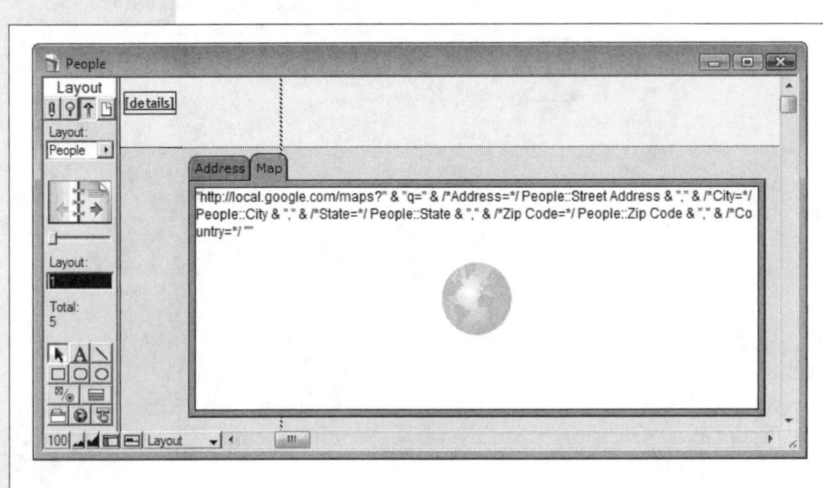

***Figure 6-44:** You'll need to make the Web viewer smaller to fit it in the tab control. It may seem counter-productive to make it smaller, when the whole point of adding the tab control was to make more room. But remember that the layout represents your minimum window size. Once you configure your anchors correctly, when you switch to Browse mode, the Web viewer can fill almost the entire layout.*

6. **Using the View → Object Info palette, anchor the Web viewer on the top, bottom, right, and left.**

   This way, FileMaker makes the Web viewer bigger when the window gets bigger.

7. **Select the tab control itself (by clicking any of its tabs) and anchor it to the top, bottom, right, and left as well.**

   Since objects on a tab are *in* the tab control, they won't grow with the window unless the tab control does too. And at any rate, it makes sense for the tab control to get bigger with the window.

8. **Drag the entire tab control to the left so it's in the space the fields used to occupy.**

   All the fields you've moved onto the tabs are now firmly attached to the tab control. If you move it (by dragging from an empty spot or by one of the tab labels), all the fields move along with it, so there's no need for fancy selection techniques. Just drag the tab control to a new location, and you're golden. You can even copy the whole panel and paste it onto another layout. It works just as it did in the original location.

9. **Make the line between the header and the body a little longer so it goes just past the width of the tab control.**

   The tab control made your layout wider, so you need to adjust this decorative line accordingly.

10. **Move the "Go to List" button up so it's just under the tab control, and reduce the size of the body appropriately.**

    These last changes will return the layout to its original svelte size. You can see it in Figure 6-45.

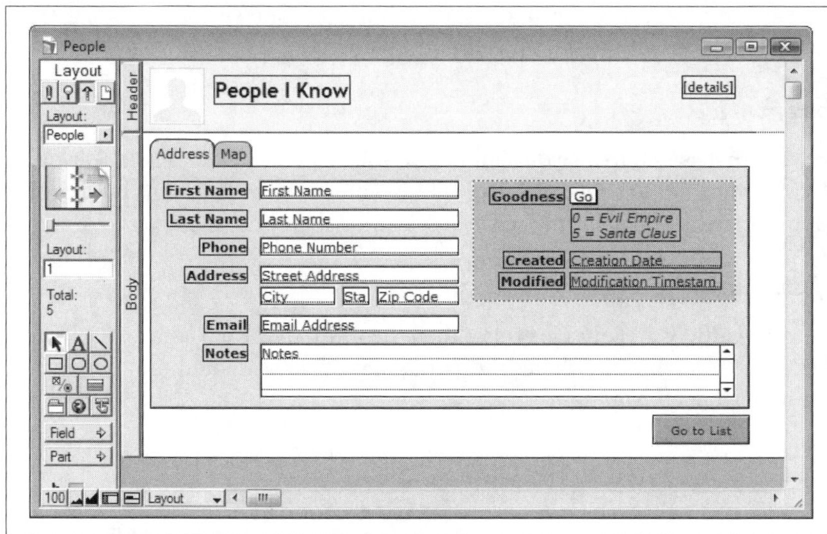

Figure 6-45: *Once you complete the steps above, your layout should look something like this. It includes all the elements it had before, but thanks to tab controls, the whole thing is much more manageable. In this particular case, each tab in the tab control has its background color set to a lighter gray and the body has been filled with white.*

11. **Switch to Browse mode to test your panel.**

    Click the panels to see how the fields appear and disappear along with their panels.

Note: If some of your fields or labels unexpectedly appear on all tabs, you may have bumped into a common problem: FileMaker considers an object to be on a particular tab only when it's *completely* enclosed by the rectangular region of the tab control. The objects that are misbehaving are probably hanging off one edge or another, perhaps by just a pixel or two. Also, make sure your tab control doesn't sneak up into the Header part of your layout. If even one pixel of the tab control is in the header, it won't work properly.

Editing Tab Controls

You can edit a tab control by double-clicking it to summon the Tab Control Setup dialog box. From there, you have many options to control the look and behavior of the tab control.

Adding, removing, and reordering tabs

In the Tab Control Setup dialog box, you can add new tabs anytime by typing a name and clicking Create. The new tab appears at the end of the list of tabs, and the right of the existing tabs in the control. You can also rename an existing tab: select it in the list, enter a new name, and then click Rename.

To delete a tab you no longer need, select it in the list and click Delete. When you delete a tab, you delete all the objects on that tab. (FileMaker warns you of this fact first, and asks whether you're sure you know what you're doing.)

Finally, you can control the order of the tabs from left to right. FileMaker draws the tabs left to right in the order they appear in the Tabs list. Rearrange the items in the list using the arrows to the left of each name. (You've used a similar technique in FileMaker with fields, value lists, and more.)

Default front tab

When you first switch to a layout but before you've clicked a tab, FileMaker needs to decide which tab to show automatically. You tell it what you want by choosing the appropriate tab name from the Default Front Tab pop-up menu.

Tab justification

If the total width of all your tabs is less than the width of the tab control itself, FileMaker lets you choose where the grouping of tabs should be positioned. Figure 6-46 shows the options.

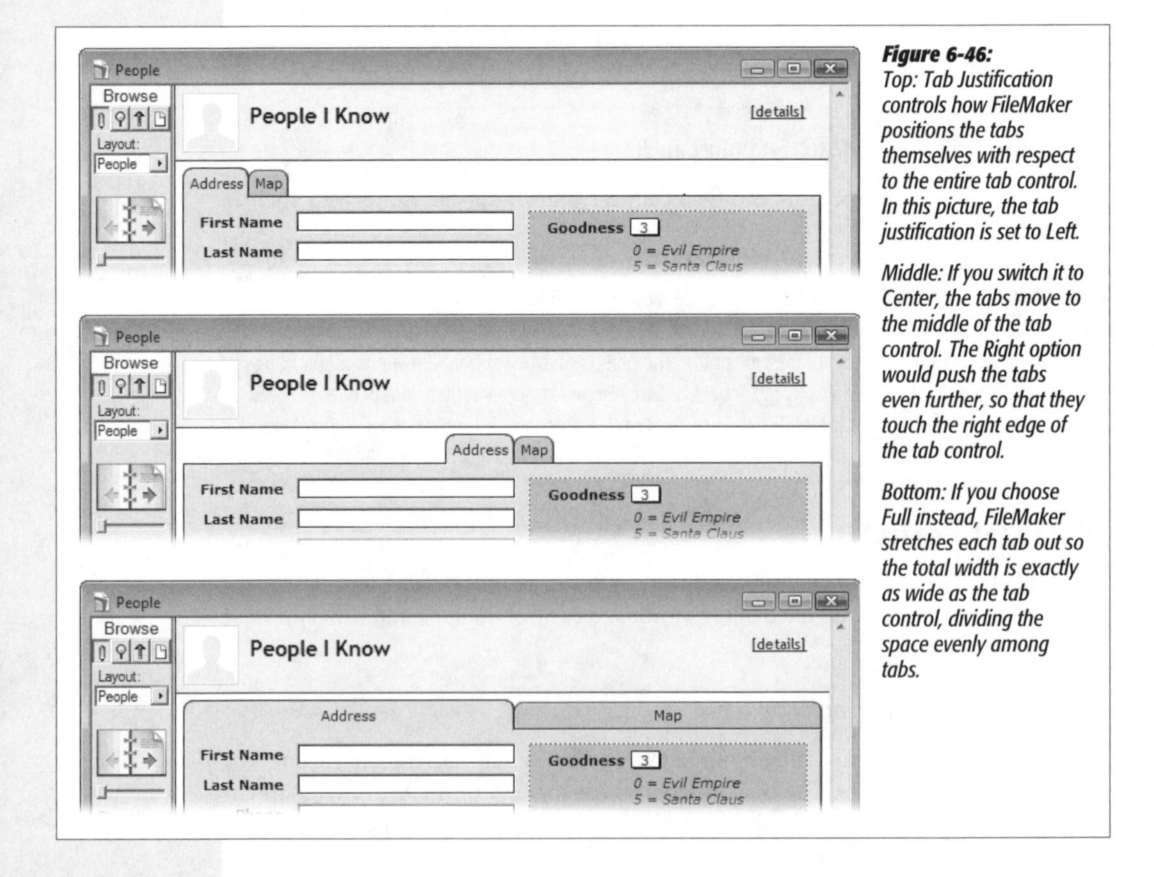

Figure 6-46: *Top: Tab Justification controls how FileMaker positions the tabs themselves with respect to the entire tab control. In this picture, the tab justification is set to Left.*

Middle: If you switch it to Center, the tabs move to the middle of the tab control. The Right option would push the tabs even further, so that they touch the right edge of the tab control.

Bottom: If you choose Full instead, FileMaker stretches each tab out so the total width is exactly as wide as the tab control, dividing the space evenly among tabs.

Note: If you have more tabs than can fit given the size of the tab control, FileMaker simply doesn't show the extras. You can either force the tabs to be narrower using the Tab Width option (see below), make the tab control itself bigger, or make the tab names shorter.

Appearance

Like buttons, FileMaker can draw tabs with rounded or square corners. As before, this is a purely cosmetic configuration, so make your choice freely from the Appearance pop-up menu.

Tab Width

The Tab Width pop-up menu has several choices to influence the width of the tabs:

- Choose **Label Width** if you want each tab to be just wide enough to hold its label. (If you also choose Full from the Alignment pop-up menu, the tabs will stretch wider than their labels nonetheless.)
- **Label Width + Margin of** works a lot like Label Width, except that you can add some additional space around the label text, in that FileMaker makes the tab wider and centers the label text within it.
- If you prefer all your tabs to be the same width, choose **Width of Widest Label.** FileMaker figures out which label is biggest, sizes its tab appropriately, and then matches that size for all the others.
- If you'd like all your tabs to be a nice consistent width, but stretch to accommodate the odd long label, choose **Minimum of.** You can enter a minimum width (75 pixels, say), and every tab uses it, unless the label is too big to fit, in which case FileMaker makes the tab wider so the label fits.
- If you want the utmost in control and uniformity, choose **Fixed Width of** and enter a width in the box. Every tab will be exactly that width. If the label is too big, FileMaker simply cuts it off at the end.

POWER USERS' CLINIC

Tab in a Tab

If your layouts have more doodads than the bridge of the Enterprise, take heart. You can put a tab control on another tab for even more space savings. That's right. You can put tabs inside tabs inside tabs. So long as the new control sits entirely *inside* an existing tab, it behaves just like any other object on a panel. It sits there quietly behind the scenes and doesn't make an appearance until you click its enclosing panel. Then, up the new panel pops, in all its tabbed glory.

Needless to say, the more you use the tab-within-a-tab technique, the more complex your layout becomes—and the more potentially confusing to anyone using your database. Use it sparingly.

Dismissing the Tab Control Setup dialog box

When you're done poking around, click OK, and all your changes are instantly reflected on the layout.

Or, if you make a set of changes and realize you've made a mistake, just click Cancel. All changes you've made to the tab panel since you opened the dialog are swept away, even if you deleted some panels, added some, and rearranged the furniture while you were in there. But once you click OK, your changes are written in stone—at least until you revisit the Tab Control Setup dialog box.

Formatting a tab control

Out of the box, tab controls are medium gray, embossed, with a think black border. But you can make yours striped purple with a thick yellow border instead if you want. Just use the fill and border tools in the status area to make your selections. You can customize the look of a tab control further by adjusting its fill color and pattern, and tweaking its border color, pattern, and thickness.

When you do, you'll probably quickly discover another unexpected reality: You can color and style each *tab* individually. The choices you make apply only to the currently selected tab. If you want to adjust all the tabs at once, use the rubber band selection technique (see page 156) to select them all. (You have to rubber band around the entire tab control, not just the tab labels at the top.)

Deleting a Tab Control

If you don't want a tab control after all, just select it and choose Edit → Clear, or tap Delete or Backspace. FileMaker warns you that it's about to delete all unlocked objects on the tab panel as well. If that's the way you want it, click OK. If you need to keep fields or objects on the tab panels, though, click Cancel, and then move the keepers off the panel (way to the right of your layout, perhaps) for safekeeping.

Reports and Summary Fields

A database excels at keeping track of things—itsy bitsy teeny tiny details about hundreds, thousands, even millions of little things. But people aren't so good at dealing with all that detail (hence the invention of the database). They like to see the *big picture.* If you want to understand your customer's music tastes, a report of 200,000 individual CD sales won't do you much good: The information is in there somewhere, but your feeble mind stands no chance of ferreting it out. But a report that divides that information into 25 *music genres*, each with sales totals, both in aggregate and by gender, helps you interpret all those reams of data at a glance. In other words, a well-designed report *summarizes* the data for you. FileMaker's not only fantastic at showing you information, it also excels at helping you see what it all *means.*

In Chapter 5, you learned how to create reports that show lists of records, but they don't include any so-called summary data. They show only the details. To get summary information, you need *summary fields.*

Summary Fields

In Chapter 3, you learned that a summary field isn't associated with records like the other field types (see page 104). Instead, summary fields gather up and process data from several records. Creating summary fields is much easier than describing what they do, as you can see from the following example.

1. **In the People database, choose File → Manage → Database.**

   You're about to add a field that counts the people in your database. This action is one of the most common ways to summarize database information.

2. **In the Manage Database window, choose the Fields tab. Then, in the Field Name box, type *Count of People*.**

   A summary field, like any other, has a name. You're going to use this summary field to count the people in your database.

3. **From the Type pop-up menu, choose Summary, and then click Create.**

   The "Options for Summary Field" window appears (Figure 6-47).

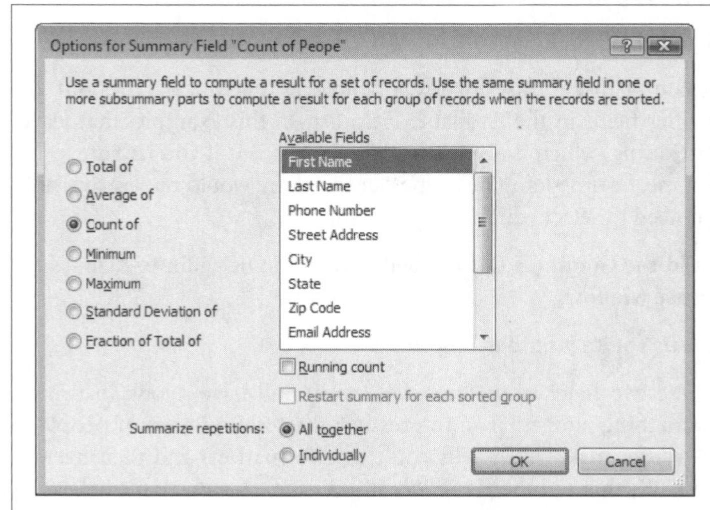

Figure 6-47: *The "Options for Summary Field" dialog box appears when you make a new summary field. Unlike the field types you've used so far, a summary field has options that must be set for it to be usable, so FileMaker shows you those options right away. This window also shows up if, in the Manage Database window, you select a Summary field and click Options.*

4. **Choose the "Count of" radio button.**

   A summary field can perform one of seven summary calculations. In this case, you want it to *count* things.

5. **From the Available Fields list, choose First Name.**

   A summary field is always based on some other field in the database. For example, this field counts the First Name field. What does that mean? Simple: If a record has something in the First Name field, it gets counted, but if the First Name field is blank, FileMaker skips the entire record. Since every person has a first name, this field counts every record. But beware—if you forget to type somebody's first name in a new record, that person doesn't get included in the count.

Note: In a simple database like this one, counting the First Name field is enough to make reasonably certain that you're counting all the records. But in the real world, you want to be certain *every* customer is counted–even if the First Name field isn't filled in. You'll learn about more complex databases and their need for a field that's never empty (called a primary key field) in Part 4.

6. **Click OK.**

   FileMaker adds the new field to the field list.

You now have a field that helps you find out how many people are in the database. That piece of information is much more useful than it sounds; you'll be using it to find out interesting things soon. It would also be nice to be able to summarize the Goodness Rating information. In this case, an *average* makes sense.

1. **In the Field Name box, type *Average of Goodness Rating.***

   Remember, field names can be about as long as you want.

2. **With Summary selected in the Type pop-up menu, click Create.**

   The "Options for Summary Field" dialog box makes its second appearance.

3. **Select the "Average of" radio button.**

   Since averages don't make sense for text or pictures, FileMaker grays out any text and container fields in the Available Field list. In this example, that leaves only Goodness Rating, which is automatically selected. But if you had any other number, date, time, or timestamp fields in your file, those would remain available, too, and you'd need to select which one you want.

4. **Click OK to add the Goodness Rating field, and then OK again to dismiss the Manage Database window.**

   FileMaker returns you to your database window.

If you squeeze these two fields onto the detail layout and have a look in Browse mode, you see something altogether unimpressive: the total number of people in the database (the status area already tells you this information) and their average Goodness Rating (OK, this number is *mildly* impressive). If you don't believe it, have a look at Figure 6-48.

Creating a Summary Report

This section began by talking about how useful it can be to summarize your data. It specifically mentions a report that shows sales by Zip code and genre for a music retailer. When you hear something like that, you're sure to think that a Summary field should have some kind of a "by what" option. In other words, how do you tell that Total Sales field to summarize by Zip code? Alas, there's no such choice in the "Options for Summary Field" dialog box.

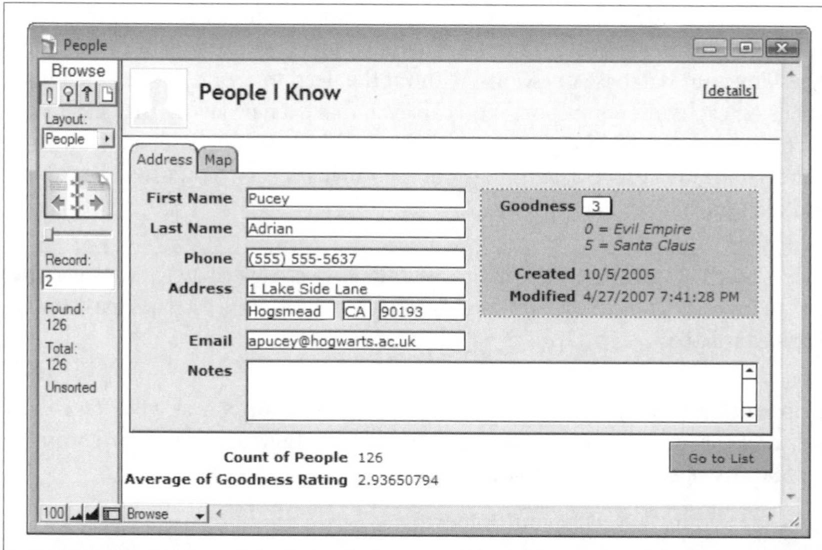

***Figure 6-48:** Showing your new summary fields on the detail layout isn't terribly exciting. You don't need a field to tell you how many records you have (the status area does this job just fine). Next you see the average Goodness Rating of all people in the database, which is only mildly interesting. For the real power, see page 288.*

POWER USERS' CLINIC

Stop That

Normally when you add a field to the database, FileMaker automatically adds it to the layout you were just on. This feature is nice in the same way those child safety bottle lids are nice: It's probably good for kids. But big people like you find it terribly annoying.

First of all, FileMaker can't possibly know where you want the field, so it just sticks it at the bottom of the layout. This place might be the right spot, and the living room floor might be the right place for your 8-year-old's shoes. Of course, you can just move it, but if the Body part had to grow to accommodate it, you'd have to reduce it again.

What's more, it usually doesn't use the right font and formatting (your new Notes field is probably formatted like the text under the Goodness Rating field shown in Figure 6-48: small, gray, and right-aligned). Putting it right is tedious. It's usually easier to duplicate an existing field and change it to show your new field.

This way, you get all the right formatting in one step. Finally, if you have several layouts in your database, you don't necessarily want the new field on the *current* layout—and its existence there is just something you have to go fix.

To teach FileMaker that you're a big boy or girl now, just do this:

1. In Windows, choose Edit → Application Preferences; in Mac OS X, choose FileMaker Pro → Preferences. The Application Preferences window pops up.
2. Switch to the Layout tab. This tab is the place you set Layout mode preferences. You've already seen the Color Palette settings.
3. Turn off "Add newly defined fields to current layout."

If you someday decide to stop thinking for yourself, you can always ask Winston to turn this setting back on.

A Summary field is, by nature, abstract. You tell it which field to summarize, and that's about it. You could have one that counts people, another that totals orders, and a third that shows the standard deviation of the Height field. You then design your layouts to produce the specific groupings you want. For example, you can make that Total Orders field display totals *per customer* on one layout, *per product* on another, and *per month* on a third. This field gives you tremendous flexibility when asking your database questions, without the need to create different fields for the totals on each different report. You can even make a new layout that slices your data a brand-new way without ever revisiting the Manage Database window. Once you understand this process, defining summary fields is easy. You usually need just a handful at most.

Tip: Some aspects of sub-summary reporting are easier to show than to explain. You can see them in action in at *www.missingmanuals.com*. The screencast uses the same database but shows you details that aren't covered in the book.

To help you understand how to tailor a layout to a report's best advantage, how about adding a new report to the People database that uses the new summary fields? Start by opening the database and switching to Layout mode.

1. **Choose Layouts → New Layout/Report.**

   The now-familiar New Layout/Report window returns.

2. **In the Layout Name box, type *Summary Report*, and then, in the "Select a layout type" list, choose Blank Layout.**

   You're going to build this layout by hand.

3. **Click Finish.**

   FileMaker creates its basic blank layout: empty header, empty body, empty footer.

First things first: This layout is a report, and as such it's going to be printed. A lot. In this case, it makes sense to fix page margins so the printed output looks as nice as possible.

1. **Choose Layouts → Layout Setup. In the dialog box that opens, click the Printing tab.**

   This panel should look familiar.

2. **Turn on "Use fixed page margins."**

   If you leave this option *off*, FileMaker automatically prints things as close to the edge of the page as your printer allows. When *on*, you get to edit the four margin boxes (Top, Bottom, Left, Right).

3. **In each of the boxes for Top, Bottom, Left, and Right, type *1*, and then click OK.**

   Back in Layout mode, you may notice that the page break lines have moved to reflect the printable area considering the new margins.

Note: If the Layout Setup dialog box is showing Centimeters (cm) or Pixels (px) instead of Inches, just type an equivalent value. For example, 72 pixels, or 2 centimeters.

4. **Choose File → Print Setup (Windows) or File → Page Setup (Mac OS X) and make sure the paper size is correct and the orientation is set to the normal portrait.**

   The page break lines may move once again to show the new size and shape of the paper.

Since your layout now has fixed margins, you may want to see them in Layout mode so you have a feel for how things fit on the page. Just choose View → Page Margins.

Note: Showing page margins in Layout mode is not a substitute for Preview mode. FileMaker doesn't attempt to show the page at the proper size. Instead, the margins in Layout mode help you get a feel for the space around your layout objects on the printed page. For example, without them, you can avoid putting text at the very top of the layout. But the margins remind you that this text will *actually* sit an inch below the top of the page. You can switch to Preview mode at any time for a more accurate look.

Now it's time to design the Body part.

1. **Add a new field to the layout by dragging the field tool into the Body part.**

   FileMaker instantly asks you which field you want.

2. **Select the First Name field in the Specify Field list, turn off "Create field label," and then click OK.**

   The First Name field is now on the layout, although it may not be formatted properly. You're going to format it, and then use it as the basis for the rest of the fields in this layout—a great timesaving trick.

3. **Change the field's font to Verdana 10-point regular. Make sure the field content aligns to the left (Format → Align Text → Left). Also, if necessary, set the fill color of the field to clear and the text color to black.**

   The field now looks something like those in Figure 6-49. Now that the field is properly formatted, you can copy it to produce the other needed fields.

4. **While pressing the Alt (Option) key, drag the First Name field to the right a few inches.**

   When you Alt-drag (or, on the Mac, Option-drag), FileMaker makes a copy of whatever you're dragging. See page 170 for more cool dragging tricks.

5. **When the Specify Field window returns, choose the Last Name field from the list, and then click OK.**

   You now have a First Name field *and* a Last Name field on the layout.

6. **Repeat steps 4 and 5 six times to add these fields: Phone Number, Email Address, Street Address, City, State, Zip Code.**

   You now have eight fields on the layout.

7. **Arrange the fields in the Body part to match Figure 6-49.**

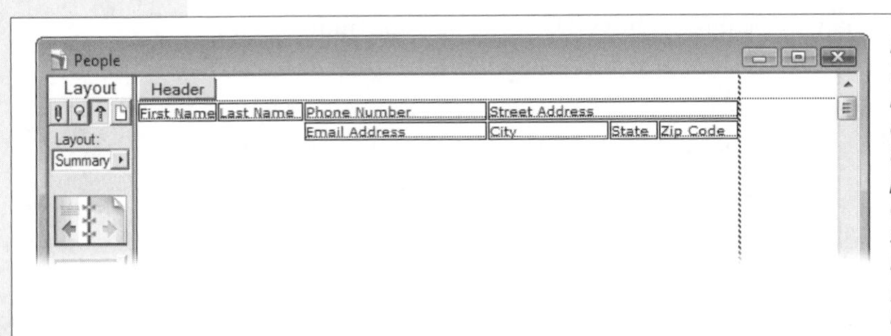

Figure 6-49: *The fields on your new layout should be arranged something like this. You'll add titles, page numbers, decorations, and so forth shortly. You also need to resize the parts and work your new summary fields in there somewhere.*

   If you stop and view this layout in Browse mode now, it looks sparse, but the data's there. You may notice, though, that the address portion is "spaced out" in an unpleasant way. You can fix this problem with sliding. (And if you don't remember what sliding is, see page 210.)

8. **In Layout mode, select these fields: First Name, Last Name, City, State, and Zip Code.**

   Remember to press Shift as you click to select more than one item. *All* these fields need to slide to the left.

9. **Choose Format → Sliding/Printing, turn on "Sliding left," and then click OK.**

   Again, sliding only affects Preview mode and printing, so you don't see any change in Layout mode.

Next, you can add the summary fields to the layout. Since they summarize data, they really don't belong in the Body part, which repeats for every record on every printed page.

FREQUENTLY ASKED QUESTION

Seen: Sliding

Is there any way I can tell which items have sliding turned on?

Yep. Choose View → Show → Sliding Objects. Every object that is set to slide gains a small black arrow pointing in the sliding direction.

If you're just curious about a particular object, and don't want to clutter your view of the layout, there's another way. Select the object in question and choose Format → Sliding/Printing. The Set Sliding/Printing window appears with the settings for the selected object.

Adding a summary part

You need to show them only once—probably *after* all the data. There's a part type that does exactly this: Trailing Grand Summary. When you start with a brand-new layout, it has a body, a header, and a footer, but it doesn't automatically have any summary parts. You have to add them yourself:

1. **Choose Insert → Part. When the Part Definition dialog box appears, select Trailing Grand Summary, and then click OK.**

   FileMaker adds a Trailing Grand Summary part to your layout, between the body and the footer.

Note: If you prefer to have your summary information *before* the data in the report, use a *Leading* Grand Summary part instead, which appears between the body and the header. Whether you want your grand totals at the top of your report or at the bottom is a Coke/Pepsi sort of thing.

---

2. **Add the two summary fields to the new part, along with meaningful labels.**

   Refer back to page 161 for instructions if you need a refresher on adding fields.

Next up, you need to reduce the size of the Body part so it shows a slim row, add a title and any lines you feel would look nice, and add a page number in the footer. You could also use separate Title Header and Header parts so you can put a *smaller* header on every page after the first. Finally, since this is a report, intended for printing, you can skip setting autoresize anchors. After all, the size of the printed page doesn't change. If you want, though, you can use anchors to make the report print properly on different paper sizes or page orientations. You can see one way to format this report in Figure 6-50.

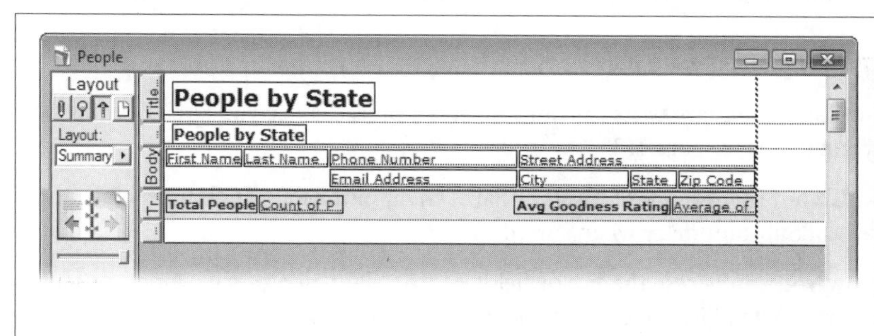

***Figure 6-50:** Here's one way you could lay out your report. The "Count of People" and Average Goodness Rating fields are in a Trailing Grand Summary part, which shows just below the body. Switch to Preview mode and click the last page to see the summary fields in action.*

Note: If you use Find mode to find only a few records (you have to switch to the detail layout first), the summary fields change to reflect only the records in the found set. Of course, the printed report also includes only the data in the found set.

Sub-summary parts

Your People database already uses summary fields to show the total number of people in the database and the average Goodness Rating. Right now they live on a Trailing Grand Summary part, where they count and average everything in the found set. That's great if all you're interested in are sweeping generalizations. But what if you want to examine your information on a slightly finer level? For example, what if you'd like to know how many people you have in California? Of course, you could do a find for California, and then run the report on just that found set, but that's a lot of work. Instead, you can use a sub-summary part, which shows summary information about a *subset* of the records in the found set.

You tell it what kind of groups you want by associating it with a field. A sub-summary part that is hooked to the State field will show totals for each state. Connect it to the Zip Code field instead to get per-Zip-code totals. When you add a sub-summary part to a report, it acts like a cross between a Trailing (or Leading) Grand Summary and a Body part. It doesn't repeat for every record, but it does repeat: It shows once for each *group* of records. Any summary fields you put on a sub-summary part automatically calculate based only on the subset of records in question. Since the sub-summary part appears in the report multiple times, you get multiple subtotals. In other words, you can put the *same* fields in *different* parts to see different results.

Sub-summary parts are unique in two ways. First, they show up only in Preview mode. You never see a sub-summary part in Browse or Find modes. Second, they show up only when the data is *sorted* by the field they're associated with.

In the People database, for instance, you could add a sub-summary part to this report based on the State field and set it to appear above the summarized records. The result would look something like Figure 6-51.

Creating a sub-summary part

Adding sub-summary parts to your layout is a breeze, since you already know how to create parts (see page 151).

1. **In Layout mode, choose Insert → Part. Then, in the Part Definition dialog box, select "Sub-Summary when sorted by."**

   Now you can access the list of fields on the right side of this window. This is where you tell FileMaker which field you'll be summarizing by.

2. **Scroll down to State in the field list and click it.**

   You've just told FileMaker to use the State field to group records.

3. **Click OK.**

   FileMaker asks if you want to print the part *above* or *below* the records it summarizes.

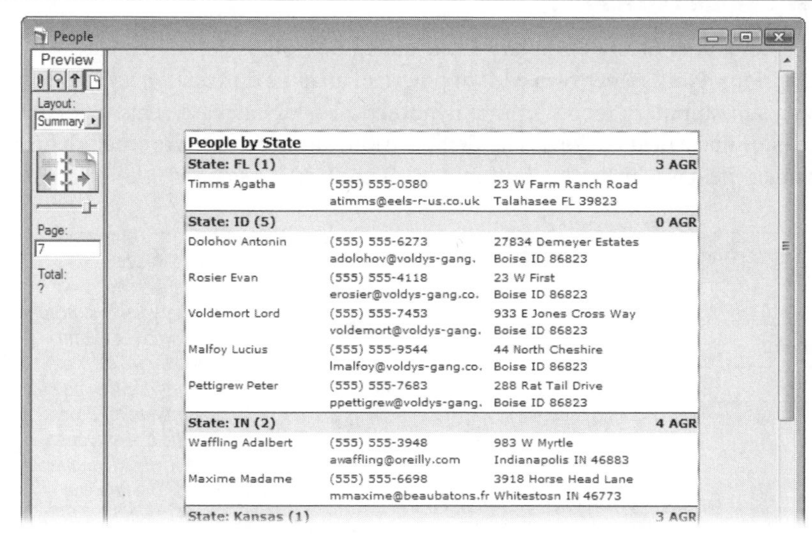

Figure 6-51: *This version of your report includes a gray-colored sub-summary part based on the State field. The part includes the State field itself, as well as the two summary fields. As you can see, the summary field values reflect just the group under them. In other words, they sub-summarize (clever, huh?).*

4. **To get the result shown in Figure 6-51, click Print Above.**

   A new sub-summary part appears between the header and the body.

5. **Add the State, "Count of People," and "Average of Goodness Rating" fields to the new part.**

   You can also decorate this part any way you see fit.

To see the results of your labors, sort the records by the State field and switch to Preview mode.

POWER USERS' CLINIC

Sub-summary Power

You can actually put *two* sub-summary parts associated with the same field on a layout at the same time, as long as one's set to print above the records and the other below.

You can also put several sub-summary parts on the same layout with each associated with a different field. This way you can create nested sub-groupings, each with their own summarization data. When you create them, you need to be extra careful with the sort order. For sub-summary parts that print *above* the records, you should sort the fields in the order of the sub-summary parts themselves. If your sub-summary parts are *below* the records, you should sort first by the field associated with the *bottommost* part, and then by the next one up, and so on.

If you don't include a field in the sort order, FileMaker simply excludes the sub-summary part(s) for that field from the report. In this way, you can have a single layout that reports on data with different groupings based only on the sort order.

You can even make a layout with sub-summary parts, but no Body part. A layout set up like this just shows group summaries, without individual record details. For example, if you remove the Body part from the report you just made, you see the people count and Goodness Rating for each state in a simple list, but you don't see individual people.

Other Summary Field Types

The Options area of the Summary Field dialog box offers several choices. Using these options, you can perform a lot of powerful analysis on your data. Figure 6-52 shows a sub-summary report from a hypothetical sales database. This report uses several summary field options. The first decision you need to make when defining a summary field is which radio button to turn on. Here's what each choice does:

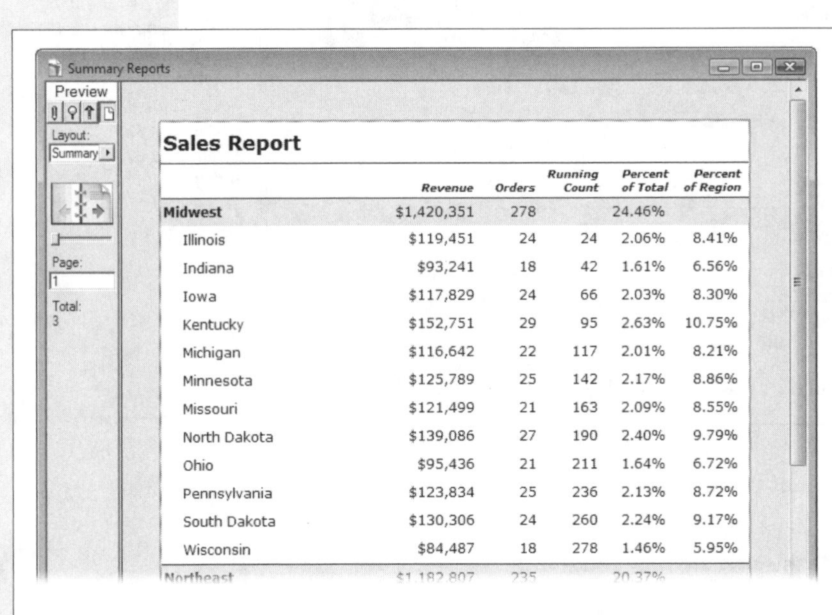

	Revenue	Orders	Running Count	Percent of Total	Percent of Region
Midwest	$1,420,351	278		24.46%	
Illinois	$119,451	24	24	2.06%	8.41%
Indiana	$93,241	18	42	1.61%	6.56%
Iowa	$117,829	24	66	2.03%	8.30%
Kentucky	$152,751	29	95	2.63%	10.75%
Michigan	$116,642	22	117	2.01%	8.21%
Minnesota	$125,789	25	142	2.17%	8.86%
Missouri	$121,499	21	163	2.09%	8.55%
North Dakota	$139,086	27	190	2.40%	9.79%
Ohio	$95,436	21	211	1.64%	6.72%
Pennsylvania	$123,834	25	236	2.13%	8.72%
South Dakota	$130,306	24	260	2.24%	9.17%
Wisconsin	$84,487	18	278	1.46%	5.95%
Northeast	$1,182,807	235		20.37%	

***Figure 6-52:** This report shows summary fields in action. The Revenue column uses a "Total of" type summary field to add up sales numbers. Orders uses the Count type to show the total number of orders. The Running Count column, on the other hand, continues to count up the orders from one state to the next. Finally, two Percent fields use the "Fraction of Total" summary field type to determine how much each state contributes to its region, and how much each region contributes to the total. You'll learn about all these options on the next few pages.*

Total of

Use the "Total of" option to *sum* (add) number fields. In Figure 6-52, the Revenue field is a total of the Sales Amount field. For each group (state or region) you see its total.

When you have this option selected, a "Running total" checkbox appears below the Available Fields list. When you use a summary field on one of those magical layouts (like the one you create on page 287) that produces grouping—total sales by Zip code, total sales by state, and so on—you normally see just the totals for each group in the report. If you turn on "Running total," FileMaker changes things slightly. Instead of individual totals for each group, the totals add up from group to group, much like the Balance column in your checkbook register.

Average of

Obviously, the "Average of" choice calculates the average of the values in a number field. This time, you see a "Weighted average" checkbox. When you turn it on, another field list appears (see Figure 6-53). From this list, you choose the field by which to *weight* your average.

You would use a weighted average when the things you are averaging have an associated quantity. For example, suppose your database has a record for each product sale. It records which product was sold, how many were sold, and the unit price. If you want a summary field that calculates the average sale price, you probably want to turn on the "Weighted average" checkbox. Imagine you have these sales figures:

- You sold three laptop computers for $2,500 each.
- You sold 18 more laptops for $2,200 each.
- You sold a single laptop for $2,800.

If you use a simple average, FileMaker tells you the average sale price for laptops is $2,500 ($2,500 + $2,800 + $2,200, divided by three). But that's not exactly right. You sold *18* of those laptops at just $2,200 each, but it only counts *once* in the calculation. In fact, you really sold 22 laptops in all, at three different prices. To calculate the correct average, you need to take quantities into consideration. In FileMaker, turn on the "Weighted average" checkbox and choose the Quantity field in the "Weighted by" list. Now it reports the correct average: $2,268.18.

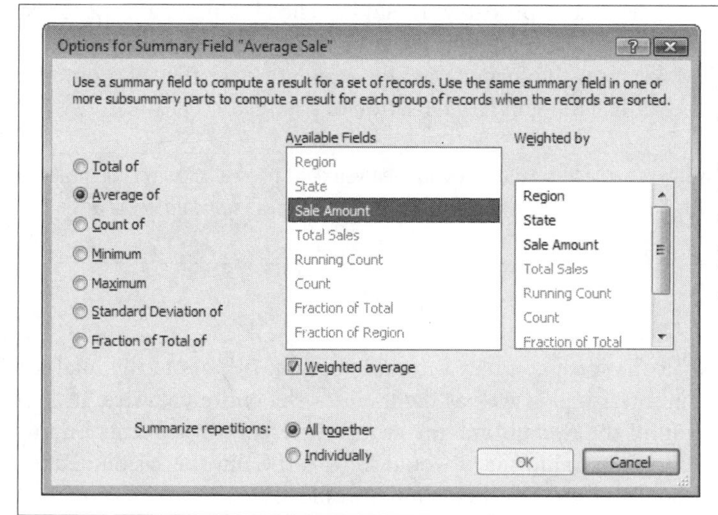

Figure 6-53: *When you turn on the "Weighted average" checkbox, FileMaker adds a second field list–'Weighted by"–to the window, where you can pick another number field. FileMaker averages the data in the first field, and weights each record's input by the second field. If you're not a statistician, see the explanation in "Average of" on page 297.*

Count of

Choose "Count of" to *count* items without totaling them. Since this option doesn't involve actual math, you can pick *any* field type, not just numbers. FileMaker counts each record in which that field isn't empty. If it's empty, it simply doesn't contribute to the count. Choose a field that is *never* empty if you want to be sure you count *every* record. You can use this property to your advantage, though. If you wanted your count to reflect just the records that are flagged, count the Flag field instead. In Figure 6-52, the Orders column uses this option.

This option gives you a "Running count" checkbox. It works like running total but has an option that running total doesn't offer. When you turn on "Running total," the "Restart summary for each sorted group" checkbox becomes available. This option lets you produce a column like Running Count in Figure 6-52. This column counts up with each state, keeping a running count. But it is set to restart numbering based on the Region field. Notice that the running count starts over with each new region.

Minimum and Maximum

If you want to know the *smallest* or the *largest* value in a group, use Minimum or Maximum. Both are very simple: Just pick the number field you want to look at. No checkboxes, no extra lists. You can use these to see the largest Goodness Rating in your database, or the price of the least expensive product.

Standard Deviation of

If you're into statistics, use "Standard Deviation of." It gives you a field that calculates its namesake for the selected number field. It also has a "by population" checkbox, which is a little oddly named (it probably should be called "of population"). Turn this checkbox on if your records represent the entire population in your particular domain, and FileMaker uses the formula for the standard deviation of a population. Turn it off to calculate the standard deviation of a *sample*.

Note: If none of this makes sense to you, then rest assured you don't need to know what it means to use summary fields. But if you're cursed with a curious mind, Google *define:standard deviation* and go to town.

Fraction of Total

'Fraction of Total" is the most complex summary option. It looks at the total for the *group* you're summarizing, as well as the total for the entire database. It then reports what portion of the overall total the group represents, as a decimal number. If all your sales were in California, it would show *1*. If California accounted for only 5 percent of your sales, on the other hand, it would say *.05*.

The "Subtotaled" checkbox that comes along with this option is also a little confusing. When you turn it on, FileMaker lets you pick another field from a list called "When sorted by." The name of this list serves to inform you that you must *sort* the record by the selected field for this summary field to work. If you don't sort the records yourself before you view the report, the field stays empty.

Note: That problem's not as big as it may seem at first. As you learned on page 298, you have to sort records to do a lot of things with summary fields.

FileMaker looks at the selected field, figures out which records have the *same* value in them as in the current record, and calculates the fraction based only on the total of *those* records. In Figure 6-52, the "Percent of Total" column is a normal "Fraction of Total" field, while the "Percent of Region" column uses "Fraction of Total" subtotaled by Region.

Summarizing repetitions

When you summarize a repeating field (see page 119), you have another choice to make. Do you want *one* summary value that aggregates every repetition, producing a single value? If so, choose "All together." If you want a repeating summary value that aggregates each repetition individually instead, choose Individually.

Tip: If you have sharp eyes, you may notice that the "Summarize repetitions" radio buttons are available all the time, although they don't do anything unless you've selected a repeating field. Don't waste your time clicking them unless you're working with a repeating field. Just one of those FileMaker mysteries for the cocktail-party circuit.

Part Three: Multiple Tables and Relationships

3

CHAPTER

7

Multiple Tables and Relationships

Up until now, you've been working with the simplest kind of database imaginable—it has just one table. In the real world, one table is almost never enough. In your private investigator business, for example, you probably need to keep track of more than just people. You need to record the time you spend working for your customers, the invoices you send them, and the payments you receive.

You can certainly create a separate database for each of these needs. But that's far from ideal, since you don't use each kind of information in isolation. You need all these different kinds of information to work in harmony, like a well-rehearsed orchestra. In database terms, what you need is a single, integrated file that keeps all your various lists, files, and records in one place, so you can arrange and rearrange them according to your needs—a *relational database.*

Relational Databases Explained

Before you dive head first into relational databases, it will be helpful to review some vocabulary. First, a *database* is a collection of tables, layouts, and other things that forms an organized system. A *table* holds information about one kind of thing, like people, orders, products, or suppliers. A *field* holds one attribute of something: the person's first name, the order date, the color of a product, or the supplier's address. (An *attribute* simply means an individual characteristic. For example, a bicycle might have several attributes: color, height, style, and price. In a database, each of these attributes gets its own field.)

In the previous chapters, you've created a database whose tables and fields track various attributes of people. You could repeat the process and build any number of individual databases for organizing your time, creating invoices, and logging payments. But that approach has real problems, like the following:

- When you log some billable work, you have to type in the customer information. Then, when you create an invoice, you have to type the customer information all over again in the invoice file. When you receive a payment, you have to type it a third time in the payment file. Since the databases aren't connected in any way, they can't share that information with one another.
- Suppose you want to see how much you've billed a customer over the years. You could use the Invoices database and run a summary report by, say, the customer's name. But duplicate names, misspellings, and name changes would render the information useless. You could use the People database instead. After all, the total amount billed (or the outstanding balance) is, in some sense, an attribute of a customer. But to have that information ready when you need it, you'd have to create a field for it in the People database and retype the invoice information there every time. You know you have all the information somewhere, but because the system isn't integrated, it can't help you put all the pieces together.

Even if you could live with these limitations, you're certain to run into trouble when you try to create the Invoices database. An invoice typically encompasses information about two different entities: the *invoice* itself, and each *line item*. There's simply no good way to track invoices without involving at least two tables. Your solution to all these problems? Hook multiple tables together into one big database.

Note: Database developers use the word *entity* to mean "one kind of thing." *Person* is an entity, and so is *Invoice*. Remember, though, that one specific thing isn't an entity–Bill Gates isn't an entity, and neither is Invoice #24601.

Not only can you put more than one table in a database—and track more than one kind of thing in the process—but you can also tell FileMaker how the data fits together. You can say, for example, that invoice records have attached line item records, or that each payment record is associated with a particular customer record.

In database parlance, you create *relationships* among the data. A relationship is a connection from one table to another, along with the rules that define how records in the tables go together. For example, suppose you have two tables—Invoices and Line Items—as shown in Figure 7-1.

To figure out which line items belong to each invoice, you need to understand the relationship between these tables. Notice that the Line Item table has a field called *Invoice Number*. This field holds (surprise!) the invoice number for each line item. You can also show this relationship with a picture, just like the one in Figure 7-2. By defining this relationship, you've created a mechanism to hook together an Invoice record and a line item record.

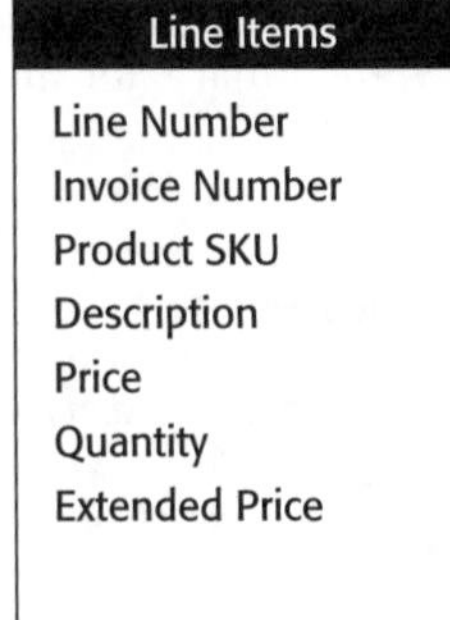

Figure 7-1:
Each box in this picture represents a table. The name of the table is on top of the box. The fields are listed inside each box. When you design a multitable database, as you'll learn later in this chapter, you can use boxes just like this to map out your plan.

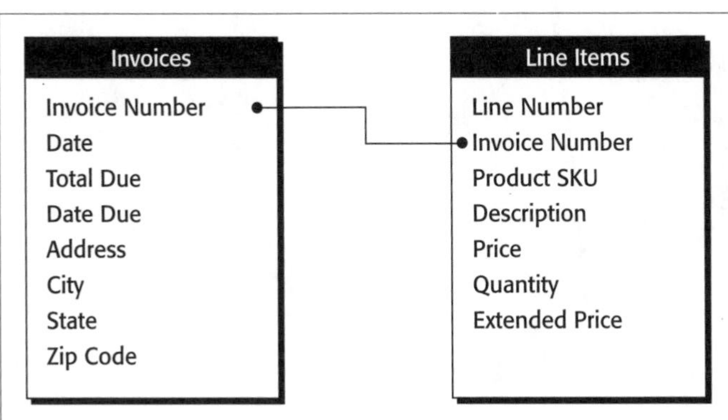

Figure 7-2:
This picture shows the same tables, but it also shows how they're related to one another. The line between the tables represents the relationship. In this case, it shows that the Invoice Number field in the Invoices table is connected to the Invoice Number field in the Line Items table.

Modeling Your Database

When you set out to design a relational database, you need to do a little upfront planning. You need to decide what entities you'll be tracking, which ones deserve a table, and how they relate to one another. It's easier to create the right tables and connections the first time than to go back and change them. You can create your own "blueprint" to follow as you build your database—what the pros call an *entity relationship diagram.*

Choosing Entities

Your first step in designing the database is deciding what tables you need and how they fit together. Since every table holds data about a single entity, you normally start by figuring out all the entities in your system. You probably won't be able to list them all in one shot. Everybody forgets some that are less obvious, so start with blank paper or a word processor, and list all the things the database will need to *do*. This list will help you identify entities.

Now's the time to stretch your mind and think of every possibility. What tasks do you do every day? What do you *wish* you could do—and what information do you need to do it? What do you want your computer to show you when you sit down first thing in the morning?

When your workflow hits a wall, what piece of information would get you moving again? What questions do people keep asking you—and how could FileMaker answer them for you? The more your initial plan matches your real needs, the more quickly you'll be up and running. You can see a list like this in Figure 7-3.

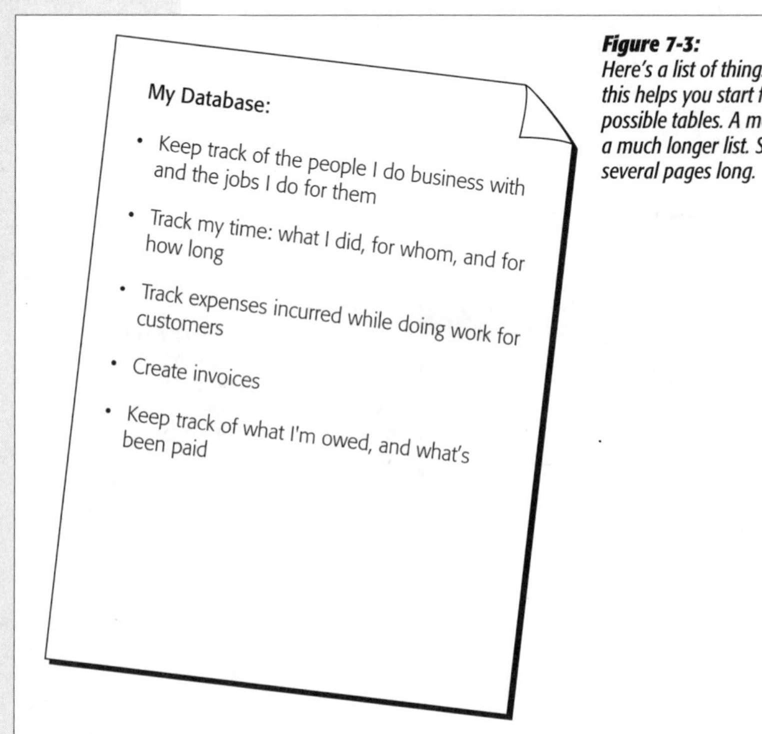
My Database:
Keep track of the people I do business with and the jobs I do for them
Track my time: what I did, for whom, and for how long
Track expenses incurred while doing work for customers
Create invoices
Keep track of what I'm owed, and what's been paid

Figure 7-3:
Here's a list of things your database will do. A list like this helps you start figuring out your entities and possible tables. A more complex database could have a much longer list. Some big systems start with a list several pages long.

With this list in hand, you can start to figure out what *entities* your database needs to track. For each item on your list, think of all the *things* it involves. Figure 7-4 shows a possible list.

Most real-world problems have lots and lots of entities, so the second step is to figure out which ones matter. You'll use a process of elimination to remove extraneous items from your list. You might eliminate items for any of four major reasons:

- **They're already covered.** The list in Figure 7-4 includes Checks and Payments. A check is really just a kind of payment, so you don't need to track them separately in your database. Since a payment is more general than a check, you can eliminate Checks. Then, when you build your Payments table, you could add a field called Type and put Check, Cash, or Credit Card in that field.

- **They're too specific.** Sometimes you'll have things in your list that aren't general enough. This list shows Airline Tickets, Hotels, and Film. But you don't really need to track the details of each of these items. Instead, you're just interested in expenses in general—what they were, how much they cost, and what job they were for. To fix this problem, think of a more general word that encompasses all three things—something like Expenses. Add that to the list and remove the more specific versions.

My Database:

- Keep track of the people I do business with and the jobs I do for them
  Customers, Jobs, Companies,
- Track my time: what I did, for whom, and for how long
  Tasks, Services
- Track expenses incurred while doing work for customers
  Expenses, Airline Tickets, Hotels, Film
- Create invoices
  Invoices, Line Items, Addresses
- Keep track of what I'm owed, and what's been paid
  Payments, Checks, Outstanding Balances

Figure 7-4:
You've now added some entities to your list. Don't worry too much about whether the entities you think of are good ones or not–right now you're just trying to get it all down so you won't leave anything out. You can start with all the nouns in the list–People, Time, Invoices–and try to think of nouns that cover other aspects of your work.

- **They're really just attributes of another entity.** Do you really need an entity called Outstanding Balances? You do need to know how much each customer still owes you, but maybe you already have that information somewhere else. A customer has an outstanding balance because one or more invoices are unpaid. So to see who owes you money, you really just want to look at the balance due on any unpaid invoices. Scratch Outstanding Balances off the list. For the same reason, you can also remove Companies—they're just attributes of a customer. (For more detail, see the box on page 310.)

Note: Just because you're crossing things off your list doesn't mean those things aren't important, or don't apply to your database. It just means they don't qualify as entities that need their own table. These things may show up as *fields* in other tables (like Company), or they may just be one *type* of a more general entity, like Check. Either way, you can still track these items in your database. See the box on page 310.

- **They're not important enough to track in your database.** Suppose your list has an item called Services. These services are the kinds of things you do for your customers: Check into a cheating spouse, find a lost dog, recover a stolen computer, or whatever. You could create a Services table in your database, and put all these kinds of services in it. But what value would it add? What kind of information are you tracking about a service? Probably just its name—which doesn't really need to be *tracked*. So, as an entity, leave out Services. Figure 7-5 shows an example of a well-edited Entities list.

My Database:
Keep track of the people I do business with and the jobs I do for them
Customers, Jobs, ~~Companies~~
Track my time: what I did, for whom, and for how long
Time, ~~Services~~
Track expenses incurred while doing work for customers
~~Airline Tickets, Hotels, Film~~ Expenses
Create invoices
Invoices, Line Items, Addresses
Keep track of what I'm owed, and what's been paid
Payments, ~~Checks, Outstanding Balances~~

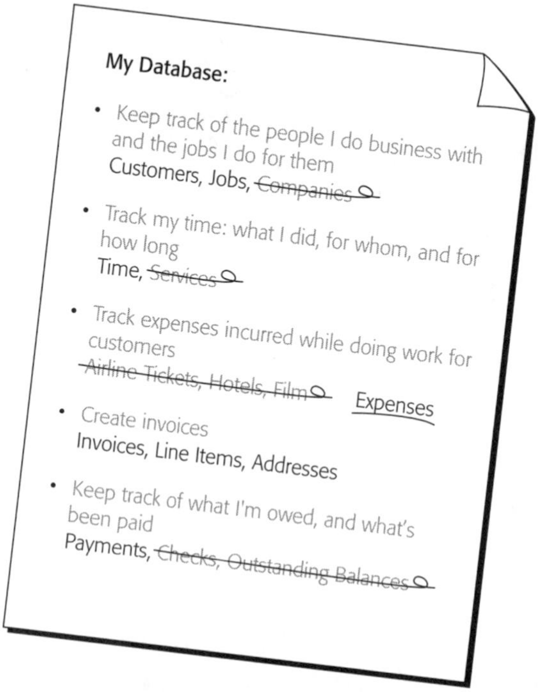

Figure 7-5:
After thinking about each entity on your list, you can remove some and possibly add some new ones. When you're through with this step, you have a pretty good list of the entities–and tables–in your database.

UP TO SPEED

Many for One and One for Many

Relationships tell FileMaker which records in two tables go together. Conceptually, relationships come in three flavors: one-to-many, many-to-many, and one-to-one.

In a one-to-many relationship, one record in the first table relates to several records in the second. For example, one invoice record has several line items, so it's a one-to-many relationship. (Likewise, several line items belong to one invoice, so you could say that line items and invoices have a many-to-one relationship. Since relationships work both ways, a one-to-many is *always* a many-to-one as well.) Figure 7-7 shows a one-to-many relationship, where one invoice has many line items.

A many-to-many relationship means something slightly different. Suppose you have a Products table and an Orders table. Each time you sell some products, you create a new order. These tables have a many-to-many relationship: A person orders multiple products, and each product can be ordered many times.

Finally, you can have two tables that are locked in a one-to-one configuration. If your database held pictures of each product you sell, you could create a Pictures table. It would have one record for each product. But the Products record also has one record for each product. In fact, each product record is related to exactly one picture record, and vice versa.

You create any of these relationships with exactly the same steps in FileMaker. But each has its own set of considerations that affect the way you design your database. These concepts are discussed on page 311.

Finding Relationships

Now that you have a list of entities, you need to figure out how they relate to one another. To get started, just pick two of your entities—Customers and Jobs, for example—and ask yourself how they go together (if you need some guidance, see the box on page 314.) You might come up with this answer: *A customer hires me to do jobs, and a job is done for a customer*. That sentence tells you two important things:

- Customers and jobs are related.
- One customer has many jobs, but each job only has one customer.

By comparing different entities in this way, you can figure out how each relates to another, if at all. Your notes as you consider these relationships might look something like Figure 7-6.

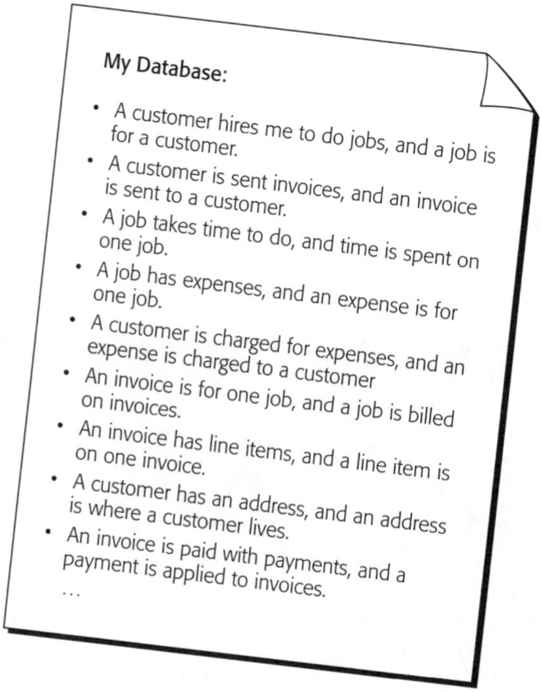

My Database:

- A customer hires me to do jobs, and a job is for a customer.
- A customer is sent invoices, and an invoice is sent to a customer.
- A job takes time to do, and time is spent on one job.
- A job has expenses, and an expense is for one job.
- A customer is charged for expenses, and an expense is charged to a customer
- An invoice is for one job, and a job is billed on invoices.
- An invoice has line items, and a line item is on one invoice.
- A customer has an address, and an address is where a customer lives.
- An invoice is paid with payments, and a payment is applied to invoices.

...

Figure 7-6: *Here's a list of relationships between entities on your list. (You may have worded things differently, or come up with some that aren't on this list.) If you follow the advice in the box on page 314, these sentences will usually exactly describe each kind of relationship.*

You can easily translate most of the items on that list into database relationships. Each tells you about two entities in your list, and how they relate in each direction. You can usually translate these directly into database-ese, as shown in Figure 7-7. That picture is one example of a diagram representing each of these relationships.

A glance at Figure 7-7 shows you how entities like Payments, Invoices, and Customers relate to one another, but the relationship with the Time entity isn't so obvious. Is "Time" plural? For that matter, if Time is an entity, then it must be a thing, so what is a *time*? You've just discovered one of the common challenges to good relational design—choosing good names.

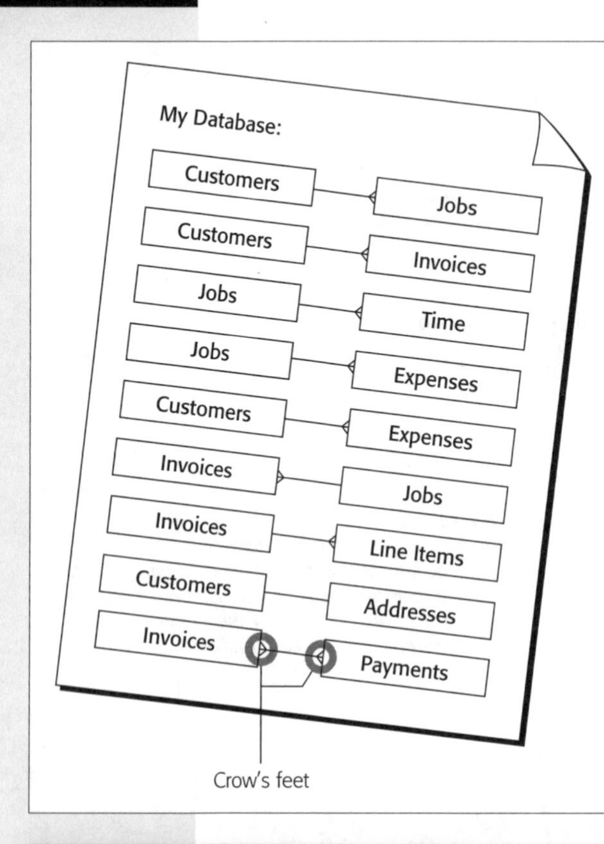

Figure 7-7:
In this picture, boxes represent entities, and the lines between them indicate relationships. The little forked end on the relationship lines (called a crow's foot) means "to-many" as in "one-to-many." If the line doesn't have a crow's foot, it's to-one. So the relationship between Payments and Invoices is many-to-many, while that between Customers and Invoices is one-to-many.

FREQUENTLY ASKED QUESTION

No Companies?

Why is Companies just an attribute of Customers? What if my customer is a company? Don't I need to be able to keep track of that?

Your decisions about entities depend on how you intend to use the database. In this database, you're assuming that *people* hire you. Even if they hire you on behalf of some business, you'll put the actual person you're working for in the database, along with the name of the company that employs her.

In a different database, you may decide companies are important enough to be in their own table. If it were important to see all the people who work for one particular company, or to keep track of lots of people from each company, then you would probably want a Companies table.

You added *Time* to your list of entities because you spend time working on a job. That's a little ambiguous, though, so think about what exactly you'll be putting in the database. You'll be logging the time you spend working: what you're doing, when you started, and when you finished. You could call it a *work log entry* but that's pretty cumbersome. Because this kind of entity is quite common, database types have made up a name for it—*timeslip*. A timeslip is sort of like one entry on a timesheet. It says what you were doing for one period of time.

Using this language, your relationship description becomes clearer:

- A job has timeslips, and a timeslip is for a job.

Now it's a lot more obvious: This relationship is one-to-many.

One-to-many relationships

Most of the relationships in your diagram are one-to-many, which is normal. One-to-many relationships outnumber all other types by a large margin in almost any system. See the box "Many for One and One for Many" on page 308 for a description of the various types of relationships.

One-to-one relationships

Your list of entities and relationships shows a one-to-one relationship between Customers and Addresses. For the purposes of this database, one customer can certainly have one address, and vice versa. But if that's the case, are they really separate entities? In fact, Address is just an attribute of the Customer entity. That makes it a prime candidate for entity-elimination. Put the address *fields* in the Customers table instead. You might argue that despite the conflict of interest, you *could* work for two people in the same household and would therefore have to type the same address twice in your Customers table if you didn't have an Address table. The best answer to an argument like that is: big deal. This situation won't arise often enough to justify a more complicated database just to eliminate duplicating one or two addresses. Even without a separate Address table, you can still separately handle all other tasks for these two clients.

On the other hand, if you're managing a high school, and it's important to know which students share a home, and which parents they belong to, then an Addresses (or more likely, a Households) entity might make sense.

Tip: If you expect to have to track several addresses for each customer, then you could create a one-to-many relationship between Customers and an Addresses entity. For the current example, though, you'll stick to a single address built right into the Customers table.

As a general rule, unless you can articulate a good reason for its existence, a one-to-one relationship is a mistake: It is just two tables where one would suffice. (For some clarification, see the box on page 316.) You'll almost always want to combine entities like people and their addresses into one table.

Many-to-many relationships

Many-to-many relationships pose a special challenge. Normally, FileMaker knows which records are related to one another because they have something in common. For example, the Invoice table and the Line Item table both have an Invoice Number field. But you can put only *one* invoice number in a line item record. Luckily, Invoices and Line Items have a one-to-many relationship. If they had a many-to-many relationship, you'd be in trouble.

FREQUENTLY ASKED QUESTION

Only One Attribute

So, I'm supposed to eliminate Services as an entity because it has only one attribute (page 307). Is that another rule? Should I remove all entities that have just one attribute?

Not necessarily. There are times when an entity has only one attribute, but you still want to give it a table. For one thing, tables can help promote consistent data entry. Say your new database is going to track jobs, among other things. A job may have just one attribute–the Job Name–so you could just put the job name on each expense, time entry, and invoice. But what if you misspell the job name? Then you'll have expenses that should go together but don't, because FileMaker sees different job names. By creating a Jobs table, you have a central place to enter job names and use it as a value list. With a Jobs table, instead of typing the job name everywhere, you simply choose it from a list.

Wait–all you need to do that is a list. Why have a table if it has just one column?

OK, wise guy. You *could* leave out the Jobs table and the job names themselves. Instead, you could just attach each expense, time log entry, or invoice to a customer. But what happens when the same customer hires you six different times? All those expenses, invoices, and entries are lumped together under that customer, and you lose the ability to track them back to the individual jobs. Sometimes a one-attribute entity exists because it gives your database greater powers of organization or categorization. (See the box on page 234 for more details–and a warning–about using a single-attribute table for a value list.)

To fix things, you need to chop your many-to-many relationships in half, turning each into two separate one-to-many relationships. You always need to add a new special-purpose entity in the middle. Your database has only one unhandled many-to-many relationship: Invoices and Payments. To split it up, you need to introduce a special entity. Since it doesn't have a decent name, just call it *Invoice Payment* (as in "This record represents one invoice payment—one payment on one invoice"). Now, instead of "An invoice is paid with payments, and a payment is applied to invoices," you can say these two things:

- An invoice is paid with invoice payments, and an invoice payment is applied to one invoice.
- A payment is divided into invoice payments, and an invoice payment is part of one payment.

Figure 7-8 shows the updated diagram.

The Entity-relationship Diagram

Now that you have a list of entities and their relationships, you're ready to assemble your master plan: the entity relationship (ER) diagram. An *ER diagram* is a picture that shows all the entities in your database and the relationships between them. Unlike the diagram you've already drawn (in Figure 7-8), each entity appears only once in an ER diagram.

It has two purposes: to help you find relationships you missed, or relationships that don't belong, and to serve as a roadmap for your database. You'll use it when you actually create this database in FileMaker, and when you go back to make changes later. (Yes, you *will* get to use FileMaker again…pretty soon.)

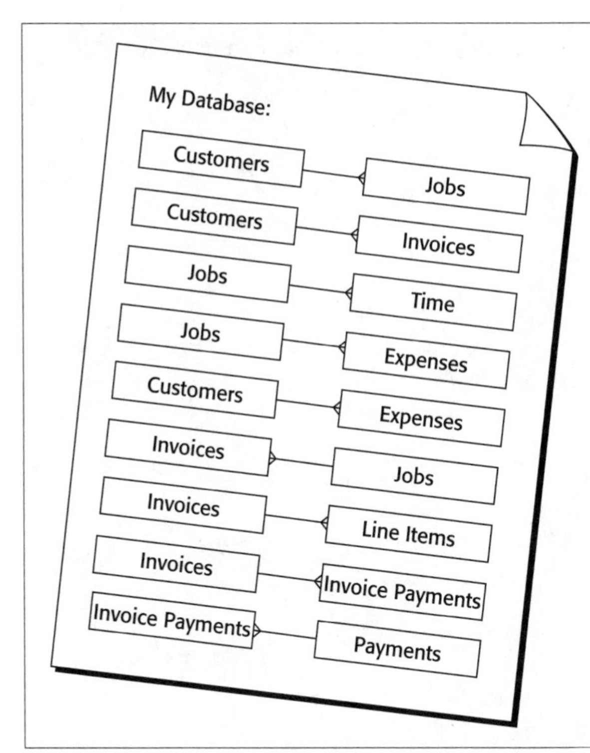

Figure 7-8:
In this updated version of the diagram, the Customers and Addresses relationship has been removed, and the Invoice Payments join entity has been added. Now you have only one-to-many relationships–perfect.

Note: The diagram you're about to create isn't, in the most technical sense, a *real* ER diagram. The real kind deals with all kinds of technical details that simply don't matter in FileMaker. Nevertheless, some database big shot may chastise you for calling your beautiful picture an ER diagram. Never mind–just be glad FileMaker doesn't make you *care* about all that mumbo jumbo.

Creating an ER diagram

When you assemble an entity relationship diagram, you must put all your entities and relationships together in one big picture. Your goal is to have each entity in the picture just *once*, and all the lines necessary to explain the various relationships.

Your ER diagram is crucial to a successful database designing experience. You'll almost always find ways to improve your database when you put it in a picture. When you set out to actually *build* the database, the ER diagram guides you through the process. Finally, six years from now, when you need to add more to your database design, the ER diagram will bring you—or your successor—up to speed on how your database fits together.

You can start by making one box for each entity you've identified. Try to place the boxes on the page so there's some open space in the middle where your lines can roam free. Then start drawing lines to represent each of the relationships you've come up with. For a simple database, you can usually get the lines in the picture

UP TO SPEED

Think Relational

If you're dazed and confused trying to figure out how different entities relate, you're not alone. Understanding relational database design takes practice, plain and simple. Here are some ideas to improve your thought process:

- **Don't get hung up on technicalities.** At this point in your design, you shouldn't be thinking about database tools like primary keys, foreign keys, or join tables. Those are all *implementation details* that you can work out later. Right now, just focus on the kinds of things you're keeping track of and how they fit together.
- **Use familiar words.** If you're trying to figure out how customers and jobs should be related, use words familiar to you, for example: "A customer hires me to do jobs," not "A Customer entity is related to a Job entity in a one-to-many configuration." As you get the hang of it, you'll discover that the simple sentences you use every day say a whole lot about relationships. For example, if a customer hires you to do *jobs* (note the plural), then you probably have a one-to-many relationship between customers and jobs.
- **Consider individual items first.** Don't think about what *customers* do. Instead, think about what *one customer* does. That will tell you whether a single customer has many jobs, or just one job. Then turn it around. Once you've decided a customer hires you to do jobs, ask yourself what a job has to do with customers. "I do a job for a customer." This process tells you that each job is connected to just *one* customer. (If you didn't follow this advice, and thought "I do *jobs* for customers," you wouldn't be any closer to understanding the relationship.) By combining these results, you discover that a customer has many jobs, while a job has just one customer. That means Customers and Jobs have a one-to-many relationship.
- **One last tip.** Don't let the word "many" hang you up. It's just a standard term to help keep things simple. (Otherwise, you could have a *one-to-quite-a-few* relationship between Jobs and Invoices, a *one-to-a-handful* relationship between Customers and Jobs, and a *usually-just-one-or-two-to-rarely-more-than-three* relationship between Payments and Invoices. Yikes!) "Many" doesn't have to mean "lots." It might mean "exactly six" or "no more than three." The only time the relationship isn't one-to-many is when it's one-to-*exactly*-one.

without much difficulty. But creating a larger diagram without the right tools can be a real pain. If you work on paper, you end up starting half a dozen times before you get a good arrangement. If you use a typical drawing program (the drawing capabilities in Word, for example), then you spend copious hours reconnecting lines and entities, reshaping lines, and hand drawing crow's feet as you move things around. See the box on the next page for some suggestions to solve this problem.

When you're done, you should have a single, unified diagram with each entity showing up only once, and every relationship indicated by a line.

When you're thinking about relationships with just pairs of tables, you don't get the big picture. The ER diagram shows you how *everything* comes together, and when that happens, you often discover tangles of relationships just like those in Figure 7-9. Tangles like these aren't inherently bad; they're just usually completely unnecessary. Take the first tangled group—Expenses, Jobs, and Customers. The diagram tells you that customers have jobs, jobs have expenses, and customers have expenses.

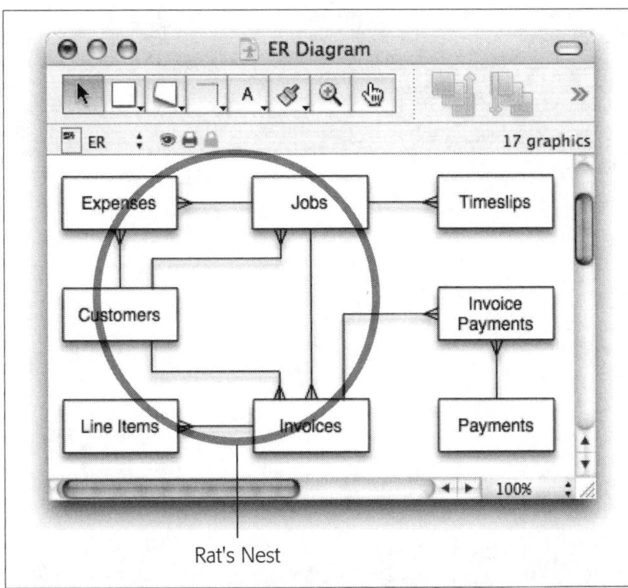

Figure 7-9: *This diagram (created in OmniGraffle) doesn't look all that bad–except for one thing. The area labeled Rat's Nest has a lot of lines between just a few tables. Expenses, Customers, and Jobs are all interrelated–there is a relationship between Jobs and Customers, another between Customers and Expenses, and a third between Expenses and Jobs. If you look closely, the same situation exists for Customers, Jobs, and Invoices. In both cases, there's a better way.*

POWER USERS' CLINIC

It's All About the Tools

If you plan on doing this more than once, you're best off buying a proper diagramming program. Two excellent choices are Microsoft Visio for Windows and OmniGraffle for Mac OS X. These tools *understand* ER diagrams. They can hook entities together with ease, draw crow's feet on your behalf (lots of programs just don't understand crow's feet), and keep everything connected as you tinker with the arrangement.

If you give Visio a run, don't be tempted by its built-in database diagramming features–they're too complex for FileMaker work. Instead, create a basic diagram and use Rectangles and Dynamic Connectors from the Basic Shapes library. With the Format → Lines command, you can put crow's feet on your lines.

Both of these tools do more than you'll need for your ER diagrams, but the time you save is well worth the expense (about $200 for Visio and $80 for OmniGraffle). You can find free trial versions at *http://office.microsoft.com/visio*, and at *www.omnigroup.com/applications/omnigraffle/*.

If you're an unrepentant cheapskate, here's a tip: Write the entity names on a piece of paper and cut out each one. Then arrange them on paper, draw lines, and see how it looks. You can slide the entity scraps around a few times to find a decent arrangement, and then commit the whole thing to a clean piece of paper.

But in point of fact, you don't need all those lines to understand all the relationships, and neither does FileMaker. It turns out that the line between Customers and Expenses is entirely superfluous. Even if it weren't there, you could still see all the expenses charged to a certain customer. Just find all that customer's *jobs* first (by following the line from Customers to Jobs). Once you've found those, you can look at the expenses for each job. Since customers only incur expenses by way of jobs, you'll get exactly what you want. In other words, if two entities are connected by a path along relationship lines—even *through* other entities—then

WORKAROUND WORKSHOP

When to Go One-to-One

When two things–like people and addresses–have a one-to-one relationship, it usually means you've got an entity you don't need (as in the example in Figure 7-7). There are exceptions to every rule, though. Here are some of the reasons you may see a one-to-one relationship in a database:

- FileMaker uses record locking to prevent two people from editing the same record at the same time. (Yes, Virginia, two people can use a database at the same time–see Chapter 18 to learn how.) Imagine you have a table of products and every time you sell something, you reduce the product's Quantity In Stock field by one. What happens if someone else is modifying the product description at the same time? FileMaker won't let you enter the inventory adjustment because the record is locked. Should you cancel the order? Allow the Quantity in Stock field to be wrong? Force your customer to wait while you ask your associate to get out of the record? A better solution is to put the inventory levels in a separate table. Each product has a Product record and an Inventory record, so two seemingly conflicting processes no longer lock each other out of your system.
- Sometimes you'll want to divide data you store about an entity among several tables. A database of stock photography might include high-resolution photographs in container fields. These photos make the database very large. By putting the photos in one table, and the information about the photos in another, you make working with the information easier. You can back up the information to a CD, and the photographs to your high-capacity backup system. (This technique requires keeping each table in a separate file–something you'll learn about in the next chapter.)
- Imagine you have customers and employees. Employees don't place orders or make payments, and customers don't have a time sheet. But they both have addresses, phone numbers, and email addresses. What's more, you like to send holiday cards to all of them every year. In a situation like this, you can create three tables: People, Customers, and Employees. The People table holds all the information that customers and employees have in common–names, addresses, and so forth. Information unique to an employee (Social Security number, hire date, and such) goes in the Employee table, and information only a customer could love (referral source, membership level, and so on) stays in the Customers table. You would have a one-to-one relationship between People and Employees, and another between People and Customers. When it comes time to send those cards, you can print envelopes right from the People table, and get customers and employees in one shot.

they're related as far as FileMaker's concerned. It can show you the expenses for a customer just as easily as it can show the jobs for that customer. Figure 7-10 illustrates this concept.

When you're thinking about these implied relationships, pay attention to the crow's feet. If, when moving from one entity to another along the relationship lines, you *ever* go through a to-many relationship, then the larger implied relationship is itself to-many. This isn't just a clever trick; it's actually intuitive. If a customer has more than one job, and each job has expenses, then clearly a customer can have more than one expense.

When you make your ER diagram, you should get rid of redundancy in your relationships. In other words, remove lines that show direct relationships when the relationship is already implied by other entities and relationships. In your diagram,

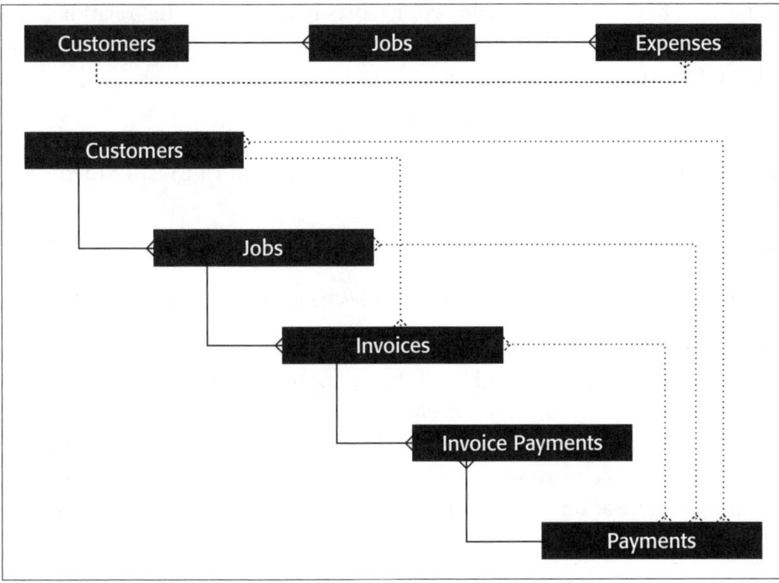

Figure 7-10:
In this picture, the solid lines represent relationships you've identified among the entities. The dotted lines show relationships you don't have to explicitly create–they are implied. As long as there is a path–any path–from one entity to another, they are related. You don't have to have a direct path.

you can remove the relationship between Customers and Expenses. You can also axe one between Customers and Invoices because Customers can find their Invoices by way of Jobs. With this revision, the ER diagram now looks like Figure 7-11.

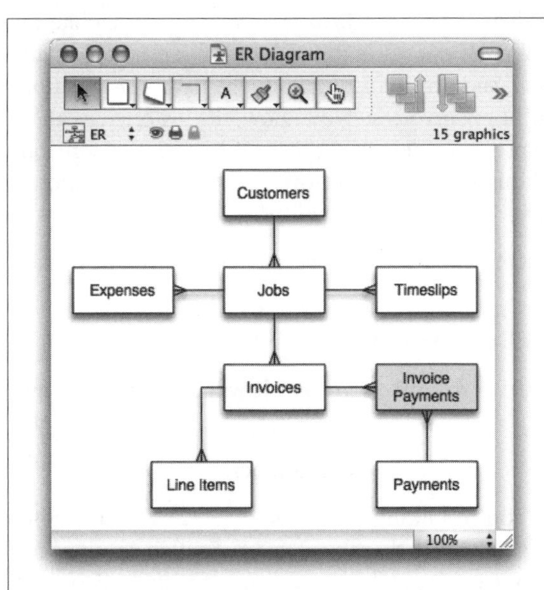

Figure 7-11:
Here's the final ER diagram that you'll use as the roadmap for creating your database. Notice that every entity is related to at least one other entity in some way. Stray, unrelated entities are so rare in a real database system that if you see one in your diagram, you should check to make sure everything belongs.

Next, you need to figure out what fields your tables need to make the relationships work. But before you get to that step, take one last chance to look over your ER diagram. Keep these points in mind as you check for errors:

- You should have no undivided many-to-many relationships.
- If you have any one-to-one relationships, make sure you can justify them (see the box on page 316 for some ideas).
- Make sure you don't have any unnecessary entities hanging out all by themselves.
- Be certain you don't have any unnecessary lines or rat's nests.

If you discover an entity that has no relationships, you may not need it in your database at all. Read back on page 305 and see if that item might belong inside one of the other tables. Or if your diagram has two or more groups of related entities and no relationships *between* the groups, you might've forgotten to draw in a relationship, or again, you might have one or more entities that your system doesn't need. Go back and make sure you're clear on your one-to-many and many-to-many relationships.

Keys

In a diagram, you can show relationships by simply drawing a line. FileMaker, however, knows what records are related because you tell it to expect them to have some data in common. It's time to look more closely at how that works. Take, for example, the typical Invoice table and its little brother, Line Items. The Invoice table probably contains fields like Due Date, Balance Due, and Terms—all attributes of the invoice itself. Then there's the *Invoice Number* field. Unlike the other fields, it's a made-up number. It does one thing—identify an invoice—and does it very well. Without it, you and your customers might have conversations like this: "I need a refund on one of my invoices…you know, the big one…yeah, in February…right, with three items…no, the other one…." As soon as someone mentions an invoice number, though, everybody knows exactly which invoice to look at. More important, FileMaker knows which invoice it is, too.

The invoice number is good at identifying an invoice because it has three important characteristics:

- **It's unique.** No two invoices will ever have the same invoice number.
- **It's unchanging.** Invoice #24601 is #24601 today and it will be tomorrow, and the next day, and the next day.
- **It's consistent.** All invoice records have an invoice number.

Since it's a unique number, if you're talking about invoice #24601, and your customer is talking about invoice #24601, there's no question that you're both referring to the same invoice. Since it's unchanging, you can go back weeks, months, or even years later and find the invoice every time. And since it's consistent, you'll never have lonely invoices hanging out there without an identifying number. In database terms, the invoice number is called a *key*. A key is a field whose value uniquely, unchangingly, and consistently identifies one record.

As far as FileMaker's concerned, any field that you use to link one table to another is a key field. Although FileMaker doesn't differentiate between key types, in the larger world of database theory there are two types of keys: primary and foreign. Understanding how the two types of keys work helps you choose appropriate ones for your databases.

Choosing a good key field

Like the Invoice Number field in your database, a primary key is most often a made-up number. You can add a new field to your table, and tell FileMaker to automatically make up a unique value for it each time you create a record (using the Serial Number option Auto-Enter tab of the Field Options dialog box, as shown on page 324). This kind of primary key, based on purely made-up data, is called a *surrogate key*.

Note: Unless you generate the value in your database, it's not a surrogate key, even if somebody else made it up. A surrogate key is made up *by your database*.

Occasionally, your table will have a real value that meets the requirements for a key. For example, if your Product database has a field for your internal Inventory Control Number, you may be able to use that field as the primary key. If you use some real piece of data as a key, then it's called a *natural key*. Surprisingly, though, the vast majority of tables don't have a field that meets the criteria for a natural primary key. Take, for example, the Phone Number field in a contact database of people. Phone numbers are *usually* unique, and don't change *all that often*. But words like "usually" and "often" have no business in a discussion about good key fields.

In fact, in most cases the only fields that meet the requirements for a natural key are, in reality, surrogate keys from somebody else's database. For example, Social Security number is a value that everybody (in America) has, never changes, and is always unique. It has these characteristics because it's a surrogate key made up by some database at the Social Security Administration. But that's okay—FileMaker databases frequently deal with information that's generated somewhere else. Your database might contain employee numbers that come from your company's payroll system, part numbers from your supplier's catalog, or document numbers from your corporate knowledge base. All of these are surrogate keys in some system somewhere, but they're natural keys to you.

Primary and foreign keys

When a key field is in the same table that holds the records it identifies, it's called a *primary key*. In the Invoice table, the Invoice Number field is the primary key because the invoice number identifies an invoice record. If you put the invoice number in some other table (like, say, the Line Items table) it's not a primary key there. Instead, it's called a *foreign key*. Foreign keys identify records in other tables.

FREQUENTLY ASKED QUESTION

Going Natural

Should I try to find natural keys for the tables in my database if I can?

This question has generated an eternal debate in the broader database world. Some ivory-tower theorists are convinced that natural keys are superior to surrogate keys for two primary reasons: First, they're *meaningful*: When you look at a natural key in your own database, it means something to you. Second, if a key is also real honest-to-goodness meaningful data, then, in a relational database situation, your table always has at least one piece of good information from the table it relates to. If that happens to be the snippet you need, you save the software the trouble of going to another table and finding the right record. Thus, the theory goes, natural keys make database programs run a little faster.

But for the kinds of databases you are likely to build with FileMaker, neither of these concerns comes up very often. If a surrogate key isn't all that meaningful to the database user, just don't put it on the layout. And as for performance, the minuscule increase in speed is almost never significant enough to matter for typical databases.

And there's a much more significant argument against trying to find an acceptable natural key: It's usually impossible. There's almost never a normal piece of data in a record that meets all the criteria for a good primary key.

Even natural keys that really seem like great choices often turn out to be problematic. Suppose you work for a company that assigns an employee ID to each employee. You're building a database to keep track of employee stock options. Just like Social Security number, employee ID is a surrogate key to somebody but it's a natural key to you. You decide to make it your primary key. Then you discover you need to track stock options for employees even if they quit and then return to the company. When they do this, their employee ID changes, and your database can't track them properly without some inconvenient upkeep. If you had used your own surrogate key instead, you wouldn't have this problem.

The penalty for a bad key choice can be huge: anything from lost connections in your data to the need for a major overhaul of the system. By contrast, surrogate keys are *easy* and *always work*. Once you accept the fact that your database will have an extra field that serves no other purpose but to be the primary key, the choice becomes a no-brainer. Don't bother with natural keys.

But where do you *put* these foreign keys? In the Invoices database, how did you decide to put the Invoice Number field in the Line Items table? Why not create a Line Item Key field in the Line Items table, and put it in the Invoices database? Wouldn't that accomplish the same thing? At first glance, it might seem like both methods would produce an identical relationship. After all, they sure *look* the same in a picture (Figure 7-12).

Think about what a primary key means. Each value identifies one, and only one, record in the table. If you build a relationship based on a Line Item key, then each invoice can have only one line item. If it had two, there would be two line items with the same line item ID. When you have a one-to-many relationship, you must put the foreign key in the table on the *many* side. Luckily, keeping this information straight in your head is a breeze. Since foreign keys belong on the to-many side of a relationship, just remember this rule: When you see a crow's foot on your ER diagram, you need a foreign key in the table to which it's attached. (But if you're getting confused, Figure 7-11 should clear things up.)

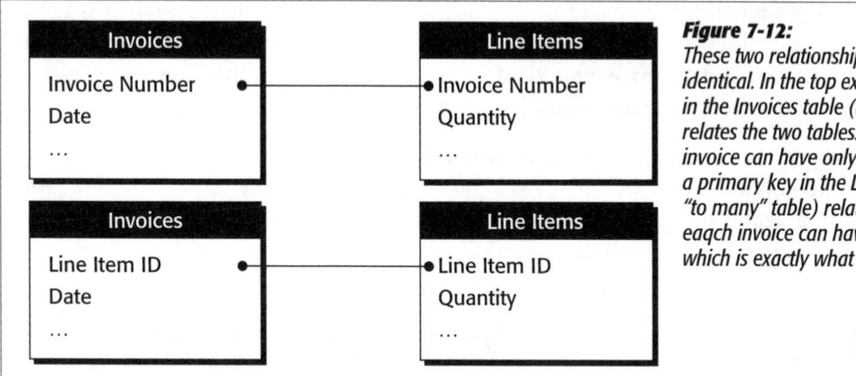

Figure 7-12: *These two relationships look almost identical. In the top example, a primary key in the Invoices table (the "one" table) relates the two tables. As a result, each invoice can have only one line item. Below, a primary key in the Line Items table (the "to many" table) relates them. This time, eaqch invoice can have many line items, which is exactly what you want.*

Note: That rule bears repeating: *Whenever you see a crow's foot in your ER diagram, put a foreign key in the table it's attached to*. The key will refer to whatever table is on the other end of the line. There are very few absolute hard-and-fast rules in relational database design, so cling to this singular bit of simplicity when you start to have doubts.

Later, you'll learn how to tell FileMaker to match records based on a foreign key in one table and a primary key in another.

Join Tables

A many-to-many relationship is more complicated than its one-sided brethren. Imagine your database tracks payments from your customers. A customer could easily send a check to cover *two* invoices. On the other hand, another customer might send a check to cover just *part* of an invoice, with the promise to send another later. So an invoice can have multiple payments, and a payment can be for multiple invoices: many-to-many.

How do you build a relationship like this? If you put the Payment ID in the Invoices table, then a payment can be applied to more than one invoice (just put the same Payment ID in each invoice record). But an invoice can have only one payment since it has just one Payment ID field. If you put the Invoice Number field in the Payments table, you get the same problem in the other direction. You may be tempted to try putting a foreign key field in *both* tables. In other words, add a Payment ID field to the Invoice table, and an Invoice Number field to the Payments table. Dig a little deeper and you'll see that this has a whole *host* of problems:

- An invoice now has a field called Payment ID, but that field *doesn't* identify the payments for that invoice. To find the payments for an invoice, you have to open the Payments database and use the Invoice Number field. That's just plain confusing.

- Instead of one bidirectional relationship, you have two unidirectional relationships. The Payment ID in the invoice matches the Payment ID in the Payments table, but this tells you only which invoices belong to each payment. You need the other relationship (based on Invoice ID) to figure out which payments belong to each invoice. If you connect a payment to an invoice by putting the invoice number in the payment record, you also have to put the Payment ID in the invoice record. If you forget, your data is no longer valid.

Luckily, there's a better way to accomplish a many-to-many relationship. You need something called a *join table* (see Figure 7-13). A join table doesn't usually represent a real entity. Instead, each record represents a relationship between two records in the related tables.

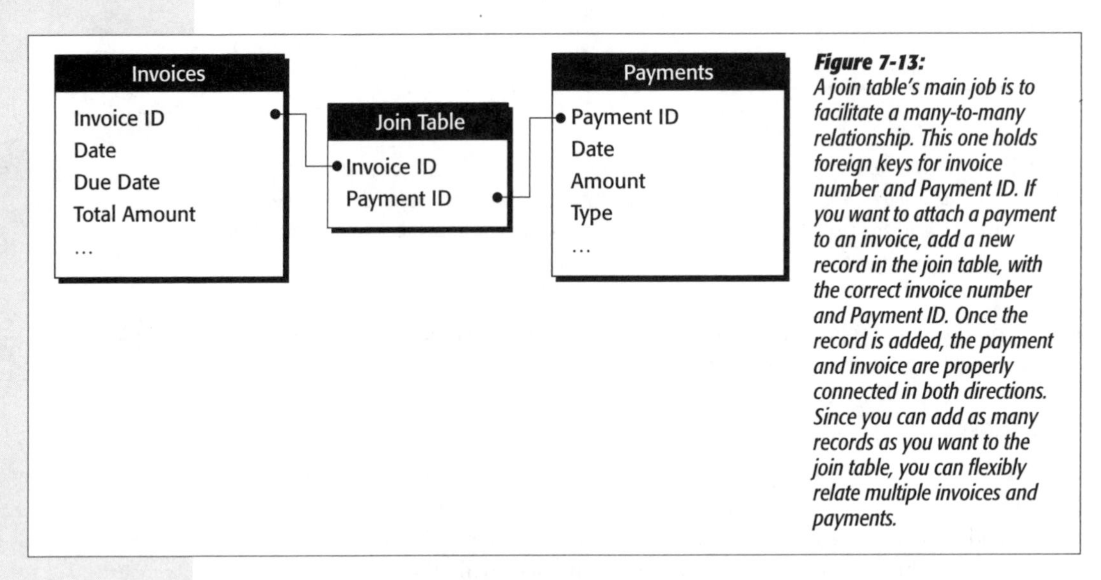

Figure 7-13: *A join table's main job is to facilitate a many-to-many relationship. This one holds foreign keys for invoice number and Payment ID. If you want to attach a payment to an invoice, add a new record in the join table, with the correct invoice number and Payment ID. Once the record is added, the payment and invoice are properly connected in both directions. Since you can add as many records as you want to the join table, you can flexibly relate multiple invoices and payments.*

If it helps, think of join tables this way: Invoices and Payments both have a one-to-many relationship to the join table. So one invoice can connect to many join records, each of which connects to one payment. Likewise, one order can connect to many join records, each of which connects to one invoice. So you get many related records in both directions. A join table always contains *two* foreign keys, one from each table it's joining. If your database has many-to-many relationships, you may have to create a join table to hold just these two keys, but sometimes your database may already have a real table that can act as a join table. Figure 7-14 shows an example.

Other times, you can use a join table to hold fields that don't quite belong in any other table. Suppose you wanted to record what portion of a payment was applied to each invoice. For example, if a customer hands you a check for $100 and you have two outstanding invoices for that customer, for $80 and $30, you may want to decide how to allocate the payment. Perhaps you apply $80 to the first invoice and $20 to the second. This dollar amount applied to each invoice can't be stored in the Invoice table because an invoice can have several payments. It can't be stored in the Payment table because you have *two* amounts and only one payment record. The best place for it is right in the join table itself.

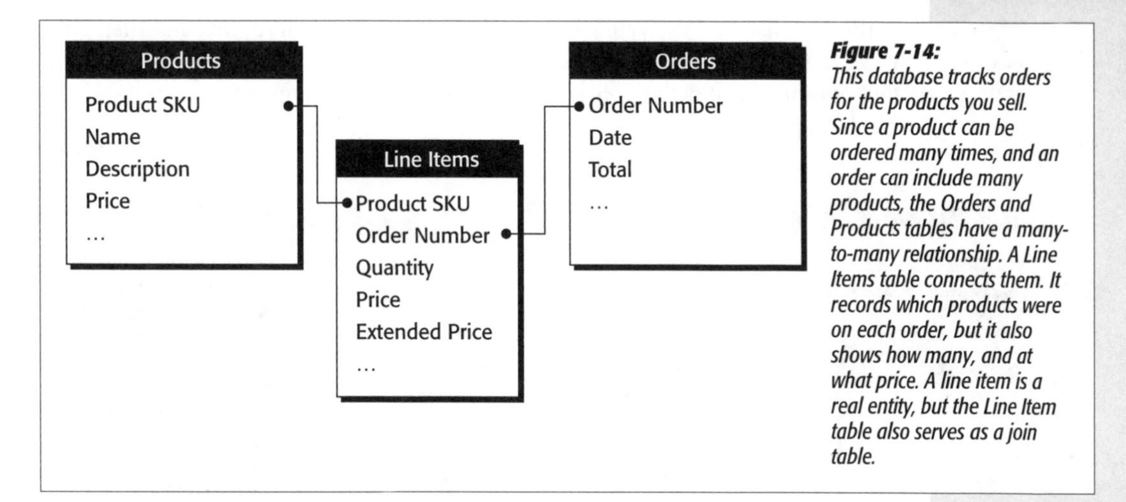

Figure 7-14: *This database tracks orders for the products you sell. Since a product can be ordered many times, and an order can include many products, the Orders and Products tables have a many-to-many relationship. A Line Items table connects them. It records which products were on each order, but it also shows how many, and at what price. A line item is a real entity, but the Line Item table also serves as a join table.*

At this point, you have a good ER diagram, you've eliminated many-to-many relationships by adding join tables, and you understand what foreign keys you'll need to make it all work. You're (finally) ready to actually build your database.

Creating a Relational Database

The tedious planning is finally over. Now comes the fun part—actually making the database. And believe it or not, this part will go *much* more smoothly with your plan in place. You create a relational database in three steps. First, you tell FileMaker what tables you want, and then you add the fields to each table. Finally, you add relationships. Don't be alarmed if you forget a table or miss a field: You can go back at any time and make changes—even six months from now when your tables are loaded with data.

Relational databases start out like any other. Go to FileMaker and choose File → New Database. Name your new database, pick the folder to save it in, and click Save.

Note: If you see the FileMaker Quick Start dialog box (the window with all the Starter Solutions) when you choose File → New, turn on "Create empty database," and then click OK. You can then name and save your new database.

Creating the Tables

When you first create a database, FileMaker shows you the Manage Database window's Field tab (you first saw this on page 95). Without your knowledge, it has already created a table for you with the same name as the database itself. FileMaker assumes you just want one table, and it's ready for you to add fields to that table.

This time, though, you *don't* want just one table, so click the Tables tab (you can see it in Figure 7-15). Your first job is to remove the table FileMaker added for you since it doesn't match one of the entities in your ER diagram. Just select the table in the table list, and then click Delete. FileMaker asks if you're sure, and then gives you the option to "Also remove occurrences of these tables in the graph." Turn this option on, and then click Delete. (You'll learn about occurrences and the graph on page 362.)

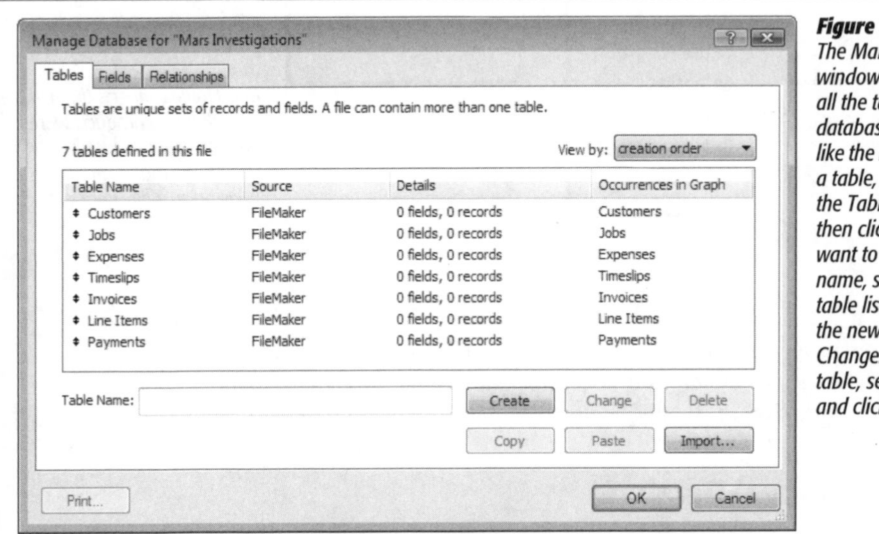

Figure 7-15: *The Manage Databases window's Tables tab lists all the tables in your database. It works a lot like the Fields tab: To add a table, type its name in the Table Name box, and then click Create. If you want to change a table's name, select it in the table list first, then type the new name, and click Change. To delete a table, select it in the list and click Delete.*

Now that you've deleted the starter table, you're ready to add your own carefully planned tables. Grab the ER diagram and create a table for each entity. The diagram has eight tables in all, so make sure you create all of them. At this point you're just adding tables. You'll start adding fields once all the tables have been created.

Warning: Deleting a table is a *dangerous* operation. Right now there's no risk because you're working in a brand-new database. But imagine you come to this window two years from now. If you accidentally delete a table, you lose *all* the data in it. You'll also have a lot of work to do putting your relationships and layouts back together. FileMaker warns you before it lets you delete the table, but it's worth an extra measure of caution.

Creating the Fields

With the tables in place, you're ready to add fields. Click the Manage Database window's Fields tab (see Figure 7-16). You choose which fields to add to each table the same way you learned to in Chapter 3, with one caveat: key fields. *Every* table needs a primary key. In this database, you'll be using surrogate (made-up) keys in each table.

Adding primary keys

To keep things consistent, each primary key field will match the name of the entity, with the word "ID" added to the end. For example, the primary key in the Customers table should be called Customer ID. This technique is so common, in fact, that you can often spot the primary keys in any database by looking for the letters "ID."

The easiest way to make a surrogate key in FileMaker is to use a *serial number*. The process is simple:

1. **Click the Fields tab in the Manage Database dialog box, if necessary. Then, from the Table pop-up menu, select Customers.**

   You're now ready to add a field to the Customers table. You'll start with the primary key.

2. **In the Field Name text box, type *Customer ID*. In the Type pop-up menu, choose Number.**

   Key fields can be any type, but number is usually the best choice because it's the easiest to match exactly.

Warning: Although FileMaker has no trouble matching up records no matter what field type you use, when you search for a record using the Find command–or, more importantly, in a script, as you'll see in Part 4–a text-based search just isn't precise enough. For example, you may get customer ID XY13374 when you're looking for customer ID XY133. To avoid even the possibility of error, stick with a number field.

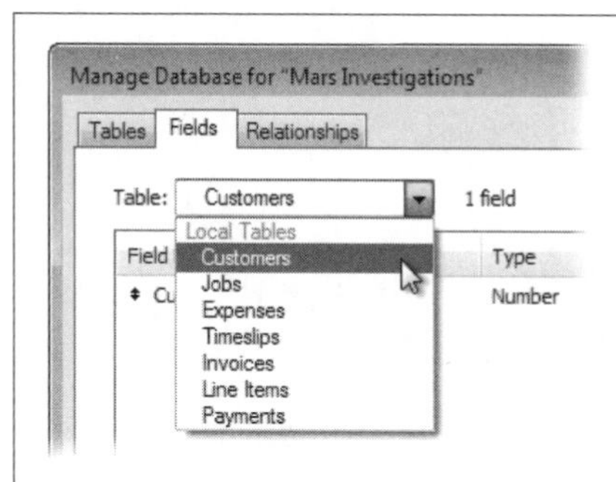

Figure 7-16: *When you have multiple tables, they all show up in the Tables pop-up menu. When you choose a table from the menu, its fields show in the field list. When you add a field, it gets added to the selected table. You can also double-click a table in the Tables tab to jump straight to its field definitions.*

3. **Click Create.**

   FileMaker adds your new field to the field list. But so far all you have is a normal text field.

4. **Click Options, and make sure the Auto-Enter tab is selected, as shown in Figure 7-17.**

   To be a good primary key, this field needs a unique value on every record. That sounds like a job for a computer.

5. **Turn on the "Serial number" checkbox.**

   When you tell FileMaker to auto-enter a serial number, it automatically makes up a new unique number every time you create a record. It sets the field to a number one bigger than the *last* value it created. Since the number always grows, it never repeats.

6. **Make sure the "On creation" radio button is turned on.**

   When you make a field a serial number, you get to choose when the serial number gets entered. It can happen when you create the record, *or* when you commit it. In other words, FileMaker can automatically put the serial number in the field for you right away, when you first create the record, and most of the time, that's exactly what you want. (As you'll see on page 352, FileMaker lets you set up your layout so you can create related records automatically while editing a record; you need the serial number for that to work.)

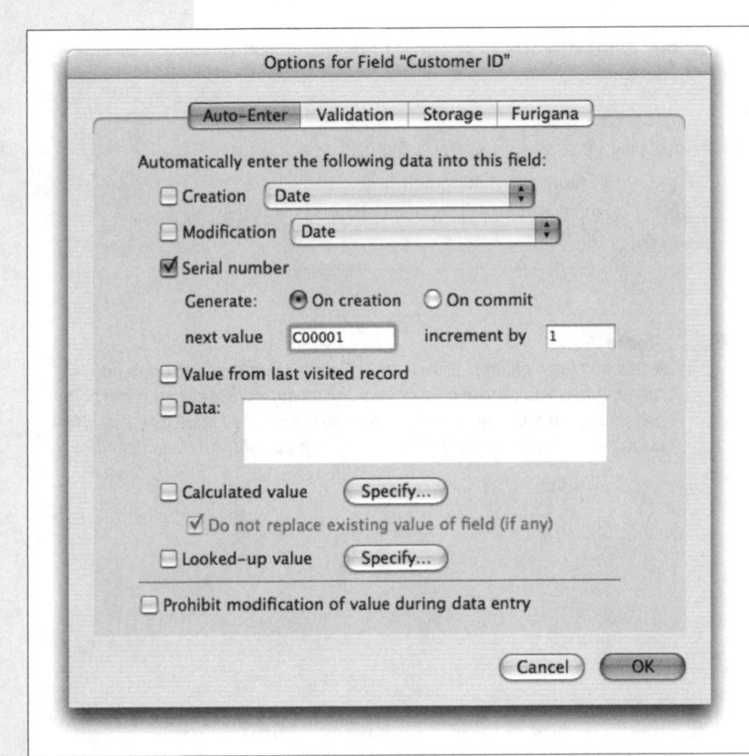

Figure 7-17: *Here's the Field Options window's Auto-Enter tab, in case you've forgotten what it looks like. Pretty slick, huh? In the next few steps, you'll be setting up those "Serial number" options.*

   Alternatively, you can have FileMaker wait until you finish entering data and actually commit the record. You might choose "on commit" if, for instance, you have a complex, automated database that adds new people to your database from lists you get from other offices. You can have the database add a person record *first*, and then see if it's a duplicate before committing the record. That way, you don't skip serial numbers. (And if you know how to do that, you probably should be the one *writing* this book.)

7. **In the "next value" text box, type *1*. Make sure the "increment by" box reads "1."**

   You've just established your starting serial number and told FileMaker how to continue. Your first customer record will have the Customer ID 1, your second will be 2, and so on.

8. **Select the "Prohibit modification of value during data entry" option.**

   Since key fields provide the links between your tables, relationships would break and other database disasters could ensue if key values got changed. When you turn on this option, you prevent that unhappy fate.

Click OK to return to the Manage Database window. You'll get a chance to test that Serial Number field in a few minutes. First, though, you need to follow those steps again for each table. You can, of course, add any field to any table at any time, but here you'll create tables, then primary keys, then foreign keys, and finally other fields. It's not the quickest way, but creating a relational database requires lots of steps, and you don't want to forget anything, so an organized approach pays off.

Note: If you have FileMaker Pro Advanced, you can save time by copying and pasting. Just select the Customer ID field in the list, and then click Copy (or choose Edit → Copy). Switch to the next table in the Table pop-up menu. Now click Paste. FileMaker adds a Customer ID field to this table. You'll need to change its name, but it already has the right type and auto-enter options defined, saving you several clicks.

POWER USERS' CLINIC

Serial Text

As funny as it sounds, you can auto-enter serial numbers into text fields and the values *themselves* can contain text. FileMaker looks at the text you've specified for "next value" and tries to find a number in it somewhere. When it comes time to generate a new value, it pulls that number out, increments it, and stuffs it back in its place.

Say your "next value" is C000LX, and "increment by" is set to 10. The first record you create will get C000LX. The second will get C010LX, and then C020LX, and so on. When you get to C990LX, FileMaker doesn't just give up. Instead, it makes more room: C1000LX.

If your "next value" has more than one embedded number (C000LX22, for example), FileMaker uses the last number only. Likewise, if you don't have a number at all, it simply adds one to the end.

Adding foreign keys

Adding foreign keys requires a little more thought than the primary keys, but not much—you already did the hard part by creating an ER diagram (see page 312). To decide where the foreign keys go, just look for the crow's feet. Figure 7-18 offers a refresher.

Since your primary key fields are all number fields, your foreign key fields should be, too—after all, the foreign keys hold primary key values. Following the crow's feet, you come up with these foreign keys (remember that a foreign key is always just a primary key from another table):

- In the Expenses table, add a field called Job ID.
- In the Jobs table, add a field called Customer ID.
- In the Timeslips table, add a field called Job ID.
- In the Line Items table, add a field called Invoice ID.

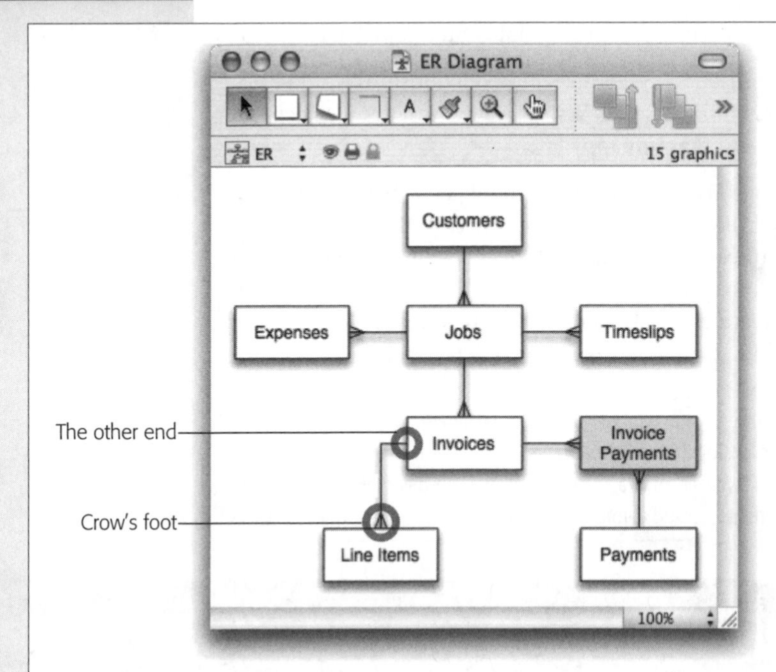

Figure 7-18: *Each crow's foot in your ER diagram indicates the need for a foreign key. Each table with a crow's foot stuck to it needs a foreign key inside it. What should the field be called? Simple: Find the other end of the line. That's the entity the foreign key points to, so name it appropriately. For example, the Line Items table needs a field called Invoice ID.*

- In the Invoices table, add a field called Job ID.
- In the Payments table, add a field called Invoice ID.
- In the Invoice Payments table, add two fields: Invoice ID and Payment ID.

Go ahead and add the foreign keys now.

Note: Because these are foreign key fields, they don't need to be unique. They're just plain old text fields. So you don't need to tell FileMaker to auto-enter serial numbers in these fields, and you don't need to turn on the "Prohibit modification during data entry" option.

Defining the Relationships

With tables and keys, you have everything you need to create some relationships. In other words, you tell FileMaker how the tables in your database fit together by matching up keys. As usual, FileMaker manages to make a tricky task seem kind of fun. You get to work with a visual, intuitive picture of the relationships between your tables—the *relationship graph*. In the Manage Database window, click the Relationships tab, which is reproduced in Figure 7-19.

Your table occurrences (TOs) may not be in precisely the same order as Figure 7-19; they appear in the order you created them. If you want to move them around, just drag them by the solid-colored border along the top (where the name appears). But if you click *inside* a table occurrence (where the fields are listed) and drag, you'll discover the secret to easily creating relationships:

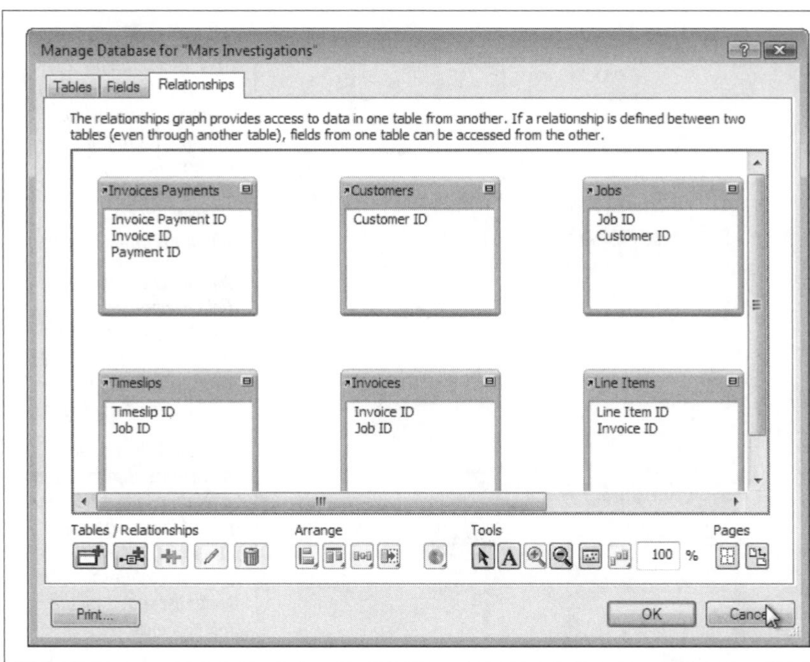

Figure 7-19: *The Manage Database window's Relationships tab is a stark departure from the other tabs. Gone are the list, Create button, Change button, and Delete button. Instead, you get a relationship graph where you can draw your relationships. FileMaker also gives you a myriad of tiny tools to help you lay out the graph. The boxes in the graph are called* table occurrences. *(There's a reason why they aren't called* tables *in this case; see page 362.)*

1. **Point to the Customer ID field in the Jobs table occurrence and press your mouse button.**

   The field name highlights and the mouse arrow changes shape indicating you're about to join (relate) two tables together.

2. **With the mouse button held down, drag the arrow over the Customer ID field in the Customers table.**

   As you drag, FileMaker draws a line starting from the first Customer ID field. When your cursor is over the second Customer ID field, it, too, highlights. If there are tables in the way, just drag straight past them. FileMaker won't do anything drastic until you let go of the mouse button.

   If you make a mistake and start dragging the wrong field, just point to some empty space in the graph before you let go of the mouse button. FileMaker notices that you didn't complete the connection and doesn't create a relationship. Then you can just start over.

3. **Release the mouse button.**

   Poof! You have a relationship. The Customers and Jobs table occurrences change in appearance slightly: FileMaker adds a new panel to each box, and shows the connected key fields in this space. You can see each step, and the end result, in Figure 7-20.

With the technique mastered, you can now create the rest of your relationships. You can refer to your ER diagram at this point, or use this handy cheat sheet. (In these examples, the stuff before "::" is the table name, and the stuff after is the field name. You'll see this notation a lot from now on.)

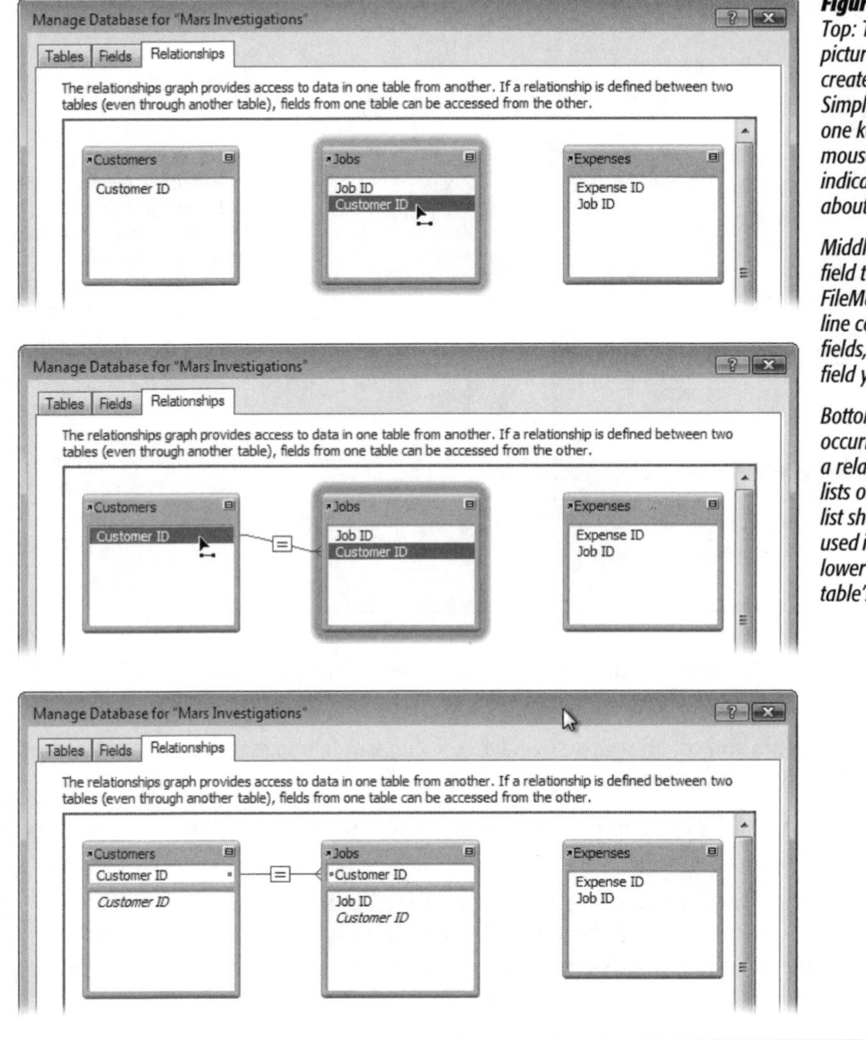

Figure 7-20:
Top: This sequence of pictures shows how you create a relationship. Simply click and hold one key field. Your mouse arrow changes to indicate that you're about to connect things.

Middle: Drag this key field to another. FileMaker creates the line connecting the two fields, and highlights the field you're dragging to.

Bottom: When a table occurrence is involved in a relationship, it has two lists of fields. The upper list shows just the fields used in relationships. The lower list shows all the table's fields.

- Drag Expenses::Job ID to Jobs::Job ID.
- Drag Invoices::Job ID to Jobs::Job ID.
- Drag Line Items::Invoice ID to Invoices::Invoice ID.
- Drag Invoice Payments::Invoice ID to Invoice ID.
- Drag Invoice Payments::Payment ID to Payments::Payment ID.
- Drag Timeslips::Job ID to Jobs::Job ID.

Note: It doesn't actually matter which direction you go. You can drag the Expenses::Job ID field to the Jobs::Job ID field. Or you drag the one from Jobs over to Expenses. Both ways are equally valid.

When you're done, you can spot-check your work by counting the lines in the relationship graph. Including the one between Customers and Jobs, you should have seven, and the graph should look like the one in Figure 7-21.

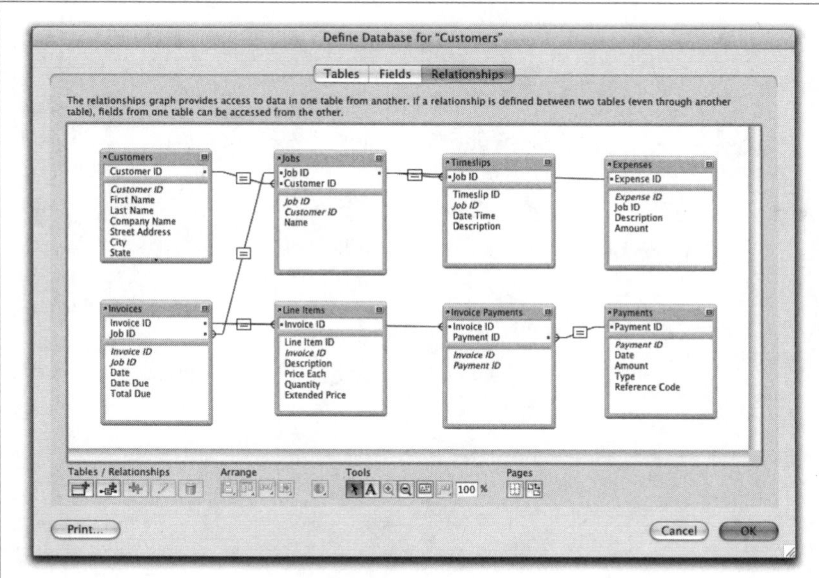

Figure 7-21: *Here's how your relationship graph looks with all the relationships created in the previous steps. These relationships work OK, but the graph is now a little hard to read. First, there's no logical order to the tables. Even worse, there are lines running under table occurrences (the line connecting Timeslips and Jobs, for instance). You can do a little manual rearranging and fix this up.*

Cleaning Up the Relationship Graph

Although this relationship graph is small and easy to understand, chances are it will grow as you power up your database by adding more tables (and even as you add new features, as you'll see through the course of the next few chapters). As it grows, your graph can easily get messy and hard to decipher. To make your graph manageable, first get rid of unnecessary information. Right now your graph shows *every* field in each table occurrence (in fact, it shows some fields *twice*, and a healthy dose of empty space, too). But you don't need to see every field here, that's what the *Fields* tab is for. Figure 7-22 shows how to reclaim the wasted space.

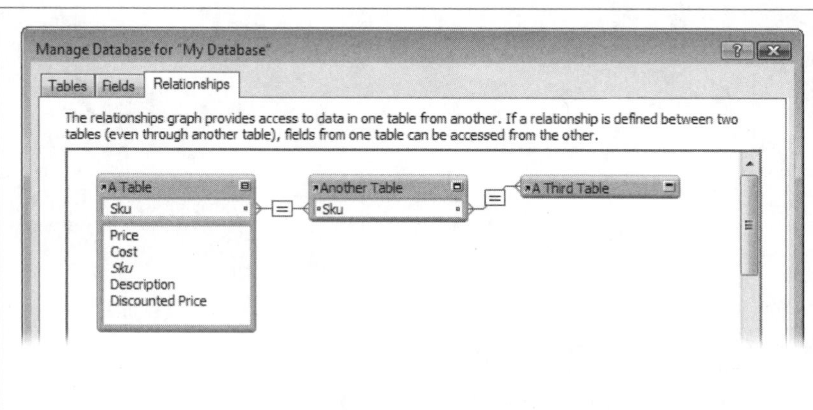

Figure 7-22: *Each table occurrence in the graph has a little button in the top-right corner. When you click it, the format of the table occurrence changes to one of the structures shown here. The first time you click, the bottom section disappears, leaving only the fields used in relationships. Another click makes all the fields disappear.*

DON'T PANIC

Lost and Found Again

You may not see table occurrences in the relationships graph for all the tables you create. Remain calm. You have all the right table occurrences; you just can't see them all at once. Chances are you just need to scroll the graph to the right. Unfortunately, it can be tricky to drag between two fields if you can't get them both on the screen at once. (You can do it, mind you. When you approach the edge of the graph while dragging, FileMaker automatically starts scrolling. It's just a little tedious.)

If you have a big enough computer screen, you can simplify things by making the entire window bigger by dragging the bottom-right corner. If you still can't fit everything in, even when the window is as big as it can get, you can zoom out on the window. Click the "Shrink to Fit" button (you can see all the tools mentioned in this box in Figure 7-24) and FileMaker shrinks everything so it all fits on the graph at once. In this reduced view, you can still drag relationships. When you're ready to see things full-size again, just type *100* in the Zoom Level box, and then press Tab.

(Don't press Enter or Return after changing the zoom level or FileMaker will think you meant to click the OK button and make the Manage Database window go away. If you do close it accidentally, just choose File → Manage Database again.)

You can zoom in on certain parts of the graph with the zoom in tool. First, click the tool, and then click anywhere in the graph. Use the zoom out tool instead if you want to zoom back out again. Unlike the zoom controls on a database window, these controls don't let you zoom in past 100 percent, but you can zoom way out–to 1 percent if you want. At that level, your tables are reduced to undifferentiated goo in the corner of the graph.

When you're done zooming, be sure to choose the selection tool again so you can drag relationships or table occurrences.

To make your graph more efficient, switch every table occurrence to show only the fields used in relationships (one click should do it, but if you go too far, just keep clicking and it will come back around again a few clicks later). Now a lovely graph is just a few drags away: You can move the table occurrences around so they form a pleasing arrangement that's easier to understand than the mess you had before. Figure 7-23 shows the result.

FREQUENTLY ASKED QUESTION

FileMaker's Sixth Sense: Crow's Feet

I haven't done anything to tell FileMaker what kind of relationships I created. How does it know where to put the crow's feet?

You never have to tell FileMaker about the types of relationships because it doesn't really matter. The work FileMaker performs to deal with a one-to-many relationship is no different than what it does for a one-to-one, so it doesn't care about the distinction.

However, it's useful to you as the database designer to know what kind of relationships you have. (It helps you decide whether an invoice should have room for one line item or a whole list of them, for example.) FileMaker tries its best to figure out where the crow's feet go, as a special service to you. It assumes every end of every line needs a crow's foot unless it finds evidence to the contrary.

Such evidence includes:

- The field used in the relationship is a serial number.
- The field used in the relationship has the Unique validation option turned on.

A line that connects to a field that meets either of these conditions will *not* have a crow's foot. Since all your primary keys are serial numbers, FileMaker has no trouble figuring out where to leave off the crow's feet.

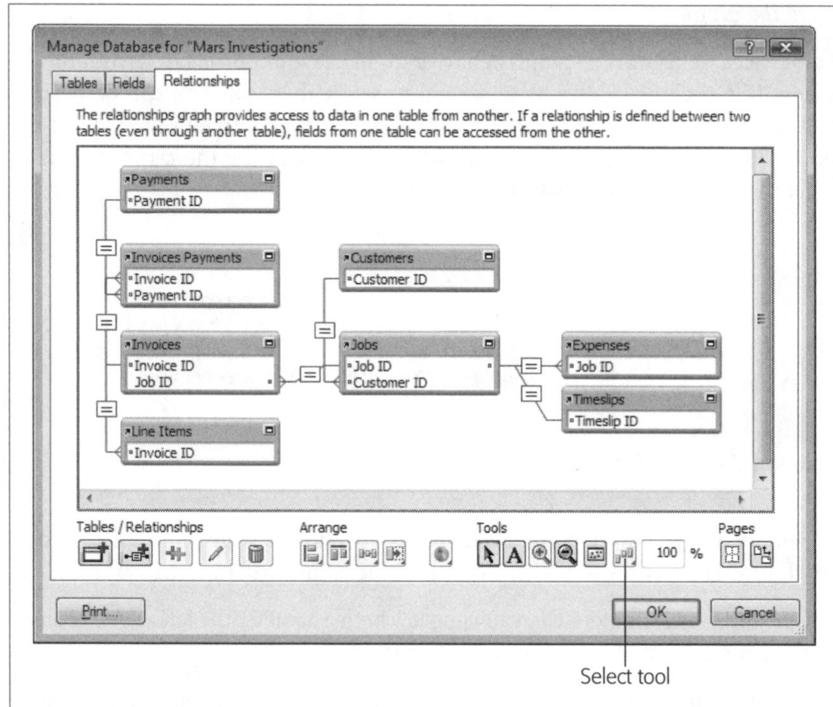

Figure 7-23: *It's amazing what a little straightening up can do. Now you can clearly see every relationship. The table occurrences are arranged in logical groupings (Invoices, Line Items, and Payments; Customers and Jobs; Timeslips, and Expenses).*

Instead of closing up the table occurrences, you can resize them. Hover the mouse over any of a table occurrence's four edges and the pointer changes to a double-headed arrow. Drag with the arrow to resize.

Note: If you have a stray table occurrence (named the same as the database itself) on your relationships graph, just select it and press Delete. It's a useless artifact from the table you deleted when you first added tables to this file. Since this table occurrence is not part of your ER diagram, you can safely ignore FileMaker's protestations that deleting it will break things.

Selection tools

The relationship graph has a few selection tricks that aren't available in Layout mode. First up, to help with selecting an entire group of connected objects, you can select just one. Then click the select tool (Figure 7-23) and choose "Select related tables 1-away." FileMaker automatically adds every table that's directly connected to this one to your current selection. You can choose this same command again to extend the selection one more notch on the graph.

If you have multiple table occurrences that have the same underlying base table (you'll learn why on page 362), you can then choose "Select tables with same source table" from the Select tool instead. FileMaker highlights all the table occurrences that match those you've selected.

Arrange the graph

The table occurrences in the graph behave a lot like layout objects in Layout mode. You can Shift-click or rubber band several to select them all. You can even press Ctrl+A (⌘-A) to select *all* the table occurrences. Just click into empty space on the graph to deselect. Once you have some selected, you can use the arrange tools to line them up. Figure 7-24 shows them close up.

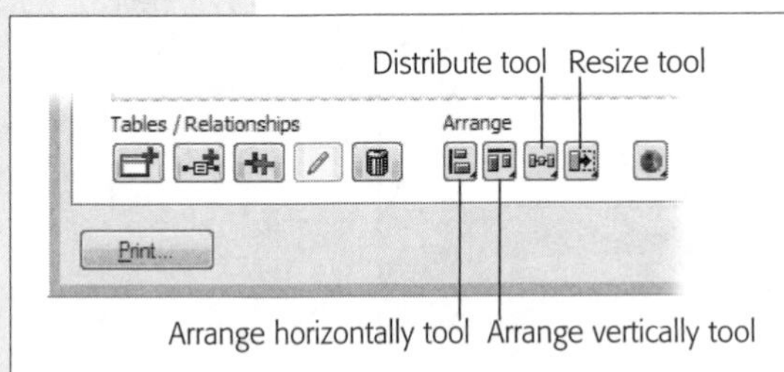

Figure 7-24:
When you select more than one table occurrence, the alignment tools become available. Each tool has a tiny triangle in the bottom-right corner to show that you get to make a choice about how that tool does its work.

Once you've dragged a few table occurrences around on your graph, it can look pretty sloppy. Here's how to use the tools to inflict some order on the graph:

- The **arrange vertically** tool lets you choose whether to align the left edges, centers, or right edges of any highlighted table occurrences.
- The **arrange horizontally** tool lets you align the top edges, centers, or bottom edges of the highlighted table occurrences.
- The **distribute** tool makes the space between selected table occurrences uniform. You can choose horizontal or vertical distribution.
- The **resize** tool makes short work of getting those manually resized table occurrences back in parade dress. Select some table occurrences, and then click the resize tool to tell FileMaker whether you want all the highlighted table occurrences resized to the smallest width or height, the largest width or height, or both (as in both height and width, not both smallest and largest, as cool as that would be).

Color your table occurrences

You can also change the color of the selected table occurrences. This won't affect the database's behavior at all. It's just there to help you organize your graph. (Organizing the graph is something that will seem a lot more important once you start to add more power to your database.) Just select one or more table occurrences, and then use the color tool as explained in Figure 7-25.

Adding notes

To notate your graph, select the note tool, and then drag on the graph to create the note. The Edit Note dialog box appears. There you type the text of the note and set its font, size, text, and background colors. If you want to edit a note, double-click it and the dialog reappears, ready to do your bidding (Figure 7-26).

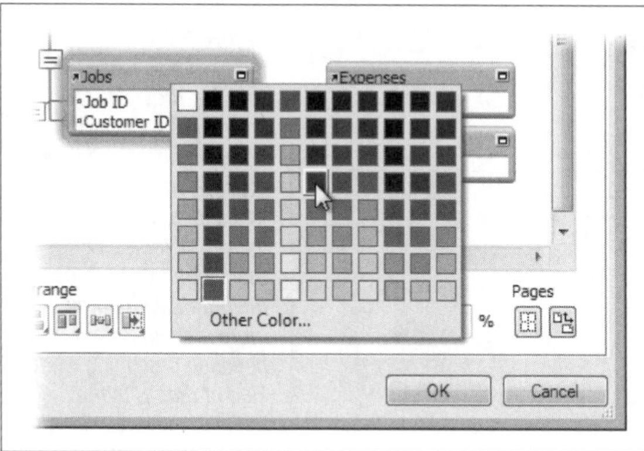

Figure 7-25:
When you click the color tool, FileMaker shows a menu of color choices, just like you see in Layout mode. Pick a color and all the selected table occurrences change to match it.

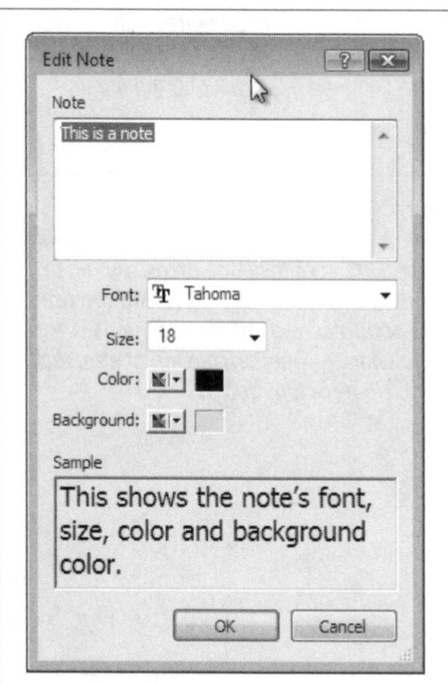

Figure 7-26:
When you use the note tool (it looks like the text tool in Layout mode: a big letter A), FileMaker shows you the Edit Note dialog box. You can pick font, size, and color, and type any text you want. You can see the note itself in Figure 7-27.

Printing the graph

Last but not least, FileMaker offers some tools to help you print the graph. Since the graph is a roadmap to your tables, some people like to print it and tape it up beside the computer for quick reference while building layouts. Figure 7-28 shows how to lay out the graph so you can print without surprises.

Deleting relationships

If you accidentally connect the wrong fields, or later decide you don't want a relationship you already created, you can easily delete it. Just click the relationship line itself to select it. Then click the Delete Relationship button or press the Delete key on the keyboard. You can see a selected relationship and the button in Figure 7-29.

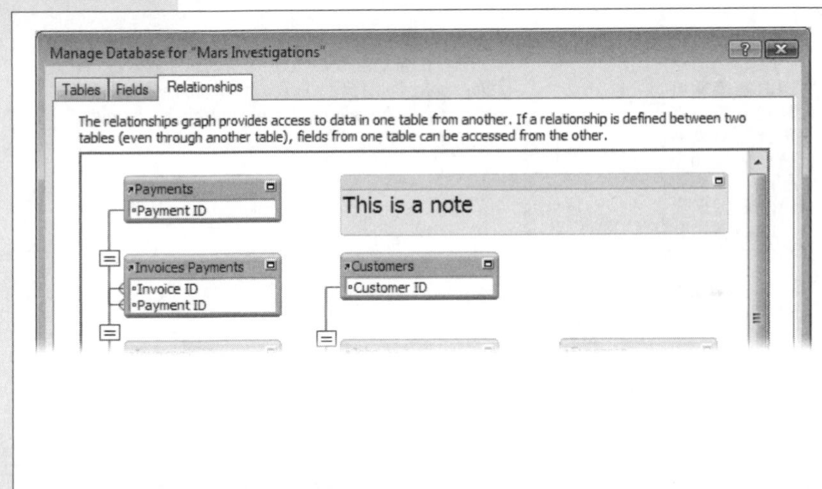

Figure 7-27:
It looks like a lowly text tool, but the notes tool lets you place floating notes anywhere on your graph. You can make detailed notes about individual tables, or make notes as wide as the graph, with nothing more in them than a headline describing what kind of data is in the table occurrences directly underneath. You can even drag your table occurrences right on top of a note, creating a sort of visual grouping.

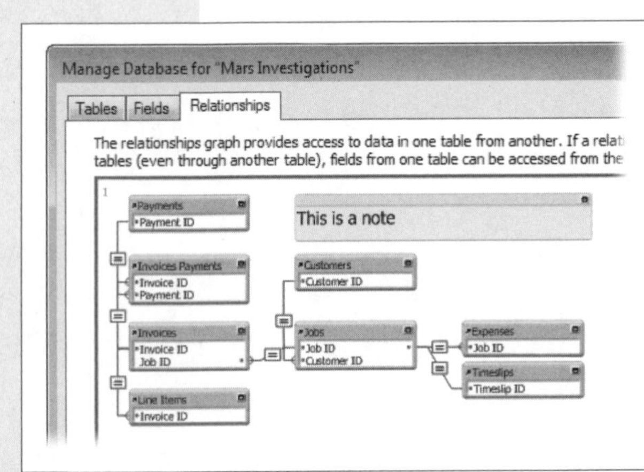

Figure 7-28:
Before you print, you want to see how the graph will fit on the page. First, click the Page Breaks button to show page-break lines on the graph. (If you can't see all your table occurrences clearly, zoom out as necessary.) To change paper orientation or size, click the Print Setup (Page Setup) button.

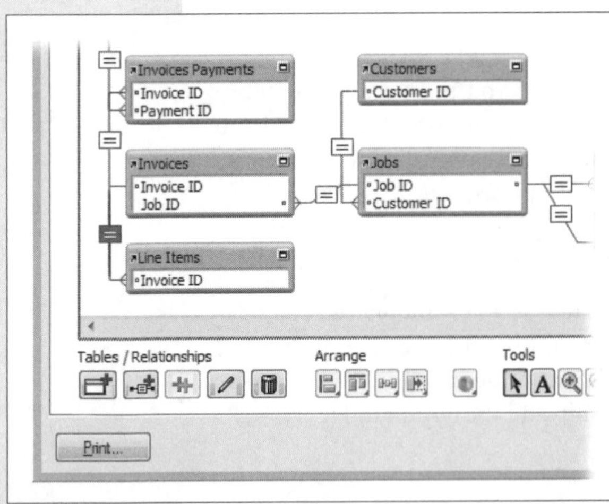

Figure 7-29:
Selecting a relationship line can be tricky because the line is so thin. It's easiest to click the "=" in the middle of the line, and it works just as well. You can tell you have it selected because its line is thicker and its equal sign is highlighted (like the relationship between Invoices and Line Items here). When a relationship is selected, you can delete it with the Delete Relationship button, or the Delete key on the keyboard.

Finishing the Field Definitions

Now that your relationships are in place, you can add the rest of the fields to your tables. Since you already know how to create fields, there's no need to bore you with the gory details. Below is a list of all the fields needed to complete this database.

Note: To save time, you can find the completed database with all fields in place on the "Missing CD" page at *www.missingmanuals.com/cds*. If you choose the ready-made option, you can skip ahead to page 339 and start learning how to use a relational database.

Customers table fields

Create the following fields in the Customers table:

- A text field called First Name
- A text field called Last Name
- A text field called Company Name
- A text field called Street Address
- A text field called City
- A text field called State
- A text field called Zip Code
- A text field called Phone Number
- A text field called Email Address

Jobs table fields

In the Jobs table, you need only one more field: a text field called Name. Of course, you could call this field Job Name, so that at a glance you could tell what table it comes from. But in FileMaker such redundancy is unnecessary. Almost everywhere the program shows field names, it includes the table occurrence name as well—*Jobs::Name*, for example. The exception, inexplicably, is Layout mode, where related fields look like this: *::Name*. You can always double-click a field to see where it comes from, but that gets boring after about the 79th time. To spare yourself the tedium, you have permission to change any field names listed here.

Expenses table fields

The Expenses table needs three new fields:

- A text field called Expense
- A number field called Amount
- A text field called Company Name

Timeslips table fields

Timeslips also needs three fields:

- A timestamp field called Date Time
- A number field called Duration
- A text field called Work Description

Note: You may be tempted to call the Date Time field *Date and Time* instead, but if you try to do it, FileMaker sternly warns you against putting the word "and" in a field name. You can create fields that break the naming rules, but you'll have to jump through hoops to use them in calculations (Chapter 9). It isn't usually worth the hassle. Pick a safe name instead.

Invoices table fields

The Invoices table is easy, too, with just three new fields:

- A date field called Date (as in the date of the invoice)
- A date field called Date Due
- A number field called Total Due

Line Items table fields

Add four new fields to the Line Items table:

- A text field called Description
- A number field called Price Each
- A number field called Quantity
- A number field called Extended Price

Payments table fields

The payments table is easy, too, with just three new fields:

- A date field called Date (as in the payment date)
- A number field called Amount
- A text field called Type
- A text field called Reference Code (this will hold a check number, direct deposit transaction number, Credit Card transaction ID, or other appropriate value)

Click OK in the Manage Database window, and FileMaker shows you your database. After all that work, the result is wholly uninspiring; it looks exactly like the single-table database you already created. But take a peek at the Layouts pop-up menu (or Figure 7-30). Surprise: FileMaker has made *several* layouts for you—one for each table occurrence on your relationship graph. At this point, everything you know about using a FileMaker database still applies. The only difference is that each layout is attached to a different table.

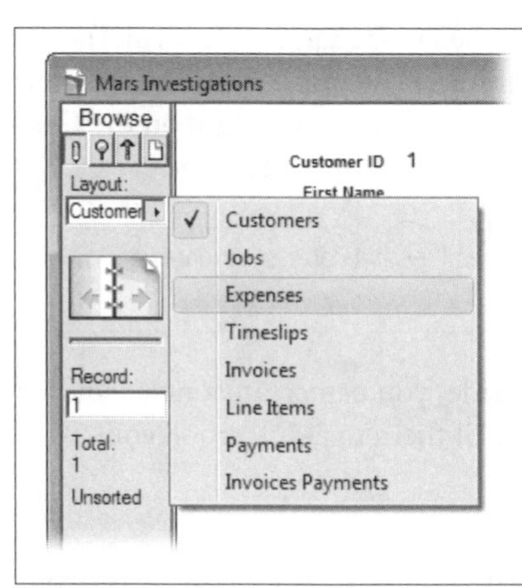

Figure 7-30:
When your database has multiple tables, FileMaker still makes ugly layouts for you–it just makes more of them. Remember, you can always review Chapter 4 for advice on beautifying layouts.

Relational Databases

The essence of a relational database is its multiple tables. But every database you've worked with up to this point has had just one table. Now you need to learn how multiple tables affect the FileMaker concepts you're familiar with: editing records, finding records, and building layouts.

One Table Occurrence, One Found Set

The most important thing to understand when using a multitable database is that each layout sees the entire database from a different perspective. You'll want to do a little exploration to see this concept in action. A layout is attached to an occurrence on the graph, and that's how it sees the world. This means when you're looking at a record on the Customers layout, you're seeing a customer. If you switch to table view (View → "View as Table"), you'll see a list of customers. You won't see payments at all. To see those, you need to use the Layout pop-up menu (or choose View → "Go to Layout" → Payments) to switch to the Payments layout.

Since each table holds different data, the concept of a found set changes a little as well. Whenever you initiate a find, the layout you're on determines which table FileMaker searches. Your newfound set is associated with that table occurrence, too. Just like when you had only a single table, the found set stays the same until you perform another find, or you tell FileMaker to show you all the records for that table occurrence (Records → "Show all records"). But if you switch to a different layout (one tied to a different table occurrence), your found set no longer applies.

For example, if you find the six customers from Texas, and then switch to the Expenses layout, you won't have six records in your found set anymore. Instead, you have a separate *Expenses* found set. Switch back to Customers and you'll see the six Texans again. FileMaker remembers one found set for each table occurrence. It also remembers the *current record* for each table occurrence, so if you switch to a different layout, and then come back, you'll still be on the same record that was active when you left that layout.

Of course, you can have more than one layout attached to the same table occurrence—Customer List and Customer Detail, for example. The found set and current record are associated with the *table occurrence*, not the layout, so a find on the Customer List layout will affect the found set on the Customer Detail layout.

Note: If you want more than one found set or current record in the same table occurrence, you can use multiple windows, just like you learned in Part 1.

If you want to see two kinds of records side by side, you can create a new window (Window → New Window), and then switch one of them to a different layout.

Viewing Related Fields

Having each table occurrence completely segregated from the rest on its own layout is a good starting place, because you will probably want separate lists of all your entities, but it's hardly ideal for a fully functional database. After all, if you wanted to view everything separately you could have created individual databases and saved yourself all the trouble of drawing all those lines.

So think of the layouts FileMaker made for you as starting points. It's time to put those relationships to work. For starters, you'd like to show the customer name when you view a Job record. But the Job table doesn't have a Customer Name field. Instead, you'll use the fields from the Customers table and let FileMaker find the correct *related* data using the relationships you created.

1. **In the Jobs layout, choose View → Layout Mode.**

   So far everything looks familiar. You've certainly seen Layout mode before (see Part 2).

2. **In the status area, use the Field tool and drag a new field onto the layout, somewhere below the existing fields.**

   As soon as you release the mouse button, FileMaker asks you what field you want.

3. **In the Specify Field dialog box, click the Table Occurrence pop-up menu (see Figure 7-31).**

   Here's where you venture into unfamiliar waters. This menu lets you pick any table occurrence on your graph.

4. **Choose Customers from the pop-up menu, and then, from the field list, select the First Name field. Click OK.**

   FileMaker adds the Customers::First Name field to the layout. It just says "::First Name" on the layout, but it does belong to the Customers table occurrence.

Note: If you forget which table occurrence a field comes from, just double-click it. The Field/Control dialog box reappears, and you can read the source table from the "Display data from" bit. Just make sure you dismiss the dialog box without making any changes. To be safe, click Cancel.

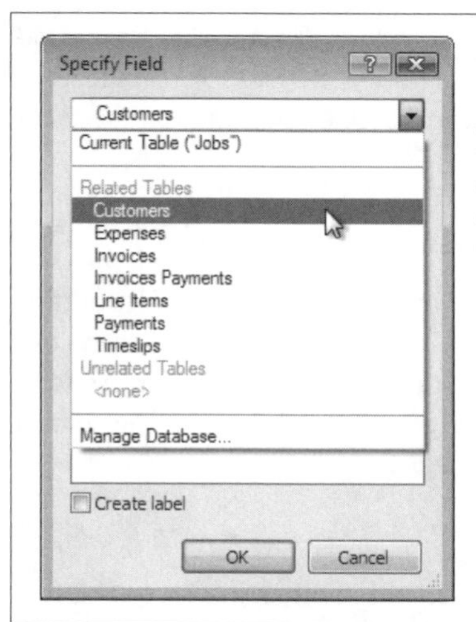

Figure 7-31:
The Specify Field window has always had a Table Occurrence pop-up menu; you've just been told to ignore it until now. This menu shows a list of all the table occurrences on the graph. FileMaker is smart enough to know which ones are related from the current layout's perspective. It breaks the list into two groups: related tables and unrelated tables. Right now you don't have any unrelated tables because the entire graph is connected in one group.

5. **Change the field label FileMaker created for the new field to Customer First Name. Then, add the Customers::Last Name field to the layout too.**

   Change its name, too, so you can remember what these fields are for.

When you're finished, switch back to Browse mode, saving your layout changes when prompted. In Browse mode, the new field doesn't look all that impressive yet. That's because you don't have any data in your database. Time to fix that.

Adding or Editing Data with Relationships

You'll really see the magic of relationships once you add some data and let FileMaker start making connections. Start with some customers. Open your database and go to the Customers layout.

Note: Making different records connect by key is going to seem really tedious in this example. You'll learn many techniques for streamlining this process later in this chapter.

1. **If the status area shows there are no records, choose Records → New Record.**

   FileMaker creates one record for you automatically, but only in the first table you added. Unless you happened to create this table *first*, you'll need a new Customer record.

2. **Name this customer *Francis Capra* by filling out the First Name and Last Name fields. Then, create a second customer record with the name *Logan Echolls*.**

   Notice that FileMaker has already filled in the Customer IDs for you—*1* and *2*. Time to add a job or two.

3. **Switch to the Jobs layout, and, if necessary, create a new record. In the Name field, type *Find the Missing Cash*.**

   Now you have one job record, but it isn't attached to a customer yet, so the Customer First Name field is empty.

Note: If you try clicking in the Customer First Name field right now, you'll get another surprise: FileMaker won't let you. It *looks* like a field, it *smells* like a field, but it doesn't *work* like a field. You're seeing the First Name field from the related Customer record, but there is no related customer record. No record, no field: No click.

4. **In the Customer ID field, type *2*, and then press Tab.**

   The 2, if you recall, is the ID of the second Customer record you added. By putting 2 in this field, you tell FileMaker that's the Customer record this job record relates to. Or, in English, that's the customer you're doing this job for. As soon as you leave the Customer ID field, FileMaker goes to work finding the correct Customer so it can show you his name. Like magic.

Editing Related Data

To see how editing works in a relational database, add another Job record. Using the same steps as above, name it "Find Lynn," and attach it to Customer 2 as well. It should then show the same customer name. Now try this:

1. **Change the value in the Customer First Name field on the Job layout to Trina.**

   Now the Find Lynn job is attached to "Trina Echolls." But who's the "Find the Missing Cash" job attached to?

2. **Switch to the first Job record using the book icon in the status area.**

   Drum roll… "Find the Missing Cash" is Trina Echolls', too.

3. **Switch to the Customers layout, and then switch to the first record.**

   Ta da! The customer record itself *also* now says Trina Echolls.

If you don't think that's cool, you need your geek level adjusted. You can now change this customer record back to Logan Echolls. It will, of course, be corrected on the Job layout as well.

You've seen a *relational* database in action. From a Job record, you can view data from the related Customer record. You can even edit that customer data directly from the Job record. The power of a relational database is all about working directly with related data like this, instead of copying information back and forth.

Note: If you want to protect your data so it doesn't get changed out of context, set the related field's behavior so that it can't be entered in Browse mode. Switch to Layout mode and choose Format → Field/Control → Behavior (page 236).

Portals

Adding the customer name field to the Job layout makes good sense because a job is attached to exactly *one* customer (it's a one-to-one relationship). But what if you want to go the other way? Suppose you put the Job::Name field on the Customers layout. How would that work since a customer can have more than one job? (In fact, Logan Echolls has *two* jobs right now.)

There are two answers to this question. The less interesting answer is that you can go right ahead and put that field on the Customers layout if you want. It will work fine. Since FileMaker can't show two values in one field, it just shows the *first* related record—in this case, Find the Missing Cash. (You can try for yourself if you want.)

The more interesting answer is *portals*. A portal is a layout object that makes viewing, editing, and even deleting multiple related records possible. The portal shows a list of records from a related table right on the layout. It can show as many rows (records) as you want, and you can even add a scroll bar so you can scroll through lots of related records in a small space. You can also edit related field data right inside the portal. When you add a portal to your layout, you get to decide which records it shows, how they're sorted, and what the portal looks like. For example, you can add a border to your portal, or change the background color of each row.

(See the box on "Editing fields through a portal" for details on all the options available for portals.) The Customers table has a to-many relationship to Jobs, so it's a perfect candidate for a portal.

The following steps take you through an example in the Customers database:

1. **In the Customers layout, switch to Layout mode. Drag the Body part a few inches down.**

   The Customers layout is a full one. You'll need more room for your portal.

2. **Click the Portal tool in the status area.**

   You can see what it looks like in Figure 7-32.

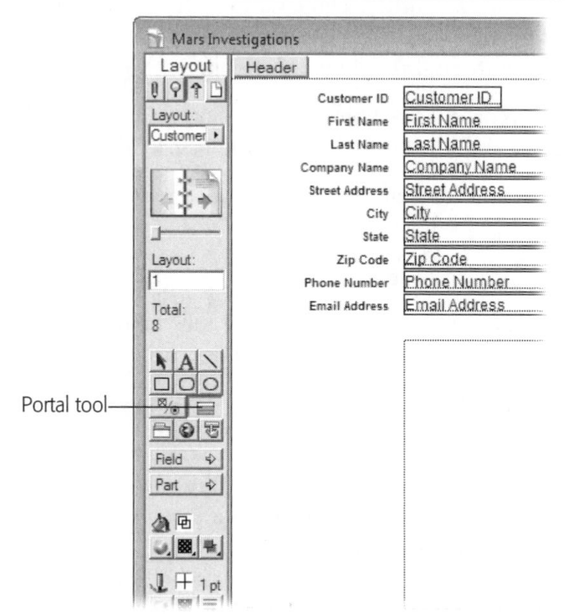

Figure 7-32: *The Portal tool is the one Layout mode tool you've never used. It works like the Shape and Button tools. Select it first, and then drag a rectangle on the layout. FileMaker creates a new portal inside that rectangle. You can also use this picture as a guide to show how much extra space you should make for your portal to live in.*

3. **Drag a large rectangle in the space below the Customer fields. (You can use Figure 7-32 as a guide, but don't worry too much about the size; you can always resize the portal later.)**

   When you release the mouse, FileMaker displays the Portal Setup dialog box. It's displayed in Figure 7-33.

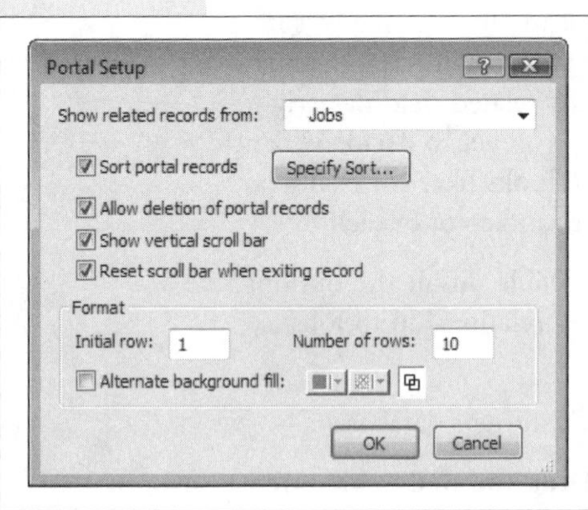

Figure 7-33:
In the Portal Setup dialog box, you can choose which table you want to show records from and how those records should be sorted. You can also decide which related records to show and adjust the look of the portal. See the box on page 347 for details on all these options.

4. **From the "Show related records from" pop-up menu, choose Jobs.**

   You're telling FileMaker to show data from the Jobs table occurrence—in this case, all the Jobs for the customer. Here's how it works: Whenever FileMaker looks at a related table occurrence (Jobs in this case), it *always* sees it from the perspective of the current layout. Working from the Customers layout, FileMaker looks at Jobs related to the customer. You could say that the Customers table is your current *context*. The idea of context is sometimes confusing, but it's important, and you'll encounter it throughout this book.

5. **Turn on the "Sort portal records" checkbox. In the Sort dialog box that appears, add the Name field to the Sort Order list, and then click OK.**

   When FileMaker shows Job records for a customer, they'll be sorted alphabetically by job name.

6. **Turn on "Allow deletion of portal records."**

   With this option turned on, you can delete records in the Jobs table right from the Customers layout, saving yourself a trip to the Layout pop-up menu.

7. **Turn on "Show vertical scroll bar."**

   A portal has a fixed size on the layout. If you have more records than fit in the allotted space, two things can happen: It can either ignore the additional related records, or you can put a scroll bar on the portal. With a scroll bar, you'll be able to view all the related jobs, no matter how many exist.

8. **Turn on "Reset scroll bar when exiting record."**

   If you've scrolled way down in a lengthy list of related records, the first records don't show up anymore, naturally. By selecting this option, you're telling the portal to go back to the first record anytime you click out of (or exit) the portal.

9. **Click OK.**

   The "Add Fields to Portal" window takes the Portal Setup window's place. From here, you get to pick which fields from the job table should be displayed in the portal.

10. **From the Available Field list, select the Name field, and then click Move.**

    FileMaker adds Jobs::Name to the Included fields list. Click OK again.

Your layout now has a portal. It looks just like the one in Figure 7-34.

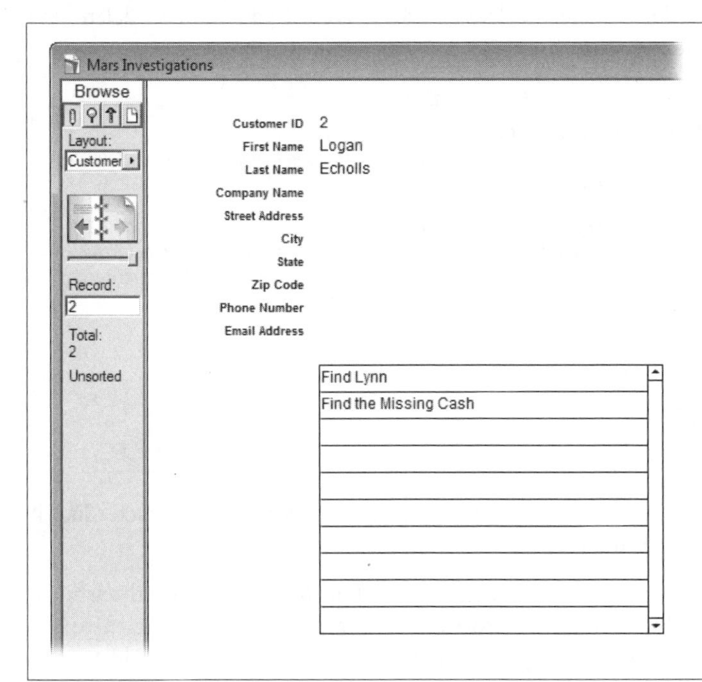

***Figure 7-34:** Every portal is made up of rows. The more rows a portal shows, the more related records you can see at one time. A row can have any other layout object inside it. In this example, the portal row has just one field. Each portal also shows what table occurrence it's associated with, and which rows it shows. Finally, if you ask for it, a portal has a scroll bar so you can scroll through lots of related records.*

Editing fields through a portal

Switch to Browse mode to see your portal in action. If you look at Logan Echolls' record, you'll see both his jobs listed in the portal. Like any related field, you can click into either Job Name field and edit the data therein. When you do, the Job record itself is updated.

You can also delete records through the portal. Click the Find Lynn row in the portal. When you do, you'll either enter the field itself or select the portal row. Figure 7-35 shows the difference.

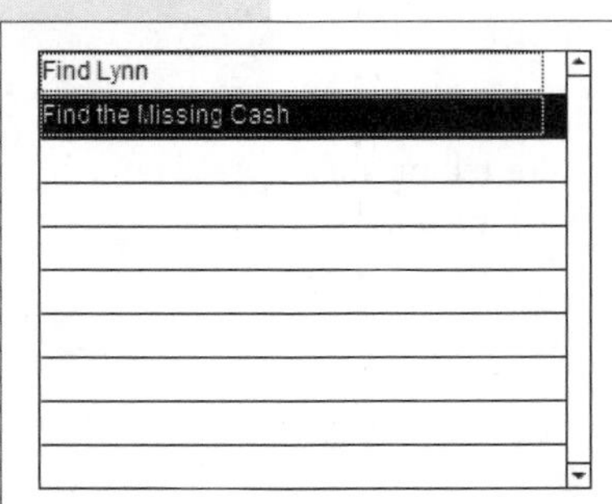

Figure 7-35:
When you click a portal row, one of two things happens. If you click into an enterable field, you'll go right into that field. You would say you're on the first portal row, and in the Jobs::Name field. If you click in a portal row somewhere other than in a field, you select the portal row instead–the entire row highlights as shown here. You're still on the first portal row, but you're not in any field this time.

When you're on a portal row, the Delete Record command takes on new meaning. If you have an entire portal row selected, FileMaker assumes you want to delete the *related* record—the one in the portal—not the so-called *master* record (the Customer record in this case). If you're in a field on the portal row when you choose the command, FileMaker instead asks you which record you want to delete: the Master record or the Related record. Figure 7-36 shows each message.

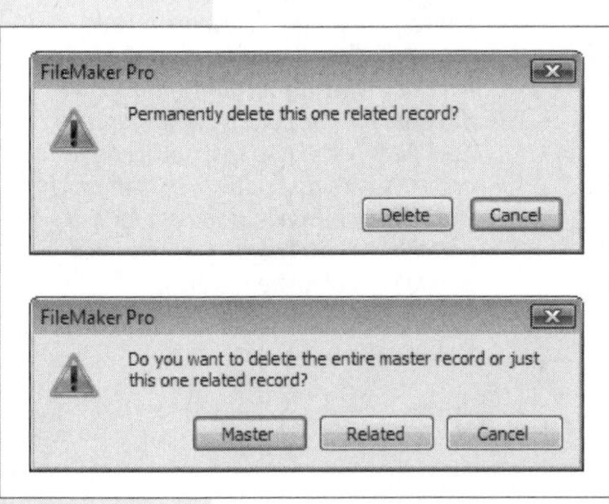

Figure 7-36:
Top: If you select a portal row, the Delete Record command deletes the related record.

Bottom: If you're in a field on the portal row when you choose the command, you get this message instead. This time you get to pick which record is deleted. Click Master to delete the Customer record, and Related to delete the Job record.

If you're not on a portal row, the Delete Record command works exactly like it does on a layout that has no portals.

You've covered a lot of ground in this chapter. You now have a full-fledged relational database, and a good idea of how it works. But manually typing arcane customer numbers into foreign key fields and bouncing from layout to layout to add a job is not your idea of efficiency. In the next chapter you'll learn how to harness *all* the power of the FileMaker features you've learned so far: Value lists, field formats, buttons, and additional relationship options all combine to make data entry a breeze, even in a complex database with several tables.

UP TO SPEED

Portal Power

In Figure 7-33, you learned a little about how the Portal Setup dialog box works. Now it's time to dig a little deeper.

To see the settings for your portal, select it in Layout mode and choose Format → Portal. (A double-click on the portal itself will get you there, too.) Portals work a lot like repeating fields. The main differences are:

- Portals work with related data, which is the way the database gods intended multiple values to be stored. In other words, portals aren't troublemakers like repeating fields.
- Portals can have a scroll bar. Got 326 items on that invoice? No problem.
- Each row in a portal can hold more than one field. In addition to the Job Name, you could show the Job Start Date if you had one. Adding objects to a portal is a breeze: Just drag them into the first row in Layout mode. When you add a field, FileMaker will show its correct value on each portal row. You can also add lines, shapes, pictures, and even buttons. You'll do some of this in the next chapter, and you'll learn how to troubleshoot when the data isn't showing up correctly.

In addition to these differences, portals have more options affecting the way they look and work. As you've already seen, you can tell FileMaker to sort the records in a portal. Whenever you view the Customers layout, for example, the job list is sorted alphabetically.

This has no effect on the sort order of the records on the Jobs layout. It just sorts the Jobs portal in the Customers layout. You can even put another Jobs portal on a different layout and set it to use a different sort order.

You can also assign an "Alternate background fill" to a portal. This works just like its counterpart in the Part Setup dialog box. When you turn it on, every even-numbered portal row will have a different background color and pattern. You can make every other row green, for example. The *odd*-numbered rows will have whatever background color you assign to the portal itself on the layout.

Finally, portals have the same partitioning power as repeating fields. Normally, a portal starts with the first related record (which record that is, exactly, depends on the sort order assigned to the portal). If you change the "Initial row" value, though, the portal will skip some rows. For example, if you put *5* in this text box, the portal will show rows 5 through 14 instead of records 1 through 9.

If it suits your needs, you can put the same portal on your layout more than once, and give it different initial rows. Your layout could show the first five jobs in one column, and jobs 6 through 10 in a second column, for instance. Portals also have specal autoresize powers (page 172).

If you make a portal grow vertically, you get to decide whether filemaker *adds more rows* or just *makes each row bigger*. Here's the trick: if anying *in* the portal is anchored on the bottom, the portal rows will get bigger. Otherwise, FileMaker keeps the rows the same size, and adds more of them as necessary.

CHAPTER
8

Advanced Relationship Techniques

FileMaker 9 was built to work with related data and make it seem easy. Related fields, for example, work just like ordinary fields. Not only can you put them on layouts, but you can use them in Find mode and the Sort dialog box too.

Now you're ready to learn how to take advantage of FileMaker's relational capabilities to make the best database system possible. You can make data entry a breeze, minimize double-entry, show data from different tables side by side, and easily move from one kind of data to another. You can also give each relationship you create special powers to make creating, deleting, and displaying related records easier. This chapter shows you how to do all these things.

Creating Related Records

The first thing you probably noticed with the database you worked on in Chapter 7 is that getting the records to relate is a tedious affair. To add a job record, for example, you go to the Customers layout, copy the Customer ID, and then go to the Jobs layout, add the record, and paste in the ID. That's a pain. Since FileMaker is all about relieving the pain of working with databases, it gives you a better way—a couple of better ways, in fact. In the last chapter you learned how to use a portal to *display* related records. Here you'll learn how a portal can also *create* related records. But first, you'll learn how to create a value list to help you enter appropriate data into a key field.

Value Lists Based on Fields

You've already seen value lists based on field values—on page 115, you attached a value list to the City field to make sure folks enter only valid state names. In a relational database, valid data entry is even more critical, since relationships work only when the key fields in each table match. Similarly, you can use a value list in the table on the "to-many" side of a relationship to make sure that the key field in the table on the "one" side of the relationship only accepts valid key values. When you make this change to your layout design *once*, you save hours of data entry work down the line. Good database design is all about this kind of up-front work. In the Customers database, for example, you may want to create a value list that ensures the entry of valid Customer ID numbers. Just follow the steps below:

Tip: You can download this chapter's sample database from the "Missing CD" page at *www.missingmanuals.com/cds*.

1. **In the Mars Investigations database, choose File → Manage → Value Lists, and then click New.**

   Name your new value list *All Customers*. You want this list to automatically show all the customers in the Customers table.

2. **Turn on the "Use values from field" radio button.**

   When you click this radio button, the "Specify Fields for Value List" window appears. (You can see an example in Figure 8-1.)

3. **In the pop-up menu under "Use values from first field," choose Customers.**

   Way back in the dark ages, when you had only one table, FileMaker put that table in the pop-up menu for you. Now that you have multiple tables, you get to choose which table you want.

4. **In the list of fields, select Customer ID.**

   When you use this value list, you want to choose a Customer ID for the job record, so you're basing the value list on this field.

5. **Turn on the "Also display values from second field" checkbox. Then, from the right-hand field list, choose First Name.**

   Since you're trying to avoid having to remember Customer IDs, you display another field value too, so that you can more easily find the Customer ID. The second field's data won't be entered into the field, though—it's just for show. In this case, the value list shows the customer ID and the customer's first name.

Note: Of course, showing first *and* last name is the best way to find the right customer, but the dialog box lets you pick only one field. See page 406 for a calculation that lets you show the first and last name in one field.

6. **In the "Sort values using" radio button set, turn on the "Second field" option.**

   After all, you'd probably prefer a list of customers in alphabetical order to one ordered by ID. Figure 8-1 shows the proper settings for this dialog box.

7. **Click OK, then OK again, and one more time.**

   It took three clicks to get here, so it takes three more to get back out.

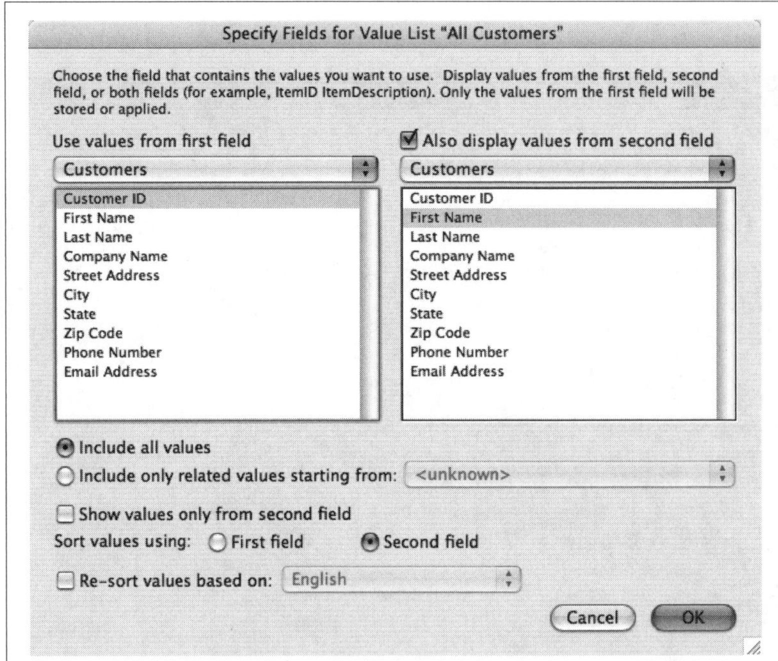

Figure 8-1: *The "Use values from field" option in the Specify Fields for Value List window gives your value lists superhero-like shape-shifting power: Instead of a dull list that never changes, your value lists automatically update as your data changes.*

Now that you've created the value list, you can attach it to the Customer ID field on the Jobs layout. To do that, you need to go back to the layout:

1. **Switch to the Jobs layout, and then go to Layout mode. Select the Customer ID field, and then choose Format → Field/Control → Setup.**

   The Field/Control Setup dialog box appears.

2. **In the "Display as" pop-up menu, choose Pop-up Menu.**

   You want to let your employees pick the customer ID from a menu. (You could use a Drop-down List instead if you want, as discussed on page 226.)

3. **From the "Display values from" pop-up menu, choose All Customers.**

   In other words, choose the value list you just created.

4. **Click OK, then switch back to Browse mode.**

Now, when you click the Customer ID field, you get a list of customers to choose from. You can see it in Figure 8-2.

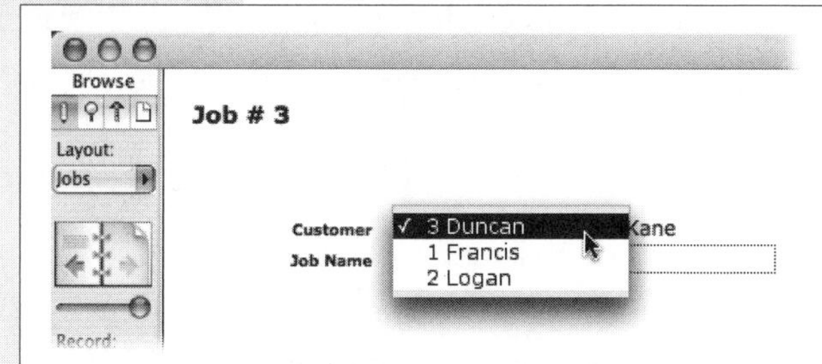

Figure 8-2:
Here's the Jobs layout after a little prettying up. To attach a job to a customer, you can now select the customer from a pop-up menu. When you do, FileMaker places the ID of the customer you choose in the Jobs::Customer ID field for you. The name is there to help you pick the right ID.

POWER USERS' CLINIC

Related Value Lists

A value list doesn't have to be a static list. It can change dynamically, based on the values in a field in your database. But you can also decide whether the list includes values from every record in the entire table, or only from the related records. First and most important, you need to choose *which* field the value list is based on. The pop-up menu under "Use values from first field" lets you pick a table occurrence. When you do, the list below it shows all the table's fields. Simply select the field you want.

You can also elect to show a *second* field in the value list. To show a second field, just turn on the "Also display values from a second field" checkbox and pick the field from the list (see step 5 on page 350). You can choose a field from any table occurrence–if the second value isn't from the same table as the first field, FileMaker uses the value from a related record. Display options let you choose how the list should be sorted: by the first field or the second field.

When the "Include only related values" radio button is turned on, FileMaker looks only at the records related to the one you're sitting on. For this method to work, FileMaker has to know which table occurrence you're coming *from*. In other words, if you ask for only the related Jobs, do you mean jobs related to the Customer record or to the Invoice record?

You make that choice in the pop-up menu below these radio buttons. (When you create a value list like this, it works properly only when it's attached to a field on a layout associated with the same table occurrence selected in this menu. If you try to use it on a different layout, FileMaker doesn't know which record to start from and the value list won't show the right values.)

Finally, you can tell the list to display values from only the second field–an ideal use for a pop-up menu. This option is really handy when you're using the value list to enter key field values, and you don't want users to be confused by a number that might not mean much to them. They see only the value in the second field, even though the field really stores the key value.

Creating Related Records Through a Portal

As a database designer, you have to think about how and where (on which layout) data gets entered. Sometimes choosing a related record's primary key from a menu doesn't make sense. The Invoices and Line Items tables illustrate this scenario. To use the pop-up menu you just created in Jobs, you'd have to add it to the Line Items layout. In that scenario, here's how you'd create an invoice:

1. **Create the invoice record.**
2. **Go to the Line Items layout.**
3. **Add every line item, choosing the correct invoice ID each time.**

Again, FileMaker has a better way. You edit your relationship so that it lets the program create new records, and then add a portal to the Invoice layout. Portals do more than just show related records. In this case, the portal also helps you create them. The first benefit is that you don't have to leave the Invoice layout to enter all the line items you need. Second, when you create the related records without leaving the Invoice layout, FileMaker automatically adds the correct Invoice ID to each line item for you.

Preparing the relationship

When you first drag a relationship into existence in the relationships graph, it starts off pretty plain vanilla. But there are three special properties that you can set to make your workflow more efficient. You get to set whether a relationship lets FileMaker create or delete related records and whether it sorts those records before it displays them. To make these changes, visit the Edit Relationship dialog box:

1. **In the Mars Investigations database, choose File → Manage → Database. If necessary, click the Relationships tab.**

   FileMaker remembers which tab you were in the last time you were here, so Relationships may already be selected.

2. **Select the relationship between Invoices and Line Items table occurrences.**

   Click the = signs in the middle of the line for an easy target.

3. **Click the Edit Relationship button (see Figure 8-3).**

   The Edit Relationship dialog box appears, as shown in Figure 8-4. (You can also double-click a relationship to open this box, saving the trip to the button.)

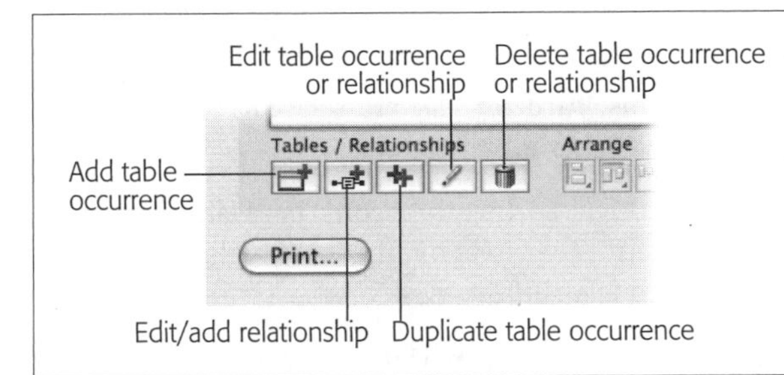

Figure 8-3: *The buttons at the lower left of the Manage Database window open the dialog boxes where most of the relationship work in this chapter is done. You can always back out of your mistakes…er, experiments by clicking the Trash can (Delete) icon.*

4. **In the set of checkboxes under Line Items, turn on "Allow creation of records in this table via this relationship".**

   Now if you put the Line Items::Description field on the Invoices layout, FileMaker lets you type in the field even when there is no related Line Item record. When you do, FileMaker immediately creates a new Line Item record for you and automatically enters the correct value in its Invoice ID field to make the two records related.

Tip: Since a relationship goes in two directions, you get to pick from the same three options for *both* table occurrences involved in a relationship. If you need a portal to display records through that relationship, then that's the side that needs to allow record creation.

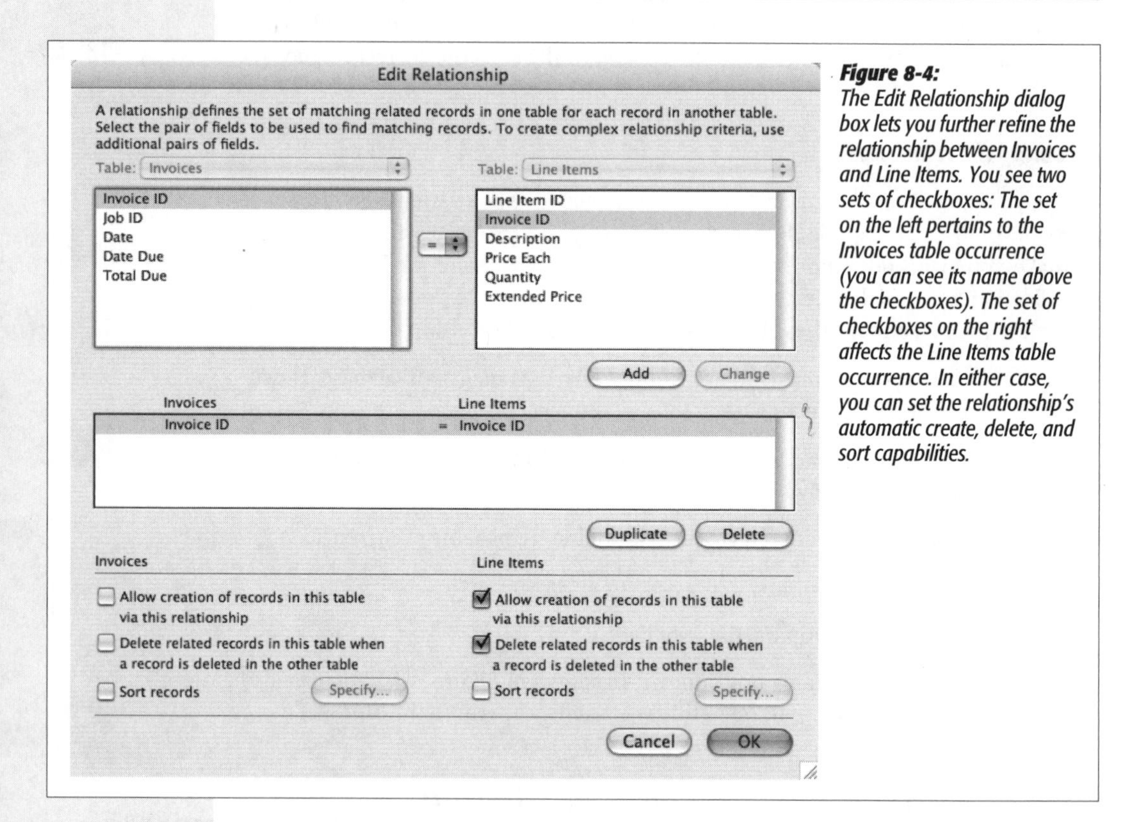

Figure 8-4: *The Edit Relationship dialog box lets you further refine the relationship between Invoices and Line Items. You see two sets of checkboxes: The set on the left pertains to the Invoices table occurrence (you can see its name above the checkboxes). The set of checkboxes on the right affects the Line Items table occurrence. In either case, you can set the relationship's automatic create, delete, and sort capabilities.*

5. **In the checkboxes under Line Items, turn on "Delete related records in this table when a record is deleted in the other table".**

   With this option turned on, if you delete an Invoice record, FileMaker automatically deletes all the related Line Item records for you. This is what you want, since a Line Item without an Invoice is meaningless.

6. **Click OK a couple of times to dismiss the Manage Database window.**

Adding a portal to a layout

In the last tutorial, you edited the relationship to allow FileMaker to create records from Invoices to Line Items. Now you're ready to fix up your Invoices layout to use that edited relationship. You're set to build a portal to display the Line Items from the relationship you've just edited.

In the Customers database, you want to create a portal on the Invoices layout. Switch to Layout mode, and then, using the portal tool (Figure 8-5), drag out a large portal on the layout.

UP TO SPEED

Cascading Deletes

The "Delete related records" option can be dangerous for a couple of reasons. First, if you turn it on accidentally, you can find yourself in an odd situation: Records keep disappearing for no apparent reason. You'll get frustrated if you don't realize how this option works.

But even if you *want* it on, keep this fact in mind: FileMaker can't bring back a record you delete. It's one thing if someone accidentally deletes a Jobs record—you just have to look up the Job Name and enter it again, being careful to give the job the same ID it had before.

It's something else entirely if you also have Delete turned on in the Jobs-to-Customers relationship, and the Customers-to-Invoices relationship, and again in the Invoices-to-Line Items relationship. You've set up the Towering Inferno scenario called *cascading deletes*. Because now, when you delete one job record—perhaps thinking that the job is finished and you don't need the record anymore—FileMaker also obeys your "hidden" instructions and deletes the Customer record attached to that Job record, *all* the Invoices attached to the Customer, and *all* his line items, too!

Some people decide it's not worth the risk and leave the delete option off even when it *should* be on. For a better solution to the cascading deletion problem, read up on security in Part 6.

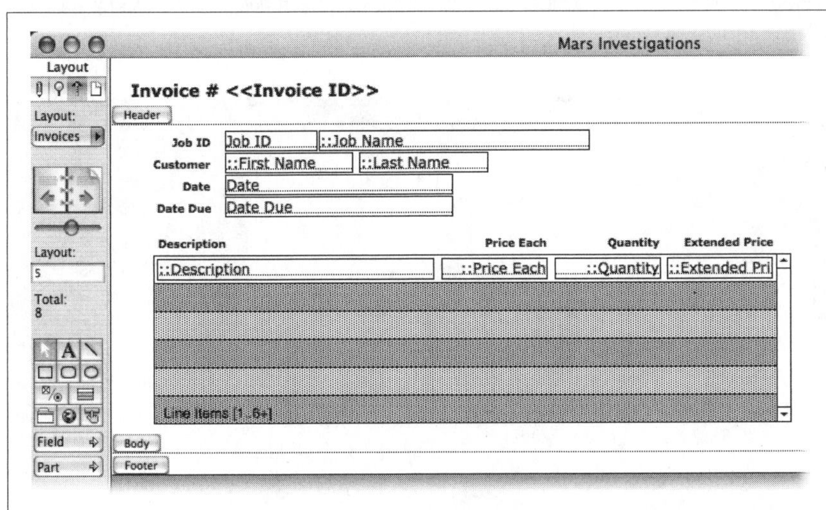

Figure 8-5: *This layout shows a portal like the one created in the steps on page 344. It needs to be wide enough to hold four fields, and tall enough to show several rows. Use this illustration to tweak your layout, or let your own design sense run wild.*

After you draw a portal, FileMaker shows the Portal Setup dialog box so you can specify which data to show in it. Proceed as follows:

1. **From the "Show related records from" pop-up menu, choose Line Items.**

   Your new Invoice record needs some Line Items, so that's the table you'll display in this portal.

2. **In the Portal Setup window, turn on "Show vertical scroll bar" and "Allow deletion of portal records." Click OK when you're done.**

   Turn them both on, since you never know how many items you'll add to an invoice—or take off.

The "Add Fields to Portal" window appears.

3. **Add the fields Description, Price Each, Quantity, and Extended Price to the "Included fields" list.**

   Notice the pop-up menu under Available fields. Because you selected the Line Items relationship three steps ago, FileMaker assumes that's where the fields are, too.

4. **Click OK.**

   FileMaker adds your portal to the layout, and divides the available space among the four fields.

You don't get field headings to help you see which field is which, and you may need to tweak the relative widths of your fields, but FileMaker's done the bulk of the work for you.

Tip: The "Alternate background fill" option in the Portal Setup dialog box lets you add color and/or a fill pattern to every other row of your portal. A subtle color really helps make it easier to read across each line. Test colors on a variety of monitors and light conditions, so you don't end up making your data harder to read instead of easier.

FREQUENTLY ASKED QUESTION

How Do I Know Where to Sort?

In the last chapter I set the sort order for a portal when I was adding it to my layout. Now you're saying I can set the sort order in the relationship. What's the difference? Does it matter?

When you set a sort order in the Edit Relationship dialog box (Figure 8-4), it applies to the relationship itself. Any time you use that relationship, the sort order applies: in portals on any layout, when showing a single related field, and when finding a set of related records (that's covered in the next section).

A portal's sort order (page 344), on the other hand, applies only to the portal itself. If you don't tell the portal to sort, FileMaker uses the relationship's sort order–if any–instead.

If you know that every time you look at your related data it should be shown in a specific order, set the relationship to sort. But if you think the related data ought to be sorted different ways in different contexts (and thus in different portals), don't sort the relationship because you add some overhead. FileMaker has to sort the records for the relationship, then sort them a different way for your portal. (You don't see this process happening, but FileMaker's doing it behind the scenes.) So when you're planning on viewing data in lots of different orders, rely on sorted portals instead of sorted relationships.

Adding records in a portal

Now that you've edited a relationship to allow the creation of related records, and provided a portal on the Invoice layout for viewing the records, you're ready to try out some Auto-creation goodness:

1. **On the Invoice layout, switch to Browse mode.**

   The portal is empty because you have no line items. You probably don't have an invoice record yet either.

2. **If necessary, create a new record.**

   Once you have a record, you see that the four fields in the portal are ready for a click. There isn't a related record yet, but FileMaker is offering you the chance to create one.

3. **Click the first (left-most) field in the portal and type *Investigate Lilly's red light incident.***

   As soon as you start typing, a *second* row of fields appears in the portal. That second row is FileMaker showing you that it's ready to make another new record for you. Figure 8-6 explains.

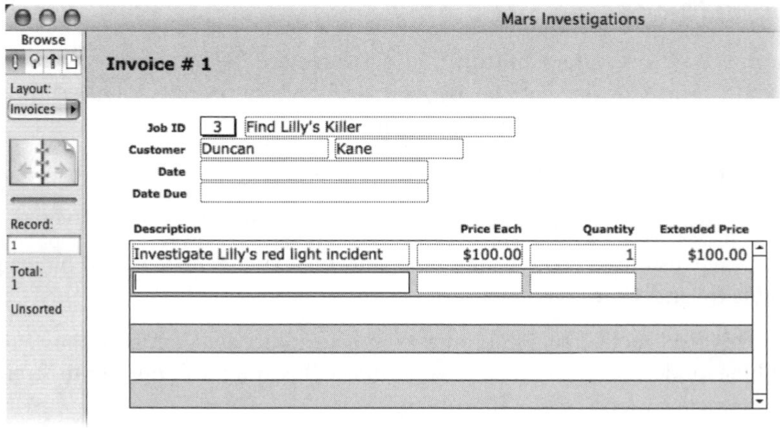

Figure 8-6: *In this example, someone's just typed the first line item on an invoice. The cursor is standing at attention in the second row waiting for a new line item to be entered. Notice that as soon as you fill out any field on the first portal row, a second row appears.*

You can fill out the remaining fields if you need the exercise. You can even add more line items: Just keep clicking into the last portal row. You can test the auto-deletion setting that you added in step 5 on page 354 by deleting the invoice you just created. When you do, the line item records should also go away. If you have two windows open, one showing the Invoice layout and another showing the Line Items layout, you see this action happen live.

Note: The last portal row is *not* a new record until and unless you type something in it, and then commit the portal record. (See page 30 for a refresher on committing records.)

Of course, the Invoices to Line Items relationship isn't the only relationship in your database that can benefit from the use of portals. For an exercise in thinking like a designer, take a look at your relationships graph and think about where else you could put portals to make data viewing and record creation easier. There's no right or wrong answer. That's the beauty of FileMaker—you can use its tools to create virtually any system your business needs.

Navigating Between Related Records

With pop-up menus and auto-creating records, adding data to your new database is now a joy. But you still have to do some serious work to navigate the system. For example, if you're looking at an invoice and you want to see details about the related customer, you have to note the Customer ID, switch to the Customers layout, and then find the customer. That's two steps too many.

Simplify this process with a button (page 258) on the layout—one that uses the *Go to Related Record* command. This command (affectionately called GTRR by FileMaker gurus) does the obvious, plus a little more. It goes to the related record to be sure. But it also changes the layout appropriately, and it can find all the related records and then sort them (if the relationship you're using has a sort specified). It can create a new window, while it's at it. That's a lot of work for one little command. If that weren't enough ways to use this little powerhouse, you can also set an option that includes the use of a found set.

Go to Related Record

Here's one way to create a button that activates the "Go to Related Record" command. In the Customers database, you already have people's names showing on a layout—just waiting to be made into buttons.

1. **Switch to the Jobs layout and then go to Layout mode.**

   You've already added the related field Customers::First Name on this layout.

2. **Select the Customers::First Name field, and then change its color to blue and its style to Underline.**

   Now this field looks like a link on a Web page. Since it's common knowledge that blue, underlined text is a link, you can use this graphical shortcut to "train" your users to click on certain bits of text.

3. **With the field still selected, choose Format → Button Setup.**

   The Button Setup dialog box appears.

4. **From the Navigation section of the list, select the "Go to Related Record" script step. When the Options section of the window appears, click its Specify button.**

   The "Go to Related Records" Options dialog box appears (Figure 8-7).

5. **From the "Get related record from" pop-up menu, choose Customers.**

   When you pick a table occurrence, you determine which table the button goes to. Notice that FileMaker shows you only the layouts that use the table occurrence you just selected.

6. **From the "Show record using layout" pop-up menu, choose Customers.**

   If you're going to a related record, it's usually from a different table occurrence. Your current layout can't show you related data, because it doesn't have the required fields. So you need to tell the button which layout to use.

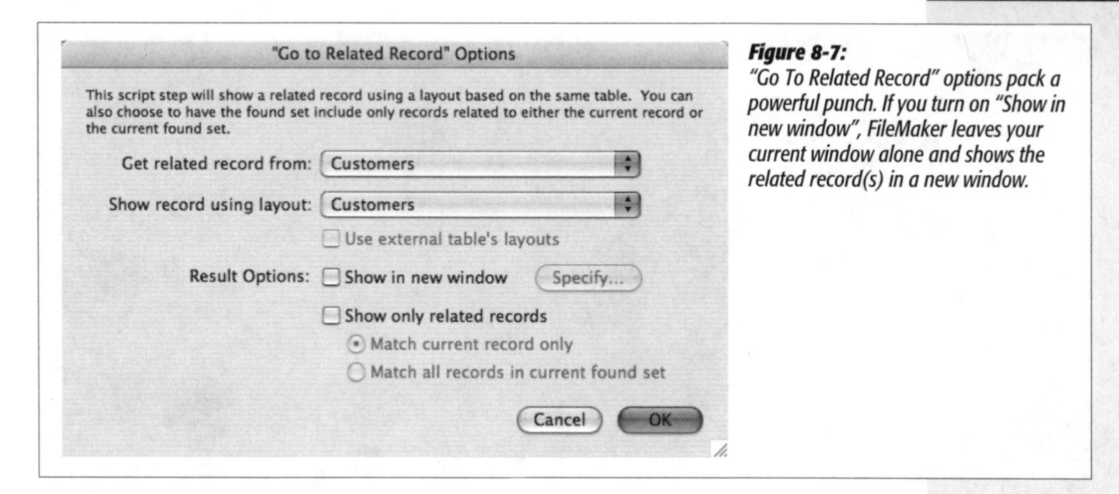

Figure 8-7:
"Go To Related Record" options pack a powerful punch. If you turn on "Show in new window", FileMaker leaves your current window alone and shows the related record(s) in a new window.

7. **Click OK, then OK again to return to your layout.**

   Now give your creation a trial run.

Switch to Browse mode. Make sure you have a customer related to this job. If you don't, click the Customer ID field and choose one. When you assign a customer, your button works. Click the Customer's name and you're transported directly to that customer's record. Figure 8-8 shows what it looks like.

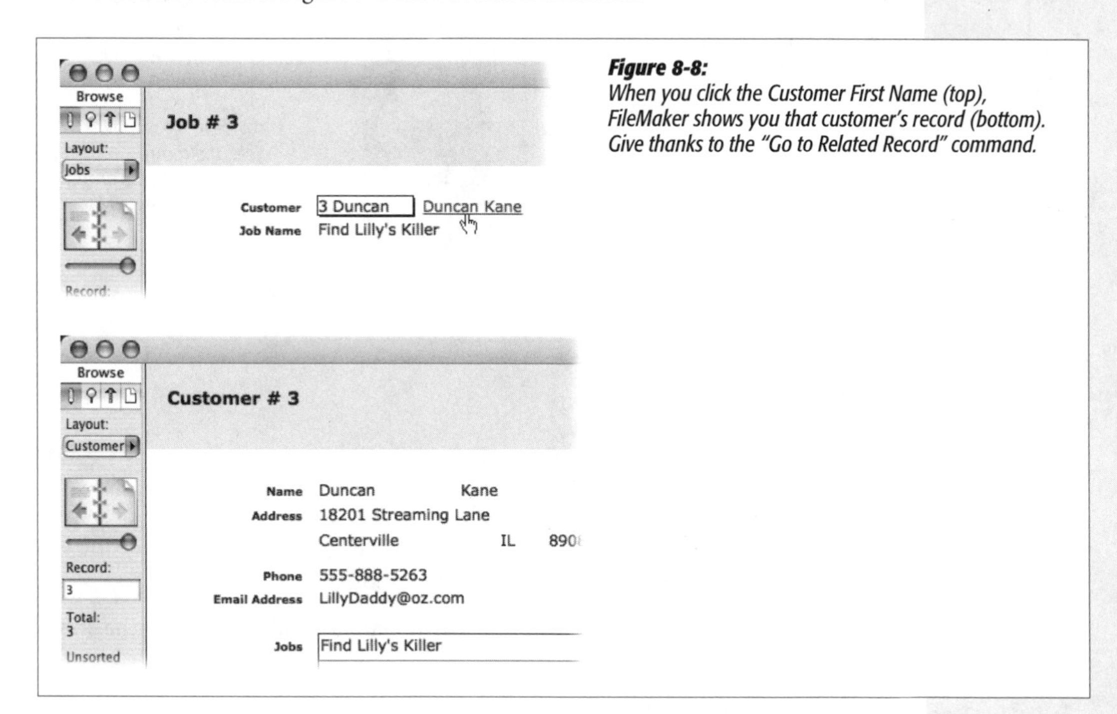

Figure 8-8:
When you click the Customer First Name (top), FileMaker shows you that customer's record (bottom). Give thanks to the "Go to Related Record" command.

Tip: The "Use external table's layouts" option applies only when you're linking multiple *files* together. You'll learn about that later in this chapter.

POWER USERS' CLINIC

Auto Creation Without a Portal

You don't have to have a portal to get automatic creation of related records. Auto creation works when you type in *any* related field as long as the relationship is set up to allow it. Suppose you have a one-to-one relationship with one table for Book Resources and another for book information. Both tables have a Book ID field, but only the Books::Book ID field is a serial number. Finally, you tell FileMaker to allow creation of related Book Resources records.

You might wind up with a database that looks like the one shown in Figure 8-9. There aren't any portals in sight. (Who needs them with just a one-to-one relationship?)

But since the relationship is set to auto-create Book Information records, you can add a new picture of the book's cover in the Resource field, and then just type a name right in the Book field. FileMaker creates the related record for you.

If you don't have Auto-creation turned on, you can't click into the Resource field. FileMaker shows the dotted field outline, but doesn't let you in.

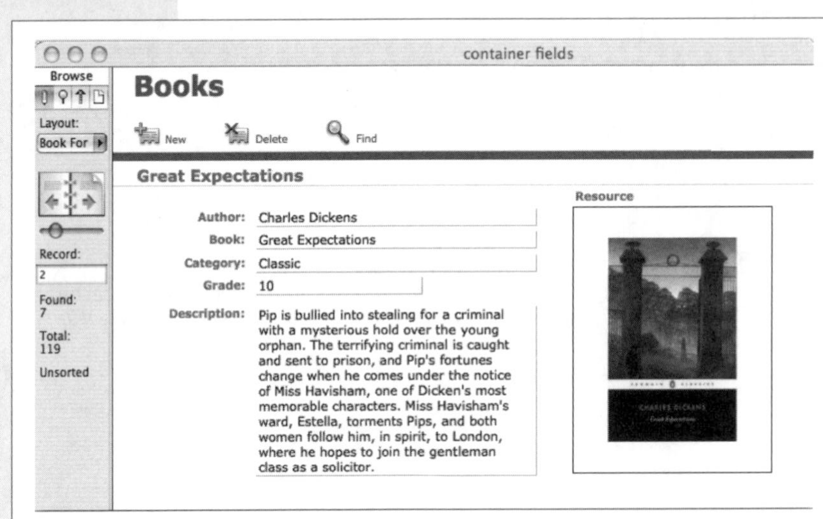

***Figure 8-9:** You can create related records without a portal if the related field is displayed on a layout. In this illustration, the Resource field is a container. If you place a picture–in this case, the artwork for a book's cover–in the container field, the record, complete with the proper key field, is created for you.*

GTRR with a found set

If you're looking at a customer record, you can see all that customer's jobs because they're right there in the Jobs portal. But what if you want to see those jobs (and only those jobs) in a sorted list on the Jobs layout? It would take a bunch of steps if you had to do it manually. But the "Go to Related Record" command does all those steps for you—when you add a few new options to the mix.

1. **On the Customers layout, switch to Layout mode, and then select the Jobs:: Name field.**

   It's the one in the jobs portal.

2. **Choose Format → Button Setup. In the Button Setup dialog box, select the "Go to Related Record" command from the list, and then click Specify.**

   The "Go to Related Record" Options window pops up.

3. **From the "Get related record from" pop-up menu, choose Jobs. From the "Show record using layout" pop-up menu, choose Jobs.**

   You need a layout that shows you meaningful data from the Jobs table. So far, this process is just like creating a related record button without a found set. The next steps make all the difference.

4. **Turn on "Show only related records".**

   When you turn on "Show only related records", FileMaker changes the found set, showing just the related records. You land on the desired record, and you have all the other records in the found set. If the relationship has a sort order, FileMaker sorts the found set, too.

   For now, leave "Match current record only" turned on. (Selecting "Match all records in the current found set" lets you go from one found set of records to another. See the box on page 363 for more detail.)

5. **Click OK, and then OK again.**

   You're looking at your layout again.

6. **For good measure, make the Jobs::Name field blue and underlined as well, using FileMaker's editing tools (page 155).**

   It's good to provide some kind of clue that the field is clickable.

Now you have a "Go to Related Record" button *in* a portal. Switch to Browse mode to see what happens. First, use the book icon to navigate to a customer record that has more than one related job. Click the *second* portal record. Because you're on the second row, the button takes you to the second record in your found set, not the first one. Then click the Customer name button again.

Note: If you didn't download the sample files, you might not have any customers with multiple jobs. Just switch back to the Jobs layout and fix that: Attach a few jobs to one customer. Then go to the Customers layout again and find that customer.

As you switch back and forth, you can see another difference: the portal changes the button's context (Figure 8-10). That is, the records related in a portal are already a set, unlike the single field you made into a button in the previous tutorial. In other words, when you click the GTRR button on the Jobs layout, you expect to see only the single Customer that's related to your job. When you click the button in the Jobs portal, you get a found set of only the job records that you just saw in the portal.

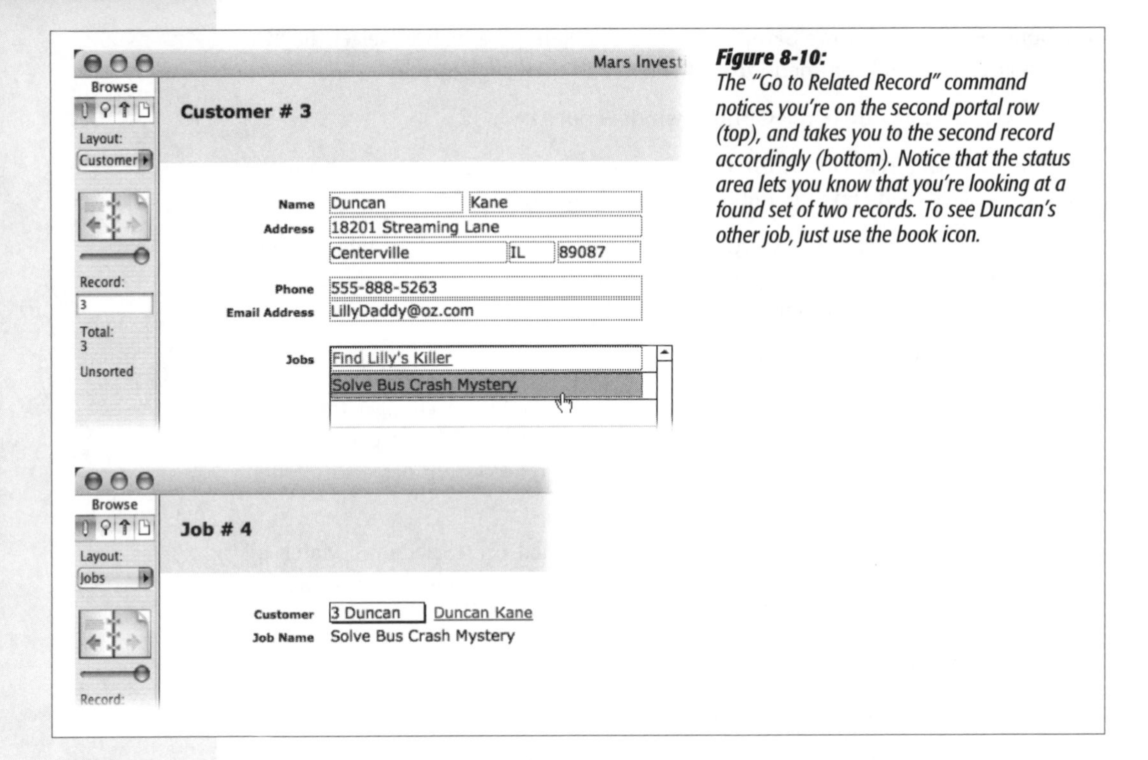

Figure 8-10: *The "Go to Related Record" command notices you're on the second portal row (top), and takes you to the second record accordingly (bottom). Notice that the status area lets you know that you're looking at a found set of two records. To see Duncan's other job, just use the book icon.*

Table Occurrences

In Chapter 7, you learned that a relationship graph doesn't really depict tables—it shows *table occurrences* (also known as *TOs*). They're just graphical representations of the underlying table. Because these occurrences are representations, you can make new occurrences of a table without duplicating it (and all its data). FileMaker's not trying to confuse you; it's actually helping you relate to the same table in different ways.

When you create a very simple database, you have only one table occurrence on the graph for each table, so it's tempting to think of them as the tables themselves. But as you add new and more powerful features to your databases—and the relationships to make them work—sooner or later you'll need to graph the same table multiple times so you can keep everything straight.

Understanding Table Occurrences

Few databases can manage all their tasks without multiple occurrences of the same table. Your Customers database is no exception. Here's an example: Your database has expenses to record what you buy to service your customers. It also has line items to record what you charge your customers for. Right now these are connected only by way of jobs. Figure 8-11 illustrates how your tables are currently related.

POWER USERS' CLINIC

GTRR On Steroids

With the "Show only related records" option, you can use "Go to Related Record" to display a found set of records (from a related table) in a portal. But what if you want to do something really cool and complicated, like find a couple of invoices that don't have anything in common other than being unpaid, and somehow see the customer records in a set without performing a complicated search?

Here's how you do it: Make a button on your Invoice layout and give it a GTRR step that goes to the Customers table occurrence using the Customers layout.

Then, in the Options window, select "Show only related records" *and* "Match all records in current found set." Do a regular find to show Invoices from just Duncan and Logan—they're always late payers. You can omit Francis Capra, who pays as soon as he gets his invoice, thank you very much. Click the GTRR button to see a new found set in the Customer table that shows only Duncan's and Logan's records.

Apply GTRR (on steroids) liberally throughout your database, and your users won't need to do as many complicated searches to find the data they're looking for.

You can do better than connecting expenses and line items via jobs, however. When you do connect them this way, it means you don't know *which* line item is actually billing for a particular expense—so you can't be sure you've actually billed for that expense yet. In other words, when you look at a line item, you can't tell which expense it's billing for.

Of course you can type that information into the Line Items::Description field, but this does nothing to help FileMaker know how these two things are connected. What you really need is a whole new relationship—one that directly connects expenses and line items. This new relationship lets you use "Go to Related Record" commands to toggle between expenses and invoices, for example.

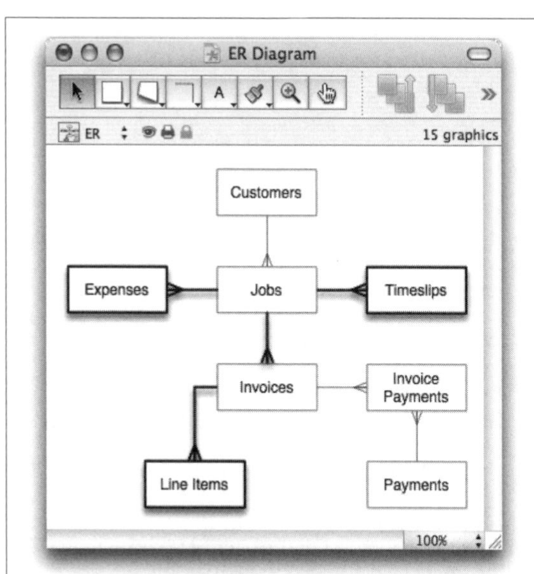

Figure 8-11: *In this version of the ER diagram, the Expenses, Timeslips, and Line Items tables have been emphasized, along with the relationships that connect them. The only relationship between an expense (which you need to be reimbursed for) and a line item (which allows for reimbursement) is through the Jobs table and the Invoices table.*

Tip: Later, when you learn more about calculations (Part 4) and scripting (Part 5), you can use this relationship to have FileMaker tell you exactly what has been billed and what hasn't.

One-to-one relationships are fairly rare birds. One example you've seen in this book is a table of books and a table of resources for each book, with a one-to-one relationship between each. Each image file had one corresponding description. This new one-to-one relationship—expenses to line items—is even rarer, in that it connects two completely different *types* of data. It's also unusual in that it's not integral to your database's structure. Unlike the other relationships in this database, you could delete it and your system would still work just fine. This relationship exists for one purpose only: to give your database a new ability.

However, as Figure 8-12 shows, when you add that relationship to the existing graph, you create ambiguity in FileMaker's digital mind. You can relate line items to the Expenses table, but to avoid interacting with existing relationships to line items, you need to create a new occurrence of that table.

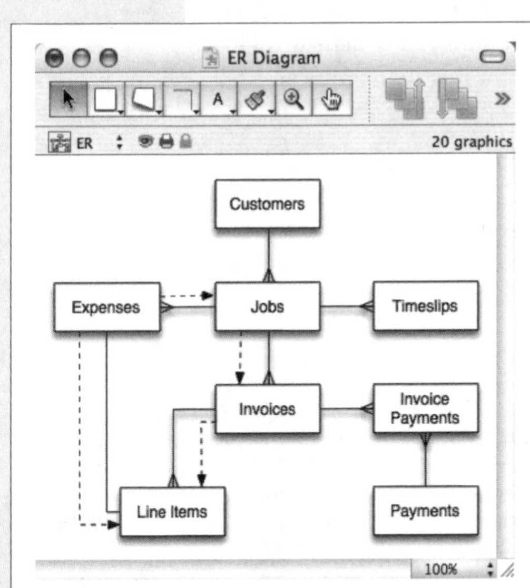

Figure 8-12: *This revised ER diagram now includes a relationship between expenses and line items. It's a one-to-one relationship because an expense is billed only once, and a line item bills only for one expense. Notice, too that you now have two relationships between expenses and line items–one direct, and one through jobs and invoices. FileMaker can't deal with that kind of ambiguity, which is why you create a new table occurrence to represent the relationship (page 366).*

To create this relationship and really make it work, you need three things:

- A new primary key (page 319) to hook the two tables together.
- A way to represent the new relationship in your relationship graph without throwing the whole thing into disarray. That's right—a new table occurrence.
- New fields on one of your layouts (the Expenses layout in this case), to use the newly related data.

To put these new database elements into play, you need to acquire some new skills and learn new twists on some old ones. The next section covers the entire process.

Relationships with Table Occurrences

FileMaker doesn't require you to follow a set order when you create new table occurrences, relationships, and layouts. Sometimes you create a new layout thinking it's just for displaying a set of data and only later realize you need a new relationship—and a new table occurrence—to make it work. Fortunately, FileMaker makes it easy to switch modes so that you move freely from one part of the program to another, creating and arranging various bits and pieces to make your new features work. In this section, you'll create a new key field and a new table occurrence, and then add fields to a layout so you can assign invoice items to the proper expense item. The following sections take you through the process in one possible, and logical, order.

Adding a new key field to a table

Before you can hook up table occurrences in a new way, you've got to make sure both tables have the proper key field for the new relationship. In this case, the Expenses table needs a Line Item ID. (See the box below for more detail.)

In the Customers database, choose File → Manage Database and switch to the Fields tab and the Expenses table. Create a new number field called Line Item ID, and click OK when you're done. You'll use this new field to relate the Expenses table to line items.

Note: You may be tempted to create your new relationship now by dragging the new Line Item ID field to the Expenses table. In fact, you may have already tried that–and gotten a confusing error message. To find your way out of that conundrum, see the box on page 369.

FREQUENTLY ASKED QUESTION

Putting New Keys in New Key Fields

I need to add a new key field to a table, but it's already got a lot of records in it. Since my serial numbers are created only when I create new records, am I stuck?

No, you're not. Lots of people need to "retrofit" key fields and add serial numbers after the data's already in a table. First, create a new field and give it the auto-enter serial number option. Put it on a layout that's tied to one of that table's table occurrences. If you have only one table occurrence for that table, so much the better–you don't have to make a choice.

Choose Records → Show All Records to make sure that all your records are in the found set. Then click in your new key field and choose Records → Replace Field Contents. Select the "Replace with serial numbers" option. FileMaker figures that you'll have to do this stuff pretty regularly when you're designing, so the values in the "Initial Value" and "Increment by" fields are already set correctly for this task. Select "Update serial number in Entry Options?" and then click the Replace button. FileMaker does the hard work of giving each record a unique serial number. It even updates the serial number so that the next *new* record you create has its own serial number. (See page xx for the full story on creating key fields.)

So, in a pinch, you *can* go back and add key fields, and key field data, to tables after the fact. But it's much better practice to create a key field as the first order of business each time you add a table to your database. It saves time and annoyance later.

Adding a table occurrence

You need to make a new relationship between the Expenses TO (table occurrence) and the Line Items TO using your new Expenses::Line Items ID key field. Since you want to access line item details while you're on the Expenses layout, you'll create a new TO for the Line Items table. In general, it's the information that you're using in a new way (the line items data, in this case) that gets the new table occurrence. The Expenses table is fine as it is. (See the box on page 364 for more detail on how to make that decision.)

Figure 8-13 shows a picture of what that relationship might look like with the new Line Items TO. With the new graph in mind, here's how to create that additional TO in your Customers database.

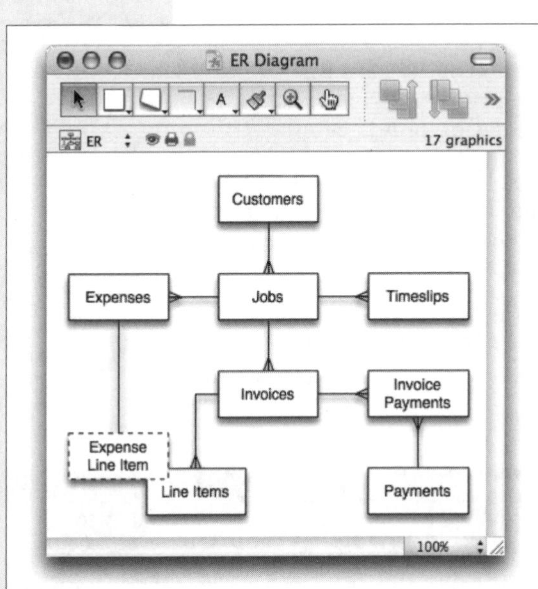

Figure 8-13: *You can use a new table occurrence to achieve the new relationship between expenses and line items, while avoiding the problem of ambiguity shown in Figure 8-12. This diagram shows you how to set up this relationship in FileMaker's relationship graph. Although you have only one Line Items table, you tell FileMaker it has two meanings: a line item on an invoice, and a line item that bills for an expense.*

1. **On the Relationships tab of the Manage Database dialog box, click the Add Table Occurrence button.**

   You see the Specify Table dialog box shown in Figure 8-14.

2. **Select the Line Items table from the list, and then, in the Name box, enter** ***Expenses_LINE ITEMS.***

   You want a descriptive name so you can pick it out of a lineup later.

3. **Click OK.**

   FileMaker adds the new table occurrence to the graph and selects it for you.

4. **Drag the Expenses::Line Item ID field to the Expenses Line Items::Line Item ID field.**

   FileMaker creates the relationship.

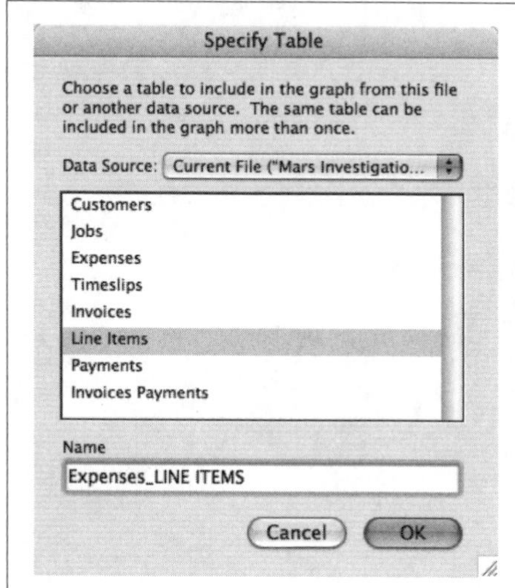

Figure 8-14: *The Specify Table box lets you tell FileMaker what table you want to use when you make a new table occurrence. You also get to give the new occurrence a name. When you name a new table occurrence, the goal is to help you remember the source table for the new table occurrence. The new TO's name is Expenses_LINE ITEMS. The "Expenses" part of the name tells you why you made the new TO–to help tie invoice line items to the proper expense records. "LINE ITEMS" is in all caps, so you can remember that the new TO comes from the Line Items table. Use whatever naming scheme you want, but use it consistently.*

Tip: If you don't see the Line Item ID field, it may be because your table occurrences are collapsed and they show only fields used in relationships. Click the little button in the upper-right corner of the TO to expand it. Since the TO cycles through three states, you might have to click twice before you see all the fields.

Now that you have both relationships created, you can switch the table occurrences back to their just-the-key-fields modes if you want, and arrange the graph however it suits you. When you're done, click OK to dismiss the dialog box. Now it's time to add fields from your new table occurrence to the Expenses layout, because if you don't put fields on at least one layout to access the Expenses_LINE ITEMS table occurrence you just created, it won't do you a bit of good.

Adding fields for new table occurrences

To put your new relationship to work, switch to Layout mode and go to the Expenses layout. As discussed on page 364, you want to add a couple of fields so you can see invoice line items and assign them to the corresponding expenses. That's the whole point of all the trouble you've gone to these last few pages.

Tip: Adding the fields using the Expenses_LINE ITEMS table occurrence is like adding any other fields, but make sure you're using the Expenses_LINE ITEMS table occurrence, not the original Line Items table occurrence.

Here's how to add the fields that do the trick:

1. **Drag a new field onto the layout. When the Specify Field dialog box appears, in the pop-up menu at the top, choose Expenses_LINE ITEMS.**

   The fields from the Line Items table appear (remember, this is an occurrence of the Line Items table, just like the Line Items occurrence itself).

UP TO SPEED

Deciding Which Table Needs a New Occurrence

Once you know that you need a new table occurrence, as in the Expenses_LINE ITEMS example on page 367, you face another challenge: Of which table do you make a new occurrence? To answer that question, ask yourself this one: Which table has the information I need? Here are the three possible scenarios; see which one you think makes the most sense:

- If you create a new occurrence of the Line Items table, you're giving that table a new meaning in the relational structure of your database. You can access this new TO–Expenses_LINE ITEMS–from any table occurrence in the system. In particular, you can add Expenses_LINE ITEMS details to the Expenses layout. (You *can't* put fields from Expenses on the Line Items layout because that layout is attached to the Line Items table occurrence, not the Expenses_LINE ITEMS occurrence.)
- If you decide to create a new occurrence of the Expenses table instead, then the opposite is true: You can't view line item information from the Expenses layout, but you *can* view expense information from the Line Item layout. In this case you've given expenses a new meaning (billed expenses, perhaps).
- If you want, you can create new occurrences of *both* tables. If you do, you can see expense information from a line item *and* line item information from an expense. But unless you plan to use your data that way, you're only creating more work for yourself.

2. **Choose the Invoice ID field from the list, and then click OK.**

   This field lets you view the Invoice ID on which this expense was billed.

3. **Add the Expenses::Line Item ID field to the layout as well.**

   This field lets you assign a line item from that invoice to the expense. Again, make sure you pick the Expenses::Line Item ID field, *not* the Line Items::Line Item ID field.

If you switch to Browse mode, you can start entering expenses. Make some expense records, and put the ID of a line item in the Line Item ID field. You see the associated invoice number through the relationship. (If you haven't created invoices yet, make a few, or else the fields can't show you any data.)

Managing Data with Data Tunneling

In the first part of this chapter, you learned how to manage data that's in a table only one relationship away from your source table. For example, earlier in this chapter, you learned how to create line items through a portal in an invoice record. (Remember from the graph in Figure 8-13 that the Invoice table occurrence is directly connected to the Line Items table occurrence.)

But you can also manage data that's stored farther away on the relationships graph. For example, your Invoice table occurrence is also related to the Expenses table occurrence all the way on the other end of the graph because there's a continuous

WORKAROUND WORKSHOP

When Dragging Doesn't Do It

When you first learned to create relationships, it was by dragging fields on the relationships graph (page 329). Since there's a clear path from the Expenses table to the Line Items table, you may be tempted to drag the Line Item ID field to connect them. You may have already tried it–and gotten the nasty message shown in Figure 8-15.

FileMaker's not trying to be difficult. It's just letting you know that what you're trying to do doesn't work, and it's even going out of its way to suggest a solution. FileMaker's offering to create a new Line Items table occurrence right now. FileMaker makes this choice because you dragged *from* Expenses *to* Line Items. (If you had dragged the other way, it would be suggesting a new Expenses table occurrence instead.)

In the "Name of Occurrence" box, type *Expenses_LINE ITEMS* and click OK. Whenever you see this message box, you *could* click Cancel and try to figure out how your ER diagram conflicts with FileMaker's relationships graph. But it's easier to just let FileMaker create the new TO for you. A new TO may not be what you had in mind, but you can rest assured that FileMaker's doing what it needs to do to make your new relationship work.

When you click OK, FileMaker adds the new table occurrence–which you can move to a less intrusive place on the graph–and creates the relationship using the key fields you dragged before you were so rudely interrupted.

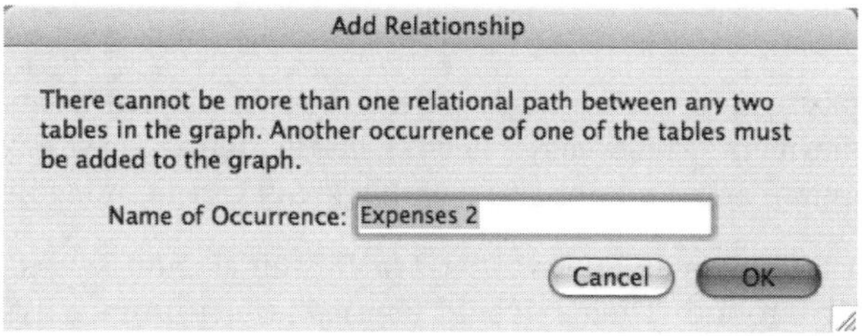

Add Relationship

There cannot be more than one relational path between any two tables in the graph. Another occurrence of one of the tables must be added to the graph.

Name of Occurrence: Expenses 2

Cancel | OK

Figure 8-15:
If you try to create a new relationship between table occurrences when there's already an existing path between your chosen TOs, you'll see this warning. Most often, you should type a new name for your TO, then click OK. See the box above.

line of table occurrences connecting them through their respective relationships (Figure 8-16). Even though they aren't directly connected, you can still work with data that's several TOs away from your current table.

Database nerds like to use the term "data tunneling" to describe how you can manage data that's multiple hops away on your relationships graph. This concept means that you don't have to navigate over to a layout based on the table where your data's stored to create or display it. If there's a path to the table occurrence you need on the relationship graph, you can stay right where you are and tell FileMaker to tunnel through your graph and bring back the data you need. In this section, you'll learn how to create layouts and arrange table occurrences to bridge the distance between you and the data you need.

Understanding Data Tunneling

Relationships like the one between expenses and line items you created in the last section are *functional*, but they aren't very easy to work with yet. You can create a value list that lets you choose from all your invoice line items and connect them to

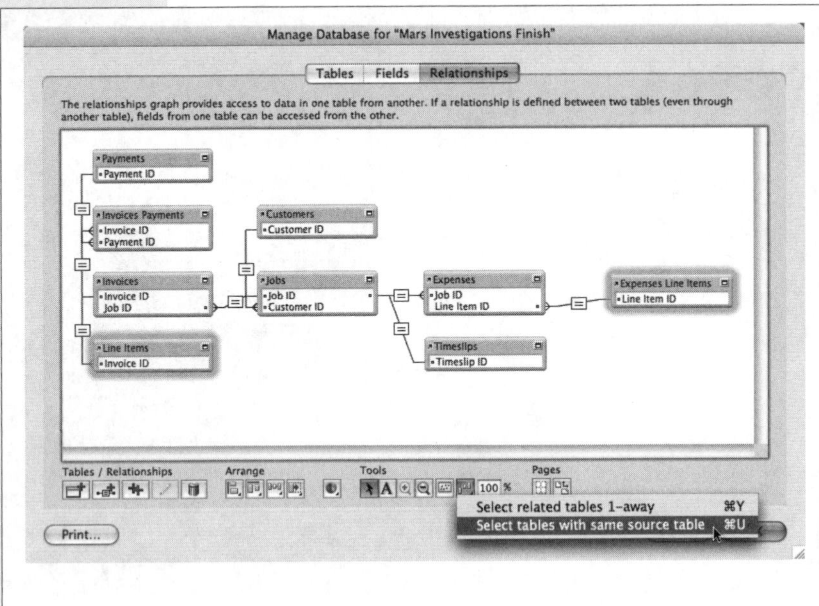

Figure 8-16: *Use the select tool to learn more about the structure of your relationships graph. Select the Line Items table occurrence, and then choose "Select tables with same source table". If you choose the other option, "Select related tables 1-away", you'll see all TOs that are directly connected to the original Line Item table occurrence. Use the Select tool again to add table occurrences two hops away to the selection. You can see that adding more items to a selection starts to confuse the message, so this option is most useful in small doses.*

expenses, but as your database grows, so can the problems. First of all, your database could have *thousands* of line items. And even if it doesn't, line items don't have a very good name—their descriptions aren't unique and their IDs aren't very meaningful.

It would be better if you could type in an Invoice ID *first*. After all, you're used to throwing invoice numbers around. Then it would be easy to pick from a list of items on just that one invoice. A new layout (like the one shown in Figure 8-17) uses data tunneling to let you manage line item data from the Expenses table.

What you need in your data tunneling interface

The Assign Line Items layout provides a special set of tools, or an *interface* to expedite a certain *process*. In this case, the process is matching line item records to expense records so you can track whether or not they've been billed. For the new interface to work, you need a few basic supplies. They're listed here to avoid confusion as you start creating them; you'll learn more about the role each item plays as you build the interface. You need:

- **A field to type in the Invoice ID.** Since this field doesn't hold information about any particular entity in your database, it's a good candidate for *global* storage. Global fields, as you remember from page 118, have the same value across every record of their table.

Note: The Assign Line Items layout needs fields to show the job name and line item description as well, but you can create them any time. In this example, you add them last (see Figure 8-17).

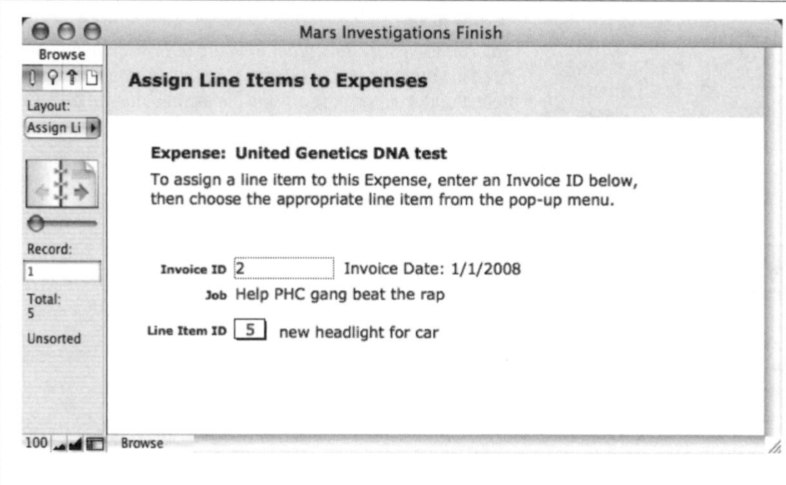

Figure 8-17: *This layout provides a nice interface for assigning line items to an expense. First, you fill out the Invoice ID field. Then, from the pop-up menu (it only shows line items on the invoice you ID'd), you choose a line item. You can download a real live copy of the database from the "Missing CD" page at www.missingmanuals.com/cds. Use the file to see how the finished process works and as a reference as you go through the exercises that create your new layout.*

- **A value list that shows line items on that invoice.** Value lists based on fields come in two forms: those that show *all* records, and those that show *related* records. Since you don't want to pick from every line item in the database, you need the second type.
- **A relationship for the value list.** This relationship needs to show the line items that match the Invoice ID in the new global field.

To get these three elements to work together, you first have to revisit your relationship graph and decide which table occurrences to connect. Read on.

Understanding Table Occurrence Groups

Since data tunneling involves relating existing table occurrences in multiple new ways, you can easily get tangled in a mass of arrows (Figure 8-19). Since you can create as many occurrences of each table as you want, FileMaker makes it easy to create an entirely *new* group of occurrences, called a *table occurrence group* (also known as a *TOG*), somewhere *else* in the graph. You can assemble and wire these together in any way that makes sense for your new interface, without complicating the existing group.

Note: Remember, table occurrences aren't tables. You can create as many groups as you like without making your database any bigger. The groups are for your convenience only, each showing you a "snapshot" of your database from a different angle.

To figure out which table occurrence you need to use to make the new layout in Figure 8-17 work, think about what you need it to do. You're looking at an expenses record on the Expenses layout and you want to attach it to a line item.

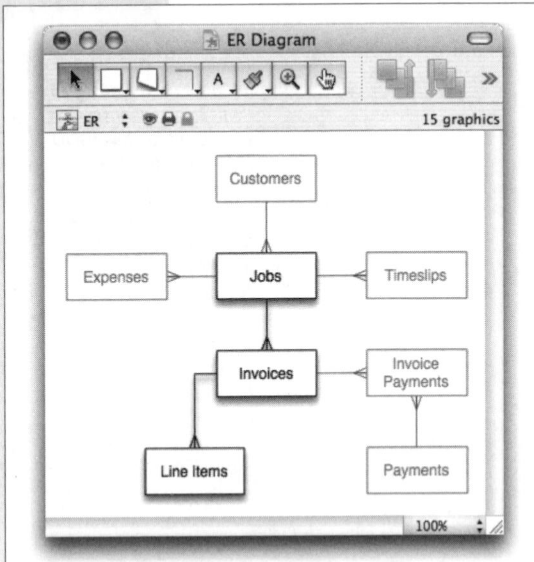

Figure 8-18:
You can use your ER diagram to figure out which tables you need in your new group, and how they go together. In your new group, you recreate just the highlighted portion of the diagram.

You need to get to the new Assign Line Items layout—via a button, perhaps. After you choose the line item (quite easy with the help of the new layout), FileMaker puts a value in the Line Item ID field—right there on the original expense record. Every step of the way, the interface takes place from the viewpoint of an expense record.

Tip: FileMaker mavens prefer the term *context* to refer to the viewpoint of a layout. Just so you know.

Since your new layout is all about modifying an expense record, you must attach it to an occurrence of the *Expenses* table. The other tables you need are Jobs, Invoices, and Line Items. As shown in Figure 8-18, those tables already have relationships to all the other tables in your database. There's no problem in creating new relationships to the Expenses table, too—at least not for FileMaker. But if you start dragging to create those relationships, you'll need a map, a GPS system, and a six-pack of aspirin to untangle all the table occurrences (see the box above).

Instead, you can create new TOs for that entire group of tables, and position the new group below your other table occurrences, as shown in Figure 8-19. This graph lets you work with the two distinct "sets" of relationships separately. Since the two groups share no relationships, FileMaker can put the relevant table occurrences in the Assign Expenses group, and separate everything else in the unrelated tables group. See Figure 8-19, bottom, for details.

Note: There is a downside to this approach for the database developer: Since each layout is attached to a single table occurrence, if you create a new group, you need a new layout to use it. But it's a small price to pay for the simplicity granted to the database's users.

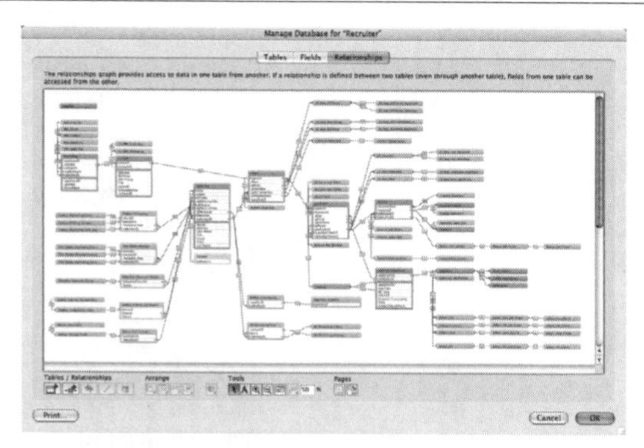

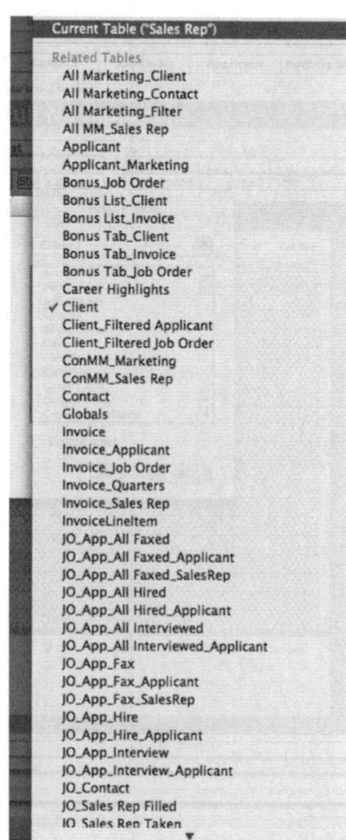

Figure 8-19:
You don't even need to be able to read the TO names in this relationships graph (top) to see how quickly good databases become the stuff of nightmares. Although the TOs are named reasonably well (bottom), so that similar TOs are grouped together alphabetically, the list won't even fit on the computer's screen. If the relationships graph were redesigned with separate table occurrence groups, all the related tables would be at the top of this list, and there'd be no need to scroll through dozens of tables that aren't pertinent to the task at hand. See Figure 8-20 for a better way to organize your graph, and your TO menus.

Managing the Relationships Graph

ER diagrams are great for helping you understand which table contains the data you need. But if you carry this concept into FileMaker's relationships graph in a complex database, you can get into trouble (Figure 8-20). With only 19 tables, the graph is as neatly ordered as it can be, given that it has almost 100 TOs, but the only thing missing from this labyrinth is a hungry minotaur. The database works just fine, but when it needs troubleshooting or updating, any developer (even if that's *you*) will have a hard time figuring out what's going on.

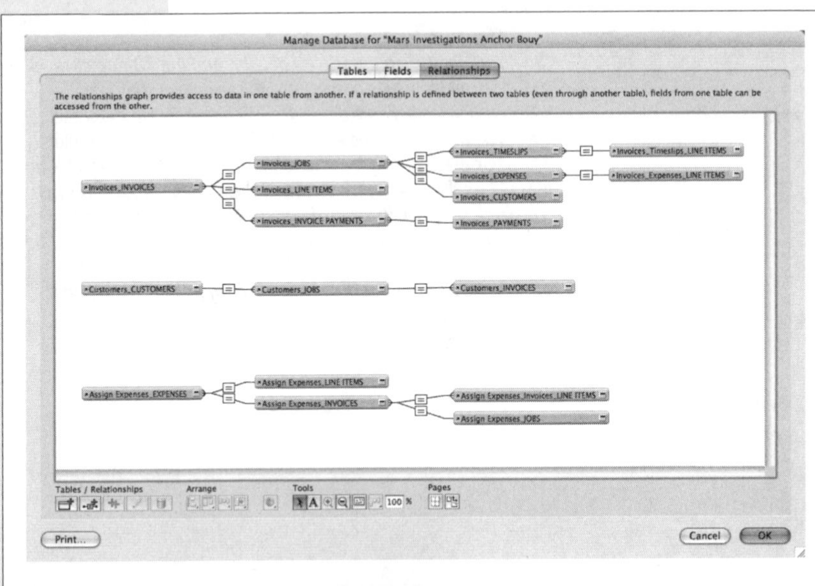

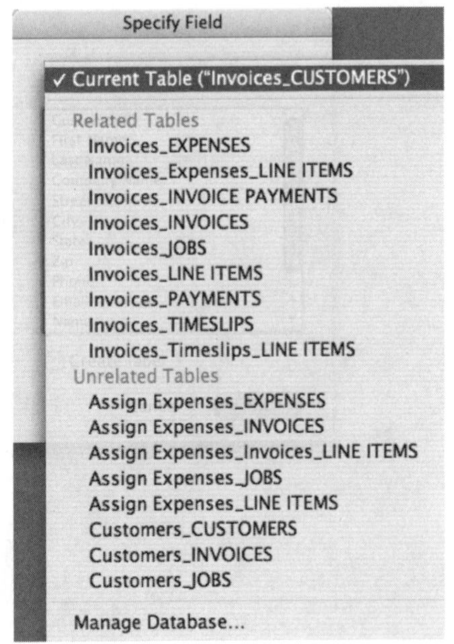

Figure 8-20: *Here's what your graph would look like if you converted the whole thing to the Anchor-Buoy model. Each new group of table occurrences (top) handles a new set of data entry and management tasks. More TOs can actually reduce the overall confusion because now they aren't lumped together in a long list, as in the Specify Field dialog box (bottom). They're grouped by Related and Unrelated Tables (note though, that this menu should really say "Table Occurrences" and not "Tables").*

Even worse, since every table occurrence relates to every other one, the table occurrence menu is nearly useless (Figure 8-19, bottom). And the table occurrence names, though descriptive, aren't grouped consistently, so they don't help you find the TO you need. So in a database of even moderate complexity, it's better to think in terms of Anchor-Buoy table occurrence groups (Figure 8-20, top) when you're building the relationships graph. With an Anchor-Buoy graph, you'll create only the table occurrences you need to display specific data on each layout.

The *Anchor* is a TO at the left of the TOG, and it's the one that determines the context (page 372) of the layout. The *Bouys* are all the other TOs trailing along in its wake. (Admittedly, the nautical metaphor doesn't work completely, so some flippant folk prefer to use the term *squid* for this kind of graph management. There's a head at the left, and a lot of dangly tentacles at the other end.)

Whichever term you prefer, when you're building an Invoice layout, you'll want to display data from almost all your tables (see the top TOG in Figure 8-19). That way, when you're looking at any specific Invoice record, you can use the power of data tunneling to see:

- The job for which the invoice was created (directly from the Invoices_JOBS table occurrence).
- All timeslips related to the job (through the Invoices_JOBS table occurrence).
- All timeslip line items related to the timeslip (through the Invoices_JOBS table occurrence and the Invoices_TIMESLIPS table occurrence).
- All expenses related to the job (through the Invoices_JOBS table occurrence).
- All expenses line items related to the job (through the Invoices_JOBS table occurrence and the Invoices_Expenses_LINE ITEMS table occurrence).
- The customer who is related to the job (through the Invoices_JOBS table occurrence).
- All the line items for the invoice (directly from the Invoices_INVOICES table occurrence).
- All invoice payment line items for the invoice (through the Invoices_INVOICE PAYMENTS table occurrence).

The TO names (Invoices_JOBS, and so on) look geeky at first glance, but their meanings are easy to decipher. The "Invoice" part of the top group tells you what layout the TO is used on, and the part in all-caps tells you the source table for the TO. Therefore, all TOs with the "Invoice" prefix are meant to do invoice layout display work or invoice data management; the prefix indicates the context. So, if you wanted to display customer data on the Invoice layout (which has the context of the Invoice_INVOICE TO), you'd look for the Invoice_CUSTOMER table occurrence and place a field from it on your layout. See the box on page 381 for tips on managing the TOs themselves.

Note: This naming scheme is one of many out there. Many developers use a similar scheme, but abbreviate the layout names/prefix part of the TO name or the table name, so the names won't get too unwieldy. Others refuse to use spaces in their TO names and use camel case instead (AssignExpensesINVOICE, for example). Feel free to make up your own scheme. Just use it consistently–it's your breadcrumb trail home.

If you don't need to see a lot of data on a layout, a simpler TOG will suffice. Look at the middle TOG in Figure 8-19. It lets you find a customer record, using the

Customer layout, and see customer details, all jobs performed for that customer, and all invoices for the jobs done for that customer. If you also wanted to see the individual line items for an invoice, you'd add an occurrence of the Line Items table, name it, and then put a field from the new TO on the Customer layout. The bottom TOG in Figure 8-20 shows the TOG you'll build in the next section with your new relationship graph taming skills.

Building a Data Tunneling Interface

Finally, it's time to start the actual construction. Start with the new global field. It's an easy place to begin, and logical too, since you need the global field for all the subsequent steps.

Creating a Global Field

Since the context of your interface is the Expenses table, that's where you add the field. Open the Customers database and proceed as follows:

1. **Choose File → Manage Database and switch to the Fields tab. From the Table pop-up menu, choose Expenses.**

   FileMaker shows the fields in the Expenses table.

2. **In the Field Name text box, enter *Global Invoice ID*, change its type to Number, and then click Create.**

   The new field appears in the field list. (See the box on page 378 to see why you've put the word "global" in this field's name.)

3. **Click Options and then, in the Field Options dialog box, click the Storage tab.**

   FileMaker shows you the field storage options. You first saw these on page 118.

4. **Turn on "Use global storage (one value for all records)," and then click OK.**

   FileMaker creates the field, and it now appears in the Field list.

You use this new global field as a key field in the next section.

Creating a New Table Occurrence Group

Before you start throwing new TOs on the graph, review your goals for the new layout. Its purpose is to show you an invoice based on data you enter in a global field, and to show the job name and a list of line items related to that job.

Since the Assign Line Items layout needs the context of the Expenses table, you'll create a new Expenses TO. You also want to be able to show the line item attached to that expense, so you need a new TO for line items. Finally, you'll use the global field you created in the Expense table to hook up to another new table occurrence of the Invoice table. With these TOs, you'll be able to see and manage the following information:

- The name of the job associated with an invoice.
- The line items attached to that invoice.

A quick glance back to Figure 8-19 reveals all the new table occurrences you need to create. Remember, the naming scheme helps you figure out which table each occurrence needs to come from.

The steps are simple if you take it one table at a time:

1. **If necessary, click the Relationships tab of the Manage Database window.**

   You need to see your existing relationship graph.

2. **Click the Add Table Occurrence button (see page 353). When the Specify Table window appears, select the Expenses table.**

   When you create your layout later, it will have the context (or viewpoint) of the Expenses table. Therefore, it's the Anchor in your Anchor-Buoy TOG, so it makes sense to create it first.

3. **In the "Name of Table Occurrence" box, type *Assign Expenses_EXPENSES*, and then click OK.**

   The *Assign Expenses* bit says that this new table occurrence was created especially for the process of assigning expenses. *EXPENSES* (in all caps) indicates the TO's source is the Expenses table.

   When you click OK, FileMaker adds the new table occurrence to the middle of the graph. Move it out of the way to get ready for the next steps.

4. **Add an occurrence of the Invoices table called Assign Expenses_INVOICES; an occurrence of the Line Items table called Assign Expenses_LINE ITEMS; a second occurrence of the Line Items table called Assign Expenses_Invoices_LINE ITEMS; and an occurrence of the Jobs table called Assign Expenses_JOBS.**

   You now have five new table occurrences on your graph. Since the names are so long, you might have to stretch your new TOs so you can tell them apart. See page 334 for tips on resizing TOs.

Tip: When TO names are lengthy, it's often easier to just copy a TO that has nearly the right name, copy the lengthy name from the Name field, reassign the TO to the new table, paste the old name, and then edit it. It's harder to read about than it is to do. Try it.

5. **Create a relationship between Assign Expenses_EXPENSES and Assign Expenses_LINE ITEMS using the Line Item ID field as keys.**

   You drag and drop; FileMaker draws the lines.

6. **Create another relationship, this time between Assign Expenses_EXPENSES and Assign Expenses_INVOICES, using Global Invoice ID and Invoice ID as keys.**

   The necessary relationships are falling into place. See Figure 8-21 to complete the relationships you need between your new TOs.

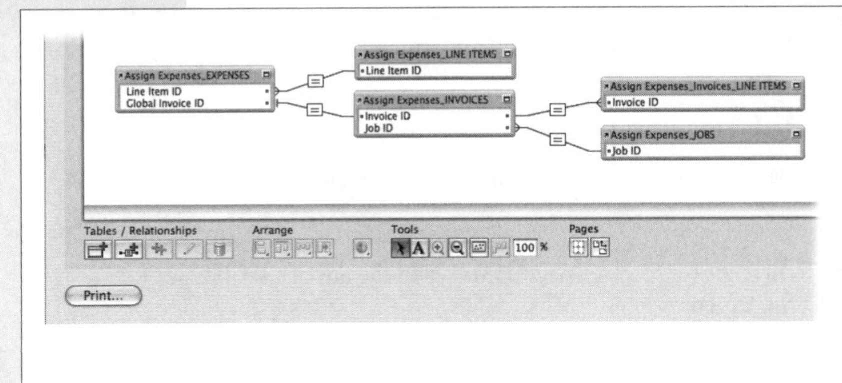

***Figure 8-21:** You can start to see how this new layout will work. When someone puts an invoice ID in the Global Invoice ID field, it instantly matches one invoice record. You can then show fields from the Assign Expenses_INVOICE table occurrence on the layout, and see data from the invoice you need to use to assign expenses. Use other relationships to show the invoice's line items and the job's name.*

When you create Anchor-Buoy TOGs on your own, the process probably won't be as straightforward as this exercise might lead you to believe. FileMaker is flexible enough to let you create part of a TOG, go design your layout, then dive back into the graph to add more TOs later. In fact, real-world development is rarely as rigid as these exercises, since you'll often realize that you need a bit of data only while you're deep in the white hot creativity of breathing life in to your database.

Now that the occurrences and relationships are in place, you can move them to a new spot on the graph where they have some breathing room. FileMaker gives you nearly infinite space down and to the right, so pick a spot that you like.

Tip: Remember, if you like things lined up nice and neat, you have Arrange tools in the relationships graph that let you resize and align a selected group of TOs together (page 334).

POWER USERS' CLINIC

One (Global) Field to Rule Them All

You know that fields set with global storage have the same value across every record in the table that holds them. Since they're so different from other fields, many database designers give them special names so that the fields stand out in a list. That way, it's less likely that they'll get used inappropriately–say in a context where they don't have much meaning, or plopped down on a layout where someone can edit the values when they should stay static.

You can just preface the names of all your global fields with the word "global," like you did in the exercise on page 376.

But in the real world, people commonly just use a lower-case "g" as a prefix. With this scheme, you can name your global field "gInvoice ID" and save a few keystrokes. Plus, you look like a guru.

Some developers also use the lower-case "g" in the names of their TOs, to indicate that the relationship uses a global field as a key. It can be a handy reminder that the relationship doesn't work bidirectionally, as fields that are based on normal fields do. The relationships graph also reminds you that a global relationship isn't bidirectional, as you can see by the connector between Global Invoice ID and the regular Invoice ID fields.

Building a Global Field Layout

Now that you've finished the new table occurrence group and hooked up its relationships, you're ready to create the "Assign Line Item to Expense" layout you first saw way back in Figure 8-17. With the graph defined, this process is surprisingly simple. First, create a new, blank layout based on your Assign Expenses_EXPENSES table occurrence, and call it "Assign Line Items to Expenses." (See page 186 if you need a refresher on creating layouts.) Then check out Figure 8-22 for layout suggestions.

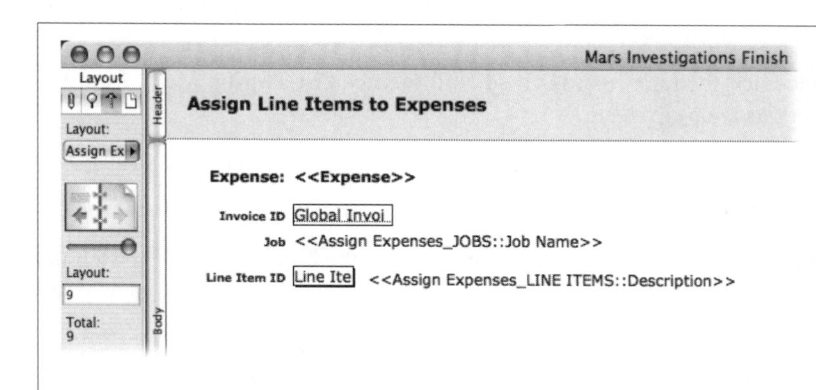

***Figure 8-22:** Your smallish TOG has two TOs from the Line Items table. One is related directly to Expenses through the Line Item ID field. The other is related through the Invoice table and its Invoice ID field. The one related directly lets you create a merge field on your layout. You'll use the second in a related values value list in the steps on page 380.*

Now add these fields to the layout:

- Assign Expenses_EXPENSES::Expense.
- Assign Expenses_EXPENSES::Global Invoice ID.
- Assign Expenses_EXPENSES::Line Item ID.
- Assign Expenses_JOB::Name.
- Assign Expenses_LINE ITEMS::Description.

Note: Remember, this layout is associated with the Assign Expenses_EXPENSES table occurrence. When you choose fields for the list above, from the top of the pop-up menu in the Specify Field dialog box, select *Current* Table.

Using a global pop-up field to change the display in a value list

By definition, a global field has the same value in all its tables' records. Therefore, you can change the data in a global field without affecting any of your "real" data for those records. When your global field is used in a relationship, and you change the value in the global field, the relationship changes and so do the records that are related to your current record.

You use this technique to create a value list that's based on the global relationship between your new Expenses TO and the new Invoice TO. When that global relationship changes, FileMaker tunnels in the new table occurrence group from Expenses to Invoices to Line Items to get the line item that's related through the value in your global. Refer to your relationships graph to refresh your memory on how those TOs hook up, if this technique doesn't make sense without a visual aid.

This advanced technique is just like searching for records, without all the hassle of going to Find mode and actually performing a search. You need to make the Line Item ID field into a pop-up menu first. Here are the steps:

1. **Double-click the Line Item ID field, and then choose Pop-up Menu from the "Display as" pop-up menu.**

   The "Display values from" pop-up menu appears, with <unknown> displayed.

2. **From the "Display values from" pop-up menu, choose Manage Value Lists.**

   You need a new value list based on the values in the Line Item ID field from the Assign Expenses_Invoices_LINE ITEMS table occurrence you made a few pages back.

3. **Click New and type *Invoice Line Items* as the value list name.**

   Even though you're about to assign your new value list to a field, you want the name to be descriptive so you can remember your thought process later on.

4. **Turn on the "Use values from field" radio button.**

   This option sets that field's data to show up in your new value list.

5. **Choose Assign Expenses_Invoices_LINE ITEMS from the Specify Fields window's drop-down list. Then click the Line Item ID field. Select "Include only related values starting from" and, from the drop-down list, choose Assign Expenses_EXPENSES.**

   The idea is to keep your users from assigning an expense to a line item from the wrong invoice, or from assigning an invalid Line Item ID. This option tells the value list to display only line items that are related to the invoice that matches the value in your Global Invoice ID field. Since that field is on the Assign Expenses_EXPENSES table occurrence, that's where the value list relationship is "starting from." To understand how this works, remember the concept of context (page 372).

6. **Turn on the "Also display values from second field" checkbox and, from the list, choose the Description field.**

   Since a Line Item ID isn't very meaningful by itself, you want to show the description too.

7. **Turn on the "Sort by second field" radio button and click OK until the dialog boxes are gone.**

   You're back on your Attach Line Items layout and your Line Item field is formatted with your new value list.

Switch to Browse mode and try out your new layout (see Figure 8-23). If you type "*1*" in the Global Invoice ID field, you should be able to pick a line item from the pop-up menu. When you do, the Expense Assign: Expense Line Item::Description field should show the selected line item's description. Create a few new invoices and see how the values in the pop-up menu change when you change the value in the Global Invoice ID field.

Note: If you type an Invoice ID and see that your value list is empty (it says <no values defined>), then you're either using an Invoice ID that doesn't exist, or it doesn't have line items yet.

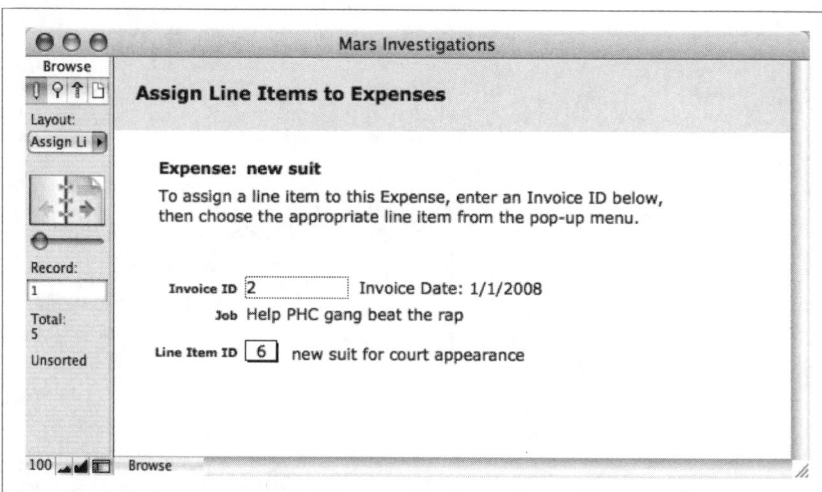

Figure 8-23: *Here's a dressed-up version of the layout you just created. It uses a mix of merge fields and field controls to draw your users' attention to the fields where they should enter data. And if that weren't enough, some simple instructions have been added to make it really clear what to do.*

UP TO SPEED

Managing Table Occurrences

When you use descriptive names for your TOs, they can get pretty long. Fortunately, you can easily resize any table occurrence so its entire name is visible. No matter how the table occurrence is configured, you can drag the right or left edge to make it wider or narrower. If it's set to show all its fields, you can also drag the top or bottom edge to change its height. A table occurrence that's too short to show all its fields has little arrow icons above and below the field list. Click these arrows to scroll through the list. (When a table occurrence is set to show just the key fields or no fields at all, its height is fixed.)

To see which table an occurrence represents, just point to the arrow icon to the left of the occurrence name. FileMaker pops up an information window that tells you everything you need to know. And if long names and pop-up tips aren't enough, you can use the note tool (it's the tool marked with the letter "A"). Use the note as a reminder of the purpose of your new table occurrences that's more detailed than a naming prefix. Notes behave themselves, staying in the background behind all your TOs, so some designers make large notes that enclose a new TO group to visually unite them on the graph.

Connecting Databases

In FileMaker, you can make two databases work together as easily as you work with multiple tables. Using the data tunneling techniques discussed in the previous section, you connect tables from another file (often called an *external database*) without the overhead of copying all that data into your file. You simply put a table occurrence from your external file onto your relationship graph, which defines its perspective in relation to all your other tables.

For example, suppose you want to connect the People database you created in Chapter 3 to your new system. You'd like a portal on the Customers layout to show all the people in the People database who live in the same state as that customer. After all, you never know when one of your leads will come in handy.

POWER USERS' CLINIC

The Secret Life of GTRR

The layout in Figure 8-23 is pretty slick, but there's one problem. Suppose you're on the *Expenses* layout looking at an expense. You decide you want to assign an invoice line item to it, so you switch to the "Attach Line Item to Expenses" layout. Unfortunately, when you do, you don't see the same record. Remember that each table occurrence has its own current record, found set, and sort order. You're forced to find the same record again.

It turns out the "Go to Related Record" command has an unexpected power: It can transfer a found set—complete with current record and sort order—from one table occurrence to another. The "Go to Related Record" Options window has a "Get related record from" pop-up menu that shows every table occurrence in the database. When you select an occurrence, you get a list of layouts to switch to. But this list isn't restricted to layouts attached to the selected table occurrence. It shows layouts attached to any occurrence of the same table. In other words, when you ask to go to a record in the Expenses table occurrence, you can pick the "Attach Line Item to Expenses" layout, even though it's associated with a different occurrence of the Expenses table.

When you use this technique, FileMaker shows the records dictated by the relationship, but uses the layout you choose. To make the connection, add a button to the Expenses layout that runs the "Go to Related Record" command. When you set up the button, choose the Expenses table occurrence and the "Attach Line Item to Expenses" layout. Also, make sure you turn on "Show only related records." FileMaker does all the rest of the work for you.

You can also add a button to the Attach Line Item layout that transports you *back* to the Expenses layout. This time you configure the "Go to Related Record" command to use the Assign Expenses_EXPENSES table occurrence and the Expenses layout.

Adding a Table Occurrence from Another File

Creating a cross-database relationship is as easy as adding a table occurrence. Once you have the People table on the relationships graph (in the Manage Database dialog box), it begins to act like a first-class citizen in its new environment: You can create relationships to it, attach layouts to it, and just about anything else you can do with the tables in this database. Here's how:

1. **In the Mars Investigations database, bring up the Relationships tab of the Manage Database window. Click the Add Table Occurrence button.**

   The Specify Table dialog box appears.

2. **From the File pop-up menu, choose Add FileMaker Data Source.**

   A standard Open File dialog box appears—just like you see when you're opening a database. To use a table from another file, you have to add a *file reference*. A file reference is just a way to tell FileMaker where you store the external databases it needs to interact with.

3. **Browse to the People database, select it, and click Open.**

   Use a copy of People from Chapter 1, or download a copy at *www.missingmanuals.com/cds*. The Specify Table dialog box now shows tables from the People database (it has only one).

Note: File references aren't dynamic. That is, if you move the files from the location in your file reference, then you need to manually update the reference for the new location so FileMaker can find it. Just choose File → Manage File References and double-click the file reference to edit it.

4. **Select the People table, rename the new TO "Other Leads", and then click OK.**

   FileMaker adds the new occurrence to the graph. As Figure 8-24 attests, you can tell at a glance that it's an occurrence of what FileMaker calls an *external* table because it shows you the table occurrence's name in italics.

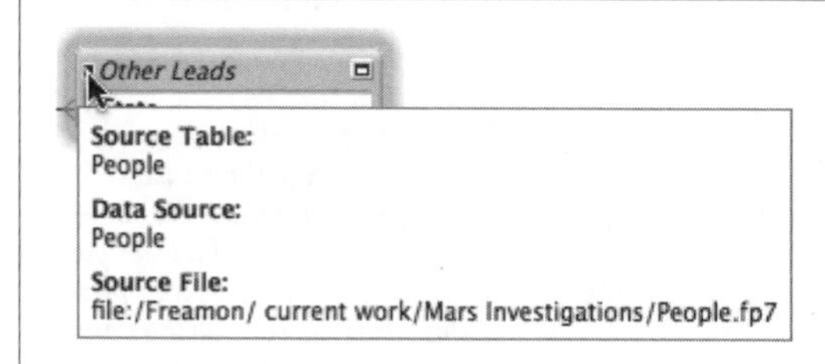

Figure 8-24: *External tables' names display in italics. To find out which database it comes from, point to the little arrow to the left of the name to show the information window. FileMaker displays the source table's name, the Data Source (or filename) and the path.*

Tip: You can double-click the People table occurrence and change its name to Other Leads to better reflect its meaning in this table occurrence group.

5. **In the relationship graph, drag the State field from the People table to the Customers::State field.**

   Now that the People table is in the graph, attaching it to the Customers table works just like every other relationship you've ever created.

You can use this relationship like any other. For example, you could create a portal, as shown in Figure 8-25.

Defining Data Sources Using a Path

Normally you create a file reference by choosing the file from your hard drive. If you want, though, you can type in a *path* instead (choose File → Manage → External

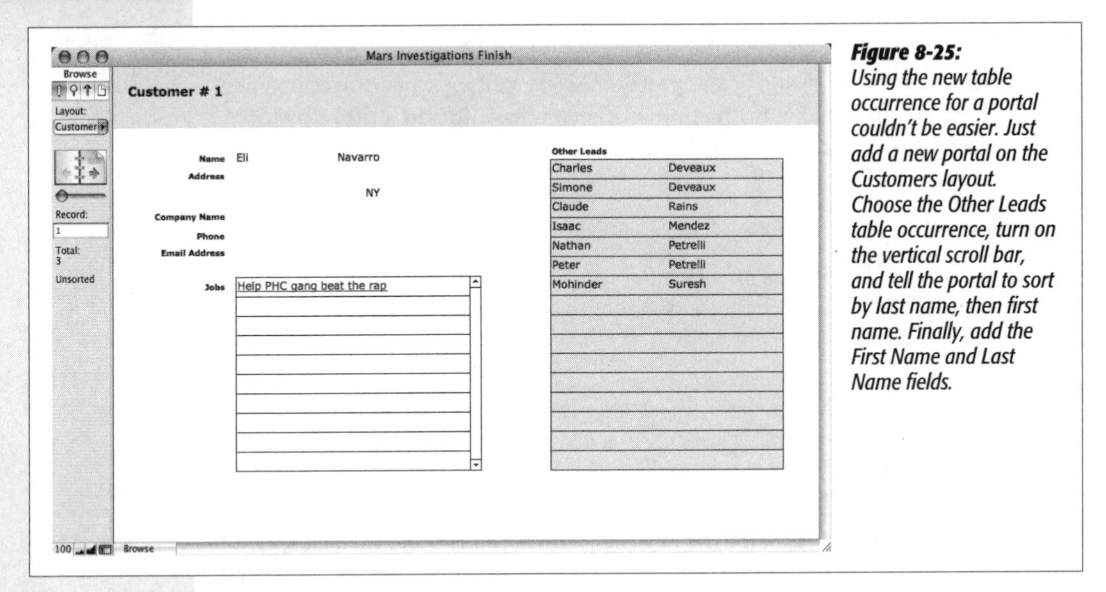

Figure 8-25: *Using the new table occurrence for a portal couldn't be easier. Just add a new portal on the Customers layout. Choose the Other Leads table occurrence, turn on the vertical scroll bar, and tell the portal to sort by last name, then first name. Finally, add the First Name and Last Name fields.*

Data Sources, then click New). FileMaker looks for the file at the specified location. The format of a path varies depending on what platform you're using and how you're accessing the file. FileMaker gives you an example of each path format at the bottom of the Manage External Data Source dialog box (Figure 8-26).

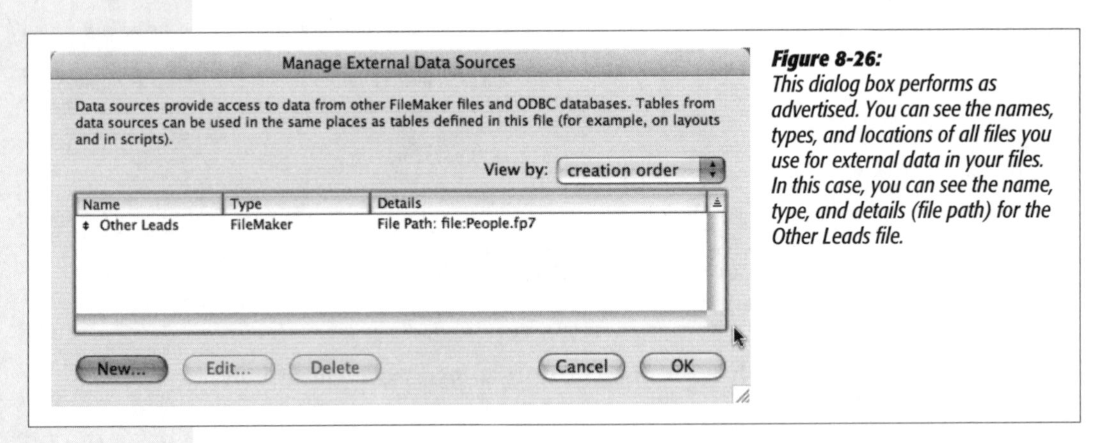

Figure 8-26: *This dialog box performs as advertised. You can see the names, types, and locations of all files you use for external data in your files. In this case, you can see the name, type, and details (file path) for the Other Leads file.*

You can even give a file reference more than one path. When you do, FileMaker looks for the file at the first path. If it doesn't find the file, it tries the second path. The search continues until it finds the file or tries every listed path. (If it never finds the file, you'll see an error message.) Using this technique, you can have a database that opens files from different locations depending on which computer it's opened on. Or you can ask FileMaker to use your local copy of the People database if it finds one, and to use the network copy otherwise. (You'll learn about sharing databases on a network in Chapter 16).

POWER USERS' CLINIC

Systems with More than One Database

Even if you're building a brand-new system from scratch, there's no rule that says every table has to be in the same database. In fact, you have many good reasons to divide your system across multiple files (Figure 8-27). The last chapter talked about one of those reasons: You might be storing large images or other files in your database. You can keep these files in an external table so the database file itself isn't so large. Then you can back up, copy, and email the information about the images without including the images themselves.

Here are some other reasons to use more than one file:

- **You can create a database for each kind of interface you need.** For example, if you need to track sales, you can create a database with the tables you need to store the actual data: orders, line items, customers, shipments, products, and so forth. You can use this database in two ways, though: sales entry (creating and managing orders) and reporting (daily, monthly, and quarterly sales reports, trend and promotion analysis, and so on). To keep your system as simple as possible, you can create these separate interfaces as two distinct databases. Since they share the tables from the central sales database, the reporting data stays up-to-date as FileMaker processes new sales. But since they're in two databases, the layouts you need for order entry don't get in the way of the reporting layouts, and vice versa.
- **One company usually has many database needs.** You might have Sales, Marketing, and Engineering departments in your organization. Each of these departments has unique needs and wants a database to match them. But the Marketing department might be very interested in sales data, and the Sales department needs access to engineering information. You can create a separate database for each department, but share some tables between systems. This way you get an interface tailored to each group, but the important data is shared.
- **When you can use external table occurrences, you have a very flexible design metaphor.** A database—or file—can hold interface elements (layouts, scripts, value lists) or data (tables and fields) or both. You can construct the database in almost any way you see fit: one file for each table, all tables in one file, or tables in logical groupings; all the interface in one database, or several databases to break things up. A FileMaker file is a very flexible unit of organization: Use it as you see fit.

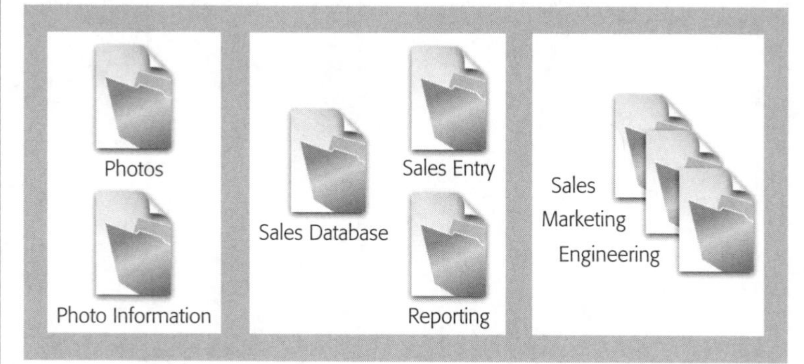

***Figure 8-27:** The great thing about separating tables into different files is that you can keep file sizes smaller and more manageable. In this arrangement, photo files, which take up lots of space, are in a separate file. Even the data for each photo is in a separate table. That way, the Photo table doesn't have to be backed up as often as other files. See the box above for rules of thumb for dividing data into multiple files.*

Lookups

Since you have a relationship between the Jobs and Customers tables (page 329), you don't have to enter customer information on each job record. Instead, FileMaker shows the same customer fields for each related job. If you update the customer's first name, the new name automatically shows on the Jobs layout. This dynamic updating of related data is the essence of a relational database. However, many times you *don't* want a piece of information to change; you want FileMaker to remember the way it was at a certain point in time. *Lookup fields*, which use relationships as a source for a sort of one-time copy-and-paste action, let you take a piece of data from a table *and* protect it from future updates.

Take a look at the Invoices table, for example. When you create an invoice, you attach it to a job. The job is in turn attached to a customer. When it comes time to mail the invoice, you could easily put the address fields from the Customers table occurrence on the Invoice layout and see the customer's address. But this method is a bad idea for two reasons:

- **It doesn't allow for special circumstances.** If a customer tells you he's going to be in Majorca for a month and to please send his next invoice there, you have no way to enter an alternate address on just one invoice. You have to change the address in his customer record, send the invoice, and then change the address back.
- **It destroys relevant information.** When you *do* update the customer record with his original home address, you lose any record of where you sent the invoice. If you go back to the special-case invoice two years from now, it will *look* like you sent it to his home address. But that's not correct.

UP TO SPEED

Empty Lookups

Lookup options give you some control over what happens when there's no matching related record. Normally, if FileMaker tries to find a related record to look up data from and it can't find one, it just leaves the lookup field alone.

That's what happens when you turn on "do not copy" in the "If no exact match, then" group of radio buttons. Here's what the others do:

- The "copy next lower value" option looks at the closest *lower* related record. For example, if you turn it on for the Invoices::Street Address field and there's no matching related customer, FileMaker copies the address of the customer with the next lower Customer ID alphabetically. In this case, it makes absolutely no sense.

But what if you were looking up price information based on quantity? If the customer orders 38, but you have pricing for 30 or 40, you might want to get the price for 30 items, the next lower value.

- The "copy next higher value" option works just like its similarly named counterpart. It just copies the value from the next *higher* related record instead. People don't use these two options a lot, but they sometimes come in very handy.
- The "use" option lets you specify any value you want to substitute for a missing related value. For example, if you're looking up customer age information and you don't have an age for one person, you can tell FileMaker to use "N/A" instead.

These problems arise because invoice data is *transactional*—an invoice represents a single business transaction at one point in the past. But your customer record doesn't represent a single transaction with your customer. Instead, it represents an association you have with that customer. In general, transactional data should *never* change once the transaction is complete. Lookup fields solve the problem of saving transactional data.

While related fields automatically show new data, lookups use a semi-automatic approach. If you change a customer record, it *won't* affect the fields in the Invoices record at all. But if you change the Job ID on an *invoice* record, the lookup triggers again, and FileMaker fetches the new customer's data. Additionally, you can *change* the data in a field formatted with Auto-Enter lookup at any time—for a one-time address change, for example. This semi-automatic approach to updating data turns out to be just the right thing for transactional data like address fields on invoices: When you change the *transaction* record, its fields update appropriately, but when you change *source* records (the address fields in your customer record), FileMaker leaves the transaction alone.

POWER USERS' CLINIC

Going to External Records

Now that you've got a file reference and a table occurrence from an external file, what do you do with it? You *could* create a new layout attached to the Other Leads table occurrence and fill it with fields from the People table. But you already have a great layout for viewing the details of a People record: the Detail layout in the People database.

Once again, "Go to Related Records" comes to the rescue (see Figure 8-28). First, turn the First Name and Last Name fields on the Other Leads portal into a button that performs the "Go to Related Record" command. In the "Go to Related Record" Options window, choose the Other Leads table occurrence. Since this is an occurrence of an external table, the "Use external table's layout" checkbox comes to life.

When this checkbox is turned on, the "Show record using layout" pop-up menu lists layouts from the People database rather than this database. Turn the checkbox on and choose the Detail layout. Don't forget to turn on "Show only related records".

Now when you click a person's name, the People database pops up and shows you the correct person. Like magic!

Creating Lookups

To create a lookup, you define a field normally but add an Auto-Enter option called *Looked-up value*. You can also add a lookup to an existing field. Simply click the field in the fields list, and then click the Options button. The following steps explain how to create a new lookup field:

1. **In the Customers database, choose File → Manage Database. On the Fields tab, choose Invoices from the Table pop-up menu.**

   You see the fields in the Invoices table—and you're ready to add a new one. You start by adding a lookup field for the customer's street address.

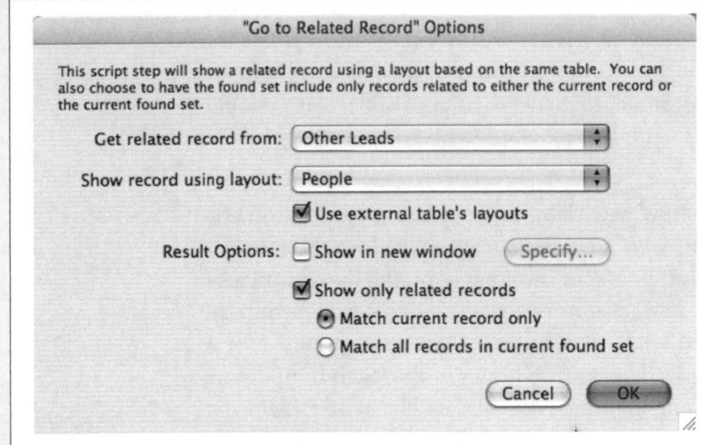

Figure 8-28: *The "Use external table's layouts" option packs a lot of punch in your "Go To Related Record" commands. You can access work you've already done by showing data in its original form—its native layout in its source file. If you also choose the "Show in new window" option, you can leave the found set showing in your original window while you scour the external file to mine its treasures.*

2. **In the Field Name box, enter *Street Address* and make sure the Type pop-up menu is set to Text. Click Create.**

   FileMaker adds the new field to the field list. Right now, though, it's just an ordinary field.

3. **Click the Options button. In the Field Options dialog box, click the Auto-Enter tab.**

   The Options dialog box appears. You'll create the lookup here.

4. **Turn on the "Looked-up value" checkbox.**

   The Lookup dialog box appears (Figure 8-29).

Lookup for Field "Street Address"

Use a lookup to copy a value from a field in another table based on the relationships defined between these tables:

Starting with table: Invoices

Lookup from related table: Customers

(When a new entry is made in the field "Job ID", this lookup will copy the value from the first matching related record in the table "Customers".)

Copy value from field:

::Customer ID
::First Name
::Last Name
::Company Name
::Street Address
::City
::State
::Zip Code
::Phone Number

If no exact match, then:

do not copy
copy next lower value
copy next higher value
use

Don't copy contents if empty

Cancel
OK

Figure 8-29: *This is what your Lookup dialog box looks like when you're done. There are lots of ways to use lookups. Imagine you have a table of currency exchange rates. Some of the currencies don't have data available the day you gather the rates, so those rate fields are blank. If you use a lookup to refresh exchange rates in your Products database, you don't want to wipe out the previous exchange rate, which you entered last week. Instead, you'd rather keep last week's value, so you turn on the "Don't copy contents if empty" option.*

5. **Make sure the "Starting with table" pop-up menu is set to Invoices.**

   It almost certainly is set properly, because in this case, the context is clear. You're defining a field in the Invoices table, so that's the field's context. If you have a table on the graph multiple times, you might have to change the "Starting with table" pop-up, and doing so will influence how the lookup finds related data.

6. **From the "Lookup from related table" pop-up menu, choose Customers.**

   As soon as you choose a table, the "Copy value from field" list is populated with all the fields in the Customers table. You're interested in the Street Address field's value.

7. **In the "Copy value from field" list, choose Street Address. Turn off the "Don't copy contents if empty" checkbox.**

   When you turn off "Don't copy contents if empty," FileMaker dutifully copies the empty value, wiping out data in the lookup field. If you turn this option on instead, FileMaker leaves the lookup field untouched—its value before the lookup remains in place.

8. **In the "If no exact match, then" group, turn on the "use" radio button and leave the associated text box empty.**

   If there is no customer record, the street address field should be blank. If you leave this set to "do not copy", any existing address (for a different customer perhaps) is left in the field. (See the box on page 386 for other "If no exact match, then" options.)

You're done. Click OK three times to back out of all the dialog boxes. Now switch to the Invoices layout and add the new field to it (page 193). When you choose a job from the Jobs table, the Invoices address field now looks up the appropriate address from the Customer table, provided you've entered addresses for your customers.

Note: If you're not using the version of this database from the Missing Manuals Web site that's pre-populated with data (download it at *www.missingmanuals.com/cds*) and you want to see this in action, give one of your customers some address information and a job.

To finish your Invoices improvements, add lookup fields for the following customer information. Use the same options as in the steps on the previous pages, or—to save clicks—duplicate the Street Address field, change its name, and then just change the field from which it looks up. You get all the other lookup settings for free. When you're done, you can arrange your Invoices layout like the one in Figure 8-30.

- Company Name
- First Name
- Last Name

- City
- State
- Zip Code

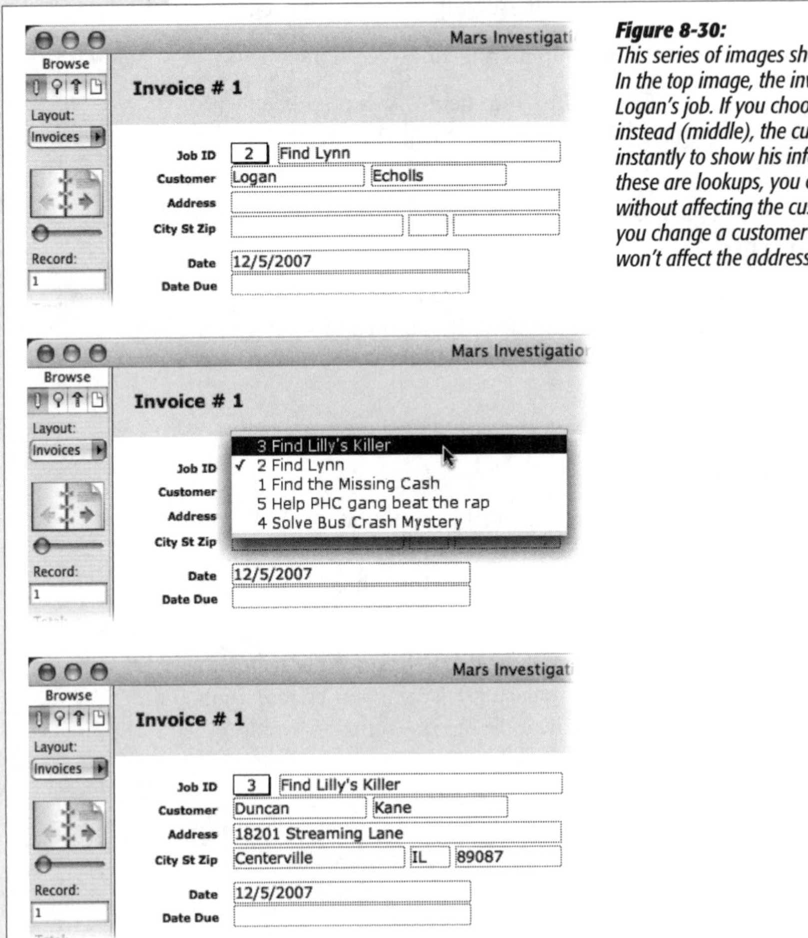

Figure 8-30: *This series of images shows your lookups in action. In the top image, the invoice is associated with Logan's job. If you choose a job tied to Duncan instead (middle), the customer fields update instantly to show his information (bottom). Since these are lookups, you can change them right here without affecting the customer record itself. And if you change a customer's address in the future, it won't affect the address on this invoice.*

Triggering a Lookup

Normally you trigger a lookup whenever you change the data in the key field on which the relationship is based. That's why changing the Job ID field makes FileMaker look up the address information again.

Sometimes you have a reason to cause a lookup to occur *without* changing the key field. For example, suppose a new customer hires you. You do work for her for three months, but never receive payment—despite sending three invoices. You finally decide it's time to ask her what's up, and that's when you discover you've been sending them to the *wrong address*. You mistyped her address in the Customers layout and now all your invoices are incorrect, too.

She agrees to pay you as soon as you mail the invoices to her correct address. You can correct her address in the Customers table, but that doesn't affect the old invoices. Luckily, you can easily fix them, too—with the Relookup Field Contents command. To use it, you click inside the field that normally triggers the lookup—the Job ID field in this case. Then you choose Records → Relookup Field Contents command. You see the message shown in Figure 8-31.

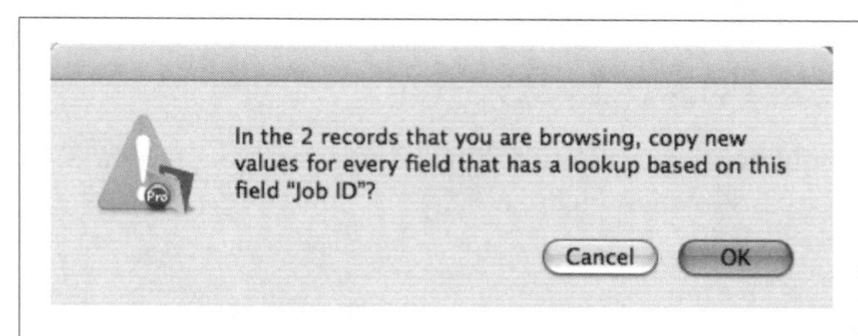
In the 2 records that you are browsing, copy new values for every field that has a lookup based on this field "Job ID"?
Cancel
OK

Figure 8-31: *When you run the Relookup Field Contents command, FileMaker shows this message. It's careful to let you know just how many records you'll be updating. That's because you can't undo this action. If you lookup new address information into old invoices accidentally, you lose historical data. If you're sure you want to proceed, click OK.*

Tip: To get into the Job ID field, just click it and be sure to choose the job that's already selected. After you make your choice, the Relookup Field Contents command works as expected.

Advanced Relationships

In this chapter and the previous one, you've only created simple relationships with one rule and keys that match exactly. But you can create relationships that go far beyond those basic concepts. And even if you don't have a very complicated database, you should know how these advanced relationships work.

For example, you might have a table of Student Test Scores that contains all the tests for every kid in your school. You can view a classroom's scores on a specific test by making a relationship that matches two key fields: the Classroom ID and the Test ID. You can also find all the kids who're failing by matching every test score that's less than 70 points. Sure, you can perform a search in your Test Scores table and add some summary fields to a report to do the same tasks, but you're limited by the fact that the subsummary parts and their fields don't show up in Browse mode, and by the need to perform the search again every time you want to see the data. With the techniques below, you can make this data available with just the switch of a layout or a "Go to Related Record" command (page 358).

Relationships with More than One Criterion

First, you can assign more than one rule to a relationship. For instance, you already added a relationship between Customers and People that matches based on state. Suppose you want to be more restrictive: You want to show only people who live in the same *city* and state.

It's easier than it sounds:

1. **In the Mars Investigations database, go to the Manage Database window's Relationships tab (page 329), and select the relationship line between Customers and Other Leads.**

   The easiest way to select a relationship is to click the "=" box in the middle of the line (it provides a nice big target). When you select the relationship, the line gets slightly thicker and the box gets highlighted.

2. **Click the Edit Relationship button** (page 353).

   You can also just double-click the relationship. Either way, you see the Edit Relationship dialog box, as shown in Figure 8-32.

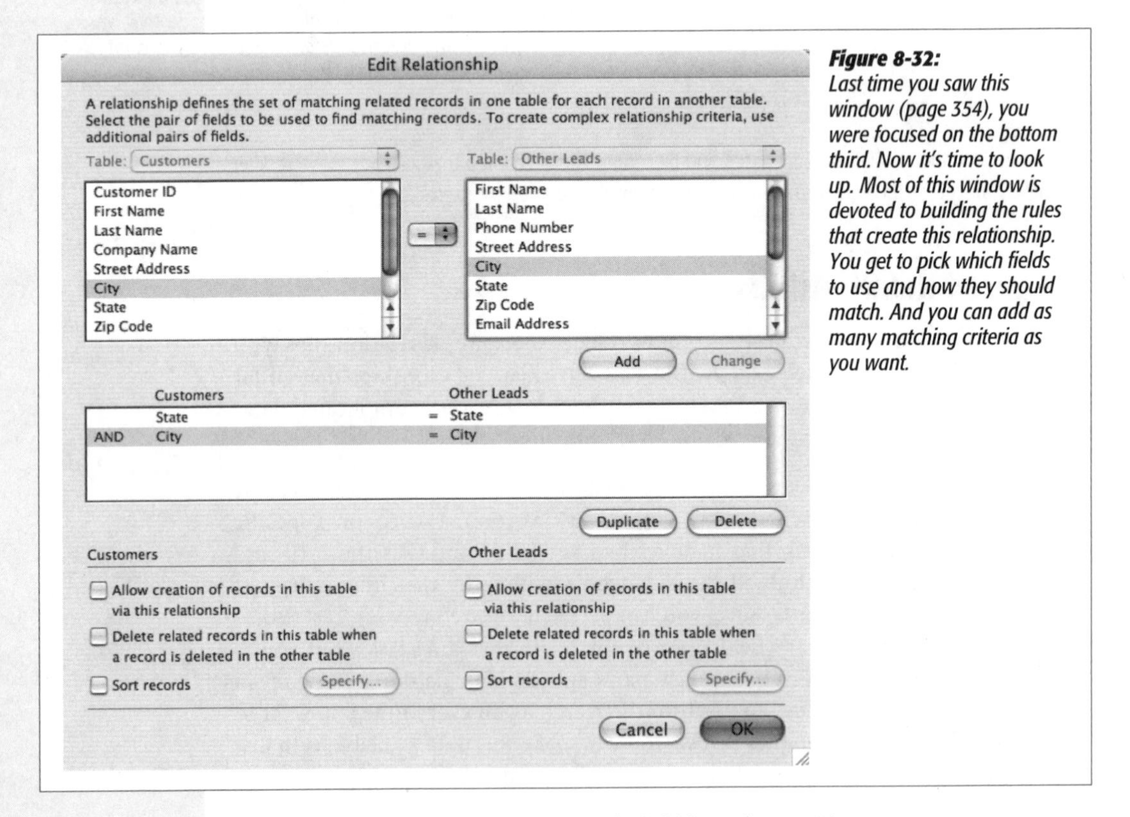

Figure 8-32: *Last time you saw this window (page 354), you were focused on the bottom third. Now it's time to look up. Most of this window is devoted to building the rules that create this relationship. You get to pick which fields to use and how they should match. And you can add as many matching criteria as you want.*

3. **In the Customer table occurrence's field list, choose City.**

   The City field gets highlighted.

4. **In the Other Lead table occurrence's field list, choose City.**

   You've now described a new criterion for your rule: *Customers::City = Other Leads::City*

Note: The Edit Relationship dialog box tries to mimic the layout you've created on your relationships graph. That is, if your Customers TO is to the left of your People TO in the graph, that's how they'll appear in the dialog box. If two TOs are on top of one another (vertically aligned), then the table on top appears at the left of the dialog box. The order shown in these lists has no effect on how the TOs relate to one another, but if you're having trouble reading this dialog box, close it, rearrange your graph, and reopen it.

5. **Click the Add button.**

   FileMaker adds this criterion to the criteria list. You now have *two* criteria for this relationship:

   ```
   Customers::State = Other Leads::State
   AND
   Customers::City = Other Leads::City
   ```

6. **Click OK.**

   FileMaker uncovers the relationship graph.

You've just created a relationship with *two* criteria, sometimes called a *multi-key relationship* because it uses two key fields. In order for two records to relate, they must meet *both* criteria. In other words, a person must be in the same city *and* the same state as a customer to show up in his portal. Figure 8-33 shows the new relationship in the graph.

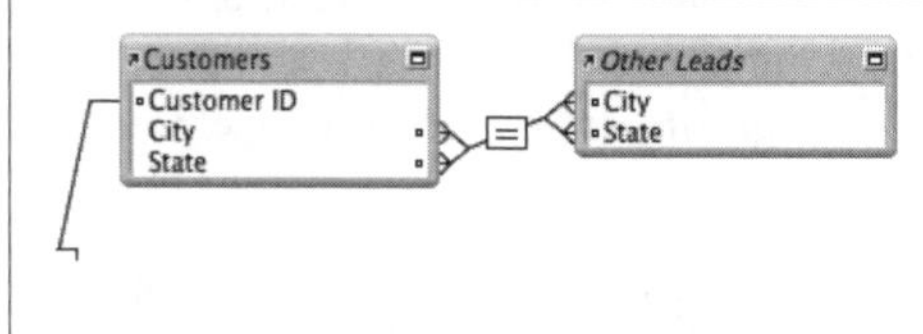

Figure 8-33: *When a relationship is based on more than one criterion—like this one between Customers and Other Leads—FileMaker forks the relationship line on each end. From this line, you can see that City matches City and State matches State. The = sign in the box in the middle of the line tells you that the data in both fields must match exactly.*

If you test your Other Leads portal now, it shows only people living in the customer's city.

Other Relationship Operators

In addition to adding more rules to a relationship definition (by defining multiple criteria), you can also base relationships on different *kinds* of rules. Each relationship in your ER diagram for your database mandates that the fields on either side match exactly. This type of relationship is called an *equijoin*, in honor of the = sign that defines it. Sometimes, though, you want to relate records without an exact match. When you make a non-equijoin relationship (don't you just love technical terms?), you use FileMaker's other comparative operators:

- **Equals (=).** The keys on both sides of the relationship match exactly.
- **Not Equals (≠).** All records but those with matching keys relate to one another.

- **Less Than** (<). Keys in the table on the left side of the dialog box must be less than keys in the table on the right side.
- **Less Than or Equal To** (≤). Keys in the table on the left side of the dialog box must be less than or equal to the keys on the right side of the table.
- **Greater Than** (>). Keys in the table on the left side of the dialog box must be greater than keys in the table on the right side.
- **Greater Than or Equal To** (≥). Keys in the table on the left side of the dialog box must be greater than or equal to the keys on the right side of the table.
- **Cartesian Join** (x). All records in the table on the left are related to all records in the table on the right, regardless of the value in their key fields.

As you work with your database, you might decide you need a quicker way to find invoices. You often want to see every invoice in a specified date range, and sometimes only those that are above a certain total amount due. Using relationships, you can create a new layout that makes it easy for you to see the invoices you want. You enter a start date and an end date into global fields, and a portal displays every matching invoice.

Creating the Invoice Finder

To set up your new relationship, you need to use the two new global fields you created on page 376. Since the global fields aren't associated with any particular table, you can create a *new* table to hold them. You also need a new relationship that matches fields in the Invoices table with these global fields. This is the sort of job that benefits from its own table occurrence group, as you saw on page 374. Call this group *Invoice Finder*.

To get the portal to show the right invoices, you need a relationship that uses your new global fields, and it'll have slightly more complicated rules than you've seen before:

```
Invoice Finder: Globals::Start Date ≤ Invoice Finder: Invoices::Date
AND
Invoice Finder: Globals::End Date ≥ Invoice Finder: Invoices::Date
```

These rules say that an invoice should match if its date is *on or after* (≥) the global start date, and if the date is *on or before* (≤) the global end date.

Below are the steps for creating a new table, defining some global fields in that new table, and then using your creations in a new table occurrence group.

You've done most of this stuff before in other tutorials, so although there are a lot of steps, they should all be pretty familiar:

1. **In the Customers database, go to the Manage Database window's Tables tab. Create a new table called Invoice Finder.**

   FileMaker adds the new table to the table list.

FREQUENTLY ASKED QUESTION

Globals and Relationships

I don't get it. I thought relationships were supposed to hook different records together, but a global field isn't associated with any record at all. How come you keep using global fields to create relationships?

When you set out to design your database in Chapter 7, you learned how to organize your information into tables and construct the relationships that make them work together. But relationships can do a whole lot more.

As the Invoice Finder example (page 394) and the "Assign Line Item to Expense" example (page 376) illustrate, relationships can be part of an overall interface (or layout) that performs a specific task. For example, when you use a global field in a relationship, it works just fine. Put an ID in the global field and FileMaker makes matches to one or more records on the other side.

This kind of relationship doesn't create a connection between records—rather, it just gives you temporary access to related records.

Since global fields can't be indexed, the relationship doesn't work in the other direction. As Figure 8-34 shows, FileMaker doesn't connect the relationship line in the graph directly to the global field. This visual cue lets you know this relationship works only one way.

One last point: If you want to use a global field from another table just to display some data on a layout, you don't need a relationship at all. Since global fields aren't associated with any record, you can view and modify them from anywhere. For example, you can put the Global Invoice ID field on any layout in the entire database, and it works just fine.

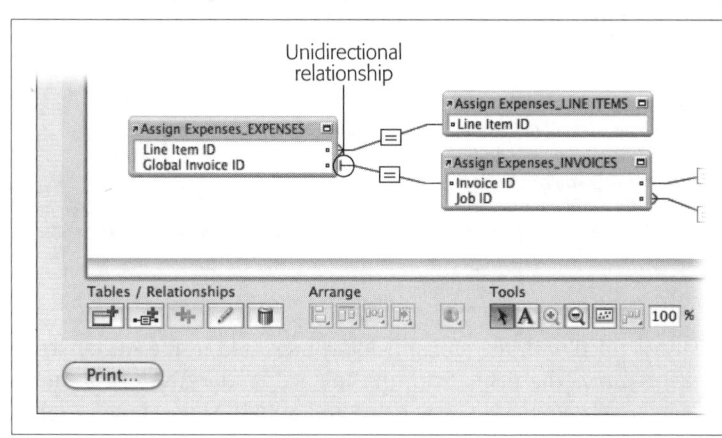

Figure 8-34: *FileMaker does its best to give you visual information about the relationships between your table occurrences. Here, the line on the Assign Expenses_EXPENSES side of the expenses-to-invoice relationship has a short gap and a bar, instead of a connected line or "fork." This tells you that the relationship will work from the Expenses side, looking over to the Invoice side, but not in reverse.*

2. **Click the Fields tab. Then, in the Field name box, enter *Start Date*. Make the field a Date type, and then click Create.**

   This field holds the starting date you're searching for.

3. **Click the Options button. When the Field Options dialog box appears, click the Storage tab and turn on the "Use global storage" checkbox. Click the OK button.**

   Since this field isn't holding data about an entity, but is used to change the records that display in a portal, you need to use a global field.

4. **Repeat steps 2–3 to create another global date field called End Date.**

   You've finished creating your global fields.

5. **Switch to the Relationships tab. Drag the Invoice Finder table occurrence down below your existing TOGs. Then double-click on it and change its name to Invoice Finder_INVOICE FINDER.**

   This new TO will become the anchor in a new TOG, so place it on the graph accordingly. You may also need to stretch the TO so its whole name appears.

6. **Add a new occurrence of the Invoices table called Invoice Finder_INVOICES, and a new occurrence of the Jobs table called Invoice Finder_JOBS.**

   Since your portal will show invoices and the job associated with each invoice, you need these tables in your group as well.

7. **Drag the Invoice Finder_INVOICES::Job ID field onto the Invoice Finder_ JOBS:: Job ID field to create a relationship.**

   You've just told FileMaker that the Job ID field relates these two tables.

8. **Click the Add/Edit Relationship button (Figure 8-35) to open the Edit Relationship dialog box. From the left table's pop-up menu, choose Invoice Finder_INVOICE FINDER. Then, from the right table's pop-up menu, choose Invoice Finder_INVOICES.**

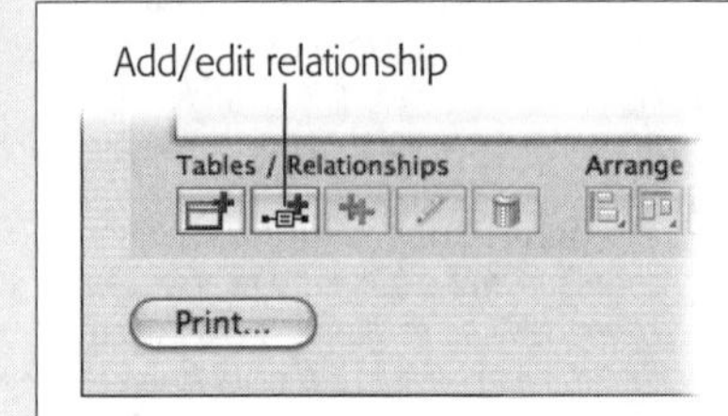

Figure 8-35:
You haven't used the Add/Edit Relationship button before because you've always used the drag-and-drop method to create relationships. But if the relationship you're creating is more complex, this button skips the drag altogether and goes straight to the Edit Relationship dialog box, so you don't have to delete or edit the equijoin relationship that FileMaker creates when you drag.

   The left-hand list is filled with the global fields you created in the earlier steps; the right-hand list shows the fields from the Invoice Finder_INVOICES table occurrence. Next, you select the two key fields and tell FileMaker how to relate these TOs.

9. **From the left-hand table field list, choose Start Date. From the Operator pop-up menu (it's between the two field lists), choose ≤.**

   This symbol tells FileMaker you want the field on the left to match when it's *less than or equal* to the field you select on the right side.

10. **From the right-hand table field list, choose Date, and then click Add.**

   The Date field tells the relationship what value to compare to the Start Date in the Globals table. In other words, you want the relationship to match only when the Start Date is *before* the Invoice Date.

Later on, you'll create a portal that uses this relationship to display only certain records. The criteria you chose tell the portal to show only invoice records that are dated on or after the date entered in the global Start Date field.

11. **Repeat the last two steps, but this time, from the left-hand table field list, choose the End Date field. From the right-hand table field list, choose the Date field, and from the Operator pop-up menu, choose the ≥. Finally, click Add.**

    When you click Add, FileMaker adds the second criteria to the list. This part tells the portal to display records that are on or before the date in the global End Date field. The relationships between the Start Date and End Date fields together determine the range of records the portal displays.

    FileMaker returns you to the graph. It should look like Figure 8-36.

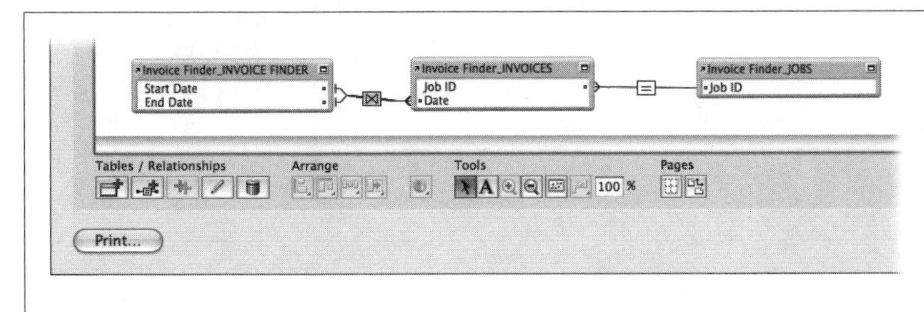

***Figure 8-36:** The relationship between Invoice Finder_INVOICE FINDER and Invoice Finder_INVOICES connects two fields to one. The box in the middle of the line now has an X instead of an equal sign, since you're using multiple operators in your relationship. If you want to refresh your memory on this multicriteria relationship, double-click on the "X" to see the Edit Relationships dialog box.*

To test your new relationship, create a new layout and attach it to the Invoice Finder_INVOICE FINDER occurrence. Add the two global fields and a portal based on the Invoice Finder_INVOICES relationship. When you put values in the two global fields, the portal updates to show the matching invoices. You can see it in action in Figure 8-37.

Note: The Invoice Finder table has no records. You might think this lack of records would be a problem, but it isn't. However, if you're not using FileMaker Pro 9, you might have a problem. In older versions, portals don't work properly when there are no records. To clear this problem up, just create a new empty record.

So what has all this work gotten you? As a designer, this technique of using global fields in a complex relationship to populate a portal has improved your understanding of relationships and tested your skill in applying that knowledge. People who use your database benefit most. Now they can see a group of invoices at a glance, without having to do a search. Next, you'll learn some techniques that you can apply to make this layout even handier. You'll learn how to create a calculation field that summarizes the value of the invoices in your portal (page 403).

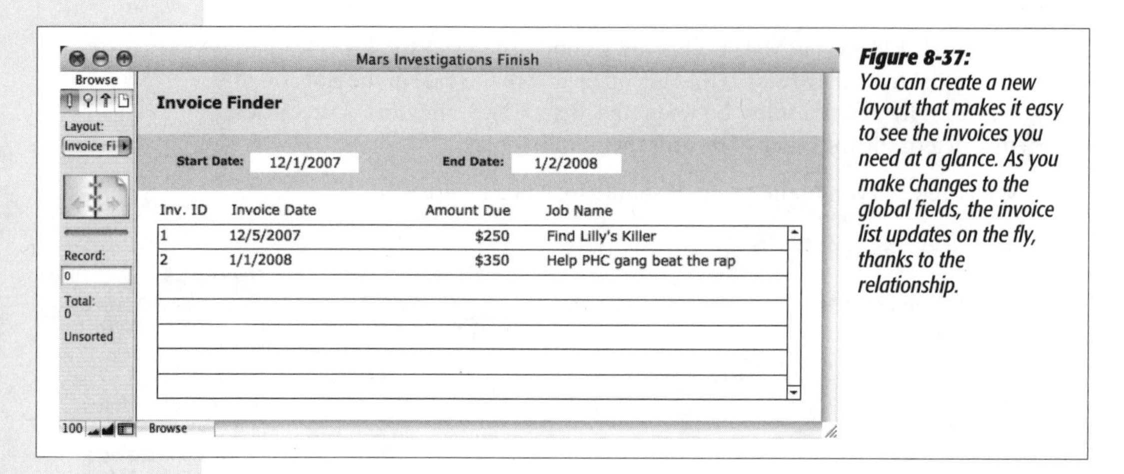

Figure 8-37: *You can create a new layout that makes it easy to see the invoices you need at a glance. As you make changes to the global fields, the invoice list updates on the fly, thanks to the relationship.*

4

Part Four: Introduction to Calculations

CHAPTER

9

Introduction to Calculations

Fields and layouts form the basis of every database: You can't have a FileMaker database without them. Using just what you know so far, you can build all kinds of useful systems that store data, from an address list to a catalog of products.

But if you want to do the really useful stuff with your data—total an invoice, analyze trends, compare figures—you need specific tools. For those tasks, FileMaker provides *calculation fields* and a whole drawer full of functions that let you examine, compare, and combine field values. And calculations aren't just limited to number-crunching tasks. You can use them to find out about the computer your database is running on, track who's logged into the system, monitor their privileges, and then perform logical tests based on what you find. You'll start by learning how FileMaker handles calculations, and then you'll see how some common functions can take your database up to a new level of power.

Understanding Calculations

A calculation is a mathematical formula: It shows how different things combine to come up with an answer. But even if you hated algebra class, don't close the book yet! Instead of the Xs, Ys, and Zs of the math world, FileMaker lets you use your own fields to supply your formula with data—a much more intuitive approach.

FileMaker calculations can also do more than just math. For starters, you can do calculations on time, date, timestamp, container, and text fields, too. (See the box on page 405 for an example.) Way back in Chapter 3, you learned that FileMaker can create *calculation fields* (see page 104). Calculation fields work just like any other FileMaker field, except that you can't type data into them. Instead, they use a calculation to determine their own value.

You can use a calculation field just like any other field: Put it on a layout, use it in Find mode, and even use it in *other* calculation fields. But as a calculation field, its value always stays up-to-date automatically. If the price or quantity changes, the calculation updates the data in your field without you doing anything. Figure 9-1 shows where calculation fields could benefit your invoices' layout.

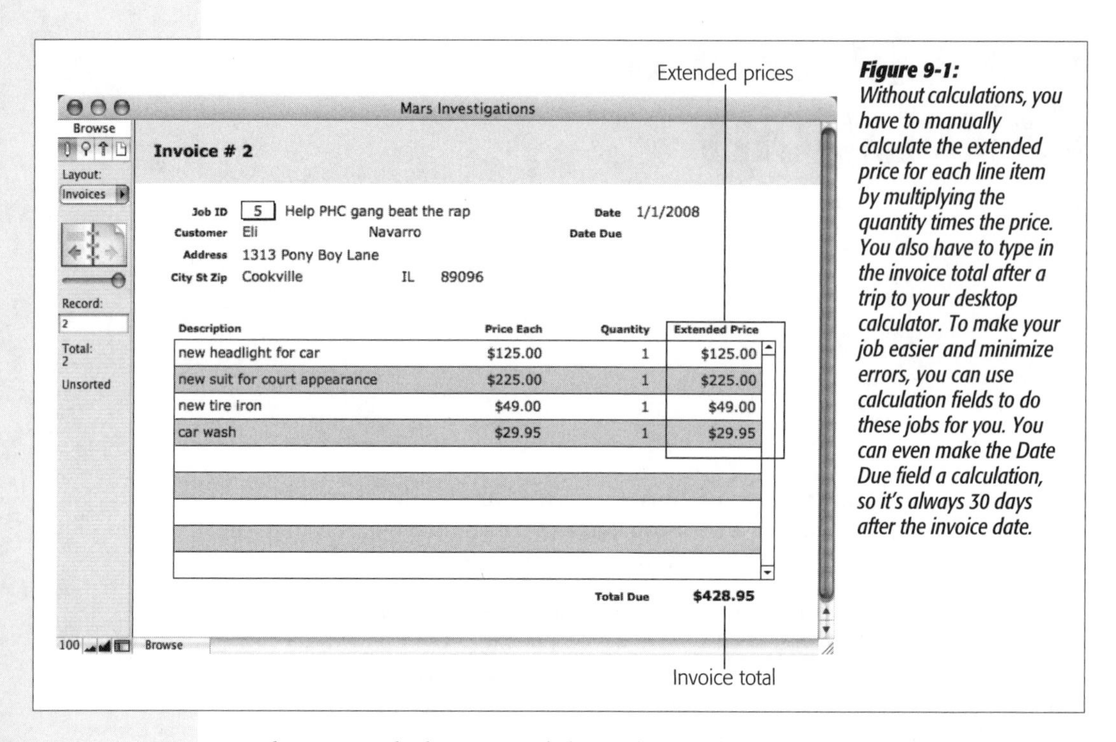

Figure 9-1: *Without calculations, you have to manually calculate the extended price for each line item by multiplying the quantity times the price. You also have to type in the invoice total after a trip to your desktop calculator. To make your job easier and minimize errors, you can use calculation fields to do these jobs for you. You can even make the Date Due field a calculation, so it's always 30 days after the invoice date.*

Furthermore, calculations aren't limited to working inside fields. Once you understand the basic concept of calculations, you gain all kinds of new FileMaker skills. For example, you can use calculations with the Records → Replace Field Contents command (see page 56). Instead of replacing the data in every record with the *same* value, the calculation can produce a unique value for each record. You can start using the Auto-Enter Calculation and Validation Calculation field options, making those features much more powerful. Scripts, as you'll learn in Part 5, use calculations a lot. And finally, if you're using FileMaker Advanced, you can use calculations to create custom menus and custom menu commands (see page 724).

Creating a Calculation

A simple example speaks louder than several pages of explanation, so you start off by adding a *calculation* to an existing number field to the database you built in Chapters 7 and 8. As your database now stands, when you add line items to an invoice, you have to type the quantity, price for each item, *and* the extended price, as shown in Figure 9-1. But since the extended price is always the price times the quantity, why not let FileMaker handle the repetitive work while you do the creative stuff?

Note: To work through the examples in this chapter, you can download the Mars Investigates database from the "Missing CD" page at *www.missingmanuals.com*.

Here's how you add a calculation to a number field:

1. **In the Mars Investigations database, choose File → Manage Database, and make sure you're on the Fields tab. From the Table pop-up menu, choose Line Items.**

   That's the table with your Extended Price field in it.

2. **In the field list, select the Extended Price field. From the Type pop-up menu, choose Calculation, and then click Change.**

   FileMaker warns you that when it converts the field, it changes (read: deletes) any information already in the field. See Figure 9-2.

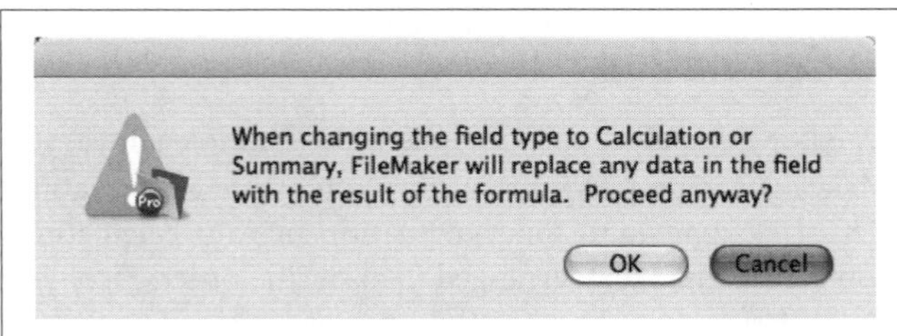

Figure 9-2: *This warning is serious. Your new calculation overwrites existing data. But even if you write a calculation, there's a way out, so long as you haven't OK'd the Manage Database dialog box. Just click its Cancel button, and you'll get the chance to discard all the changes you've made in the dialog box.*

3. **Click OK.**

   As shown in Figure 9-3, FileMaker asks you what calculation you have in mind.

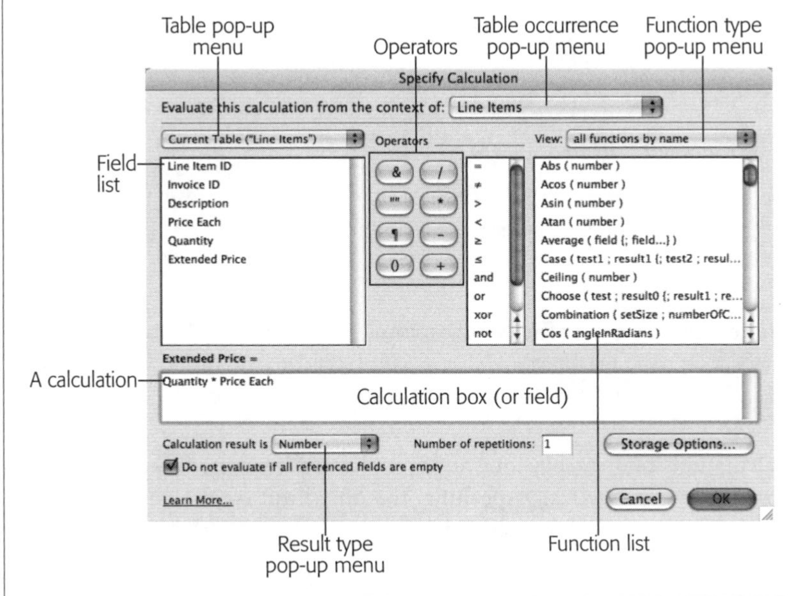

Figure 9-3: *Any time you edit a calculation, you see a window just like this one. There are lots of tools here, all focused on helping you create a calculation. You'll learn how to use all these options in the rest of this chapter.*

4. **In the Calculation Box, type *Price Each * Quantity*.**

   Although case doesn't matter, spelling and spacing do. You've just added a brand-new calculation that multiplies the contents of the Price Each by the contents of the Quantity field.

5. **In the Manage Database window, click OK, and then OK again.**

   You're now back in your database. Switch to the Invoices layout and add a line item. You see that the Extended Price field updates *automatically* to reflect the proper price.

Tip: If FileMaker complains about not being able to find a field when you click OK, check the spelling of your field names. And if you hate to type, you can double-click the fields in your field list and have FileMaker handle the tedious stuff.

The Structure of a Calculation

If you accidentally mistyped or misspelled a field name in the example above, you already know that FileMaker is a little picky about how you create a calculation. Clearly, syntax (the order of elements and the punctuation in your calculation) matters. Still, a calculation is really just text, arranged in a specific order. Here you learn the basic parts of a calculation through a couple examples.

Note: Calculations are often called *calcs* for short, or *formulas*. Although there are some slight differences between a calculation and a formula, people usually use the terms interchangeably. Sometimes, a formula is so useful, or common, that FileMaker defines it as a reusable formula, also known as a *function* (see page 412).

A calculation can be short and simple:

```
Pi * Diameter
```

Or it can be more complicated:

```
Case ( Shape = "Circle" ; Pi * (Diameter/2) ^ 2 ;
Shape = "Rectangle" ; ShapeLength * Width ;
)
```

Note: FileMaker won't let you give a field the same name as an existing function. The field containing the length of a rectangular object has the unwieldy name "ShapeLength" to avoid confusion with FileMaker's *length* function. The field name "Width" is fine, because there's no width function.

In fact, calculations can be *really* long and complicated if you need them to be—up to 30,000 characters. Practically speaking, the only limit on the complexity of a calculation is your patience for creating it.

FREQUENTLY ASKED QUESTION

Text Calculations?

Aren't calculations just for numbers?

Many people see the Manage Database window's Calculation field type and assume it's for numbers. Too bad, because calculations can do all this:

- Calculations can pick apart *text* and put it together in different ways (in the next chapter, you'll use a calculation to make a Web address that links to a customer's address map). You can even modify fonts, sizes, colors, and styles (turn every occurrence of the word "FileMaker" to bold text, for instance).
- You can do math on *dates, times*, and *timestamps*. You can find out how old someone is based on their birth date, figure out how long you worked on a job, or see which payment came first.
- Using calculations, you can use summary values (page 286) without switching to Preview mode.
- If you've stored a reference to a file in a *container* field, you can use a calculation to retrieve the *path* to the original file.

You can even convert one kind of value into another when you use calculations. For example, if you have a text field that contains *12/29/2001*, you can use a calculation to turn that date into a proper date value.

So you see, calculations can do much more than add a few numbers together.

Regardless of its complexity, a calculation, or formula, is made up of three different elements: *field references, constants*, and *operators*. In the first example, "Pi" is a constant, "*" is an operator, and "Diameter" is the name of a field. The second example uses a function, called a case statement. In that example, "Shape" and "Diameter" are field references, "Circle" and "2" are constants, and "=," "*," and "^" are operators.

Field references have *values* that FileMaker replaces in the formula once it goes to work on your formula. First, all the values are replaced, then the operators tell FileMaker what to do to those values, and finally, FileMaker returns a *result* in your field.

You'll see these terms again in the next few chapters. Here are some helpful definitions:

- **Field References** are just what they sound like. They refer FileMaker to the data in the field you're referring to. Since the data inside those fields may change on each record in your database, the values that get replaced in each record are different and may yield a different result.
- **Constants** stay the same each time FileMaker does the calculation. See page 406 for details.
- **Operators** tell FileMaker how to treat the values in the calculation. See page 408 for a listing of operators and what they do.
- FileMaker has more than 180 defined **Functions** that you can use as shortcuts when you create your formulas. You learn about some of the most common functions later in this chapter. Chapter 11 introduces you to more advanced functions, and in Chapter 12 you learn how FileMaker Advanced lets you create your own reusable functions, called *Custom Functions*.

- Each calculation has a **Result**. This result is, in a sense, the "answer" to the calculation. The result of the first calculation above is the circumference of the circle. The second calculation is a little more complex: Its result is the area of a circle *or* a rectangle, depending on the value in the Shape field. (Don't worry if this calculation doesn't make sense to you. It will before too long.)

  The result of a calculation has a **type** (just like every field has a type). The type can be any of the standard field types—text, number, date, time, timestamp, or container—or a type called *Boolean*. A Boolean value has only two possible results: yes or no. (Chapter 10 goes into more detail about calculations and data types.)

Note: Sometimes people call a Boolean value "True or False" or "One or Zero" instead. Which term you use doesn't matter much if you just remember that there is a yes-like value and a no-like value. See page 460 for more on Boolean values.

Fields

The most exciting thing about calculations is learning all the new things you can do with the fields that hold all your data. But the underlying principle is simple: When you reference a field in a calculation, FileMaker takes the data stored in the field and uses its value when it determines the calculation's result. For example, let's say a field has this calculation:

```
First Name & " " & Last Name
```

When FileMaker performs (or *evaluates*) the calculation, it replaces the First Name and Last Name field names with the person's first and last names from a given record. The field type determines the value's type: A number field has a number value, a text field has a text value, and so forth.

Note: FileMaker uses the value *stored* in (not displayed in) a field. So if you have a number field with 3.1415926 as the stored value, and you've formatted the field on the layout to display only two decimal places, FileMaker uses all seven digits of the stored value to do its math. If you don't want it to use all those digits, use the *round* function (see page 455).

Constants

As handy as it is to refer FileMaker to a field to find the values in your calculations, you don't want to have to store everything in fields just to use it in a calculation. When a value is going to be the same for every record, it's time to call in a constant. You simply include that value right in the calculation.

Number constants

Sales tax is one of the most common constants. If you need to add sales tax to your order, you can just type the percentage right in the calculation, since it's the same for everybody:

```
Order Total * 1.0625
```

POWER USERS' CLINIC

Evaluating Calculations: Now or Later

When you use a calculation, you're asking FileMaker to do something with your fields, constants, and operators and come up with a result. In technical lingo, FileMaker *evaluates* the calculation. *When* the evaluation takes place depends on *where* in your database FileMaker encounters the calculation. Sometimes FileMaker evaluates right away, as when you're calculating an Extended Price. As soon as you type in either a price or a quantity, FileMaker tries to multiply the value. But because one of the fields is empty, the Extended Price calculation has a result of zero (because any value times zero equals zero). When you provide the second value, FileMaker immediately does the math and shows you your result.

If you create a new calculation field after you already have data in your database, FileMaker spends some time updating the calculation as soon as you go to the Manage Database dialog box and click OK. You may see a progress bar if you have a slower computer and a lot of records.

When you run the Records → Replace Field Contents command, for example, FileMaker evaluates the calculation you specify once for every record as soon as you click OK. As above, this may take a couple seconds, but it's happening just as soon as FileMaker can plow through your found set.

- Validation calculations evaluate whenever you change the field, or exit the record (you get to decide). See page 426 for more on these.
- Calculations used in scripts evaluate whenever you run the script. Part 5 of this book is all about scripts.

You can enter numbers in any of the formats supported by number fields:

- 37
- .65
- 28.3
- 6.02E23

Text constants

You can also use a constant to have FileMaker plunk some text in with your results. If you want a text value instead of a number, put it in quotes:

```
Age & " years old"
```

Everything within the quote marks is a *text constant* (some people call it a *string* as in "string of characters"). Those quote marks are very important (see the box on page 409). Suppose you have a field called First Name, and a calculation like this:

```
"This is my First Name"
```

The quote marks enclose the text that is also a field name, so the result of this calculation is always (*constantly*) "This is my First Name." FileMaker makes no connection whatsoever between the First Name field and the words "First Name" in the text, because the text is in quote marks.

Forgetting quote marks around a text string, or putting them in the wrong place, can make FileMaker whiny. If you make the following calculation:

```
"This is" my First Name
```

FileMaker shows you a warning message that says, "The specified field could not be found," when you try to click OK to close the Manage Database dialog box (Figure 9-4). The characters "my First Name" are highlighted in your calculation so you can tell exactly which part of the calculation confuses FileMaker. Move your quotes appropriately, and FileMaker stops telling you that it can't find your field reference. Here's the correct answer:

```
"This is my " & First Name
```

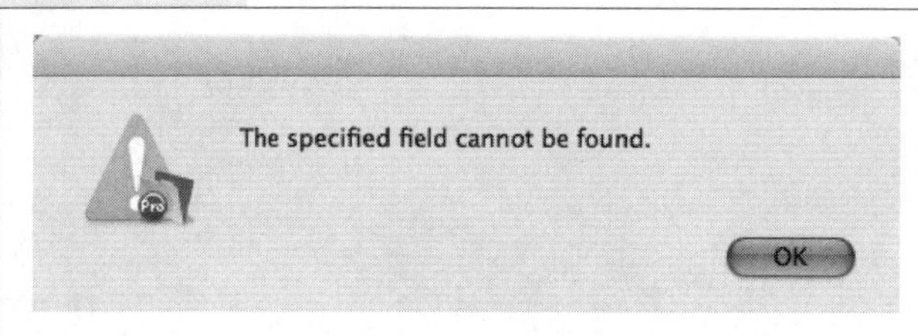

Figure 9-4: *When you click OK, FileMaker tries to evaluate your calculation. If it finds any part of the text that seems like it should be a field name, but there's no field with that name, you'll see this error message. Sometimes, you've made a typing error, but sometimes, the field you want is in another table. See page 419 for more info on referring to fields in a related table.*

Operators

If a calculation could contain only one thing, it wouldn't be much good: How often do you want to calculate a field value, number, or text value you already know? The power of calculations comes from their ability to combine different values to come up with a new and meaningful value. This situation is where *operators* come in. An operator takes the values on either side of it (the *operands*) and *does something* (operates) with them.

A special symbol or word stands for each operator. This calculation uses the + (addition) operator:

```
3 + 2
```

In this case, the + operator is given 3 and 2 as operands. When the calculation evaluates, the operator and its operands combine to produce a single value.

Operators come in three flavors:

- **Mathematical and logical operators** combine two values into one. The + operator is a good example; It takes two number values and adds them together. Its resulting value is the sum of the two numbers.
- **Comparison operators** compare two values. For example, the = operator tells you if two values are exactly the same. This kind of operator always produces a Boolean value.

- **Parenthesis** operators are used to group parts of a calculation together. Remember your eighth grade math teacher carrying on about the "order of operations"? FileMaker remembers, too, and it uses those same rules to figure out how to evaluate calculations. If the rules don't work for you, parentheses let you take more control.

FREQUENTLY ASKED QUESTION

Quotes in Quotes

You're saying that I should use quote marks to incorporate a word or a phrase into the results of a calculation. But what if I want to put a quote mark inside my text?

You're out of luck.

No, just kidding. Just put a backslash ("\") in front of the quote mark, and FileMaker pretends it doesn't exist when it analyzes your calculation. When a quote is preceded with a backslash, you say it's escaped, and "\" is called the escape character: When you put the escape character in front of another character, it tells FileMaker to ignore any special meaning that character might have and treat it as ordinary text. It looks like this:

```
"My line was, \"There's a lady with slacks
on lying in the gutter! Who does she
belong to?\" Can you believe that?"
```

This calculation is just one long text constant. The two quote marks inside it are escaped.

If you're a real troublemaker, your next question is, "What if I want to put a real backslash *and* quote mark inside my text constant?"

Luckily, that's easy, too. Just escape the backslash and then escape the quote:

```
"I really want this: \\\" inside my text"
```

This calculation evaluates to:

```
I really want this: \" inside my text
```

Note: Two buttons in the Operators section of the Specify Calculation window aren't really operators at all. The ¶ is a special character that tells FileMaker you want a new line in your calculation result, and the quote marks are for entering text values, as explained in the box above.

Mathematical operators

The most obvious use for a calculation is to do a little math. Maybe your database of products includes fields for dimensions (Length, Width, and Height), and you want to know the volume. This calculation does the trick:

```
Length * Width * Height
```

It consists of three field values and two copies of the * (multiplication) operator. The result is just what you'd get if you used a calculator to multiply the three field values together.

FileMaker includes operators for basic math:

- + for addition
- - for subtraction

- * for multiplication
- / for division
- ^ for exponentiation ("to the power of" a value)

The concatenation operator

While the mathematical operators combine numbers, the & (concatenation) operator works with text. It hooks together two text values:

```
Length & " inches"
```

If the Length field contains 36, the result of this calculation is *36 inches*.

Tip: FileMaker is such a good friend that it can mix numeric values and text together in the same calculation. If you use a number value or field in a place where FileMaker is expecting text, it just converts the number into text and gets on with its business.

Comparison operators

You often need to compare two values to learn about them. For example, you may need to add an additional shipping charge if the total weight of an order is more than 20 pounds. All comparison operators result in a Boolean value (see page 460).

FileMaker can compare things in several ways:

- = tells you if two values are the same.
- ≠ or <> tells you if the two values are different.
- > tells you if the first value is bigger than the second.
- < tells you if the second value is bigger than the first.
- ≥ or >= tells you if the first value is bigger than or equal to the second.
- ≤ or <= tells you if the second value is bigger than or equal to the first.

Logical operators

The logical operators evaluate values and come up with a Boolean (Yes/No) result (page 460). Unlike the other operators, most of them are recognizable words.

- The *and* operator tells you if both values are Yes. The calculation below uses the *and* operator. It evaluates to Yes if the length is more than 3 *and* the height is more than 5.

  ```
  Length > 3 and Height > 5
  ```

- The *or* operator tells you if *either* value is Yes. The *or* calculation below evaluates to Yes if the length is more than 3 *or* the height is more than 5.

  ```
  Length > 3 or Height > 5
  ```

- The *xor* operator's function is as offbeat as its name. It stands for *exclusive or*. The *xor* operator tells you when *only one* of your two choices is Yes. Put another way, if you find yourself thinking, "I want one of two things to be true, but *not both* of them," then *xor* saves the day. For instance, you may want to track whether you've billed a customer *or* you've marked her character rating below 3. That formula would look like this:

```
Invoice Sent = Yes xor Character Rating < 3
```

Note: If you can't think of a use for *xor*, don't worry. Most of the time when you need an "or" calculation, you can handle it with plain old *or* and not *exclusive or*.

- The last logical operator, *not*, stands alone: It works only on one value, not two like every other operator. It simply reverses the Boolean value that comes after it. So the calculation below would evaluate to Yes if the length is *not* more than 3.

```
Not Length > 3
```

Note: The comparison and logical operators are usually used with the *logical functions*. Those are covered in Chapter 10.

The ^ Operator

The last—and probably least used—operator is the exponentiation, or ^ operator. This lets you calculate exponents:

```
Pi * Radius ^ 2
```

This calculation uses the exponentiation operator and squares the value in the Radius field.

Parentheses

FileMaker uses standard mathematical rules to decide in what order to evaluate things. The order of evaluation is exponentiation, then multiplication/division, then lastly addition/subtraction. If you need FileMaker to do part of your calculation *first*, before moving onto any other operators, put it in parentheses. The parentheses tell FileMaker to treat everything between them as a single unit.

In the calculation below, FileMaker multiplies 3 and 2 before adding 4, and gives you a result of 10.

```
4 + 3 * 2
```

Even though the + operator comes first in the calculation, FileMaker follows the order of calculation. If you want to add 4 and 3 before multiplying, you need to use parentheses:

```
(4 + 3) * 2
```

Thus, it sees that it needs to add 4+3 first, then multiply by 2, for a result of 14. You can see the value of parentheses in calculations like the one below, which calculates the interest on the sum of the balance and service charge. Without the parentheses, FileMaker would calculate the interest on only the service charge and then add that to the balance due, with an entirely different result:

```
(Balance Due + Service Charge) * Interest Rate
```

Note: If you have trouble remembering (nay, understanding) the order of calculation, just use parentheses when in doubt. It certainly doesn't hurt to be *too* explicit.

Functions

Values, fields, and operators alone make for a pretty powerful combination. But if you stop there, you've only scratched the surface. The meat of calculations is found in the Function list (which you saw briefly back in Figure 9-3). A *function* is simply a predefined formula, and FileMaker's list covers most common calculation purposes. If you find a function that already does what you want to do—like average all invoices over a specific time period—use it. When you add these tried-and-true formulas to your calculations, you save time and even help prevent errors.

For example, if you didn't know about functions, you could find your average with a series of fields. First, you'd need to create a calculation field to total all the invoices in your found set. Then you'd need another field to count the invoices in the set and a third one that divides the first field by the second. It would work, but it'd be clumsy and inefficient, since you've created at least two fields that you didn't really need.

Because you often need to find averages, FileMaker gives you a *function* that handles the math in a given field. All you have to do is tell FileMaker *which* field you want to average. The function takes care of figuring out the total of the found set and how many records there are. It looks like this:

```
Average ( Line Item::Quantity )
```

The word "Average" is the function's name. "Line Item::Quantity" is a reference to a related field (see the box on page 414 on aggregate functions). This field reference is called a *parameter*. Parameters tell the function how to perform its specific calculation. The *average* function has only a single parameter, but many functions have two or more.

Parameters are always enclosed in parentheses. (A few functions—most notably, Random—don't need any parameters, so you leave the parentheses off all together.) When there's more than one parameter, they're separated by a semicolon, as in the date function below:

```
Date ( Month ; Day ; Year )
```

FileMaker has more than *180* functions, divided into 16 groups, as described below. Later in this chapter, you'll learn how to use some of the more common functions. (Functions come into play in Chapters 10 and 12, as well.)

Note: FileMaker has a lengthy help file (Ctrl-? or ⌘-?) that lists each function and some sample uses. If you want to explore a function that isn't covered here, open Help, and then type in the function's name.

Text functions

Dozens of *text* functions let you work with text values. You can compare them, convert them into other types (like numbers), split them up in various ways, count the number of letters, words, or lines, change case, and replace parts of them with new text values. If you're trying to slice, mix, or examine words, look here first.

Text formatting functions

Text formatting functions let you adjust the font, size, style, and color of all or part of a text value. For instance, you could make the account balance for a customer turn red if it's over $100. See page 459 for another way to format data conditionally.

Number functions

Number functions do everything with numbers—from the mundane (rounding) to the esoteric (combinatorics). In between, you can get rid of the decimal part of a number, calculate logarithms and square roots, convert signs, generate random numbers, and perform modulo arithmetic.

Date functions

Date functions make working with dates a breeze. You can safely create date values without worrying about the computer's date settings. You can also pick date values apart (for example, get just the *month* from a date), convert day and month numbers into proper names, and work with weeks and fiscal years.

Time functions

Time functions are few: They create time values from hours, minutes, and seconds, and split times up into the same parts. You use these values most frequently when you're trying to find out how long something took. For instance, if you bill your services hourly, you can create Start Time and Finish Time fields. Then, in a Duration field, you can subtract finish time from start time to find out how long you worked on a project.

Timestamp functions

There's only one *timestamp* function: It lets you build a timestamp value from a separate date and a time. If you're creating your own data, you already know that FileMaker needs both a date and a time for a valid Timestamp field and you've planned accordingly. But you may receive data from an outside source in which the date and time aren't already in a single field. No problem, just use the timestamp function.

Aggregate functions

Aggregate functions calculate statistics such as average, variance, and standard deviation. They can also count things, sum things, and find minimums and maximums. By definition, aggregate functions *gather up* multiple values and find results based on the group as a whole. (See the box below for more detail.)

UP TO SPEED

Aggregate Functions

Usually when you perform a calculation on a group of related records, you use an aggregate function. These functions take multiple values and combine them in some useful way:

```
Sum ( 10 ; 20 ; 30 ; 40 )
```

But if you refer an aggregate function to even one related field, FileMaker aggregates that field's values from *every* related record:

```
Sum ( Line Items::Extended Price )
```

Finally, you can also reference a single repeating field. When you do, FileMaker combines each repetition into a single value.

This special behavior for related or repeating fields works only if you use a single parameter. You can't, for example, sum two sets of related fields as one like this:

```
Sum ( Line Items::Extended Price ; Line
Items::Shipping Charge )
```

If you refer to more than one field in a sum function, it looks at only the *first* related value or repetition for each field. Of course, if you did want to total two related fields, you could do so by calling Sum twice and adding their results:

```
Sum ( Line Items::Extended Price ) +
Sum ( Line Items::Shipping Charge )
```

Summary functions

There's only one *Summary* function—GetSummary. Its primary purpose is to let you use the value of a summary field (page 104) in your calculations. In the olden days, before FileMaker was the robust relational database it is now, the GetSummary function was the best way to sort and summarize certain kinds of data. Now that FileMaker is relational, you'll usually use calculations through table occurrences to do that work.

Repeating functions

Repeating functions work with repeating fields, and some of them work with *related* fields as well (see Part 4). You can make non-repeating fields and repeating fields work together properly in calculations, access specific repeating values, or get the *last* non-empty value. Since repeating fields have limited uses in these days of related tables within files, so do these functions. However, there are a few valid uses, as you'll learn in Chapter 11.

Financial functions

Financial functions make the MBAs in the audience feel right at home. Calculate present value, future value, net present value, and payments. Non-MBAs could calculate the cost of competing loans with these functions.

Trigonometric functions

Trigonometric functions, on the other hand, bring back terrible memories from high school math. If you're making a business-related database, don't worry; you don't even have to look at these functions. But engineers and scientists will know what to do with this bunch: sine, cosine, and tangent. They can also convert between radians and degrees. And because everybody has trouble remembering it, you get Pi out to 400 decimal places.

Logical functions

Logical functions are a powerful grouping. These functions can make *decisions* based on calculated values (if the due date is more than six months ago, double the balance due). There are functions to evaluate *other* calculations inside your calculations; functions to figure out if fields are empty or contain invalid data; performance enhancing functions to create and use variables (page 475); and functions to perform lookups inside calculations (page 471). Chapter 11 is where you learn when and how to use these big dogs of the function world.

Get functions

Get functions pull up information about the computer, user, database, or FileMaker Pro itself. They make up the largest group (70 in all). You can, for example, find out the computer's screen resolution, the current layout's name, the computer's network address, the current user's name, or the size of any database window. This list just scratches the surface, though. If you're looking for information about the current state of FileMaker, the computer, or the user, you can probably find it with a get function.

Design functions

Design functions tell you about your database's structure. You can get a list of tables, fields, layouts, or value lists, or details about any of these items. You won't need most of these functions until you become an advanced database designer indeed. But one notable exception is ValueListItems, which gives you a list of the values in a value list, separated by paragraph breaks.

Custom functions

If you have FileMaker Pro Advanced, you can create your very own *custom* functions and have them show up on the list. Once you have them, you (or anyone you let create fields in your database) can choose them just like the built-in functions. (See Chapter 12 for details on creating and using custom functions.)

External functions

If you're not using plug-ins or FileMaker Server, your *external* functions category is empty. If you've installed any plug-ins ("mini-programs" that add extra features to FileMaker), they probably brought along some functions for their own use. FileMaker stores them in this category. FileMaker Server also uses plug-ins, ironically to help you update your third-party plug-ins. (External plug-ins are covered on page 487.)

Expressions

Expression is a fancy name for a subsection of a calculation—one or more fields, functions, or constants, each connected with operators. When you made the first calculation in this chapter (page 403), you multiplied the contents of the field called Price Each by the contents of the field called Quantity. That's a calculation, but it's also an example of an *expression*.

An expression always reduces to a single value when you combine its individual values according to the operators. If you can't boil it down to a value, it's not an expression. That's an important point, because it means you can use expressions as function parameters (page 412) just like any individual values—fields and constants. When used in a function, these expressions are called *sub-expressions*.

Here are some examples of expressions:

The following is a simple expression, which reduces to the value 6.

```
3 + 3
```

Below is a more complex expression. It might turn into something like "Shrute, Dwight K."

```
Last Name & ", " & First Name & " " & Middle Initial & "."
```

The following calculation is a function *and* it's an expression, because it reduces down to a single value.

```
Average(L1 * W1 * H1 ; L2 * W2 * H2 ; L3 * W3 * H3)
```

But if you look at just the stuff in parentheses, you have this:

```
L1 * W1 * H1 ; L2 * W2 * H2 ; L3 * W3 * H3
```

That's *not* an expression because it doesn't reduce down to one value. It has three expressions in all, each separated by a semicolon. Each expression reduces to a single value—three values in all that become parameters passed to the average function.

You can put *any valid expression* in place of a parameter in a function. In the trade, that's called *nesting* expressions. For example, the expression `3 + 3` above could be rewritten like this:

```
( 1 + 1 + 1 ) + 3
```

In this case, the sub-expression `( 1 + 1 + 1 )` has replaced the original value `3`. The whole thing is a new expression, and it contains one sub-expression. This idea comes in particularly handy when you work with functions. Instead of using individual fields or constants in a function, you can pass along whole expressions. You can even nest functions within other functions (see page 448).

Creating a Calculation Field

The invoice line items now calculate their extended prices automatically, because you created a calculation at the beginning of the chapter to handle that. But you still have to add up the extended price of each line item and enter the total amount due on the invoice itself. Another calculation solves this problem.

1. **In the Mars Investigations database, choose File → Manage → Databases and go to the Fields tab. From the Table pop-up menu, choose Invoices.**

   The field list shows all the fields in the Invoices table.

2. **Select the Total Due field in the list.**

   The Field Name, Type, and Comment at the bottom of the window update to show information about this field.

3. **From the Type pop-up menu, choose Calculation, and then click the now highlighted Change button. When FileMaker asks if you're sure you want to make this change, click OK.**

   The Specify Calculation dialog box pops up. (See page 419 for details on its many features.)

4. **From the "Evaluate this calculation from the context of" pop-up menu, choose Invoices.**

   The Invoices table has multiple occurrences on the graph, but since you'll be displaying the Total Due field on the Invoices layout, you want the calculation to evaluate from this context.

Note: When you manage your relationships graph using Anchor Buoy table occurrence groups, it's a lot easier to figure out the context of your calculations. You'll create most calculations in the source table for the Anchor TO and they'll evaluate from that same context. (See page 372 to learn about context and page 373 to learn about Anchor Buoy TOGs.)

5. **From the View pop-up menu (above the function list), choose Aggregate Functions.**

   The function list now shows just the functions FileMaker uses to calculate various kinds of totals and averages. You're looking for the sum function.

6. **Double-click the "Sum (field {; field…})" function in the list.**

   FileMaker copies the full function example into the calculation box. To save you an extra step, it even selects everything between the parentheses (see Figure 9-5). The next thing you type or click becomes the first parameter to the function.

Tip: Anything within curly braces in a function is optional. In the sum function above, you could reference several fields that all get summed up into one glorious total. But that doesn't make sense when you're trying to summarize line items on an invoice, so you're just replacing all the highlighted material with a single field reference.

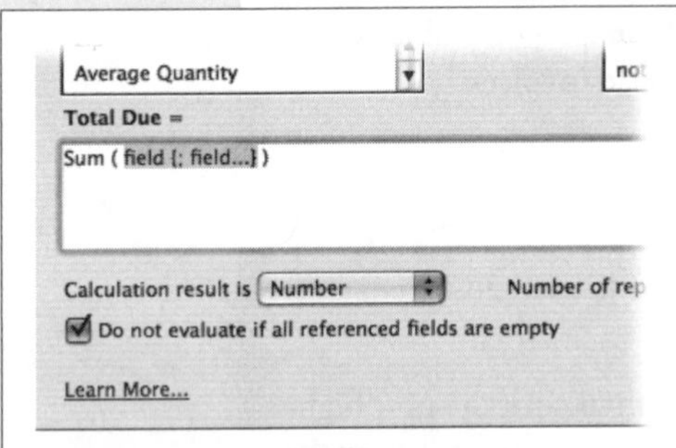

Figure 9-5: *FileMaker gives you a handy syntax reference for each function you choose from the function list. When you double-click to place the function in the calculation box, FileMaker even highlights the parameters for you, so you can start building right away. If you aren't sure what to do, click the "Learn More..." link at the bottom left of the dialog box for context-sensitive help.*

7. **From the pop-up menu above the field list, choose Line items, and then, in the list of line item fields, double-click the Extended Price field.**

   FileMaker adds this field to the calculation, placing it between the parentheses that surround the parameters to the sum function. Your calculation should now read:

   ```
   Sum ( Line Items::Extended Price )
   ```

Tip: If you prefer the keyboard, you can use the Tab key to move from the calculation box to the field list, then the operator list, then the function list. Once you're in one of these lists, use the up and down arrow keys to select an item (or type the first few letters of the item's name). Finally, press the Space bar to add the selected item to the calculation box.

8. **From the "Calculation result is" pop-up menu, choose Number.**

   This calculation is based on number fields and produces a number, too.

9. **Click OK.**

   If you've done everything right, the Specify Calculation window disappears.

Your Total Due field should now work perfectly. Since you modified an existing field that's already on your layout, you don't need to do anything else. Every layout that shows the Line Items::Extended Price now shows the new calculated value.

Switch to the Invoices layout to try for yourself. As you change the Price Each or Quantity fields on a line item, the Extended Price field changes automatically to reflect the correct total.

The Specify Calculation Dialog Box

As you saw in the steps on the previous pages, whenever you create a new calculation field, FileMaker shows the Specify Calculation window (Figure 9-3). This window is where you tell it what calculation to use. This window is loaded with options, making it seem a bit daunting—but all those buttons are there to help you. FileMaker shows you the table occurrences, fields, operators, and functions, and all you have to do is point and click to build any calculation you have in mind.

Once you learn how this box works, you can write calculations like a pro without memorizing complicated functions and/or typing out long field names. The following pages give you a guided tour of each element in the window.

Table occurrence context

This pop-up menu lists every occurrence of the current table—the one you're adding a field to—on the relationship graph. In the last chapter, you learned that FileMaker sees your entire database from the perspective of one table occurrence at a time. This list is where you tell FileMaker how to view the database when it evaluates this calculation. (If the calculation doesn't reference any related data, you can skip this menu.)

Field list

Since most calculations include fields, and field names are often long and hard to remember, FileMaker lets you pick field names from a list. The Table pop-up menu shows every table occurrence in the graph, with the related tables at the top of the pop-up, and the unrelated tables in a group below. The list below the pop-up shows the fields in the selected table occurrence. A calculation can refer to any related field in the database: FileMaker follows the appropriate relationships to grab the data it needs.

Note: You can use global fields from unrelated tables in your calculations. But if you try to use a regular field from an unrelated table, you'll get a warning message when you try to close the Specify Calculation dialog box.

If you want to put a field in the calculation itself, just double-click its name in the list, and FileMaker does the typing for you. See step 7 on page 418 for a prime example of when *not* to type a long field name.

Note: When you double-click a field from the list of table occurrences, you create what FileMaker calls a "fully-qualified field reference," which contains the Table name, two colons, and the Field name (Invoices::InvoiceID). Because you might have similar field names in several tables, a fully qualified name makes sure you reference the right one.

TROUBLESHOOTING MOMENT

Think Like a Machine

If you've jumped right in and started making perfect calculations every time, you can skip this bit of arcana. But if FileMaker throws up a warning dialog box every time you try to make a halfway complex calculation, or if the syntax seems fine, but you just aren't getting the math to work out right, you might have to try thinking like FileMaker thinks. To understand how fields, constants, functions, and operators come together to produce a single result, you have to think very logically and in a straight line that inexorably leads to the end of a problem. When FileMaker evaluates a calculation, it looks for something it can do to simplify it–fetch a field value, perform a function, or evaluate an operator.

The calculation shown in Figure 9-6 has a function (average), several operators (* and &), a constant ("cubic inches"), and six fields (L1, W1, H1, L2, W2, H2). You might think the average function is the right place to start, because it comes first. But you quickly realize you can't compute the average until you figure out what its parameters are by performing the multiplication. The * operators multiply values on either side to produce a new value–but FileMaker needs to replace these fields with their values before it can do anything else.

In Step #1, FileMaker identifies six fields. Step #2 shows how the calculation looks once FileMaker replaces them with values.

Now the * operators are all surrounded by values, and FileMaker is ready to do some multiplication (Step #3). Step #4 shows the calculation once all the multiplication is finished.

At last, the average function has two parameters (Step #5), which is just what it needs, so FileMaker performs this function, and the new calculation looks like Step #6.

There are no more fields to replace and no more functions to perform, but there's one last operator. The & operator takes two text values and puts them together, but this & operator has a number on one side. FileMaker notices this fact in Step #7 and fixes it in Step #8. Finally, the & operator is evaluated, and Step #9 shows the calculation result.

If you apply the concepts outlined here to your problem calculations–find the answer to each step, then plod along to the next one–you can always figure out where your calculation has gone astray.

Figure 9-6: *Taking a complex calculation one bite at a time helps you get the results you expect. Just chip away at the parts, and check your logic at each stage to make sure you and FileMaker are in concert.*

Operators

To help you remember all those operators, FileMaker shows them in the Operators area. Eight buttons represent the most common operators—just click one to insert it. Other operators appear in a scrolling list, which requires a double-click.

Function list

Some functions are so short and sweet that it's faster to type them than to hunt through this very lengthy list. Or you may come to memorize the functions you use most often. But you can't beat the Function list for convenience. It shows every function FileMaker understands *and* all the parameters each function expects, in the right order. (See the box on page 422 for more detail.)

As usual, double-click a function to add it to the calculation. If you don't fancy an alphabetical list of every function, you can narrow down your choices using the View pop-up menu. You can pick a specific function type and see a list of just those functions. The pop-up menu also includes three special categories. The first, "all functions by type" reorganizes the functions in the list. You can see the effect in Figure 9-7.

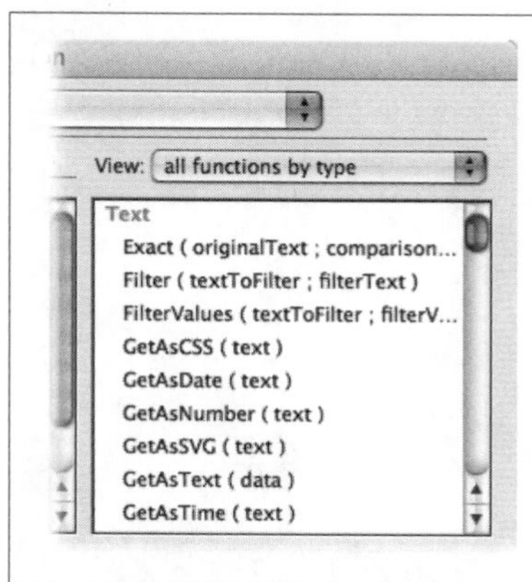

Figure 9-7:
When you choose "all function by type" in the function list, FileMaker groups the functions by their type, and sorts them by name in each group. The type itself is shown in bold above each group. This method is the easiest way to explore the list of functions when you're not quite sure what you're looking for.

Tip: You can always switch back to "all functions by name" to see every function in one alphabetical list. This choice comes in handy when you know a function's name, but not its category.

Result type

Just as you specify field types when you create fields (page 94), you also specify result types for your calculations. You use the Result Type pop-up menu to tell FileMaker what kind of data this field holds. You can easily figure out result type. If you're using a text calculation, your result is probably going to be *text*. If it's a number calculation, the result type is *number*. Surprisingly though, you can also make calculations that are *container* types (see page 457).

Calculation box

Your calculation itself goes in the Calculation box in the middle of the window (it has the field name above it as a label). You can type right into the calculation box if you're a codehead, but mere mortals usually use the field list, operators, and function list, and let FileMaker assemble their calculations for them. When you're getting started, you probably mostly point and click, but as you get more familiar with

UP TO SPEED

The Function List

The function list doesn't show just a list of meaningless names–it also shows an example of how to use the function. The example includes everything you need to call the function in a calculation: name, the necessary parentheses, and a placeholder for each parameter. You just need to replace the placeholders with fields, constants, functions, or expressions.

Most functions are simple, and have a simple example to match:

```
Date ( month ; day ; year )
```

This function, called Date, expects three parameters: a month, day, and year. (If you're curious, it returns a date value based on the three numbers passed to it. See Chapter 10 for more details.

Many functions aren't quite so simple. Some functions don't have a predetermined number of parameters. The average function needs *at least* one parameter, but you can pass as many as you want. It looks like this in the Function list:

```
Average ( field {; field...} )
```

The first "field" parameter shows that you must specify at least one value. The second one is inside curly braces, meaning it's optional. And it's followed by "…" meaning you can add more copies if you want.

The case function shows up like this:

```
Case ( test1 ; result1 {; test2 ; result2
; ... ; defaultResult} )
```

This shows that you can add additional test and result parameters, and you can put a final defaultResult parameter on the end if you want.

Finally, a few functions actually accept more than one value for a single parameter. The Evaluate function is an example:

```
Evaluate ( expression {; [field1 ; field2
;...]} )
```

It always expects one parameter, called an expression (see page 416). You can also specify a field to go with it. The brackets around the field show you that it can take two parameters, but the second can be a bracketed list of multiple values. In other words, you can call this function in three ways:

```
Evaluate ( "<some expression>" )
Evaluate ( '<some expression>" ; A Field )
Evaluate ( "<some expression>" ; [Field 1
; Field 2 ; Field 3] )
```

In the first case, it receives only one parameter. In both the second and third cases, you're passing *two* parameters. In the third case only, the second parameter is actually a list of values. Functions like this are rare, but a few exist.

formulas and functions, you start typing more often. Most people end up using a hybrid of typing and clicking to create their calculations.

Tip: You can also copy and paste into the Calculation box. If you have a calculation in another table file that's the same or similar, you can paste and then update it for its new home, saving yourself some typing. See the Self function on page 463. It can reduce or eliminate editing when you reuse a calculation.

Repetitions

Like any field, a calculation field can be a repeating field (see page 119). FileMaker provides this option for the rare occasion when you need to calculate repeating fields. Suppose you have a repeating field that holds five quantities, and another with five prices. You can write a calculation that multiplies the two fields, and then turn on this box. FileMaker takes care to match all the repetition numbers for you,

FREQUENTLY ASKED QUESTION

Result Type

Why do I have to tell FileMaker my calculation has a number result? I'm multiplying two numbers together, so isn't it obvious?

You're right; FileMaker can figure that out for itself. In fact, in a calculation where you're performing simple math, the field always has a number result. But the ability to set the result type for a field gives you a good measure of control.

For one thing, you and FileMaker may have different ideas about what type a result *should* be. Take this calculation, for example:

```
1 & 1 * 3
```

Because you're mixing concatenation (&) and math (*) operators, it's not terribly obvious *what* that calculation will produce. A number? Or just a numerical text value? So FileMaker lets you say what you *want* it to produce. If it doesn't do what you expect, you can easily fix the calculation, but at least you don't have to wonder what type of field you have.

Furthermore, setting the type explicitly prevents FileMaker from changing it later. Imagine if a simple change to your calculation accidentally changed the result type from number to text. If you tried to reference this field in a calculation or a relationship, you'd get strange results. And it might take you a while to figure out that the problem is due to FileMaker calculating a text value instead of a number, rather than a mistake in your calculation.

If you've set a result type and your calculation doesn't naturally produce the correct type, FileMaker converts it for you before it stores the final result. Thus, you can always tell exactly what type the field is just by looking at the Result Type pop-up menu.

so the third repetition of the calculation multiplies the third price and the third quantity, for instance. (You're more likely to have related tables, and use a standard single calculation to do the totals, but the option to calculate on repetitions is there if you need it.)

POWER USERS' CLINIC

Do Not Evaluate If All Referenced Fields Are Empty

When you create calculation fields (like the Extended Price and Total Due fields in this chapter), you may notice a long-winded checkbox labeled "Do not evaluate if all referenced fields are empty." FileMaker always turns this option on when you first specify a calculation. Here's what it does:

Say you create a new invoice record. It's completely empty, no line items yet. If the Total Due field's "Do not evaluate if all referenced fields are empty" checkbox is turned on, that field is also completely blank, as shown in Figure 9-8. After all, there are no referenced fields (line items), so FileMaker skips the calculation, as the checkbox says.

To be perfectly accurate, however, the value of the total due isn't a blank oblivion—it's zero dollars and zero cents, or $0.00. And indeed, if you turn off the "Do not evaluate" option, FileMaker goes through the calculation even when the invoice's fields are empty. For a newly created invoice, FileMaker shows the correctly formatted Total Due result: $0.00. You're free to choose whichever result you prefer.

There are other types of calculations where you'd want FileMaker to keep its paws off empty fields, though. Suppose you had a calculation like this:

```
Height & " inches"
```

If FileMaker evaluates that calculation and the Height field is empty, the result is " inches," which is pretty meaningless, and annoying to boot. In cases where something is worse than nothing, the "Do not evaluate if all referenced fields are empty" option saves you from worry.

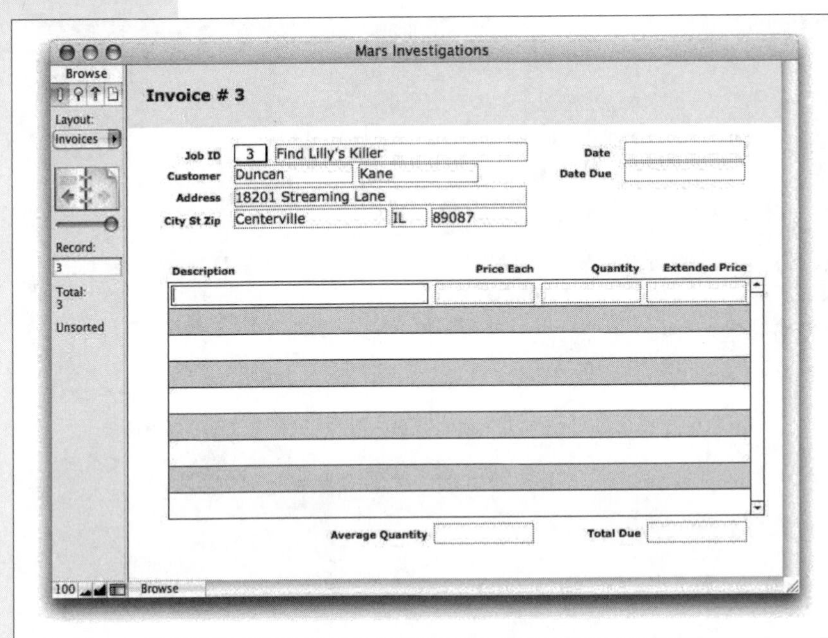

***Figure 9-8:** When you first create a record, the fields that are referred to in your calculations are usually empty, so your calculation results are blank, too. But is the field blank or is there a "0" in the field? The box on page 423 explains when and why it matters.*

Auto-Enter Calculations

Calculation fields are fantastic—they save time and ensure error-free results. But they have one serious limitation: You can't *change* their values. Of course, you can adjust the calculation itself, or the fields the calculation depends on, but sometimes you need to be able to override a field's calculated value on a record-by-record basis.

For example, it would be nice if your invoice's Date Due field automatically showed a date 30 days after the date of the invoice itself. But sometimes you may want to make an invoice due earlier or later, based on special circumstances (like a holiday). If you make the Date Due field a calculation field, you don't have this flexibility. The solution is to use a normal Date field with an *Auto-Enter calculation* (see the box on page 425).

Like all the Auto-Enter options (page 105), an Auto-Enter calculation automatically fills in a field's value, but leaves it changeable. You can get all the accuracy and time savings of a calculation field, plus the power to change your mind. Here's how to put it to use:

1. **Bring up the Manage Database window and switch to the now-familiar Fields tab. From the Table pop-up menu, choose Invoices.**

   The fields from the Invoices table appear.

2. **Select the Date Due field in the list, and then click Options.**

   The Field Options dialog box makes an appearance.

3. **On the Auto-Enter tab, turn on the Calculated Value checkbox.**

   The Specify Calculation window appears. It looks just like it did before, but this time you're *not* creating a calculation field. Instead, you're specifying the calculation used to determine the auto-enter value.

4. **Create the calculation *Date + 30*.**

   You can use any method you want to build this calculation: Click the field and operators, or type them. Notice that the calculation result is set to Date, and there's no pop-up menu to allow you to change that. Your calculation must resolve to a valid date, or FileMaker will squawk at you.

5. **Click OK three times to dismiss all the dialog boxes.**

   You return to the database itself.

POWER USERS' CLINIC

Do Not Replace Existing Value

Auto-Enter calculation fields don't act *exactly* like other calculation fields. If you *change* the invoice date, the due date doesn't update to reflect the change. Instead, it keeps its original value, as in the example on the previous page. That's normally the way Auto-Enter calculations work: Once the field gets a value, the calculation never changes it. It acts only when the field is empty.

Often, though, you don't want this behavior. Instead, you want it to change the field value every time any field used in the calculation is changed, just like a normal calculation. You can easily get this modified behavior by turning off the "Do not replace existing value of field (if any)" checkbox in the Field Options dialog box (shown in Figure 9-9). When you turn this checkbox *off*, FileMaker dutifully updates the field value whenever the calculation evaluates–in other words, when any field it uses changes.

Which option you should choose depends on the situation. For the Date Due field, you probably want to turn this option off. After all, if you're changing the date of an invoice, it's reasonable to assume you want to rethink the due date as well.

But suppose you have a database of products, and you use an Auto-Enter calculation to copy the distributor's product code into your internal product code field. If you then change the internal product code to something unique to you, you probably *don't* want it to change again if you switch to a different distributor. In that case, you would leave the "Do not replace existing value (if any)" option turned on, ensuring that once you've put in your own special value, it never changes.

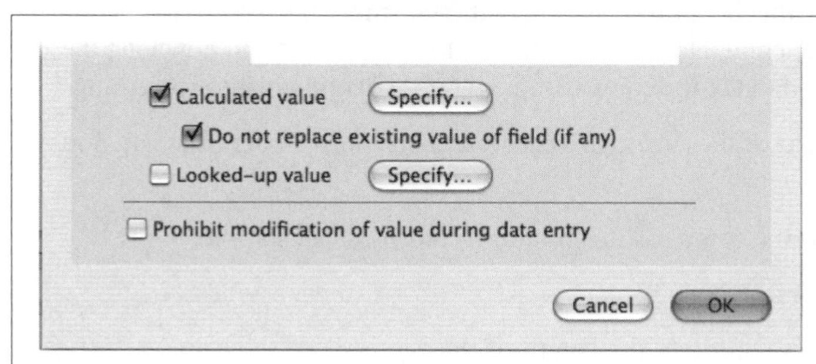

Figure 9-9:
Auto-enter calculations let you protect data that's already in a field if you change the field the calculation refers to. The verbose setting here, "Do not replace existing value for field (if any)" is turned on for you. But if want an Auto-Enter calculation to update any time the field(s) it refers to changes, uncheck this option.

Now you can create a new invoice and test out your field. When you enter a date for the invoice, the Date Due field updates instantly with the date 30 days from now. Notice that you can still change the Date Due field if you want. See the box on page 428 for more on Auto-Enter calculations.

Validate Data Entry with a Calculation

In Chapter 3 you were introduced to several ways to validate data entered into a field. But what if the Validation tab in the Field Options dialog box doesn't have a checkbox to meet your needs? For example, you may want to use validation on the Zip Code field in the Customers table. A valid Zip code has *either* five characters *or* 10 characters (in other words, it can look like this: 90210, or this: 90210-1100). The closest validation option you'll find is "Maximum number of characters"—close, but not right.

This situation is just the kind where the "Validate by calculation" option comes in handy. Your job is to create a calculation with a Boolean result. It should return True when the data is valid, and False otherwise. Here's how it works:

1. **View the field definitions for the Customers table (In File → Manage Database). Select the Zip Code field, and then click Options.**

   The Field Options dialog box pops up.

2. **Click the Validation tab, and turn on "Validate by calculation."**

   The Specify Calculation window appears, ready for you to enter your validation calculation.

3. **From the View pop-up menu, choose "Text functions."**

   The function list updates to show just the text functions.

4. **In the function list, double-click "Length (text)."**

   The function appears in the calculation box. Notice that "text" is already highlighted, ready to be replaced. The length function returns the length of a text value. You use it here to see how many characters are in the Zip Code field.

5. **In the field list, double-click the Zip Code field.**

   FileMaker puts this field inside the parentheses, where it becomes the parameter to the length function. Now that you have a function to tell you how long the Zip code is, you need to use the comparison operator to compare it to something.

6. **Click to the right of the closing parenthesis. Then, in the operators list, double-click "=".**

   FileMaker adds the comparison operator (=) to your calculation.

7. **After the = operator, type *5*.**

   Your calculation compares the length of the Zip code to the value 5. If they're equal, it returns True. But you also want to accept a Zip code with *10* characters.

8. **In the operator list, double-click "or."**

   The "or" operator is added to the end of the calculation. Remember that this operator connects two Boolean values and returns True if *either* value is true. Next, you set up the second value.

9. **Double-click the length function again, then double-click the Zip Code function again, and then double-click the = operator.**

   This second check should also compare the length to some other value.

10. **In the calculation box, type *10*.**

    Your calculation is complete. It should look like the one in Figure 9-10.

11. **Click OK, then OK again, and then a third time.**

    You're now back in your database and ready to test. Try giving a customer a few different Zip codes and make sure the validation works.

Most validations occur as soon as you leave the field, even if you're just moving to another field in the record. But some validation types—including most validation calculations—don't happen until you exit the *record*.

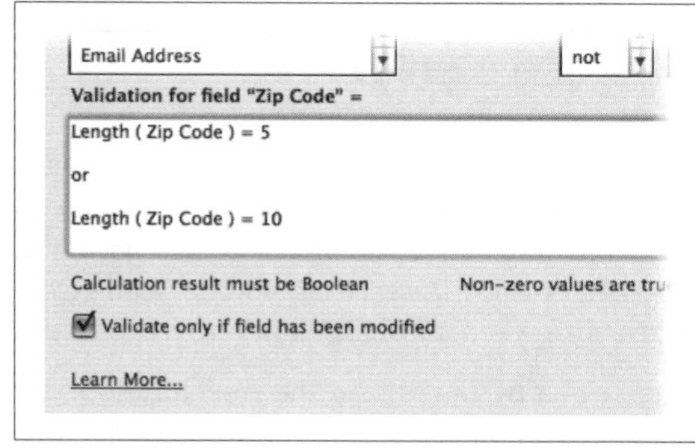

Figure 9-10: *Now you have two comparisons in your calculation. One comparison checks to see if the length is five, while the other looks for a length of 10. If either is True, your calculation is True as well, and FileMaker accepts the Zip code. If both conditions fail, the calculation result is False, and FileMaker shows you an error message.*

Tip: If you're dying to know what determines when your validation occurs, here's the skinny: If, when validating a field, FileMaker looks at the data only *in the field itself*, it performs the validation immediately. If it has to look at data in *other fields* or *other records*, then it waits until you commit the record before validating.

Replacing Data Using a Calculation

You can use calculations productively with the Records → Replace Field Contents command. This command tells FileMaker to visit every record in the found set, replacing the contents of one field with something new. When you first saw this command in Chapter 2, you entered a single value in every record. Sometimes, though, it's more useful to have FileMaker use a calculation to figure out what should go in each record.

FREQUENTLY ASKED QUESTION

Validate Only If Field Has Been Modified

What is the "Validate only if field has been modified" checkbox for? I don't remember seeing this in the Specify Calculation window before. For that matter, where did the Result Type pop-up menu go?

Good eye. The Specify Calculation window can show up in lots of places–when defining a calculation field, when specifying an Auto-Enter calculation, and so on–and it can change slightly in each case.

First, the Result Type pop-up menu shows up only when you're defining a calculation field, since it can produce any data type. Since a validation calculation always has a Boolean result, there's no need to ask you here.

In place of this pop-up menu, you often see some new option specific to the calculation type–like the "Validate only if field has been modified" checkbox in Figure 9-10.

Normally when you edit a record, FileMaker validates only the fields you actually change. Any field in the record that hasn't been changed is accepted even if it violates the validation rule. This can happen when you have your field set to validate "Only during data entry" and the records have been set some other way–from an import (page 657) or a script (page 493). If you want to validate this field whenever you edit the record, not just when the field itself changes, turn off this checkbox.

Tip: Replace Field Contents is a huge timesaver, but since it works on a found set of records, you can't undo it. Improperly used (bad calculation or the wrong found set), it can be destructive. See page 713 to learn how the Data Viewer in FileMaker Pro Advanced helps you preview the results of a calculation before you make that one-way trip through the Replace Field Contents dialog box.

Imagine you attended the International Private Investigators conference in South Dakota, where you picked up 73 business cards you'd like to add to your database. Rather than type them yourself, you told your 13-year-old nephew you'd give him a gumball for each card he typed in. After the cards are tossed and the gum given, you discover he has an aversion to the Shift key—none of the names are capitalized.

You could go through all the records one by one, fixing the capitalization and regretting the cost of the gumballs. But if you use the Replace Field Contents command, you can do all your records with just one command, using a calculation. You use the Proper function, which capitalizes the first letter of each word it encounters. Here's how:

1. **From Browse mode, click the First Name field.**

   The Replace Field Contents command operates on the field you're in when you run it. So click to start in the correct field first.

2. **Choose Records → Replace Field Contents. In the Replace Field Contents window, select the "Replace with calculated result" radio button.**

   As soon as you make this choice, your old friend the Specify Calculation window appears.

3. **Choose "Text functions" from the View pop-up menu (above the function list).**

   The list updates to show only text functions.

4. **Double-click "Proper (text)" in the function list.**

   FileMaker inserts the proper function in the calculation box. Since it has only one parameter, it's already selected. You just have to tell it what text to perform its magic on.

5. **Double-click the First Name field in the field list.**

   FileMaker inserts *First Name* as the parameter for the proper function.

6. **Click OK to close the Specify Calculation dialog box. Then, in the Replace Field Contents window, click Replace.**

   Notice—and beware—that the Cancel button in this dialog box is automatically highlighted. If you hit Enter too quickly, or accidentally click Cancel, you have to start all over, because the dialog box doesn't remember your calculation. It's worth taking an extra second to make sure you're clicking the appropriate button.

If you have a lot of records, you see a progress dialog box. Normally, though, the replacement happens quickly enough that you don't even notice.

Tip: FileMaker has two other functions for changing case: Upper and Lower. It probably goes without saying that Upper converts all the text to uppercase, and Lower converts it to lowercase.

Comments

Everything you can put in a calculation has some kind of value—unless it's a *comment*. Comments are chunks of text whose sole purpose is to help guide you through long calculations. Professional database developers, like all good programmers, provide lots of comments for the benefit of people who might work on the computer code months or years later. Once you have a few sets of parentheses or nested function calls, you may have trouble understanding even your *own* FileMaker calculation when you have to go back and make changes. When it evaluates the calculation, FileMaker ignores all comments completely—it's as if they weren't there. (But you'll be glad they are.)

Note: You may have noticed that this book shows some extras spaces and paragraph returns that FileMaker doesn't throw into your functions automatically. These spaces are for ease of reading, and lots of developers type them into their calculations. Like comments, FileMaker ignores those spaces, as long as all the other syntax is correct.

You can use two different styles for your comments. First, any text that comes after two consecutive slash marks (//) is considered a comment. This kind of comment goes all the way to the end of the line.

```
// this is a comment
3.14 * Diameter // and so is this
```

A comment is also any text that comes between the symbols /* and */. This symbol pair comes in handy in two places. It saves typing if you need to type a long comment across multiple lines:

```
/* this is a comment that runs across multiple
lines. To make life easier, you can use the second
comment style */
```

Also, this comment style lets you add comments *within* a line:

```
3 /*sprocket size*/ * 10 /*sprocket count*/ * 57 /*tooth count*/
```

In addition to comments, you can—and should—use white space to make your calculations easier to read. Calculations don't have to be strung together in one long line, even though that's the way FileMaker does it in the Specify Calculation dialog box. Press the Return key or Space bar to add space anywhere, except in a field name, function name, text constant, or number. Comments and white space can make a world of difference. Here's a long calculation that doesn't make use of either:

```
Let([NewText=":" & Path & ":"]; Case(Item < 0; Let([TextLen=
Length(NewText); Pos=Position(NewText;":";TextLen;Item-1)+1; Len=
Position(NewText; ":";TextLen;Item)-Pos];Middle(NewText;Pos;Len));
Let([os=Position(NewText;":";1;Item)+1;Len=Position(NewText;":";
1;Item+1)-Pos];Middle(NewText;Pos;Len))))
```

Ten points to the first person who can make sense of that mess. Now here's the same calculation, written with more care:

```
// Parsing is easier if we can be sure we have delimiters
// on both ends of the text
Let( [NewText = ":" & Path & ":" ];
    Case(
        // If the item number is negative, we count from the end
        Item < 0;
        Let( [TextLen = Length( NewText);
            Pos = Position ( NewText ; ":" ; TextLen; Item - 1) + 1 ;
            Len = Position ( NewText ; ":" ; TextLen; Item) - Pos ] ;
            Middle ( NewText ; Pos; Len)
        );
        // If the item number is positive, we count from the
        // beginning
        Let( [Pos = Position ( NewText ; ":" ; 1 ; Item ) + 1 ;
            Len = Position ( NewText ; ":" ; 1 ; Item + 1 ) - Pos ] ;
            Middle ( NewText ; Pos ; Len )
        )
    )
)
```

It may not be a picnic to run through in your head, but it's a lot easier to follow than before.

CHAPTER

10

Calculations and Data Types

The last chapter introduced the terminology and concepts behind FileMaker's calculations. You learned how to create them using the Specify Calculation dialog box's tools. Functions, as you saw in the previous chapter, play a big role in good calculation construction. In this chapter, you'll learn the details about the most common functions for the various data types—text, number, date, time, timestamp, and container—and when to use them. As in your FileMaker design life, if you want to test a calculation, just create a calculation field and start building it using the techniques you've learned so far. If it doesn't work the way you expect, or if you don't need it after your experiment is done, just delete the field.

Number Crunching Calculations

Although they don't come first in the function list, number functions are the most obvious application of calculations. Since most people easily understand them, number functions are a logical place to start. A lot of the concepts you'll learn for number functions apply to other functions as well.

Number Operators

Operators, along with fields, constants, and functions, are one of the basic building blocks of a calculation. FileMaker has five operators that specifically apply to numerical calculations, the same five that you probably already know:

- + is for addition
- - is for subtraction
- * is for multiplication

- / is for division
- ^ is for exponentiation ("to the power of")

"Text constants" explains how to use these operators in detail. In your day-to-day work with FileMaker, you usually use these operators to calculate the numerical values in your fields.

Note: If you're new to calculations, you'll want to get a handle on the material in this chapter before proceeding. But if you've worked with logical tests before, you can skip straight to Chapter 11.

Say you're an event planner and you always plan for 10 percent above the expected number of attendees. Use this calculation to find your fudge factor:

```
Confirmed Attendees * 1.1
```

Number Function Types

FileMaker also gives you dozens of functions that do special things to numbers. Because there are so many number functions, the function list breaks them up into smaller groups. The groups have descriptive names, so you can drive right to the group you need (or skim by them without looking, if you might be traumatized by accidentally seeing a sine or cosine function). The functions you use with your numeric data are:

- Number functions
- Aggregate functions
- Financial functions
- Trigonometric functions

As you saw on page 413, every number function expects one or more parameters, each a number value, and all the number functions return a number result. Here's how to put them to work:

Note: This book doesn't cover the financial and trigonometric functions, which have highly specialized uses. If you need to use these brawny functions, you probably have the mental muscle to decipher the technical terms in FileMaker's Help file, where you'll find them explained.

Precision

Some calculations demand a high degree of precision, like those that track radioactive isotopes or other scientific data with lots of places following the decimal point. FileMaker comes prepared with the SetPrecision function. This function extends FileMaker's default precision of 16 decimal places, up to a maximum of 400. If you need more precision, you add a SetPrecision function to the calculation that produces the value that requires precision. You can use SetPrecision with all other numeric functions, except trigonometric functions, which don't accept this extended precision (see Figure 10-1).

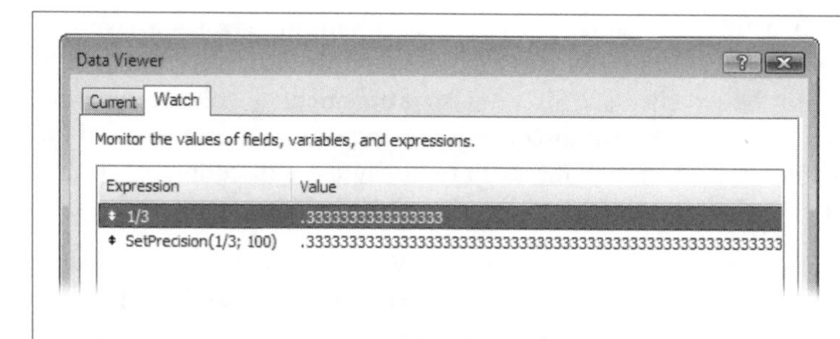

Figure 10-1:
The first item in this window shows how FileMaker normally evaluates the formula 1/3. In the second, the SetPrecision function lets you request more decimal places. You can see the formula on the left, and the result on the right. (This window is the Data Viewer, which you'll learn more about on page 713.)

The SetPrecision function requires two parameters. The first parameter is a number, or any expression that results in a number. The second is the number of decimal places you want to see.

This calculation would return Pi with three decimal places:

```
SetPrecicion( Pi ; 3 )
```

This version would show 100 decimal places:

```
SetPrecision( Pi ; 100 )
```

Note: The SetPrecision function affects your calculation's result, but not necessarily the way FileMaker displays it. To save space on your layout, you can format a very precise calculation to show only a few decimal places until you click the field, when you see the stored value (Figure 10-1).

Going Beyond Basic Calculations

In the last chapter you created two very simple calculation fields using numbers: Extended Price and Invoice Total. But those calculations were very simple. Now, you build on those basic concepts to see how you can make a set of calculations that fit an upcoming sales promotion.

Preparing the Data

You've decided to start reselling personal security products to your customers. To help you keep track of things, you need to add a Products table to your database. The table should have these fields:

- A text field called SKU
- A text field called Description
- A number field called Cost
- A number field called Price

Note: See page 323 for advice on creating tables.

Once you've created this new table, FileMaker automatically creates a layout—Products. Switch to that layout now and create a few product records. To help drive sales to your larger clients, you want to implement a volume discount scheme; they should get a 5 percent discount if they buy enough. But some of the products you sell don't have enough mark-up to justify these discounts. You want to be sure the discount never reduces your mark-up below 20 percent.

First, you add a line to your marketing materials: "Volume discounts not available for all products." You can make this line as small as humanly possible and hide it way down in the corner. Next, you need to fix your database so it tells you the discount price for each product.

Building the Calculation Fields

To implement this discount scheme, take what you need to know and translate it into calculation terms.

- First, calculate 95 percent of the price (a 5-percent discount):

  ```
  Price * .95
  ```

- Second, you also know the cost (in the Cost field) and you can figure out the lowest price by adding 20 percent to this cost:

  ```
  Cost * 1.2
  ```

- Finally, the discounted price is either the calculated discount price, *or* the cost + 20-percent price, whichever is *greater*. Put another way, you want the *maximum* of these two values:

  ```
  Max ( Price * .95 ; Cost * 1.2 )
  ```

Using the max function, the previous calculation results in either the discounted price, or the minimum price, whichever is greater (see the box on the next page). That result is *almost* perfect. But suppose you have a product whose *normal* price is less than 20 percent above cost (hey, it's a competitive market). If you use the Max calculation as it is now, the new discounted price is *more* than the normal price. You need to go back and add to your calculation so that it takes the regular price into account, and uses *that price* if it's lower than the calculated discount. Read on to learn how to think through this calculation quandary.

Constructing the Calculation

When calculations start to get complicated like this discount price example, imagine that you have a field that contains the value you already want. You can use this pretend field in your new calculation, and then, when you're all finished, put the old calculation in place of the pretend field. In this case, just pretend you have a field called Calculated Discount that holds the discount price. With that imaginary field in mind, you can fix your problem with this calculation:

```
Min ( Calculated Discount ; Price)
```

UP TO SPEED

The Max and Min Functions

Many times, you need to know either the highest or lowest value in a series. The max function and its twin sister, min, fulfill these needs, and you find them in the function list's aggregate functions category. Like all the aggregate functions, they expect at least one parameter, and are glad to get more. Every parameter should be a number. Your parameters can be:

- Constant data
- Fields within a record
- Repeating fields
- Related fields

The max function looks at every number referenced and returns whichever is largest. Min, on the other hand, returns the smallest value.

For example, look at this calculation:

```
Max ( 10 ; 3 ; 72 ; 19 ; 1 )
```

Its result is 72, since that's the largest of the parameters.

If you had a repeating field called Distances that held the distances from your office to each Krispy Kreme store, you could use this calculation to find the closest sugar fix:

```
Min ( Distances )
```

The same is true for *related* fields too. This calculation finds the most expensive line item:

```
Max ( Line Items::Price )
```

With both repeating fields and related fields, you pass just *one* field to the min or max function, but FileMaker considers *all* the values in that field. If the field is a repeating field, FileMaker considers every repetition. If it's a related field, its value from every related record is considered.

The result of this calculation is either the calculated discount or the regular price, if it's lower. Now, just put the old calculation in place of the words "Calculated Discount" (since the old calculation *results in the calculated discount*):

```
Min ( Max ( Price * .95 ; Cost * 1.2 ) ; Price)
```

The entire max function, complete with its two parameters, is now the min function's first parameter. You might think it looks a little confusing at first, but with practice you become accustomed to looking at functions-inside-functions like this.

If it helps, you can add white space and comments to clarify the calculation, as Figure 10-2 shows.

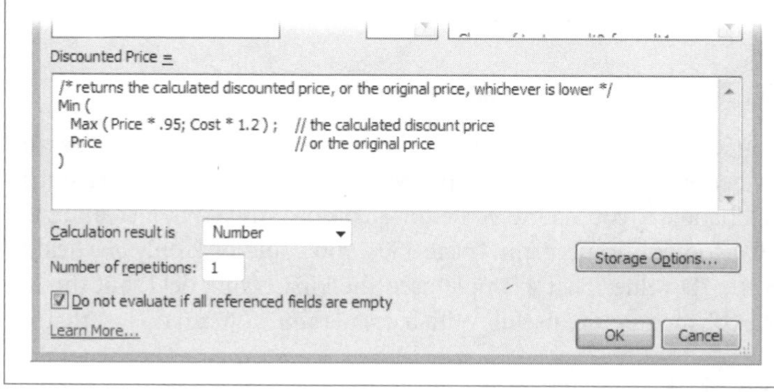

***Figure 10-2:** You may find it hard to write nested calculations, and hard to read them if you need to come back later and tweak them. In this case, though, a savvy person formatted the calculation with copious white space and plenty of comments. Chances are you'll understand this version better than the one shown above.*

To use the calculation, just create a new calculation field (call it *Discounted Price*) with the calculation above. It automatically adjusts and shows you an appropriate discounted price.

If you want to test a complicated calculation, spot-check a few records where you know the result. Sometimes the math is so complex that you just have to work it out on paper and enter dummy records to check the calculation. Usually, if a calculation isn't working, you can figure out how to fix it when you compare your math to the value in the field.

Text Parsing Calculations

Although most people think of functions for doing dry stuff like math in a spreadsheet, you can also use functions in your database's text fields. Just as you can add and subtract numbers with number functions, you can use text functions to slice and dice the words in your database. For example, you might receive data from an outside source that needs major cleanup before you can use it. This data has people's first and last names in the same field; it's even got entire email messages crammed into a field—address, subject, and body—when all you need is the email address. You can equip a temporary database with fields and text calculations to *parse* (think of it as sifting) the data into the form your better-designed database expects.

Note: Fixing data this way usually means that you do a find for a certain kind of bad data–if only some records have two email addresses in the same field, say. Use a calculation with the Records → Replace Field Contents command. Do a find first, and then do a calculated Replace Field Contents that fixes the error.

The Concatenation Operator

In contrast to the wide variety of mathematical operators for working with numbers, there's only one that pertains specifically to text—the *concatenation* operator. Represented by the & sign (ampersand), it strings bits of text together. (When you need to chop and divide your text in order to parse it, you use a function instead of an operator, as described on page 436.)

To use this operator, put it between units of text, as in the expression below:

```
"This is a " & "test"
```

The result of this calculation is *This is a test.*

The concatenation operator lets you combine text from two different fields and make them work better together. For example, when you set up the jobs layout in your database in Chapter 8, you had to settle for a compromise. When creating the value list for the Customer pop-up menu (page 350), you could pick only *one* field to show along with the ID value. That example used the First Name field, but the full name would make the menu more useful. With a calculation, you can do just that.

POWER USERS' CLINIC

Repeating Fields for Multiple Results

What if one discount price isn't enough? Suppose you want to give your customers 5 percent off on orders of five or more, 10 percent off on orders of 10 or more, 15 percent off on orders of 15 or more, and so on. You could create more calculation fields with slight variations on the calculations you've already specified:

- Discounted Price for 10:

```
Min ( Max ( Price * .90 ; Cost * 1.2 ) ;
Price)
```

- Discounted Price for 15:

```
Min ( Max ( Price * .85 ; Cost * 1.2 ) ;
Price)
```

If you want seven price breaks, you have to create seven fields. And if you want to change the calculation slightly (for example, to give an additional 2 percent discount per break instead of 5 percent), you have to change every single field's calculation.

This example is one of those cases where repeating fields come in handy. When you create a repeating calculation field, you have only *one* calculation, but you get multiple results. With only one calculation, though, FileMaker doesn't show you an obvious way to provide different discount rates. The secret ingredient is the *Get(CalculationRepetitionNumber)* function. It returns the repetition number being calculated at the moment. For example, when FileMaker goes to calculate the *third* value in your repeating field, this function returns 3.

With this function in mind, you can devise a single calculation that uses different discount rates depending on the repetition number:

```
Min (
 Max (
  Price[1] * (1 -
  Get(CalculationRepetitionNumber) * .05);

  Cost[1] * 1.2
 ) ;
 Price[1]
)
```

In this calculation, you replace the constant discount rate by the expression:

```
(1 - Get(CalculationRepetitionNumber) *
.05)
```

You also need to add [1] to the end of each mention of the Price and Cost fields since they aren't repeating fields (this tells FileMaker to grab the *first* repetition–the only one with anything in it).

If you test this calculation with a few numbers, you see it results in an extra 5 percent discount for each subsequent repetition. Once you've created a field like this, a lot of things become really easy:

To add *more* price breaks, just change the number of repetitions in the Specify Calculation dialog box:

- Going from seven breaks to 20 is a 5-second change.
- To change the discount rates for *every* break, just change one number–the .5–and you affect every calculated value.

Create a new field that shows what you want in your value list. Add a new calculation field to the Customers table, called *Full Name*. Use this calculation:

```
Last Name & ", " & First Name "
```

Some results might be "Trout, Kilgore" or "Pilgrim, Billy." Note that the calculation includes a comma and the appropriate spaces for separating data between your fields. Now you can modify the All Customers value list to take advantage of the new field. Just change it to use the new Full Name field instead of the First Name field. Figure 10-3 shows the result.

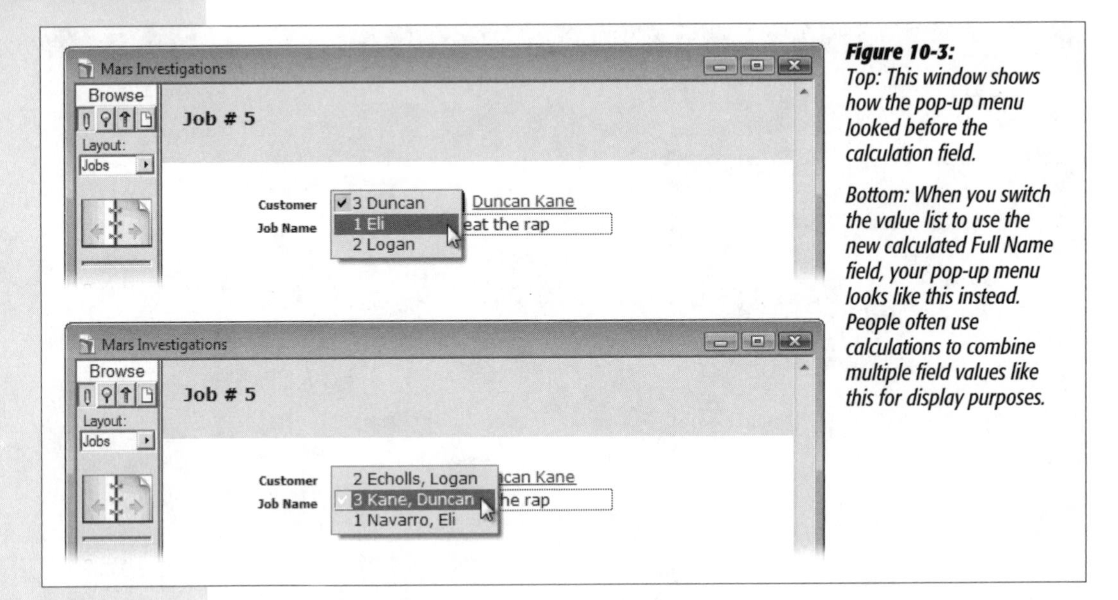

Figure 10-3: *Top: This window shows how the pop-up menu looked before the calculation field.*

Bottom: When you switch the value list to use the new calculated Full Name field, your pop-up menu looks like this instead. People often use calculations to combine multiple field values like this for display purposes.

Text Function Types

FileMaker's text-handling functions come in two flavors: *text functions* and *text formatting functions*. Text functions handle tasks like the parsing mentioned above, or finding whether a particular string of characters occurs in a field. You can change all instances of specific characters within a field, or count text length, with text functions.

Text formatting functions change the way your text looks, like making a part of the text in a field bold and red. These functions are a lot more flexible than just making a field bold and red on your layout, because you can tell the calculation to search *inside* the field, find just the characters "Propane Sale!," and make them red, while it leaves all the surrounding text untouched.

Text Functions

Many of the text functions exist to help you *parse* text—split it apart in useful ways. Sometimes one text value contains multiple useful pieces of information, and you need to look at them individually. If you're lucky, the information comes in a form that FileMaker already understands. If you're not so lucky, you have to do some extra work to tell FileMaker exactly how to divide the text value.

FileMaker can automatically break up text in three ways: by *characters*, *words*, or *values*. When it does the dividing, it gives you three ways to decide which parts you want: *left*, *middle*, or *right*.

Character functions

Parsing by character comes in handy when you have data that's in a well-known format and you need to access pieces of it. You can use functions to grab the first three digits of a Social Security number, the last four digits of a credit card number, or the style code buried inside a product number.

POWER USERS' CLINIC

Advance Web Viewer URLs

In Chapter 6 you learned about the Web viewer, a full-featured Web browser you can stick right on a layout. When you add a Web viewer to your layout, FileMaker lets you configure it to use any of a handful of helpful Web sites just by filling in the blanks. But if you want to go beyond the basics, you have to code your own custom URL into the Web viewer, and that almost always requires calculations. Now that you know all about the concatenation operator (&), you're ready to take your Web viewer expertise to the next level.

In the Web Viewer Setup dialog box (which you can open by creating a new Web viewer, double-clicking an existing one, or following the instructions back on page 272), the first item in the "Choose a Web Site" list is Custom Web Address. Choose it. When you do, the configuration options on the right side of the window disappear, and your sole focus is the Web address box at the bottom of the window.

To calculate a custom Web address, click Specify. FileMaker presents the Specify Calculation dialog box, and you can use all the tools available to a calculation to custom-craft a Web address. (You must delete all the text FileMaker puts in first.)

Now the sky's the limit. Almost every Web page in the world has a unique URL that includes all the information you need to pull it up. Your job is to look at that URL in your browser, find the parts that are based on changing data, and convert it to a calculation. Here are a few examples:

- In the simplest case, you can actually store a Web address in your database. For example, suppose you have a Home Page field in your Company database that holds the URL for a company's home page. If that's the case, just use this simple calculation to display the home page in your Web viewer:

  ```
  "http://" & Company::Home Page
  ```

- If you look up a stock symbol on Yahoo Finance, the address box in your browser shows something like this:

  ```
  http://finance.yahoo.com/q?s=MSFT
  ```

- In this case, the URL shows stock information for Microsoft, whose stock symbol is *MSFT*. To make the Web viewer show the correct page for any symbol in your database, use this calculation (which assumes you have a field called Stock Symbol):

  ```
  "http://finance.yahoo.com/q?s=" & Company:
  :Stock Symbol
  ```

- Finally, suppose you use the Basecamp project management system (*http://basecamphq.com*), and you want to show the project overview page in your FileMaker billing database. Basecamp's URL looks like this:

  ```
  https://myaccount.com/projects/12345/
  project/log
  ```

If you look closely, you'll come to the conclusion that the "12345" bit is a unique identifier for the project. Everything else looks pretty generic. So you can store just that identifier in your FileMaker database, and use this calculation to show any project in a Web viewer:

```
"https://myaccount.com/projects/" &
Project::Basecamp ID & "/project/log"
```

Using the power of calculations, you can integrate just about any Web content into your layout. You're no longer limited to the list of sites FileMaker provides.

FileMaker can work with individual characters inside a text value. The first letter in a text value is number one, the second is number two, and so on. Then you can ask for the first few characters, or the last few, or just the fifth, sixth, and seventh.

Note: Every letter, number, punctuation mark, space, tab, carriage return, or other symbol counts as a character.

- The **left** function returns the first few letters of a text value, eliminating the rest. You *pass* (that is, tell) the calculation the actual text value, and the number of letters you want. For example, to get a person's initials, you can use a calculation like this:

  ```
  Left ( First Name ; 1 ) & Left ( Last Name ; 1 )
  ```

  To get the first three digits of a Social Security number, you can use this calculation:

  ```
  Left ( SSN ; 3 )
  ```

- The **right** function does the same thing but starts from the other end of the text value. If you want to record the last four digits of someone's credit card number, you can do it like this:

  ```
  Right ( Credit Card Number ; 4 )
  ```

- If the information you want isn't on either end, you may need to use the **middle** function instead. This function is a little different: It expects *three* parameters. Just as when using left and right, the first parameter is the text value FileMaker's inspecting. The second parameter is the starting position. Finally, you tell FileMaker how many characters you want.

  For example, suppose you have a product database that uses a special coding system for each item. The code "SH-112-M" indicates shirt style 112, medium size. To pull out just the style number (that 112 in the middle of the product code), you want your calculation to grab three characters from the Product Number field, starting with the fourth character.

  ```
  Middle ( Product Number ; 4 ; 3 )
  ```

Word functions

FileMaker also understands the concept of words. With word functions, you don't have to bother dealing with every single character.

In FileMaker's mind, a *word* is any stretch of letters, numbers, or periods that doesn't have any other spaces or punctuation in it. Most of the time, this definition means FileMaker does exactly what you expect: It sees the real words in the text. For example, each of the following is one word:

- FileMaker
- ABC123
- This.is.a.word

Any sequence of other characters isn't part of a word at all. Each of these has two words:

- FileMaker Pro
- ABC 123

POWER USERS' CLINIC

A Calculation in a Button

In Chapter 6, you learned how to create buttons on a layout and program them to perform all kinds of database duties at a click (page 258). The only problem is, the more features you give your database, the more buttons you have to make. And some of the folks using your database need a completely different assortment of buttons than others. Fortunately, most button commands have one or more options you can set with a calculation. The calculation can adjust what the button does based on field data, user information, the current date or time, and so forth.

Suppose you have two different layouts to view the people in your People database. One is for the people who are *customers* and the other is for *employees*. In Chapter 5, you added a button to the list layout of a database that takes you to the detail layout. You might think with two different detail layouts you would need two buttons. But you can summon the power of calculations to make one button do double duty.

If you take a peek at the options for the "Go to Layout" button action, you'll see that in addition to all the layouts in your database, the pop-up menu includes two options you haven't used before: "Layout Name by calculation" and "Layout Number by calculation."

If you pick either of these options, FileMaker presents the Specify Calculation dialog box. You simply write a calculation that evaluates to the correct layout name (or number if that's your persuasion) and FileMaker will go to the right one. For example:

```
If ( Person::Type = "Customer", "Customer
Detail", "Employee Detail" )
```

- A-Test
- Two *** Words

Warning: If your text value doesn't have normal words (like a long URL, for example), you may have to pay special attention to the letters-numbers-periods rule to get the results you expect.

Along the same lines as the character functions, FileMaker has three word-oriented functions called LeftWords, RightWords, and MiddleWords. Each takes two parameters, including the text value to examine, and a number or two to tell FileMaker which words you're interested in. You can use a word function to parse a person's first and middle name if you ever get a file with all three names unceremoniously dumped into a single field.

- **LeftWords** returns all the text before the end of the specified word. For instance, this function:

  ```
  LeftWords ( Preamble ; 3 )
  ```

  might return *We the People*. But if Preamble contained "This *** Is *** a *** Test," it would return *This *** Is *** A* instead. In other words, it doesn't just return the words. It returns *everything* before the end of the third word.

- Likewise, **RightWords** returns everything *after* the specified word's *beginning*, counting from the end. This calculation:

  ```
  RightWords ( Revelations ; 1 )
  ```

  would return *Amen*.

FREQUENTLY ASKED QUESTION

The Middle Way

It looks like you can tell the middle function to isolate characters anywhere in a text field, just by telling it which characters to count. So why do we need left and right functions when you can do the same thing with middle?

As the example on this page suggests, the middle function indeed provides all the power you need to pick text values apart character by character. For example, instead of:

```
Left ( Model Number ; 3 )
```

You could do this:

```
Middle ( Model Number ; 1 ; 3 )
```

It gets a little tougher to mimic the right function, but it's possible.

There are *lots* of places where one function can do the same thing as another (or a few others).

For example, you can use left and right instead of middle if you want. This calculation:

```
Middle ( Product Number ; 4 ; 3 )
```

Can be rewritten like this:

```
Right ( Left ( Product Number ; 7 ) ; 3 )
```

The good news is, there's no *right answer*. You can write your calculations any way you want, as long as they work. In fact, FileMaker developers have a grand tradition of finding creative ways to do something with less typing. Bear in mind, though, that sometime in the future you'll probably have to figure out what you were doing in a calculation so you can change it, fix it, or use it somewhere else. If a few extra keystrokes makes the calculation easier to understand, they may well be worth it.

- What would LeftWords and RightWords be without **MiddleWords**? You can probably guess how this function works: You pass in a text value, a starting word, and the number of words to return. It then returns everything from the beginning of the starting word through the end of the finishing word. The following calculation shows how it works; it returns "or not" because they are the third and fourth words.

```
MiddleWords ( "To be, or not to be" ; 3 ; 2 )
```

Text value functions

How can *text* have a *value*? Well, to FileMaker, values are what fields hold, so a field's text *is* its value. If a field holds more than one chunk of text, each on its own line, FileMaker considers each a separate value, hence the term *return-separated values*. You can think of these bits of text as *lines* or *paragraphs*. Text value functions let you use those line breaks to parse text. This trick comes in handy more often than you think.

Here's a simple example to show how it works. Suppose you have a field called Colors with lists like this:

- Red
- Green
- Blue

- Orange
- Yellow

FileMaker tells you this field contains five values, and you can work with them just like characters and words. For example, this LeftValues formula returns "Red" and "Green."

```
LeftValues ( Colors ; 2 )
```

Use the GetValue function when you need to parse just one value from a list. The value you need has to be in a predictable place in the list, as in the whole-email-slammed-into-one-field example at the beginning of this section. Say the email comes to you like this:

- Email From
- Email To
- Subject
- Body

You could grab the Email To address with this function:

```
Get Value ( Email ; 2 )
```

FileMaker has RightValues and MiddleValues functions, too. See the box on page 444 for ideas on how to use them.

Text counting functions

Another way to work with text is to simply count its individual parts. FileMaker has three related functions for finding out *how much* text your fields contain:

- The **length** function returns the length of a text value by counting characters.
- The **WordCount** function tells you how many words are in a text value.
- Using the **ValueCount** function, you can find out how many lines a field has.

These functions become powerhouses in combination with the various left, right, and middle functions. When the fields you're parsing contain varying amounts of text, you can have FileMaker count each one so you don't have to. For example, to return all but the last letter in a field, you can use this calculation:

```
Left ( My Field ; Length ( My Field ) - 1 )
```

It uses the left function to grab characters from the field, and the length function (minus one) to find out how many to get. Just change the number on the end to chop off any number of junk characters from the end of a field. You're welcome.

POWER USERS' CLINIC

Outsmarting the Smarties

LeftValues and RightValues are helpful when you need to pull some items from a return-separated list. But they're also helpful when you want to protect your database from people who know a few workarounds. Say you have a sales promotion going, where your best customers get to pick one free premium from a list of four items. So you've set up a field with a value list and a set of radio buttons. Everybody knows that you can choose only one item from a radio button set, right? Apparently not, because you've got some salespeople who know they can beat the system by Shift-clicking to select multiple radio buttons. (Those folks read page 230.)

All you have to do is add an Auto-Enter calculated value to your Premiums field. Make sure you uncheck the "Do not replace existing value (if any)" option. Here's how the calculation goes:

```
RightValues (Premiums ; 1 )
```

Now your savvy salespeople can wear out their Shift keys, but they still can't select more than one item in the premium field, because your calculation holds the field to a single value.

You can even add smarts to a Checkbox Set with a similar technique. Make this calculation:

```
LeftValues ( Premiums ; 2 )
```

People using the program can't select more than two checkboxes. FileMaker knows the first two items they selected, and just keeps putting those same two back into the field, no matter how many checkboxes the salespeople try to select. For another twist, change the calculation to:

```
RightValues ( Premiums ; 2 )
```

Now FileMaker remembers the last two items that were selected and very cleverly deselects the oldest value, so that the field always contains the last two items selected from the Checkbox Set.

Other text parsing functions

FileMaker includes dozens of text functions, but a few of them are worth special mention because you see them throughout the rest of this section, and because they're so useful for cleaning up messy data.

- The **substitute** function performs a find-and-replace within a text value. For example, if you want to turn all the Xs to Os in your love letter (maybe you felt like you were coming on too strong), you can do this:

  ```
  Substitute ( Love Letter ; "X" ; "O" )
  ```

  A few FileMaker functions support a special *bracketed syntax* and substitute is one of them. If you want to perform *several* replacements on a piece of text, you can do it with one substitute function. Each pair in brackets represents one search value and its replacement value. Here's how you can show a field value with all the vowels removed. You can do this:

  ```
  Substitute ( My Field ; ["a" ; ""] ; ["e" ; ""] ; ["i" ; ""] ; ["o" ; ""] ;
  ["u" ; ""] )
  ```

Note: This example shows another nice fact about the substitute function: You can use it to *remove* something. Just replace it with empty quotes: "".

- While the substitute function can be used to change or remove what you specify, **filter** can remove everything you *don't* specify. For example, suppose you want to strip any non-numeric characters from a credit card number. You can *try* to think of all the possible things a person might type in a Credit Card Number field (good luck!), or you can use the filter function instead:

  ```
  Filter ( Credit Card Number ; "0123456789" )
  ```

  This calculation tells FileMaker to return the contents of the Credit Card Number field with everything except the numerals removed. In other words, simply put the characters you'd like to *keep* in the second parameter.

WORKAROUND WORKSHOP

When Data Doesn't Comply

Sometimes the text you need to break up doesn't come in pieces that FileMaker automatically recognizes, like characters or words. For example, suppose you have a file path:

```
C:\My Documents\Product Shots\Tools\Large
    Hammer.jpg
```

You need to get the name of the file (Large Hammer.jpg) and its parent folder (Tools). Unfortunately, this text value isn't divided into characters, words, or values. It's divided into *path components*, each with a backslash in between.

When you're faced with something like this, your best bet is to make it look like something FileMaker *can* deal with. If you can turn every backslash into a new line symbol (¶), then you can simply use the RightValues function to pull out the last value. In other words:

```
Substitute ( File Path ; "\ " ; "¶" )
```

The result of this expression is the list of path components, each on its own line:

C:

My Documents

Product Shots

Tools

Large Hammer.jpg

To get just the file name, you can do this:

```
RightValues ( Substitute ( File Path ; "\
" ; "¶" ) ; 1 )
```

Unless your data already contains multiple lines, you can always use the substitute function to turn any kind of delimited list into a list of values. Bear in mind, though, that the substitute function is *case sensitive*. You can read more about case sensitivity on page 469.

Text Formatting Functions

Normally when you see data in a calculation field, it's displayed in the format (font, size, style, color, and so on) you applied in Layout mode. Every character in the field shares the same format, unless you want to manually search through all your records selecting the words "Limited Time Only" in your Promotion Notes field, so you can make that bold and red every time it appears. Not only does that method waste your precious time (especially if you're on salary), it also plays havoc with your design when you try to print the field.

FileMaker's text formatting functions let you specify exactly what bit of text you want in 18-point, boldfaced, red Verdana. And you don't have to visit a single record in person. You just write a calculation and FileMaker does the drudgework for you, without tampering with the real data.

FileMaker has six text formatting functions, as described below.

Note: Since that big heading above clearly reads "*Text* Formatting Functions," any reasonable person would assume that this formatting applies only to text. Luckily, the unreasonable people rule the world. You can apply text formatting to any data type, as you'll see later in this chapter.

TextColor and RGB

The TextColor function takes two parameters: some text, and a color. It returns the text you send it in the right color. Like many computer programs, FileMaker thinks of colors in RGB code, which defines all colors as combinations of red, green, and blue as expressed by numerical values. The second parameter to the TextColor function is (almost) always the RGB function (and FileMaker automatically adds it when you add TextColor to your formula).

This function returns a color based on three parameters: red, green, and blue. For example, if you want to change the Full Name field to show the first name in bright red, and the last name in bright blue, you use this calculation:

```
TextColor ( First Name ; RGB ( 255 ; 0 ; 0 ) )
& " " &
TextColor ( Last Name ; RGB ( 0 ; 0 ; 255 ) )
```

Note: For a crash course in RGB code–including how to avoid using it–see the box below.

TextFont

To change the font in a calculation result, use the TextFont function. In its simplest form, this function is, well, simple. You just pass it the text you want to format, and the name of the font to use. FileMaker returns the same text with the font applied:

```
TextFont ( "Dewey Defeats Truman!" ; "Times New Roman" )
```

TextFont also has a third optional parameter called fontScript. Most people can simply ignore this option. It tells FileMaker which *character set* you're interested in, and to select an appropriate font. (The character set determines which languages the font can be used for.) FileMaker accepts the following fontScript values:

- Roman
- Greek
- Cyrillic
- CentralEuropean
- ShiftJIS
- TraditionalChinese

UP TO SPEED

Color My World (With 16M Colors)

FileMaker has a basic conflict over color. After all, it's a computer program that works with data, which comes in a limited number of types, like text value, number, date, and time. So what kind of data type is a *color*? The explanation isn't very, er, colorful. FileMaker understands 16,777,216 distinct colors, each subtly different from the one before, and numbered from 0 to 16,777,215. Unfortunately, *learning* all those colors by number is beyond the reach of even the most bored developer. So FileMaker uses a standard (albeit entirely unintuitive) method of specifying a color as a mixture of component colors–red, green, and blue–with varying intensities.

Each parameter to the RGB function is a number, from zero to 255. The number says how intense–or bright–the component color should be. A zero in the first parameter means red doesn't enter into the equation at all. The number 255 means FileMaker should crank the red component to the max. The RGB function returns a number, identifying one of those 16-odd million choices. To make it doubly confusing for anyone who doesn't have a degree in computer programming or television repair, the RGB system deals with red, green, and blue as sources of *light*, not the more intuitive red-yellow-blue primary colors of paints and pigments. When colored lights mix (like those little pixels on a monitor), red and green make…yellow. In other words, to FileMaker and other RGB experts, it makes perfect sense to see bright yellow as the following:

```
RGB (255 ; 255 ; 0)
```

So what's a person to do? Don't use RGB codes. Find some other tools.

If you use Mac OS X, you have just such a tool in the Utilities folder (in your Applications folder). It's called Digital Color Meter. Launch the application and choose RGB As Actual Value, 8-bit from the pop-up menu in its window. Now the little blue numbers show proper red (R), green (G), and blue (B) values for any color you point to on your screen. For example, in the status area (in Layout mode), pop open the Fill Color menu and point to any of the colors there to see the RGB equivalent.

On Microsoft Windows, you can see RGB colors in the standard color picker window. Just go to Layout mode, and in the status area, click the Fill Color button. Choose Other Color. When you click a color, you see the red, green, and blue values listed in the bottom-right corner of the window.

- SimplifiedChinese
- OEM
- Symbol
- Other

Note: Unlike the font name, which is simply a text value, the script value shouldn't be in quotes. It's not a text value. Instead, you must specify one of the above values exactly, with no quotes.

If FileMaker can't find the specific font you've asked for, it selects another font in the specified script, so if you're on an English-based system and need to select a Chinese font, this parameter can help. (If you don't specify a script, FileMaker automatically uses the default script on your computer. That's why you rarely have to worry about it—you automatically get what you probably want.)

TextSize

The TextSize function is simple in every case. Just pass some text, and the point size you'd like (just like the sizes in the Format → Size menu in Browse mode). FileMaker returns the resized text.

TextStyleAdd and TextStyleRemove

Changing text *styles* (bold, italic, and so on) is a little more complicated. After all, a piece of text can have only *one* color, *one* font, or *one* size, but it can be bold, italic, and underlined all at the same time. With text styles, you don't just swap one style for another; you need to do things like take italic text and add bold formatting or even take bold-titlecase-strikethrough text and un-strikethrough it, leaving everything else in place.

To solve these problems, FileMaker gives you *two* functions for dealing with style: TextStyleAdd and TextStyleRemove. You use the first to add a style to a piece of text:

```
"Do it with " & TextStyleAdd ( "style" ; Italic )
```

Likewise, the TextStyleRemove function removes the specified style from the text.

```
TextStyleRemove ( My Text Field ; Italic )
```

The text style parameter goes in the calculation without quotes, just like the examples above. You can use any and every text style in FileMaker: Plain, Bold, Italic, Underline, Condense, Extend, Strikethrough, SmallCaps, Superscript, Subscript, Uppercase, Lowercase, Titlecase, WordUnderline, and DoubleUnderline. And then there's AllStyles. When you use the AllStyles parameter, it adds (or removes) *all* existing styles.

With these two functions and all these style options, you can do any kind of fancy formatting footwork imaginable. Here are some guidelines:

- When you add a style to some text using TextStyleAdd, it doesn't change any style that you've already applied. The new style's simply layered over the existing styles.
- Plain style's the notable exception to the above point. Adding Plain style effectively *removes* any other styling. This style comes in handy when you need to remove a mess of styling and apply something simpler. Say your fields contain the words "Past Due," styled in uppercase, bold, italic, and double underlined, and you decide that modest italics would work just fine. Nesting the TextStyleAdd function with the Plain parameter does the trick:

```
TextStyleAdd ( TextStyleAdd ( "past due" ; Plain ) ; Italic )
```

Note: As you may suspect, using TextStyleRemove with the AllStyles parameter does the exact same thing as TextStyleAdd with Plain. They both remove existing styling, but as you can see above, when you add Plain, you can write neater expressions.

- When you add more than one style parameter, FileMaker applies them all to the text. You can use nesting, as shown in the previous point, or simply stack them up with + signs:

```
TextStyleAdd ( "WARNING" ; Bold+Italic )
```

- If you take a bit of text that was formatted with a text formatting function, and then send it to another calculation as a parameter, the formatting goes along with the text. With the substitute function, for example, you can format text that hasn't even been typed yet. If you add this function to a text field into which people can type letters to customers, it changes every occurrence of "for a limited time" to bold italics.

```
Substitute ( Letter ; "for a limited time" ; TextStyleAdd ( "for a limited
time" ; Bold+Italic )
```

Date and Time Calculations

FileMaker can be a little esoteric about dates and times. If you don't understand how they work, you can end up wasting a *lot* of time trying to do things that FileMaker can easily do for you. For example, you may need to know the first day of the month following the date an invoice is due. You can spend ages writing a calculation that takes leap years and the different number of days in each month into account. You'd be sweaty, tired, and proud when you were done—six hours after you started. But if you know how dates work in FileMaker, you can just type this single line:

```
Date ( Month ( Invoice Due Date ) + 1 ; 1 ; Year ( Invoice Due Date ) )
```

How FileMaker Looks at Time

Before you start writing date and time calculations, you need to know how FileMaker actually keeps track of dates and times. FileMaker internally stores any date or time value as a single number that makes sense to it. Then, when it needs to display a date or time, it converts the number to a value people recognize as a date or time, like "11/7/2007" or "10:23 AM." As with other numbers that it stores one way and displays another, FileMaker does the math on the stored value, and then converts it for your convenience. Here's how FileMaker keeps track of time:

- It stores a *date* as the number of days since the beginning of the year 1 A. D.
- It stores a *time* as the number of seconds since midnight.
- It stores a *timestamp* as the number of seconds since midnight at the beginning of the year 1 A. D. (a really big number).

This secret to date and time storage isn't just a technicality. It actually tells you a lot about how you can use dates and times in calculations. In the next few sections, you'll see how you can use simple math to do temporal magic.

Math with Dates and Times

Because FileMaker looks at dates and times as numbers, you're free to use them right along with other numbers and operators in all kinds of mathematical functions. By adding, subtracting, multiplying, and dividing dates, times, timestamps, and numbers, you can come up with meaningful results.

Dates

You can use the information in your database's date fields to have FileMaker figure out due dates, anniversaries, and so on. You can use date fields and numbers interchangeably. FileMaker's smart enough to figure out that you want to add whole days to the date value it's storing. Here are some general principles:

- To get a date in the future or past, add or subtract the number of days. For example, if your policy is that payments are due 10 days after invoices are presented, use this calculation:

  ```
  Invoice Date + 10
  ```

- Of course, you aren't limited to adding constant numbers to dates. You can add a number field to a date field just as easily. If your video rental database holds the checkout date and the rental duration, you can find the due date with this calculation:

  ```
  Checkout Date + Rental Duration
  ```

- To get the number of days between two dates, subtract them.

  Imagine your registration database holds arrival and departure dates. You can find the duration of the stay (in days) using this calculation:

  ```
  Departure Date-Arrival Date
  ```

Note: When you're adding a number to a date, the result is a brand new date, and you should set the result type of your calculation accordingly. On the other hand, if you're subtracting two dates, the result is a number–the number of days between the two dates. In this case, set your calculation to return a number result.

Times

Although FileMaker's internal clock counts time as the number of seconds since midnight, a time value doesn't always have to be a time of day. Depending on the field format (page 253 in Chapter 6), a time value can be a time of day, like 2:30 PM, or a *time* (as in duration, like 3 hours, 27 minutes).

Note: FileMaker is savvy to the concept that time passes, but not all programs are. For instance, if you're exporting data to Excel, you should first convert time fields containing durations to plain old number fields.

In both cases, times have a numeric value, in hours:minutes:seconds format. When considered a time of day, 14:30:05 represents 5 seconds after 2:30 PM, but if you look at it as a duration, it represents 14 hours, 30 minutes, and 5 seconds. If the time has fractional seconds (a decimal point), the numerical value does too.

You can record how long your 5-year-old takes to find her shoes (34:26:18), or how long she takes to find the Halloween candy (00:00:02.13).

The key to doing math with any kind of time value is to remember you're always adding and subtracting amounts of *seconds*. Here are the guidelines:

- To get a time in the future or past, add or subtract a number of seconds or a time value. If you know when a student finished her exam, and you know how long the exam took in minutes (1 minute = 60 seconds), you can figure out when she started:

```
Finish Time-(Exam Duration * 60)
```

- To get the number of seconds between two times, subtract one from the other. Your Test Reporting database stores start and finish times for each exam. To find the duration, use this calculation:

```
Finish Time-Start Time
```

- To get a time of day value in the future or past, add or subtract the number of seconds or a time value. Suppose you have a database of movie show times for your theater business. You use a timestamp field to record the date and time when each showing starts. You also use a time field to keep track of how long each movie is. Now you need to know when each movie *ends*:

```
Showtime + Duration
```

Note: If you store the date and time the movie starts in separate date and time fields, the movie time calculation is much more difficult. Suppose a movie starts at 11:30 p.m. and runs for two hours. Adding these together, you get 25:30, which is a perfectly valid time value, but not a valid *time of day*. When you add to time values, they don't "roll over" after midnight. Timestamps, on the other hand, work as expected: You get 1:30 a.m. on the next day.

- To get the number of seconds between two timestamp values, subtract one from the other. For example, you use timestamps to record the date and time you start and finish a job. To find out how long the job took, in minutes, use this calculation:

```
(Finish Time Stamp-Start Time Stamp) / 60
```

- To increase or decrease a time duration value, add or subtract the number of seconds, or another time duration. Say you have a related Songs table with a Song Lengths field to hold the length of each song on a CD. This calculation tells you how long the entire CD is:

```
Sum ( Songs::Song Lengths )
```

- To double, triple, halve, or otherwise scale a time duration, multiply or divide it by a number.

  If chilling your microbrew always takes twice as long as cooking, you can determine the chilling time with this calculation:

  ```
  Cooking Time * 2
  ```

Parsing Dates and Times

Just as you can parse bits of text from text fields, FileMaker lets you pull out parts of a date or time value. For example, you can keep track of all your employees' birthdays in a normal date field, but you're trying to get statistical data from the year they were born, so you're not concerned about the month or date part of that value. You have six functions at your disposal to pick those individual components from a date, time, or timestamp value. They are:

- Year
- Month
- Day
- Hours
- Minutes
- Seconds

With a date value, you can use Year, Month, and Day. If you have a time, Hours, Minutes, and Seconds apply. You can use all six functions with a timestamp value.

These functions all have the same form. Each takes a single parameter—the value—and returns a numerical result. For example, the day function returns the day portion of a date. This calculation returns 27:

```
Day ( "7/27/2006")
```

UP TO SPEED

From Numbers to Times

If you can treat dates and times like numbers, it only makes sense that you can go the other way, too. Suppose you have a field called Race Time that holds each athlete's race time as a number of seconds. If you'd rather view this time in the Hours:Minutes:Seconds (or Minutes:Seconds) format, you can easily use a calculation to convert it to a time value:

```
GetAsTime(Race Time)
```

When you pass it a number value, the GetAsTime function converts that number into the equivalent time. (If you view this on a layout, you can use the time formatting options to display hours, minutes, and seconds in just about any way you want, as shown on page 253.) The GetAsTime function has another purpose: It can convert *text values* into times. If someone puts "3:37:03" into a text field, you can use GetAsTime to convert that text into a valid time value.

FileMaker has GetAsDate and GetAsTimestamp functions, too, which work just the same.

Note: For advice on how to display the results of month and day values in plain English, see the box below.

UP TO SPEED

Name the Day (or Month)

Even when you're using the month number to group your data, you may prefer to see months by *name*. For example, if you produce a report of sales by month, you probably want the groupings labeled January, February, March, and so on, instead of 1, 2, and 3. You can use the MonthName function to get this effect:

```
MonthName ( Invoice Date )
```

This calculation returns "March."

You can still sort all your invoices by the date field to get them in order, but you use your new MonthName value to display in the sub-summary part. See "Summarizing repetitions" on page 294 for details on using sub-summary parts in reports.

Sometimes you need to see the day name (Monday, Tuesday, or Wednesday, for example). The DayName function does just that. To get its numerical equivalent, use DayOfWeek instead, which returns 1 for Sunday, 2 for Monday, and so forth.

Calculations that Create Dates and Times

Almost every database in existence has fields that create date and time values—otherwise, folks would still sit around pecking out business forms with a typewriter, an adding machine, and a wall calendar. It sounds quaint, but there was one advantage—the human brain. Without even being aware of it, people do incredibly complex math every time they glance at a paper calendar or analog clock. When the boss said, "I want these invoices to go out two days before the end of next month," a human clerk knew exactly what to do.

When you work with dates and times in FileMaker, sometimes you can get away with simple math as in the previous section, plugging date and time values into basic calculations. But how do you tell a computer to put "two days before the end of next month" in the Invoice Date field? FileMaker provides three functions to assist the translation:

- The **date** function accepts three parameters—Month, Day, and Year—and returns the appropriate date value. For example, to put a date value of January 21, 2006 in a calculation, you use the date function like this:

  ```
  Date ( 1 ; 21 ; 2006 )
  ```

- The **time** function wants three parameters as well, this time Hours, Minutes, and Seconds. It returns the time value. (The Seconds parameter can have a decimal point if necessary.) For example, you can construct the time value "8:00 PM" like this:

  ```
  Time ( 20 ; 0 ; 0 )
  ```

Note: For time-of-day values, the time function doesn't let you specify AM or PM, so you have to use 24-hour notation.

- The **timestamp** function takes just two parameters: Date and Time. It combines the two into a single timestamp value. It shows January 10, 2006 at 8:30 PM like this:

```
Timestamp ( Date ( 1 ; 10 ; 2006) ; Time ( 20 ; 30 ; 0 ) )
```

  In this example, you use all three functions: the date function to produce the correct date value, the time function for the time value, and the timestamp function to put them together.

FREQUENTLY ASKED QUESTION

Why Functions?

Why can't I just put "1/10/2006" in my calculation, just like I'd put it in a date field?

Because "1/10/2006" is a text value, not a date value. When you're entering data in a date field, FileMaker knows it's a date field, and is nice enough to convert text like this into a date for you. In a calculation, though, FileMaker may not know you want a date, so it treats what you put in as text instead.

You can use the GetAsDate( ) function to convert text values like this into dates:

```
GetAsDate ( "1/10/2006" )
```

But even this isn't advisable. Remember that dates are interpreted depending on how you've configured your computer. On one computer, this calculation could produce the date value January 10, 2006, while on another machine it might result in October 1 instead. In other words, there's no safe way to ensure you get the date you really want when you use GetAsDate with a text value, unless you're using text the user supplied.

The date function always expects the month, then the day, then the year. Computer settings don't affect it. So the date function is the safest way to record dates in calculations.

The secret powers of date

Although FileMaker doesn't look at calendars the way people do, that's not all bad. You see a calendar in absolute terms: April 30 belongs to April, May 1 belongs to May, and that's that. FileMaker, however, thinks of dates in relative terms and sees no such limitations. You can use this flexibility to your advantage in calculations—big time. You can give seemingly illogical parameters to the date function, and have FileMaker produce a valid date anyway.

For example, this calculation actually produces a valid date:

```
Date ( 5 ; 0 ; 2006 )
```

You see a nonsense result—May 0, 2006. But FileMaker looks at the same code and says, "No problem. Zero comes before 1, so you must mean the day that comes before May 1." And so it returns April 30, 2006.

These same smarts apply to the month as well:

```
Date ( 15 ; 11 ; 2006 )
```

That calculation produces March 11, *2007*. In other words, three months into the next year, since 15 is three months more than one year.

This behavior comes in super handy when you're trying to fiddle with dates in calculations. Suppose you have order records, each one with an order date. You bill on the last day of the month in which the order was placed, so your calculation needs to figure out that date, which could be 28, 30, or 31, depending on the month, or even 29 if it's February in a leap year. That calculation would take an entire page in this book. But here's a much easier approach: Instead of calculating which day each month ends, use the fact that the *last* day of *this* month is always the day *before* the *first* day of *next* month. To start with, you can calculate next month like this:

```
Month ( Order Date ) + 1
```

So the date of the first day of next month is:

```
Date ( Month(Order Date) + 1 ; 1 ; Year(Order Date) )
```

To get the day before, just subtract one from the whole thing:

```
Date (
    Month(Order Date) + 1;     // the _next_ month
    1;                   //the _first_ day
    Year(Order Date)     // the same year
)- 1                   // subtract 1 to get the day before
```

It may look a little confusing at first, but it's much shorter than a page. And it works perfectly every month of every year.

Aggregate Calculations

The min and max functions you learned about on page 435 are part of a collection of functions called *aggregate functions*. Aggregate functions work differently from other FileMaker functions when you use related fields because they look at all the *related* records. For example, consider this calculation:

```
Round(Line Items::Price, 2)
```

It uses the *round* function to round a related Price field's value to two decimal places. If you have three related line item records, this calculation returns the rounded value from only the *first* record. After all, it really only makes sense to round a single value. But aggregate functions are, by their nature, all about working with lots of values. This calculation returns the largest price across all three related line item records:

```
Max(Line Items::Price)
```

Min and max are two of the most common aggregate functions, but FileMaker offers several, from the obvious, to the obscure, to the unexpected. You can see them all by selecting "Aggregate functions" from the View pop-up menu in the Specify Calculation dialog box.

Numerical Aggregate Functions

The most basic aggregate functions operate on numbers and perform fairly common operations. The common ones include:

- **Min** returns the smallest of the values passed to it.
- **Max** returns the largest value instead.
- **Average** calculates the statistical average of all the values. (In other words, it adds the values, counts them, and divides the total by the count.)
- **Sum** adds all the values and returns the total.

One more aggregate function, called *count*, is also very common. It counts the number of values passed to it. If one of the related values is empty, then it isn't counted. So you can use this function to count all the related records (by passing a field that will never be empty, like the ID field):

```
Count(Line Items::Line Item ID)
```

Or you can count how many records have a value for a certain field. This calculation tells you how many customers have no company name:

```
Count(Customers::Customer ID) - Count(Customers::Company Name)
```

In addition to these everyday numerical functions, FileMaker offers a few more powerful statistical functions for number crunchers (you know who you are):

- **Stdev** and **StDevP** calculate standard deviations. Use the first for the standard deviation of a sample, and the second for the population. Or ignore this sentence completely and be glad you don't know what it means.
- **Variance** and **VarianceP** perform a statistical *variance* calculation. Again, you get a sample and population version.

The List Function

One aggregate function has nothing to do with numbers at all. The list function typically operates on text values. It gathers up all the values passed to it and returns them in one long list. For example, this calculation uses the list function:

```
List(Line Items::Description)
```

It might return something like this:

```
35mm Film
1GB USB Flash Drive
Labor
```

This calculation returns each description from the related line item records, with one record's value on each line. The list function allows you to suck related data into a single block for easy display, reporting, or manipulation. It comes in particularly handy when trying to quickly show related data in a tooltip, which you'll learn about on page 723 (Chapter 19).

Containers in Calculations

Although it isn't a typical calculation data type, you can do a few interesting things with container fields in calculations. You don't have the same vast options you do with other types. It would be great if you could subtract Cousin Clem.jpg from Family Reunion.jpg to get the scoundrel out of the picture, but alas, the technology's not quite there yet. Nevertheless, FileMaker doesn't leave containers entirely out in the cold when it comes to calculations.

Calculations with Pictures, Sounds, Movies, and Files

When you create a calculation field, you can set its result type to Container. You can't *create* container data in a calculation, but you *can* refer to other container fields. When you do, the picture, sound, movie, or file in the referenced container field shows in the new calculation field.

You can, for example, make a calculation field that shows the contents of one container field when you're in Browse mode and another in Preview mode. This field lets you use low-resolution images when you view on the screen, and higher resolutions when you view in print. (You'll learn to do that in the next chapter, when you learn about calculations with that kind of decision-making ability.)

You may also want to use container fields in a calculated replace. Suppose you have a found set of 30 records that don't have a low-resolution image. You have to have something in that field, so you decide to take the hi-resolution image for those few records and plunk them down in the low-resolution image field. Choose Records → Replace Field Contents and perform this calculated replace:

```
Graphics::High Resolution Image
```

The entire calculation consists of a reference to a field of that name in the Graphics table. The calculation does the grunt work of copying the high-resolution image into the low-resolution field in each record.

Calculations with References

If a container field holds a reference to a picture, movie, sound, or file, instead of the object itself (page 80), you can do even more. When you treat such a field as *text*, FileMaker gives you some information about the referenced file.

If you have a field called Product Shot that holds a reference to a photograph file, you can use this calculation:

```
GetAsText ( Product Shot )
```

The result of this calculation looks like this:

```
size:266,309
image:../../../../../quilt database/sale quilt pix/batik squares.jpg
imagemac:/babycakes/current work/quilt database/sale quilt pix/batik squares.
jpg
```

FileMaker tells you the size (width and height in pixels) and location of the file (if this weren't a picture, you wouldn't see the "size:" line).

You can use this calculation to help you keep track of a set of images that the whole company needs to use. You really need two container fields for this purpose. One holds the graphic itself, or a low-resolution copy, if you don't want the file size to balloon. Then, when you place the graphic as a reference in the second container field, the calculation stores the graphic's original location. The calculation's not dynamic, however, so the path serves as a reference of where the file *should* be, not where it really is. Company policy about putting things back where you found them has to reinforce your good data practices.

CHAPTER

11

Advanced Calculations

In the previous two chapters, you learned loads of ways calculations can make your databases work harder for you. But the functions you've learned so far can't make your databases work much *smarter*. For example, what if you want to add a five-percent delinquency charge to invoices over a month old? You could do it in any number of ways, from sorting invoice records to creating a special "past due balance" field. But they all either make extra work for the person using the database, or give you yet another field to worry about every time you tweak, troubleshoot, or repurpose the database. The most elegant solution is to let the database figure out for itself when an invoice is past due. In other words, you want to create a calculation that makes a *decision* based on current data, whatever it may be. This chapter shows you how to give your calculations that brainpower by using logical functions and other advanced techniques.

Note: Before you read on, now's a good time to download a fresh copy of the working database. This chapter refers to some layouts and fields that your copy may not have. download a copy of this chapter's sample file at *www.missingmanuals.com/cds.*.

Conditional Formatting

The whole point of a database is to make it easier to find and use information. Using conditional formatting, you can make important data more visible on your layouts, so it's easier to see what you need to know with a quick glance. For example, when your collections department has to call your client's accounting department, it would be easier for them to find information they need if you make the Due Date and Amount Due fields turn bold and bright red if the invoice hasn't been paid.

Back on page 238, you learned how to use conditional formatting to change the way fields or text objects display data. You dipped your toe into the power of the Condition pop-up menu (Figure 11-1) by choosing "Formula is," and then typing a simple calculation. Now it's time to wade in a little further.

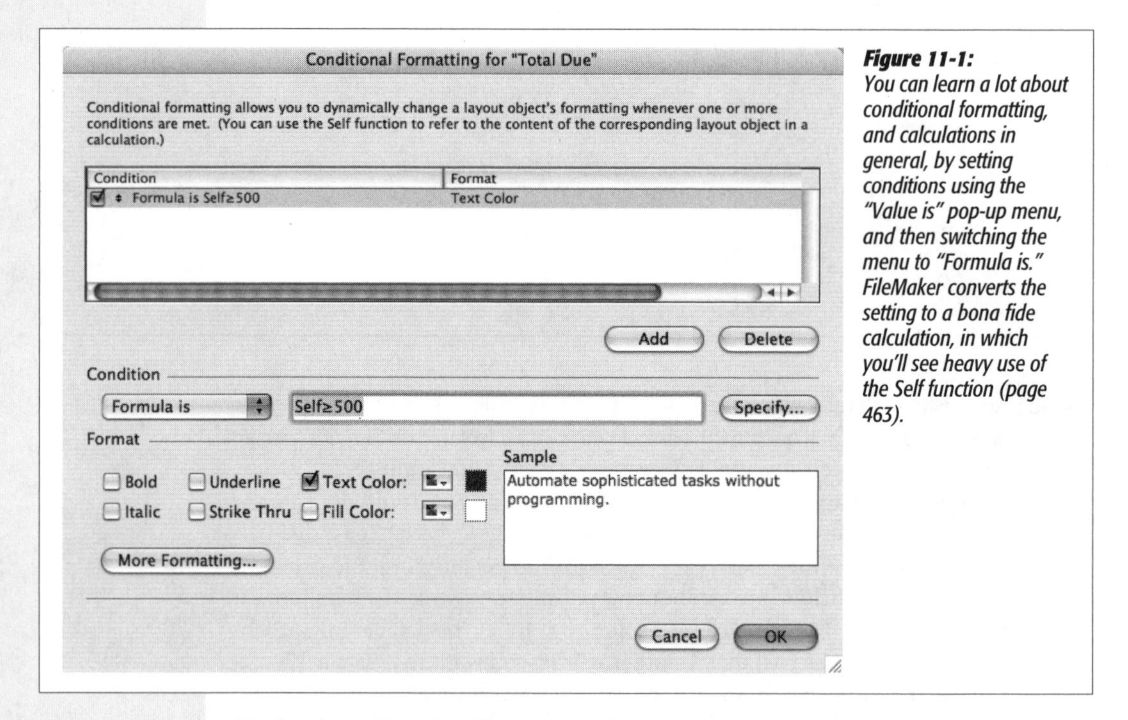

Figure 11-1: *You can learn a lot about conditional formatting, and calculations in general, by setting conditions using the "Value is" pop-up menu, and then switching the menu to "Formula is." FileMaker converts the setting to a bona fide calculation, in which you'll see heavy use of the Self function (page 463).*

Understanding Boolean Functions

You can't write just any calculation, though. The result of any conditional formatting calculation must be a Boolean value. But Boolean isn't a choice in the "Calculation Result is" pop-up menu. Instead, you have to write an equation that produces a Boolean result. Booleans aren't really hard to understand, so long as you look at the world through their eyes. To Booleans, everything is either black or white. Things are either "true" or "false," "yes" or "no," "not empty" or "empty." There are no shades of grey in the Boolean world; there's no "maybe," and there are no glasses that are half full.

For example, these statements are true, as most any modern schoolchild can tell you:

$4 > 3$

$6 * 6 = 36$

$E = mc^2$

In Boolean terms, they are "True." So are the values:

```
1
True
T
Yes
Y
```

If you turn a Boolean loose on these statements, they'll evaluate as "False."

```
0
False
F
f
No
N
n
Blank or ""
```

It's that last item in the list that can make things a little murky. Typing the word *blank* in a field doesn't make it evaluate as false; *leaving* it blank does. And that's what the "" (empty quote marks) mean. For example, in a record for Lance Armstrong, even the value of "couch potato" in the "Amount of Daily Exercise" field means "True" to a Boolean statement. If the entry isn't "0" or "False" or another item in the list above, all the Boolean cares about is whether there's a value in the field. You've already used this fact to your advantage on page 263 when you used a calculation to format the text of an Email button as gray if the Email Address field was empty:

```
Customers::Email Address = ""
```

This calculation is explicit about what it's looking for. It checks the contents of the Email Address field for contents that are blank. The statement evaluates to "True" when the field is blank, and to "False" when there's data in the field.

Note: Just remember that the Boolean calculation is not checking the validity of the email address. You can write a calculation that tests the email address for its essential parts (ude the PatternCount function) or use a plug-in (page 487) to send an email and actually test the address.

Even though it's more explicit to add the equals sign and the empty quote marks, it isn't necessary because "empty" means "False" in the Boolean world. Plus, some developers don't like the inverted logic required when you check for the presence of nothing in a field. That's why you'll often see Booleans written more simply, like so:

```
Customers::Email Address
```

Unlike the first example, this calculation evaluates to "True" when there is data in the field, and to "False" when it's empty. But you can reinvert the logic by putting a "not" in front of a calculation:

```
not Customers::Email Address
```

This syntax means that the result is "True" when the field is empty and "False" when the field contains data.

So is one method better than another? Probably not. But when you look at other developers' calculations, you may see all these forms, so it helps to know how they work. If you're the only developer working on your files, then you're free to use the construction that makes most sense to you. But when you develop in a team, you might want to develop a standard for constructing your Boolean calculations. In either case, it's a good idea to comment your Boolean calculations, so those who follow you can save time trying to retrace your logic.

GEEKILY ASKED QUESTION

Separating Formatting from Data

Why would a math major like me use lowly, layout-based conditional formatting when I can make a whole bunch of very cool, very complicated calculations using text formatting functions?

It's true that conditional formatting, which was introduced in FileMaker 9, doesn't give you a whole bunch of new options that you didn't already have in text formatting functions. What you do get, though, is a giant leap closer to something that's been difficult to do in FileMaker–separating the presentation layer from the data layer of your file.

In programmer-speak, the *presentation layer* is anything having to do with showing you your data. It's the layout and all the stuff you put on a layout to make your data easy to understand. Even the fact that you can move fields around in relation to one another is part of FileMaker's sophisticated presentation layer. Boldface fields, portals, buttons, and Web viewers are presentation tools, as well. Custom menus (page 724) and tooltips (page 723), which help you help your users work with their data, are also a form of presentation.

The *data layer* is just what it sounds like–the tables and fields (or rows and columns) of actual information. Most calculations also fall onto the data layer. For example, when you multiply the Quantity and Price Each fields together, using a calculation in the Extended Price field, that's data. So is adding a five percent surcharge to late payments. Adding another five percent 30 days later, when those deadbeats have come up with more excuses, is still data.

But when you use number formatting to display the results of any of those calculations with dollar signs, commas, and decimal places, that's presentation-layer territory. And if you use a text function to display the late penalty in red, boldface at 18 points, you're treading in the presentation layer, even if you use a sophisticated calculation to see if the penalty is due before you apply the format. Those calculations are difficult to adapt if your business rules change or troubleshoot if something goes wrong.

Furthermore, when you rely solely on calculations for formatting, you've got to add more *complexity* to your calculations to *simplify* some layouts. Say you use a text formatting function to display unpaid invoice totals in red after 30 days. The field *always* displays the red text, even if that's not the purpose of the layout. For example, if the marketing department needs a list of invoices over $500 to decide who gets special offers, the red invoice amounts make no sense–and may violate customers' privacy. But if you separate presentation and data using conditional formatting, you can apply the format on a layout-by-layout basis. So all in all, it makes life easier down the road if you confine your use of calculations to mathematical operations *on* your data and use conditional formatting to handle the display *of* your data.

Using the Self Function

You got a peek at the Self function back in Figure 11-1. The Self function simply returns the contents of the object it's applied to. Without a Self function, you'd have to use the Object Info palette to name the object you wanted to format conditionally, and then reference the formatted object by name in your calculation. But that's just too much work, so FileMaker's engineers created the Self function to make that process easier. The good news is that you can use the Self function in your own calculations to make them portable—that is, you won't need to retrofit them if you move them from one field or object to another.

Here's one example of how it works. The five volunteer data entry folks keeping up with your theater group's subscription and donor list are expressing their artistic temperament by using different formats for phone numbers. So when you print out the contact list, you've got (800) 555-1212, 800-555-1212, 800.555.1212, 555-1212, and every other variation under the sun.

FileMaker's Auto-Enter calculations can help you transform self-expression into standard formats. To straighten things out, you could add this calculation to your Phone field:

```
"(" & // start with an open paren sign
Left ( Filter ( Phone ; "0123456789" ) ; 3 ) & // grab the area code
") " & // finish the area code with a close paren
Middle ( Filter ( Phone; "0123456789" ) ;  4 ; 3 ) & // grab the exchange
"-" & // give me a hyphen
Middle ( Filter ( Phone ; "0123456789" ) ; 7 ; 4 ) // the last four digits
```

This calculation takes the data entered into the Phone field and imposes its own order onto the data. As the comments show, one part of the phone number format is assembled from each line of this nested calculation.

Note: This formula uses several techniques that were covered in Chapters 9 and 10: The Filter function (page 445); Left, Middle, and Right functions (page 440); and nested functions (page 448). Also, the Customer field in the sample database at *www.missingmanuals.com/cds* shows you the Self version of the formula in action.

This calculation solves the problem for the Home Phone field, but what if all your records contain three Phone fields? Plus, you've got three Phone fields in your Employees and Vendors databases, too. To transfer this calculation, you'd have to paste it into each field's Auto-Enter calculation dialog box, select each instance of "Phone," and change it to "Mobile" or "Work Phone" so the calculation can work properly in each new context. Don't you have *real* work to do?

With the Self function, which takes no parameter, and therefore doesn't need its own set of parentheses, you can write the calculation this way instead:

```
"(" &
Left ( Filter ( Self ; "0123456789" ) ; 3 ) &
") " &
Middle ( Filter ( Self; "0123456789" ) ;  4 ; 3 ) &
"-" &
Middle ( Filter ( Self ; "0123456789" ) ; 7 ; 4 )
```

The Self function knows that it's referring to the field it's in, so you can copy and paste this function until the digital cows come home, and you never have to edit it for its new context. Good as it is, this calculation still has a couple loopholes. See the box on page 478 for another way to clean up stray data entry in a Phone field.

Stored, Unstored, and Global Fields

When you defined calculation fields in Chapters 9 and 10, you may have wondered about the Specify Calculation dialog box's Storage Options button (Figure 11-2). You learned about indexing and other storage options back in Chapter 3 (see page 117). When you use similar options in your calculations, you exercise more control over the information your functions work with.

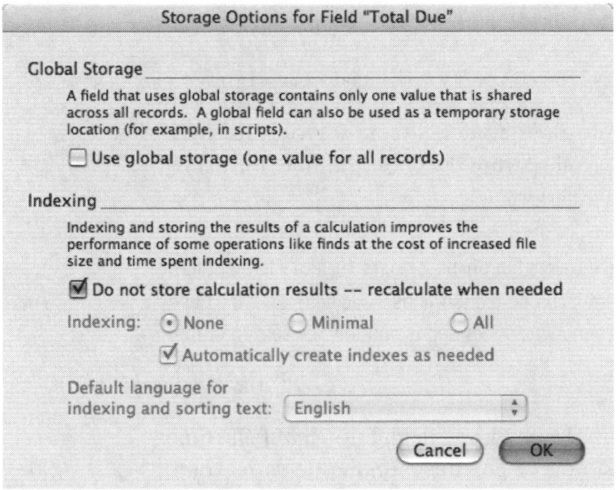

Figure 11-2: *When you click the Storage Options button in the Specify Calculation dialog box, you can set global storage and indexing options, just like any other field type. You also get a choice you haven't seen before: "Do not store calculation results." With this option, you can make your calculations save information as a kind of snapshot or use the most up-to-date information as your database changes. This example shows the storage options for the Invoice::Total Due field, which is not stored because you want FileMaker to update if you add or edit any line item on the invoice. Notice though, that unstored calculations can't be indexed. That means finds will be a little slower and you can't use an unstored calculation as a key field (page 318).*

Stored and Unstored Calculation Fields

Normally, a calculation field holds a value just like any other field. *You* can't edit the value, because FileMaker creates it for you from the calculation. When you use this field on a layout, for example, FileMaker simply displays its results. Depending on whether you turn on the "Do not store calculation result" option in

Figure 11-2, FileMaker either grabs saved (stored) results from a table or calculates the value *on the fly* whenever necessary. For example, when you have an unstored calculation field on a layout, FileMaker recalculates the value as soon as you switch to the layout. In fact, whenever an unstored field is showing onscreen, FileMaker updates it automatically any time something causes its value to change.

At the same time, whenever the data in a field changes, FileMaker also works behind the scenes, finding all the *stored* calculation fields that depend on the changed field, and *recalculates* them (even if they're aren't on your current layout), storing the new value in the field. Whether it's stored or unstored, a calculation field usually changes because a field used in the calculation has changed, as you'll see next. Understanding *when* fields recalculate and how dependencies work can help you avoid future mistakes.

Note: When you use a field in a calculation, you can say the calculation *depends* on the field (or, in other words, it has a *dependency* on the field).

Field dependencies

Take a look at the example in Figure 11-3 to see how FileMaker knows when to recalculate fields. It's very common for calculation fields to use other calculation fields in complex arrangements, as this hierarchy of field dependencies illustrates.

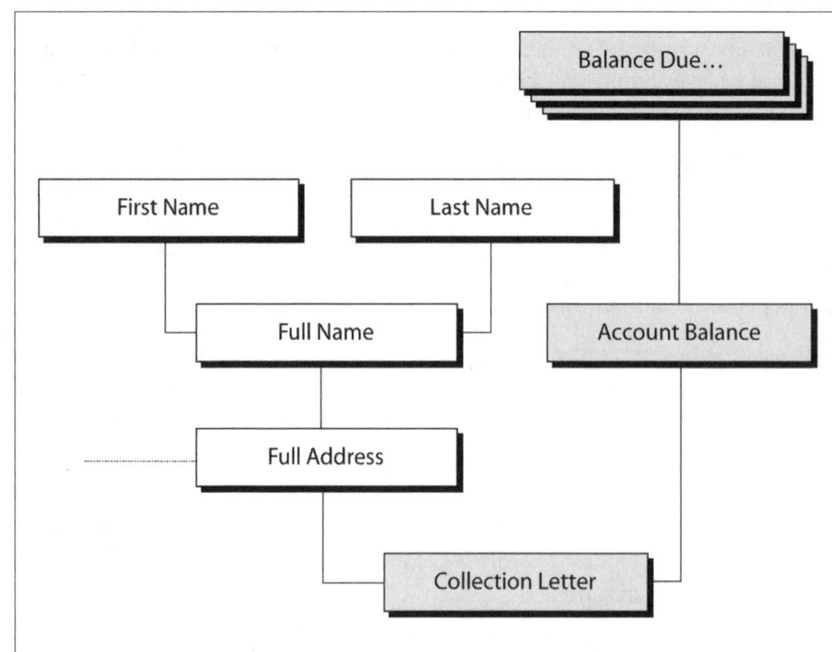

Figure 11-3: *This picture shows a series of interdependent fields. The Full Name field is a calculation field that uses First Name and Last Name. The Full Address field uses Full Name (and some others not shown here). The fields in gray are unstored calculation fields. Collection Letter uses Account Balance and Full Address. Account Balance in turn uses Balance Due. Since an account can have several invoices, each with a balance due, Account Balance actually uses several balance due values—one from each related invoice.*

First Name and Last Name are the only editable fields in Figure 11-3. When someone edits one of these fields, FileMaker looks at the field dependencies to see if it needs to do any extra work. The program sees that it needs to recalculate Full Name and then store that Full Name value, which in turn triggers more work. FileMaker must recalculate and store the Full Address value as well. In a sense, that one change trickles down through all the dependent fields as FileMaker calculates and stores, calculates and stores. All this recalculating happens as soon as the user exits the First Name field after making the change.

By contrast, since Collection Letter is an *unstored field and it's not shown on this layout*, FileMaker *doesn't* recalculate it right away. (There's no reason to recalculate since you aren't *displaying* the value anywhere on the current layout.) Instead, the program waits until someone brings up the field onscreen, *then* it runs the calculation on the current data and displays the result.

At that time, more things change. To calculate the Collection Letter value, FileMaker grabs the stored value for the Full Address field. But it also needs the Account Balance, which is not stored. As such, it has to first calculate *that* field. Doing so requires calculating the Balance Due on each invoice in turn, and then adding them up to get an Account Balance. Finally, it has the values it needs to show you the Collection Letter. Thus, when you use *unstored* calculations, FileMaker pulls the data it needs down through the hierarchy of dependencies on an as-needed basis.

Deciding when to store

When you first create a calculation field, FileMaker makes it a stored field automatically, *if possible*. Some field values aren't eligible for storage. These are the situations when a calculation field must be unstored:

- If it depends on any other unstored fields
- If it depends on any global fields
- If it depends on any related fields
- If it depends on any summary fields

If your calculation meets any of these criteria, FileMaker automatically turns on the "Do not store calculation results–recalculate when needed" option for you, and it doesn't let you turn it off. Otherwise, FileMaker automatically stores the field.

- An unstored field has to be recalculated every time it appears onscreen, in a layout, or in a report. All that recalculation can slow your database down, especially if the unstored field is part of a summary field or a calculation that aggregates many records. So it's best to store a field unless you need and expect a freshly calculated value every time.
- If you perform a find based on an unstored calculation field, FileMaker has to go through all your records one-by-one, calculating each one as it goes. The result is a slow search process. If you plan on searching a field, store it. (For more detail, see the box on page 467.)

Even if FileMaker can store a certain value, you may not always want it to. Here are some reasons you might turn *on* that "Do not store" box:

- Stored fields automatically recalculate as needed when *other fields* change. But FileMaker has no such automatic behavior for other kinds of information. For example, when you use the Get(CurrentDate) function in a calculation, FileMaker doesn't recalculate it when the date changes. In general, when you use any of the Get functions (page 415), you usually want to make your field unstored to "get" the most up-to-date information.
- A stored field takes up space on disk, while an unstored field doesn't. FileMaker 9 files can hold 8 terabytes of data, so space isn't a major consideration for most people. But if you're into slim and trim files, you can save space by making calculations unstored.
- Lots of stored calculation fields can really slow down *record creation*. That's usually not a big deal, but if you often import data (Chapter 17) or use a script to regularly create lots of records, you can speed things up by reducing the number of stored calculations.

Tip: Obviously, there's some gray area here. When in doubt, store the field. You can always make it unstored later. Choose File → Manage Database, then select your field from the list and click Options, and then Storage Options to find the "Do not store calculation results–recalculate as needed" option.

FREQUENTLY ASKED QUESTION

I Want to Store My Field

What if I want to search on a field that FileMaker won't let me store?

Just because you can't store a field doesn't mean you don't wish you could. For example, in your Invoices layout, you probably do want to be able to search for invoices with a balance due. But since that field uses related data, it's not storable.

The good news is, you don't have to store a field in order to search it; the search is just a little slower. You won't notice the slowdown until you've amassed *lots* of invoice records. Sadly, there's no easy way to speed it up.

One remedy is to change the way people work with your database. You have to make your Invoice Detail layout *read only*–meaning users can't change data on the invoice directly (see page 619). Instead, they use a special layout and a script to make invoice changes.

When they're finished, your script can calculate the balance due and update a number field on the invoice appropriately. This way, the Balance Due field is a normal, nonrelated field, eligible for indexing and quick searches.

Also, remember that FileMaker can't search a field based on related data very quickly, but it can search the related data *itself* with lightning speed. For example, to find an invoice that has payments applied to it, don't search the Amount Paid field in the invoice. Instead, search for invoices where Payments::Amount is greater than zero. That search turns up every invoice with a related payment record that's not negative. You get exactly what you want, and FileMaker can carry it out using indexed fields.

Note: With the exception of global fields and unstored fields, you can set indexing for calculation fields just like any other field, as discussed on page 464. The available options and their effects depend on the result type of the calculation: text, number, date, or time.

Global Calculation Fields

A calculation field can use *global storage* (page 118) just like any other field. When you're in the Storage Options window and you turn on "Use global storage," FileMaker calculates just one value for the entire table, rather than a value for each record. If your calculation uses other global fields—and *no* other fields—then it works just as you expect. That is, when you modify one of the global fields it depends on, FileMaker automatically recalculates its value.

If the calculation uses non-global fields, on the other hand, things get a little tricky. Whenever you change one of the fields referenced in the calculation, FileMaker recalculates the global calculation field using the values from the current record. For example, if you turn on "Use global storage" for your Full Name field, it shows the name of the person you're looking at when you dismiss the Define Database window. If you were on the first record, that's whose name you see in the field, just as expected. But as you flip through the records, you see that first user's name on every record. You're changing records, but with global storage, the Full Name value stays the same. That's because nothing it depends on has changed.

Now imagine you switch to the *last* record. If you then change the First Name field, Full Name recalculates. This new value displays the first and last name from the last record, since FileMaker reevaluates the calculation in its entirety.

This behavior may seem kind of odd, but there's a really cool use for it. If you need to track the data in the last record you *changed*—maybe you need an informal audit of which record just got changed while you're scanning through other records—throw a global calculation field on your data entry layout. Then, no matter which record you're looking at, you see the value of the last *edited* record in that field.

Logical Functions

The logical function group is a diverse and powerful lot. You get functions for making decisions (called *conditional functions*), learning about field values, and even evaluating calculations *inside* other calculations. This section covers all those possibilities. Along the way, you learn how to define and use *variables*, which act as placeholders while complex calculations go through their many steps.

Conditional Functions

This chapter began by posing an interesting challenge: You have a calculation field in the Invoices table called Total Due. It calculates the total amount due on an invoice by subtracting the sum of all payments from the total amount of the invoice. Can you modify the Total Due calculation to add a five-percent penalty when an invoice is past due?

The answer lies in the three conditional functions. Each one lets you specify more than one possible result. The functions require one or more parameters—called *conditions* or *conditional expressions*—that tell them which result to pick. The conditional functions—If, Case, and Choose—differ in how many possible results they support and what kind of conditions they expect.

The If function

The first and most common conditional function is simply called *If*. The If function is the basic unit of decision making in FileMaker calculations. It's the ticket when you have to decide between two choices, based on some criteria.

It looks like this:

```
If ( Condition ; True Result ; False Result )
```

When you use the If function, FileMaker evaluates the condition looking for a Boolean result (True or False). If the condition has a True value, the function returns its second parameter (True result). If the condition is False, though, it returns the False result instead. Here's an example:

```
If ( First Name = "Dominique" ; "Free" ; "$299.00" )
```

For example, this calculation returns Free if the First Name field matches "Dominique." If it *doesn't* match, then it returns $299.00 instead.

FREQUENTLY ASKED QUESTION

Matching Text Values

What do you mean by "First Name field matches 'Dominique'?" What constitutes a match?

When you use the = operator with text values, FileMaker compares the two values on each side, letter by letter. If every letter, number, space, punctuation and so on matches, you get a True result. But the comparison isn't case sensitive. In other words, this expression has a True result:

```
"TEXT" = "text"
```

If this function is too forgiving for your needs, you can use the *Exact* function instead.

Exact takes two text parameters, compares them, and returns True if they match exactly–including case. This expression has a False result:

```
Exact ( "TEXT" ; "text" )
```

It's perfectly legal to use the Exact function (or any other function, field, or expression) as the first parameter of the If function, like this:

```
If ( Exact ( First Name ; "Dominique" ) ;
"Free" ; "$299.00" )
```

This version of the calculation would return "$299.00" if the First Name field contained "dominique," since the case on the letter D doesn't match.

The Case function

Sometimes you need to pick from more than just two choices. Luckily, the If function has a cousin named *Case* that simply excels at such problems. For example, suppose you want to show one of these four messages on the top of your layout:

- Good Morning
- Good Afternoon
- Good Evening
- Go To Bed

You obviously need to choose between these messages based on the time of day. The If function doesn't work very well for this problem because If only allows one condition and two possible results. You *can* nest If statements one inside the other, so that the False result is really another If statement. But nested If functions are really hard to read and even harder to tweak, so if you find that your business rules require a change in your calculation, you may rue the day you decided to use 12 nested Ifs to decide which discount your customers should get.

The Case function has this form:

```
Case ( test1 ; result1 ; {test2 ; result2 ; ... ; defaultResult } )
```

You can add as many parameters as you want, in pairs, to represent a condition and the result to be returned if that condition is True. Because the conditions and results are sequential and not nested, you can easily read a Case statement, no matter how many conditions you pile on. You can even add an optional parameter after the last result. This parameter represents the *default* result—the one FileMaker uses if none of the conditions were true.

Note: Since the Case function accepts several conditions, it's entirely possible that more than one condition is true at the same time. If so, FileMaker chooses the *first* True condition when it picks a result.

To implement the greeting message, a calculation using the Case function might look like this:

```
Case (
  Get ( CurrentTime ) > Time ( 4 ; 0 ; 0 ) and Get ( CurrentTime ) < Time (
  12 ; 0 ; 0 ) ;
  "Good Morning" ;

  Get ( CurrentTime ) > Time ( 12 ; 0 ; 0 ) and Get ( CurrentTime ) < Time (
  18 ; 0 ; 0 ) ;
  "Good Afternoon" ;

  Get ( CurrentTime ) > Time ( 18 ; 0 ; 0 ) and Get ( CurrentTime ) < Time (
  22 ; 0 ; 0 ) ;
```

```
        "Good Evening" ;

        "Go To Bed"
    )
```

In this calculation, the Case function checks first to see if the current time is between 4:00 AM and 12:00 PM. If it is, the "Good Morning" value is returned. If not, it then checks whether the time is between 12:00 PM and 6:00 PM, which would produce the "Good Afternoon" message. Finally, it checks to see if it's between 6:00 PM and 10:00 PM. If so, the user sees "Good Evening."

You don't need to specify a condition for the last result—"Go To Bed"—because if all the previous conditions are false, it *must* be time for bed. In other words, if it *isn't* the morning, and it *isn't* the afternoon, and it *isn't* the evening, then it must be late at night. (If you need further help deciphering the above calculation, see the box below. On the other hand, if you're so far ahead that you can see a better way to do it, see the box on page 473.)

UP TO SPEED

A Complex Case

The Case function expresses a familiar concept–do Plan A in one case, do Plan B in a different case, and so on. But you might not immediately know how you get from that simple idea to the more complicated calculations shown in this chapter. Here's how it breaks down:

Remember that semicolons separate the parameters you pass to a function. So the first parameter is *all* of this:

```
Get(CurrentTime) > Time(4;0;0) and
Get(CurrentTime) < Time(12;0;0)
```

That whole expression forms the first condition. Remember from Chapter 9 that the *and* operator works on two Boolean values. It returns a True result if the values on each side are *both true*.

So really, you can split this condition in two. First, this must be true:

```
Get(CurrentTime) > Time(4;0;0)
```

If that's true, FileMaker checks to see if this expression is true, too:

```
Get(CurrentTime) < Time(12;0;0)
```

These sub-expressions are much simpler. Each has the same form, comparing the current time to a time you construct with the Time function. The first makes sure it's after 4:00 AM. The second makes sure it's *before* 12:00 PM. The other two conditions in the calculation are exactly the same–except they look at different times.

The Choose function

The *Choose* function is sort of the forgotten third member of the conditional trio. People don't immediately grasp how to use it—so they don't. But if you think of it as a value list with the choices coded into a calculation, you see how the Choose function can turn an awfully ugly Case function into a specimen of neatness.

It looks like this:

```
Choose ( Condition ; Result Zero ; Result One ; Result Two ... )
```

Unlike the other conditional functions, Choose doesn't expect a Boolean expression for its condition. Instead, it looks for a *number*. The number tells it which of the results to choose: If Condition is zero, the function returns Result Zero; if it's one, it returns Result One; and so on.

Imagine you have a Student table, and one of its fields is called *GPA*. This field holds the student's current grade point average, as a number. You'd like to turn this number into a letter grade on the printed report.

Many FileMaker developers would immediately jump to the Case function to solve this problem. They'd do something like this:

```
Case (
 GPA < 0.5; "F";
 GPA < 1.5; "D";
 GPA < 2.5; "C";
 GPA < 3.5; "B";
 "A"
)
```

While this calculation gets the job done, you can do it more succinctly with the Choose function:

```
Choose ( Round(GPA; 0); "F"; "D"; "C"; "B"; "A" )
```

When you turn the GPA value into an integer (using the Round function), it becomes a candidate for the Choose function. When the GPA is 3.2, FileMaker rounds it to three, and selects the result that represents the number 3: "B." (Remember that the first result is for *zero*, so number three is actually the *fourth* result parameter. For more detail, see the box on page 474 called "Total Due calculation #1: Using the If function".)

Note: This calculation uses the Round function, which you haven't seen before. Round takes two numbers as parameters. It rounds the first value to the number of decimal places specified in the second parameter.

Constructing a Conditional Calculation

Now that you've seen the three conditional functions, it's time to take a stab at that calculation way back from the beginning of this chapter: Add a five-percent penalty when the due date has passed.

When you're trying to come up with a logical calculation, think about what information FileMaker needs to make the decision, and what action you want FileMaker to take after it decides. Then consider how best to do that using your database's existing fields and structure. Your first decision is which conditional function to use.

POWER USERS' CLINIC

Clever Case Conditions

If you were one of those students who handed in homework early and always sat in the front row, you may be jumping up and down in your chair right now, waving your hand in the air. What you're *dying* to say is, "I can make that Case function simpler!" Well, you're probably right. In fact, this calculation does the same job:

```
Case (
  Get(CurrentTime) <= Time(4;0;0) or
  Get(CurrentTime) > Time(22;0;0);
  "Go To Bed";

  Get(CurrentTime) < Time(12;0;0);
  "Good Morning";

  Get(CurrentTime) < Time(18;0;0);
  "Good Afternoon";

  "Good Evening"
)
```

This version takes advantage of the fact that the Case function returns the result associated with the *first* True condition. FileMaker looks at the first condition, which checks to see if it's before 4:00 AM or after 10:00 PM. If either's true (note the "or" operator), the function returns *Go To Bed*. If both *aren't* true, FileMaker moves on to the second condition, which asks if it's earlier than 12:00 PM. If so, it returns *Good Morning*. (What if it's three in the morning? That *is* earlier than 12:00 PM, but you don't see "Good Morning" because FileMaker never gets this far. If it's 3:00 AM, the search for truth stops after the first condition.)

If it still hasn't found a true condition, FileMaker moves on to the next: Is it before 6:00 PM? Again, the structure of the case statement *implies* that it must be after noon at this point since any time before noon would've been caught in the previous conditions. So this condition is *really* looking for a time between noon and six, even though it doesn't say so in so many words.

If you're comfortable with this kind of logic, you can save yourself some clicks and a little typing. (Technically you also make a more efficient calculation, but unless you're using the abacus version of FileMaker, you won't see a speed increase.)

Many people, on the other hand, find a calculation like this one utterly confusing. In that case, just use the longer version and find something else in your life to brag about.

Total Due calculation #1: Using the If function

Most people's first thought would be to use the If function, since the calculation needs to check *if* one condition is true:

- Is the value of the Date Due field earlier than today's date?

The calculation then takes the result of the If function and returns one of two possible results:

- If it's *true* that the due date has passed, add five percent (.05) of the Total Due to the value in Total Due.
- If it's *not true* that the due date has passed, display the Total Due normally.

In plainer English, the If condition checks to see if the due date has passed. If so, it adds five percent to the Total Due amount; if not, it returns the Total Due amount.

The full calculation might look like the following:

```
If (
   // Test
Get ( CurrentDate ) > Date Due
   and // Calculate the total due here to make sure it's not zero
Sum ( Line Items::Extended Price ) > Total Paid ;

// True Result
   Sum ( Line Items::Extended Price ) + ( Sum ( Line Items::Extended Price )
   * .05 ) ;

   // False Result Display the Total Due normally
      Sum ( Line Items::Extended Price )
)
```

To put this calculation to work in your sample database, delete the calculation currently in the field definition for Total Due and type in this one. When the due date has passed, the value in your newly smarter Total Due field changes reflects a late payment penalty.

Note: Since the Total Due field already calculates the due balance, you may be tempted to create a *new* field that calculates five percent of every invoice, and then only adds that value in if the invoice is past due. But that would clutter your database with a superfluous field. Also, it's far better to have all your math in one place in case your business rules change.

FREQUENTLY ASKED QUESTION

No Zero

The Choose function insists that the first parameter should be for a zero condition. What if I don't want zero? My condition values start with 1.

You're in a common predicament. Luckily, there are two equally easy ways to get what you want from the Choose function. Perhaps the most obvious is to simply add a dummy zero result:

```
Choose ( Door ; "" ; "European Vacation" ;
"New Car" ; "Wah Wah Wah" )
```

In this calculation, there is no Door number zero, so you just stick "" in the spot where the zero result belongs. You could just as well put "Dennis Kucinich" there, since it never gets chosen anyway. Just make sure you put something there, so your first real result is in the number-one spot.

If you just don't like having that dummy result in your calculation, you can take this approach instead:

```
Choose ( Door-1 ; "European Vacation" ;
"New Car" ; "Wah Wah Wah" )
```

This version simply subtracts one from the Door number. Now Door number one gets the zero result, and Door number two gets the one result. This approach becomes more appealing when your choices begin with an even higher number:

```
Choose ( Year - 2000 ; "Dragon" ; "Snake";
"Horse" ; "Sheep" )
```

Since this calculation uses the year as the condition, it would be a real drag to enter 2000 dummy values. Instead, you just subtract enough to get your sequence to start with zero.

Total Due calculation #2: Using the Case function

Lots of people like the Case function so much that they always use it, even in places where the If function is perfectly competent. You might choose to use Case if there's any chance you'll want to add some conditions to the statement later on. Instead of editing an If expression later, you can save time by using Case from the start.

The same calculation using Case (and minus the helpful comments above) would look like this:

```
Case (
   Get ( CurrentDate ) > Date Due and Sum ( Line Items::Extended Price ) >
   Total Paid ;
   Sum ( Line Items::Extended Price ) + ( Sum ( Line Items::Extended Price )
   *  .05 )
   Sum ( Line Items::Extended Price )
)
```

Tip: With a single condition and default result, the syntax for If and Case are the same. So if you do need to change an If statement to Case later, simply change the word "If" to "Case" and add the conditions.

This calculation works as advertised, but it has a couple weak points. First, it has to calculate the total amount due *three times*. That makes for three times as many chances to introduce typos and three times as many places to edit the "Sum (Line Items::Extended Price)" expression if you change the calculation later.

Second, Total Paid is an unstored calculation based on the sum of related records. That's one of the slowest things you can ask a calculation to do. It may not matter much in this example, but in a more complicated situation, a calculation like this could slow FileMaker to a crawl.

In the next section, you'll learn how FileMaker helps you write leaner calculations that are easier for you to read—and quicker for FileMaker to work through.

The Let Function and Variables

The *Let* function creates a temporary holder for a value, called a *variable*, which can be plugged into a calculation over and over again. You'll do a little more work upfront to set up a variable, but that effort pays off with faster calculations that are easier to read, edit, and troubleshoot.

Defining Calculation Variables

In your Let function, you define a value and give it a name, and then use that name as often as you need throughout the calculation. In this case, you can calculate the amount due once, and store the result in a variable called Amount Due.

The Let function is unique among functions because it controls the way you write your calculation, not the result. Here's an example:

```
Let ( [ L = 5 ; W = 10 ; H = 3 ] ; L * W * H )
```

Like the Substitute function described on page 444, Let uses bracketed notation. It really takes just two parameters. The first is a list of variable definitions. Each variable gets a name and a value using this format:

```
Name = Value
```

Tip: FileMaker uses the terms "var" for Name and "expression" for Value in its manual and help files. The terms mean the same things, but "var" and "expression" sound much more impressive.

If you have more than one variable to define (as in the example above), put a semicolon between each one, and put them all between a pair of square brackets. You can use any calculation expression as the value.

In fact, the expression that determines the value of a variable can even use other variables that were defined earlier. For example, the next calculation is perfectly legal. Its Hours variable has a value of 240: 24 times the value of the Days variable:

```
Let (
 [ Days = 10 ;
   Hours = 24 * Days ;
   Minutes = 60 * Hours ];

 Minutes & " Minutes"
)
```

The second parameter can be any calculation expression. This parameter is special because you can use any of the variables you've defined inside the expression, just like fields. In the first example above, there are three defined variables (L, W, and H); the expression then multiplies them together.

When FileMaker evaluates the Let function, it determines the value of each variable just once, and then plugs this value into the expression every time that variable is used. The result of a Let function is simply the result of its expression.

Total Due calculation #3: Using the Let function

Your Total Due calculation can use the Let function to solve all its problems. Just put the Amount Due in a variable and use it throughout the calculation:

```
Let ( AmountDue = Sum ( Line Items::Extended Price ) ;
 If (
    Get(CurrentDate) > Date Due and AmountDue > 0;
     AmountDue + ( AmountDue * .05 );
    AmountDue
 )
)
```

This version of the calculation is simpler, easier to change, and more efficient. You can't beat that.

The Life of a Variable

Most variables last only as long as it takes FileMaker to work through the calculation, and then they're gone. This type of variable is called a *local variable* because they aren't valid outside the Let function that calls them into existence. But you can also create a special variable called a *global variable*, which lives beyond your calculation. Read on to see when to use each type.

Local variables

The variables you've written so far have all been local variables. Now it's time to learn that local variables having shockingly short memories.

Local variables can lose their values even before a calculation is finished. If you write:

```
Let ( AmountDue = Sum ( Line Items::Extended Price ) ;
 If (
    Get(CurrentDate) > Date Due and AmountDue > Total Paid;
     AmountDue + ( AmountDue * .05 );
    AmountDue
 )
) & If ( AmountDue < 0 ; "CR" ; "" )
```

The calculation tries to use the Amount Due variable after the end parenthesis in the Let function. Anything that happens after that in the calculation is outside the Let function's *scope*, so when you try to close the Specify Calculation dialog box on this calculation, FileMaker complains that it doesn't know what that last Amount Due is supposed to be. One way to rewrite that calculation using a local variable is:

```
Let ( AmountDue = Sum ( Line Items::Extended Price ) ;
 Case (
 Get ( CurrentDate ) > Date Due and AmountDue > Total Paid;
     AmountDue + ( AmountDue * .05 ) ;
     AmountDue < 0 ; "CR" ; ""
     )
)
```

In this example, you're including the last test condition within the scope of the Let function, and you've switched to a Case function, so that you don't have to read a set of nested If functions.

If you want the local variables you set inside calculations to follow the same naming conventions as variables you set in scripts (see Chapter 15), prefix their names with "$." In that case, you'd write the calculation you just saw like this:

```
Let ( $AmountDue = Sum ( Line Items::Extended Price ) ;
 Case (
 Get ( CurrentDate ) > Date Due and $AmountDue > 0;
     $AmountDue + ( $AmountDue * .05 ) ;
     $AmountDue < 0 ; "CR" ; ""
     )
)
```

Note: When you create a variable with a "$" prefix in a calculation that runs during a script, you extend its lifespan beyond the Let function. In this case, the variable's scope is now the script. See page 578 for more information on how variables work in scripts.

Notice that you have to include the prefix in the Let function *and* in the formula that follows it.

POWER USERS' CLINIC

Field Formatting Calculations

Now that you understand most of FileMaker's calculation power features, you're ready to see something really powerful. To clean up phone number data when it's entered, just add an Auto-Enter calculation to the Phone Number field. This calculation, which consolidates a lot of techniques you've covered in this section, does the trick:

```
Let(
 cleanPhone = Filter ( Self; "0123456789"
) ;

 Case (
  Length( Self ) = 10 ;

  "(" & Left ( cleanPhone ; 3 ) & ") " &
  Middle ( cleanPhone ; 4 ; 3 ) &
  "-" &
  Right ( cleanPhone ; 4 ) ;

  Self
 )
)
```

First, the calculation uses the Filter function to remove any non-numeric characters from the entered phone number, and puts the result in a variable called "cleanPhone." Then, if cleanPhone has exactly 10 digits, the calculation breaks it apart according to the format you want. Otherwise, it just returns the phone number the way the person entered it.

To make the calculation work properly, be sure you turn off "Do not replace existing value (if any)" in the Field Options dialog box.

Global variables

But just as FileMaker gives you global fields, it also gives you *global variables*. Unlike local variables, global variables hold their results after the Let function is finished. To create a global variable, add a "$$" prefix to its name. Here's the same calculation rewritten with a global variable:

```
Let (
 $$AmountDue = Sum ( Line Items::Extended Price ) ;
 Case (
  Get ( CurrentDate ) > Date Due and $$Amount Due > 0;
  $$AmountDue + ( $$AmountDue * .05 ) ;
  $$AmountDue < 0 ; "CR" ; ""
 )
)
```

The only difference you can see in the calculation is the $$ prefix. But the practical difference is vast: Global variable values remain until you change them (through another calculation or through a script), or until you close the file.

Tip: As with local variables, scope changes if global variables are created within scripts. FileMaker Pro Advanced's Data Viewer (page 713) eliminates guesswork by letting you check the contents of variables, whether you create them in calculation fields or from scripts.

You could run a script that checks to see if a payment was made within 10 days of the invoice date, and if it was, apply a one-percent discount to the $$Amount Due field. Sure, you can do something similar with a straightforward calculation field, but in that case, it gets a little trickier to apply the discount to some of the records, but not to others. With a script, you can find the records you want to give a spur-of-the-moment discount, run the script on that found set, and you're done.

Nesting Let Functions

As with other functions, you can nest Let functions inside each other. In fact, you can define a variable once, and then *redefine* it inside a nested Let function. The variable's value changes while inside the nested Let function, and then changes back when it ends. By the same token, you can define a variable with the same name as a *field*, and FileMaker uses the variable's value while inside the Let function.

Here's a very simple example of a Let function *inside* another Let function:

```
Let ( X = 3 ; // only X is defined here
 Let ( Y = 4 ; // X and Y are both defined here
  X * Y
 )
 // Only X is defined here too
)
```

You can also use the Let function more than once in a single calculation without nesting:

```
Let ( X = 3; Y = 4 ; X * Y ) &
Let ( units = "inches" ; " " & units )
```

CHAPTER

12

Extending Calculations

As you've seen in the past three chapters, FileMaker's calculation functions can do everything from text processing to financial analysis. Since calculations show up in so many different places in FileMaker, you might want to use the *same* calculation more than once. It would be a shame to have to type it in every time—and then make changes in several places the next time you need to modify it. In fact, a creative person like you may make extensive use of a unique calculation to do something FileMaker, Inc. never thought of.

For these situations and more, FileMaker provides *two* ways to extend the calculation system. The first, called *custom functions*, lets you design your own calculation functions using the same syntax you use to create a calculation. You can then use these functions in any calculation in the same FileMaker file.

The second way is more complex, and thus more powerful. You (or someone you hire) can create a FileMaker *plug-in* in a programming language like C++. The plug-in also adds new functions to FileMaker's Specify Calculation window. The difference is that those functions can do *anything* a programmer wants them to do.

Note: To *create* custom functions *or* plug-ins, you need FileMaker Pro Advanced, a special version of FileMaker that has extra tools for developers. (You can find out more in Chapter 19.) Once you've created a custom function or plug-in, though, it can be *used* in any version of FileMaker. Read on to find out more.

Custom Functions

Often, you need to use a particular calculation more than once. Perhaps you have several tables that hold information about people and you want to write that "Full Address" calculation only *once*, and then use it in each table. Or you might find yourself wondering why FileMaker doesn't have a function to do some incredibly useful thing. Maybe you frequently need to calculate your custom sprockets' weight, and FileMaker (for some odd reason) doesn't have a MySprocketWeight function. In all these cases, you can define your own functions to get the job done.

Defining a Custom Function

To get started, you'll add a new function that can calculate the circumference of a circle. You may not actually need to calculate circumferences in your own databases much, but this example illustrates important concepts common to creating any custom function.

Note: If you don't have the FileMaker Advanced edition, you'll have to sit these next few exercises out, as explained in the previous Note.

1. **In FileMaker Pro Advanced, choose File → Manage → Custom Functions.**

   You see the window shown in Figure 12-1. If you've never created your own function before, the list is blank—but not for long.

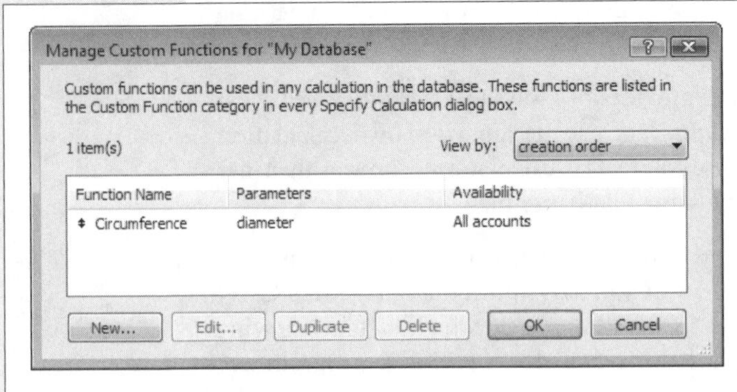

Figure 12-1: *The Manage Custom Functions window (File → Manage → Custom Functions) is where you go to create your own functions. It shows a list of custom functions that are already defined. You also get buttons to edit, duplicate, or delete a custom function, or to make a new one. As usual, you can sort the list by making a choice from the "View by" pop-up menu. Finally, when you're all done, click OK to save all your changes, or Cancel to close the window and ignore any changes you've made.*

2. **Click the New button.**

   The Edit Custom Function window appears. You can see it in Figure 12-2.

3. **In the Function Name box, type *Circumference*.**

   You've just given your function a name, which you'll call upon later when you want to *use* this function in calculations.

4. **In the Function Parameters box, type *diameter*.**

   Most functions need parameters (page 412), and this box is where you tell FileMaker which parameters your function needs. If you have more than one parameter, you have to enter them one at a time.

5. **Click the Add Parameter button (see Figure 12-2).**

   FileMaker moves "diameter" into the parameter list. This action means "diameter" is now officially a parameter of the Circumference function.

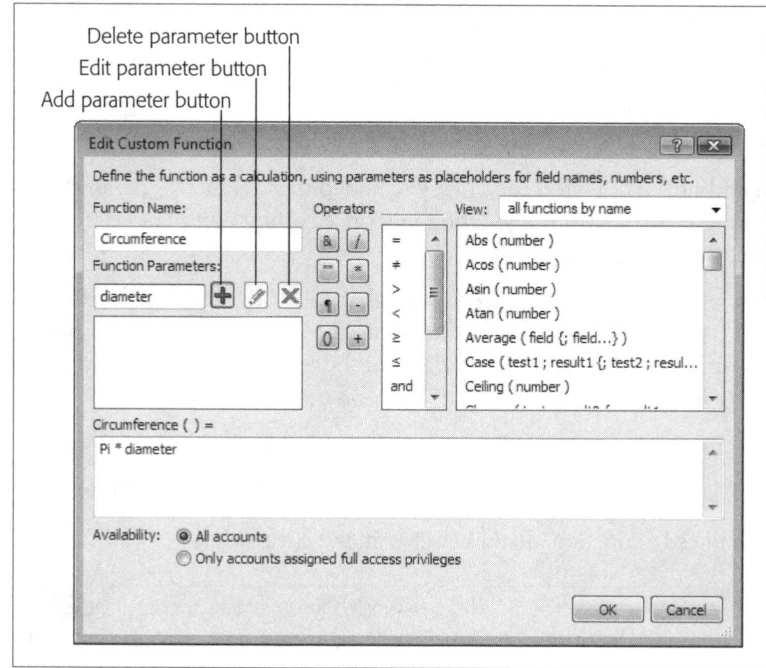

Figure 12-2: *The Edit Custom Function window is where you actually create the function. It looks a lot like the Specify Calculation dialog box you've seen so much of lately. But instead of fields, it has a list of function parameters (which is empty right now). Aside from this distinction, it works a lot like the Specify Calculation dialog box.*

Note: When you add more than one parameter to the Function Parameters list, you can use the arrow icon by each item to move it up or down in the list. The order here is important: It determines the order in which you want the parameters to pass to the function (page 412).

6. **From the View pop-up menu (above the function list), choose "Trigonometric functions."**

   The function list changes to show just the relevant options.

7. **In the function list, double-click the Pi function, then click the * operator button (or type *).**

   The function calculation area now reads *Pi **.

8. **Finally, in the parameter list, double-click "diameter."**

   FileMaker adds the word *diameter* to the end of the calculation, like so: *Pi * diameter*.

When you're done, click OK, and then OK again to close the Edit Custom Function and Manage Custom Functions dialog boxes. The database has a brand new function called Circumference. You can see your handiwork in the Specify Calculation dialog box's Functions list.

Editing Custom Functions

You probably feel like a pro at the Manage Custom Functions window already, since it works a lot like other FileMaker dialog boxes. But even you could end up with a custom function that needs adjustment or repair. To edit an existing custom function, either double-click its name, or select it from the list and click Edit. In the Edit Custom Function window (Figure 12-2), you can modify the definition of a function as follows:

- To change its name, just type a new name in the Function Name box.
- You can add new parameters, just like you added the "diameter" parameter in the Circumference function. If you no longer need a function parameter, select it and click the Delete Parameter button.
- To change a parameter's name, you must first select it in the parameter list. When you do, FileMaker puts the parameter in the Parameter Name box, where you can edit it. When you're done, click the Edit Parameter button to apply your change to the one in the list.
- You can reorder parameters by dragging them up or down in the list.
- If you click Duplicate, FileMaker makes an exact copy of the selected function.
- If you don't need a function anymore, select it and click Delete.

Warning: Be careful adding, reordering, or deleting parameters for an existing function. If the function is being used in a calculation somewhere, that calculation breaks because it no longer passes the right parameters back to the function. On the other hand, it's safe to *rename* a function or its parameters–FileMaker fixes any existing calculations when you do.

Recursion

As described in the box on page 485, you can create custom functions that call other custom functions, creating whole strings of mathematical wizardry that perform to your exact specifications. Even more interesting, a custom function can *use itself*, a technique known as *recursion*. With recursion, you can create calculations that repeat a process over and over again until they reach a result—called *iterative calculations*.

Note: Recursion is a notoriously complicated topic, and many *very* capable FileMaker developers are stymied by it. Fortunately, recursion is rarely the only solution to a given problem, so you can certainly get by without it. For example, consider using a script instead.

UP TO SPEED

Using Custom Functions

You can use custom functions just like any of FileMaker's built-in functions. When you're in the Specify Calculation dialog box, choose Custom Functions from the View pop-up menu to access the functions you've made. (When you create a custom function, you're adding it to the FileMaker file you're working in. It isn't available in other files unless you add it to them as well.)

Just like other functions, custom functions can also use *other* custom functions to do their job.

For example, if you want to add a new function that calculates the surface area of a cylinder, it can take two parameters (diameter and height) and it can use your custom Circumference function, like so:

```
Circumference(diameter) * Height
```

With this in mind, you can create functions that build upon one another–to keep each one simple, or to provide different but related capabilities.

Imagine you need a function that removes duplicate lines from a list. For example, if a field contains a list of colors, you want a new list with each *unique* color name, even if it appears in the original list several times. You can't do that with a normal calculation, because you just don't know how many words you need to pull out. A recursive function solves the problem by repeating its work until it takes care of all items (colors).

While the concept of a recursive function is simple, creating one can be tricky. To implement a recursive function, you're best off tackling the calculation in three distinct steps. First, solve the initial problem; second, call that first formula over and over again (that's the recursive part); and third, tell the formula how to stop.

Note: If you're having trouble getting through the following recursion example on your own, you can download a sample database from the Missing CD page at *www.missingmanuals.com*.

Step 1: Solve the first case

Rather than think about how to solve the entire problem, just figure out how to deal with the *first* line in the list. If you have a field called Values, for example, and you want to make sure the *first* line appears only once in the list, you can use this calculation:

```
LeftValues ( values ; 1 ) & Substitute ( values ; LeftValues ( values; 1 ) ;
"" )
```

Suppose the Values field contains:

```
Red
Green
Orange
Red
Orange
Yellow
```

The Substitute part of this expression does the lion's share of the work, so start with that to figure out how the formula works. The Substitute function sees that "Red" is the first item in the Values field and takes it out of the field everywhere it occurs. If Substitute were the whole shooting match, "Red" would disappear entirely from the Values field. But the "LeftValues (values ; 1) &" piece of the expression also notices that "Red" is the first item in the Values field and it puts "Red" back at the top of the list. When both are put together (using &), the result is the first item in the list, then the rest of the list with the Red is removed. Here's the result you'd see if you made a calculation field with the formula above:

```
Red
Green
Orange
Orange
Yellow
```

Now you're ready to move on to the rest of the function, where you call the same action over and over again—and things start to get interesting.

Step 2: Assume your function already works, and use it

You're ready to take the *recursion leap of faith*. A recursive function, by definition, calls itself. So at some point, it depends on its own resources to work. But when you're *writing* the recursive custom function, it obviously doesn't work yet. You'll be at a total impasse if you don't *assume* it already works and just get on with writing.

So since you're writing a new custom function called RemoveDuplicates, write its syntax as if you already have a function called RemoveDuplicates that does what you want. If such a function did exist, you could use it in the above calculation like this:

```
LeftValues ( values ; 1 ) & RemoveDuplicates ( Substitute ( values ;
LeftValues ( values ; 1 ); "" ) )
```

This new version works a lot like the last one. It first pulls the first item from the list and adds it to the result. It also removes duplicates of the first item from the rest of the list (using Substitute). But instead of adding that to the result, it sends the entire remaining list through RemoveDuplicates. If you assume RemoveDuplicates already works, then it will remove duplicates from the rest of the list. You take care of the *first* line using your calculation skills. Then you rely on the function itself to take care of all the rest. Notice that the new list that's passed to RemoveDuplicates starts with the *second line* of the original list. So when the function runs again, the second line becomes the first, and the function takes care of it. Unfortunately, this process will go on forever, which is probably not exactly what you want.

Step 3: Find a stopping point

You now have two of the three critical components of a recursive function: You're manually doing the *first* part of the job, and you're telling recursion to do the rest. If you leave the function like this, though, you're in trouble. If RemoveDuplicates calls RemoveDuplicates, which in turn calls RemoveDuplicates (ad infinitum), you have a problem: This function just keeps going forever.

Note: When you work on recursive functions, you inevitably create such *loops* accidentally. When you do, you'll see FileMaker think for several seconds, and then give up and return *invalid* (a question mark). If FileMaker seems to be hung, give it some time; it gives up eventually.

To avoid ending up in a loop, you need to figure out when to *stop* calling Remove-Duplicates. Think about what happens after this function calls itself several times. Each time it's called with a slightly smaller list than the time before (because the first item—along with any copies of it—has been removed). Eventually it's going to get called with just one item (or zero items). When that happens, you no longer need the services of RemoveDuplicates. Instead, you can just return that last word by itself since it obviously has no duplicates. You use an If function to help the recursion figure out when to stop. The final function looks like this (with comments added):

```
// Start the result with the first item in the list
LeftValues ( values ; 1 ) &

// If there are more items in List...
If ( ValueCount ( values ) > 1;
 // ...then remove duplicates from the remaining items
 RemoveDuplicates ( Substitute ( values ; LeftValues ( values ; 1); "") );
 // ...otherwise we're done
 ""
)
```

Now all you have to do is create the RemoveDuplicates custom function shown above. RemoveDuplicates needs one parameter, which is the values from which you're sifting duplicates. A descriptive name, like "values," helps you remember what this parameter does. Finally, create a calculation field using your new custom function and create a reference to the field containing the list of duplicated values.

Figure 12-3 illustrates an example of a recursive calculation calling the Remove-Duplicates custom function to remove all duplicate colors it finds in the list. (It takes four iterations to remove all the duplicates and return a unique instance of each item in the list, in the order in which they occur.)

Plug-ins

Some things just can't be done (or can't be done *well*) using calculations and custom functions. When you run into this situation, you may consider looking into *plug-ins*, which are tiny applications that live inside FileMaker to help it do specific tasks that it can't do on its own.

Many plug-ins focus on doing certain things: processing credit card transactions; creating charts; performing certain jobs based on a schedule; or interacting with special devices like cameras, barcode readers, and so on. Although plug-ins work through calculation functions, scripts (which the next section covers) generally control them.

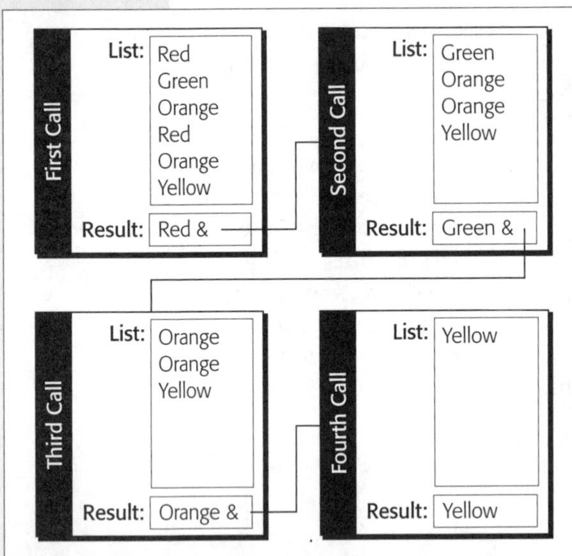

Figure 12-3:
The box in the top-left corner shows how RemoveDuplicates is first called. It receives a list of colors as its one parameter. It returns the first item in the list and the result of the second call. This time, though, Red has been removed from the list. The second call returns Green and the results of the third call. This progresses until the fourth call, when the script passes a single item to RemoveDuplicates. This time RemoveDuplicates simply returns the item without calling itself again. When it returns, the third call has all it needs, so it returns as well. This process goes back up the chain until the first call is reached, and the final result is returned. If you join up the results of each call, you see the correct list.

WORKAROUND WORKSHOP

When There's No Return

RemoveDuplicates works great for finding unique values in a list, so long as the last item in the list has a ¶ (paragraph return) following it. If it doesn't, the function gets confused and may leave the last line in even if it's a duplicate. You can adjust for lists that don't have a trailing ¶ by adjusting your calculation field slightly:

```
RemoveDuplicates ( values & "¶" )
```

You could also modify the custom function itself to guard against this possibility. Doing so makes the formula more complex, but here it is in case you want a challenge:

```
Let (
   [cleanList = if ( Right ( values, 1 ) =
"¶", values, values & "¶" );
    first = LeftValues ( cleanList, 1 )];

first &
if ( ValueCount(cleanList) > 1;
    RemoveDuplicates(cleanList);
    ""
)
)
```

Some plug-ins, though, are perfect candidates for calculations. Plug-ins can convert, resize, and otherwise modify images in container fields, or perform complex mathematical, scientific, or financial calculations that would be difficult or inefficient in a calculation. Although this book doesn't cover any specific plug-ins, this section shows you how to access the functions provided by any plug-in you install.

Installing Plug-ins

A plug-in comes in a file bearing a special FileMaker Plug-in icon (shown in Figure 12-4). In order to use plug-ins, FileMaker needs to *load* them—that is, it has to put the plug-in code into its own memory. Every time you launch the program, it searches for plug-ins in a folder called Extensions, which is inside its own folder, and loads all that it finds.

Figure 12-4:
FileMaker plug-ins come in many varieties–with many names–but they all look like this. (Some plug-ins have a .fmx filename extension, some have .fmplugin, and some have no extension at all.) Your job is to put the file where FileMaker can find it.

Installing a plug-in is thus a simple matter of making sure it's in the right folder:

- On Windows, it's typically C: → Program Files → FileMaker → FileMaker Pro 9 → Extensions.
- On Mac OS X, it's usually Applications → FileMaker Pro 9 → Extensions.

Note: If you're using FileMaker Pro Advanced, the FileMaker folder is called FileMaker Pro 9 Advanced, not FileMaker Pro 9.

Once you've found the folder, just drag the plug-in file into it and restart FileMaker. You won't see anything on your screen to let you know it worked. To see which plug-ins FileMaker has actually loaded, you need to visit the application preferences (FileMaker Pro → Preferences on Mac OS X, Edit → Preferences on Windows). In the Preferences window, click the Plug-ins tab, or look to Figure 12-5.

Once you've installed plug-ins, you can use their functions from the External functions section of the list in the Specify Calculation dialog box (page 419). For details on how to use these functions, consult their developer's manuals or Web sites.

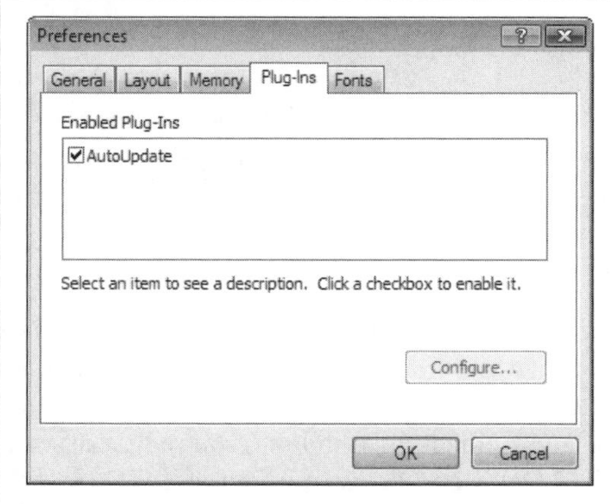

Figure 12-5:
The Plug-ins tab in FileMaker's Preferences dialog box shows you all the plug-ins you've installed. Disable a plug-in by turning off the checkbox by its name. If a plug-in requires any configuration, select it in the list and click Configure. When you have a plug-in selected, you see a description of it below the list.

Old and New Plug-ins

There are actually two kinds of plug-ins for FileMaker: older FileMaker 4-style plug-ins and newer FileMaker 7+-style plug-ins. FileMaker 9 works with *both* types of plug-ins, but it's a good idea to ask your plug-in provider which type you're getting, since the FileMaker 4 plug-ins have limited abilities:

- The functions provided by FileMaker 4 plug-ins always expect *one* parameter. Even if the function doesn't need a parameter, you have to pass "", which is just an empty parameter. If the function really needs more, consult the documentation that came with the plug-in to find out how to accommodate it.
- This single parameter's type is *always* text in a FileMaker 4 plug-in's function. If you want to pass a date, time, timestamp, or number, you have to convert it to text first, using GetAsText.

Newer FileMaker plug-ins give you a lot more options. Functions can have as many parameters as their creator cares to give them. They can also deal with all data types, including pictures, movies, and files stored in container fields. Thankfully, these days almost all available FileMaker plug-ins use the new capabilities.

Finding Plug-ins

Most FileMaker developers lack the know-how to build their own plug-ins. Although you can hire a programmer to make one to your specifications, you can often find one on the market that already does what you want. You can find a comprehensive list of available plug-ins on FileMaker's Web site. Just choose Products → "Made for FileMaker." Then look for the Plug-ins link on the right side of the page.

You can also visit the more prolific FileMaker plug-in vendors' Web sites:

- 24U Software (*www.24usoftware.com*)
- New Millennium Communications (*www.nmci.com*)
- Troi Automatisering (*www.troi.com*)

New vendors come up with great products all the time so if you don't see what you want, head over to Google and get your search on.

Creating Your Own Plug-ins

If you're feeling adventurous (or have helpful programmer friends), you can create your own plug-ins. To do that, you first need FileMaker Advanced (it's the only version of FileMaker that includes the *Plug-in Software Development Kit* or SDK). You also need a C++ development environment. In Windows, you're best off with Visual C++ or Visual Studio.NET. On Mac OS X, you can use XCode (it's included with the Developer Tools that came with your computer, although you have to install it yourself from the CD). Plug-in SDK includes sample projects for each of these environments—and sample plug-in code—to get you started.

Part Five: Scripting

5

CHAPTER

13

Scripting Basics

Calculation fields let you tell FileMaker how to automatically update and validate the *data* in your database. But *working with the database* is still a manual affair. If you often need to print a summarized report, you have to perform a find, sort the records, switch layouts, print, and then switch back to the original layout manually. Once you've done it 27 times, you start wishing you could click a button and have the report print itself. Well, you can: Just tell FileMaker the same series of steps you've been doing over and over again, and attach the list to a button (page 504). That's the essence of scripting.

A *script* is a series of steps bundled together. When you run the script (by clicking a button, say), FileMaker carries out all the steps on your behalf, one after the other. Scripts can be simple—just the same five steps you'd go through if you printed a report manually. Or they can be much more complicated—and can handle tricky or tedious tasks you wouldn't want to do manually. Advanced scripts can even incorporate calculations (Chapter 9) to do different things in different situations by making simple decisions based on the data in your database, the current time or date, or any other condition you want to test.

Note: If you've worked with other scripting environments–like Visual Basic for Applications, AppleScript, or JavaScript–FileMaker's script-building tools are pleasantly familiar.

Your First Script

To get a feel for how scripting works, you'll create a really simple script. Suppose you want to find all invoices with a balance due and view them in a sorted list. The following pages show how to go about preparing your database, planning, creating, and polishing the script, and finishing off with a way to run it.

Preparing the Database

FileMaker is flexible enough to let you create fields and layouts on the fly, at the same time as you write a script, but it's easier to focus on the script if you create all the supporting material you need before you even open ScriptMaker. In this example, you'll need a layout that shows a list of invoices, so create that first:

1. **Switch to Layout mode in your database and choose Layout → New Layout/Report.**

   The New Layout/Report window appears.

2. **From the "Show records from" pop-up menu, choose Invoices. In the Layout Name box, type *Invoice List*.**

   Since you'll tell the script which layout it needs to use, it helps to name the layout appropriately so you can pick it from the list of layouts later.

3. **In the "Select a layout type" list, select "Columnar list/report," and then click Next. Leave the "Columnar list/report" radio button turned on, click "Constrain to page width," and then click Next again.**

   These options save time when you rearrange your fields.

4. **Click to add the following fields to the "Layout fields" list: Invoice ID, Jobs::Name, Date, Date Due, and Balance Due. When you're finished, click Next, then a second time to skip the Sort Records panel.**

   FileMaker asks how you want the list sorted. Since this list isn't a report, you can simply ignore this setting. The "Select a Theme" panel appears.

5. **Choose a theme that pleases you, and then click Next, then a second time.**

   The second click skips the Header and Footer Information panel without setting any options. You want to end up on the "Create a Script for this Report" panel.

6. **Choose "Do not create a script", and then click Next.**

   You're going to write your own script, thank you very much. The final screen asks if you'd like to view the layout in Preview mode or Layout mode.

7. **Select "View the report in Layout mode," and then click Finish.**

   FileMaker creates your new layout and shows it to you.

Feel free to decorate the layout now if you want, using any of the features described in Chapter 4. But for writing your script, you can leave the layout as it is.

Planning Your Script

Before you dive in and create the script, you should review what you want it to do. A script is just a series of steps that FileMaker repeats for you. When you're planning a script, it often helps to go through the process the script should do first, so you can see whether it works. This trial run helps you clarify the steps you're scripting. Plus, some scripts are easier to write if you do the steps manually beforehand, since dialog boxes retain their settings until you change them. So if your script needs to sort records, the dialog box will already have the settings you need when you're actually creating the script.

So go through the steps necessary to find the balance due, and take notes. You probably end up with something like the following:

- **Switch to the Invoice List layout.** This layout has the fields the script needs to create the invoice list. It's also going to display the final list, so you want to make sure the script runs in this layout.
- **Choose View → Find Mode.** The script needs to *find* all invoices with a balance due. Scripts can't click a button or even choose a menu command, but you know you need a script step that puts FileMaker into Find mode.
- **In the Balance Due field, enter ">0", and then press Enter.** This step tells FileMaker what to find and puts it into action. When the script runs this step, FileMaker performs the find and shows the correct records, just as if you'd performed the find yourself.

Note: If none of your invoices has a balance due, just click Cancel when the error message pops up, and then choose Records → Show All Records so you can do the next step. Jot down that your script needs to account for this message box if it pops up when someone runs your script. See Chapter 15 to learn ways to make your script account for errors like these.

- **Choose Records → Sort and sort the records ascending by Date Due.** You should now see your final list, properly sorted. Once you have the results that you want the script to produce, you know everything you need to know to build it.

Now that you know all the steps involved, you're ready to get acquainted with ScriptMaker.

Creating Your Script

You create, edit, run, and delete scripts in FileMaker using *ScriptMaker*. It's the first item in the Scripts menu and is available except while a script is running. When you choose this command, you see the window shown in Figure 13-1. Your window may not have scripts in it yet, but otherwise, it's the same.

Now it's time to build the script. First, tell FileMaker to repeat each of the steps you went through when you planned the script. Here's how:

1. **Choose Scripts → ScriptMaker, or choose File → Manage → Scripts. When the Manage Scripts window appears, click New.**

   The Edit Script window appears (Figure 13-2). Make sure to click the New button, and not the pop-up menu. You'll learn how and when to use the pop-up menu later.

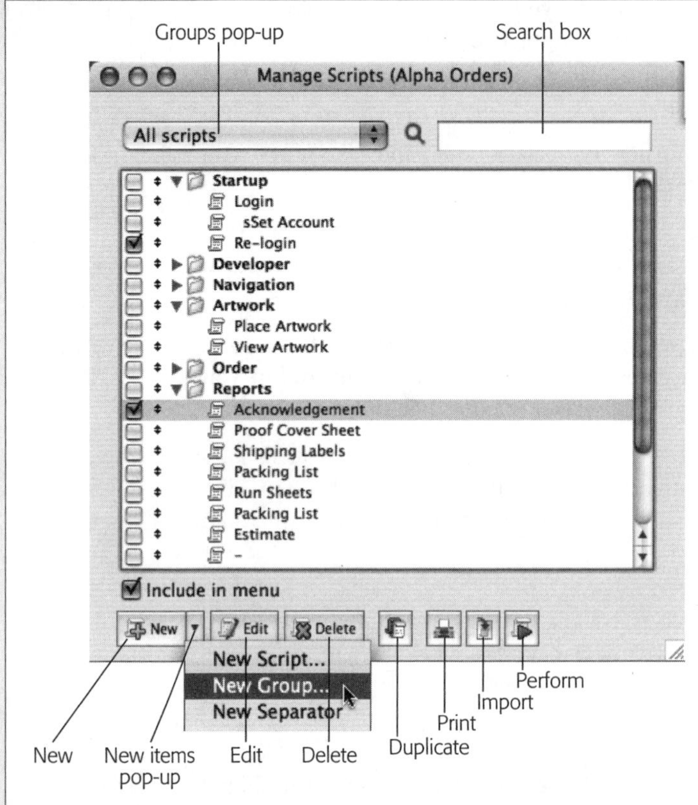

***Figure 13-1:** The Manage Scripts window, more affectionately known as ScriptMaker, is a blank canvas–in a file with no scripts. Scripts appear in the list as you create them. Tools along the bottom let you create and manage your scripts. The New pop-up menu lets you create Groups (or folders) to organize your scripts. Separators show up as hyphens in the script list and as menu separators in the ScriptMaker menu. You'll learn more about these options in the next sections.*

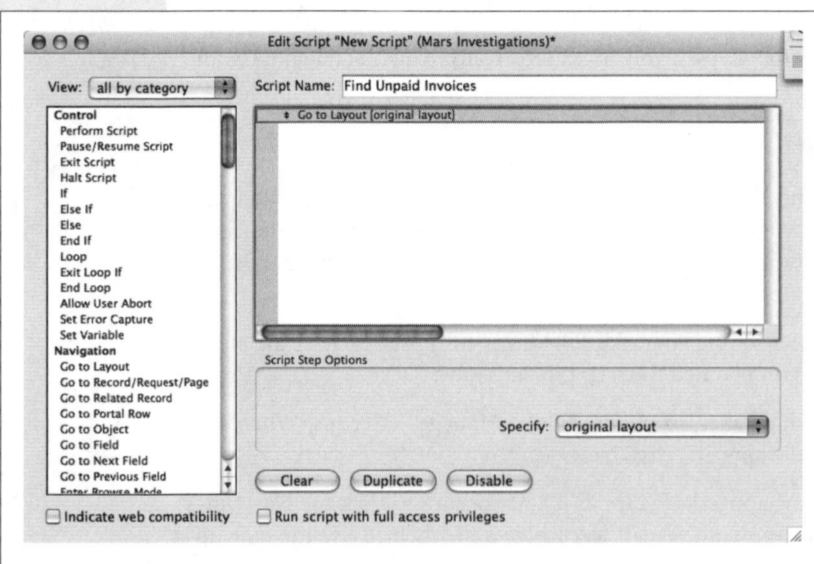

***Figure 13-2:** In the Edit Script window, you build your script by choosing steps from the Available Script Steps list and use the Move button to add them to your script. Or double-click a step to move it. Once moved, you can configure script steps using buttons, checkboxes, and radio buttons that appear in the Script Step Options area. In this figure, you can see the Specify pop-up menu for telling FileMaker which layout you want the script to go to.*

2. **In the Script Name box, type *Find Unpaid Invoices.***

   Your script's name is important. It's how you'll identify it when you want to run it later.

3. **A little more than halfway down the list, just below the Navigation headline, choose the "Go to Layout" step, and then click the Move button.**

   The Move button doesn't become available until you've clicked a script step. When you click Move, FileMaker adds (and selects) a "Go to Layout" step to the list of current steps.

Tip: You can double-click a step in the list to avoid the trip to the Move button. When the script step list is active, you can type the first part of a step's name to scroll to it, and then press the Space bar to add it. If the script step list isn't active, use the Tab key to move between the script step list, the current steps list, and the Script Name box.

4. **From the Specify pop-up menu (in the Script Step Options area), choose Invoice List.**

   This layout is the one you want FileMaker to go to when the script runs. Now your script has just one step, or line. If you run it as is, it would simply take you to the Invoice List layout. (If you were *already* on the Invoice List layout, it wouldn't do anything.)

5. **From the View pop-up menu (top-left corner), choose "all by name" to sort the script steps alphabetically, and then double-click Enter Find Mode.**

   FileMaker adds a second line to your script. The Script Step Options area now has new options (those that make sense with the Enter Find Mode step). Notice that the Pause option at the left side of the Script Step Options area is turned *on*.

6. **Turn off the Pause option.**

   Turning off this option tells the script not to wait for user input when it's run. (You'll learn more about pausing a script on page 547.)

7. **Add a Set Field script step to the script.**

   Use the scroll bar to skip down to the steps that start with "s," and then double-click Set Field, or click it, and then click Move.

   The Set Field step lets you put (or set) data in a field. You can use Set Field in Browse or Find mode. In Browse mode, it enters data; in Find mode, it specifies find requests. Since this Set Field step comes right after an Enter Find Mode step, you're specifying a find request for the invoices.

8. **In the Script Step Options area, turn on "Specify target field".**

   You can save a step by clicking the top Specify button. Here you tell FileMaker *which* field to set. As soon as you turn on this option, FileMaker shows a slightly different Specify Field window (Figure 13-3).

Note: If you *don't* turn on the Specify target field option, the Set Field step modifies whichever field happens to be active when the step is carried out.

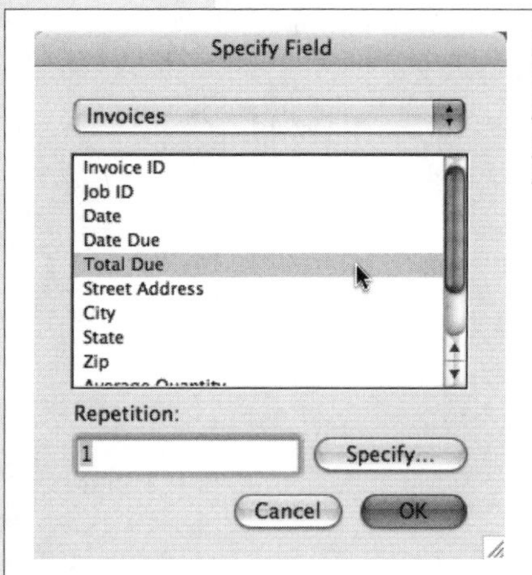

Figure 13-3:
This Specify Field dialog box looks almost exactly like the one you've seen in Layout mode. The only difference is the Repetition box at the bottom. If you select a repeating field (page 119), you can use this box to tell FileMaker which repetition to set.

9. **In the field list, select Balance Due, and then click OK.**

   The Set Field step in your script (Figure 13-4) shows the option you've selected. In the Script Step Options area, click the bottom Specify button (the one beside "Calculated result").

   FileMaker shows you the Specify Calculation dialog box, the same one you used to build calculation fields in the previous chapters. Here you'll use a calculation to tell FileMaker what to put in the Invoices::Balance Due field. Remember, you're in Find mode when this script runs, so the Set Field step tells FileMaker what records you want to find.

10. **In the Calculation box, enter "*>0*" (including the quotes), and then click OK.**

    This bit of computerese sets the Invoices::Balance Due field to the appropriate value for finding unpaid invoices. FileMaker now shows the calculation beside the Set Field step as well. (Spoken out loud, this step reads, "Set the Invoices::Balance Due field to greater than zero.")

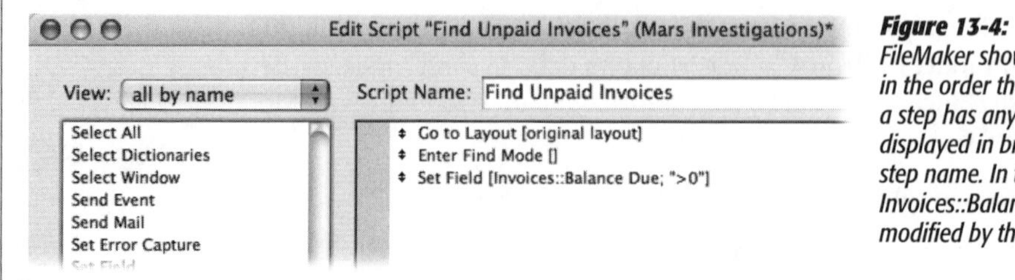

Figure 13-4:
FileMaker shows your script steps in the order they're performed. If a step has any options, they're displayed in brackets after the step name. In this example, the Invoices::Balance Due field is modified by the Set Field step.

11. **Add the Perform Find script step to your script.**

    Don't specify any options. This step carries out the find operation. It's the equivalent of clicking Find or pressing Enter if you were doing it yourself.

12. **Add the Sort Records script step to your script. Then, in the Script Step Options area, select "Perform without dialog".**

    This tells FileMaker you want the script to go ahead and sort, instead of opening the Sort dialog box every time it runs. That way, the sort will be the same every time you run the script.

13. **Turn on the "Specify sort order" checkbox.**

    If you went through the script-planning phase, as described on page 494, the Sort dialog box is already configured properly. When you add a Sort Records step to your script, FileMaker configures it to match the *last* sort you performed. If you skipped the dry run, set the dialog box to sort by Date Due, in ascending order.

14. **Click OK in the Sort Records window.**

    Unlike some other script steps, Sort Records doesn't show its settings. It just says "Restore". But if you forget, you can always click the Specify dialog box and check it out.

15. **Click the Edit Script window's close button, and then click the Save button.**

    There's no Save button in the Edit Script window, but when you close it, you'll always see a warning dialog box that lets you save your scripts.

16. **Click the Perform button.**

    It's the one with a green triangle at the bottom right. FileMaker runs your script.

You should see the correct list of invoices, or—oops!—a message telling you no records were found. In the next section, you'll refine your script to help deal with these message boxes if they pop up when someone runs the script. (See the box on page 502.)

Note: You can adapt the basic structure of this script for a host of purposes. Just edit the script's find or sort criteria and specify a different layout.

Improving Your Script

On the preceding pages, you created a script that mimics what you would do to get an unpaid invoice list, step by step. But ScriptMaker has a lot of options to make writing scripts fast and easy. Often, a script can get the results you want with *fewer* steps than it would take to do it yourself. For example, to see your unpaid invoice list, the steps boil down to the following:

- Switch to the Invoice List layout.

- Find the right invoices.
- Sort the records.

This version has just *three* steps instead of five because it assumes you can "find the right invoices" in one step. Luckily, ScriptMaker's Perform Find script step *really can* find what you want in one step. Here's how to revise your script to use the simpler form:

1. **Choose Scripts → ScriptMaker. In the Manage Scripts window, select the Find Unpaid Invoices script, and then click Edit.**

   Or you can double-click the script instead. The Find Unpaid Invoices script pops up in the Edit Script window.

2. **Select the second and third steps in your script (Enter Find Mode and Set Field).**

   You can select both by clicking Enter Find Mode in your script, and then Shift-clicking Set Field.

Note: You should select the steps in your script (in the window on the right), not the steps in the available script steps list (on the left side of the window).

3. **Click the Clear button.**

   FileMaker removes the two selected steps from the script. It now has two steps that look a lot like the simplified process above. Also notice that the Perform Find step is already highlighted, since FileMaker automatically selects the *next* step when you clear one or more steps from the script.

4. **Select the "Specify find requests" checkbox in the Script Step Options area.**

   The Specify Find Requests dialog box appears, and, like the Sort script step in the previous tutorial, it's already set with the find you did when you planned your script. Since that's exactly what you want, you don't need to do anything in the Specify Find Requests window. But if you skipped the recommended planning work on page 494, you'll have to set your find request manually now, as described in steps 5–7. If, on the other hand, you followed instructions, you can skip to step 8.

5. **Click New.**

   The Edit Find Request dialog box appears.

6. **In the "Find records when" pop-up menu, choose Invoices, if necessary, and then scroll through the list until you see the Balance Due field. Click to select it.**

   The Balance Due field is highlighted so you can remember which field you're telling FileMaker to search.

7. **Type *>0* in the Criteria list box, and then click OK.**

   Your search is entered in the Action box at the top of the dialog box (Figure 13-5). You wouldn't have all this trouble if you'd followed directions.

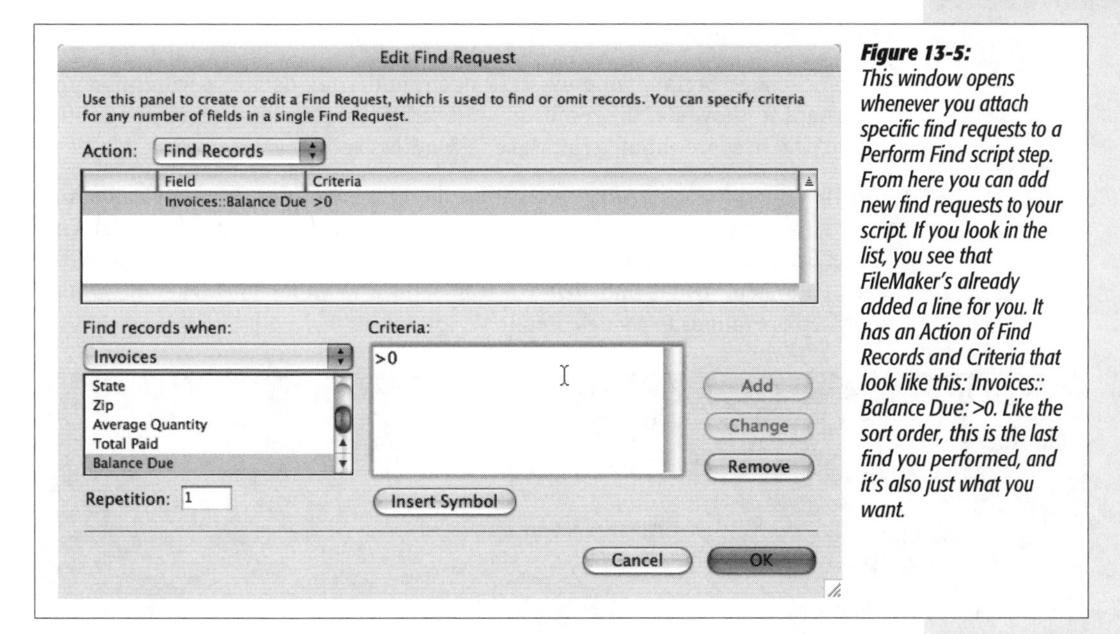

***Figure 13-5:** This window opens whenever you attach specific find requests to a Perform Find script step. From here you can add new find requests to your script. If you look in the list, you see that FileMaker's already added a line for you. It has an Action of Find Records and Criteria that look like this: Invoices:: Balance Due: >0. Like the sort order, this is the last find you performed, and it's also just what you want.*

8. **Click OK until you're back in Edit Script.**

   The Perform Find script step now has options set (Figure 13-6). Notice that the Edit Script window has a * (or star) at the end of its name. That tells you you've made changes to the script that haven't been saved. Whenever you close an Edit Script window that has a star, FileMaker asks if you want to save changes to your script.

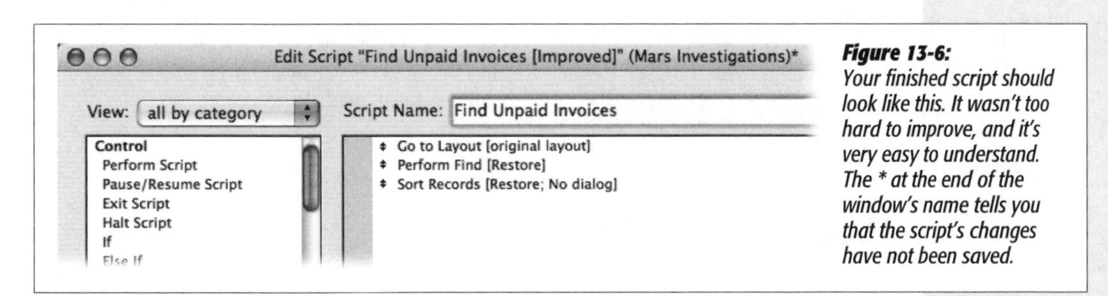

***Figure 13-6:** Your finished script should look like this. It wasn't too hard to improve, and it's very easy to understand. The * at the end of the window's name tells you that the script's changes have not been saved.*

9. **Close the Edit Script window, and then click the Save button in the dialog box that follows.**

   Or, press Ctrl+S (Windows) or ⌘-S (Mac), which saves the script and leaves the Edit Script window in front.

Note: The Scripts menu also has a Save All Scripts command and a Revert script command. They have no keyboard shortcuts, but you don't have to click the Close box on an Edit Script window to handle your save/revert chores.

10. **Click the Perform button.**

    The Manage Scripts window stays open, and your database window comes forward to show you the results of your script. Later in this chapter (page 507), you'll learn more about ScriptMaker's windows and how they work.

This new, simpler script does everything the first script did. It's simpler because you didn't have to script all the steps involved in performing a find: Enter Find Mode; Set Field; Perform Find. Instead, you let FileMaker do all that in one Perform Find step. You'll find that you can reduce *many* of FileMaker's common multistep operations to a single step in ScriptMaker.

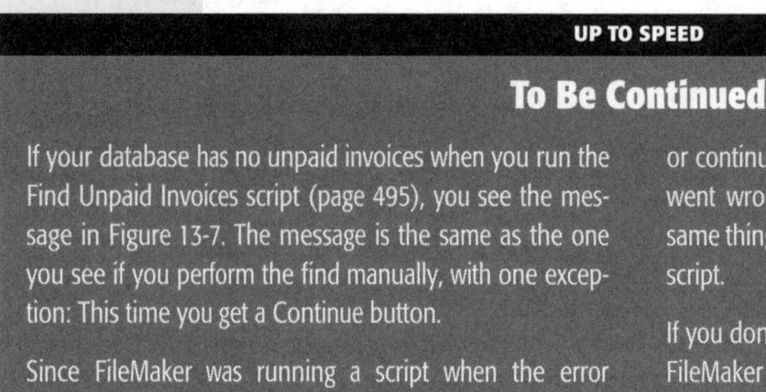

UP TO SPEED

To Be Continued

If your database has no unpaid invoices when you run the Find Unpaid Invoices script (page 495), you see the message in Figure 13-7. The message is the same as the one you see if you perform the find manually, with one exception: This time you get a Continue button.

Since FileMaker was running a script when the error occurred, it gives you the choice to cancel the script (in other words, stop in the middle and return control to the user) or continue the script (or keep going and pretend nothing went wrong). In this case, Cancel and Continue do the same thing since the error happened on the *last* step in the script.

If you don't want the user to make this choice, you can tell FileMaker to *capture* the errors as they happen and let you deal with them inside the script. You'll learn about this process on page 581.

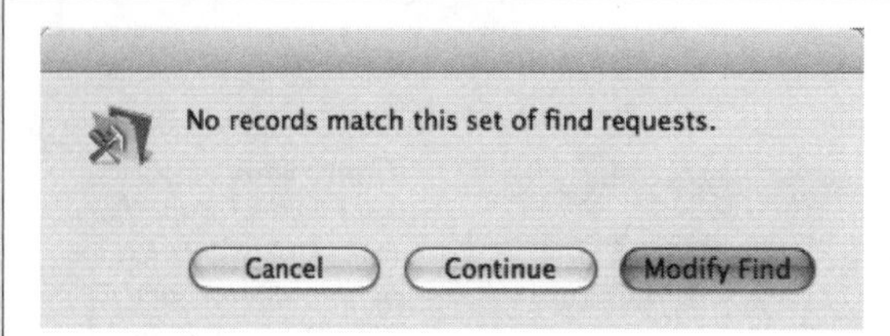

Figure 13-7: *If your scripted find, like either of the ones you've just created, can't find records that match your request, you'll see this dialog box. The Modify Find button lets you try another search, but the Continue button finishes your script with a found count of zero records.*

The Importance of the Layout

In a script, the active layout is very important, since it's what determines the script's *context*. Context is critical when you do things like delete records. If you write a script that simply deletes a record, without checking for context, it deletes the current record from whatever layout the user happens to be on. That may not be the right record at all. You could end up deleting a record from the Customer table instead of the single invoice record you meant to delete!

Take the script you've created in this chapter, for example. Before it does anything else, your Find Unpaid Invoices script goes to the Invoice List layout—but what would happen if you left that step out? Figure 13-5 shows the options ScriptMaker gives you for the Perform Find script step. See if you can spot what's *missing*.

You can see that Perform Find—like every other script step—makes absolutely no mention of which table it should act upon. Just because you're asking it to "Find records when Invoices::Invoice ID > 0," doesn't mean you're looking for *invoice* records. You could be looking for customers whose attached invoices have a balance due. Or you could be looking for any line items that are on an unpaid invoice. The only way FileMaker can tell what you're looking for is by the context of the layout you're on. That's why the first step in the script goes to the Invoice List layout. That layout is attached to the Invoices table occurrence. This tells FileMaker which records to look through (those in the Invoices table) and from what perspective to resolve relationships (the Invoices table occurrence on the relationship graph).

When to Switch

Now that you've dutifully absorbed the lesson in the previous paragraphs, don't get lured into the idea that you *always* have to switch to a layout for your script to work. The fact that a script can do something useful from more than one context can be a good thing. In general, you have three choices when you write a script, and here are some guidelines on when to use each:

- **Switch to a layout associated with the table you want to work with.** The "Go to Layout" script step makes sense when you're showing certain results (like the Find Unpaid Invoices script) or when your script always makes sense, but only from one particular context. If necessary, you can then switch *back* to the original layout at the end of the script ("Go to Layout" has an Original Layout option).
- **Don't include a "Go to Layout" script step at all.** Just let the script go about its business, whatever the context. If you use this approach, you have to make sure the script works and makes sense from any perspective. For instance, a script could switch to Preview mode, resize the window to show the whole page, and then ask the user if he'd like to print. This script can run on nearly any layout and still do something useful: print. See the box on page 504 for one example of context independent scripting.
- **Prevent the script from running on the wrong layout.** As you'll see on page 517, you can make it so a script won't run at all if it's not designed to work properly on the current layout. This alternative is your best bet when switching layouts within the script isn't feasible. For example, suppose you have a Refund Invoice script that carries out the steps necessary to pay someone back. Using "Go to Layout" to switch to the Invoices layout would ensure the right layout, but not the right *invoice*. It's best if this script runs only when the user is *already* open to the Invoices layout—presumably looking at the invoice she wants to refund.

Tip: When a script can do damage to your database if it's run from the wrong layout, use the failsafe of the third option even if you're the only person who uses your database. If your mouse hand slips when you're insufficiently caffeinated, the script can show you an error message rather than running at the wrong time (page 567).

POWER USERS' CLINIC

Context Independence

You may be wondering why the Send Email to Customer script you create on page 512 doesn't go to the Customers layout first. After all, doesn't it only make sense from this context? Actually, this script is a perfect candidate for *context independence* (page 503). If you run this script from the Jobs layout, it creates a new email message addressed to the *related customer*. The same holds true from the Invoice layout. In fact, you can run this script from *any* layout and get a useful result: FileMaker finds the related customer record and addresses the message to her.

But what if you have more than one related customer record? If you just run the script from the Scripts menu, FileMaker automatically selects the *first* related customer based on the active record on the current layout. Remember, the Send Email to Customer script is set to send only one email, even though the Send Mail script step lets you send multiple emails to all customers in a found set. If the relationship to Customers is sorted in the Relationships tab of Manage Databases, it'll be the customer that sorts to the top. Otherwise, you get the oldest customer record.

But if your layout has a portal of related customers, you can put a button inside the portal row. Then, when you click this button, the script automatically addresses the email to the appropriate related customer, even if he's not the customer in the first related record.

The point is, you can put a button just about anywhere and tell it to run this script. FileMaker does something a little different depending on where the button is. So this example is one of those scripts that you *don't* want to associate with a specific layout.

Running Scripts

At this point you're probably starting to see how scripts can be really useful in your database. The fact is, most large database systems are *loaded* with scripts that do all kinds of things. But the only way you've seen to run a script is pretty tedious: Chose Scripts → ScriptMaker, select the script, and then click Perform. That's lots of clicks to run a script that's supposed to *save* you time! Thankfully, there are a few *other* ways to run scripts that are more convenient, and you can set them up when you first create a script.

The Scripts Menu

You can show some or all of your scripts right in the Scripts menu. If you have a script or two that you want quick access to from *anywhere*, then it makes sense to put it in the Scripts menu. That way, anyone can run it by simply choosing it from the menu. There are even keyboard shortcuts for the first 10 scripts in the Scripts menu: Ctrl+1 (⌘-1) through Ctrl+9 (⌘-9) for the first nine, and Ctrl+0 (⌘-0) for number 10. Since only the top 10 scripts will get keyboard shortcuts, you'll want to put frequently used scripts up at the top, so you can save time using the keyboard instead of the mouse. Figure 13-8 shows how to assign a script to this menu in the Manage Scripts dialog box.

Defining Buttons

When you use the Button tool (see Figure 13-9, left), to draw a button on a layout, FileMaker shows you a list of script steps like the ones you get in ScriptMaker

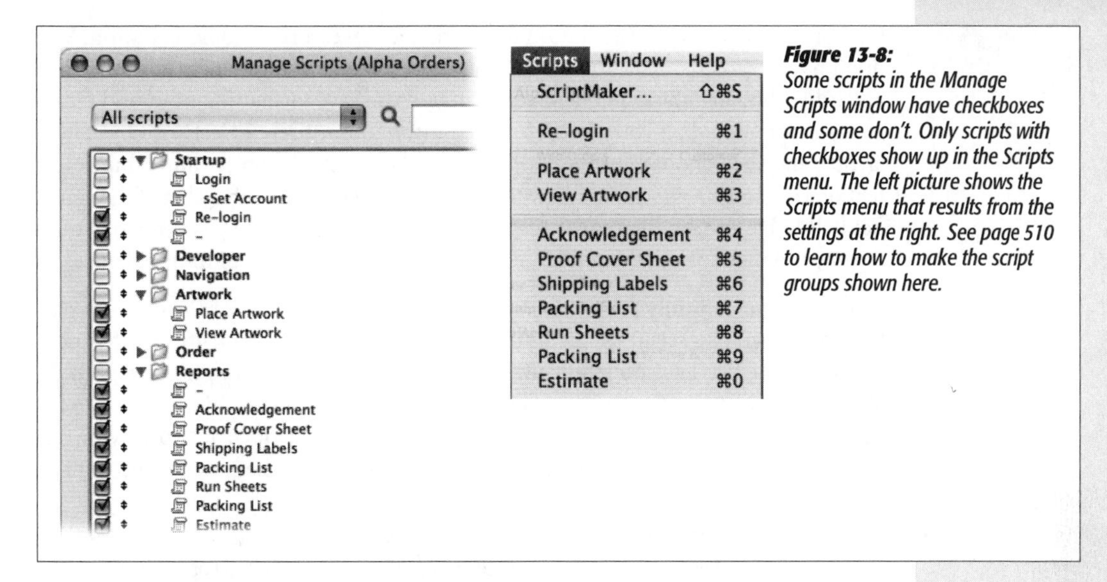

Figure 13-8: *Some scripts in the Manage Scripts window have checkboxes and some don't. Only scripts with checkboxes show up in the Scripts menu. The left picture shows the Scripts menu that results from the settings at the right. See page 510 to learn how to make the script groups shown here.*

(Figure 13-9, right). You can attach any single script step from that list to a button. See the box on page 507 to help you decide whether one script step is the right choice.

Note: Not all script steps are available in this list, though. Some script steps, like If and End If (page 512) don't make sense when used alone, so they aren't included.

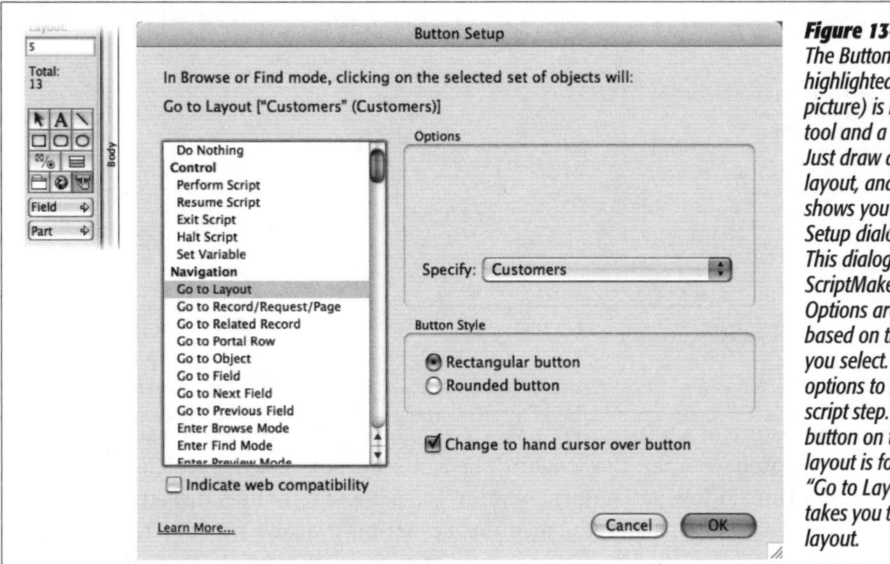

Figure 13-9: *The Button tool (the highlighted tool in the left picture) is both a drawing tool and a scripting aid. Just draw a button on any layout, and FileMaker shows you the Button Setup dialog box (right). This dialog box is a lot like ScriptMaker. There's an Options area that changes based on the script step you select. Use those options to format your script step. In this picture, a button on the Invoice layout is formatted with a "Go to Layout" step that takes you to the Customers layout.*

One of the downsides of the Button tool is that it makes a retro-looking button. You don't have to accept the factory-set button style, though. You can format buttons like any other drawing object in FileMaker. But you can save formatting time, and create a more custom look, if you just bypass the Button tool entirely. Select any object on a layout, and then choose Format → Button Setup to turn the object into a button. A text object can be a good candidate; for example, you can make the label of the Email field clickable for sending email (page 512). You can also place custom icons on a layout, and then format them to do your will through the power of Button Setup.

Although you can only attach one script step to a button, the Perform Script step lets you assign any script to any button. Perform Script, conveniently located near the top of the list, lets you tell FileMaker, via the Current Script option, what to do about any script that's running when your new button is clicked (see page 573 for details). And the Specify Button lets you decide which script runs, plus you can attach a script parameter to the script (page 575) to change the way it runs.

Tip: The Specify Script dialog box lets you perform scripts in other files (Figure 13-10). Just make sure you have a File Reference for the file (page 383) so you can choose it from the top pop-up menu. Just like a native script list, an external file shows you a list of all that file's scripts.

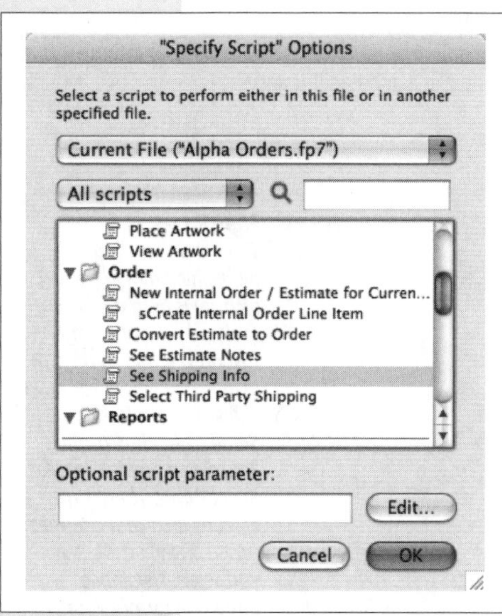

Figure 13-10:
The Specify Script Options dialog box lets you choose the script that runs when you click your new button. The Current File pop-up menu lets you run scripts from another file. The All Scripts pop-up menu lets you filter the list of scripts using script groups (page 510), and the search box lets you type search criteria to find scripts by their names. See page 575 to learn how to use optional script parameters.

One feature of a button that makes it so useful is that it lives on a specific layout. So if you have script that ought to be run only from the Invoice Layout (like the Find Unpaid Invoices script), a button is a better choice than displaying the script in the menu. By default, the menu makes scripts available no matter which layout you're looking at. But if you attach invoice-related scripts to buttons on the Invoices layout and payment-related scripts to buttons on the Payment layout, then you're adding another layer of assurance that FileMaker runs your scripts only from the right context.

Tip: If you want the ultimate in control over who gets to see which scripts, and even which layout they can see them in, take a look at the Custom Menus section (page 724) in Chapter 19. You need FileMaker Pro Advanced to create custom menus, but for many situations, this powerful feature alone is worth the price of admission.

UP TO SPEED

A Button or a Script?

Even if many of your buttons do only one thing, you'll often save time in the long run if you create a single line script and attach that to your button instead. Yes, it's a little more work upfront, but scripts have a lot more flexibility over the long haul. Here's why.

Lots of the initial development work in a database has to do with helping the users get around. So, many of the first buttons you create will just go to a layout, or to a set of related records. But what if your business rules change—like from now on, only managers will be able to see a customer's payment history? Your task is to figure out how to stop unauthorized folks from seeing payment data. With an If statement (page 512) that checks Get (PrivilegeSetName), a script can see who's logged in to the file before it allows the "Go to Layout" to run. So you have to write the script, and then find all the 14 places you created a button with a plain vanilla "Go to Layout" script action. If you'd written a "Go to Layout" script, and attached that to your 14 buttons, you could handle this new wrinkle just by editing the script. No time spent finding all your "Go to Layout" [Payments] script action buttons, or worrying about what happens if you missed one, because it's all handled by the script.

Opening and Closing Scripts

Finally, you can tell FileMaker to run a script automatically when someone opens or closes the file. The opening script runs when you first open the file. You can use this script if you want to be greeted with the list of unpaid invoices first thing every morning. The closing script runs when you close the *last window* for an open file. This option is a little less common, but it has its uses: If you want to make sure other related files close whenever the main file closes (even if they have open windows), then you could write a script to close them all whenever you close the main file.

To make the selection, you need to visit the File Options dialog box (File → File Options). In the File Options window, make sure the Open/Close tab is selected. In this window, you first turn on one of the "Perform script" checkboxes (there's one under "When opening this file" and another under "When closing this file"). Then you can select one of your scripts from the associated pop-up menu. Figure 13-11 shows the result.

Understanding ScriptMaker's Windows

When you created the Find Unpaid Invoices script (page 495), you learned to save your script by closing Edit Script and then clicking the Save button in the dialog box that follows. If you're upgrading from a previous version of FileMaker, you may find this behavior unusual. It's a result of a change deep in the heart of ScriptMaker. To understand what's going on, you need to understand a technical concept called *mode*.

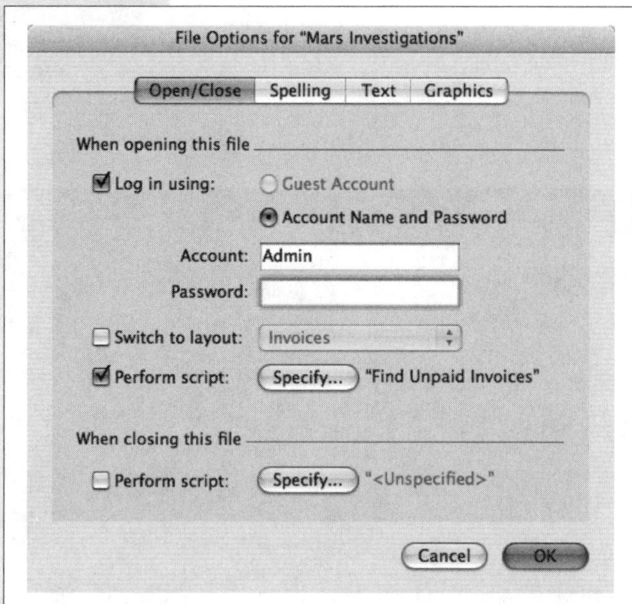

***Figure 13-11:** The Open/Close tab of the File Options window (File → File Options) lets you tell FileMaker what to do when a user opens or closes a file. Most of this window is devoted to the things that happen when a file opens. Only the last checkbox (under "When closing this file") has to do with which script should run when the file closes.*

You already know about FileMaker's main modes: Browse, Find, Preview, and Layout. When you're in Layout mode, you can't see your data, and when you're in Preview mode, you can't interact much with it. In other words, you enter a specific mode to do a specific task, and other modes' tasks aren't available to you. In its old incarnations, ScriptMaker behaved like a mode (as nerds would say, it was modal), even though it didn't advertise itself in the View menu. So, when you were creating or editing scripts, you were restricted to performing only certain tasks related to scripts. And in big organizations, where there was more than one developer working on a file, ScriptMaker's modality meant that only one person could edit scripts. The second developer had to wait until the first one closed ScriptMaker's dialog box to get her work done.

In FileMaker 9, ScriptMaker has shuffled off its modal coil. You can leave the Manage Scripts window, plus an Edit Script window (or two or three) open, and return to your database and do normal database work, like edit or find records. Heck, you can even close Manage Scripts, but leave a couple of Edit Script windows open. So if you're hard at work on a hairy script, and you get an emergency phone call about getting a report ready right away, you don't have to close ScriptMaker and potentially forget which script you were working on. Just click the database window behind the Edit Script window, do your work, and then pick up scripting right where you left off. Plus, with this new non-modal behavior, more than one person can edit scripts at the same time (although only one person can work on any individual script at once). And just like any other window, you can minimize ScriptMaker, hiding it in your taskbar (Windows) or Dock (Mac).

These benefits warrant a few warnings, though. Because there's no Save button in either the Manage Scripts or Edit Script window, scripts behave somewhat—but not exactly—like documents. When either a Manage Scripts or an Edit Script window is active, you'll see Save-related commands in the Scripts menu:

- Save Script saves the script in the active Edit Script window.
- Save All Scripts saves any script that isn't already saved.
- Revert Script reverts the script in the active Edit Script window.

If you aren't a menu fan, you can just close an active Edit Script window, and FileMaker gives you a dialog box that lets you choose what to do. Click Save if you want to save your work, or click Don't Save to revert the script to the way it was before your last bout of editing. But if you try to test a script you've edited, FileMaker gives you a warning dialog box (see Figure 13-12).

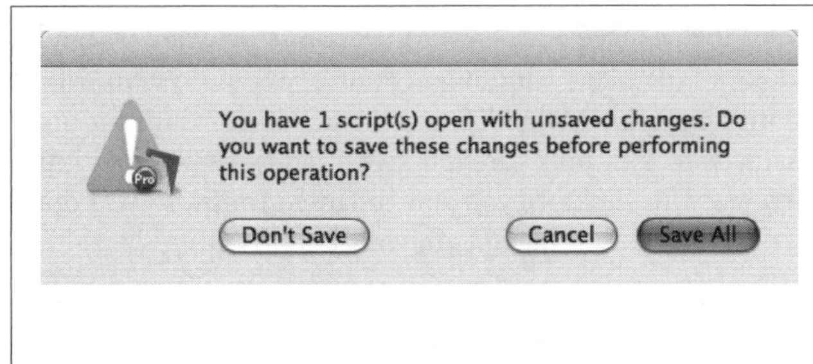

Figure 13-12:
If you make changes in a script, but forget to save it before you run it, FileMaker asks what you want it to do. In this case, the decision is easy. You've got only one unsaved script–the one that's running now. Most likely, you want to click Save All. But what would you do if the dialog had more than one unsaved script? You might save something you'd prefer to revert. In that case, click either Don't Save, which runs the script in its old form, or Cancel, which cancels the running script and doesn't save anything.

And if you like to work with lots of windows open, you may have trouble finding the right one, even using the Window menu (see Figure 13-13). If you use Windows (you know Windows XP, Vista—that kind of Windows) and like to work with your applications' windows maximized, then ScriptMaker's windows will be maximized, too. You may find this change frustrating. In the old days, when ScriptMaker was modal, it was easy to work in ScriptMaker and peek around it to the database below. Now that writing scripts is non-modal, the Manage Script and Edit Script windows open full-size on your screen, making it hard to see both your data and your script steps. You may have to make a tradeoff in your work habits and stop using that Maximize Window button.

Organizing Your Scripts

Most mature databases end up with dozens, or even hundreds, of scripts that make life a lot easier for the folks who use it. But developers don't usually have the luxury of creating scripts in an order that makes sense for display in the Manage Scripts window. That's why FileMaker gives you a suite of tools you can use to organize your scripts.

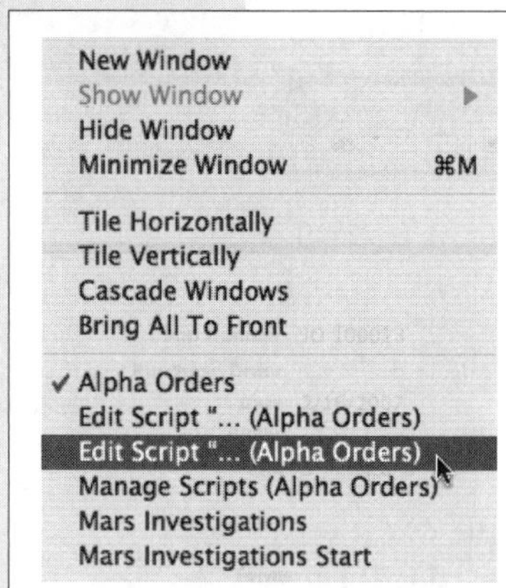

Figure 13-13:
The Window menu displays the names of all FileMaker's open windows. Database windows usually have the same name as their file, so it's easy to choose the one you need. But Edit Script windows lose a bit of meaning when the menu truncates their names, as you can see here. When you have multiple Edit Script windows open, be prepared. You may not get the window you want the first time. If you think about the windows like a deck of cards, it may help you remember which one is which. When two windows appear to have the same name, the one closest to the top of the deck will be higher in the Window menu.

Creating Script Groups

In Figure 13-14, you can see the Manage Scripts window from a database with a lot of scripts. The window looks a little like a window on your operating system, where documents are organized in folders. FileMaker lets you create New Groups for organizing your scripts that same way. Not only can you give a new group a descriptive name, but also, like folders on your desktop, you can collapse groups, so you don't have to scan a lengthy list of scripts to find the ones in your Reports group.

Script groups make the Manage Scripts window nice and tidy, but they also organize the Scripts menu. Any scripts inside a script group appear in a hierarchical (or pop-out) menu when you click the Scripts menu.

To see how all this works, you'll need to create a few extra scripts in your sample file. Just select your Find Unpaid Invoices script, and then click the Duplicate button in the Manage Scripts window a few times.

1. **In the Manage Scripts window, select the top script in your list, and then click the triangle at the right edge of the New button** (see Figure 13-1).

   The New item pop-up menu appears.

2. **Choose New Group.**

   The Edit Group dialog box appears.

3. **Type *Reports* in the Group Name box.**

   Just like everything else in FileMaker, a descriptive name helps you figure out what's what. "Reports" is a little arbitrary, since this is a theoretical exercise, but it's still a good habit to use descriptive names.

4. **Click OK.**

   The Reports group folder appears as the second item in your list. A new group always appears below any selected item in the list.

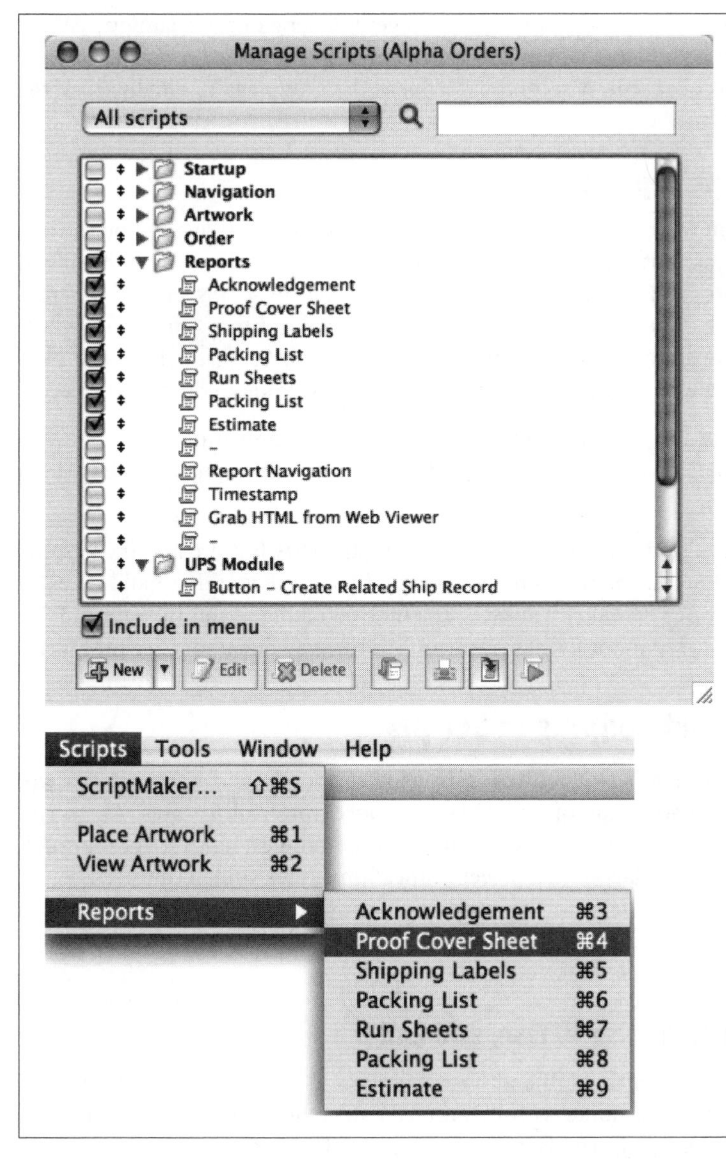

Figure 13-14:
You can name new groups according to any organizing scheme that makes sense to you. Since lots of scripts have to do with creating reports, most databases could stand to have a group named Reports. Move scripts that create reports into this folder, and then close it up when you're done. That way, when you're looking for Report scripts, you can jump right to them in the menu. The top figure shows the settings in the Manage Scripts dialog box and the bottom figure shows what you'll see in your script menu. Notice that the folder called Reports is now a hierarchical menu, and each nested script appears as a nested menu command.

5. **Drag the double arrow to the left of a script to move it into the Reports group folder.**

   The motion can be a little twitchy until you get used to it. Drag straight up or down to move a script to a new position in the list. But drag toward the *right* to move a script into a group. If the new group is directly above the scripts you're moving, then it's easiest to move the first script under the group right, then move each successive one right, also.

Move a few scripts into the Reports group to get the hang of the technique. When you have some scripts in the new group, click the gray triangle to the left of the group name to collapse it. A second click opens the group again. Finally, click the Scripts menu to see how script groups work there.

Creating Menu Separators

Groups help you when you're plowing through a list of scripts trying to find the one you need to tweak. But you can also help your database's users by giving them menu separators. It's a good idea to use them to organize sets of scripts that do different things. To create a menu separator, click to select the script that's just *above* where you want the separator to appear, and then choose New Separator from the New item pop-up menu. If a separator isn't where you want it, you can drag it into place.

You can also use the Duplicate button to copy a whole bunch of separators with just a few clicks. Each new separator appears just below the original; just drag them into place.

Finally, you can also create separators by clicking the New button, and then typing a single hyphen for the name of the new script. Make sure you don't add an extra space at the end, or FileMaker will list it as a funny-looking script. In Figure 13-13, you can see how a separator looks in a menu. It's the gray line under ScriptMaker.

Branching and Looping in Scripts

Now that you have a basic foundation in what scripts do and how you can run them, it's time to see some of ScriptMaker's more powerful features. The script you created at the beginning of this chapter was the simplest kind: It goes through a series of steps from start to finish every time. Sometimes your script needs more smarts. You can add steps to the script that cause it to take different actions depending on the situation (called *branching*), or make it do the same thing over and over again (called *looping*).

Branching with If, Else If, Else, and End If

If you're comfortable with the If and Case functions in calculations (see page 468), then you'll feel right at home with this topic. You've noticed that you often look someone up in the Customers layout, copy his email address, and then go to your mail program to send him an email. You'd like to add a button to the Customers layout that creates the email directly, saving you all the trouble of copying, switching, and pasting.

You can use FileMaker's Send Mail script step, which is just like the File → Send Mail command, to accomplish this task. First, create the script:

1. **Choose Scripts → ScriptMaker, and then, in the Manage Scripts dialog box, click New.**

   The Edit Script window pops up.

2. **In the Script Name box, type *Send Email to Customer*.**

   When you want to *run* this script, you choose this name from the Scripts menu.

3. **In the list of available script steps, select Send Mail, and then click Move.**

   FileMaker adds the script step to the script.

Note: The Send Mail script step is under Miscellaneous near the bottom of the list. If you don't like looking through this long list, choose Miscellaneous from the View pop-up menu to see just the steps in this category. Whenever you're *not* sure which category holds the step you want, choose "all by name" from the menu to see every step in alphabetical order.

---

4. **In the Script Step Options area, turn on the "Perform without dialog" checkbox.**

   This tells FileMaker you *don't* want a window that lets you enter or edit the Send Mail Options dialog box when the script runs. In this case, you just want it to do its work as you specify in the script step.

5. **Click Specify, and then, when the Send Mail Options dialog box appears, click the pop-up menu to the right of the To field. Choose Specify Field Name.**

   You now see a Specify Field dialog box. Here, you *tell* FileMaker where to find your customer's email address. Make sure "One email using data from the current record" is selected or you could get some dicey results, like sending an email about a customer's recent invoice to all the customers who happen to have records in your found set.

6. **Switch to the Customers table, if necessary, and then choose the Email address field. Click OK.**

   FileMaker closes the Specify Field window and shows you the Send Mail Options window again. Now, though, it shows your Email Address field reference in the To field. You can also add field references or calculations for CC, BCC, Subject, or even the body of your email message in those fields. This dialog box even lets you choose a file to attach to your email. But for now, just leave all these options blank.

   You now see your single line script in the Edit Script dialog box again, with the Send Mail options [No dialog; To Customers::Email Address] listed as a reference.

Tip: Turn on the "Multiple emails (one for each record in found set)" option to use this script step to send email to more than one person at a time. But remember, use this option for good, never for evil. You'd never send spam emails, would you?

---

7. **Close the Edit Script window, and then click the Save button.**

   You don't have to close the Edit Script window to save your script. Choose Scripts → Save Script, or press Ctrl+S (Windows) or ⌘-S (Mac).

At this point you have a working script. If you run it, it indeed creates a new email addressed to the current customer. But what happens if you *don't* have an email address for this customer? If the Customers::Email Address field is *empty*, your script tries to send an email without a valid address to your email program, which complains mightily. Fortunately, you can head off this problem at the pass. If the Email Address field is empty, you'd rather have your script tell you about it and skip the Send Mail step entirely. This is a job for the If step, so add it as follows:

1. **In the Edit Script dialog box, add the If step to your script.**

   FileMaker adds this step *after* the Send Mail step. It also adds a third step: End If. You can't have an If without an End If, so you get both automatically.

Note: If you accidentally delete the End If step from your script, FileMaker shows an error message when you try to save the script. To fix the error, you need to add the End If step back to your script and drag it to its proper place.

2. **Using the double-pointed arrow to the left of the If step, drag the step up above the Send Mail step.**

   By rearranging the steps in your script, you're telling FileMaker what order they should run in. (A script won't work as intended if you've got a step above something that needs to happen *first.*)

   Also, notice that the Send Mail script step is now indented. Everything between If and End If indents automatically to remind you that you're inside an If condition.

3. **Select the If step and, in the Script Step Options area, click Specify.**

   FileMaker shows you a standard Specify Calculation dialog box like the one shown on page 403. You use a calculation to define the *condition* of this If step. If the calculation evaluates to True, FileMaker does the steps after the If. If the calculation evaluates to False, FileMaker skips to the End If and continues running the script from there.

4. **In the calculation box, type Not IsEmpty(Customers::Email Address), and then click OK.**

   This calculation evaluates to *True* and sends your customer an email only if the Email Address field isn't empty. See the box on page 517 for details on how this calculation makes these decisions.

   Your script now checks to see if the Email Address field has something in it before running off to create the email message. But what happens when you run the script and the Email Address field is empty? Right now, nothing at all. FileMaker evaluates the If condition, sees that it's False, and skips to the End If. There's nothing after the End If, so the script just stops and your user waits in suspense, until he finally realizes that the requested email message simply isn't coming and investigates the problem on his own—or chucks his computer out the window.

In the interest of preventing property damage, it's better for your script to tell the user *why* nothing's happening. For example, you can have your script open a message box when the If condition is false, saying, "You can't email this customer, since there's no email address on file," or whatever. You can get exactly what you want with the Else step:

1. **Select the Send Mail script step in your script.**

   When you add a *new* step, FileMaker inserts it after the selected step. You want the Else step to go right after the Send Mail step, so you select that step first.

2. **Add the Else step to the script.**

   FileMaker inserts an Else step between Send Mail and End If.

Note: Don't click the Else If step by mistake. You want the step called just Else. If you added the wrong step, select it, click Clear, and try, try again.

---

3. **Right after the Else step, add the Show Custom Dialog script step to the script.**

   This step is also under Miscellaneous. Its job is to pop up a dialog box for the user. You get to decide what the box says, which buttons it includes, and which fields—if any—it should show.

4. **Click the Specify button in the Script Step Options area.**

   The "Show Custom Dialog" Options window appears (Figure 13-15).

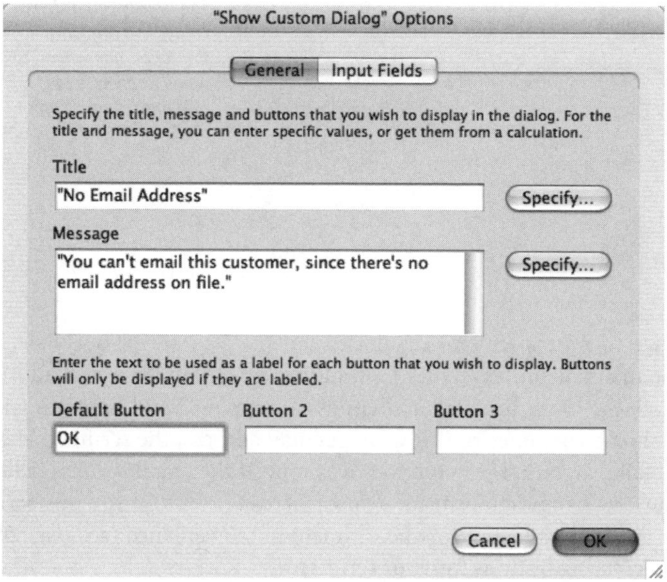

Figure 13-15:
The Show Custom Dialog script step, lets you provide feedback, like why an email script isn't behaving as expected. You can give your dialog box a title, a message, and up to three buttons for the user to click. You can also add input fields to the dialog box by visiting the Input Fields tab. You'll learn about these on page 568.

5. **In the Title box, type *No Email Address.***

   Whatever you type in this box will appear in the title bar along the top of your custom dialog box. Punctuation marks like commas and periods look odd in title bars, but you're welcome to include them.

6. **In the Message box, type *You can't email this customer, since there's no email address on file.***

   This tells FileMaker what to put *inside* the dialog box.

7. **From the Button 2 box, select and delete the word *Cancel.***

   A custom dialog box can have up to three buttons. In this case, you want only one: an OK button. (If you don't type anything in the Button 2 and Button 3 boxes, those buttons won't show up.)

8. **Click OK.**

   Your script should now look like the one shown in Figure 13-16.

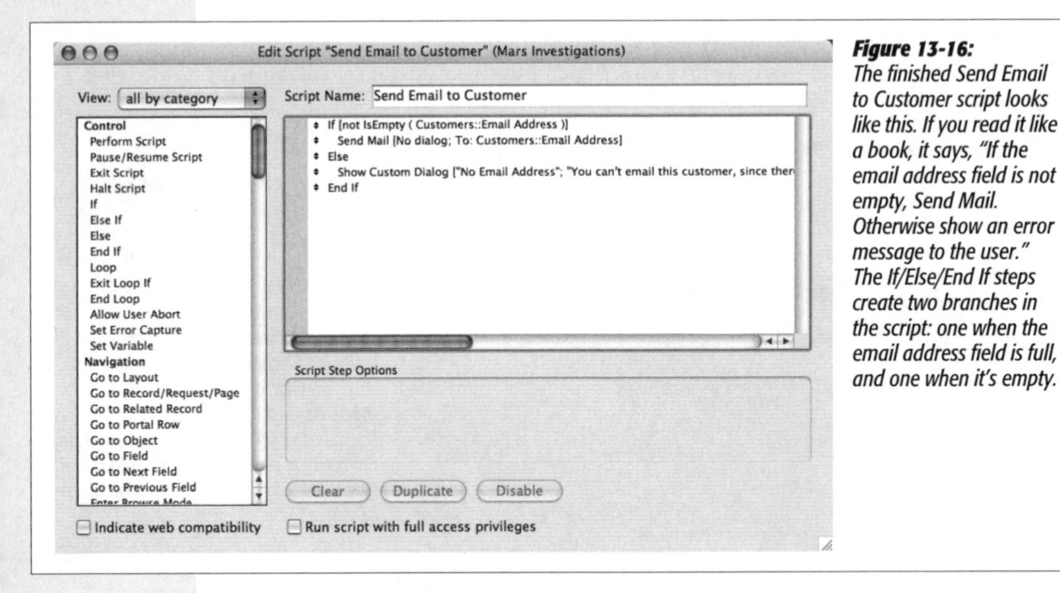

Figure 13-16: *The finished Send Email to Customer script looks like this. If you read it like a book, it says, "If the email address field is not empty, Send Mail. Otherwise show an error message to the user." The If/Else/End If steps create two branches in the script: one when the email address field is full, and one when it's empty.*

Just click OK twice to return to your database, and try your script out: Select a customer without an email address (enter Find mode, type *>0* in the Email address field, and then click the Omit button), and choose Scripts → "Send Email to Customer." If you look at a customer record with an email address, the script creates a message in your mail program, ready for you to fill out. If the email address field is empty, you see an error message instead. You can create a button for this script and add it to the Customers layout for the ultimate in convenience (see page 504 for more detail on creating buttons for your scripts).

UP TO SPEED

Not What?

FileMaker lets you create calculations that involve layers of Boolean logic. In the script you wrote on page 512, the If script step runs the indented steps only when the whole calculation evaluates to True. To figure out when that happens, you have to deconstruct the calculation itself.

By itself, the IsEmpty function returns True when the value you pass to it is completely empty—in other words, when the Email Address field is empty:

```
IsEmpty ( Customers::Email Address )
```

But that doesn't help you because you want the email sent only when there *is* data in the email field. If you have no email address entered, the calculation above returns True, and causes the Send Email step to run. If the email address field is filled in, on the other hand, the calculation's result is False and FileMaker skips the Send Mail step.

This behavior is exactly the opposite of what you want. To flip the result of the calculation around, you use the Not operator. It looks at the Boolean value to its right, and turns a True to a False, or a False to a True. Here's the calculation you need:

```
Not IsEmpty ( Customers::Email Address )
```

You can easily tell if you've got the right construction by reading the If step like a sentence: "If not is empty Email Address." It may not be grammatical perfection, but it does get the logic right.

Testing Multiple Conditions

If you have more than one condition to consider, you can use the Else If script step. It works a lot like the Case function in a calculation. You could have a script like this, for instance:

```
If [ Get ( CurrentTime ) < Time ( 12 ; 0; 0 ) ]
 Show Custom Dialog [ "Good Morning!" ]
Else If [ Get ( CurrentTime ) < Time ( 18 ; 0 ; 0 ) ]
 Show Custom Dialog [ "Good Afternoon!" ]
Else
 Show Custom Dialog [ "Good Evening!" ]
End If
```

When this script runs, it tests each condition in turn, deciding which custom dialog box to show your user, based on the actual current time. If the current time is before noon, your user sees a "Good morning" message, and the script jumps to the end (the End If script step) without needing to test the second condition.

If it isn't before noon, the script does a second test to see if it's before 6 PM. If it is, the user sees a "Good Afternoon" message, and the script jumps to the end. But if both tests fail, no third condition is tested, and the Else just shows the "Good Evening" message, like a default condition in a Case statement. However, you can add other Else Ifs to test other conditions.

You can add as many Else If steps as you want, but they must come between the If and End If steps. Each Else If can test a different condition. If you have an Else step, it should come after the If and every Else If, but before the End If. You can think of the Else condition as the default condition in a Case or an If statement when you write a calculation (page 468).

Tip: For a really cool way to tell which of the conditions in your scripts are evaluating as True and which ones evaluate as False, see the section on Script Debugger (page 706).

Looping

Sometimes you want to do the same thing over and over again, until you reach some kind of end point. For example, people often write a script that does something to every record in the found set, one after another. This kind of scripting is called *looping*. You make a script *loop through records* using the Loop script step.

Like the If step, the Loop step has a necessary partner called End Loop. When you put script steps between Loop and End Loop, FileMaker simply repeats them over and over, forever.

So how does a script like this end? Simple: You tell FileMaker to *exit the loop* at the right time. To this end, FileMaker has a script step called Exit Loop If. Like the If step, Exit Loop If has an associated calculation. If the calculation evaluates to True, FileMaker immediately skips ahead to the End Loop step, and continues with the step that follows. As such, a loop usually looks like this:

```
Loop
 # Do some stuff
 Exit Loop If [ // some condition ]
End Loop
```

Using what you've learned in this chapter and about calculations in Part 4, you can easily build a script like this. For "some condition," just use a calculation that describes the condition when the loop should stop repeating itself. read on to page xx, you can see an example of a looping script that stops when every record in a found set has been used up.

Using Go to Record/Request/Page to exit a loop

If you've used loops in other programs, you may think you have to devise some kind of test to figure out when you've reached the last record in your found set. You may be tempted to write a loop like this:

```
 Loop
  # Your script's work goes here.
  Go to Record/Request/Page [ Next ]
  Exit Loop If [ Get ( FoundCount ) = Get (RecordNumber) ]
 End Loop
# Your script's work goes here. Again!
```

This script starts with a loop that does your task on the current record, and then moves to the next record (just as if you'd clicked the right-hand page in the book icon). If the number of the record you're now on *equals* the current found count, FileMaker exits the loop. But there's a problem with this approach. The Exit Loop If step exits when you *first* reach the last record. You have to add another set of script steps to do your loop's work on the last record of the found set. It's not a very elegant arrangement, especially if the loop is just a part of a longer script. But the "Go to Record/Request/Page" script step has a trick that lets you eliminate the Exit Loop If conundrum. When you choose the Next option (telling it to go to the *next* record), a new checkbox appears in the Script Step Options area (Figure 13-17).

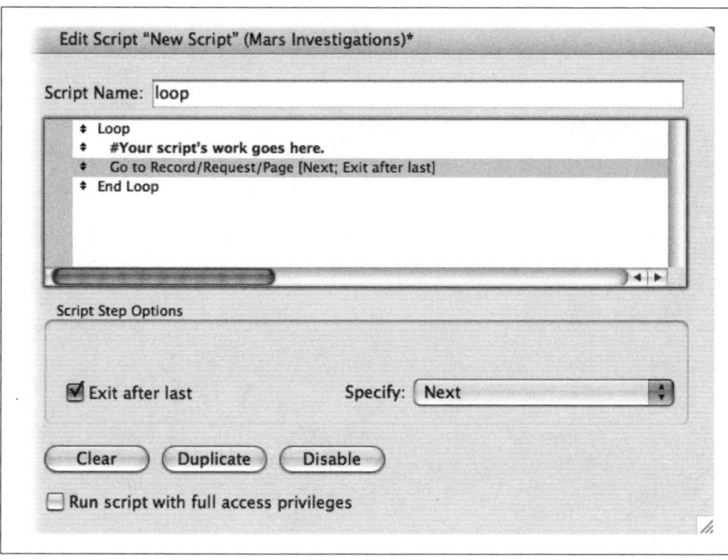

Figure 13-17: *The "Exit after last" option of the "Go to Record/Request/Page" script step tells FileMaker you want it to automatically exit the loop after the last record. In other words, FileMaker exits the loop when the "Go to Record/Request/Page" step runs and you're on the last record.*

This kind of scripting is good for two reasons. First, you can forget about using the Exit Loop If step in your script, since FileMaker exits the loop for you, compliments of "Exit after last." Second, just as advertised, the exit happens *after* the last record; there's no need to add a duplicate set of script steps after the Exit Loop. The revised—and tidy—script looks like this:

```
Loop
 # Your script's work goes here.
 Go To Record/Request/Page [ Next, Exit after last ]
End Loop
```

CHAPTER

14

Script Steps

Now that you know how to create scripts (you did read the previous chapter, didn't you?), it's time to expand your repertoire. FileMaker has a script step for just about everything you can do from the menus and status area. You can use any combination of these steps with script techniques like looping, branching, custom dialog boxes, and more to automate just about anything FileMaker can do. Major areas of scripting include working with field data and records, finding, sorting, working with windows and files, and printing. This chapter is a compendium of steps—and boatloads of scripting possibilities.

Go to Layout

The "Go to Layout" script step was introduced on page 497. Its purpose is simple: Change layouts. It works just like making a choice from the Layout pop-up menu in the status area, except that the script can go to *any* layout (even if it doesn't show in the menu).

"Go to Layout" has just one option, a pop-up menu labeled Specify. In addition to every layout in your database, this menu also has three special choices:

- The **original layout** option causes FileMaker to switch to the layout your user was on when the script started. After all, you can run lots of scripts anywhere, especially if they're on the Script menu. Since scripts often change layouts as they run, this option makes sure folks end up back where they started.
- The **Layout Name by calculation** option lets you specify a typical FileMaker calculation. The result of the calculation must be text, and it should exactly match the *name* of one of the layouts in the database. When the script runs, FileMaker evaluates the calculation and switches to the layout with the correct name.

- The **Layout Number by calculation** option is similar. You specify a calculation with a *number* result. FileMaker numbers every layout sequentially, in the order in which they're listed in Layout mode. The result of the calculation determines which layout to visit by number.

Note: Layout numbers don't necessarily correspond to their position in the Layout pop-up menu. Remember that not all layouts show in this list and you can reorder them manually. To find out a layout's number reliably, switch to Layout mode first. Then go to the layout and look at the Layout box in the status area. It shows which layout number you're on.

See the box below to learn when to use "Go to Layout" with Layout Name and when to use Layout Number.

FREQUENTLY ASKED QUESTION

Specifying a Layout

There are three ways to tell the "Go to Layout" step which layout to visit. Which one should I use?

The easiest way is to choose the layout from the Specify pop-up menu (see page 497). When the script runs, FileMaker goes to your chosen layout, period (that is, unless somebody deletes the layout).

The other two options–specifying a layout by name or number–are trickier, for a couple of reasons. First, they're a pain: You have to write a calculation when you could just pick from a menu. Second, both calculation methods have soft underbellies. If you specify a layout name using a calculation, and later rename the layout, even just by adding an accidental space somewhere in the name, the script can't find the layout any more. If you use the layout number, and then add or delete a layout, or rearrange your layout list (page 218), the script goes to the wrong layout.

Still, these options give you greater flexibility. For example, if you use "Go to Layout" and specify by Layout Name, you can use script parameters to name any layout in your database. With this technique, you can create a single navigation script and use it in all sorts of routine database tasks.

If you want to create a scripted process that's like a wizard or an assistant in some programs, the Layout Number is a godsend. Create the layouts that control your process, and make one Next button that you copy onto each layout. The button gets a "Go to Layout" script step, specifying a Layout Number that's one more than the current layout number (Get(LayoutNumber) + 1). Now, no matter how you rearrange the layouts, the button always takes your user to the next one in the Set Layout Order list–and you've used only one script step.

Scripting for Fields

Most people using FileMaker spend *a lot* of their time working with field data, so it's no surprise that script steps devoted to fields abound. You can put the user in a specific field, select field text, and even play sounds and movies from container fields. You can perform a find and replace operation, run the Replace Field Contents command, and export field contents to a file. Finally, you get more than 10 ways to put data into a field.

Navigating Fields

FileMaker offers a couple of ways to field-hop—pressing Tab to move to the next field in order, or just clicking the desired field. It has script steps that mimic both techniques.

Go to Field

The simplest field navigation script step is called "Go to Field." It's really a two-purpose step, with two checkboxes to prove it. In its simplest form, you turn on the "Go to target field" checkbox and pick the field you want to go to. When the script runs, FileMaker puts the user in the specified field (provided it's on the layout).

Tip: When you use "Go to Field" in a script, FileMaker dutifully ignores the field behavior specified on the layout and puts the user right into the field. You can use this fact to create a field that users can get to only by using your script.

The step also has a checkbox called "Select/perform." When this option is turned on, the script either *selects* the contents of the field it goes to or *does* what's in the field—if possible. For example, if the step goes to a *container* field that holds a sound or a movie, FileMaker *plays* the contents instead. If the container field holds a *reference* to a picture or a file, FileMaker *opens* the correct file, using the appropriate program.

The mildly weird thing about "Go to Field" is you can turn on "Select/perform" and *turn off* "Go to target field." With the options set this way, "Go to Field" doesn't go to a field at all. Instead, it simply selects or performs the contents of the field you happen to be in when the script runs.

Go to Next Field and Go to Previous Field

To mimic the process of tabbing through fields, FileMaker has two more script steps. The first, called "Go to Next Field," just tabs to the next field in the tab order. You probably already figured out that "Go to Previous Field" goes to the *previous* field in the tab order. These steps don't have a "Select/perform" option—they just go to the field.

Tip: To get the effect of "Select/perform," use "Go to Next Field" or "Go to Previous Field" to get to the field you want, and then use "Go to Field" to select/perform it. When you add the "Go to Field" step, don't turn on "Go to target field," and it acts on the field you're already in.

Editing Commands

FileMaker has all the classic commands in its Edit menu: Undo, Cut, Copy, Paste, and Clear. It also has a script step for each of these commands. The Undo step is the simplest. It has no options at all, and has exactly the same effect as choosing Edit → Undo. It's rare that you want to undo something you just scripted, so you'll rarely use this script step. It's quite handy, though, if you use custom menus (page 724) to control users' access to certain menu commands.

Cut, Copy, and Clear are slightly more complicated, with two options each. The first, "Select entire contents," lets you decide which part of a field's value gets cut, copied, or cleared. If you turn this option on, FileMaker selects the entire field before acting. If this option's turned off, FileMaker cuts/copies/clears whatever happens to be selected in the field. (But see page 525 to learn why you should rarely use these commands.) You also get a "Go to target field" option, through which the script can tell FileMaker *which field* to act on. If it's not turned on, it uses the *current field*—the one the user's in when the step runs.

The Paste step is the most complicated of these four. In addition to specifying the field you want, and whether or not to select everything in the field before pasting, you get an option to "Paste without style." When you turn this option on, FileMaker pastes the text on the clipboard, but throws away any style information. If you're in Windows, you get a fourth option: "Link if available." If the data on the clipboard comes from a source that supports object linking, FileMaker embeds the linked object. Changes to the original data show up in FileMaker. Turn this option off if you just want the script to paste a *copy* of the data.

Selecting Text

FileMaker has two script steps to help you select text. The first, called Select All, selects everything in the current field, just like the Edit → Select All command. If you need more control, use Set Selection instead. This step has two options. First, you can specify a target field so that FileMaker operates on the current field. The step also has a separate Specify button (below the one associated with "Go to target field") that brings up the Specify Set Selection window (Figure 14-1).

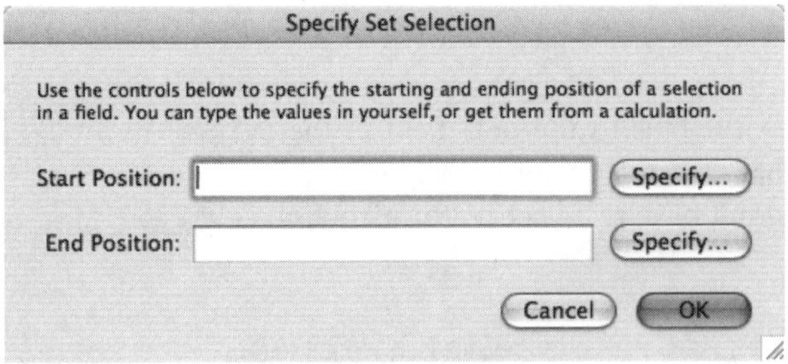

Figure 14-1: *This window lets you tell FileMaker exactly what text you want the script to select. You can type numbers directly in the Start Position and End Position boxes, or click either Specify button to bring up the Specify Calculation dialog box.*

If you imagine the text in your field as a string of letters, numbers, spaces, and punctuation, then you can pretend each of these is numbered. For instance, the word "Missing" has letters numbered one through seven. You first tell FileMaker where the selection should *start* by putting the number of the first character in the Start Position box. Next, you put the number of the *last* character in the End Position box. When the step runs, FileMaker selects these two characters and everything in between.

POWER USERS' CLINIC

Positioning the Insertion Point

You can use the Set Selection script step to put the insertion point anywhere in a field, too. The trick is to make sure *nothing* gets selected. When you specify a Start Position and an End Position, FileMaker selects the characters at each position, plus anything in between. If these two numbers are the same, FileMaker selects just one character.

But what if the End Position comes *before* the Start Position? When you set the End Position one number lower than the Start Position, FileMaker doesn't select anything. Instead, it puts the little flashing insertion point right before the Start Position. Using this technique, you can get your script to put the user anywhere you want inside a field, say at the beginning of a Notes field, so they can just start typing, without needing to move the cursor.

Editing Field Data

Editing field data is such an important part of FileMaker that there are more than 10 ways to put stuff in fields with a script step. On page 499, you learned that the scripted process for creating a printed report could actually be shorter and more efficient than the manual process. Editing field data via scripts is also different from manually editing data, and the following sections cover those differences.

The first thing to understand is that, except for Set Field, the steps in this section *work only if the field is on the current layout.* This property is no problem for scripts you use to structure a user's data entry, but it can be a roadblock in other cases. Suppose you have a script that sets a "Paid in Full" flag on an invoice. You want this script to work no matter what layout you're on (as long as it's one that shows invoice records), and whether the field is on that layout or not. In that case, you need to understand the Set Field script step (page 526).

Avoiding Cut, Copy, and Paste

Your first inclination might be to use Cut, Copy, and Paste in a script to move data from one field to another, and it does work. You can, for example, have a script copy the Customer ID field, and then go to the Invoices layout, create a new invoice, and paste it into the Customer ID field there.

But most developers don't use this approach for two reasons. First, many people consider the user's clipboard to be sacred ground. They argue you should *never* change what's on the clipboard unless the user asks you to. So it would be OK to have a Copy button by the Address fields, for example, that copies the address to the clipboard because the user would know exactly what is going into the clipboard. But what if the user manually copies a long product description to the clipboard, and then runs the "Create Invoice for Customer" script? She then tries to paste the description in the invoice line item, only to find that the description's gone, replaced by the Customer ID for some odd reason. To keep from frustrating the user (or yourself), you should generally avoid Cut and Copy.

Also, these steps don't work if the field isn't on the layout. People often show the customer's *name* on an invoice, but not his *ID*. But if you delete the Customer ID field from the Invoices layout, any scripts that use Cut, Copy or Paste and the Customer ID field break. That's where Set Field steps in to save the day.

Set Field

The one field-editing power step that doesn't care a whit about what fields are on the layout is called Set Field. This step replaces the contents of a field with the result of a calculation. Its two options let you specify the field to set, and the calculation to use. The calculation result must be the same type as the field you've specified. For Text, Date, Time, and Timestamp fields, Set Field is usually the step of choice: It's flexible and reliable, no matter what's on the layout.

Note: As with many other FileMaker processes, be aware of context when you use a Set Field script step. You can edit data through a relationship using Set Field, but make absolutely certain the context is what you intend. If you aren't careful, you can edit data in the wrong record.

Like many of the steps you've seen so far, you don't have to specify a field at all. When you do, Set Field changes the field it's in *at the moment the step runs*. (The current-field method works only with text results; otherwise, you have to specify the field so FileMaker knows what type you have in mind.)

Insert Calculated Result

Set Field's one weakness is that it *always* overwrites a field completely (but see the tip below). Another step, Insert Calculated Result, lets a script put data in a field while keeping the data that's already there. It has three options. First you can specify a target field. You can also choose "Select entire contents" in the field first (in which case it overwrites the entire field, just like Set Field). Finally, you get to specify the calculation. Here are some variations on these options:

- If you *don't* turn on the "Select entire contents" option, FileMaker inserts the calculation result *after* whatever's already in the field.
- If you *don't* specify a field at all, and you *don't* turn on "Select entire contents," then FileMaker inserts the result of the calculation into the current field. If you select data when the script step runs, the calculation result overwrites whatever's highlighted. Otherwise, the text goes in wherever the insertion point happens to be, just as though you'd typed it from the keyboard.

Tip: You can use Set Field to append results to existing data: Just include the field's data in the calculation. If you want to add "Esquire" to the end of the customer's last name (in the Last Name field), just use this calculation in your Set Field step:

```
Last Name & ", Esquire"
```

Inserting other values

FileMaker has six other *Insert* script steps that work like Insert Calculated Result. Each step lets you specify a target field and select the field contents if you want. They differ only in what gets inserted:

- **Insert Text** lets you specify any static text value and add it to the field verbatim. Use this if you know ahead of time what you want your script to put in the field, and don't need to calculate it.
- **Insert from Index** makes your script show the same View Index window just like choosing Insert → From Index in Browse or Find mode. The user picks a value from the list, and FileMaker inserts it into the field. This option's especially valuable in Find mode, both to keep your user from having to type a value (and possibly making a typo) *and* to make sure the search always finds records, since if a value's in the index, it's in a record somewhere.
- **Insert from Last Visited** is an interesting step. It grabs the value from the *same* field on the *last visited* record and inserts it. This step is particularly useful on data entry layouts. Imagine, for example, you have to enter 300–person records from 15 different companies. You could use this step to create a button that pops in the *last* company you typed into the Company Name field, rather than type it over again.

Note: You can't just take a peek at a record and call it visited, though. The record must be entered or opened (page xx). An Open Record/Request script step helps insure you get the record you intend.

- **Insert Current Date** and **Insert Current Time** do just as they say. Unfortunately, there's no Insert Current Timestamp step; use Insert Calculated Result and the Get (CurrentTimeStamp) function instead.
- **Insert Current User Name** puts the user name of the person using FileMaker into the field. Your operating system normally determines this user name, but you can easily change it from FileMaker's Preferences' General Tab.

See the box on page 528 for advice on when to use Set Field and when to use an Insert step.

Putting data in container fields

In Part 4, you learned that calculations can work with container data. Set Field and Insert Calculated Result are no exception: You can use either of them to move pictures, movies, sounds, and files from one container field to another. You can also use Cut, Copy, and Paste to work with container fields, provided you're willing to live with the caveats for intruding on your user's clipboard described on page xx.

But FileMaker has special commands in the Insert menu to get container data into your database in the first place, and these commands have script step equivalents:

- **Insert Picture** lets you specify the file to insert, and whether you want to "Store only a reference" (see page 80 for a refresher on references). If you don't specify a file, FileMaker asks the user to pick one when the step runs.

Note: The dialog box the user sees when he's asked to pick a picture file includes the "Store only a reference" checkbox, regardless of how you set this option on the script step itself. In a sense, your choice in the script becomes a *suggestion* to the user: It determines how the checkbox is set when the dialog box pops up. The user's free to change it.

- **Insert QuickTime** has only one option: the file you want to insert. Again, if no file is selected, the user gets to pick one when the script runs. Since QuickTime files are *always* stored as a reference, you don't get that choice this time.
- **Insert File** has the most options of all. Of course, you get to pick the file to be inserted. You also get a "Store only a reference" checkbox. This time, though, you also get a "Go to target field" checkbox. You can use it to tell FileMaker which field to put the file in.

Insert Picture and Insert QuickTime don't have an option to tell FileMaker *which field to use*, which probably seems odd. They're designed to put things in the current container field the user clicks before the script runs. If you want more control, just use "Go to Field" first, specifying the appropriate field, and then use Insert Picture or Insert QuickTime to insert into that field.

POWER USERS' CLINIC

Set Field vs. Insert

FileMaker's field editing script steps have a lot of overlap (page 525). For example, Set Field with no target field does exactly the same thing as Insert Calculated Result with no target field and the "Select entire contents" checkbox turned on. And you can use Insert Calculated Result with the appropriate calculation to do the same thing as Insert Date, Insert Time, Insert Text, and Insert Current User Name. In general, it doesn't matter one bit which one you use.

But you should think twice about using the Insert script steps with a target field specified *and* the "Select entire contents" checkbox turned on. With both options set, these script steps simply overwrite the value in some field—exactly what Set Field does.

Since these steps need the field on the layout, though, they're more *fragile*: The script can break if you make changes to a layout. You'll probably save yourself a headache tomorrow if you just use Set Field today.

Of course, if you're inserting *into* a field (without "Select entire contents" turned on), then you *must* use an Insert step. Luckily, with settings like this one, a step makes sense only if the user's already in the field–and thus the field's obviously on the layout.

Finally, you can't accomplish some of the Insert steps from a calculation. Specifically, you can't access the last visited record or the View Index dialog box from a Set Field step.

A Field Script in Action

Suppose you decide to add a Notes field to the Customer table in your database. You use this field to hold any arbitrary information you think is important about the customer. Unfortunately, you soon realize this field is a little *too* unorganized. You have no idea if the note that says, "Customer already paid" is from last Tuesday or last year. What you need is a consistent way to keep track of *who* left a note, and *when*. You decide everybody should record this information along with any note they leave. To make things even easier, you want to be sure people add *new* notes *above* older notes. Thus, when a customer record has been around for a while, the Notes field would look something like this:

```
--- 12/11/07 @ 3:30 PM by Jim ---
Called the customer, confirmed both orders were received. Placed a copy of
the order in Jello, along with Dwight's stapler, in the top drawer of his
desk.

--- 12/01/07 @ 1:25 PM by Dwight ---
Customer called saying he never got his order. I checked and we have no
record of shipment because some people are so lax! I'm shipping again.

--- 11/28/07 @ 4:58 PM by Jim ---
Order came in really close to quittin' time. I'll finish the paperwork
Monday.
```

In this example, you create a script that "forces" all added comments into that format. This script adds a separator line with the date and time (plus a couple blank lines) and leaves the insertion point under the separator. You also create a button next to the Notes field that runs this script. All the user has to do is click and type.

Note: Like almost every problem you ever solve with a script, you can do this process in *about* 24,601 ways. One way's described below, and another in the box on page 532. You may prefer a different way, and that's OK.

Before you start creating your script, think about what you need to do in sequence. Here's a breakdown:

- Put the insertion point at the start (top) of the Notes field.
- Insert two blank lines—to create some space before the previous comment.
- Put the insertion point back at the start, and add the separator line with the date and time.
- At that point, the script ends and the user can start typing.

Your next mission is to translate these plain-English steps into ScriptMaker steps, which you'll do in the next section.

Building the script

If your Customers table doesn't already have a Notes field, create one before you write the script. Then proceed as follows:

1. **Choose Scripts → ScriptMaker. Create a new script called *Add Note Separator*.**

   Develop the habit of giving your scripts descriptive names so you can remember what you want them to do.

2. **Add a Set Selection script step to the script.**

   You can find this step under Editing in the list, or you can choose "all by name" from the View pop-up menu to see an alphabetical list. When you add the step, it appears in your script.

3. **Turn on the "Go to target field" checkbox. If necessary, choose Customers from the table pop-up menu, and then choose the Notes field, and click OK.**

   The Set Field step in your script updates to show the target field.

4. **In the Script Step Options area, click the second Specify button.**

   It's not labeled, but it's *below* the first Specify button. When you click it, the Specify Set Selection window appears.

5. **In both boxes (Start Position and End Position), type *0* (zero).**

   Zero in both boxes tells FileMaker you want the insertion point right at the start of the field, and you don't want any text selected. (Positioning at the start of a field is the single exception to the box on page 525, which discusses how to set the insertion point without selecting text.)

6. **Add an Insert Text step to the script and turn off the "Select entire contents" option.**

   You don't want the two blank lines you're about to insert to replace everything in the field.

7. **Click the bottom Specify button.**

   A window called simply Specify appears (Figure 14-2).

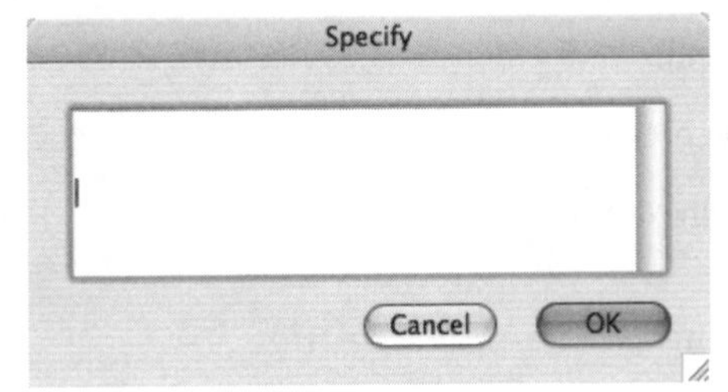

Figure 14-2: *The Specify dialog for Insert Text seems puzzling, because there aren't any options for you to click. You just type the exact text you want the script step to insert. Note that this box isn't a calculation dialog box. It allows only the insertion of literal text. Use Insert Calculated Result if you need to insert dynamic text with a script step.*

8. **In the Specify window, add two empty lines (press Return or Enter twice), and then click OK.**

   That's the regular Enter key, not the one in the numerical keypad: In this dialog box, that key just clicks the OK button. Anyway, after pressing it twice, you don't see the returns you've typed in the dialog box, but you do see two blank spaces inside quotes in the Insert Text script step. Those returns tell FileMaker to add two blank lines to the top of the Notes field.

9. **Select the Set Selection step at the top of the script, and then click the Duplicate button at the bottom of the window.**

   FileMaker adds a second copy of the Set Selection step, right below the first.

10. **Drag either Set Selection step to the bottom of the script.**

    Mouse junkies can use Ctrl+down arrow (⌘-down arrow) to move script steps.

    Your script now has Set Selection, then Insert Text, and then Set Selection again. It doesn't matter *which* Set Selection step you drag, as long as one's on top and the other on the bottom when you're done.

11. **Add the Insert Calculated Result step to the script and turn off the "Select entire contents" option.**

    Make sure the step lands *after* the last Set Selection script. If it doesn't, move it there. Turning off the selection option ensures that the calculation goes right in the middle of the text, not on top.

12. **Click the Specify button to the right of "Calculated result," and enter this calculation in the Specify Calculation window:**

    ```
    "--- " & Get(CurrentDate) & " @ " & Get(CurrentTime) & " by " &
    Get(UserName) & " ---¶"
    ```

    You can use any method you want to enter the calculation, as long as it does the same thing as this one.

13. **Save the script.**

    Your new script is ready to test.

Now you just need to add the Notes field to the Customers layout, and a button by it that runs the new script. When you click the button, FileMaker adds the separator to the field, and puts the insertion point in place. Your users can now type notes that are nicely organized and separated.

Other Steps That Work with Fields

Lots of times, you want to be able to write scripts that work on multiple records. You may need to change values across a found set of records, or you may want to let FileMaker handle the serial numbering of all the records in a table. The next script steps let you manage data in lots of records without lots of hassle.

Perform Find/Replace

The Perform Find/Replace script step brings all the power of the Find/Replace command (page 60) to your scripts. You can include the find parameters in the script step, or create a calculation to determine the parameters on the fly, as shown in Figure 14-3.

GEM IN THE ROUGH

Fewer Steps, Bigger Calculations

The Add Note Separator script described on page 529 is easy to create, but it has one weakness: It uses four steps where two could accomplish the same thing. A more concise approach would be to first put the separator and a few blank lines at the top of the Notes field, and *then* use the Set Selection script step to put the insertion point after the separator. The drawback here is that you have much more complex calculations to write. The choice is yours.

In the Insert Calculated Results step, you need a calculation that builds the separator line, adds two blank lines after it, and finally adds the *old* contents of the Notes field to the end:

```
"--- " & Get(CurrentDate) & " @ " &
Get(CurrentTime) & " by " & Get(UserName)
& " ---¶¶¶" & Customers::Notes
```

To keep the contents of your field from being duplicated, make sure you leave the "Select entire contents" option on this time.

Now you need to get the insertion point in place after the first line, using the Set Selection script step. Use the same technique as before: Set Selection with an End Position that's *smaller* than the Start Position. FileMaker puts the insertion point *before* the character at the Start Position. Since you want it *after* the end of the first line, you need to find the first new line symbol, add *1* to it, and put *that* in the Start Position. Here's the calculation that does the trick:

```
Position ( Customers::Notes, "¶", 1, 1 )
+ 1
```

Put this same calculation, but without the last *+1*, into the End Position field and you're ready to test your script. You can use this script with or without the "Go to Target Field" option, as described in step 3 on page 523.

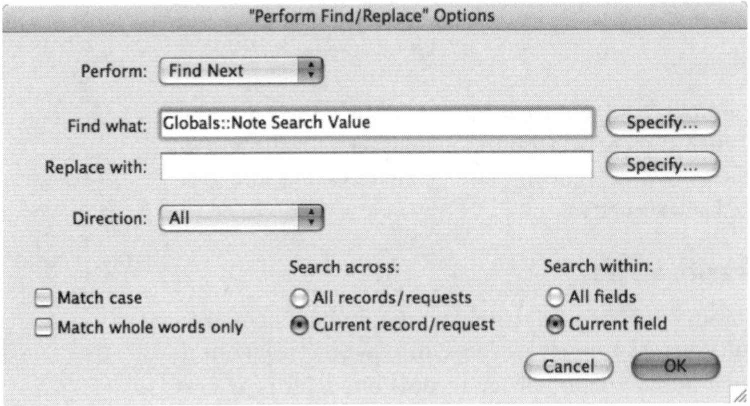

"Perform Find/Replace" Options		
Perform: Find Next		
Find what: Globals::Note Search Value	Specify...	
Replace with:	Specify...	
Direction: All		
	Search across:	Search within:
☐ Match case	○ All records/requests	○ All fields
☐ Match whole words only	◉ Current record/request	◉ Current field
	Cancel	OK

Figure 14-3: *The window behind the Specify button on a Perform Find/Replace script step looks a lot like the normal Find/Replace window. But this version has a new pop-up menu (called Perform) and a couple new Specify buttons that let you specify calculated values for what you're looking for and what you want to replace the found results with. This picture shows the settings you'll use in the steps on page 533.*

When you use this step, you pick which action you want to perform from the Perform pop-up menu. Your choices are Find Next, "Replace and Find," Replace, and Replace All (these correspond with the buttons you use to dismiss the normal Find/Replace dialog box). The "Find what" and "Replace with" boxes each have a Specify button by them. If you know exactly what you're looking for, you can type it right in these boxes. If you click Specify, you get to use a calculation to set these values instead.

For example, say your Notes field is such a smashing success, you find some customers have *pages* of notes—and it's becoming a problem to find what you want.

You'd like a quick way to search the material in the Notes fields. Figure 14-4 shows one solution: Add a button to the Customers layout that runs a Find script.

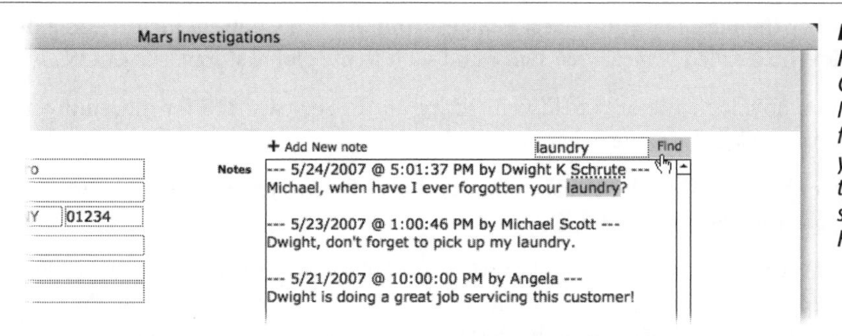

Figure 14-4: *Here's one idea for a Customers layout with a Notes field and a search field added. To find what you're looking for, you'll type something in the search field and click Find.*

The script is simple. It just needs to go to the Notes field and use the Perform Find/Replace script step. You need a field to type the search value into, which you could create before opening ScriptMaker, but in real life you probably think of that after you start writing your script. FileMaker makes it easy to create fields without leaving the warmth and protection of ScriptMaker, as you'll see in the following steps.

Here's how to make the script. Call it *Search Notes Field*:

1. **Add "Go to Field" as your first script step. Set it to go to the Customers::Notes field.**

   First things first: You want to make sure the script searches the correct field. Now you create the Find script itself.

2. **Add the Perform Find/Replace step to the script, and turn on the "Perform without dialog" option. Click the Specify button.**

   You see the Perform Find/Replace Options window.

3. **Make sure the Perform pop-up menu is set to Find Next, and then click the Specify button to the right of the "Find what" box.**

   The Specify Calculation window appears.

4. **From the pop-up menu above the field list, choose Manage Database.**

   It makes sense for this field to use global storage, and since it doesn't really belong to a customer, you add a new table for it as well. You can do that right here in the Manage Database window.

Note: Scripts often make use of global fields, so FileMaker lets you create a quick table to hold them without cluttering or interfering with your relationship graph (see page 331).

5. **Click the Tables tab and add a new table called *Globals*.**

   This table holds global fields that aren't tied to specific tables. You don't need a relationship to a table to grab the value from a global field, so a table like this makes them very easy to find. If you're working in the file you used back in Chapter 8, you may already have a table for your globals. If so, add your new global fields there.

6. **Click the Fields tab, and select Globals from the Table pop-up menu. Add a new text field called *Note Search Value* and set it to use global storage. Click OK.**

   You now have the only field your script needs. See page 118 for more information on global storage fields.

7. **Double-click the Globals::Note Search Value field to create its field reference as your calculation. Click OK.**

   This calculation tells FileMaker where to look when it runs the Perform Find/Replace step—whatever's in the new field, in this case. Clicking OK when you're done returns you to the Perform Find/Replace Options window.

8. **In the Direction pop-up menu, choose All.**

   This options tells FileMaker to look through the entire Notes field.

9. **Turn on the "Current record/request" and "Current field" radio buttons. Click OK until you're back in your database.**

   You don't want the search to spill into different fields or records. These options restrict it to just the record the user's viewing. Since the script first goes to the Notes field, FileMaker searches only that field.

To finish the job, add the new global field and a Find button, formatted with your new script, to the Customers layout (as shown in Figure 14-4). Then type a value into the search field, and click your script button to test your new script.

POWER USERS' CLINIC

A Reusable Notes Separator Script

The mark of a FileMaker power-scripter is someone always on the lookout for the opportunity to write *one* script that can be used in *several* places. After all, who wants to spend his life in ScriptMaker? The fact is, you're probably so happy with your new Notes field and its separator script that you want to use it in other places–on a Job, an Invoice, a Payment, and so forth.

It would be much nicer if the Add Note Separator script could add a note separator (and place the insertion point) in *any* field you wanted. You could then tell the user to click the Notes field before running the script.

The only thing tying your script to the Customers::Notes field is the "Go to target field" checkbox on the Set Selection steps. If you edit the script and turn this option off for *both* Set Selection steps, it works on whatever field is active when the script runs.

If you don't like to have to click the field before running the script, then you can fix it in two ways, but both require information you haven't learned yet. See page 580 for a continuation of this technique.

Replace Field Contents and Relookup Field Contents

It's probably no surprise that you can execute the Replace Field Contents and Relookup Field Contents commands from a script. These steps let you specify a field to act upon. If you *don't* specify a field, they act on the current field. You also get the typical "Perform without dialog" checkbox. When you turn this checkbox on, the action happens immediately when the step runs. If you leave this option off with the Replace Field Contents step, the user sees the typical Replace Field Contents dialog box (with all the settings you specified in the script). With the Relookup Field Contents step, the user just sees a confirmation message first, asking if she really wants to perform the relookup operation.

Set Next Serial Value

The Set Next Serial Value script step is invaluable—in the rare cases when anyone actually uses it. It's a one-trick pony: If a field auto-enters a serial number, this step changes the "next value" stored in the Field Options dialog box. In other words, if you want to start your customer ID values over again, you can use Set Next Serial Value to do it from a script. (See the box on page 536 for an example.)

Warning: Use extreme care when you change a field that's used as a key in a relationship. You risk leaving related records orphaned if you don't change their key fields, too. See the box on page 605 for a script that helps you change key fields without losing related records (or your sanity).

The step has two options. First, you can specify the field to update. As usual, if you don't specify a field, it works on the current field. You tell FileMaker what to set the "next value" to by entering a calculation.

Working with Records

You can get only so far with your scripts by working with field values. Eventually you need to deal with more than one *record*. Thankfully, FileMaker has script steps for creating, duplicating, and deleting records; navigating among existing records; and even managing the process of opening and editing a record, and saving (committing) or reverting the changes. You can also work directly with portal rows on the current layout—and the records they represent.

Creating, Duplicating, and Deleting Records

New Record/Request and Duplicate Record/Request have no options, and do exactly what you'd expect. The first script step creates a new record, just like the Records → New Record menu command. The second duplicates the current record. In either case, the *new* record becomes the current record, just like when you do it manually. You use these steps most often on buttons, when you're taking away menu commands from people and providing them with buttons that appear only on the layouts where you want your users to be able to create records.

POWER USERS' CLINIC

Why Set Next Serial Value

The previously used Set Next Serial Value script step may seem odd to you. After all, if you want to set the next serial value for a field, you can just do it yourself from the Manage Database window. But this step can come in very handy in some situations.

Imagine you're in the auto parts business and you have 200 stores around the country. Each office has its own copy of your database, which gets updated periodically. The main office sends a new empty database to each store with all the latest enhancements, and the folks at each store have to *import* all the data from their old database into the new one (you'll learn about importing and exporting data in Chapter 17).

Now suppose this database includes an Orders table with an Order ID field. After the old orders have been imported, the database may have orders with IDs from one to 1000. But since no *new* records have been created yet, the Order ID field still has a "next value" of *1*. The store's first thousand orders use IDs that are *already used by other records*. That's a big no-no.

The solution's obvious: You need to fix the "next value" on the Order ID field after the import's finished. To save the store manager the trouble, you can put a script in the database to fix this glitch for her. (In fact, you can make a script that does *all* the work of importing old data and fixing next serial values in every table.)

Note: Duplicating a record from a script step works just like doing it manually–that is, the script duplicates the static values in the record, too. If calculations depend on those static values, they also get duplicated, but will change if you edit the static values later. Some Auto-Enter calculations, like serial numbers, are *not* duplicated but are recalculated at the time the duplicate record is created.

The Delete Record/Request script step deletes the current record. If you turn on its "Perform without dialog" option, the delete happens automatically with no warning. When this option is turned off, the user sees the same "Are you sure" message box he'd see when deleting a record manually.

Note: Each of these three script steps also works for *find requests* when a script runs in Find mode.

Navigating Among Records

There are two ways to change to a different record. You can move to it with the "Go to Record/Request/Page" script step, which works a lot like the book icon in the status area. Or you can switch to a related record, or a set of related records, using the "Go to Related Record" script step.

Go to Record/Request/Page

FileMaker has one script that handles changing *records*, *find requests*, and *pages*. This may seem strange at first, but it makes sense because it's exactly how the book icon in the status area works: If you're in Browse mode, the step goes to a different record. If you're in Find mode, it switches find requests instead. Finally, if you're in Preview mode, it flips through pages.

Note: You can't run scripts when in Layout mode, and a script *can't* go to Layout mode, so it doesn't apply here.

The "Go to Record/Request/Page" step has just one option. You get to pick *which* record, request, or page to go to from a simple list:

- First
- Last
- Previous
- Next
- By Calculation

When you lock your users out of the usual interface and control everything they do through the script (see the box on page 558), the First, Last, Previous, and Next options let you provide your own customized replacement for the status area and book icon. For example: Make four buttons and arrange them in a horizontal line (like those on a tape recorder or CD player). Give each button a "Go to Record" step and set them up in the following order, so they mimic the tape recorder concept:

- Leftmost button – "Go to Record/Request/Page" [First]
- Second button – "Go to Record/Request/Page" [Previous]
- Third button – "Go to Record/Request/Page" [Next]
- Rightmost button – "Go to Record/Request/Page" [Last]

This visual concept is so common that your users are likely to know how the buttons work without any instructions. But you can add a tooltip (page 723) to each button if you want to provide that extra boost.

Another common, but more advanced use of this step is to provide a way for a looping script to end. When you choose the Next or Previous option, a new checkbox appears in the Script Step Options area, called "Exit after last." When it's turned on, FileMaker knows to exit the loop after it's finished with the last record (when you choose "Go to Record" [next]) or after the first record (when you choose "Go to Record" [previous]). (When to exit a loop is no small matter, as page 518 explains.)

When you choose By Calculation, you get the chance to specify a calculation with a number result. FileMaker goes to exactly that record, request, or page. You could use this option if the record number's in a field, or if you want to skip ahead *25* records each time the script is run, for example. This technique is more useful than it sounds. For example, it's an ideal way to show records in a list using Instant Web Publishing (IWP), which you'll learn about in Chapter 18. In IWP, FileMaker limits the list to 25 records at a time, so you have to give your Web users some way to see the next patch of records.

Go to Related Record

You were first introduced to this power step when learning about relationships (see page 358). It can go to a different record, found set, layout, window, and even file—all in one step. This step's job is simple: It takes you to a related record. But carrying out that job *isn't* so simple. When you click the Specify button, you get a wealth of choices, as shown in Figure 14-5. To go to a related record, you need to tell FileMaker which related table occurrence you're interested in, by selecting it from the "Get related record from" pop-up menu. For example, if you're on the Customer layout and you want to see a related invoice, you should choose Invoices from the menu.

With this done, FileMaker can find the right record. But how should it *show it to you*? If you're visiting related records, chances are you can't view them directly on the current layout (since the layout is associated with the wrong table occurrence). So a "Go to Related Record" command almost always involves changing layouts. You pick the layout you want from the "Show record using layout" pop-up menu.

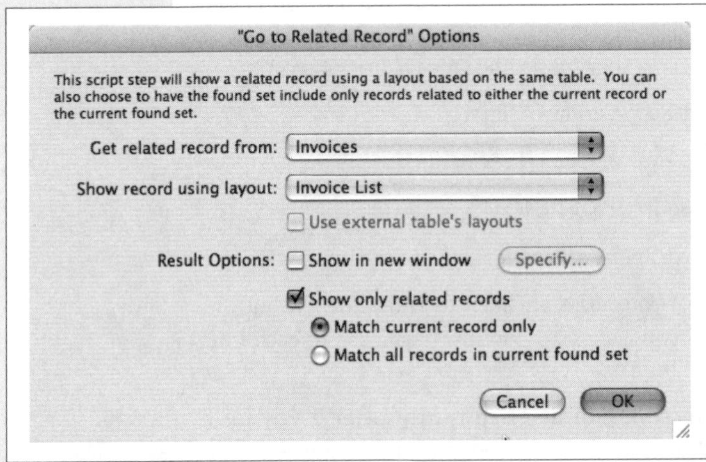

Figure 14-5: *This window's the same one you saw when you attached a "Go to Related Record" script step to a button back on page 358. But inside a script you wield a whole new level of power when you tie this command to other processes, like printing a report from a found set that changes based on whichever record a user's on when running the script.*

At first you may be surprised by the menu choices. It shows all the layouts associated with the table occurrence in the first pop-up menu, as you might expect. But it *also* shows layouts associated with any *other* occurrence of the same table. FileMaker uses the specified table occurrence to find the right related record, and the specified layout to show it to you. You can show an invoice record from any layout that shows records from the Invoices table, no matter what *occurrence* it uses:

- If the table occurrence you picked in the first menu is an occurrence of a table from a *different* file, you can turn on "Use external table's layout" to see layouts in the file the table comes from. When you use this option from a button, FileMaker switches to a window for the other file instead of showing records in the current window. If you use this option in a script, though, you'll need to add a Select Window script step (page 554) if you want the external file's window to be active.

- If you want a *new* window (whether you're using an external table or not), turn on the "Show in new window" checkbox. When you do, you see the New Window Options dialog box, which is explained alongside the New Window script step on page 553.

Finally, you get to decide how to deal with the found set when the script step finishes. See the box below to help you decide when each option makes sense.

- If you don't turn on "Show only related records," FileMaker goes to the related table, but you see all the records in the related table, not just those that are children of the formerly active record. The first related record is active in your new found set. So, from the Customer layout, GTRR without "Show only related records" shows all your invoices, and the active record is the first one for the customer that you're viewing when the GTRR script step runs.
- If you turn on "Show only related records" and "Match current record only," FileMaker returns a found set of only those records that match the active parent record. The customer invoice GTRR set, as described above, shows you a found set of just the invoices for the customer record that was active when the script step ran. The first related record would be the active one.
- Choosing "Show only related records" and "Match all records in current found set," is most useful when you have a found set selected before the GTRR script step runs. In this scenario, FileMaker shows a new found set in which all the records are related to at least one of the records in the old found set. So, in the Customers layout, you've found your two highest volume customers. Use GTRR, matching all records in the current found set to find all the invoices related to either of these two customers. The first record that's related to the customer record that's active when the GTRR script step runs is the active record in the new found set.

FREQUENTLY ASKED QUESTION

To Show or Not to Show

How do I decide when to turn on "Show only related records" and when to leave it off?

The "Show only related records" option is useful when you use Go to Related Record as a navigational aid for your users, or when you really want all the related records, not just one. For example, if the user clicks a button on the Invoice portal, it makes good sense to show not just the invoice he clicked, but also the other related invoices. The user can then just use the book icon to flip through the rest of the records. Likewise, if your script is going to loop through all the related invoices to do its job, then you want to show just the right records before starting the loop.

The tradeoff is performance. When you turn this option off, FileMaker simply shows the record. It doesn't worry about the found set or the sort order. With the option turned on, though, FileMaker has to find the correct records first, and then show the one you asked for. If your relationship is sorted, FileMaker even sorts the records for you. This sorting takes more time. If your script just needs to visit a specific related record, do something to it, and then come right back, you can leave this option turned off to make your script run more quickly.

Opening, Reverting, and Committing Records

When you use your database in Browse mode, FileMaker does a lot of things automatically. When you start typing in a field, it locks the record. When you exit the record—click outside any field or press Enter—it commits the record. When you use a script, though, you're not really clicking fields and pressing Enter. So how does FileMaker know when to lock a record and when to commit? You have to tell it, by including the appropriate script steps: Open Record/Request, Revert Record/Request, and Commit Record/Request.

Open Record/Request

The Open Record/Request step tells FileMaker you're about to start editing a record. If the record is already open it does nothing—that is, it doesn't automatically commit the record first. It just locks it if it isn't locked already. But if the record is already open (by you, via another window, or by another user), then you'll get a record-locking error. (See page 581 to see how you can check for errors while a script is running.)

Commit Record/Request

Whether you've used the Open Record/Request step or just let FileMaker lock the record for you, you can explicitly commit the record with the Commit Record/Request step. It has two options:

- The "Skip data entry validation" option tells FileMaker to commit the record even if it violates field validation. This option works only when you turn on the "Only during data entry" radio button in the Validation options for the field. If you have set the validation to happen "Always," then the script *can't* get around it.
- When the "Perform without dialog" option is turned off, and you turn *off* "Save record changes automatically" in the Layouts → Layout Setup window's General tab, FileMaker shows the message in Figure 14-6 when the step runs.

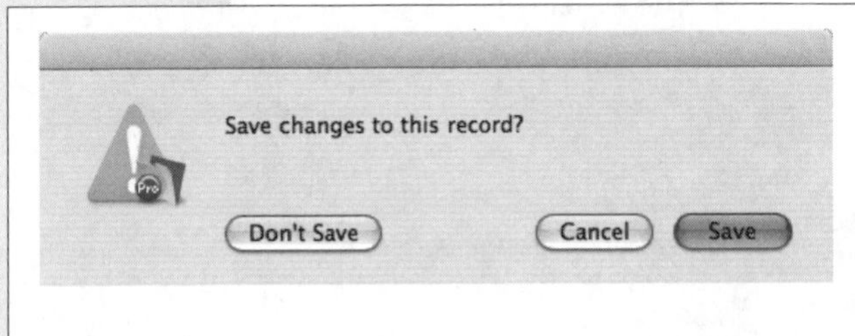

Figure 14-6: *If the layout is set not to save record changes (page 146), and you don't turn on the "Perform without dialog" checkbox, you see this warning when the Commit Record/Request step runs. Click Save to commit the record. If you click Don't Save, FileMaker reverts the record instead. The Cancel button leaves the record open and locked.*

Tip: You know how to handle dialog boxes when they come up, but they often confuse your users. Most database designers try to avoid requiring their users to interact with FileMaker's normal dialog boxes while scripts are running, especially when the user could make a choice that circumvents the purpose of the carefully crafted script.

Revert Record/Request

The Revert Record/Request step has only one option: "Perform without dialog." When this option is turned off, the user sees the message in Figure 14-7. Otherwise, FileMaker reverts the record immediately when the script runs.

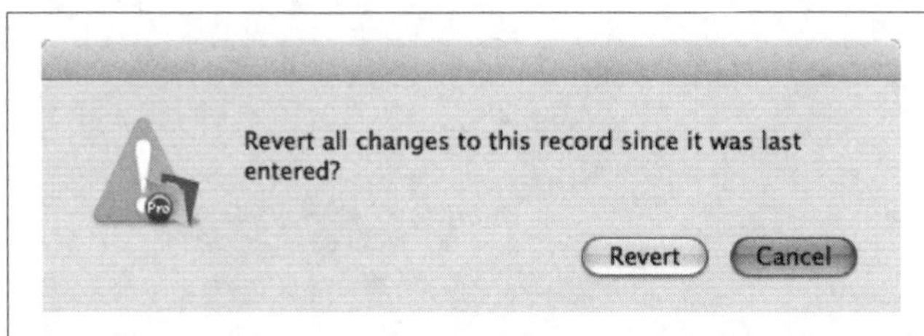
Revert all changes to this record since it was last entered?
Revert
Cancel

Figure 14-7:
Unless you turn on the "Perform without dialog" option, your users see this dialog box when the Revert Record/Request step runs. If a user clicks Cancel, FileMaker leaves the record open and locked, which is probably not your intention.

These script steps are relatively easy to understand, but *when* to use them is hard to figure out. Here are some things to keep in mind when you're trying to decide when you need to open or commit a record in a script:

- When you use a script step that *inserts* data into a field (and leaves the user in the field), then FileMaker locks the record when the step runs, but doesn't commit the change. You can then do *more* work with fields if you want. FileMaker commits the record later, when the user exits the record.
- If your script changes to a different layout, switches to Find or Preview mode, or closes the window, FileMaker automatically commits the record if needed.
- If you use a script step that modifies several records—Replace Field Contents, for example—FileMaker locks, edits, and commits each record in turn, as it goes.
- If you perform a series of Set Field steps in a script, and you are *not* in the record when the script runs, FileMaker locks the record and makes the field changes. When the script is done, you're not in the record (no field is active), but the record's still locked and uncommitted. In other words, you can use the Records → Revert Record command to revert all the changes made by the script, which probably isn't what you want to happen. Add a Commit Records/Requests script step at the *end* of the script to avoid losing the data your script enters.
- If your script changes some records and includes a step to revert them if something goes wrong, you should probably make sure to commit any changes your user was making before your script changes anything. That way, the script doesn't undo any of the user's work. Thus, put a Commit Records/Requests step at the *beginning* of your script.

And if you're still not sure if your script really needs an Open or Commit step, go ahead and open the record at the beginning of your script and commit it at the end. Sure, it takes a nanosecond or two extra to run a couple steps that may not strictly be needed. But what's a nanosecond on the grand scale of time when your data may be at risk?

FREQUENTLY ASKED QUESTION

Why Open a Record?

Why would I ever use the Open Record/Request step? Doesn't FileMaker automatically lock a record as soon as my script starts editing it?

For simple scripts, this step is almost always unnecessary. FileMaker does, indeed, do the right thing. But as you'll learn in Chapter 18, you can set up your FileMaker database so multiple people can use it at the same time, each on her own computer. When you set up FileMaker this way, lots of interesting things can start happening.

For example, a record can change while you're looking at it. Suppose a new area code is added in your area, and you write a script that looks at the phone number and decides, based on its exchange code, whether or not to change the area code. The script might look like this:

```
If [ "Exchange Code = 555 or Exchange Code
= 377" ]
        Set Field [ Area Code, "602"]
End If
```

You probably find this hard to believe, but technically, someone could change the Exchange Code field after the If step runs but before the Set Field happens. (Remember that other people are editing records on other computers, so they're free to make changes while the script is running on your computer.) If this scenario happens, you end up assigning the customer an incorrect phone number.

To fix this, you need to lock the record before you start looking at it:

```
Open Record/Request
If [ "Exchange Code = 555 or Exchange Code
= 377" ]
    Set Field [ Area Code, "602"]
    Commit Record/Request [No Dialog]
Else
    Revert Record/Request [No Dialog]
End If
```

Now, somebody else can't edit the Exchange Code field because the record is locked. In general, if your database has multiple users, you should open a record before you start looking at it in a script.

This script reverts the record when it didn't make any changes. FileMaker does this reverting for two reasons. First, committing a record means saving the data, and that's unnecessary here. Second, suppose a field has had validation turned on since this record was created. It's possible that this unmodified record has now-invalid data. If you try to commit this data back, you get a validation error. Reverting avoids this error since nothing's being saved. Moral of the story: Try to commit a record *only* when necessary.

Copying Records

FileMaker has two record-related script steps that do something you can't easily do manually in Browse mode: copy an entire record to the clipboard. One version copies just the current record, while the other copies every record in the found set at once.

Copy Record/Request

The first, called Copy Record/Request, copies data from *every* field on the layout and puts it on the clipboard. FileMaker puts a tab character between each field value.

If any field has *more* than one line, FileMaker converts the new line character into a funny character called a *vertical tab*. Some programs, like Microsoft Word, convert these characters back into new lines when you paste in a copied record.

Figure 14-8 shows the result of pasting a customer record into Text Edit. In that example, the new line character is an "ã;" and the data's strung into one long line. Your mileage may vary.

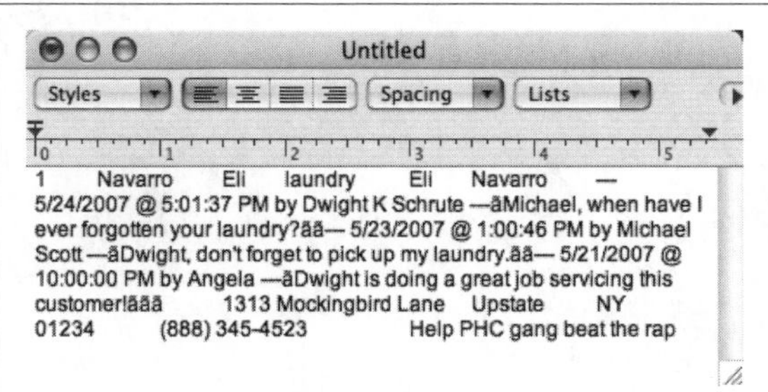

Figure 14-8: *This picture shows what you get when you copy a customer record, and then paste it into a word processor that's not great at rendering vertical tabs. You see the first and last name twice because those fields appear on the layout twice (once in the header, and again in the editable fields). You even get the contents of your global and related fields. Although this block of text needs some serious cleanup, it's often easier to copy/paste it all in one shot than to copy each field value individually.*

Tip: As usual with FileMaker, there's more than one way to get things done. See page 638 for two other ways to export data. Remember, using a scripted Copy, Cut, or Paste command violates your sacred trust not to mess with the contents of your user's clipboard unless he knows it's happening.

Copy All Records/Requests

While Copy Record/Request copies the entire *current* record, its brother—Copy All Records/Requests—copies *every* record in the found set. Each individual record is added to the clipboard in the same format as the Copy Record/Request command produces, and FileMaker puts one record on each line.

Suppose, for example, you want to get all the Invoice IDs for a particular customer and put them in an email to a coworker. Or perhaps you're compiling a list of all the Zip codes in Phoenix where you have customers. Using Copy All Records/Requests, you can do this job with ease.

The trick is to create a *new* layout that has only one field on it. For example, make a new layout with just the Invoice ID field, or just the Zip Code field. Write a script that switches to this layout, and run the Copy All Records/Requests command to get a simple list of values on the clipboard.

Working with Portals

FileMaker has a script step specifically designed to go to a certain portal row. Why would you want to do that? First, when you use the "Go to Field" script step to target a field in a portal, it goes to the *first* portal row, which may not have anything to do with what the user needs at that point. If you want to put the user in the field on a *different* row, you need to go to that row first.

When you use data from a related field, or put data in a related field, and there are *multiple* related records, FileMaker grabs the value from the *first* record. If you want to tell FileMaker to work with a different related record instead, use a portal and go to the right row. See the box below for tips (and a warning) on working with portals.

GEM IN THE ROUGH

Beware the Portal

Technically, it's possible to do all kinds of things through a portal using a script–but it's not always wise. For example, if you wanted to discount every line item on an invoice by 10 percent, you could write a looping script. It would start by visiting the first portal row and applying the invoice. It could then go to each additional row, applying the discount as it goes. In each pass through the loop, you'd be modifying the Line Items::Price field; the active portal row determines which line item is changed. Unfortunately, the active portal row is too transient to be relied upon. A script can do all kinds of things that make FileMaker forget which portal row you're on (change modes, change layouts, go to another field, commit or revert the record, and so forth).

If you accidentally do confuse FileMaker like this at some point inside your loop, you end up looping forever because you never reach the end of the portal.

It's much safer to find the appropriate records and work with them directly. You can get the same effect by using the "Go to Related Records" script step to find all the line item records, and then looping through the records directly with "Go to Record/Request/Page," avoiding the perils of the portal.

Go to Portal Row

The "Go to Portal Row" script step works a lot like the "Go to Record/Request/Page" step. You can go to the First, Last, Previous, or Next portal row, or specify the row *number* with a calculation. It even has an "Exit after last" option to help when looping through portal rows.

This step includes an option you can use to make what's happening onscreen a little more obvious to your users: "Select entire contents." When you turn this checkbox on, FileMaker highlights the whole portal row. Otherwise, it goes to the portal row without highlighting it onscreen. (After all, you don't always want your user to see what's going on.)

One setting you *won't* find with "Go to Portal Row" is *which portal to use*. The guidelines below are how FileMaker knows which portal you have in mind:

- If the current layout only has one portal, FileMaker uses it automatically.
- If the layout has more than one portal, it assumes you want the portal that's currently active.
- If you're writing a script and you want to be sure you go to a row in the right portal, just use "Go to Field" first, targeting a field that's displayed in the portal.

Note: In general, a portal is active whenever a person (or a script) puts the cursor in one of its fields. If you aren't sure what your user will be doing before your script runs, throw in a "Go to Field" script step, just to be safe.

Finding Records

FileMaker has three nearly identical script steps to handle the grunt work of finding records. You can let your user tell the script what to find, you can decide what the script finds (a *hard-coded* find), or you can script a dynamic find using calculations.

Deciding which one to use depends on whether your users know what they're looking for—or how much work you want to save them. The upcoming sections go into this topic in detail. You'll also see a find script in action, and learn how to make a script pause and wait for information.

Performing the User's Find Requests

The first, Perform Find, is the equivalent of a visit to Find mode, followed by a click of the Requests → Perform Find menu command. Perform Find's single option lets you specify what find requests to use, but, surprisingly, you can skip it entirely. If you *don't* turn this option on, then Perform Find assumes you're already in Find mode with one or more requests, and works just like the Requests → Perform Find menu command (and the Find button in the status area). It looks for records that match the already defined find requests. All the matching records become the new found set.

But where do those find requests *come from*? Either the user creates them, or your script does. For example, many developers like to add special "Find" layouts to their databases. These layouts can show just the right fields, along with helpful text, to make things easier for the user. Figure 14-9 shows a Find layout for the Customers table.

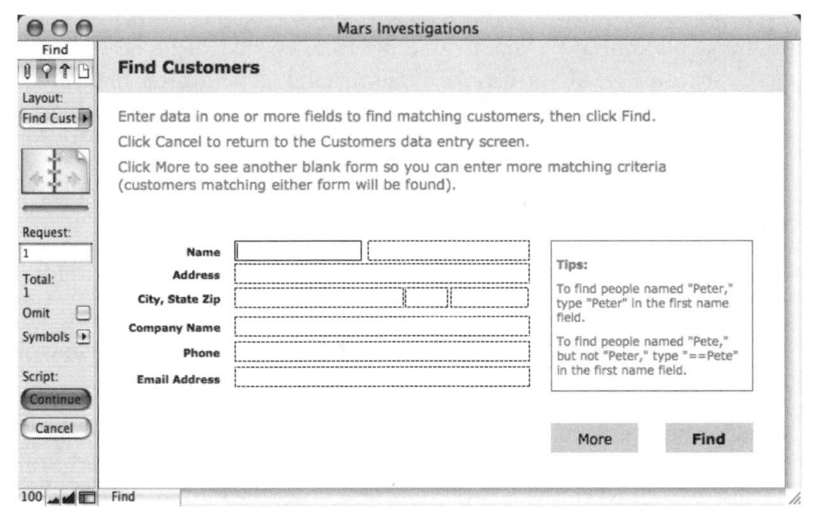

***Figure 14-9:** This layout is designed specifically for Find mode. Two sets of instructions help people figure out what to do. The Find button resumes your script. The More button runs a New Record/Request script step. Since this layout is for Find mode only, make sure the user's in Find mode when she gets here, and take her to a different layout when she's done. That calls for a script like the one shown on page 546.*

To get your user to this new layout, add a Find button on your normal Customers layout. When the user clicks this button, it runs a script that goes to the Find layout and puts the user in Find mode. The script then *pauses* (see the box on page 547), giving the user a chance to enter find requests. When she's done, she clicks a button to *Continue* the script, which performs the find and switches back to the Customers layout.

Tip: The finished file for this chapter has the layout created for you. Download it at *www.missingmanuals.com/cds*.

To set this process up yourself, first create a Find Customers layout like the one shown in Figure 14-9. Then visit the Manage Scripts window, click New, and name the script appropriately. Follow these steps to create the script itself:

1. **Add the "Go to Layout" script step, targeting the Find Customers layout.**

   You want to make sure the user's in the right context—the new Find Customers layout—before the script enters Find mode.

2. **Add the Enter Find Mode script step to the script.**

   The step already has its Pause option turned on and its "Specify find requests" option turned off. That's just what you want. This step switches to Find mode *and* pauses the script.

Tip: If you want to start the user off with some basic criteria, you can specify them right in the Enter Find Mode step. FileMaker doesn't perform the find now. It just puts the user in Find mode and creates the requests you specify. The user's then free to *modify* or *delete* them as necessary.

3. **Add the Perform Find script step to the script.**

   Once the script continues, you assume the user has added the necessary find requests, so you're ready to use the Perform Find step with no find requests specified. (Be careful not to choose the Perform Find/*Replace* script step, which doesn't work in this script.)

4. **Add another "Go to Layout" script step to the script. This time, pick the Customers layout.**

   This step takes the user back to the Customers layout once FileMaker finds the correct records.

After you follow these steps, your completed Find Customer script should look like the one in Figure 14-10.

To complete your layout, create a Find button on the Find Customers layout. You don't even have to write a script for this button. Since the user's always in the middle of a paused script when she sees this layout, just set the button with a Resume Script action. If you're feeling adventuresome, you can also create a More button with a New Record/Request script step and type some helpful instructions right on the layout.

Tip: It's probably a good idea to hide the Find Customers layout from the Layouts pop-up menu so users don't accidentally switch to it without running your script. In the Layout Setup dialog box, turn off the "Include in layouts menu" checkbox (page 145).

Edit Script "Find Customers" (Mars Investigations)

Script Name: Find Customers

```
Go to Layout ["Find Customers" (Customers)]
Enter Find Mode [Pause]
Perform Find []
Go to Layout ["Customers" (Customers)]
```

Figure 14-10:
This is how your Find Customer script will look if you've been following the steps on page 546. It takes the user to the new Find Customers layout and switches to Find mode. Notice that the Enter Find Mode has its Pause option turned on–FileMaker automatically pauses the script after this step. When the user's finished adding find requests and continues the script, FileMaker runs the Perform Find step (with no find requests specified, so it uses the ones the user created) and switches back to the Customers layout.

POWER USERS' CLINIC

Pausing a Script

Normally when you run a script, FileMaker performs its steps one by one as fast as it can. When they're all finished, the script's done. But sometimes a script should pause, usually to wait for the user to do something, like enter Find criteria, or to show the user something, like a Preview mode for a report. The Pause/Resume Script step, and some other steps (like Enter Find Mode) can pause the script automatically when their Pause option is turned on. When FileMaker gets to a step like this, it stops executing the script, but remembers where it left off. Later, the script continues, starting with the next step in line. While a script is paused, you're free to edit records, switch modes, change layouts, and so forth, You *can't* open the Manage Database, Manage Value Lists, Manage Custom Functions, or Manage Scripts windows, though, until the script finishes running.

While a script is paused, FileMaker adds two new buttons to the status area (shown in Figure 14-9). The Continue button causes the script to continue immediately (pressing the Enter key does the same thing). The Cancel button tells FileMaker you don't want to run the rest of the script. Your script stops and you get back full control of the program.

If you want to, you can tell FileMaker how long to pause by clicking the Specify button in the Script Step Options area when the Pause/Resume Script step is selected. The dialog box that appears has two choices: Indefinitely and For Duration. If you choose For Duration, you get to enter the number of seconds you want the script to pause, or you can click *another* Specify button to use a calculation to set the number of seconds. In either case, your pause duration can be fractional–like *4.5 seconds*–if needed. If you have set the script to pause for a specific duration, you can still do things with your database while the script is paused, including click the Continue or Cancel buttons.

With a name like "Pause/Resume Script" you'd think this step can also *resume* a paused script. But then again, if the script is paused, then how can the step possibly execute? Don't be fooled: This step can only pause.

Static Find Requests

With the script you created on the previous few pages, your users can search for just about anything they want, by entering find requests. More often than not, you *don't* want to make users enter the find requests manually. After all, the whole point of a script is to have FileMaker do things so people don't have to. If you know ahead of time exactly what you want the script to find, use the Perform Find step all by itself: Just turn on the "Specify find requests" option and put those requests right in the dialog box; the search options stay the same each time the script runs. When you specify find requests in a script, you see the window shown in Figure 14-11.

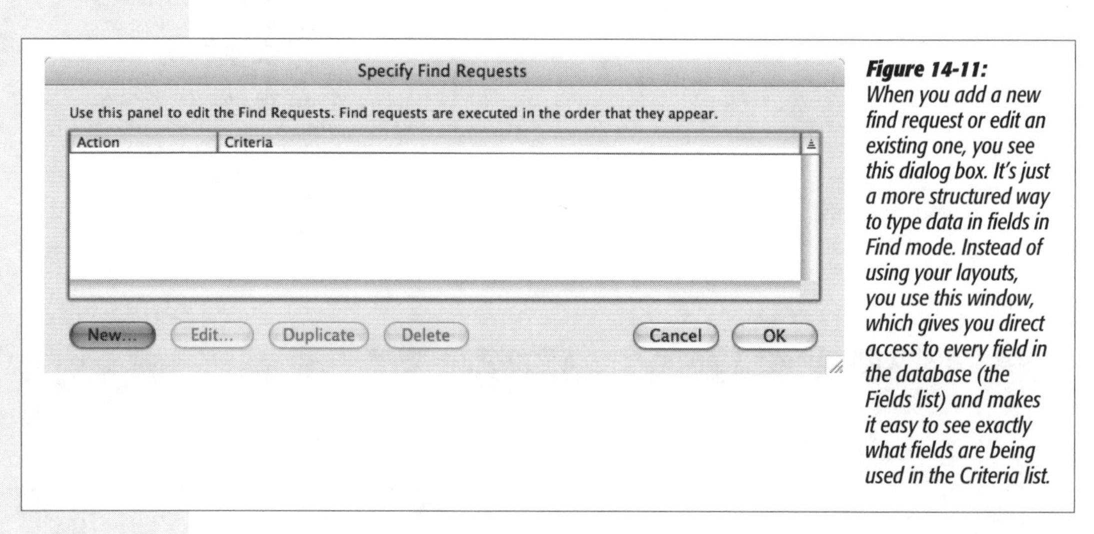

Figure 14-11: *When you add a new find request or edit an existing one, you see this dialog box. It's just a more structured way to type data in fields in Find mode. Instead of using your layouts, you use this window, which gives you direct access to every field in the database (the Fields list) and makes it easy to see exactly what fields are being used in the Criteria list.*

This window is pretty straightforward. To add a new find request, click New. To edit an existing request, select it first, and then click Edit. You can also delete or duplicate the selected step using the Delete and Duplicate buttons. Using the Specify Find Requests and Edit Find Request windows (Figure 14-12), you can tell the Perform Find step to do any find you can do from Find mode.

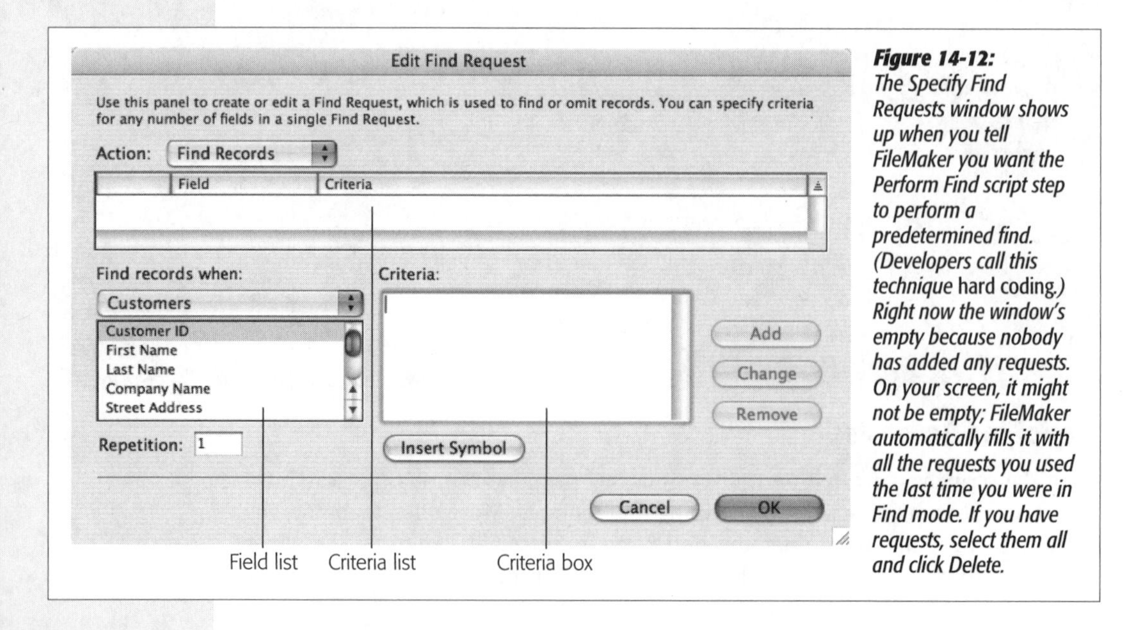

Figure 14-12: *The Specify Find Requests window shows up when you tell FileMaker you want the Perform Find script step to perform a predetermined find. (Developers call this technique* hard coding*.) Right now the window's empty because nobody has added any requests. On your screen, it might not be empty; FileMaker automatically fills it with all the requests you used the last time you were in Find mode. If you have requests, select them all and click Delete.*

Tip: The Edit Find Requests dialog box is confusing until you get used to it. But there's a way you can learn how it translates requests into its own particular syntax. Perform a find manually, and then write a test script with a Perform Find script step. FileMaker sets the dialog box with the criteria for the search you just did.

To create a find request, select a field from the "Find records when" list (if it's a repeating field, you can specify the repetition number in the Repetition box), and then enter text in the Criteria box. The Insert Symbol button gives you quick access to the same symbols you see in the status area in Find mode, and the Criteria box accepts all the standard symbols. Once you've finished entering the criteria, click Add to add it to the Criteria list.

- To edit an existing item in the criteria list, select it. When you do, FileMaker automatically selects the matching field in the Field list and puts the criterion in the Criteria box. You can then make any changes necessary, and click Change.
- To remove a criterion from the list entirely, select it and click Remove.
- Finally, you get to choose whether this request should be used to *find* matching records, or to *omit* them (see page 550). To turn this into an omitting find request, choose Omit Records from the Action pop-up menu.
- When you've finished adding criteria, click OK. Just like Find mode, you can add more find requests if you want. In the Specify Find Requests window, just click the New button a second time. When you're all finished adding requests, click OK again.

Dynamic Find Requests

As dependable as static finds are, you may not always be able to predict what the user wants to find. Or the criteria for finding the same thing over and over can change, like when you're searching in a date field. For example, suppose you want to find all the invoices created one week ago. You can easily do so in Find mode: Just put the date from a week ago in the Invoices::Date field. But what you put in that field *changes every day*. For example, if today is November 7, and you create a script to find invoices from a week ago, you could attach this request to the Perform Find step:

```
Invoices::Date = "10/31/2007"
```

Unfortunately, as soon as November 8 rolls around, this script *won't* find week-old invoices. It always finds invoices from October 31, 2005. When you're faced with a situation like this, you do have an option: Make the script build the find request the same way you would in Find mode. In other words, tell your script to go to Find mode, have *it* put the right date in the field, and then perform the find. You can use the Set Field script step to put the date in the Invoices::Date field since it conveniently lets you use a calculation to determine the actual date.

The script would look like the one in Figure 14-13.

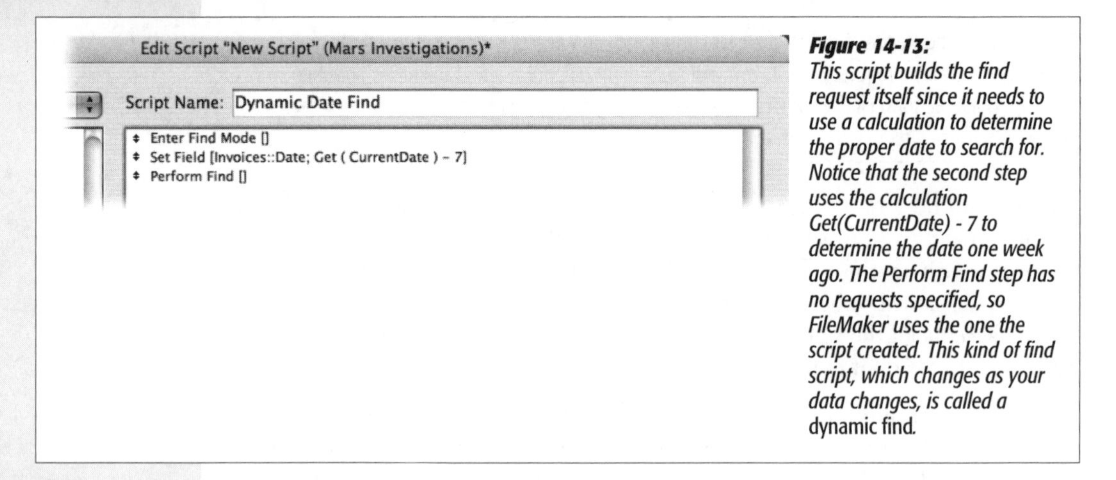

Figure 14-13: *This script builds the find request itself since it needs to use a calculation to determine the proper date to search for. Notice that the second step uses the calculation Get(CurrentDate) - 7 to determine the date one week ago. The Perform Find step has no requests specified, so FileMaker uses the one the script created. This kind of find script, which changes as your data changes, is called a* dynamic find.

Note: If your find request can be handled using the *symbols* supported by Find mode (page 48), then you can use Perform Find all by itself. For instance, to find invoices created today, tell Perform Find to find records with Invoices::Date = //. Since "//" stands for "today's date," it works on any day.

Constraining and Extending the Found Set

You may have already noticed that Perform Find doesn't have an option for the Requests → Constrain Found Set and Requests → Extend Found Set commands. That's because each of these is a separate script step. It makes sense, really, because to constrain or extend a find, you have to *have* a find first. In other words, this process always takes two separate steps to complete.

The Extend Found Set and Constrain Found Set script step options work *exactly* like Perform Find. Everything you just learned about Perform Find still applies: You can hard-code the find requests, pause the script and let the user enter them, or build them in the script.

Omitting Records

The Omit Record script step lives a dual life. If you're in Browse mode when it runs, it simply omits the current record from the found set. If you're in Find mode, on the other hand, it turns on the Omit checkbox in the status area.

Omit Multiple Records works only in Browse mode and does the same thing as the Records → Omit Multiple command. As usual, you can specify the number of records to omit in the script, either as a number or a calculation. You also get a "Perform without dialog" option so you can decide whether or not the user gets to enter the number of records to omit.

Finally, the Show Omitted Only script step has the same effect as the Records → Show Omitted menu command.

GEM IN THE ROUGH

Mix and Match

You have three basic options when performing a find in a script: You can let the user enter the find requests, hard-code the requests right in the Perform Find step, or build the requests bit by bit using script steps. But these aren't mutually exclusive choices: You can mix and match techniques.

For example, suppose you need a relatively complex set of find requests that, for the most part, never change, but one value in one field on just one request needs to be based on the current date. It would be tedious to have to add dozens of Set Field and New Record/Request steps to your script when all but one use a hard-coded value.

Other times, it would be nice to let the user specify the find requests, but add a little more to it when they're done. You can start by turning on the "Specify find requests" option on the Enter Find Mode script step. This step tells FileMaker to go to Find mode *and* load it up with the requests you specify in a Specify Find Requests dialog box.

Once you're in Find mode, though, you're free to use Set Field, New Record/Request, and "Go to Record/Request" to modify the prefab requests to your heart's content. Just go to the right request and use Set Field to work the dynamic date value into it.

Suppose you want to let the user search for invoices. You create a Find Invoices layout and a script just like the one for Find Customers. But this time, you want to restrict users to invoices created only in the last year. Before the Perform Find step, you can add these two steps:

```
New Record/Request
Omit
Set Field [Invoices::Date; "..." &
Get(CurrentDate) - 365]
```

Now the script finds just what the user asks for, but omits records more than 365 days old. You've used the script to add a new request to the ones the user created. What's more, your user doesn't even know you've controlled her find.

Modify Last Find

The simplest find-related script step is Modify Last Find. It has exactly the same effect as the Records → Modify Last Find command: It puts you in Find mode with the same requests you created the *last* time you were in Find mode.

Save Records as...

Now that you've mastered the scripted find, you can keep right on going and automate the process of putting your found set to good use—outside FileMaker. The Save/Send Records commands (covered in full in Chapter 17) let you export records into formats other programs can understand.

Save Records as Excel

As with its manual counterpart, your users will need export privileges (page 614) to run the "Save Records as Excel" script step. (Actually, any user with full access privileges can do it.) You need to make the same choices in this script step as you do from the menu command, but the options are divided among the various dialog boxes a little bit differently. The "Save Records as Excel" script step has three options:

- **Perform without dialog** lets you control the step's options without input from your users. Don't turn on this option if you want users to be able to specify all the options they'd normally see in the "Save Records as Excel" dialog box.

- The **Specify output file** option lets you determine where the file is saved. You can click the Browse button to select a location through the Open dialog box, or simply type a file path. You also have access to the **Automatically open file** and **Create email with file as attachment** options.
- The **Specify Options** dialog is almost the same as the one you see when you choose this command manually and click the Options button. You can set a Worksheet name, and a document Title, Subject, and Author. Here's also where you specify whether you want to save the **Records being browsed** or just the **Current Record.**

Note: It'd be great if you could suppress one of these dialog boxes and leave the other one open for business, but you can't. If you tell the step to "Perform without dialog," *both* dialog boxes get shut down. You can, however, set up the options you want, show your users the dialog boxes, and instruct them that they should change only certain items. (Use of the phrase "under pain of reprisal" while you deliver these instructions is entirely optional.)

Save Records as PDF

Like its popular Excel twin, the Save Records as PDF script step is the automated version of a menu-driven counterpart. It requires printing privileges (page 614) or Full Access privileges to do its work. Similarly, you can control all the step's myriad options by choosing the "Perform without dialog" option, or you can open the script up to input from your users. Check out the full instructions for "Save/Send as PDF" on "Portable Document Format (PDF)" to see the ramifications of the full option set. The Specify Options button lets you choose output options appropriate to creating a PDF:

- The Save pop-up menu lets you choose between **Records being browsed** and the **Current Record.**
- The Options button produces a three-tabbed dialog box:
  - **Document.** Set the Title, Subject, Author, Keywords, Compatibility, and page numbers here.
  - **Security.** Set passwords and access on this tab.
  - **Initial View.** Choose the setup your users see when the PDF is first opened.

Sorting Records

After all that fuss about finding records, the sorting script steps are refreshingly simple. There're only two of them, and you already know how to use both. The Sort Records script step behaves in a now-familiar way. All by itself, it brings up the Sort dialog box when the script runs. If you turn on its "Specify sort order" option, you can preload the sort dialog box with a specific sort order. Finally, turn on the "Perform without dialog" option to sort the records without bothering the user with a dialog box at all.

If the records are already sorted, you can *unsort* them from a script. For instance, you might sort records for a report, but you want to return them to their unsorted order when the report is finished so your users don't get confused. Just use the Unsort Records script step. It does its job with no options.

Working with Windows

Scripts give you complete control over the database windows on the screen. You can create new windows, close existing windows, bring any window to the front, and move or resize any window. (Why would a script need to monkey with someone's onscreen windows? See the box on page 558 for some ideas.)

Creating Windows

To make a new window on the screen, you use the New Window script step. With this step selected in your script, you see a Specify button in ScriptMaker's Script Step Options area. Clicking this button brings up the New Window Options dialog box, pictured in Figure 14-14.

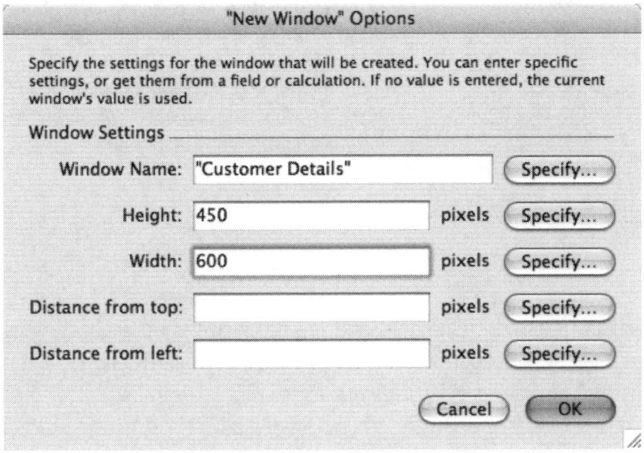

Figure 14-14:
The Window Options dialog box lets your script open and close windows and move them around the screen. You can use it to make annoying coworkers think they have poltergeists in their PCs, or just make windows behave properly when your scripts run. See the box on page 555 for advice.

The first box—Window Name—gives your script control over the name of the window. (Window name is something you can control *only* from a script. When you create the window from the Window menu, FileMaker assigns it a name for you.) You can also tell FileMaker how big the window should be (Height and Width), and where to put the window on the screen ("Distance from top" and "Distance from left").

Here are some tips on using the New Window Options dialog box:

- If you leave any of the values blank, FileMaker uses the same value from the *current* window (it adds a number to the end of the window name so the new name is different). For example, if the current window is called "My Database" and you run the New Window script step without specifying a name, the new window's name is "My Database – 2."

- If you also don't specify a size and position, FileMaker puts it right over the top of the current window (with the same size and position).

Tip: To avoid confusing your user, it's usually best to offset the new window at least a little so he can see that there's a new window on top of his old one.

- You can set each value directly by typing in the box in the New Window Options dialog box, or set them from a calculation by clicking the Specify button by any box. See the box on page 555 for more detail.

Bringing a Window to the Front

In ScriptMaker parlance, you bring a window to the front by *selecting* it. As such, you use the Select Window script step. It has one option, which lets you specify a window by name, or select the current window, as shown in Figure 14-15. You also use the Select Window script step to show a hidden window and bring it to the front.

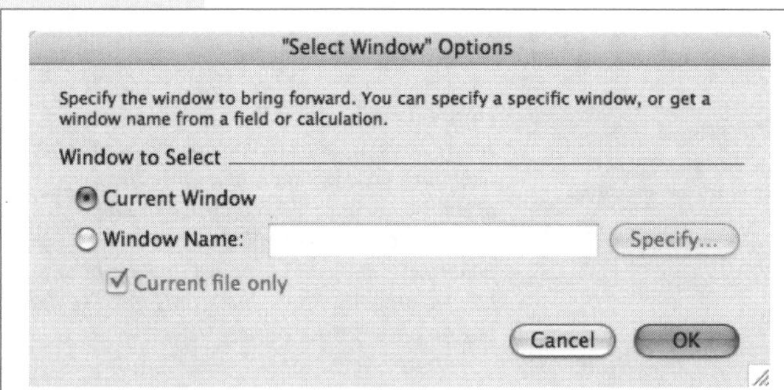

Figure 14-15: *This window appears when you click the Specify button with a Select Window script step selected. From here, you can specify the Current Window, or choose Window Name and put the name of the window you want in the box. As usual, you can use a calculation to determine the window name as well.*

Note: Usually, the current window is already in the front, and you don't have to worry about this step. But when you run scripts that involve more than one database, as you'll learn in Chapter 15, you may need this step to bring forward the current window from *another file*.

Closing a Window

The Close Window script step has the same options as Select Window. You tell FileMaker which window to close: the current window, or one you specify by name.

Moving and Resizing Existing Windows

FileMaker has three ways to move and resize a window. You can opt for one of its canned window maneuvers, or you can set the exact pixel size and location of the window just like you can with the New Window step. You can also *hide* the current window.

POWER USERS' CLINIC

Window Size and Position Calculations

The fact that you can set a new window's size and position using a calculation may seem a little strange. After all, do you really need a bigger window for someone named Bill? Do you want your windows in a different place on Thursdays?

In fact, though, you can do a lot of interesting things with window size and position calculations. FileMaker provides a handful of functions that let you find out about the size and position of the current window, and of the computer screen, and use that information in calculations:

- The Get (WindowHeight) function, for instance, returns the height of the current window, in screen pixels (the little dots on your screen). Its brother, Get (WindowContentHeight) returns the height of just the content area of the window; that is, the area inside the title bar, scroll bars, and status area. The Get (WindowHeight) and Get (WindowContent-Height) functions are similar.
- Get (WindowTop) and Get (WindowLeft) functions tell you where the window is on the screen. The first returns the distance from the top of the window to the top of the screen. The second tells you the distance from the left edge of the window to the left side of the screen. Both distances are measured in pixels.
- The Get (WindowDesktopHeight) and Get (WindowDesktopWidth) functions tell you how much desktop space you have. On Windows, it's the area of FileMaker's main application window. On Mac OS X, it's the size of the desktop.
- Finally, Get (ScreenHeight) and Get (ScreenWidth) tell you how big the screen is. (If you have more than one screen, they tell you about the screen the current window is on.)

By combining these functions in creative ways, you can make your scripts smart about how they size and position windows. For example, to make the new window appear slightly offset from the current window, use these settings:

- Distance from top: Get (WindowTop) + 20
- Distance from left: Get (WindowLeft) + 20

If you're paranoid, and you want to make sure the new window never hangs off the bottom of the screen, use this calculation for the "Distance from top" value:

```
Let (
   [Limit = Get(WindowDesktopHeight) -
Get(WindowHeight);
   Offset = Get(WindowTop) + 20;
   Best = Min(Limit; Offset)];

Best
)
```

Similarly, you can use the "Distance from left" value to make sure it doesn't hang off the screen's right edge. Just substitute WindowDesktopWidth, WindowWidth, and WindowLeft for WindowDesktopHeight, WindowHeight, and WindowTop.

Adjust Window

The Adjust Window script step always operates on the current window, and it gives you just five simple choices:

- Choose **Resize to Fit**, and FileMaker makes the window exactly the right size to fit its contents.
- Choose **Maximize** to make the window as large as possible.

- Choose **Minimize** to shrink the window to a little bar (Windows) or a Dock icon (Mac OS X).
- Choose **Restore** to switch the window back to the *last* size it was, just before it was most recently resized.
- Choose **Hide** to hide the window (just like the Window → Hide Window command).

Note: The Maximize options have slightly different behavior on Mac OS X and Windows. For example, when you maximize a window in Windows, and then select a different window, the second window also gets maximized. On Mac OS X, the second window keeps its original size. Also, a maximized window on Mac OS X fills as much of the screen as possible. On Windows, it fills FileMaker's outer application window, whatever size it may be, and there's no way to adjust the application window from a script.

Arrange All Windows

The Arrange All Windows script step is the equivalent of the four window arrangement options in the Window menu. You can tile windows horizontally or vertically, or cascade them (see page 41). On Mac OS X, you can also bring all FileMaker windows to the front.

Move/Resize Window

For the ultimate in window control, call upon the Move/Resize Window script step. It can move and/or resize any window with pixel-perfect precision. Its Specify button shows the dialog box in Figure 14-16, where you can choose the window's size and position. As with New Window, you can leave any of the size or position values empty. When you do, FileMaker leaves that part of the window's size or position alone. For example, if you specify a new value for Width but leave Height blank, FileMaker makes the window wider or narrower, but its height doesn't change.

Note: Move/Resize Window also *selects* the window it acts on, which always brings the window to the front, and, if it's a hidden window, shows it.

Other Window-related Script Steps

FileMaker has a handful of other window-related script steps, listed below. They come in handy if you need to exert more control over what your users see (not to imply that you're a control freak or anything).

- **Freeze Window** tells FileMaker to stop showing changes in the window while the script runs. For example, if your script is looping through all the records in the found set, you normally see each record on the screen as it runs. If you add a Freeze Window script step before the loop, the user sees only the first record while it runs. When the script is finished, FileMaker updates the window again. Looping scripts that have to visit lots of records run decidedly faster when the window is frozen.

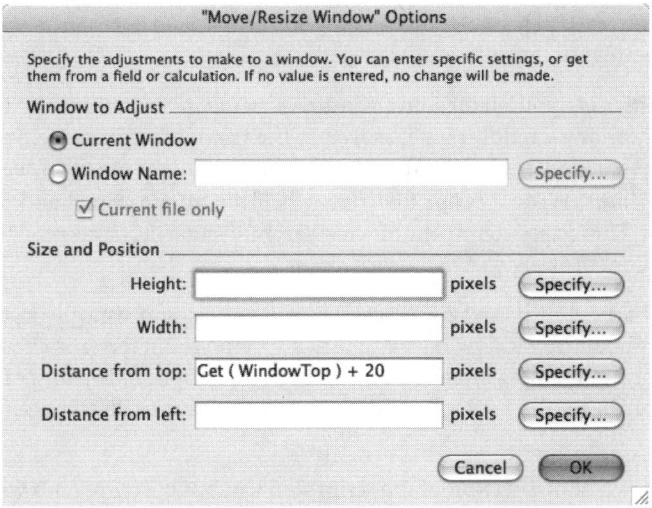

Figure 14-16:
The Move/Resize Window settings look like a combination of the Select Window settings and the New Window settings. First, you pick which window you want to work on (Current Window, or a window selected by name). You then specify the new size and position for the window.

- **Refresh Window** forces FileMaker to update what's inside the window when it normally wouldn't. This can be because you previously ran the Freeze Window step, or because FileMaker's simply being conservative. If you want to make sure the user sees a particular record or field value on the screen while a script is running, add a Refresh Window step after making the change.

- **Scroll Window** lets you simulate a vertical scroll bar click in a window. You can scroll to the Home (top) or End of a window, or move up or down one screenful. You also get a To Selection option, which scrolls the window so that the selected record and field value both show. You'll design most of your window so that scrolling isn't necessary, which means you may never need this step.

- **Show/Hide Status Area** lets you decide if the user should see the status area or not. You can explicitly show or hide the status area, or ask that it be *toggled* (shown if it's hidden, and hidden if it's showing). You can also turn on the Lock option to prevent the user from manually changing the status area. For example, if you never want the user to see the status area at all, hide and lock it in the script that runs when your database opens. Then the status area is locked, and its toggle icon and menu command are grayed out. More commonly, though, the status area's turned off and locked during a process, such as a scripted find. You don't want your users using the Cancel button during a Pause step to cancel a script, and then end up dumped on a layout that you meant them to see only while a script is running. If you hide the status area, though, you should provide a button that cancels the process, in case users change their minds. That way, they don't have to go all the way through a process if they get an urgent phone call and need to do something different than the script's agenda.

- **Show/Hide Text Ruler** can toggle, show, or hide, the Text Ruler. Unlike Show/Hide Status Area, this step doesn't have a Lock option. The user can always override your setting, so this step is rarely worth the trouble.
- **Set Window Title** lets you change any window's name. You can specify the current window, or any window name, as well as the window's new name. FileMaker normally names a window with the file's name, but you can tailor each window to your user. Write a script that runs when the file is opened and use the Set Window Title script step with this calculation: Get (FileName) & " " & Get (AccountName). See page 626 to learn about Account Names.
- **Set Zoom Level** sets the window zoom level, just like the zoom controls in the bottom-left corner of the window. You can pick a specific zoom level, or choose to zoom in or out to the next level. Again, you get a Lock option. If you set the zoom level and turn on the Lock checkbox, the user can't manually change the zoom level.
- **View As** is in the Windows section of the script step list, but it isn't really a window-related step. It changes the view option for the current *layout*. You can pick form view, list view, or table view. You also get a choice called Cycle that tells FileMaker to switch to the *next* view setting in the list. If you really want to control how your users see your database, use Layout → Layout Setting (View Tab) to turn off the views you don't want them seeing. You can then let users override those settings with this script step.

POWER USERS' CLINIC

Controlling the Interface

If you want to pull out all the stops, you can use a combination of layouts, custom menus (page 724), tooltips (page 723), and scripting to almost completely take over control of your database. You can hide and lock the status area, and then give the user buttons to go to the next, previous, first, and last records. You can make it so that when you click a customer on the list layout, a new detail window pops up named after that particular customer. You can even make your script so smart that it selects an existing detail window for the customer if one exists, and makes a new one otherwise.

In this way, you give the user the impression that each customer has his own window, and you make comparing customers side by side a breeze.

This kind of high-level window management takes a fair amount of work, so most people stick with the normal every-layout-in-one-window approach and let the user create windows as needed. Which approach you use depends entirely on how much time you want to spend writing scripts and how important the multiple-window interface is to you.

Working with Files

The Files section in the Script Step list contains some of the *least often used* script steps in all of FileMaker. But if you work in a school, say, the day may come when you need to automate the process of formatting files or saving backup copies for every student in a class. You can also script the process of converting older databases to FileMaker .fp7 format and recovering damaged databases, but these are sensitive processes that are better handled manually.

Opening and Closing Files

The Open File script step lets you open another *FileMaker* file. You can pick any of your existing file references (see page 382) or create a new file reference if necessary. When the step runs, the specified file opens and appears in a new window. If the file has a script set to run when it opens, it runs.

If you want the file to open, but you don't want to see a window on the screen, turn on the "Open hidden" option for this step. The file opens, but it's listed in the Show Window submenu of the Window menu, with its name in parentheses.

The Close File script step closes any open file. When you add the step, you get to pick any file reference or add a new one. You can also choose Current File to close the file the script is in. If the file is open when the script runs, all its windows close and its closing script runs.

Note: In general, FileMaker is very smart about when to open and close files. It opens a file when it needs to and closes it again when it no longer needs it. You usually don't need to open and close files from a script, but there's one important exception: when the file has an opening script that should run before the user can see the file. If you jump directly to a related record in another file, FileMaker bypasses the opening script, so use an Open File script step to ensure that the open script runs.

Save a Copy As

If you need to make a copy of an open database, use the "Save a Copy As" script step. It works just like the File → "Save a Copy As" command. When you're working on a set of files and want to back them up without a lot of manual muss and fuss, just add a "Save a Copy As" script to each one. Then, from your main file, call that script in each file, and you've made a backup with one script.

Note: This script step (or menu command, for that matter) doesn't work on files that are shared using FileMaker Server. See page 697 to learn how to create automatic backups.

Other File-Related Script Steps

The rest of the file-related script steps are almost never used, but that doesn't mean *you* won't find a good reason to use them.

- **Convert File** lets you convert an older FileMaker database to a FileMaker 7 database. Since this process requires so much preparation and manual checking, there is very little reason to do this from a script.
- **Set User System Formats** toggles the Use System Formats file option on or off. When you first create a database, FileMaker remembers how your system expects dates, times, and numbers to be formatted. If someone opens the file on a computer with different settings (usually a different language), FileMaker has to decide if it should use the original format settings for the file, or those specified by the new system. You usually set this choice in the Edit → File Options window.

- **Recover File** runs FileMaker's automatic file repair process on a selected database. Recovering a file is a rare thing in general since FileMaker is careful to avoid damaging databases even when your computer crashes. It's even more rare, and even inadvisable, to do this on the same database so often you'd need a script to do it for you.

Printing

Printing typically involves two specific commands on Windows or Mac OS X: File → Print Setup or File → Page Setup and File → Print. ScriptMaker sees it this way, too.

You use the Print Setup script step to set the options in the Print Setup or Page Setup dialog box. Turn on "Specify print setup" or "Specify page setup" to see the standard dialog box. You can pick the option you want to associate with the script step. When the script runs, FileMaker restores these same options. You can also turn on a "Perform without dialog" checkbox. When this option is off, the user sees—and gets a chance to configure—the dialog box when the script runs. If you just want to set the options without user intervention, turn on "Perform without dialog."

The Print script step works very similarly. You can specify the exact print options (number of pages and so forth) or let the user make the choice. Either way, when the step runs, FileMaker prints the current record or found set.

Note: Many of the options you can set in the Print dialog box are specific to a particular printer model. For example, some printers let you pick color or black-and-white printing or have settings for different kinds of paper. If someone uses your database and script on a different printer, these options don't work.

Other Script Steps

You've now seen most of the often-used script steps (and a few of the not-so-often used ones). You'll see even more as they come up in the next few chapters. The rest of this chapter covers a few oddball steps that don't seem to fit in anywhere:

Open URL

You first saw the Open URL script step as a button command when learning about text calculations. When FileMaker runs this step, it asks your computer's operating system to open the URL you specify. Most often the URL is a Web address (HTTP), but it can be any URL type your computer supports, including FTP, MAILTO, SSH, and even FMP7 (to open a file on a network server). As usual, you can specify the URL or let the user do it, and you can use a calculation if needed.

Dial Phone

The Dial Phone script step tells your modem to dial the telephone using a phone number you provide. You can use a calculation to specify the phone number or enter it directly.

Note: This script step doesn't work on Mac OS X.

Set Web Viewer

Web viewers are pretty cool on their own, but the Set Web Viewer script step (Figure 14-17) can make your FileMaker layouts look even more like a Web browser. With this flexible script step, you can make a series of buttons:

- **Reset** sets the Web viewer back to the Web address that's specified in its Web Viewer Setup dialog box.
- **Reload** gets you a fresh copy of the Web page you're currently viewing.
- **Go Forward** lets you move forward through your Web page history.
- **Go Back** lets you move backwards through the Web pages you've been browsing.
- **Go to URL…** lets you specify any new Web address via the Specify Calculation dialog box.

But to use this script step, you have to refer to your Web viewer by name. Check out the screencast at *www.missingmanuals.com* for a refresher on naming layout objects using the Info palette. One cool thing about referring to a Web viewer by name is that you can display more than one Web viewer on a layout and choose which one your scripts affect.

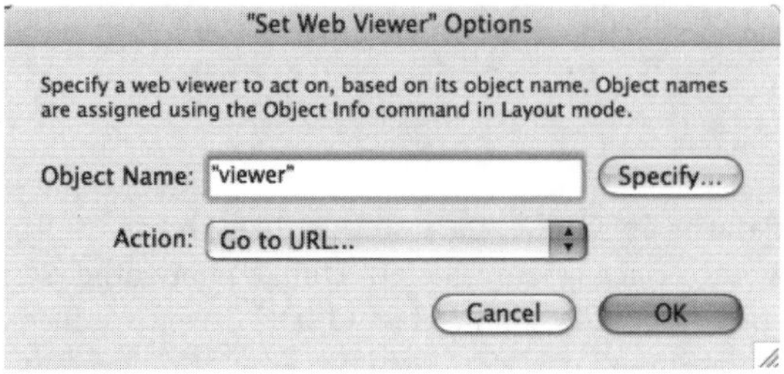

Figure 14-17:
This Set Web Viewer dialog box is set to work on a Web viewer with the prosaic name of "viewer." When you select the "Go to URL…," option, you'll see the same Set Web Viewer dialog box that comes free with every Web viewer.

Send Email

If you have an email program set up on your computer, FileMaker can use it to send email from a script. The Send Email script step has two options: the standard "Perform without dialog" checkbox, and a Specify button. Clicking Specify shows the Send Mail Options window in Figure 14-18.

Figure 14-18:
You saw many of the options for this script step back on page 513. But here's a new wrinkle: You can pick a single file to include as an attachment. Each email you send gets the same attachment, but it's a good way to send a marketing or informational piece out to a select group of customers–or to every one of them.

Although you probably wouldn't guess it, you can use a calculation for each of the values in the Specify Mail dialog box. When you click the little button to the right of each entry box, you see a menu with two choices:

- Specify Field Name.
- Specify Calculation.

Whatever you specify for the To, CC, and BCC values, you can also select the associated "Get values from every record in found set" checkbox. When you turn on any one of these boxes, FileMaker creates one outgoing email message for each found record. Each message uses field data specific to one of the records. With this setting, you can email all your customers in one shot, addressing each one individually, and including a custom-crafted email message for each.

The "Perform without dialog" option for this script step has an unexpected behavior. Instead of showing the user FileMaker's Specify Mail dialog box when this option is turned off, FileMaker opens her email program, creates the message, and opens it onscreen. The user can then modify the message as needed and send it. If you turn on "Perform without dialog," FileMaker puts the message directly in your email program's outbox with no user interaction. Just make sure your email program is set to send out emails periodically, if you want the whole process handled automatically.

Execute SQL

If you need to manipulate data in an ODBC data source, like Oracle, SQL, or MySQL, this script step is at your service (Figure 14-19). Unlike many other script steps, this one requires some prior setup. You'll need an OBDC driver installed on any computer that will run an Execute SQL script. Each driver is a bit different, so use the drivers' documentation for installation and setting up data sources. Finally, if you don't write SQL queries, you'll need help from someone who does, to make sure you get to the data you want. See page 641 to learn how you can use SQL data almost as easily as native FileMaker data.

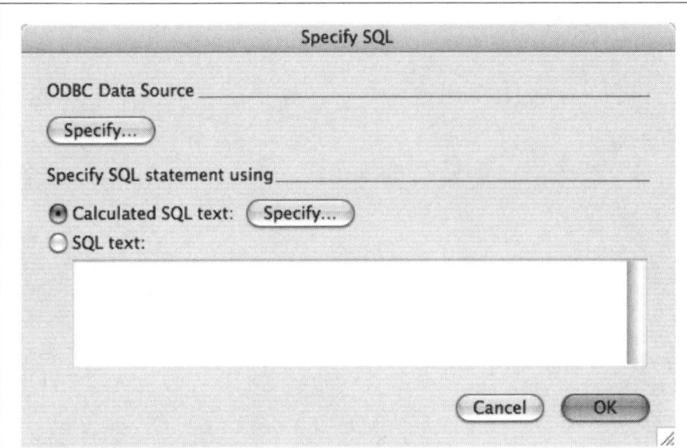

Figure 14-19:
This picture shows the Specify SQL dialog box in its unvarnished state. Once you prepare your computer, and select an ODBC Data Source, the source name shows up beside the top Specify button. Then, you can use the Calculations dialog box to assemble a query, or just type directly in the SQL text field.

Flush Cache to Disk

Any time changes are made to a record, FileMaker records those changes in your computer's memory first, and writes the change to the hard drive later—when it gets some free time. If you want to *force* the changes to be written to disk immediately, you can run the "Flush Cache to Disk" script step. For instance, you might add this script step after a script that creates a new customer order. That way, if your computer crashes while you're busily taking orders, you lose only the last order you were working on.

Exit Application

Last but not least, you can have a script exit or quit the FileMaker application on your behalf. Of course, this causes every open window and file to be closed as well. People usually use this when they have just one database, and they never use FileMaker unless they're in that database. They add the Exit Application step to the very end of their database's closing script so that when they close the last database window FileMaker goes away, too. (Of course *you* find FileMaker so useful you *never* want to close it, right?)

CHAPTER

15

Advanced Scripting

Familiarity with FileMaker's lengthy list of script steps is a great foundation, but putting together a workable script takes practice. Although some scripts are simple five-line affairs, sometimes a script requires a lot of forethought, planning, and organization. FileMaker gives you tools to help you write scripts and to troubleshoot them when they aren't working. Plus, you can organize and document your work as you go. In this chapter you'll pull these concepts together to learn how to write and manage complex scripts.

Commenting Scripts

When you look at a script someone else created—or you created a long time ago—it isn't always obvious what it's trying to do. To help keep things clear, add comments to your script. You add each comment using a Comment script step. This step has just one option: the text of the comment itself. The comment step is special for two reasons. First, it doesn't *do* anything. Second, it shows in bold when you view your script in the Edit Script window. You can see a commented script in Figure 15-1.

Use comments to document anything important about the script. Here are some things you may want to include in a comment or set of comments:

- What the script does
- Who wrote the script
- The date the script was written
- The date, if any, the script was last edited
- Who edited the script

- Anything special about how or when the script should be run, like whether only some database users can run it, or if the script requires parameters to do its work (see page 575).

Documenting scripts is standard operating procedure among programmers, for a couple reasons. First, if something's wrong with the script, or it needs to be changed, you've got extra information that could help. You know exactly what the script should do, plus you have a list of people who've worked on it and can give you background or pointers. Second, the date can help identify whether a particular business rule was in effect that made certain parts of a script necessary. If you see that script is really old, you may decide to rewrite it with some of FileMaker's newer features. Comments don't take up much space or slow down your scripts, so commenting scripts as you create them saves you time later.

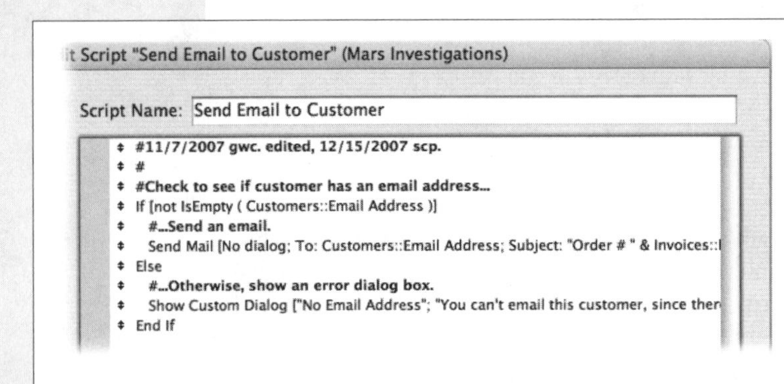

Figure 15-1: *Here's the Send Email script you worked with in Chapter 14, with comments added. The first comment lets you know who created and edited the script, and when those monumental events happened. The second one is blank and serves only to make a little space. The three comments inside the script explain what it's supposed to do at critical junctures. The comment lines appear with a # symbol at the start, and in bold text.*

Note: There's another way to help indicate what your scripts are doing: Put comments in any embedded calculations. When a script has an If statement that uses a complex calculation for its condition, you're free to put comments in the calculation itself (page 429).

Asking and Telling the User

Sometimes a script needs to tell your users something—"There are no records to include in this report"—or ask the user a question—"How many copies of the report do you want?" To this end, the Show Custom Dialog script step can display a dialog box that you control. Calling it a "Custom" dialog box may be a bit too generous (you don't have much say in how it looks), but you do get to give information to people using your database, and ask them simple questions.

When you add the Show Custom Dialog step to your script and click its Specify button, you see the window shown in Figure 15-2.

The Show Custom Dialog script step has three basic purposes. First, it can display a simple message. In a script that finds all overdue invoices, for example, you can have a message that says, "No invoices are overdue" if FileMaker finds nothing.

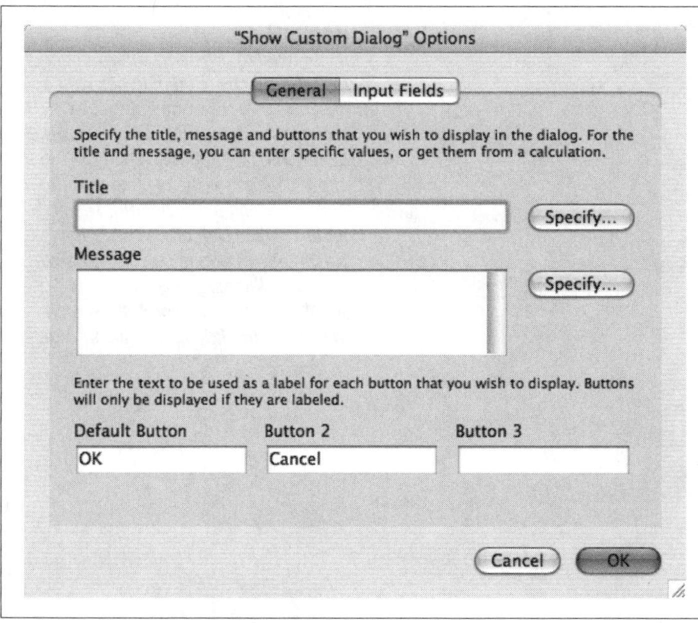

Figure 15-2: *The Show Custom Dialog Options window has two tabs. Here you see what's under the General tab: Title, Message, and the buttons. In its most basic form, a custom dialog box shows a message with just one, two, or three buttons. Figure 15-3 shows how each of these settings affects the dialog box the user sees.*

Second, you can create a dialog box that asks a simple question. Say you have a script that posts a customer payment. Before launching into the process, your custom dialog box can ask, "Are you sure you want to post a payment?," and include Post Payment and Cancel buttons for your users' feedback. Finally, you can use this script step when you need to ask your users to enter some data, not just click a button. For example, a script that runs a sales report might start by asking what date range to report on. Here's how to create all three types.

Showing a Simple Message

In its simplest form, the Show Custom Dialog script step just delivers a message to the user. Figure 15-3 shows how to configure a box like this, and how the final result looks.

You can generate the title and message from a calculation to make it more dynamic. For instance, if someone wants to see all open invoices for a particular client, but there aren't any, you can show a calculated custom message that says, "Nathan Petrelli's account is paid in full," instead of something equally true but less helpful, like "No records were found."

Using a custom dialog box like this in a script is simple. Just use the Show Custom Dialog step wherever you want in your script. When the dialog box pops up, your script waits for the user to click the button, and then continues with the next step.

Asking a Simple Question

To ask the user a simple question (with either two or three possible responses), just add more buttons to the dialog box by filling in the Button 2 and Button 3 boxes

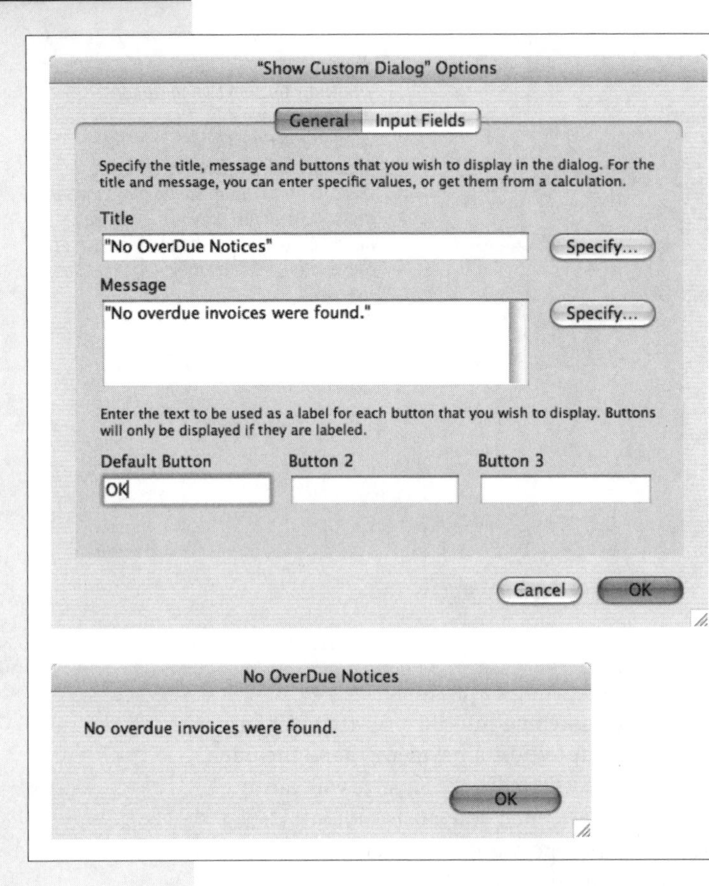

Figure 15-3: *If you need to give users information, format your custom dialog box with a title, message, and one button like the top picture. The Custom Dialog Box is below. The title appears along the top of the dialog box, the message inside, and the button at the bottom. The first button (called Default Button in the Show Custom Dialog Options window) is the one that users can "click" by simply pressing Enter or Return–or, if they insist, by clicking with the mouse.*

in the Show Custom Dialog Options window. You can see this process in action in Figure 15-4.

When a dialog box like this appears, your script waits for a click of one of its buttons, and then continues. Although FileMaker knows whether button 1, 2, or 3 got clicked, you have to add logic to your script to tell the program what to *do* in each case. For that, you use the Get (LastMessageChoice) function and If statements based on its results. (The function returns *1* for the default button, *2* for Button 2, and *3* for Button 3.) The script in Figure 15-5 uses Get (LastMessageChoice) to take action only if the user clicks the Post button in the custom dialog box. Nothing happens if she clicks the Default button, or hits the Enter key.

Note: To make the script shown in Figure 15-5 carry extra weight, you could put the invoice's balance due amount in your new payment record. There are a few ways to move data between tables, and you'll learn about them later in this chapter.

Asking a Not-so-simple Question

If you need user input that goes beyond two or three simple choices, you can venture into the second tab—Input Fields—in the Show Custom Dialog script step

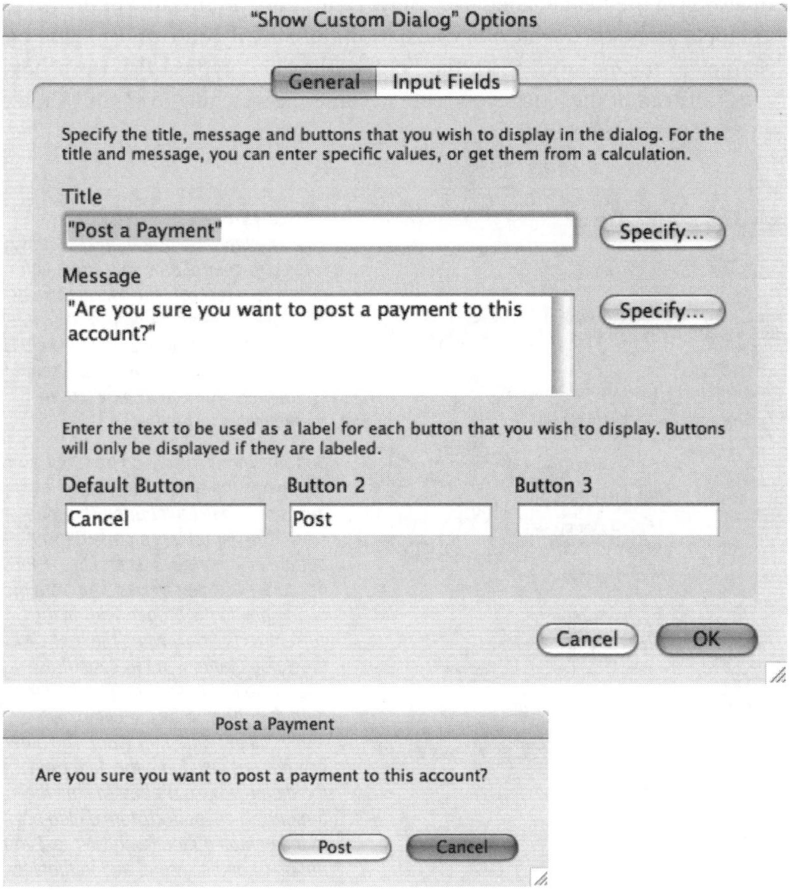

***Figure 15-4:** This custom dialog box asks a question and offers two user choices (Cancel and Post). Notice that Cancel is the default button (botton), acting as a safety device, since people often reflexively hit the Return or Enter key when they see a dialog box. By making Cancel the default button, you can prevent potentially destructive processes when someone fails to read instructions.*

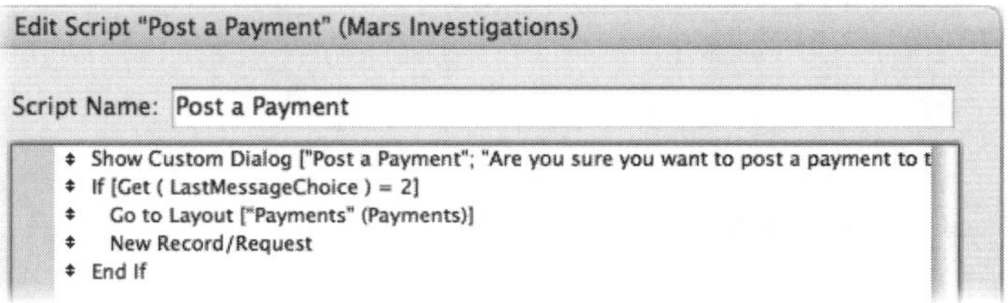

***Figure 15-5:** This script asks the user a question, then an If statement with a Get (LastMessageChoice) function decides what to do. If the user has clicked Post, then function result is a "2," and the script goes to the Payment layout and creates a new record. If the user has clicked the Default button, or hits the Enter key, nothing happens.*

(Figure 15-6). The "Show Custom Dialog" Options window's Input Fields tab lets you add fields to your custom dialog box. To add a field to a custom dialog box, turn on one of the "Show input field" checkboxes in the Input Fields tab of the "Show Custom Dialog" Options window. When you do, FileMaker shows a Specify Field dialog box, in which you can pick the field to use. (If you want to change the field later, click the Specify button).

You can also give the field a label, like "Start Date" and "End Date" in Figure 15-6 (top). A label can be the result of a calculation. Finally, if you turn on "Use password character" for an input field, the field works like a typical Password box: It shows * or • instead of the letters you type, so someone watching over your shoulder can't see what you're entering.

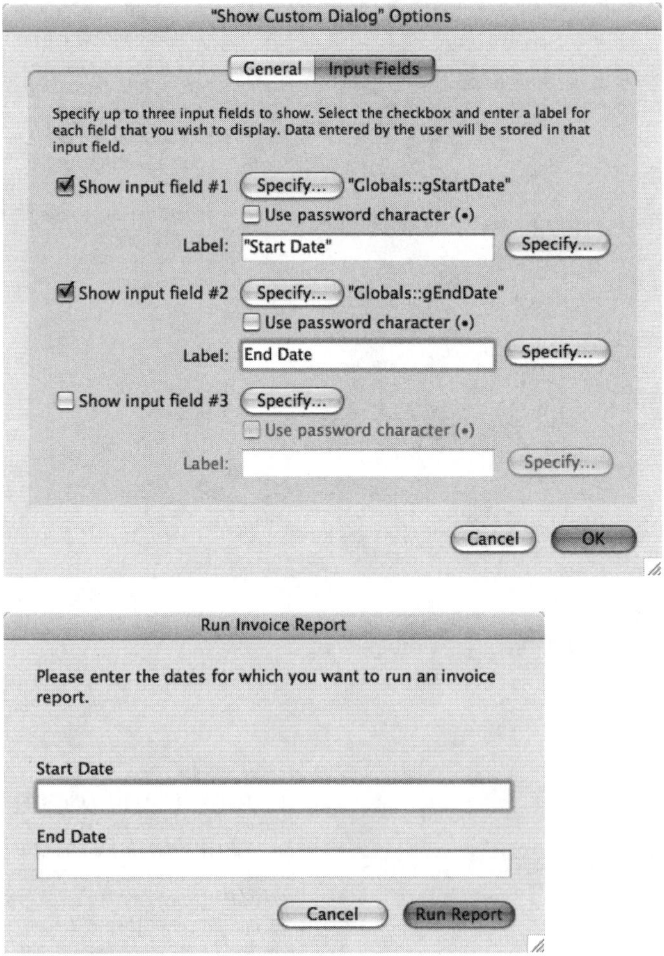

Figure 15-6:
Top: The Input Fields tab makes it easy for you to control how your users enter data into a record. (The specified fields have geeky developer names–a lowercase "g" prefix tells you the field is a global, but may confuse your users. Fortunately, you can display a user-friendly label instead.)

Bottom: This is the dialog box your user sees when the script runs. Notice that in this case, the default button (this one says "Run Report") is not the Cancel button, as is normal best practice. That's because FileMaker moves data from the dialog box to the proper fields in the current record only *when the user clicks the default button. In this case, those users who just automatically click the default button, or hit the Enter key really will get what they want. The other two buttons just dump the data from the dialog box, so it's best to limit the buttons on an input custom dialog box to the default button (whatever text you put on it) and a second button that lets your user cancel data entry and the script.*

The fields you add to a custom dialog box have some limitations, including the ones listed below. (For other alternatives, see the box on page 571.)

- As far as data entry goes, Show Custom Dialog can have only free-entry fields like those shown in Figure 15-6. You can't use radio buttons, checkboxes, or pop-up menus. You also have no control over the size of the field, so short fields for dates, or tall fields for lots of text, aren't an option.

- "Data-entry only" validation doesn't apply to fields in custom dialog boxes. If you use a dialog box to gather data for a record, either use the Always option in the field validation, or check the validity of the data in your script (page 585).
- You must use the OK button as the default when you're using input fields in a custom dialog box or the data won't be entered into a record. Consequently, you have to trust people to read the dialog box when they need to enter data in it.

WORKAROUND WORKSHOP

Really Custom Dialog Boxes

If the window created by the Show Custom Dialog script step (Figure 15-4) doesn't meet your needs, all is not lost. You have two options. For professional-level needs (*real*, resizable dialog boxes with text you can calculate, progress bars, and multiple input fields), get a third-party plug-in made for the task. See page 487 for more information on how to use plug-ins and where to find them.

But for light duty, you can get a similar effect by assembling your own dialog box from a window, a layout, and a script.

First, you need a layout that shows what you want. You can use text objects on the layout to show messages, fields of any kind to gather input, and layout buttons in any quantity and configuration. Once you've got the layout just the way you like it, you need a script to show it.

To get the effect of a typical dialog box, a few things need to happen. First, the new layout should appear in its own window. It probably shouldn't have the status area showing. And while the window is up, your users shouldn't be able to switch to a different window. Here's how to do all these things in a script:

- Use the New Window script step to make a new window. Then use Show/Hide Status Area to hide and lock the status area, and use Adjust Window with the 'Resize to Fit" option to make the new window just the right size.
- To keep the window frontmost, pause the script once the window is showing. When a script is paused, the user can't switch windows. For added assurance, add the Allow User Abort script step with the Off option before you pause the script. This step prevents the user from doing anything that would cancel the script.
- If the user presses Enter, FileMaker continues the script, so make one of the buttons look like a default button, and have the script take its action when it continues. To handle other buttons, you can have them set a variable (see page 578) and resume the script. The script can then check the variable when it continues to see what action it should take.
- After the pause script step, take any steps you need to deal with the user's input, and then close the window with the Close Window script step.

This layout-based approach has some drawbacks–most notably, it lacks the convenient default Cancel button of FileMaker's built-in custom dialog boxes. If you want this behavior in a layout-based box, you have to take special measures to avoid losing valuable data if someone clicks the wrong button. For instance, you could put entered data into global fields, and then move the entered data into the real fields only when the script continues.

Organizing Complex Scripts

Sometimes you need a script that does a *lot*. At the end of this chapter you'll build a script that generates an invoice for a selected job. As you'll see, this process involves many steps across several tables. To do all this work in one long script can be cumbersome, especially when several levels of If and Loop steps get mixed up with each other.

In other situations, you may need two or more scripts that do similar things. In fact, sometimes, entire sections of two scripts are identical with only minor differences. You may have a script that finds unpaid invoices so it can print a statement, and another that finds unpaid invoices to send email payment reminders.

If you build these two scripts independently, you have two problems. First, you have to write all the "find the unpaid invoices" stuff twice, which is a waste of time. More importantly, next month when you realize you need to exclude voided invoices from the list, you'll have to remember to make the change in *both* places. A database that's been growing for years can be a real bear to manage if the same general business logic is implemented over and over in dozens of different scripts.

In both these situations, you can improve your prospects by dividing your scripts into smaller parts. That way, you can break up a complex script into simpler scripts that each do part of the job. Also, you can make one script that finds unpaid invoices and use it in another script that prints a statement and/or sends an email payment reminder. This technique of writing scripts in small pieces that you can then reuse in other scripts is called *modular scripting*.

The Perform Script Script Step

The key to modular scripting is the *Perform Script* script step. It lets one script run another script—a *subscript*, to use another bit of programming lingo. When you add the Perform Script step to your script, you get only one option: a Specify button. Figure 15-7 shows how to use the Specify Script dialog box to tell your script which subscript script you want to run and what file to find it in.

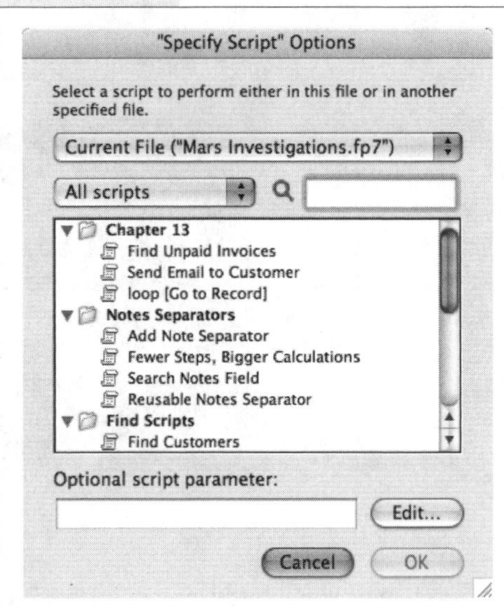

Figure 15-7:
The "Specify Script" Options dialog box is where you tell the Perform Script step what script to run. You can pick any file you have a reference to from the File pop-up menu (or choose Add File Reference to add a reference to another file). The script list shows every script in the selected file, complete with its groups and separators. Just select the script you want and click OK. See page 575 for details on script parameters.

When one script runs another, it waits for the subscript to finish before continuing. Imagine you have a script called Find Unpaid Invoices, and you want to make a new script to print statements for all your customers. The Print Statements script might start off by performing the Find Unpaid Invoices script. Once that's done, the main script can sort and print the invoices.

When you perform a script from another file, FileMaker uses that file's frontmost window (which is behind the user's window). If it doesn't have any windows, FileMaker automatically creates one. In either case, you're in a unique scripting situation: The window you're working with in your script isn't the one in front. Here's where the Current Window option in the Select Window script step comes in handy.

Halt Script and Exit Script

Normally a script ends when its last step runs. But you can force a script to end early if you want to. FileMaker actually has *two* script steps that end a script prematurely: Exit Script and Halt Script. These two steps do exactly the same thing if you run a script yourself directly. But if the current script was run by *another script*—via the Perform Script step—then they do different things. The Exit Script step tells FileMaker to stop the current script and continue the script that ran it. Halt Script, on the other hand, causes *all* script execution to stop immediately, no matter how the current script was started. (To learn more about these ominously powerful steps and when to use them, see the next page.)

Exit Script (Result)

Exit Script also has a powerful option that Halt Script doesn't have: a script result (see Figure 15-8). With a script result, you can tie all the power of the calculation dialog box to Exit Script. Then your main script can check the script result and decide how to proceed based on the results of the test. For example, you don't want to bother going through a sort and print process if your script doesn't find any invoices. An Exit Script step at the end of Find Unpaid Invoices will help the Print Invoices script figure out whether it should sort and print. Here's how to add an Exit Script step to an existing script:

1. **In the Manage Scripts window, double-click the Find Unpaid Invoices script.**

   The Edit Script window opens. The Exit Script step is always added to your subscript.

2. **Double-click the Exit Script step.**

   The step is added to your list. If necessary, move it to the bottom of the list. (You don't want the script stopping before all the work is done.)

3. **Click the Specify button.**

   The Specify Calculation dialog box appears.

4. **In the View pop-up list, choose the Get (FoundCount) function.**

   The function appears in the calculation field, so the script will record the number of unpaid records it finds.

5. **Choose Scripts → Save Script.**

   You want to keep your work, don't you?

Exit Script Result doesn't do much on its own. You also need to test those results in the main script. Use an If test, with a Get (Script Result) function to see if any records were found that should be sorted and printed. See Figure 15-8 for a script that calls Find Unpaid Invoices and then checks its results.

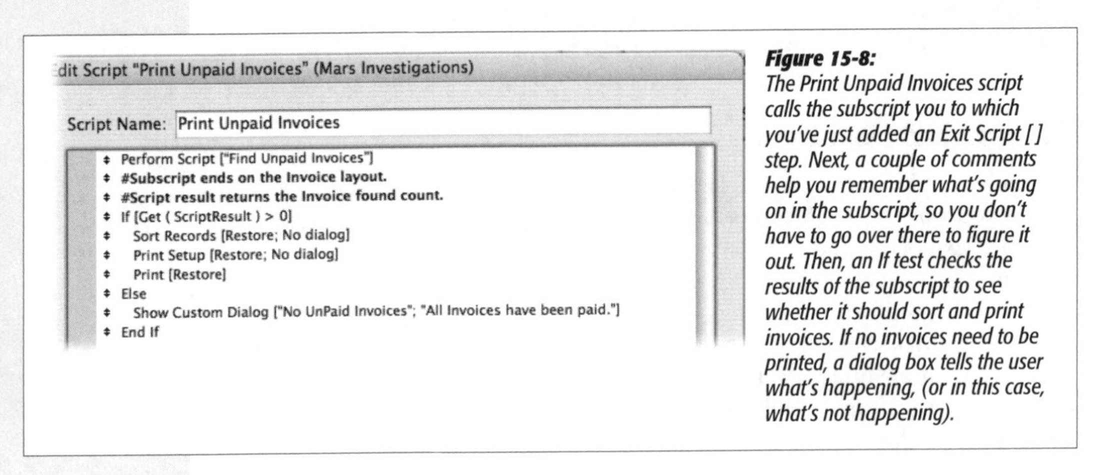

Figure 15-8: *The Print Unpaid Invoices script calls the subscript you to which you've just added an Exit Script [ ] step. Next, a couple of comments help you remember what's going on in the subscript, so you don't have to go over there to figure it out. Then, an If test checks the results of the subscript to see whether it should sort and print invoices. If no invoices need to be printed, a dialog box tells the user what's happening, (or in this case, what's not happening).*

Organizing scripts that use Halt or Exit Script

The Halt Script and Exit Script steps are useful exit strategies when you want to abort a script's execution because some problem has come up. But more often than not, you're better off without them. Take, for example, the two scripts shown in Figure 15-9.

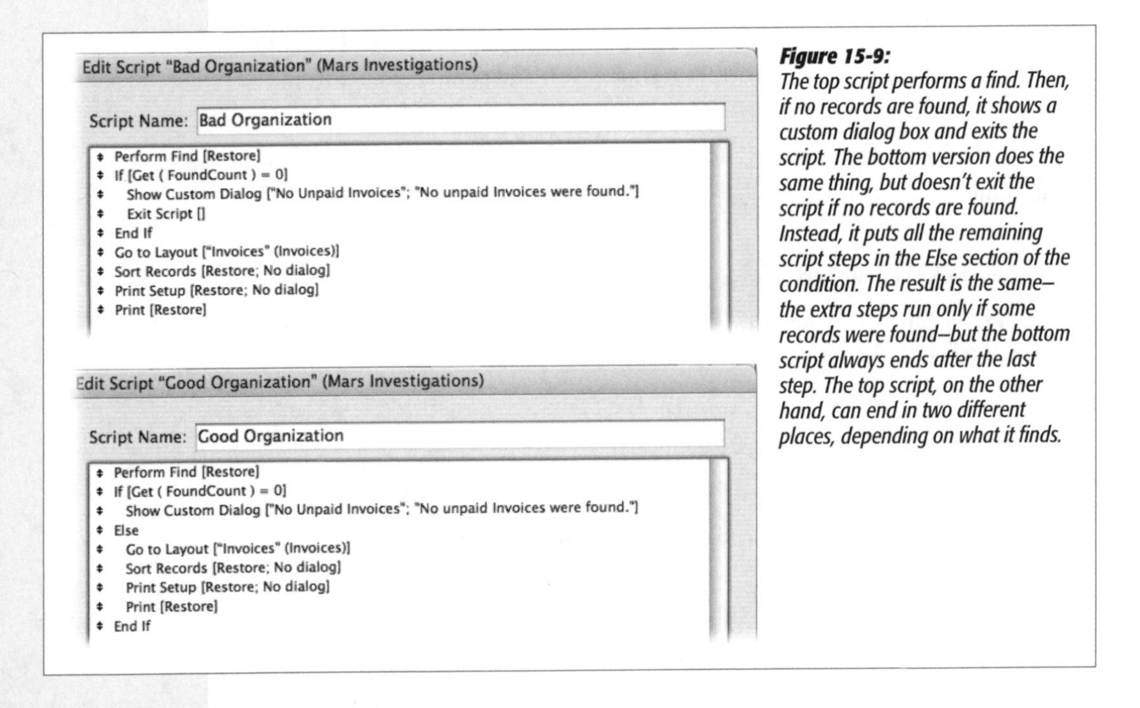

Figure 15-9: *The top script performs a find. Then, if no records are found, it shows a custom dialog box and exits the script. The bottom version does the same thing, but doesn't exit the script if no records are found. Instead, it puts all the remaining script steps in the Else section of the condition. The result is the same–the extra steps run only if some records were found–but the bottom script always ends after the last step. The top script, on the other hand, can end in two different places, depending on what it finds.*

Suppose you revisit this process later and want to add some more steps to the end that should happen *last*, every time the script runs—not just when records are found.

If your script looks like the one on top, you have a problem. You either have to add your new steps to the script *twice* (once before the Exit Script, and again at the end of the script), or reorganize the entire script to support the changes. But the script on the bottom is easy to fix: Just add the new steps to the end. In general, if a script ends in more than one place, it will come back to bite you later.

You're much better off organizing your script so it always reaches the same ending place.

Note: Halt Script has an even bigger downside. Since scripts can run other scripts, and most databases grow and change over time, you never know for sure if the script you're writing today is going to be run by another script some day in the future. It's rarely acceptable to run another script that could halt before reaching its normal end. It gives your new script no opportunity to recover if something goes wrong, so use this step sparingly.

Script Parameters

When you call a script using the Perform Script step or attach the script to a button, the Specify Script window shows a box labeled "Optional script parameter." You can type a static value in the box, or you can click Edit to create a dynamic calculation that FileMaker evaluates when the script starts to run. FileMaker stores the value, and you can check it anywhere inside the script, and then branch based on the value of the parameter.

As shown in Figure 15-10, you might make a script that can sort the records in three different ways. That way, four different buttons can run the same script, with different results. The script parameter that's attached to each button tells the script which sort order to use. Then, your script uses the Get (ScriptParameter) function to check the value stored when the script is run.

Note: A script parameter is not automatically passed to subscripts. If the subscript needs to know what's in your main script's parameters, you don't have to resort to any funky workarounds. Just use Get (Script-Parameter) as the subscript's optional parameter.

Suppose you wanted buttons to sort your Customer records by Name, City and State, or Zip Code. By using script parameters, you can get the job done with just one script. Each button passes a different parameter to the script, which takes the appropriate action. Before you can create the buttons, you need to create the script they'll run:

1. **Create a new script called *Sort Customers* (see page 495 for a refresher on creating scripts). Add the If step to the script.**

   FileMaker adds two new lines (If and End If) to your script.

2. **Click the Specify button. From the View pop-up menu, choose "Get functions".**

   The function list now shows all the Get functions.

3. **Find Get (Script Parameter) in the list and add it to your calculation.**

   You can choose "Get functions" or "all functions by name" from the View menu to help you narrow the search. The Get (ScriptParameter) function returns the parameter value specified when this script was called. If the parameter was a calculation, it returns the *result* of the calculation. It's now in the calculation box.

4. **After Get (ScriptParameter) in the calculation box, type = *"Name"*, and then click OK.**

   You're back in the Edit Script window, where the If step shows your calculation. Your calculation should look like this: *Get (ScriptParameter)* = "Name". Its result is true if the parameter sent to this script is "Name", and false otherwise.

5. **Add the Sort Records script step to the script, and then turn on the "Perform without dialog" option.**

   Insert it *after* the If step and *before* the End If step. (If yours is somewhere else, move it between these two steps.)

Tip: New script steps are inserted just below any highlighted step. If no script step is highlighted, then the new script step lands at the end of your script.

---

6. **Turn on the "Specify sort order" checkbox, add the Last Name field, then First Name field to the Sort Order list, and then click OK.**

   Your first test is written. The rest of the script will be variations on this theme.

7. **Add the Else If script step to the script.**

   You want Else If to come after the Sort Records step and before the End If step. (If it doesn't land there, move it.)

8. **Click Specify. In the Specify Calculation box, type *Get (ScriptParameter)* = *"City and State"*, and then click OK.**

   You're setting up a new test, this time checking to see if "City and State" is the script parameter. If it is, then you want a Sort step following this parameter to sort by—you guessed it—city and state.

Tip: Sometimes, it's quicker to copy one If test, and then paste and edit it in the Else If steps.

---

9. **Add another copy of the Sort Records script step to the script. Turn on "Perform without dialog." Set the sort order to State, then City, and then click OK.**

   Your second test, and what to do if that test is true, is now complete.

Tip: Another shortcut is to select the Else If and its Sort, and then use the Duplicate button to make copies of both steps. Then, edit the Else If test and the Sort order.

10. **Add one more copy of the Else If script step, this time with *Get (ScriptParameter)* = "Zip Code" as the calculation.**

    If the first two tests fail, your script makes this third test.

11. **Add another Sort Record step, this time set to sort by the Zip Code field. Then click OK until you're back in the database.**

    Your finished script should look something like Figure 15-10.

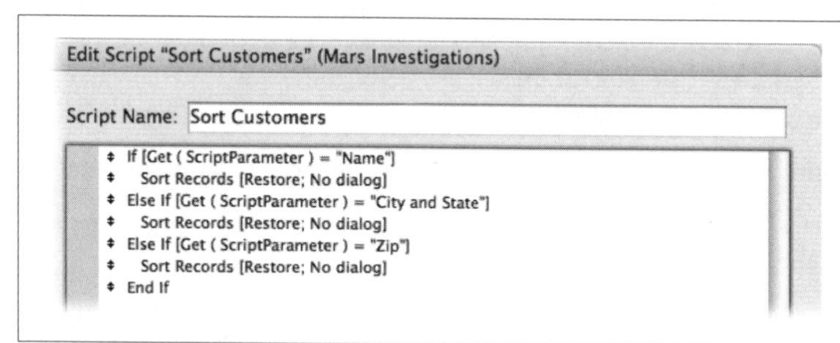
Edit Script "Sort Customers" (Mars Investigations)
Script Name: Sort Customers
If [Get (ScriptParameter) = "Name"]
Sort Records [Restore; No dialog]
Else If [Get (ScriptParameter) = "City and State"]
Sort Records [Restore; No dialog]
Else If [Get (ScriptParameter) = "Zip"]
Sort Records [Restore; No dialog]
End If

Figure 15-10: *Here's how your finished sort script should look. It has three branches (one for each of the possible sort orders). Now you just need to add buttons on the Customer layout to run this script.*

Note: When you're making a series of tests like the ones in this script, it's more efficient to put the condition that most often tests as true at the top. That way, the script doesn't have to test conditions that usually fail.

Now it's time to add buttons to the Customers layout to make it easy for your users to run the script. You need three buttons, one for each sort in the script you just wrote.

1. **Add a new button to the Customers layout.**

   Use the button tool (you know, the one that looks like a finger pushing a button). FileMaker shows you the Specify Button dialog box.

2. **Choose the Perform Script button command, and then click Specify. In the "Specify Script" Options list, select Sort Customers.**

   This is the script you created on page 575.

3. **In the "Optional script parameter" box, type *Name*, and then click OK until you're back on the Customers layout.**

   The first test of the Sort Customers script (Get (ScriptParameter) = "Name") is true when the users run it by clicking this button. Back on the layout, your button awaits its new name.

Note: If you check the text in the Optional script parameter box, you see that FileMaker put double quotes around Name for you. That's because it considers "Name" a text constant. If you like to be thorough, you can type the quote marks yourself, or you can rest easy knowing FileMaker will do it for you.

4. **Name the button *Sort by Name*.**

   You now have one button on your layout. Test it. It always sorts by name.

Time to work on the second button. To do so, you can save time by starting from a copy of the one you already have.

1. **Duplicate the Sort by Name button and double-click the new copy. In the dialog box's Options section, click the Specify button.**

   The Specify Script Options window pops up.

2. **Change the "Optional script parameter" box so it contains City and State.**

   Type carefully, since you're telling the script to exactly match what's in the Else If statement. Case doesn't matter, but spacing does. The second test of the Sort Customers script (Get (ScriptParameter) = "City and State") is true when the users run it by clicking this button.

3. **Click OK until you're back on the Customers layout and can rename your button.**

   Now you have two appropriately named buttons, and you can switch the sort order back and forth by clicking each button in turn.

To add the third button, follow steps 1 through 3 again. This time, set the parameter to "Zip Code," and name the button *Sort by Zip Code*.

Note: You don't have to write the script first, and then create your buttons. Lots of developers prefer to create buttons first, complete with the appropriate parameters, and then write scripts later. The order doesn't matter. Just make sure both tasks get done and that the parameters set on your buttons match up with the tests in the script.

These three buttons each call the same script, but the script parameters attached to each button allow the script to do double, even triple duty. To make this script even more flexible, you could keep adding Else If and Sort steps, and then make a button with a script parameter that matches each new test. See the box on page 580 for a way to use script parameters to extend the flexibility of the Add Note Separator script you wrote back in Chapter 14.

Script Variables

Global fields are great for storing a value that's not tied to a specific record in a table. Script variables are similar; use them when you need to store a value for your script to use, usually when you're testing a condition. But variables are better than globals in one important way: You don't have to add a field to a table to use them. Instead, variables are created as a script is running, and can vanish again when the script is finished, leaving no impact on your data's structure. (See page 475 for a refresher on using calculations to create variables.) Figure 15-11 shows you how to create a variable.

POWER USERS' CLINIC

Passing Multiple Parameters

A script can have only one parameter, and its result type is always text. But the parameter itself can be multiple values, if you're willing to use your calculation skills. To pass multiple parameters, string your values together with a separator character, and then pull them apart again in the script.

For example, if you want a script to have a pair of static values, you could type this text as the script parameter:

```
Molly¶Walker
```

Since the separator is the "¶", each value is on its own "line" and that makes it easy to grab the bits you need using the GetValue function. A calculation to pull "Molly" out from the script parameter would look like this:

```
GetValue ( Get ( ScriptParameter ) ; 1 )
```

Here's how to assemble a set of dynamic values into one script parameter:

```
Customer::First Name & "¶" & Customer::
LastName & "¶" & Customer::Phone & "¶" &
Customer::Email
```

The GetValue () function above could pull apart the pieces of your multivalue parameter.

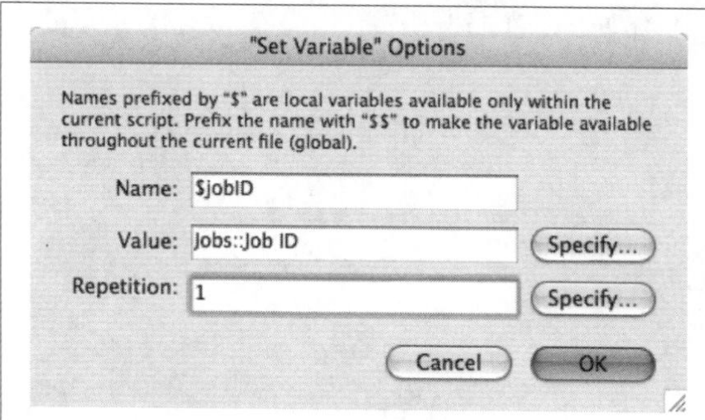

Figure 15-11:
*The "Set Variable" Options dialog box is full of useful information. First you create a variable by giving it a name. Since you can use variables inside calculations, their naming rules are similar to those of field names. Basically, you don't want to use characters, like a comma, +, -, *, or any other symbol that has a mathematical meaning and would therefore confuse the calculation that uses your variable. See page 592 for a tutorial using a variable.*

The Set Script Variable script step has three options:

- **Name.** Choose a short, descriptive name. All script variable names require a $ prefix. If you forget to type the prefix, ScriptMaker adds it for you. But you should get in the habit of typing the prefix, since it determines how long the value in the variable is available. A single $ means the variable is local and lasts only while your script is running. If you set a local variable, and then perform a subscript, the local variable isn't sent to that subscript. But if you need a global variable (the value persists through subscripts and even after all scripts have finished running), prefix the variable's name with $$. Global variables are cleared when you close the file.
- **Value.** This is the value you want to store in the variable. Values can be static text or the dynamic result of a calculation.
- **Repetition.** Repetitions are optional. You can make a variable store multiple values, similar to the way a repeating field stores multiple values. Most of the time, though, you don't set a repetition.

Since you can pass the value in a local variable with either a script result or a script parameter, there is rarely a reason to use a global variable. Programmers consider global variables sloppy housekeeping, because once the script finishes running, variables just lay around your database full of values that don't have meaning outside a script.

Warning: Global variables are potential security risks, since the Data Viewer (page 713) in FileMaker Pro Advanced will reveal their values to anybody who knows their names and has enough privileges to run scripts. If security is a big consideration at your business, make sure you don't leave sensitive data laying around in global variables by resetting their values to "0" or "" when the script is done. In practice, though, it's usually a lot easier, and cleaner, to use only local variables and rest assured that FileMaker is cleaning up after you.

UP TO SPEED

Note Separators Revisited

In the previous chapter, you learned how to make the Add Note Separator script work with any field (see page 534). The only drawback was that you had to click the field you wanted to work with before running the script. With script parameters, though, you can easily fix this problem. Just add a series of If and Else If script steps to the top of the script. Each one checks for one of the Notes field types (Invoice, Job, Customer, and so on) in the script parameter.

For instance, if the script parameter is "Invoice," then the script should use the "Go to Field" script step to go to the Invoices::Notes field first.

With these conditions in place, you just need to pass the right parameter from your Add Notes button. Just add tests to check the script parameter, and then use an appropriate "Go to Field" script step, depending on which button the user clicks. Use the script you wrote back on page 512 to see how to do this kind of branching.

Now if you want to add a new Notes field, you just need to add an Else If and a "Go to Field" step to this script. If you want to change the way the note separators look, you can change it in one place and the change applies to every Notes field in the database.

Handling Errors

As discussed on page 495, when an error occurs during a script (a Perform Find finds no records, for instance), FileMaker shows an error message almost like the one it would if you were doing the steps manually. The one difference is a button called Continue, as Figure 15-12 explains.

If the user clicks a Cancel button in an error message, the script stops immediately, and leaves the user wherever the script was when it stopped. If he clicks Continue instead, FileMaker ignores the error and moves on with the script. In the Perform Find example, for instance, the script continues with no records in the found set. Some errors (like the one in Figure 15-12) give the user a third choice. If the user clicks Modify Find, for instance, FileMaker takes him to Find mode on the current layout and pauses the script.

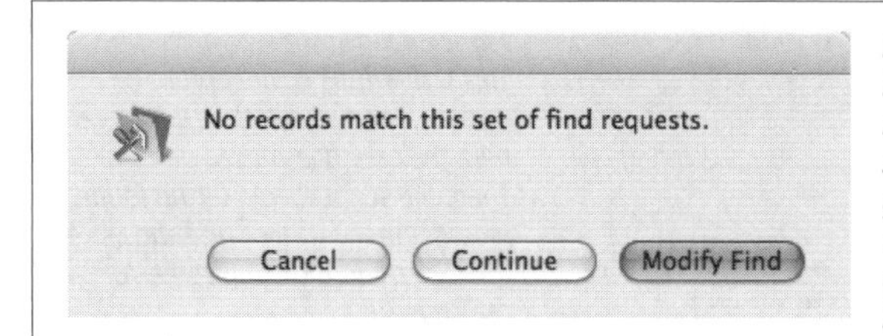

Figure 15-12:
Here's the warning you'll see if FileMaker can't find records that match your request if you search within a script. When an error occurs during a script, FileMaker gives the user all the normal choices he'd usually see in a warning dialog box, plus the option to ignore the error and continue the script. In this case, the Continue button is added to the normal mix.

Sometimes this error-handling approach is just fine. If the script is simple and everyone using it knows a little about FileMaker, it isn't too big a problem. But often, you need more control:

- If your system is complex and/or your users inexperienced with FileMaker, all sorts of confusion can result. First, the error message may make absolutely no sense to the user. The message complains, for instance, about not finding any records. But the user thinks, "I just wanted to create a new invoice for this job. Who said anything about finding records?" Even worse, if the user clicks Cancel, he could wind up just about anywhere: some layout in some window on some record. It could be a layout (like the Line Items layout) that he's never even seen before.
- If an error happens in the middle of a larger multistep process, it might be really important that the script know about it and deal with it appropriately. But it's the *user*, not the *script*, that decides whether to continue or cancel. You may want to make sure the script *always* continues, so it can get on with important work.

Luckily, you can opt for more control over error handling if you want it. FileMaker gives you three functions for finding and dealing with errors that may occur when scripts run.

The Set Error Capture Script Step

The Set Error Capture script step lets you turn on *error capture*. That way, instead of displaying potentially confusing error messages to your database's users, FileMaker keeps track of error information (*captures* it) so you can pull it into your script and handle it there. Although error capturing is a great feature, it's not part of FileMaker's normal behavior. You have to activate it by adding the Set Error Capture step to your script, and choosing the On option. At any time in the script, you can turn it back off again by using the step a second time and switching the option off.

If a script turns error capture on, and then uses the Perform Script step to run another script, the second script also runs with error capture on. In other words, the error capture setting sticks around as long as scripts call other scripts. But as soon as script execution stops for good, FileMaker turns off error capture. Understanding this behavior helps you determine when you need an error capture script step and when it would just be redundant. Figure 15-13 shows a script that turns error capture on before performing a find, then turns it back off when it's done.

Edit Script "Find" (Mars Investigations)

Script Name: Find

```
Set Error Capture [On]
Perform Find [Restore]
Set Error Capture [Off]
If [Get ( FoundCount ) = 0]
  Show Custom Dialog ["No Records Found"; "No Unpaid Invoices were found"]
  Show All Records
End If
```

Figure 15-13: *This script turns error capture on, and then performs a find. If the find fails, the user doesn't see an error. Then, the script checks for no found records (in the If step) and shows the user a more customized error message.*

As discussed in the box below, you could just turn error capture on so that your script ignores any and all errors—but that's not good script writing. The best way to use Set Error Capture is hand-in-hand with the Get (LastError) function, described next, to achieve error-free results.

WORD TO THE WISE

Keep It Off

Using Set Error Capture to eliminate those pesky dialog boxes sounds so cool, you may be tempted to turn it on at the start of every script. You can't anticipate every error, but at least you can keep FileMaker from casting doubt on your database skills by throwing error messages in your users' faces. But if all your script does is turn on error capture, and then never checks to see which errors are happening, you're not doing your users—or yourself—any favors.

If odd error messages pop up, your users probably let you know about it (perhaps via cell phone, while you're trying to relax on the beach), giving you a chance to figure out the problem and improve your script. With error capture turned on, a script might seem to be working because no warning dialog box shows up, but really, something's gone kablooie and error capture suppresses the dialog box that would have explained what happened.

You have little hope of figuring out what went wrong—especially if no one realizes there's been a problem until long after the script has run.

Usually, you find errors when you're developing your scripts, and you can use a custom dialog box (page 566) or error capture to deal with them. Don't turn error capture on unless you've already anticipated an error and figured out how your script can handle it; then turn it off again. That way, *unanticipated* errors don't get swept under the rug. In general, you should have just a few steps between Set Error Capture [On] and Set Error Capture [Off].

The Get (LastError) Function

When error capture is on, FileMaker doesn't just *ignore* the errors. Rather, it remembers which error occurred and gives you the chance to ask about it if you're interested. The script in Figure 15-13, for example, *isn't* interested. It doesn't ask if an error occurred at all. Instead, it just checks to see if the find worked by counting the records in the found set.

But sometimes you can use such error information within your script, much like any other value, to trigger other script steps. To check an error, use the Get (LastError) function to find out what happened. This function returns an *error code*, which is always a number. If there was no error in the previous step, Get (LastError) returns a zero. In other words, it doesn't return the number of the last

error that occurred. Instead, it returns the error number for the *last step* that ran. You wouldn't, therefore, put a *comment* step before the step that checks the last error, since the comment step itself always sets the last error back to zero. The same goes for End If and even Set Error Capture [Off].

In FileMaker, just about everything that could possibly go wrong has its own error number. This feature gives you a lot of flexibility, but it also makes it a real pain to figure out which errors you should check for. A complete list of error numbers is found in Appendix B. Luckily, most of these errors are pretty obscure, and chances are you'll never have to worry about them. Here's a list of the more common error numbers you may actually be interested in:

- **Error 9, 200 - 217, 723 - 725:** Assorted security-related errors (see Chapter 16).
- **Error 112:** Window is missing (you get this error if you try to select, close, or move/resize a window that doesn't exist).
- **Error 301:** Record is in use by another user (you get this error when you try to modify a record that is locked in another window or by another user).
- **Error 400:** Find criteria are empty (if you let users enter find criteria during a script, the Perform Script step gets this error if they don't enter anything).
- **Error 401:** No records match this request (this is the actual error that happens when no records are found; most people choose to check Get (FoundCount) instead since it's easier to understand).
- **Errors 500 -507:** Assorted field validation errors (you get these errors when you try to modify a field in a way that violates its validation setting and it is set to "always" validate).
- **Errors 718 and 719:** XML processing errors (see Chapter 17).
- **Errors 1200 -1219:** Calculation-related errors (you see these errors in conjunction with the EvaluationError and Evaluate functions).
- **Errors 1400 - 1413:** Assorted ODBC errors (see Chapter 17).

Tip: To capture an error by number, try this: Turn on error capture before the step that's producing the error, and then add a Show Custom Dialog step right after the offending step. Set the dialog box to show Get (LastError). When you run the script, instead of the error message you've been seeing, you'll see a custom dialog box with the real error number. You can then modify the script to handle this particular number. But it's even easier to use FileMaker Pro Advanced, which has a script debugger (see page 706). It automatically shows you error numbers as they occur–no need to write junk steps into your scripts that you just have to strip out again.

The Allow User Abort Script Step

One more script step has ramifications when dealing with errors: Allow User Abort. This step lets you turn off a user's ability to cancel the script. Allow User Abort has only two options: on and off. Its normal state is to be turned on, unless

you specifically turn it off with the script step. Like Set Error Capture, when you turn user abort off or back on within a script, the setting carries through any subscripts called by the main script. Allow User Abort always turns back on again when the script finishes running.

If you turn user abort off, but leave error capture on, the Cancel button in error messages is removed, so the user is forced to continue the script. Turning off user abort also prevents the user from pressing Escape (Windows) or ⌘-period (Mac OS X) to cancel a running script. Finally, if the script pauses, the user doesn't get a Cancel button in the status area. Instead, the only choice is to continue.

Note: When a script turns off user abort and pauses, the user also can't switch to a different window, close the window, or quit FileMaker.

Putting a Complex Script Together

Building a complicated script takes time and planning. Given the flexible nature of scripting, you could script a given process many different ways, and outside the artful application of your business's rules to your database, there is no one way. Your job is to find a *good* way.

In this section, you'll make a script that generates an invoice for a job. It gathers all the unbilled expenses and timeslips for the job, and adds appropriate line items for them to the invoice. To make a script like this, you need to cover all your bases:

- **Planning.** Without writing the actual script, what will your general approach be? Can you outline all the things your script will do, and in the right order? This process usually evolves from very general to somewhat specific. The most specific version is the script itself, when you'll tell FileMaker *exactly* what to do.
- **Exceptions.** What kinds of things can go wrong? How do you check for, and prevent, those problems?
- **Efficiency.** Are you doing the same things several places in the script? Are there other reasons to break your script into multiple smaller scripts?

Tip: The rest of this chapter is one long exercise. Here, you'll get a chance to put some theoretical concepts into practical use. Since each section builds on the one before it, this complex script is best digested if you work straight through from here to the end—without skipping parts or jumping around.

Also, you can see the process of building *and testing* this script in a screencast at *www.missingmanuals.com*.

Planning the Script

Planning a big script is usually an iterative process. You start by outlining the steps the script will take in very general terms. You can then go in and fill in more and more detail with each pass. When you're done adding detail, you know exactly what steps your script will use. Using the invoicing script as an example, you'll see how FileMaker gives you the tools to plan and execute your new script.

You can do this planning on paper, or in a word processor, or with any other tool you choose. But one good place you may *not* think of is ScriptMaker itself. Since the planning process involves a series of steps, and since it naturally produces the finished script when it's done, ScriptMaker is an ideal candidate. Just start with comments explaining each general step. You can then replace a comment line with some real script steps, and perhaps more comments. You never get lost or forget essential parts of the process because you always have a comment to tell you exactly what you still need to add, and exactly where it should go. When you're done, the script is written and it's already commented for posterity.

For this script, begin your planning by creating the script shown in Figure 15-14.

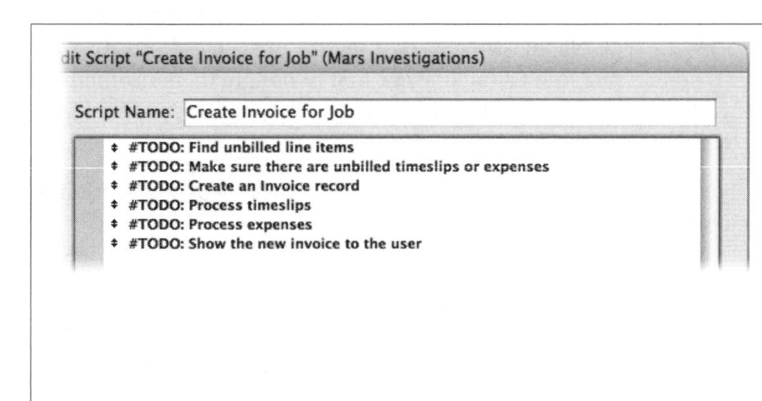

Figure 15-14: *This first rough-cut of your script doesn't do anything yet. Instead, it's just a series of comments that map out, at the most general level, what the script is going to do. You'll add more and more details as you go. Since these comments are just placeholders for real steps and comments yet to come, each one starts with the word TODO. You're welcome to use any marker you want, but it helps if you can easily tell these placeholder comments apart from the real comments you'll add later.*

Considering Exceptions

Many people forget one of the most critical steps in script writing—planning for exceptions. The old saw, "A stitch in time saves nine," truly applies. Spend a few minutes now, thinking ahead to what might go wrong and planning how to prevent problems. These minutes can save you hours of troubleshooting and repair work on your data later.

Look at what your script is supposed to do and try to think of reasonable *exceptions*—situations where your script might not be able to do its job. Thinking of exceptions is important for two reasons:

- **If your script always assumes ideal circumstances, it can wreak havoc if your assumptions are wrong when it runs.** The last thing you need is a wild script running amok in your data, changing and deleting the wrong things.
- **If a script gets halfway through its job, and then discovers that it can't continue, you may be left with half-finished work.** It's usually best to look for the problems up front so the script can simply refuse to run if it won't be able to finish. (For more detail, see the box on page 587.)

For example, the Invoice creation script could run into two potential problems. The problems, and their solutions, are as follows:

- **How does the script know which job to create an invoice for?** This problem is easy to solve. Make the script available only through a button that's on the Job layout. That way, your users can run only the script from the right context. The script will always run on the job record the user is looking at. Make a comment at the top of your script that reminds you how the script is run.
- **What if the job has no timeslips or expenses that haven't been billed?** You'd wind up with an invoice that has no line items, and you don't want to send *that* to your customer. You could go ahead and create the invoice, and then delete it if it's empty. But this approach uses up an invoice number, and it means your script has to go through all the work of creating an invoice only to throw it away when it's done. Your script should check first to be sure there's something to bill. Then, it can show the user an informative message and skip all the hard work when there's nothing to bill.

Figure 15-15 shows how to edit your script to take these two problems into account. Also note that the edited script has other changes.

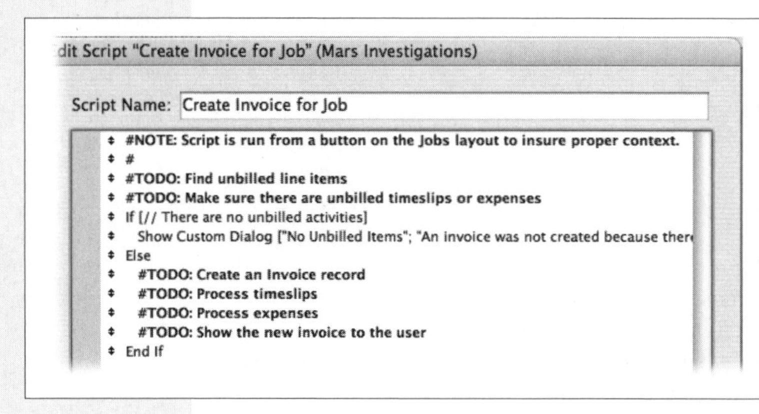

Figure 15-15: *Your first pass at editing the script shows where you'll put the test that determines whether an invoice needs to be created. And since you want to show the user a message if no invoice is made, add the Show Custom Dialog script step to the If part of the test.*

- **The If step doesn't need a fully realized test yet.** Put a commented calculation (page 429) as your test for now, just to remind yourself what needs to be tested. You can put the real test in later.
- **Add feedback for the user by putting a custom dialog step in the true part of the If step.** If you don't give the user feedback here, he may become confused, since nothing happens. The dialog box should tell your user why FileMaker doesn't create any invoice.
- **Add an Else step.** Since you don't want to create an invoice if there aren't any billable items for the job, put the last three TODO items in an Else step. The End If for this test should be just above the final End If in the script.

GEM IN THE ROUGH

The Problem with Problems

Although detecting problems up front is usually best, it isn't always possible. Sometimes you can't find out about problems until your script has run partway through.

Most database systems handle this problem with something called *transactions*, a chunk of work that's held in limbo until you tell the database to make it permanent. In a nutshell, you open a transaction, and then you're free to do anything you want, but your changes don't get saved until you commit the record. If you decide you don't want the changes after all, you undo the transaction.

FileMaker uses this transaction concept under the hood to handle record changes, but unfortunately there's no easy way to tap into the transaction system from a script. Here's why. When you first enter a record–using the Open Record/Request script step, for instance–FileMaker begins a transaction for you. When you exit the record–Commit Record/Request–FileMaker commits the transaction, writing all changes to the database. If you revert the record instead–Revert Record/Request–FileMaker essentially rolls back the transaction, leaving the database untouched. Just remember that each transaction is linked to a record. For example, you can't begin a transaction, then make changes to five different customer records and eleven invoices, and then roll back all those changes.

But if you create, edit, or delete records *in portal rows* while you're still in the record, all your changes happen in one transaction. Try this exercise in the Customers file to explore how this works. Have two windows open–one showing the Invoice layout and the other showing line items. Create a new invoice record and add a few line items. Notice that FileMaker creates the new line item records when you add items to the Line Item portal on the Invoice layout. Being very careful not to commit the record (that is, don't hit the Enter key or click anywhere outside the fields onto your layout), choose Records → Revert Record. The parent invoice record disappears, *and* all the child line items disappear, too. You've just witnessed FileMaker's version of transactions.

Knowing this, you can use the Open Record/Request script step on an invoice record, and then make changes to dozens of line items. Then if your script detects a problem, you can revert the invoice record, and all your line item changes are tossed out as well. If you absolutely, positively must have control over your transactions, arrange your scripts so they do everything through relationships from one single record.

Creating Subscripts

Now that you've figured out how to solve problems your script might encounter, you've come to a fork in the road. You could write a script containing all the necessary steps, but it would be long and hard to follow. For example, the End If steps at the end of the script would be a long way from their If and Else counterparts, making it hard to figure out where they belong. Alternatively, you may decide to break this script into smaller, more manageable pieces.

When you're trying to decide whether to write one long script, or several shorter ones, you might consider a few other things. If you have several small scripts, you can run any one of them individually. This method gives you the chance to try out parts of the script to see if they work properly. Also, since you can pass parameters to scripts when you run them, using subscripts to do some jobs often saves you the trouble later on, since you can pass errors, or script results (page 573), via script parameters (page 575). But in the end, either approach is perfectly valid. Some people really like short, simple scripts, even if it means more of them and more opening and closing of the Edit Script window. Others find this multiple-script song and dance far worse than a script that needs a little scrolling.

For this example, you'll be creating subscripts. Figure 15-16 shows a repeat of your script-in-progress with places for subscripts clearly identified. Each of these scripts is relatively short and easy to understand, but you'll have *five* scripts in all. (See the box on page 590 for some tips for breaking up long scripts into subscripts.)

Creating subscript placeholders

You can use the comments steps you wrote earlier to figure out what subscripts you'll need. Then you can create placeholders for them by putting Perform Script steps underneath the appropriate comments. Figure 15-16 shows your edited script.

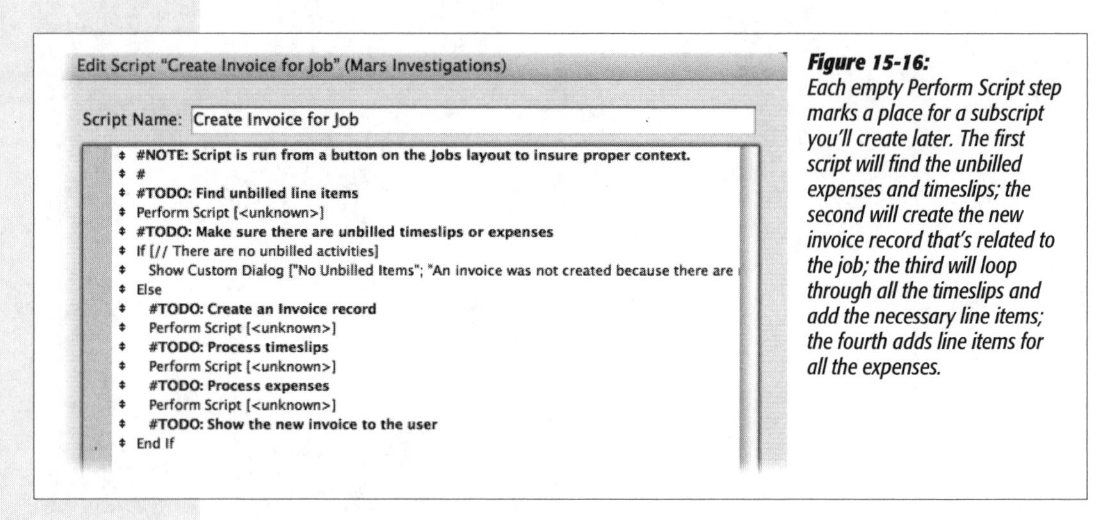

Figure 15-16: *Each empty Perform Script step marks a place for a subscript you'll create later. The first script will find the unbilled expenses and timeslips; the second will create the new invoice record that's related to the job; the third will loop through all the timeslips and add the necessary line items; the fourth adds line items for all the expenses.*

The "Create Invoice for Job" script performs four subscripts at the right time to pull everything together. Even though the script doesn't do much work at this point, you have a very good roadmap for the rest of the script-writing process. If you get lost, or interrupted, your main skeleton script contains everything you need to pick up right where you left off.

Creating skeleton subscripts

Next, you'll create all the subscripts you need—but that doesn't mean writing them all yet. You just need to create scripts in the Manage Scripts window and make some placeholder comments to remind you what they should do.

Tip: Using *naming conventions* can help keep your script list organized. In this book, all subscripts start with a dash and use all lowercase letters. It's also helpful to arrange all your subscripts right under the main script, in the order in which they run. That way, ScriptMaker helps you remember the structure of the main script, without delving into Edit Script.

Start by adding a new script called "-find unbilled activity." The dash and use of lowercase reminds you that the script is always performed by another script, and is not one you should expect to work on its own. You can see the "-find unbilled activity" script in its planning stage form in Figure 15-17.

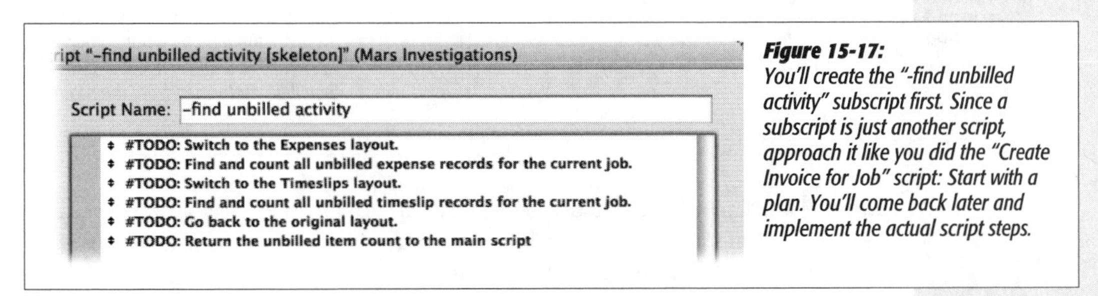

Figure 15-17: *You'll create the "-find unbilled activity" subscript first. Since a subscript is just another script, approach it like you did the "Create Invoice for Job" script: Start with a plan. You'll come back later and implement the actual script steps.*

The "-process expenses" and "-process timeslips" scripts are almost exactly the same. The context is different, because the data is in different tables and the data each script moves is different. But the process you'll use to find and process totals is very similar, so your comments notes can be the same for now. You'll create the custom pieces for each script in later exercises. Create the two subscripts shown in Figure 15-18 now.

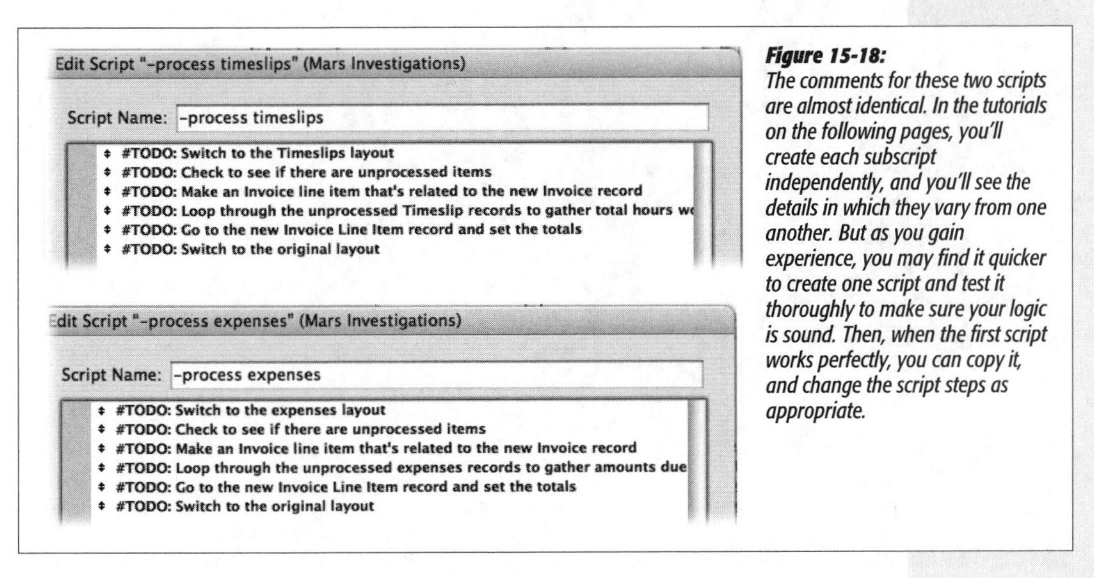

Figure 15-18: *The comments for these two scripts are almost identical. In the tutorials on the following pages, you'll create each subscript independently, and you'll see the details in which they vary from one another. But as you gain experience, you may find it quicker to create one script and test it thoroughly to make sure your logic is sound. Then, when the first script works perfectly, you can copy it, and change the script steps as appropriate.*

Finally, you'll create the comments for the "-create invoice record" subscript. Like the others, it switches to the proper layout, and then gets on with its work. This script makes a new invoice record, then switches back to the original layout and sends script results back to the main script (Figure 15-19).

dit Script "-create invoice record" (Mars Investigations)

Script Name: -create invoice record

```
#TODO: Switch to the Invoices layout
#TODO: Make a new record related to the Job ID
#TODO: Switch to the original layout
#TODO: Return script results to the main script
```

Figure 15-19: *Here's the skeleton "-create invoice record" script. Since nothing actually happens in your comments, and you aren't running them until they're done, you won't mess anything up by writing your subscripts in a different order than they'll be performed from the main script.*

Tip: Now that all your skeleton subscripts are finished, you could go back to your main script and change each empty Perform Script step to specify its proper subscript. But if you hook up each subscript as you finish it, the main script serves as a To Do list. You can tell at a glance which scripts you've done and which ones still need attention.

UP TO SPEED

The Right Way to Create Subscripts

When you think about ways to break your script into smaller pieces, you should be thinking about *tasks*. It makes good sense to create a smaller script to do one of the tasks needed in the larger script. It doesn't make sense to simply take a long script and break it in two, so that the last step in the first script simply performs the second script. Breaking scripts up that way has all the disadvantages of multiple scripts (more windows to work in, more scripts to scroll through) and none of the advantages (neither script is particularly simple or self-contained, and neither can be run individually for testing purposes). Also, as you look for places to use subscripts, you should also be looking for opportunities for reuse. In other words, you should look for things the script has to do more than once in two different places. It almost always makes sense to use a subscript in this situation.

In almost every case, the right way to subdivide a script is to create one master script that starts *and* finishes the process. The "Create Invoice for Job" script does just that. It starts by finding unbilled line items, and finishes by showing the invoice. Along the way, it relies on other simple scripts to get the whole job done.

This isn't to say that a subscript should never have subscripts of its own. In fact, subscripts often do. But you should structure the entire set of scripts so that the top-level script implements the highest-level logic and behavior of the entire script itself. Each subscript should, in turn, do some particular task from start to finish. If the task is particularly complex, then the subscript itself might implement only the highest level of logic, calling on more subscripts to handle parts of the task. Since scripts are named by the mini-task they carry out, they provide helpful overviews of what's going on. When the "Create Invoice for Job" script is finished, you see that even though it's somewhat complex, its structure makes it easy to follow. The script almost reads like a book, describing exactly what it's doing.

Finishing the Subscripts

You've created a series of subscripts that have placeholder comments to remind you what process the script will perform. Now it's time to finish your subscripts and turn them into working scripts by replacing those comments with real script steps.

The "-find unbilled activity" subscript

Before you leap into finishing this script, a short refresher about what you're trying to accomplish is in order. This subscript is the first step in the "Create Invoice for Job" master script. As the name says, it finds unbilled activity by searching the Timeslips and Expenses tables for items related to this job. It runs when a user clicks a button on the Job layout. You'll use a script parameter to send a Job ID to the script, so it can find the right items.

The first TODO item inside the script is a cinch: Just use the "Go to Layout" script step to switch to the appropriate layout. Next, for the current job, you need to find expenses that don't have a line item ID. You'll use a combination of Enter Find [Restore], Set Field with the Job ID (from your script's parameter), and Perform Find, to make sure you don't get items that have already been billed. Then, the script will count the found items so it can send that value back to the main script. Finally, you'll do the same thing for the Timeslips table.

1. **In ScriptMaker, double-click the "-find unbilled activity" script to edit it. Add the "Go to Layout" script step to the script.**

   If necessary, drag the "Go to Layout" step just below your first comment. Remember, if a script step is selected, any new step you create lands just below it.

2. **From the "Go to Layout" Script Step Options area's Specify pop-up menu, choose Expenses. Select the first TODO comment, and then add an Enter Find Mode script step. Click the Specify button. Turn off the Pause checkbox and turn on the "Specify find requests" option.**

   The Enter Find Mode script step lands below your second comment, and then the Specify Find Requests dialog box opens.

3. **If any requests are showing in the list, click Delete until they're all gone. Click the New button.**

   The Edit Find Request window appears.

4. **From the "Find records when" pop-up menu, choose Expenses, and then click the Line Item ID field.**

   The selected field is now highlighted.

5. **Click the Insert Symbol button and choose "== field content match" from the resulting menu. Click the Add button. Then click OK, and click OK again to get back to your script.**

   FileMaker puts "==" in the Criteria box. If you prefer, you can just type "==". Two equal signs, used alone, tell FileMaker you want records where the Line Item ID field matches *nothing*. These are all your expenses that haven't been billed.

6. **Add the Set Field script step to the script, and then turn on the "Specify target field" checkbox. Select the Expenses::Job ID field and click OK.**

   The step should appear after the Enter Find Mode step. If it doesn't, move it there now. Make sure you get the right Job ID field: You need to pick the Expenses table from the pop-up menu first.

7. **Click the Specify button to the right of "Calculated result." In the calculation box, type "==" & *Get (ScriptParameter)*. Click OK.**

   This calculation puts the Job ID (from the script parameter) into the field, with "==" before it, telling FileMaker you want to find records that match this ID exactly. Together with the find request above, the script finds unbilled activity for the current job.

8. **Add the Set Error Capture script step to the script and make sure its "On" option is selected.**

   You're about to perform a find, and you don't want the user to see an error message if there are no unbilled expenses.

9. **Add the Perform Find script step to the script.**

   The script step belongs below the Set Error Capture step. Make sure you don't select Perform Find/Replace by accident.

10. **Add another copy of the Set Error Capture step to the script, this time with the "Off" option selected.**

    You can select the existing Set Error Capture step, then click the duplicate button, then drag the new step into place, and set the option to "Off." Once the Perform Find step is finished, you want FileMaker to stop capturing error messages.

11. **Add a Set Variable script step below Set Error Capture [Off]. Name the variable *$unbilledItems*. Set its value to Get (FoundCount). Save the script.**

    Remember, you want to make sure you have unbilled items for this job before you create an invoice. By grabbing this value now, and passing it to the main script later on, the main script will have the information it needs to decide whether to create an invoice.

Your script should now look like the one in Figure 15-20.

You can refine your script further by removing the "TODO" from your first two comments, so you can see that they're now explanations of what should be happening, instead of reminders of what you still need to do.

Copying and editing existing script steps

Since the timeslips half of the script is almost a duplication of what you did in the last tutorial, you could repeat all those steps above and you'd be done. But it's a lot

it Script "-find unbilled activity" (Mars Investigations)*

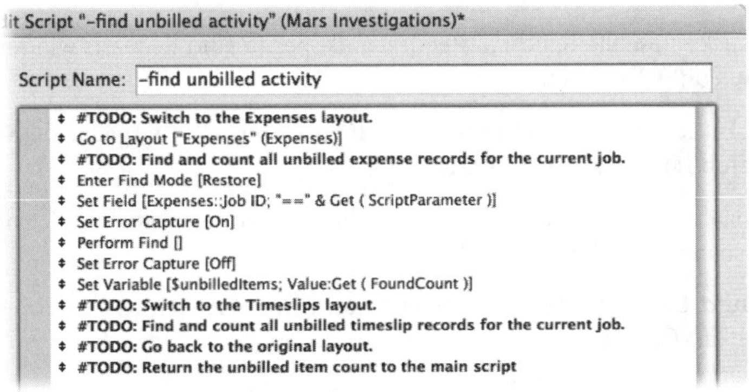

Script Name: -find unbilled activity

```
#TODO: Switch to the Expenses layout.
Go to Layout ["Expenses" (Expenses)]
#TODO: Find and count all unbilled expense records for the current job.
Enter Find Mode [Restore]
Set Field [Expenses::Job ID; "==" & Get ( ScriptParameter )]
Set Error Capture [On]
Perform Find []
Set Error Capture [Off]
Set Variable [$unbilledItems; Value:Get ( FoundCount )]
#TODO: Switch to the Timeslips layout.
#TODO: Find and count all unbilled timeslip records for the current job.
#TODO: Go back to the original layout.
#TODO: Return the unbilled item count to the main script
```

Figure 15-20: *The "-find unbilled activity" script is half done. You've got helpful comments, plus the steps to find unbilled line items that should be billed to the job for which you're creating an invoice.*

faster to duplicate those steps, and then make a few changes so that your duplicated steps operate on the Timeslips table, not on the Expenses table. Here's how:

1. **Click the "Go to Layout" top line in the script. With the Shift key held down, click the Set Variable step, and then click Duplicate.**

   FileMaker creates an exact copy of all the selected steps. They all wind up below the first set.

2. **Delete "TODO:" from the TODO: Switch to the Timeslips layout comment, and then move it up above the duplicated script steps. Then edit the "Find and count…" comment to read "timeslips" instead of "expenses."**

   While it may seem like overkill to keep a comment that seems to repeat what's happening in the "Go to Layout" step that follows, it serves as a very visible divider between the first and second parts of your script. In the next steps, you'll edit your duplicated script steps to work on the Timeslips table.

Tip: You can Ctrl-click (Windows) or ⌘-click (Mac) items in a selected list to exclude them so you won't copy them in the first place.

3. **Select the next step—"Go to Layout"—and, from Script Step Options area's pop-up menu, choose Timeslips.**

   This time you want to work with Timeslips records, so you need to go to the Timeslips layout.

4. **Double-click the next step: Enter Find Mode. Double-click the find request in the list. Select the only criterion in the list. From the "Find records when" pop-up menu, choose Timeslips, and, in the field list, select Line Item ID. Finally, click Change.**

   You're changing the find request so that it searches for empty Line Item IDs in the Timeslips table instead of in Expenses. The line in the criteria list changes to show *Timeslips::Line Item ID* instead of *Expenses::Line Item ID.*

5. **Click OK, and then OK again.**

   These two clicks close the Edit Find Request and Specify Find Requests windows, respectively. You're back in the script.

6. **Double-click the next Set Field step, and then change the targeted field to Timeslips:: Job ID instead of Expenses::Job ID.**

   Your Calculated result is just fine and so are the Set Error Capture and Perform Find steps, so you skip ahead to the last step.

7. **Select the next Set Variable step (the last non-comment step), and click the Specify button. Change the value calculation to read: *$unbilledItems + Get (FoundCount)*. Then click OK.**

   This time you don't want to *replace* the value in the script variable, so this calculation simply adds your new count to it.

8. **Select the duplicated "TODO: Find and count..." comment and delete it. Remove the "TODO:" from the other two.**

   When you're getting started writing complex scripts, more comments are better. As you get more experience, you may prefer to have fewer comments.

9. **After the "Go back to the original layout" comment, add a "Go to Layout" step and set it to go to "original layout."**

   Once the script is done finding things, it needs to return to the layout it started on so the script that ran this one won't be surprised by a layout change. It's usually best when a subscript puts things back the way they were when it started.

10. **Add an Exit Script step at the end of the script. Click the Specify button, and then type *$unbilleditems* in the calculation box. Don't forget to save your script.**

    You're telling the subscript to pass the value in the $unbilledItems variable back to the main script.

Whew! Finally, the "-find unbilled activity" script is finished. It should look just like the one in Figure 15-21. When you're done looking, click the OK button.

Adding a Script Parameter to a Perform Script Step

You already know you can set a script parameter for a button as it runs a script. You can also set a script parameter when you run a script with a Perform Script step. Back when you started creating the "-find unbilled activity" script, you learned that it needs to find all the activity for the *current* job, using that job's ID. Since the "Create Invoice for Job" script is performing this script from the Jobs layout, it can put the Job ID in a script parameter so it'll be available when subscripts move to other contexts.

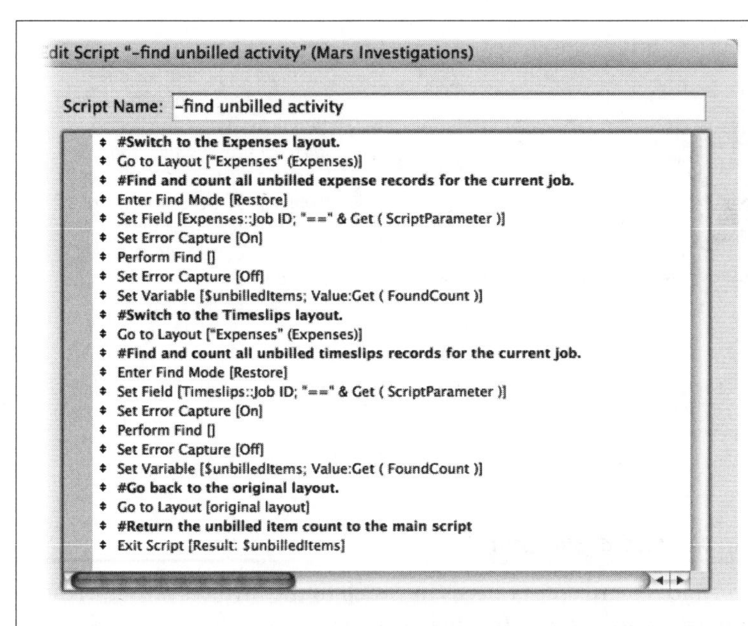

Figure 15-21: *This is the completed "-find unbilled activity" subscript. It finds and counts the expenses, and then the timeslips. This serves two purposes in the final process: The $unbilled items variable helps the "Create Invoice for Job" script decide if it should create an invoice or not, and FileMaker uses the found sets later to create line items.*

Also, now that you know what the subscript is doing to check for unbilled activity (it's setting a variable called $unbilledItems), you can grab the subscript's result and finish the If step with the proper test.

1. **In ScriptMaker, double-click the "Create Invoice for Job" script to edit it. Select the first Perform Script [<unknown>] step.**

   The Script Step Options area shows a Specify button.

2. **Click Specify. Select the "-find unbilled activity" script. In the "Optional script parameter" box, type *Jobs::Job ID*.**

   If you don't like typing field names, click Edit instead and add the field in the Specify Calculation window. Then close the Specify Calculation window by clicking OK.

3. **Add a Set Variable step below the first Perform Script set. Name the variable *$unbilledItems*, and set its value to *Get (ScriptResult)*.**

   This step completes the job of passing the variable's value from the subscript up to the main script.

4. **Double-click the If test to edit it. Set its calculation to *$unbilledItems = 0*.**

   This tells the script to test the count of found items made by the subscript.

5. **Save your script.**

   Now the script can find and count unbilled activities for the current job and then perform a test on the count so it can decide whether to create an invoice, or tell the user that no invoice is necessary (Figure 15-22).

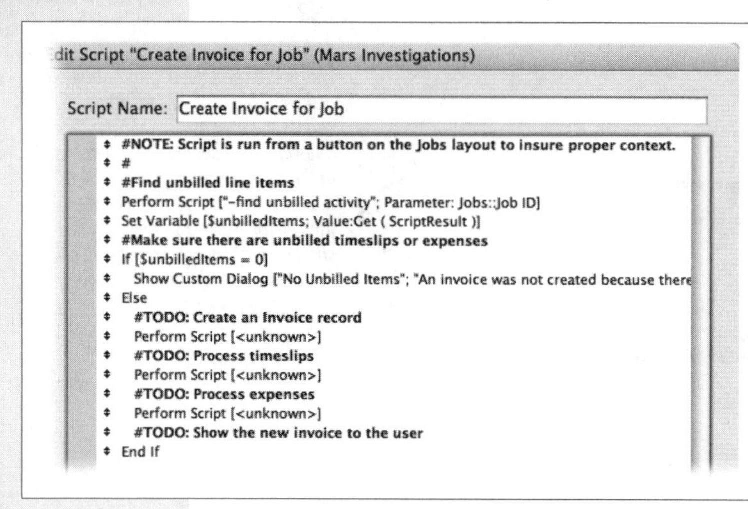

Figure 15-22: *The main script now has one completed subscript with a script parameter. It also tests the subscript's results and branches based on the value it finds. The remaining TODO comments and Perform Script [<unknown>] steps give you a perfect roadmap of the work ahead.*

The "-create invoice record" subscript

The "- create invoice record" script needs to switch to the Invoices layout, create a new record, attach it to the job (by filling in its Job ID field), grab the new Invoice's ID, and then switch back to the original layout. And like the last subscript, this one needs the Job ID in its script parameter, when you hook it up.

Since you're used to removing the "TODO:" part of your existing comments and placing the appropriate script steps just below them, the remaining tutorials in this chapter will skip those instructions for simplicity's sake. Now you're ready to polish off the "-create invoice record" script itself:

1. **Double-click the "-create invoice record" script in ScriptMaker to edit it. Select the first line: "TODO: Switch to invoices layout."**

   The next step you add appears *after* this comment.

2. **Add the "Go to Layout" script step to the script. From the Specify pop-up menu, choose Invoices.**

   You can't add an invoice record from the Jobs layout, so you're switching to a layout attached to the Invoices table first.

3. **Select the second comment step: "TODO: Create invoice record and set Job ID field." Add the New Record/Request step to the script.**

   The step appears after the second comment.

4. **Add the Set Field step to the script. The target field is the *Invoices::Job ID* field in the list, and the calculated result is *Get (ScriptParameter).***

   You're matching the new invoice to the Job ID that was set as the script's parameter way back when the script began running.

5. **Add a Set Variable script step after the Set Field. Name the variable *$invoiceId,* and set its value to *Invoices::InvoiceID.***

   You're grabbing the new invoice's ID, so you can put it in the line item records later. You have to grab it now, before you return to the script's original context.

6. **Add the "Go to Layout" step to the script.**

   Subscripts should always return the database to its previous state, so the main script doesn't get confused about its context.

7. **Add an Exit Script step at the end of your script. Its result is $invoiceId. Save the subscript.**

   Since you set the new invoice's ID in a local variable, you'll pass it back to the main script with a script result.

8. **In the "Create Invoice for Job" script, set the first Perform Script step under the Else to run the "-create invoice record" subscript, with a script parameter of Jobs::Job ID.**

   You're passing the Job ID to the subscript, so it knows which job it's creating an invoice for.

9. **Add a Set Variable script step below Perform Script ["-create invoice record"; Parameter: Jobs::Job ID]. Name the variable *$invoiceId,* and set its value to *Get (ScriptResult).* Save the script.**

   The subscript will pass the ID for the invoice it's just created back to the main script so it can create related line items in the next subscripts.

You can see the finished "-create invoice record" subscript in Figure 15-23. Now that your script creates a new invoice, you're ready to write the subscripts that create its line items.

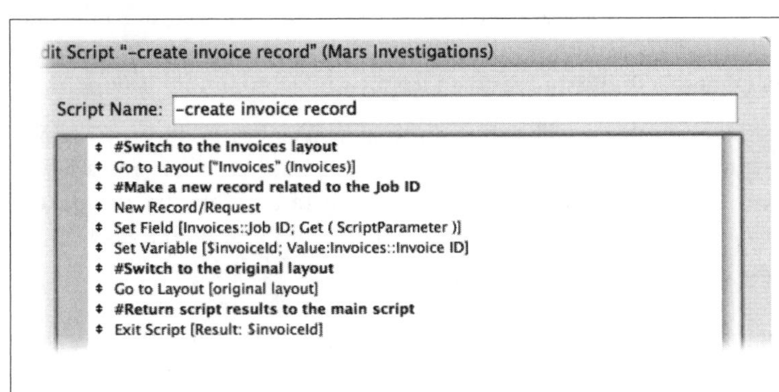

Figure 15-23: *The finished "-create invoice record" subscript has almost as many comments as it has working script steps, yet its task is relatively simple. It makes a new invoice record for a specific job. But even if you understand the process perfectly, it's good to leave comments intact. Someone else who doesn't have your experience may take over the database some day, and your comments will serve as a tutorial.*

THINK LIKE A PROGRAMMER

Testing Multiple Conditions Redux

Back on page 517, you learned how to write a script that tested multiple conditions. Now that you're familiar with setting variables, it's time to learn how to take a more advanced approach to the same problem. Instead of calling three different custom dialog boxes that are each hard-coded, you can set your message in a *local variable*, and then call a single custom dialog box that changes based on which condition tested as true.

Why go to all that trouble? It's certainly not because File-Maker gives you a limited number of Show Custom Dialog boxes and you have to ration their use.

The rationale behind this exercise is to give you a taste of the software engineer's approach to FileMaker's variables. By thinking in terms of storing data that doesn't need to last inside a local variable (which itself has a very short shelf-life), instead of as an option in a dialog box, you're well on the way to solving more advanced problems as they arise. And if you've come from another programming background, you'll be glad to see that FileMaker handles variable storage like some of the big toys in the programming world.

Here's how it looks:

```
If [ Get(CurrentTime) > Time(4; 0 ; 0) and
Get(CurrentTime) < Time(12 ; 0 ; 0) ]
    Set Variable [ $customMessage ; Value:
"Good morning!" ]
Else If [ Get(CurrentTime) > Time(12 ; 0 ;
0) and Get(CurrentTime) < Time(18 ; 0 ; 0)
]
    Set Variable [ $customMessage ; Value:
"Good afternoon!" ]
Else
    Set Variable [ $customMessage ; Value:
"Go to bed" ]
End If
Show Custom Dialog [ Title: "Greetings" ;
Message: $customMessage ; Buttons:
"Thanks" ]
```

The "-process timeslips" subscript

Now you'll tackle the subscript that processes your unbilled timeslips. This script creates a line item record and then moves a lot of data around. First the script puts the Line Item ID into an unbilled timeslip, so it's related to the line item record and won't be found *next* time you run the script." (Remember, your -find unbilled activity script looks for all timeslip and expense records that don't have a Line Item ID.) Then the script grabs the time worked from the record, so the data can be put into the new line item record. Finally it'll loop through the found set of unbilled timeslips and grab the time worked from each record, until it's done.

Some steps in these scripts are variations on what you've been doing—switching layouts, doing If tests, creating records, and setting data into records from variables. You'll get them out of the way so you can concentrate on the harder part—processing the data in the found set. To get started, replace your first few TODO items with appropriate steps, per Figure 15-24.

Creating a looping script. As you learned back in Chapter 13, you can use a loop to run a set of script steps over and over again. But there's more to a loop than just cramming steps between a loop and an end loop pair. Most times, you have to do a little prep work to get the database ready to enter the loop. And you must always have a way for the loop to stop. In this case, since you're working on a found set of records, you'll use a "Go to Record" step that exits after the last record (see page 518).

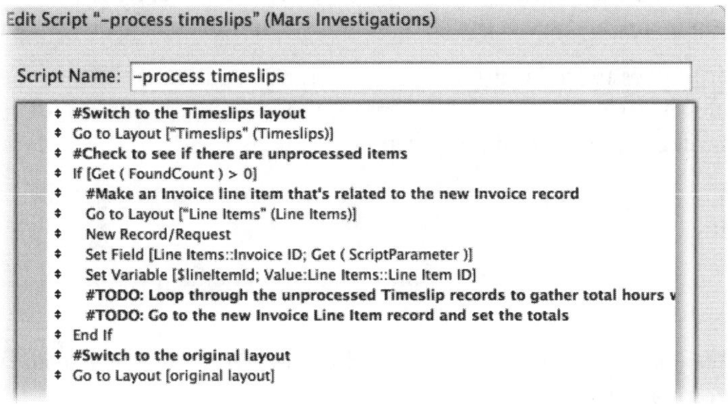

```
Edit Script "-process timeslips" (Mars Investigations)

Script Name: -process timeslips

#Switch to the Timeslips layout
Go to Layout ["Timeslips" (Timeslips)]
#Check to see if there are unprocessed items
If [Get ( FoundCount ) > 0]
    #Make an Invoice line item that's related to the new Invoice record
    Go to Layout ["Line Items" (Line Items)]
    New Record/Request
    Set Field [Line Items::Invoice ID; Get ( ScriptParameter )]
    Set Variable [$lineItemId; Value:Line Items::Line Item ID]
    #TODO: Loop through the unprocessed Timeslip records to gather total hours v
    #TODO: Go to the new Invoice Line Item record and set the totals
End If
#Switch to the original layout
Go to Layout [original layout]
```

Figure 15-24: *The "-process timeslips" subscript goes to the Timeslips layout to see if the earlier subscript found any records. If there are records in the found count, the script switches to the Line Items layout and makes a new record with the Invoice ID that is passed via the subscript's parameter. Finally, it puts the new line item's ID in a variable so that you can put the ID into each timeslip record.*

Here's what to do:

1. **Add a "Go to Layout" step below the Set Variable step. Specify Timeslips for the target layout.**

   The script was just on the Line Items layout, so you need to make sure the loop will happen in the proper context.

2. **Add a "Go to Record/Request/Page" step below "Go to Layout."**

   You want to make sure your loop starts with the first record in your found set.

3. **Add a Set Variable step below "Go to Record." Name the variable *$totalHours*, and set its value to *0*.**

   This variable helps the script add up hours as it loops through the found set of timeslip records.

4. **Add a Loop step below the Set Variable step.**

   ScriptMaker also gives you a matching End Loop step. The next few script steps will go between this pair.

5. **Add a Set Field step as the first step of your loop. The target field is Timeslips:: Line Item ID, and the calculated result is $LineItemId.**

   When you put a Line Item ID into a timeslip record, you're relating the Line Item and Timeslips table. Now you can look at any timeslip record and see any line item related to it, and you can look at a line item record and see any timeslip related to it. You'll use this relationship later on to move dates without switching layouts.

6. **Add a Set Variable step below the Set Field step. Name the variable *$total-Hours*, and set its value to *$totalHours + Timeslips::Duration*.**

   The script will add the hours worked on each timeslip record to the value that's already in the variable. On the first record, the variable will have 0 in it, so the result of the first calculation will be the same as the duration. But every time the loop runs again, the value in the variable will increment by the amount in the current record.

7. **Add a "Go to Records/Request/Page" step after the Set Variable. Specify Next in the pop-up menu, and select the "Exit after last" option.**

   Now the script goes to the next record in the found set. It exits the loop automatically after it performs the looped steps on the last record. The rest of your script steps will go after the End Loop step.

8. **Add a "Go to Layout" step below the End Loop step. Set it to go to the Line Items layout.**

   You're putting the data you gathered into your new line item record, so make sure you're back on the Line Item layout.

9. **Add a Set Field step next. Set the target field to *Line Items::Price Each*, and set the calculated result to *20*.**

   This step tells the line item record how much money to charge for each hour worked. When you get your private investigator's license, you can change this calculation to reflect your new status, and it won't change any old invoices.

10. **Add a second Set Field step below the first one. Set the target field to *Line Items::Quantity*, and set the calculated result to *$totalHours*.**

    This step tells the line item record how many hours were worked on the job.

11. **Add a third Set Field step below the second one. Set the target field to *Line Items::Description*, and set the calculated result to *Labor*. Edit your TODO items and save the script.**

    Your time line items are labeled with static text describing the charge, and your looping script is finished.

Your finished script should look like the top picture in Figure 15-25. Then take a gander at the box on page 602 to see some other ways you might've handled the problems presented in this script.

The "-process expenses" subscript

You'll apply lessons learned in the "-process timeslips" subscript to this script, but there are some important differences. First, although this example assumes your business rules say that all labor is combined into one line item per invoice, you'll create a line item record for each expense in the found set. So the steps that create a new line item will fall inside this script's loop. Second, you're gathering more bits of data for each expense, so the steps that set data into Line Item fields are different from what you did for Timeslips. But the overall process is still very similar. Here's what to do:

1. **Add a "Go to Layout" step below your first comment. Set the target layout to *Expenses*.**

   You need to be on a layout tied to the Expenses table so you can check to see if any records need to be processed.

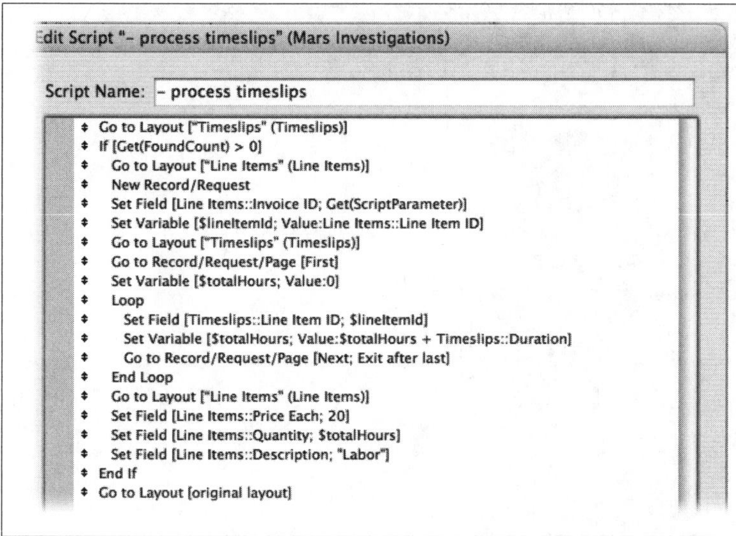
Edit Script "- process timeslips" (Mars Investigations)
Script Name: - process timeslips
Go to Layout ["Timeslips" (Timeslips)]
If [Get(FoundCount) > 0]
Go to Layout ["Line Items" (Line Items)]
New Record/Request
Set Field [Line Items::Invoice ID; Get(ScriptParameter)]
Set Variable [$lineItemId; Value:Line Items::Line Item ID]
Go to Layout ["Timeslips" (Timeslips)]
Go to Record/Request/Page [First]
Set Variable [$totalHours; Value:0]
Loop
Set Field [Timeslips::Line Item ID; $lineItemId]
Set Variable [$totalHours; Value:$totalHours + Timeslips::Duration]
Go to Record/Request/Page [Next; Exit after last]
End Loop
Go to Layout ["Line Items" (Line Items)]
Set Field [Line Items::Price Each; 20]
Set Field [Line Items::Quantity; $totalHours]
Set Field [Line Items::Description; "Labor"]
End If
Go to Layout [original layout]

Figure 15-25: *Your finished "-process timeslips" script would look like this if you deleted all your comments. Keep your comments intact if it'll help you remember what the script is doing, or if somebody else might need to figure out what the script is doing. Remember, comments don't take up computer processing power, but they can help you save brain processing power because you don't have to reinvent the wheel months down the road if your business rules change and you have to adapt your script to the new paradigm.*

2. **Add an If test and set its calculation to *Get (FoundCount) > 0.***

   You don't want to go to any trouble if there are no expenses for the current job.

3. **Add a "Go to Record/Request/Page" step between the If and End If steps. Set the "Go to Record" option to *First.***

   You want to make sure the loop begins with the first record in the found set so nothing gets missed.

4. **Add a Loop step below the "Go to Record" step.**

   You'll also get an End Loop step. Most of the rest of your script's steps will go between the Loop and End Loop steps.

5. **Add a Set Variable step as the first step in the loop. Name the variable *$description*, and set its value to *Expenses::Expense.***

   You're grabbing data to put into the new line item record you'll be creating later in this script. The remaining steps should be set in the order you see below.

6. **Add a Set Variable step. Name the variable *$amount*, and set its value to *Expenses::Amount.***

   You're grabbing more data.

7. **Add a "Go to Layout" step. Set it to go to the Line Items layout.**

   The context has to be right to create your new record.

8. **Add a New Record/Request step.**

   It doesn't have any options.

POWER USERS' CLINIC

Other Right Ways

Back when you were planning your complex script, you saw that there's no single right way to accomplish a particular task. Your job is to find a *good* way. To be sure, there are best practices–tried and true methods that scripters rely on–but if your script does what you need it to do, and your users can't find a way to make it break, then you've got a winner. Still, it pays to have a variety of tools in your scripting toolbox. Here are some things you can do differently in the "-process timeslips" subscript.

- **You don't have to go to a layout to move data.** If you have a relationship between two records in your script, you can use the relationship to "push" data into the right record. In this case, you'd have to make a special table occurrence (page 366) for this purpose, but it would be worth doing if something happened to change the active line item record during your script. Remember, you *can* use a "Go to Layout" script step in "-process timeslips" and trust it to find the new line item record you've just made, because your script doesn't do anything to change the active record. But sometimes your script needs to change the active record. Pushing data is just the thing in that situation.
- **You can push more data through a relationship.** The subscript increments a variable with the amount of time spent working on a job for each record in the found set. But if the relationship is valid when you enter the loop, you could just increment the Timeslip::Duration value in the line item record directly. That way, you can save the $TotalHours variable if you want.
- **You can create the relationship and push no data at all.** You can use a Sum calculation (page 414) in the Line Item table to add up related line items' Duration fields. It means creating a new field in Line Items, but it would be dynamic, unlike the Set Field step, which produces a static value. That is, if you run the "Create Invoice for Job" script, and then find out that the Duration amount on a timeslip record is wrong, then you can't just change the timeslip and expect it to update on the line item. (If your business rules require one line item for each expense, as covered on page 600, then this calculation won't fill the bill.)
- **Local variables don't have to be initialized.** In this chapter, you set the subscript's $totalHours variable to 0 before you entered the loop that increments its value. In other words, by setting its value to 0 before you add any data to it, you *initialized* the variable. Initializing the variable is considered a best practice for working on complex scripts. It's perfectly possible to use the same variable for different parts of a lengthy script, but if you do, you can get unexpected results if the variable already has some other value in it. So initializing a variable (resetting it to 0) heads off problems before they occur. But, if you're sure the script won't ever create or set a variable with the same name, you can save a Set Variable script step by not initializing the variable before you put data in it.

9. **Add a Set Field step. The target field is *Line Items::Invoice ID* and the calculated result is *Get (ScriptParameter)*.**

   You'll need to remember to set this script's parameter when you hook it up to the main script later.

10. **Add a Set Field step. The target field is *Line Items::Description* and the calculated result is "Expense: " & $description.**

    You want the calculation to set the static text *Expense:* into the field, and then add the contents of your $description variable, so be sure to include text quotes around the text part of the calculation.

11. **Add a Set Field step. The target field is *Line Items::Price Each* and the calculated result is *$amount*.**

    The amount is how much you spent.

12. **Add a Set Field step. The target field is *Line Items::Quantity* and the calculated result is *1*.**

    Don't include the quotes this time, since 1 is a number. You need the value so your Extended Price can perform its math properly.

13. **Add a Set Variable step. Name the variable *$lineitemID*, and set its value to *LineItems::Line Item ID*.**

    You're grabbing the Line Item ID now so you can put it into the expense record next. This step creates the relationship between the Line Item and Expenses tables, and it insures that the next time you run the script, this same expense record won't be found again.

14. **Add a "Go to Layout" step. Set it to go to the Expenses layout.**

    The script will return to the expense record it started the loop on.

15. **Add a "Go to Record/Request/Page" step. Specify Next in the pop-up menu, and select the "Exit after last" option.**

    This step makes sure you're working through the found set, and can get out of the loop after the script has worked on the last record.

16. **Add a "Go to Layout" step at the end of your script. Set it to go to "original layout." Edit your TODO comments, move them into place, and save the script.**

    You always want a subscript that changes context to return to the settings it started with.

Compare your script with Figure 15-26.

Finishing the main script

As your last bit of housekeeping, you'll need to hook up your Perform Script [<unknown>] steps and set their parameters.

1. **Open the "Create Invoice for Job" script, and then double-click the unfinished Perform Script below the TODO: Process timeslips comment.**

   The "Specify Script" Options dialog box opens.

2. **Choose the "-process timeslips" script, and set its script parameter to *$invoiceId*.**

   The subscript uses this value to relate its new line item to the proper invoice record.

3. **Double-click the last unfinished Perform Script step, and then choose the "-process expenses" script. Set its script parameter to $invoiceID.**

   This subscript needs the same value, and for the same purpose as the one above.

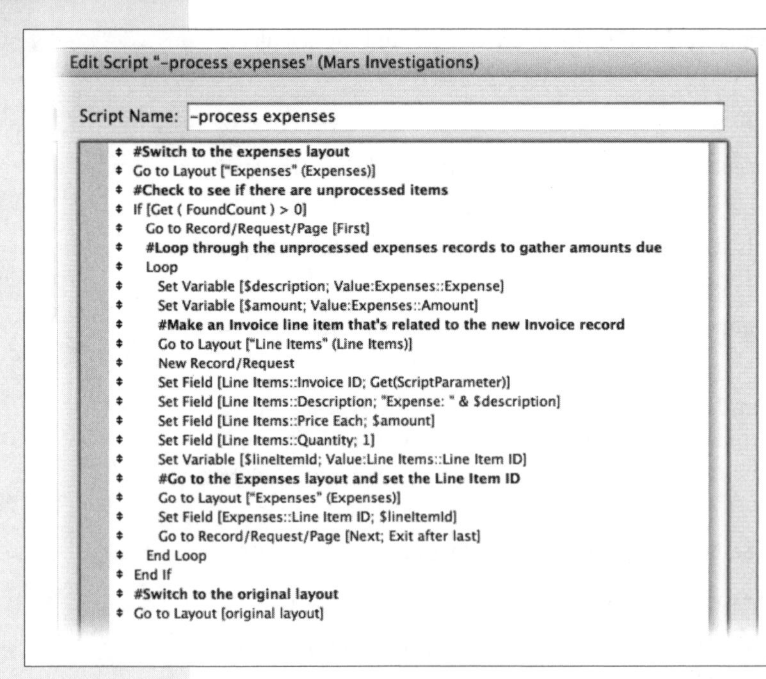

Figure 15-26: *This is what the "-process expenses" script should look like when you're finished. These are suggestions for revised comments, if you're the type who likes to keep them to remind yourself what you were thinking when you wrote a complicated script.*

4. **Add a "Go to Layout" step before the End if step. Set it to go to the Invoices layout.**

   You want the database user to see the fruits of your labor, don't you?

Compare your finished script with Figure 15-27.

Testing Scripts

To test your script, first go to a job record that has unbilled timeslips and expenses (or create a new job record, plus new unbilled timeslips and expenses, if necessary). Once you're on the job record, run the "Create Invoice for Job" script. To make your testing as much like the conditions your users will see, create a button for running the script.

In a flash, you should see a new invoice, properly assigned to the customer and containing line items for each unbilled item. You may be a little miffed that it took you *hours* to build the script, and FileMaker runs the whole thing in seconds. Cheer up, though; think how much time it will save you *in the future*.

Tip: If the script doesn't work, you have a few options. First, check your data to make sure you have appropriate timeslips and expenses for the script to work on. Second, you can surf over to *http://www.missingmanual.com/cds* and compare your scripts to the ones in this chapter's finished file. But if you have FileMaker Pro Advanced, you should also read about the Debug Scripts and Data Viewer tools in Chapter 19. These gems can make hunting down script problems a breeze. Few serious scripters work for long without the debugger and Data Viewer.

POWER USERS' CLINIC

Referential Integrity

By now, it's ingrained in your developer's brain that relationships work because there's a match between key fields in the related tables. But what if you absolutely, positively *have* to change the value in a key field? You know it'll wreak havoc with your related records, because as soon as you change the value in the "one" side of the relationship, all the "to-many" records are no longer related to their parent records (or to any other record). In other words, they're orphaned.

If you changed the value in key fields manually, it'd be fairly easy to figure out how to keep this from happening. You use the existing relationship to find the child records, change their keys, and only then, go back to the parent record and change its key. The record family is reunited and everybody's happy.

Here's a script that handles that grunt work for you:

```
Allow User Abort [ Off ]
Go to Layout [ "Customers" (Customers) ]
Set Variable [ $newID; Value:Customers::
NewCustomerID ]
Go to Related Record [Show only related
records ; From table: "Jobs"; Using
layout:
"Jobs"
(Jobs) ]
Loop
      Set Field [ Jobs::Customer ID;
$newID ]
      Go to Record/Request/Page [ Next;
Exit after last ]
End Loop
Go to Layout [ "Customers" (Customers) ]
Set Field [ Customers::Customer ID; $newID
]
```

There's still some brainwork that this script doesn't handle, like making sure your NewCustomerID value is unique before you try to use it. If you're changing your key field value, it's probably not a surrogate key, so you'll have to know how your business policy creates and insures unique key values, and then apply that logic to your script. And you need to ensure that each related record is unlocked and available for your script to change. (See the box on page 683 for the scoop on record locking.) Only you can decide whether changing a key field is something you want to hand over to your users or if you'll manage this task yourself. Whichever way you go, this skeleton script will get you started.

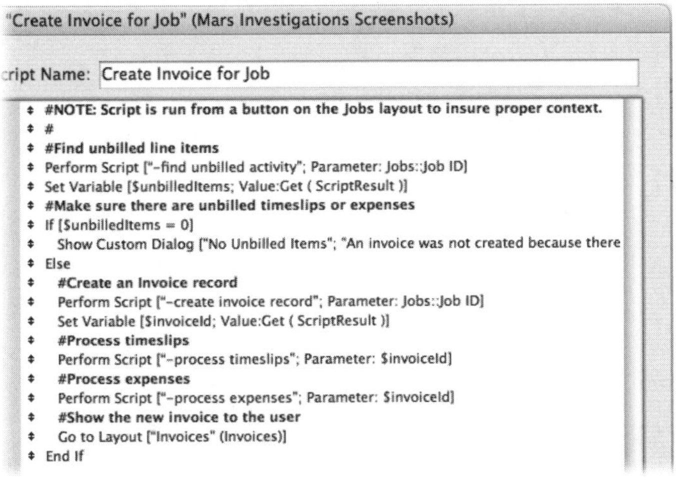

```
"Create Invoice for Job" (Mars Investigations Screenshots)
Script Name: Create Invoice for Job
#NOTE: Script is run from a button on the Jobs layout to insure proper context.
#
#Find unbilled line items
Perform Script ["-find unbilled activity"; Parameter: Jobs::Job ID]
Set Variable [$unbilledItems; Value:Get ( ScriptResult )]
#Make sure there are unbilled timeslips or expenses
If [$unbilledItems = 0]
   Show Custom Dialog ["No Unbilled Items"; "An invoice was not created because there
Else
   #Create an Invoice record
   Perform Script ["-create invoice record"; Parameter: Jobs::Job ID]
   Set Variable [$invoiceId; Value:Get ( ScriptResult )]
   #Process timeslips
   Perform Script ["-process timeslips"; Parameter: $invoiceId]
   #Process expenses
   Perform Script ["-process expenses"; Parameter: $invoiceId]
   #Show the new invoice to the user
   Go to Layout ["Invoices" (Invoices)]
End If
```

***Figure 15-27:** You're finished! You may find that there are just too many comments for your taste. Feel free to delete any you find extraneous; the script doesn't need them to work. And after all, a well-named subscript–like "- create invoice Record" or "-process timeslips"–doesn't need many comments, since its name explains what it's meant to do. But the top comment, about context, could be important for troubleshooting later. If problems arise, or if you need to tweak the script later because your business rules have changed, you can skim this main script to remind yourself how it works before you dive in and make changes.*

In this exercise, you walked through a lengthy task where the steps and outcome were known. Out there on the mean streets of development, you won't always have a road map. Still, the concepts you learned when you started thinking in terms of planning, execption handling, and efficiency will get you out of a lot of sticky script situations.

When you're first scripting, or if you're attempting to do something that you aren't quite sure will work, following a similar approach will serve you well. In addition to creating your scripts in comment and subscript form, you can break scripting down even further. Create a few script steps, and then test them to make sure they behave as you expect. If they don't work properly, tweak them until they do. Then add a few more script steps and test again. If a new problem arises, you know it's in the new steps you've just added.

Finally, don't forget that the state of your database can influence what happens when you test a script. For example, a button on the Jobs layout insures that your users can run only the "Create Invoice for Jobs" script from the proper context. But in the heat of testing, you might accidentally run the script from ScriptMaker while you're on the wrong layout. If you do, your script parameter won't be set properly, and all kinds of havoc will be loosed in the script.

As you gain experience, you'll find that planning, finding exceptions, and subscripting will become second nature. You'll start envisioning scripts of increasing complexity, and soon you'll be making them your own way, without following a rigid plan.

6

Part Six: Security and Integration

CHAPTER
16

Security

Easy access to information is what FileMaker's all about. But that's a double-edged sword. As it stands now, every person who uses your database has unrestricted access. Of course, you can take all the usual precautions (give your computer a password, install virus protection software, lock your door, and so on). But eventually, you'll probably want to let other people work in your database, and that brings up all kinds of security challenges. Mike in Accounting is free to rename all your scripts if he so desires. And Kelly in Sales can delete all those "old" order records that are getting in her way. Fortunately, FileMaker has features of its own that give you a finer level of control, so you can let selected people use your database to the fullest, while keeping important information out of harm's way.

You may be tempted to think you don't have to worry about security. But the best time to think about protecting your data is *before* you have a problem. If you wait until your database grows big and complex before considering security, it'll take you longer to build in later.

How Security Works

FileMaker's security system has two levels of control: *who* can get into your database in the first place and *what* they can do once they're there. You determine who gets access to your database by setting up *user accounts*, and you control what each person can do by assigning *privilege sets* to each account.

Who Gets Access

FileMaker understands that different individuals access your database. The *who* part of security is important for several reasons. For instance, Malcolm and Lois each need access to the database, but their manager Craig doesn't. You get to decide who gets access. With individual accounts, you can keep track of who's in the file. If Lois leaves the company, you need to keep her from accessing the database in the future. Likewise, when Lois's replacement is hired, you need to give him access, too.

In FileMaker, you create an account for each person who accesses the database. Just like any password-protected document, an account has a user name and a password. When people open the database, they have to type a name and password to get in. If they don't know the right combination, they can't see your database. If they get the password right, FileMaker assumes they are who they say they are.

Note: When FileMaker asks for an account name and password, propeller-heads say it's *authenticating* the user. In other words, it's making sure the user's for real. The actual window that pops up on the screen is called the *Authentication dialog box*, and the whole process is called *authentication*. This book, for the most part, dispenses with this jargon.

POWER USERS' CLINIC

Spying by Script

When you've set up database accounts, FileMaker remembers the account name of whoever's currently signed in. In fact, by using a script, you can find out who it is with the Get (AccountName) function. For example, if you want to record the account name in a Notes field when someone runs a particularly important script, you could include a script step like this:

```
Set Field [Notes;Notes & Get(AccountName)
& " ran THE script on " & Get
(CurrentDate) & " at " & Get
(CurrentTime)]
```

Then every time the script runs, FileMaker looks up the name and password of whoever's using the file at the moment, and puts the person's account name and the date and time in the Notes field.

Along with the account name, FileMaker remembers the name of the privilege set when someone logs in. You can use the Get (PrivilegeSetName) function to find out what it is.

What They Can Do

But who gets into your database is only half the story. You also control *what* they can do. Now then, while all people are unique, you probably don't need to grant each person the privilege to use individual layouts or scripts on a case-by-case basis. Instead, FileMaker assumes you have just a few different types of users, and lets you create privilege sets for each type. A privilege set is simply a list of things a user's allowed to do, and in effect it creates a level of privilege. For example, you may have one privilege set for Accounting and another for Sales. People with the Accounting privilege set can run reports, but they can't enter new orders. People with the Sales privilege set can enter and edit data, but they can't run reports.

You can make as many—or as few—privilege sets as you need. And you can give 50 accounts the same privilege set, or make a privilege set just for one account. When you create a privilege set, you get lots of control over what it can do. A privilege set can prevent people from editing scripts, or it can let them edit just certain scripts. It can stop a salesperson from editing any order entered more than five days ago, or prevent accountants from editing orders at all.

Privilege Sets

Generally, you create your privilege sets *first*, and then add accounts for each user, as you'll see in the following sections. When you add an account, FileMaker asks you to pick a privilege set to control that person's access. But true to the FileMaker way, if you start to create an account, and don't yet have an appropriate privilege set, you can easily create one right then and there, before you save the account.

All the work of creating and maintaining accounts and privilege sets is done in the Manage Accounts & Privileges window (Figure 16-1). You can get there by way of the File → Manage → Accounts & Privileges command.

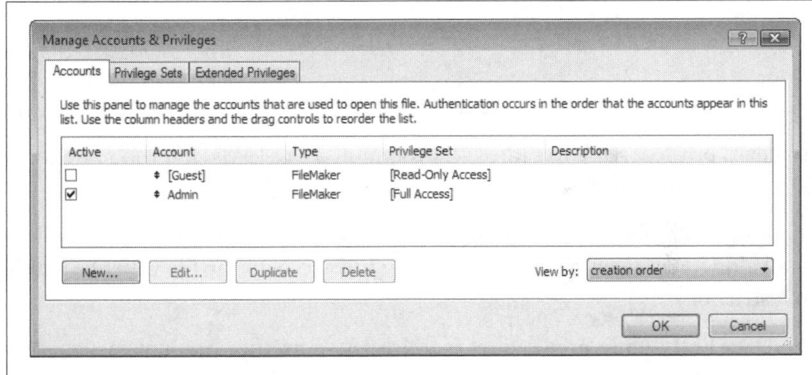

Figure 16-1: *The Manage Accounts & Privileges window (File → Manage → Accounts & Privileges) has three tabs: Accounts, Privilege Sets, and Extended Privileges. You'll learn about extended privileges on page 630, but the first two tabs are where you go to manage accounts and privilege sets, respectively.*

When you're creating privilege sets, there's a big temptation to give people too much power. The more folks can do on their own, the less often they'll come bugging you, right? Unfortunately, this attitude invites trouble. For instance, if your database holds credit card numbers along with order records, and your Order Entry privilege set lets users export data, you may one day find yourself the subject of an FBI investigation. To be on the safe side, if you aren't *sure* someone needs a privilege, don't give it to him.

There's a practical component to this rule as well. If someone has access to a feature he shouldn't have, it's very unlikely he'll complain. He probably won't even notice, and neither will you until someone abuses it. However, if you lock someone out of a capability she needs, you can bet you'll hear about it right away. You can easily add the needed power when it comes up. In other words, if your privilege sets start out too restrictive, they'll naturally grow to the right level of power over time based on user feedback.

Managing Privilege Sets

To create or edit privilege sets, click the Privilege Sets tab. The first thing you notice is that you already have some privilege sets. Every FileMaker database has three built-in privilege sets: [Full Access], [Data Entry Only], and [Read-Only Access] (the brackets help to remind you that these privilege sets are special). You can see the Privilege Sets tab in Figure 16-2.

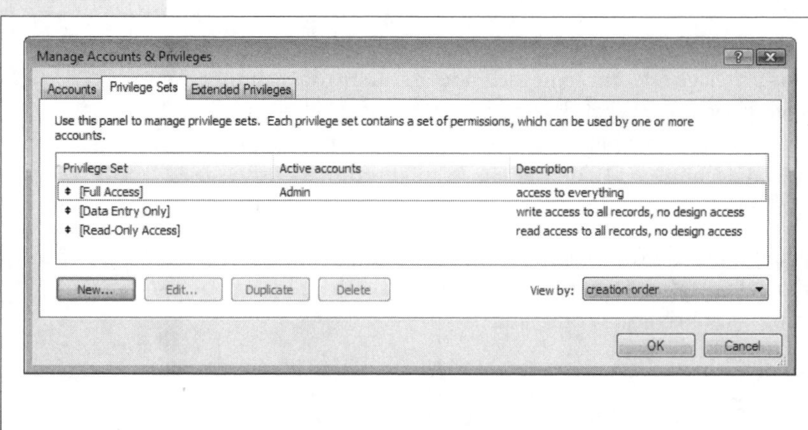

Figure 16-2: *The Privilege Sets tab of the Manage Accounts & Privileges dialog box lists all the privilege sets in your database. Each privilege set has a name (in the Privilege Set column) and a description. The list also shows you all the accounts that are assigned each privilege set. In this case, only the [Full Access] privilege set is actually being used–by the Admin account.*

The standard privilege sets cover three very common access levels, and you're welcome to use them if you want:

- Although you probably didn't realize it, you've been using the **Full Access** privilege set all along. As the name says, it gives you full access to the file with absolutely no restrictions.
- The **Data Entry Only** privilege set is much less powerful. Accounts assigned to this privilege set can't create or modify tables, field definitions, scripts, or layouts. But they can add, edit, and delete records in any table, and they can export data.
- The least powerful built-in privilege set is **Read-Only Access**. Not only does it prevent developer activities, but it also prevents modification of the data. Accounts with this privilege set can't create, edit, or delete records. They can only *view* the data that's already there.

These built-in privilege sets provide basic security, but they don't give you a full range of possibilities. Using just FileMaker's default privilege sets, you can't give Malcolm full control of some tables, but let him just enter data in others. In developer's lingo, you don't get a lot of *granularity*.

Note: Think of granularity as a medium for sculpture. If you're building a statue from boulders, you can't create delicate details like the nose or eyelashes. If you're building with grains of sand (get it?), you can work at a much finer level. Similarly, granularity in security lets you control specific access to very specific aspects of your database.

In FileMaker, you can exercise precise, granular control over security by creating your own privilege sets and assigning them to certain people or groups.

Creating a new privilege set

Before you create a new privilege set, you have a decision to make: Do you start from scratch, or do you take a shortcut? If you click New, FileMaker makes a new privilege set with absolutely no privileges. In other words, accounts attached to this set—if left alone—can't do *anything* in the database. You have to turn on exactly the privileges you think the user should have.

To save time, you can start by duplicating the [Data Entry Only] or [Read-Only Access] privilege set, and then add or remove privileges as necessary. This way is usually a little faster, but it does open up the possibility that you'll accidentally leave something turned on that shouldn't be.

Note: You can't duplicate the [Full Access] privilege set. This is FileMaker's way of encouraging you to really think about the privileges you assign, and it should encourage you to give users the least access possible for them to do their jobs. If you want a privilege set that grants *almost* full access, you have to build it up by hand.

To develop a full understanding of how privilege sets work, why not try building one from scratch? To get started, click New. FileMaker pops up the Edit Privilege Set dialog box (Figure 16-3). Your first job is to give the privilege set a name and a description. In the Privilege Set Name box, type *Project Manager*, and in the Description box, type *create and edit jobs, create new invoices*.

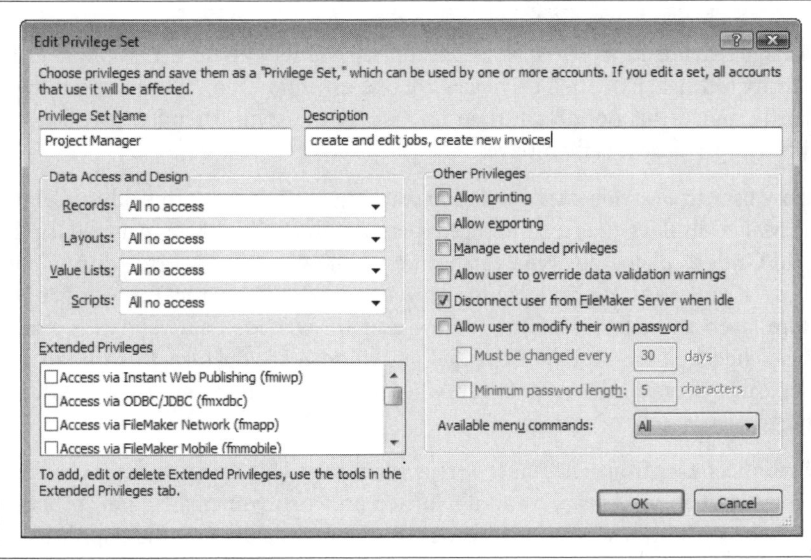

***Figure 16-3:** When you create a new privilege set, FileMaker shows you a window where you can choose its settings. Notice how many things aren't turned on, or say "All no access." This set offers very few privileges.*

This dialog box has a lot of options, divided into three primary sections:

- In the **Data Access and Design** section, you control access to the data (records and layouts). You also decide what kinds of developer operations the user can perform. For example, can she create new layouts? Or edit your scripts? Numerous dialog boxes and dozens of options live behind the pop-up menus in this section.
- **Other Privileges** includes a block of simple checkboxes controlling access to assorted database-wide features like printing, exporting, and password restrictions.
- The **Extended Privileges** section shows a scrolling list of checkboxes. For the most part, these are added by FileMaker to control access to your data from other applications, but you can also add your own custom extended privileges.

You'll learn more about each of these sections in the following pages.

Other Privileges

Draw your attention to the Other Privileges area. Here's where you decide on some basic FileMaker features:

- **Allow printing.** Turn this option on, and the user can print layouts. If you turn this option off, the Print menu command is grayed out, and the Print script step fails.
- **Allow exporting.** This option lets people access the Export Records command. Again, if it's off, the menu command is grayed out, and the Export Records script step doesn't work.

Note: There's a workaround to let scripts do things the active privilege set doesn't let them do (see page 634).

- **Manage Extended Privileges.** Normally, only accounts with full access can manage security settings. Extended privileges are one exception. You'll learn about these shortly, but if this option's turned on, users can assign extended privileges to different privilege sets themselves.
- **Allow user to override data validation warnings.** When you use field validation, FileMaker displays an error message if people enter invalid data in a field. In the Field Options dialog box, you can turn on "Allow user to override during data entry" if you want to give folks the power to ignore this error. But you get one more layer of control with the "Allow user to override data validation warnings" checkbox in the Edit Privilege Set window. If you turn this option off, they can't override the errors even when the field options say they should be able to.
- **Disconnect user from FileMaker Server when idle.** This isn't actually a privilege. It's more of an *un-privilege*, and it's turned on when you create a new privilege set. When it's on, users are kicked out of a shared database if they don't use it for a while (you get to decide how long when you configure FileMaker Server). Turn it *off* if you want to give these users the power to stay connected right through their lunch breaks.

- **Allow user to modify their own password.** FileMaker lets you implement some typical password management features. First, you get to decide if someone can change his account password at all. If you want to give him this power, turn this option on. Once it's on, you can choose "Must be changed every" and enter a number of days to force the user to change his password periodically. You can also enforce a minimum password length.

Note: You probably want to turn this option off if people *share* accounts in the same database. If you have just one account for each group, for instance, you don't want one wisenheimer changing the password on everybody else just for laughs.

- **Available menu commands.** A brand-new privilege set gets full access to the menu bar. Of course most menu commands don't actually *do* anything unless you turn on the appropriate privileges. If you don't want your users running menu commands willy-nilly, you can change the "Available menu commands" pop-up menu. Choose "Editing only" to give these people access only to the Edit menu and basic formatting commands. Choose "None" to turn off every menu command that affects the current database.

Your privilege set needs a few of these options turned on.

1. **For the Project Manager privilege set you're defining, turn on these checkboxes:**
   - Allow printing
   - Allow user to override data validation warnings.
   - Disconnect user from FileMaker server when idle
   - Allow user to modify their own password
2. **Set the "Available menu commands" pop-up menu to "Editing only".**

   That's it for the Other Privileges part of the dialog box. But if you leave the Project Manager privilege set with these settings, your users can't do anything very useful. Next, you'll look at the section where all the granularity is hiding so you can start adding real privileges to the list.

Note: You may have noticed there's no checkbox for "Allow user to manage the database," or "Allow user to create tables." Only accounts with full access can open the Manage Database window and use its features. The same goes for the Accounts and Privilege Sets tabs in the Accounts & Privileges window.

Data Access and Design Privileges

The "Data Access and Design" section of the Edit Privilege Set dialog box is where you control access to your specific database elements. The window has a pop-up menu for Records, Layouts, Value Lists, and Scripts. Right now, the Project Manager privilege set doesn't allow access to any of these. To start adding privileges, click the Records pop-up menu. Figure 16-4 shows all your choices.

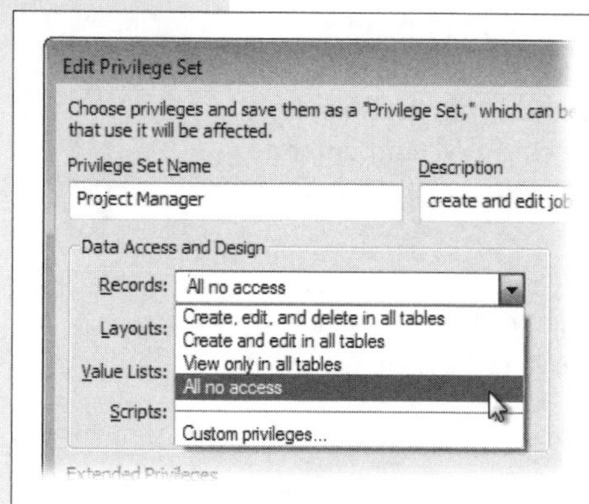

Figure 16-4: *When you click the Records pop-up menu in the Edit Privilege Set window, these are your choices. Like privilege sets themselves, you get a few canned options (the first four). The brave at heart choose "Custom privileges" instead, where even more options await, as discussed below.*

Record privileges

If the three built-in privilege sets form the first level of granularity in the security system, then the options in this pop-up menu are part of the *second* level.

Without much fuss, you can pick one of the prebuilt options:

- **Create, edit, and delete in all tables** is the level you're accustomed to. It lets these people do anything they want with the records—including delete them all.
- **Create and edit in all tables** is almost as good. It just prevents the users from *deleting* records.
- **View only in all tables** is for the browsers among you. They can *see* anything they want, but they can't *change* anything.
- If, for some reason, you want to give somebody access to your *database* but not your *data*, then keep **All no access** selected.

Each of these options applies to *every* record in *every* table. But you may want to let some users "Create, edit, and delete" only in *some* tables, and let them "View only" in others. For instance, you can let part-timers create new customer records, but not tamper with the Expenses table. For that kind of control, choose "Custom privilege" (Figure 16-5).

To modify privileges for a particular table, you first have to select it. But don't waste time: You can select *several* tables if you want to, and then modify the settings for all of them at once. FileMaker even gives you a Select All button so you can easily make a change to *every* table.

For the Project Manager privilege set, you want to give *at least* View access to every table:

1. **From the Records pop-up list, choose Custom Privileges, and then click Select All.**

   FileMaker selects every table in the list.

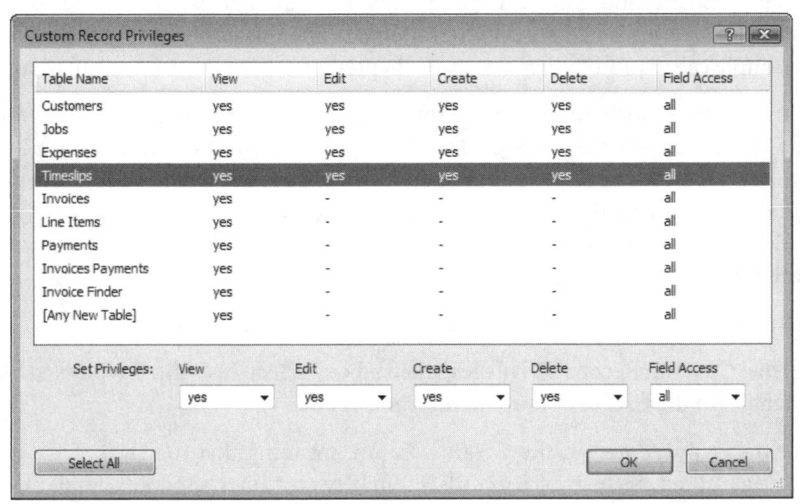

Figure 16-5: *Now you're starting to see some real granularity. The Custom Record Privileges window lets you control view, edit, create, and delete privileges on each individual table. You can also control exactly which fields the users have access to by choosing options from the Field Access pop-up menu.*

2. **From the View pop-up menu, choose Yes.**

   The word "yes" appears in the View column for every table. Accounts with the Project Manager privilege set can see data in every table in the file.

3. **From the Field Access pop-up menu, choose all.**

   This time, "all" appears in the Field Access column. Now project managers can see the contents of every field in all the tables. Project managers need to work with customers, jobs, expenses, and timeslips, so you'll give them access to those tables next.

4. **Click in the list to deselect the group, and then select only the Customers, Jobs, Expenses, and Timeslips tables by holding the Control key (Windows) or ⌘ key (Mac) while you click each one.**

   Managers should be able to create, edit, and delete in those tables, not just view them.

5. **With all four tables selected, choose "yes" from the Edit pop-up menu, the Create pop-up menu, and the Delete pop-up menu.**

Creating record-level access

Invoice privileges are a little more complicated. You want project managers to be able to "create invoices," but invoices involve multiple tables and processes, which you have to translate into a set of privileges. They need to create invoice records, of course, but they also need to be able to create line item records. And once they've added items to an invoice, they should also be able to edit those items. You decide, however, that they *shouldn't* be able to edit items on invoices from last year. In fact, they probably shouldn't change any invoice that isn't dated today. You can handle even a complicated security requirement like this easily in FileMaker: Just add a simple calculation to the mix. (See Chapter 9 for a refresher on calculations.)

When you choose to limit access like this, FileMaker lets you use a calculation to decide which records the users can edit. This calculation gives you tremendous control over the security system. You can use data from the record itself, information about the current date, time, or account name, and even global field or global variable values. Your calculation must return a Boolean result: True if the record should be editable, and False if it shouldn't.

Here are the steps to set up the invoice privileges described above:

1. **In the Custom Record Privileges dialog box, select just the Invoices table. Then, from the Create pop-up menu, choose Yes.**

   FileMaker puts "yes" in the Create column, meaning that managers with this privilege set can create invoice records. From here on, things get more complicated.

2. **From the Edit pop-up menu, choose limited.**

   You don't want the user to be able to edit *any* invoice record. Instead, you're giving them *limited* edit privileges. Your old friend, the Specify Calculation dialog box, appears.

3. **In the calculation box, enter *Date >= Get (CurrentDate)*.**

   This calculation returns a true result when the invoice date is on or after the current date. It's false for invoices dated before today, so FileMaker lets project managers edit only today's invoices.

   You're going to use the exact same calculation shortly, so why bother retyping?

Note: This security calculation has a significant weakness: The user can simply change the date on his computer and bypass the restriction. Luckily, in most cases, a secured multiuser database is shared with FileMaker Server (Chapter 18). When that's the case, you can use a more robust calculation: *Date >= GetAsDate (Get (CurrentHostTimestamp))*. This version uses the Get (CurrentHostTimestamp) function, which gets the date and time from the server computer. Since you, or your IT folks, control this computer, ordinary users can't fiddle with its clock.

4. **Select the entire calculation, and choose Edit → Copy, and then click OK to close the calculation box.**

   Unsurprisingly, you're back in the Custom Record Privileges window. The word "limited…" shows in the Edit column for Invoices.

5. **From the Delete pop-up menu, choose Limited.**

   The Specify Calculation dialog box returns. This time, you're going to limit the managers' ability to delete invoice records. The rule is the same: They can delete only *new* invoices.

6. **Choose Edit → Paste to use the calculation from step 3 here.**

   FileMaker adds the calculation to the calculation box. Click OK when you're done.

   Repeat the above steps for the Line Items table. In this case, though, you want to let managers edit or delete line items when the invoice they're attached to contains today's date. So use the following in steps 3 and 6:

   Invoices::Date ≥ Get (CurrentDate)

   Project managers at your company have no business creating or editing payments or products, so you can leave Edit, Create, and Delete set to "no" for Invoice Payments, Payments, and Products.

Note: FileMaker shows a "–" instead of the word "no" when you turn off a privilege. The dashes make the denied privileges easier to spot when you're looking at a long list.

Field-level access

Suppose you added a field to the Payments table for Credit Card Number. This type of information falls into the *need-to-know* category: Unless someone *needs* it to do his job, he has no business seeing it. Even though project managers can view payment records, you can still control access to individual *fields* in that table. You're about to exercise field-level granularity:

1. **Select the Payments table, and then, from the Field Access pop-up menu, choose Limited.**

   The Custom Field Privileges window appears (Figure 16-6). FileMaker offers three field-level privileges: *modifiable* means users can see *and* edit the field data; *view only* means they can see the information in the field, but can't change it; and *no access* means they can't even see it.

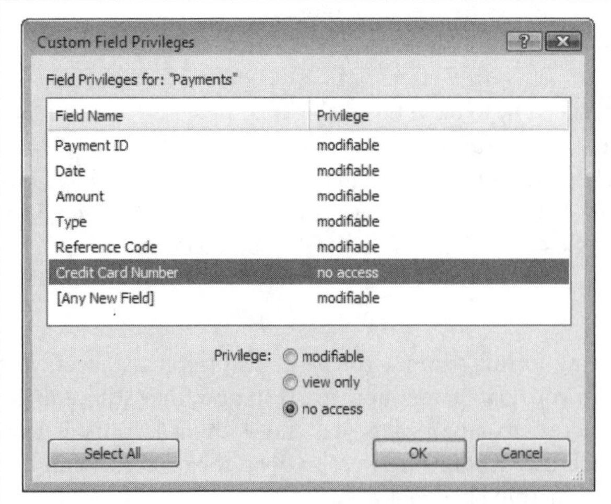

Figure 16-6: *The Custom Field Privileges window lets you control access to individual fields. Select the fields you want to change, and then select one of the Privilege radio buttons. FileMaker dutifully changes every selected field accordingly. Click Select All to quickly select every field.*

2. **Select the Credit Card Number and Credit Card Expiry fields. When they're both highlighted, select the "no access" radio button.**

   And indeed, the words "no access" appear in the Privilege column for the selected fields. Click OK.

Note: Even though the other fields in this list say "modifiable," the entire record isn't editable for these people, so they can't change field data. The record-level security settings effectively trump those at the field level.

The Invoice Finder table has global fields only, so it doesn't need records at all. But you still need to turn on the Edit privilege, so the managers can change values in the globals. Select it and choose "yes" from the Edit pop-up menu. When you're finished, your Custom Record Privileges dialog box should look a lot like the one in Figure 16-7.

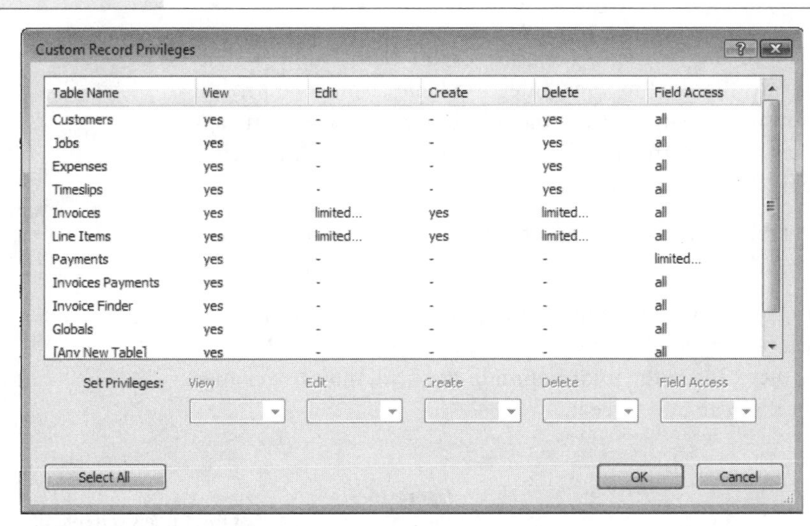

Table Name	View	Edit	Create	Delete	Field Access
Customers	yes	-	-	yes	all
Jobs	yes	-	-	yes	all
Expenses	yes	-	-	yes	all
Timeslips	yes	-	-	yes	all
Invoices	yes	limited...	yes	limited...	all
Line Items	yes	limited...	yes	limited...	all
Payments	yes	-	-	-	limited...
Invoices Payments	yes	-	-	-	all
Invoice Finder	yes	-	-	-	all
Globals	yes	-	-	-	all
[Any New Table]	yes	-	-	-	all

Figure 16-7: *The record privileges for the Project Manager privilege set look like this. Project managers have wide-open access to some tables, limited access to others, and view-only access to a few. Record privileges represent the most granular level of FileMaker's security system.*

When you're done looking, click OK to close this dialog box. Because you just made a set of complex choices, FileMaker sums up everything you just did by displaying "Custom privileges" in the Records pop-up menu in the Data Access and Design section of the Edit Privilege Set dialog box. To review or edit the record-level or field-level access you've set, click "Custom Privileges" in the pop-up menu again.

Layout privileges

If you've been following along in this section, you've given project managers just the right access to the data in your database. But if you stop now, they still can't get very far. They don't have access to any *layouts* yet, and without layouts, a FileMaker database isn't of much use. If someone were to open the database with this privilege set now, she'd see something like Figure 16-8.

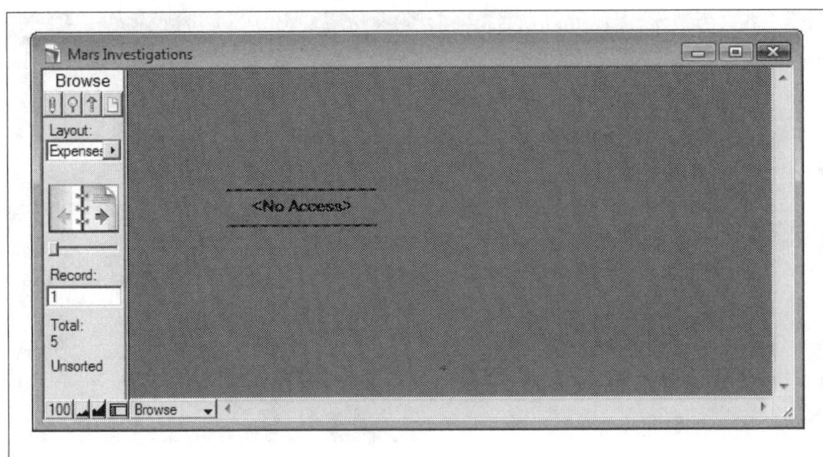

Figure 16-8: *When people try to view a layout they don't have access to, this blank screen is what they see. FileMaker tries hard to avoid this, though; it removes layouts the user can't access from the Layouts pop-up menu. But your scripts can still put them somewhere the user doesn't belong. And in this case, they don't have access to any layout, so FileMaker doesn't have much choice.*

FileMaker uses layouts to display your file's data, which means you'll need to add layout access to your privilege sets. To give your users all-important access to the various database layouts, use the Edit Privilege Set window's Layouts pop-up menu:

- **All modifiable** means the users can use *and* edit every layout. (Here, "edit" means "add fields, delete portals, resize parts, and the whole nine yards.")
- **All view only** gives the users access to every layout, but won't let them change any.
- **All no access** prevents *any* layouts from showing, as shown in Figure 16-8.

The final option—Custom Privileges…—lets you exercise the greatest control over access to specific layouts. Because layouts are a vehicle for the other database items *on* the layout, there are two distinct layers of privilege.

- **Layout.** These privileges control the users' ability to view or edit the layout itself. They're basically the same as the All layout privileges described above, but they apply only to the selected layout. Choose *modifiable* if you want to let people edit the layout (enter Layout mode and move fields and things around), *view only* if you want them only to see it, and *no access* if you want them to see that gray screen thing in Figure 16-8 instead.
- **Records via this layout.** Use this option to determine whether or not the users should be able to see or edit data in fields on a particular layout. If you make records from the Customer layout "view only," you can still edit them from the Customer List layout.

Note: If you want to prevent editing of customer data altogether, it'd make more sense to use the record-level privileges instead. The "Records via this layout" setting is available just in case you want to restrict editing from one particular layout, even though the data in the table can be edited elsewhere.

UP TO SPEED

Any New Anything

Both the table list in the Custom Record Privileges window and the field list in the Custom Field Privileges window have an unusual last item: [Any New Table] and [Any New Field]. These items don't really exist in your database. Instead, when you set privileges for them, you're telling FileMaker how this privilege set should treat any new items that are added later.

Most FileMaker databases are living creatures that grow and adapt constantly. You might add new fields, layouts, scripts, and even tables at any time, so it would be foolhardy to give everybody access to any and every new item. Instead, you'll be more secure assuming that no one gets access to anything new, until you set the new privileges specifically. To implement this more strict security rule, turn off all privileges for the [Any New…] items. In fact, FileMaker already has "any new" turned off whenever you make a new privilege set.

Figure 16-9 shows the Custom Layout Privileges dialog box. This window has something else that didn't exist on the Custom Record Privileges dialog box: The "Allow creation of new layouts" checkbox lets you decide if these people can create their own new layouts. In fact, you can let users who can't even add or edit data create layouts. For example, you might have a whole class of people—the Accounting Department, say—who shouldn't be editing customer records or adding product information, but they need to create monthly and annual reports (read: layouts) *from* that data.

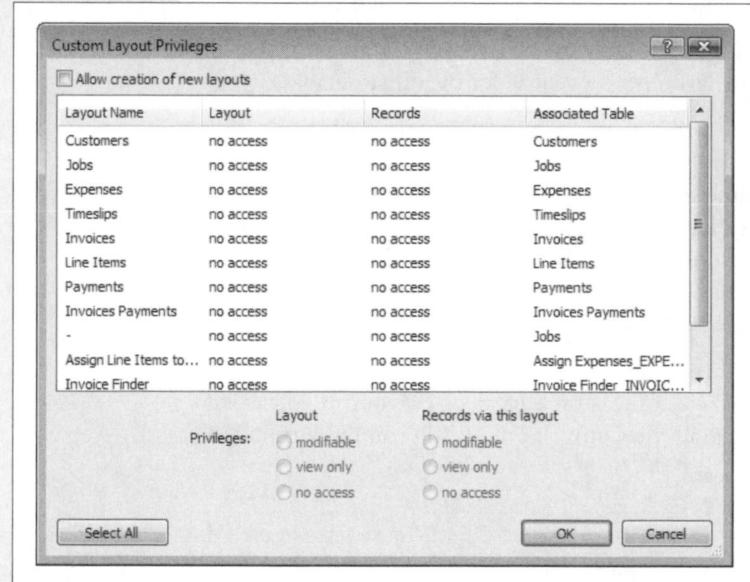

Figure 16-9:
The Custom Layout Privileges window looks a lot like its records counterpart. You get a list of layouts and some privilege choices. Thankfully, there are fewer things to do here, and thus fewer things to learn. As usual, select the layout (or layouts) first, and then make changes.

In the current example, you want project managers to be able to use any layout (and edit records through them). But you also want them to be able to create their own layouts in case they need to do some custom reporting. These new layouts should, of course, be editable.

1. **If you're looking at the Custom Layout Privileges window, click OK to dismiss it and return to the Edit Privilege Set dialog box. Then, from the Layouts pop-up menu, choose "All view only."**

   You really intend to make custom privilege settings, but when you first visit the Custom Layout Privileges dialog box, everything is turned off. Since you want most options on, save your wrist by choosing "All view only," and FileMaker turns them all on for you. In the next step, you'll just turn a few options off.

2. **From the Layouts pop-up menu, choose "Custom privileges."**

   The Custom Layout Privileges window reappears. This time, though, every layout is set to "view only" with "modifiable" records.

3. **Turn on "Allow creation of new layout", and then select the [Any New Layout] item in the layout list.**

   You may have to scroll down to see it, as it's always at the bottom of the list.

4. **Turn on the "modifiable" radio button under Layout.**

   This action tells FileMaker you want new layouts to be modifiable. Click OK when you're done.

If you had tried to click OK without making new layouts modifiable, FileMaker would complain that it doesn't make sense to let someone make a new layout he can't edit. Now, any user with the Project Manager privilege set can edit any new layouts he creates.

Value list privileges

Value lists may not seem as critical a security choice as records and layouts, but since value lists help your users enter consistent data, you want to pay attention to these choices. If you put a pop-up menu on a field to limit data input, but then you give those same users the ability to modify the value list underlying the pop-up menu, they have a way to circumvent your control.

You can see the Custom Value List Privileges window in Figure 16-10. This window lets you assign any of three privileges to each value list: modifiable, view only, or no access. You can also let the user create new value lists with an "Allow creation of new value lists" checkbox, and set the privileges to be assigned to any new value lists.

You can control access to value lists in much the same way you manage record and layout privileges. And like record and layout privileges, you have three canned choices in the pop-up menu, plus Custom privileges:

- **All modifiable** means the users can use and edit every value list.
- **All view only** lets the users see and select from your value lists, but not change them.
- **All no access** prevents the users from seeing value lists at all.
- **Custom privileges** gives you a dialog box where you can create your own set of privileges.

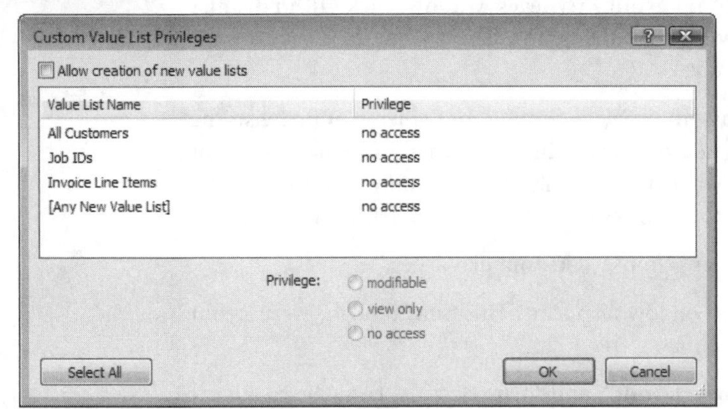

Figure 16-10:
The Custom Value List Privileges window is even simpler than the Custom Layout Privileges version. It works just like the others: Select a value list or two, and then choose a privilege.

In the business rules you're applying to your database, project managers should have view-only access to all value lists, so click Cancel and choose "All view only" from the Value Lists pop-up menu. The Value List access you assign to a privilege set overrides layout designs. That is, even if you set up a pop-up menu with the option of "Include 'Edit…' item to allow editing of value list," users with the Project Manager's privilege set can't edit values in the list.

Script privileges

The final option under 'Data Access and Design" lets you control access to your scripts. As with layouts, it's possible to have a class of users who can create new scripts, but can't edit data. If it's the accountants mentioned in the example on page 611, they need to write scripts to run the reports on the layouts you're letting them create. You could also create a privilege set that lets a level of users run most scripts, but doesn't let them run certain scripts that do destructive activities like deleting sets of records. You could save those scripts for higher-level users instead. Figure 16-11 shows the control choices you have.

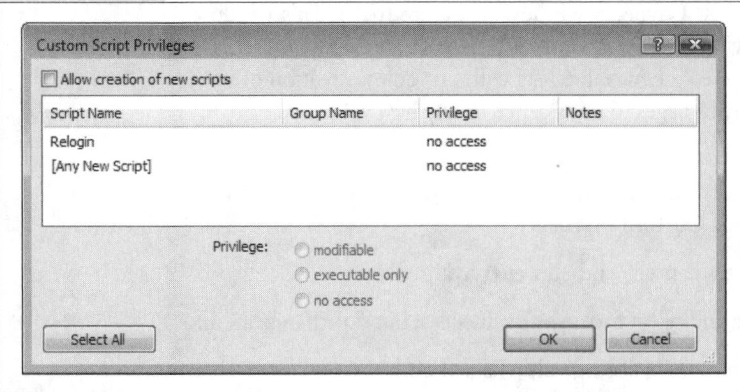

Figure 16-11:
The only thing unexpected in the Custom Script Privileges window is the Notes column in the script list. Since you can't assign notes to a script, you might wonder what exactly this column is for. In fact, it tells you when a script is set to "Run with full access privileges." You'll learn about this later in this chapter.

Again, the pop-up menu gives you three canned choices and a custom option:

- **All modifiable** means the users can run *and* edit any script.
- **All executable only** lets the users *run* scripts, but not edit them.
- **All no access** keeps users from running any scripts at all.
- **Custom Privileges** brings up the now-familiar Custom Privileges dialog box.

For the Project Managers set, choose "All executable only" from the Scripts pop-up menu. With this change, you've finished creating your privilege set. Your window should look just like Figure 16-12.

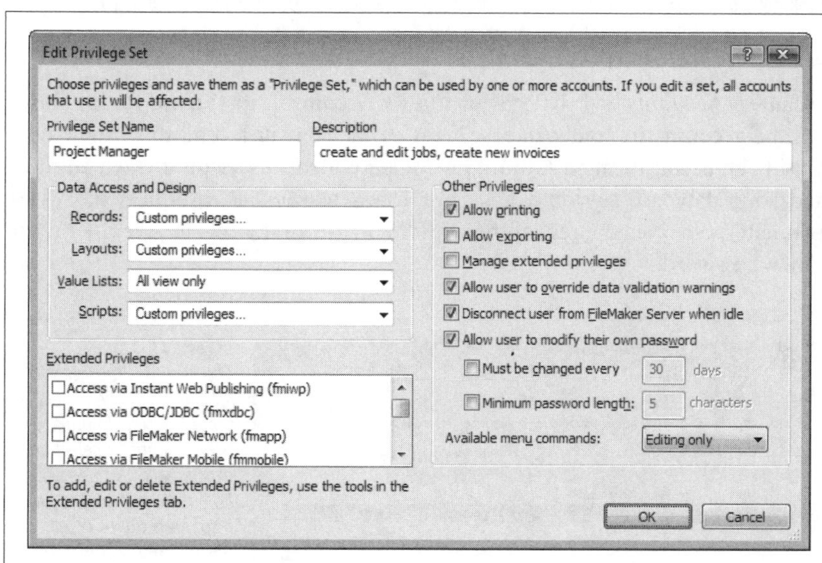

Figure 16-12: *When your privilege set is finished, it looks like this. Sadly, you can't see all your settings in one screen, but the "..." in the Records and Layouts pop-up menus lets you know there's more detail to be seen if you need it.*

To save your new privilege set, click OK. FileMaker adds Project Manager to the list of privilege sets in the Manage Accounts & Privileges window (Figure 16-1).

Note: When you give an element—a record, field, layout, value list, or script—the "no access" setting, it literally disappears from the user's view. Scripts disappear from the Scripts menu, layouts from the Layouts pop-up menu, fields from sort dialog boxes, and records from lists and portals. Your users won't be tempted to run a script or go to a layout they don't have access to.

Editing a privilege set

If you need to make changes to this privilege set later, just come back to this window, select it in the list, and click Edit. You see the Edit Privilege Set window again, and you're free to change anything you want.

You can't edit FileMaker's built-in privilege sets. If you want to change one, duplicate it first and then change the duplicate. Remember, though, that you can't duplicate [Full Access].

Managing Accounts

At the start of this chapter, you learned that there are two facets to FileMaker security: *who* can get in and *what* they can do. So far, you've created a privilege set called Project Manager, which handles the what part of the security equation. But a privilege set has no effect until you tell FileMaker who gets those privileges. You handle the who part by assigning a privilege set to an account. As you can see in the Manage Accounts & Privileges window's Privilege Sets tab, your new privilege set has no "Active accounts" assigned to it. This section covers creating and managing accounts.

Note: You can have privilege sets that don't have active accounts, but you can't create an account without assigning a privilege set to it. If you start creating an account first, and then realize you need a custom privilege set for it, that's OK. Just choose "New Privilege Set…" and create it on the fly.

The Manage Accounts & Privileges window's Accounts tab (Figure 16-13) shows you all the accounts in your database. You never knew it, but all this time you've been using an account called Admin. FileMaker added this account when you first created your database so you'd have full access to the file without a password. Unfortunately, so does the rest of the world. So your first job is to give the Admin account a password.

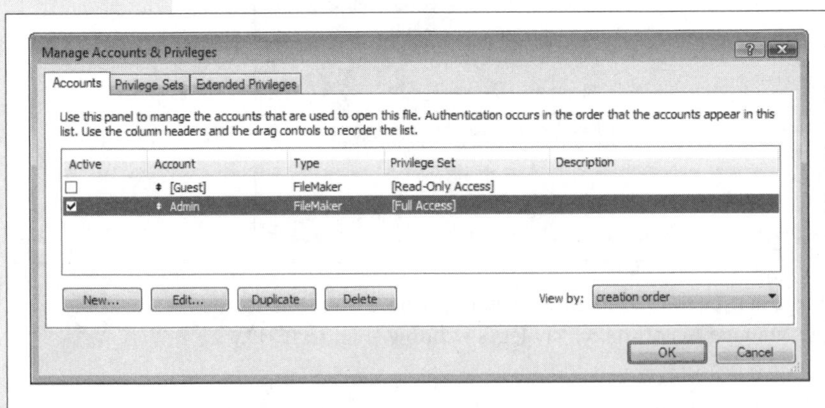

Figure 16-13: *The Accounts tab works a lot like the Privilege Sets tab. Click New to make a new account, or select an existing account and click Edit to change it. You can also duplicate or delete the selected account. Every account has a name (in the Account column), a type, an assigned privilege set (page 611), and an optional description.*

To assign a password to the Admin account, select it from the list on the Accounts tab in the Manage Accounts & Privileges window, and then click Edit (or double-click the Admin account). The Edit Account window appears (Figure 16-14). Type any password in the Password field. Passwords can take any mix of alphanumeric characters and uppercase and lowercase characters you like. (Just remember, although account names aren't case sensitive, passwords are.) Click OK when you're done. Now that you've assigned a password to the Admin account, the next time you open this file, FileMaker will ask you for an account name and password.

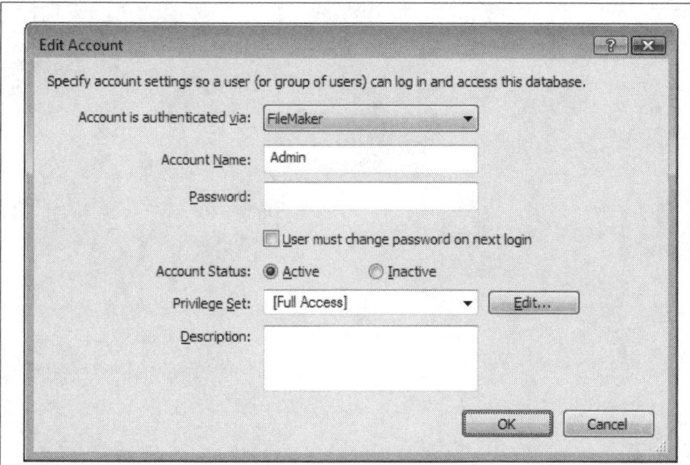

Figure 16-14:
After creating a privilege set, the Edit Account window is refreshingly simple. It's even simpler when you consider that you can completely ignore the "Account is authenticated via" pop-up menu for now. You get to edit the account name and password, make an account inactive (when an account is inactive, FileMaker doesn't let users log in), assign a privilege set, and edit the description.

If you want, you can change the name of the Admin account, too. There's no reason you must have an account called Admin. On the other hand, you're required to have an account with full access. If you try to dismiss this dialog box without one, FileMaker complains. Finally, whenever you click OK in the Manage Accounts & Privileges window, FileMaker wants to make sure you know an account name and password with full access, so it asks you to enter them. If you don't get it right, FileMaker doesn't let you save your changes. This password box is the final layer of protection from losing your file forever.

Warning: Make sure you don't forget your Full Access password. FileMaker uses industry-standard and ultra-secure techniques to manage passwords, and there's simply no way to bypass them. FileMaker, Inc. may be willing to change the password in the file, but the process takes several weeks and is not guaranteed.

If you forget a more restricted password, on the other hand, the fix is simple. Just open the database with a Full Access password, visit the Manage Accounts & Privileges dialog box, and change the forgotten password.

Adding a New Account

Adding a new account is almost as easy as editing an existing one. Since it's so easy to add accounts, there's no reason not to follow best security practices and give everyone an individual account, complete with a unique name and password combination. It's even possible to give people more than one account. For example, you can designate some people as super-users who mostly do data entry and editing but sometimes need to create layouts. As much as you trust them, you just want to make sure they don't inadvertently damage layouts and scripts while they're doing other work. So you require them to log in with higher-level access when switching from data entry to tasks that require more care, like database design. (See page 636 for more detail on re-login.)

FREQUENTLY ASKED QUESTION

Automatic Login

If I've been using the Admin account all this time, how come FileMaker never asked me to log in? Does it just skip the authentication dialog box when some account has no password?

Actually, FileMaker's been logging in for you. Every new database is set up to log in automatically using the Admin account and a blank password. Once you give the Admin account a password for a given database, automatic login stops. But you can set your database to log in with any account automatically, or you can turn off automatic login entirely, which is a much more secure option.

The setting is behind the File → File Options command. When you choose this command, you see the File Options dialog box Turn off the "Log in using" checkbox to stop the automatic login process. Alternately, you can type a different account and/or password in the appropriate box to log in a different way. Finally, you can have FileMaker automatically log in to the file using the guest account (see the box below).

If you set your file to automatically log in with an account that doesn't have full access, including the guest account, you can't come back to this window to turn it off. You may think you've just locked yourself out of your file completely. But you haven't. If you hold down the Shift key (Option key on a Mac) while a file opens, FileMaker asks you for an account name and password even if the file's set to automatically log in.

To create a new account, click New. In the Edit Account window, give the account a name and a password and assign a privilege set. If you don't see a suitable privilege set, choose New Privilege Set from the Privilege Set pop-up menu. You can also edit the selected privilege set by clicking Edit.

If you let each person manage his or her own password, you can turn on "User must change password on next login." When you turn this option on, you can create an account for someone with a generic password, and then email the account information to her, with instructions to create a more secret password when she first opens the database.

UP TO SPEED

The Guest Account

FileMaker has one built-in account called [Guest] that you can't rename or delete. Normally it's assigned to the [Read-Only Access] privilege set, but you can change it to any privilege set you want. The [Guest] account is also normally *inactive*. In other words, it exists, but doesn't work until you turn it on.

If you want to let some people access your database even if they don't have an account, you should activate the guest account by turning on the checkbox by its name. (Or you can bring up the Edit Account dialog box and, in the Account Status option, choose "Active," but that's a lot more work.) When the guest account is enabled, the normal Log In dialog box includes a Guest Account radio button.

Someone can choose this option, and then click OK without entering an account name or a password. FileMaker gives her access according to the privilege set you assigned to the guest account.

Note: If your colleague forgets his password, you can't retrieve it for him because FileMaker masks it as soon as you click OK in the Edit Account dialog box. You can *change* his password, though, so long as you have an account with full access to the file.

You can also make an account inactive. When you do, FileMaker keeps the account—and all its information—in the Accounts list, but it won't let the user open the database. You can make an account inactive if someone leaves the company for an extended period of time, but plans to return. You can easily reactivate the account when you need to. You can also use this option to create accounts for new employees before they start.

Create a new account with the name and password of your choosing. Assign it to the Project Manager privilege set, and then close and reopen the file. When prompted, enter the new account name and password. Now experiment. Try modifying or deleting old invoices, or editing product records. You should see your new security settings in action. When you're done, close the file again and open it one more time. This time use the Admin account to log in.

External Authentication

If you work for an organization that uses Windows Active Directory or Open Directory in Mac OS X, you can take advantage of the fact that your coworkers *already* log in to their computers each morning. Since everybody already has a company-wide user name and password, you can use *external authentication*, which tells FileMaker to hand off the chore of identifying users. This setup has two advantages. First, you can save yourself the trouble of creating scads of accounts in all your database files. And when your IT department creates a new user, or removes someone who's left the company, access to FileMaker is automatically adjusted as well. Additionally, on Windows your users can take advantage of Single Sign-on: They don't have to enter a password to access FileMaker if they already logged in to their computer with their own user name and password.

Note: On Mac OS X, the system-wide Keychain handles automatic login for FileMaker just like every other program. You don't need to use external authentication to speed past the password dialog box. Just click "Add to keychain" the first time you log in instead.

Since these external accounts aren't actually stored in FileMaker, you don't need to add the accounts themselves to your database. Instead, you tell FileMaker which *groups* in the external system should be granted access. For example, if your Windows Active Directory already has a group for Accounting and another for Customer Service, you can tell FileMaker what privileges people in each of these groups have.

If you don't have appropriate groups in the external system, you can have the system administrator add a new group (or several new groups) just for you. You can then assign a privilege set to each group that should be given access, and the system administrator assigns individual users to each group.

To assign a privilege set to an external group, you create a single account in FileMaker. But instead of entering a user name and password, choose External Server from the "Account is authenticated via" pop-up menu. The Account Name and Password boxes disappear, and a new Group Name box appears instead. Just type the name of the Active Directory or Open Directory group in this box.

You can set up external authentication in two ways, but both require a working directory server and FileMaker Server (see Chapter 18):

- **Local accounts on your FileMaker server.** You can manage account names and passwords on the server itself, and have them apply to every database. This method saves you the trouble of creating individual FileMaker accounts in every file.
- **Domain accounts.** FileMaker Server communicates with the directory server on your company's network to authenticate users. This approach centralizes account management *and* lets people log in with the same account name and password they use for every other computer system on your network.

Both methods require coordination with your IT department. Consult them (or the documentation for your directory server) for more information on setting up and maintaining external authentication.

Note: You're free to use a mixture of normal FileMaker accounts and external authentication accounts. In fact, you *must* have at least one full access FileMaker account in every file. If you need to extend access to someone who's not in the directory server, you can add a FileMaker account for that person, too. Users from the directory server will be able to log in, and so will this special person.

Extended Privileges

Extended privileges come in two flavors. There's a set of default extended privileges that lets you determine how your users interact with shared databases. These privileges control how your database works with other FileMaker products (primarily FileMaker Server) so they're covered in Chapter 18. You can also create custom extended privileges of your own. Each extended privilege can be turned on or off for each privilege set you define.

These custom extended privileges don't actually add any capability on their own. Instead, using scripts, you can check to see whether the active privilege set has an extended privilege before you let the user do anything important or irreversible. To use this feature fully, write your scripts with extended privileges in mind. Then, when you need to temporarily give extra power to a particular privilege set, you just turn on a checkbox in the Edit Privilege Set window and all your scripts do the right thing. The next section takes you through one example.

Creating an Extended Privilege

Suppose you've decided to let project managers delete records directly, and you give them that power in their privilege set. When other people try to delete a customer record, you want FileMaker to *flag* the record instead, so that a manager can find and delete the flagged records later. To automate the process, you write a Delete script, using the Get (PrivilegeSetName) function to check whether the person's a manager before deleting the records.

Here's how to set up the extended privileges so you can use them in the script. Open the Manage Accounts & Privileges window, click the Extended Privileges tab, and then click New. You see the Edit Extended Privilege window on your screen. It's also in Figure 16-15. This extended privilege controls a user's ability to directly delete customer records, so put "Directly delete customer records" in the Description box. For the keyword, enter *delcust* as an abbreviation. While you're here, turn on the checkbox next to [Full Access]. For now, only those people with full access can delete customer records. When you're done, click OK.

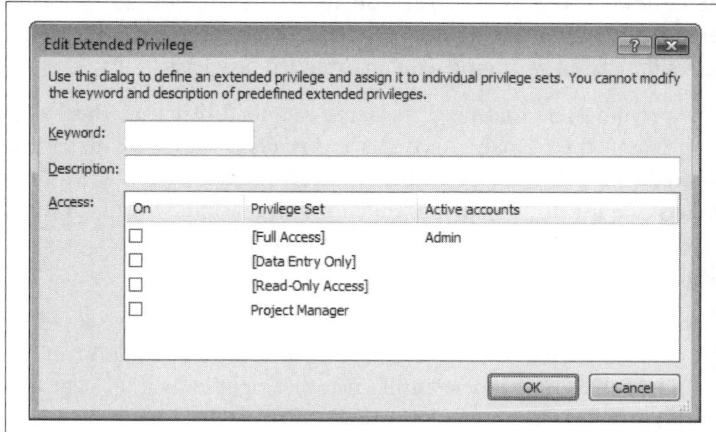

Figure 16-15: *The Edit Extended Privilege window lets you give your extended privilege a keyword and a description. The description should say what the extended privilege is for. The keyword can be anything you want; it's what you'll look for in your scripts, so once you start using an extended privilege, you probably don't want to change its keyword. You can also tell FileMaker which privilege sets have this extended privilege turned on by clicking the Access list's checkboxes.*

Checking for an Extended Privilege

Now you need to write your script. You'll use the Get (ExtendedPrivileges) function to ask FileMaker for the list of extended privileges turned on for the active privilege set. The script checks to see if this list includes "delcust," and takes the appropriate action. While creating this script, you need to add a new text field called Delete Flag to the Customers table. You can see the finished script in Figure 16-16.

Try out your script by running it from the Customers layout. Assuming you're working in the Admin account, the script should delete the customer record, since you have the [Full Access] privilege set. Then close the database and open it again. This time, log in as someone assigned the Project Manager privilege set. Project Manager *doesn't* have the "delcust" extended privilege turned on, so when you run the script this time, it sets the Delete Flag field instead of deleting the record.

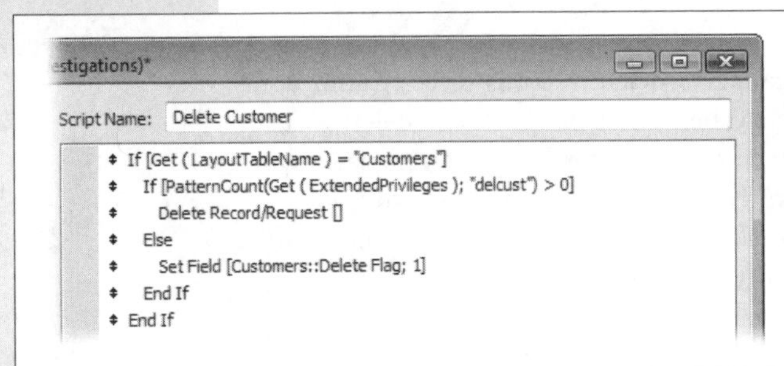

Figure 16-16:
This script first checks to make sure you're on a layout associated with the Customers table occurrence. If not, it refuses to run. If you're on the right layout, it then checks your extended privileges to see if you have the "delcust" privilege turned on. If you do, it deletes the record. If you don't, it sets the Delete Flag field instead.

Assigning Extended Privileges

To give project managers the ability to delete customers directly, which is the whole point of the script you just wrote, you have two options: First, you can edit the Project Manager privilege set itself. The Edit Privilege Set window has a list of extended privileges in the bottom-left corner where you can control which extended privileges are turned on (see Figure 16-17). To give project managers the power to delete customer records, just turn on the checkbox next to "Directly delete customer records." If you're adding it to only a privilege set, editing the privilege set itself is the easiest way to turn on an extended privilege.

If you have a few privilege sets that need the same extended privilege, there's an alternate method: Go to the Manage Accounts & Privileges window's Extended Privileges tab and edit the "delcust" extended privilege instead. This way, you see all the Privilege Sets in a list. In the Edit Extended Privilege window, you can turn the extended privilege off or on for any privilege set by clicking the checkboxes in the list of privilege sets.

To test the "delcust" extended privilege, turn it on for the Project Manager privilege set and close the database. Then open it, log in as a project manager, and run the Delete Customer script. This time it deletes the customer right away. (See page 636 to see how the re-login script step can make testing security settings easier.)

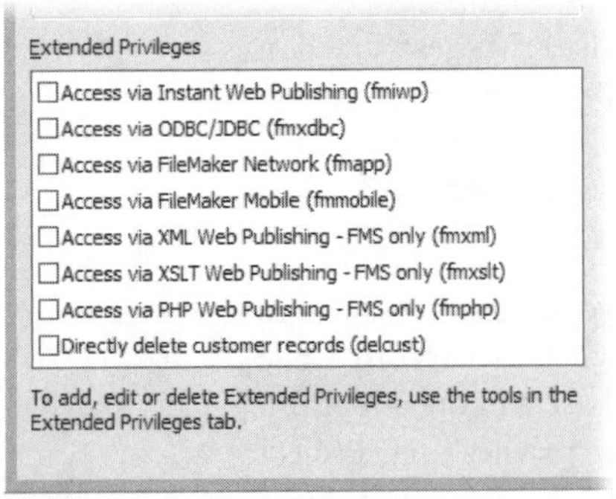

Extended Privileges

- [ ] Access via Instant Web Publishing (fmiwp)
- [ ] Access via ODBC/JDBC (fmxdbc)
- [ ] Access via FileMaker Network (fmapp)
- [ ] Access via FileMaker Mobile (fmmobile)
- [ ] Access via XML Web Publishing - FMS only (fmxml)
- [ ] Access via XSLT Web Publishing - FMS only (fmxslt)
- [ ] Access via PHP Web Publishing - FMS only (fmphp)
- [ ] Directly delete customer records (delcust)

To add, edit or delete Extended Privileges, use the tools in the Extended Privileges tab.

Figure 16-17:
The list of extended privileges in the Edit Privilege Set window shows every extended privilege in the database, each with a checkbox beside it. If you turn one of these checkboxes on, you're giving this privilege set access to everything controlled by that extended privilege.

Scripts and Security

Security and script writing intersect in two areas. First, you need to take into account the level of access people have, and whether or not your scripts will override some or all of their privileges. (The previous section describes one way of doing so with extended privileges.) Second, FileMaker lets you automate some of the security features described earlier in this chapter with scripting. ScriptMaker has a handful of steps dedicated to security-related tasks, and this section shows you how to use them.

Detecting Privileges in a Script

The first way to handle security in your scripts is to deal with it directly. In the last section you learned how to check for extended privileges and take appropriate actions. If you want, you can check for specific privilege sets, or even specific account names.

- To check the privilege set, use the **Get (PrivilegeSetName)** function. It returns the name of the privilege set assigned to the current user. Bear in mind that if you change the name of a privilege set, you have to modify any scripts that use this function.
- If you must restrict an action to a particular account, use **Get (AccountName)** instead. As you probably expect, it returns the name of the account with which the user logged in. The same warning applies here: Beware of renamed accounts.

Note: If the user logged in with external authentication, then Get (AccountName) will give you their real account name in the external directory server.

- Finally, FileMaker has one more tempting function: **Get (UserName)**. This function normally returns the user name from the computer's operating system (the name you use to log in to the computer itself). If you use shared accounts in FileMaker, you may want to use the user name to find out who's actually doing something. Bear in mind, though, that most users can change their user name setting to anything they want, so it isn't useful for security-related purposes.

These functions are easy to use, but they have some drawbacks. Chances are that, at some point in the future, you'll need to change the account names, privilege sets, or users that can do certain things. Every time you do, you have to check and probably edit all your scripts.

Furthermore, the Get (UserName) function has a *severe* limitation: Anybody can change it at any time. In FileMaker's Preferences window, under the General tab, FileMaker lets anyone type in any name they want. This characteristic means it's *easy* for someone to pretend to be someone else. For this reason, you should never rely on the user name for security purposes. If you want to secure a scripted process, the extended privilege feature described on page 630 is safer and makes it much easier to update accounts and privilege sets.

Handling Security Errors

If your script tries to do something the user isn't allowed to do, FileMaker shows the error message in Figure 16-18. If you turn error capture on in your script, this error doesn't show on the screen. Instead, you can use the Get (Last-Error) function to check for an error (see page 582). That way, you can have the script display a custom message box, or email you the name of the misbehaving person, or take some other action. The most common security-related error is number 200: "Record Access is Denied." (If you're interested in learning more about error codes, check out the resources in Appendix B.)

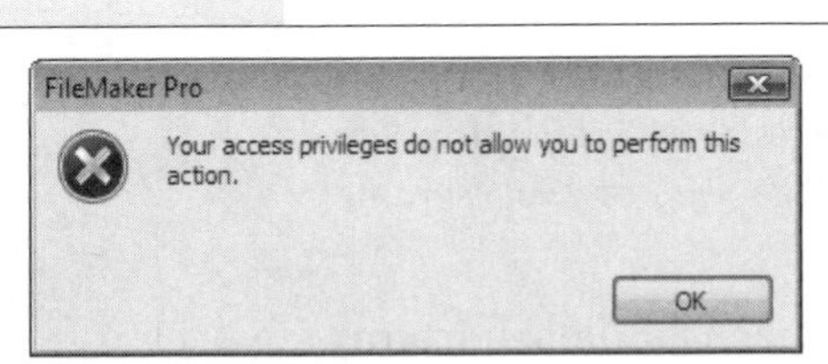

Figure 16-18:
When someone tries something your security setup doesn't allow, he sees this message—even if it's a script that's breaking the rules. Unfortunately, FileMaker doesn't tell him—or you—what the script is trying to do.

Running Scripts with Full Access Privileges

Sometimes you *want* the script to do its duty even though the user doesn't have the necessary privileges. For example, you may want to remove an accountant's ability to delete invoice records since she's not supposed to delete any orders. But you may still want to let her run a script that finds old completed invoices, exports them to an archive, and then deletes them. Since this script is careful to delete only invoices that are ready to go, the accountants can safely run it when necessary.

For those kinds of circumstances, FileMaker lets you specify when a script should run with full access privileges for *anyone*. In other words, the script overrides the normal restrictions you set up in the user's privilege set. At the bottom of the Edit Script dialog box, just turn on the "Run script with full access privileges" option. With this option turned on, the script dutifully deletes the invoices even though the accountant running it isn't allowed to delete records in the Invoice or Line Item tables herself.

Even when you set a script to run with full access privileges in this way, you can still prevent some folks from running it by switching it to "no access" in the Custom Script Privileges window for a privilege set (page 611). You can also make the script check for an extended privilege and take appropriate actions for different people.

Managing Security with Scripts

ScriptMaker's Edit Script window (Figure 13-2) has an entire section called Accounts. It includes six steps that give you some control over the security system from your scripts. All these steps require full access privileges to work. If you don't manage a lot of accounts in your database, you might not find much use for these steps. But if you have a large organization, or one that has lots of turnover—like a school system that's constantly adding new teachers or graduating a whole class of students who no longer need access to databases for class work—these script steps can save tons of time and effort.

Add Account

FileMaker actually lets you add new accounts to a database from a script—and for good reason. If you build a system that uses several databases, and you can't use external authentication, the Add Account step is your best friend. Instead of adding each account to all your files manually, try this: Write a script that asks for the account name and password with a custom dialog box, and stores them in global fields. Then use scripts in each file to add the same account to every file at once. When you're all done, be sure to clear the password from the global field to protect it from prying eyes.

Or, if you have to populate your brand-new file with a huge number of users when you're first installing your database, you save tons of time creating accounts if you have an electronic list of user names and passwords. Import them (page 657) into a table, and then use a looping script to create hundreds of accounts in a few seconds. The Add Account step lets you specify the account name and password using calculations, but you have to select a specific privilege set for all users in the loop. If you want to script the creation of accounts with different privilege sets, use the If/Else If steps and several copies of the Add Account step.

Delete Account

If you're going to create accounts with a script, why not delete them, too? The Delete Account script needs only an account name—and you can supply it with a calculation. With this script, you can build the other half of your multifile account management system.

Warning: If you write a script that adds or deletes accounts, pay special attention to its security settings. It's all too easy to give a database the tightest security FileMaker allows, and then leave a gaping security hole through a script. Customize privilege sets so that only you (or a trusted few) can run it, and *don't* put it on the Scripts menu.

Reset Account Password

If lots of people use your database, forgotten passwords will undoubtedly become your worst nightmare. You could spend all day changing passwords for people. Why not write a script that can reset a password to something generic and then email it to the user? If you set the script to run with full access privileges, you can even delegate password resetting to someone else. The Reset Account Password step needs an account name and a new password to do its job.

Change Password

This odd step doesn't see the light of day very often. After all, folks can change their own passwords with the File → Change Password command (it shows only in accounts that don't have full access). You could use this step to create a Change Password button if you have users who aren't very good at remembering where menu commands are either.

Enable Account

Once you've created a bunch of new accounts using the Add Account step, the Enable Account step lets you turn them on and off at will. That way, you can create accounts for, say, an entire class of students, and later turn on accounts for those who've arrived on campus. This step does the same thing as *make active* and *make inactive* in the Edit Accounts dialog box, and it works only when there's a valid account name.

Re-Login

The most exciting step in the Accounts section is Re-Login. It provides a function that doesn't exist anywhere else in FileMaker. Namely, it lets you switch to a different account without closing the file, which gives you almost superhuman ability to test security settings. Instead of opening and closing the files until your mouse button wears out, just run a Re-Login script. Add steps in the script that set global fields on pertinent layouts to Get (AccountName) and Get (PrivilegeSet) so you can keep track of what you're testing as you re-login over and over.

You can also use Re-Login when someone inevitably calls you to his desk to show you a problem in the database. Just re-login as an account with full access and then you can poke around and find out what's happening *on his computer*. When you re-login, you're not just saving time by not closing and reopening the file. You can actually work in the same window, on the same record, with the same found set and sort order without all the trouble of recreating the situation back at your desk. Again, since you can re-login only from a script, consider adding a Re-Login script to the Scripts menu in every database you create.

CHAPTER 17

Sharing Data with Other Systems

You may have forgotten it by now—building a big database can make you feel like a slave to your computer—but the point of a database is to make managing information more efficient. Nothing illustrates this point more quickly than FileMaker's ability to suck data into your database from various sources, and dump it back out again in assorted ways.

If you have data in almost any kind of program—spreadsheets full of figures, lists of names and phone numbers, electronic orders in XML, folders full of pictures or text documents—FileMaker can *import* it directly into your database. If your data is already in FileMaker, then you can *export* it to lists, other databases, XML, or almost any other format imaginable. FileMaker takes a wonderfully flexible approach: It lets you handle simple imports and exports with just a click or two, and provides the features to tackle the most complex cases as well—if you (or some hired help) are willing to do the necessary work.

If your company uses one of the vast corporate databases—Oracle, Microsoft SQL Server, or MySQL—FileMaker Pro 9 can integrate directly with them, bringing its powerful (and easy) developer tools to bear on their complex-yet-oh-so-speedy data. You can put your corporate SQL data right on the FileMaker layout, perform FileMaker finds, write scripts, and even add calculation fields, all without writing a single line of SQL code.

Sharing Your Data with Others

Most database systems don't live in a vacuum. Chances are your information is important to someone else, or important to you some*where* else. You may want to transfer job information to your Accounting software, or send the sales report to your associate across town. Luckily, FileMaker provides options for getting the data out of your database in copious forms.

Save/Send Records As

If your data is destined for a *person* (rather than some other computer program), then you want a format that's easy to look at and to work with on almost any computer. FileMaker lets you save your data in two ubiquitous formats: an Excel spreadsheet and a PDF document. Choose Excel if you want to be able to work with the data (perform analysis, combine it with other data, create graphs, and so forth). But if you want the output to look just like it looks in FileMaker, and you don't need it to be editable, then a PDF is the perfect choice.

Saving as Microsoft Excel

If people need to work with the data you send them, but they aren't lucky enough to have FileMaker, you can create an Excel file for them. (And presumably, if they're working with data, they either have Excel or a program that can open Excel spreadsheets.) Just choose File → Save/Send Records As → Excel. When you do, FileMaker shows the window in Figure 17-1.

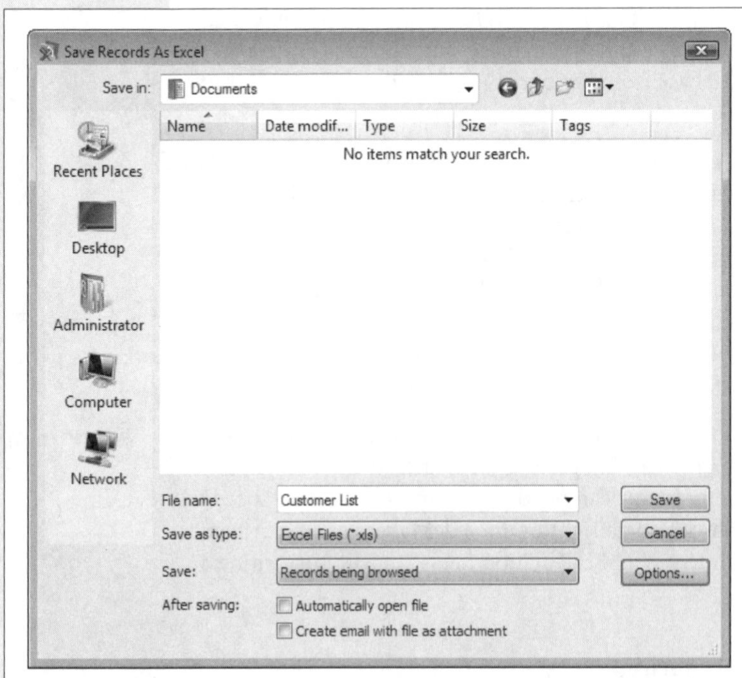

Figure 17-1: *The Save Records As Excel window lets you tell FileMaker where to save the spreadsheet file. It also gives you the option of automatically opening the file you're creating, so you don't have to go rummaging around your hard drive looking for it.*

The Save pop-up menu lets you choose whether you want to save all the "Records being browsed" (that is, the found set) or just the "Current Record." Turn on "Automatically open file" if you want to see the spreadsheet as soon as FileMaker finishes saving it. When you do, FileMaker automatically launches Excel and shows you the spreadsheet. You also have the option to "Create email with file as attachment," so it's easy to check your work and create a quick email with the data your boss just asked to email her. Once you save, FileMaker will create a new email message in your email program, attach the spreadsheet, and pop it up on your screen so you can add recipients, a subject, and any body text you want.

If you click Options, you can set up some basic details for your new Excel file. For example, you can choose whether you want your FileMaker field names put in the first row of the spreadsheet. You can also type in a worksheet name and a title, subject, and author (each of which appear in the spreadsheet in the appropriate places).

Saving as Portable Document Format (PDF)

PDF files are viewable by just about anybody with a computer. With PDF files, you get to choose exactly how the data looks, since this format preserves your beautifully crafted layouts. With FileMaker's layout tools, your keen design sense, and the "Save/Send Record as PDF" command, you could use email to distribute invoices, product catalogs, sales brochures, or annual reports. You can even send vision-impaired people a file their software can read out loud. Even if all you need to do is send people data they can see but can't change, then a PDF file is just what the software engineer ordered.

Note: The most common PDF viewer, Adobe Acrobat, is a free download at *www.adobe.com/products/acrobat/readstep2.html*. Mac OS X also comes preloaded with its own PDF viewer, called Preview.

The basic choices are the same as for Excel. You choose between sending just the current record or the whole found set. You can have the file opened in a PDF viewer or attached to a new, blank email just as soon as FileMaker's created it. But behind the Options button you'll find a much richer set of choices. There are three tabs—Document, Security, and Initial View. Starting with the Document tab, you can set:

- **Title.** This title isn't the name you give the file in the dialog box. It's an additional title that becomes part of the properties of the document. Most, but not all, PDF viewer programs let you see a file's properties.
- **Subject.** This document property helps you tell a series of similar documents apart from each other.
- **Author.** This document property is usually your name, but may also be the name of your company or department. Again, it helps you organize a bunch of similar files.

- **Keywords.** Some file management programs can search these keywords to locate documents.
- **Compatibility.** Choose from "Acrobat 5 and later" or "Acrobat 6 and later." Choose the lower number if you think your recipient might not have the latest and greatest PDF viewer.
- **Number pages from.** You can make a different numbering system than the one you have in FileMaker.
- **Include.** You can set a limited page-number range with these options, so that only a part of the found set is included in the PDF file. You may have to go to Preview mode in FileMaker first, though, to help you set the page range properly.

Note: You can see the PDF file's Title, Subject, and Author in Adobe Acrobat's PDF viewer's Document Properties Summary window. In Mac OS X's Preview program, choose Tools → Get Info instead.

In the Security Tab, you can decide how much access you give your recipients when they receive your file. You can choose:

- **Require password to open the file.** Click the checkbox to turn this option on, and then enter a password. This checkbox is useful if you're selling a catalog and provide passwords only to people who've paid to receive it. Then, of course, there's the standard use; you just don't want every Malcolm, Reese, and Dewey poking around in your PDF files.
- **Require password to control printing, editing and security.** Click the checkbox to turn this option on and enter a password. You might want your PDF freely distributed, but not so freely used. If so, don't require a password to open the file, but lock it down so nobody without a password can use the material without your permission. With this option checked, a whole raft of new options becomes available. You can set:
- **Printing.** Choose from Not Permitted, Low Resolution (150 dpi), or High Resolution. These options would protect photographic or other artwork images that you want to send in a catalog but don't want people to reprint freely. You also may want someone to *see* your document onscreen, but not print it and risk having it fall into the wrong hands.
- **Editing.** Although PDF files are generally considered view-only, with the right software, they can actually be edited. If you don't want to allow this (or want to restrict what can be done), choose options from this pop-up menu. For example, if you're sending a contract for review, and you want to be sure no new clauses are snuck in while it's away, you can choose **Not permitted.**
- **Enable copy of text, images and other content.** With this option checked, recipients can copy and paste material from your PDF file.
- **Allow text to be read by screen reading software.** This option lets people with vision or reading problems have their screen reading programs read your document out loud.

The final tab in the PDF Options window is probably the one you'll use the least. But if you like to control which PDF viewer options are visible when your recipient first opens your PDF file, then Initial View is the panel for you:

- **Show.** Your choices include **Page Only** (just the FileMaker layout, with no extra tools or panels), **Bookmarks Panel and Page**, or **Pages Panel and Page** to offer viewers some navigation options.
- **Page Layout.** Control the way the PDF viewer displays multipage documents. If you choose *Default*, your recipients' preferred view remains in force. But you can also specify **Single Page**, **Continuous**, or **Magnification**.

Note: These Initial View options may or may not actually take effect, depending on what program and what version of that program the PDF is opened with.

External SQL Sources

If you don't know MySQL from MySpace, and have no interest in taking your humble FileMaker skills to the hard-core level of IT professionals, then feel free to skip right past this section. For those of you who *do* have to cross between these worlds, or who need to bring the power and capability of industrial-grade database servers into your systems, FileMaker's new *External SQL Sources* (or ESS) feature will seem like magic.

In a nutshell, you point your FileMaker database in the general direction of an Oracle, Microsoft SQL Server, or MySQL (pronounced "my sequel") database (heretofore referred to as a SQL database). FileMaker then absorbs information about that database, learning all it needs to know to make those normally complicated systems almost as easy to use as FileMaker. You can create table occurrences in your relationship graph that are actually references to the tables in the SQL database. You can draw relationship lines between SQL tables, or even between your FileMaker tables and the SQL tables. You can create a layout based on a SQL table, drop a few fields on the layout, and then jump to Find mode, from which FileMaker will search the real honest-to-goodness SQL data and show you a found set of records.

With few exceptions, a SQL table works just like any other FileMaker table. But instead of storing the data on your hard drive, the SQL database stores and manages the data. You don't need to know a lick of SQL programming to make this work. When you add a record using the Records → New Record command, FileMaker sends the right secret code that adds the record to the SQL database. Just type in a field and press Enter, and FileMaker updates the SQL database. It doesn't get more seamless this.

Setting Up ODBC

Before you can take advantage of ESS, you need to set up a few things. This business of getting things installed and configured is the hardest part—and it's not FileMaker's fault.

The SQL database server

First of all, you need a SQL database. To integrate as seamlessly as it does, FileMaker needs to know exactly which database you're using:

- Microsoft SQL Server 2005
- Microsoft SQL Server 2000
- Oracle 10g
- Oracle 9g
- MySQL 5.0 Community Edition

If your SQL database isn't in this list, you'll need to upgrade or migrate to one of these. Trying to make a different type of database work is futile—just ask someone who's tried. Luckily, this list represents recent versions of three very popular database systems. If you don't have a SQL database, but you want to get one, you'll need to do some research to decide which is best for you. But if you just want to experiment, start with MySQL. For most purposes (including real commercial use), it's completely free. To get MySQL for Mac OS X or Windows, visit *www.mysql.com* and look for the MySQL Community Server link.

The rest of this section assumes you have a working SQL database server, and that you have access to at least one database on that server.

Installing the ODBC driver

In order for FileMaker to communicate with the SQL database, you need an ODBC driver. This software acts as the bridge between programs on your computer and the SQL database server software. The driver is specific to your database server. If you're using Oracle, you need an Oracle ODBC driver, for instance. If you use Microsoft Windows, this step is usually a breeze. Each of the supported SQL databases has an ODBC driver provided by the manufacturer. Just visit their Web site and find out how to get the driver you need.

Note: If you're not sure what you need, try searching the Web for *microsoft sql server odbc driver download*. The first site listed will probably be the download page you need. (Substitute *oracle* or *mysql* for *microsoft sql server*, as appropriate.)

Mac OS X users aren't so lucky. The big database developers don't provide free ODBC drivers for the Mac. Instead, head over to *www.actualtechnologies.com*, and purchase the right driver (they're cheap and work beautifully). FileMaker, Inc. worked directly with Actual to ensure maximum compatibility, and they provide the drivers of choice. (For MySQL, choose the driver called *ODBC Driver for Open Source Databases*.)

Once you've acquired the correct driver, install it on your computer. After you've installed the driver, you need to do some configuration.

Configuring the data source

Your computer's operating system has the ODBC system built in. You use a special program on your computer to tell it which SQL databases you want to work with. The configuration process is entirely different on Mac OS X and Windows, so go directly to the section that applies to you.

Configuring data sources on Windows. You configure your Windows machine for ODBC in the Control Panel (Start → Control Panel). The control panel looks a little different in various Windows versions:

- On Windows Vista, you may see a category called "System and Maintenance." Open this category, and click Administrative Tools at the bottom of the list. If you don't see "System and Maintenance," look for Administrative Tools in the Control Panel window and open it.
- On Windows XP, you may see a category called "Performance and Maintenance." Open this category and click Administrative Tools. If you don't have "Performance and Maintenance," look for Administrative Tools right in the Control Panel window and open it.

Assuming you've found the Administrative Tools window, look inside it and open Data Sources (ODBC). You should see something on your screen that looks like Figure 17-2.

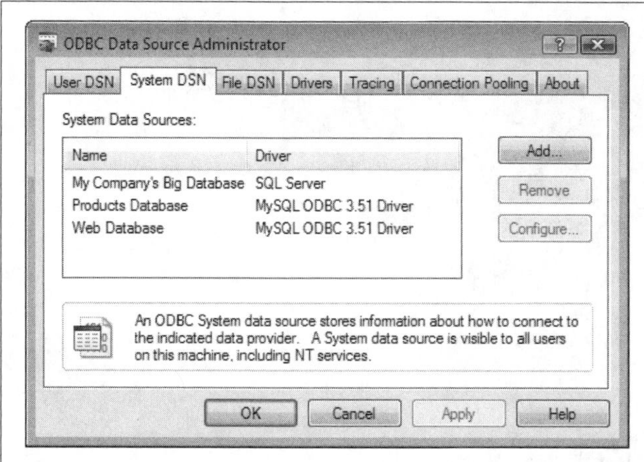

Figure 17-2:
The ODBC Data Source Administrator on Windows lets you configure the SQL databases your computer has access to. The acronym DSN stands for Data Source Name, since you name each data source you define here, and then refer to it by name in FileMaker.

In this window, you add a *DSN (data source name)* for each SQL database you want FileMaker to work with. A DSN can be one of two flavors: A *System* DSN is available to all users on your computer; and a *User* DSN is available only to the person who creates it. FileMaker works only with the System DSN variety, so to get started, switch to the System DSN tab. Unfortunately, you may not have permission to define these computer-wide data sources on your work computer. If Windows won't let you add a system DSN, contact your system administrator.

Once you're on the System DSN tab, click Add. Windows shows you a list of available ODBC drivers. Select the appropriate one and click Finish. (Don't get too excited by the label on this button; you're nowhere near finished.)

Note: The list of available drivers on Windows can be a little confusing. First, you may see many drivers whose names are apparently in a foreign language. Just scroll right past them. Also, you may be tempted to select the driver called SQL Server. After all, every database FileMaker works with could legitimately be called a SQL database server. But this driver is specifically for *Microsoft* SQL Server. If you use one of the other database systems, keep looking.

WORKAROUND WORKSHOP

The Case of the Missing Driver

A bug in the MySQL ODBC driver installer can leave your ODBC system in a confused state where it stops showing new ODBC drivers you've installed (even non-MySQL drivers). If you installed your driver but it isn't in the list, don't beat yourself up. You didn't do anything wrong.

The fix requires a trip to the RegEdit program, where non-technical folks rarely dare to tread. Luckily, the steps are straightforward. Just follow them exactly, and you'll be fine. If you're worried, show this page to your nerdiest friend (or anyone under 20) and ask for help.

1. Run the RegEdit program.

   On Windows Vista, click the Start button and, in the search panel, type *regedit*. Then click regedit.exe at the top of the Start menu. On Windows XP, click Start → Run, type *regedit* in the box that pops up, and then click OK.

2. Choose File → Export and save your current registry someplace safe.

   On the off chance you mess up here, you can restore your old settings by running RegEdit again and using the File → Import command.

3. In the folder list on the left side of the window, click the plus signs to expand each of these folders in succession: HKEY_LOCAL_MACHINE, SOFTWARE, ODBC, and ODBCINST.INI.

   The Windows registry works like a hierarchy of folders, and you're digging your way down to the thing you need to change.

4. Select the ODBC Drivers folder inside ODBCINST.INI.

   RegEdit fills the list on the right with what looks a lot like the list of ODBC drivers.

At this point, you need to look for the problem. At the top of the list on the right side, you see an entry called "(Default)" (with parentheses and all). In the Data column for that line, it should say "(value not set)." If the top row of the data column is empty, or has a pair of quotation marks, then you're a victim of the bug. Just select the "(Default)" item and press the Delete key on your keyboard. The words "(value not set)" should appear where they weren't before.

Close RegEdit and, if prompted, agree to save the changes. Now exit the Data Sources control panel and open it again. You should see your driver.

From this point forward, configuration works a lot like Mac OS X. Skip ahead to "Finishing data source configuration" on page 645.

Configuring data sources on Mac OS X. On Mac OS X, you configure ODBC data sources using an application called ODBC Administrator. You can find this program in your Applications → Utilities folder. When you launch the program, you see the window in Figure 17-3.

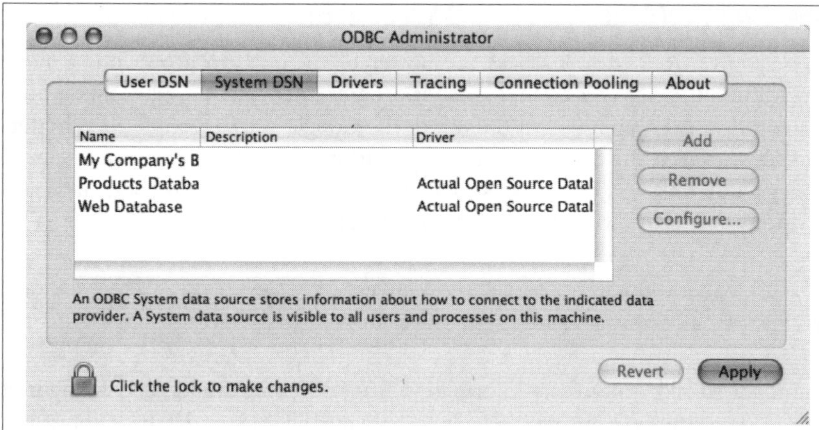

Figure 17-3: *The ODBC Administrator on Mac OS X lets you create ODBC data sources. You need to be logged in to your computer as an administrator to be able to create the kind of data source FileMaker needs. You also may need to click the padlock icon in the bottom-left corner of this window before you can make changes.*

When you open ODBC Administrator, first click the padlock icon in the bottom-right corner to unlock it. Then click the System DSN tab. (FileMaker works only with system-wide data sources.) Next, click Add. A sheet slides down showing a list of ODBC drivers installed on your computer. Select the one you want, and then click OK.

At this point, the exact configuration will vary based on the driver you're using.

Finishing ODBC data source configuration. The exact setup procedure varies with each ODBC driver, but a few things remain constant:

- On Mac OS X, even though you're in the System DSN tab, you'll be given the option to create either a *user* or a *system* DSN. Make sure you choose *system*.
- Give the data source any name you like. You'll use this name later when you connect FileMaker to the database. But bear in mind if you *change* a name here, you'll have to update every FileMaker database that uses it or the connections will break.
- The description is not important. Leave it blank, or leave a note for yourself.
- You need to know the address (IP address or host name) of the database server, as well as a user name and password. You also need to know the name of the database you're connecting to (not Oracle or MySQL, but the name of the actual database on the server, like Products or Financial).
- Your driver may ask lots of questions, but you can usually accept the pre-entered answers for most of them. If you're not sure, talk to your database administrator. If you don't have a database administrator, make friends with one.
- On the last page of the setup process, you get a chance to test data source. Click this button—it tells you whether all the info you just entered is correct. Better to find out now than when FileMaker gets confused later on.

Once you're finished, you see your data source listed in the System DSN tab of your ODBC configuration program. Go ahead and close the window. Your configuration work is finished.

Connecting FileMaker to a SQL Data Source

Suppose you've decided to harness the power of the Web to grow your private investigation business. You hired a hotshot programmer to build you a sweet little Web site that's sure to put you at the top of the Google search results. Even better, visitors to your Web site can fill out an inquiry form asking for your help. The programmer set up the site so the form submissions go directly into a MySQL database. Now you want to work with that data in FileMaker.

Tip: You can see a screencast of attaching a FileMaker database to a MySQL from a Web site that gathers sales leads. Visit *www.missingmanuals.com*.

You've acquired all the necessary information from the programmer, and configured an ODBC data source. Your next step is to tell your FileMaker database about the SQL database:

1. **Open the FileMaker database you've been building, or download a copy from the Missing Manual Web site. Then choose File → Manage → External Data Sources.**

   Here's where you tell your database about other places it can find data. You used this same window to connect one FileMaker database to another (see page 383). This time, though, you're going to connect to a non-FileMaker database.

2. **Click New.**

   FileMaker shows you the Edit Data Source window.

3. **In the Name box, type *Web Leads*.**

   You can name the data source anything you want. This name will show up when you're choosing tables to add to the Relationship graph.

4. **Click the ODBC radio button below the Name box.**

   FileMaker revamps the dialog box so it looks like the one in Figure 17-4.

5. **Click Specify.**

   You see a list of all the system ODBC data sources defined on your computer.

6. **Choose the data source you want to connect to, and then click OK.**

   FileMaker puts the data source name in the box next to DSN.

At this point you have a decision to make. When you (or one of your users) opens this database, should it automatically connect to the SQL database with no further user interaction? If so, you need to tell FileMaker what user name and password to log in to the SQL database with. If you don't set the user name and password here, you'll have to enter it every time you open the file. (That's the preferred setup, though, if each user of your database has different permissions in the SQL database.)

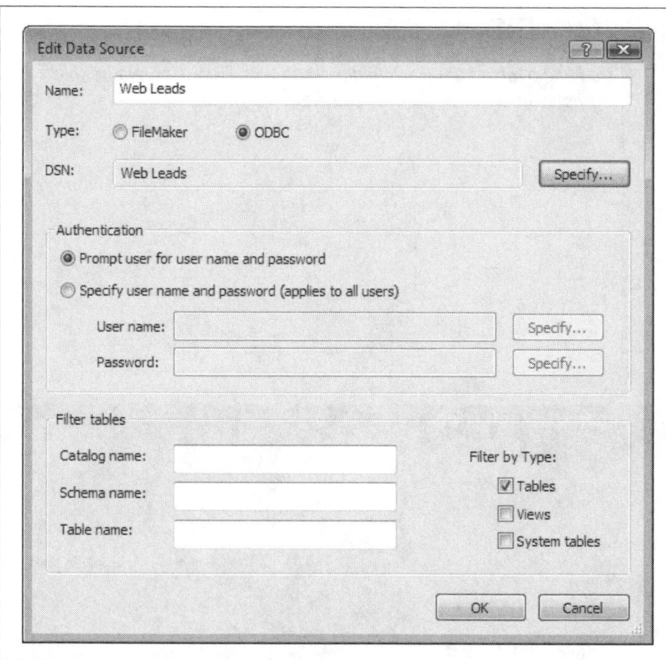

Figure 17-4: *When you turn on ODBC, the Edit Data Source window takes on a whole new look. Instead of just the path to a FileMaker database, you tell FileMaker which ODBC data source to connect to, the user name and password to use, and which SQL objects you want to see. Don't worry if these terms don't make sense yet. You'll learn about them later in this chapter, and many of them don't matter much.*

Note: You may be wondering why you have to enter a user name and password here at all, since you already typed them in when you created the ODBC data source. It turns out the ODBC system just really wants that information so it can test your data source and ease configuration. It doesn't actually *use* that login info when you open the database.

In this case, turn on "Specify user name and password (applies to all users)," and type the user name and password for your SQL database. Click OK to tell FileMaker you're done. Click OK again in the Manage External Data Sources window to get back to your database.

Adding SQL Tables to a FileMaker Database

Your database now has a pipeline to the tables in a SQL data source. But you haven't told it what to do with those tables yet. Your next stop is the Relationships tab of the Manage Database window, where you can fold the SQL database tables into your overall system.

Choose File → Manage → Database, and switch to the Relationships tab. Then click the Add Table button, just as though you were adding a normal FileMaker table occurrence. But this time, when the Specify Table window pops up (Figure 17-5), click the Data Source pop-up menu and choose Web Leads (or the name of *your* SQL data source).

The list below the pop-up menu changes to show all the available tables in the SQL database. Choose the table you're interested in, adjust the table name as necessary (in the Name box at the bottom of the window), and then click OK.

***Figure 17-5:** Once you've worked through the complexity of ODBC configuration, adding a table from a SQL database to your FileMaker relationship graph works exactly the way you'd expect: simple.*

POWER USERS' CLINIC

Advanced ODBC Data Source Options

At the bottom of the Edit Data Source window, you see a section labeled "Filter tables" (Figure 17-4). These settings are entirely optional, but may prove very useful if you are connecting to a complex database system. These settings tell FileMaker which tables you consider important, and which ones it can safely ignore. Doing so means you don't have to look at very long lists as you build your database, and helps FileMaker keep things running as quickly as possible.

Database terminology is inconsistent from one system to another. The "Filter tables" section gives you three empty boxes to fill in, some with mysterious names. Here's how it shakes out:

- If you use Oracle, the Catalog box is irrelevant: leave it empty. In the Schema box, you can enter a user name. When you do, FileMaker will only look at tables owned by that user.
- If you use Microsoft SQL Server, you can put the name of a particular database in the Catalog box to limit FileMaker to only tables in that database. If you use schemas, or collections of tables and views, you can also restrict FileMaker to just one schema.
- If you use MySQL, the Catalog box has no bearing on things, so you can leave it empty. If you want to see only tables for a particular user, enter the user name in the Schema box.Whatever your database, if you care only about one particular table, enter its name in the Table Name box. FileMaker will then show that table alone.

To the right of these three boxes, FileMaker offers three checkboxes. In the world of SQL databases, there are two or three *different* things that all act like tables.

- **Tables** are real honest-to-goodness tables, a lot like their FileMaker counterpart.
- **Views** are sort of like smart folders in iTunes or your mail program: They show portions of one or more tables based on criteria defined on the database server. If you're accessing a complex database, and you need read-only access to a specific portion, you might consider asking your database administrator to create a view that includes just the data you need. This will make things simpler for you down the road.
- **System tables** are tables the database system creates itself for various purposes. (MySQL doesn't have this kind of table, so don't fret about it if you're a MySQL user.)

Your job is to turn on the checkbox for each type you want FileMaker to show. You can also turn off all three checkboxes, and FileMaker will show everything it can.

If you don't know what any of this means, try leaving every box blank, and turning on Tables and Views. If FileMaker takes a long time showing tables to pick from, if the table you want is not in the list, or if you feel like you're seeing loads of tables you don't want to see, consult your database administrator for help.

Creating relationships

When you're viewing a record from the Web Leads table, you might want FileMaker to show you if that person is already in your Customers table. To make this possible, you need some kind of connection between Customers and Web Leads. When you add a table from an external data source, FileMaker puts a table occurrence right on the relationship graph, so making the connection is easy. The table occurrence looks, smells, and functions just like a FileMaker table. For example, it would make sense to connect it to the Customers table by Email Address, since they both have that information in common. Just drag the email_address field from the Web Leads table to the Email Address field in the Customers table. FileMaker now knows how they relate.

You're free to relate tables in any combination you want: Connect a FileMaker table to a SQL table, or connect two SQL tables together. Connect a SQL table to a FileMaker table, which then connects to another SQL table. You can even connect tables from two *different* SQL databases.

Shadow tables

If you switch to the Tables tab in the Manage Database window, you may see something unexpected. FileMaker includes every SQL table you've added to your graph in the Tables list (in stark contrast to tables from other FileMaker databases, which never show in the Tables tab).

Note: No matter how many *table occurrences* you create for a particular SQL table, the underlying table is listed only once. Also, SQL tables are always shown in italics so they're easy to spot.

The italicized entry in the Tables tab is called a *shadow table*. In other words, it isn't the table. Rather, it's a representation of the real table. It reflects information about the real table, and even lets you add a little FileMaker magic to an otherwise bare bit of computer science.

If you double-click the table (or switch to the Fields tab and select the table from the Table pop-up menu), you'll see the fields (sometimes called *columns* by non-FileMaker database folks) from the SQL table listed in italics as well. You can do certain things to these italicized fields:

- You **can't** rename a field or change its type. That sort of thing is controlled on the SQL database side of things.
- You **can** add a field comment if you want.
- You **can** click Options and set Auto-Enter and Validation options for the field. Remember, though, that the rules you set here apply only when you add or edit records *in FileMaker*. Other systems that interact with the database are restricted only by settings in the SQL database.

- You **can** delete a field. You're not actually deleting the field from the SQL table. Rather, deleting a field tells FileMaker you simply don't want to see that field in FileMaker anymore. (You can always get it back later by clicking the Sync button, as explained below.)

SQL databases tend to be more restrictive about acceptable values than FileMaker itself. For instance, a text field in a SQL database usually has a maximum size that is relatively small, compared to FileMaker's 2 GB field limit. If you select a field, click the Options button, and visit the Validation tab, then you'll see that the "Maximum number of characters" option is turned on, and you can't turn it off. Right by the checkbox, FileMaker also shows how many characters the field can hold.

Perhaps most important, you can *add new fields* to the shadow table. Specifically, you can add unstored or global calculation fields and summary fields. Neither of these field types is supported by SQL databases, but both are super important to FileMaker developers. By adding them to the shadow table, you can treat the SQL tables a little more like normal FileMaker tables. For example, you can add summary fields so you can do complex reporting on the SQL data, or add a calculation field to show a subtotal on a FileMaker layout.

Note: Remember, the fields you add to the shadow table aren't in the real table. They live only in FileMaker.

Finally, if the underlying SQL table changes in some way (perhaps the database administrator added a new column you're particularly interested in seeing), click Sync at the top of the window. This button tells FileMaker to go back to the SQL database and find out if any columns have been added, removed, or adjusted in an important way.

Syncing has nothing to do with the *data* in the database, though. FileMaker always interacts with the SQL database directly to show up-to-the-moment data as you perform searches or make changes. The Sync button synchronizes only the field definitions from the SQL table.

Using SQL Tables

There's no secret to using a SQL table. As you've probably guessed, it works just like any other FileMaker table. You can create a new layout to show records from the SQL table. You can view those records in list view, form view, or table view. You can write scripts that loop through SQL records, or use the "Go to Related Record" script step to find the records associated with a particular customer.

Everything you know about FileMaker still applies. But there are a few points to keep in mind as you develop your database around SQL tables:

- You can configure access to a SQL table using privilege sets just like any other FileMaker table. But a privilege set can't overrule the underlying SQL database. If the user name and password you're using to connect to the SQL database don't provide permission to delete records, FileMaker can't delete them, no matter how hard you try. FileMaker does its best to give meaningful error messages in such situations.

- Speaking of error messages, since SQL databases are more restrictive than FileMaker, you may see error messages in places you wouldn't normally expect them. For example, a Name field might be limited to 30 characters. If you try to enter more than that, FileMaker will let you, but you won't be able to commit the record. It would be nice if FileMaker simply stopped you from typing in too many letters, but it doesn't. It's up to you to go back and delete enough to make it happy.
- FileMaker does some powerful computing magic to make these SQL tables work. So if you have a large amount of data in your SQL table, it can take a long time for FileMaker to get ready to show you data. You'll just have to be patient and grateful for FileMaker's efforts.
- FileMaker may have trouble performing some finds efficiently. If you include only fields from one table in your find request, then it should move quickly. But if you search in related fields, and there are thousands of matches in the related table, FileMaker can take a very long time to sort things out. If you find that SQL tables aren't performing well, and you can't simplify your find requests, consider enlisting the help of a SQL expert (or learning it yourself). It may be possible to offload some of the heavy lifting to the SQL database server, where ready access to the data makes things faster. For example, a complex find in FileMaker could be converted to a SQL view that is super-snappy. This same advice applies to large summary reports. If you are dealing with lots of records, it may be much faster to let the SQL database server calculate the subtotals and averages for FileMaker.

You can use ESS to get direct access to enterprise data, interact with the back end of your Web site, or even replace chunks of FileMaker data with a set of tables that is more open to other applications. This powerful feature may need a little setup and some new expertise, but if you have big needs, it can be an incredibly powerful option.

Exporting Data

The Save/Send Records As options (page 638) make good sense when you just want to send FileMaker data to an associate. But sometimes your recipient is a computer. You might be sending your customer information to a mailing house to be printed on postcards, or loading it into QuickBooks. In cases like this, you'll *export* the data.

When you export data, FileMaker needs to know *what* data to export. You tell it with the Export dialog box (Figure 17-6). The Table pop-up menu shows you what FileMaker considers the *current table*—in this case, Customers. Below it, the field list shows every field in the current layout for that table. But click the pop-up menu, and you'll see that you can choose Current Table, which shows you all the fields in the current table, instead of just the fields on the layout. You're also welcome to pick other tables from the pop-up menu and see their fields. When you choose fields from other tables, you're still exporting Customer records. If you include fields from other tables, FileMaker gets the values from the first record related to each customer record.

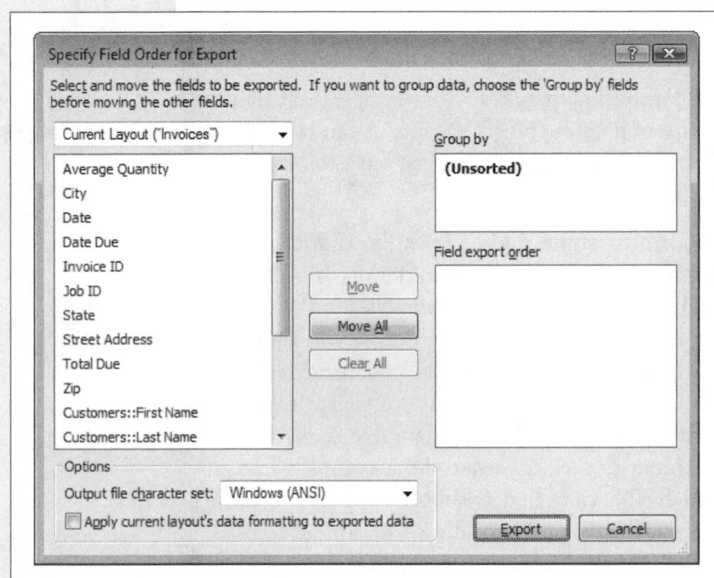

Figure 17-6:
When FileMaker exports the data, it includes each field in this list in the export file. The order of the fields in this list determines their order in the export file, and you can change it by dragging fields up or down in the list. To add every field in the field list to the field export order list, click Move All. Likewise, to remove all fields from the export order, click Clear All.

To choose a field for export, select it and click Move. FileMaker adds the field to the "Field export order" list, but doesn't actually move it there. Rather, the field stays in the list because you may want to export the same field *twice* in the same export file. Imagine, for example, you are creating an export file that needs the billing address info in the first four fields, and the shipping address info in the next four fields. Since your database has only one set of address fields, you can export them twice so the resulting file has the right number of fields. (Unfortunately, you can't ask FileMaker to export a blank field. If you often export to a format that needs fields you don't have, and leaving them blank is OK, just export an empty global field in each one's place.)

Note: If a field isn't on the current layout, it doesn't show up in the export field list, so if you're wasting time scrolling through fields that you don't need, switch to a simpler layout from the same table. But if you can't find a field that you *know* is in the table, use the pop-up menu to choose Current Table. That way, you'll get a list of all the fields in the table, regardless of which ones are on the current layout.

At the bottom of the window, the Character Set pop-up menu lets you tell FileMaker how to *encode* characters in the export file so the receiving computer can read them properly. For instance, if you're using Mac OS X and you know the person receiving the export file is using Windows, it probably makes sense to choose the Windows (ANSI) choice. Unfortunately, the conversion from Macintosh to

Windows or Windows to Mac is imperfect, so some less common characters may be switched out for others in the output file. Unicode is the best choice, assuming your recipient can accept it, because it can handle *all* the characters you may have in your database (even foreign language characters like Chinese and Korean).

Finally, the checkbox called "Apply current layout's data formatting to exported data" is a little misleading. It has nothing to do with font, size, style, or color. Rather, when you turn this option on, FileMaker formats numbers, dates, times, and timestamps according to the formatting options for each field on the layout: number of decimal places, date formats, and so forth. If you leave this option off, FileMaker exports the data exactly as it was originally entered.

Note: The "Group by" list lets you sort data as you export it. You'll learn how this feature works on page 654.

Here's an example of a typical database export. You've hired a printing company to print, address, and mail personalized cards to all your customers at holiday time. To do the job, the card company needs a list of names and addresses. Instead of typing all your customer info by hand, you can produce the list by exporting it from your database in the appropriate format. Often, plain text is fine, so that's what this example uses.

1. **Switch to the Customers layout.**

   Like many FileMaker features, the Export command is layout-based—that is, it decides which table to export (and from which table occurrence to find related data) by looking at the current layout. To export customer records, you need to be on a layout associated with the Customers table.

2. **Choose Records → Show All Records.**

   If this command is grayed out, then all records are already showing. Otherwise, take this step to ensure that you export *every* customer.

3. **Choose File → Export Records. If the command isn't available, you're probably in Find mode, so switch to Browse mode.**

   You can also export from Layout and Preview modes, too, should the need arise. The "Export Records to File" dialog box appears. It looks a lot like a normal Save dialog box, except that it has a pop-up menu at the bottom called *Type*.

4. **Name the file *Holiday Card List.txt*, and choose any location you want.**

   When FileMaker exports data, it creates a new file and puts the data in it. You use this window to tell FileMaker what to call the file and where to put it.

5. **From the Type pop-up menu, choose Comma-Separated Text, and then click Save.**

   You'll learn what each of these types means in the next section. The "Specify Field Order for Export" window appears (Figure 17-6).

6. **While pressing Ctrl (Windows) or ⌘ (Mac), select these fields in the field list: First Name, Last Name, Company Name, Street Address, City, State, and Zip Code. Then click Move.**

   FileMaker adds the highlighted fields to the field export order list.

Note: If you want to export most of your fields, but not quite all of them, it may be faster to click the Move All button, and then clear the few you don't want from the Field export order list.

7. **Click Export.**

   FileMaker creates the file and returns you to your database.

So what just happened? If you open the Holiday Card List file you just created, you see names, company names, and addresses from your customers file. Dig a little deeper and you notice a few things:

- Each *record* is on its own line. (If the program you're viewing the file in wraps lines, it might look like a record goes across two or more lines, but there's a return character at the *end* of each record, and nowhere else.)
- Each field value is in quotes, and there are commas between them.

These factors are important because this file conforms to a *standard*. Other programs—including the program used by the card printing company—that support files in the Comma-Separated Text format can read this file and grab the data.

Grouped exports

You may have noticed the "Group by" list in the "Specify Field Order for Export" dialog box. Under normal circumstances, you see "(Unsorted)" in this list. But if you sort the records in the found set *before* choosing the Export Records command, you see instead a list of the fields in your sort order, each with a checkbox by its name. You can see this in action in Figure 17-7.

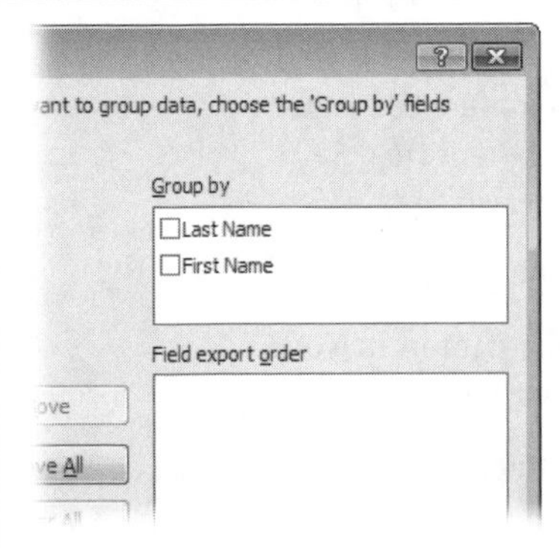

Figure 17-7: *When your data is sorted, FileMaker shows the sort fields in the "Group by" list. By turning on one or more of these checkboxes, you tell FileMaker you want to group the data in the export file.*

If you opt to group the data, you get just one record in the export file for each *unique* value in the "group by" field. For example, if you export 300 people records, grouped by state, you get one record for each state. Why would you ever want to do this? Because you can include *summary* fields in your export list, and FileMaker properly summarizes all the records represented by each group. You could see, for example, how many people you have in each state.

You're free to select as many fields as you want in the "group by" list. If you select more than one, you get a hierarchical list of records, similar to a sub-summary report (Chapter 6). For example, if you sort first by state, then by city, and turn on the checkbox next to both fields in the "group by" list, you get a list of states, and below each state, you see one record for each city in that state. Again, summary fields included in your export show proper totals for both the state as a whole, and each city.

Export formats

When exporting data, you always create a file, but you get to decide in what *format* the file should be. In the last example, you exported your data to a Comma-Separated Text file. This example is one of the many file formats FileMaker can produce when it exports. Most formats exist simply because computer software has put forth a lot of standards in the last 50 years, and FileMaker wants to be as flexible as possible. Some formats do have unique advantages, though.

The first question you need to ask is, "Where is the data going?" Your export format choice almost always depends on what the person you're sending it to needs, and most of the available formats are uncommon types you use only if the person on the other end asks for it. These include SYLK, DBF, DIF, Lotus 1-2-3, and Basic.

The remaining formats are explained below:

- **Tab-Separated Text** and **Comma-Separated Text** are very common formats for database data. They put each record on its own line. With tab-separated text, you get a tab between each field value, while comma-separated text has quotes around field values, and commas between them. Almost every program in the world that can import data supports one of these formats. If you're not sure, try Tab-Separated Text first—it's the most common.

Note: Sometimes the Comma-Separated Text format is called *Comma-Separated Values* in other programs. They're the same thing.

- The **Merge** format is just like Comma-Separated Text format, with one difference: The first line of the file shows individual field names. The advantage is that when you import this file in another program, you can see what each field is called, making it easier to get the right data. Unfortunately, most programs don't expect this extra line, and treat it as another record. People most often use this format for mail merge in word processing programs.

- If you want to put the data on a Web page, use **HTML Table**. The resulting file isn't suitable for importing into another program, but it can be displayed nicely in a Web browser. You can also open the file, copy the HTML table from inside it, and paste it into another Web page.

UP TO SPEED

Where's My Style?

Most of FileMaker's export formats are *text based*. In other words, what gets produced is just a normal, plain text file. The structure of this file determines which format it is, but you can open them all in Notepad or TextEdit and read them directly. A side effect of this reality is that none of them support *styles*. In other words, if you go to great lengths to change the first names in all your records so the font matches the customer's personality, you can kiss your hard work goodbye when you export.

In addition to the font, you lose the size, style, and color of the text. The notable exception to this rule is the FileMaker Pro format. Since this export format creates another FileMaker Pro database, all the formatting you painstakingly put in place is preserved.

If you *must* have text styles in your exported data, there is an option, but it ain't pretty. FileMaker has two calculation functions designed to aid this process: GetAsCSS and GetAsSVG.

Each function takes a single text parameter and returns a snippet of ordinary text with style information embedded using special *tags*. GetAsCSS produces text that can be put on a Web page. When viewed in a Web browser, the text takes on its original fonts, sizes, styles, and colors. GetAsSVG works the same way, but uses a different tagging scheme: the one used in the SVG, or Scalable Vector Graphics format.

To take advantage of these functions, you'd need to create a calculation field with a formula something like this:

```
GetAsCSS ( First Name )
```

You would then export *this* field instead of the First Name field. If you do this with the HTML Table export format, you get properly formatted text on your Web page. More realistically, you'd use these along with the XML format and a special XSLT style sheet that produces a Web page or an SVG image. You'll learn more about this option at the end of this chapter.

- The **FileMaker Pro** format is your best choice if your data is destined to go back into FileMaker some day, or if you just want to view and work with the exported data directly. When you choose this format, FileMaker creates a brand new database with just one table and only the fields you choose to export. This format is the *only* one that preserves font, style, size, and color in field data (see the box above) and one of the few that supports repeating fields (see page 119).

Note: Usually, if you just want to export records from one FileMaker file to another, you don't have to export them first. Just go to the database where you want the data to end up and import them directly (page 657). Of course, if one database is in South Africa and the other is in Tibet, then by all means export them first.

- For the ultimate in flexibility, choose **XML**—the un-format. When you export XML, you get to apply something called an XSLT style sheet. An XSLT style sheet is a document written in a programming language all its own that tells FileMaker exactly how the exported data looks. If you need to produce an export format that FileMaker doesn't support directly, XSLT is the way to do it. But be forewarned: XSLT is *not* in the same league as FileMaker itself, ease-of-use-wise. Here is where you may need some hired help. XSLT is introduced briefly at the end of this chapter.

Note: Although it applies to *one field value* and not a set of records, don't forget about the Edit → Export Field Contents command. This command lets you export the data in the current field to a file. Text, number, date, time, and timestamp fields are exported to a plain text file. Container fields create a file whose type is appropriate for the data in the field.

- Last but not least, you can choose **Excel** to create a bona fide spreadsheet. When you choose this format, FileMaker opens an extra dialog box, which lets you put FileMaker's field names in the first row of your new spreadsheet. You can even give your Excel file a worksheet Name, document Title, Subject, and Author if you so desire.

Regardless of which format you choose, the "Export Records to File" dialog box has two options that let you determine what happens to the file after FileMaker creates it. Choose "Automatically open file" to avoid hunting down the file on your hard drive and launching it yourself. And "Create email with file as attachment" does just what it promises: opens your email program and creates a new message with your fresh new document attached. To share your date, you just need to supply the email address, add a subject line, and click Send.

Importing Data

Sometimes, the data you need is already somewhere else. You just need to get it into FileMaker. Before you start lamenting your lackluster words-per-minute typing skills, consider doing an *import*. Chances are FileMaker can load the data directly into its tables with just a little help from you to tell it where things go.

FileMaker can handle the most common data types—and quite a few lesser-known ones—with a straightforward process. You tell FileMaker which file contains your incoming data, and then show it how you want to match the incoming data (the source) with the fields in your file (the target). This procedure is called *field mapping*, and it's the only time-consuming part of any import. See Figure 17-8 for a preview of the Import Field Mapping dialog box.

This window lists all the fields in the source file on the left, and the fields in your table on the right. FileMaker will transfer the data, field by field and record by record, into your database. The first field in the Source Fields list goes into the first field in the Target Fields list.

Unfortunately, FileMaker can't always tell which fields match. You might be importing records from a system that uses different field names, for example. How is FileMaker supposed to know that *t_fname* is the First Name field in your old contact manager software? Worse still, many data formats have no field names, so all you have to work with is the data itself.

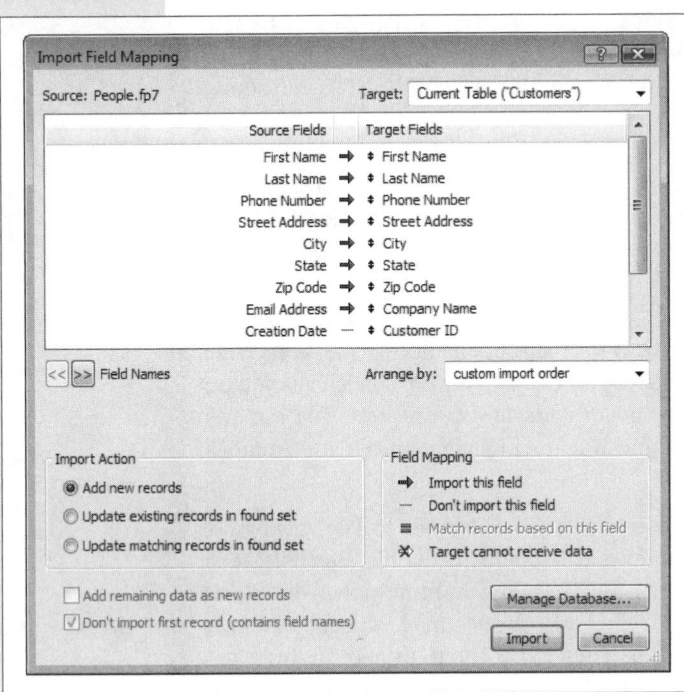

Figure 17-8:
Use this dialog box to tell FileMaker what data to import and where to put it. In the top-left corner of the window, FileMaker tells you where this data is coming from (in this case, a file called People.fp7). To the right, you see where the data's going (the Customers table). The arrows down the middle show you what data will go where. Creation Date, for instance, has no arrow, so FileMaker won't import it.

Using the Import Field Mapping dialog box, your job is to tell FileMaker which source fields match with each of the target fields. The concept is simple, but the procedure can be a real drag. First of all, you can't rearrange the fields in the Source Fields list at all. They match the order in which they appear in the file you're importing and that's that. So instead, you move the target fields up or down so they line up next to the appropriate source fields. (You move them just like you do fields and tables in the Manage Database window—by dragging the little arrows.)

If you don't have many fields, this process is quick and painless. If you have lots of fields, it can be tough for a few reasons:

- Since the whole point of this operation is to put the target field list in a very particular order, you can't simply sort the list by name whenever you're having trouble finding a field. If you're looking for First Name in a long list, there's no way to find it short of looking through the list field by field. If this process proves overwhelming, here's a trick: Click Manage Database, and in the familiar Manage Database window it summons, rename the field with a whole lot of X's at the end of its name. When you close the Manage Database window, the field in question will stand out from the list.
- As you drag fields up and down, if you have to drag beyond the visible list (because your destination has scrolled past the top or bottom), FileMaker sometimes scrolls the list by so quickly while you drag that you easily overshoot your destination, repeatedly. To avoid this runaround, don't drag. Instead, click

FREQUENTLY ASKED QUESTION

Making It Fit

A lot of FileMaker's Export formats use special characters for important things. For instance, the Tab-Separated Text format uses a return character to separate records. What happens if I have a return character in my field?

Good question! Special characters are one of those problems with no ideal solution. But FileMaker does the best it can within the limitations of each export file type. For a file to be called Tab-Separated Text, for example, you simply can't have return characters inside records. It's just against the rules. In this particular case, FileMaker turns the return character into something else, called a *vertical tab*, which is a standard but rarely-used character left over from when computers had green screens. Presumably, you don't have any of these in your fields (you can't type them, so it is a pretty safe bet you don't), so it's easy enough to turn vertical tab characters back into return characters when you open the file in another program. In fact, that's exactly what happens when you *import* a Tab-Separated Text file into FileMaker.

Another character of concern is the quote mark. If you have these in your fields, and you export a Comma-Separated Text file, FileMaker has to do something with them so they don't interfere with the quotes around field values. In this case, FileMaker turns your quote mark into two quote marks together.

That doesn't sound like a solution, but it is. If you assume any quote mark that is immediately followed by a second one is really just data, and not the end quote mark for a field value, you can figure out which is which in the export file. Most programs that support Comma-Separated Text understand this convention. (You might think commas would also be a problem with Comma-Separated Text, but they're not. Since every field value is in quotes, commas are OK. Only the commas between quoted values are considered field separators.)

The HTML and XML formats have all kinds of special characters, but each has a special *entity* form that's used if they're supposed to be treated as ordinary data. FileMaker converts any such characters appropriately, and every program that processes these formats understands the conventions.

Finally, FileMaker has a data-structure concept that most formats simply don't understand: repeating fields. The idea that one field could hold several values is foreign to most database programs. When you export repeating fields, FileMaker pulls another freaky character out of its hat: the Group Separator, which is used to separate each value. Thankfully, this action is almost never a problem because you generally don't export repeating field data to a file that needs to be read by a program that doesn't understand repeating fields. One last note: The FileMaker Pro export format *does* directly support repeating fields.

the field you want to move to select it. Then hold down the Control key (⌘), and use the up or down arrow keys to move the field. As long as you hold the appropriate modified key down, you can move the field up or down as far as you want by repeatedly pressing the arrow keys. This more controlled method may go a little slower, but it makes it easy to hit the right spot.

- Finally, if you accidentally drop a field in the wrong spot, the field you're moving changes places with the one you dropped it on top of. If the one you replaced was already in the right spot, it is now far away, and will need to be repositioned once you correctly place the first field. In other words, an accidental drop leaves *two* fields in the wrong place. The only solution to this problem is to be careful (and use the keyboard trick from the previous paragraph to minimize mistakes).

Sometimes you don't care about some of the fields in your source file (maybe it includes a Fax Number for each customer, and you simply don't need to keep that particular value). Between each source and destination field, you see one of two symbols: an arrow or a line. The arrow means FileMaker plans to import the data on the left side into the field on the right. A line tells FileMaker to ignore this particular piece of data in the import file. Click an arrow to change it to a line, or vice versa. Just make sure there's a line next to the field or fields you don't want to import. (You sometimes see *other* symbols between fields, but they show up only when you change the Import Action setting. You'll learn about that on page 662.)

Note: If you forget what the importing icons mean, never fear. The Import Field Mapping window has a legend at the bottom right.

UP TO SPEED

Mapping Out Your Options

FileMaker's smart, but when it comes to something as picayune as deciding which field to put where, there's no substitute for human input. As you can see in Figure 17-8, the Import Field Mapping dialog box looks a trifle crowded, but every tool, button, and gizmo has saved a life (or a career, anyway).

For example, your input data source may or may not include field names. If it doesn't, the Source Fields list shows you the first record in the import file instead. Or, even if your data already has named fields, you may *want* to see some of the data being imported so you can see what's really in that field called Q1GPFnw. Either way, FileMaker lets you check as many records as you wish before you import, by providing arrow buttons below the list. As you click, FileMaker replaces items in the source field list with data from the next (right) or previous (left) record. When field names are included, you see them as the *first* record. Occasionally, the format you're importing doesn't accommodate field names, but the import file has them anyway, as the first record. When this happens, turn on "Don't import first record" so FileMaker doesn't treat that record as data.

The "Arrange by" pop-up menu lets you bulk-reorder the target fields in the list. Most choices are obvious (alphabetical by field name, and by field type), but others aren't so clear. If you choose "matching names," FileMaker tries to match fields up by matching their names. If your input file has the same field names as your database, this option sets the right order for you. The "last order" choice restores the field order you used the last time you imported data. Choose "creation order" to see the fields in the order in which you created them. Finally, if you manually drag the fields in the list, FileMaker switches to the "custom import order" choice. If you decide to try one of the other arrangements, you can get back to the order you were working on by choosing "custom import order" yourself.

Finally, just like the export dialog box, this window lets you specify a character set ("Exporting a File"). This time, though, you don't decide what you *want* it to be. Rather, you need to tell FileMaker what it *is*. If you're lucky, this pop-up menu is grayed out, meaning FileMaker was able to figure out the encoding itself. Otherwise, you need to make sure you make the right choice so special characters in the import file come through intact. You'll want to choose either Windows (ANSI) or Macintosh 99 percent of the time. And for typical data (letters, numbers, and basic punctuation), the choice is largely irrelevant.

For the sake of illustration, here's the simple rundown on how importing works:

1. **Choose File → Import Records → File.**

   FileMaker can import data from all kinds of sources. In this case, you're telling it you want to import records from a *file*. When you choose this command, the standard Open File dialog box appears.

2. **Choose the file you want to import, and then click Open.**

   The Import Field Mapping dialog box pops up.

3. **Drag the fields in the target field list so they line up properly with the input data.**

   As you drag, you can ignore the arrows completely. You can fix them once you've got the fields in the right order.

Note: If your data source has a field that doesn't match any existing field in your target table, and you decide you want to import that field anyway, just click the Manage Database button to create a new field, and then return to your field mapping. See page 664 (below) for how to handle an entire *table* that's missing.

4. **Click the arrows or lines between fields until each matching field has an arrow, and each remaining field has a line.**

   This process is the time-consuming part. Just take it slow and be glad you don't have to type all this data.

5. **Make sure the "Add new records" radio button (in the Import Action area) is turned on.**

   This action tells FileMaker you want a new record created in the Customers table for each record in the import file. (The Import Field Mapping dialog box has more features, but you don't need them right now. See the box on "Importing Data" for full detail.)

6. **Click Import. When the Import Options dialog box appears (Figure 17-9), turn on "Perform auto-enter options while importing."**

   You want to make sure the new customers have valid customer IDs, and those come from Auto-Enter serial numbers.

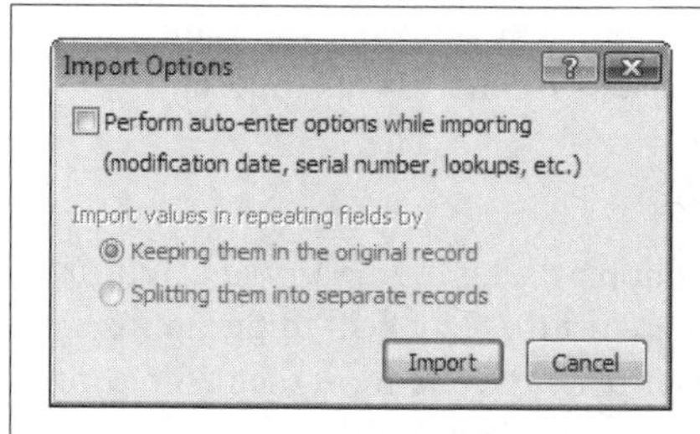

Figure 17-9:
If you have any Auto-Enter fields, or you're importing repeating fields, you see this window after clicking Import. Turn off "Perform auto-enter options while importing" if you don't want FileMaker to auto-enter data in your records as they're created. When importing repeating fields, you usually want to choose "Keeping them in the original record." If you don't, FileMaker makes a new record for each repetition that has data in it.

Note: If you import into a field that has Auto-Enter options set, and you tell FileMaker to perform Auto-Enter options when importing, you might wonder *which* value will wind up in the field: the auto-entered data or the imported data. In almost every case, the imported data wins. The one exception: If a field is set to auto-enter a looked-up value, FileMaker performs the lookup and thus overrides the imported value.

When you're done, click Import. After a very short delay, the Import Records Summary dialog box appears (Figure 17-10). Click OK to make it go away.

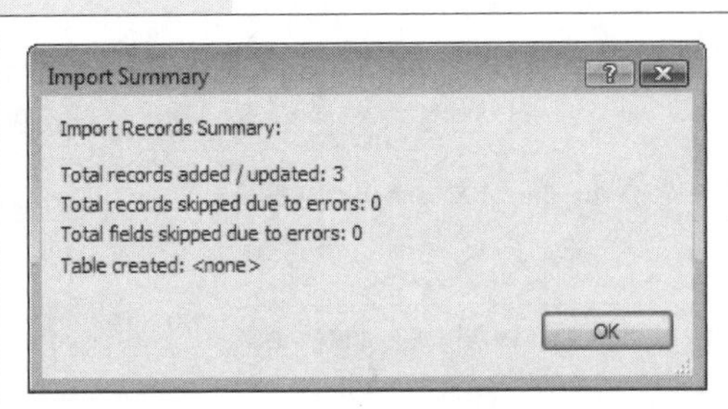

Figure 17-10:
This window appears after FileMaker completes the import operation. It tells you important information about your import, including how many records were imported. Sometimes problems can occur during import (for instance, some data in the import file may violate your field validation settings). When this happens, FileMaker may skip certain fields or whole records. This window also tells you when that happens (although it doesn't tell you which fields or records were skipped).

After the import's complete, FileMaker shows you a found set of just the records it imported. But don't reach for the Show All Records command yet: The fact that it's a found set is your safety net. If something goes wrong with your import (the wrong records came through, field mapping doesn't look right, or whatever), just delete the found set and start over. You can scan through the data and make sure you got what you wanted and that the data went into the fields you intended. You can also take this opportunity to perform other actions (like use the Replace Field Contents command) on every imported record.

Importing Over Existing Data

When you import data into a file that already has some records in it, the Import Action section of the Import Field Mapping dialog box (page 658) gives you three ways to specify how you want to deal with that existing data. Normally, it starts out with the "Add new records" setting turned on, meaning that FileMaker simply adds imported records to your database. Sometimes, though, you want to update existing records instead. For example, suppose your database holds shipping rates for every state you ship to. When your freight company updates its rates, it sends you a new file with one record for each state, and the new rates in a Rate field. If you add these records to your database, you end up with *two* records for each state, which is probably not what you want. So FileMaker gives you two other choices that let you update records as you import.

Update existing records in found set

To avoid creating duplicate records as in the shipping rates example, you can turn on "Update existing records in found set," and map just the Rate field to the appropriate field in your table. When you import, FileMaker takes the rate from the first record in the import file and puts it in the first record in the found set. It then copies the second rate into the second record. This process continues until it has imported every rate.

If your import file has more records than the found set, FileMaker simply skips the extra records. If you'd rather import *all* the records (adding new records once all those in the found set have been updated), turn on "Add remaining data as new records."

Warning: This import action is useful only if you're certain the records in the import file are in the *same order* as those in the export file. If they're not, FileMaker updates the wrong records, leaving you with incorrect data. If you aren't positive the records are in the right order, use "Update matching records in found set" instead.

Update matching records in found set

"Update matching records in found set" works much the same way. When you import with this action, FileMaker updates data in existing records by copying it from the import file. This time, though, you get to tell FileMaker how to figure out which records in the import file match each record in the found set. You tell FileMaker this by specifying one or more *matching fields*, as described in Figure 17-11.

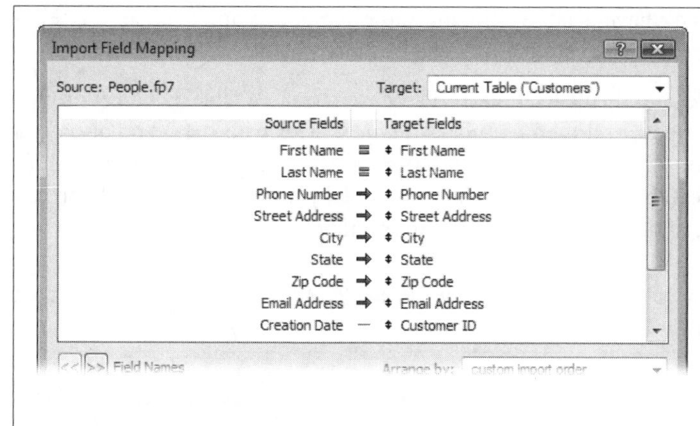

Figure 17-11: *When you turn on "Update matching records in found set," FileMaker lets you use a new symbol between source and target fields. In this picture, the First Name and Last Name fields have an "=" symbol beside them. This symbol tells FileMaker to match records based on first and last name. In other words, when it imports the first record, it finds a record in the found set with the same name. FileMaker then updates that record's data based on the import file. If FileMaker doesn't find a match, it skips the import record. It's safest to use a key field for import matching.*

Warning: Pay special attention to this command's name: "Update matching records in *found set*." FileMaker notes your found set when it starts the import. When looking for matches, it looks only at the records in the found set. If you have a customer with a matching first and last name, but that customer is not in the found set, FileMaker will either skip that record, or add a new duplicate. In most cases, you want to do a Records → Show All Records operation before starting this kind of import.

To get the new symbol in the field mapping list, just click the spot between fields. FileMaker now toggles between the three possible symbols: Import, Don't import, and Match. (If you forget what each symbol means, the Field Mapping area in the window reminds you.) Again, if you'd rather have FileMaker import every record in the import file, adding new records when no match is found, turn on "Add remaining data as new records."

Creating Tables on Import

All the importing you've learned about so far assumes that your tables and fields are already created. In other words, your target table is already in place when you choose your source file. But when you're doing a big conversion job (say, upgrading from 15 over-extended Excel spreadsheets to a smooth-running FileMaker dream system), it'll take quite some time to create all those tables and fields. And even though you have access to the Manage Database dialog box while you're importing, this process isn't quick or easy when you've got hundreds of fields coming in from dozens of files. FileMaker's already thought of that, and offers to handle the tedious work of table and field creation for you.

Choose Import → File and select a data source. In the Import Field Mapping window, there's a handy pop-up menu called Target. Click it, and you see the current table (remember that's based on the layout that was active when you chose the Import command), all your other tables (grayed out, so you can't choose them), and a very useful command, New Table (Data Source). The stuff in parentheses is the name of your data source and the name FileMaker gives the new table it creates for you. (If you already have a table with the same name as your data source, FileMaker appends a number to the end of the new table's name.)

Choose New Table, and then click Import. FileMaker creates a table and an appropriate set of fields for you, and then populates the new fields with data. You also get a simple form layout for your new table and a table occurrence on your relationships graph. You can treat this table just like one you created yourself. For example, you can start hooking it up to other table occurrences in meaningful relationships.

Note: See "Importing Tables and Fields to see how FileMaker Pro Advanced lets you import tables and fields *without* the data that normally comes with them.

When you let FileMaker create fields for you, it does its best to create the field types you want. For instance, if the data source is a FileMaker file, your new fields match the old file's field names and field types. But if the source is a plain text file with no formatting information to go by, FileMaker doesn't have any names to go by, so the new fields become text fields and get the prosaic names of f1, f2, f3, and so on. In either case, you should check the fields in your new table to make sure you get the names and field types you want. You have to manually create any calculations you need.

Creating a New Database from an Import File

If you have a file full of data, and you want a brand new database built around it, FileMaker has an even simpler option than creating a database and importing the data. Just choose File → Open and select the file you want to convert. You can also use drag and drop: On Windows, drag it to the open FileMaker Pro window. FileMaker promptly converts the file to a database for you. On the Mac, drag a file onto FileMaker's application icon.

Note: If you can't see the file you want in the Open dialog box, or it is grayed out, change the option in the "Files of Type" (Windows) or "Show" (Mac) pop-up list. If your file is one of the formats FileMaker supports, you can select it once you identify its type.

If FileMaker finds data with a first row that looks like field names, it asks you if you want to use those when FileMaker creates fields. If it can't find anything that looks like field names, you get those old standbys, f1, f2, f3. In addition to a single table and the appropriate number of fields (complete with data, of course), you get two very plain layouts. One is a generic form layout, showing one record at a time, and the other is a simple columnar list.

Converting Older FileMaker Files

Use this same process (the Open file command) if you're converting files from very old versions of FileMaker (FileMaker 3, 4, 5, 5.5, or 6) to the more capable format used by FileMaker 7, 8, 8.5, and 9. FileMaker will do its best to carry all the data, scripts, layouts, and so forth from the old file into the modern era. But if the original file was complex, you'll almost certainly have some work to do to get things up to snuff. Converting old files is a huge topic and most people find that conversion requires a certain amount of retrofitting, either to make scripts and other things that break during conversion whole again or to take full advantage of the .fp7 multiple-table-per-file power. (FileMaker offers two excellent white papers on this subject for download at *www.filemaker.com/support/whitepapers.html*. Look under Migration Topics.)

Import Data Sources

You've learned about the most common importing task—when your data's coming in from a single file. But you have other needs and FileMaker's got other choices. File → Import is an entire submenu, with commands to suit even the most demanding database manager. From there, you get to pick where the data should come from (the data source), and you get several choices.

File

The File → Import → File command shows an Open File dialog box. Select any file that matches one of the export formats explained earlier in this chapter. You see your old friend, the Import Field Mapping dialog box (Figure 17-8). Match your source to your target, and away you go.

You can also use a similar command when you have to move data from one table to another within the same file. Go to your target layout and choose File → Import Records → File. In the dialog box, choose the database you're in, and you see the Import Field Mapping dialog box. Select the table that's your data source from the Source pop-up menu and you're ready to go.

Folder

Using this command, you can pick any folder, and FileMaker imports the contents of each appropriate file in that folder. It creates *one* record for each file it imports, and puts the file into the field you specify. In other words, if you have a folder full of letters you've written, you can import them into a Letters database using this command. The complete text of each letter would go in a field, with one record per letter. (Remember, though, that FileMaker only supports pictures, movies, and plain text files when importing. If your letters are in Microsoft Word format, for example, you're out of luck.)

Choosing File → Import → Folder summons the "Folder of Files Import Options" dialog box shown in Figure 17-12.

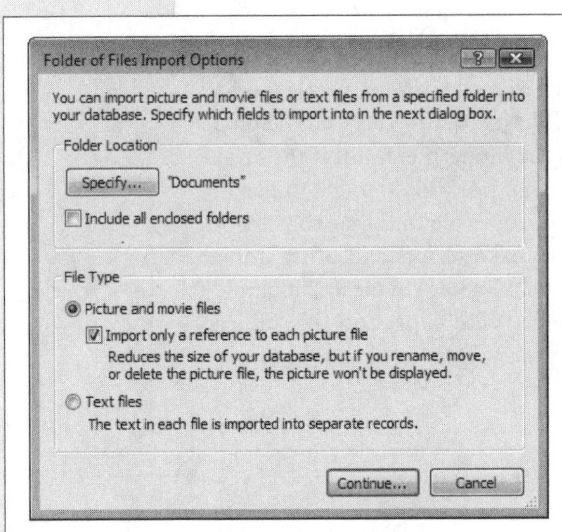

Figure 17-12:
This window is what you see when you choose the File → Import → Folder command. In the top part of the window, you get to choose which folder to import (click Specify). In the bottom half, you decide what kind of files you're interested in.

Normally, FileMaker finds only files directly inside the folder you pick; it ignores any other folders contained inside. You have to turn on "Include all enclosed folders" to make FileMaker look inside those folders, too. With this option turned on, it digs as deep as necessary to find every file.

Once you've picked a folder, you get to decide what kind of files to import. You have only two choices: "Picture and movie files" and "Text files." In the first case, FileMaker ignores every file that isn't a supported picture or movie type. You choose whether the files themselves are inserted in the container field or just references to them. If you choose the "Text files" option instead, it seeks out only plain text files.

Importing a folder of pictures or movies

When you choose the "Pictures and movie files" option and click Continue, you may be in for a bit of a wait. Depending on the number of files FileMaker has to look through, you may see a progress dialog box for as long as several minutes. When the import is complete, you see the now-familiar Import Field Mapping dialog box. But the list of source fields looks entirely unfamiliar—in a good way.

As outlined in Figure 17-13, FileMaker translates the file information into logical field types, perfect for database use.

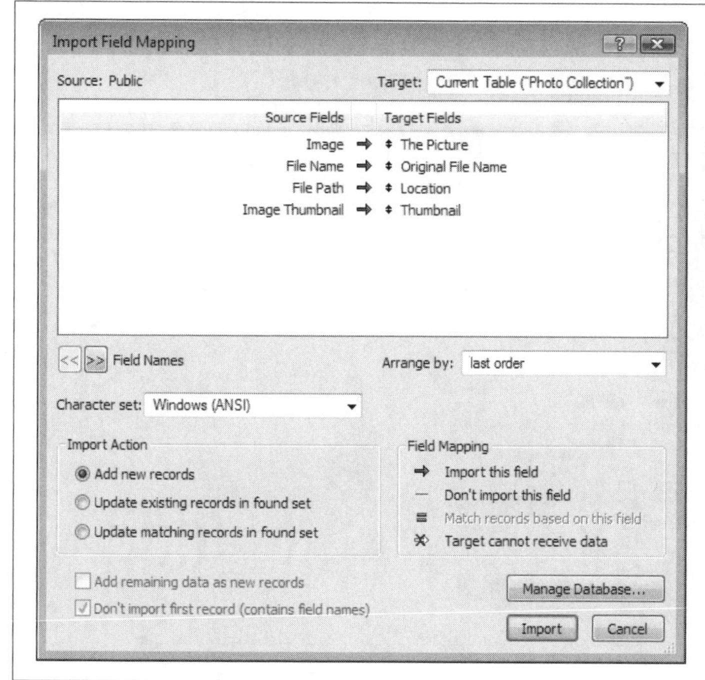

Figure 17-13: *When you import a folder full of pictures, FileMaker practically reads your mind. It not only lets you dump the picture into a container field, but it also offers you the chance to put the file name and full path into text fields. Best of all, FileMaker can shrink the picture down to a thumbnail and put that into a container field, too, which saves space by reducing size and resolution. The thumbnails appear even when the original images aren't available (if a network drive is unavailable, for instance).*

Importing a folder of text files

When you choose to import text files, you still get an Import Field Mapping dialog box. This time, the source field list includes Text Content, File Name, and File Path. Each expects to be imported into a text field.

Digital Camera

If you're using Mac OS X, the File → Import Records menu has a Digital Camera option. Unfortunately, this option relies on a feature unique to Mac OS X, so you can't import directly from a camera on Windows. You have to download the images to your computer first, and then import them. (There's a workaround if you can set up your camera to show up as a USB disk on Windows. In that case, use the Import → Folder command to import images directly from the camera.)

When you first plug your camera into your Mac, chances are iPhoto launches and prepares to import the images. To avoid any potential confusion, quit iPhoto first (or be careful not to click Import in iPhoto while FileMaker's working with the camera).

Note: If you import from your camera to FileMaker a lot, you can tell iPhoto to get out of the way: Just launch Image Capture (in your Applications folders) and in its Preferences → Camera tab, select FileMaker. If you use iPhoto sometimes and FileMaker others, choose No Application in the pop-up menu instead. That way, you get to decide what program each time.

With the camera connected, choose File → Import Records → Digital Camera. The verbosely titled FileMaker Pro Photo Import Options dialog box appears (Figure 17-14).

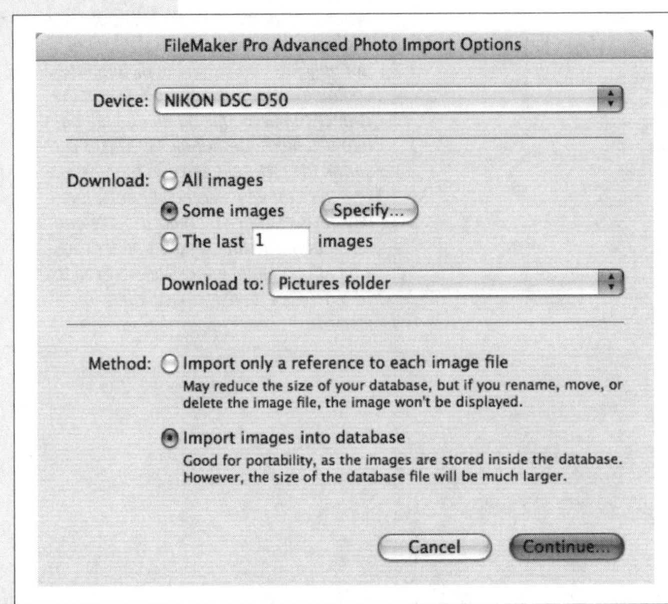
FileMaker Pro Advanced Photo Import Options
Device: NIKON DSC D50
Download: All images
Some images
Specify...
The last 1 images
Download to: Pictures folder
Method: Import only a reference to each image file
May reduce the size of your database, but if you rename, move, or delete the image file, the image won't be displayed.
Import images into database
Good for portability, as the images are stored inside the database. However, the size of the database file will be much larger.
Cancel
Continue...

Figure 17-14:
This dialog box appears when you import from a digital camera in Mac OS X. The device pop-up menu lets you pick which camera to import from (on the off chance you have several connected). You also get to decide which images to import, where to put them (more on these options in a moment), and whether or not you want to store just references to the pictures.

If you want to import *everything* on the camera, turn on "All images." But if you just want, for example, the last five shots you took, turn on the last radio button—"The last [blank] images"—and put the right number in its box. Finally, you can choose "Some images," and click Specify to see a list of image thumbnails to choose from.

Even if you want to import all the images, the "Some images" choice can come in handy. It's the only place you can *rotate* the images before you import them. There's no direct way to rotate an image once it's in the container field. You have to export it, rotate it in another program, and then insert it again.

Even if you're importing the images directly into FileMaker (rather than just a reference), it still puts them in the folder you specify in the "Download to" pop-up menu. If you want to, you can simply delete them when you're done. (If you're storing references, though, the folder you pick becomes very important. If you import the pictures and then move them to a different folder, the references are wrong, and the pictures don't display in FileMaker.)

When you're through making choices, click Continue. The Import Field Mapping window that appears next is loaded with source fields this time. FileMaker lets you import loads of image data along with the pictures, including dimensions, resolution, shot date and time, and all that photographer-speak stuff you see when you accidentally put your camera in advanced mode.

At this point, you're in familiar territory. Just match up the fields and click Import. Be prepared for a wait as it takes FileMaker longer to import full-color digital pictures than, say, Zip codes.

XML Data Source

Because there are so many programs and data formats out there, the World Wide Web Consortium (W3C) created the XML format to make data exchange more predictable. FileMaker uses a special subset of XML's code, called FMPXML-RESULT, to facilitate import. If your data source was created by another File-Maker Pro database, it already uses FMPXMLRESULT, and you can import that data straight up, no chaser. But if the XML document doesn't use FileMaker's Document Type Definition (DTD), you'll need an Extensible StyleSheet Language (XSLT) document to tell FileMaker how to make the XML file work with File-Maker. In fact, with the help of XSLT style sheets, FileMaker can import *any* XML file in any form. An XSLT style sheet converts the XML you're importing into FMPXMLRESULT.

Tip: You can learn to write your own XSLT style sheets, and thereby turn FileMaker's XML into just about anything, from specialized XML your accounting software uses, to an HTML Web page, to a standard RSS news feed. XML and XSLT are complex languages and this book can't cover them in full. If you're ready for a challenge, check out the book *Learning XSLT* by Michael Fitzgerald (O'Reilly). You can also find dozens of premade style sheets on FileMaker's Web site at *www.filemaker.com*.

To import XML data, choose File → Import Records → XML Data Source. When you do, you'll see the window in Figure 17-15. Here, you tell FileMaker where to get the XML data, and optionally what XSLT style sheet to apply. (If you don't apply a style sheet, FileMaker assumes the data is already in its special FMPXML-RESULT format.)

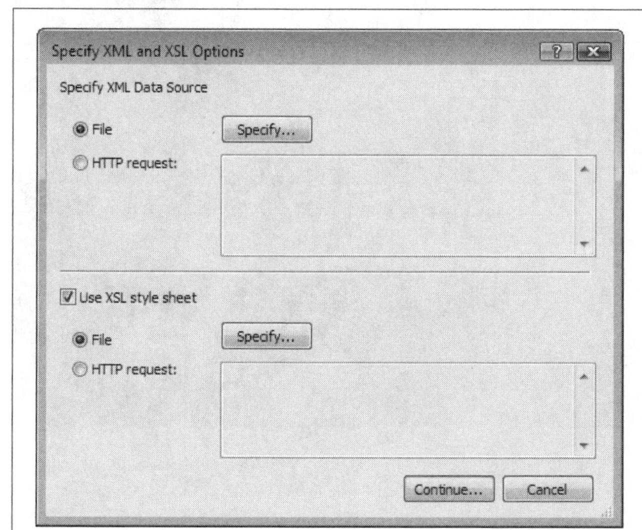

Figure 17-15: *When you import from an XML data source, FileMaker first asks you where to get the data from, and how to process it. You can instruct FileMaker to look in any XML file on your computer, or to fetch the XML data from a Web server (see the box on the next page).*

Unlike the typical import command, when you import XML data, you don't actually have to have a *file* to import from. This window also lets you specify an "HTTP request," which is just a fancy way of saying "Web page." Type the URL of a Web page here, and FileMaker will go out over the Internet, grab the page, and pull it down for you. Believe it or not, a lot of XML data is available hot off the Web like this. Likewise, you can choose to fetch the XSLT template from the Web as well.

When you're finished choosing XML and XSL options, click Continue. FileMaker processes the XML and XSLT (which may take a few minutes), and then shows you the Import Field Mapping dialog box. From there, you can proceed like any import, as described earlier in this chapter.

XML export

When you export to XML, FileMaker exports the data in the FMPXMLRESULT format, and then applies the style sheet. You create the style sheet to translate this XML into the appropriate format for your intended recipient. You have slightly more flexibility when exporting than when importing: XSLT can translate only XML documents, but it can *produce* any text-based format. So although you can import only XML files, you can export just about anything.

POWER USERS' CLINIC

XML and HTTP

Sometimes the XML data you want to import is in a file on your computer. But a big part of the XML data source feature's power is that FileMaker can also get XML data from other computers using *HTTP*, or Hyper-Text Transport Protocol. You probably recognize this acronym because it usually sits in front of Web addresses (as in *http://www.missingmanuals.com*). HTTP is the way Web browsers talk to Web sites, but it's used for a lot more than that. Often, companies make important information available on HTTP servers in XML format. It's this kind of information that FileMaker wants to let you tap into:

Many news-oriented Web sites make headlines and article excerpts available in XML formats called RSS or Atom. Using the XML Data Source feature in FileMaker, you could import news directly into your FileMaker database.

You can grab current or historical exchange rates from various sources to perform accurate currency conversions in FileMaker.

Some shippers let you track packages by downloading XML data. You can build package tracking right into FileMaker Pro.

FileMaker's XML import does have two significant limitations. First, it can't access data that's available only over a secure connection (in other words, it doesn't support HTTP over SSL, or HTTPS). If the data you need to access is available only in this form, you need to find another way.

Second, some XML data sources need information passed to them as *post arguments*—the equivalent of form fields on some Web pages. FileMaker can't send post arguments with the URL. Luckily, most data sources let you pass this information as part of the URL instead. Refer to the documentation for your data source for details.

ODBC Data Sources

The last import data source is called ODBC. This data source is a popular standard to let programs access information stored in database systems. For instance, if your company has an Oracle, Sybase, or Microsoft SQL Server database to manage orders, you can extract data directly from that database and import it into your FileMaker Pro database (perhaps you want to make your own reports with FileMaker).

Note: Although you can *import* data from other big database systems, FileMaker also offers a much more powerful means to interact with some of them: External SQL Sources, or ESS (page 641), which lets you work directly with data from Oracle, Microsoft SQL Server, and MySQL in FileMaker. ESS is often a simpler and more powerful choice unless you're just after a one-shot copy of the data.

ODBC is the most complex import data source to set up. It's a two-step process:

- First, you need to install an **ODBC driver** for the kind of database you're connecting to. For example, if your corporate database is in Oracle, you need an ODBC driver for Oracle. These drivers are platform specific, and most vendors supply only drivers for Microsoft Windows. If you're using Mac OS X, you can buy high-quality FileMaker-compatible drivers from Actual Technologies at *www.actualtechnologies.com/filemaker.php*. (When you visit their site, make sure you get the version that is appropriate for the number of simultaneous users you will have.)
- Next, you need to set up an **ODBC data source**. FileMaker doesn't connect to the database directly. Rather, it uses a data source that's been specified in the ODBC system on your computer. So you have to set up that data source first. In Microsoft Windows, you do this setting up in the ODBC control panel. In Mac OS X, you use the ODBC Administrator application in your Utilities folder.

Once you have a driver installed and a data source set up, you can use the File → Import Records → ODBC Data Source command. When you do, you see the Select ODBC Data Source window (Figure 17-16).

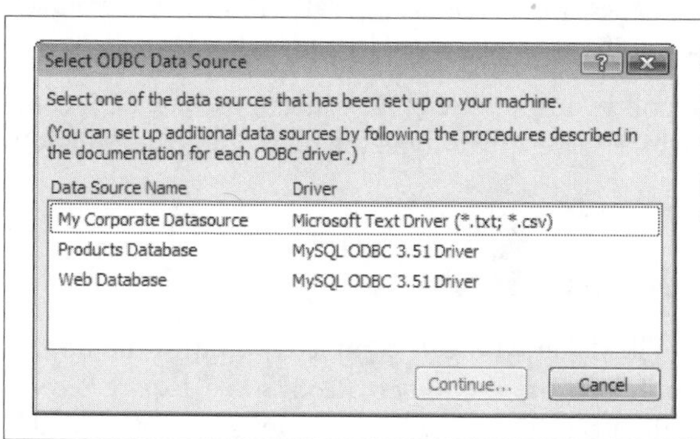

Figure 17-16:
When you tell FileMaker you want to import from an ODBC data source, it first asks you which source to use. This window shows every data source you've created in your ODBC system. You just highlight the one you want and click Continue.

When you click Continue in this window, you probably need to enter a user name and password for the database you're connecting to. You need to get this information from the database administrator, unless you created it in the ODBC software yourself.

Next, FileMaker shows the SQL Query Builder dialog box (Figure 17-17). When you extract data from *most* databases (FileMaker being the notable exception), you have to use a special programming language called Structured Query Language, or SQL (often pronounced *sequel*). Writing an SQL *query* (or program) is a complicated affair. Luckily, in most cases, FileMaker can do it for you—you just make the right choices. (For more detail, see the box on page 673.)

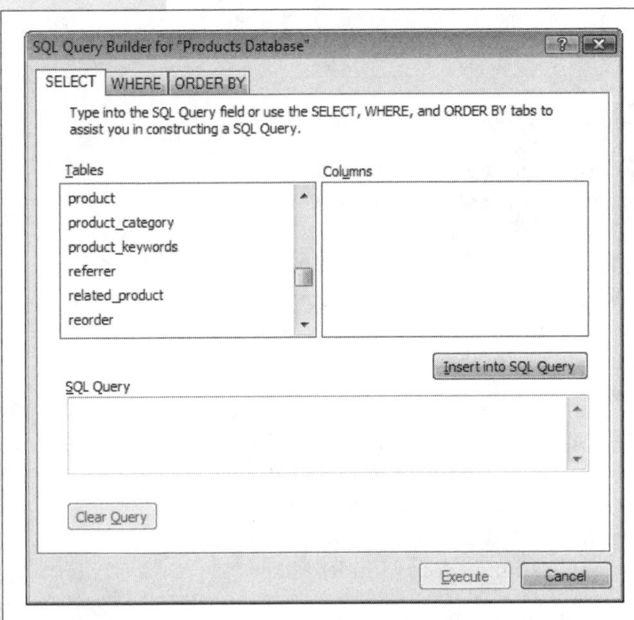

Figure 17-17: *In the SQL Query Builder dialog box's Select tab, the Tables list shows every table available from the database you're connecting to. When you select a table, FileMaker lists all its fields (called columns in most database systems) in the Columns list. Select a field and click "Insert into SQL Query" to include that field in the data you're importing. If you're a SQL pro, you can simply type in the SQL Query box instead.*

When you're all finished building your query, click Execute. FileMaker performs the query, gathers the data from the data source, and shows the same Import Field Mapping dialog box you always see when importing data. If you find yourself doing a lot of ODBC imports, you may be well served by a good book on SQL.

Although the query builder supports only a little SQL, you can use any SQL commands supported by your database server if you type the query directly. And SQL can do *a lot*.

Importing and Exporting in a Script

Like almost everything else in FileMaker, you can completely control the import and export process from a script. You use the *Import Records* and *Export Records* scripts, which you can find in the Records section of the script steps list. You also find script steps for "Save Records as Excel" and "Save Records as PDF," with similar options.

POWER USERS' CLINIC

SQL Queries

To make use of FileMaker's query builder, you need to know just a little bit about SQL. A SQL query is made up of *clauses*, each of which influences the results you receive from the database server. Although SQL understands several clauses, the query builder window supports just three of them: SELECT, WHERE, and ORDER BY. The window has a tab for each of these.

The SELECT clause is where you tell the database what *fields* you want to import. You can include fields from more than one table if necessary. A SELECT clause alone imports every record in the table. If you include fields from more than one table, you get a result that may surprise you: Every record from each file is mixed in every possible combination. In other words, you import lots of records (multiply the record counts from each table to figure out how many).

The WHERE clause's job is to control which *records* get imported and how the tables are related. To specify certain records, you build find criteria into the WHERE clause. First, select a table and column from the pop-up menus. Then select something from the Operator pop-up menu. You can match this field with a value you type yourself (turn on the Value radio button) or with another field (turn on the Column radio button). Either way, enter or select the correct value. Finally, select either the And radio button or the Or radio button and turn on Not if you want to *omit* the matching records. When you're finished defining the criteria, click "Insert into SQL Query."

Relationships in SQL are probably the most confusing. SQL databases don't have a relationship graph like FileMaker, so the database doesn't know how things relate to one another at all. Each time you build a query, it's your job to tell it how to relate records from one table to those in another. You do this job by matching field values in each table in the WHERE clause.

For instance, you might pick the Customer ID field from the Customers table, the "=" operator, and the Customer ID field from the Orders table. When you add criteria like this to your WHERE clause, you've told the database how Order and Customer records relate. You can add as many criteria in this way as you need.

The last tab is called ORDER BY. This clause lets you specify a sort order for your data. It works just like FileMaker's normal Sort dialog box: Just add the fields to the Order By list, selecting Ascending or Descending as appropriate. When you've given it the order you want, click "Insert into SQL Query" again.

As you do these things, FileMaker builds the actual query in the SQL Query box at the bottom of the window so you can see how it comes together. If you feel adventurous, you can manually change this query at any time.

Save Records Script Steps

To automate the creation of Excel spreadsheets, use the "Save Records as Excel" script step. Not surprisingly, there's a "Save Records as PDF" script step as well. Each of these lets you specify all the options the standard menu commands offer, so you can completely automate the process.

As an added bonus, the "Save Records as PDF" script step includes one option you don't get when you run the command manually: an "Append to existing PDF" checkbox. When you turn this option on, if the file you're saving already exists, FileMaker adds the new pages to the end of the existing file. This scheme makes it possible to lump together several reports, or data from several different layouts into one complete PDF package for printing or distribution.

The Import Records Script Step

This script step has three options. First, you get to specify the data source to import from. Your choices match those in the File → Import Records menu: File, Folder, Digital Camera (Mac OS X only), XML Data, and ODBC Data. Whichever option you choose, FileMaker asks you for more information (*which* file to import, or *which* ODBC data source to use, for instance). When specifying a file, you get the standard path list dialog box. In other words, you can specify several paths if you want; FileMaker imports the first one it finds. (If you don't specify a source, your users have to do it as they run the script, in a potentially confusing series of dialog boxes. Since you're presumably providing a script to make things easier for people, it's best to store source files in a safe place and have the script escort your users to them.)

Once you've specified the source, you can turn on "Specify import order" to record the import field mapping, and other import options. Finally, you can turn on "Perform without dialog" if you want FileMaker to import the data directly, with no input from your users. If you leave this option off, FileMaker displays the Import Field Mapping dialog box when the script runs, so folks can make changes to any field mapping you specified.

The Export Records Script Step

The Export Records script step offers similar options. You can specify the output file and export order, and you can choose "Perform without dialog" if you don't want your users to see the export dialog box.

When you specify the output file, you may be surprised to see an Output File Path list. In other words, FileMaker lets you specify *more than one file*. This choice doesn't mean FileMaker exports more than one file, though. Instead, it exports to the first file path that is *valid*. If the first path in the list includes a folder name that doesn't exist, for example, FileMaker skips it and tries the next one.

CHAPTER

18

Sharing Your Database

You've now got a solid foundation for building even the most complex database systems in FileMaker Pro. But your databases have so far been limited to just one user: you. Only the smallest small business, though, has only one person. Most databases are *multiuser databases*, used by lots of people, all at the same time. It's easy to set up any FileMaker database for lots of people to use; you simply turn on a checkbox or two. In this chapter, you'll learn about those settings, plus some of the things you can expect from FileMaker when you're sharing databases.

Before you dive in and start changing settings, consider where you're going to keep the shared file and how other people's computers connect to it. There are three types of sharing: Internet, Network, and FileMaker Server.

- **FileMaker Network.** This type of file sharing is also called *peer-to-peer*—that is, you don't use a server or any special software. You just use your ordinary computers to share files. Peer-to-peer sharing is limited to nine users at once. If more than nine people need to use the database at the same time, use FileMaker Server.
- **Internet Sharing.** Internet sharing has its own set of benefits and tradeoffs. On the plus side, people who need access to your files don't need a copy of FileMaker. All they need is an Internet connection and a recent-model browser. On the downside, not everything you can do in FileMaker translates to the Web, so you may have to live with fewer features. FileMaker uses a type of Internet sharing called **Instant Web Publishing** (IWP). It translates your layouts to Web language according to settings you specify.

- **FileMaker Server** is the Big Daddy of FileMaker database sharing. FileMaker Server offers protection for your files in case of a crash, automated backups, and tremendous speed and stability boosts over peer-to-peer sharing. It also lets 250 (that's right, *two hundred and fifty*) people use the database all at once.

Note: Another type of Internet sharing, called *Custom Web Publishing (CWP)*, offers more features than IWP. Using XML/XSLT or PHP, you can build incredibly powerful Web-based databases. With add-on software, you can even use other web technologies like Ruby on Rails (www.sixfriedrice.com/wp/products/rfm) or Lasso (www.lassosoft.com). But there are steep learning curves to these technologies–plus, they're beyond the scope of this book.

FileMaker Network Sharing

The easiest way to share your data is with *FileMaker Network Sharing*. If you already have a network in your office, and a few copies of FileMaker, you're ready to share your database. First, you put all your databases on one computer. Then open those files, change a few settings in each file, and call that computer the *host*. Each computer that opens those files is called a *guest*, since it opens the same databases that are on the host. Up to nine guests can connect to one host.

Once you're set up, all nine people can work in the database at the same time, adding, editing, and deleting records, performing finds, printing, and running scripts. No two people can work in the same *record* at the same time, though. Once you're sharing files, you need to revisit the topic of record locking. See the box on page 683 for a refresher.

Note: You can do more than just browse data in a shared database. If your privilege set allows it, you can add or modify tables and fields, manage relationships, work in Layout mode, and even write scripts. When you do, the same one-at-a-time concept applies: Only one person can edit a particular script or layout at a time, and only one person can use the Manage → Database window. As soon as one person saves the layout or script or closes the Manage Database window, someone else is free to hop in.

Setting Up a Host Computer

To set up the host, open the databases you want to share on one computer, and then choose Edit → Sharing → FileMaker Network. Either way, you see the FileMaker Network Settings dialog box: command central for all file sharing. Choose the database you're setting up from the list at left (if it's not there, make sure the file's open). Then, as described in Figure 18-1, turn sharing on.

Once you've turned on network sharing for the host computer, you need to tell FileMaker which databases to share. The dialog box shows a list of each open database (if you don't see the one you want, click OK, open the database, and then

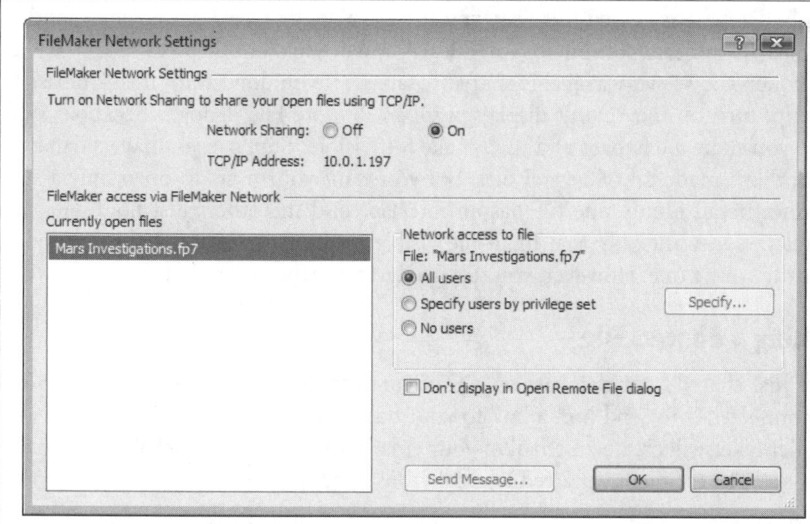

Figure 18-1: *The FileMaker Network Settings dialog box lets you set up your database host. The first step is to turn on the Network Sharing option by clicking the On radio button. When you do, FileMaker shows the computer's TCP/IP address, if it's connected to the network. (If you don't see a valid TCP/IP address, you may have network problems.)*

choose File → Sharing → FileMaker Network again). You must turn on network access for at least one privilege set in each file you want to share. First, select a database from the "Currently open files" list. Then choose one of the following three settings to control who gets access to the file:

- **All Users** means that anybody on your network with a copy of FileMaker and a valid account can get in, so long as only nine people are on at a time.
- **Specify users by privilege set.** When you choose this option, you see a dialog box listing all your privilege sets (see page 611). Click the checkbox to the left of each privilege set that should have access to the file.
- **No users.** If a file needs to be open on the host, but you don't want it shared, choose this option.

When you make changes to these settings, FileMaker is actually making changes to the privilege sets in the selected file. When you turn on "All users," FileMaker simply turns on the "Access via FileMaker Network" extended privilege for every privilege set. Likewise, if you choose "No users," it turns this extended privilege off for every set. When you specify people by privilege set, you get to decide which privilege sets have this extended privilege turned on. If you prefer, you can make these changes manually in the Extended Privileges tab of the Manage Accounts & Privileges window (File → Manage → Accounts & Privileges). Look for the [fmapp] extended privilege if you're setting access manually (page 630).

Note: You can control the access settings for each file even if you don't turn on network sharing. The settings you make to a file stick with that file even when you move it to another computer, so you can use this window to set the sharing options for a file *before* you send it to the host computer.

When a database is shared this way, you use the File → Open Remote command to open it from another computer (you'll learn how to do so in the next section). FileMaker then shows every available shared database. If you don't want this database to show up, turn on the "Don't display in Open Remote File dialog" checkbox. Why would you share a database and then make it invisible? Suppose you have a database system that's made up of several files, but you want your users to open only a specific one (because only one file has an interface and the others just hold data, for example). You want only that main file visible in the Open dialog box, so nobody opens the wrong one. However, you still need to *share* the other files.

Opening a Shared File

If you just shared your database so a colleague can access it, the easiest way to get him connected is to send him a link to your database. Just choose File → Send Link, and FileMaker will create an email in your email program with a clickable link to the database. (The recipient will need FileMaker installed for the link to work.)

But FileMaker has a more direct route to opening shared files, too. Launch FileMaker Pro on another computer on the network, and then follow these steps:

1. **Choose File → Open Remote.**

   If you're already looking at the Open File dialog box, click the Remote button instead. Either way, you see the Open Remote File dialog box (Figure 18-2).

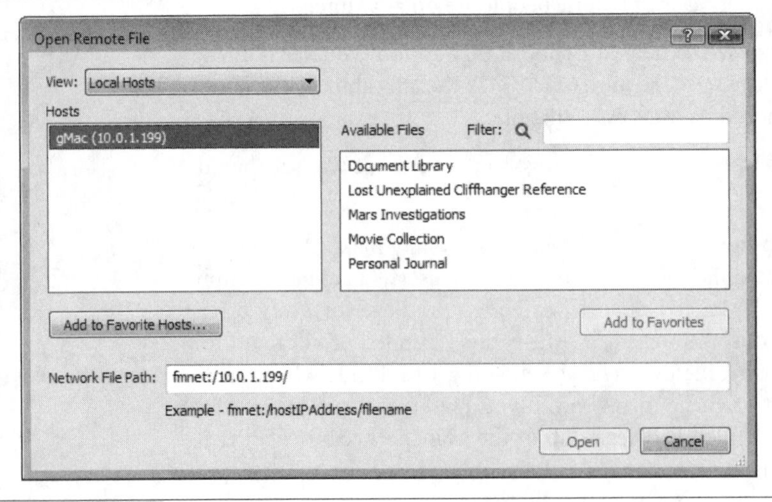

Figure 18-2: *The Open Remote File dialog box lets you find files that are shared on the network. This box lists all the hosts it can find in the Hosts list. Select a host to see all the available files in the list to the right. If you like the typing thing, you can enter exactly what FileMaker needs in the Network File Path box.*

2. **Select the appropriate host from the Hosts list.**

   The shared files show in the Available Files list. (If the host computer you're looking for isn't listed, see "Choosing a host computer" below for advice.)

3. **Select the file you want to open from the Available Files list, and then click Open.**

   If you've added accounts to the file, FileMaker asks you for an account name and password. When you give it what it needs, the database opens.

Note: When a database opens from a host, FileMaker puts the host name in parentheses in the window title bar to help you keep things straight. If you don't like seeing host names in your window's title bars, use the Set Window Title step to change that name in a script that runs when the file is opened (page 558).

The Open Remote File Dialog Box

The Open Remote File dialog box (File → Open Remote) has even more tricks up its sleeve, mostly geared towards folks with a lot of databases. If you're perfectly happy with the previous instructions, you have permission to skip this section.

Choosing a host computer

The first task when opening a remote file is to choose the host computer. The View pop-up menu above the Hosts list offers three choices:

- Choose **Local Hosts**, and FileMaker searches your local network and lists any host computers it finds. This view is usually the easiest way to share files in the office (or house or wherever all your computers are in one place). You can see each computer's name and IP address.

  Unfortunately, the Local Hosts option has a few weaknesses. First, it can be a little slow, which may drive you crazy if you can't stand to waste a single second. Worse, sometimes FileMaker can't find the host you want, usually because the guest computer and the host computer aren't on the same network (you might have a host computer at the office, and need to access it from home, for instance).

- If Local Hosts doesn't do the trick, choose **Favorite Hosts** from the View pop-up menu instead. When you do, FileMaker doesn't show anything in the Hosts list at first. Click the Add button to summon the Edit Favorite Host dialog box, and type the host computer's information, as shown in Figure 18-3.

  When you're done setting up the favorite host, click Save. FileMaker now shows the computer in the Hosts list. Now, whenever you visit the Open Remote File dialog box, FileMaker will have Favorite Hosts preselected, with all your favorites instantly available.

  Of course, you can change a favorite at any time (just select it and click Edit) or remove it from the list when you don't need it anymore (select it and click Remove).

Tip: When you add a host to your favorites, FileMaker also shows it in the Quick Start dialog box (page 21). Click the Open Database icon in that window, and you'll see your host listed in the box on the left.

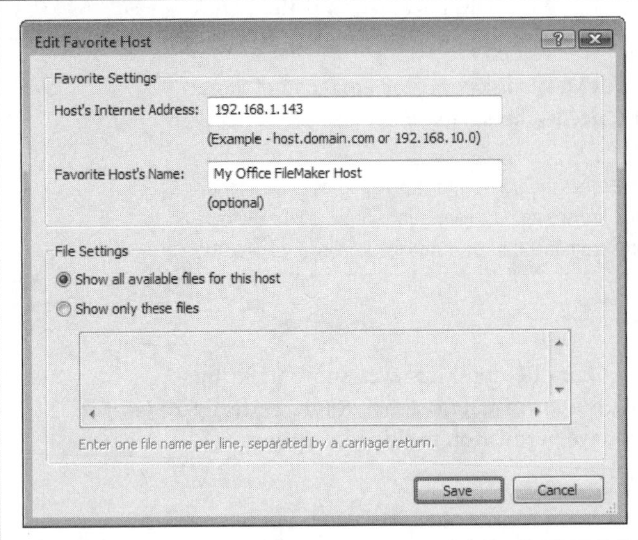

Figure 18-3: *When you add (or edit) a host in the Favorite Hosts list, FileMaker shows this window. Type the host computer's address in the first box. You can use the IP address, or if the computer has a name (like filemaker.mycompany.com), you can type that instead. Next, give it any descriptive name you want in the Favorite Host's Name box. Normally FileMaker shows every visible database from a host. You can enter specific database names if you want, though (if you routinely use just one database from a host with dozens, say). Just turn on "Show only these files," and then type one name on each line in the big box below it.*

- The **Hosts Listed by LDAP** option is for the big guys. If you have a lot of FileMaker servers, and you don't want end users to have to manage their Favorites list manually, you can set up an LDAP server with available host information. Refer to the FileMaker Server documentation for details on this not-so-common option.

Choosing a file

Once you've made your host selection, you get to choose the file you want to open. Typically, each shared file is listed in the Available Files list on the right side of the window, and you can just double-click one to open it (or select it and click Open).

If the Available Files list has *lots* of databases, you can find the one you want by typing in the Filter box. FileMaker reduces the list to show each file whose name contains the letter or phrase you enter. For example, if you type *mars*, you'll probably see only the Mars Investigations file.

If you find yourself opening the same files often (a pretty common thing), select a file and click "Add to Favorites." When you do, FileMaker adds this file to the list of favorite files in the Quick Start dialog box (page 21).

Finally, on some occasions you may need to open a file that doesn't show in the list. For example, you might have an ancillary file that you've configured to share but not show in the Open Remote dialog box. That setup is fine for your users, who never need to open this file directly. But you, O wise developer, may need to open the file to look under the hood.

1. **Select the host computer from the Hosts list if you haven't already.**

   In addition to showing files from the host, FileMaker adds the host's address to the Network File Path box at the bottom of the window. For example, if you select a host with the address 192.168.1.10, FileMaker puts *fmnet:/192.168.1.10/* in the box.

2. **Add your database name to the end of the network file path (after the "/").**

   Since the file you want doesn't show in the list, you have to type its name directly. You're actually creating a FileMaker network file path, which FileMaker will use to open the file for you.

3. **Click Open.**

   If you typed the name correctly, FileMaker opens the file.

If you get an error, check to make sure you spelled the file name correctly, and that the file really *is* shared and open on the host computer.

Note: You don't need to put the ".fp7" in the network file path. FileMaker knows you're looking for a FileMaker database.

Sharing over the Internet

FileMaker Network Sharing is the easiest way to share your database. Folks simply open the file, and it works *exactly* like a file on their hard drive. The catch is that they need a copy of FileMaker Pro on whatever computer they're using to connect. (Of course, when you consider how cool FileMaker Pro is, you're probably doing them a favor.) If you want to open up your database to people who don't have FileMaker—and you're willing to live with a less elegant interface—you can use Instant Web Publishing. This feature turns your computer into its own Web server. Like magic, it turns all your layouts into Web pages and lets anybody with an up-to-date Web browser search, sort, and edit your data directly.

Turning on Web Sharing

Enabling Instant Web Publishing (IWP for short) is just as easy as turning on FileMaker Network Sharing. First, choose File → Sharing → Instant Web Publishing, and then click On. Once IWP starts up, FileMaker shows you the URL by which people access your databases. (You also get to pick a language for your Web pages. This action doesn't translate the information in your database, though. Instead, it controls what language all of FileMaker's built-in buttons, labels, and links use in the Web browser.)

Advanced Web Publishing Options

The Advanced Web Publishing Options window lets you configure FileMaker's built-in Web server. You get to pick a *port* (more on that next) and restrict access to only certain computers, among other settings. Clicking Advanced Options in the Instant Web Publishing window opens the dialog box (Figure 18-4).

Network servers set up shop at a *TCP/IP Port Number*, and once you turn on IWP, your computer is a network server, too. The usual Web publishing port is 80 and, if you have no other Web services running on your computer, that's the one you'll

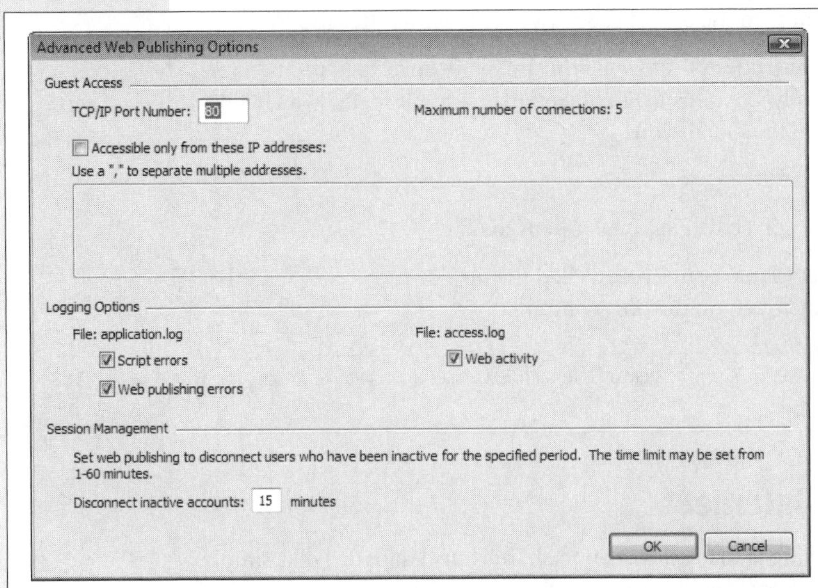

Figure 18-4: *In the Advanced Web Options dialog box, you get to decide which information FileMaker records in log files (you can refer to these files if you have problems or are curious who's using the database). Also, you can tell FileMaker to forget about users who haven't clicked the Web page for a while by setting the "Disconnect inactive accounts" value.*

usually use. But if you do need to set up your Web server with multiple services, you can change FileMaker's port number to avoid a conflict. As you can see in the figure above, FileMaker has registered its very own port number just for Web publishing (591). If you stick with port 591, chances are no other program's using it, and you'll avoid conflicts even if you need to add other services later on. When you assign any other port other than 80, FileMaker automatically adds the port number to the URL it displays in the Instant Web Publishing dialog box, as a reminder of the link your browser uses to connect to your site.

Note: When you use port 80, links to your site don't need to include the port number, but if you're using any other port number, you'll have to make sure they do. In a URL, the port number comes right after the server name, with a colon in front, like this: *http://mycomputer:591/*.

If you don't want just anybody trying to connect to your databases, you can turn on "Accessible only from these IP addresses." You then have to list the network address of each computer you want to allow (with commas in between). If you have a large intranet, you don't have to type dozens of IP addresses, though. You can specify a range of addresses using an asterisk. For example, 192.168.15.* lets everyone whose IP address matches the first three sets of numbers access the file.

While IWP is running, it can keep track of activity and errors. FileMaker keeps this information in log files in its Web Logs folder. The "Web activity" log records each time someone interacts with the database. The log includes the network address of the user, and the URL she requested. The "Script errors" log records errors in your FileMaker scripts. The "Web publishing errors" log holds other errors that occur in IWP, like invalid requests and missing databases. You can use these logs to see if

UP TO SPEED

Record Locking Revisited

Back in Chapter 2, you learned about *record locking*. When you start editing a record, FileMaker locks it, so it can't be changed in another window until you commit it in the first. At the time, this scenario probably seemed like a pretty obscure situation: How often do you try to edit the same record in two different windows? But when several people start sharing the same database, record locking takes on a whole new meaning. Now, when you start editing a record, *nobody else* can edit it. If you type a few lines in the Notes field, and then go home sick without clicking out of the record, you keep it locked all day.

When you try to edit a locked record, FileMaker warns you with a message box. It tells you the record's locked, and *who* has it locked (including the user name on their computer, *and* the account name they've logged in with).

If you'd like to politely ask them to get out of the record, click Send Message. You see the "Send Message to Conflicting Users" window. Enter any message you want and click OK. A window will pop up on the other user's screen with your message.

While record locking can be a minor annoyance to the user, it can be a real problem for the database developer. If you've designed all your scripts with the mistaken notion that you'll *always* be able to edit *any* record you want, you might get an unpleasant surprise the first time a script tries to modify a locked record.

Even worse, sometimes you build a process that simply doesn't work for multiple users. For example, suppose you expect people to flag a series of records, and then run a script that does something to all the ones they flagged. If the script *finds* the flagged records and loops through them, FileMaker gets utterly confused when two people try to use the same script at once. The script sees everyone's marked flags, unless you take special care to make each person's flag unique. It's anybody's guess how your poor records will wind up. In this example, you could mitigate the problem by entering the user's account name in the flag field. The script could then find just that user's flagged records.

In general, you should think about how the script you write works if a record can't be edited, or if several people are using it at the same time. Or, to avoid the issue altogether, make it so only one person can use certain scripts, and use privilege sets to keep everybody else away from them.

you need to fix your scripts, or to see who's been using the databases and what problems they've encountered. If you use IWP a lot, these logs can get large. Turn any or all of them off to keep FileMaker from recording this information.

Web browsers don't work exactly like FileMaker itself. Someone has to explicitly log out to tell FileMaker he's disconnecting. If he doesn't—for example, if he just quits his browser or goes to a different Web site—FileMaker doesn't know he's left your site. To keep people from tying up connections forever, FileMaker automatically disconnects anyone who hasn't requested a page in a while. You get to decide how long "a while" is. A smaller setting (like 15 minutes) ensures that people don't hold connections long if they forget to log out. But if they spend more than 15 minutes looking at a single record (reading a long Notes field, for instance), then they're disconnected even though they're still using the database. If you have situations like this one, set the "Disconnect inactive accounts" value to something larger (the maximum is 60 minutes).

Configuring file access

Just like FileMaker Network Sharing, you get to decide which files are shared by IWP, and which privilege sets have Web access. In fact, the settings are identical: Select an open file, and then choose the appropriate access level. Finally, you manage IWP access using the [fmiwp] extended privilege.

Connecting from a Web Browser

Not all Web browsers are created equal. They aren't all good at showing you Web sites that use Cascading Style Sheets (CSS). And since FileMaker translates your layouts into CSS when you share them via IWP, you must have a browser that understands CSS to use databases on the Web, like one of the following:

- Microsoft Internet Explorer 6.0 or higher in Windows
- Safari 1.2 or higher in Mac OS X 10.3
- Safari 2.0 or higher in Mac OS X 10.4 or Windows
- Firefox 1.0 or higher in Mac or Windows

To connect to the database from a Web browser, you need to know the URL in the Instant Web Publishing dialog box. Type this URL into the Location box in your Web browser. The resulting Web page looks like the one in Figure 18-5.

Figure 18-5: *This screen is the first thing you see when you connect to Instant Web Publishing in your Web browser. The page has a link for each shared database. You just click the link to open the database.*

When you click a database link on the Web page, FileMaker asks you to log in to the database—even if you haven't set up accounts on your database. If you've created accounts, enter a valid account name and password. Otherwise, enter *Admin* for the user name, and leave the password box blank. After you log in, you see what probably looks a *lot* like your real database displayed right inside the Web page (Figure 18-6).

The most noticeable difference is the status area: It's bigger and has more options, as Figure 18-6 attests. When you view your data in List view or Table view, the Web page shows only a few records at a time. To see more, click the pages in the book icon or type a record number in the Current Record box, and then click the "Go to Record" button in the status area. Since you're working on the Web, you *must* click this button to reload the page with the desired record.

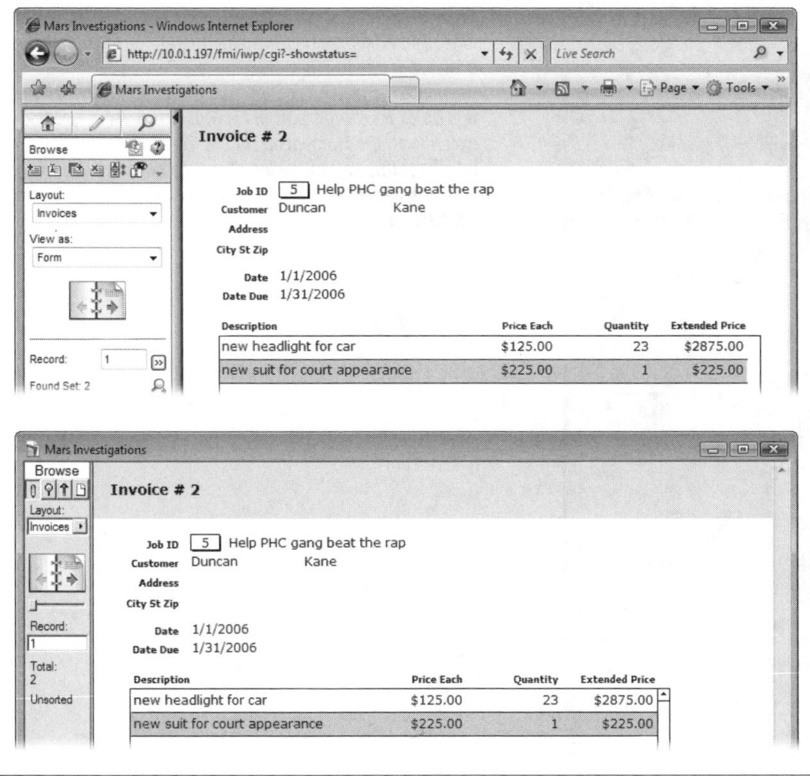

Figure 18-6: *Top: When you view a layout in the browser, it looks almost identical to the original, except for a radically redesigned status area.*

Bottom: Here's the original window. FileMaker goes to heroic lengths to make the Web page match this layout.

The process of editing records is also different in IWP. When you first click an editable field (or click the Edit Record button in the toolbar), FileMaker reloads the page in editable form. The status area also changes: Submit and Cancel buttons appear, while all other tools become unavailable. After you've made changes, you have to click Submit or FileMaker doesn't save them. If you don't want to keep your changes, click Cancel instead.

The toolbar in the status area has icons for common database activities. The icons change if you switch to Browse mode, and if you hold your mouse arrow over a button for a few seconds, a label pops up telling you what the button does. You can see the Browse mode and Find mode toolbars in Figure 18-7.

Custom Home Page

The IWP home page, shown in Figure 18-5, gets the job done, but it's not likely that it matches your corporate identity. And some users find it a bit confusing, since it doesn't provide them with a lot of clues about what your IWP database does. But you can make a Custom Home Page to replace it. First, take the HTML file you want to use for the home page and name it *iwp_home.html*. Then put it in

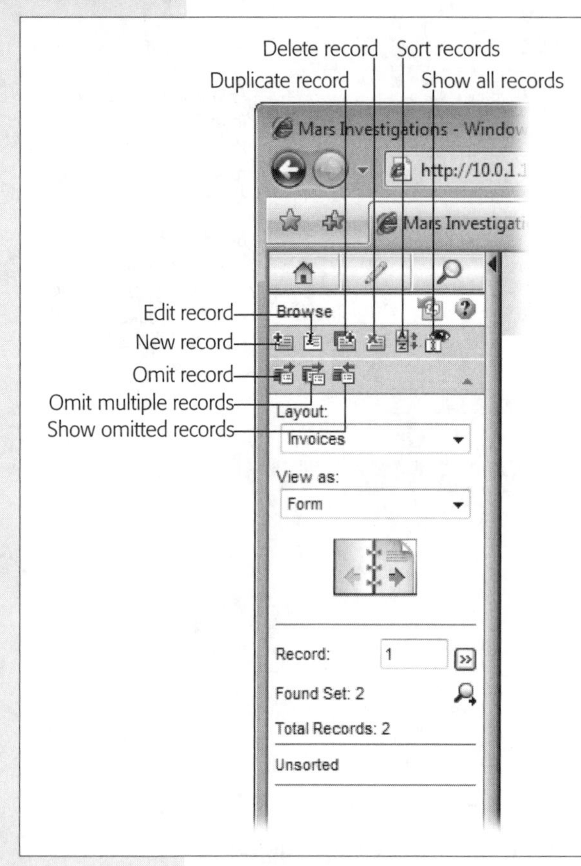

Figure 18-7:
Since FileMaker can't control the menu bar in your Web browser, it has to cram everything it thinks you'll ever need into the status area instead. Almost everything here has an exact counterpart in FileMaker Pro itself. Notable exceptions: the Home icon (in the top-right corner), which returns you to the list of shared databases, and Log Out, which tells FileMaker you're done using the connection.

FileMaker's Web folder. On Windows, you'll find it at Program Files → FileMaker → FileMaker Pro → Web. On Mac OS X, it's at Applications → FileMaker Pro 9.0 → Web. If FileMaker sees a file with this name, it automatically shows it instead of the normal IWP home page.

Of course, you'll want to include links to your databases on this page. Direct links to an IWP database look like this:

```
/fmi/iwp/cgi?-db=Database Name&-startsession
```

Just replace "Database Name" with the name of your database.

FileMaker Server

Using FileMaker Pro on an ordinary desktop computer to host your files is easy and decidedly inexpensive, but it has some pretty severe drawbacks. First, it can handle no more than nine guests at once. If you have more, you have to find a better way.

There are some less obvious problems as well, including the following:

- If somebody's working on the host computer, chances are they're doing more than just FileMaker. The more you do on a computer, the more likely it is to crash—especially after you contract the next email virus. The host in a peer-to-peer setup can sometimes be unstable. You probably don't want your database server interrupting your office workflow. But more serious than that, databases that crash often are likely to get corrupted. And that's not safe for your data.
- FileMaker Pro is designed for *using* databases, not hosting them. It does an admirable hosting job, but it simply wasn't built for speed or large numbers of simultaneous users.
- As you remember from Chapter 1, you should close databases before you back them up. But if they're open on a host computer, you have to disconnect all the guests before closing the files. This necessity makes midday backups a little inconvenient.

The answer to all these problems—and more—is FileMaker Server. It's a special piece of software designed for one thing: turning a dedicated computer into a lean, mean, and *stable* database host. When FileMaker Server hosts your databases, you can have *250* guests connected at once. Since it runs on a dedicated server, it tends to be much more stable (and you can put it in the closet, where nobody will pull the plug or close the files accidentally). From a performance perspective, you *can't* launch FileMaker Server and use the database directly. In fact, it has no windows, menus, or dialog boxes at all (there is an administration tool through which you can monitor the server and make changes to it, though). Instead, it's a true *server* (sometimes called a *service* or a *daemon*), designed specifically to share data over the network. Finally, it's loaded with special server-only features, including an automatic backup feature that can safely back up files while people are connected.

So what's the catch? Money. FileMaker Server costs $999, while another copy of FileMaker Pro is only $249. Don't be fooled, though. This cash is money well spent if your database is at all important to your business.

Note: FileMaker Server comes in two flavors: *FileMaker Server* and *FileMaker Server Advanced*. Both do a fine job with FileMaker Network Sharing, but only the Advanced version does those *other* kinds of sharing–Instant Web Publishing. (Regular Server can do Custom Web Publishing too, if that's your need. But you'll need Advanced for ODBC and JDBC support.) If you're not sure you need Advanced just yet, don't sweat it. You can buy FileMaker Server today, and then trade it up to Advanced later if the need arises. This book doesn't cover the Advanced version. If you're interested in getting into big-time Web publishing, check out the resources in Appendix A.

File Compatibility

As you learned back near the beginning of this book, the file extension for database files created with version 7, 8, and 9 is "fp7." Therefore, you can do a fair amount of version mixing between FileMaker Server, FileMaker Developer, and

FileMaker Pro, and still get good results. You can develop files on FileMaker Pro Advanced 8, put them on a FileMaker 9 Server, and let your users with FIleMaker Pro 7 share them. You can mix-and-match versions 7-9 at will.

Note: The files will open just fine across versions 7, 8, and 9. However, some features, like Tab controls, script variables, conditional formatting, and External SQL Sources (ESS) won't work properly in version 7 or 8, so take care how you mix versions if you're using these recent additions.

However, files prior to version 7 have to be converted before you can use them with any FileMaker product that's version 7 or above. But those good folks at FileMaker, Inc. have been careful to provide support for conversion. FileMaker 9 can convert files from as far back as FileMaker 3. You *can* convert even older versions, but it's tricky. You have to find someone with FileMaker 5 first, and use it to convert older files to the fp5 format. Once the files have been updated, FileMaker Pro 8 can take over and get you up to .fp7-land.

If you have files to convert, be sure to check out two excellent documents on migration: "Migration foundations and methodologies" and "How to migrate existing solutions." Look for them in the Migration Topics section at *www.filemaker.com/support/whitepapers.html.*

POWER USERS' CLINIC

Global Fields and Multiple Users

When many people share a single database, you might be worried about global fields. If one user changes a global field, does it change for *everybody*? In a word, "no." FileMaker keeps global field information on the *guest* computer. If you change what's in the global field, it has no effect on what's in that global field for other people.

This characteristic is, in general, a very good thing. But it does have an annoying side effect. Since everyone has his or her own globals, you *can't* change them for other people even when you want to. If you open a shared database, change a global, and then close it, you lose your changes. The next time you open the database, the globals have the same values as the *host* computer.

If you're using peer-to-peer sharing, you can change the globals on the host directly to make them stick. Since FileMaker Server has no real interface, there's no way to directly modify the initial value for a global field. You have to close the files on the server, move them to another computer, open them with FileMaker Pro, make the change, and then copy them back to the server. In other words, it's a pain.

If you have globals you often need to change permanently in a multiuser system, then it's often easier to simply set them from a script that runs when the database opens. Then you're sure they have the right value, and you can always modify the script if you want to change the starting value while the databases are still hosted.

Installing FileMaker Server

If you decide a FileMaker Server is the right thing for your database, your first step is to install the software. (Although you may want to buy a good server computer first. See "Server Hardware" on page 701 for some guidelines.) FileMaker Server (in both its standard and Advanced versions) includes an installer program that takes care of the basic complexities of configuration for you. When you run the installer (and after you accept the terms of the license agreement) FileMaker asks you a simple question, as shown in Figure 18-8.

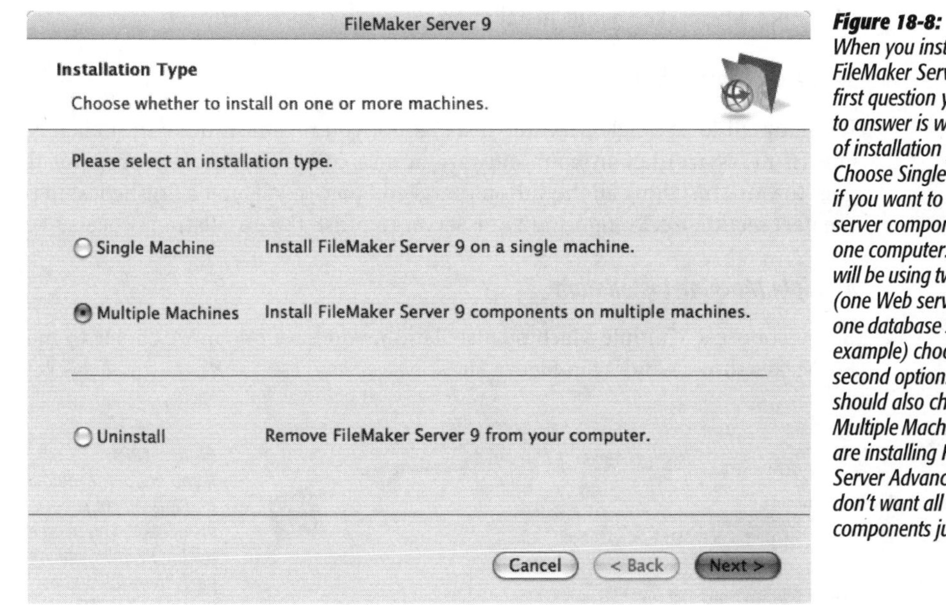

Figure 18-8: *When you install FileMaker Server, the first question you have to answer is what type of installation you want. Choose Single Machine if you want to install all server components on one computer. If you will be using two servers (one Web server and one database server, for example) choose the second option. You should also choose Multiple Machines if you are installing FileMaker Server Advanced but don't want all the Web components just yet.*

If your database will be heavily used (by dozens or even a couple hundred people) and you plan on using the Web publishing capabilities of FileMaker heavily, it probably makes sense to install different portions of the server setup on different machines. Three configurations are typical:

- **FileMaker Server and Web Server.** Install FileMaker Server and the Web Publishing Engine on one computer, and use an ordinary Web server computer as the "front end" for your web publishing. This configuration works well if you already have a Web server in your organization, and you want to add some FileMaker based Web content. You can keep all the FileMaker parts together in one place, with minimal impact on the Web server computer.
- **Web Server and Database Server.** Install FileMaker Server on one computer, and the Web Publishing Engine on another. The database server will handle all your pure data serving needs. The Web Server will handle both ordinary Web pages and the FileMaker Web publishing system.
- **Web Server, Web Publishing Engine, and Database Server.** Install the FileMaker Server on one computer, the Web Publishing Engine on another, and use a third as a Web server. In this configuration, the load of the Web Publishing Engine does not interfere with ordinary Web server tasks, and does not slow down the FileMaker Server. This configuration is generally the fastest for maximum load.

Note: If you aren't using FileMaker Server Advanced or you don't need plan on doing any Web publishing, your decision is simple. Just do a Single Machine installation on the server computer and you're done.

If you plan on using any of these multi-computer configurations, choose Multiple Machines when asked about Installation Type, then click Next.

Single Machine Installation

If you opted for a Single Machine installation, you're almost done. Just click Next and (if necessary) key in your software license code. The installer program then goes to work installing all the various parts and pieces. When it's finished, skip past the next section to Configuring Your Server to finish the installation process.

Multiple Machine Installation

If you choose a Multiple Machine installation, you have one more choice to make. FileMaker shows window in Figure 18-9.

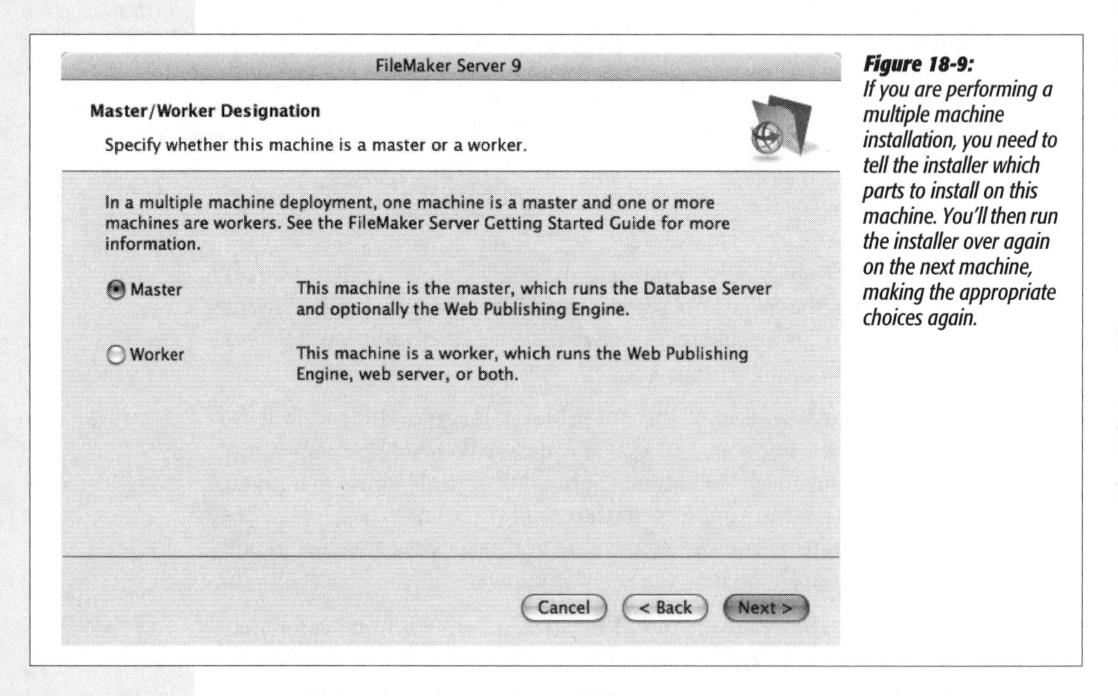

***Figure 18-9:** If you are performing a multiple machine installation, you need to tell the installer which parts to install on this machine. You'll then run the installer over again on the next machine, making the appropriate choices again.*

To install the FileMaker Server itself (for sharing your database) choose Master. The installer places the FileMaker Server and Web Publishing software on your computer (although you don't have to run the web publishing portion if you don't want).

If you are setting up a Web publishing server of some kind, choose Worker instead. The installer will install the Web Publishing Engine software on the server, and configure its Web server appropriately. You may have to perform this installation on *two* different computers if you have a three-server setup.

Configuring Your Server

Once the installer has finished putting software on your computer, it will ask if you want to start the Deployment Assistant. This step is necessary since otherwise, the software will sit dormant on your computer. Click Continue, and your Web browser opens to show the page in Figure 18-10.

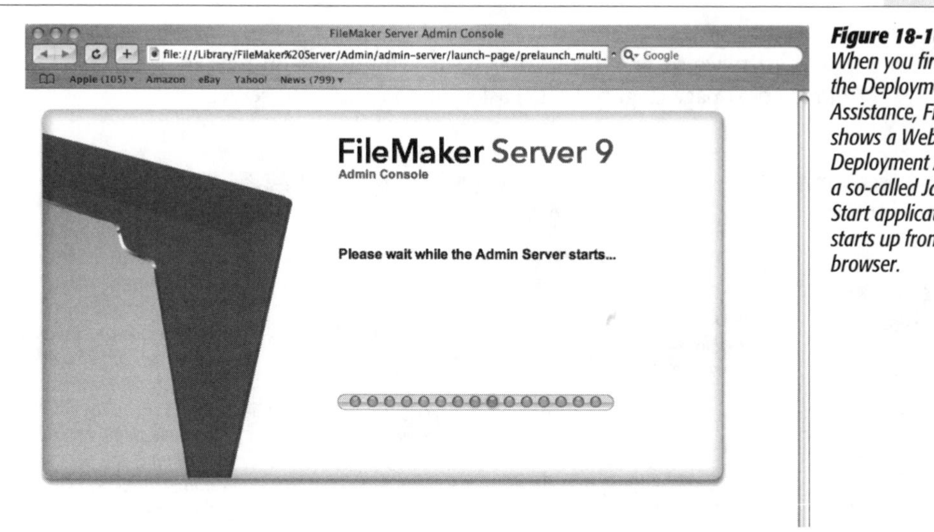

***Figure 18-10:** When you first launch the Deployment Assistance, FileMaker shows a Web page. The Deployment Assistant is a so-called Java Web Start application, so it starts up from your web browser.*

When you first start the Deployment Assistant, it can take several minutes. FileMaker has to start up its server software, download the configuration tools to your computer, and start up the admin application. But if you exercise some patience, you'll eventually see the first screen of the Deployment Assistant, as shown in Figure 18-11.

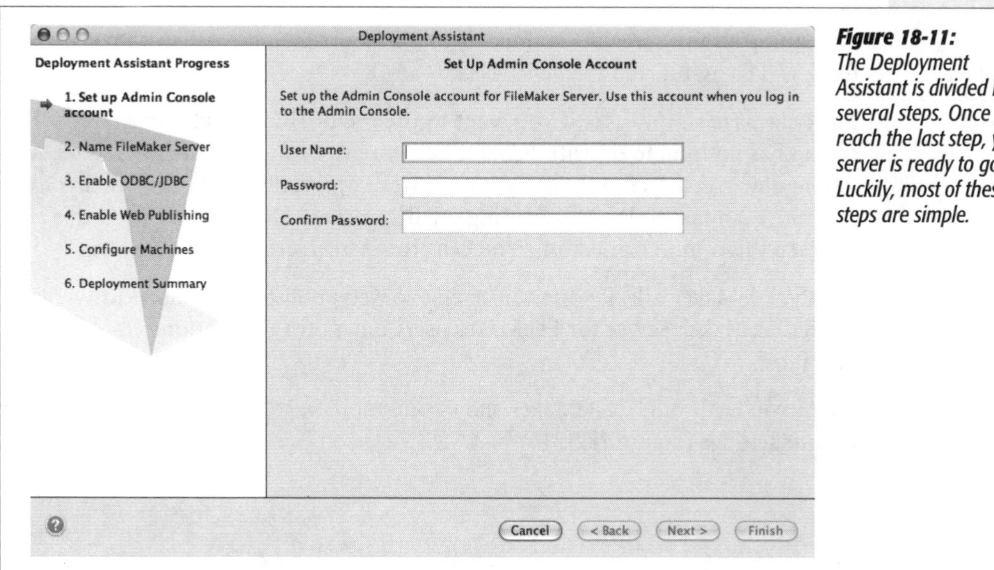

***Figure 18-11:** The Deployment Assistant is divided into several steps. Once you reach the last step, your server is ready to go. Luckily, most of these steps are simple.*

In the first screen, you're asked to set up an "admin console account." When you interact with your FileMaker Server in the future, you'll use the Admin Console application. It can tweak configuration settings, install new databases, perform backups, and more. And it can do all this from any computer on the network. To prevent unauthorized users from working with your server, you set up an account (with a name and password) for authorized administrators.

Just enter the User Name and Password you want to use. You have to type the password twice so FileMaker can be sure you didn't mistype it. Then click Next, and the next page (Figure 18-12) asks you to name your server.

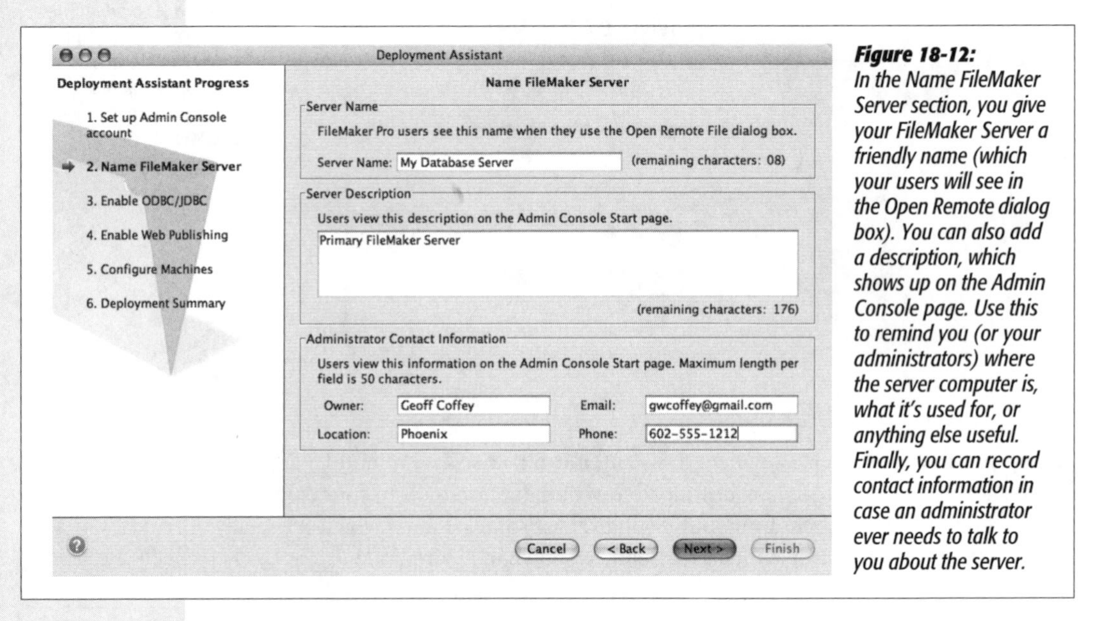

Figure 18-12: *In the Name FileMaker Server section, you give your FileMaker Server a friendly name (which your users will see in the Open Remote dialog box). You can also add a description, which shows up on the Admin Console page. Use this to remind you (or your administrators) where the server computer is, what it's used for, or anything else useful. Finally, you can record contact information in case an administrator ever needs to talk to you about the server.*

Everything on this screen is optional except the Server Name. Fill out the parts you think will be useful, and then click Next.

The next page simply asks if you want to use ODBC/JDBC with your server. This option has nothing to do with ESS, ODBC Import, or the Execute SQL script step: You're *always* free to use these features. Instead, this setting controls whether *other* programs can talk to FileMaker using ODBC or JDBC. If you don't need this ability, keep this option turned off. (You can always turn it on at any time later.)

Finally, FileMaker asks if you want to enable web publishing. If this is just a plain-vanilla FileMaker Server for FileMaker users only, turn this option off. Otherwise, turn it on.

When you're through, FileMaker shows one more page, with a summary of your various settings (Figure 18-13).

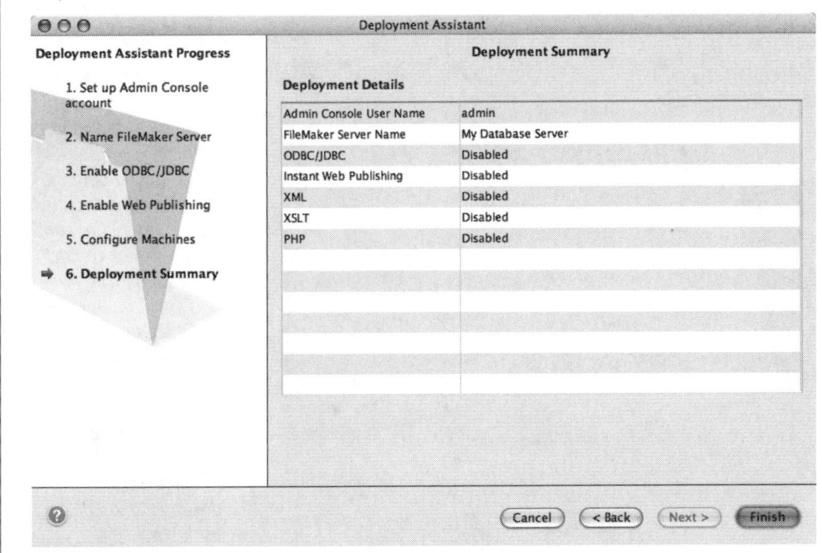

***Figure 18-13:** Before it goes about deploying servers, FileMaker gives you a concise overview of the options you've selected. You can click Back if you want to change some of your choices.*

When you're confident you have the server set up the way you want, click Finish. The assistant then configures all the parts of your server, and launches the Admin Console for you.

Administering FileMaker Server

Once you have a server installed and configured, you can administer it at any time using the Admin Console. On the computer you performed the installation, you'll see a shortcut on your desktop that takes you to the FileMaker Server Admin Console Start Page (Figure 18-14). But you can visit this page from *any computer on your network* so you don't have to leave your desk to work with your server. If this is the first time you've accessed this page on your computer, you'll have to type the URL directly. It looks like this:

```
http://myserver:16000/
```

In other words, use the name of your server, followed by ":16000". This URL tells your browser to access FileMaker Server's start page directly.

From the start page, you can launch the Admin Console itself. Just click the icon next to Start Admin Console. Again, the first time you use the Admin Console (Figure 18-15), it takes a few minutes to configure the software on your computer. (Later, when you come back to the Admin Console, it will be faster).

The sidebar in the Admin Console includes several important sections:

- **Clients.** All the people who are connected to your server. Generally, they're folks who have one of your shared databases open, or are using Instant Web Publishing. You can see their FileMaker account name, the type of connection

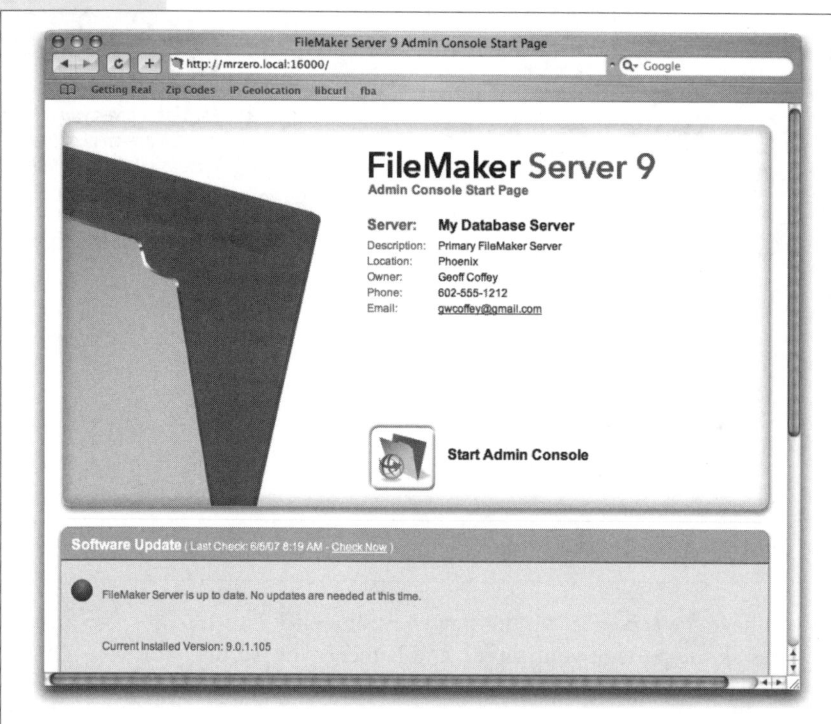

***Figure 18-14:** The FileMaker Server Admin Console Start Page is a one-stop shop for server information. At the top, you see information about the server itself, including its name, description, and administrator contact information. The page tells you if an update is available for your FileMaker Server software (bottom). You can't see it in this picture, but if you scroll down, you also get links to online server documentation and useful tools.*

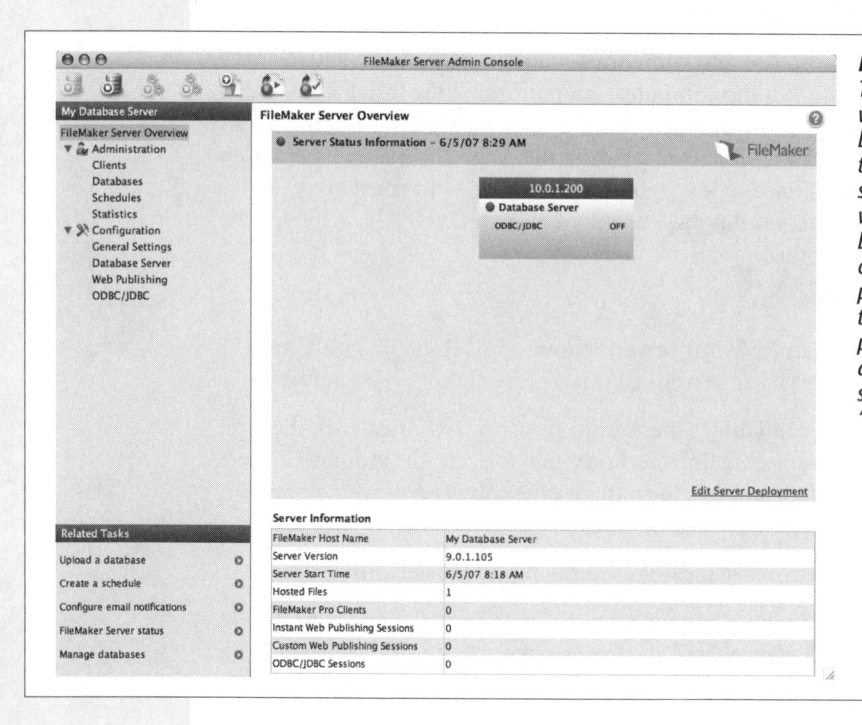

***Figure 18-15:** The Admin Console is a vast application. The bar along the left side of the window lets you switch between the various sections. At the bottom of this bar, you can click links to perform important tasks. For example, you probably want to install a database on your server. To do that, click "Upload a database."*

they have, their computers' network address, and even which version of FileMaker they're using. You can also send them a message, or disconnect them from the server. To do so, first select a user in the list, then pick from the Actions pop-up menu and click Perform Action.

- **Databases.** A list of databases being shared with this server. You can see which databases are being shared, and in what ways. And just like with Clients, you can select a database and perform any of several actions.
- **Schedules.** Gives you high level information about scheduled tasks on your server. You can schedule three different things on FileMaker Server: backups, scripts, and messages. The most important of these are backups, and you'll see how to create a backup schedule on page 697.
- **Statistics.** Tells you about your server. The myriad numbers presented on this screen give your (or FileMaker's tech support staff) information about how much load your server encounters, and how it's performing.
- **General Settings.** Includes all the configuration options you set when you set up your server, plus some additional options. Here, you can rename your server (in the Server Information tab), tell the server to email you important information periodically (in the Email Notifications tab), change the administrator password (in the Admin Console tab) and decide if the server should start automatically when the computer boots (in the Auto Start tab).
- **Database Server.** Shows configuration options specific to the database server portion of FileMaker Server. In addition to numerous parameters like how many users can connect to the server and how many databases can be installed, you can also decide where database backups are stored.
- **Web Publishing** and **ODBC/JDBC** let you configure these optional portions of the FileMaker Server.

Below this list of console screens, the Admin Console has a list of common tasks. You will probably visit each of these when you first set up your server.

Installing a Database

When you first install your server, it is like a well of untapped potential. Although the server is ready to go, you don't have any *databases* installed. Your first job is to install at least one shared database so you can take advantage of FileMaker Server's high performance capabilities.

1. **Click Databases in the Admin Console sidebar.**

   FileMaker shows you the Databases section of the admin console, including an Actions pop-up menu.

2. **From the Actions pop-up menu, choose Upload, then click Perform Action.**

   The Upload Database Assistant appears (Figure 18-16).

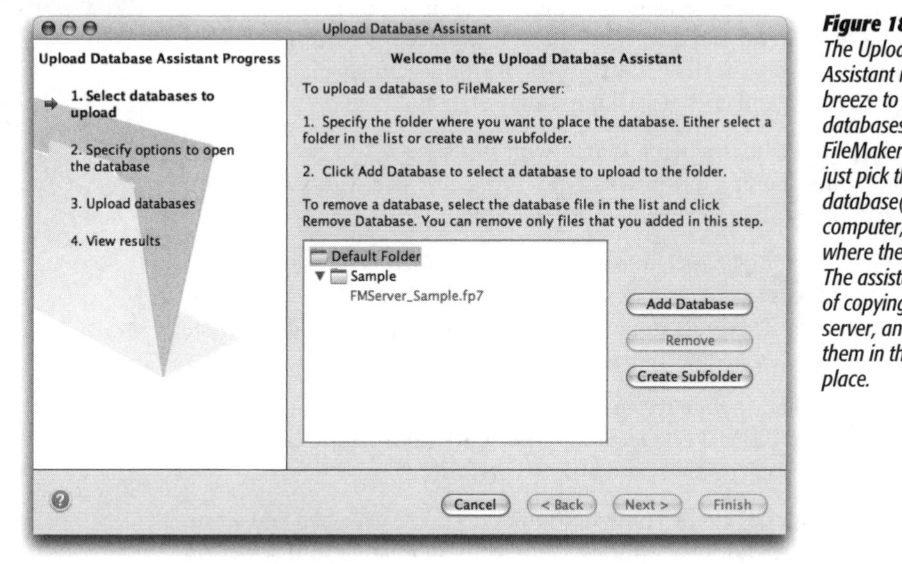

Figure 18-16: *The Upload Database Assistant makes it a breeze to install databases on your FileMaker server. You just pick the database(s) from your computer, and decide where they should go. The assistant takes care of copying them to the server, and installing them in the appropriate place.*

3. **Click Create Subfolder and, in the box that pops up, enter "My Database System," then click OK.**

   FileMaker Server organizes shared databases in folders. This step is entirely optional, but if your database system has several files, or you want to share different database systems, it's helpful to keep related databases together in one folder.

4. **Click Add Database.**

   You see a standard Open File dialog box. Here's where you pick the file you want to share.

5. **Navigate to the file you want to share, select it, and click Open.**

   Make sure the database isn't already open in FileMaker Pro before you try to upload it. When you've made your choice, FileMaker adds it to the list in the assistant window. If you have other databases to share, select a folder and click Add Database again.

6. **Click Next.**

   FileMaker inspects your files to be sure they're ready to share, then asks if you want to open the files once they're uploaded. (A file can be opened and closed on the server just like on your own computer. An open file is shared and ready to be opened by other users. A closed file is on the server, but can't be accessed by users.)

7. **Leave "Automatically open databases after upload" turned on and click Next.**

   The Upload Assistant uploads the databases (it shows a progress bar as they're copied) and then reports that the "Upload has completed successfully."

8. **Click Next.**

   The Upload Assistant shows you the status of each uploaded file. Generally, each file will indicate "File uploaded successfully and opened." This means your database is shared and ready to be accessed in FileMaker Pro using the File → Open Remote dialog box.

When you're done uploading, click Finish. You return to the Admin Console window, where you can see your database in the Databases section.

Scheduling a Backup

One of the primary advantages of a true FileMaker Server is the ability to perform database backups easily. The importance of this step can't be underestimated. Some day your server will crash, perhaps because a hard drive fails, or the power goes out, or for any of a dozen other reasons. When this happens, your best course of action is to take your lumps, restore from backup, and re-enter any missing data. The more often you back up, the less difficult this is.

If you want, you can configure FileMaker Server to back up to a different location than the main hard drive on your server computer. It makes good sense, for example, to back up on a second hard drive. This way if the main hard drive fails you don't lose your database *and* your backup.

But you should also make off-line backups that are stored in a remote location. This protects against the "office burns down" type scenarios, where all the computers and drives in your office are lost. FileMaker's automated backup will get the files cleanly copied to a drive of your choice, but it is up to you to copy those backups to tape, CD, DVD, or over the network so they're stored off site.

To configure the backup location, Database Server in the Admin Console sidebar. Then switch to the Default Folders tab. At the bottom of this window, you see the backup folder location (Figure 18-17).

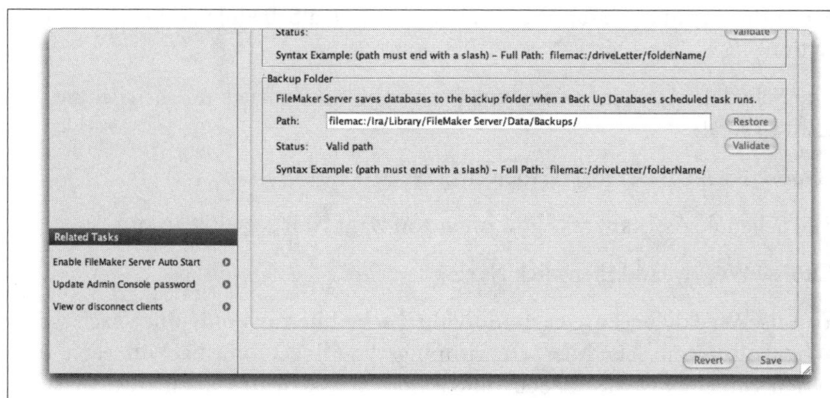

***Figure 18-17:** On the Default Folders tab, you tell FileMaker where you want to store backup files. You can enter any valid path on your computer (following the syntax example). You're best bet is a path on a hard drive other than the one your databases are stored on.*

In the Path box, type the full path to the folder where you want backups stored. The path must start with filewin: (Windows) or filemac: (Mac OS X) and must end with a slash. When you're done typing, click Validate and FileMaker will tell you if your path is valid.

Once you've set the backup location, you're ready to schedule the backup. Like many things in FileMaker, you can do this the easy way if your needs are basic, or you can peek under the hood and make numerous configuration choices to get exactly what you want. In fact, if you want the most basic backup (every file, every night) you don't have to do anything. FileMaker Server comes pre-configured to run just such a backup automatically. (You can see it in the Schedules section of the Admin Console, labeled Daily.)

If you want more frequent backups, turn off Daily and turn on Hourly instead (you turn on a schedule using the checkbox by its name). Alternately, you can turn on Weekly if you just want backups every week.

But suppose you want something a little more advanced. You want a daily backup, but you want to *keep* old backups for 7 days. Normally, FileMaker replaces the old files each time the backup runs. This is just fine if you're only worried about unexpected crashes. But sometimes problems can crop up in your database that you don't notice right away. (Imagine an employee accidentally deletes older archived order data, and you don't notice for a couple of days). To schedule daily backups like this, you need a custom schedule.

1. **Create seven folders in your backup folder, called Monday, Tuesday, Wednesday, etc.**

   These are your daily backup folders. You'll create seven schedules (one for each day) that back up files to these folders.

2. **In the Admin Console, switch to the Schedules section in the sidebar.**

   You see a list of schedules on your server.

3. **From the Actions pop-up menu, choose Create a Schedule and click Perform Action.**

   The Schedule Assistant window appears, and asks what kind of schedule you want to create.

4. **Choose Back Up Databases, then click Next.**

   The Schedule Assistant asks how often you want your schedule to run.

5. **Choose Weekly, and then click Next.**

   You use Weekly because each individual schedule runs only once each week. When all seven schedules are running, you'll get one backup each day. When you click Next, the Schedule Assistant asks which databases you want to back up.

6. **Turn on All Databases, and then click Next.**

   The Schedule Assistant now asks where you want the backup files stored. It shows the backup path you've set for this server, but you're free to make changes.

7. **Add "Monday/" to the end of the backup path, then click Validate.**

   You want this schedule to put files in the Monday folder you created in step 1. When you click Validate, the Status line should say "Valid path." If it does not, correct your path and click Validate again.

8. **Turn on Verify Backup Integrity.**

   If you're going to all the trouble to back up your data, you would like to know if it didn't work. When you turn this on, FileMaker will email you if it has any problems backing up later.

Note: In order for email notifications to work, you need to set up Email Notifications in the General Settings section of the Admin Console.

9. **Click Next.**

   The Schedule Assistant now asks you for details about *when* the backup should run. You already told it you wanted a weekly schedule, but you need to tell it when during the week.

10. **Under "Select the days of the week you would like the schedule to run," turn on Monday and turn off every other day.**

    This tells FileMaker Server to run this backup only on Mondays. The schedule is already configured to run at 11:00 PM. (You can change the time in the box by "Once per day from.")

11. **Click Next again.**

    You now get the chance to name your schedule. Every schedule has a unique name so you can tell them apart at a glance.

12. **In the Schedule Name box, enter "Monday backup." Then click Next.**

    Finally, the Schedule Assistant asks you what email address to send status reports to.

13. **Enter your email address, then click Next.**

    The Schedule Summary appears, showing all your schedule options.

14. **Make sure "Enable this schedule" is turned on, and click Finish.**

    You are back at the Schedules section of the Admin Console, and your new "Monday backup" schedule is in the list.

15. **Select "Monday backup" in the list, then from the Actions pop-up menu, choose Duplicate a Schedule and finally click Perform Action.**

    FileMaker creates an exact copy of the new schedule, called "Monday backup Copy." You'll now modify this copy to do Tuesday's backup.

16. **Select "Monday backup Copy". From the Actions pop-up menu, choose Edit a Schedule, and then click Perform Action.**

    The Schedule Assistant reappears.

17. **Click Next.**

    Since this schedule is a copy of the first one, most of its settings are correct. You only need to make three changes. When you click Next, the Schedule Assistant asks you where to store the backups.

18. **Remove "Monday/" from the end of the backup path, and add "Tuesday/" instead. Then click Next.**

    You now need to tell the schedule to run on Tuesday instead of Monday.

19. **In the "Select the days of the week you would like the schedule to run" section, turn off Monday and turn on Tuesday. Then click Next.**

    Finally, you need to give this schedule a more meaningful name.

20. **In the Schedule Name box, enter "Tuesday backup." Then click Finish.**

    The Schedule Assistant closes and you now have a "Tuesday backup" in the schedule list.

Repeat steps 14 through 19 again for Wednesday, Thursday, Friday, Saturday, and Sunday. When you're done, you'll have seven schedules, each configured to run once a week and tuck the backup files away in a safe place. Now you have seven days worth of backed up data to refer to in case of emergency.

Testing Your Server

You can test your FileMaker Server's various components at any time to be sure they're configured correctly and working. To do so, first go to the FileMaker Server Admin Console Start Page (page 693). On this page, click the FileMaker Server 9 Technology Tests link under Troubleshooting. You'll see the page in Figure 18-18.

From this page, each section tells you if the particular sharing technology is turned on and working. You can click the link in each section to go to a test page or database. The test pages use the appropriate technology to load data from a database, so if they display successfully, you can be confident your server is ready to publish your content.

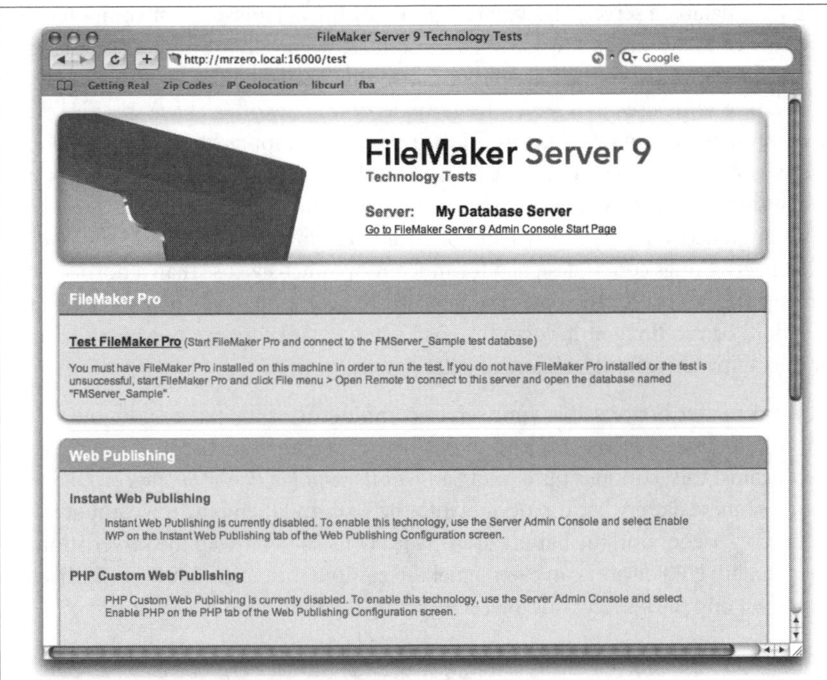

Figure 18-18: *The Technology Tests page includes a section for each of FileMaker Server Advanced's main technologies (FileMaker Sharing, Instant Web Publishing, PHP Custom Web Publishing, and XSLT Custom Web Publishing).*

Server Hardware

While you're spending money, why not get a better *computer*, too? If you have lots of users or lots of data (or both), your database server needs all the power you can give it. After all, FileMaker Server performs finds, edits records, sorts, imports, exports, and otherwise constantly busies itself with the work of *every user*.

The most important thing you can do to make FileMaker Server faster is give it faster access to the data on the disk. At the very least, this increased speed means you should *never* store the files on a file server. Instead, they should always be on a hard drive in the host computer. If you still find things aren't as fast as you'd like them, your best upgrade is often a faster disk system—something called a RAID, or Redundant Array of Inexpensive Disks. You can ignore the "Redundant" part and the "Inexpensive" part, though. A RAID is an *array* of hard disks. By putting several disks together, you can get faster access to your data than you would with just one disk. As important, you can get *more reliable* access as well, since the same data can be stored in more than one place in case a disk drive fails, as outlined in the box on the next page.

In addition to a fast disk system, you should consider adding plenty of RAM to the host computer. The least important component is the CPU speed itself (but that's not to say it doesn't matter; don't expect a fast server with a 500 MHz processor).

If you find all this terribly confusing, be comforted by the fact that most major computer companies sell specially configured server computers. Let them know you're setting up a database server, and you can probably buy a fantastic host computer with RAID, lots of RAM, and a fast CPU—all in one box. For all but the most basic multiuser purposes, you absolutely should consider a dedicated computer designed by the manufacturer to be used as a server. Dell, Apple, and many others have specific server-class computers. It may *seem* like one of their desktop computers has the same specs as the servers for less money, but appearances can be deceiving. Server computers may have the same processors, amount of memory, and hard drive space, but they generally use upgraded versions of key components. Everything from the hard drive to the fan that keeps things cool is designed for much more intensive use than a normal desktop computer. Consider the cost of a good server computer part of your FileMaker installation, or you'll regret it down the road when you experience poor performance, poor reliability, or (worst of all) loss of data.

Finally, no matter how reliable your server computer is, if the power goes out, it will crash. And a crashed server can lead to database corruption and a lot of lost time. To protect against this, consider purchasing an *Uninterruptible Power Supply*, or UPS. You plug one of these battery backup devices into the wall, and then plug the computer into it. If the power goes out, the battery automatically kicks in to keep the server running. Higher-quality UPS devices can even signal the computer to safely shut down when the power is out and the battery runs low, eliminating the possibility of a crash.

POWER USERS' CLINIC

RAID Overview

RAID is just a generic term for any assemblage of several disks that look, to the computer, like just one disk. But the devil is in the details. It turns out there are several different *kinds* of RAID out there, and each serves a different purpose.

If speed is all you care about, there's something called *striping*. With striping, the data's spread across all disks so that when FileMaker Server reads or writes, it can usually do it to every disk at once. In general, a four-disk array with striping can shuffle data four times faster than just one disk. The trouble with striping is that every doubling of performance also produces a halving of reliability. In other words, if you expect one drive to fail sometime in the next four years, then one of the drives in your array will fail in the next year, on average. Since the data is spread across the disks, when one disk fails, you can permanently lose data (sometimes all of it).

On the other end of the spectrum is *mirroring*. This model gives you *maximum* reliability, but with no speed benefit. In a mirrored array, every piece of data is written to every drive at the same time. If one drive fails, the system can simply switch to another drive without losing any data. But you often need more performance than a mirrored array can give.

Unless you are certain you know what you're doing, you should never use just striping. The idea of maximum performance can be appealing, but data integrity and reliability are paramount. Generally, the best bet is a combination of mirroring and striping. Ideally, you'd create a few mirrored sets of disks, and then connect these sets into a striped super-set. If you use RAID, you should look for a system that lets you set up this kind of *striping over mirroring* configuration for the maximum in reliability and performance. You get to decide how much reliability you want (by picking the number of disks in each mirrored set) and how much speed you want (by choosing the number of mirrored sets to create).

Another type of RAID (called RAID 5) gives you a performance boost and redundancy with fewer disks. It does this through magic only a computer scientist would appreciate. RAID 5 tends to be cheaper than the mirroring and striping systems because you can buy fewer hard drives. But RAID 5 gives you a performance boost only for *reading* data. Writing data to the drive is actually slower than a normal disk. You're better off spending a little more money to get a mirrored and striped system.

CHAPTER 19

Developer Utilities

FileMaker Pro takes you from your first simple database all the way into power-user territory. It lets you create complex relational databases with ease, design virtually any layout imaginable, and add features of your own invention with buttons and scripts. With it, you can create any database you may need for a small business or organization. Once you have more than a handful of people using your database, you may eventually outgrow even FileMaker Pro's abilities and need to buy another FileMaker product. In Chapter 18, for example, you can see how FileMaker Server lets more than five users work in a database at once—something FileMaker Pro simply can't handle. FileMaker offers another upgrade, called FileMaker Pro Advanced. This version doesn't make your database run better, or accept more users, or hold more data. Rather, with Advanced, you can be a more productive *developer*.

For a couple hundred dollars more ($299 for Pro versus $499 for Advanced), you get a whole raft of developer tools that will make your life easier and your databases better. If you find yourself troubleshooting long, complex scripts, Script Debugger may save your sanity and your valuable time. The analysis tools are indispensable if you're in a consultant role, working on databases that other people created. And most FileMaker developers have longed for an easy way to keep their more adventuresome users away from potentially destructive menu commands (including but not limited to Delete All Records). Finally, a new feature called Custom Menus gives them—and you—the godlike power to determine which commands are available to a database's users. If you spend a good portion of your time building FileMaker databases, FileMaker Pro Advanced is an extra $200 well spent.

Copying and Pasting Database Structure

Since a large percentage of a database designer's work is fairly repetitive, FileMaker Pro Advanced provides some tools that let you take shortcuts through the tedious process of creating tables, fields, and scripts. By copying work you've already done, you can spend less time defining fields or recreating complex scripts and more time doing the creative work of designing a database. You can import tables and fields without copying data between tables in the same file and between different files.

FileMaker also provides Copy and Paste buttons in several major dialog boxes so you can reuse fields in the Manage Database window, scripts and script steps in Script Maker, and even entire tables or groups of table occurrences. (You need full access privileges in both the source file and the target file to import or copy and paste elements from file to file.)

Importing Tables and Fields

If you have a handful of tables in one file that would also be useful in another, you can *import* the table and field information. Importing tables doesn't copy the data inside them. Rather, it copies the tables' design and structure, with all their fields, including their names, types, comments, calculations, and so on. Start by choosing File → Manage Database and clicking the Table tab. Click Import, and then locate the file that contains the table you want to copy.

Next, tell FileMaker which specific tables to import in the dialog box shown in Figure 19-1. When FileMaker Pro Advanced has finished importing the tables and fields, it displays a dialog box similar to the one you see when you import data. You see a summary of how many tables and fields were created during the import.

Figure 19-1:
You see a simple list of all tables in the source file you've chosen to import tables from. Turn on the checkbox by all the tables you want to import. You don't get to specify which fields are imported–they all come in. So if there are a few you don't need, delete them when the import's finished.

Note: When FileMaker Pro Advanced builds your new tables and fields, it saves a record of its progress in a log file. If you see an error in the summary window, click the Open Log File button to see what went wrong. Things might go wrong if you have calculation fields that reference table occurrences that don't exist yet, for example. When this happens, FileMaker puts the calculation in comments so you can reconstitute it later once you've added table occurrences.

Copying and Pasting Tables

If you prefer, you can copy and paste tables in the Manage Database dialog box instead of using the Import button. Just select a table in the Tables tab, and then click the Copy button. If you want an exact copy in the same file (since your new table will contain common fields like ID, Creation Date, and so on), just click Paste. Alternatively, you can dismiss the Manage Database window, go to a different file, bring up its Tables tab, and paste the table there. As usual, you can use the Shift key to select several items next to each other in the table list. Use the Ctrl key (⌘) to select tables that aren't right next to each other.

Warning: When you copy a table into another database, it may include calculation fields that FileMaker can't successfully copy. For example, a calculation may reference a table occurrence that doesn't exist in the new file. In such cases, FileMaker keeps the field, but puts the entire calculation in comments (like /* this */). Be sure to check all calculation fields after pasting.

Copying and Pasting Fields

If you have complex calculations that you want to reuse in another table within the same file, or in a different file, use the Copy and Paste buttons on the Manage Database dialog box's Fields tab. Just like with tables, select one or more fields, and then click Copy. Then open the table where you want to create the new fields, and finally click Paste to do the deed.

When you copy *calculation* fields, your results may vary depending on whether you also copy the fields it references. It usually saves time to plan ahead and make sure the field references already exist in the target table before you copy and paste. But you can always paste the calculation fields and clean up the references later, especially if you intend to use different field names anyway. Here are some general rules:

- If fields matching the references in your copied calculation don't exist in the target table, FileMaker pastes the calculation as a comment (`/*Amount * Quantity*/`), since it can't find matching fields in the new table. Simply edit the calculations with the new field references, and then click OK.
- To save yourself some editing work, *first* paste into the target table (or create) fields with names that match the ones in the calculation you're transferring. Then, when you paste the calculation, FileMaker resolves the field references automatically.

- If the field references are local (that is, they refer to other fields within the same table), you can copy the fields referenced in the calculation *and* the calculation field at the same time. When you paste the set of fields, FileMaker resolves the field references automatically, and you have nothing to edit.
- If you're copying a calculation field that contains a fully qualified field reference (containing both a table name and a field name, like Expenses::Job ID), the calculation again transfers just fine, assuming there is a table occurrence with the same name in the target file.

Copying Scripts and Script Steps

You can use the Import button in the Manage Scripts dialog box to import whole scripts from other files, but if you have FileMaker Pro Advanced, you can avoid that cumbersome process. Simply open the file that contains the scripts you want to copy, and then use the Copy and Paste buttons in the Manage Scripts dialog box. Copy the scripts you want to reuse, then open the Manage Scripts dialog box in the *target* file, and finally click Paste. Check all pasted scripts to see if any field, layout, or other reference needs to be pointed to another element in its new location. Copying or importing scripts works best when you need the whole script, and all the elements referenced in your script were already in place, so that no script steps break on the way in.

You can also copy script steps individually or in chunks. In the Edit Script dialog box, select just the script steps you want, and then click Copy. Then you either create a new script or open the script that needs your copied steps. Highlight the script step just above where you want the next steps to land, and then click Paste. Your recycled steps appear in your script. Fix any broken references as needed.

You don't even have to move to a new script to find Copy and Paste useful. Sometimes it's faster to copy and paste a series of steps and then edit them so they work slightly differently than to type them from scratch. Sure, you could use the Duplicate button, but then you have to move each step down into place one by one. With Copy and Paste, you get to place the new steps right where you want them.

Note: FileMaker doesn't include break points when you import or copy and paste scripts or script steps.

Script Debugger

When you write a script using FileMaker Pro, your testing and troubleshooting routine is pretty simple. You perform the script and wait to see what happens at the end. In a simple script, like one that prints a report, it's easy enough to see what went wrong and fix it: Your script just went to the wrong layout, perhaps. But when you're creating a complex script that sets variables and works with different sets of records that you can't verify before the next script step whizzes past, it's devilishly hard to figure out where your script veers off course. Even simple scripts can go wrong in puzzling ways that you can't detect by reading over your steps.

That's where Script Debugger comes in. When you run scripts with Script Debugger turned on, FileMaker performs scripts at human speed, so you can see exactly what's happening, each step of the way.

Note: To run Script Debugger, it's best to be logged in to the file with a password that has script-editing privileges (see page 624). But if you need to figure out how a script runs for lesser accounts, you can log in as someone else, then use the Authenticate/Deauthenticate button (see page 709).

To see the Script Debugger, choose Tools → Script Debugger. When you do, the Script Debugger window appears on the screen (Figure 19-2). Left to its own devices, the Script Debugger window doesn't do much. It consists of a couple blocks of empty space and several buttons you can't click.

But it shows its true colors when you run a script. As soon as you do, it swings in to action. It shows the name of the script you're running near the top, and the complete contents of that script just below. You can even see the value of any parameter that was passed to the script. But more important than all this, you can *control* the script as it runs. You can run just one line of the script at a time, dig into subscripts or back out to the calling script, skip over some steps completely, back up and run some steps over again, or stop the script in its tracks.

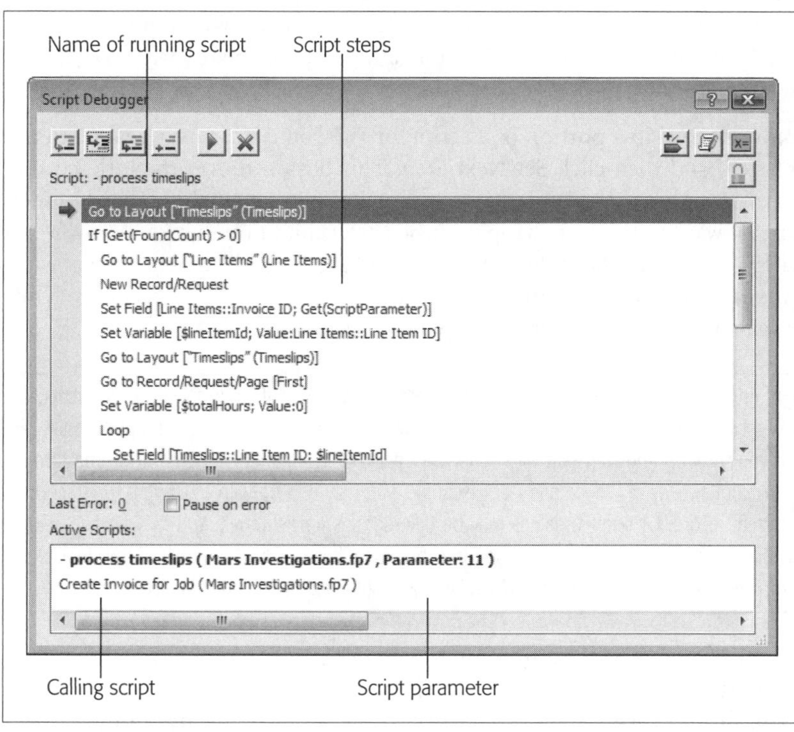
Name of running script
Script steps
Script Debugger
Script: - process timeslips
Go to Layout ["Timeslips" (Timeslips)]
If [Get(FoundCount) > 0]
Go to Layout ["Line Items" (Line Items)]
New Record/Request
Set Field [Line Items::Invoice ID; Get(ScriptParameter)]
Set Variable [$lineItemId; Value:Line Items::Line Item ID]
Go to Layout ["Timeslips" (Timeslips)]
Go to Record/Request/Page [First]
Set Variable [$totalHours; Value:0]
Loop
Last Error: 0
Pause on error
Active Scripts:
- process timeslips (Mars Investigations.fp7 , Parameter: 11)
Create Invoice for Job (Mars Investigations.fp7)
Calling script
Script parameter

Figure 19-2: *The Script Debugger window's loaded with information about the current script. You can see the name of the script at the top, and all its steps in the middle. At the bottom, you can see the script that called this script (if any). Since scripts can call scripts that call scripts, FileMaker lists the complete history here, showing which called this one, and below it, the one that called it. If a parameter was passed to any script, it shows up in the bottom list as well.*

Tip: You can see the script debugger in action in a screencast at *www.missingmanuals.com*.

Controlling Script Execution

Unlike most dialog boxes, Script Debugger stays on top of your work, giving you constant feedback about running scripts. As long as Script Debugger's window is open, when a script starts running, it immediately shows up in the Script Debugger, and is essentially paused. FileMaker is asking you for permission to perform the first step. You control the running script using the buttons at the top of the window. You can see them in Figure 19-3, and read about them here:

- Click **Step** to execute the current script step. (FileMaker marks the current step with a blue arrow along the left edge of the script steps.) FileMaker runs that one step, moves the arrow to the next one, and then stops, waiting for further instruction from you.
- **Step Into** works just like Step, with one caveat. If the current step happens to be a Perform Script script step, Step Into will go into that script and stop at its first line. This way you can step through the subscript line by line. The Step button, on the other hand, just executes the subscript in its entirety and takes you to the next line in the calling script.
- When you click **Step Out,** FileMaker runs the current script to completion, takes you back to the script that called it, and then stops. If the script you're running was not called by another script, Step Out just finishes the script normally. Use Step Out if you accidentally step into a script you don't need to see in full detail, or if you're finished investigating a subscript and want to get back to the calling script quickly.
- If you want to skip a portion of a script, or run some steps over again, select a script step, and then click **Set Next Step**. This button moves the little current step arrow to the selected step without actually running anything. For instance, if you just want to test what happens inside an If condition that you know won't be satisfied, you can move the current step into the If and run its contents without the If step itself being run. You can also back up and run a section of code over again by moving the current step up in the list.

Warning: Any time you use the Set Next Step button, you're changing the normal flow of the script. The results you get when you use it may not match what would happen if you ran the script normally. For instance, if you back up and start part of a script over again, things may be different this time through because the script already did those parts. For example, you may end up with a different found set or a different current record. Or script variables may be different this time through. You may be bypassing If conditions that would otherwise apply. And you may be on a different layout from which the steps would normally run. Be careful, or you may end up sending the script in an inappropriate direction.

- If the script is stopped, waiting for you to click a button, you can click **Run/Pause** to start it running normally. It will no longer stop at each step. Instead, it will run through every step in sequence. If the script is already running, clicking this button will stop the script and let you control its flow again. (To find out how to stop the script exactly where you want, read about *breakpoints* in the next section.)

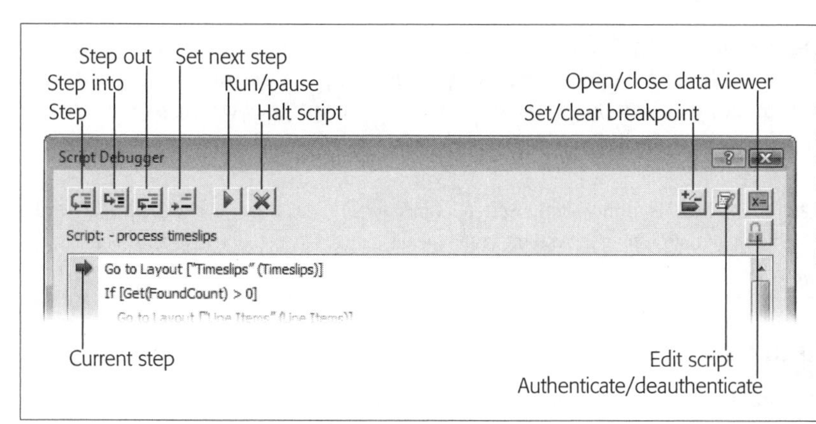

***Figure 19-3:** The Script Debugger window includes a row of unlabeled buttons across the top. The buttons on the left control the running script. The buttons on the right give you quick access to other debugger features.*

- If you've decided you've seen enough and you just want to stop the script completely, click **Halt Script**. The Script Debugger window empties of its script-specific information and FileMaker returns to normal Browse mode behavior. The Halt Script button does not let the script finish running. Instead, it stops the script in its tracks, just like the Halt Script script step.
- You use the **Set/Clear Breakpoints** button to add or remove breakpoints in your script. You'll learn about these shortly.
- One of the handiest buttons in the Script Debugger is the **Edit Script** button. If you're debugging a script that isn't quite working, and while it's running in the debugger you spot the problem, just click Edit Script. FileMaker will open the Edit Script window for the running script, and take you straight to the step that's next in line (the one with the arrow pointing to it in the debugger window). You can easily make the change and then run the script again to test it.

Note: When you click the Edit Script button, FileMaker opens the script for editing, but keeps it running in the Script Debugger. You're free to jump back to the Script Debugger and click any of the buttons to step the script forward further. So you can also use the Edit Script button to see more details about a script (like the exact calculation in a Set Field script step) while you are debugging. However, if you actually save a change to the script, FileMaker tells you it needs to halt the running script before it can apply the change.

- The **Open/Close Data Viewer** button shows FileMaker Pro Advanced's Data Viewer window, which is explained on page 713.
- The **Authenticate/Deauthenticate** button lets you debug a script you would normally not have access to (because of restrictions imposed by your privilege set). Sometimes a script you create will behave differently for your users (who don't have full access to the database) than they will for you. You can log in to your database as one of these restricted users to test the script, but then you can't see the contents of the script in the debugger. If you click the Authenticate/Deauthenticate button (and enter your full access account name and password), though, FileMaker lets you see and debug the script. Importantly, the script *runs* as though you're still the restricted user. You can see exactly how it behaves for your users and hunt down the problem.

By using the buttons in the Script Debugger, you can watch your script in action, performing each step one by one, and examining the results as it goes. This approach makes it infinitely easier to see where a script goes wrong as you try out various iterations, squashing bugs along the way.

Note: Each of the buttons in the Script Debugger window has a menu command counterpart in the Tools → Debugging Controls menu. If you prefer the menus, or want to learn the keyboard shortcuts, this menu is your friend.

Breakpoints

In some situations, the click-the-step-button-for-each-step approach can become unacceptably tedious. For example, you may have a long script, and you know the problem part is near the end. To make your life simpler, the Script Debugger includes *breakpoints*. You set a breakpoint on any line you want, and then click the Run/Pause button. FileMaker immediately begins cruising through the script steps, running them at full speed. When it reaches the step with the breakpoint, it immediately stops so you can begin stepping manually.

You can set a breakpoint three different ways:

- Select the script step in the Script Debugger window, and then click the Set/Clear Breakpoint button.
- In the Script Debugger window, click next to the script step in the gray stripe along the left edge of the script steps.
- In FileMaker Advanced, the same gray stripe appears in the Edit Script window. You can click next to any step when editing a script to set a breakpoint. Using this method, you can set a breakpoint in a deeply nested subscript, before you debug the main script. Then, if you click Run/Pause, FileMaker will run through the script and its subscripts until it hits your breakpoint, saving you a lot of clicking.

No matter how you get it there, the breakpoint is indicated by a red arrow to the left of the script step. To remove an existing breakpoint, just click it again (or select the line in the Script Debugger and click the Set/Clear Breakpoint button again). The arrow disappears.

When you click the Run/Pause button, FileMaker runs to the *next* breakpoint it encounters (even if it's in one of the subscripts this script calls). If you find you've hit a breakpoint before the one you want, just click Run/Pause again to jump to the next one. In fact, adding breakpoints at key places in a complex script (and leaving them there) can make it easy to quickly debug the script later, as you Run/Pause your way through the major chunks, stopping to step through only the parts that currently interest you.

POWER USERS' CLINIC

Conditional Breakpoints

Some programs have a feature called *conditional breakpoints* that let you tell the debugger to stop on a certain line only when some condition is met. For example, you may want to stop only if the $count variable is bigger than 100, or if the found count is more than 1000.

FileMaker doesn't have built-in conditional breakpoints, but you can easily set up a similar scheme. Just add an If script step to your script that checks a meaningful condition. Then put a comment inside the If block and set a break point on the comment. FileMaker will go into the only If block when the condition is met; otherwise it'll skip right past it and the breakpoint it contains.

For example, you might add this to a long loop in your script, so you can break only after the loop has run 100 times:

```
If [$count > 100 ]
# break here
End If
```

If you set a breakpoint on the line with the "break here" comment, you'll get the desired effect.

Examining Errors

In Chapter 15 you learned about checking for errors using the Get(LastError) function. The Script Debugger helps you tackle this job as well. As you step through your script line by line, the debugger constantly updates the Last Error display just below the list of script steps (Figure 19-4). Normally this function shows 0 (zero) because most script steps don't produce an error. But if you *do* encounter an error, the error number appears right after the step runs, making it a breeze to see what error number a certain situation produced so you can handle it in your code.

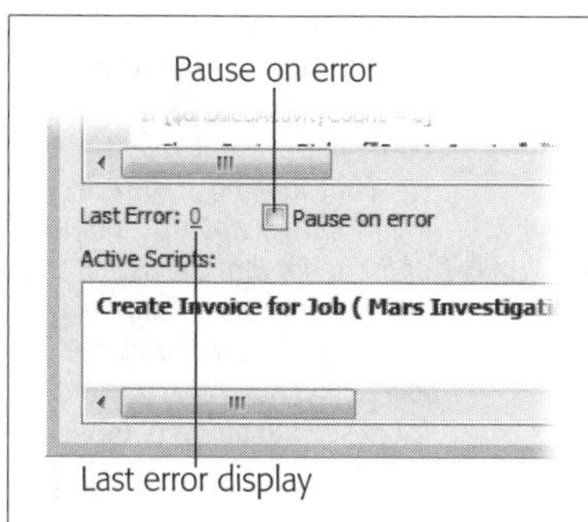

Figure 19-4: *As you step through your script, the debugger constantly updates the last error number. You can instantly see when an error happened, and what the error code is. Best of all, this error number shows up when error capture is turned on (so you can spot an otherwise silent error)* and *when it is turned off (so you can see the code behind the error message). So if you're looking for error numbers, watch this space. If error capture is turned on, it's the only place you can view the error condition.*

You can even click right on the error number, which happens to look like a Web link, and FileMaker shows you the online help page that explains each error code.

Pause on Error

If you know your script is producing an error *somewhere* (perhaps because an error message pops up when you run it), but you don't know where it's coming from, the "Pause on error" checkbox is your friend. Just turn this option on, and then click Run/Pause. FileMaker runs the script full speed until any step produces an error.

When that happens, it stops so you can examine your place in the script, see the error number, and use the debugger controls to manipulate execution. You can also click the Edit Script button to jump to the trouble spot in the Edit Script window.

This feature also works whether or not error capture is turned on, so it may spot errors you're already handling. If that happens, just click Run/Pause again to run to the next error. Keep going as necessary until you find the error you're looking for.

Active Scripts

The bottom part of the window shows you detail about the *active* script—in other words, the script that's running right now. It shows the name of the script, the file it lives in, and the value, if any, of the script parameter that was sent to it.

But why's this box so big if it just shows a few facts about one script? Because it can actually show a few bits about *lots* of scripts. Every time a script performs another script, it moves down in the list to make room for the new script's information. FileMaker puts the topmost—and current—script in boldface at the top of the list. Below it, you see the script that came before. If *that* script was itself run by another script, the first script's then third in the list. You can see how this looks in Figure 19-5.

Click a script in the list to switch the debugger's view to the new script. The Current Position arrow changes color (white with blue outline) to indicate you're viewing a script that doesn't include the current script step.

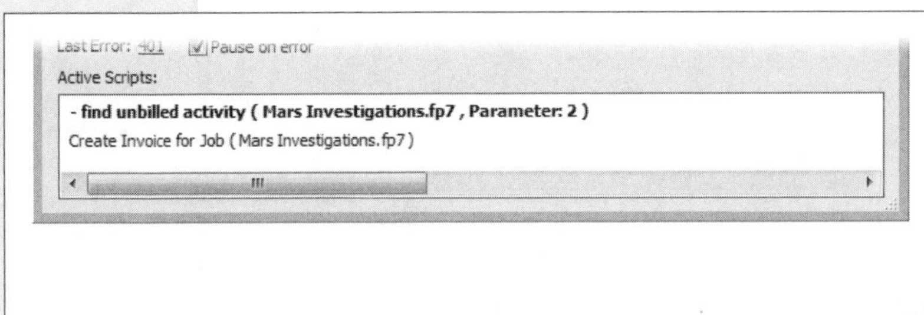

Figure 19-5: *When scripts call other scripts, FileMaker stacks the script names up in the Active Scripts list. On top–and in bold lettering–you see the name of the script you're currently looking at. Directly below each script is the name of the script that called it. If you have scripts calling scripts with more than three levels, you have to scroll the list to see the oldest ones.*

Working with the Debugger Window

The debugger window doesn't work like FileMaker's other dialog boxes. When it's open on the screen, you can still interact with your database window. Even when a script is running (but paused waiting for you to step), you can move database windows around, switch layouts, and even type data into records. That way, you can poke around in your database while the script runs to see how things are progressing. It also lets you totally mess up your script by putting it in a state it would normally never reach, like an inappropriate layout, or a mussed-up global field. And although you can edit existing records, you can't create new records, delete records, or create new windows.

Since all this window manipulation is possible, you're free to arrange the debugger and database windows on the screen so you can see as much as possible while your script runs. You can also resize the debugger window at any time to make more space.

Note: Before you get too hung up trying to fit your layouts on the screen so you can see field values and the like, read about the Data Viewer in the next section. It's often a better choice if you're trying to watch the data or variables change.

As long as the Script Debugger window is showing, FileMaker debugs any script that runs (even if it runs from clicking a button, or automatically when a file opens or closes). If you choose Tools → Script Debugger, the debugger window disappears and script execution goes back to normal. You can also simply close the debugger window to turn it off.

The Data Viewer

The *Data Viewer* grants you under-the-hood access to field data, variables, and calculations. It's usually the easiest way to watch things change as your script runs in the debugger. To show the Data Viewer, just choose Tools → Data Viewer and it will appear on your screen. You can also click the Open/Close Data Viewer button in the Script Debugger window. No matter how you get to it, though, it looks just like Figure 19-6.

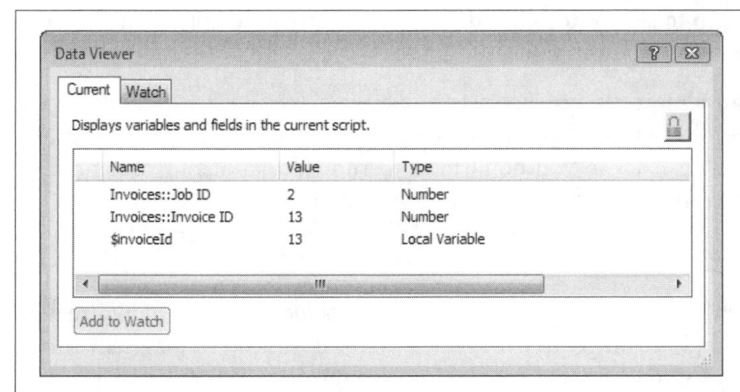

Figure 19-6: *The Data Viewer has two tabs, Current and Watch. Current shows information related to the script that's currently running in the debugger. Under Watch, you can tell FileMaker exactly what you want to see.*

The Current Tab

If you open the Data Viewer (Tools → Data Viewer) and switch to the Current tab, FileMaker strives to show you the most pertinent information about the script you're debugging. When a script starts to run in the debugger, the Data Viewer lists every field that the script uses in any way. For instance, if you use the Set Field script step to modify a field anywhere in the script, that field appears in the list in the Current tab. Likewise, if you use a field in an If condition, that field shows up, too. In addition to the name of each important field, the Data Viewer shows its current value (in the Value column) and its data type.

As you step through the script, the Data Viewer updates the value column appropriately, so it always reflects the current field value. It also helps to draw your attention to fields you should be watching, as Figure 19-7 attests.

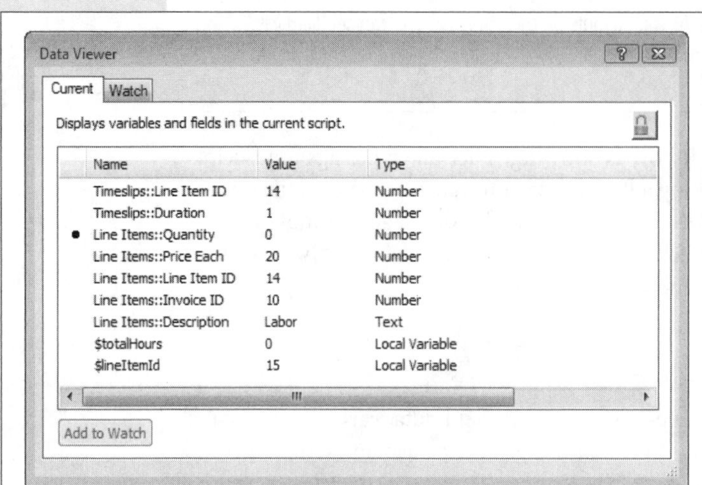

Figure 19-7: *As you step through your script in the Script Debugger, the Data Viewer keeps its list of fields up to date. Whenever you step to a new script, a little black dot appears next to any fields that are referenced in the current script step. You can take note of their values before moving on.*

The Current tab also shows information about script variables. Instead of showing every variable the script uses as soon as the script starts, the window shows a new line for each new variable as it's created. For example, the first time you use the Set Variable script step to set a $customerId variable, $customerId appears in the Data Viewer, along with its type and value.

The Current tab almost always shows you just what you need to see while you debug. It can be a huge timesaver, pointing out everything your script is using and what it's doing with data, so you don't have to run calculations in your head or scramble around different layouts. Open it early and often.

The Watch Tab

The second tab in the Data Viewer, called Watch, shows the same kind of information as the Current tab, but you get to configure it yourself. Instead of magically showing the fields and variables your script is using, it shows the fields and variables you tell it to show. And it can show the result of arbitrary calculation expressions as well. You can see a sample Watch list in Figure 19-8.

To add an item to the Watch list, click the Add button (shown in Figure 19-8). When you do, FileMaker shows you the Edit Expression dialog box (Figure 19-9). This window is almost an exact copy of the Specify Calculation dialog box, except it has an extra text box at the bottom labeled Result, and it has two new buttons: Evaluate and Monitor.

Differences aside, you can do anything here that you can do in the ordinary Specify Calculations dialog box. Just enter any formula you want in the Expression box.

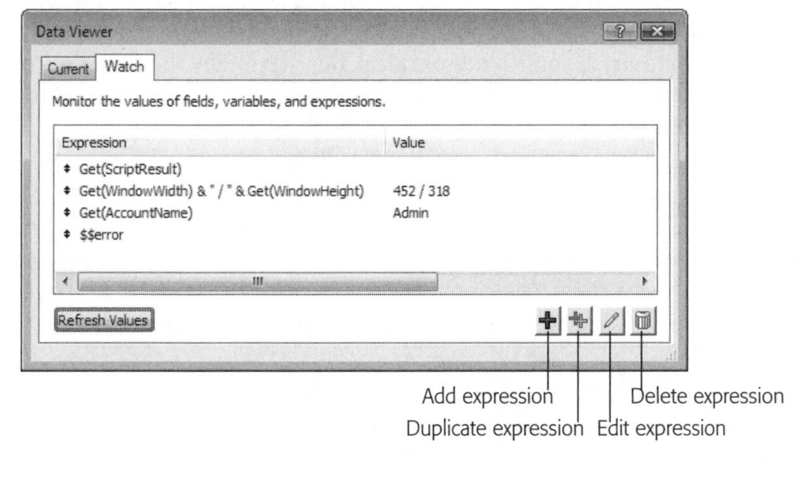

Figure 19-8: *The Data Viewer's Watch tab shows what you want to watch. You load it up with various calculation expressions, and it keeps tabs on their results for you. If you want to see a field value, just put the field all by itself in the expression. Variables work the same way. But unlike the Current tab, you can even put complex calculations here, and watch them as things change. In this window, the second line shows the height and width of the current database window. If you resize a window, click Refresh, and the new size appears instantly.*

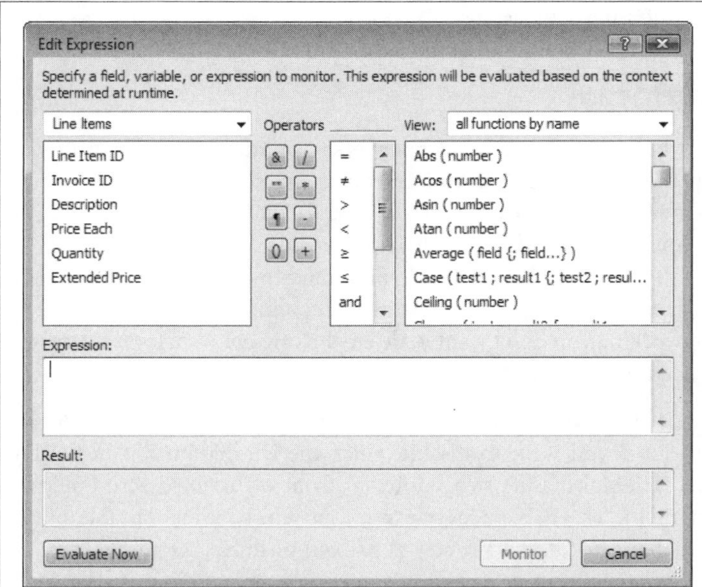

Figure 19-9: *The Data Viewer's Edit Expression window should look familiar—it's almost an exact replica of the Specify Calculation window. But this version can run the calculation in place and show you the result (just click Evaluate Now).*

When you click Evaluate, FileMaker performs the calculation and shows the result in the Result box at the bottom of the window. You can use this handy feature to test a calculation and correct it without jumping in and out of the dialog box.

When you're satisfied with the formula, click Monitor. FileMaker adds the expression to the Watch list, with its value beside it. FileMaker attempts to keep the values up to date, but it can't refresh some kinds of calculations (typically those that use Get functions). If necessary, you can click Refresh Values to automatically recalculate each Watch expression.

Note: You don't *have* to click Monitor in the Edit Expression window. It's sometimes handy to use this window when you're trying to write a calculation, even if you don't need to keep an eye on the results. Just click the Add button and fiddle with the formula until you have it right (clicking Evaluate Now whenever you need to see how it's doing). When you're done, copy the formula (Edit → Copy) and click Cancel. You can now paste the tested-and-working formula into a field calculation or a script step.

Data Viewer isn't attached to any particular file, so its Watch list contents don't change when you open and close files. The viewer can even be open while you have no databases open. Since all files and scripts share the same Watch list, it can quickly get long and hard to monitor. Select items you aren't using, and then click the trash can icon to delete them.

Finally, if you need to see how certain calculations behave for users who don't have full access, log in as the user in question. In the Data Viewer, click the Authenticate icon to unlock its powers. You can now monitor values and edit expressions even though you don't have full access.

Disable Script Steps

The Set Next Step button in the Script Debugger lets you manually skip script steps while debugging, but it's not much help unless *you* remember to click it at the right time. Sometimes you have a script step (or several) that you always want FileMaker to skip. You could just delete them, but maybe you're not quite ready to. Perhaps it's code that isn't working yet and you intend to come back later to fix it. Or perhaps you're moving the code somewhere else, and until you're sure you've got it moved and working you don't want to delete the original. Whatever the reason, you may want to temporarily disable a group of steps.

To disable a script step (see Figure 19-10), open the script in ScriptMaker, and then highlight the step you want to disable. Click the Disable button in the Edit Script dialog box. FileMaker puts two slashes in front of disabled script steps so you can identify them. To enable a step again, first select it. The Disable button changes to say Enable; click it and the step is back in business. As always, you can select *multiple* script steps at once, and disable or enable them all in one shot.

Disabling script steps is useful for debugging, but it can have long-term use, too. Any step you disable in FileMaker Pro Advanced gets skipped whenever someone runs it—even in FileMaker Pro. So, say your company has a semi-regular promotion that creates discounts for a limited period.

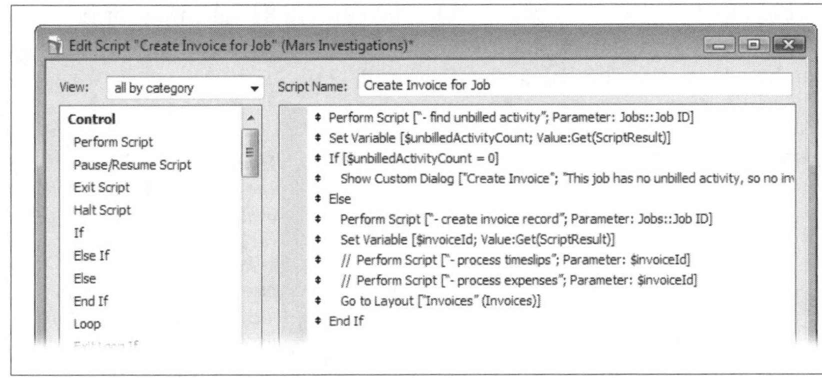

Figure 19-10: *Two steps (the Perform Script steps) in this script have been disabled, as you can see by the double slashes in front of the names. When a disabled script step is highlighted, the Disable button reads "Enable." FileMaker skips disabled steps when the script runs.*

You don't have to write two different scripts, one with the discount and one without, and then worry about some kind of test to make them available on a button or in the script menu at the proper times. Write one script, making sure the discount creation steps are separate from the main process. Then you can enable the pertinent steps when the promotion starts and disable them when it's over, with very little fuss.

The Database Design Report

Sometimes you inherit a large database from somebody else, and you simply don't see how it comes together. (OK, be honest. Sometimes *you* create a large database and still don't understand how it's put together.) While FileMaker's point-and-click interface makes it easy to build databases, teasing things out later is a different story. You can look at a script, field, layout, table occurrence, or even an entire table in FileMaker Pro, and have no idea whether the database actually uses or needs it.

If you've shelled out for FileMaker Pro Advanced, however, you've got help. Its built-in internal analysis tool, the Database Design Report (affectionately called DDR), gives you an overview of your database, where you can easily see how database items are connected and other details, all in one place. You run the report, tell it what kinds of things you're interested in, and FileMaker presents the information in a series of Web pages.

Unlike the reports discussed in Chapter 6, the DDR is a report about the structure of your database, not about the data inside. It tells you what tables and fields you have, which fields are used on each layout, and so on, but nothing about the information in your records and fields.

Generating the DDR

The Database Design Report window lets you tell FileMaker exactly what you want it to report on. You get to pick which files and table occurrences to include, what kinds of things you want to report on, and what format you want the report to use.

You also get to decide whether you want to open the report right away, or just save it for later use. To get started, choose Tools → Database Design Report. Up pops the Database Design report dialog box (Figure 19-11).

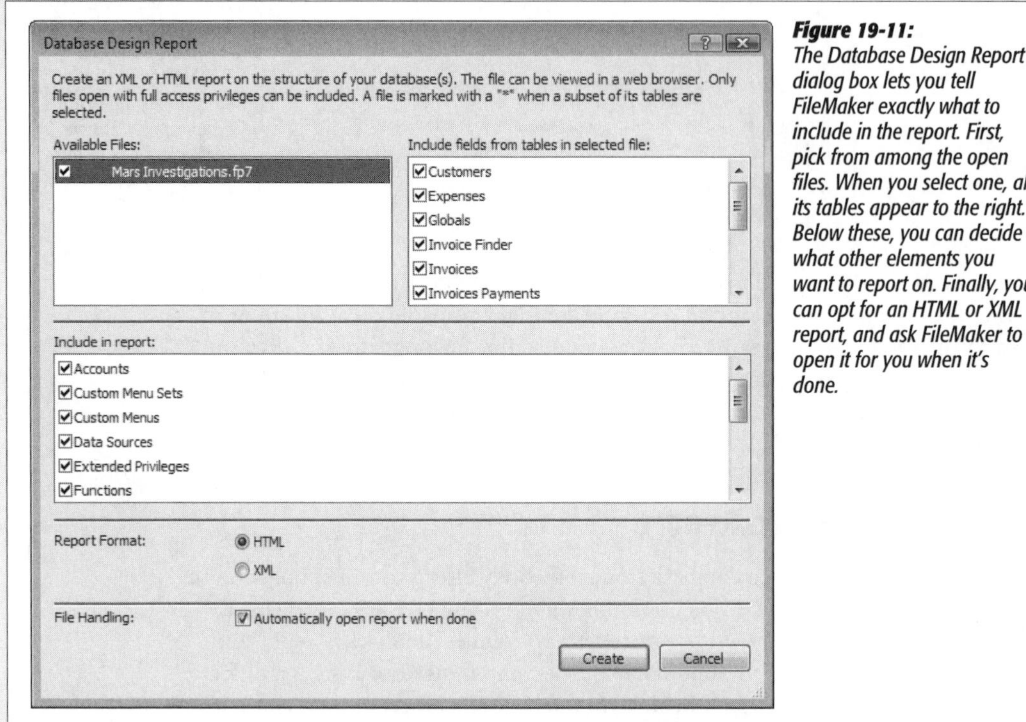

***Figure 19-11:** The Database Design Report dialog box lets you tell FileMaker exactly what to include in the report. First, pick from among the open files. When you select one, all its tables appear to the right. Below these, you can decide what other elements you want to report on. Finally, you can opt for an HTML or XML report, and ask FileMaker to open it for you when it's done.*

The Available Files list in this window shows every open file. To include a file in the report, turn on the checkbox by its name. FileMaker assumes you want every file at first, so you may have to do more turning off than on.

Note: If you have a lot of files to turn off, you can Shift-click to select groups. Then if you turn off one file's checkbox, every selected file turns off as well. This same approach applies to tables in the list on the right.

The report will include field information for tables in each file. Select a file in the list to see all its tables in the "Include fields from tables in selected file" list. Again, you can use the checkboxes in this list to tell FileMaker which tables you want included in the report.

In the "Include in Report" section, there's a checkbox for each kind of database element the DDR can report on. Again, FileMaker assumes you want everything, but you're free to limit the report to just certain information. The less you report on, the faster the report runs, and the smaller the final files.

Normally, FileMaker saves the report in HTML format so you can read and navigate it in any Web browser, but it also offers a more structured XML format. XML files aren't easy for *humans* to read, but with the help of other software, you can process the XML and integrate information about your database into other systems. Furthermore, some companies make DDR analysis tools that process the XML version of your DDR and provide extra tools for browsing, finding, and reporting on the information it contains. (See the box on page 721 for more information on these third-party tools.)

When you're done making decisions, click Create. FileMaker asks you where to save the report. The DDR is made up of several files, so you probably want to make a new folder to hold the report. The more complex your files, the longer it takes to create the DDR. In a file with dozens of tables, each of which may have dozens or even hundreds of fields, this could take a minute or more. FileMaker displays a progress bar for you, so you can gauge how long the process will take.

Note: A DDR is a snapshot of the database at the moment you create it. So it's good to make periodic DDRs as your database evolves. You can create a record of when you added or changed various parts of the database. A DDR can also help with troubleshooting broken elements.

Using the DDR

If you checked "Automatically open report when done" when you created the DDR, FileMaker launches your browser and shows you the DDR Report Overview (Figure 19-12) as soon as the progress bar disappears.

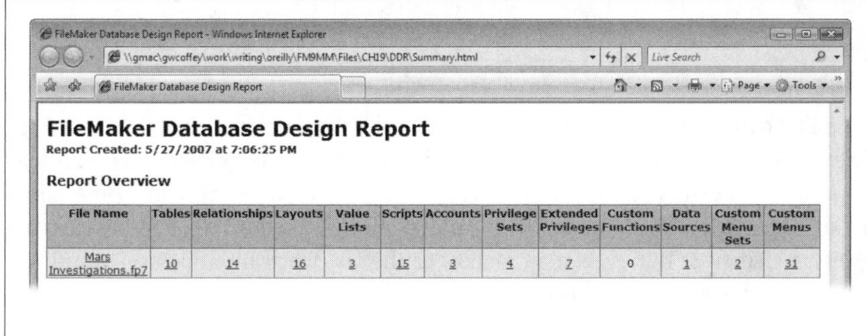

FileMaker Database Design Report

Report Created: 5/27/2007 at 7:06:25 PM

Report Overview

File Name	Tables	Relationships	Layouts	Value Lists	Scripts	Accounts	Privilege Sets	Extended Privileges	Custom Functions	Data Sources	Custom Menu Sets	Custom Menus
Mars Investigations.fp7	10	14	16	3	15	3	4	7	0	1	2	31

Figure 19-12: *Report Overview is the first thing you see when you open a DDR. It's a table, with one row for every file you included in the report, and a column for each option you checked when you created the DDR. Each "cell" contains a link leading to more information. Each DDR lists the time and date of its creation, so you can tell if the report matches the current state of your database.*

This is the main report file, and it has URL links that bring up the detail pages. To view the DDR later, go to where you saved it and open the file called Summary, or Summary.html. (You also see a folder named for each file you selected when you created the DDR.)

On the overview page, the DDR tells you which elements you chose when you created the DDR. If you click a file name, you see the file detail page (Figure 19-13), with lots of information about that file. The links in each column go to the same file detail page, but each link scrolls you to the relevant section. On large databases, with lots of fields, this option can save you a lot of time scrolling through the page, looking for what you want. For instance, if you click the number in the Relationships column, you see the Relationships section of the file detail page.

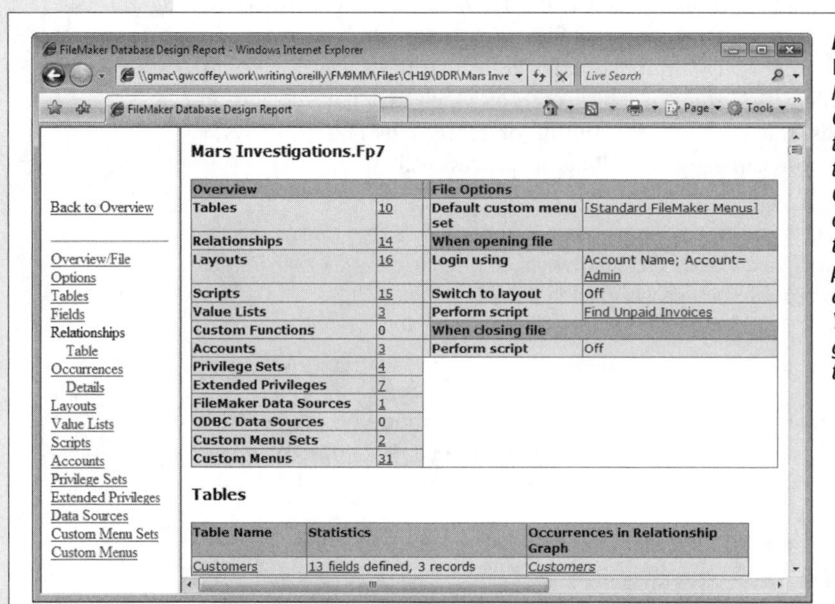

Figure 19-13: *When you click the File Name link on the Report Overview page, you see this page. The top link on the left leads back to the Overview page. All the others just scroll the page to various important parts. The report itself is also loaded with links. You can click any link to go to more details about that item.*

Use the DDR to help you figure out what parts of your database can safely be edited or deleted. Since it's so easy to create tables, fields, and layouts in FileMaker, you may well end up with extras that you don't need when your database reaches completion. You can make your database easier to understand and more efficient by deleting these extra elements. But even if a database is the last word in efficiency, running a DDR is one of the best ways to trace the designer's thinking process.

To see if—and how—a particular element is used, look at its detail. Suppose you have a bunch of fields you'd like to delete from your database, and you want to find out whether it's safe to do so. First, click the Tables link; fields are part of tables. You see a list of tables, with information about how many fields each table contains, along with a list of occurrences of each table in the Relationship Graph (Figure 19-12). Click the link for a table's fields, and you see a list of all the fields in that table.

Details appear in the Field Name, Type, and Options columns for every field. Comments, if there are any, show up in the Comments column. Any layouts or scripts that use the field are listed in the Layout and Script columns, respectively. You see the information in the Relationship column only if it's a key field. Fields used in layouts, relationships, and scripts are called *dependencies* of those elements.

POWER USERS' CLINIC

Getting the Most from the DDR

At first glance, you may not appreciate the true value of the DDR. It appears to tell you the same things you can find out in other FileMaker windows, like Manage Database, ScriptMaker, and so on. But once you run your first DDR, you understand it has powers those flimsy boxes never dreamed of.

For example, the DDR information for a script helps you determine how the script functions in and interacts with the rest of the database. In a neat chart, you can see every field, layout, table, table occurrence, and custom function the script uses. More importantly, you can see every script or layout button that runs this script. That kind of information would be very hard to nail down without the DDR. You'd basically have to go to each layout in your database, click anything that might be a button, and see if the script you're interested in is attached to it. If you've created custom menus, you'd have to check them individually, too. The DDR gathers up all that information for you—not just for scripts but for tables, layouts, value lists, and other kinds of database elements as well.

If you want even more power, consider acquiring a DDR analysis tool. One such tool—Inspector from FMNexus (*www.fmnexus.com*)—lets you search your DDR, quickly hotlink from element to element, and print any number of reports. It can even compare two different DDRs and tell you what you've changed. Best of all, Inspector automatically detects problems in your database (like scripts that look at fields you've since deleted). It marks each problem with a conspicuous red dot, and lets you report on problems, mark them fixed, and even keep notes.

Note: Even if you don't use a "Go to Field" script step for a specific field, a field may be listed in the scripts column. "Go to Related Record," or any other step that uses a relationship, also requires the use of that relationship's key field, so it also has that field as a dependency.

Finding Broken Elements with the DDR

Suppose you've deleted a field, unaware that it's used in a script. Your script could be run numerous times, not *quite* working without your knowledge. The DDR is a great way to check for errors like this. Take, for example, the "-find unbilled activity" script you wrote back in Chapter 15. It searched in the Expenses::Job ID field for all unbilled expenses, but you've deleted the Job ID field.

If you examine that script in ScriptMaker, you can see the words "<Field Missing>" right in the script.

```
Set Field [Expenses::<Field Missing>; "==" & Get (ScriptParameter)]
```

To spot every error like this, though, you'd have to open every script and read through it. FileMaker has no facility to let you search through your scripts.

But you *can* search the DDR page in your Web browser. (Pressing Ctrl+F or ⌘-F does the trick in most browsers.) Type the text you're looking for in the Find field, and then click Next (or whatever button your browser uses) to start the search. You see the first instance of your search criteria highlighted. Click the button again to find other instances.

The whole list of errors you might search for appears below. If you have any inkling what kind of error you're looking for, start with that one:

- **<Missing Field>**. Referenced field is missing.
- **<Missing Table Occurrence>**. Referenced table occurrence set is missing.
- **<Missing Base Table>**. Referenced base table is missing.
- **<Missing File Reference>**. Referenced file reference is missing.
- **<Missing Layout>**. Referenced layout is missing.
- **<Missing Valuelist>**. Referenced value list is missing.
- **<Missing Custom Function>**. Referenced custom function is missing.
- **<Missing Script>**. Referenced script is missing.
- **<Missing Account>**. Referenced account is missing.
- **<Missing Privilege Set>**. Referenced privilege set is missing.
- **<Missing Extended Privilege>**. Referenced extended privilege is missing.
- **<Missing Custom Menu>**. Referenced custom menu is missing.
- **<Missing Custom Menu Set>**. Referenced custom menu set is missing.

Once you find a broken element, return to your database and fix it manually. The DDR won't update itself to show your fix until you run another one. And since you can't mark the electronic version of your DDR, a good way to keep track of your work is to print it out, and then mark off each item as you fix it. Then, when all the broken elements are fixed (or you've deleted all the unused stuff), run another DDR. This time it should be clean, but if it's not, you've got the tools to fix it.

POWER USERS' CLINIC

Prevention is Worth a Pound of Cure

Why use the DDR to fix your mistakes when you can prevent them in the first place? Here's a technique you can use next time you want to delete a field, script, layout, or any other important element. If you're not completely certain you don't need the element, you can use the DDR to check for you.

First, in FileMaker, *rename* every element you plan to delete. Put something noticeable and consistent in each name. For example, you might put "TO_BE_DELETED" before each element's name.

Once you've renamed every doomed element, run a fresh DDR. Choose the HTML type. When the report is finished, search it for the code words you put in each name ("TO_BE_DELETED," in this example). FileMaker should find each element you've marked for deletion. But it'll also find this element in the list of dependencies if it's still in use. For example, a field you're pondering deleting might show up in a script. Unless that script is also marked for deletion, you have a situation you need to investigate further. Once you're sure the things you're deleting are not used by anything else, you can delete them with confidence.

Tooltips

Training people, either when you first launch a new database, or when new employees come into your workforce, is a big part of making your database successful. You can have beautiful layouts, bulletproof privilege sets, and complex, well-thought-out scripts, but if folks don't know how and when to use them, they'll miss out on the benefits. To spare you the wrath of confused (or worse, frustrated) users, FileMaker Pro Advanced has a feature called *tooltips*. Like the onscreen labels that pop up in Windows and many other programs, tooltips can help guide people through the features you've created for them, and maybe even cut down on training time.

You can attach tooltips to any object, or group of objects, that you can select on a layout: fields, text, or graphics. Although you need FileMaker Pro Advanced to *create* tooltips, they work in any version of FileMaker, and even in the Web browser when you use Instant Web Publishing.

To create a tooltip, go to Layout mode and choose the object you want decorate. Then choose Format → Set Tooltip. Enter the text for your tooltip, and then click OK. Now people see the tooltip when the mouse hovers over the object in Browse mode. Just like tooltips in other applications, the tooltip doesn't appear immediately, so as not to inconvenience more advanced users. You can see a tooltip in action in Figure 19-14.

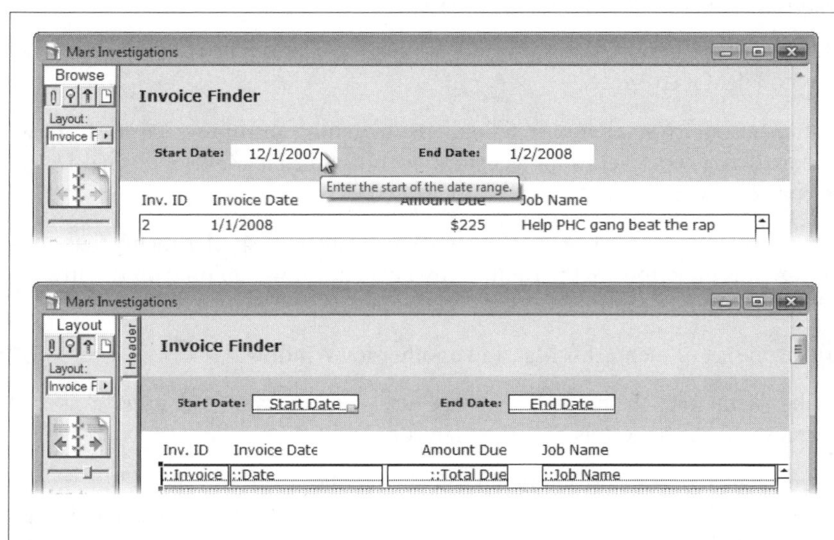

Figure 19-14: *Top: With a tooltip in place, your user only needs to point at the Start Date field and wait a moment to get a little help. The tooltip shows just below the mouse arrow.*

Bottom: In Layout mode, you can choose View → Show → Tooltips to see which elements have a tooltip assigned. In this example, the Start Date field has a little note icon in the bottom-right corner, indicating there's an assigned tooltip.

The Specify Tooltip dialog box has a Specify button. Click this button and you get all the power of calculations. The result of the calculation becomes the text of the tooltip. (If the calculation has an empty result, FileMaker doesn't show the tooltip, so you can use the If function to make the tooltip show up only when it's relevant.)

Custom Menus

FileMaker's menus are all about power. Through them, you can control—and limit—your users' access to the whole feature set. As the developer, you need all those commands to do your design and development of your database, but there are plenty of commands that give too much power to your users, particularly folks who don't have much computer experience or who aren't shy about experimenting with commands, even if they aren't sure what might happen at the other end of a dialog box.

Luckily, with FileMaker Pro Advanced, you can completely customize the menus your users see. You can remove the Delete All Records and the Replace Field Contents commands for all your users, or you can remove them only from certain users' privilege sets. If you're the type of developer who likes to take charge of the user interface, custom menus are your dream come true.

Here are just a few of the things you can do:

- Remove potentially destructive items from menus: Delete All Records, for example.
- Edit menu commands: Change Modify Last Find to read Repeat Last Find, perhaps.
- Add, edit, or remove keyboard shortcuts: If you can't remember that Ctrl+S (⌘-S) does *not* mean Save in FileMaker, then you can at least prevent that pesky Sort dialog box from popping up every time.
- Remove entire menus, like the Window menu, which can be confusing for folks new to FileMaker Pro.
- Run a script from a new or edited menu item: Substitute a custom Delete Record script (complete with a custom warning) for FileMaker's normal Delete Record command.
- Change menus when a user changes layout: Create a special menu that runs commands or scripts that pertain to invoices and shows up only on the Invoice layout.
- Make one set of menus for Mac and another for Windows.
- Make menu sets that match privilege sets: Give admin-level users a special menu showing the scripts only they can run.

You can create and edit custom menus only in FileMaker Pro Advanced, but anyone can use them. These menus don't transfer to files you publish on the Web, though (Chapter 17). When you create custom menus for a database, you may want to provide a User Guide or similar documentation explaining what your custom commands do, since your users won't be able to look up the commands you add in FileMaker's online help.

You can use custom menus to supplement, and even go beyond, privilege set features. For example, if you want to limit data entry people to using the copy and paste buttons that run your scripts, remove the Edit menu for users with that privilege set. They won't be able to use keyboard shortcuts to cut, copy, or paste. Removing the View menu prevents the Mode pop-up menu, toolbar, and all related keyboard shortcuts from working. (But you'll need to do some work providing replacement commands in your buttons and menus.)

Note: As powerful as custom menus are, they're no substitute for good security practices, as discussed in Chapter 16. For example, just because you don't see a Delete command right in front of your face doesn't mean you can't delete records. (Try creating a new database, and adding an occurrence of the table into *that* database. If your privilege set allows deletion, you can use the menus in the new database to empty out the table.) If you need to prevent a user from doing something, *you must restrict it by privilege set.*

Editing a Menu

All new files you create use FileMaker's standard menu set unless you tell them to use a custom set. Just as each new file contains three default privilege sets, you get one set of custom menus that you can edit to suit your needs. And as with privilege sets, some items are in brackets and cannot be edited or duplicated, but you're free to create new menus with the same name and customize them.

Your goal for this exercise in customizing menus is to remove menu items that may confuse your users. When people are just learning FileMaker, simplified menus are less intimidating than masses of unfamiliar commands. You can also help protect your database from damage by someone unwittingly choosing the wrong command. You start the process by editing the View menu so that only a few items show up.

1. **In FileMaker Pro Advanced, choose File → Manage → Custom Menus.**

   The Manage Custom Menus dialog box appears (Figure 19-15).

2. **Click "View copy" in the Custom Menu list, and then click Edit.**

   Or you can double-click an item to edit it. The Edit Custom Menu window appears (Figure 19-16). This is where you tell the custom menu what it should look like and how it should behave.

3. **Click the checkbox beside the Override Title field, and then type *Switch* in the field.**

   The Override Title option changes what the user sees in his menu bar. You changed it to Switch since the word "View" is too vague for beginning users. Plus, you don't want them getting confused if they pick up FileMaker's manual (or this book) for help. The changed menu name should clue people in that they need to look at your custom documentation for help.

   The menu's name *in this dialog box* remains View Copy; that's how you know it originated from the normal View menu, not from scratch.

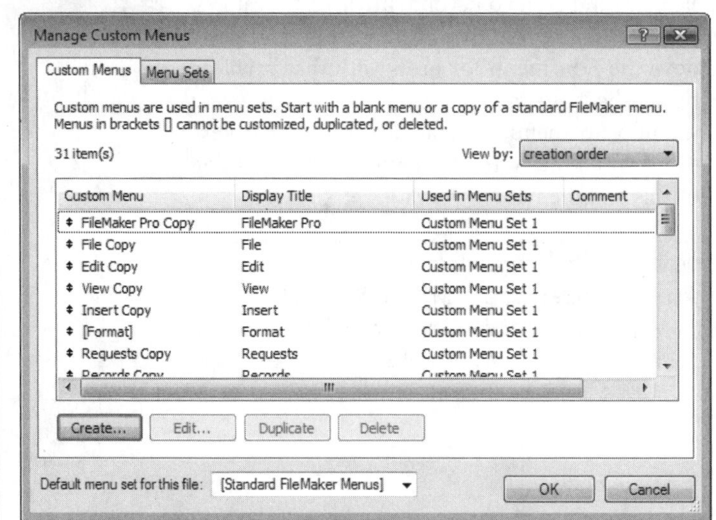

Figure 19-15: *You can reorder the items in the Custom Menu list with the "View by" pop-up menu. You can also click each of the four column heads to sort the list. Probably this window's most important item is the small pop-up menu at the bottom. You can do all the editing of custom menus you like, but unless you remember to switch to your custom set, you don't see any change in your file.*

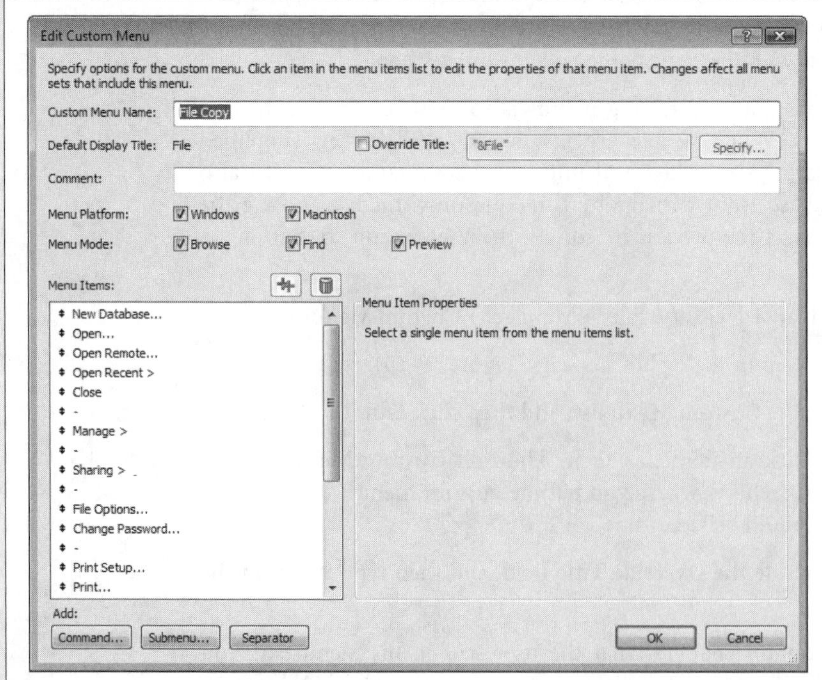

Figure 19-16: *This dialog box has many splendors. You can specify that a menu appears only when your user's on a Mac, or only when she's in Find mode. You can add, change or remove keyboard shortcuts. You can even take the liberty of replacing a command's normal action with a script.*

Warning: If you customize menus even in the slightest, consider turning off the built-in Help menu as well. It opens FileMaker's online help file, which can't answer people's questions about *your* custom menus. If you need documentation, you can add your own Help menu that leads people to the custom-crafted help on your web site, for instance.

4. **Select the first hyphen below "Go to Layout >" in the Menu Items list, and then press Shift as you select the last item in the list. Click the trash can icon. Then select Layout mode and delete it.**

   All highlighted items disappear when you click the trash can icon (those hyphens represent divider lines in menus). You should have only three mode menu items, a hyphen, and a Go to Layout menu (a total of five items) remaining in the list.

5. **Click the Browse mode menu item. As with View mode in step 2, turn on the override checkbox, and change the title to "Browse".**

   This menu item title replaces the text that appears in the list. Your users will see a command called *Browse*, not Browse mode. Notice the quotation marks around "Browse." If you forget (or refuse) to type the quotes, FileMaker obstinately puts them back in for you. That's your indication that FileMaker considers that text a character string, and that's a further cue that the Specify button gives you access to the calculation dialog box.

6. **Repeat the previous step for Find mode, Preview mode, and "Go to Layout>." Change Find mode's title to "Find," change Preview mode's title to "Print Preview," and change the title of "Go to Layout>" to "Show." When you've made these changes, click OK.**

   Use terms that are easy for folks to comprehend. Most people already understand what Print Preview does, but the meaning of Preview mode is a little murky.

7. **Choose "Custom Menu Set 1" from the Default menu set for this file pop-up menu, and then click OK.**

   You've just told FileMaker to display the customized version of your View menu.

   The View menu now says "Switch." When you click it, there are only four items. Notice that the Layout tool is grayed out, and Layout mode has disappeared from the Layout pop-up menu at the bottom of your screen. Also, the commands in the pop-up menu match the changes you made in the View custom menu.

By editing menus to suppress items that might confuse those who haven't had in-depth FileMaker training, you've made your database a friendlier place to work. But don't stop there: In the next section, you'll learn how to create menus that show lists of commands you *do* want people to see, like your scripts.

Creating a New Menu

Using the steps described in the previous tutorial, you can edit FileMaker's menus to your heart's content, renaming them, and deleting extraneous commands to make room for new ones. If you don't necessarily want to delete any existing menus or commands, or even if you do, you can always create *additional* menus from scratch.

1. **In Manage Custom Menus, click Create. In the Create Custom Menu window that appears, choose "Start with an empty menu." Click OK.**

   If an existing menu is similar to what you need, you can use it as a template when you create new menus. But in this case, you don't need any existing menu commands because you'll attach your scripts to a new menu. When you click OK, the Edit Custom Menu window appears, just as in Figure 19-16. This time, though, you won't edit it; you'll build the menu from the ground up.

2. **Type "Invoices" in the Custom Menu Name fields. Also type "Invoices" in the Override Title field.**

   Since you started with an empty menu, FileMaker assumes you want a custom name. If you don't type a name, the word "Untitled" appears in your menu bar.

3. **Turn off the Menu Mode options for Find and Preview modes.**

   You don't want your scripts run from either Find or Preview modes, so by telling the menu not to even *show up* in those modes, you're adding another layer of security.

4. **Click the Command button. In the Specify FileMaker Command dialog box, choose the "No command assigned" option above the list of available commands, and then click OK.**

   This action creates a new command, but doesn't use one of FileMaker's canned actions. You could use this method to build a new menu that picks and chooses from various default menus, but in this instance, you're going to run your scripts from the new Invoices menu.

5. **In the Title field, type *Create invoice for unbilled expenses*, and then click Specify (to the right of the Action pop-up menu). From the list in the Specify Script Options window, choose the "Create Invoice for Job" script, and then click OK.**

   The Specify Script Options shows all the scripts you've created in this database file. To add more scripts to this menu, repeat the last two steps until you've created new commands for all the scripts you want. The arrows to the left of each item let you rearrange them. Click the Separator button to create a divider line in the menu.

6. **Click the Menu Sets tab of the Manage Custom Menus dialog box. If necessary, select "Custom Menu Set 1" in the list, and then click Edit.**

   The Edit Menu Set window appears.

7. **Scroll through the list of Available Custom Menus until you see Invoices. Select it, and then click the Move button. Click the arrow to the left of the Invoices menu and move it up, so that it appears above [Scripts]. Click OK until you're back in your database.**

   The Invoices custom menu is now a part of the new custom menu set, and it appears between the Records and Scripts menus.

So far, you've simplified one of FileMaker's menus and created a custom menu from scratch. Now you need to get rid of a menu that strikes fear even in the hearts of experienced FileMaker users: You're going to *completely* suppress the Windows menu.

Removing a Menu

At first glance through the Manage Custom Menus dialog box, you may think you just click an item in the Custom Menu list, and then click Delete to remove it. But you'll run into problems if you do. First, if you highlight menus with brackets around their names, the Delete button is inactive. And if you select an item where the Delete button remains active (Help), and then delete it, you get a nasty surprise when you click OK and return to your file. You see the text "Missing Menu" inserted in the menu bar, and the Help menu stays right where it was. Despite these obstacles, you *can* remove an entire menu; you just have to dig a little deeper to do it.

Note: Troubleshoot a file for missing menu items by running a DDR (page 717), or by checking Get (Last-Error) after you load a menu set in a script.

The Window menu can cause problems for new users. For example, the Show command lists files they may not know are open. Hiding and showing windows is also perilous for new users if they don't understand how FileMaker manages windows. Instead of bothering people with stuff they don't need to know, you can just suppress this menu entirely by removing it from the menu bar.

1. **In the Manage Custom Menus dialog box, click the Menu Sets tab. Select Custom Menu Set 1, and then click Edit.**

   The Edit Menu Set dialog box appears.

2. **In the Menu Set Name field, type "Data Entry".**

   This descriptive name helps you remember the menu set's purpose. If you like, type additional information in the Comment box.

3. **In the "Menus in 'Data Entry'" list, click the [Window] menu. Click Clear, and then click OK until you're back in your database.**

   Usually brackets on a list item indicate you can't delete it. But you *can* delete it from the display list, as you've just done. The [Window] menu remains in the Available Custom Menus list at left. If you change your mind, you can move it back into the display list to restore it.

Back in your database, the Window menu is gone entirely from the menu bar. This menu configuration is ideal for your data entry people, but not so great for administrative users, who understand the Window menu and use it all the time. Read on to find out how to tailor *sets* of menus for people with different privilege levels.

Installing Custom Menu Sets

FileMaker Pro Advanced lets you create a set of custom menus (see Figure 19-17) and use it as the *default* for a file, meaning everyone who uses your database sees it, every time. But since the people using your database may have different levels of skill (and trust), you may want your custom menus to adapt accordingly. In fact, if you've read this book's chapters on layouts and privilege sets, you have all the tools you need to make the right menus appear to the right people at the right time. It's a simple matter of assigning menu sets to these existing features. You can conceal certain menus and commands from people who don't need them, but keep them available for everybody else. Or maybe you just want menu items to show up when they make sense for the active layout.

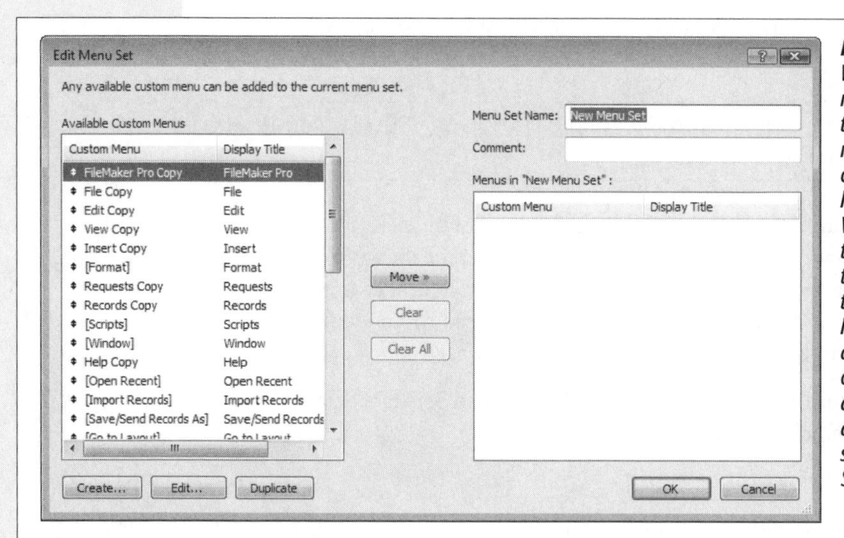

***Figure 19-17:** When you're editing menu sets, the field on the left lists the custom menus attached to the current set. Look in the list to see your edited View menu. The list on the right is a subset of the list on the left. Menus that aren't in the right-hand list are not displayed when this custom menu set is active. The Move, Clear, and Clear All buttons are similar to the ones in the Sort dialog box.*

Once you've created menu sets using the steps outlined earlier in this chapter, you can install them in any of several ways:

- **As the default for a file.** That's what you did in the tutorial in the "Editing a Menu" section on page 725. Unless you tell FileMaker otherwise, everybody gets the same custom menus. This option works great for a runtime file, or any situation where all users are at the same level.
- **On individual layouts.** In this scenario, when someone switches layouts, either by menu command or through a script, the menu set changes to a layout-specific one of your choosing. Choose Layout → Layout Setup to attach a custom menu set to a layout.
- **By mode.** This option offers the ultimate in elegance. It lets you do things like create a set with only one menu and just a few items, and make it the *only* menu people see when they're in Find mode. Instead of a gaggle of buttons to perform and cancel finds, write the appropriate scripts and display them in the one menu, short and sweet.

- **When a script is run.** By checking the privilege set in a script that runs when someone logs into your file, you can load a set of menus customized to that person's level of privilege. Use the Get (PrivilegeSetName) step to check privileges (page 633) and the Install Menu Set script step to specify which menu set installs. (If you have a re-login script, you need to make sure the right menu set is installed each time users re-login.)

Warning: Since you're effectively removing features for your users when you customize menus, thorough testing is a critical part of the process. Be sure to test menus with all affected layouts, privilege sets, and scripts, and across platforms. In FileMaker Pro Advanced, choose Tools → Custom Menus to switch among sets as you test them.

Developer Utilities

The Tools → Developer Utilities command looks insignificant and benign to the unsuspecting person, but behind it lurks a vast array of powerful features. There are developer utilities for the following techniques:

- Rename one file in a system of interconnected files, and have every file reference in the *other* files automatically update to the new name.
- Turn your database into a *kiosk* system. You can use this feature to make interactive programs that run on publicly accessible computers. In this setup, FileMaker hides the menu bars, the Windows taskbar or Macintosh Dock, and all other screen decorations that aren't part of your layouts.
- Create a *runtime solution*—a special version of your database that anyone can use, even if they don't have FileMaker Pro.
- Permanently remove full access to files so you can send your database to people you don't know, and be sure they can't tamper with your hard work, including your scripts, table and field definitions, and relationship graph.
- Create an error log to help you troubleshoot problems that occur when FileMaker generates runtimes.

In fact, you can (and often want to) do several of these things at once. Here's an example: You build a beautiful interactive product catalog, complete with pictures and an easy-to-use ordering screen. You then want to set up a kiosk computer at a trade show where attendees can use the database to see what you have and place their orders. Using the developer utilities, you could do all this:

- Add "Kiosk" to the end of every file name, so you can keep this copy separate from the one you use in the office.
- Make the database run in Kiosk mode so users at the trade show won't be able to exit FileMaker, switch to other programs, or otherwise cause mischief.

- Make the whole thing run by itself so you don't have to bother installing FileMaker on the computer you're renting just for this job.
- Lock out full access so if someone manages to steal a copy of your database while you're not looking, they can't see how it works or steal your product's beauty shots.

Using the Developer Utilities

The most confusing thing about the developer utilities is that you have to *close* your files before you work with them—just the opposite of every other command in FileMaker. So close the files you want to modify, and then choose File → Developer Utilities. You behold the Developer Utilities window (Figure 19-18).

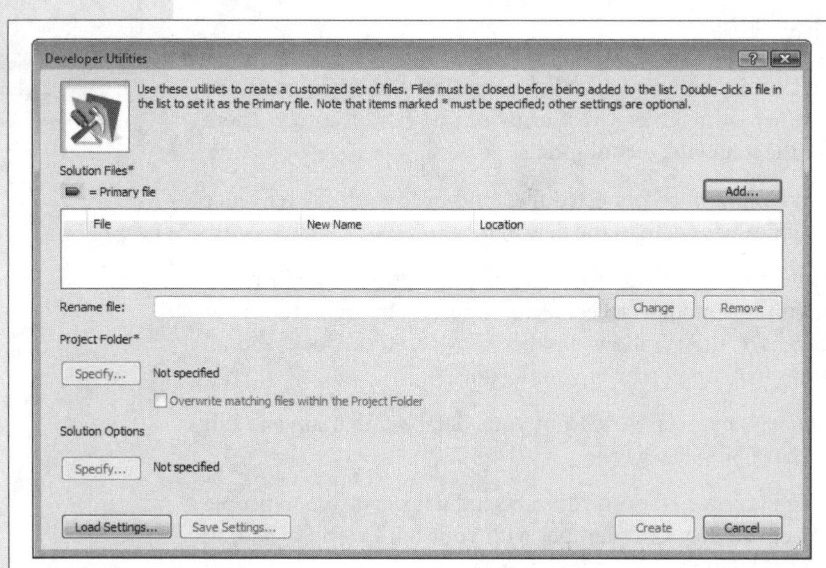

Figure 19-18: *The Developer Utilities window (File → Developer Utilities) lets you gather the files you want to change, and then tell FileMaker what changes to make. When you're done, click Create, and FileMaker builds new versions of your files (in a new location) with all the changes in place.*

In the Developer Utilities window, you first choose which files you want to work with. Click Add to put a file on the list. You can select several files at once in the Open File dialog box using your Shift and Control (⌘) keystrokes. Keep on adding until every file you want to change is in the list. If you accidentally add the wrong file, select it and click Remove.

You have to pick one file to be your *main* file. This file is the one that opens first if you create a runtime solution, for example. To set the main file, just double-click it in the list. FileMaker shows a red square—it looks surprisingly like a script breakpoint—by the main file.

Renaming files

Of course, you can always rename a file in Windows Explorer or the Mac's Finder. But those interfaces let you change *only* the file name. Developer Utilities makes that look like child's play. When it changes a file name, it also looks inside the file and updates any internal file references to match the file's new name. If you've ever tried to open two versions of a multiple file solution at the same time (to test some scripts that delete data and on a copy of the files, say), you know FileMaker sometimes gets confused and keeps multiple copies open even after you try to close one set. You can eliminate the crossover problem by renaming one set in Developer Utilities. You can test your scripts without a problem, since the scripts in the copy files automatically inherit the correct new file names.

To rename a file or set of files, add them to the Solution File list (Figure 19-18). Select a file, type the new name in the "Rename file" box, and then click Change. FileMaker shows the new name in the New Name column.

Next, you need to pick the *project folder*. This folder is the one where FileMaker saves the finished files. Just click the Specify button under "Project Folder" and pick any folder you wish. If the folder already contains files with the same names as the ones you're about to create, you get an error message—unless you turn on "Overwrite matching files within the Project Folder." When you click Create, FileMaker Pro Advanced makes copies of the files with their new names, leaving the originals untouched.

To complete the example above (your kiosk product catalog), you would turn on "Create Runtime solution application(s)," "Remove admin access from files permanently," and "Enable Kiosk mode for non-admin accounts." Only the first option needs to be configured.

Create Runtime Solution application(s)

To create Runtime Solutions, add the files to the Solution Files list, and then select a project folder, just as you did above. Don't type a new name for the runtime in this window, though. Click the Specify button under Solution Options. You see the Specify Solution Options dialog box, as shown in Figure 19-19.

When you tell FileMaker you want to build a runtime solution, it generates a special program you need to include with your databases. This program can do most of what FileMaker Pro can do, but it can't modify tables, fields, layouts, or scripts. You get to decide what this program is called—just type it in the Runtime Name box. Along with the runtime program, FileMaker creates new copies of each of your files to go with it, and changes all the file name extensions to something other than .fp7. Tell FileMaker what extension to use in the Extension field.

Warning: Your computer's operating system uses file name extensions to figure out which program files belong to. The Developer Utilities let you assign any extension you want, but you should avoid common extensions like .doc, .jpg, .mp3, and so on. You know computers—they get confused easily.

The new files don't just have a new name; they're also modified internally so they're *bound* to the runtime program, and the runtime program in turn can open only properly bound files. In other words, when you send people a runtime program, they can't use it to open any old FileMaker Pro file.

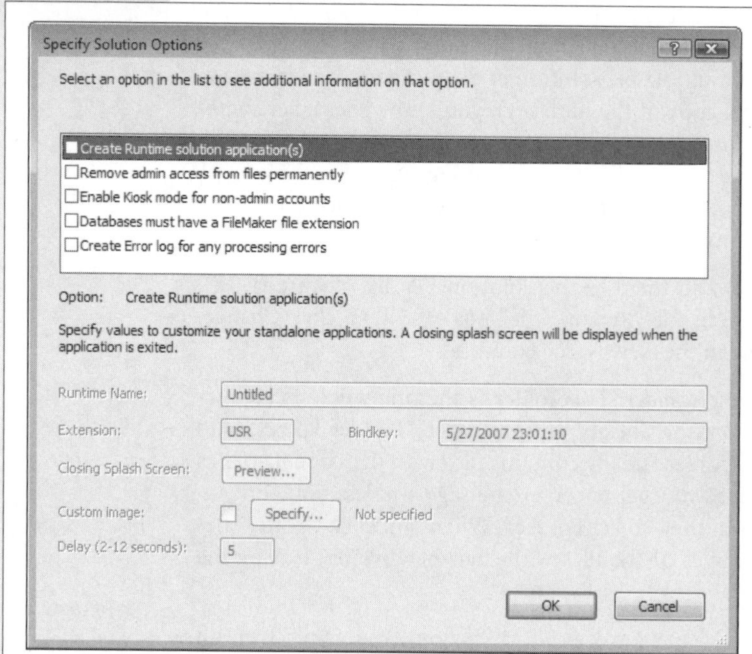

Figure 19-19: *The Specify Solution Options window lets you tell FileMaker what you want done to the files. Turn on a checkbox in the options list to tell FileMaker you want that thing done to your files. Most options need to be configured, and when you select an item in the list, the bottom half of the window lets you change the appropriate settings.*

To facilitate the binding process, FileMaker asks you to provide a *bindkey*. FileMaker stores this value in both the runtime program and any database files in the Developer Utilities window. The value you use for the bindkey is entirely unimportant, and there's no need to keep it secret. But if you later want to bind *new* databases to the same runtime program, you'll have to use the same bindkey.

Finally, when users exit the runtime program (in other words, when they close your database system), they see a "Made with FileMaker" splash screen. Normally, this screen looks like the one in Figure 19-20. You can also control how long the splash screen shows by putting the number of seconds in the Delay box. Unfortunately, you can't make it go away entirely.

Figure 19-20: *When you quit a runtime solution, this window pops up for a few seconds. You can't get rid of the "Made with FileMaker" logo, but you can change the big FileMaker graphic to anything you want. Just turn on "Custom image" and pick a picture file from your hard drive. FileMaker stretches the picture to fit in the window, so to avoid distortion, you should create a picture that is exactly 382 pixels wide and 175 pixels high.*

Remove admin access from files permanently

The "Remove admin access from files permanently" option doesn't actually remove the accounts that have full access. Instead, it modifies the [Full Access] privilege set so it no longer truly has full access. If you log in with an account that normally has full access, it doesn't have access to the Manage Database window, Layout mode, or ScriptMaker, and its access to Accounts & Privileges is limited to the Extended Privileges tab. This option has no settings.

Enable Kiosk mode for non-admin accounts

If you turn on Kiosk mode and then open the new file using an account that has full access, you don't see any changes. But if you log in with a lesser account, *everything* changes. The screen goes completely black, except for the content area of your database window. You can see an example in Figure 19-21.

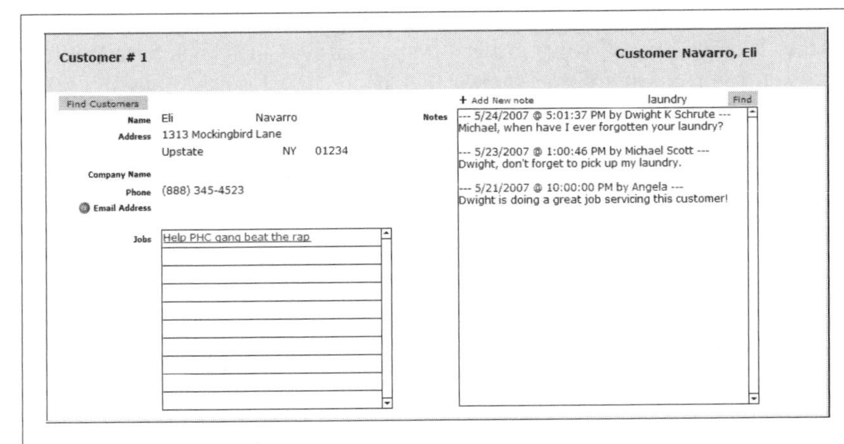

Figure 19-21: *When you open a database in Kiosk mode with an account that doesn't have full access, it looks like this example. Everything on the screen is completely black outside your layout. You can still switch layouts and otherwise interact with your database, but you can't make new windows, resize the window, exit FileMaker, or switch to other programs. You also can't print, enter Find mode, or otherwise use FileMaker's features unless buttons on the layout let you.*

When you use Kiosk mode, you typically hide the status area and let people control everything using the buttons on layouts. Alternatively, you can use custom menus (page 724) to hide all the menus and commands that would let nosy people poke around in your file. Remember to troubleshoot your file before creating a custom runtime from it, because any problems in your file (broken links, missing data, bad scripts) also show up in the runtime. But once you've suppressed all the normal FileMaker commands, folks have no way of getting around these problems.

Databases must have a FileMaker file extension

Sometimes people, Mac types especially, create databases without the .fp7 file extension, only to regret that decision later. An extension is the computers' most compatible way to identify a file. So turn on "Databases must have a FileMaker file extension," and FileMaker adds ".fp7" to the end of every file name that doesn't already have it.

Create error log for any processing errors

While FileMaker processes your files, applying your options, building runtime programs, or renaming files, it may encounter problems. Turn on "Create error log for any processing errors" so you can see what went wrong. FileMaker saves error messages in a file on your hard drive (you get to pick where it goes and what it's called).

Loading and saving settings

If you maintain a database system that other people use, you may well run your files through Developer Utilities every time you send out a new version. To save you the tedium of configuring the Database Utilities dialog box again and again, FileMaker lets you save all your settings to a special file—just click Save Settings. Later, when you're ready to process your files again, click Load Settings and select the same file. FileMaker sets up everything in the dialog box for you. All you have to do is click Create.

Delivering a Runtime Solution

If you build a runtime solution with FileMaker Pro Advanced in Mac OS X, it runs *only* in Mac OS X. Likewise, if you build from Windows, your runtime solution is limited to Windows. If you need a runtime solution for *both* platforms, you must buy FileMaker Pro Advanced for Mac OS X *and* for Windows and build a separate runtime solution on each kind of computer.

File Maintenance

The File Maintenance utility doesn't come into play as you're developing a database. Instead, you use it periodically on existing, actively used databases—with good reason. As people add, remove, and modify records in a database, FileMaker has to go to great lengths to make room for things in the file on your hard drive. For the sake of speed, the program avoids actions that require massive reorganization of the data on disk. As FileMaker shuffles things around, information from one record can spread to different parts of the file, and sections of the file can be wasted—too small to hold anything useful, but stuck there in the middle of the file anyway.

The Tools → File Maintenance command tidies up such scattered data and frees unused disk space. When you choose it, you see the File Maintenance dialog box (Figure 19-22).

The Compact File option goes through the file from top to bottom seeking out the wasted space. When it finds some, it moves everything *else* in the file a little bit so the wasted space is gone. In the end, you have a file that's as small as possible.

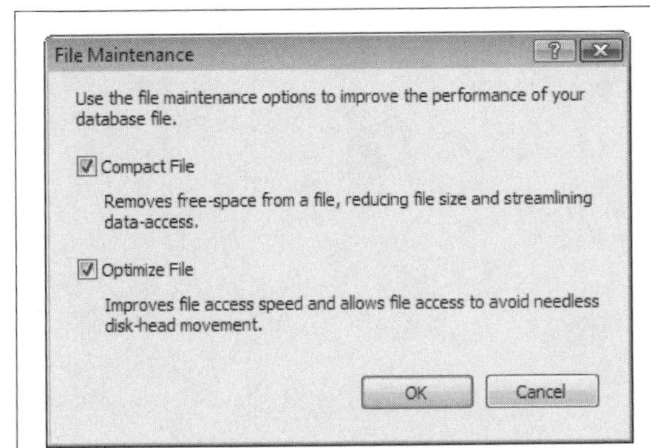

Figure 19-22:
The File Maintenance dialog box (File → File Maintenance) lets you compact and optimize your files. You get to decide which to do by turning on or off the appropriate checkboxes. You're free to do either of these, or do both at once. Each takes quite a bit of time on a large file, so plan ahead.

The Optimize File option works differently. It goes through the records, layouts, scripts, and other elements of your database and makes sure all the information for each element is together. Instead of searching all over your large file to get the entire Customer list, FileMaker can stay within a consecutive block of information in a small area of the file. Everything in the database works just a little bit faster.

Part Seven: Appendixes

7

APPENDIX

A

Getting Help

This book provides a solid foundation in FileMaker and takes you well into power user territory, but it doesn't cover everything there is to know about this vastly versatile program. (You wouldn't be able to lift it if it did.) This appendix is a guide to the many resources available to help you plumb the depths of FileMaker database design and development.

Getting Help from FileMaker Itself

The installation CDs for FileMaker Pro and FileMaker Pro Advanced include online help files, electronic documentation, templates, and example files. The installer program *always* installs online help, but the others are optional. When you choose the Easy Install option in the Install panel of the installation wizard, you get *everything* installed. Choose Custom Install instead to pick and choose which of the optional files you want installed. And if FileMaker's already installed on your computer, but the helpers listed below are missing, you can perform a Custom Install and choose the helper files you need without having to uninstall and reinstall FileMaker itself.

On Windows you can find these helpers at Program Files → FileMaker → FileMaker Pro 9 → English Extras. And on the Mac, look in Applications → FileMaker Pro → English Extras.

The Learning Center

Your next best stop for FileMaker assistance is the FileMaker Learning Center. Just choose Help → Learning Center. In a new window, FileMaker takes you to a special Web site covering many FileMaker topics. Unlike an ordinary online help system, which dryly enumerates everything about a piece of software at a mind-numbing pace, the Learning Center is actually fun to use. It covers real-world cases with video demonstrations and point-by-point guidance. It covers a limited number of topics, but covers them thoroughly.

FileMaker Pro Help

If you *prefer* something less stimulating, you can read FileMaker's onboard help files by choosing Help → FileMaker Pro Help. You can also simply press F1 (⌘-?). If you launch Help while no dialog boxes are open, it opens to the Contents page (Figure A-1).

If what you need help with is the dialog box that's open in front of you, whatever you do, don't close it! Instead, leave the dialog box open, which tells FileMaker you want context-sensitive help. For example, if you choose File → Manage → Database, then click the Relationships tab, and *then* choose Help → FileMaker Pro Help, the file opens to the detail page called "Working with related tables and files."

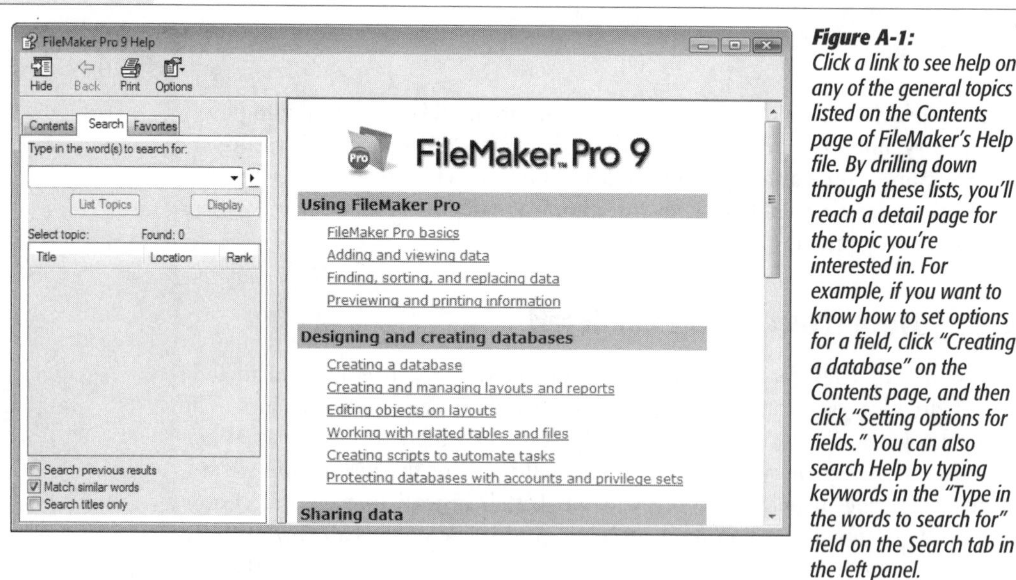

Figure A-1: *Click a link to see help on any of the general topics listed on the Contents page of FileMaker's Help file. By drilling down through these lists, you'll reach a detail page for the topic you're interested in. For example, if you want to know how to set options for a field, click "Creating a database" on the Contents page, and then click "Setting options for fields." You can also search Help by typing keywords in the "Type in the words to search for" field on the Search tab in the left panel.*

Detail pages within the help system provide assistance with technical terms. When you see underlined words or phrases, click those links for a short definition. At the bottom of each page is a list of related topics for further reading.

One of the most useful parts of the Help file is a comprehensive list of FileMaker's functions. As in the Specify Calculation dialog box, the functions are listed two ways: by type and alphabetically. The detail page for each function gives you the function name, parameter(s), data type returned, and a description of what the function does. Use these pages to help you when you're using a function for the first time.

Templates

You got a glimpse of these starter solutions in Chapter 1, when you created your first new file from the Contact Management template. You see all these template files listed in the FileMaker Quick Start dialog box—unless you've previously checked that dialog box's option to "No longer show this dialog." If you've turned this option on, but want to see the templates listed again, choose FileMaker Pro → Preferences (Mac) or Edit → Preferences (Windows), and then turn on the Show FileMaker Quick Start Screen option on the General tab of the Preferences dialog box. The next time you choose File → New Database, FileMaker's templates will be listed. Pick the template you want, and FileMaker creates a new copy of the file for you. You can add data, create and edit scripts, or delete objects you don't need without affecting the original template.

Note: If you prefer, you can navigate to the Templates folder and launch the template you want just like any other file. When you launch a template file directly, though, you're opening the *original* template file, and any changes you make to the template will be reflected in any new copies you make when you choose File → New Database.

These basic file templates are great for getting you up and running with basic data management tasks without wasting time figuring out how things work in FileMaker's universe. But they also serve another purpose—as an introduction to good database design. They have a clean, uncluttered look you can adapt for your own purposes. Feel free to copy the design as is or use it as a jumping-off point for your new database.

Each template stores different kinds of data, so it's helpful to explore several templates to get ideas for arranging and grouping your data effectively. In general, there's usually an easy-to-read name at the top of the layout, which serves to orient your users to the task at hand. Underneath the name, you'll find a couple of rows of navigation tools and buttons grouped together by function. The largest portion of the layout is dedicated to a logical arrangement of data fields.

Finally, FileMaker's templates contain ideas you can use for creating relationships, buttons, and scripts that will make your own databases more powerful. For instance, the Contact Management template contains a script that lets you swap a contact's main address data with the secondary address data. By studying these files, you can pick up tips about how the pros use FileMaker's power to make data management easier.

XML Examples

Example files, including a database and sample XML and XSLT files, are in a folder aptly titled Examples. These simple files serve as a primer for working with FileMaker and XML. To get started, open the database file (xml example.fp7), then run each script to see how XML import and export work. Then take a look at the steps that make up each script, paying particular attention to the options set for the Import Records and Export Records steps. Finally, take a look at the files that are imported and the files that are created by the export scripts. In them you'll see how your XML pages should be structured.

Getting Help from FileMaker, Inc.

FileMaker's Web site has the usual marketing materials you'd expect from a great software company. But there's lots of substance there, too. Look for "Support" in its main navigation menu, where you'll find free and fee-based help.

Updaters and Downloads

Like most programs, FileMaker's latest software versions are those found on the software company's Web site. You'll find software updates and support files, like localized language packs at *www.filemaker.com/support/downloads/*. Trial software and development tools, including an XLST library and a list of recently released plug-ins, are also available from this page.

If your installation is missing some (or all) its templates, click the Starter Solutions link to download new copies. You can also download a free, ready-made business solution called FileMaker Business Tracker. It's an invoicing system that lets you track sales, contacts, and product data. Even if your business doesn't do sales, you'll find this product useful for study purposes. It was written as a demo file for FileMaker 7, and it's full of developer tricks of the trade you can analyze. When you've mastered all the secrets there, you're ready to leave the monastery, Grasshopper.

Documentation and Publications

You can reach this list from the Downloads page above, but it's so jam-packed that it deserves a headline all its own.

- **Product Documentation.** You'll find all the documentation that came with your product here, plus any updates to those guides. There are also tutorial files and some extra guides on topics like security, Windows 2000 Terminal Services, and Citrix.
- **White Papers.** Here you'll find shorter papers on specific subjects, like migrating your older files to .fp7 format and custom Web publishing with server-side scripting. If you want to make the case for FileMaker's power and simplicity to higher-ups in your organization, check out the Industry sections, where you'll find such topics as Information Management and Cost of Ownership studies on FileMaker.
- **Technical Briefs.** These are usually longer documents than the white papers, so they cover similar topics in more depth. Unlike product documentation, which has explanations and step-by-step instructions, technical briefs focus more on methods and benefits of FileMaker's newest technologies, like improved security and the server and Web publishing models.

- **FileMaker Resource Guide.** The Resource Guide lists FileMaker's complete product line, third-party products, trainers, and consultants.
- **Knowledge Base.** Find FAQs, bug alerts, workarounds, errata, and the official word on topics that don't fit into FileMaker's other document categories. You can either search the Knowledge Base with keywords, or peruse the most recent topics to see what's new. A button at the bottom of each page lets you request email notification if the page is updated, so you can stay on top of developments with ease. A clickable list of related topics helps you wander around in case the main topic didn't fill the bill.

Technical Support

FileMaker supports the current version of its software and one version prior. If your files are older than that, you'll need to get help from a third party, usually a consultant or a user group. See the section below to find out how to find those animals.

You can't start making databases until FileMaker's installed, so everybody who purchases FileMaker gets unlimited tech support phone calls regarding installation. Plus, you get one free troubleshooting call for each product you buy, which is helpful when you have a bunch of staffers on FileMaker Pro, a copy or two of FileMaker Server, and your very own copy of FileMaker Pro Advanced. The tech support is free, but you'll pay for the phone call, so break out those free long-distance minutes. Dial (408) 727-9004 for the free stuff.

Paid tech support is available by calling (800) 965-9090. Get out your credit card when you call, and then decide how you want to pay. You can choose a $45 flat fee and they'll solve a single issue for you, or you can roll the dice (and get multiple problems solved at once) by choosing the $3 per minute rate, with a $75 maximum. Phone tech support is available 7:00 AM to 5:00 PM PT weekdays.

With Premium 800 Support, you prepay $180 for a five-pack of access codes that let you make the calls when the trouble arises. Codes are good for one year. Call (800) 325-2747 for the bulk discount.

Professional Support costs $899 per year. You nominate one person from your company who can call a special toll-free number as many times as needed for twelve months. Add $699 for each additional person who needs the same access. Download the order form at *www.filemaker.com/downloads/pdf/prof_support_form.pdf.*

Note: Technical Support deals with technical problems, like when a feature isn't working as advertised and you need help figuring out why. Teaching you how to create databases or writing your calculations and scripts for you are not considered technical support issues.

File corruption isn't common with FileMaker, but it's devastating when it happens. FileMaker offers file recovery services at $500 per file. Go to *www.filemaker.com/downloads/pdf/filerecovery.pdf* for more information.

FileMaker Applications

If you find yourself without the time or inclination to create a new database, you may be able to purchase one of these ready-made systems, professionally designed by FileMaker staff. Like FileMaker's Starter Solutions (aka templates), FileMaker Applications are fully unlocked and customizable. But they go a lot further than the Starter Solutions, and you may find that they meet many of your needs straight out of the box. Prices range from $69 to $448. These applications let you manage tasks like employment recruiting, tracking donors and donations, managing meetings, and work requests. See *www.filemaker.com/products/applications/* for a complete list. Click the link for each solution to get more information about each product and to see online demos.

Developer Programs

FileMaker runs two programs to help developers keep in touch with each other, and with FileMaker, Inc. itself. The FileMaker Technical Network (*www.filemaker.com/technet/*) gets you access to an email discussion forum crawling with FileMaker experts swapping ideas and helping one another. You also get access to exclusive technical white papers on important FileMaker topics. Finally, TechNet subscribers get free FileMaker add-on software and a special developer version of FileMaker Server Advanced for testing purposes. To call yourself a member, you only need to pay the dues: $99 per year.

If you're a professional FileMaker developer (meaning you build FileMaker databases for other companies for pay), you may qualify to join the FileMaker Business Alliance (FBA) instead. In addition to online discussions, technical info, and free software, FBA members get outstanding software perks. You can purchase FileMaker products for your own use (or your company's use) for deep discounts. You can also get discount pricing on FileMaker products, which you can then resell to your customers. The FBA has many more perks, and costs $500 per year. Find out more at *www.filemaker.com/fba/*.

Getting Help from the Community

Even outside the members-only programs, the FileMaker developer community is a congenial bunch. You'll find lots of resources on the Internet, including free newsgroups and Web sites. Many independent consultants' sites have free or low-cost resources, too, like lists of custom functions free for the taking or sample files that demonstrate specific techniques.

Mail Lists and Newsgroups

A listing of email lists is available at *www.filemaker.com/support/mailinglists.html*, but new sites are cropping up all the time, and URLs change even on established sites. So use the link above, or check your favorite search engine, to get the latest links for these groups. To get your feet wet, try general lists, like the one run by

Dartmouth University or FileMaker Today. Fmpug.com is a membership-based, online user group with forums, reviews, and resources, including podcast interviews with subject-matter experts. For more specialized topics, have a look at FileMaker XML Talk, FileMaker Pro CGI Talk, and Troi FileMaker Plug-in Talk.

Training/Consultants

FileMaker's Web site lists trainers and consultants who are members of the FBA. And the FileMaker Resource Guide also lists the FBA group, plus it takes paid advertisements. Your favorite search engine will yield hundreds of results. FileMaker has a certification program, so look for the FileMaker Certified Developer logo or ask the consultant if they've been certified as part of your selection process.

DevCon

If total FileMaker immersion is what you seek, the annual Developer's Conference (DevCon) is the way to go. Each day you can attend as many as seven sessions on about 30 different topics, ranging from running a FileMaker consulting firm to Web publishing, so you're sure to come away from the three-day conference with a brain-pan full of new ideas. For details, see *www.filemaker.com/developers/devcon/index.html.*

APPENDIX B

FileMaker Error Codes

The following table (Table B-1) lists the error codes that may pop up when FileMaker detects something out of whack in your database, especially when you're writing or running a script. Like many things written by and for computer programmers, these official descriptions may not make much sense in English, but they may provide a little more guidance than the error number alone.

Error codes marked with an asterisk (*) pertain only to Web-published databases.

Table B-1. *Error Codes*

Error Number	Description
-1	Unknown error
0	No error
1	User canceled action
2	Memory error
3	Command is unavailable (for example, wrong operating system, wrong mode, and so on)
4	Command is unknown
5	Command is invalid (for example, a Set Field script step does not have a calculation specified)
6	File is read-only
7	Running out of memory
8	Empty result
9	Insufficient privileges
10	Requested data is missing

***Table B-1.** Error Codes (continued)*

Error Number	Description
11	Name is not valid
12	Name already exists
13	File or object is in use
14	Out of range
15	Can't divide by zero
16	Operation failed, request retry (for example, a user query)
17	Attempt to convert foreign character set to UTF-16 failed
18	Client must provide account information to proceed
19	String contains characters other than A–Z, a–z, 0–9 (ASCII)
100	File is missing
101	Record is missing
102	Field is missing
103	Relationship is missing
104	Script is missing
105	Layout is missing
106	Table is missing
107	Index is missing
108	Value list is missing
109	Privilege set is missing
110	Related tables are missing
111	Field repetition is invalid
112	Window is missing
113	Function is missing
114	File reference is missing
115	Specified menu set is not present
116	Specified layout object is not present
117	Specified data source is not present
130	Files are damaged or missing and must be reinstalled
131	Language pack files are missing (such as template files)
200	Record access is denied
201	Field cannot be modified
202	Field access is denied
203	No records in file to print, or password doesn't allow print access
204	No access to field(s) in sort order
205	User does not have access privileges to create new records; import will overwrite existing data
206	User does not have password change privileges, or file is not modifiable

Table B-1. *Error Codes (continued)*

Error Number	Description
207	User does not have sufficient privileges to change database schema, or file is not modifiable
208	Password does not contain enough characters
209	New password must be different from existing one
210	User account is inactive
211	Password has expired
212	Invalid user account and/or password; please try again
213	User account and/or password does not exist
214	Too many login attempts
215	Administrator privileges cannot be duplicated
216	Guest account cannot be duplicated
217	User does not have sufficient privileges to modify administrator account
300	File is locked or in use
301	Record is in use by another user
302	Table is in use by another user
303	Database schema is in use by another user
304	Layout is in use by another user
306	Record modification ID does not match
400	Find criteria are empty
401	No records match the request
402	Selected field is not a match field for a lookup
403	Exceeding maximum record limit for trial version of FileMaker Pro
404	Sort order is invalid
405	Number of records specified exceeds number of records that can be omitted
406	Replace/Reserialize criteria are invalid
407	One or both match fields are missing (invalid relationship)
408	Specified field has inappropriate data type for this operation
409	Import order is invalid
410	Export order is invalid
412	Wrong version of FileMaker Pro used to recover file
413	Specified field has inappropriate field type
414	Layout cannot display the result
415	One or more required related records are not available
416	Primary key required from data source table
417	Database is not supported for ODBC operations

Table B-1. Error Codes (continued)

Error Number	Description
500	Date value does not meet validation entry options
501	Time value does not meet validation entry options
502	Number value does not meet validation entry options
503	Value in field is not within the range specified in validation entry options
504	Value in field is not unique as required in validation entry options
505	Value in field is not an existing value in the database file as required in validation entry options
506	Value in field is not listed on the value list specified in validation entry option
507	Value in field failed calculation test of validation entry option
508	Invalid value entered in Find mode
509	Field requires a valid value
510	Related value is empty or unavailable
511	Value in field exceeds maximum number of allowed characters
512	Record was already modified by another user
513	Record must have a value in some field to be created
600	Print error has occurred
601	Combined header and footer exceed one page
602	Body doesn't fit on a page for current column setup
603	Print connection lost
700	File is of the wrong file type for import
706	EPSF file has no preview image
707	Graphic translator cannot be found
708	Can't import the file or need color monitor support to import file
709	QuickTime movie import failed
710	Unable to update QuickTime file reference because the database file is read-only
711	Import translator cannot be found
714	Password privileges do not allow the operation
715	Specified Excel worksheet or named range is missing
716	A SQL query using DELETE, INSERT, or UPDATE is not allowed for ODBC import
717	There is not enough XML/XSL information to proceed with the import or export
718	Error in parsing XML file (from Xerces)
719	Error in transforming XML using XSL (from Xalan)
720	Error when exporting; intended format does not support repeating fields

Table B-1. *Error Codes (continued)*

Error Number	Description
721	Unknown error occurred in the parser or the transformer
722	Cannot import data into a file that has no fields
723	You do not have permission to add records to or modify records in the target table
724	You do not have permission to add records to the target table
725	You do not have permission to modify records in the target table
726	There are more records in the import file than in the target table. Not all records were imported
727	There are more records in the target table than in the import file. Not all records were updated
729	Errors occurred during import. Records could not be imported
730	Unsupported Excel version. (Convert file to Excel 7.0 [Excel 95], Excel 97, 2000, or XP format and try again)
731	The file you are importing from contains no data
732	This file cannot be inserted because it contains other files
733	A table cannot be imported into itself
734	This file type cannot be displayed as a picture
735	This file type cannot be displayed as a picture. It will be inserted and displayed as a file
736	Too much data to export to this format. It will be truncated
800	Unable to create file on disk
801	Unable to create temporary file on System disk
802	Unable to open file
803	File is single user or host cannot be found
804	File cannot be opened as read-only in its current state
805	File is damaged; use Recover command
806	File cannot be opened with this version of FileMaker Pro
807	File is not a FileMaker Pro file or is severely damaged
808	Cannot open file because access privileges are damaged
809	Disk/volume is full
810	Disk/volume is locked
811	Temporary file cannot be opened as FileMaker Pro file
813	Record Synchronization error on network
814	File(s) cannot be opened because maximum number is open
815	Couldn't open lookup file
816	Unable to convert file
817	Unable to open file because it does not belong to this solution
819	Cannot save a local copy of a remote file
820	File is in the process of being closed

Table B-1. *Error Codes (continued)*

Error Number	Description
821	Host forced a disconnect
822	FMI files not found; reinstall missing files
823	Cannot set file to single-user, guests are connected
824	File is damaged or not a FileMaker file
900	General spelling engine error
901	Main spelling dictionary not installed
902	Could not launch the Help system
903	Command cannot be used in a shared file
905	No active field selected; command can only be used if there is an active field
906	Current file must be shared in order to use this command
920	Can't initialize the spelling engine
921	User dictionary cannot be loaded for editing
922	User dictionary cannot be found
923	User dictionary is read-only
951	An unexpected error occurred (*)
954	Unsupported XML grammar (*)
955	No database name (*)
956	Maximum number of database sessions exceeded (*)
957	Conflicting commands (*)
958	Parameter missing (*)
1200	Generic calculation error
1201	Too few parameters in the function
1202	Too many parameters in the function
1203	Unexpected end of calculation
1204	Number, text constant, field name or "(" expected
1205	Comment is not terminated with "*/"
1206	Text constant must end with a quotation mark
1207	Unbalanced parenthesis
1208	Operator missing, function not found or "(" not expected
1209	Name (such as field name or layout name) is missing
1210	Plug-in function has already been registered
1211	List usage is not allowed in this function
1212	An operator (for example, +, -, *) is expected here
1213	This variable has already been defined in the Let function
1214	AVERAGE, COUNT, EXTEND, GETREPETITION, MAX, MIN, NPV, STDEV, SUM, and GETSUMMARY: expression found where a field alone is needed

Table B-1. *Error Codes (continued)*

Error Number	Description
1215	This parameter is an invalid Get function parameter
1216	Only Summary fields allowed as first argument in GETSUMMARY
1217	Break field is invalid
1218	Cannot evaluate the number
1219	A field cannot be used in its own formula
1220	Field type must be normal or calculated
1221	Data type must be number, date, time, or timestamp
1222	Calculation cannot be stored
1223	The function is not implemented
1224	The function is not defined
1225	The function is not supported in this context
1300	The specified name can't be used
1400	ODBC driver initialization failed; make sure the ODBC drivers are properly installed
1401	Failed to allocate environment (ODBC)
1402	Failed to free environment (ODBC)
1403	Failed to disconnect (ODBC)
1404	Failed to allocate connection (ODBC)
1405	Failed to free connection (ODBC)
1406	Failed check for SQL API (ODBC)
1407	Failed to allocate statement (ODBC)
1408	Extended error (ODBC)
1409	Error (ODBC)
1413	Failed communication link (ODBC)

Index

Symbols

A

B

C

D

E

F

G

H

I

Q

R

S

T

U

V

W

X

Z